PRENTICE HALL MATHEMATICS

ALGEBRA 1

Allan E. Bellman

Sadie Chavis Bragg

Randall I. Charles

William G. Handlin, Sr.

Dan Kennedy

PEARSON

Prentice
Hall

Needham, Massachusetts
Upper Saddle River, New Jersey

Authors

Series Authors

Dan Kennedy, Ph.D., is a classroom teacher and the Lupton Distinguished Professor of Mathematics at the Baylor School in Chattanooga, Tennessee. A frequent speaker at professional meetings on the subject of mathematics education reform, Dr. Kennedy has conducted more than 50 workshops and institutes for high school teachers. He is co-author of textbooks in calculus and precalculus, and from 1990 to 1994 he chaired the College Board's AP Calculus Development Committee. He is a 1992 Tandy Technology Scholar and a 1995 Presidential Award winner.

Randall I. Charles, Ph.D., is Professor Emeritus in the Department of Mathematics and Computer Science at San Jose State University, San Jose, California. He began his career as a high school mathematics teacher, and he was a mathematics supervisor for five years. Dr. Charles has been a member of several NCTM committees and is the former Vice President of the National Council of Supervisors of Mathematics. Much of his writing and research has been in the area of problem solving. He has authored more than 75 mathematics textbooks for kindergarten through college.

Dorling Kindersley (DK) is an international publishing company that specializes in the creation of high-quality, illustrated information books for children and adults. Dorling Kindersley's unique graphic presentation style is used in this program to motivate students in learning about real-world applications of mathematics. DK is part of the Pearson family of companies.

ISBN 0-13-052316-X

13 14 15 16   08 07 06 05

Algebra 1 and Algebra 2 Authors

Allan E. Bellman is a Lecturer/Supervisor in the School of Education at the University of California, Davis. Before coming to Davis, he was a mathematics teacher for 31 years in Montgomery County, Maryland. He has been an instructor for both the Woodrow Wilson National Fellowship Foundation and the T^3 program. Mr. Bellman has a particular expertise in the use of technology in education and speaks frequently on this topic. He was a 1992 Tandy Technology Scholar.

Sadie Chavis Bragg, Ed.D., is Professor of Mathematics and Vice President of Academic Affairs at the Borough of Manhattan Community College of the City University of New York. Dr. Bragg is a past president of the American Mathematical Association of Two-Year Colleges (AMATYC), is co-director of the AMATYC project to revise the standards for introductory college mathematics before calculus, and is an active member of the Benjamin Banneker Association. Since 1976, she has co-authored more than 50 mathematics textbooks from kindergarten through college.

William G. Handlin, Sr., is a classroom teacher and Department Chairman of Technology Applications at Spring Woods High School in Houston, Texas. Awarded Life Membership in the Texas Congress of Parent and Teachers Association for his contributions to the well-being of children, Mr. Handlin is also a frequent workshop and seminar leader in professional meetings throughout the world.

Geometry Authors

Laurie E. Bass
Fieldston, the Grades 7–12 Division of the Ethical Culture Fieldston School
Riverdale, New York

Art Johnson, Ed.D.
Professor of Mathematics
Boston University
Boston, Massachusetts

Reviewers

Algebra 1 Reviewers

Mary Lou Beasley
Southside Fundamental
  Middle School
St. Petersburg, Florida

Blanche Smith Brownley
Washington, D.C., Public
  Schools
Washington, D.C.

Joseph Caruso
Somerville High School
Somerville, Massachusetts

Belinda Craig
Highland West Junior High
  School
Moore, Oklahoma

Jane E. Damaske
Lakeshore Public Schools
Stevensville, Michigan

Stacey A. Ego
Warren Central High School
Indianapolis, Indiana

Earl R. Jones
Formerly, Kansas City
  Public Schools
Kansas City, Missouri

Jeanne Lorenson
James H. Blake High School
Silver Spring, Maryland

John T. Mace
Hibbett Middle School
Florence, Alabama

**Ann Marie Palmieri-
  Monahan**
Director of Mathematics
Bayonne Board of Education
Bayonne, New Jersey

Marie Schalke
Woodlawn Middle School
Long Grove, Illinois

Julie Welling
LaPorte High School
LaPorte, Indiana

Sharon Zguzenski
Naugatuck High School
Naugatuck, Connecticut

Geometry Reviewers

Marian Avery
Great Valley High School
Malvern, Pennsylvania

Mary Emma Bunch
Farragut High School
Knoxville, Tennessee

Karen A. Cannon
K–12 Mathematics
  Coordinator
Rockwood School District
Eureka, Missouri

Johnnie Ebbert
Department Chairman
DeLand High School
DeLand, Florida

Russ Forrer
Math Department Chairman
East Aurora High School
Aurora, Illinois

Andrea Kopco
Midpark High School
Middleburg Heights, Ohio

Gordon E. Maroney III
Camden Fairview High
  School
Camden, Arkansas

Charlotte Phillips
Math Coordinator
Wichita USD 259
Wichita, Kansas

Richard P. Strausz
Farmington Public Schools
Farmington, Michigan

Jane Tanner
Jefferson County
  International
  Baccalaureate School
Birmingham, Alabama

Karen D. Vaughan
Pitt County Schools
Greenville, North Carolina

Robin Washam
Math Specialist
Puget Sound Educational
  Service District
Burien, Washington

Algebra 2 Reviewers

Josiane Fouarge
Landry High School
New Orleans, Louisiana

Susan Hvizdos
Math Department Chair
Wheeling Park High School
Wheeling, West Virginia

Kathleen Kohler
Kearny High School
Kearny, New Jersey

Julia Kolb
Leesville Road High School
Raleigh, North Carolina

Deborah R. Kula
Sacred Hearts Academy
Honolulu, Hawaii

Betty Mayberry
Gallatin High School
Gallatin, Tennessee

John L. Pitt
Formerly, Prince William
  County Schools
Manassas, Virginia

Margaret Plouvier
Billings West High School
Billings, Montana

Sandra Sikorski
Berea High School
Berea, Ohio

Tim Visser
Grandview High School
Cherry Creek School District
Aurora, Colorado

Content Consultants

Courtney Lewis
Mathematics
Prentice Hall Senior National Consultant
Baltimore, Maryland

Deana Cerroni
Mathematics
Prentice Hall National Consultant
Las Vegas, Nevada

Kim Margel
Mathematics
Prentice Hall National Consultant
Scottsdale, Arizona

Sandra Mosteller
Mathematics
Prentice Hall National Consultant
Anderson, South Carolina

Rita Corbett
Mathematics
Prentice Hall Consultant
Elgin, Illinois

Cathy Davies
Mathematics
Prentice Hall Consultant
Laguna Niguel, California

Sally Marsh
Mathematics
Prentice Hall Consultant
Baltimore, Maryland

Addie Martin
Mathematics
Prentice Hall Consultant
Upper Marlboro, Maryland

Rose Primiani
Mathematics
Prentice Hall Consultant
Brick, New Jersey

Loretta Rector
Mathematics
Prentice Hall Consultant
Foresthill, California

Charlotte Samuels
Mathematics
Prentice Hall Consultant
Lafayette Hill, Pennsylvania

Margaret Thomas
Mathematics
Prentice Hall Consultant
Indianapolis, Indiana

Contents in Brief

Tools of Algebra

Solving Equations

Solving Inequalities

Solving and Applying Proportions

Chapter 5

Graphs and Functions

Linear Equations and Their Graphs

Student Support

Systems of Equations and Inequalities

Exponents and Exponential Functions

Polynomials and Factoring

Quadratic Equations and Functions

Chapter 11

Radical Expressions and Equations

Student Support

Rational Expressions and Functions

Student Support

Take It to the Net

Throughout this book you will find links to the Prentice Hall Web site for *Algebra 1*. Use the Web Code provided with each link to gain direct access to online material.

Here's how to **Take It to the Net:**
• Go to **PHSchool.com**.
• Enter the Web Code.
• Click Go!

For a complete list of online features, use Web Code aek-0099

Lesson Quiz Web Codes

There is an online quiz for each lesson. Access these quizzes with Web Codes aea-0101 through aea-1209 for Lesson 1-1 through Lesson 12-9. See page 8.

88 Lesson Quizzes
Web Code format: aea-0204
02 = Chapter 2   04 = Lesson 4

Chapter Resource Web Codes

Chapter	Vocabulary Quizzes See page 67.	Chapter Tests See page 70.	Dorling Kindersley Real-World Snapshots See pages 130–131.	Chapter Projects
1	aej-0151	aea-0152		aed-0161
2	aej-0251	aea-0252	aee-0253	aed-0261
3	aej-0351	aea-0352		aed-0361
4	aej-0451	aea-0452	aee-0453	aed-0461
5	aej-0551	aea-0552		aed-0561
6	aej-0651	aea-0652	aee-0653	aed-0661
7	aej-0751	aea-0752		aed-0761
8	aej-0851	aea-0852	aee-0853	aed-0861
9	aej-0951	aea-0952		aed-0961
10	aej-1051	aea-1052	aee-1053	aed-1061
11	aej-1151	aea-1152		aed-1161
12	aej-1251	aea-1252	aee-1253	aed-1261
End-of-Course		aea-1254		

Additional Resource Web Codes

Data Updates Use Web Code aeg-2041 to get up-to-date government data for use in examples and exercises. *See page 27.*

Algebra at Work For information about each Algebra at Work feature, use Web Code aeb-2031. *See page 94.*

A Point in Time For information about each A Point in Time feature, use Web Code aee-2032. *See page 53.*

Graphing Calculator Procedures There are 27 procedures available online. Use Web Code aee-2100 for an index of all the procedures, or Web Codes aee-2101 through aee-2127 to access individual procedures. *See page 45.*

Using Your Book for Success

Welcome to Prentice Hall *Algebra 1*. There are many features built into the daily lessons of this text that will help you learn the important skills and concepts you will need to be successful in this course. Look through the following pages for some study tips that you will find useful as you complete each lesson.

Instant Check System
An *Instant Check System*, built into the text and marked with a ✔, allows you to check your understanding of skills before moving on to the next topic.

✔ Diagnosing Readiness
Complete the *Diagnosing Readiness* exercises to see what topics you may need to review before you begin the chapter.

✔ Check Skills You'll Need
Complete the *Check Skills You'll Need* exercises to make sure you have the skills needed to successfully learn the concepts in the lesson.

New Vocabulary
New Vocabulary is listed for each lesson so you can pre-read the text. As each term is introduced, it is highlighted in yellow.

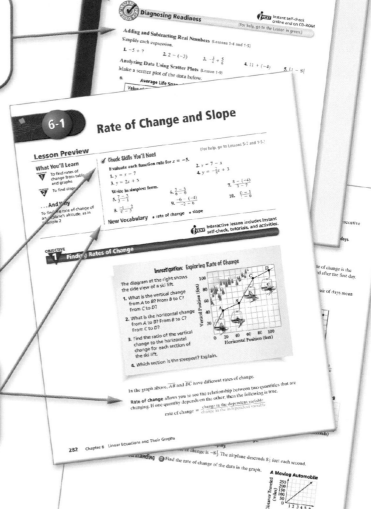

Need Help?

Need Help? notes provide a quick review of a concept you need to understand the topic being presented. Look for the green labels throughout the text that tell you where to "Go" for help.

Reading Math

The *Reading Math* hints help you to use mathematical notation correctly, understand new mathematical vocabulary, and translate mathematical symbols into everyday English so you can talk about what you've learned.

✓ Check Understanding

Every lesson includes numerous *Examples,* each followed by a *Check Understanding* question that you can do on your own to see if you understand the skill being introduced. Check your progress with the answers at the back of the book.

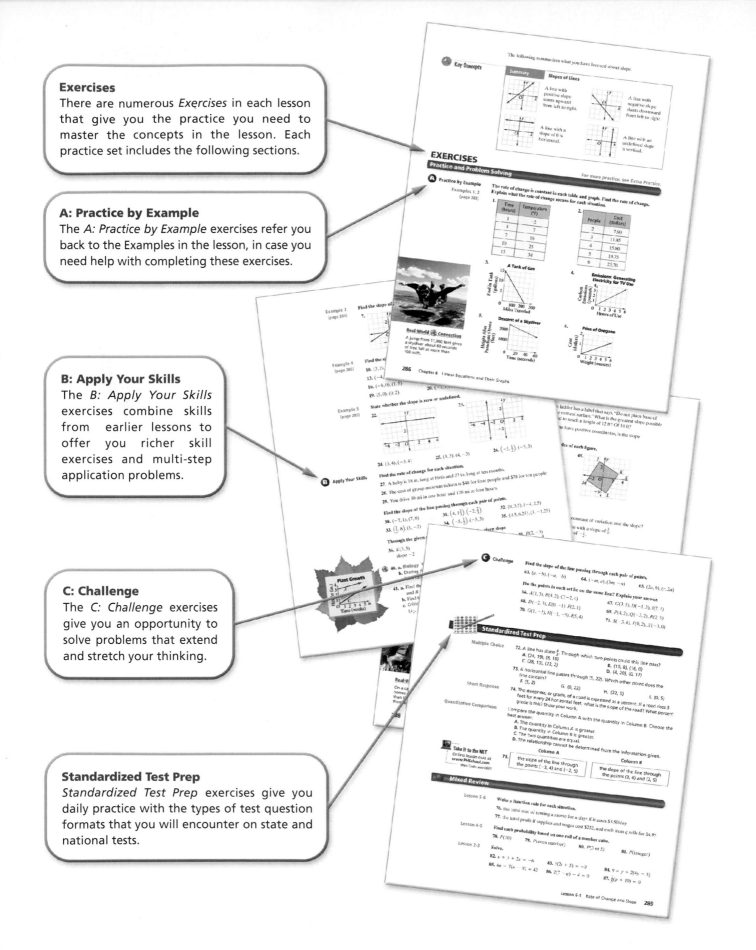

Exercises

There are numerous *Exercises* in each lesson that give you the practice you need to master the concepts in the lesson. Each practice set includes the following sections.

A: Practice by Example

The *A: Practice by Example* exercises refer you back to the Examples in the lesson, in case you need help with completing these exercises.

B: Apply Your Skills

The *B: Apply Your Skills* exercises combine skills from earlier lessons to offer you richer skill exercises and multi-step application problems.

C: Challenge

The *C: Challenge* exercises give you an opportunity to solve problems that extend and stretch your thinking.

Standardized Test Prep

Standardized Test Prep exercises give you daily practice with the types of test question formats that you will encounter on state and national tests.

Preparing for Tests

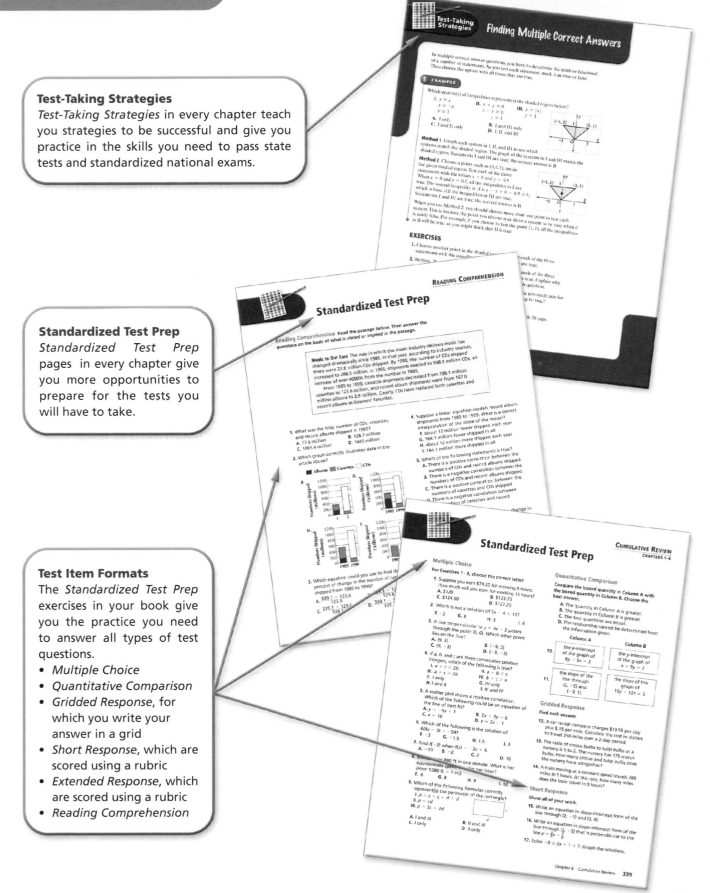

Test-Taking Strategies
Test-Taking Strategies in every chapter teach you strategies to be successful and give you practice in the skills you need to pass state tests and standardized national exams.

Standardized Test Prep
Standardized Test Prep pages in every chapter give you more opportunities to prepare for the tests you will have to take.

Test Item Formats
The *Standardized Test Prep* exercises in your book give you the practice you need to answer all types of test questions.
- *Multiple Choice*
- *Quantitative Comparison*
- *Gridded Response*, for which you write your answer in a grid
- *Short Response*, which are scored using a rubric
- *Extended Response*, which are scored using a rubric
- *Reading Comprehension*

Reading to Learn

In addition to the Reading Math hints shown on page xxi, your *Algebra 1* text provides even more ways for you to develop your ability to read mathematically so that you are successful in this course and on state tests.

Reading Math lessons
Reading Math lessons focus on a variety of topics to help you read more effectively, so that you can write, speak, and think mathematically.

Reading Math exercises
Reading Math exercises in the Chapter Review help you to understand and correctly use the vocabulary presented in the chapter.

English/Spanish Illustrated Glossary
While you are learning, use your *English/Spanish Illustrated Glossary* as a handy reference for all the vocabulary in the book. Not only is there a written explanation, but you will also find an illustrated example of each term to help you understand and remember.

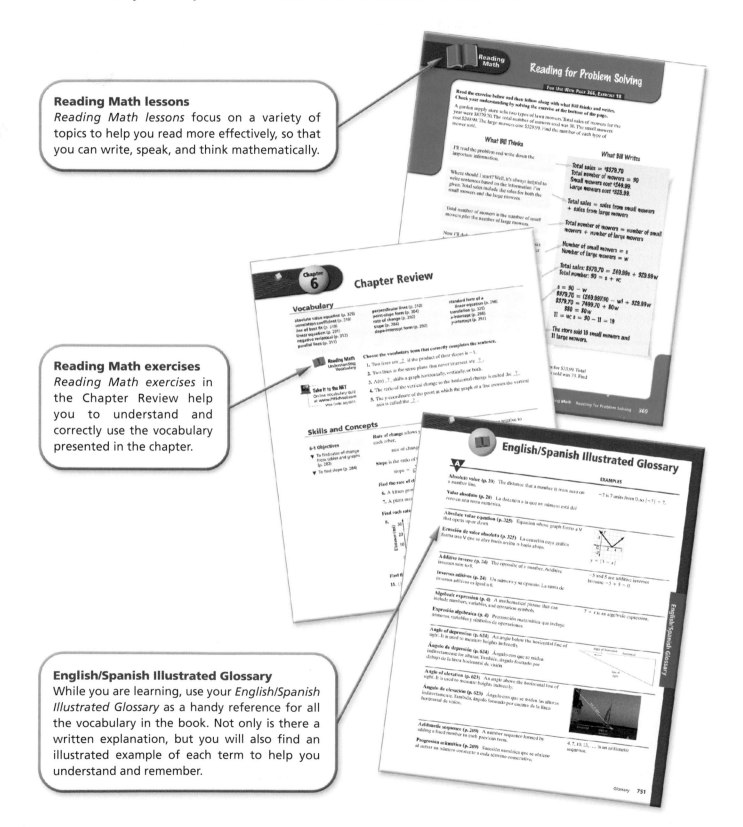

Real-World Snapshots

The *Real-World Snapshots* feature applies the exciting and unique graphic presentation style found in Dorling Kindersley books to show you how mathematics is used in real life.

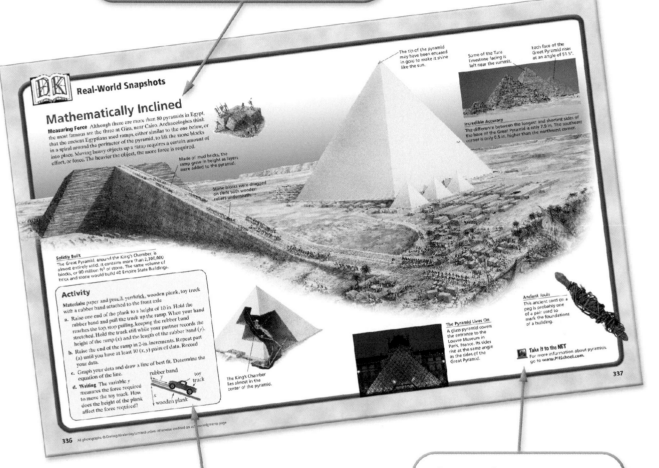

Activities

Using data from these pages and data that you gather, complete the hands-on *Activities* to apply the mathematics you are learning in real-world situations.

Take It to the Net

Take it to the Net for online information you can use to learn more about the topic of the feature.

Dorling Kindersley (DK) is an international publishing company that specializes in the creation of high-quality, illustrated information books for children and adults. DK is part of the Pearson family of companies.

Where You've Been

In previous courses, you learned

● to perform calculations involving addition, subtraction, multiplication, and division with whole numbers, fractions, and decimals

● to compare numerical expressions using inequality and equality symbols

● to read and interpret graphs

 **Diagnosing Readiness**

iTEXT Instant self-check online and on CD-ROM

(For help, go to the Skills Handbook.)

Simplifying Fractions (Skills Handbook page 724)

Write in simplest form.

1. $\frac{12}{15}$ 2. $\frac{20}{28}$ 3. $\frac{33}{77}$ 4. $\frac{8}{56}$ 5. $\frac{48}{52}$

Adding and Subtracting Fractions (Skills Handbook page 726)

Add or subtract. Write each answer in simplest form.

6. $\frac{1}{8} + \frac{1}{6}$ 7. $\frac{27}{33} - \frac{6}{22}$ 8. $\frac{3}{4} + \frac{7}{10}$ 9. $\frac{12}{13} - \frac{1}{3}$

10. $5\frac{7}{10} + 6\frac{7}{8}$ 11. $7\frac{5}{6} - 3\frac{1}{4}$ 12. $3\frac{5}{12} - 1\frac{7}{12}$ 13. $4\frac{5}{7} + 8\frac{3}{4}$

Exponents (Skills Handbook page 729)

Write using exponents.

14. $9 \cdot 9 \cdot 9 \cdot 9 \cdot 9$ 15. $8 \cdot 7 \cdot 7 \cdot 7 \cdot 7 \cdot 7 \cdot 7$ 16. $2 \cdot 2 \cdot 3 \cdot 3 \cdot 3 \cdot 3 \cdot 3 \cdot 3$

Analyzing Graphs (Skills Handbook page 738)

Use the graph at the right.

17. What was the approximate difference in the voting-age populations of Texas and of Florida in 1988?

18. Between 1992 and 1996 which state had the greater increase in voting-age population? Estimate that increase.

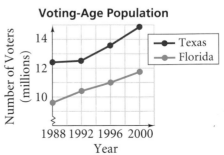

Voting-Age Population

Number of Voters (millions)

— Texas
— Florida

1988 1992 1996 2000
Year

Tools of Algebra

Key Vocabulary

- absolute value (p. 20)
- coefficient (p. 49)
- constant (p. 49)
- coordinates (p. 59)
- equation (p. 5)
- exponent (p. 9)
- integers (p. 17)
- like terms (p. 49)
- ordered pair (p. 59)
- order of operations (p. 10)
- origin (p. 59)
- rational number (p. 17)
- real numbers (p. 18)
- reciprocal (p. 41)
- variable (p. 4)

Where You're Going

- In this chapter, you will use variables to transform English phrases into mathematical expressions.

- You will extend your ability to calculate with whole numbers, decimals, and fractions to include integers.

- You will use the order of operations and the distributive property to simplify expressions.

- You will show the relationship between two sets of real-world data, using a scatter plot.

 Real-World Connection You will use addition of integers to find the height of a mountain that has a base below sea level, on page 26.

1-1

Using Variables

Lesson Preview

What You'll Learn

OBJECTIVE 1
To model relationships with variables

OBJECTIVE 2
To model relationships with equations and formulas

. . . And Why

To model the relationship between the number and the cost of CDs, as in Example 3

✓ Check Skills You'll Need

Write the operation (+, −, ×, ÷) that corresponds to each phrase.

1. divided by   2. difference   3. more than   4. product

5. minus   6. sum   7. multiplied by   8. quotient

Find each amount.

9. 12 more than 9   10. 8 less than 13   11. 16 divided by 4   12. twice 25

New Vocabulary
- variable
- algebraic expression
- equation
- open sentence

Interactive lesson includes instant self-check, tutorials, and activities.

OBJECTIVE 1

Modeling Relationships With Variables

Reading Math

Each expression below means 6.50 multiplied by h.

$6.50 \times h$

$6.50 \cdot h$

$6.50(h)$

$(6.50)h$

$6.50h$

$(6.50)(h)$

If you earn an hourly wage of $6.50, your pay is the number of hours you work multiplied by 6.5.

In the table at the right, the variable h stands for the number of hours you worked. A **variable** is a symbol, usually a letter, that represents one or more numbers. The expression $6.50h$ is an algebraic expression. An **algebraic expression** is a mathematical phrase that can include numbers, variables, and operation symbols. Algebraic expressions are sometimes called variable expressions.

Hours Worked	Pay (dollars)
1	6.50×1
2	6.50×2
3	6.50×3
h	$6.50 \times h$

1 EXAMPLE   Writing an Algebraic Expression

Write an algebraic expression for each phrase.

a. seven more than n

$n + 7$ **"More than"** indicates addition. Add the first number 7 to the second number n.

b. the difference of n and 7

$n - 7$ **"Difference"** indicates subtraction. Begin with the first number n. Then subtract the second number 7.

c. the product of seven and n

$7n$ **"Product"** indicates multiplication. Multiply the first number 7 by the second number n.

d. the quotient of n and seven

$\dfrac{n}{7}$ **"Quotient"** indicates division. Divide the first number n by the second number 7.

✓ **Check Understanding**   **1** Write an algebraic expression for each phrase.

a. the quotient of 4.2 and c **b.** t minus 15

To translate an English phrase into an algebraic expression, you may need to define one or more variables first.

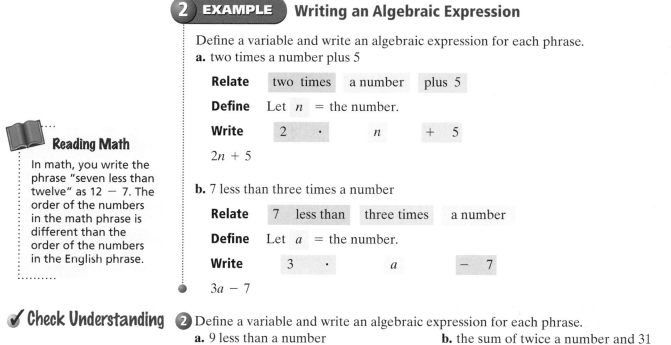

2 EXAMPLE Writing an Algebraic Expression

Define a variable and write an algebraic expression for each phrase.

a. two times a number plus 5

| **Relate** | two times | a number | plus 5 |

Define Let n = the number.

| **Write** | 2 | · | n | + | 5 |

$2n + 5$

b. 7 less than three times a number

| **Relate** | 7 | less than | three times | a number |

Define Let a = the number.

| **Write** | 3 | · | a | − | 7 |

$3a − 7$

✓ Check Understanding **2** Define a variable and write an algebraic expression for each phrase.
a. 9 less than a number
b. the sum of twice a number and 31
c. the product of one half of a number and one third of the same number

OBJECTIVE

2 Modeling Relationships With Equations and Formulas

Real-World Connection

More than 940 million CDs were sold in the United States in the year 2000.

You can use algebraic expressions to write an equation. An **equation** is a mathematical sentence that uses an equal sign. If the equation is true, then the two expressions on either side of the equal sign represent the same value. An equation that contains one or more variables is an **open sentence.** In everyday language, the word "is" often suggests an equal sign in the associated equation.

3 EXAMPLE Writing an Equation

Music Track One Media sells all CDs for $12 each. Write an equation for the total cost of a given number of CDs.

| **Relate** | The total cost | is | 12 times | the number of CDs bought. |

Define Let n = the number of CDs bought.

Let c = the total cost.

| **Write** | c | = | 12 | n |

$c = 12n$

✓ Check Understanding **3 a.** Suppose the manager at Track One Media raises the price of each CD to $15. Write an equation to find the cost of n CDs.
b. Critical Thinking Suppose the manager at Track One Media uses the equation $c = 10.99n$. What could this mean?

When you write an equation for data in a table, it may help to write a short sentence describing the relationship between the data. Then translate the sentence into an equation. Be sure to tell what each variable represents.

4 EXAMPLE **Real-World Problem Solving**

Sales Write an equation for the data in the table.

Relate   Change   equals $20.00   minus   cost of purchase.

Define   Let c = cost of item purchased.
         Let a = amount of change.

Write a =   20   − c

● $a = 20 - c$

Cost of Purchase	Change From $20
$20.00	$0
$19.00	$1.00
$17.50	$2.50
$11.59	$8.41

✓ **Check Understanding**   ④ Write an equation for the data in the chart.

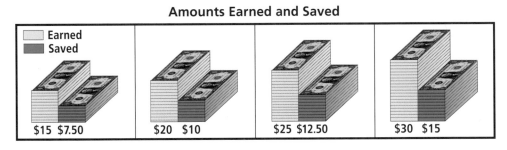

Amounts Earned and Saved

□ Earned
■ Saved

$15 $7.50 $20 $10 $25 $12.50 $30 $15

EXERCISES

For more practice, see *Extra Practice.*

Practice and Problem Solving

A Practice by Example

Example 1
(page 4)

Write an algebraic expression for each phrase.

1. 4 more than p **2.** y minus 12
3. 12 minus m **4.** the product of c and 15
5. the quotient of n and 8   **6.** the quotient of 17 and k
7. 23 less than x **8.** the sum of v and 3

Example 2
(page 5)

Define a variable and write an expression for each phrase.

9. 2 more than twice a number   **10.** a number minus 11
11. 9 minus a number   **12.** a number divided by 82
13. the product of 5 and a number   **14.** the sum of 13 and twice a number
15. the quotient of a number and 6 **16.** the quotient of 11 and a number

Example 3
(page 5)

Define variables and write an equation to model each situation.

17. The total cost is the number of cans times $.70.
18. The perimeter of a square equals 4 times the length of a side.
19. The total length of rope, in feet, used to put up tents is 60 times the number of tents.
20. What is the number of slices of pizza left from an 8-slice pizza after you have eaten some slices?

Example 4
(page 6)

Define variables and write an equation to model the relationship in each table.

21.

Number of Workers	Number of Radios Built
1	13
2	26
3	39
4	52

22.

Number of Tapes	Cost
1	$8.50
2	$17.00
3	$25.50
4	$34.00

23.

Number of Sales	Total Earnings
5	$2.00
10	$4.00
15	$6.00
20	$8.00

24.

Number of Hours	Total Pay
4	$32
6	$48
8	$64
10	$80

B **Apply Your Skills**

Write an expression for each phrase.

25. the sum of 9 and k minus 17

26. 6.7 more than 5 times n

27. 9.85 less than the product of t and 37

28. the quotient of $3b$ and 4.5

29. 15 plus the quotient of 60 and w

30. 7 minus the product of v and 3

31. the product of m and 5, minus the quotient of t and 7

32. the sum of the quotient of p and 14 and the quotient of q and 3

33. 8 minus the product of 9 and r

Write a phrase for each expression.

34. $q + 5$ **35.** $3 - t$ **36.** $9n + 1$ **37.** $\frac{y}{5}$ **38.** $7hb$

Define variables and write an equation to model the relationship in each table.

39.

Number of Days	Change in Height (meters)
1	0.165
2	0.330
3	0.495
4	0.660

40.

Time (months)	Length (inches)
1	4.1
2	8.2
3	12.3
4	16.4

41. Use the table at the right.
  a. Does each statement fit the data in the table? Explain.
    i. hours worked = lawns mowed · 2
    ii. hours worked = lawns mowed + 3
  b. Writing Which statement in part (a) better describes the relationship between hours worked and lawns mowed? Explain.

Lawns Mowed	Hours
1	
2	
3	6

42. a. Money Write an equation to show how the amount of money in a bag of quarters relates to the number of quarters in the bag.
  b. The bag contains 13 quarters. How much money is this?

Real-World Connection

In 1998, people in the United States spent more than $8.5 billion on lawn care.

C Challenge 🌐 Physics **The table at the left shows the height of the first bounce when a ball is dropped from different heights.**

43. **a.** Write an equation to describe the relationship between the height of the first bounce and the drop height.
   b. Suppose you drop the ball from a window 20 ft above the ground. Predict how high the ball will bounce.

44. Suppose the second bounce is $\frac{1}{4}$ of the original drop height. Write an equation to relate the height of the second bounce to the drop height.

Open-Ended Describe a real-world situation that each equation could represent. Include a definition for each variable.

45. $d = 5t$ 46. $a = b + 3$ 47. $c = \frac{40}{h}$

Drop Height (ft)	Height of First Bounce (ft)
1	$\frac{1}{2}$
2	1
3	$1\frac{1}{2}$
4	2
5	$2\frac{1}{2}$

Standardized Test Prep

Multiple Choice

48. Which is an algebraic expression for "six less than k"?
   A. $\frac{6}{k}$ **B.** $\frac{k}{6}$ **C.** $6 - k$ **D.** $k - 6$

49. Which is an algebraic expression for "the product of a and 10"?
   F. $a + 10$ **G.** $a - 10$ **H.** $10a$ **I.** $\frac{a}{10}$

50. Which is an algebraic expression for "9 more than v"?
   A. $v + 9$ **B.** $v - 9$ **C.** $9 - v$ **D.** $9v$

51. A container of milk contains 64 ounces. Which equation models the number n of ounces remaining after you have drunk m ounces?
   F. $m - 64 = n$ **G.** $64 - m = n$ **H.** $n - 64 = m$ **I.** $n - m = 64$

52. Which equation models the relationship in the table if r represents the row number and t represents the number of tulips?
   A. $r = 3t$ **B.** $\frac{r}{t} = 3$
   C. $t = r + 3$ **D.** $t = 3r$

Row Number	Number of Tulips
1	3
2	6
3	9
4	12

53. Which is an algebraic expression for "the quotient of $r + 5$ and b"?
   F. $\frac{r + 5}{b}$ **G.** $\frac{r}{b + 5}$ **H.** $\frac{b}{r + 5}$ **I.** $\frac{b}{r} + 5$

Take It to the NET
Online lesson quiz at
www.PHSchool.com
Web Code: aea-0101

Mixed Review

Pre-Course

Add, subtract, multiply, or divide.

54. $0.2 + 0.7$ 55. $0.13 + 0.91$ 56. $0.6 + 0.75$ 57. $1.09 + 0.37$

58. 0.9×0.7 59. $0.58 - 0.49$ 60. $0.8 - 0.66$ 61. $1.32 - 0.39$

62. 2×0.5 63. $0.69 \div 3$ 64. $0.6 \div 0.2$ 65. $1.21 \div 11$

66. List four prime numbers between 20 and 50.

1-2 Exponents and Order of Operations

Lesson Preview

What You'll Learn

OBJECTIVE 1 To simplify and evaluate expressions and formulas

OBJECTIVE 2 To simplify and evaluate expressions containing grouping symbols

. . . And Why

To find the total cost of sneakers including sales tax, as in Example 3

✓ Check Skills You'll Need

Find each product.

1. $4 \cdot 4$ **2.** $7 \cdot 7$ **3.** $5 \cdot 5$ **4.** $9 \cdot 9$

Perform the indicated operations.

5. $3 + 12 - 7$ **6.** $6 \cdot 1 \div 2$

7. $4 - 2 + 9$ **8.** $10 - 5 - 4$

9. $5 \cdot 5 + 7$ **10.** $30 \div 6 \cdot 2$

New Vocabulary
• simplify • exponent • base • power • order of operations • evaluate

---

OBJECTIVE 1

Simplifying and Evaluating Expressions and Formulas

TEXT Interactive lesson includes instant self-check, tutorials, and activities.

Problem Solving Hint
Drawing a diagram may help you understand the problem.

w [rectangle diagram] ℓ

Investigation: Order of Operations

⬛ **Geometry** Two formulas for the perimeter of a rectangle are $P = 2\ell + 2w$ and $P = 2(\ell + w)$.

1. The length ℓ of a rectangle is 8 in. and its width w is 3 in. Find the perimeter of the rectangle using each of the formulas.

2. When you used $P = 2\ell + 2w$, did you add first or multiply first?

3. When you used $P = 2(\ell + w)$, did you add first or multiply first?

4. Which formula do you prefer to use? Why?

To **simplify** a numerical expression, you replace it with its simplest name. The simplest name for $2 \cdot 8 + 2 \cdot 3$ and for $2(8 + 3)$ is 22.

Expressions may include exponents. Using an exponent provides a shorthand way to show a product of equal factors.

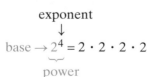

$$\text{base} \rightarrow 2^4 = 2 \cdot 2 \cdot 2 \cdot 2$$

An **exponent** tells how many times a number, the **base,** is used as a factor. A **power** has two parts, a base and an exponent.

You read the expression 2^4 as "two to the fourth power." To simplify 2^4, you replace it with its simplest name, 16. There are special names for 2^3, "two cubed," and 2^2, "two squared."

Look at the expression below. It is simplified in two ways.

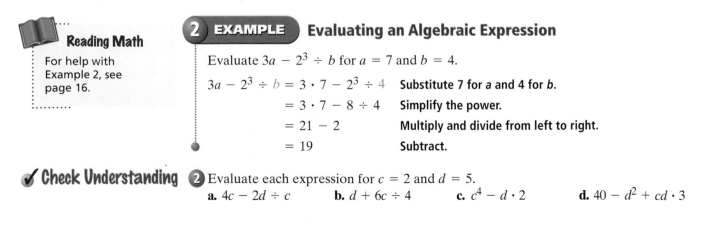

To avoid having two different results when simplifying the same expression, mathematicians have agreed on an order for doing operations.

 Key Concepts

Summary	Order of Operations

1. Perform any operation(s) inside grouping symbols.

2. Simplify powers.

3. Multiply and divide in order from left to right.

4. Add and subtract in order from left to right.

1 EXAMPLE Simplifying a Numerical Expression

Simplify $25 - 8 \cdot 2 + 3^2$.

$25 - 8 \cdot 2 + 3^2 = 25 - \underline{8 \cdot 2} + 9$ **Simplify the power:** $3^2 = 3 \cdot 3 = 9$.

$= \underline{25 - 16} + 9$ **Multiply 8 and 2.**

$= 9 + 9$ **Add and subtract in order from left to right.**

$= 18$ **Add.**

✓ Check Understanding **1** Simplify each expression.

a. $6 - 10 \div 5$ **b.** $3 \cdot 6 - 4^2 \div 2$ **c.** $4 \cdot 7 + 4 \div 2^2$ **d.** $5^3 + 90 \div 10$

You **evaluate** an algebraic expression by substituting a given number for each variable. Then simplify the numerical expression using the order of operations.

Reading Math

For help with Example 2, see page 16.

2 EXAMPLE Evaluating an Algebraic Expression

Evaluate $3a - 2^3 \div b$ for $a = 7$ and $b = 4$.

$3a - 2^3 \div b = 3 \cdot 7 - 2^3 \div 4$ **Substitute 7 for a and 4 for b.**

$= 3 \cdot 7 - 8 \div 4$ **Simplify the power.**

$= 21 - 2$ **Multiply and divide from left to right.**

$= 19$ **Subtract.**

✓ Check Understanding **2** Evaluate each expression for $c = 2$ and $d = 5$.

a. $4c - 2d \div c$ **b.** $d + 6c \div 4$ **c.** $c^4 - d \cdot 2$ **d.** $40 - d^2 + cd \cdot 3$

You can use expressions with variables to model many real-world situations.

3 EXAMPLE Real-World 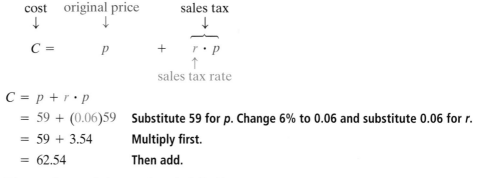 Problem Solving

Sales Find the total cost of the sneakers shown. Use the formula below.

$$\underset{\uparrow}{\text{cost}} \qquad \underset{\uparrow}{\text{original price}} \qquad \underset{\uparrow}{\text{sales tax}}$$

$$C = \qquad p \qquad + \qquad \overbrace{r \cdot p} \\ \underset{\uparrow}{\text{sales tax rate}}$$

$C = p + r \cdot p$

$\quad = 59 + (0.06)59$ **Substitute 59 for *p*. Change 6% to 0.06 and substitute 0.06 for *r*.**

$\quad = 59 + 3.54$ **Multiply first.**

$\quad = 62.54$ **Then add.**

The total cost of the sneakers is $62.54.

✓ **Check Understanding** ③ A shirt costs $24.95 plus sales tax of 5%. Find the total cost of the shirt.

OBJECTIVE

2 **Simplifying and Evaluating Expressions With Grouping Symbols**

When you simplify expressions with parentheses, work within the parentheses first. Inside parentheses, use the order of operations.

4 EXAMPLE Simplifying an Expression With Parentheses

Simplify $15(13 - 7) \div (8 - 5)$.

$15(13 - 7) \div (8 - 5) = 15(6) \div 3$ **Simplify within parentheses first.**

$\qquad\qquad\qquad\qquad\quad = 90 \div 3$ **Multiply and divide from left to right.**

$\qquad\qquad\qquad\qquad\quad = 30$ **Divide.**

✓ **Check Understanding** ④ Simplify each expression.

   a. $(5 + 3) \div 2 + (5^2 - 3)$ **b.** $8 \div (9 - 7) + (13 \div 2)$

The base for an exponent is the number, variable, or expression directly to the left of the exponent. For $(cd)^2$, cd is the base. For cd^2, d is the base. Grouping symbols show which part of the expression is the base of the power.

5 EXAMPLE Evaluating Expressions With Exponents

Evaluate each expression for $c = 15$ and $d = 12$.

a. $(cd)^2$ **b.** cd^2

$\quad (cd)^2 = (15 \cdot 12)^2$ ← **Substitute 15 for *c* and 12 for *d*.** → $cd^2 = 15 \cdot 12^2$

$\qquad\quad\; = (180)^2$ ← **Simplify within parentheses.** $= 15 \cdot 144$

$\qquad\quad\; = 32{,}400$ ← **Simplify.** → $= 2160$

✓ **Check Understanding** ⑤ Evaluate each expression for $r = 9$ and $t = 14$.

   a. rt^2 **b.** r^2t **c.** $(rt)^2$

You can also use brackets [ ] as grouping symbols. When an expression has several grouping symbols, simplify the innermost expression first.

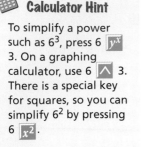
6 EXAMPLE Simplifying an Expression

Simplify $2[(13 - 7)^2 \div 3]$.

$$
\begin{aligned}
2[(13 - 7)^2 \div 3] &= 2[(6)^2 \div 3] &&\text{First simplify (13 − 7).} \\
&= 2[36 \div 3] &&\text{Simplify the power.} \\
&= 2[12] &&\text{Divide within the brackets.} \\
&= 24 &&\text{Multiply.}
\end{aligned}
$$

✓ **Check Understanding** ⑥ Simplify each expression.

    a. $5[4 + 3(2^2 + 1)]$ **b.** $12 + 3[18 - 5(16 - 13)]$ **c.** $5 + [(2 + 1)^3 - 3]$

A fraction bar is also a grouping symbol. For an expression like $\frac{2 + 8}{5 - 3}$, do the calculations above and below the fraction bar before simplifying the fraction.

7 EXAMPLE Real-World 🌐 Problem Solving

Urban Planning A neighborhood association turned a vacant lot into a park. The park is shaped like the trapezoid below. Use the formula $A = h\left(\dfrac{b_1 + b_2}{2}\right)$ to find the area of the lot.

$$
\begin{aligned}
A &= h\left(\frac{b_1 + b_2}{2}\right) \\[4pt]
&= 130\left(\frac{100 + 200}{2}\right) &&\text{Substitute 130 for } h, \\
& &&\text{100 for } b_1 \text{, and 200 for } b_2. \\[4pt]
&= 130\left(\frac{300}{2}\right) &&\text{Simplify the numerator.} \\[4pt]
&= 130(150) &&\text{Simplify the fraction.} \\[4pt]
&= 19{,}500 &&\text{Multiply.}
\end{aligned}
$$

$b_1 = 100$ ft

$h = 130$ ft

$b_2 = 200$ ft

The area of the park is 19,500 ft^2.

✓ **Check Understanding** ⑦ Find the area of a trapezoid with height $h = 300$ ft and bases $b_1 = 250$ ft and $b_2 = 170$ ft.

EXERCISES

For more practice, see *Extra Practice*.

Practice and Problem Solving

A Practice by Example

Simplify each expression.

Example 1
(page 10)

1. $5 + 6 \cdot 9$ **2.** $40 - 2 \cdot 3^2$ **3.** $8 + 12 \div 6 - 3$

4. $8 \cdot 4 + 9^2$ **5.** $5 \cdot 3^2 - 13$ **6.** $21 + 49 \div 7 + 1$

Example 2
(page 10)

Evaluate each expression for $a = 5$, $b = 12$, and $c = 2$.

7. $a + b + 2c$ **8.** $2b \div c + 3a$ **9.** $b^2 - 4a$

10. $ca + a$ **11.** $abc + ab$ **12.** $5a + 12b$

Example 3
(page 11)

Sales Use the formula $C = p + r \cdot p$ to find the total cost of each purchase, where C is the total cost, p is the price, and r is the sales tax rate written as a decimal.

13. A coat costs $34.99. The sales tax is 6%.

14. A camcorder costs $329. The sales tax is 5.5%.

Example 4
(page 11)

Simplify each expression.

15. $2(5 + 9) - 6$ **16.** $(17 - 7) \div 5 + 1$ **17.** $(2 + 9) \cdot (8 - 4)$

18. $(7^2 - 3^2) \div 8$ **19.** $17 - 5^2 \div (2^4 + 3^2)$ **20.** $(10^2 - 4 \cdot 8) \div (8 + 9)$

Example 5
(page 11)

Evaluate each expression for $s = 11$ and $v = 8$.

21. sv^2 **22.** $(sv)^2$ **23.** $s^2 + v^2$ **24.** $(s + v)^2$

25. $s^2 - v^2$ **26.** $(s - v)^2$ **27.** $2s^2v$ **28.** $(2s)^2v$

Example 6
(page 12)

Simplify each expression.

29. $6[13 - 2(4 + 1)]$ **30.** $[3(7 + 4) - 2]6$ **31.** $20 - [4(3 + 2)]$

32. $1^{11} + 3\left[\left(\frac{22}{11} + 8\right) \div 5\right]$ **33.** $27[5^2 \div (4^2 + 3^2) + 2]$ **34.** $9 + [4 - (10 - 9)^2]^3$

Example 7
(page 12)

Evaluate the formula $V = \frac{Bh}{3}$ for each pair of values.

35. $B = 4 \text{ cm}^2, h = 6 \text{ cm}$ **36.** $B = 21 \text{ in.}^2, h = 13 \text{ in.}$

37. $B = 7 \text{ ft}^2, h = 9 \text{ ft}$ **38.** $B = 8.4 \text{ cm}^2, h = 10 \text{ cm}$

39. $B = 500 \text{ ft}^2, h = 90 \text{ ft}$ **40.** $B = 118 \text{ m}^2, h = 66 \text{ m}$

B Apply Your Skills

Simplify each expression.

41. $(2 + 3)^2 - 10$ **42.** $2^3 + 3^2 - 10$ **43.** $(2^3 + 3)^2 - 10$

44. $(2^3 + 3^2) - 16$ **45.** $3 + 6 \cdot 8$ **46.** $(5.2 - 1) \cdot 12$

47. $3 \cdot 9^2 - 1$ **48.** $5 + (24 \div 3) \cdot 7^1$ **49.** $(9.8 \cdot 2) + 6.5 \cdot 8$

50. $4\frac{1}{3} + 6 \cdot 9$ **51.** $\frac{8^2 - 4}{72}$ **52.** $28 \div [(19 - 7) \div 3]$

53. $1 + 2(3 + 4) \div (5 \cdot 6)$ **54.** $4^3 \div 8 - 1 + 5 \div 8$

55. A student wrote that $(a + b)^2 = a^2 + b^2$.
   a. Evaluate each side of the equation for $a = 0$ and $b = 1$.
   b. Evaluate each side of the equation for $a = 1$ and $b = 1$.
   c. Open-Ended Choose another pair of values for a and b. Evaluate each side of the equation for those values.
   d. Writing An equation is true if each side of the equation simplifies to the same value or expression. Is the equation $(a + b)^2 = a^2 + b^2$ true? Explain.

Evaluate each expression for $m = 3, p = 7,$ and $q = 4$.

56. $mp - q$ **57.** $m(p - q)$ **58.** $mp^2 - q$ **59.** $m(p^2 - q)$

60. $(mp^2) - q$ **61.** $m(p - q)^2$ **62.** $m \div q + 2p$ **63.** $qp^2 + pq^2$

—2 in.

—2 in.

64. a. Framing The frame at the left is 2 in. wide. The outer height h is 17.5 in., and the outer width w is 14 in. Use the formula $A = (h - 4)(w - 4)$ to find the area of the picture.
   b. Critical Thinking Why is 4 subtracted from the height and from the width in the formula in part (a)?

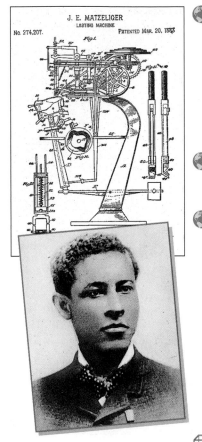

65. History In 1883, Jan Matzeliger invented the shoe-lasting machine to attach the upper part of a shoe to its sole. Before that, each shoe was assembled and sewn by hand. You can estimate the wages at that time using the formula $w = 0.34\frac{p}{t}$, where w is the hourly wage in dollars, p is the price of a pair of shoes in dollars, and t is the time in minutes to assemble a pair of shoes.

In 1891, a worker who used the shoe-lasting machine could assemble one pair of shoes in two minutes. A pair of shoes cost about $.94. Estimate the worker's hourly wage to the nearest cent.

66. Sports The formula for the volume of a sphere with radius r is $V = \frac{4\pi r^3}{3}$. Find the volume of a croquet ball that has radius 4.6 cm. Round your answer to the nearest hundredth.

67. a. Food Use the formula for the volume of a sphere in Exercise 66. Find the volume of a seedless orange with radius 5 cm.
   b. Suppose the peel of the orange is 0.5 cm thick. What volume of the orange is edible?
   c. Express the edible part of the orange as a percent of the whole orange. Round your answer to the nearest percent.

Evaluate each expression.

68. $(5h^2 - 4) - h$, for $h = 3$

69. $[(5.2 + a) + 4]10$, for $a = 3.5$

70. $\frac{p + 4q}{3}$, for $p = 7$ and $q = 5$

71. $[x \div (y + 1)]y$, for $x = 12$ and $y = 5$

72. $h + (34 - g^2) \div g$, for $h = 2$ and $g = 3$

73. a. Geometry The formula for the volume of a cylinder is $V = \pi r^2 h$. What is the volume of the cylinder below? Round your answer to the nearest hundredth of a cubic inch.

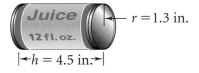

$r = 1.3$ in.

$h = 4.5$ in.

   b. Critical Thinking About how many cubic inches does an ounce of juice fill? Round your answer to the nearest tenth of a cubic inch.
   c. The formula for the surface area of a cylinder is $SA = 2\pi r(r + h)$. What is the surface area of the cylinder? Round your answer to the nearest hundredth of a square inch.

74. Writing Suppose you have a numerical expression. Is there only one number that is the simplest form of the expression? Explain.

C Challenge   **Use grouping symbols to make each equation true.**

75. $10 + 6 \div 2 - 3 = 5$

76. $14 - 2 + 5 - 3 = 4$

77. $3^2 + 9 \div 9 = 2$

78. $6 - 4 \div 2 = 1$

79. a. Simplify $12 + (3 + 7)$ and $(12 + 3) + 7$.
   b. Does it seem that the placement of the parentheses affects the value of an expression when only addition is involved? Explain.

80. a. Simplify $(12 - 3) + 7$ and $12 - (3 + 7)$.
   b. Does it seem that the placement of the parentheses affects the value of the expression when both addition and subtraction are involved? Explain.

81. Open-Ended Use the numbers 1, 2, 4, and 5 in any order to write expressions to equal each integer from 1 to 20. Examples:

$$(2 \cdot 4) + 1^5 = 9 \qquad 4(5 - 2) + 1 = 13$$

82. a. Geometry A trapezoid has height $h = 8$ ft, and bases $b_1 = 4$ ft and $b_2 = 5.5$ ft. Use the formula $A = h\left(\dfrac{b_1 + b_2}{2}\right)$ to find the area of the trapezoid.

b. Critical Thinking Does the area of the trapezoid double if the height doubles? If one base doubles? If both bases double? Explain your answers.

Multiple Choice

83. Simplify $5^3 - 15 \div 2 + 2$.
A. 2   B. 57   C. 112   D. 119.5

84. Simplify $8(5 - 3)^3 + 9$.
F. 73   G. 57   H. 40   I. 22

85. Evaluate $2ab + c$ for $a = 3.3$, $b = 4.5$ and $c = 2$.
A. 18.4   B. 31.7   C. 32.8   D. 41.6

86. Evaluate $(r - s)^2$ for $r = 9$ and $s = 6.5$.
F. 2.5   G. 3.5   H. 6.25   I. 12.25

87. A shirt is on sale for $25 at the local department store. There is also a 4% sales tax. What is the total cost of the shirt, including the sales tax?
A. $25   B. $26   C. $29   D. $35

88. You can find the distance d an object falls in feet for time t in seconds using the formula $d = 16t^2$. Suppose a ball is dropped out of a window of a tall building. How far will the ball fall in 3 seconds?
F. 144 ft   G. 96 ft   H. 48 ft   I. 16 ft

Take It to the NET
Online lesson quiz at
www.PHSchool.com
Web Code: aea-0102

Mixed Review

Lesson 1-1

Write an expression for each phrase.

89. 2 more than c

90. the product of m and 36

91. the difference of t and 21

92. the quotient of y and 5

Pre-Course

Write each decimal as a percent.

93. 0.5   **94.** 0.34   **95.** 0.95   **96.** 1.45   **97.** 0.06

Find each percent.

98. What is 50% of 86?

99. What is 18% of 105?

100. What is 0.5% of 250?

101. What is 67% of 90?

Open-Ended **Write three multiples of each number.**

102. 8   **103.** 5   **104.** 11   **105.** 30   **106.** 13

The description below explains how to read an example. Follow each step carefully. Then do the exercise at the bottom of the page to check your understanding.

Above an example there is usually a paragraph that will help you understand what the example is teaching. On page 10, the paragraph above Example 2 tells you that to evaluate an algebraic expression, you do the following:

- Substitute a given number for each variable and
- Simplify the numerical expression using the order of operations.

Examples show you how to use the concepts taught in each lesson. In an example, the steps are on the left and the explanations are in **bold** on the right. As you read an example, make sure you understand each step and its explanation. Checking the math in an example as you read it is one way to help you make sure you understand the concepts being taught.

EXAMPLE **Evaluating an Algebraic Expression**

Evaluate $3a - 2^3 \div b$ for $a = 7$ and $b = 4$.

Read the problem and locate the variables.

$3a - 2^3 \div b = 3 \cdot 7 - 2^3 \div 4$ **Substitute 7 for a and 4 for b.**

The text in **bold** explains what is being done. Each variable is shown in color to help you see the substitution.

$= 3 \cdot 7 - 8 \div 4$ **Simplify the power.**

To evaluate the expression, locate the power in the previous step. Check that it was simplified correctly by making sure that 2^3 is 8.

$= 21 - 2$ **Multiply and divide from left to right.**

Check that $(3 \cdot 7)$ and $(8 \div 4)$ were simplified correctly.

$= 19$ **Subtract.**

Check that $21 - 2$ was simplified correctly.

EXERCISE

After every example, you will see this heading. The problems in this section help you check how well you understand the concepts and techniques illustrated in the example. Try the one on page 10 under Example 2, which is shown below.

Evaluate each expression for $c = 2$ and $d = 5$.

a. $4c - 2d \div c$ **b.** $d + 6c \div 4$ **c.** $c^4 - d \cdot 2$ **d.** $40 - d^2 + cd \cdot 3$

1-3

Exploring Real Numbers

Lesson Preview

What You'll Learn

OBJECTIVE 1 To classify numbers

OBJECTIVE 2 To compare numbers

...And Why

To determine which sets of numbers are appropriate for real-world situations, as in Example 2

✓ Check Skills You'll Need

(For help, go to Skills Handbook page 725.)

Write each decimal as a fraction and each fraction as a decimal.

1. 0.5   **2.** 0.05   **3.** 3.25   **4.** 0.325

5. $\frac{2}{5}$ **6.** $\frac{3}{8}$ **7.** $\frac{2}{3}$ **8.** $3\frac{5}{9}$

New Vocabulary

- natural numbers
- whole numbers
- integers
- rational number
- irrational number
- real numbers
- counterexample
- inequality
- opposites
- absolute value

OBJECTIVE 1

Classifying Numbers

*i*TEXT **Interactive lesson includes instant self-check, tutorials, and activities.**

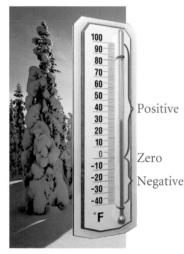

The thermometer shows positive numbers, zero, and negative numbers.

Each of the graphs below shows a set of numbers on a number line. The number below a point is its coordinate on the number line.

Natural numbers   1, 2, 3, . . .

Whole numbers   0, 1, 2, 3, . . .

Integers   . . . −2, −1, 0, 1, 2, . . .

As you can see, the set of integers has negative numbers as well as zero and positive numbers. There are also numbers that are not integers, such as 0.37 or $\frac{1}{2}$, which are rational numbers. A **rational number** is any number that you can write in the form $\frac{a}{b}$, where a and b are integers and $b \neq 0$. A rational number in decimal form is either terminating, such as 6.27, or repeating, such as 8.222 . . . , which you can write as $8.\overline{2}$.

All integers are rational numbers because you can write any integer n as $\frac{n}{1}$.

1 EXAMPLE   Classifying Numbers

Name the set(s) of numbers to which each number belongs.

a. $-\frac{17}{31}$ rational numbers

b. 23   natural numbers, whole numbers, integers, rational numbers $\left(\frac{23}{1}\right)$

c. 0   whole numbers, integers, rational numbers $\left(\frac{0}{1}\right)$

d. 4.581   rational numbers $\left(\frac{4581}{1000}\right)$

✓ Check Understanding

1 Name the set(s) of numbers to which each number belongs.

a. −12   **b.** $\frac{5}{12}$ **c.** −4.67   **d.** 6

You may need to determine the set of numbers that is reasonable for a given situation. For example, suppose 110 students are going on a field trip. Each bus can hold 40 students. To find the number of buses needed, divide 110 by 40. The answer is a rational number, 2.75. However, it is not the number of buses you would need. You would need a whole number of buses, or 3 buses.

2 EXAMPLE __Real-World__ 🌐 __Problem Solving__

Which set of numbers is most reasonable for each situation?

a. the number of students who will go on the class trip   whole numbers

b. the height of the door frame in your classroom   rational numbers

✓ **Check Understanding** **2** Which set of numbers is most reasonable for the cost of a scooter?

📖 **Reading Math**

π represents the ratio $\frac{\text{circumference}}{\text{diameter}}$ of a circle. This is not a rational number because either the circumference or the diameter is not rational.

An **irrational number** cannot be expressed in the form $\frac{a}{b}$, where a and b are integers. Here are three irrational numbers.

$$0.101001000\ldots \qquad \pi \qquad \sqrt{10}$$

Decimal representations of each of these are nonrepeating and nonterminating.

Together, rational numbers and irrational numbers form the set of **real numbers.**

The Venn diagram below shows the relationships of the sets of numbers that make up the real numbers.

🔑 **Key Concepts**

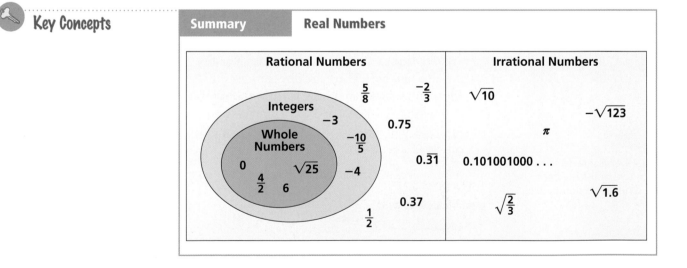

Suppose a friend says that all integers are whole numbers. You respond that -3 is an integer but not a whole number. You are using a counterexample to prove that a statement is false.

Any example that proves a statement false is a **counterexample.** You need only one counterexample to prove that a statement is false, while a proof to show that a statement is true may be more complicated.

Is each statement *true* or *false*? If it is false, give a counterexample.

a. All whole numbers are rational numbers.
Every whole number can be written in the form $\frac{n}{1}$, so all whole numbers are rational numbers. The statement is true.

b. The square of a number is always greater than the number.
The square of 0.5 is 0.25, and 0.25 is *not* greater than 0.5. The statement is false.

✓ **Check Understanding** **3** Critical Thinking Is each statement true or false? If it is false, give a counterexample.
  a. All whole numbers are integers.   **b.** No fractions are whole numbers.

OBJECTIVE

2 Comparing Numbers

An **inequality** is a mathematical sentence that compares the value of two expressions using an inequality symbol, such as < or >.

When you compare two real numbers, only one of these can be true:

$a < b$	or	$a = b$	or	$a > b$
is less than		**is equal to**		**is greater than**

There are three other symbols that compare two values.

$a \leq b$	or	$a \neq b$	or	$a \geq b$
is less than or equal to		**is not equal to**		**is greater than or equal to**

Reading Math

You can read the inequality 3 < 5 from right to left as "5 is greater than 3." Thus 3 < 5 and 5 > 3 are identical in meaning.

The number line below shows how values of numbers increase as you go to the right on a number line.

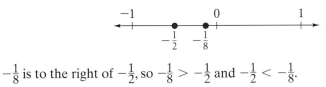

$-\frac{1}{8}$ is to the right of $-\frac{1}{2}$, so $-\frac{1}{8} > -\frac{1}{2}$ and $-\frac{1}{2} < -\frac{1}{8}$.

To compare fractions, you may find it helpful to write the fractions as decimals and then compare the decimals.

4 EXAMPLE Ordering Fractions

Write $-\frac{3}{8}$, $-\frac{1}{2}$, and $-\frac{5}{12}$ in order from least to greatest.

$-\frac{3}{8} = -0.375$ **Write each fraction as a decimal.**

$-\frac{1}{2} = -0.5$

$-\frac{5}{12} = -0.4166\ldots = -0.41\overline{6}$

$-0.5 < -0.41\overline{6} < -0.375$ **Order the decimals from least to greatest.**

From least to greatest, the fractions are $-\frac{1}{2}$, $-\frac{5}{12}$, and $-\frac{3}{8}$.

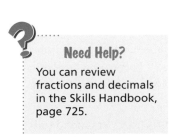

Need Help?

You can review fractions and decimals in the Skills Handbook, page 725.

✓ **Check Understanding** **4** Write $\frac{1}{12}$, $-\frac{2}{3}$, and $-\frac{5}{8}$ in order from least to greatest.

Two numbers that are the same distance from zero on a number line but lie in opposite directions are **opposites**.

3 units   3 units

−4 −3 −2 −1 0 1 2 3 4

−3 and 3 are the same distance from 0.
So −3 and 3 are opposites.

The **absolute value** of a number is its distance from 0 on a number line. Both −3 and 3 are 3 units from zero. Both have an absolute value of 3. You write "the absolute value of −3" as $|-3|$.

5 EXAMPLE Finding Absolute Value

Find each absolute value.

a. $|12|$ 12 is 12 units from 0 on a number line. $|12| = 12$

b. $\left|-\frac{2}{3}\right|$ $-\frac{2}{3}$ is $\frac{2}{3}$ units from 0 on a number line. $\left|-\frac{2}{3}\right| = \frac{2}{3}$

c. $|0|$ 0 is at 0 on a number line. $|0| = 0$

✓ **Check Understanding** ⑤ Find each absolute value.

a. $|5|$ b. $|-4|$ c. $|-3.7|$ d. $\left|\frac{5}{7}\right|$

EXERCISES

For more practice, see *Extra Practice*.

Practice and Problem Solving

A **Practice by Example**

Example 1
(page 17)

Name the set(s) of numbers to which each number belongs.

1. -1 2. $\frac{1}{3}$ 3. -4.8 4. 7 5. $-\frac{32}{95}$

6. $-\frac{20}{4}$ 7. 0 8. -7.34 9. $\frac{7}{1239}$ 10. $\sqrt{5}$

Open-Ended Give an example of each kind of number.

11. negative integer   12. whole number   13. positive real number

Example 2
(page 18)

Are *whole numbers, integers,* or *rational numbers* the most reasonable for each situation?

14. your shoe size

15. the number of siblings you have

16. a temperature in a news report

17. the number of quarts of paint you need to buy to paint a room

18. the number of quarts of paint you use when you paint a room

Example 3
(page 19)

Is each statement *true* or *false*? If the statement is false, give a counterexample.

19. All integers are rational numbers.

20. All negative numbers are integers.

21. Every multiple of 3 is odd.

22. No positive number is less than its absolute value.

23. No negative number is less than its absolute value.

Example 4
(page 19)

Use <, =, or > to compare.

24. $\frac{2}{3}$ ■ $\frac{1}{6}$ **25.** $-\frac{2}{3}$ ■ $-\frac{1}{6}$ **26.** $\frac{15}{8}$ ■ $1\frac{6}{8}$ **27.** $\frac{3}{5}$ ■ 0.6

Order the numbers in each group from least to greatest.

28. $2.01, 2.1, 2.001$ **29.** $-9\frac{2}{3}, -9\frac{7}{12}, -9\frac{3}{4}$ **30.** $-\frac{5}{6}, -\frac{1}{2}, \frac{2}{3}$

31. $-1.01, -1.001, -1.0009$ **32.** $\frac{7}{11}, 0.63, 0.636$ **33.** $\frac{22}{25}, \frac{8}{9}, 0.8888$

Example 5
(page 20)

Find each absolute value.

34. $|4|$ **35.** $|-9|$ **36.** $\left|\frac{-9}{14}\right|$ **37.** $|-0.5|$

38. $\left|\frac{3}{5}\right|$ **39.** $|0|$ **40.** $|-1295|$ **41.** $\left|-\frac{4}{5}\right|$

B Apply Your Skills

**Write each number in the form $\frac{a}{b}$ using integers to show that it is a
rational number.**

42. 0.2 **43.** 5 **44.** 21.3 **45.** 1.034 **46.** -4

Name the set(s) of numbers to which each number belongs.

47. $\left|\frac{93}{3}\right|$ **48.** $|-782|$ **49.** $|-1.93|$ **50.** $\left|\frac{37}{59}\right|$

Use <, =, or > to compare.

51. $|19|$ ■ $|-19|$ **52.** $|-18|$ ■ $|-17|$ **53.** $\left|\frac{1}{2}\right|$ ■ $|-0.51|$

54. $|-3.121|$ ■ $|3.12|$ **55.** $\left|\frac{-8}{10}\right|$ ■ $\left|\frac{-16}{20}\right|$ **56.** $\left|\frac{1}{3}\right|$ ■ $|-0.333|$

Simplify each expression. (Hint: Absolute value symbols are grouping symbols.)

57. $4 + |3 - 1|$ **58.** $|41 - 38| + 6$ **59.** $|a - a| + a$

60. $|24| + |-4|$ **61.** $|12| \cdot |-4|$ **62.** $|-6 + 4| + |3|$

63. a. Math in the Media In the cartoon below, what type of number is pi (π)?
   b. Will the football ever be hiked? Explain.

Real-World Connection

Careers Cartoonists may
draw syndicated cartoons,
such as the one at the
right, that appear daily
in newspapers.

FoxTrot   by Bill Amend

Critical Thinking Use the number
line for Exercises 64–66.

64. If the coordinates of P and T are opposites, what is the coordinate of S?

65. If the coordinates of Q and T are opposites, is R positive or negative? Explain.

66. Reasoning If the coordinates of R and T are opposites, which point has the
   coordinate with the greatest absolute value? Explain.

67. Open-Ended Choose a real number. Find the sum of the absolute value of the number and the absolute value of its opposite.

Determine whether each statement is *sometimes*, *always*, or *never* true.

Problem Solving Hint
Test each statement using a variety of numbers.

68. The difference of two rational numbers is an integer.

69. The product of two numbers is greater than either number.

70. The opposite of a number is less than the number.

71. The quotient of two nonzero integers is a rational number.

72. Writing Are natural numbers, whole numbers, and integers also rational numbers? Explain.

C **Challenge** **Evaluate each expression for $c = 5$, $d = 1$, and $e = 6$.**

73. $-|c + d|$ **74.** $2e + \left|\frac{c}{d}\right|$ **75.** $\frac{|e - d|}{c}$ **76.** $|d + 2| + |-7|$

77. a. Science Use the formula $d = \frac{m}{v}$ to find the density d of each substance in the table below.

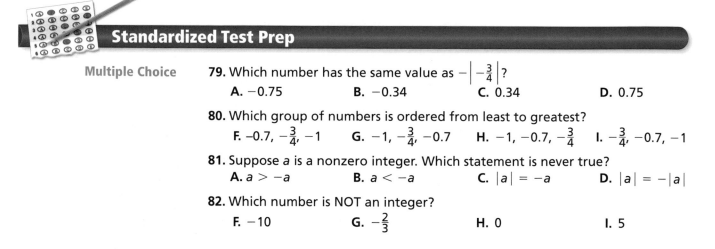

Densities of Some Substances

	Mass (*m*)	Volume (*v*)	Density (*d*)
Aluminum	38.5 g	14 cm³	■
Gold	38.6 g	2 cm³	■
Silver	42 g	4 cm³	■
Diamond	1.75 g	0.5 cm³	■

b. List the substances from least to greatest density.

78. a. Open-Ended Find a number between -2 and -3 on a number line.
   b. Find a number between -2.8 and -2.9.
   c. Find a number between $-2\frac{1}{16}$ and $-2\frac{3}{8}$.
   d. Make a Conjecture On a number line, is it possible to find a number between any two different given numbers? Explain.

Standardized Test Prep

Multiple Choice

79. Which number has the same value as $-\left|-\frac{3}{4}\right|$?
   A. -0.75 **B.** -0.34 **C.** 0.34 **D.** 0.75

80. Which group of numbers is ordered from least to greatest?
   F. $-0.7, -\frac{3}{4}, -1$ **G.** $-1, -\frac{3}{4}, -0.7$ **H.** $-1, -0.7, -\frac{3}{4}$ **I.** $-\frac{3}{4}, -0.7, -1$

81. Suppose a is a nonzero integer. Which statement is never true?
   A. $a > -a$ **B.** $a < -a$ **C.** $|a| = -a$ **D.** $|a| = -|a|$

82. Which number is NOT an integer?
   F. -10 **G.** $-\frac{2}{3}$ **H.** 0 **I.** 5

83. Use the double bar graph below. In which year was there the least difference between the numbers of metal workers and of textile workers?

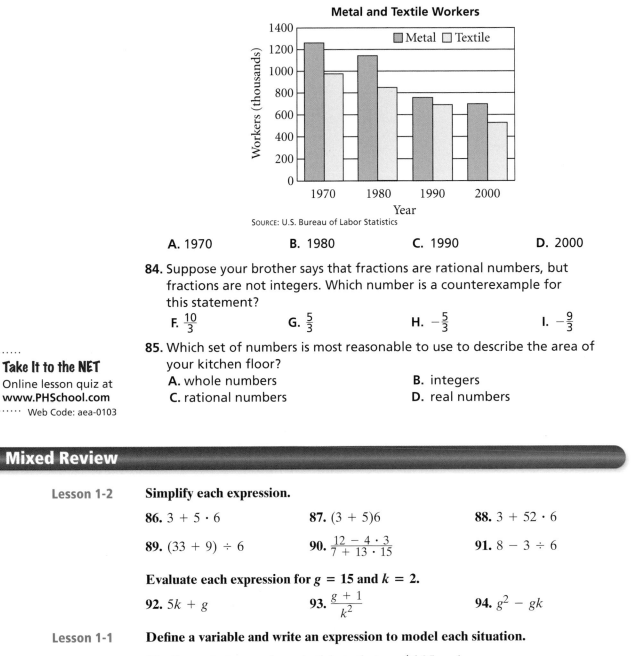

Metal and Textile Workers

SOURCE: U.S. Bureau of Labor Statistics

A. 1970   **B.** 1980   **C.** 1990   **D.** 2000

84. Suppose your brother says that fractions are rational numbers, but fractions are not integers. Which number is a counterexample for this statement?

F. $\frac{10}{3}$ **G.** $\frac{5}{3}$ **H.** $-\frac{5}{3}$ **I.** $-\frac{9}{3}$

85. Which set of numbers is most reasonable to use to describe the area of your kitchen floor?
A. whole numbers   **B.** integers
C. rational numbers   **D.** real numbers

Take It to the NET
Online lesson quiz at
www.PHSchool.com
Web Code: aea-0103

Mixed Review

Lesson 1-2

Simplify each expression.

86. $3 + 5 \cdot 6$ **87.** $(3 + 5)6$ **88.** $3 + 5^2 \cdot 6$

89. $(33 + 9) \div 6$ **90.** $\frac{12 - 4 \cdot 3}{7 + 13 \cdot 15}$ **91.** $8 - 3 \div 6$

Evaluate each expression for $g = 15$ and $k = 2$.

92. $5k + g$ **93.** $\frac{g + 1}{k^2}$ **94.** $g^2 - gk$

Lesson 1-1

Define a variable and write an expression to model each situation.

95. the cost of several movie tickets that are $6.25 each

96. the total cost of an item with a shipping fee of $3.98

Define variables and write an equation to model the relationship in each table.

97.

Number of Hours	Distance Traveled
1	7 mi
2	14 mi
3	21 mi
4	28 mi

98.

Number of Books	Total Cost
1	$3.50
2	$7.00
3	$10.50
4	$14.00

Adding Real Numbers

Lesson Preview

What You'll Learn

OBJECTIVE 1 To add real numbers using models and rules

OBJECTIVE 2 To apply addition

...And Why

To use integers to represent yards gained and lost in a football game, as in Example 3

✓ Check Skills You'll Need

(For help, go to the Skills Handbook page 726.)

Find each sum.

1. $4 + 2$
2. $10 + 7$
3. $9 + 5$
4. $27 + 32$
5. $0.4 + 0.9$
6. $5.2 + 0$
7. $4.1 + 6.8$
8. $7.6 + 9.5$
9. $\frac{1}{5} + \frac{3}{5}$
10. $\frac{4}{9} + \frac{7}{9}$
11. $\frac{1}{2} + \frac{3}{4}$
12. $\frac{3}{8} + \frac{1}{4}$

New Vocabulary • Identity Property of Addition • additive inverse • Inverse Property of Addition • matrix • element

---

iTEXT Interactive lesson includes instant self-check, tutorials, and activities.

OBJECTIVE

1 Adding Real Numbers

In previous math courses, you learned that the sum of a number and 0 is the original number. This is true for any number, whether it is positive or negative.

 Key Concepts

Property	Identity Property of Addition
For every real number n, $n + 0 = n$.	
Examples $\quad 0 + 5 = 5 \qquad -5 + 0 = -5$	

The opposite of a number is its **additive inverse.** The number line shows the sum of $4 + (-4)$.

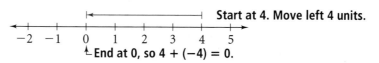

Start at 4. Move left 4 units.

End at 0, so $4 + (-4) = 0$.

The additive inverse of a negative number is a positive number. The number line below shows the sum of $-5 + 5$.

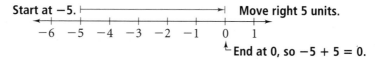

Start at -5.   Move right 5 units.

End at 0, so $-5 + 5 = 0$.

Key Concepts

Property	Inverse Property of Addition
For every real number n, there is an additive inverse $-n$ such that $n + (-n) = 0$.	
Examples $\quad 17 + (-17) = 0 \qquad -17 + 17 = 0$	

You can use number lines as models to add real numbers.

1 EXAMPLE Using a Number Line Model

Simplify each expression.

a. $2 + 6$ Start at 2. ⊢——————→ Move right 6 units. $2 + 6 = 8$

0　2　4　6　8　10

b. $2 + (-6)$ ⊢←——————⊣ Start at 2. Move left 6 units. $2 + (-6) = -4$

−8　−6　−4　−2　0　2

c. $-2 + 6$ Start at −2. ⊢——————→⊣ Move right 6 units. $-2 + 6 = 4$

−4　−2　0　2　4　6

d. $-2 + (-6)$ ⊢←——————⊣ Start at −2. Move left 6 units. $-2 + (-6) = -8$

−10　−8　−6　−4　−2　0

✓ **Check Understanding** ❶ Use a number line to find each sum.

a. $-6 + 4$ **b.** $4 + (-6)$ **c.** $-3 + (-8)$ **d.** $9 + (-3)$

You can also find the sums in Example 1 using rules. Recall that numbers being added are called addends.

🔑 **Key Concepts**

Rule	Adding Numbers With the Same Sign

To add two numbers with the same sign, *add* their absolute values. The sum has the same sign as the addends.

Examples $2 + 6 = 8$ $-2 + (-6) = -8$

Rule	Adding Numbers With Different Signs

To add two numbers with different signs, find the *difference* of their absolute values. The sum has the same sign as the addend with the greater absolute value.

Examples $-2 + 6 = 4$ $2 + (-6) = -4$

2 EXAMPLE Adding Numbers

Simplify each expression.

a. $-5 + (-6) = -11$ Since both addends are negative, add their absolute values. The sum is negative.

b. $13 + (-34) = -21$ The difference of the absolute values is 21. The negative addend has the greater absolute value, so the sum is negative.

c. $3.4 + 9.7 = 13.1$ Since both addends are positive, add their absolute values. The sum is positive.

d. $-1.5 + 3.4 = 1.9$ The difference of the absolute values is 1.9. The positive addend has the greater absolute value, so the sum is positive.

✓ **Check Understanding** ❷ Find each sum.

a. $-7 + (-4)$ **b.** $-26.3 + 8.9$ **c.** $-\frac{3}{4} + \left(-\frac{1}{2}\right)$ **d.** $\frac{8}{9} + \left(-\frac{5}{6}\right)$

You can use negative numbers to model real-world situations.

3 EXAMPLE **Real-World** **Problem Solving**

Football A football team gains 2 yd and then loses 7 yd in two plays. You express a loss of 7 yd as −7. Use addition to find the result of the two plays.

$$2 + (-7) = -5$$

● The result of the two plays is a loss of 5 yd.

✓ **Check Understanding** **3** **Temperature** The temperature falls 15 degrees and then rises 18 degrees. Use addition to find the change in temperature.

OBJECTIVE

2 **Applying Addition**

You can evaluate expressions that involve addition. Substitute a value for the variable(s). Then simplify the expression. The expression −n means the opposite of n. The expression −n can represent a negative number, zero, or a positive number.

4 EXAMPLE **Evaluating Expressions**

Evaluate −n + 8.9 for n = −2.3.

$$-n + 8.9 = -(-2.3) + 8.9 \quad \textbf{Substitute −2.3 for } n.$$
$$= 2.3 + 8.9 \qquad \textbf{− (−2.3) means the opposite of −2.3, which is 2.3.}$$
$$= 11.2 \qquad \textbf{Simplify.}$$

✓ **Check Understanding** **4** Evaluate each expression for t = −7.1.
    a. $t + (-4.3)$ **b.** $-2 + t$ **c.** $8.5 + (-t)$ **d.** $-t + 7.49$

You can write and evaluate expressions to model real-world situations.

5 EXAMPLE **Real-World** **Problem Solving**

Climbing A rock climber climbs a mountain. The base of the mountain is 132 ft below sea level.
a. Write an expression to represent the climber's height below or above sea level.

    Relate   132 ft below sea level   plus   feet the route rises

    Define Let h = feet the route rises.

    Write   −132   + h

    −132 + h

b. Find the climber's height above sea level when he is 485 ft above the base of the mountain.

$$-132 + h = -132 + 485 \quad \textbf{Substitute 485 for } h.$$
$$= 353 \qquad \textbf{Simplify.}$$

● His height is 353 ft above sea level.

✓ **Check Understanding** **5** **Temperature** The temperature one winter morning is −14°F. Define a variable and write an expression to find the temperature after it changes. Then evaluate your expression for a decrease of 11 degrees Fahrenheit.

Real-World  **Connection**

Rock climbers use helmets, harnesses, ropes, and a variety of other devices to help them ascend steep routes.

U.S. School Enrollment (millions)

Level	Public	Private
Elementary	29.3	3.1
High School	14.6	1.2
College	12.1	3.3

SOURCE: *Statistical Abstract of the United States.*
Go to **www.PHSchool.com** for a data update.
Web Code: aeg-2041

You can use matrices to add real numbers. A **matrix** is a rectangular arrangement of numbers in rows and columns. The plural of matrix is matrices (pronounced MAY-truh-seez). The matrix below shows the data in the table.

$$
\begin{array}{cc}
& \text{Public} \quad \text{Private} \\
\begin{array}{c} \text{Elementary} \\ \text{High School} \\ \text{College} \end{array} &
\left[\begin{array}{cc} 29.3 & 3.1 \\ 14.6 & 1.2 \\ 12.1 & 3.3 \end{array} \right] \leftarrow \text{row} \\
& \uparrow \\
& \text{column}
\end{array}
$$

You identify the size of a matrix by the number of rows and the number of columns. The matrix above has 3 rows and 2 columns, so it is a 3×2 matrix. Each item in a matrix is an **element.**

Matrices are equal if the elements in corresponding positions are equal.

$$
\begin{bmatrix} -1 & 2 \\ 4 & 0 \end{bmatrix} = \begin{bmatrix} -1 & \frac{4}{2} \\ \frac{20}{5} & 0 \end{bmatrix}
$$

You add matrices that are the same size by adding the corresponding elements.

6 EXAMPLE **Adding Matrices**

Add $\begin{bmatrix} -5 & 2.7 \\ 7 & -3 \end{bmatrix} + \begin{bmatrix} -3 & -3.9 \\ -4 & 2 \end{bmatrix}$.

$$
\begin{bmatrix} -5 & 2.7 \\ 7 & -3 \end{bmatrix} + \begin{bmatrix} -3 & -3.9 \\ -4 & 2 \end{bmatrix} = \begin{bmatrix} -5 + (-3) & 2.7 + (-3.9) \\ 7 + (-4) & -3 + 2 \end{bmatrix} \quad \textbf{Add corresponding elements.}
$$

$$
= \begin{bmatrix} -8 & -1.2 \\ 3 & -1 \end{bmatrix} \quad \textbf{Simplify.}
$$

✓ **Check Understanding** **6** Find each sum.

a. $\begin{bmatrix} 5 \\ 3.2 \\ -4.9 \end{bmatrix} + \begin{bmatrix} -9 \\ -1.7 \\ -11.1 \end{bmatrix}$

b. $\begin{bmatrix} -4 & \frac{7}{8} \\ \frac{3}{4} & 0 \end{bmatrix} + \begin{bmatrix} -5 & -\frac{3}{4} \\ \frac{1}{2} & -1 \end{bmatrix}$

EXERCISES

For more practice, see *Extra Practice.*

Practice and Problem Solving

A **Practice by Example**

Example 1
(page 25)

Write the expression modeled by each number line. Then find the sum.

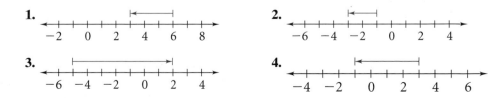

1.

2.

3.

4.

Example 2
(page 25)

Simplify.

5. 3 + 12

6. −7 + (−4)

7. −8.7 + (−10.3)

8. 5.04 + 7.1

9. 5 + (−9)

10. −8 + 13

11. −27 + 19

12. 45 + (−87)

13. −2.3 + 4.5

14. −8.05 + 7.4

15. 9.51 + (−17)

16. 3.42 + (−2.09)

17. $\frac{4}{5} + \frac{2}{15}$

18. $-\frac{5}{9} + \left(-\frac{1}{3}\right)$

19. $2\frac{1}{4} + 3\frac{15}{16}$

20. $-4\frac{3}{8} + \left(-1\frac{3}{4}\right)$

21. $-\frac{2}{3} + \frac{4}{6}$

22. $\frac{1}{9} + \left(-\frac{5}{6}\right)$

23. $-5\frac{7}{12} + 10\frac{3}{4}$

24. $\frac{9}{7} + \left(-2\frac{3}{14}\right)$

Example 3
(page 26)

25. A diver dives 47 ft below the surface of the water and then rises 12 ft. Use addition to find the diver's depth.

26. On two football plays, a team gains 8 yd, and then loses 5 yd. Use addition to find the result of the two plays.

27. The temperature at 6 A.M. is −6°F. The temperature rises 13 degrees Fahrenheit by noon. Use addition to find the temperature at noon.

Example 4
(page 26)

Evaluate each expression for $n = 3.5$.

28. 5.2 + n

29. −5.2 + n

30. −n + 5.2

31. −n + (−5.2)

32. 9.1 + n

33. −9.1 + n

34. −n + 9.1

35. −9.1 + (−n)

Example 5
(page 26)

36. Temperature The temperature one winter morning is −8°F. Define a variable and write an expression to find the temperature after each change below. Then evaluate your expression for each change.
a. a rise of 7°F
b. a decrease of 3°F
c. a rise of 19°F

37. Money You have $74 in a checking account. Define a variable and write an expression to find the balance in your account after each deposit or withdrawal below. Then evaluate your expression for each change.
a. a deposit of $18
b. a withdrawal of $29
c. a withdrawal of $47

Example 6
(page 27)

Simplify.

38. $\begin{bmatrix} 7 & -8 \\ -12 & 6.2 \end{bmatrix} + \begin{bmatrix} -8 & 9.4 \\ -9 & 17 \end{bmatrix}$

39. $\begin{bmatrix} -7.2 \\ 3.2 \\ -4.9 \end{bmatrix} + \begin{bmatrix} -11 \\ 8.4 \\ 24 \end{bmatrix}$

40. $\begin{bmatrix} \frac{1}{2} \\ 8 \\ -9 \end{bmatrix} + \begin{bmatrix} -\frac{1}{2} \\ 17 \\ -3 \end{bmatrix}$

41. $\begin{bmatrix} 1.3 & 26 \\ \frac{1}{8} & -2 \end{bmatrix} + \begin{bmatrix} 0.5 & -4 \\ -\frac{5}{8} & 9 \end{bmatrix}$

B **Apply Your Skills**

Simplify.

42. 2.4 + (−8.7) + 3.6

43. −13.2 + 7 + (−6.8)

44. 0.9 + 6.4 + (−0.7)

45. $\frac{1}{6} + 12 + \left(-\frac{3}{8}\right)$

46. |−4| +(− 4) + 4

47. $1\frac{4}{7} + \left(-8\frac{1}{5}\right) + 3$

48. −17 + (−1.7) + 0.17

49. 2.47 + (−9.8) + (−13.5)

50. −8.02 + |−5.9| + 0.4

51. $-\frac{1}{3} + \frac{1}{4} + \left(-\frac{1}{5}\right)$

52. $-\frac{5}{12} + 1\frac{5}{8} + \left(-6\frac{3}{10}\right)$

53. |−0.1| + |−0.7|

54. |−2| + $\left(-\frac{2}{3}\right)$ + 3

55. −4.3 + 1.2 + (−5.7)

Real-World  **Connection**

The art of photography is changing because of the development of digital cameras.

 Art Use the table for Exercises 56–59.

Number of People Who Participate in Art Activities (millions)

Ages	Drawing	Pottery	Weaving	Photography	Creative Writing
18–24	9.2	5.0	5.2	6.6	7.6
25–34	7.2	6.8	10.0	7.2	5.2
35–44	6.8	8.2	13.1	8.2	5.4
45–54	4.4	6.1	9.8	6.1	3.4
55–64	1.9	2.1	6.1	2.1	1.0

SOURCE: *Statistical Abstract of the United States*

56. How many people aged 18 to 34 participate in photography?

57. How many people aged 45 to 64 draw?

58. Which of the activities is most popular? Explain how you found your answer.

59. a. Write a fraction to compare the number of people aged 25 to 34 who weave to the number of people aged 18 to 64 who weave.
  b. Write your answer from part (a) as a decimal to the nearest hundredth.
  c. What percent of the people who weave are aged 25 to 34?

Evaluate each expression for $a = -2$, $b = 3$, and $c = -4$.

60. $-a + 2 + c$ **61.** $-|a|$ **62.** $a + b$ **63.** $a + (-b)$

64. $a + 3b$ **65.** $c + 3b$ **66.** $c + a + 5$ **67.** $-(c + a + 5)$

68. Writing Without calculating, which is greater, the sum of -227 and 319 or the sum of 227 and -319? Explain.

69. Reasoning Explain what is wrong with the reasoning in the statement: *Since 20 is the opposite of -20, then $20°F$ must be very hot, because $-20°F$ is very cold.*

Evaluate each expression for $b = -3.5$.

70. $b + 3.2$ **71.** $-9 + b + (-1.2)$ **72.** $b + |-2.9|$

73. $8.5 + b + 3.7$ **74.** $|b| + (-3.4)$ **75.** $-5.6 + b + 7.2$

TWO ATOMS TALKING

ARE YOU SURE YOU'VE LOST AN ELECTRON?

I'M POSITIVE!

76. Chemistry A charged atom of magnesium has 12 protons and 10 electrons. Each proton has a charge of $+1$, and each electron has a charge of -1. What is the total charge of the atom?

77. Open-Ended Write a 2 × 3 matrix.

78. Error Analysis A student added two matrices as shown. What error did the student make?

$$\begin{bmatrix} 4 & -1 \\ -3 & 2 \\ 1.5 & 6 \end{bmatrix} + \begin{bmatrix} -2 & 2.3 & 0 \\ 7 & -4 & 5.1 \end{bmatrix} = \begin{bmatrix} 11 & -3 \\ -7 & 4.3 \\ 6.6 & 6 \end{bmatrix}$$

79. Math in the Media In the cartoon below, does the total "12 27" make sense? Explain.

Frank and Ernest

© 1980 Thaves / Reprinted with permission. Newspaper dist. by NEA, Inc.

Number of Employees

Saturday Schedule

Shift	Hourly Wage			
	$6.25	$6.50	$7.00	$7.50
Day	8	3	5	1
Evening	10	2	2	1
Night	4	1	0	1

Sunday Schedule

Shift	Hourly Wage			
	$6.25	$6.50	$7.00	$7.50
Day	5	2	1	1
Evening	8	2	0	1
Night	2	1	0	1

 80. Jobs Use the data in the tables at the left.
  a. Write the data in each table as a matrix.
  b. Add the matrices to find the total number of workers in each pay category for each work shift.
  c. How many weekend employees on the evening shift earn $6.50 per hour?
  d. How many weekend employees work the night shift?
  e. Critical Thinking Suppose all employees work 8-hour shifts both Saturday and Sunday. How would you use the matrix to find the total wages of the weekend employees?
  f. Find the total wages of the weekend employees.

81. Suppose you overdrew your bank account. You have a balance of −$34. You then deposit checks for $17 and $49. At the same time the bank charges you a $25 fee for overdrawing your account. What is your balance?

82. a. What is the value of $-n$ when $n = -4$?
  b. What is the value of $-n$ when $n = 4$?
  c. Reasoning For what values of n will $-n$ be positive? Negative?

C Challenge

Simplify the elements in each matrix.

83. $\begin{bmatrix} \frac{5}{6} \div \frac{2}{3} & -4 + 2\frac{1}{2} \\ \left(3\frac{1}{3}\right)\left(\frac{3}{4}\right) & \frac{1}{2} + \left(\frac{2}{5}\right)\left(\frac{5}{4}\right) \end{bmatrix}$

84. $\begin{bmatrix} 8 + 2 \div 4 & 2^5 & -12 + (-15) \\ -45 + 5(13) & \frac{10 + 16}{4} & 4 - 2^2 \end{bmatrix}$

Simplify each expression.

85. $\frac{w}{5} + \left(-\frac{w}{10}\right)$

86. $-\frac{c}{4} + \left(-\frac{c}{4}\right)$

87. $3\left(\frac{a}{7}\right) + 7\left(\frac{a}{3}\right)$

88. $-1\left(\frac{b}{9}\right) + \left(-\frac{b}{9}\right)$

89. $\frac{-x}{4} + \frac{x}{3}$

90. $\frac{x}{4} + \left(-\frac{x}{3}\right)$

91. $\frac{2t}{3} + \frac{-3t}{6}$

92. $\frac{-m}{2} + \left(\frac{-m + 1}{4}\right)$

93. $\frac{m}{6} + \left(-\frac{m}{18}\right)$

Tell whether each sum is *positive*, *negative*, or *zero*. Explain.

94. n is positive and m is negative. $n + (-m)$ is __?__.

95. n is positive, and m is negative. $-n + m$ is __?__.

96. $|n| = |m|$, n is positive, and m is negative. $n + (-m)$ is __?__.

97. $|n| = |m|$, n is positive, and m is negative. $-n + (-m)$ is __?__.

98. $n = m$, and n and m are negative. $n + (-m)$ is __?__.

Multiple Choice

99. Simplify $10 + |-3| + (-3)$.

A. 16   **B.** 10   **C.** 7   **D.** 4

100. Evaluate $(3a + b) + (-20)$ for $a = 5$ and $b = -1$.

F. -6 **G.** -2 **H.** 20   **I.** 22

101. Which expression has a value different from the others?

A. $-7 + 3$ **B.** $5 + (-9)$ **C.** $-8\frac{2}{3} + 4\frac{2}{3}$ **D.** $-9 + 13$

102. In a 12-hour period, the temperature rose from $-12°F$ to $18°F$. Find the increase in temperature in degrees.

F. 30   **G.** 6   **H.** -6 **I.** -30

103. The value of $-(-(-27))$ is NOT the same as which expression?

A. $-29 + 2$ **B.** $-12.8 + (-14.2)$

C. $-42 + 17$ **D.** $8 + (-35)$

104. Suppose you have $95 in your checking account. You pay for a $34 sweater using your debit card. Then you deposit a $32 check. Later, you withdraw $16 at the supermarket. What is the balance in your account?

F. $145   **G.** $81   **H.** $77   **I.** $13

Take It to the NET
Online lesson quiz at
www.PHSchool.com
Web Code: aea-0104

Mixed Review

Lesson 1-3

Use $<$, $=$, or $>$ to compare.

105. $-1.23 \blacksquare -1.18$

106. $1\frac{2}{4} \blacksquare 1\frac{5}{10}$

107. $|-5| \blacksquare |-6|$

108. $|-4.1| \blacksquare |-3.9|$

109. $\left|-\frac{3}{10}\right| \blacksquare \left|\frac{2}{9}\right|$

110. $|1.2| \blacksquare \left|-\frac{6}{5}\right|$

Lesson 1-2

Simplify each expression.

111. $(5 - 2)^2$ **112.** $-4 + 3.1(2)$ **113.** $9[5 + (-3)]$ **114.** $4^2 + 3^2 - 2^2$

✓ Checkpoint Quiz 1   Lessons 1-1 through 1-4

TEXT Instant self-check quiz online and on CD-ROM

Write a variable expression for each phrase. Then evaluate the expression for $a = 3$, $b = -2$, and $c = 2.5$.

1. the sum of b and 4

2. the quotient of c and 2

3. the product of a and 4.3

4. b plus c plus twice a

5. 17 more than b

6. three times c

7. the difference of 24 and a

8. the sum of b and twice a

9. Is the statement "A number is always greater than its opposite" true? Explain.

10. What set of numbers is reasonable to use for the number of loaves of bread a bakery bakes in one day?

Subtracting Real Numbers

Lesson Preview

What You'll Learn

OBJECTIVE 1 To subtract real numbers

OBJECTIVE 2 To apply subtraction

. . . And Why

To find stock prices, as in Example 6

✔ Check Skills You'll Need (For help, go to Lessons 1-3 and 1-4.)

Find the opposite of each number.

1. 6 **2.** −7 **3.** 3.79 **4.** $-\frac{7}{19}$

Simplify.

5. $3 + (-2)$ **6.** $9.5 + (-3.5)$ **7.** $13 + (-8)$ **8.** $\frac{2}{3} + \left(-\frac{1}{6}\right)$

OBJECTIVE 1 — Subtracting Real Numbers

🄸 TEXT **Interactive lesson includes instant self-check, tutorials, and activities.**

You have learned to add real numbers and to find the opposite of a number. You can use these two concepts to understand how to subtract real numbers.

1 EXAMPLE Using a Number Line Model

Find $4 - 7$.

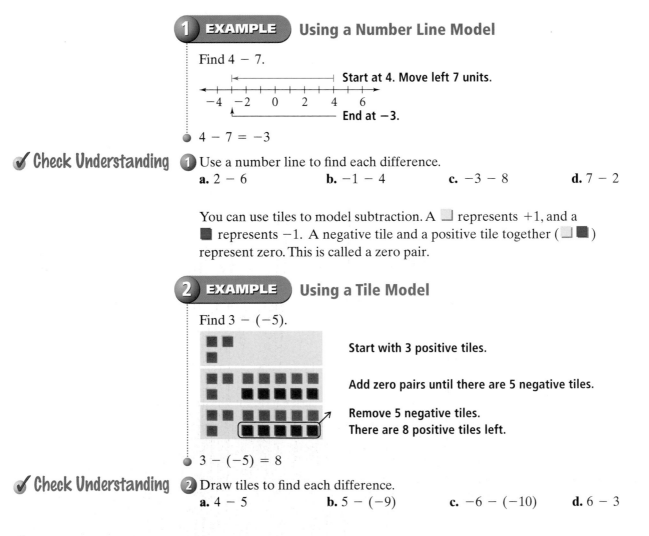

Start at 4. Move left 7 units.

End at −3.

$4 - 7 = -3$

✔ Check Understanding ① Use a number line to find each difference.
   a. $2 - 6$ **b.** $-1 - 4$ **c.** $-3 - 8$ **d.** $7 - 2$

You can use tiles to model subtraction. A ▢ represents +1, and a ■ represents −1. A negative tile and a positive tile together (▢ ■) represent zero. This is called a zero pair.

2 EXAMPLE Using a Tile Model

Find $3 - (-5)$.

Start with 3 positive tiles.

Add zero pairs until there are 5 negative tiles.

Remove 5 negative tiles.
There are 8 positive tiles left.

$3 - (-5) = 8$

✔ Check Understanding ② Draw tiles to find each difference.
   a. $4 - 5$ **b.** $5 - (-9)$ **c.** $-6 - (-10)$ **d.** $6 - 3$

The number line below models the sum $2 + (-6)$ *and* the difference $2 - 6$.

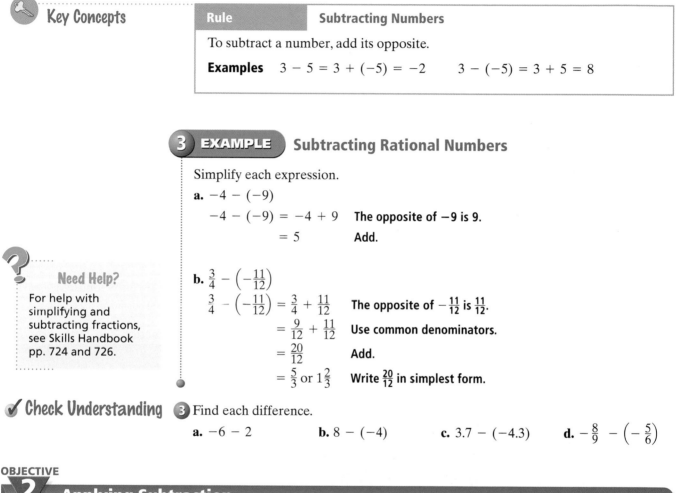

Start at 2. Move left 6 units.

Both $2 + (-6)$ and $2 - 6$ have the same value, -4. This illustrates the following rule for subtracting real numbers.

Key Concepts

Rule	Subtracting Numbers

To subtract a number, add its opposite.

Examples $3 - 5 = 3 + (-5) = -2$ $3 - (-5) = 3 + 5 = 8$

3 EXAMPLE   Subtracting Rational Numbers

Simplify each expression.

a. $-4 - (-9)$

$-4 - (-9) = -4 + 9$ **The opposite of -9 is 9.**

$\qquad\qquad = 5$ **Add.**

Need Help?

For help with simplifying and subtracting fractions, see Skills Handbook pp. 724 and 726.

b. $\frac{3}{4} - \left(-\frac{11}{12}\right)$

$\frac{3}{4} - \left(-\frac{11}{12}\right) = \frac{3}{4} + \frac{11}{12}$ **The opposite of $-\frac{11}{12}$ is $\frac{11}{12}$.**

$\qquad\qquad = \frac{9}{12} + \frac{11}{12}$ **Use common denominators.**

$\qquad\qquad = \frac{20}{12}$ **Add.**

$\qquad\qquad = \frac{5}{3}$ or $1\frac{2}{3}$ **Write $\frac{20}{12}$ in simplest form.**

✓ **Check Understanding**   **3** Find each difference.

a. $-6 - 2$ **b.** $8 - (-4)$ **c.** $3.7 - (-4.3)$ **d.** $-\frac{8}{9} - \left(-\frac{5}{6}\right)$

OBJECTIVE

2 Applying Subtraction

Recall that when you simplify an expression, you work within grouping symbols first. Absolute value symbols are grouping symbols, so find the value of an expression within the absolute value symbols before finding the absolute value.

4 EXAMPLE   Absolute Values

Simplify $|5 - 11|$.

$|5 - 11| = |-6|$ **Subtract within absolute value symbols.**

$\qquad\quad = 6$ **Find the absolute value.**

✓ **Check Understanding**   **4** Simplify each expression.

a. $|8 - 7|$ **b.** $|7 - 8|$ **c.** $|-10 - (-4)|$ **d.** $|-4 - (-10)|$

You evaluate expressions that involve subtraction by substituting for the variable. Then simplify the expression.

5 EXAMPLE Evaluating Expressions

Evaluate $-a - b$ for $a = -3$ and $b = -5$.

$$-a - b = -(-3) - (-5) \quad \text{Substitute } -3 \text{ for } a \text{ and } -5 \text{ for } b.$$
$$= 3 - (-5) \quad \text{The opposite of } -3 \text{ is } 3.$$
$$= 3 + 5 \quad \text{To subtract } -5, \text{ add its opposite, } 5.$$
$$= 8 \quad \text{Add.}$$

✓ **Check Understanding** **5** Evaluate each expression for $t = -2$ and $r = -7$.
a. $r - t$ **b.** $t - r$ **c.** $-t - r$ **d.** $-r - (-t)$

You can write expressions to model real-world situations.

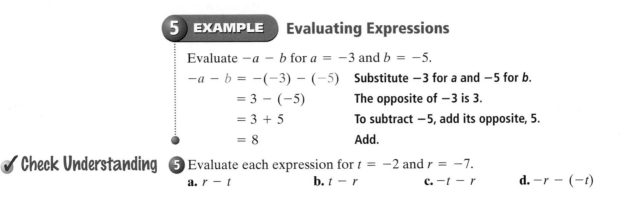

C3

STOCK PRICES

	Thurs	
Stock	Close	Change
ABC	32.79	0.32
PQR	14.23	-1.23
XYZ	17.37	-0.87

6 EXAMPLE Real-World Problem Solving

Stock Price Find the closing price of stock XYZ on Wednesday by subtracting the change in price from the closing price on Thursday.
$$17.37 - (-0.87) = 17.37 + 0.87 \quad \text{Add the opposite.}$$
$$= 18.24 \quad \text{Simplify.}$$
The closing share price on Wednesday was $18.24.

✓ **Check Understanding** **6** **Stock Price** Find the closing price of stocks ABC and PQR on Wednesday.

EXERCISES

For more practice, see *Extra Practice*.

Practice and Problem Solving

A **Practice by Example**

Examples 1, 2
(page 32)

Draw a number line or tiles to model each difference. Then find each difference.

1. $1 - 2$ **2.** $7 - 9$ **3.** $-4 - 2$ **4.** $-2 - 3$
5. $-5 - (-6)$ **6.** $-3 - 8$ **7.** $5 - (-9)$ **8.** $-1 - (-4)$

Example 3
(page 33)

Simplify each expression.

9. $3 - 7$ **10.** $2 - (-9)$ **11.** $-4 - 6$ **12.** $-5 - (-1)$
13. $6.2 - 8.3$ **14.** $-7.4 - 1.8$ **15.** $5.3 - (-8.4)$ **16.** $-3.6 - (-7.1)$
17. $\frac{1}{3} - \frac{1}{2}$ **18.** $-\frac{2}{5} - \frac{7}{10}$ **19.** $\frac{2}{12} - \left(-\frac{3}{4}\right)$ **20.** $-\frac{5}{12} - \left(-\frac{1}{10}\right)$

Example 4
(page 33)

21. $|5 - 2|$ **22.** $|-7 - 1|$ **23.** $|4 - 10|$ **24.** $|-3 - (-5)|$
25. $|-6 - 7|$ **26.** $|8 - 6|$ **27.** $|3 - 9|$ **28.** $|-11 - (-8)|$

Example 5
(page 34)

Evaluate each expression for $x = 3$, $y = -4$, and $z = 6$.

29. $y - z$ **30.** $x - y$ **31.** $-y - x$ **32.** $-x - y$
33. $z - x$ **34.** $2x - z$ **35.** $x + y - z$ **36.** $-z + y - x$

Example 6
(page 34)

37. On Friday, the closing price of a KJL company share was $51.72. It had risen $1.08 from the previous day. Find the closing price of KJL on Thursday.

Evaluate each expression for $a = -2$, $b = 3.5$, and $c = -4$.

38. $a - b + c$ **39.** $-c - b + a$ **40.** $-|a|$ **41.** $|a| + |b|$

42. $|a + b|$ **43.** $-|3 + a|$ **44.** $4b - a$ **45.** $-4b - |a|$

46. $|c + a - 5|$ **47.** $|c + a + 5|$ **48.** $|a - c| - |c|$ **49.** $|a| + |3b|$

Real-World Connection

Careers Archaeologists uncover and study the remains of ancient cultures. Archaeologists may look for remains in remote locations, underground, in caves, or underwater.

50. Archaeology Archaeologists found a 1500-year-old ship at the bottom of the Black Sea. The ship is well preserved because oxygen could not make the ship decay. The ship is at a depth of 1000 ft below the surface. This is about 350 ft below the boundary between surface water, which has oxygen, and water below, which does not have oxygen. At what depth is the boundary?

51. Open-Ended Write two matrices with the same dimensions. Find the difference of the two matrices.

Decide if each statement is always true. If the statement is not always true, give a counterexample.

52. The difference of two numbers is less than the sum of those two numbers.

53. The difference of two numbers is less than either of those two numbers.

54. A number minus its opposite is twice the number.

55. a. Sports Write the data in each table below as a matrix.

Participation in Sports Activities (millions)

	Sport	Ages 7–11	Ages 12–17	Ages 18–24
	Basketball	5.5	8.2	4.9
1992	Tennis	1.4	3.2	3.9
	Soccer	4.2	3.8	1.3
	Volleyball	1.6	5.2	5.1

	Sport	Ages 7–11	Ages 12–17	Ages 18–24
	Basketball	6.8	7.9	4.9
1997	Tennis	1.0	1.8	1.7
	Soccer	5.6	4.1	1.3
	Volleyball	1.8	4.9	2.9

b. Subtract the 1992 matrix from the 1997 matrix to find the changes in participation in sports activities.

c. Writing Suppose you invest in sporting goods. In which sport would you invest? Use elements from your matrix to explain.

Subtract.

56. $\begin{bmatrix} -3 & 4 \\ 0 & -1 \end{bmatrix} - \begin{bmatrix} -5 & 6 \\ 9 & -4 \end{bmatrix}$ **57.** $\begin{bmatrix} \frac{3}{8} & \frac{1}{5} & 4 \end{bmatrix} - \begin{bmatrix} \frac{5}{8} & \frac{2}{10} & 7 \end{bmatrix}$ **58.** $\begin{bmatrix} \frac{1}{4} \\ -3 \end{bmatrix} - \begin{bmatrix} \frac{2}{3} \\ -2 \end{bmatrix}$

59. Critical Thinking Use examples to illustrate your answers.
    a. Is $|a - b|$ always equal to $|b - a|$?
    b. Is $|a + b|$ always equal to $|a| + |b|$?

Simplify each expression.

60. $1 - \frac{1}{2} - \frac{1}{3} - \frac{1}{4} - \frac{1}{5} - \frac{1}{6}$

61. $1 - \left(\frac{1}{2} - \left(\frac{1}{3} - \left(\frac{1}{4} - \left(\frac{1}{5} - \frac{1}{6}\right)\right)\right)\right)$

62. $5x - 7x + 6 - 2x - 5 + 8$

63. $-8t - 5m + 3m - 7t - (-3t) + m$

64. $\frac{7r - 8}{4} - \left(\frac{-r + 3}{16}\right)$

65. $\frac{-5w - 2 + w - 1}{3} - \frac{w - 3w + 4w - 1 + w}{9}$

66. Order $|x + y|$, $|x - y|$, $|x| - |y|$, and $x - y$ from least to greatest for $x = -8$ and $y = -10$.

Standardized Test Prep

Multiple Choice

67. Evaluate $-|a - b| + |c|$ for $a = -3$, $b = 4$, and $c = -4$.
   A. 11   **B.** 3   **C.** −3   **D.** −11

68. Which expression has a value different from the others?
   F. $-7 - 12$ **G.** $17 - 12$ **H.** $12 - 7$ **I.** $12 + (-7)$

69. Find the next number in the pattern 11, 8, 5, 2, . . .
   A. 1   **B.** 0   **C.** −1   **D.** −2

70. Use the bar graph at the right. Estimate the average hourly earnings of U.S. nonfarm workers in 2005.

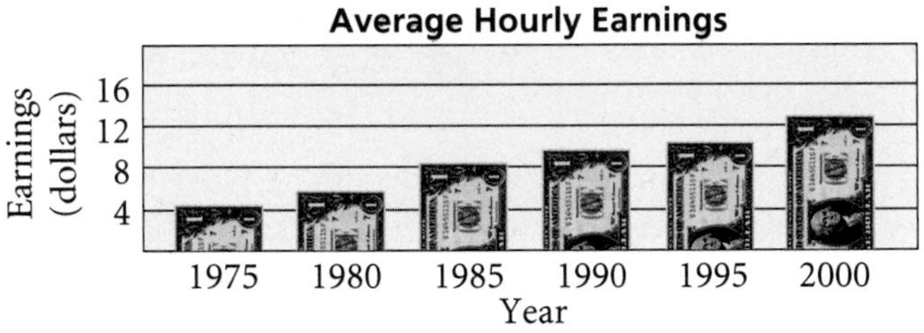

Average Hourly Earnings

   F. $12.00   **G.** $13.50   **H.** $15.00   **I.** $20.00

71. One January day, the temperature at noon is 8°F. During the afternoon, the temperature drops 5 degrees. By dawn, the temperature has fallen another 9 degrees. What is the temperature at dawn?

   A. −22°F   **B.** 12°F   **C.** −4°F   **D.** −6°F

Take It to the NET
Online lesson quiz at
www.PHSchool.com
Web Code: aea-0105

Mixed Review

Lesson 1-4

Simplify each expression.

72. $6 + (-2)$ **73.** $-5 + (-4)$ **74.** $-3.4 + 2.7$ **75.** $5.9 + (-10)$

Simplify.

76. $\begin{bmatrix} 3 & -8 \\ 2 & 11 \end{bmatrix} + \begin{bmatrix} 1 & 8 \\ -2 & 5 \end{bmatrix}$

77. $\begin{bmatrix} 1.3 \\ -6.7 \\ 7.1 \end{bmatrix} + \begin{bmatrix} -0.1 \\ 4.2 \\ -1.9 \end{bmatrix}$

78. $\begin{bmatrix} \frac{1}{2} & -1 \\ 6 & \frac{2}{3} \end{bmatrix} + \begin{bmatrix} -4 & \frac{1}{3} \\ \frac{1}{3} & -5 \end{bmatrix}$

Lesson 1-1

Define variables and write an equation to model each situation.

79. The total cost equals the number of pounds of pears times $1.19/lb.

80. You have $20. Then you buy a bouquet. How much do you have left?

81. You go out to lunch with five friends and split the check equally. What is your share of the check?

1-6 Multiplying and Dividing Real Numbers

Lesson Preview

What You'll Learn

OBJECTIVE 1 To multiply real numbers

OBJECTIVE 2 To divide real numbers

. . . And Why

To find the change in temperature with an increase in altitude, as in Example 3

✔ Check Skills You'll Need

(For help, go to Lessons 1-4 and 1-5.)

Simplify each expression.

1. $-2 + (-2) + (-2) + (-2)$ **2.** $-5 + (-5) + (-5) + (-5) + (-5)$

3. $-6 - 6 - 6 - 6$ **4.** $-12 - 12 - 12 - 12 - 12 - 12$

Write the next three numbers in each pattern.

5. $2, 4, 6, \blacksquare, \blacksquare, \blacksquare$ **6.** $6, 4, 2, \blacksquare, \blacksquare, \blacksquare$

7. $12, 9, 6, \blacksquare, \blacksquare, \blacksquare$ **8.** $-18, -12, -6, \blacksquare, \blacksquare, \blacksquare$

New Vocabulary

- Identity Property of Multiplication
- Multiplication Property of Zero
- Multiplication Property of -1
- Inverse Property of Multiplication
- multiplicative inverse • reciprocal

OBJECTIVE 1 Multiplying Real Numbers

ⓘTEXT Interactive lesson includes instant self-check, tutorials, and activities.

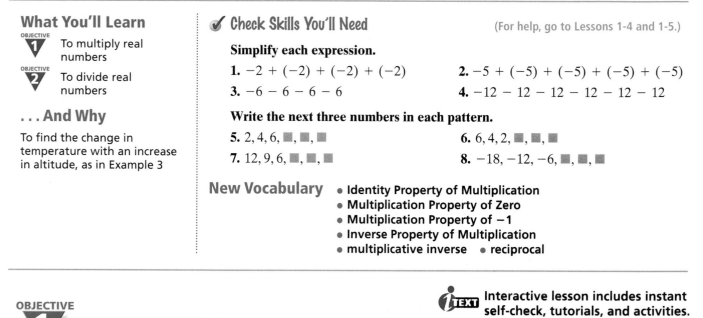

Investigation: Multiplying Integers

1. Patterns Use patterns to complete each statement.

a. $2 \cdot 3 = \blacksquare$ b. $3(-2) = \blacksquare$
  $2 \cdot 2 = \blacksquare$ $2(-2) = \blacksquare$
  $2 \cdot 1 = \blacksquare$ $1(-2) = \blacksquare$
  $2 \cdot 0 = \blacksquare$ $0(-2) = \blacksquare$
  $2(-1) = \blacksquare$ $-1(-2) = \blacksquare$
  $2(-2) = \blacksquare$ $-2(-2) = \blacksquare$
  $2(-3) = \blacksquare$ $-3(-2) = \blacksquare$

2. Make a Conjecture From the patterns you found in Question 1, what seems to be the sign of the product of a positive number and a negative number?

3. Make a Conjecture From the patterns you found in Question 1, what seems to be the sign of the product of two negative numbers?

The product of a number and 1 is the original number. It does not matter whether the original number is positive or negative. The product of 0 and a number is 0. The product of -1 and a number is the opposite of the original number.

Key Concepts

| Property | Identity Property of Multiplication |

For every real number n, $1 \cdot n = n$.

Examples $\quad 1 \cdot 5 = 5 \qquad 1 \cdot (-5) = -5$

| Property | Multiplication Property of Zero |

For every real number n, $n \cdot 0 = 0$.

Examples $\quad 35 \cdot 0 = 0 \qquad -35 \cdot 0 = 0$

| Property | Multiplication Property of -1 |

For every real number n, $-1 \cdot n = -n$.

Examples $\quad -1 \cdot 5 = -5 \qquad -1 \cdot (-5) = 5$

From the examples for the properties above, you can see a pattern for multiplying positive and negative numbers.

Multiplying Numbers With with the Same Sign

$$1 \quad \cdot \quad 5 \quad = \quad 5$$
positive · positive = positive

$$-1 \quad \cdot \quad (-5) \quad = \quad 5$$
negative · negative = positive

Multiplying Numbers With Different Signs

$$1 \quad \cdot \quad (-5) \quad = \quad -5$$
positive · negative = negative

$$-1 \quad \cdot \quad 5 \quad = \quad -5$$
negative · positive = negative

This pattern also holds true when multiplying by numbers other than 1 and -1.

Key Concepts

| Rule | Multiplying Numbers With the Same Sign |

The product of two positive numbers or two negative numbers is positive.

Examples $\quad 5 \cdot 2 = 10 \qquad -5(-2) = 10$

| Rule | Multiplying Numbers With Different Signs |

The product of a positive number and a negative number, or a negative number and a positive number, is negative.

Examples $\quad 3(-6) = -18 \qquad -3 \cdot 6 = -18$

---

1 EXAMPLE **Multiplying Numbers**

Simplify each expression.

a. $-9(-4) = 36$ **The product of two negative numbers is positive.**

b. $5\left(-\frac{2}{3}\right) = -\frac{10}{3}$ **The product of a positive number and a negative number is negative.**

$\qquad\qquad = -3\frac{1}{3}$ **Write $-\frac{10}{3}$ as a mixed number.**

✓ **Check Understanding** ❶ Simplify each expression.

a. $4(-6)$ **b.** $-10(-5)$ **c.** $-4.9(-8)$ **d.** $-\frac{2}{3}\left(\frac{3}{4}\right)$

You can evaluate expressions involving multiplication. To simplify expressions with three or more negative numbers, you must be careful to account for all of the negative signs as you multiply.

2 EXAMPLE Evaluating Expressions

Evaluate $-2xy$ for $x = -20$ and $y = -3$.

$-2xy = -2(-20)(-3)$ **Substitute -20 for x and -3 for y.**

$\quad\quad = -120$ **$-2(-20)$ results in a positive number, 40. $40(-3)$ results in a negative number, -120.**

✔ **Check Understanding** ② Evaluate each expression for $c = -8$ and $d = -7$.
 a. $-(cd)$ **b.** $(-2)(-3)(cd)$ **c.** $c(-d)$

You can use expressions involving multiplication to model real-world situations.

3 EXAMPLE Real-World 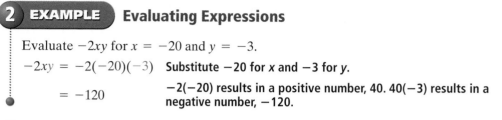 Problem Solving

Temperature You can use the expression $-5.5\left(\frac{a}{1000}\right)$ to calculate the change in temperature in degrees Fahrenheit for an increase in altitude a, measured in feet. A hot-air balloon starts on the ground and then rises 8000 ft. Find the change in temperature at the altitude of the balloon.

$-5.5\left(\frac{a}{1000}\right) = -5.5\left(\frac{8000}{1000}\right)$ **Substitute 8000 for a.**

$\quad\quad\quad\quad = -5.5(8)$ **Divide within parentheses.**

$\quad\quad\quad\quad = -44$ **Multiply.**

● The change in temperature is -44 degrees.

✔ **Check Understanding** ③ **a.** Find the change in temperature if a balloon rises 4500 ft from the ground.
 b. Suppose the temperature is 40°F at ground level. What is the approximate air temperature at the altitude of the balloon?

8000 ft

The expression -3^4 means the opposite of 3^4. The exponent 4 applies to the base 3. The negative sign is not part of the base. In the expression $(-3)^4$, the negative sign is part of the base -3. The exponent 4 applies to the base -3.

4 EXAMPLE Simplifying Exponential Expressions

Use the order of operations to simplify each expression.
a. -3^4
 $-3^4 = -(3 \cdot 3 \cdot 3 \cdot 3)$ **Write as repeated multiplication.**
 $\quad\quad = -81$ **Simplify.**
b. $(-3)^4$
 $(-3)^4 = (-3)(-3)(-3)(-3)$ **Write as repeated multiplication.**
 $\quad\quad\quad = 81$ **Simplify.**

✔ **Check Understanding** ④ Simplify each expression.
 a. -4^3 **b.** $(-2)^4$ **c.** $(-0.3)^2$ **d.** $-\left(\frac{3}{4}\right)^2$

The rules for finding the sign when dividing real numbers are the same as the rules for finding the sign when multiplying real numbers.

Key Concepts

Rule	Dividing Numbers With the Same Sign

The quotient of two positive numbers or two negative numbers is positive.

Examples $6 \div 3 = 2$ $-6 \div (-3) = 2$

Rule	Dividing Numbers With Different Signs

The quotient of a positive number and a negative number, or a negative number and a positive number, is negative.

Examples $-6 \div 3 = -2$ $6 \div (-3) = -2$

You can use the rules for dividing numbers to simplify expressions.

5 EXAMPLE **Dividing Numbers**

Simplify each expression.

a. $12 \div (-4) = -3$ **The quotient of a positive number and a negative number is negative.**

b. $-12 \div (-4) = 3$ **The quotient of a negative number and a negative number is positive.**

✓ Check Understanding **5** Simplify each expression.
  a. $-42 \div 7$ **b.** $-8 \div (-2)$ **c.** $8 \div (-8)$ **d.** $-39 \div (-3)$

You can evaluate expressions that involve division.

Reading Math

You can indicate division using a fraction bar.
$\frac{15}{5}$ means $15 \div 5$.

6 EXAMPLE **Evaluating Expressions**

Evaluate $\frac{-x}{-4} + 2y \div z$ for $x = -20, y = 6,$ and $z = -1$.

$\frac{-x}{-4} + 2y \div z = \frac{-(-20)}{-4} + 2(6) \div (-1)$ **Substitute -20 for x, 6 for y, and -1 for z.**

$= -5 + (-12)$ **Divide and multiply.**

$= -17$ **Add.**

✓ Check Understanding **6** Evaluate each expression for $x = 8, y = -5,$ and $z = -3$.
  a. $3x \div 2z + y \div 10$ **b.** $\frac{2z + x}{2y}$ **c.** $3z^2 - 4y \div x$

A number and its multiplicative inverse have a special relationship.

Key Concepts

Property	Inverse Property of Multiplication

For every nonzero real number a, there is a **multiplicative inverse** $\frac{1}{a}$ such that $a\left(\frac{1}{a}\right) = 1$.

Examples $5\left(\frac{1}{5}\right) = 1$ $-5\left(-\frac{1}{5}\right) = 1$

The **multiplicative inverse,** or **reciprocal,** of a nonzero rational number $\frac{a}{b}$ is $\frac{b}{a}$. Zero does not have a reciprocal. Division by zero is undefined.

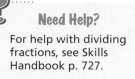

Need Help?

For help with dividing fractions, see Skills Handbook p. 727.

7 EXAMPLE **Division Using the Reciprocal**

Evaluate $\frac{x}{y}$ for $x = -\frac{3}{4}$ and $y = -\frac{5}{2}$.

$\frac{x}{y} = x \div y$ Rewrite the expression.

$\quad = -\frac{3}{4} \div \left(-\frac{5}{2}\right)$ Substitute $-\frac{3}{4}$ for x and $-\frac{5}{2}$ for y.

$\quad = -\frac{3}{4}\left(-\frac{2}{5}\right)$ Multiply by $-\frac{2}{5}$, the reciprocal of $-\frac{5}{2}$.

$\quad = \frac{3}{10}$ Simplify.

✓ Check Understanding   **7** Evaluate the expression in Example 7 for $x = 8$ and $y = -\frac{4}{5}$.

EXERCISES

For more practice, see *Extra Practice.*

Practice and Problem Solving

A Practice by Example

Example 1
(page 38)

Simplify each expression.

1. $3(-5)$ **2.** $5(-3)$ **3.** $3(5)$

4. $-3(-5)$ **5.** $8(-4.3)$ **6.** $9\left(-\frac{5}{18}\right)$

7. $10(-12)$ **8.** $7(-15)$ **9.** $-4(20)$

10. $-20(-4)$ **11.** $13(-6)$ **12.** $-9(-9)$

Example 2
(page 39)

Evaluate each expression for $m = -4, n = 3,$ and $p = -1$.

13. mn **14.** $-mn$ **15.** $3m - n$

16. $-5p$ **17.** $2m$ **18.** $7p - 2n$

19. $8p \cdot (-2n)$ **20.** $p \cdot (m + n)$ **21.** mnp

22. $m \cdot (3 + p)$ **23.** $4n^3 \cdot m$ **24.** $m \cdot p + (-n)$

Example 3
(page 39)

Evaluate each expression for $x = -12$ and $y = 4$.

25. $xy - 4y$ **26.** $2xy + 9$ **27.** $x + 4y$

28. $-x + 3y$ **29.** $3y - 2x$ **30.** $6y + x$

🌐 **31. Weather** The expression $-39 + \frac{3}{2}t$, where t is the actual air temperature, gives the approximate wind chill temperature when the wind speed is 20 mi/h. Find the approximate wind chill temperature for the given air temperatures with a 20 mi/h wind.
     a. $10°F$ **b.** $-24°F$ **c.** $-8°F$ **d.** $5°F$

Example 4
(page 39)

Simplify each expression.

32. $(-1)^5$ **33.** $-(-2)^3$ **34.** -5^2 **35.** $(-9)^2$

36. -9^2 **37.** $3(-4)^3$ **38.** $-5(-1)^4$ **39.** $-5^2(-3)^3$

Example 5
(page 40)

Simplify each expression.

40. $\frac{6}{-3}$ **41.** $\frac{-36}{9}$ **42.** $\frac{3-14}{-2}$ **43.** $-18 \div (-3)$

44. $-121 \div 11$ **45.** $-64 \div (-5)$ **46.** $2^3 \div (-4)$ **47.** $-56 \div (4+3)$

Example 6
(page 40)

Evaluate each expression for $x = -2, y = 3,$ and $z = 3.5.$

48. $(y + 3x) \div y$ **49.** $4z \div x$

50. $4x^3 - \frac{2z}{x}$ **51.** $(3x + 2y) \div (2x + 3y)$

52. $(2z + 7) \div y$ **53.** $8 + 6x \div (4y) - \frac{3z}{y}$

Example 7
(page 41)

Evaluate each expression.

54. $\frac{x}{y}$, for $x = \frac{2}{5}$ and $y = \frac{3}{10}$ **55.** $\frac{-3m}{t}$, for $m = \frac{5}{6}$ and $t = \frac{1}{6}$

56. $\frac{r}{-3s}$, for $r = -\frac{1}{8}$ and $s = \frac{3}{4}$ **57.** $\frac{3x}{5y}$, for $x = \frac{1}{5}$ and $y = -\frac{1}{2}$

B   **Apply Your Skills**   **Simplify each expression.**

58. $\frac{10}{-5}$ **59.** $-3(-6)$ **60.** $\frac{2}{3} \div \left(-\frac{4}{3}\right)$

61. $\frac{2}{3}\left(-\frac{4}{5}\right)$ **62.** -5^3 **63.** $2.25 \div 3$

64. $(-3)^3$ **65.** $-7.2(-3.1)$ **66.** $|4 + 8(-6)|$

67. $|-6(-9)| \div (-2)$ **68.** $(-6)(-2)(-5)$ **69.** $(-2)(5)(-3)$

70. a. Find each product.
     i. $(-1)(-2)$ **ii.** $(-1)(-2)(-3)$
     iii. $(-1)(-2)(-3)(-4)$ **iv.** $(-1)(-2)(-3)(-4)(-5)$
   b. Patterns For an even number of negative factors, the product will be __?__.
   c. For an odd number of negative factors, the product will be __?__.
   d. Writing For a product that includes negative and positive factors, do the positive factors affect the sign of the product? Explain.

71. Suppose a and b are integers.
   a. When is the product ab positive?
   b. When is the product ab negative?

Evaluate each expression for $a = -\frac{3}{4}, b = \frac{1}{3},$ and $c = -\frac{2}{5}.$

72. $a - 2b$ **73.** $b \div c$ **74.** $\frac{a}{c}$ **75.** $-2abc$

Evaluate each expression for the given value(s).

76. $\frac{3}{4}w - 7$, for $w = 1\frac{1}{3}$ **77.** $\frac{x}{2y}$, for $x = 3.6$ and $y = -0.4$

78. $\frac{n}{m}$, for $n = -\frac{4}{5}$ and $m = 8$ **79.** $\frac{3a}{b} + c$, for $a = -2, b = -5,$ and $c = -1$

Open-Ended Use $a = -3, b = 2,$ and $c = -5$ to write an algebraic expression that has each value.

80. 17   **81.** 0   **82.** -1 **83.** 1   **84.** 7

85. History A toll bridge in Maine in the early 1900s charged 2¢ per person and $6\frac{1}{4}$¢ for a dozen sheep. How much would the toll for 3 people and 4 dozen sheep have been?

86. Reasoning Does $|ab|$ always equal $|a| \cdot |b|$? Explain.

87. a. Simplify each expression.

$$(-2)^2 \quad (-2)^3 \quad (-2)^4 \quad (-2)^5$$
$$(-3)^2 \quad (-3)^3 \quad (-3)^4 \quad (-3)^5$$

    b. Make a Conjecture Do you think a negative number raised to an even power will be positive or negative? Explain.

    c. What is the sign of a negative number raised to an odd power? Explain.

88. Is -10 or 0.1 the multiplicative inverse of 10? Explain.

89. Explain why the reciprocal of a nonzero number is *not* the same as the opposite of the number.

In *scalar multiplication*, **you multiply the elements in a matrix by a number, called a *scalar*. Find each product.**

Sample $3 \begin{bmatrix} 4 & -1.5 \\ \frac{1}{2} & -6 \end{bmatrix} = \begin{bmatrix} 3 \cdot 4 & 3 \cdot (-1.5) \\ 3 \cdot \frac{1}{2} & 3 \cdot (-6) \end{bmatrix}$ **Multiply each entry by the scalar.**

$$= \begin{bmatrix} 12 & -4.5 \\ \frac{3}{2} & -18 \end{bmatrix} \quad \textbf{Simplify.}$$

90. $-2 \begin{bmatrix} 11 & -5 \\ -9 & 6 \\ -4 & 3 \end{bmatrix}$ **91.** $\frac{3}{5} \begin{bmatrix} -25 & 35 \\ \frac{10}{9} & -15 \end{bmatrix}$ **92.** $-0.1 \begin{bmatrix} -47 & 13 & -7.9 \\ 0.2 & -64 & 0 \end{bmatrix}$

93. $-4 \begin{bmatrix} 3 & \frac{2}{3} \end{bmatrix}$ **94.** $2 \begin{bmatrix} -4 & -5.3 & 2 \\ 3.1 & 0 & 6 \end{bmatrix}$ **95.** $\frac{1}{4} \begin{bmatrix} -1 & \frac{3}{4} \\ \frac{8}{9} & 0 \end{bmatrix}$

155 ft

96. Entertainment As riders plunge down the hill of a roller coaster, you can approximate the height h, in feet, above the ground of their roller-coaster car. Use the formula $h = 155 - 16t^2$ where t is the number of seconds since the start of the descent.

    a. How far is a rider from the bottom of the hill after 1 second? 2 seconds?

    b. Critical Thinking Does it take more than or less than 4 seconds to reach the bottom? Explain.

97. a. Sales The table at the left shows the monthly sales in March and October for three departments of a clothing store. Organize the data into a matrix.

	Dept. Sales		
March	180	210	200
October	170	230	190

    b. Use a scalar to find the matrix for each month's average daily sales. Assume the store is open every day. Round to the nearest tenth.

    c. Each department hopes sales in March and October increase by 10% next year. Find the matrix that shows the projected sales for these months.

98. Temperature Scales The formula $C = \frac{5}{9}(F - 32)$ changes a temperature reading from the Fahrenheit scale F to the Celsius scale C. What is the temperature measured in Celsius if the Fahrenheit temperature is $-10°$ degrees? Round to the nearest degree.

C Challenge   Evaluate each expression for $b = -\frac{1}{2}$.

99. b^3 **100.** b^4 **101.** b^5 **102.** b^6 **103.** $-b^6$

104. What is the greatest integer n for which $(-n)^3$ is positive and the value of the expression has a 2 in the ones place?

Rewrite each expression using the symbol ÷. Then find each quotient.

Sample $\dfrac{\frac{-7}{12}}{4} = \dfrac{-7}{12} \div 4$ Rewrite as $\dfrac{-7}{12} \div 4$.

$= \dfrac{-7}{12} \cdot \left(\dfrac{1}{4}\right)$ Multiply by $\frac{1}{4}$, the reciprocal of 4.

$= -\dfrac{7}{48}$

105. $\dfrac{\frac{5}{4}}{9}$ **106.** $\dfrac{\frac{3}{8}}{\frac{-2}{3}}$ **107.** $\dfrac{\frac{-5}{6}}{8}$ **108.** $\dfrac{\frac{-2}{5}}{\frac{-4}{5}}$

Standardized Test Prep

Multiple Choice

109. Simplify $(-3)(-3)(2)(2)(-1)$.
     A. -36 **B.** -6 **C.** 6   **D.** 36

110. Evaluate $-ac + bc$ for $a = -2$, $b = 6$, and $c = -3$.
     F. -24 **G.** -6 **H.** 6   **I.** 24

111. A Mach number M indicates the speed of a supersonic airplane. You can find an airplane's speed a in miles per hour using the formula $a = Ms$ where s is the speed of sound at the altitude of the airplane. Find an airplane's speed in miles per hour if the airplane travels at Mach 2.5 at an altitude where the speed of sound is 710 mi/h.
     A. 177.5 mi/h   **B.** 284 mi/h   **C.** 1775 mi/h   **D.** 2840 mi/h

112. Which expression does NOT have the same value as $-11 + (-11) + (-11) + (-11)$?
     F. -44 **G.** $4(-11)$ **H.** $(-11)^4$ **I.** $33 - 77$

113. Use the table below. What was the average temperature for the week?

Day	Mon.	Tues.	Wed.	Thur.	Fri.	Sat.	Sun.
Temperature	$-3°F$	$4°F$	$-2°F$	$-5°F$	$-3°F$	$1°F$	$1°F$

     A. $-7°F$ **B.** $-1°F$ **C.** $1°F$ **D.** $4°F$

Take It to the NET
Online lesson quiz at
www.PHSchool.com
Web Code: aea-0106

Mixed Review

Lesson 1-5

Subtract.

114. $6 - 8$ **115.** $-3 - 17$ **116.** $-2.3 - (-3.1)$

117. $7 - (-2.8)$ **118.** $1\frac{3}{4} - \left(-\frac{1}{2}\right)$ **119.** $-\frac{7}{8} - \left(-\frac{8}{9}\right)$

Lesson 1-3

Find each absolute value.

120. $|4.95|$ **121.** $|-56|$ **122.** $|-4.59|$ **123.** $\left|-\frac{3}{4}\right|$

Lesson 1-2

Evaluate each expression for $a = 4$ and $b = 7$.

124. $a^2 + b$ **125.** $(a + b)^2$ **126.** ab^2

127. A sweater costs $32.95. The sales tax rate is 6%. Find the total cost.

Matrices

FOR USE WITH LESSON 1-6

You can use a graphing calculator to add and subtract matrices and to multiply a matrix by a number, or scalar.

Take It to the NET
Graphing Calculator procedures online at **www.PHSchool.com**
Web Code: aee-2113

1 EXAMPLE Matrix Operations

Let $A = \begin{bmatrix} 3 & 7 & 1 \\ 2 & -4 & 9 \end{bmatrix}$ and $B = \begin{bmatrix} 5 & 0 & -8 \\ 6 & 2 & 2 \end{bmatrix}$. Find $A + B$ and $5A$.

A calculator names the matrices using brackets [A] and [B] to remind you that you are working with matrices.

Step 1 To enter the first matrix, access the MATRX feature of your calculator. Use the arrow keys to highlight EDIT at the top of the screen. Press ENTER. Matrix A is a 2×3 matrix, so revise the numbers at the top of the screen, if necessary. Press ENTER to access the first entry of the matrix. Enter the values given for matrix A. Use (-) for negative.

Step 2 To enter the second matrix, access the matrix screen again. Use the arrow keys to highlight EDIT. Use the arrow keys to move down to [B]. Press ENTER. Change the dimensions and enter the values for matrix B.

Step 3 To find $A + B$, use the NAMES list on the matrix screen to select [A] or [B]. The calculator will display the matrix sum as shown at the right.

Step 4 To find $5A$, press 5, select [A] from the NAMES list, and ENTER. The result is also shown at the right.

```
[A] + [B]
            [[8  7 −7]
             [8 −2 11]]
5[A]
            [[15  35 5 ]
             [10 −20 45]]
```

EXERCISES

For $A = \begin{bmatrix} 4 & -2 \\ 8 & 6 \end{bmatrix}$, $B = \begin{bmatrix} -5 & 12 \\ 0 & 3 \end{bmatrix}$, and $C = \begin{bmatrix} 3 & 15 \\ 9 & -10 \end{bmatrix}$, find each of the following.

1. $A + B$ **2.** $B + C$ **3.** $C - A$

4. $A + C$ **5.** $B - C$ **6.** $3B$

7. $-4C$ **8.** $2A + B$ **9.** $-2B + C + A$

For $A = \begin{bmatrix} 4 & 7 & 3 \\ 8 & 2 & 1 \\ -7 & 5 & -2 \end{bmatrix}$, $B = \begin{bmatrix} -1 & 0 & 6 \\ 2 & -3 & 4 \\ 1 & 15 & 8 \end{bmatrix}$, and $C = \begin{bmatrix} 2 & 0 & 0 \\ 0 & -3 & 6 \\ 4 & 6 & 9 \end{bmatrix}$, find each of the following.

10. $A + 2B$ **11.** $C + B - A$ **12.** $2A + 5B - C$

13. $-4A + 5C$ **14.** $-4A - 5C$ **15.** $A + B - 2C$

The Distributive Property

From Lesson 1-5, you know that ▢ represents $+1$ and ■ represents -1. The tile ▮ represents a variable.

You can use tiles to represent an expression like $x + 5$.

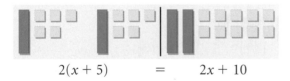

$$x + 5$$

Write the expression represented by each group of tiles.

1.  **2.**   **3.**

Represent each expression using tiles.

4. $x + 1$ **5.** $2x + 4$ **6.** $3x - 5$

The expression $2(x + 5)$ indicates two groups of tiles, as shown below on the left. You can add the variable tiles together and the unit tiles together to simplify the expression, as shown below on the right.

$$2(x + 5) \quad = \quad 2x + 10$$

The tiles show that the product $2(x + 5)$ equals $2x + 10$. This illustrates the Distributive Property.

Write an equation for each model.

7. **8.**

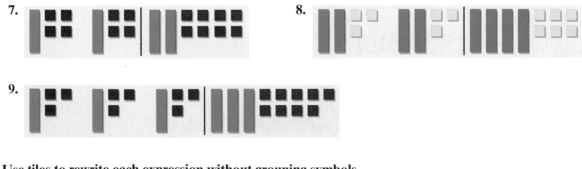

9.

Use tiles to rewrite each expression without grouping symbols.

10. $3(x + 1)$ **11.** $2(x + 4)$ **12.** $3(2x - 1)$

13. Critical Thinking Does $5(2x - 3)$ equal $10x - 3$ or $10x - 15$? Explain.

1-7

The Distributive Property

Lesson Preview

What You'll Learn

OBJECTIVE 1 To use the Distributive Property

OBJECTIVE 2 To simplify algebraic expressions

...And Why

To calculate costs when shopping, as in Example 2

✔ Check Skills You'll Need

(For help, go to Lessons 1-2 and 1-6.)

Use the order of operations to simplify each expression.

1. $3(4 + 7)$ **2.** $-2(5 + 6)$ **3.** $-1(-9 + 8)$

4. $-0.5(8 - 6)$ **5.** $\frac{1}{2}t(10 - 4)$ **6.** $m(-3 - 1)$

New Vocabulary

• Distributive Property   • term   • constant   • coefficient   • like terms

---

OBJECTIVE

1 Using the Distributive Property

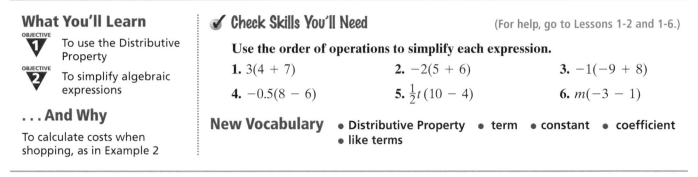

TEXT Interactive lesson includes instant self-check, tutorials, and activities.

You can use the Distributive Property to multiply a sum or difference by a number.

🔑 Key Concepts

Property	Distributive Property

For every real number a, b, and c,

$a(b + c) = ab + ac$ $(b + c)a = ba + ca$

$a(b - c) = ab - ac$ $(b - c)a = ba - ca$

Examples $5(20 + 6) = 5(20) + 5(6)$ $(20 + 6)5 = 20(5) + 6(5)$

           $9(30 - 2) = 9(30) - 9(2)$ $(30 - 2)9 = 30(9) - 2(9)$

You can use the Distributive Property to multiply some numbers using mental math. For instance, you can think of 102 as $100 + 2$ and 98 as $100 - 2$.

1 EXAMPLE   Simplifying a Numerical Expression

Use the Distributive Property to simplify $34(102)$.

$34(102) = 34(100 + 2)$ **Rewrite 102 as 100 + 2.**

         $= 34(100) + 34(2)$ **Use the Distributive Property.**

         $= 3400 + 68$ **Simplify.**

         $= 3468$

✔ Check Understanding

1 Simplify each expression.

a. $13(103)$ **b.** $21(101)$ **c.** $24(98)$ **d.** $15(99)$

You can also use the Distributive Property and mental math to calculate costs.

2 EXAMPLE **Real-World** **Problem Solving**

Shopping Find the total cost of 8 sandwiches that cost $2.99 each.

$8(2.99) = 8(3 - 0.01)$ **Rewrite 2.99 as 3 − 0.01.**

$\qquad = 8(3) - 8(0.01)$ **Use the Distributive Property.**

$\qquad = 24 - 0.08$ **Simplify.**

$\qquad = 23.92$

● The total cost of 8 sandwiches is $23.92.

✓ **Check Understanding** **2** Find the total cost of 6 pairs of socks that cost $2.95 per pair.

OBJECTIVE

2 Simplifying Algebraic Expressions

You can use the Distributive Property to simplify an algebraic expression. An algebraic expression in simplest form has no grouping symbols.

3 EXAMPLE **Simplifying an Expression**

Simplify each expression.

a. $2(5x + 3)$

$2(5x + 3) = 2(5x) + 2(3)$ **Use the Distributive Property.**

$\qquad = 10x + 6$ **Simplify.**

b. $(3b - 2)\left(\frac{1}{3}\right)$

$(3b - 2)\left(\frac{1}{3}\right) = 3b\left(\frac{1}{3}\right) - 2\left(\frac{1}{3}\right)$ **Use the Distributive Property.**

$\qquad = b - \frac{2}{3}$ **Simplify.**

✓ **Check Understanding** **3** Simplify each expression.

a. $6(m + 5)$ **b.** $2(3 - 7t)$ **c.** $(0.4 + 1.1c)(3)$

To simplify an expression like $-(6x + 4)$, rewrite the expression as $-1(6x + 4)$, using the Multiplication Property of -1.

4 EXAMPLE **Using the Multiplication Property of -1**

Simplify $-(6x + 4)$.

$-(6x + 4) = -1(6x + 4)$ **Rewrite the expression using −1.**

$\qquad = -1(6x) + (-1)(4)$ **Use the Distributive Property.**

$\qquad = -6x - 4$ **Simplify.**

✓ **Check Understanding** **4** Simplify each expression.

a. $-(2x + 1)$ **b.** $-(7 - 5b)$ **c.** $(3 - 8a)(-1)$

In an algebraic expression, a **term** is a number, a variable, or the product of a number and one or more variables.

$$6a^2 - 5ab + 3b - 12 \leftarrow \text{A } \textbf{constant} \text{ is a term that has no variable.}$$

A **coefficient** is a numerical factor of a term.

Think of $3b - 12$ as $3b + (-12)$ to determine that the constant is -12.

Like terms have exactly the same variable factors.

Like Terms	Not Like Terms
$3x$ and $-2x$	$8x$ and $7y$
$-5x^2$ and $9x^2$	$5y$ and $2y^2$
xy and $-xy$	$4y$ and $5xy$
$-7x^2y^3$ and $15x^2y^3$	x^2y and xy^2

An algebraic expression in simplest form has no like terms. You can use the Distributive Property to combine like terms when simplifying an expression. Think of the Distributive Property as $ba + ca = (b + c)a$.

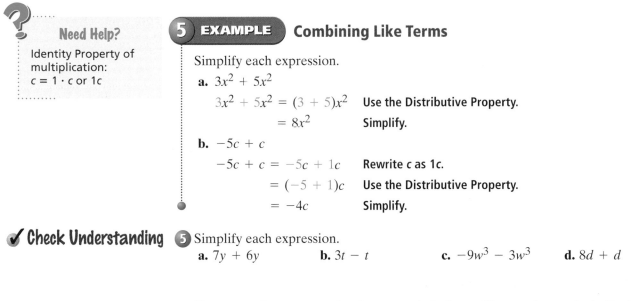

Need Help?

Identity Property of multiplication:
$c = 1 \cdot c$ or $1c$

5 EXAMPLE **Combining Like Terms**

Simplify each expression.

a. $3x^2 + 5x^2$

$3x^2 + 5x^2 = (3 + 5)x^2$ **Use the Distributive Property.**

$= 8x^2$ **Simplify.**

b. $-5c + c$

$-5c + c = -5c + 1c$ **Rewrite c as 1c.**

$= (-5 + 1)c$ **Use the Distributive Property.**

$= -4c$ **Simplify.**

✓ **Check Understanding** ⑤ Simplify each expression.

a. $7y + 6y$ **b.** $3t - t$ **c.** $-9w^3 - 3w^3$ **d.** $8d + d$

You can write an expression from a verbal phrase. The word *quantity* indicates that two or more terms are within parentheses.

6 EXAMPLE **Writing an Expression**

Write an expression for "3 times the quantity x minus 5."

Relate   3   times   the quantity x minus 5

Write   3   · $(x - 5)$

$3(x - 5)$

✓ **Check Understanding** ⑥ Write an expression for each phrase.

a. -2 times the quantity t plus 7

b. the product of 14 and the quantity 8 plus w

EXERCISES

For more practice, see *Extra Practice*.

Practice and Problem Solving

A Practice by Example

Example 1
(page 47)

Simplify each expression using the Distributive Property.

1. 12(201)   **2.** 51(13)   **3.** 11(499)   **4.** 8(306)

5. 7(98)   **6.** 3(999)   **7.** 41(502)   **8.** 24(1020)

Example 2
(page 48)

Mental Math Use the Distributive Property to find each price.

9. 4($.99)   **10.** 6($1.97)   **11.** 5($5.91)   **12.** 7($29.93)

13. The school librarian got money to buy new reference works. She bought three new CD-ROMs for $32.99 each. How much did she spend in all?

14. You stopped on your way to basketball practice and bought four cans of fruit punch for $.69 each. How much did you spend in all?

Example 3
(page 48)

Simplify each expression.

15. $7(t - 4)$ **16.** $-2(n - 6)$ **17.** $3(m + 4)$

18. $(5b - 4)\frac{1}{5}$ **19.** $-2(x + 3)$ **20.** $\frac{2}{3}(6y + 9)$

21. $0.25(6q + 32)$ **22.** $(3n - 7)(6)$ **23.** $(8 - 3r)\frac{5}{16}$

24. $-4.5(b - 3)$ **25.** $\frac{2}{5}(5w + 10)$ **26.** $(9 - 4n)(-4)$

Example 4
(page 48)

27. $-(x + 3)$ **28.** $-(x - 3)$ **29.** $-(3 + x)$ **30.** $-(3 - x)$

31. $-(6k + 5)$ **32.** $-(7x - 2)$ **33.** $-(2 - 7x)$ **34.** $(4 - z)(-1)$

Example 5
(page 49)

35. $4t - 7t$ **36.** $12k^2 + 8k^2$ **37.** $9x - 2x$ **38.** $w + 23w$

39. $-18v^2 + 23v^2$ **40.** $7m - m$ **41.** $13q - 30q$ **42.** $x - 46x$

Example 6
(page 49)

Write an expression for each phrase.

43. 3 times the quantity m minus 7

44. -4 times the quantity 4 plus w

45. twice the quantity b plus 9

46. the product of -11 and the quantity n minus 8

47. 2 times the quantity 3 times c plus 9

48. the quantity 3 plus r times the quantity r minus 7

B Apply Your Skills

Simplify each expression.

49. 9(4998)   **50.** 8(299)   **51.** 7(2.003)

52. 12(7.001)   **53.** 6(1.97)   **54.** 4(3.998)

55. $7(4.3 + x)$ **56.** $\frac{10}{14}d(8 - 10h)$ **57.** $2(6.4 - 0.5n)$

58. $144\left(\frac{15}{16}b + \frac{8}{9}\right)$ **59.** $3(6.2 + 5m)$ **60.** $\frac{7}{8}\left(\frac{10}{14}d - 48\right)$

61. $-(8.4 + 300g - 512h)$ **62.** $-(12k + 5m - 62)$

63. $\frac{2}{5}p(15 - 35q + 75w)$ **64.** $9(4x + 1.2y - 8.1)$

Write an expression for each phrase.

65. $2\frac{1}{4}$ times the quantity $5\frac{1}{2}$ minus k

66. $6\frac{7}{100}$ times the quantity 8 plus $\frac{4}{3}p$

67. the product of $\frac{11}{20}$ and the quantity b minus $\frac{13}{30}$

68. 17 divided by the quantity z minus 34

69. $4\frac{1}{3}$ times the quantity x minus $\frac{11}{12}$

70. Geometry Write an expression for the perimeter of the figure below. Simplify the expression.

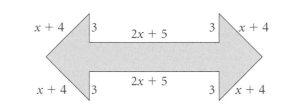

Problem Solving Hint

For Exercise 71, test positive and negative values of a and b as well as zero before writing your conclusion.

71. Writing Does $2ab = 2a \cdot 2b$? Explain.

72. Error Analysis A student rewrote $4(3x + 10)$ as $12x + 10$. Explain the student's error.

73. Open-Ended Write a variable expression that you could simplify using the Distributive Property. Then simplify your expression.

Simplify each expression.

74. $4.78d + 0d$

75. $-21p - 76p^2 - 9 + p$

76. $3.3t^2 + 8.7t - 9.4t^2 + 5t$

77. $1.5m - 4.2m - 12.5v + 4.2m$

78. $\frac{6}{7}n + n^3 - \left(-\frac{5}{6}n\right)$

79. $-\frac{16}{15}k + \frac{3}{20}h + \frac{7}{40}k$

80. $8m^2 - 5mz + 4mz - m^2 + 4$

81. $9 - 4t + 6y - 3t + 10$

82. $1.4b - 3b^2 + 4c - 2b^2 + c$

83. $8xyz + 4xy - 12yzx + 2xy$

84. Identify the terms, the coefficients, and the constant(s) in the expression $-7t + 6v + 7 - 19y$.

85. Sports A high school basketball court is 84 ft long by 50 ft wide. A college basketball court is 10 ft longer than a high school court but has the same width.

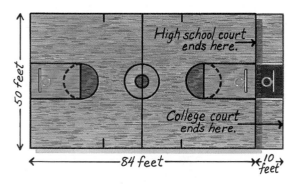

Real-World Connection

Basketball is one of the ten most popular sports activities in the United States, based on participation.

a. Write an expression using parentheses for the area of a college basketball court.

b. Simplify your expression.

86. A student searched the pockets of his jeans before doing laundry and found the following numbers of coins: 4 pennies, 2 nickels, and a quarter; 3 quarters and 6 pennies; 1 dime and 5 nickels. How many of each type of coin does the student have?

 87. Shopping Suppose you buy 4 cans of tomatoes at $1.02 each, 3 cans of tuna for $.99 each, and 3 boxes of pasta at $.52 each. Write an expression to model this situation. Then use the Distributive Property to find the total cost.

C **Challenge** **Simplify each expression.**

88. $9(5 + t) - 6(t + 3)$ **89.** $4(r + 8) - 5(2r - 1)$

90. $-(m + 3) - 2(m + 3)$ **91.** $a[2 + b(2 + c)]$

92. $7b[8 + 6(b - 1)]$ **93.** $-[-5(y + 2z) - 3z]$

94. Critical Thinking If $y = 3x - 10$, what is an expression for $\frac{y}{3}$?

95. a. Evaluate $(a + b) \div c$ and $a \div c + b \div c$ for $a = -10, b = 6,$ and $c = -2$.
    b. Evaluate each expression for $a = -9, b = -3,$ and $c = 6$.
    c. Reasoning Does it appear that $(a + b) \div c = a \div c + b \div c$? Explain.

96. a. Evaluate $a \div (b + c)$ and $a \div b + a \div c$ for $a = -60, b = 3,$ and $c = -5$.
    b. Evaluate each expression for $a = -24, b = -4,$ and $c = 2$.
    c. Reasoning Does it appear that $a \div (b + c) = a \div b + a \div c$? Explain.

Standardized Test Prep

Multiple Choice

97. Which expression is another form of $14x - 21x$?
    A. $-7x^2$ **B.** $7x^2(2 - 3x)$ **C.** $7x(2x - 3)$ **D.** $-7x$

98. Which expression is another form of $-6(k - 5)$?
    F. $-6k^2 - 30k$ **G.** $-6k + 30$ **H.** $-6k^2 - 5$ **I.** $-6k^2 + 5$

Use the table below for Exercises 99–102.

Competitors in the Ultra-Marathon 2000

Category	130-Mile Race		350-Mile Race	
	Number Started	Number Finished	Number Started	Number Finished
Bicycle	51	41	24	16
Foot	43	37	11	9
Ski	9	6	3	3

99. Which category had the most competitors in each race?
    A. bicycle   **B.** foot   **C.** ski   **D.** all of them

100. What percent of the competitors on bicycles completed the 350-mile race?
    F. 67%   **G.** 75%   **H.** 80%   **I.** 82%

101. What percent of the competitors completed the 130-mile race?
    A. 67%   **B.** 75%   **C.** 80%   **D.** 82%

102. Rocky Reifenstuhl won the 130-mile race on his bicycle. He finished in 11 hours and 45 minutes. What was his average speed in miles per hour?

    F. 11.8   **G.** 11.4   **H.** 11.1   **I.** 10.8

103. Simplify $7q + 8pq - 4qp - 9q$.

    A. $-2q + 12pq$ **B.** $16q + 4pq$
    C. $-2q + 4pq$ **D.** $16q + 12pq$

Take It to the NET
Online lesson quiz at
www.PHSchool.com
Web Code: aea-0107

104. A notebook costs $1.89 at the school store. How much would notebooks for a class of 30 students cost?

    F. $59.70   **G.** $59.67   **H.** $57.30   **I.** $56.70

Mixed Review

Lessons 1-5, 1-6

Simplify each expression.

105. $8(-7) + 4(-3)$ **106.** $8 + (-4) \cdot 3$ **107.** $(-3)^2 + (-5)$

108. $(9^2 - 60) \div 3$ **109.** $\dfrac{-7 + 5}{-7 - 5}$ **110.** $\dfrac{7 - 2}{-12 + 8}$

111. $\dfrac{1 + (-4)}{21 - 6}$ **112.** $\dfrac{8 - 5}{16 - 17}$ **113.** $-3^4 \div 9 - 4 \cdot 2$

Lesson 1-4

Simplify each expression.

114. $6.034 + (-8.42)$ **115.** $9.73 + 2.397$ **116.** $-54.1 + 99.4$

117. $|-28.2| + 17.5$ **118.** $-6.45 + |-9.02|$ **119.** $3.02 + (-2.1)$

120. $-5.7 + (-3.9)$ **121.** $-12.5 + 4.8$ **122.** $14.7 + |-8.3|$

Lesson 1-1

123. **a.** Write an expression for the phrase "4 more than the quotient of m and 3."
    b. Evaluate your expression for $m = 9, m = 3,$ and $m = 12$.

A Point in Time

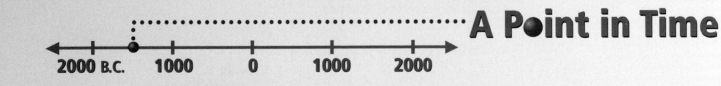

2000 B.C.   1000   0   1000   2000

A papyrus scroll discovered in Egypt shows that Egyptians were using symbols for "plus," "minus," "equals," and "unknown quantity" more than 3500 years ago. Named for the scribe who copied it, the Ahmes Papyrus is 18 ft long and 1 ft wide. It is also known as the Rhind Papyrus, after the British Egyptologist who bought the papyrus. It is a practical handbook containing 85 problems that include work with rational numbers. In the Ahmes Papyrus, rational numbers are written as sums of unit fractions. A unit fraction has 1 as its numerator. Here are some examples.

$$\frac{3}{4} = \frac{1}{2} + \frac{1}{4} \qquad \frac{3}{8} = \frac{1}{4} + \frac{1}{8} \qquad \frac{21}{30} = \frac{1}{6} + \frac{1}{5} + \frac{1}{3}$$

Take It to the NET For more information about the Ahmes Papyrus, go to **www.PHSchool.com**.
Web Code: aee-2032

1-8

Properties of Real Numbers

Lesson Preview

What You'll Learn

OBJECTIVE 1 To identify properties

OBJECTIVE 2 To use deductive reasoning

...And Why

To use mental math when buying multiple items, as in Example 2

✔ **Check Skills You'll Need** (For help, go to Lessons 1-4 and 1-6.)

Simplify each expression.

1. $8 + (9 + 2)$ **2.** $3 \cdot (-2 \cdot 5)$ **3.** $7 + 16 + 3$

4. $-4(7)(-5)$ **5.** $-6 + 9 + (-4)$ **6.** $0.25 \cdot 3 \cdot 4$

7. $3 + x - 2$ **8.** $2t - 8 + 3t$ **9.** $-5m + 2m - 4m$

New Vocabulary • deductive reasoning

OBJECTIVE 1

Identifying and Using Properties

🅘TEXT Interactive lesson includes instant self-check, tutorials, and activities.

The properties of real numbers allow you to write equivalent expressions and simplify expressions. The summary below reviews properties of real numbers that apply to both addition and multiplication.

🔑 **Key Concepts**

Property	Properties of Real Numbers
For every real number a, b, and c,	
Commutative Property of Addition $a + b = b + a$	**Example** $3 + 7 = 7 + 3$
Commutative Property of Multiplication $a \cdot b = b \cdot a$	**Example** $3 \cdot 7 = 7 \cdot 3$
Associative Property of Addition $(a + b) + c = a + (b + c)$	**Example** $(6 + 4) + 5 = 6 + (4 + 5)$
Associative Property of Multiplication $(a \cdot b) \cdot c = a \cdot (b \cdot c)$	**Example** $(6 \cdot 4) \cdot 5 = 6 \cdot (4 \cdot 5)$
Identity Property of Addition $a + 0 = a$	**Example** $9 + 0 = 9$
Identity Property of Multiplication $a \cdot 1 = a$	**Example** $6 \cdot 1 = 6$
Inverse Property of Addition For every a, there is an additive inverse $-a$ such that $a + (-a) = 0$.	**Example** $5 + (-5) = 0$
Inverse Property of Multiplication For every a $(a \neq 0)$, there is a multiplicative inverse $\frac{1}{a}$ such that $a\left(\frac{1}{a}\right) = 1$.	**Example** $5 \cdot \frac{1}{5} = 1$

The following summary reviews some additional properties of real numbers.

Key Concepts

Property	Properties of Real Numbers

For every real number a, b, and c,

Distributive Property   **Examples**

$a(b + c) = ab + ac$ $5(4 + 2) = 5 \cdot 4 + 5 \cdot 2$

$a(b - c) = ab - ac$ $5(4 - 2) = 5 \cdot 4 - 5 \cdot 2$

Multiplication Property of Zero

For every real number n, $n \cdot 0 = 0$. $-35 \cdot 0 = 0$

Multiplication Property of -1

For every real number n, $-1 \cdot n = -n$. $-1 \cdot (-5) = 5$

---

1 EXAMPLE   **Identifying Properties**

Name the property that each equation illustrates. Explain.

a. $9 + 7 = 7 + 9$ Commutative Property of Addition, because the order of the addends changes

b. $(d \cdot 4) \cdot 3 = d \cdot (4 \cdot 3)$ Associative Property of Multiplication, because the grouping of the factors changes

c. $t + 0 = t$ Identity Property of Addition, because the sum of a number and zero is the number

d. $-q = -1q$ Multiplication Property of -1, because the opposite of a value is the same as -1 times the value

✓ Check Understanding   **1** Name the property that each equation illustrates. Explain.

a. $1m = m$ **b.** $(-3 + 4) + 5 = -3 + (4 + 5)$ **c.** $3(8 \cdot 0) = (3 \cdot 8)0$

d. $2 + 0 = 2$ **e.** $np = pn$ **f.** $p + q = q + p$

You can also use the properties to reorganize the order of numbers in sums or products so that you can calculate more easily.

2 EXAMPLE   **Real-World**   **Problem Solving**

Shopping Suppose you buy the school supplies shown at the left. Find the total cost of the supplies.

$0.85 + 2.50 + 5.15 = 2.50 + 0.85 + 5.15$ **Commutative Property of Addition**

$= 2.50 + (0.85 + 5.15)$ **Associative Property of Addition**

$= 2.50 + 6$ **Add within parentheses first.**

$= 8.50$ **Simplify.**

● The total cost of the supplies is $8.50.

✓ Check Understanding   **2** **Shopping** At the supermarket, you buy a package of cheese for $2.50, a loaf of bread for $2.15, a cucumber for $.65, and some tomatoes for $3.50. Find the total cost of the groceries.

Deductive reasoning is the process of reasoning logically from given facts to a conclusion. Using deductive reasoning, you justify each step in simplifying an expression with reasons such as properties, definitions, or rules.

3 EXAMPLE Justifying Steps

Simplify each expression. Justify each step.

a. $-4b + 9 + b$

Step	Reason
$-4b + 9 + b = -4b + 9 + 1b$	Identity Property of Multiplication
$= -4b + 1b + 9$	Commutative Property of Addition
$= (-4 + 1)b + 9$	Distributive Property
$= -3b + 9$	addition

b. $7z - 5(3 + z)$

Step	Reason
$7z - 5(3 + z) = 7z - 15 - 5z$	Distributive Property
$= 7z + (-15) + (-5z)$	definition of subtraction
$= 7z + (-5z) + (-15)$	Commutative Property of Addition
$= [7 + (-5)]z + (-15)$	Distributive Property
$= 2z + (-15)$	addition
$= 2z - 15$	definition of subtraction

? Need Help?

To use the Commutative Property of Addition, write subtraction as addition of the opposite.

✓ **Check Understanding** **3** Simplify each expression. Justify each step.
a. $5a + 6 + a$
b. $2(3t - 1) + 2$

EXERCISES

For more practice, see *Extra Practice*.

Practice and Problem Solving

A Practice by Example

Example 1
(page 55)

Name the property that each equation illustrates. Explain.

1. $-\frac{6}{7} + 0 = -\frac{6}{7}$ **2.** $8 + 43 = 43 + 8$ **3.** $1 \cdot \frac{21}{23} = \frac{21}{23}$

4. $(-7 + 4) + 1 = -7 + (4 + 1)$ **5.** $-0.3 + 0.3 = 0$

6. $9(7.3) = 7.3(9)$ **7.** $5(12 - 4) = 5(12) - 5(4)$

8. $8(9 \cdot 11) = (8 \cdot 9) \cdot 11$ **9.** $-0.5 \cdot (-2) = 1$

Example 2
(page 55)

Mental Math Simplify each expression.

10. $47 + 39 + 3 + 11$ **11.** $25 \cdot 74 \cdot 2 \cdot 2$ **12.** $4.75 + 2.95 + 1.25 + 6$

13. $10 \cdot 6 \cdot 7 \cdot 10$ **14.** $2(5 - 3.5) - 8$ **15.** $6\frac{1}{2} + 4\frac{1}{3} + 1\frac{1}{2} + \frac{2}{3}$

🌐 **16. Shopping** You buy 3 grapefruits for $1.50, a pound of apples for $.79, some grapes for $2.50, and some bananas for $1.21. Find the total cost of the fruit.

Example 3
(page 56)

Give a reason to justify each step.

17. a. $3y - 5y = 3y + (-5y)$ ___?___

   b. $\qquad\quad = [3 + (-5)]y$ ___?___

   c. $\qquad\quad = -2y$ ___?___

18. a. $3 \cdot (12 \cdot 10) = 3 \cdot (10 \cdot 12)$ ___?___

   b. $\qquad\qquad\quad = (3 \cdot 10) \cdot 12$ ___?___

   c. $\qquad\qquad\quad = 30 \cdot 12$ ___?___

   d. $\qquad\qquad\quad = 360$ ___?___

Simplify each expression. Justify each step.

19. $25 \cdot 1.7 \cdot 4$

20. $-5(7y)$

21. $8 + 9m + 7$

22. $12x - 3 + 6x$

23. $29c + (-29c)$

24. $43\left(\frac{1}{43}\right) + 1$

B Apply Your Skills

Simplify each expression. Justify each step.

25. $2 + g\left(\frac{1}{g}\right)$

26. $36jkm - 36mjk$

27. $(3^2 - 2^3)(8759)$

28. $(7^6 - 6^5)(8 - 8)$

29. $4 + 6(8 - 3m)$

30. $5\left(w - \frac{1}{5}\right) - w(9)$

31. Shopping Suppose you are buying soccer equipment: a pair of cleats for $31.50, a soccer ball for $14.97, and shin guards for $6.50. Use mental math to find the total cost.

Tell whether the expressions in each pair are equivalent.

32. $6m + 1$ and $1 \cdot 6 + m$

33. $9y$ and $9 + y$

34. $mp + nq$ and $mq + np$

35. $-(5 - 9)$ and $9 - 5$

36. $8 - 4c$ and $4c - 8$

37. $3(5 + z)$ and $15 + z$

38. $6t - 4$ and $2[(2 + 1)t - 2]$

39. $vwx \cdot yz$ and $v \cdot w \cdot zxy$

Reasoning Explain your answer to each question.

40. Is subtraction commutative?

41. Is subtraction associative?

42. Is division commutative?

43. Is division associative?

44. Give a reason to justify each step.

   a. $5t + 6 + 3(t + 2) = 5t + 6 + 3t + 6$ ___?___

   b. $\qquad\qquad\qquad\quad = 5t + 3t + 6 + 6$ ___?___

   c. $\qquad\qquad\qquad\quad = 5t + 3t + (6 + 6)$ ___?___

   d. $\qquad\qquad\qquad\quad = 5t + 3t + 12$ ___?___

   e. $\qquad\qquad\qquad\quad = (5 + 3)t + 12$ ___?___

   f. $\qquad\qquad\qquad\quad = 8t + 12$ ___?___

45. Reasoning The Distributive Property states that $a(b + c) = ab + ac$. Use this and the other properties to explain why $(b + c)a = ba + ca$ is also true.

46. Writing Suppose you make a peanut butter and jelly sandwich. Do you think it tastes the same regardless of whether the jelly is on top or the peanut butter is on top? Relate your answer to one of the properties of real numbers.

C Challenge

Critical Thinking The *closure properties* for a set of numbers assure that the sum and product of two numbers in a given set of numbers are also in the set of numbers. Determine whether each set of numbers is closed for addition, for multiplication, or for both. If not, give a counterexample.

47. rational numbers

48. integers

49. whole numbers

50. negative numbers

51. odd numbers

52. even numbers

Multiple Choice

53. Simplify $-4 + 17 - 29 + 4 + 29 - 3$.
  A. 14   **B.** 20   **C.** 22   **D.** 72

54. Which of the following has the same result as dividing a number by $\frac{5}{2}$ and then multiplying by $\frac{1}{2}$?
  F. multiplying by 2   **G.** dividing by 2
  H. multiplying by 5   **I.** dividing by 5

55. In the formula $A = \pi r^2$, if the value of r is doubled, then what is the value of A multiplied by?
  A. $\frac{1}{4}$ **B.** $\frac{1}{2}$ **C.** 2   **D.** 4

56. The variable a is an integer. Which of the following could NOT equal a^3?
  F. -27 **G.** -16 **H.** 8   **I.** 64

57. What is the total cost if you buy 3 goldfish for $1.90 each, 3 angelfish for $6.10 each, and 12 neon tetras for $1.53 each?
  A. $39.36   **B.** $42.36   **C.** $60.36   **D.** $66.36

58. Simplify $-2h - (5 - 3h)$.
  F. $h - 5$ **G.** $-5h - 5$ **H.** h **I.** $-4h$

Take It to the NET
Online lesson quiz at
www.PHSchool.com
Web Code: aea-0108

Mixed Review

Lesson 1-7

Simplify each expression.

59. $5(1.2 + k)$ **60.** $\frac{1}{3}(33 - b)$ **61.** $-2.5(4p + 14)$

62. $4(7 - n)$ **63.** $-(-7.4m + 0.05)$ **64.** $(3v - 5.2)(-6)$

Lesson 1-6

Write an expression for each phrase.

65. 7 plus the sum of m and -17 **66.** 8 minus the quantity 9 minus t

67. one half of the quotient of b and 4   **68.** one third of the sum of x and 5.1

Lesson 1-4

Simplify.

69. $12 + (-5)$ **70.** $9.2 + (-27.5)$ **71.** $\frac{5}{8} + \left(-\frac{7}{8}\right)$

72. $-4\frac{6}{10} + 3\frac{2}{5}$ **73.** $-11 + (-124)$ **74.** $|-2.4| + |6.8|$

Checkpoint Quiz 2   Lessons 1-5 through 1-8

TEXT Instant self-check quiz online and on CD-ROM

Simplify each expression.

1. $7 + 4t + 6 + t$ **2.** $(5 \cdot 16) \cdot 2$ **3.** $(5 + 16)2$

4. $(-4)^3 + (-3)(-5)$ **5.** $-3(4 + w) - 6w$ **6.** $-(-5 - 4m)$

7. $|43.7 + (-45.2)|$ **8.** $9 \div (-3) - 4 \div (-8)$ **9.** $3x + 6y - 8x - y$

10. a. Simplify the expression $9t + 3(t + 4)$. Justify each step.
   b. Evaluate the expression for $t = -3$.

Graphing Data on the Coordinate Plane

Lesson Preview

What You'll Learn

OBJECTIVE 1 To graph points on the coordinate plane

OBJECTIVE 2 To analyze data using scatter plots

. . . And Why

To analyze car age and price data, as in Example 5

✔ **Check Skills You'll Need** (For help, go to Lesson 1-3.)

Graph each number on a number line.

1. 6   **2.** −5   **3.** 2.7   **4.** 0

Write the coordinate of each point on the number line below.

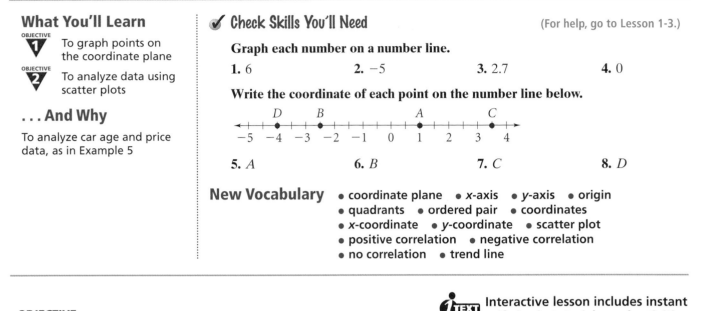

5. A   **6.** B   **7.** C   **8.** D

New Vocabulary
- coordinate plane
- x-axis
- y-axis
- origin
- quadrants
- ordered pair
- coordinates
- x-coordinate
- y-coordinate
- scatter plot
- positive correlation
- negative correlation
- no correlation
- trend line

OBJECTIVE 1

iTEXT Interactive lesson includes instant self-check, tutorials, and activities.

Graphing Points on the Coordinate Plane

Real-World 🌎 Connection

To find a street on a map, you look in a region between grid lines. To locate a point on a coordinate plane, you look at the intersection of grid lines.

Two number lines that intersect at right angles form a **coordinate plane.** The horizontal axis is the **x-axis** and the vertical axis is the **y-axis.** The axes intersect at the **origin** and divide the coordinate plane into four sections called **quadrants.**

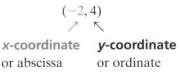

An **ordered pair** of numbers identifies the location of a point. These numbers are the **coordinates** of the point on the graph. Point B has coordinates $(-2, 4)$.

$$(-2, 4)$$

x-coordinate   **y-coordinate**
or abscissa   or ordinate

The x-coordinate tells you how far to move right (positive) or left (negative) from the origin. The y-coordinate tells you how far to move up (positive) or down (negative) from the origin.

1 EXAMPLE Identifying Coordinates

Name the coordinates of point Z in the graph.

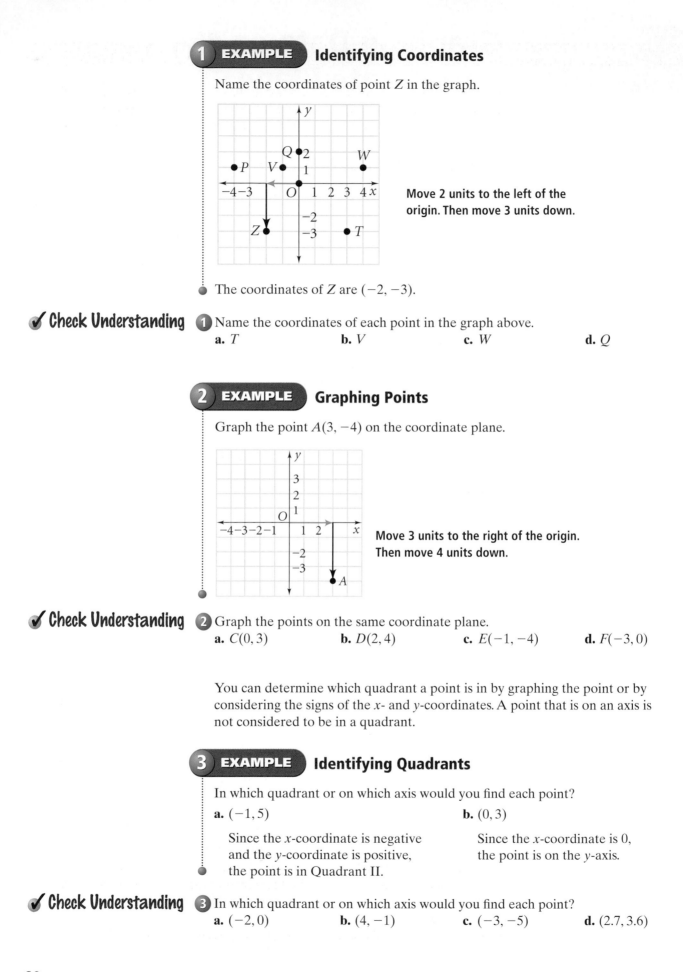

Move 2 units to the left of the origin. Then move 3 units down.

The coordinates of Z are $(-2, -3)$.

✓ Check Understanding **1** Name the coordinates of each point in the graph above.
a. T **b.** V **c.** W **d.** Q

2 EXAMPLE Graphing Points

Graph the point $A(3, -4)$ on the coordinate plane.

Move 3 units to the right of the origin. Then move 4 units down.

✓ Check Understanding **2** Graph the points on the same coordinate plane.
a. $C(0, 3)$ **b.** $D(2, 4)$ **c.** $E(-1, -4)$ **d.** $F(-3, 0)$

You can determine which quadrant a point is in by graphing the point or by considering the signs of the x- and y-coordinates. A point that is on an axis is not considered to be in a quadrant.

3 EXAMPLE Identifying Quadrants

In which quadrant or on which axis would you find each point?
a. $(-1, 5)$ **b.** $(0, 3)$

Since the x-coordinate is negative and the y-coordinate is positive, the point is in Quadrant II.

Since the x-coordinate is 0, the point is on the y-axis.

✓ Check Understanding **3** In which quadrant or on which axis would you find each point?
a. $(-2, 0)$ **b.** $(4, -1)$ **c.** $(-3, -5)$ **d.** $(2.7, 3.6)$

A **scatter plot** is a graph that relates two groups of data. To make a scatter plot, plot the two groups of data as ordered pairs. Most scatter plots are in the first quadrant of a coordinate plane, because the data are usually positive numbers.

4 **EXAMPLE** **Making a Scatter Plot**

Data Collection The table at the left shows data students collected on their test scores and the number of hours they watched television the previous day. Make a scatter plot of the data.

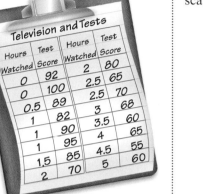

For 2 hours of television watched and a test score of 80, plot (2, 80).

The highest score is 100. So a reasonable scale on the vertical axis is 0 to 100 with every 20 points labeled.

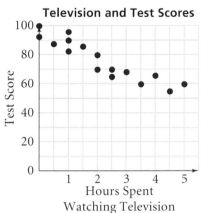

Television and Test Scores

✔ **Check Understanding** **4** Use the data in the table at the right. Make a scatter plot of the data.

Media in the United States

Year	Daily Newspaper Circulation (millions)	Number of Households With Television (millions)
1950	54	4
1960	59	46
1970	62	59
1980	62	76
1990	62	92
2000*	55	101

*estimated

You can use scatter plots to look for trends in data. The three scatter plots below show the types of relationships two sets of data may have.

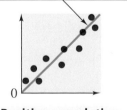

Positive correlation
In general, both sets of data increase together.

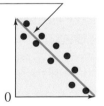

Negative correlation
In general, one set of data decreases as the other set increases.

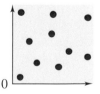

No correlation
Sometimes data sets are not related.

A **trend line** on a scatter plot shows a correlation more clearly.

5 EXAMPLE   Real-World Problem Solving

Cars Use the scatter plot below. Is there a *positive correlation*, a *negative correlation*, or *no correlation* between the age of a used car and the asking price of the car?

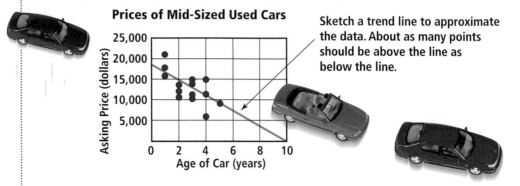

Prices of Mid-Sized Used Cars

Sketch a trend line to approximate the data. About as many points should be above the line as below the line.

As the age of a car increases, the asking price generally decreases. There is a negative correlation between the age and asking price of a car.

✓ **Check Understanding** 5 **a. Critical Thinking** In the graph above, what does the data point at (4, 14,900) represent?

b. Use the graph to predict the asking price of a 7-year-old car.

EXERCISES

For more practice, see *Extra Practice*.

Practice and Problem Solving

A **Practice by Example**

Example 1
(page 60)

Name the coordinates of each point on the graph at the right.

1. *A*   **2.** *F*

3. *D*   **4.** *I*

Example 2
(page 60)

Graph the points on the same coordinate plane.

5. $(3, 0)$ **6.** $(-1, 8)$

7. $(-2, -3)$ **8.** $(7, -7)$

Example 3
(page 60)

In which quadrant or on which axis would you find each point?

9. $(-10, 6)$ **10.** $(-12, 0)$ **11.** $(8, -18)$ **12.** $(0, 30)$

Complete each statement.

13. If the *x*-coordinate and the *y*-coordinate of an ordered pair are positive, the ordered pair is in Quadrant __?__.

14. If the *x*-coordinate of an ordered pair is negative, and the *y*-coordinate is positive, the ordered pair is in Quadrant __?__.

15. The *x*-coordinate is 0 and the *y*-coordinate is negative. Is the point in Quadrant III? Explain.

Example 4
(page 61)

16. Make a scatter plot of the data below.

Gasoline Purchases

Dollars Spent	10	11	9	10	13	5	8	4
Gallons Bought	6.3	6.1	5.6	5.5	8.3	2.9	5.2	2.7

Example 5
(page 62)

Describe the trend in each scatter plot below.

17. 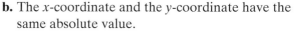   **18.**   **19.**

B **Apply Your Skills**

Mental Math **Write the coordinates of each point.**

20. the point 3 units to the left of the *y*-axis and 4 units above the *x*-axis

21. the point 5 units to the right of the *y*-axis and on the *x*-axis

22. the point 6 units to the right of the *y*-axis and 6 units below the *x*-axis

23. What are the coordinates of the points on the calculator screen at the right? Assume tick marks on the axes are separated by one unit.

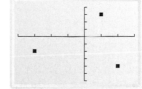

24. Open-Ended Write the coordinates of three points that satisfy each condition.
   a. The *x*-coordinate is the opposite of the *y*-coordinate.
   b. The *x*-coordinate and the *y*-coordinate have the same absolute value.

Geometry **Graph and connect the points in the order given. Connect the last point to the first. Describe the figure.**

25. $(4, 4), (-1, 1), (2, -4), (7, -1)$ **26.** $(-3, 0), (0, 5), (3, 0), (0, -5)$

27. $(-2, 1), (2, 4), (5, 0)$ **28.** $(5, -3), (2, -7), (-6, -1), (-3, 3)$

Critical Thinking **Would you expect a *positive correlation*, a *negative correlation*, or *no correlation* between the two data sets? Explain why.**

29. the amount of free time you have and the number of classes you take

30. the air pollution levels for a city and the number of cars registered in that city

31. length of a baby at birth and the month in which the baby was born

32. the number of calories burned and the time spent exercising

33. Open-Ended Describe three situations: one that shows a positive correlation, one that shows a negative correlation, and one that shows no correlation.

34. a. Think about the weather and its effect on voters. What correlation would you expect between the amount of precipitation and voter turnout? Explain.
   b. Reasoning Should candidates in an election be concerned about the weather forecast? Explain.

35. During one month at a local deli, the number of pounds of ham sold decreased as the number of pounds of turkey sold increased.
  a. Is this an example of a *positive correlation*, *negative correlation*, or *no correlation?*
  b. Reasoning Is it reasonable to conclude that fewer pounds of ham were sold because the deli sold more pounds of turkey? Explain.

36. a. Nutrition Draw a scatter plot of the data below. Graph the grams of fat on the *x*-axis and the number of calories on the *y*-axis.

Calories Per Serving of Some Common Foods

Food	Grams of Fat	Number of Calories	Food	Grams of Fat	Number of Calories
Whole Milk	8	150	Eggs	6	80
Chicken	4	90	Ham	19	245
Corn	1	70	Broccoli	1	45
Ground Beef	10	185	Cheese	9	115

  b. Draw a trend line on the scatter plot. Describe the correlation, if any, between calories and grams of fat.
  c. Writing Write a statement describing the relationship between calories and grams of fat.
  d. A serving of ice cream has 14 grams of fat. Predict the number of calories a serving of ice cream has.

Challenge

37. Geometry Find the perimeter and area of a rectangle whose vertices have coordinates $(4, 1)$, $(-3, 1)$, $(-3, -2)$, and $(4, -2)$.

38. Geometry Find the area of a triangle whose vertices have coordinates $(-1, 2)$, $(-1, -1)$, and $(-6, 2)$.

39. Points with the coordinates $(0, 3)$, $(2, 5)$, $(4, 3)$, and $(2, 1)$ lie on a circle with center $(2, 3)$. Find another circle with center $(2, 3)$, such that there are at least eight points on the circle with integers for the *x*- and *y*- coordinates. What are the coordinates of the eight points?

40. a. Transportation In the scatter plot below, what does a point on the scatter plot represent?

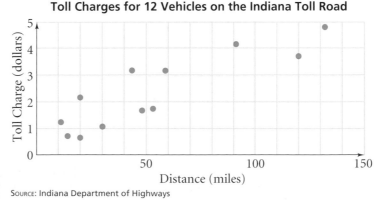

Toll Charges for 12 Vehicles on the Indiana Toll Road

Source: Indiana Department of Highways

  b. How can you tell if some vehicles traveled the same distance?
  c. How can you tell which vehicles paid the same toll charge?
  d. Is there a correlation between distance traveled and toll charges? Explain.

Multiple Choice

41. In which quadrant on the coordinate plane is $(-3, -1)$?

    A. I   **B.** II   **C.** III   **D.** IV

42. What are the coordinates of the point that is on the *y*-axis 6 units above the *x*-axis?

    F. $(0, -6)$ **G.** $(0, 6)$ **H.** $(6, 0)$ **I.** $(-6, 0)$

43. The point (q, r) is in Quadrant II. The value of *q* must be __?__ . The value of *r* must be __?__ .

    A. positive, negative   **B.** negative, negative
    C. positive, positive   **D.** negative, positive

44. The coordinates of three vertices of a rectangle are $(-2, -1)$, $(2, -5)$, and $(9, 2)$. What are the coordinates of the fourth vertex?

    F. $(4, 3)$ **G.** $(5, 6)$ **H.** $(5, 5)$ **I.** $(6, 6)$

45. Suppose you take a survey of all the schools in your state. What would you expect the relationship between the number of students and the number of teachers in each school to be?

    A. positive correlation   **B.** negative correlation
    C. no correlation   **D.** none of the above

46. Which sets of data would most likely have a negative correlation?

    F. the population of Detroit over a 10-year period and the population of Kansas over the same 10-year period
    G. the height of a person and that person's shoe size
    H. the number of times a car stops to fill its gas tank and the amount of gas the tank can hold
    I. the size of an animal and the amount of food it needs each day

Take It to the NET
Online lesson quiz at
www.PHSchool.com
Web Code: aea-0109

Mixed Review

Lesson 1-8

Simplify each expression. Justify each step.

47. $x - 4(2x + 1) - 3$ **48.** $5(8t) + 4(9 - t) - 37$

49. $8b + 7a - 4b - 9a$ **50.** $3m^2 - (10m + 3m^2)$

Lessons 1-4, 1-5

Find each sum or difference.

51. $\begin{bmatrix} 3 & -5 \\ 4 & -1 \end{bmatrix} + \begin{bmatrix} 6 & -8 \\ 15 & 0 \end{bmatrix}$ **52.** $[12 \quad -27 \quad 0 \quad -3] - [-4.5 \quad 2 \quad -1 \quad 6.5]$

53. $\begin{bmatrix} -2.9 & 5 & 17 \\ 0 & -4.7 & 3.9 \\ 1 & -8 & 15 \end{bmatrix} - \begin{bmatrix} -6 & 5.7 & -4 \\ 4.9 & 0 & 6 \\ 2 & -1 & 7 \end{bmatrix}$ **54.** $\begin{bmatrix} \frac{1}{2} & -\frac{3}{5} \\ 6 & -9 \\ 4 & 16 \end{bmatrix} + \begin{bmatrix} -12 & \frac{1}{10} \\ \frac{9}{2} & -8 \\ 1 & 14 \end{bmatrix}$

Lesson 1-3

Decide whether each statement is *true* or *false*. If the statement is false, give a counterexample.

55. All positive integers are natural numbers.

56. A number cannot have a value equal to its square.

57. All integers are rational numbers.

Writing Gridded Responses

Some standardized test questions require you to enter a number answer on a grid. The number can be a fraction or a decimal.

1 EXAMPLE

What is $\frac{1}{2} + \frac{3}{4}$?

The sum can be written as $\frac{10}{8}$, $\frac{5}{4}$, or 1.25. Write your answer in the spaces at the top, and fill in the corresponding bubbles below. These three forms of the answer are shown at the right.

Note:

- Write a mixed number as an improper fraction. For example, do not put the mixed number $1\frac{1}{4}$ in the grid because the test-scoring computer will read "1 1/4" as $\frac{11}{4}$.

- Fractions do not have to be simplified.

2 EXAMPLE

How many feet are in $\frac{1}{7}$ mile? Round to the nearest foot.

There are 5280 feet in a mile, so there are $5280 \div 7 \approx 754.3$ feet in $\frac{1}{7}$ mile.

Rounded to the nearest foot, the answer is 754 feet. Enter 754 on the grid.

Do not enter the units.

EXERCISES

Which number should you grid for each answer?

1. What is 14% of 0.4?

   A. 0.56   **B.** 0.006   **C.** 0.056   **D.** 0.05

2. What part of a mile is 2200 feet? Round to the nearest hundredth of a mile.

   F. 0.40   **G.** $\frac{40}{100}$ **H.** 0.41   **I.** 0.42

3. What is the value of $\frac{(x+2)^2}{x+3}$ when $x = 1$?

   A. 0.75   **B.** 1.25   **C.** $\frac{3}{4}$ **D.** $\frac{9}{4}$

4. What is the value of x^3 when $x = 0.2$?

   F. 8   **G.** 0.8   **H.** 0.6   **I.** 0.008

Chapter Review

Vocabulary

absolute value (p. 20)	integers (p. 17)	quadrants (p. 59)
additive inverse (p. 24)	irrational numbers (p. 18)	rational numbers (p. 17)
algebraic expression (p. 4)	like terms (p. 49)	real numbers (p. 18)
base (p. 9)	matrix (p. 27)	reciprocal (p. 41)
coefficient (p. 49)	multiplicative inverse (p. 41)	scatter plot (p. 61)
constant (p. 49)	natural numbers (p. 17)	simplify (p. 9)
coordinate plane (p. 59)	negative correlation (p. 61)	term (p. 49)
coordinates (p. 59)	no correlation (p. 61)	trend line (p. 61)
counterexample (p. 18)	open sentence (p. 5)	variable (p. 4)
deductive reasoning (p. 56)	opposites (p. 20)	whole numbers (p. 17)
element (p. 27)	ordered pair (p. 59)	*x*-axis (p. 59)
equation (p. 5)	order of operations (p. 10)	*x*-coordinate (p. 59)
evaluate (p. 10)	origin (p. 59)	*y*-axis (p. 59)
exponent (p. 9)	positive correlation (p. 61)	*y*-coordinate (p. 59)
inequality (p. 19)	power (p. 9)	

Reading Math
Understanding
Vocabulary

Take It to the NET
Online vocabulary quiz
at **www.PHSchool.com**
Web Code: aej-0151

Choose the term that correctly completes each sentence.

1. A (constant, term) is a number, a variable, or the product of a number and one or more variables.

2. You (evaluate, simplify) an algebraic expression by substituting a given number for each variable.

3. A mathematical phrase that uses numbers, variables, and operation symbols is an (algebraic expression, equation).

4. The number $-\frac{5}{8}$ belongs to the set of (irrational, rational) numbers.

5. The (absolute value, opposite) of a number is its distance from 0 on a number line.

6. A (coordinate plane, matrix) is a rectangular arrangement of numbers in rows and columns.

7. Dividing by a nonzero number is the same as multiplying by its (coefficient, reciprocal).

8. You express the fraction of a pizza you have eaten using a(n) (rational number, integer).

9. In an ordered pair, the first number is the (*x*-coordinate, *y*-coordinate), which tells how far to move to the left or right of the origin as you graph the point represented by the ordered pair.

10. A (coordinate plane, scatter plot) is a graph that relates data from two different sets.

11. When one set of data increases while another set of data decreases, there is a (positive correlation, negative correlation) between the two sets of data.

12. You simplify a(n) (power, exponent) by multiplying the base by itself the indicated number of times.

Skills and Concepts

1-1 and 1-2 Objectives

▼ To model relationships with variables (p. 4)

▼ To model relationships with equations and formulas (p. 5)

▼ To simplify and evaluate expressions and formulas (p. 9)

▼ To evaluate expressions containing grouping symbols (p. 11)

A **variable** represents one or more numbers. To **evaluate** a variable expression, you substitute a given number for each variable. Then you simplify the expression using the **order of operations.**

Order of Operations

1. Perform any operation(s) inside grouping symbols.

2. Simplify powers.

3. Multiply and divide in order from left to right.

4. Add and subtract in order from left to right.

Define a variable and write an expression for each phrase.

13. the sum of 5 and three times a number

14. 30 minus a number

15. the quotient of 7 and a number

16. the product of a number and 12

Evaluate each expression for $a = 3, b = 2,$ and $c = 1$.

17. $2a^2 - (4b + c)$ **18.** $9(a + 2b) + c$ **19.** $\frac{2a + b}{2}$ **20.** $4a - b^2$

1-3 Objectives

▼ To classify numbers (p. 17)

▼ To compare numbers (p. 19)

Real numbers can be classified as either rational numbers or irrational numbers. A **rational number,** like $\frac{5}{8}$, is a ratio of two integers. An **irrational number,** like π or $\sqrt{2}$, cannot be written as a ratio of integers. Rational numbers include **natural numbers** $(1, 2, 3, \dots)$, **whole numbers** $(0, 1, 2, 3, \dots)$, and **integers** $(\dots, -2, -1, 0, 1, 2, \dots)$.

Name the set(s) of numbers to which each number belongs.

21. -3.21 **22.** $\sqrt{7}$ **23.** $-\frac{1}{2}$ **24.** 18 **25.** $\frac{35}{5}$

1-4, 1-5, and 1-6 Objectives

▼ To add real numbers using models and rules (p. 24)

▼ To apply addition (p. 26)

▼ To subtract real numbers (p. 32)

▼ To apply subtraction (p. 33)

▼ To multiply real numbers (p. 37)

▼ To divide real numbers (p. 40)

To add two real numbers with the same sign, add their absolute values. The sum has the same sign as the addends. To add two real numbers with different signs, find the difference of their absolute values. The sum has the sign of the addend with the greater absolute value. To subtract a real number, add its opposite.

The product or quotient of two real numbers that have the same sign is positive. The product or quotient of two real numbers with different signs is negative.

Simplify each expression.

26. $(-13) + (-4)$ **27.** $-12 - (-7)$ **28.** $-12.4 + 22.3$

29. $|54.3 - 29.4|$ **30.** $5 - 17$ **31.** $-3^2 + (-3)^2$

32. $4 - 3(-2)$ **33.** $5(4)(-2)$ **34.** $\left(\frac{5}{6}\right)\left(-\frac{2}{3}\right)$

35. $\frac{4 - (-2)}{3}$ **36.** $\frac{5}{6} \div \left(-\frac{2}{3}\right)$ **37.** $\frac{5}{6} + \left(-\frac{2}{3}\right)^2$

1-7 Objectives

▼ To use the Distributive Property (p. 47)

▼ To simplify algebraic expressions (p. 48)

Terms with exactly the same variable factors are **like terms.** You can combine like terms and use the Distributive Property to simplify expressions.

Distributive Property For all real numbers $a, b,$ and $c, a(b + c) = ab + ac$ and $a(b - c) = ab - ac$.

Simplify each expression.

38. $9m - 5m + 3$ **39.** $2b + 8 - b + 2$ **40.** $-5(w - 4)$ **41.** $9(4 - 3j)$

42. $-(3 - 10y)$ **43.** $-2\left(r - \frac{1}{2}\right)$ **44.** $(7b + 1)(5)$ **45.** $7 - 16v - 9v$

46. $\frac{3}{5}(15t - 2)$ **47.** $(6 - 3m)(-3)$ **48.** $-(4 - x)$ **49.** $0.5(20g + 3)$

1-8 Objectives

▼ To identify properties (p. 54)

▼ To use deductive reasoning (p. 56)

Use properties of real numbers to simplify expressions. Use the Commutative Property to change order. Use the Associative Property to change grouping.

Which property does each equation illustrate?

50. $62 + 15 + 38 = 62 + (15 + 38)$ **51.** $62 + 0 + (15 + 38) = 62 + (15 + 38)$

52. $50 \cdot 17 \cdot 2 = 50 \cdot 2 \cdot 17$ **53.** $9(2^3 - 4^2) = 9(2^3) - 9(4^2)$

Simplify each expression. Justify each step.

54. $19 + 56\left(\frac{1}{56}\right)$ **55.** $-12p + 45 - 7p$ **56.** $24abc - 24bac$ **57.** $4 \cdot 13 \cdot 25 \cdot 1$

1-9 Objectives

▼ To graph points on the coordinate plane (p. 59)

▼ To analyze data using scatter plots (p. 61)

A **coordinate plane** is formed by the intersection of two number lines. The *x*-axis and the *y*-axis divide the coordinate plane into four **quadrants.** An **ordered pair** gives the coordinates of a point. The *x*-coordinate shows how far to move left or right from the origin. The *y*-coordinate shows how far to move up or down from the origin.

A **scatter plot** is a graph that relates two sets of data.

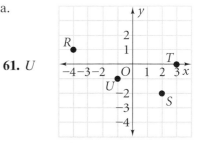

Write the coordinates of each point.

58. R **59.** S **60.** T **61.** U

Graph each point on the coordinate plane.

62. $J(-6, 4)$ **63.** $K(0, -8)$ **64.** $L(7, 4)$

65. a. Make a scatter plot of the data below.

Height (meters)	1.5	1.8	1.7	2.0	1.7	2.1	1.6	1.9	1.9
Arm Span (meters)	1.4	1.7	1.7	1.9	1.6	2.0	1.6	1.8	1.9

b. Is there a *positive correlation*, a *negative correlation*, or *no correlation* between the sets of data?

Chapter Test

Take It to the NET
Online chapter test at
www.PHSchool.com
Web Code: aea-0152

Define variables and write an equation to model the relationship in each table.

1.
Number	Cost
1	$2.30
2	$4.60
3	$6.90

2.
Payment	Change
$1	$9
$2	$8
$3	$7

Simplify each expression.

3. $3 + 5 - 4$

4. $8 - 2^4 \div 2$

5. $\dfrac{2 \cdot 3 - 1}{3^2}$

6. $36 - (4 + 5 \cdot 4)$

Evaluate each expression for $x = 3$, $y = -1$, and $z = 2$.

7. $2x + 3y + z$

8. $-xyz$

9. $-3x - 2z - 7$

10. $-z^3 - 2z + z$

11. $\dfrac{xy - 3z}{-5}$

12. $x^2 + (-x)^2$

Find each sum or difference.

13. $\begin{bmatrix} 3 & 2 \\ -1 & 5 \end{bmatrix} + \begin{bmatrix} 8 & -5 \\ 3 & 0 \end{bmatrix}$

14. $\begin{bmatrix} 1 & 9 & -4 \\ 5 & 2 & -1 \\ -6 & -2 & -1 \end{bmatrix} - \begin{bmatrix} 2 & -6 & 7 \\ -8 & 3 & -3 \\ 4 & -7 & 9 \end{bmatrix}$

Explain why each statement is true or false.

15. All rational numbers are integers.

16. The absolute value of a number is always positive.

Simplify each expression.

17. $(7 - 42a)\left(-\dfrac{3}{7}\right)$

18. $6(2d - 5)$

Simplify each expression. Justify each step.

19. $10x + 3\left(\dfrac{1}{3} - x\right)$

20. $(3^3 - 3^3)(1 - 2^2)$

Write an expression for each phrase.

21. negative ten times the quantity two minus eleven

22. five divided by the quantity m plus six

23. the quantity p minus five eighths times the quantity one fourth plus p

Simplify each expression.

24. $-7\dfrac{7}{8} + \left(-2\dfrac{1}{2}\right)$

25. $-1.8 + 12.1 + (-7.6)$

26. Writing Tell whether each of the subtraction sentences will *always*, *sometimes*, or *never* be true. Support your answer with two examples.
   a. $(+) - (+) = (+)$ **b.** $(+) - (-) = (-)$
   c. $(-) - (-) = (-)$ **d.** $(-) - (+) = (+)$

27. Open-Ended Write four rational numbers. Use a number line to order them from least to greatest.

In which quadrant or on which axis would you find each point?

28. $(0, -2)$

29. $(-3, -6)$

30. Geometry Find the area of a trapezoid whose vertices have coordinates $(-2, 1), (2, 1), (5, -3)$, and $(-5, -3)$.

31. On four plays, a football team gained 22 yd, lost 18 yd, gained 8 yd, and lost 14 yd. What is the total number of yards gained or lost on the four plays?

32. Banking Marcus had $163 in his checking account. On Monday, he wrote a check for $315. How much does Marcus need to deposit into his account to prevent the account balance from dipping below the minimum of $25?

33. Sales A CD costs $17.95 plus tax. The sales tax rate is 7.5%. Find the total cost of the CD.

Use the scatter plot below for Exercises 34–35.

34. Is there a *positive correlation, negative correlation,* or *no correlation* between daily mean temperature and latitude?

35. What is the daily mean temperature for the location at latitude 58° N?

Climate Data

36. Writing Explain why $\left|\dfrac{a}{b}\right| = \dfrac{a}{b}$ is *not* always true.

Standardized Test Prep

Reading Comprehension Read the passage below, and then answer the questions on the basis of what is *stated* or *implied* in the passage.

Travel Math Often one of the biggest complications of visiting a foreign country is doing the math. Things that would cause no problem at home are suddenly challenging because the units are different. Consider a quarter-pound hamburger. At 2.2 pounds (lbs) per kilogram (kg), what is the mass of a quarter-pound hamburger in the metric system?

Once you have ordered lunch, you have to pay for it. Let's see . . . one U.S. dollar is worth 1.53 Canadian dollars, 0.70 British pounds, or 1.07 European euros. So how much does a quarter-pound hamburger cost in other countries?

Then there is figuring out the temperature. Even if you can remember the formula Fahrenheit $= \frac{9}{5} \cdot$ Celsius $+ 32$, you must do some work to find whether 20°C is a beach day or a ski day.

Fortunately, it doesn't have to be quite so hard. If you look for some simple approximations, you can usually get around foreign countries without having to pack a calculator. As with many other aspects of travel, the trick is to think ahead, anticipate what might be coming, and have a plan for dealing with it. Before you go, figure out which formulas you will be using and come up with some simple approximations. Then you can leave your calculator home.

1. About how many kilograms are there in 10 lb?
   A. 25 kg   **B.** 20 kg
   C. 11 kg   **D.** 5 kg

2. How many kilograms correspond to a quarter pound?
   F. 0.1 kg   **G.** 0.5 kg
   H. 5 kg   **I.** 8.8 kg

3. Based on the article, which could you use to estimate an exchange of Canadian dollars and United States dollars?
   A. 1 U.S. Dollar $= \frac{1}{2}$ Canadian Dollar
   B. 1 U.S. Dollar $= \frac{2}{3}$ Canadian Dollar
   C. 2 U.S. Dollar $= 3$ Canadian Dollars
   D. 3 U.S. Dollars $= 2$ Canadian Dollars

4. Suppose you pay $3.00 for a hamburger in Canada. How much is this in United States currency?
   F. $1.95   **G.** $3.00
   H. $4.53   **I.** $4.59

5. According to the article, about how many euros could you get for 5 U.S. dollars?
   A. 0.20 euros   **B.** 1.50 euros
   C. 4.20 euros   **D.** 5.50 euros

6. Suppose you are traveling in France. You see a T-shirt for 40 euros. Is this a reasonable price? Justify your answer.

7. A taxicab ride in London costs you 15 pounds. How much is this in United States currency?

8. The formula Fahrenheit $= 2 \cdot$ Celsius $+ 30$ gives a good estimate of the temperature in degrees Fahrenheit when you know the temperature in degrees Celsius. Is 20°C a beach day? Justify your answer.

9. A foreign exchange student could use the formula Celsius $= \frac{5}{9}$(Fahrenheit $- 32$) to find the temperature in degrees Celsius when he knows the temperature in degrees Fahrenheit. Write a formula the student could use to get a good estimate of the Celsius temperature.

Where You've Been

- In previous courses, you learned to solve simple equations.

- In Chapter 1, you extended your ability to do arithmetic operations to include rational numbers.

- Also in Chapter 1, you used variables to write expressions and equations that represent real-world situations.

Diagnosing Readiness

iTEXT Instant self-check online and on CD-ROM

(For help, go to the Lesson in green.)

Writing an Equation (Lesson 1-1)

Write an equation to model each situation.

1. The total cost of n cartons of milk is \$3.60. Each carton costs \$.45.

2. The perimeter of an equilateral triangle is 3 times the length of a side s. The perimeter of an equilateral triangle is 124 in.

Using the Order of Operations (Lesson 1-2)

Evaluate each expression for $a = 4$, $b = 13$, and $c = 2$.

3. $2a + cb$ **4.** $cb - a^2$ **5.** $5c + 2a - b$ **6.** $38 - a^2 \div c$

Adding and Subtracting Integers (Lessons 1-4 and 1-5)

Simplify each expression.

7. $6 + (-3)$ **8.** $-4 - 6$ **9.** $-5 - (-13)$ **10.** $-7 + (-1)$

11. $-4.51 + 11.65$ **12.** $8.5 - (-7.9)$ **13.** $\frac{3}{10} - \frac{3}{4}$ **14.** $\frac{1}{5} + \left(-\frac{2}{3}\right)$

Multiplying and Dividing Rational Numbers (Lesson 1-6)

Simplify each expression.

15. $-85 \div (-5)$ **16.** $7\left(-\frac{6}{14}\right)$ **17.** $4^2(-6)^2$ **18.** $22 \div (-8)$

Combining Like Terms (Lesson 1-7)

Simplify each expression.

19. $14k^2 - (-2k^2)$ **20.** $4xy + 9xy$ **21.** $6t + 2 - 4t$ **22.** $9x - 4 + 3x$

Solving Equations

Key Vocabulary

- consecutive integers (p. 104)
- equivalent equations (p. 75)
- identity (p. 98)
- inverse operations (p. 75)
- literal equation (p. 111)
- mean (p. 118)
- measures of central tendency (p. 118)
- median (p. 118)
- mode (p. 118)
- outlier (p. 118)
- range (p. 120)
- solution of an equation (p. 75)
- uniform motion (p. 104)

Where You're Going

- In this chapter, you will solve equations, including equations with variables on both sides, using properties of equality.

- You will develop the ability to solve problems by defining variables, relating them to one another, and writing an equation.

- You will use measures of central tendency to describe a set of data.

 Real-World Snapshots Applying what you learn, you will do an activity involving bicycle gears, on pages 130–131.

Solving One-Step Equations

Lesson Preview

What You'll Learn

OBJECTIVE 1
To solve equations using addition and subtraction

OBJECTIVE 2
To solve equations using multiplication and division

...And Why

To model a geometric problem, as in Example 2

✓ Check Skills You'll Need

(For help, go to Lessons 1-4, 1-5, and 1-6.)

Simplify each expression.

1. $x - 2 + 2$ **2.** $n + 2 - 2$ **3.** $\frac{c}{5} \cdot 5$ **4.** $\frac{7m}{7}$

For each number, state its opposite and its reciprocal.

5. 2   **6.** −2   **7.** $\frac{3}{5}$ **8.** $-\frac{3}{5}$

New Vocabulary
- solution of an equation
- equivalent equations
- inverse operations

OBJECTIVE

1

Solving Equations Using Addition and Subtraction

🔲 **TEXT** Interactive lesson includes instant self-check, tutorials, and activities.

An equation is like a balance scale because it shows that two quantities are equal. Look at the scales and equations below. The scales remain balanced when the same weight is added to each side.

$3 = 3$ $2 + 3 = 2 + 3$

Similarly, the scales remain balanced when the same weight is taken away from each side. This demonstrates the addition and subtraction properties of equality.

🔑 **Key Concepts**

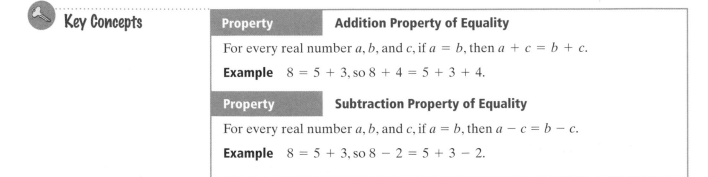

Property	Addition Property of Equality
For every real number $a, b,$ and $c,$ if $a = b,$ then $a + c = b + c.$	
Example $8 = 5 + 3,$ so $8 + 4 = 5 + 3 + 4.$	

Property	Subtraction Property of Equality
For every real number $a, b,$ and $c,$ if $a = b,$ then $a - c = b - c.$	
Example $8 = 5 + 3,$ so $8 - 2 = 5 + 3 - 2.$	

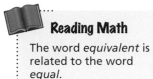
To solve an equation containing a variable, you find the value (or values) of the variable that make the equation true. Such a value is a **solution of the equation.** To find a solution, you can use properties of equality to form equivalent equations. **Equivalent equations** are equations that have the same solution (or solutions).

One way to solve an equation is to get the variable alone on one side of the equal sign. You can do this using **inverse operations,** which are operations that undo one another. Addition and subtraction are inverse operations.

1 EXAMPLE **Using the Addition Property of Equality**

Solve $x - 3 = -8$.

$x - 3 + 3 = -8 + 3$	Add 3 to each side to get the variable alone on one side of the equal sign.
$x = -5$	Simplify.

Check $x - 3 = -8$ Check your solution in the original equation.

$-5 - 3 \stackrel{?}{=} -8$ Substitute -5 for x.

$-8 = -8$ ✓

✓ **Check Understanding** **1** Solve each equation. Check your answer.

  a. $m - 10 = 2$ **b.** $y - 7.6 = 4$ **c.** $-9 = b - 5$

When you solve an equation involving addition, subtract the same number from each side of the equation.

2 EXAMPLE **Using the Subtraction Property of Equality**

Geometry The triangle below is isosceles with sides $\overline{AB}$ and $\overline{BC}$ congruent. Find the value of a.

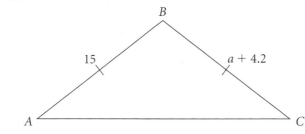

$AB = BC$	The lengths of congruent sides are equal.
$15 = a + 4.2$	Substitute.
$15 - 4.2 = a + 4.2 - 4.2$	Subtract 4.2 from each side.
$10.8 = a$	Simplify.

Check $15 = a + 4.2$

$15 \stackrel{?}{=} 10.8 + 4.2$ Substitute 10.8 for a.

$15 = 15$ ✓

✓ **Check Understanding** **2** Solve each equation. Check your answer.

  a. $x + 5 = 6$ **b.** $\frac{2}{3} + y = \frac{1}{4}$ **c.** $-18 = 6 + w$

You can write and solve equations describing real-world situations. Use estimation to check whether your solution is reasonable.

3 EXAMPLE **Real-World 🌐 Problem Solving**

Weighing a Baby A mother holds her baby and steps on a scale as shown at the left. Alone, the mother weighs 129 lb. How much does the baby weigh?

Relate baby's weight plus mother's weight equals scale reading

Define Let w = the baby's weight.

Write w +   129   =   147

$$w + 129 = 147$$
$$w + 129 - 129 = 147 - 129 \quad \textbf{Subtract 129 from each side.}$$
$$w = 18 \quad \textbf{Simplify.}$$

The baby weighs 18 lb.

Check Is the solution reasonable? The baby weighs about 20 lb, and the mother weighs about 130 lb. The baby's weight plus the mother's weight is about 150 lb, which is close to 147 lb. The answer is reasonable.

✔ **Check Understanding** **3 Banking** Brendan withdrew $25 from his bank account at an ATM. The transaction slip said his balance was then $243.19. Write and solve an equation to find Brendan's previous balance.

OBJECTIVE

2 Solving Equations Using Multiplication and Division

Multiplication and division are inverse operations. When you multiply or divide to solve equations, you use the following properties.

🔑 **Key Concepts**

Property	**Multiplication Property of Equality**

For every real number $a, b,$ and $c,$ if $a = b,$ then $a \cdot c = b \cdot c.$

Example $\frac{6}{2} = 3,$ so $\frac{6}{2} \cdot 2 = 3 \cdot 2.$

Property	**Division Property of Equality**

For every real number $a, b,$ and $c,$ with $c \neq 0,$ if $a = b,$ then $\frac{a}{c} = \frac{b}{c}.$

Example $3 + 1 = 4,$ so $\frac{3 + 1}{2} = \frac{4}{2}.$

Multiplication and division are inverse operations. When you solve an equation involving division, multiply each side of the equation by the same number.

4 EXAMPLE **Using the Multiplication Property of Equality**

Solve $-\frac{r}{4} = -10.4.$

$$-4\left(-\frac{r}{4}\right) = -4(-10.4) \quad \textbf{Multiply each side by -4 to get the variable alone on one side of the equal sign.}$$
$$r = 41.6 \quad \textbf{Simplify.}$$

✓ **Check Understanding** ④ Solve each equation. Check your answer.

a. $\frac{n}{6} = 5$
b. $\frac{x}{-3} = 18$
c. $-\frac{a}{5} = -20$

In the next example, the coefficient of the variable is a fraction. You can use reciprocals to solve the equation.

⑤ **EXAMPLE** **Using Reciprocals to Solve Equations**

Need Help?
To review reciprocals, see Lesson 1-6.

Solve $\frac{3}{4}x = 9$.

$\frac{4}{3}\left(\frac{3}{4}x\right) = \frac{4}{3}(9)$ Multiply each side by $\frac{4}{3}$, the reciprocal of $\frac{3}{4}$.

$x = 12$ **Simplify.**

Check $\frac{3}{4}x = 9$

$\frac{3}{4}(12) \stackrel{?}{=} 9$ **Substitute 12 for *x*.**

$9 = 9$ ✓

✓ **Check Understanding** ⑤ Solve each equation. Check your answer.

a. $-\frac{1}{4}m = 8$
b. $\frac{3}{8}p = -15$
c. $\frac{8}{15} = \frac{2}{5}a$

When you solve an equation involving multiplication, divide each side of the equation by the same number.

⑥ **EXAMPLE** **Using the Division Property of Equality**

Solve $4c = -96$.

$\frac{4c}{4} = \frac{-96}{4}$ **Divide each side by 4.**

$c = -24$ **Simplify.**

✓ **Check Understanding** ⑥ Solve each equation. Check your answer.

a. $3a = 12$
b. $20 = -2x$
c. $-8 = 5y$

EXERCISES

For more practice, see *Extra Practice*.

Practice and Problem Solving

Ⓐ **Practice by Example**

Solve each equation. Check your answer.

Example 1
(page 75)

1. $x - 8 = 0$
2. $n - 2 = -5$
3. $c - 4 = 9$

4. $23 = x - 17$
5. $-3.5 = m - 2.5$
6. $x - \frac{2}{3} = 5$

7. $x - \frac{4}{7} = \frac{3}{7}$
8. $28.32 = p - 32.96$
9. $c - 7.88 = 9.24$

Example 2
(page 75)

10. $b + 5 = -13$
11. $x + 2 = 6$
12. $23 + y = 16$

13. $-31 = 26 + a$
14. $k + \frac{3}{11} = \frac{8}{11}$
15. $4 = \frac{2}{3} + c$

16. $x + 2.5 = 4.5$
17. $5.25 + x = 3.75$
18. $73.35 = 4.37 + y$

Example 3
(page 76)

Write an equation to model each situation. Then solve.

19. **Measurement** A physician's assistant measures a child and finds that his height is $41\frac{1}{2}$ in. At his last visit to the doctor's office, the child was $38\frac{3}{4}$ in. tall. How much did the child grow?

20. **Sales Tax** Sales tax charged by the state of Virginia is 4.5%. This is 2.5% less than the sales tax charged by the state of Rhode Island. What does Rhode Island charge for sales tax?

Example 4
(page 76)

Solve each equation. Check your answer.

21. $\frac{y}{5} = 100$ 22. $\frac{x}{2} = 98$ 23. $\frac{m}{3} = -6$ 24. $\frac{w}{4} = -80$

25. $28 = \frac{p}{7}$ 26. $10 = \frac{a}{-2}$ 27. $-\frac{c}{7} = 35$ 28. $-\frac{r}{3} = -101$

Example 5
(page 77)

29. $-\frac{2}{3}x = 6$ 30. $\frac{2}{3}c = -18$ 31. $\frac{2}{5}a = -4$ 32. $\frac{3}{7}y = 1$

33. $\frac{7}{8}w = 14$ 34. $-\frac{2}{9}x = 10$ 35. $-\frac{1}{6}m = 12$ 36. $\frac{5}{11}n = 3$

37. $\frac{5}{8}x = 8$ 38. $-\frac{12}{17}y = 3$ 39. $\frac{4}{7}m = 8$ 40. $\frac{3}{4}n = -\frac{3}{8}$

Example 6
(page 77)

41. $5x = -75$ 42. $-7y = 28$ 43. $-8n = -64$ 44. $6p = -120$

45. $-6 = -3a$ 46. $2 = -2m$ 47. $-4k = 52$ 48. $-3x = -48$

49. $-4 = 7x$ 50. $9 = 11y$ 51. $-7m = 9$ 52. $9n = -5$

B **Apply Your Skills**

53. **Estimation** Use estimation to check whether 96.26 is a reasonable solution for the equation $m - 62.74 = 159$. Explain.

54. **Open-Ended** Write a word problem that you could solve using the equation $15n = 120$.

Solve each equation.

55. $14 + t = 16.1$ 56. $\frac{2}{3}w = 12$ 57. $b + 6\frac{1}{8} = 5\frac{3}{4}$

58. $9\frac{2}{3} = a + 19$ 59. $\frac{x}{6} = -10$ 60. $y - 3.7 = 6.93$

61. $15.9 = r + 27.3$ 62. $-\frac{a}{7} = 2.5$ 63. $-3x = \frac{5}{6}$

64. $\frac{x}{18} = 13.5$ 65. $m - 1.2 = -2.09$ 66. $0.9x = 11.7$

67. $p + \frac{1}{4} = -3\frac{1}{2}$ 68. $6.1 + m = -11$ 69. $-1\frac{3}{4} = p - \frac{1}{2}$

Write an equation to model each situation. Then solve.

**Average Annual
Precipitation**

46 in.

?

El Paso

Houston

70. **Weather** The average annual precipitation in Houston, Texas, is about 5.2 times that of El Paso, Texas. Use the information at the left to find the average annual precipitation in El Paso. Round to the nearest tenth.

71. **Sports** In 1999, 189 physical therapists ran the New York City Marathon. This was 1048 fewer than the number of engineers who ran. How many engineers ran in the marathon?

72. **a. Tourism** Annual visits to Grand Canyon National Park increased from about 106,000 in 1915 to about 4,930,000 in 1999. What was the increase in the annual number of visits?
    b. Suppose $\frac{2}{5}$ of the park's visitors in 2000 were under the age of 18. If 1,928,000 visitors were under 18, what was the total number of visitors in 2000?

73. Wages Suppose you work as a carpenter's apprentice. You earn $106.25 for working 17 hours. What is your hourly wage?

Use the cartoon for Exercises 74 and 75.

"Just a minute! Yesterday you said X equals two!"

74. Critical Thinking Explain what the student does *not* understand about using letters in algebra.

75. What property of equality did the teacher use to solve the equation?

76. a. Error Analysis By using a calculator to solve the equation $-\frac{a}{6} = 11.2$, a student got the answer 672. What error (or errors) did the student make?

b. Writing How could the student use estimation to catch the error?

Geometry In each triangle, the measure of $\angle A$ = the measure of $\angle B$. Find the value of x.

77. 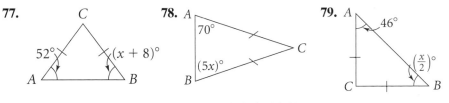 **78.** **79.**

80. Labor Costs Your bill for a car repair is $166.50.
a. One third of the bill is for labor. Write and solve an equation to find the cost for labor.
b. The mechanic worked on your car for 1.5 hours. What is the hourly charge for labor?

C Challenge

81. Geometry Two angles are supplementary if the sum of their measures is 180°. $\angle A$ and $\angle B$ are supplementary angles. The measure of $\angle A$ is 109°. What is the measure of $\angle B$?

82. a. Solve each equation.

$22 = 23 + a$ $\qquad$ $\frac{s}{4} = \frac{1}{16}$

$-a = 0.1$ $\qquad$ $2T = -33$

$f + 10 = 11$ $\qquad$ $\frac{5}{8} + t = -\frac{1}{8}$

$80h = -1288$ $\qquad$ $\frac{1}{5}u = 4$

$9 + n = 33$ $\qquad$ $w - 1\frac{1}{6} = -1\frac{5}{6}$

b. Order the ten solutions from part (a) from least to greatest and use the letters used for variables to spell a word or phrase.

83. Nutrition There are about 200 mg of calcium in 1 oz of cheddar cheese. This is only $\frac{2}{3}$ the amount of calcium in 1 c of skim milk. How many milligrams of calcium are in 1 c of skim milk?

84. a. For what value or values of x is $0 \cdot x = 0$?
  b. For what value or values of x is $0 \cdot x = 9$?

Standardized Test Prep

Multiple Choice

85. Solve $g + 7 = 28$.
  A. -21 **B.** -4 **C.** 4   **D.** 21

86. Solve $\frac{2}{3}x = 18$.
  F. 6   **G.** 12   **H.** 27   **I.** 36

87. During the first half of a basketball game, a team scored 38 points. They made only field goals, which are 2 points each. Which of the following equations could you use to find the number of field goals g the team scored?
  A. $2 + g = 38$ **B.** $2 - g = 38$ **C.** $\frac{g}{2} = 38$ **D.** $2g = 38$

88. Jessica has $50.00 she wants to spend on CDs, which are on sale for $13.50 each. Which equation could you use to find out how many CDs she can afford to buy?
  F. $c - 13.5 = 50$ **G.** $c + 13.5 = 50$ **H.** $50c = 13.5$ **I.** $13.5c = 50$

89. A meteorologist forecast that the high temperature would reach 34°F one afternoon. The low temperature for the day was −4°F. Which equation could you use to find out how many degrees d the temperature would need to rise to reach the predicted high temperature for the day?
  A. $34 - 4 = d$ **B.** $-4 + d = 34$ **C.** $34 - d = 4$ **D.** $d - (-4) = 34$

90. Which of the following is an expression that represents "6 times the difference of a number n and 2"?
  F. $6n - 2$ **G.** $6(n - 2)$ **H.** $6(n + 2)$ **I.** $6 \cdot 2 - n$

Take It to the NET
Online lesson quiz at
www.PHSchool.com
Web Code: aea-0201

Mixed Review

Lesson 1-9

Name the point in the coordinate plane with the given coordinates.

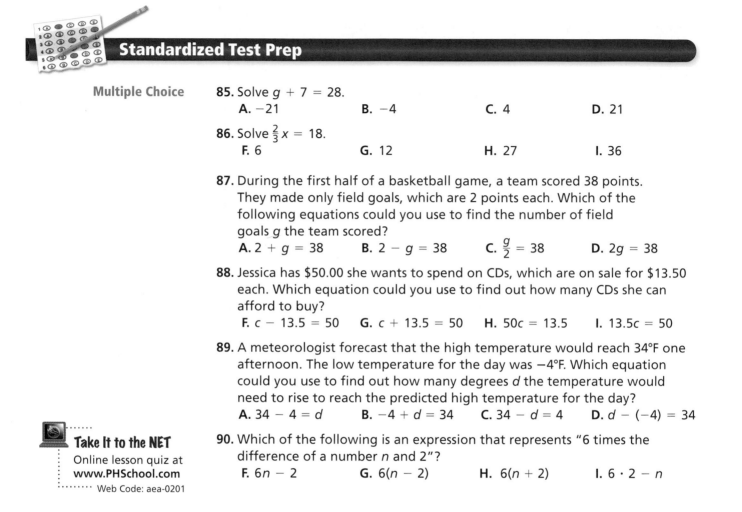

91. $(-2, 4)$ **92.** $(4, -2)$

93. $(4, 2)$ **94.** $(-2, -4)$

Lesson 1-8

Use the Distributive Property to simplify.

95. $5(a - 3)$ **96.** $(6 + y)(-2)$

97. $\frac{1}{2}(18 + m)$ **98.** $(4a - 5)(2c)$

Lesson 1-2

Simplify each expression.

99. $12 - 36 \div 6$ **100.** $5 \cdot 9 - 2^2$ **101.** $3 \cdot 2 + 13 - 4 \cdot 8$

2-2

Solving Two-Step Equations

Lesson Preview

What You'll Learn

OBJECTIVE 1 To solve two-step equations

OBJECTIVE 2 To use deductive reasoning

. . . And Why

To solve a problem involving ordering from a catalog, as in Example 2

✔ Check Skills You'll Need

(For help, go to Lesson 2-1.)

Solve each equation and tell which property of equality you used.

1. $x - 5 = 14$

2. $x + 3.8 = 9$

3. $-7 + x = 7$

4. $x - 13 = 20$

5. $\frac{x}{4} = 8$

6. $9 = 3x$

Solve each equation.

7. $10x = 2$

8. $\frac{2}{3}x = -6$

9. $x + 2\frac{3}{4} = 6\frac{1}{2}$

OBJECTIVE

1

Solving Two-Step Equations

*i*TEXT Interactive lesson includes instant self-check, tutorials, and activities.

A two-step equation is an equation that involves two operations. Models can help you understand how to find the solution of a two-step equation.

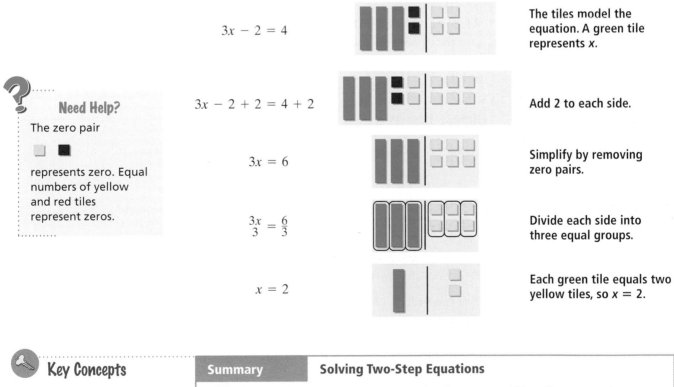

$3x - 2 = 4$

The tiles model the equation. A green tile represents *x*.

Need Help?

The zero pair

represents zero. Equal numbers of yellow and red tiles represent zeros.

$3x - 2 + 2 = 4 + 2$

Add 2 to each side.

$3x = 6$

Simplify by removing zero pairs.

$\frac{3x}{3} = \frac{6}{3}$

Divide each side into three equal groups.

$x = 2$

Each green tile equals two yellow tiles, so *x* = 2.

🔑 **Key Concepts**

Summary	**Solving Two-Step Equations**

Step 1 Use the Addition or Subtraction Property of Equality to get the term with a variable alone on one side of the equation.

Step 2 Use the Multiplication or Division Property of Equality to write an equivalent equation in which the variable has a coefficient of 1.

1 EXAMPLE **Solving a Two-Step Equation**

Solve $10 = \frac{m}{4} + 2$.

$10 - 2 = \frac{m}{4} + 2 - 2$ **Subtract 2 from each side.**

$8 = \frac{m}{4}$ **Simplify.**

$4 \cdot 8 = 4 \cdot \frac{m}{4}$ **Multiply each side by 4.**

$32 = m$ **Simplify.**

Check $10 = \frac{m}{4} + 2$

$10 \stackrel{?}{=} \frac{32}{4} + 2$ **Substitute 32 for m.**

$10 \stackrel{?}{=} 8 + 2$

$10 = 10$ ✓

✔ **Check Understanding** **1** Solve each equation. Check your answer.

a. $7 = 2y - 3$ **b.** $6a + 2 = -8$ **c.** $\frac{x}{9} - 15 = 12$

You can write two-step equations to model real-world situations. Some real-world situations require whole-number answers. So check that your answer is reasonable in the given situation.

2 EXAMPLE **Real-World 🌍 Problem Solving**

Retailing You are ordering tulip bulbs from a flower catalog. You have $14 to spend. Use the catalog page at the left to determine the number of bulbs you can order.

Relate | cost per tulip bulb | times | number of tulip bulbs | plus | shipping | equals | amount to spend

Define Let b = number of bulbs you can order.

Write $\quad 0.75 \quad \cdot \quad b \quad + \quad 3 \quad = \quad 14$

$0.75b + 3 = 14$

$0.75b + 3 - 3 = 14 - 3$ **Subtract 3 from each side.**

$0.75b = 11$ **Simplify.**

$\frac{0.75b}{0.75} = \frac{11}{0.75}$ **Divide each side by 0.75.**

$b = 14.\overline{6}$ **Simplify.**

You can order 14 bulbs.

Check Is the solution reasonable? You can only order whole tulip bulbs. Since 15 bulbs would cost 15 · $0.75 = $11.25 plus $3 for handling, which is more than $14, you can only order 14 tulip bulbs.

Tulips
Take advantage of our high quality and our low prices for your spring garden with tulips from the greenhouses that you can trust.

1 bulb $0.75
(plus $3.00 shipping)

✔ **Check Understanding** **2** Suppose tulips are on sale for $.60 per bulb. What number of bulbs can you order?

In some equations, the variable may have a negative sign in front of it, such as $-x = 3$. To help you solve these equations, recall that $x = 1 \cdot x$ and $-x = -1 \cdot x$. You can solve for x by multiplying or dividing by -1.

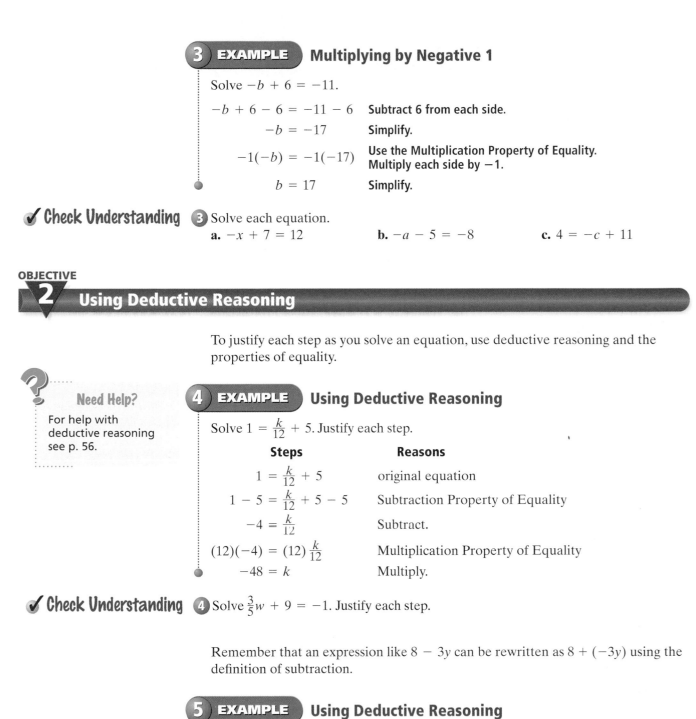

3 EXAMPLE **Multiplying by Negative 1**

Solve $-b + 6 = -11$.

$-b + 6 - 6 = -11 - 6$ Subtract 6 from each side.

$-b = -17$ Simplify.

$-1(-b) = -1(-17)$ Use the Multiplication Property of Equality. Multiply each side by -1.

$b = 17$ Simplify.

✔ **Check Understanding** **3** Solve each equation.

a. $-x + 7 = 12$ **b.** $-a - 5 = -8$ **c.** $4 = -c + 11$

OBJECTIVE

2 **Using Deductive Reasoning**

To justify each step as you solve an equation, use deductive reasoning and the properties of equality.

Need Help?

For help with deductive reasoning see p. 56.

4 EXAMPLE **Using Deductive Reasoning**

Solve $1 = \frac{k}{12} + 5$. Justify each step.

Steps	Reasons
$1 = \frac{k}{12} + 5$	original equation
$1 - 5 = \frac{k}{12} + 5 - 5$	Subtraction Property of Equality
$-4 = \frac{k}{12}$	Subtract.
$(12)(-4) = (12)\frac{k}{12}$	Multiplication Property of Equality
$-48 = k$	Multiply.

✔ **Check Understanding** **4** Solve $\frac{3}{5}w + 9 = -1$. Justify each step.

Remember that an expression like $8 - 3y$ can be rewritten as $8 + (-3y)$ using the definition of subtraction.

5 EXAMPLE **Using Deductive Reasoning**

Solve $8 - 3y = 14$. Justify each step.

Steps	Reasons
$8 - 3y = 14$	original equation
$8 + (-3y) = 14$	definition of subtraction
$8 + (-3y) - 8 = 14 - 8$	Subtraction Property of Equality
$-3y = 6$	Subtract.
$\frac{-3y}{-3} = \frac{6}{-3}$	Division Property of Equality
$y = -2$	Divide.

✔ **Check Understanding** **5** Solve $-9 - 4m = 3$. Justify each step.

EXERCISES

For more practice, see *Extra Practice*.

Practice and Problem Solving

A Practice by Example

Example 1
(page 82)

Solve each equation. Check your answer.

1. $1 + \frac{a}{5} = -1$ **2.** $2n - 5 = 7$ **3.** $-1 = 3 + 4x$ **4.** $\frac{y}{2} + 5 = -12$

5. $3b + 7 = -2$ **6.** $\frac{x}{3} - 9 = 0$ **7.** $14 + \frac{h}{5} = 2$ **8.** $-10 = -6 + 2c$

9. $\frac{m}{8} + 4 = 16$ **10.** $\frac{a}{4} - 21 = 7$ **11.** $3x - 1 = 8$ **12.** $10 = 2n + 1$

13. $35 = 3 + 5x$ **14.** $41 = \frac{2}{5}x - 7$ **15.** $-3 + \frac{m}{3} = 12$ **16.** $9 + \frac{n}{5} = 19$

Example 2
(page 82)

Define a variable and write an equation for each situation. Then solve.

17. Donations A library receives a large cash donation and uses the funds to double the number of books it owns. Then a book collector gives the library 4028 books. After this, the library has 51,514 books. How many books did the library have before the cash donation and the gift of books?

18. Cooking Suppose you are helping to prepare a large meal. You can peel 2 carrots per minute. You need 60 peeled carrots. How long will it take you to finish if you have already peeled 18 carrots?

19. Cell Phones One cell phone plan costs $39.95 per month. The first 500 minutes of usage are free. Each minute thereafter costs $.35. For a bill of $69.70, how many minutes over 500 minutes was the cell phone in use?

Example 3
(page 83)

Solve each equation. Check your answer.

20. $-b + 5 = -16$ **21.** $-p - 24 = -8$ **22.** $-7 = -c - 29$ **23.** $-y - 52 = 33$

24. $-m + 2 = 1$ **25.** $-9 = -a + 16$ **26.** $-x + 100 = 100$ **27.** $-1 = -n - 3$

28. $-y - 3 = 8$ **29.** $15 = -z + 8$ **30.** $-q + 5 = 10$ **31.** $-a + 9 = 25$

32. $-x - 4 = 20$ **33.** $-y + 10 = 25$ **34.** $5 = -z - 3$ **35.** $9 = -x + 8$

Examples 4, 5
(page 83)

Justify each step.

36.
$$\frac{x}{5} + 9 = 11$$
$$\frac{x}{5} + 9 - 9 = 11 - 9$$
$$\frac{x}{5} = 2$$
$$5\left(\frac{x}{5}\right) = 5(2)$$
$$x = 10$$

37.
$$-y - 5 = 11$$
$$-y - 5 + 5 = 11 + 5$$
$$-y = 16$$
$$-1(-y) = -1(16)$$
$$y = -16$$

38.
$$18 - n = 21$$
$$18 - n - 18 = 21 - 18$$
$$-n = 3$$
$$-1(-n) = -1(3)$$
$$n = -3$$

39.
$$12 - 2h = 8$$
$$12 - 2h - 12 = 8 - 12$$
$$-2h = -4$$
$$\frac{-2h}{-2} = \frac{-4}{-2}$$
$$h = 2$$

B Apply Your Skills

Solve each equation.

40. $\frac{5}{7}x + \frac{1}{7} = 3$ **41.** $\frac{a}{5} + 15 = 30$ **42.** $-\frac{1}{5}t - 2 = 4$ **43.** $-6 + 6z = 0$

44. $3.5 + 10m = 7.32$ **45.** $7 = -2x + 7$ **46.** $\frac{1}{2} = \frac{2}{5}c - 3$ **47.** $10.7 = -d + 4.3$

48. $0.4x + 9.2 = 10$ **49.** $4x + 92 = 100$ **50.** $-t - 0.4 = -3$ **51.** $-10t - 4 = -30$

Solve each equation. Justify each step.

52. $8 + \frac{c}{-4} = -6$ **53.** $7 - 3k = -14$ **54.** $14 = 6 - 2p$ **55.** $\frac{-y}{2} + 14 = -1$

Reading Math

For help with reading and solving Exercise 56, see p. 87.

Define a variable and write an equation for each situation. Then solve.

56. Mining Beneath Earth's surface, the temperature increases 10°C every kilometer. Suppose that the surface temperature is 22°C, and the temperature at the bottom of a gold mine is 45°C. What is the depth of the gold mine?

57. Insurance One health insurance policy pays people for claims by multiplying the claim amount by 0.8 and then subtracting $500. If a person receives a check for $4650, how much was the claim amount?

58. Library The Library of Congress in Washington, D.C., is the largest library in the world. It contains nearly 125 million items. The library adds about 10,000 items to its collection daily. How many days will it take the library to reach about 150 million items?

Solve each equation. (*Hint:* As your first step, multiply each side by the denominator of the fraction.)

59. $\frac{x + 2}{9} = 5$ **60.** $\frac{y + 1}{3} = 2$ **61.** $\frac{a - 10}{-4} = 2$ **62.** $\frac{b - 7}{2} = 6$

63. $\frac{x - 5}{2} = 10$ **64.** $\frac{x - 3}{7} = 12$ **65.** $\frac{x + 4}{3} = -8$ **66.** $\frac{x + 6}{4} = -7$

Real-World Connection

Since 1950, the size of the collections and the size of the staff of the Library of Congress have tripled.

Geometry In each triangle, the measure of $\angle A$ = the measure of $\angle B$. Find the value of x.

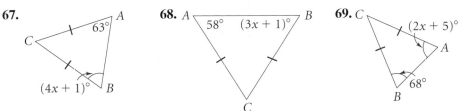

67. (triangle with $63°$ at A, $(4x + 1)°$ at B, C)   **68.** (triangle with $58°$ at A, $(3x + 1)°$ at B, C)   **69.** (triangle with $(2x + 5)°$ at A, $68°$ at B, C)

70. Writing Miles has saved $40. He wants to buy a CD player for $129 in about four months. To find how much he should save each week, he wrote $40 + 16x = 129$. Explain his equation.

Error Analysis What is the error in the work? Solve each equation correctly.

71.

$12 - 3y = 15$
$3y = 3$
$y = 1$

72.

$\frac{m}{3} - 9 = -21$
$\frac{m}{3} - 9 + 9 = -21 + 9$
$\frac{m}{3} = -12$
$m = -4$

73. Open-Ended Write a problem that you can model with a two-step equation. Write an equation and solve the problem.

74. You can find the value of each variable in the matrices below by writing and solving equations. For example, to find the value of a, you solve the equation $2a + 1 = 11$. Find the values of a, x, y, and k.

$$\begin{bmatrix} 2a + 1 & -6 \\ -7 & -3k \end{bmatrix} = \begin{bmatrix} 11 & x - 5 \\ 5 - 2y & 27 \end{bmatrix}$$

75. Critical Thinking If you multiply each side of $0.24r + 5.25 = -7.23$ by 100, the result is an equivalent equation. Explain why it might be helpful to do this.

Use the table at the right for Exercises 76 and 77.

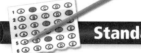 **76.** A formula for converting a temperature from Celsius C to Fahrenheit F is $F = 1.8C + 32$. Copy and complete the table. Round to the nearest degree.

Fahrenheit	Celsius	Description of Temperature
212°	■	boiling point of water
■	37°	human body temperature
68°	■	room temperature
■	0°	freezing point of water
■	−40°	

77. a. Estimation Use the formula $F = 2C + 30$ to estimate the Fahrenheit temperatures not shown in the table.

b. Critical Thinking Compare your estimated values with the actual values. How good is your formula at estimating the actual temperatures? Explain.

Solve the first equation for x. Then substitute your result into the second equation and solve for y.

78. $x + y = 8$
$2x + 3y = 21$

79. $x + 2y = 1$
$6x - y = -20$

80. $x + y = 12$
$2x + y = 17$

Standardized Test Prep

Gridded Response

81. What is the value of the expression $-\frac{3}{5}x - 2$ when $x = -6$?

82. Dana has a photograph that is 4 in. wide and 5 in. long. She has the photo enlarged so that both dimensions are tripled. How many times larger than the original area will the area of the enlargement be?

83. What is the value of the following expression? $\dfrac{3^2 \times 4 - (-5)^2}{(-2)^3 + 3 \times 4}$

84. Last season, Everett scored 48 points. This is 6 less than twice the number of points Max scored. How many points did Max score?

85. A cable television company charges $24.95 a month for basic cable service and $6.95 a month for each additional premium channel. If Sami's monthly bill is $45.80, how many premium channels is he receiving?

Take It to the NET
Online lesson quiz at
www.PHSchool.com
Web Code: aea-0202

Mixed Review

Lesson 2-1

Solve each equation.

86. $4s = 18$

87. $x - 3 = 9$

88. $\frac{m}{5} = 3$

89. $-7 = n + 2$

90. $7x = 42$

91. $3y = 99$

92. $5z = 57$

93. $8a = 48$

Lessons 1-3, 1-4

Simplify.

94. $-2 + 6$

95. $9 + (-3)$

96. $-7 + (-4)$

97. $16 + (-4)$

Read through the problem below. Then follow along with what Maria thinks as she solves the problem. Check your understanding with the exercise at the bottom of the page.

Beneath Earth's surface, the temperature increases 10°C every kilometer. Suppose that the surface temperature is 22°C, and the temperature at the bottom of a gold mine is 45°C. What is the depth of the gold mine?

What Maria Thinks

I need to read the problem carefully so that I can understand it. I'll write down the important information.

The temperature increases 10 degrees for every kilometer I go down. This means I multiply. Now I can relate the temperature and the depth.

Since I am trying to find the depth of the gold mine, I'll let d be the depth in kilometers.

Now I can use the variable to write an equation.

I can solve the equation for d. First I subtract 22 from both sides. Then I divide each side by 10, to get d by itself.

I will state my answer in a sentence. Also, I need to remember to include the units.

What Maria Writes

The temperature at the surface is 22°C. The temperature at the bottom is 45°C. The temperature increases 10°C for every kilometer you go down.

$$\text{surface temperature} + 10 \text{ times depth} = \text{bottom temperature}$$

$d = $ depth, in kilometers

$$22 + 10d = 45$$

$$22 - 22 + 10d = 45 - 22$$
$$10d = 23$$
$$\frac{10d}{10} = \frac{23}{10}$$
$$d = 2.3$$

The gold mine is 2.3 km deep.

EXERCISE

The temperature at a ski slope decreases 2.5°F for every thousand feet of elevation above the base. The temperature at the base is 28°F and the temperature at the summit is 24°F. How many thousand feet above the base is the summit?

2-3 Solving Multi-Step Equations

Lesson Preview

What You'll Learn

OBJECTIVE 1 To use the Distributive Property when combining like terms

OBJECTIVE 2 To use the Distributive Property when solving equations

. . . And Why

To solve a problem involving building a fence, as in Example 2

✓ Check Skills You'll Need

(For help, go to Lessons 1-2 and 1-7.)

Simplify each expression.

1. $2n - 3n$ **2.** $-4 + 3b + 2 + 5b$

3. $9(w - 5)$ **4.** $-10(b - 12)$

5. $3(-x + 4)$ **6.** $5(6 - w)$

Evaluate each expression.

7. $28 - a + 4a$ for $a = 5$ **8.** $8 + x - 7x$ for $x = -3$

9. $(8n + 1)3$ for $n = -2$ **10.** $-(17 + 3y)$ for $y = 6$

Interactive lesson includes instant self-check, tutorials, and activities.

OBJECTIVE

1 Using the Distributive Property to Combine Like Terms

Need Help?

You use the Distributive Property whenever you add or subtract like terms.

$x + 4x = 1x + 4x$
$= (1 + 4)x$
$= 5x$

You can solve equations that require more than two steps. They are called multi-step equations. If there are like terms on one side of an equation, first use the Distributive Property to combine them. Then use the properties of equality to solve the equation.

1 EXAMPLE Combining Like Terms

Solve each equation.

a. $2c + c + 12 = 78$

$2c + c + 12 = 78$

$3c + 12 = 78$ Combine like terms.

$3c + 12 - 12 = 78 - 12$ Subtract 12 from each side.

$3c = 66$ Simplify.

$\frac{3c}{3} = \frac{66}{3}$ Divide each side by 3.

$c = 22$ Simplify.

b. $4b + 16 + 2b = 46$

$4b + 16 + 2b = 46$

$4b + 2b + 16 = 46$ Use the Commutative Property of Addition.

$6b + 16 = 46$ Combine like terms.

$6b + 16 - 16 = 46 - 16$ Subtract 16 from each side.

$6b = 30$ Simplify.

$\frac{6b}{6} = \frac{30}{6}$ Divide each side by 6.

$b = 5$ Simplify.

✓ Check Understanding **1** Solve each equation. Check your answer.

a. $3x - 4x + 6 = -2$ **b.** $7 = 4m - 2m + 1$

c. $-2y + 5 + 5y = 14$ **d.** $-3z + 8 + (-2z) = -12$

You can model real-world situations using multi-step equations.

2 EXAMPLE Real-World 🌐 Problem Solving

Gardening A gardener is planning a rectangular garden area in a community garden. His garden will be next to an existing 12-ft fence. The gardener has a total of 44 ft of fencing to build the other three sides of his garden. How long will the garden be if the width is 12 ft?

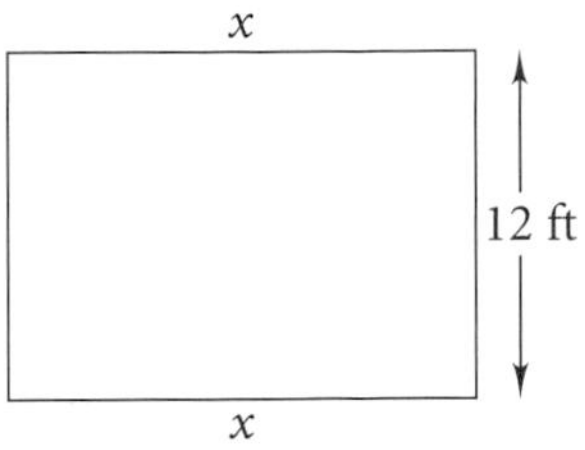

[diagram: rectangle with top side labeled x, right side labeled 12 ft, bottom side labeled x]

Relate | length of side | plus | 12 ft | plus | length of side | equals | amount of fencing |

Define Let x = length of a side adjacent to the fence.

Write x +   12   + x =   44

$$x + 12 + x = 44$$
$$2x + 12 = 44 \qquad \text{Combine like terms on the left side of the equation.}$$
$$2x + 12 - 12 = 44 - 12 \qquad \text{Subtract 12 from each side.}$$
$$2x = 32 \qquad \text{Simplify.}$$
$$\frac{2x}{2} = \frac{32}{2} \qquad \text{Divide each side by 2.}$$
$$x = 16 \qquad \text{Simplify.}$$

The garden will be 16 ft long.

✓ **Check Understanding** ❷ A carpenter is building a rectangular fence for a playground. One side of the playground is the wall of a building 70 ft wide. He plans to use 340 ft of fencing material. What is the length of the playground if the width is 70 ft?

Real-World 🌐 Connection

In the United States, there are approximately 10,000 cities with community gardens.

OBJECTIVE

2 Using the Distributive Property to Solve Equations

In the equation $-2(b - 4) = 12$, the parentheses indicate multiplication. Use the Distributive Property to multiply each term within the parentheses by -2. Then use the properties of equality to solve the equation.

3 EXAMPLE Solving an Equation With Grouping Symbols

Solve $-2(b - 4) = 12$.

$$-2b + 8 = 12 \qquad \text{Use the Distributive Property.}$$
$$-2b + 8 - 8 = 12 - 8 \qquad \text{Subtract 8 from each side.}$$
$$-2b = 4 \qquad \text{Simplify.}$$
$$\frac{-2b}{-2} = \frac{4}{-2} \qquad \text{Divide each side by } -2.$$
$$b = -2 \qquad \text{Simplify.}$$

✓ **Check Understanding** ❸ Solve each equation.
  a. $3(k + 8) = 21$ **b.** $15 = -3(x - 1) + 9$

You can solve an equation like $\frac{2x}{3} + \frac{x}{2} = 7$ by adding the fractions or by clearing the equation of fractions. To clear fractions, you multiply each side of the equation by a common multiple of the denominators.

4 EXAMPLE **Solving an Equation That Contains Fractions**

Solve $\frac{2x}{3} + \frac{x}{2} = 7$.

Method 1 Adding fractions

$$\frac{2x}{3} + \frac{x}{2} = 7$$

$$\frac{2}{3}x + \frac{1}{2}x = 7 \qquad \text{Rewrite the equation with fractions as coefficients.}$$

$$\frac{4}{6}x + \frac{3}{6}x = 7 \qquad \text{Write the fractions with a denominator of 6.}$$

$$\frac{7}{6}x = 7 \qquad \text{Combine like terms.}$$

$$\frac{6}{7}\left(\frac{7}{6}x\right) = \frac{6}{7}(7) \qquad \text{Multiply each side by } \frac{6}{7}, \text{ the reciprocal of } \frac{7}{6}.$$

$$x = 6 \qquad \text{Simplify.}$$

Method 2 Multiplying to clear fractions

$$\frac{2x}{3} + \frac{x}{2} = 7$$

$$6\left(\frac{2x}{3} + \frac{x}{2}\right) = 6(7) \qquad \begin{array}{l}\text{Multiply each side by 6,}\\ \text{a common multiple of 3 and 2.}\end{array}$$

$$6\left(\frac{2x}{3}\right) + 6\left(\frac{x}{2}\right) = 6(7) \qquad \text{Use the Distributive Property.}$$

$$4x + 3x = 42 \qquad \text{Multiply.}$$

$$7x = 42 \qquad \text{Combine like terms.}$$

$$\frac{7x}{7} = \frac{42}{7} \qquad \text{Divide each side by 7.}$$

$$x = 6 \qquad \text{Simplify.}$$

✔ Check Understanding **4** Solve each equation.

a. $\frac{m}{4} + \frac{m}{2} = \frac{5}{8}$ **b.** $\frac{2}{3}x - \frac{5}{8}x = 26$

Reading Math

$\frac{x}{2}$ and $\frac{1}{2}x$ both represent $x \div 2$.

$\frac{2x}{3}$ and $\frac{2}{3}x$ both represent $2x \div 3$.

You can clear an equation of decimals by multiplying by a power of 10. In the equation $0.5a + 8.75 = 13.25$, the greatest number of digits to the right of a decimal point is 2. To clear the equation of decimals, multiply each side of the equation by 10^2, or 100.

Need Help?

Powers of 10:
$10^1 = 10$
$10^2 = 100$
$10^3 = 1000$
$10^4 = 10,000$

5 EXAMPLE **Solving an Equation That Contains Decimals**

Solve $0.5a + 8.75 = 13.25$.

$$100(0.5a + 8.75) = 100(13.25) \qquad \text{Multiply each side by } 10^2, \text{ or 100.}$$

$$100(0.5a) + 100(8.75) = 100(13.25) \qquad \text{Use the Distributive Property.}$$

$$50a + 875 = 1325 \qquad \text{Simplify.}$$

$$50a + 875 - 875 = 1325 - 875 \qquad \text{Subtract 875 from each side.}$$

$$50a = 450 \qquad \text{Simplify.}$$

$$\frac{50a}{50} = \frac{450}{50} \qquad \text{Divide each side by 50.}$$

$$a = 9 \qquad \text{Simplify.}$$

✔ Check Understanding **5** Solve each equation.

a. $0.025x + 22.95 = 23.65$ **b.** $1.2x - 3.6 + 0.3x = 2.4$

Keep the steps in the summary below in mind as you solve equations that have variables on one side of the equation.

Key Concepts

Summary	Steps for Solving a Multi-Step Equation
Step 1	Clear the equation of fractions and decimals.
Step 2	Use the Distributive Property to remove parentheses on each side.
Step 3	Combine like terms on each side.
Step 4	Undo addition or subtraction.
Step 5	Undo multiplication or division.

EXERCISES

For more practice, see *Extra Practice*.

Practice and Problem Solving

A Practice by Example

Example 1
(page 88)

Solve each equation. Check your answer.

1. $4n - 2n = 18$

2. $y + y + 2 = 18$

3. $a + 6a - 9 = 30$

4. $5 - x - x = -1$

5. $72 + 4 - 14c = 36$

6. $13 = 5 - 13 + 3a$

7. $9 = -3 + n + 2n$

8. $7m - 3m - 6 = 6$

9. $-13 = 2b - b - 10$

Example 2
(page 89)

Write an equation to model each situation. Solve your equation.

10. Two friends are renting an apartment. They pay the landlord the first month's rent. The landlord also requires them to pay an additional half of a month's rent for a security deposit. The total amount they pay the landlord before moving in is $1725. What is the monthly rent?

11. You are fencing a rectangular puppy kennel with 25 ft of fence. The side of the kennel against your house does not need a fence. This side is 9 ft long. Find the dimensions of the kennel.

Example 3
(page 89)

Solve each equation. Check your answer.

12. $2(8 + p) = 22$

13. $5(a - 1) = 35$

14. $15 = -3(2q - 1)$

15. $26 = 6(5 - a)$

16. $m + 5(m - 1) = 7$

17. $-4(x + 6) = -40$

18. $48 = 8(x + 2)$

19. $5(y - 3) = 19$

20. $5(2 + y) = 77$

Example 4
(page 90)

21. $\frac{a}{7} - \frac{5}{7} = \frac{6}{7}$

22. $x - \frac{5}{8} = \frac{7}{8}$

23. $\frac{m}{6} - 7 = \frac{2}{3}$

24. $\frac{2}{3} + \frac{3k}{4} = \frac{71}{12}$

25. $4 + \frac{m}{8} = \frac{3}{4}$

26. $\frac{a}{2} + \frac{1}{5} = 17$

27. $\frac{1}{2} + \frac{7x}{10} = \frac{13}{20}$

28. $\frac{9y}{14} + \frac{3}{7} = \frac{9}{14}$

29. $\frac{1}{5} + \frac{3w}{15} = \frac{4}{5}$

Example 5
(page 90)

30. $3m + 4.5m = 15$

31. $7.8y + 2 = 165.8$

32. $3.5 = 12s - 5s$

33. $1.06y - 3 = 0.71$

34. $0.11p + 1.5 = 2.49$

35. $25.24 = 5y + 3.89$

36. $1.12 + 1.25y = 8.62$

37. $1.025x + 2.458 = 7.583$

38. $0.25m + 0.1m = 9.8$

Solve each equation.

39. $0.5t - 3t + 5 = 0$ **40.** $-(z + 5) = -14$ **41.** $\frac{a}{15} + \frac{4}{15} = \frac{9}{15}$

42. $0.5(x - 12) = 4$ **43.** $8y - (2y - 3) = 9$ **44.** $\frac{2}{3} + y = \frac{3}{4}$

45. $2 + \frac{a}{-4} = \frac{3}{5}$ **46.** $\frac{1}{4}(m - 16) = 7$ **47.** $x + 3x - 7 = 29$

48. $4x + 3.6 + x = 1.2$ **49.** $2(1.5c + 4) = -1$ **50.** $26.54 - p = 0.5(50 - p)$

51. Error Analysis Explain the error in the student's work at the right.

52. Critical Thinking Suppose you want to solve the equation $-3m + 4 + 5m = -6$. What would you do as your first step?

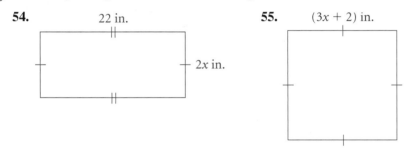

$$\frac{3}{8}x - 1 = 4$$
$$3x - 1 = 32$$
$$3x = 33$$
$$x = 11$$

53. Writing To solve $-\frac{1}{2}(3x - 5) = 7$, you can use the Distributive Property, or you can multiply each side of the equation by -2. Which method do you prefer? Explain why.

Geometry **The perimeter of each rectangle is 64 in. Find the value of x.**

54.

22 in.

$2x$ in.

55.

$(3x + 2)$ in.

CANOE RENTAL
$5.00 per hour
$2.00 life jacket

Use an equation to solve each problem.

56. John and two friends rent a canoe at a park. Each person must rent a life jacket. If the bill for the rental of the canoe and life jackets is $41, for how many hours did they rent the canoe?

57. Moving Costs The MacNeills rented a moving truck for $49.95 plus $.30 per mile. Before returning the truck, they filled the tank with gasoline, which cost $18.32. The total cost was $95.87. Find the number of miles the truck was driven.

58. Cell Phones Jane's cell phone plan is $40 per month plus $.15 per minute for each minute over 200 minutes of call time. If Jane's cell phone bill is $58.00, for how many extra calling minutes was she billed?

59. Open-Ended Write an expression with four terms that can be simplified to an expression with two terms.

Geometry **Find the value of x.** (*Hint:* **The sum of the measures of the angles of a triangle is 180°.**)

60.

$x°$

$66°$ $50°$

61.

$2x°$

$(x + 15)°$

62.

$(2x + 16)°$

$44°$ $4x°$

For Exercises 63–67, use an equation to solve each problem.

63. **Cars** You fill your car's gas tank when it is about $\frac{1}{2}$ empty. The next week, you fill the tank a second time when it is about $\frac{3}{4}$ empty. If you buy a total of $18\frac{1}{2}$ gal of gas on these two days, about how many gallons does the tank hold?

64. A work crew has two pumps, one new and one old. The new pump can fill a tank in 5 hours. The old pump can fill the same tank in 7 hours.
    a. How much of a tank can be filled in 1 hour with the new pump? With the old pump?
    b. Write an expression for the number of tanks the new pump can fill in t hours. (*Hint:* Write the rate at which the new pump fills tanks as a fraction and then multiply by t.)
    c. Write an expression for the number of tanks the old pump can fill in t hours.
    d. Write and solve an equation for the time it will take the pumps to fill one tank if the pumps are used together.

65. **Investing** Mr. Fairbanks invested half his money in land, a tenth in stock, and a twentieth in bonds. He put the remaining $35,000 in a savings account. What is the total amount of money that Mr. Fairbanks saved or invested?

66. **Business** A company buys a copier for $10,000. The value of the copier is $10,000\left(1 - \frac{n}{20}\right)$ after n years. After how many years will the value of the copier be $6500?

67. **Carpentry** Kate cut a board 2 m long into two pieces. One piece is 10 cm shorter than the other. How long is each piece? (*Note:* 1 m = 100 cm)

Standardized Test Prep

Multiple Choice

68. What is the value of the expression $-3r + 6 + r$ when $r = -2$?
    A. -6 **B.** -2 **C.** 10   **D.** 14

69. Solve $8n + 5 - 2n = 41$.
    F. $3\frac{1}{2}$ **G.** $4\frac{1}{2}$ **H.** 6   **I.** $7\frac{2}{3}$

70. If a number is increased by 3 and that number is doubled, the result is -8. What was the original number?
    A. -7 **B.** -5.5 **C.** 1   **D.** 6

71. The gas tank in Royston's car holds 12 gal of gasoline. The car averages 29 mi/gal. Royston filled up the tank and then drove 140 mi. About how many gallons of gasoline are left in the tank?
    F. 6 gal   **G.** 7 gal   **H.** 8 gal   **I.** 9 gal

72. Josie's goal is to run 40 miles each week. This week she has already run distances of 5.3 miles, 6.5 miles, and 6.2 miles. If she wants to spread out the remaining miles evenly over the next 4 days, which equation can you use to find how many miles (m) per day she must run?
    A. $5.3 + 6.5 + 6.2 + 40 = m$ **B.** $40 - 5.2 - 6.5 - 6.2 = m$
    C. $5.3 + 6.5 + 6.2 + 4m = 40$ **D.** $5.3 + 6.5 + 6.2 + m = \frac{40}{4}$

73. A cell phone company charges $.35 for the first minute but only $.10 every minute after that. Which equation can you use to find how many minutes m Eric talked if the bill for the call was $5.45?
    F. $0.35 + 0.10(m - 1) = 5.45$ **G.** $0.35 + 0.10m = 5.45$
    H. $0.10 + 0.35(m - 1) = 5.45$ **I.** $0.10 + 0.35m = 5.45$

Take It to the NET
Online lesson quiz at
www.PHSchool.com
Web Code: aea-0203

Lesson 2-3 Solving Multi-Step Equations   **93**

Lesson 2-2   Solve each equation.

74. $2y + 4 = -6$ **75.** $3x - 15 = 33$ **76.** $-4n + 20 = 36$ **77.** $-8 - c = 11$

78. $3x + 5 = 12$ **79.** $-4y - 3 = 15$ **80.** $8m - 4 = 8$ **81.** $-p + 3 = 10$

Lesson 1-8   **Mental Math** Simplify each expression.

82. $14 \cdot 4 \cdot 25$ **83.** $16 + 28 + 34 + 72$ **84.** $-8 + 15 + -9 + 2$

85. $3 \cdot 3 \cdot 10$ **86.** $2 \cdot 8 \cdot 5$ **87.** $27 + 46 - 17 - 16$

Lessons 1-4 through 1-6   Simplify each expression.

88. $2 - 6$ **89.** $-9 \cdot (-3)$ **90.** $-7 + (-4)$ **91.** $16 \div (-4)$

92. $-7 + (-3)$ **93.** $-5 - (-3)$ **94.** $-5 \cdot 6$ **95.** $-25 \div (-5)$

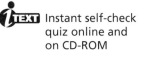

Checkpoint Quiz 1   **Lessons 2-1 through 2-3**

Instant self-check quiz online and on CD-ROM

Solve and check.

1. $x - 7 = -6$ **2.** $\frac{w}{3} = 11$ **3.** $15 = 0.75v$

4. $2t - 1 = 4$ **5.** $\frac{b}{3} - 20 = 20$ **6.** $-12 - 4x + 3 = -1$

7. $\frac{y}{8} + \frac{y}{12} = -4$ **8.** $9(n + 7) = -81$ **9.** $\frac{1}{2} = \frac{2}{3}b + \frac{1}{6}b$

10. Sales A telemarketer makes calls from her home. She earns \$240 per month plus a commission of 5% on her sales. Her employer also reimburses her for long distance telephone charges for calls made for the company. Last month she received a check for \$256.65, which included a reimbursement of \$8.95. What was the total of her sales?

Algebra at Work
⋯⋯⋯⋯⋯⋯⋯⋯⋯⋯⋯⋯⋯⋯ Airline Pilot

Airline pilots make many calculations before, during, and after a flight. Pilots study weather conditions to determine the safest altitude, route, and speed for a flight. Pilots calculate lift, which must equal the airplane's weight in pounds. An airplane's lift capabilities are calculated using the formula $L = \frac{1}{2}dv^2sa$, where L is the lift, d is the density of the air, v is the velocity of the aircraft in feet per second, s is the wing area of the aircraft in square feet, and a is a value determined by the type of airfoil the airplane has and the pitch angle of the airplane.

Take It to the NET For more information about a career as an airline pilot, go to **www.PHSchool.com**.
Web Code: aeb-2031

Modeling Equations

Models can help you understand how to solve equations that have variables on both sides.

EXAMPLE

Model and solve $3a - 2 = a + 4$.

$3a - 2 = a + 4$ 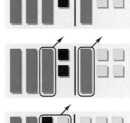 The tiles model the equation.

$3a - 2 - a = a + 4 - a$
$2a - 2 = 4$

Use the Subtraction Property of Equality. Subtract a from each side to get the variable on one side of the equation.

$2a - 2 + 2 = 4 + 2$
$2a = 6$

Use the Addition Property of Equality. Add 2 to each side. Remove zero pairs.

$\dfrac{2a}{2} = \dfrac{6}{2}$

Use the Division Property of Equality. Divide each side into two identical groups.

$a = 3$

Each green tile equals three yellow tiles, so $a = 3$.

EXERCISES

Write an equation for each model. Use tiles to solve each equation.

1.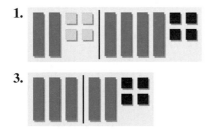

2.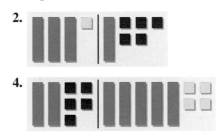

3.

4.

Use tiles to model and solve each equation.

5. $4x + 2 = 2x + 6$

6. $2y - 2 = 4y + 2$

7. $2a + 2 = a + 8$

8. $5b - 4 = 2b + 5$

9. $z - 8 = 2z - 1$

10. $4(p + 1) = 2p - 2$

11. $5n - 3 = 2(n + 3)$

12. $2(k + 1) = 5(k - 2)$

2-4

Equations With Variables on Both Sides

Lesson Preview

What You'll Learn

OBJECTIVE 1 ▼ To solve equations with variables on both sides

OBJECTIVE 2 ▼ To identify equations that are identities or have no solution

... And Why

To solve a problem involving renting in-line skates, as in Example 2

✓ Check Skills You'll Need

(For help, go to Lessons 1-5 and 2-3.)

Simplify.

1. $6x - 2x$ **2.** $2x - 6x$ **3.** $5x - 5x$ **4.** $-5x + 5x$

Solve each equation.

5. $4x + 3 = -5$ **6.** $-x + 7 = 12$

7. $2t - 8t + 1 = 43$ **8.** $0 = -7n + 4 - 5n$

New Vocabulary   • identity

OBJECTIVE 1

iTEXT Interactive lesson includes instant self-check, tutorials, and activities.

Solving Equations With Variables on Both Sides

Investigation: Using a Table to Solve an Equation

Costs for a key chain business are $540 to get started plus $3 per key chain. The cost of producing k key chains is $(540 + 3k)$ dollars.

Key chains sell for $7 each. The revenue for selling k key chains is $7k$ dollars. To make a profit, revenue must be greater than costs.

1. Copy and complete the following table.

Key Chains	Cost	Revenue
k	$540 + 3k$	$7k$
100	840	700
110	▦	▦
120	▦	▦
130	▦	▦
140	▦	▦
150	▦	▦

2. For 110 key chains, which is greater, the cost or the revenue?

3. When will the revenue be greater than the cost?

4. Use your table to estimate the solution of $540 + 3k = 7k$.

5. Explain how solving an equation can help you decide whether a business can make a profit or not.

To solve an equation that has variables on both sides, use the Addition or Subtraction Properties of Equality to get the variables on one side of the equation.

1 EXAMPLE **Variables on Both Sides**

Geometry Find the value of x in the diagram below.

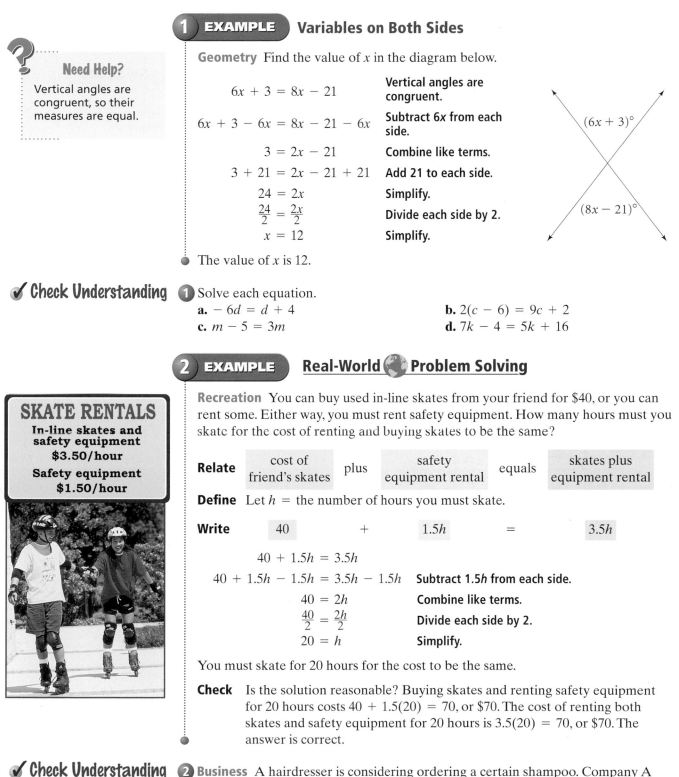

$6x + 3 = 8x - 21$	Vertical angles are congruent.
$6x + 3 - 6x = 8x - 21 - 6x$	Subtract 6x from each side.
$3 = 2x - 21$	Combine like terms.
$3 + 21 = 2x - 21 + 21$	Add 21 to each side.
$24 = 2x$	Simplify.
$\frac{24}{2} = \frac{2x}{2}$	Divide each side by 2.
$x = 12$	Simplify.

● The value of x is 12.

(6x + 3)°

(8x − 21)°

✓ **Check Understanding** **1** Solve each equation.

a. $-6d = d + 4$
c. $m - 5 = 3m$
b. $2(c - 6) = 9c + 2$
d. $7k - 4 = 5k + 16$

2 EXAMPLE **Real-World 🌐 Problem Solving**

Recreation You can buy used in-line skates from your friend for $40, or you can rent some. Either way, you must rent safety equipment. How many hours must you skate for the cost of renting and buying skates to be the same?

Relate | cost of friend's skates | plus | safety equipment rental | equals | skates plus equipment rental |

Define Let h = the number of hours you must skate.

Write   40   +   1.5h   =   3.5h

$40 + 1.5h = 3.5h$	
$40 + 1.5h - 1.5h = 3.5h - 1.5h$	Subtract 1.5h from each side.
$40 = 2h$	Combine like terms.
$\frac{40}{2} = \frac{2h}{2}$	Divide each side by 2.
$20 = h$	Simplify.

You must skate for 20 hours for the cost to be the same.

Check Is the solution reasonable? Buying skates and renting safety equipment for 20 hours costs $40 + 1.5(20) = 70$, or $70. The cost of renting both skates and safety equipment for 20 hours is $3.5(20) = 70$, or $70. The answer is correct.

SKATE RENTALS

In-line skates and safety equipment
$3.50/hour

Safety equipment
$1.50/hour

✓ **Check Understanding** **2** **Business** A hairdresser is considering ordering a certain shampoo. Company A charges $4 per 8-oz bottle plus a $10 handling fee per order. Company B charges $3 per 8-oz bottle plus a $25 handling fee per order. How many bottles must the hairdresser buy to justify using Company B?

2 Special Cases: Identities and No Solutions

An equation has **no solution** if no value of the variable makes the equation true. The equation $2x = 2x + 1$ has no solution. An equation that is true for every value of the variable is an **identity.** The equation $2x = 2x$ is an identity.

3 EXAMPLE Identities and Equations with No Solutions

a. Solve $10 - 8a = 2(5 - 4a)$.

$$10 - 8a = 10 - 8a \qquad \text{Use the Distributive Property.}$$
$$10 - 8a + 8a = 10 - 8a + 8a \qquad \text{Add 8}a \text{ to each side.}$$
$$10 = 10 \qquad \text{Always true!}$$

This equation is true for every value of a, so the equation is an identity.

b. Solve $6m - 5 = 7m + 7 - m$.

$$6m - 5 = 7m + 7 - m$$
$$6m - 5 = 6m + 7 \qquad \text{Combine like terms.}$$
$$6m - 5 - 6m = 6m + 7 - 6m \qquad \text{Subtract 6}m \text{ from each side.}$$
$$-5 = 7 \qquad \text{Not true for any value of }m!$$

● This equation has no solution.

✓ **Check Understanding** ❸ Determine whether each equation is an *identity* or whether it has *no solution.*
   a. $9 + 5n = 5n - 1$ **b.** $9 + 5x = 7x + 9 - 2x$

EXERCISES

For more practice, see *Extra Practice.*

Practice and Problem Solving

A Practice by Example

Example 1
(page 97)

Geometry Find the value of x.

1.
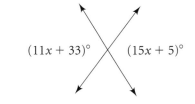
$(12x + 4)°$
$(13x - 5)°$

2.
$(11x + 33)°$ $(15x + 5)°$

Solve each equation. Check your answer.

3. $6x - 2 = x + 13$ **4.** $5y - 3 = 2y + 12$

5. $4k - 3 = 3k + 4$ **6.** $5m + 3 = 3m + 9$

7. $8 - x = 2x - 1$ **8.** $2n - 5 = 8n + 7$

9. $3a + 4 = a + 18$ **10.** $6b + 14 = -7 - b$

11. $5a - 14 = -5 + 8a$ **12.** $3 + 4x = 3x + 6$

13. $30 - 7z = 10z - 4$ **14.** $8x - 3 = 7x + 2$

15. $-36 + 2w = -8w + w$ **16.** $4p - 10 = p + 3p - 2p$

Example 2
(page 97)

Write and solve an equation for each situation. Check the reasonableness of your solution.

17. Telephone Service One telephone company charges $16.95 per month and $.05 per minute for local calls. Another company charges $22.95 per month and $.02 per minute for local calls. For what number of minutes of local calls per month is the cost of the plans the same?

18. Fitness One health club charges a $44 sign-up fee and $30 per month. Another health club charges a $99 sign-up fee and $25 per month. For what number of months is the cost the same?

19. Carpentry Peter was building a porch. Placing boards of equal length from end to end, Peter found that 4 boards were 3 ft too long for the porch length, while 3 boards were 5 ft too short. How long was each board?

20. Flying You and a pilot friend decide to rent an airplane to do some sightseeing. One service charges $100 plus $80 per hour, while another charges $250 plus $70 per hour for the same airplane. At what number of hours is the cost the same?

Example 3
(page 98)

21. a. Use the equation $9 - 6x = 3(3 - 2x)$. Substitute four different values for x and simplify.
  b. What kind of equation is $9 - 6x = 3(3 - 2x)$?

Determine whether each equation is an *identity* or whether it has *no solution*.

22. $14 - (2q + 5) = -2q + 9$ **23.** $6x + 1 = 6x - 8$

24. $-8x + 14 = -2(4x - 7)$ **25.** $y - 5 = -(5 - y)$

26. $a - 4a = 2a + 1 - 5a$ **27.** $9x + 3x - 10 = 3(3x + x)$

Ⓑ Apply Your Skills

Solve each equation. If the equation is an identity, write *identity*. If it has no solution, write *no solution*.

28. $18x - 5 = 3(6x - 2)$ **29.** $9 + 5a = 2a + 9$

30. $3(x - 4) = 3x - 12$ **31.** $6x = 4(x + 5)$

32. $\frac{3}{5}k - \frac{1}{10}k = \frac{1}{2}k + 1$ **33.** $0.5y + 2 = 0.8y - 0.3y$

34. $5m - 2(m + 2) = -(2m + 15)$ **35.** $\frac{7}{8}w = \frac{4}{8}w + \frac{6}{8}w$

36. $0 = 0.98b + 0.02b - b$ **37.** $6(6g - 2) + 8(1 - 5g) = 2g$

38. Business A toy company spends $1500 each day for factory expenses plus $8 per teddy bear, like the one shown at left. How many bears must the company sell in one day to equal its daily costs? Write an equation and solve.

39. Business A company manufactures tote bags. The company spends $1200 each day for overhead expenses plus $9 per tote bag for labor and materials. The tote bags sell for $25 each. How many tote bags must the company sell each day to equal its daily costs for overhead, labor, and materials? Write an equation and solve.

Find the value of each variable.

40. $\begin{bmatrix} 2x + 1 & a - 1 \\ w - 4 & 9y \end{bmatrix} = \begin{bmatrix} -5x - 6 & 5a \\ 3w + 4 & -3y \end{bmatrix}$ **41.** $\begin{bmatrix} a + 1 & 4b \\ 2c + 3 & 5d - 3 \end{bmatrix} = \begin{bmatrix} 7 - a & 3b + 5 \\ 3c - 4 & 63 - d \end{bmatrix}$

Find the value of each variable.

42. $\begin{bmatrix} 0.5x + 3 & w + 1.5 \\ 2.5y + 2.5 & a + 1 \end{bmatrix} = \begin{bmatrix} x + 0.5 & 2w - 1.5 \\ 5y - 2.5 & 19 - a \end{bmatrix}$

43. $\begin{bmatrix} \frac{1}{2} + a & \frac{1}{2}b + 2 \\ c - \frac{1}{3} & \frac{1}{3}d + \frac{2}{3} \end{bmatrix} = \begin{bmatrix} 6\frac{1}{2} - a & b - 1 \\ 4\frac{2}{3} & d + \frac{4}{9} \end{bmatrix}$

Error Analysis Find the mistake in the solution of each equation. Explain the mistake and solve the equation correctly.

44.
$$2x = 11x + 45$$
$$2x - 11x = 11x - 11x + 45$$
$$9x = 45$$
$$\frac{9x}{9} = \frac{45}{9}$$
$$x = 5$$

45.
$$4.5 - y = 2(y - 5.7)$$
$$4.5 - y = 2y - 11.4$$
$$4.5 - y - y = 2y - y - 11.4$$
$$4.5 = y - 11.4$$
$$4.5 + 11.4 = y - 11.4 + 11.4$$
$$15.9 = y$$

Need Help?

If triangles are congruent, then their corresponding angles are congruent and their corresponding sides are congruent.

46. **Geometry** $\triangle ABC$ is congruent to $\triangle DEF$. Find the lengths of the sides of $\triangle DEF$.

47. **Writing** Is an equation that has 0 for a solution the same as an equation with no solution? Explain.

48. **Spreadsheet** Don set up a spreadsheet to solve $5(x - 3) = 4 - 3(x + 1)$.
   a. Does Don's spreadsheet show a solution to the equation?
   b. Between which two values of x is the solution to the equation? How do you know?
   c. For what values of x is $4 - 3(x + 1)$ less than $5(x - 3)$?

	A	B	C
1	x	$5(x - 3)$	$4 - 3(x + 1)$
2	−5	−40	16
3	−3	−30	10
4	−1	−20	4
5	1	−10	−2
6	3	0	−8

C **Challenge**

Open-Ended Write an equation with a variable on each side such that you get the solution described.

49. $x = 0$

50. x is a positive number.

51. x is a negative number.

52. All values of x are solutions.

53. No values of x are solutions.

54. $x = 1$

55. Use the equations below to find the length of the pipe.

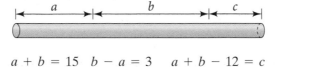

$$a + b = 15 \quad b - a = 3 \quad a + b - 12 = c$$

56. **Geometry** The perimeters of the rectangles at the right are equal. Find the length and width of each rectangle.

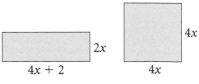

Multiple Choice

57. Solve $2y = 3y - 20$.

    A. -20 **B.** -4 **C.** 4   **D.** 20

58. Which of the following equations is NOT equivalent to the others?

    F. $-2(y - 3) = -6y$ **G.** $-2y - 6 = -6y$

    H. $y = -\frac{3}{2}$ **I.** $4y = -6$

59. Ace Truck Rental charges $54.00 a day plus 9¢ per mile. Roni's Truck Rental charges $38.00 a day plus 13¢ per mile. For how many miles will the cost of renting a truck for one day at Ace equal the cost at Roni's?

    A. 40 mi   **B.** 170 mi   **C.** 400 mi   **D.** 418 mi

60. Which equation is NOT equivalent to $3p - 2 = 6p + 4$?

    F. $3p = 6p + 6$ **G.** $-6 = 3p$

    H. $3p = 6$ **I.** $-3p - 2 = 4$

61. A record store sells CDs for $12.00 each. A music club offers 5 free CDs and charges $15.00 for each additional CD. Which equation can you use to find the number of CDs x that would cost the same under both plans?

    A. $15x - 5 = 12x$ **B.** $12x - 5 = 15x$

    C. $12x = 15(x - 5)$ **D.** $12(x - 5) = 15x$

62. Solve $2(y - 3) = 1.2 - y$.

    F. -1.6 **G.** 1.4   **H.** 1.6   **I.** 2.4

63. The perimeters of the rectangle and the triangle below are equal. Find the value of x.

    A. 6   **B.** 8   **C.** 10   **D.** 12

6 in.   6 in. $(x + 4)$ in.

$(x + 2)$ in. $2x$ in.

Take It to the NET
Online lesson quiz at
www.PHSchool.com
Web Code: aea-0204

Mixed Review

Lesson 2-3   **Solve each equation.**

64. $9 = -4y + 6y - 5$ **65.** $-2(a - 3) = 14$ **66.** $0.5m + 2.8 = 3.64$

67. $\frac{1}{2}x + 4 = \frac{2}{3}$ **68.** $4.8 = 1.25(y - 17)$ **69.** $4\left(\frac{1}{4} + x\right) = 5$

Lesson 2-2   **70. Art** An art gallery owner is framing a painting. The width of the painting to be displayed is 30 in. He wants the width of the framed painting to be $38\frac{1}{2}$ in. How wide should each section of the frame be?

Lesson 1-3   **Write the numbers in each group in order from least to greatest.**

71. $-\frac{3}{5}, -\frac{5}{8}, -\frac{4}{5}$ **72.** $5.04, 5.009, 5.043$ **73.** $8.1, 8.02, 8.3$

74. $-100, 93, -87, 500$ **75.** $0.45, -1.24, 2.24, 1.23$ **76.** $9.7, -9.8, 8.6, 0.9$

Graphing to Solve Equations

You can use a graphing calculator to check solutions of equations. One way to do this is to graph each side of the equation. The x-coordinate of the point where the graphs intersect gives the solution of the equation.

Take It to the NET
Graphing Calculator procedures online at **www.PHSchool.com**
Web Code: aee-2107

EXAMPLE

Solve $-\frac{1}{2}c = \frac{1}{2}c + 5$ using a graphing calculator.

Step 1 Press [Y=] to go to the equation screen. Delete any equation(s) that may appear on this screen by using the [CLEAR] and down arrow keys. Then for Y_1 =, enter $-\frac{1}{2}x$ by pressing [(] [(-)] [1] [/] [2] [)] [X,T,θ]. For Y_2, enter $\frac{1}{2}x + 5$ by pressing [(] [1] [/] [2] [)] [X,T,θ,n] + 5.

Step 2 Graph the equations. Use a standard graphing window, which you can find using the [ZOOM] feature.

Step 3 Find the point where the graphs intersect. Access the **CALC** feature and press 5. Move the cursor near the point of intersection. Press [ENTER] three times to find the coordinates of the intersection point. The x-coordinate of the point is the solution of the equation. The solution of $-\frac{1}{2}c = \frac{1}{2}c + 5$ is -5.

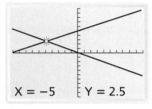

X = −5   Y = 2.5

EXERCISES

1. The graphing calculator screen at the right shows the solution of $2w - 1 = w + 1$.
   a. What two equations were graphed?
   b. What is the x-coordinate of the point where the graphs intersect?
   c. What is the solution of the equation?

2. David solved $3(a + 1) = 5a + 4$. His solution was $-\frac{3}{2}$.
   Graph $y = 3(x + 1)$ and $y = 5x + 4$. Use the **CALC** feature to find the x-coordinate of the intersection of the two lines. Is David's solution correct? If not, what is the correct solution?

Use your graphing calculator to solve each equation.

3. $2a + 5 = -a - 4$ 4. $4b - 10 = 2b$ 5. $-5.4(2n + 5) = 1.8(6 + 3n)$

6. $3p - 8 = -6 + p$ 7. $4 - 7n = n + 4$ 8. $5x - \frac{1}{2} = 4x + \frac{3}{4}$

Use your graphing calculator to check each solution. If the solution is incorrect, state the correct solution.

9. $5(q + 1) = q + 2; \frac{1}{4}$ 10. $2h - 9 = -3(h - 6); 5\frac{2}{5}$ 11. $b - 0 = -2(b + 1); 3\frac{2}{3}$

12. $6(2n - 5) = -3(7 - 3n); 3$ 13. $8x + 5 = -(2x + 8) - 2; -2.5$

Equations and Problem Solving

Lesson Preview

What You'll Learn

OBJECTIVE 1
To define a variable in terms of another variable

OBJECTIVE 2
To model distance-rate-time problems

. . . And Why

To solve real-world problems involving distance, rate, and time, as in Examples 3–5

✓ Check Skills You'll Need

(For help, go to Lesson 1-1.)

Write a variable expression for each situation.

1. value in cents of q quarters
2. twice the length ℓ
3. number of miles traveled at 34 mi/h in h hours
4. weight of 5 crates if each crate weighs x kilograms
5. cost of n items at \$3.99 per item

New Vocabulary
• consecutive integers • uniform motion

 Interactive lesson includes instant self-check, tutorials, and activities.

OBJECTIVE
1 Defining Variables

Some problems contain two or more unknown quantities. To solve such problems, first decide which unknown quantity the variable will represent. Then express the other unknown quantity or quantities in terms of that variable.

1 EXAMPLE Defining One Variable in Terms of Another

Geometry The length of a rectangle is 6 in. more than its width. The perimeter of the rectangle is 24 in. What is the length of the rectangle?

Relate The length is 6 in. more than the width.

Define Let w = the width.
Then $w + 6$ = the length.

> The length is described in terms of the width. So define a variable for the width first.

Write

$P = 2\ell + 2w$	Use the perimeter formula.
$24 = 2(w + 6) + 2w$	Substitute 24 for P and $w + 6$ for ℓ.
$24 = 2w + 12 + 2w$	Use the Distributive Property.
$24 = 4w + 12$	Combine like terms.
$24 - 12 = 4w + 12 - 12$	Subtract 12 from each side.
$12 = 4w$	Simplify.
$\frac{12}{4} = \frac{4w}{4}$	Divide each side by 4.
$3 = w$	Simplify.

The width of the rectangle is 3 in. The length of the rectangle is 6 in. more than the width. So the length of the rectangle is 9 in.

> **Problem Solving Hint**
>
> For Example 1, drawing a diagram will help you understand the problem.
>
> $w + 6$
>
> w [ ]

✓ Check Understanding
1 The width of a rectangle is 2 cm less than its length. The perimeter of the rectangle is 16 cm. What is the length of the rectangle?

Consecutive integers differ by 1. The integers 50 and 51 are consecutive integers, and so are -10, -9, and -8. For consecutive integer problems, it may help to define a variable before describing the problem in words. Let a variable represent one of the unknown integers. Then define the other unknown integers in terms of the first one.

2 EXAMPLE Consecutive Integer Problem

The sum of three consecutive integers is 147. Find the integers.

Define Let n = the first integer.
Then $n + 1$ = the second integer,
and $n + 2$ = the third integer.

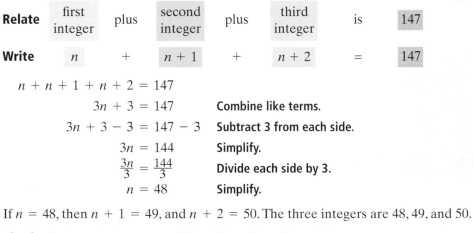

Relate | first integer | plus | second integer | plus | third integer | is | 147 |

Write | n | + | $n + 1$ | + | $n + 2$ | = | 147 |

$$n + n + 1 + n + 2 = 147$$
$$3n + 3 = 147 \qquad \text{Combine like terms.}$$
$$3n + 3 - 3 = 147 - 3 \qquad \text{Subtract 3 from each side.}$$
$$3n = 144 \qquad \text{Simplify.}$$
$$\frac{3n}{3} = \frac{144}{3} \qquad \text{Divide each side by 3.}$$
$$n = 48 \qquad \text{Simplify.}$$

If $n = 48$, then $n + 1 = 49$, and $n + 2 = 50$. The three integers are 48, 49, and 50.

Check Is the solution correct? Yes; $48 + 49 + 50 = 147$.

✓ **Check Understanding** **2** The sum of three consecutive integers is 48.
a. Define a variable for one of the integers.
b. Write expressions for the other two integers.
c. Write and solve an equation to find the three integers.

OBJECTIVE

2 **Distance-Rate-Time Problems**

An object that moves at a constant rate is said to be in **uniform motion.**
The formula $d = rt$ gives the relationship between distance d, rate r, and time t.
Uniform motion problems may involve objects going the same direction, opposite directions, or round trips.

In the diagram below, the two vehicles are traveling the same direction at different rates. The distances the vehicles travel are the same.

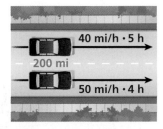

200 mi

40 mi/h · 5 h

50 mi/h · 4 h

Since the distances are equal, the products of rate and time for the two cars are equal. For the vehicles shown, $40 \cdot 5 = 50 \cdot 4$.

A table can also help you understand relationships in distance-rate-time problems.

3 EXAMPLE Same-Direction Travel

Engineering A train leaves a train station at 1 P.M. It travels at an average rate of 60 mi/h. A high-speed train leaves the same station an hour later. It travels at an average rate of 96 mi/h. The second train follows the same route as the first train on a track parallel to the first. In how many hours will the second train catch up with the first train?

Define Let t = the time the first train travels.

Then $t - 1$ = the time the second train travels.

Relate

Train	Rate	Time	Distance Traveled
1	60	t	$60t$
2	96	$t - 1$	$96(t - 1)$

Write

$60t = 96(t - 1)$	The distances traveled by the trains are equal.
$60t = 96t - 96$	Use the Distributive Property.
$60t - 60t = 96t - 96 - 60t$	Subtract 60t from each side.
$0 = 36t - 96$	Combine like terms.
$0 + 96 = 36t - 96 + 96$	Add 96 to each side.
$96 = 36t$	Simplify.
$\frac{96}{36} = \frac{36t}{36}$	Divide each side by 36.
$t = 2\frac{2}{3}$	Simplify.
$t - 1 = 1\frac{2}{3}$	Find the time the second train travels.

The second train will catch up with the first train in $1\frac{2}{3}$ h.

✓ **Check Understanding** **3** A group of campers and one group leader left a campsite in a canoe. They traveled at an average rate of 10 km/h. Two hours later, the other group leader left the campsite in a motorboat. He traveled at an average rate of 22 km/h.
a. How long after the canoe left the campsite did the motorboat catch up with it?
b. How long did the motorboat travel?

For uniform motion problems that involve a round trip, it is important to remember that the distance going is equal to the distance returning.

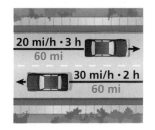

Since the distances are equal, the products of rate and time for traveling in both directions are equal. That is, $20 \cdot 3 = 30 \cdot 2$.

4 EXAMPLE Round-Trip Travel

Noya drives into the city to buy a software program at a computer store. Because of traffic conditions, she averages only 15 mi/h. On her drive home she averages 35 mi/h. If the total travel time is 2 hours, how long does it take her to drive to the computer store?

Reading Math

The total travel time is for a round trip. If it takes x out of a 2-hour round trip to get to the store, then $2 - x$ is the time it will take for the drive home.

Define Let t = time of Noya's drive to the computer store.

$2 - t$ = the time of Noya's drive home.

Relate

Part of Noya's Travel	Rate	Time	Distance
To the computer store	15	t	$15t$
Return home	35	$2 - t$	$35(2 - t)$

Noya drives $15t$ miles to the computer store and $35(2 - t)$ miles back.

Write

$15t = 35(2 - t)$	The distances traveled to and from the store are equal.
$15t = 70 - 35t$	Use the Distributive Property.
$15t + 35t = 70 - 35t + 35t$	Add **35t** to each side.
$50t = 70$	Combine like terms.
$\frac{50t}{50} = \frac{70}{50}$	Divide each side by 50.
$t = 1.4$	Simplify.

● It took Noya 1.4 h to drive to the computer store.

✓ Check Understanding ④ On his way to work from home, your uncle averaged only 20 miles per hour. On his drive home, he averaged 40 miles per hour. If the total travel time was $1\frac{1}{2}$ hours, how long did it take him to drive to work?

For uniform motion problems involving two objects moving in opposite directions, you can write equations using the fact that the sum of their distances is the total distance.

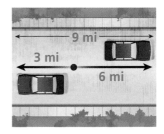

5 EXAMPLE Opposite-Direction Travel

Jane and Peter leave their home traveling in opposite directions on a straight road. Peter drives 15 mi/h faster than Jane. After 3 hours, they are 225 miles apart. Find Peter's rate and Jane's rate.

Define Let r = Jane's rate.

Then $r + 15$ = Peter's rate.

Relate

Person	Rate	Time	Distance
Jane	r	3	$3r$
Peter	$r + 15$	3	$3(r + 15)$

Jane's distance is $3r$. Peter's distance is $3(r + 15)$.

Write $3r + 3(r + 15) = 225$ The sum of Jane's and Peter's distances is the total distance, 225 miles.

$$3r + 3(r + 15) = 225$$
$$3r + 3r + 45 = 225 \qquad \text{Use the Distributive Property.}$$
$$6r + 45 = 225 \qquad \text{Combine like terms.}$$
$$6r + 45 - 45 = 225 - 45 \qquad \text{Subtract 45 from each side.}$$
$$6r = 180 \qquad \text{Simplify.}$$
$$\frac{6r}{6} = \frac{180}{6} \qquad \text{Divide each side by 6.}$$
$$r = 30 \qquad \text{Simplify.}$$

Jane's rate is 30 mi/h, and Peter's rate is 15 mi/h faster, which is 45 mi/h.

✓ **Check Understanding** ⑤ Sarah and John leave Perryville traveling in opposite directions on a straight road. Sarah drives 12 miles per hour faster than John. After 2 hours, they are 176 miles apart. Find Sarah's speed and John's speed.

EXERCISES

For more practice, see *Extra Practice*.

Practice and Problem Solving

A **Practice by Example**

Example 1
(page 103)

1. The length of a rectangle is 3 in. more than its width. The perimeter of the rectangle is 30 in.
   a. Define a variable for the width.
   b. Write an expression for the length in terms of the width.
   c. Write an equation to find the width of the rectangle. Solve your equation.
   d. What is the length of the rectangle?

2. The length of a rectangle is 8 in. more than its width. The perimeter of the rectangle is 24 in. What are the width and length of the rectangle?

3. The width of a rectangle is one half its length. The perimeter of the rectangle is 54 cm. What are the width and length of the rectangle?

4. The length of a rectangular garden is 3 yd more than twice its width. The perimeter of the garden is 36 yd. What are the width and length of the garden?

Example 2
(page 104)

5. The sum of the two consecutive integers is -35. If $n =$ the first integer, which equation best models the situation?
   A. $n(n + 1) = -35$ **B.** $n + 2n = -35$
   C. $n + (n + 1) = -35$ **D.** $n + (2n + 1) = -35$

6. The sum of two consecutive *even* integers is 118.
   a. Define a variable for the smaller integer.
   b. What must you add to an even integer to get the next greater even integer?
   c. Write an expression for the second integer.
   d. Write and solve an equation to find the two even integers.

7. The sum of two consecutive *odd* integers is 56.
   a. Define a variable for the smaller integer.
   b. What must you add to an odd integer to get the next greater odd integer?
   c. Write an expression for the second integer.
   d. Write and solve an equation to find the two odd integers.

8. The sum of three consecutive integers is 915. What are the integers?

9. The sum of two consecutive *even* integers is -298. What are the integers?

Example 3
(page 105)

10. A moving van leaves a house traveling at an average rate of 35 mi/h. The family leaves the house $\frac{3}{4}$ hour later following the same route in a car. They travel at an average rate of 50 mi/h.
  a. Define a variable for the time traveled by the moving van.
  b. Write an expression for the time traveled by the car.
  c. Copy and complete the table.

Vehicle	Rate	Time	Distance Traveled
Moving van	■	■	■
Car	■	■	■

  d. Write and solve an equation to find out how long it will take the car to catch up with the moving van.

11. Air Travel A jet leaves the Charlotte, North Carolina, airport traveling at an average rate of 564 km/h. Another jet leaves the airport one half hour later traveling at 744 km/h in the same direction. How long will the second jet take to overtake the first?

Example 4
(page 106)

12. Juan drives to work. Because of traffic conditions, he averages 22 miles per hour. He returns home averaging 32 miles per hour. The total travel time is $2\frac{1}{4}$ hours.
  a. Define a variable for the time Juan takes to travel to work. Write an expression for the time Juan takes to return home.
  b. Write and solve an equation to find the time Juan spends driving to work.

13. Air Travel An airplane flies from New Orleans, Louisiana, to Atlanta, Georgia, at an average rate of 320 miles per hour. The airplane then returns at an average rate of 280 miles per hour. The total travel time is 3 hours.
  a. Define a variable for the flying time from New Orleans to Atlanta. Write an expression for the travel time from Atlanta to New Orleans.
  b. Write and solve an equation to find the flying time from New Orleans to Atlanta.

Example 5
(page 106)

14. John and William leave their home traveling in opposite directions on a straight road. John drives 20 miles per hour faster than William. After 4 hours they are 250 miles apart.
  a. Define a variable for John's rate. Write an expression for William's rate.
  b. Write and solve an equation to find John's rate. Then find William's rate.

15. Two bicyclists ride in opposite directions. The speed of the first bicyclist is 5 miles per hour faster than the second. After 2 hours they are 70 miles apart. Find their rates.

B **Apply Your Skills**

16 a. Which of the following numbers is not the sum of three consecutive integers?
  I. 51   **II.** 61   **III.** 72   **IV.** 81
  b. Critical Thinking What common trait do the other numbers share?

17. Geometry The length of a rectangle is 8 cm more than twice the width. The perimeter of the rectangle is 34 cm. What is the length of the rectangle?

18. The sum of four consecutive *even* integers is 308. Write and solve an equation to find the four integers.

19. The sum of three consecutive *odd* integers is -87. What are the integers?

20. The tail of a kite is 1.5 ft plus twice the length of the kite. Together, the kite and tail are 15 ft 6 in. long.
    a. Write an expression for the length of the kite and tail together.
    b. Write 15 ft 6 in. in terms of feet.
    c. Write and solve an equation to find the length of the tail.

21. **Travel** A bus traveling at an average rate of 30 miles per hour left the city at 11:45 A.M. A car following the bus at 45 miles per hour left the city at noon. At what time did the car catch up with the bus?

22. Ellen and Kate raced on their bicycles to the library after school. They both left school at 3:00 P.M. and bicycled along the same path. Ellen rode at a speed of 12 miles per hour and Kate rode at 9 miles per hour. Ellen got to the library 15 minutes before Kate.
    a. How long did it take Ellen to get to the library?
    b. At what time did Ellen get to the library?

23. At 1:30 P.M., Tom leaves in his boat from a dock and heads south. He travels at a rate of 25 miles per hour. Ten minutes later, Mary leaves the same dock in her speedboat and heads after Tom. If she travels at a rate of 30 miles per hour, when will she catch up with Tom?

24. **Air Travel** Two airplanes depart from an airport traveling in opposite directions. The second airplane is 200 miles per hour faster than the first. After 2 hours they are 1100 miles apart. Find the speeds of the airplanes.

25. Three friends were born in consecutive years. The sum of their birth years is 5961. Find the year in which each person was born.

26. Two boats leave a ramp traveling in opposite directions. The second boat is 10 miles per hour faster than the first. After 3 hours they are 150 miles apart. Find the speeds of the boats.

27. **Travel** A truck traveling 45 miles per hour and a train traveling 60 miles per hour cover the same distance. The truck travels 2 hours longer than the train. How many hours does each travel?

28. **Electricity** A group of ten 6- and 12-volt batteries are wired in series as shown at the right. The sum of their voltages is 84 volts. How many of each type of battery are used?

Batteries in Series

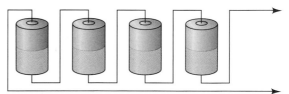

29. **Writing** Describe the steps you would use to solve consecutive integer problems.

30. **Open-Ended** Write a word problem that could be solved using the equation $35(t - 1) = 20t$.

31. a. Write and solve an equation to find three consecutive integers with a sum of 126. Let $n =$ the first integer.
    b. **Critical Thinking** In part (a), could you solve the problem by letting $n =$ the middle integer, $n - 1 =$ the smallest integer, and $n + 1 =$ the largest integer?

C Challenge 32. **Geometry** A triangle has a perimeter of 165 cm. The first side is 65 cm less than twice the second side. The third side is 10 cm less than the second side. Write and solve an equation to find the length of each side of the triangle.

33. At 9:00 A.M., your friends begin hiking at 2 mi/h. You begin from the same place at 9:25 A.M. You hike at 3 mi/h.
  a. How long will you have hiked when you catch up with your friends?
  b. At what time will you catch up with your friends?

34. Find five consecutive *odd* integers such that the sum of the first and the fifth is one less than three times the fourth.

Standardized Test Prep

Multiple Choice

35. Solve $3n - 7 + 2n = 8n + 11$.
  A. -6 **B.** $1\frac{1}{3}$ **C.** $3\frac{3}{5}$ **D.** 9

36. Which expression represents the sum of 3 odd integers of which *n* is the least integer?
  F. $n + 3$ **G.** $3n + 3$
  H. $3n + 6$ **I.** $3n + 7$

37. Which equation does NOT have -2 as its solution?
  A. $2x + 5 = 5x + 11$ **B.** $7n + 9 = 3 - 9n$
  C. $3k + 6 - 4k = k + 10$ **D.** $4 + 3q = 7q + 12$

38. A truck traveling at an average rate of 45 miles per hour leaves a rest stop. Fifteen minutes later a car traveling at an average rate of 60 miles per hour leaves the same rest stop traveling the same route. How long will it take for the car to catch up with the truck?
  F. 15 minutes   **G.** 45 minutes
  H. 1 hour 15 minutes   **I.** 3 hours

39. The perimeter of the triangle at the right is 22.6 in. What is the value of *n*?
  A. 3.5   **B.** 4.6
  C. 7.8   **D.** 9.4

Triangle with sides labeled n in., $(n + 5.2)$ in., and $(2n + 3.4)$ in.

Take It to the NET
Online lesson quiz at
www.PHSchool.com
Web Code: aea-0205

Mixed Review

Lesson 2-4

Solve each equation. If the equation is an identity, write *identity*. If it has no solution, write *no solution*.

40. $2x = 7x + 10$ **41.** $2q + 4 = 4 - 2q$

42. $0.5t + 3.6 = 4.2 - 1.5t$ **43.** $2x + 5 + x = 2(3x + 3)$

44. $4 + x + 3x = 2(2x + 5)$ **45.** $8z + 2 = 2(z - 5) - z$

Lesson 2-3

46. Brendan earns $8.25 per hour at his job. He also makes $12.38 per hour for any number of hours over 40 that he works in one week. He worked 40 hours last week, plus some overtime, and made $385.71. How many overtime hours did he work?

Lesson 1-5

Simplify.

47. $-8 - 4$ **48.** $2 - 12$ **49.** $45 - (-9)$ **50.** $18 - 15$

2-6

Formulas

Lesson Preview

What You'll Learn

OBJECTIVE
1 To transform literal equations

...And Why

To solve problems involving temperature, as in Example 4

✓ Check Skills You'll Need

(For help, go to Lessons 1-2, 1-4, and 1-6.)

Evaluate each formula for the values given.

1. distance: $d = rt$, when $r = 60$ mi/h and $t = 3$ h

2. perimeter of a rectangle: $P = 2\ell + 2w$, when $\ell = 11$ cm, and $w = 5$ cm

3. area of a triangle: $A = \frac{1}{2}bh$, when $b = 8$ m and $h = 7$ m

New Vocabulary • literal equation

OBJECTIVE
1

Transforming Literal Equations

Interactive lesson includes instant self-check, tutorials, and activities.

Investigation: Using a Transformed Formula

A track coach is calculating the average speed of each team member.

d	r	t
1500 m	■	4.98 min
800 m	■	3.08 min
800 m	■	2.93 min
400 m	■	1.18 min

1. Using the formula $d = rt$, copy and complete the table at the left.

2. Now use the formula $r = \frac{d}{t}$ to find values for r.

3. What do you notice about the two sets of values?

4. Which formula is easier to use when you need to find r? Explain.

A **literal equation** is an equation involving two or more variables. Formulas are special types of literal equations. To transform a literal equation, you solve for one variable in terms of the others. This means that you get the variable you are solving for alone on one side of the equation.

1 EXAMPLE **Transforming Geometric Formulas**

Geometry Solve the formula for the area of a triangle $A = \frac{1}{2}bh$ for height h.

$$A = \frac{1}{2}bh$$

$$2A = 2\left(\frac{1}{2}\right)bh \quad \text{Multiply each side by 2.}$$

$$2A = bh \quad \text{Simplify.}$$

$$\frac{2A}{b} = \frac{bh}{b} \quad \text{Divide each side by } b, b \neq 0, \text{ to get } h \text{ alone on one side of the equation.}$$

$$\frac{2A}{b} = h \quad \text{Simplify.}$$

✓ Check Understanding **1** Solve the formula for the perimeter of a rectangle $P = 2(\ell + w)$ for the width w.

2 EXAMPLE Transforming Equations

Solve $y = 5x + 7$ for x.

$y - 7 = 5x + 7 - 7$	**Subtract 7 from each side.**
$y - 7 = 5x$	**Simplify.**
$\dfrac{y - 7}{5} = \dfrac{5x}{5}$	**Divide each side by 5.**
$\dfrac{y - 7}{5} = x$	**Simplify.**

✔ **Check Understanding** **2** Solve $y - 4 = 3x - 8$ for x.

Sometimes an equation will only have variables. Transforming this type of equation is no different from transforming equations with numbers.

3 EXAMPLE Transforming Equations Containing Only Variables

Solve $ab - d = c$ for b.

$ab - d + d = c + d$	**Add d to each side.**
$ab = c + d$	**Combine like terms.**
$\dfrac{ab}{a} = \dfrac{c + d}{a}$	**Divide each side by a, $a \neq 0$.**
$b = \dfrac{c + d}{a}$	**Simplify.**

✔ **Check Understanding** **3** Solve $m - hp = d$ for p.

You can transform a formula so that it is in a convenient form for solving real-world problems.

4 EXAMPLE Real-World 🌐 Problem Solving

Temperature The formula $C = \frac{5}{9}(F - 32)$ gives the Celsius temperature C in terms of the Fahrenheit temperature F. Transform the formula to find Fahrenheit temperature in terms of Celsius temperature. Then find the Fahrenheit temperature when the Celsius temperature is 30°.

Step 1 Solve for F.

$C = \frac{5}{9}(F - 32)$	
$\frac{9}{5} \cdot C = \frac{9}{5} \cdot \frac{5}{9}(F - 32)$	**Multiply each side by $\frac{9}{5}$, the reciprocal of $\frac{5}{9}$.**
$\frac{9}{5}C = F - 32$	**Simplify.**
$\frac{9}{5}C + 32 = F - 32 + 32$	**Add 32 to each side.**
$\frac{9}{5}C + 32 = F$	**Simplify.**

Step 2 Find F when $C = 30$.

$\frac{9}{5}(30) + 32 = F$	**Substitute 30 for C.**
$54 + 32 = F$	**Simplify $\frac{9}{5}(30)$.**
$86 = F$	

$30°C$ is equivalent to $86°F$.

✓ **Check Understanding** ④ You can use the number of chirps n a cricket makes in one minute to estimate the outside temperature F in degrees Fahrenheit. Transform the formula $F = \frac{n}{4} + 37$ to find the number of chirps in terms of temperature. How many chirps per minute can you expect if the temperature is 60°F?

EXERCISES

For more practice, see *Extra Practice*.

Practice and Problem Solving

Ⓐ Practice by Example

Example 1
(page 111)

Solve each formula in terms of the given variable.

1. $C = 2\pi r$; r **2.** $\pi = \frac{C}{d}$; d **3.** $P = 2\ell + 2w$; ℓ **4.** $S = L + 2B$; B

5. Volume of a rectangular prism
$V = \ell wh$; h

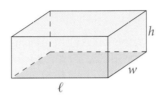

6. Perimeter of a square
$P = 4s$; s

....

Problem Solving Hint

For Exercise 7, you can solve for b_1 by letting $(b_1 + b_2) = x$. Solve for x and then solve for b_1.
....

7. Area of a trapezoid
$A = \frac{1}{2}h(b_1 + b_2)$; b_1

8. Volume of a cylinder
$V = \pi r^2 h$; h

Example 2
(page 112)

Solve each equation for y.

9. $y + 2x = 5$ **10.** $y - 6x = -1$ **11.** $y + 4x = 3$ **12.** $2y + 4x = 8$

13. $3y - 5x = 9$ **14.** $4y + 3x = 7$ **15.** $5x + 4y = 4$ **16.** $2x + 7y = 4$

Example 3
(page 112)

Solve each equation for the variable in red.

17. $dx = c$ **18.** $c = \frac{d}{g}$ **19.** $z - a = y$ **20.** $ax + by = c$

21. $A = P + Prt$ **22.** $S = C + rC$ **23.** $\frac{m}{n} = \frac{p}{q}$ **24.** $\frac{y - b}{m} = x$

Example 4
(page 112)

25. Construction Bricklayers use the formula $N = 7LH$ to estimate the number of bricks N needed to build a wall of height H and length L.
   a. Solve the equation for H.
   b. What is the height of a wall that is 30 feet long and that requires 2310 bricks to build?

26. Sports You can use the formula $a = \frac{h}{n}$ to find the batting average a of a batter who has h hits in n times at bat.
   a. Solve the equation for h.
   b. If a batter has a batting average of .265 and has been at bat 200 times, how many hits does the batter have?

Apply Your Skills 🌐 **27. a. Banking** The formula $I = prt$ gives the amount of simple interest I earned by principal p at an annual interest rate r over t years. Solve this formula for p.
b. Find p if $r = 0.035$, $t = 4$, and $I = \$420$.
c. Writing What does the value p mean in your answer to part (b)?

🌐 **28. Sales Commission** Suppose that you sell shoes and get a 5% commission on your sales. Last week, your paycheck included \$24.71 in commissions.
a. Solve the formula $C = 0.05s$ for s, where C is the amount of commission and s is the amount of sales.
b. Find your sales.

Solve each equation for the variable in red.

29. $A = bh$ **30.** $y = \frac{2}{3}x + 8$ **31.** $ap - b = r$

32. $2(p + r) = 5$ **33.** $SA = 2\pi rh + 2B$ **34.** $2x + 10 = 5y - 4$

35. $\frac{a}{b} = \frac{c}{d}$ **36.** $\frac{m + k}{h} = w$ **37.** $V = \frac{1}{3}\pi r^2 h$

38. $3y + 2 = 9x - 4$ **39.** $y = 3(w - y)$ **40.** $3m = 2(4 + x)$

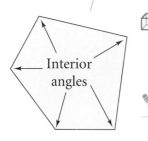
Interior angles

41. Geometry To find S, the sum of the measures of the interior angles of a polygon with n sides, you can use the formula $S = (n - 2)180$.
a. Transform the formula to find the number of sides in terms of the interior angle sum. Solve this equation for n.
b. Complete the table at the right using your new formula.

S	n
540	▦
900	▦
360	▦
1260	▦

42. Writing How is solving a literal equation similar to solving an equation that involves one variable? How is it different?

43. Open-Ended Write an equation using three variables. Solve the equation for each variable. Show all your steps.

🅒 **Challenge** 📦 **44. Geometry** To find the coordinate of the midpoint of a segment with endpoints that have coordinates a and b, you can use the formula $m = \frac{a + b}{2}$.
a. Find the coordinate of the midpoint of a segment with endpoints 8.2 and 3.5.
b. Transform the formula to find b in terms of a and m.
c. A segment has midpoint 2.1. One endpoint is -1.7. Find the other endpoint.

🌐 **45. Recreation** The aspect ratio of a hang glider describes its ability to glide and soar. The formula $R = \frac{s^2}{A}$ gives the aspect ratio R for a glider with wingspan s and wing area A.
a. Solve this formula for A.
b. Suppose you want to design a glider with a 9-ft wingspan and an aspect ratio of 3. Use the formula you found in part (a) to find the wing area.

Real-World 🌐 Connection

Careers Aeronautical engineers may design simple aircraft, like hang gliders, or complex superjets. Every aspect of design, from wingspan to the size of fuel containers, requires engineers to know and use formulas.

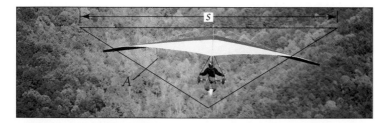

🌐 **46. Health** The volume of air an adult's lungs can hold decreases with age. The formula $V = 0.104h - 0.018a - 2.69$ estimates air volume V (in liters) of a person's lungs for someone of height h inches and age a years. Solve this formula for age a.

114   Chapter 2   Solving Equations

Multiple Choice

47. You can find the cost of renting a hot-air balloon at Tavares Balloon Rental using the formula $C = 85 + 36h$, where C is the total cost and h is the number of hours rented. Solve this equation for h.

A. $h = C - 121$ **B.** $h = \frac{C - 85}{36}$ **C.** $h = C - 85$ **D.** $h = \frac{C - 36}{85}$

48. Kelly, Ted, and Lauren opened savings accounts. Kelly started with $80 and saves $30 per month. Ted started with $50 and saves twice as much as Kelly each month. Lauren started with twice as much as Kelly and saves one third as much as Ted each month. Let m represent the number of months each has been saving. Which expression represents the total amount of money saved by Kelly, Ted, and Lauren in m months?

F. $290 + 270m$ **G.** $110 + 290m$ **H.** $270 + 290m$ **I.** $290 + 110m$

49. A rectangular table measures 36 in. by 48 in. A square game board that is 24 in. on each side is on the table. Which amount of the table's area is NOT covered by the game board?

A. 264 in.^{2} **B.** 1152 in.^{2} **C.** 1704 in.^{2} **D.** 1728 in.^{2}

50. The formula for the time that a traffic light remains yellow is $t = \frac{1}{8}s + 1$, where t is the time in seconds and s is the speed limit. If the light is yellow for 6 seconds, what is the speed limit in miles per hour?

F. 56   **G.** 40   **H.** 10   **I.** 1.75

Take It to the NET
Online lesson quiz at
www.PHSchool.com
⋯⋯⋯ Web Code: aea-0206

Mixed Review

Lesson 2-5

51. The sum of three consecutive integers is 216. Find the integers.

52. The perimeter of a rectangle is 116 cm. The length is 10 cm greater than twice the width. What is the length of the rectangle?

Lesson 1-6

Multiply.

53. $12\begin{bmatrix} -5 & \frac{3}{4} \end{bmatrix}$ **54.** $2\begin{bmatrix} 7 & -3.1 \\ \frac{1}{4} & -8 \end{bmatrix}$ **55.** $-3\begin{bmatrix} 5.2 & -9 & -1 \\ 0 & -8 & 9.5 \end{bmatrix}$

✔ Checkpoint Quiz 2   **Lessons 2-4 through 2-6**

ⓘTEXT Instant self-check quiz online and on CD-ROM

Solve each equation.

1. $7x + 3 = 15x + 9$ **2.** $\frac{3}{4}n + 5 = \frac{2}{5}n$ **3.** $-\frac{1}{5}x - 8 = 4x + 3$

4. $5(2w - 4) = 6w$ **5.** $2y - 8 = -\frac{1}{2}(3 - 5y)$ **6.** $0.3a + 0.7 = 0.5a - 0.1$

Solve each equation for y.

7. $2x + 7y = 35$ **8.** $5x - 2y = 15$ **9.** $\frac{2}{3}x + \frac{3}{4}y = 9$

10. Two cars are traveling on the same highway. The first car is traveling at an average rate of 44 mi/h. The second car leaves an hour later traveling at an average rate of 55 mi/h. How long will the cars have traveled when the second car catches up with the first car?

Developing Geometric Formulas

You can develop formulas for the surface area of prisms and cylinders using what you know about the areas of geometric shapes. Making a net of a figure can help. A net is a two-dimensional figure that you could fold to make a three-dimensional figure.

1 EXAMPLE

The figure at the right is a rectangular prism. Write a formula for the surface area of a rectangular prism.

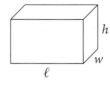

Draw a net.

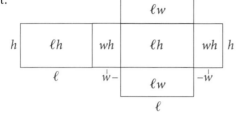

Add the areas of the six rectangles that form the net. The sum of the areas of all six faces of the net will give you the surface area *SA* of the prism.

$$SA = \ell w + \ell w + \ell h + \ell h + hw + hw$$
$$= 2\ell w + 2\ell h + 2hw \quad \textbf{Combine like terms.}$$
$$= 2(\ell w + \ell h + hw) \quad \textbf{Use the Distributive Property.}$$

The formula for the surface area is $SA = 2(\ell w + \ell h + hw)$.

EXERCISES

Use the net for each figure. Write a formula for the surface area of each figure.

1. cylinder

2. square pyramid

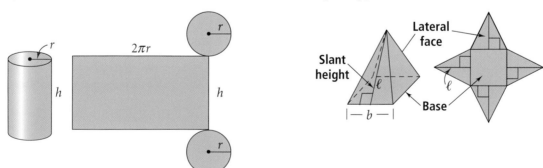

Use the formula in Example 1 and the formulas you wrote in Exercises 1 and 2 to find the surface area of each figure. Round answers to the nearest hundredth, if necessary.

3. rectangular prism with $\ell = 8$ in., $w = 5$ in., and $h = 10$ in.

4. cylinder with $r = 3$ ft and $h = 10$ ft

5. cylinder with $r = 8$ cm and $h = 100$ cm

6. square pyramid with $b = 12$ mm and $\ell = 10$ mm

7. square pyramid with $b = 100$ m and $\ell = 90$ m

8. Write a formula for the surface area of a cube with edges of length s.

In general, the formula for the volumes of rectangular prisms and cylinders is area of base × height. You make the formula more specific by including the formula for the area of the base in the formula for the volume.

2 EXAMPLE

Write a formula for the volume of a cylinder.

The base is a circle.
The area of a circle is πr^2.

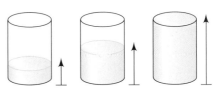

The height of a cylinder takes into account "filling" the cylinder. So the volume of a cylinder is the area of the base times the height.

● $V = \pi r^2 h$

EXERCISES

9. A rectangular prism is shown at the right. Write a formula for the volume of a rectangular prism.

Find the volume of each figure.

10. rectangular prism with $\ell = 8$ in., $w = 5$ in., and $h = 10$ in.

11. cylinder with $r = 3$ ft and $h = 10$ ft

12.

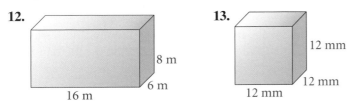

8 m
6 m
16 m

13.

12 mm
12 mm
12 mm

14. a. The volume of a pyramid is $\frac{1}{3}$ the volume of a rectangular prism with the same base and height. Write a formula for the volume of a pyramid.
  b. Use your formula to find the volume of a rectangular pyramid with base length 7 cm, width 12 cm, and height 10 cm.

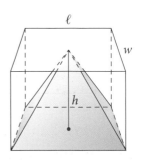

Using Measures of Central Tendency

Lesson Preview

What You'll Learn

OBJECTIVE 1 To find mean, median, and mode

OBJECTIVE 2 To make and use stem-and-leaf plots

. . . And Why

To analyze real-world employment data, as in Example 1

✔ Check Skills You'll Need

(For help, go to Lessons 1-4 and 1-6.)

Write the numbers in each group in order from least to greatest.

1. $2.4, 9.8, 3.6, 7.5, 1.9$

2. $144, 235, 98, 72, 58, 195$

3. $-12, 14, -3, -8, 7, 0$

4. $2\frac{1}{2}, -3\frac{2}{3}, -4\frac{3}{8}, 6\frac{1}{4}, -2\frac{5}{8}, 4\frac{1}{2}$

Use mental math to simplify.

5. $\dfrac{3 + 4 + 5 + 6 + 7}{5}$

6. $\dfrac{5 + 6 + 8 + 9}{4}$

New Vocabulary

- measures of central tendency • mean • outlier
- median • mode • range • stem-and-leaf plot

OBJECTIVE

1 Finding Mean, Median, and Mode

🅘TEXT Interactive lesson includes instant self-check, tutorials, and activities.

To understand a set of data, you need to organize and summarize the data using a measure of central tendency. Mean, median, and mode are all **measures of central tendency.**

You must decide which measure of central tendency best describes a set of data. Below is a review of mean, median, and mode, and where you would use each as the measure of central tendency.

🔑 Key Concepts

Review	**Mean, Median, Mode**

Mean $= \dfrac{\text{sum of the data items}}{\text{total number of data items}}$

Use the mean to describe the middle of a set of data that *does not* have an outlier. An **outlier** is a data value that is much higher or lower than the other data values in the set. The mean is often referred to as the average.

The **median** is the middle value in the set when the numbers are arranged in order. For a set containing an even number of data items, the median is the mean of the two middle data values.

Use the median to describe the middle of a set of data that *does* have an outlier.

The **mode** is the data item that occurs the most times. It is possible for a set of data to have no mode, one mode, or more than one mode.

Use the mode when the data are nonnumeric or when choosing the most popular item.

1 EXAMPLE **Real-World Problem Solving**

Wages Find the mean, median, and mode of the data in the line plot below. Which measure of central tendency best describes the data?

Hourly Wages of Employees at a Local Restaurant

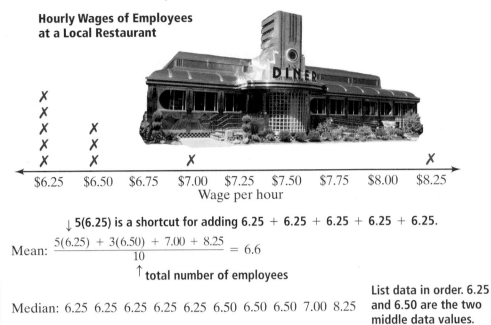

X							
X							
X	X						
X	X						
X	X		X				X

$6.25 $6.50 $6.75 $7.00 $7.25 $7.50 $7.75 $8.00 $8.25
Wage per hour

↓ **5(6.25) is a shortcut for adding 6.25 + 6.25 + 6.25 + 6.25 + 6.25.**

Mean: $\dfrac{5(6.25) + 3(6.50) + 7.00 + 8.25}{10} = 6.6$

↑ **total number of employees**

Median: 6.25 6.25 6.25 6.25 6.25 6.50 6.50 6.50 7.00 8.25   **List data in order. 6.25 and 6.50 are the two middle data values.**

$\dfrac{6.25 + 6.50}{2} = 6.375$ **The median of an even number of data items is the mean of the two middle data values.**

Mode: 6.25   **the data item that occurs most often**

The mean is $6.60, the median is about $6.38, and the mode is $6.25. The mean is greater than the salary of 8 workers. The mode is the salary of the 5 workers with the lowest salary. The median best describes the data.

✓ **Check Understanding**   **1** a. **Wages** The employee who earns $8.25 per hour resigns. She is replaced by an employee earning $7.50 per hour. Find the mean, median, and mode of the data.
   b. **Critical Thinking** Which measure best describes the data? Explain why.

Students often ask, "What grade do I need on the next test to bring up my average?" The example below shows you how to solve that kind of problem.

2 EXAMPLE **Solving an Equation**

Suppose your grades on three history exams are 80, 93, and 91. What grade do you need on your next exam to have a 90 average on the four exams?

Mean (average): $\dfrac{80 + 93 + 91 + x}{4} = 90$ **Let x = the grade on the fourth exam.**

$\dfrac{264 + x}{4} = 90$ **Simplify the numerator.**

$4\left(\dfrac{264 + x}{4}\right) = 4(90)$ **Multiply each side by 4.**

$264 + x = 360$ **Simplify.**

$264 + x - 264 = 360 - 264$ **Subtract 264 from each side.**

$x = 96$ **Simplify.**

Your grade on the next exam must be 96 for you to have an average of 90.

✓ Check Understanding **2** **Critical Thinking** If 100 is the highest possible score on the fourth exam, is it possible to raise your average to 92? Explain.

The **range** of a set of data is the difference between the greatest and least data values. The range gives you a measure of the spread of the data.

3 **EXAMPLE** **Finding the Range and Mean of Data**

Find the range and mean of each set of data. Use the range to compare the spread of the two sets of data.

25 30 30 47 28

Range: $47 - 25 = 22$

Mean: $\dfrac{25 + 30 + 30 + 47 + 28}{5}$

$\dfrac{160}{5} = 32$

34 28 31 36 31

Range: $36 - 28 = 8$

Mean: $\dfrac{34 + 28 + 31 + 36 + 31}{5}$

$\dfrac{160}{5} = 32$

Both sets of data have a mean of 32. The range of the first set of data is 22, and the range of the second set of data is 8. The second set of data is less spread out.

✓ Check Understanding **3** For the first five days in February, the low temperatures in northern Maine were 7°F, 4°F, −3°F, −6°F, and 0°F. During the same time period, the low temperatures in northern Michigan were 24°F, 15°F, −2°F, −10°F, and −5°F. Find the mean and range of the temperatures. Compare the spreads of the temperature data.

OBJECTIVE

2 Stem-and-Leaf Plots

You can use a stem-and-leaf plot to organize data. A **stem-and-leaf plot** is a display of data made by using the digits of the values. To make a stem-and-leaf plot, separate each number into a stem and a leaf. This is the stem and leaf for the number 1.54.

all digits
to the left of   last
last digit   /digit
⟶ **1.5 | 4**
↑   ↑
stem   leaf

REGULAR EXTRA PREMIUM

4 **EXAMPLE** **Making a Stem-and-Leaf Plot**

Gasoline Prices
(cost /gallon)
$1.77
$1.55
$1.58
$1.73
$1.54
$1.83
$1.63
$1.67

Make a stem-and-leaf plot for the data at the left.

Use the first two
digits for the "stems."

1.5 | 4 5 8
1.6 | 3 7
1.7 | 3 7
1.8 | 3

Use the corresponding last digits
for the "leaves." Arrange the numbers
in order.

1.8 | 3 means 1.83

✓ Check Understanding **4** Make a stem-and-leaf plot for the data below.
4.5 4.3 0.8 3.5 2.6 1.4 0.2 0.8 4.3 6.0

You can find the measures of central tendency of data displayed in a stem-and-leaf plot. The stem-and-leaf plot in the next example is a back-to-back stem-and-leaf plot. The stem is between the two bars, and the leaves are on each side. Leaves are in increasing order from the stems.

5 EXAMPLE **Using a Stem-and-Leaf Plot**

Find the mean of the city mileage and highway mileage for nine new cars.

New Car Mileage (mi/gal)

City		Highway
9	1	
9 8 3 3 0	2	7 8
4 1 1	3	0 2 2 7 8 8
	4	1

means 20 mi/gal ← 0 $\mid$2$\mid$7 → means 27 mi/gal

Mean City Mileage: $\frac{19 + 20 + 23 + 23 + 28 + 29 + 31 + 31 + 34}{9} = 26.\overline{4}$ mi/gal

Mean Highway Mileage: $\frac{27 + 28 + 30 + 32 + 32 + 37 + 38 + 38 + 41}{9} = 33.\overline{6}$ mi/gal

✔ **Check Understanding** **5 a.** Find the median of the city mileage and of the highway mileage.
b. Find the mode(s) of the city mileage and of the highway mileage.
c. Find the range of the city mileage and of the highway mileage.

EXERCISES

For more practice, see *Extra Practice*.

Practice and Problem Solving

Ⓐ Practice by Example

Find the mean, median, and mode. Which measure of central tendency best describes the data?

Example 1
(page 119)

1. weights of textbooks in ounces
    12 10 9 15 16 10

2. ages of students on math team
    14 14 15 15 16 15 15 16

3. time spent on Internet in min/day
    75 38 43 120 65 48 52

4. weights of channel catfish in pounds
    4.8 5 2.3 4.5 4.8 5.2

Example 2
(page 119)

Write and solve an equation to find the value of x.

5. 3.8, 4.2, 5.3, x; mean 4.8

6. 99, 86, 76, 95, x; mean 91

7. 100, 121, 105, 113, 108, x; mean 112

8. 31.7, 42.8, 26.4, x; mean 35

Example 3
(page 120)

Find the range.

9. 12 15 17 28 30

10. 5.3 6.2 3.1 4.8 7.3

11. −12 −15 5 3 −2 0 −7

12. $2\frac{1}{2}$ $3\frac{1}{3}$ $-5\frac{3}{4}$ $\frac{3}{8}$ $3\frac{5}{8}$

13. For each list of data, find the range and the mean.
    Use the range to compare the spread of the data.

List 1	List 2
64 43 55 28 71	48 53 61 47 52

Example 4
(page 120)

Make a stem-and-leaf plot for each set of data.

14. 18 35 28 15 36 10 25 22 15   **15.** 18.6 18.4 17.6 15.7 15.3 17.5

16. 785 776 788 761 768 768 785   **17.** 0.8 0.2 1.4 3.5 4.3 4.5 2.6 2.2

Example 5
(page 121)

Find the mean, median, mode, and range of each side of the stem-and-leaf plot.

18.

Time Spent on Homework (minutes/day)

Class A		Class B
6 6 4 3	4	1 1 4 5 7
9 8 6 4 4 4	5	0 2 2 2 4
5 2 1 0	6	4 5 8 9
8 7 6 6 4 2	7	3 6 7 9 9 9

means 43 ← 3 | 4 | 1 → means 41

19.

Growth of Two Varieties of Tulip Plants (inches/day)

Type A		Type B
6 3 3	2	
3 2 1 1	3	1 1 2
1	4	3 5 8
	5	2 4

means 0.33 ← 3 | 3 | 1 → means 0.31

B **Apply Your Skills**

Find the mean, median, mode, and range.

20. 9.8 7.2 6.3 8.7 5.8 9.4 5.1 6.2

21. 3 −12 −1 −7 −2 0 −5 −1 −4 −2

22. 42.1 46.4 58.2 67.3 49.1 40.2 22.3 46.6

23. Critical Thinking The mean of a set of data is 7.8, the mode is 6.6, and the median is 6.8. What is the least possible number of data values? Explain.

24. Wildlife Management A wildlife manager working at the Everglades National Park in Florida measured and tagged adult male crocodiles. The data he collected are at the right.

Crocodile Lengths (meters)

2.4	2.5	2.5	2.3
2.8	2.4	2.3	2.4
2.1	2.2	2.5	2.7

a. What are the mean and median lengths of the crocodiles?

b. The wildlife manager captured another crocodile. Its length was 3.3 m. What is the mean with this new piece of data? What is the median? Round to the nearest tenth.

25. Manufacturing Two manufacturing plants create sheets of steel for medical instruments. The back-to-back stem-and-leaf plot at the right shows data collected from the two plants.

Width of Steel (millimeters)

Manufacturing Plant A		Manufacturing Plant B
	4	3 5 9
8 7 4 4 2	5	2 7
4 3 1	6	3 4
	7	2

means 6.1 ← 1 | 6 | 3 → means 6.3

a. Find the mean, median, mode, and range of each set of data.

b. Which measure of central tendency best describes each set of data? Explain.

c. Reasoning Which plant has the better quality control? Explain.

26. Open-Ended Give an example of a set of data for which the mode best represents the data. Explain.

27. Sports The median height of the 21 players on a girls' soccer team is 5 ft 7 in. What is the greatest possible number of girls who are less than 5 ft 7 in. tall?

28. Writing How does an outlier affect the mean of a set of data?

Real-World 🌐 **Connection**

Careers A wildlife manager collects data about the animal and plant life of an area. Using statistical measures, the wildlife manager can make predictions about the growth of plants and animals and the ecological health of the area.

29. Make a back-to-back stem-and-leaf plot of the data below.

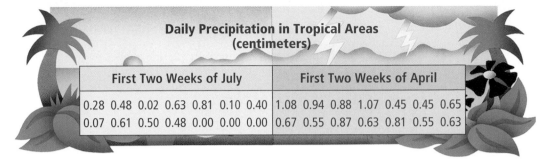

**Daily Precipitation in Tropical Areas
(centimeters)**

First Two Weeks of July	First Two Weeks of April
0.28 0.48 0.02 0.63 0.81 0.10 0.40	1.08 0.94 0.88 1.07 0.45 0.45 0.65
0.07 0.61 0.50 0.48 0.00 0.00 0.00	0.67 0.55 0.87 0.63 0.81 0.55 0.63

30. Data Collection Record the high and low temperatures in your town for one week. Make a back-to-back stem-and-leaf plot with the data you collect.

31. During the first 6 hours of a trip, you average 44 mi/h. During the last 4 hours of your trip, you average 50 mi/h. What is your average speed for the whole trip? (*Hint:* First find the total number of miles traveled.)

Standardized Test Prep

Gridded Response

32. You have a mean score of 84 after taking five 100-point tests. What do you need to score on the sixth 100-point test to have a mean score of 85?

33. Five runners on the track team have the following times in seconds for the 100-meter dash. What is the difference between the mean and the median of the following times?

| 10.2 | 10.6 | 11.9 | 9.9 | 10.6 |

34. The average speeds of the winners of the Daytona 500 from 1995 to 2000 are listed at the right. What is the mean in miles per hour of the given speeds rounded to the nearest tenth?

35. Find the sum of the mean, the median, and the mode of the following data: 22, 18, 17, 18, 25, 24, 24, 18.

36. The average low temperature for a 4-day period in January for the city of Orlando, Florida, was 58°F. After the fifth day, the 5-day average was 59°F. What was the low temperature on the fifth day?

Daytona 500

Year	Average Speed
1995	141.7 mi/h
1996	154.3 mi/h
1997	148.3 mi/h
1998	172.7 mi/h
1999	161.6 mi/h
2000	155.7 mi/h

SOURCE: *2001 Sports Almanac*

Take It to the NET
Online lesson quiz at
www.PHSchool.com
Web Code: aea-0207

Mixed Review

Lesson 2-6 **Solve each equation for *x*.**

37. $y = x + 4$ **38.** $y = -x + 3$ **39.** $y = 10x + 4$ **40.** $y = 2x + 9$

Lesson 2-1 **Solve each equation.**

41. $\frac{x}{8} = -18$ **42.** $-15n = 210$ **43.** $-a = \frac{2}{3}$ **44.** $-\frac{y}{5} = -22$

Writing Short Responses

Short-response questions in this textbook are usually worth a maximum of 2 points. To get full credit you need to give the correct answer (including appropriate units, if applicable) and justify your reasoning or show your work.

EXAMPLE

The cost for using a phone card is 35 cents per call plus 25 cents per minute. A recent call cost $12.35. Write and solve an equation to find the length of the call.

The problem is asking you to do three things: (1) use a variable to set up an equation, (2) solve the equation, and (3) find the length of the call. Below is a rubric that shows the number of points awarded for different types of answers.

Scoring Rubric

[2] The equation and the solution are correct. The call took 48 minutes.

[1] There is no equation, but there is a method to show that the call took 48 minutes.

[1] There is an equation and a solution, both of which may contain minor errors. The solution indicates the time, but does not show the units.

[0] There is no response, it is completely incorrect, or it is a correct response, but no procedure is shown.

Three responses are below with the points each received.

2 points	1 point	0 points
Let n = number of minutes. $$1235 = 35 + 25n$$ $$1200 = 25n$$ $$48 = n$$ The call took 48 minutes.	$$\frac{12.35 - 0.35}{0.25} = 48$$ 48 minutes	48 minutes

EXERCISES

Use the rubric above to answer each question.

1. Explain why each response above received the indicated points.

2. Write a 1-point response that begins with a correct equation.

3. Write a 2-point response that includes the equation $0.35 + 0.25n = 12.35$.

4. Error Analysis Suppose a student used the equation $25x + 35 = 12.35$. Explain why this equation is incorrect.

Chapter Review

Vocabulary

consecutive integers (p. 104)	mean (p. 118)	range (p. 120)
equivalent equations (p. 75)	measures of central tendency (p. 118)	solution of an equation (p. 75)
identity (p. 98)	median (p. 118)	stem-and-leaf plot (p. 120)
inverse operations (p. 75)	mode (p. 118)	uniform motion (p. 104)
literal equation (p. 111)	outlier (p. 118)	

Reading Math
Understanding
Vocabulary

Take It to the NET
Online vocabulary quiz
at www.PHSchool.com
Web Code: aej-0251

Choose the term that correctly completes each sentence.

1. A(n) _?_ is true for all values of the variable.

2. A particular value of a variable that makes an equation true is called a(n) _?_ of the equation.

3. You use subtraction to undo addition, and division to undo multiplication. These are examples of _?_.

4. _?_ have the same value.

5. The difference between two _?_ is one.

Match the correct answer in Column II with the word in Column I.

Column I	Column II
6. mean	**A.** the difference between the greatest and least items in a data set
7. mode	
8. range	**B.** the middle value in an ordered set of data
9. median	**C.** the value of a data set most likely to be affected by an outlier
	D. the item in a data set that occurs most frequently

Skills and Concepts

2-1 Objectives

▼ To solve equations using addition and subtraction (p. 74)

▼ To solve equations using multiplication and division (p. 76)

The value of a variable that makes an equation true is a **solution of the equation.** To solve an equation you can use **inverse operations,** which are operations that undo one another. Addition and subtraction are inverse operations. So are multiplication and division.

To solve an addition or subtraction equation, subtract or add the same value to each side of the equation. To solve a multiplication or division equation, divide or multiply each side of the equation by the same nonzero value.

Solve each equation. Check your answer.

10. $y - 7 = 9$
11. $\frac{x}{12} = -3$
12. $w + 23 = 54$
13. $5d = 120$

14. $9 + t = 35$
15. $c + 0.25 = 4.5$
16. $7b = 84$
17. $\frac{z}{4} = \frac{1}{2}$

2-2 Objectives

▼ To solve two-step equations (p. 81)

▼ To use deductive reasoning (p. 83)

A two-step equation is an equation that has two operations. You can use tiles to model and solve a two-step equation. To solve a two-step equation, first add or subtract. Then multiply or divide.

Solve each equation. Check your answer.

18. $5x - 8 = 12$ **19.** $7t - 3 = 18$ **20.** $\frac{c}{5} - 4 = -3$

21. $-2q - 5 = -11$ **22.** $-3m + 8 = 2$ **23.** $11y + 9 = 130$

24. $8u + 2 = 6$ **25.** $10h - 4 = -94$ **26.** $-z + 11 = -7$

27. $15 = -t + 3$ **28.** $\frac{w}{3} + 2 = 5$ **29.** $-\frac{2}{5}x + 4 = 8$

30. A state park charges admission of $6 per person plus $3 for parking. Jo paid $27 when her car entered the park. Write and solve an equation to find the number of people in Jo's car. Be sure to explain what your variable represents.

Solve each equation. Justify each step.

31. $314 = -n + 576$ **32.** $-\frac{1}{4}w - 1 = 6$ **33.** $3h - 4 = 5$

Solve each equation.

34. $10 = 35 + \frac{x}{5}$ **35.** $0 = -8t + 48$ **36.** $31 = 3 - 4k$

2-3 and 2-4 Objectives

▼ To use the Distributive Property when combining like terms (p. 88)

▼ To use the Distributive Property when solving equations (p. 89)

▼ To solve equations with variables on both sides (p. 96)

▼ To identify equations that are identities or have no solution (p. 98)

You can combine like terms and use the Distributive Property to simplify expressions and solve equations. You can also use the properties of equality to solve an equation.

An equation has no solution if no value of the variable makes the equation true. An equation is an **identity** if every value of the variable makes the equation true.

Solve each equation. If the equation is an identity or if it has no solution, write *identity* **or** *no solution***.**

37. $b + 4b = -90$ **38.** $-x + 7x = 24$ **39.** $2(t + 5) = 9$

40. $-(3 - 10y) = 12$ **41.** $x - (4 - x) = 0$ **42.** $4n - 6n = 2n$

43. $4 + 3n = 5n + 4$ **44.** $-2(r - \frac{1}{2}) = -2$ **45.** $9c + 4 = 3c - 8$

46. $3(5x - 2) - 6x = 3(3x + 2)$ **47.** $3(2t - 6) = 2(3t - 9)$

48. $\frac{3y}{4} - \frac{y}{2} = 5$ **49.** $0.36p + 0.26 = 3.86$

50. $2n + 3 + 4n = 5 + 6n - 2$ **51.** $7s - (3s + 1) = 4(3 + s)$

52. Geometry The width of a rectangle is 6 cm less than the length. The perimeter is 72 cm. Write and solve an equation to find the width and the length of the rectangle.

53. Costs for bowling at a certain bowling alley are $2.50 for shoes and $4.25 for each game bowled. Austin spent $15.25. Write and solve an equation to find how many games he bowled.

A **literal equation** is an equation that shows the relationship between two or more variables. A formula is a special type of literal equation. When you express one variable in terms of the others, you are solving the equation for that variable.

Solve each equation for the given variable.

54. $A = \frac{1}{2}bh; b$ **55.** $y = mx + b; x$ **56.** $C = \pi d; d$

57. Science Ohm's Law states that in an electrical circuit $E = IR$, where E represents the potential in volts, I represents the current in amperes, and R represents the resistance in ohms.
   a. Solve this formula for I.
   b. Find I if $E = 6$ volts and $R = 0.15$ ohms of resistance.

Write and solve an equation for each situation.

58. The Great Seto Bridge in Japan is about 7.6 mi long. How long would it take you to cross the bridge if you were walking at 4 mi/h?

59. Botany A eucalyptus tree in New Guinea grew 10.5 meters in one year. How much will this tree grow in 3.5 years if it continues to grow at this rate?

60. The sum of three consecutive integers is 582. Find the three integers.

61. The sum of three consecutive *even* integers is -198. Find the three integers.

62. Ocean Travel A supertanker leaves port traveling north at an average speed of 10 knots. Two hours later a cruise ship leaves the same port heading south at an average speed of 18 knots. How many hours after the cruise ship sails will the two ships be 209 nautical miles apart? (*Hint:* 1 knot = 1 nautical mile per hour)

63. Recreation The handicap H of a bowler whose average is A is often found by using the formula $H = 0.8 (200 - A)$. A bowler's final score for a game is the actual score plus the bowler's handicap. Find the handicap of a bowler whose average score is 135.

Mean, median, and **mode** are three measures of central tendency. The **range** of a data set is the difference between the greatest and least items. A stem-and-leaf plot is a display that organizes the data by showing each item in order.

Find the mean, median, and mode for each set of data.

64. 85, 87, 81, 92, 87, 80, 83 **65.** 24, 45, 33, 27, 24

66. 2.4, 2.3, 2.1, 2.5, 2.3, 2.2 **67.** 42, 18, 55, 37, 57, 37, 49, 47, 37

Use the stem-and-leaf plot at the right for Exercises 68–71. It shows the number of kilometers walked during a benefit walk.

68. Find the range.

69. How many data items are there?

70. How many people walked more than 19 km?

71. Find the mean, median, and mode.

Benefit Walk (km)

```
16 | 1 1 2 3 5 5
17 | 0 2 2
18 | 4 5 8 9
19 | 3 6 7 9 9 9
```

19 | 3 means 19.3

Chapter
2

Chapter Test

......
Take It to the NET
Online chapter test at
www.PHSchool.com
...... Web Code: aea-0252

Solve each equation. Check your answers.

1. $5n = -20$

2. $t + 7 = 4$

3. $\frac{r}{3} = 21$

4. $u - 8 = -15$

5. $-x + 4 = -7$

6. $-2z + 1 = -9$

7. $3w + 2 - w = -4$

8. $\frac{1}{4}(k - 1) = 10$

9. $6(y + 3) = 24$

10. $\frac{5n + 1}{8} = \frac{1}{2}$

11. If $2t + 3 = -9$, what is the value of $-3t - 7$?

12. Solve $2x - 4 = -7$. Justify each step.

Define a variable and write an equation to model each situation. Then solve.

13. Your chorus holds a car wash. They have $25.00 for making change. At the end of the car wash, they have $453.50. How much money did they make?

14. Truck Rental The rate to rent a certain truck is $55 per day and 20¢ per mile. Your family pays $80 to rent this truck for one day. How many miles did your family drive?

15. Entertainment Movie tickets for an adult and three children cost $20. An adult's ticket costs $2 more than a child's ticket. Find the cost of an adult's ticket.

Solve. If the equation is an identity, write *identity*. **If it has no solution, write** *no solution*.

16. $9j + 3 = 3(3j + 1)$

17. $2(1 - 2y) = 4y + 18$

18. $4v - 9 = 6v + 7$

19. $4p - 5 + p = 7 + 5p + 2$

20. Open-Ended Describe a situation that you can model with the equation $\frac{m}{5} = 4$.

21. A taxicab company charges each person a flat fee of $1.85 plus an additional $.40 per quarter mile.
   a. Write a formula to find the total cost for each fare.
   b. Use this formula to find the cost for 1 person to travel 8 mi.
   c. Writing Is your answer for part (b) the same cost as for 2 people in the same taxi traveling 4 miles? Explain your reasoning.

Use the table below for Exercises 22 and 23.

Percent of People Who Speak a Language Other Than English at Home

State	Percent
Connecticut	15
Massachusetts	15
Maine	9
New Hampshire	9
New Jersey	20
New York	23
Pennsylvania	7
Rhode Island	17
Vermont	6

SOURCE: U.S. Census Bureau
Go to **www.PHSchool.com** for a data update.
Web Code: aeg-2041

22. Make a stem-and-leaf plot for the data. Find the range.

23. Find the mean, median, and mode for the data.

Define a variable and write an equation to model each situation. Then solve.

24. Ticket Sales Tickets for a high school play are $3.00 each for students and $4.00 each for all others. Find the total money collected from ticket sales if 315 student tickets are sold out of a total of 518 tickets.

25. Jan is one year younger than her brother Bill and one year older than her sister Sue. The sum of their ages is 57. How old is each family member?

26. Labor Costs Mr. Gomez paid a total of $267 for the repairs on his car. The cost of the labor was two thirds of the total charge. Find the charge for labor.

27. Travel At noon, your family leaves Louisville on a trip to Memphis driving at 40 miles per hour. Your uncle leaves Memphis to come to Louisville 2 hours later. He is taking the same route and is driving 60 miles per hour. The two cities are 380 miles apart. At what time do the cars meet?

Standardized Test Prep

Multiple Choice

For Exercises 1–7, choose the correct letter.

1. Which equation is equivalent to
   $3x + 5 - 4x = 7$?
   A. $3x + 5 = 4x - 7$ **B.** $3x + 5 = 4x$
   C. $x = 2$ **D.** $x = -2$

2. Simplify the expression $15 - (6 + 3^2)$.
   F. -66 **G.** 0
   H. 18 **I.** 36

3. Evaluate $-2xy$ for $x = 3$ and $y = 4$.
   A. -234 **B.** -68
   C. -24 **D.** 24

4. Find the solution of the equation $-8k - 3 = 1$.
   F. $-\frac{1}{2}$ **G.** $-\frac{1}{4}$
   H. $\frac{1}{4}$ **I.** $\frac{1}{2}$

5. Find the difference.

   $$\begin{bmatrix} 8 & -7 \\ 3 & -5 \end{bmatrix} - \begin{bmatrix} 4 & 0 \\ -2 & -4 \end{bmatrix}$$

   A. $\begin{bmatrix} 4 & 7 \\ 5 & 1 \end{bmatrix}$ **B.** $\begin{bmatrix} 4 & -7 \\ 1 & -1 \end{bmatrix}$

   C. $\begin{bmatrix} 4 & -7 \\ 5 & -1 \end{bmatrix}$ **D.** $\begin{bmatrix} 4 & -7 \\ 1 & -9 \end{bmatrix}$

6. Choose the pair of coordinates that lie on the graph shown.

   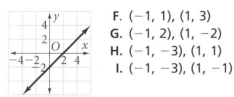

   F. $(-1, 1)$, $(1, 3)$
   G. $(-1, 2)$, $(1, -2)$
   H. $(-1, -3)$, $(1, 1)$
   I. $(-1, -3)$, $(1, -1)$

7. Which equation has -2 as its solution?
   A. $4x + 2 = 5$
   B. $4x - 2 = 5$
   C. $4x - 2 = 5x$
   D. $4 - 2x = 5x$

8. Which expression *cannot* be simplified using the Distributive Property?
   F. $3(2 + 8)$ **G.** $9(14 - 18)$
   H. $5(2 \cdot 3)$ **I.** $(18 - 25)7$

Gridded Response

9. Nice 'N' Clean Laundromat charges $1.50 to wash each load and $1.25 to dry each load. How much can a family with 8 loads expect to pay in dollars at this laundromat?

10. The advertised price for salads at a local supermarket salad bar is $3.49 per pound. Find the price in dollars of a salad that weighs 10 oz.

11. Sue's math class made the stem-and-leaf plot below. It shows each student's daily morning travel time to school. Find the mean of the data.

    Travel Time to School

0	3 5 8 8
1	0 0 0 1 1 2 2 5 6 8
2	1 2 3 7 7
3	0 5
4	5 9 9
5	
6	
7	5

    $7 \mid 5$ means 75 minutes

12. Use the formula $P = 2(w + \ell)$ to find the perimeter in centimeters of a rectangle with length 4.45 cm and width 1.3 cm.

13. Find the solution to the equation $3y = 6 - 2y$.

14. Jon is in charge of ordering eggs to make pancake batter for his school's all-you-can-eat pancake breakfast fund-raiser. Jon figures that 594 eggs will be needed to make enough pancakes for the number of tickets sold. How many cartons of eggs should Jon order if each carton contains 1 dozen eggs?

15. Four friends were born in consecutive years. The sum of their birth years is 7798. In what year was the oldest of the four friends born?

16. The Empire State Building is 1250 ft tall and it has 102 stories. It is 859 ft taller than the Park Row Building, the world's tallest building in 1900. What was the height in feet of the Park Row Building?

Real-World Snapshots

Shifting Gears

Applying Variation Gears and levers can make a job easier, but there is a trade-off for efficiency. For instance, the higher gears on a bicycle allow you to go farther with each rotation of the pedals, but the price you pay is pushing harder. Conversely, in first gear you don't have to push hard, but you also don't go very fast.

Activity 1

Materials: paper and pencil

Bicycle data: tire diameter = 26 in., chainwheel diameter = 6 in., sprocket diameter in first gear = 5 in., sprocket diameter in second gear = 4.5 in., sprocket diameter in third gear = 4 in.

a. Use the transmission equation and the bike travel equation below to find out how far the bicycle will travel in first gear when the chainwheel is turned once by the rider. Repeat the calculation for second gear and for third gear.

b. Your calculations indicate the relative speeds at which the bicycle moves in different gears. How many times faster is third gear than first gear?

Transmission Equation

$$\frac{d_1}{d_2} = \frac{N_2}{N_1}$$

N_1 and N_2 are the number of rotations of the chainwheel and the sprocket.

Bike Travel Equation
$L = \pi d_3 N_3$
N_3 is the number of rotations of the back tire.
(*Hint:* How does N_3 relate to N_2?)

d_1 = diameter of chainwheel
d_2 = diameter of sprocket
d_3 = diameter of back tire
L = distance bicycle travels

Shifting Gears

Some mountain bikes have gears you can shift with your thumb, allowing your other fingers to remain curled around the handlebars to maintain control.

Chainwheel

Crank

d_1

Sprockets

d_2

Iditasport

Three Iditasport events began simultaneously on February 17, 2002, in Alaska. Chris Van Alstine, of Anchorage, Alaska, competed in the Iditasport 130, a 130-mi race to Finger Lake, Alaska.

Activity 2

Use the bicycle data from Activity 1. Suppose you wanted to design a new gear that allowed the bicycle to travel twice as far with each rotation of the chainwheel as it does in first gear. What would the diameter of the new sprocket be?

Take It to the NET For more information about bicycles, go to **www.PHSchool.com**.
Web Code: aee-0253

Bicycles of the Future

Carbon-based materials and design differences make this bicycle more aerodynamic and therefore faster than traditional bicycles.

Where You've Been

- In Chapter 1 you learned about the real number system.

- In Chapter 1 you also learned how to add, subtract, multiply, and divide using rational numbers.

- In Chapters 1 and 2 you used this knowledge to evaluate variable expressions and solve equations.

Diagnosing Readiness

(For help, go to the Lesson in green.)

i̇TEXT Instant self-check online and on CD-ROM

Ordering Rational Numbers (Lesson 1-3)

Complete each statement with $<$, $=$, or $>$.

1. $-3 \blacksquare -5$ **2.** $7 \blacksquare \frac{14}{2}$ **3.** $-8 \blacksquare -8.4$ **4.** $-\frac{3}{2} \blacksquare -1$

Absolute Value (Lesson 1-3)

Simplify each expression.

5. $5 + |4 - 6|$ **6.** $|30 - 28| - 6$ **7.** $|-7 + 2| - 4$

Solving One-Step Equations (Lesson 2-1)

Solve each equation. Check your solution.

8. $x - 4 = -2$ **9.** $b + 4 = 7$ **10.** $-\frac{3}{4}y = 9$ **11.** $\frac{m}{12} = 2.7$

12. $-8 + x = 15$ **13.** $n - 7 = 22.5$ **14.** $-\frac{12}{7}z = 48$ **15.** $\frac{5y}{4} = -15$

Solving Two-Step Equations (Lesson 2-2)

Solve each equation. Check your solution.

16. $-5 + \frac{b}{4} = 7$ **17.** $4.2m + 4 = 25$ **18.** $-12 = 6 + \frac{3}{4}x$ **19.** $6 = -z - 4$

20. $4m + 2.3 = 9.7$ **21.** $\frac{5}{8}t - 7 = -22$ **22.** $-4.7 = 3y + 1.3$ **23.** $12.2 = 5.3x - 3.7$

Solving Multi-Step Equations (Lesson 2-3)

Solve each equation. Check your solution.

24. $4t + 7 + 6t = -33$ **25.** $2a + 5 = 9a - 16$ **26.** $\frac{1}{3} + \frac{4y}{6} = \frac{2}{3}$

27. $6(y - 2) = 8 - 2y$ **28.** $n + 3(n - 2) = 10.4$ **29.** $\frac{1}{2}w + 3 = \frac{2}{3}w - 5$

Solving Inequalities

Chapter

3

Key Vocabulary

Where You're Going

● In this chapter you will learn how to graph inequalities.

● You will solve inequalities, noting the differences from the methods
used for solving equations.

● You will write and solve compound inequalities by interpreting phrases
that use *and* or *or*.

Real-World Connection Applying what you learn, you will
solve problems involving quality control, on page 169.

133

Inequalities and Their Graphs

Lesson Preview

What You'll Learn

OBJECTIVE 1
To identify solutions of inequalities

OBJECTIVE 2
To graph and write inequalities

...And Why

To write inequalities for speed limits and starting salaries, as in Example 5

✔ **Check Skills You'll Need** (For help, go to Lesson 1-3.)

Graph the numbers on the same number line.

1. 4   **2.** -3 **3.** $\frac{9}{3}$ **4.** 0   **5.** 1.5

Complete each statement with <, =, or >.

6. $-3 \ \blacksquare \ -5$ **7.** $4.29 \ \blacksquare \ 4.8$ **8.** $(-3)(-4) \ \blacksquare \ 12$

9. $-1 - 2 \ \blacksquare \ 6 - 9$ **10.** $-\frac{3}{4} \ \blacksquare \ -\frac{4}{5}$ **11.** $\frac{1}{3} + \frac{1}{3} \ \blacksquare \ \frac{1}{2} + \frac{1}{2}$

New Vocabulary • solution of an inequality

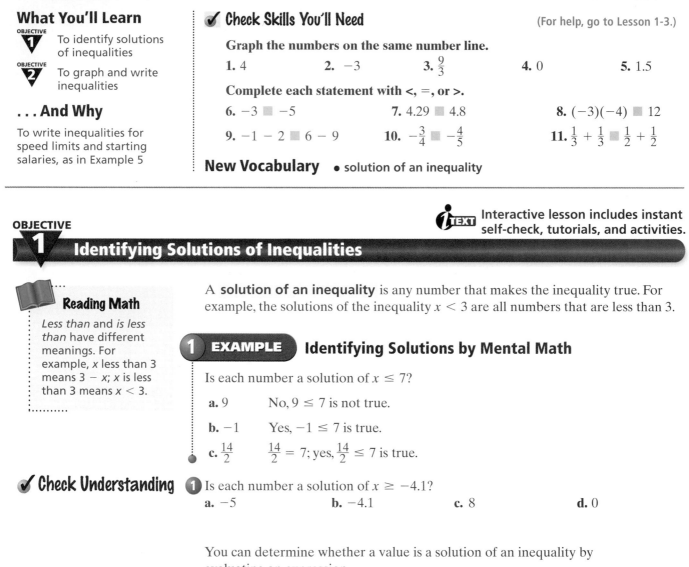

OBJECTIVE

1 **Identifying Solutions of Inequalities**

🅣TEXT Interactive lesson includes instant self-check, tutorials, and activities.

Reading Math

Less than and *is less than* have different meanings. For example, *x* less than 3 means $3 - x$; *x* is less than 3 means $x < 3$.

A **solution of an inequality** is any number that makes the inequality true. For example, the solutions of the inequality $x < 3$ are all numbers that are less than 3.

1 EXAMPLE **Identifying Solutions by Mental Math**

Is each number a solution of $x \leq 7$?

a. 9   No, $9 \leq 7$ is not true.

b. -1 Yes, $-1 \leq 7$ is true.

c. $\frac{14}{2}$ $\frac{14}{2} = 7$; yes, $\frac{14}{2} \leq 7$ is true.

✔ **Check Understanding** **1** Is each number a solution of $x \geq -4.1$?
       a. -5 **b.** -4.1 **c.** 8   **d.** 0

You can determine whether a value is a solution of an inequality by evaluating an expression.

2 EXAMPLE **Identifying Solutions by Evaluating**

Is each number a solution of $2 - 5x > 13$?
    a. 3   **b.** -4

$2 - 5x > 13$		$2 - 5x > 13$
$2 - 5(3) > 13$	← Substitute for *x*.→	$2 - 5(-4) > 13$
$2 - 15 > 13$	← Simplify.→	$2 + 20 > 13$
$-13 \not> 13$	← Compare.→	$22 > 13$

3 does not make the original inequality true, so 3 is not a solution.

-4 does make the original inequality true, so -4 is a solution.

✓ **Check Understanding** **2** Is each number a solution of $6x - 3 > 10$?

a. 1 **b.** 2 **c.** 3 **d.** 4

Graphing and Writing Inequalities in One Variable

Since the solution of an inequality is not just one number, you can use a graph to indicate all of the solutions.

Reading Math

You normally read $-1 \geq a$ as "-1 is greater than or equal to a." The inequality symbol also indicates that a is less than or equal to -1.

Inequality	Graph	
$x < 3$	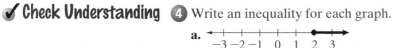	The open dot shows that 3 is *not* a solution. Shade to the left of 3.
$m \geq -2$		The closed dot shows that -2 is a solution. Shade to the right of -2.
$-1 \geq a$		The closed dot shows that -1 is a solution. Shade to the left of -1.

You can also write $-1 \geq a$ as $a \leq -1$.

3 **EXAMPLE** **Graphing Inequalities**

a. Graph $c > -2$.

The solutions of $c > -2$ are all the points to the right of -2.

b. Graph $4 \leq m$.

The solutions of $4 \leq m$ are 4 and all the points to the right of 4.

✓ **Check Understanding** **3** Graph each inequality.

a. $a < 1$ **b.** $n \geq -3$ **c.** $2 > p$

You can write an inequality for a graph.

4 **EXAMPLE** **Writing an Inequality From a Graph**

Write an inequality for each graph.

a. $x < -4$ Numbers less than -4 are graphed.

b. $x \leq 5$ Numbers less than or equal to 5 are graphed.

c. $x > \frac{1}{2}$ Numbers greater than $\frac{1}{2}$ are graphed.

d. $x \geq -1$ Numbers greater than or equal to -1 are graphed.

✓ **Check Understanding** **4** Write an inequality for each graph.

a. **b.**

You can describe real-world situations using an inequality.

5 EXAMPLE **Real-World Problem Solving**

Define a variable and write an inequality for each situation.

a.

b.

Let s = a legal speed.
The sign indicates that $s \leq 65$.

Let p = pay per hour (in dollars).
The sign indicates that $p \geq 6.15$.

✓ **Check Understanding** **5 a. Critical Thinking** In part (a) of Example 5, can the speed be *all* real numbers less than or equal to 65? Explain.
b. In part (b) of Example 5, are all real numbers greater than or equal to $6.15 reasonable solutions of the inequality? Explain.

EXERCISES

For more practice, see *Extra Practice*.

Practice and Problem Solving

A Practice by Example

Example 1
(page 134)

Mental Math Is each number following the inequality a solution of the given inequality?

1. $v \geq -5; 4$ **2.** $0.5 > c; 2$ **3.** $b < 4; -0.5$ **4.** $d \leq \frac{17}{3}; 5$

5. $g \leq \frac{12}{5}; 3$ **6.** $k < 0; -1$ **7.** $a > 3.2; 3$ **8.** $x \geq -2.5; -2.5$

Example 2
(page 134)

Is each number a solution of the given inequality?

9. $3x - 7 > -1$ **a.** 2   **b.** 0   **c.** 5

10. $4n - 3 \leq 5$ **a.** 2   **b.** 3   **c.** -1

11. $2y + 1 < -3$ **a.** 0   **b.** -2   **c.** 1

12. $\frac{4 - m}{m} \geq 5$ **a.** 0.5   **b.** 2   **c.** -4

13. $n(n - 3) < 54$ **a.** 9   **b.** 3   **c.** 10

14. $5(2q - 8) \geq 7$ **a.** -2   **b.** $\frac{9}{2}$ **c.** 6

Example 3
(page 135)

Match each inequality with its graph.

15. $x < 4$ **16.** $x \geq 4$ **17.** $x > 4$ **18.** $x = 4$

A. ←+—+—+—+—+—+—+—●—+→
    −3 −2 −1 0 1 2 3 4 5

B. ←+—+—+—+—+—+—+—●━━→
    −3 −2 −1 0 1 2 3 4 5

C. ←━━+—+—+—+—+—+—⊕—+→
    −3 −2 −1 0 1 2 3 4 5

D. ←+—+—+—+—+—+—+—⊕━━→
    −3 −2 −1 0 1 2 3 4 5

Graph each inequality.

19. $x > 1$ **20.** $s < -3$ **21.** $y \le -4$ **22.** $t \ge -1$

23. $-2 < d$ **24.** $-\frac{3}{2} \le b$ **25.** $7 \ge a$ **26.** $4.25 > c$

Example 4
(page 135)

Write an inequality for each graph.

27.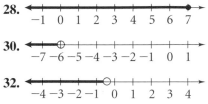

28.

29.

30.

31.

32.

Example 5
(page 136)

Define a variable and write an inequality to model each situation.

33. A bus can seat at most 48 students.

34. In many states, you must be at least 16 years old to obtain a driver's license.

35. It is not safe to use a light bulb of more than 60 watts in this light fixture.

36. At least 350 students attended the band concert Friday night.

37. Aviation The Navy's flying squad, the Blue Angels, makes more than 75 appearances each year.

Ⓑ Apply Your Skills

Write each inequality in words.

38. $n < 5$ **39.** $b > 0$ **40.** $7 \ge x$ **41.** $z \ge -5.6$

42. $4 > q$ **43.** $-1 \ge m$ **44.** $35 \ge w$ **45.** $g - 2 < 7$

46. $a \le 3$ **47.** $6 + r > -2$ **48.** $8 \le h$ **49.** $1.2 > k$

50. Writing Explain how you choose whether to draw an open or a closed dot when you graph an inequality.

Need Help?

For help with counterexamples see p. 18.

51. Error Analysis A student claims that the inequality $3x + 1 > 0$ is always true because multiplying a number by three and then adding one to it makes the number greater than zero. Use a counterexample to show why the student is not correct.

52. Critical Thinking Describe how you can display the solutions of the inequality $x \ne 3$ on a number line.

53. Open-Ended Describe a situation that you can represent using the inequality $x \ge 18$.

Rewrite each inequality so that the variable is on the left. Then graph the solutions.

54. $2 < x$ **55.** $-5 \ge b$ **56.** $0 \le r$ **57.** $5 > a$

Graph each inequality from the given description.

58. t is nonnegative.   **59.** x is positive.

60. k is no more than 3.   **61.** r is at least 2.

62. s is at most 4.   **63.** v is no less than 7.

64. Writing Explain how you interpret the phrases "at least" and "at most" in an inequality that models a real-world situation.

Use the map below for Exercises 65–66.

Real-World ⊕ Connection

There is an average of 2500 flights in and out of Chicago's O'Hare Airport each day.

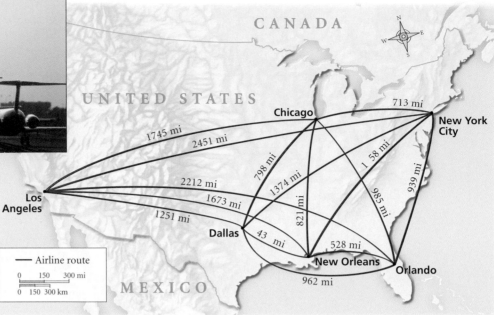

CANADA

UNITED STATES

713 mi

Chicago

New York City

1745 mi

2451 mi

798 mi

1374 mi

1158 mi

939 mi

985 mi

2212 mi

Los Angeles

1673 mi

821 mi

1251 mi

Dallas

43 mi

528 mi

New Orleans

Orlando

— Airline route

0   150   300 mi

0 150 300 km

MEXICO

962 mi

⊕ **65. Air Travel** You plan to go from New York City to Los Angeles. Let *x* be the distance in miles of any air-route between New York City and Los Angeles. The shortest route is a direct flight. Using the map, write a true statement about the mileage of any route from New York City to Los Angeles.

⊕ **66. Air Travel** Your travel agent is making plans for you to go from Chicago to New Orleans. A direct flight costs too much. Option A consists of flights from Chicago to Dallas to New Orleans. Option B consists of flights from Chicago to Orlando to New Orleans. Write an inequality comparing the mileage of these two options.

67. Critical Thinking Explain the difference between "4 greater than *x*" and "$4 > x$."

C **Challenge**

68. Critical Thinking Which is the correct graph of $-4 < -x$? Explain.

A. ⊕ number line −3 −2 −1 0 1 2 3 4 5

B. ⊕ number line −5 −4 −3 −2 −1 0 1 2 3

C. ⊕ number line −3 −2 −1 0 1 2 3 4 5

D. ⊕ number line −5 −4 −3 −2 −1 0 1 2 3

69. Reasoning Give a counterexample for this statement. If $a < b$, then $a^2 < b^2$.

70. Reasoning Describe the numbers *a* and *b* for which the following statement is true. If $a < b$, then $a^2 = b^2$.

....

Problem Solving Hint

In Exercise 70, make logical choices for values of *a* and *b*. Use positive and negative numbers as well as zero.
....

⊕ **71. Ticket Sales** Suppose your school plans a musical. The director's goal is ticket sales of at least $4000. Adult tickets are $5.00 and student tickets are $4.00. Let *a* represent the number of adult tickets and *s* represent the number of student tickets. Write an inequality that represents the director's goal.

Graph on a number line.

72. all values of *x* such that $x > -2$ and $x \le 2$

73. all values of *x* such that $x < -1$ or $x > 3$

Multiple Choice

74. Which inequality has the same solutions as $n > 5$?

    A. $n < -5$ **B.** $n < 5$ **C.** $5 < n$ **D.** $-n > -5$

75. What is the least whole-number solution of $k \geq -5$?

    F. -5 **G.** -4 **H.** 0 **I.** 1

76. Employees must work at least 20 years in a company in order to receive full benefits upon retirement. Which inequality or graph does NOT describe this situation?

    A. $y \geq 20$ **B.** $y > 20$

    C. $20 \leq y$ **D.**
```
├──┼──┼──┼──●──┼──→
0   5   10  15  20  25
```

77. Which value makes the inequality $x^2 \geq x$ false?

    F. $-\frac{1}{4}$ **G.** 0 **H.** $\frac{1}{4}$ **I.** 1

78. Fire codes require that no more than 150 persons occupy a conference room. Which graph includes a room count in possible violation of the fire codes?

    A.
```
←─┼──●──●──●──┼──→
  147 148 149 150 151
```

    B.
```
←─┼──┼──●──●──●──→
  147 148 149 150 151
```

    C.
```
←─┼──┼──┼──●──┼──→
  147 148 149 150 151
```

    D.
```
←─●──●──●──┼──┼──→
  147 148 149 150 151
```

Short Response

Take It to the NET

Online lesson quiz at
www.PHSchool.com
Web Code: aea-0301

79. A stretch of $12\frac{3}{5}$ mi of highway is being repaired. The project foreman reported that less than half of the job is complete. Draw a diagram to show the remaining miles to be repaired. Then write an inequality for the number of miles m that still need repair.

Mixed Review

Lesson 2-7

Solve for y in terms of x.

80. $2x + 3y = 6$ **81.** $5x - y + 8 = 4$

82. $-5y + 4x = 15$ **83.** $2x + 4y = -20$

Lesson 2-6

Find each measure for the following data.

    1   3   4   4   5   5   7   9   9   9   13

84. mean   **85.** median   **86.** mode

Solve for the indicated variable.

87. $V = IR; I$ **88.** $P = 2\ell + 2w; \ell$ **89.** $P = a + b + c; b$

Lesson 1-8

Name the property that each equation demonstrates.

90. $3(2 \cdot 7) = (3 \cdot 2)7$ **91.** $5 \times 1 = 1 \times 5$ **92.** $3 + 4 = 4 + 3$

Solving Inequalities Using Addition and Subtraction

Lesson Preview

What You'll Learn

OBJECTIVE 1 To use addition to solve inequalities

OBJECTIVE 2 To use subtraction to solve inequalities

. . . And Why

To solve a problem involving safe loads, as in Example 4

✓ Check Skills You'll Need

(For help, go to Lessons 1-4 and 2-1.)

Complete each statement with <, =, or >.

1. $-3 + 4 \ \blacksquare \ -5 + 4$ **2.** $-3 + 6 \ \blacksquare \ 4 + 6$ **3.** $-3.4 + 2 \ \blacksquare \ -3.45 + 2$

Solve each equation.

4. $x - 4 = 5$ **5.** $n - 3 = -5$ **6.** $t + 4 = -5$ **7.** $k + \frac{2}{3} = \frac{5}{6}$

New Vocabulary • equivalent inequalities

---

iTEXT Interactive lesson includes instant self-check, tutorials, and activities.

OBJECTIVE 1 Using Addition to Solve Inequalities

Equivalent inequalities are inequalities with the same solutions. For example, $x + 4 < 7$ and $x < 3$ are equivalent inequalities.

$x + 4 < 7$ $x < 3$

You can add the same value to each side of an inequality, just as you did with equations.

Key Concepts

Property	Addition Property of Inequality
For every real number a, b, and c, if $a > b$, then $a + c > b + c$; if $a < b$, then $a + c < b + c$.	
Examples $3 > 1$, so $3 + 2 > 1 + 2$. $-5 < 4$, so $-5 + 2 < 4 + 2$.	
This property is also true for $\geq$ and $\leq$.	

1 EXAMPLE Using the Addition Property of Inequality

Solve $x - 3 < 5$. Graph the solution.

$x - 3 + 3 < 5 + 3$ **Add 3 to each side.**

$\qquad x < 8$ **Simplify.**

-1 0 1 2 3 4 5 6 7 8 9 10

✓ **Check Understanding** ① Solve $m - 6 > -4$. Graph your solution.

Reading Math

The word *infinite* indicates that the number of solutions is unlimited. The solutions cannot be listed or counted.

An inequality has an infinite number of solutions, so it is not possible to check all the solutions. You can check your computations and the direction of the inequality symbol. The steps below show how to check that $x < 8$ describes the solutions to Example 1.

Step 1 Check the computation. See if 8 is a solution to the equation $x - 3 = 5$.

$x - 3 = 5$

$8 - 3 \stackrel{?}{=} 5$ **Substitute 8 for *x*.**

$5 = 5$ ✓

Step 2 Check the inequality symbol. Choose any number less than 8 and substitute it into $x - 3 < 5$. In this case, use 7.

$x - 3 < 5$

$7 - 3 < 5$ **Substitute 7 for *x*.**

$4 < 5$ ✓

Since the computation and the direction of the inequality symbol are correct, $x - 3 < 5$ and $x < 8$ are equivalent inequalities. So the solution of $x - 3 < 5$ is $x < 8$.

2 EXAMPLE   Solving and Checking Solutions

Solve $12 \leq x - 5$. Graph and check your solution.

$12 + 5 \leq x - 5 + 5$ **Add 5 to each side.**

$17 \leq x$ **Simplify.**

Check $12 = x - 5$ **Check the computation.**

$12 \stackrel{?}{=} 17 - 5$ **Substitute 17 for *x*.**

$12 = 12$ ✓

$12 \leq x - 5$ **Check the direction of the inequality.**

$12 \leq 18 - 5$ **Substitute 18 for *x*.**

$12 \leq 13$ ✓

✓ **Check Understanding**   **2** Solve $n - 7 \leq -2$. Graph and check your solution.

OBJECTIVE

2   Using Subtraction to Solve Inequalities

You can subtract the same number from each side of an inequality to create an equivalent inequality.

Key Concepts

Property	Subtraction Property of Inequality
For every real number a, b, and c, if $a > b$, then $a - c > b - c$; if $a < b$, then $a - c < b - c$.	
Examples $3 > -1$, so $3 - 2 > -1 - 2$ $-5 < 4$, so $-5 - 2 < 4 - 2$	
This property is also true for $\geq$ and $\leq$.	

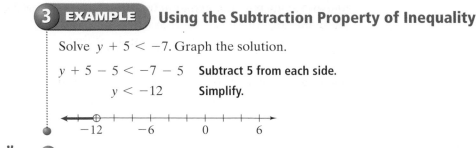

3 **EXAMPLE** **Using the Subtraction Property of Inequality**

Solve $y + 5 < -7$. Graph the solution.

$y + 5 - 5 < -7 - 5$ **Subtract 5 from each side.**

$\qquad y < -12$ **Simplify.**

✓ **Check Understanding** **3** Solve $t + 3 \geq 8$. Graph and check your solution.

You can use inequalities to model real-world situations.

4 **EXAMPLE** **Real-World Problem Solving**

Safe Load The maximum safe load of a chairlift like the one at the left is 680 lb. The weight of the person in the lift is 124 lb, and the weight of the bicycle is 32 lb. How much additional weight can the chairlift safely carry?

Relate | weight of a person and a bicycle | plus | additional weight | is at most | safe load |

Define Let w = the amount of weight that can be added to the chairlift.

Write | $124 + 32$ | + | w | $\leq$ | 680 |

$124 + 32 + w \leq 680$

$\qquad 156 + w \leq 680$ **Combine like terms.**

$156 + w - 156 \leq 680 - 156$ **Subtract 156 from each side.**

$\qquad\qquad w \leq 524$ **Simplify.**

The chairlift can safely carry an additional 524 lb.

Real-World Connection

The design of a chairlift allows for 170 lb per passenger, including equipment.

✓ **Check Understanding** **4** Your baseball team has a goal to collect at least 160 blankets for a shelter. Team members brought 42 blankets on Monday and 65 blankets on Wednesday. How many blankets must the team donate on Friday to make or exceed their goal?

EXERCISES

For more practice, see *Extra Practice*.

Practice and Problem Solving

A **Practice by Example**

Examples 1, 2
(pages 140, 141)

State what number you would add to each side of the inequality to solve the inequality.

1. $d - 5 \geq -4$ **2.** $0 < c - 8$ **3.** $z - 4.3 \geq 1.6$

Solve each inequality. Graph and check your solution.

4. $x - 1 > 10$ **5.** $t - 3 < -2$ **6.** $-5 > b - 1$ **7.** $7 \leq d - 3$

8. $s - 2 \geq -6$ **9.** $r - 9 \leq 0$ **10.** $8 < n - 2$ **11.** $-4 \geq w - 2$

12. $-1 < -4 + d$ **13.** $y - \frac{1}{2} \leq -5$ **14.** $-\frac{2}{3} > q - 4$ **15.** $x - 2 \geq 0.5$

16. $3.2 > -1.3 + r$ **17.** $-3.4 > m - 1.8$ **18.** $b - \frac{3}{8} < \frac{1}{8}$ **19.** $n - 2\frac{1}{2} > \frac{1}{2}$

Example 3
(page 142)

State what number you would subtract from each side of the inequality to solve the inequality.

20. $w + 2 > -1$ **21.** $8 < \frac{5}{3} + r$ **22.** $5.7 \geq k + 3.1$

Solve each inequality. Graph and check your solution.

23. $w + 4 \leq 9$ **24.** $m + 5 > -3$ **25.** $1 < 8 + b$ **26.** $-2 \geq 4 + a$

27. $r + 1 \geq -5$ **28.** $k + 3 \leq 4$ **29.** $3 > 4 + x$ **30.** $-5 < 1 + p$

31. $\frac{3}{5} + z \geq -\frac{2}{5}$ **32.** $7.5 + y < 13$ **33.** $\frac{1}{2} < m + 2$ **34.** $2.7 \geq a + 3$

35. $-2.9 < 4.1 + p$ **36.** $\frac{1}{4} \geq h + \frac{3}{4}$ **37.** $5.3 + d > 3.8$ **38.** $t + \frac{3}{8} < -\frac{1}{8}$

Example 4
(page 142)

39. Vacation Budget Your brother has $2000 saved for a vacation. His airplane ticket is $637. Write and solve an inequality to find how much he can spend for everything else.

40. Weekly Budget You have an allowance of $15.00 per week. You are in a bowling league that costs $6.50 each week, and you save at least $5.00 each week. Write and solve an inequality to show how much you have left to spend each week.

41. Fund-Raising A school club is selling reflectors for Bicycle Safety Day. Each member is encouraged to sell at least 50 reflectors. You sell 17 on Monday and 12 on Tuesday. How many reflectors do you need to sell on Wednesday to meet your goal?

B Apply Your Skills

State what you must do to the first inequality in order to get the second.

42. $36 \leq -4 + y$; $40 \leq y$ **43.** $9 + b > 24$; $b > 15$ **44.** $m - \frac{1}{2} < \frac{3}{8}$; $m < \frac{7}{8}$

Solve each inequality.

45. $w - 3 + 1 \geq 9$ **46.** $\frac{1}{2} + c \leq 3\frac{1}{2}$ **47.** $y - 0.3 < 2.8$

48. $-6 > n - \frac{1}{5}$ **49.** $z + 4.1 < -5.6$ **50.** $-4.1 > y - 0.9$

51. $\frac{2}{3} + t - \frac{5}{6} > 0$ **52.** $5 \leq v - 4 - 7$ **53.** $3.6 + k \geq -4.5$

54. $6 + b - 7 < 5$ **55.** $m + 2.3 \leq -1.2$ **56.** $4 \geq k - \frac{3}{4}$

57. $h - \frac{1}{2} \geq -1$ **58.** $-7.7 \geq x - 2$ **59.** $-2 > 9 + 3 + w$

60. $\frac{3}{2} + w \leq \frac{1}{3}$ **61.** $x + 4 - 7 < 13$ **62.** $3.5 < m - 2$

63. $9.4 \leq t - 3.5$ **64.** $0 > k - 2\frac{3}{5}$ **65.** $5.3 > 1.6 + n - 2.3$

66. $-7\frac{3}{4} + m + \frac{1}{2} \leq -2\frac{1}{4}$ **67.** $-1.4 + s + 2.1 > 11$

68. a. If $45 + 47 = t$, does $t = 45 + 47$?
    b. If $45 + 47 < r$, is $r < 45 + 47$?
    c. Discuss the differences between these two examples.

69. Gymnastics Suppose your sister wants to qualify for a regional gymnastics competition. At today's competition she must score at least 34.0 points. She scored 8.8 on the vault, 7.9 on the balance beam, and 8.2 on the uneven parallel bars. The event that remains is the floor exercise.
    a. Write and solve an inequality that models the information.
    b. Explain what the solution means in terms of the original situation.
    c. Open-Ended Write three scores your sister could make that would allow her to qualify for the regional gymnastics competition.

Real-World Connection

More than 71,000 athletes compete in gymnastic programs in the United States.

70. Computers Suppose your computer has nearly 64 megabytes (MB) of memory. Its basic systems require 12.8 MB. How much memory is available for other programs and functions?

71. Banking Your local bank offers free checking for accounts with a balance of at least $500. Suppose you have a balance of $516.46 and you write a check for $31.96. How much must you deposit to avoid being charged a service fee?

72. To earn an A in Ms. Orlando's math class, students must score a total of at least 135 points on the three tests. On the first two tests, Amy's scores were 47 and 48. What is the minimum score she must get on the third test in order to earn an A?

73. a. Open-Ended Use each of the inequality symbols $<$, $\leq$, $>$, and $\geq$ to write four addition or subtraction inequalities.
   b. Solve each of the inequalities in part (a) and graph your solution.

74. a. Sam says that he can solve $z - 8.6 \geq 5.2$ by replacing z with 13, 14, and 15. When $z = 13$, the inequality is false. When $z = 14$ and $z = 15$, the inequality is true. So Sam says that the solution is $z \geq 14$. Is his reasoning correct? Justify your answer.
   b. Critical Thinking Explain why substituting values into the inequality does not guarantee that your solution is correct.

Solve each inequality.

75. $4x + 4 - 3x \geq 5$

76. $-5n - 3 + 6n < 2$

77. $7t - (6t - 2) \leq -1$

78. $5k - 2(2k + 1) > 8$

79. $3(r + 2) - 2r < 4$

80. $4(r + 5) - 3r \geq 7$

81. $3a + 6 - 2a \geq -19$

82. $-5 \leq 3m - 10 - 2m$

83. $-3d + 4(d + 3) > 4$

84. $5(y - 2) - 4(y - 1) < 0$

85. $-6(a + 2) + 7a \leq 12$

86. $-2(a - 3) + 3(a + 2) < 4$

87. Geometry The Triangle Inequality Theorem states that the sum of the lengths of any two sides of a triangle is greater than the length of the third side. Following are inequalities for sides of the triangle shown.

$$a + b > c$$
$$b + c > a$$
$$a + c > b$$

   a. Write an inequality using $c - b$ and a.
   b. Write an inequality using $a - c$ and b.
   c. Write an inequality using $b - a$ and c.
   d. Writing Write a generalization about the length of the third side and the difference of the lengths of the other two sides.

Challenge

Reasoning Decide if each inequality is true for all real numbers. If the inequality is *not* true, give a counterexample.

88. $a - b < a + b$

89. If $a \geq b$, then $a + c \geq b + c$.

90. If $c > d$, then $a - c < a - d$.

91. If $a < b$, then $a < b + c$.

92. Reasoning Find real numbers x, y, z, and w for which it is true that $x > y$ and $z > w$, but it is not true that $x - z > y - w$.

Multiple Choice

93. Solve $x + 5 < 13$.

    A. $x > 8$ **B.** $x < 8$ **C.** $x > 18$ **D.** $x < 18$

94. Solve $-12 + n > 20$.

    F. $n < 32$ **G.** $n > 32$ **H.** $n < 8$ **I.** $n > 8$

95. Which graph represents all real number solutions of $x + 4 \geq 8$?

    A. ‹—+—+—+—+—+—◆—+—›
           −1 0 1 2 3 4 5

    B. ‹—⊕—+—+—+—+—+—+—›
         −5 −4 −3 −2 −1 0 1

    C. ‹—+—+—+—+—+—◆—›
           −1 0 1 2 3 4 5

    D. ‹—+—+—+—+—○—+—+—›
         −3 −2 −1 0 1 2 3

96. Which of the following is a solution for $5 < n - 0.1$?

    F. 4.99   **G.** 5.01   **H.** 5.10   **I.** 5.11

97. Hector is flying his plane. To avoid a storm, he climbs 5,500 ft without going above his plane's maximum safe altitude of 35,000 ft. The inequality $a + 5{,}500 \leq 35{,}000$ represents his original altitude a in feet. Which of the following could have been the original altitude?

    A. 40,500   **B.** 30,000 ft   **C.** 29,750 ft   **D.** 27,750 ft

Short Response

Take It to the NET
Online lesson quiz at
www.PHSchool.com
Web Code: aea-0302

98. The leading scorer in your high school basketball's division finished the season with a game average of 20 points for 25 games. As the division's second leading scorer, you have a 19.5 point per game average for 24 games. You have your last game yet to play.

How many points must you score in the final game of the season to overtake the division's leading scorer? Show your work.

Mixed Review

Lesson 3-1

Define a variable and write an inequality to model each situation.

99. An octopus can be up to 10 ft long.

100. A hummingbird migrates more than 1850 mi.

101. Your average in algebra class must be 90 or greater to receive an A for the term.

102. You must read at least 25 pages this weekend.

Lessons 2-1 and 2-2

Solve each equation.

103. $n - 4 = 9$ **104.** $8 + w = 7$ **105.** $c + 5 = -7$

106. $7 - k = 3$ **107.** $4t = 52$ **108.** $-\frac{2x}{3} = 12$

109. $\frac{k}{7} = -4$ **110.** $18 = y - 4$ **111.** $40 = \frac{5}{8}q$

Lesson 1-2

Simplify.

112. $9^2 + 17$ **113.** $4(5 - 3)^2 - 3^2$ **114.** $0.2(4.2 - 3.4) + 0.4$

115. $3 \cdot 2 + 5^2$ **116.** $3 + 7^2 - 4$ **117.** $4^3 + 3^2$

118. $6(5 - 2)^2 + 4$ **119.** $2 + 8(6 + 2^2)$ **120.** $3^3 - 2^3 + 7$

Solving Inequalities Using Multiplication and Division

Lesson Preview

What You'll Learn

OBJECTIVE 1
To use multiplication to solve inequalities

OBJECTIVE 2
To use division to solve inequalities

...And Why

To find how much food can be purchased for a food bank, as in Example 4

✔ Check Skills You'll Need

(For help, go to Lessons 2-1 and 3-1.)

Solve each equation.

1. $8 = \frac{1}{2}t$

2. $14 = -21x$

3. $\frac{x}{6} = -1$

4. $5d = 32$

5. $\frac{2}{3}x = -12$

6. $0.5n = 9$

Write an inequality for each graph.

7.
−3 −2 −1 0 1 2 3

8.
−1 0 1 2 3 4 5

OBJECTIVE

1 **Using Multiplication to Solve Inequalities**

ⓘTEXT Interactive lesson includes instant self-check, tutorials, and activities.

Investigation: Multiplying Each Side of an Inequality

Consider the inequality $4 > 1$.

1. Copy and complete each statement at the right by replacing each ■ with $<$, $>$, or $=$.

2. What happens to the inequality symbol when you multiply each side by a positive number?

3. What happens to the inequality symbol when you multiply each side by zero?

4. What happens to the inequality symbol when you multiply each side by a negative number?

$4 \cdot 3$ ■ $1 \cdot 3$	
$4 \cdot 2$ ■ $1 \cdot 2$	
$4 \cdot 1$ ■ $1 \cdot 1$	
$4 \cdot 0$ ■ $1 \cdot 0$	
$4 \cdot -1$ ■ $1 \cdot -1$	
$4 \cdot -2$ ■ $1 \cdot -2$	
$4 \cdot -3$ ■ $1 \cdot -3$	

You can multiply each side of an inequality by the same number, just as you did with equations. When you multiply each side of an inequality by a positive number, the direction of the inequality symbol stays the same. When you multiply each side by a negative number, the direction of the inequality symbol reverses.

Key Concepts

Property	**Multiplication Property of Inequality for $c > 0$**
For every real number a and b, and for $c > 0$,	
if $a > b$, then $ac > bc$;	if $a < b$, then $ac < bc$.
Examples $4 > -1$, so $4(5) > -1(5)$.	$-6 < 3$, so $-6(5) < 3(5)$.
This property is also true for $\geq$ and $\leq$.	

You can use the Multiplication Property of Inequality to solve inequalities that involve division.

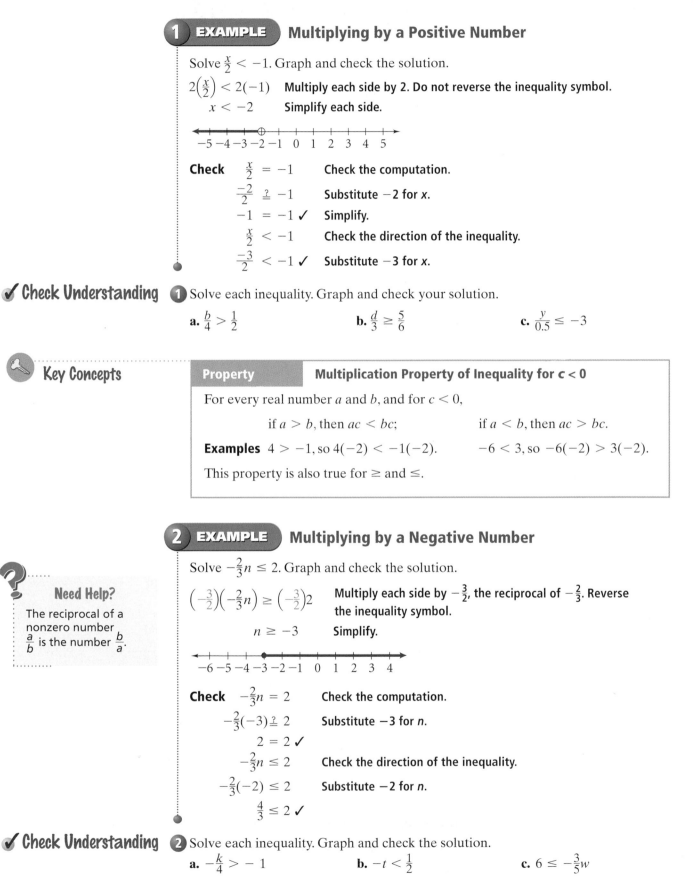

1 EXAMPLE Multiplying by a Positive Number

Solve $\frac{x}{2} < -1$. Graph and check the solution.

$2\left(\frac{x}{2}\right) < 2(-1)$ **Multiply each side by 2. Do not reverse the inequality symbol.**

$\quad\quad x < -2$ **Simplify each side.**

Check $\frac{x}{2} = -1$ **Check the computation.**

$\quad\quad \frac{-2}{2} \overset{?}{=} -1$ **Substitute -2 for x.**

$\quad\quad -1 = -1$ ✓   **Simplify.**

$\quad\quad \frac{x}{2} < -1$ **Check the direction of the inequality.**

$\quad\quad \frac{-3}{2} < -1$ ✓   **Substitute -3 for x.**

✓ Check Understanding **1** Solve each inequality. Graph and check your solution.

a. $\frac{b}{4} > \frac{1}{2}$ **b.** $\frac{d}{3} \geq \frac{5}{6}$ **c.** $\frac{y}{0.5} \leq -3$

Key Concepts

Property	Multiplication Property of Inequality for $c < 0$

For every real number a and b, and for $c < 0$,

if $a > b$, then $ac < bc$;   if $a < b$, then $ac > bc$.

Examples $4 > -1$, so $4(-2) < -1(-2)$. $-6 < 3$, so $-6(-2) > 3(-2)$.

This property is also true for $\geq$ and $\leq$.

2 EXAMPLE Multiplying by a Negative Number

Solve $-\frac{2}{3}n \leq 2$. Graph and check the solution.

$\left(-\frac{3}{2}\right)\left(-\frac{2}{3}n\right) \geq \left(-\frac{3}{2}\right)2$ **Multiply each side by $-\frac{3}{2}$, the reciprocal of $-\frac{2}{3}$. Reverse the inequality symbol.**

$\quad\quad n \geq -3$ **Simplify.**

Need Help?

The reciprocal of a nonzero number $\frac{a}{b}$ is the number $\frac{b}{a}$.

Check $-\frac{2}{3}n = 2$ **Check the computation.**

$\quad\quad -\frac{2}{3}(-3) \overset{?}{=} 2$ **Substitute -3 for n.**

$\quad\quad 2 = 2$ ✓

$\quad\quad -\frac{2}{3}n \leq 2$ **Check the direction of the inequality.**

$\quad\quad -\frac{2}{3}(-2) \leq 2$ **Substitute -2 for n.**

$\quad\quad \frac{4}{3} \leq 2$ ✓

✓ Check Understanding **2** Solve each inequality. Graph and check the solution.

a. $-\frac{k}{4} > -1$ **b.** $-t < \frac{1}{2}$ **c.** $6 \leq -\frac{3}{5}w$

Solving inequalities using division is similar to solving inequalities using multiplication. Remember that division by zero is undefined.

🔑 **Key Concepts**

Property	Division Property of Inequality

For every real number a and b, and for $c > 0$,

$$\text{if } a > b, \text{ then } \frac{a}{c} > \frac{b}{c}; \qquad\qquad \text{if } a < b, \text{ then } \frac{a}{c} < \frac{b}{c}.$$

Examples $6 > 4, \text{ so } \frac{6}{2} > \frac{4}{2}.$ $\qquad\qquad\qquad 2 < 8, \text{ so } \frac{2}{2} < \frac{8}{2}.$

For every real number a and b, and for $c < 0$,

$$\text{if } a > b, \text{ then } \frac{a}{c} < \frac{b}{c}; \qquad\qquad \text{if } a < b, \text{ then } \frac{a}{c} > \frac{b}{c}.$$

Examples $6 > 4, \text{ so } \frac{6}{-2} < \frac{4}{-2}.$ $\qquad\qquad 2 < 8, \text{ so } \frac{2}{-2} > \frac{8}{-2}.$

This property also applies to $\geq$ and $\leq$.

---

3 EXAMPLE **Dividing to Solve an Inequality**

Solve $-5z \geq 25$. Graph the solution.

$\dfrac{-5}{-5}z \leq \dfrac{25}{-5}$ **Divide each side by -5. Reverse the inequality symbol.**

$\quad z \leq -5$ **Simplify.**

$$\xleftarrow{\ \ } \begin{array}{cccccccccccc} + & + & + & \bullet & + & + & + & + & + & + & + \\ -9 & -8 & -7 & -6 & -5 & -4 & -3 & -2 & -1 & 0 & 1 \end{array}$$

✓ **Check Understanding** **3** Solve the inequality. Graph and check your solution.

a. $-2t < -8$ **b.** $-3w \geq 12$ **c.** $0.6 > -0.2n$

There are times when you must think about which types of numbers are acceptable as solutions of inequalities that represent real-world situations.

Real-World 🌐 Connection

Careers The duties of a manager of a non-profit organization, such as a food bank, include organizing and supervising volunteers.

4 EXAMPLE **Real-World 🌐 Problem Solving**

Community Service The student council votes to buy food for a local food bank. A case of 12 jars of spaghetti sauce costs $13.75. What is the greatest number of cases of sauce the student council can buy if they use at most $216 for this project?

Relate | cost per case | times | the number of cases | is at most | total cost |

Define Let c = the number of cases of spaghetti sauce.

Write | 13.75 | · | c | $\leq$ | 216 |

$13.75c \leq 216$

$\dfrac{13.75c}{13.75} \leq \dfrac{216}{13.75}$ **Divide each side by 13.75.**

$\quad c \leq 15.71$ **Simplify and round to the nearest hundredth.**

The student council does not have enough money to buy 16 cases, so they can buy at most 15 cases of sauce for the food bank.

✓ Check Understanding ④ Students in the school band are selling calendars. They earn $.40 on each calendar they sell. Their goal is to earn more than $327. Write and solve an inequality to find the fewest number of calendars they can sell and still reach their goal.

EXERCISES

For more practice, see *Extra Practice*.

Practice and Problem Solving

A Practice by Example

Examples 1, 2
(page 147)

Solve each inequality. Graph and check your solution.

1. $\frac{t}{4} \geq -1$ **2.** $\frac{s}{6} < 1$ **3.** $1 \leq -\frac{w}{2}$ **4.** $2 < -\frac{p}{4}$

5. $-2 < \frac{y}{2}$ **6.** $-\frac{v}{3} \geq 0.5$ **7.** $4 > \frac{2}{3}x$ **8.** $-5 \leq \frac{5}{2}k$

9. $0 < -\frac{7}{8}x$ **10.** $\frac{4}{3}y \geq 0$ **11.** $-\frac{5}{7}x > -5$ **12.** $6 \geq -\frac{3}{2}d$

13. $-\frac{4}{9} < \frac{2}{3}c$ **14.** $\frac{3}{4}b \geq -\frac{9}{8}$ **15.** $-\frac{5}{3}u > \frac{5}{6}$ **16.** $-\frac{5}{8} > -\frac{5}{6}n$

Example 3
(page 148)

17. $3t < -9$ **18.** $4m \geq 8$ **19.** $10 \leq -2w$ **20.** $-20 > -5c$

21. $-27 \geq 3z$ **22.** $-7b > 42$ **23.** $18d < -12$ **24.** $-3x \leq 16$

25. $-7 < 2q$ **26.** $16 > 3.2h$ **27.** $-1.5d < -6$ **28.** $3.6 \leq -0.8m$

Example 4
(page 148)

29. Fund-Raising The science club charges $4.50 per car at their car wash. Write and solve an inequality to find how many cars they have to wash to earn at least $300.

30. Earnings Suppose you earn $6.15 per hour working part time at a dry cleaner. Write and solve an inequality to find how many full hours you must work to earn at least $100.

B Apply Your Skills

Write four solutions to each inequality.

31. $\frac{x}{2} \leq -1$ **32.** $\frac{r}{3} \geq -4$ **33.** $-1 \geq \frac{t}{3}$ **34.** $0.5 > \frac{1}{2}c$

35. $-\frac{3}{4}q > 4$ **36.** $1 < -\frac{5}{7}s$ **37.** $-4.5 \leq -0.9p$ **38.** $-2.7w \geq 28$

Tell what you must do to the first inequality in order to get the second.

39. $-\frac{c}{4} > 3$; $c < -12$ **40.** $\frac{n}{5} \leq -2$; $n \leq -10$

41. $5z > -25$; $z > -5$ **42.** $\frac{3}{4}b \leq 3$; $b \leq 4$

43. $-12 < 4a$; $-3 < a$ **44.** $-b \geq 3.4$; $b \leq -3.4$

Replace each ▦ with the number that makes the inequalities equivalent.

45. ▦$s > 14$; $s < -7$ **46.** ▦$x \geq 25$; $x \leq -5$

47. $-8u \leq$ ▦; $u \geq -0.5$ **48.** $-2a >$ ▦; $a < -9$

49. $36 <$ ▦r; $r < -3.6$ **50.** $-k \leq$ ▦; $k \geq -7.5$

Problem Solving Hint

For Exercise 51, drawing a graph may help you to understand the problem.

51. Critical Thinking If $x \geq y$ and $-x \geq -y$, what can you conclude about x and y?

Estimation Estimate the solution of each inequality.

52. $-2.099r < 4$ **53.** $3.87j > -24$ **54.** $20.95 \geq \frac{1}{2}p$ **55.** $-\frac{20}{39}s \leq -14$

56. Safe Load An elevator like the one at the left can safely lift at most 4400 lb. A concrete block has an average weight of 42 lb. What is the maximum number of concrete blocks that the elevator can lift?

57. Writing Explain how solving the equation $-\frac{x}{3} = 4$ is similar to and different from solving the inequality $-\frac{x}{3} > 4$.

58. Open-Ended Write four different inequalities with $x > 3$ as their solution that you can solve using multiplication or division.

Solve each inequality.

59. $4d \le -28$ **60.** $\frac{u}{7} > 5$ **61.** $2 < -8s$ **62.** $\frac{3}{2}k \ge -45$

63. $0.3y < 2.7$ **64.** $9.4 \le -4t$ **65.** $-h \ge 4$ **66.** $\frac{5}{2}x > 5$

67. $24 < -\frac{8}{3}x$ **68.** $0 < -\frac{1}{6}b$ **69.** $\frac{5}{6} > -\frac{1}{3}p$ **70.** $-0.2m \ge 9.4$

71. $6 < -9g$ **72.** $4n \ge 9$ **73.** $-3.5 < -m$ **74.** $\frac{2}{5}z \ge -1$

Real-World Connection

Depending on its size, an elevator at a construction site can have a maximum load from 900 lb to 20,000 lb.

75. Michael solved the inequality $-2 > \frac{y}{-3}$ and got $6 < y$. Erica solved the same inequality and got $y > 6$. Are they both correct? Explain.

76. A friend calls you and asks you to meet at a location 3 miles from your home in 20 minutes. You set off on your bicycle after the telephone call. Write and solve an inequality to find the average rates in miles per minute you could ride to be at your meeting place within 20 minutes.

Reading Math

For help reading and solving Exercise 77, see page 152.

77. a. Error Analysis Kia solved $-15q \le 135$ by adding 15 to each side of the inequality. What mistake did she make?
   b. Kia's solution was $q \le 150$. She checked her work by substituting 150 for q in the original inequality. Why didn't her check let her know that she had made a mistake?
   c. Open-Ended Find a number that satisfies Kia's solution but does not satisfy the original inequality.

C Challenge

Reasoning If a, b, and c are real numbers, for which values of a is each statement true?

78. If $c < 0$, then $ac < a$. **79.** If $b > c$, then $ab > ac$.

80. If $b > c$, then $a^2b > a^2c$. **81.** If $b > c$, then $\frac{b}{a} < \frac{c}{a}$.

82. Packaging Suppose you have a plastic globe that you wish to put into a gift box. The circumference of the globe is 15 in. The edges of cube-shaped boxes are either 3 in., 4 in., 5 in., or 6 in. Write and solve an inequality to find the boxes that will hold the globe. (*Hint:* circumference = $\pi \cdot$ diameter)

83. Tiling a Floor The Sumaris' den floor measures 18 ft by 15 ft. They want to cover the floor with square tiles that are $\frac{9}{16}$ ft². Write and solve an inequality to find the least number of tiles they need to cover the floor.

Standardized Test Prep

Gridded Response

84. Solve $\frac{2}{5}x = 16$.

85. Mr. Houston expects to pay $16,800 in income taxes. This is no more than $\frac{1}{3}$ of his salary. What is his least possible earned income?

86. Five boxes of tiles will cover 30 ft². What is the least number of boxes of tiles needed to tile 320 ft²?

87. What is the greatest number of 34¢ stamps you can buy for $5.00?

88. The length of a rectangle is 90 in. Its area is less than 380 in². What is the greatest possible width of the rectangle, to the nearest inch?

89. The Environmental Club of City Middle School set a goal of collecting "one mile of cans." If the height of a typical 12 oz aluminum can is $4\frac{3}{4}$ in., what is the fewest number of cans needed to reach their goal?

Take It to the NET
Online lesson quiz at
www.PHSchool.com
Web Code: aea-0303

Mixed Review

Lesson 3-2 Solve each inequality.

90. $x + 3 \leq -4$ **91.** $\frac{5}{8} > \frac{3}{4} + w$ **92.** $t - 3.4 \geq 5.8$ **93.** $0 < d - 4$

94. $3.2 \geq m + 7.1$ **95.** $y - 2 < 6$ **96.** $-3 > a - 4$ **97.** $k + 12 \leq 15$

Lesson 2-3 Solve each equation.

98. $3t + 5 - t = 9$ **99.** $-3(2n + 1) = 9$ **100.** $\frac{3x}{4} - \frac{1}{2} = \frac{1}{4}$

Lesson 1-8 Name the property that each exercise illustrates.

101. $(-7) + 7 = 0$ **102.** $-3\left(-\frac{1}{3}\right) = 1$ **103.** $0 + 2 = 2$

104. $1x = x$ **105.** $4(2 \cdot 5) = (4 \cdot 2)5$ **106.** $4(2 \cdot 5) = 4(5 \cdot 2)$

✓ Checkpoint Quiz 1   Lessons 3-1 through 3-3

TEXT Instant self-check quiz online and on CD-ROM

Solve each inequality. Graph your solution.

1. $6 < c + 1$ **2.** $5x < -30$ **3.** $\frac{p}{3} \leq -2$

4. $y - 4 \geq -2$ **5.** $12 + g < 4$ **6.** $-3b \geq 15$

7. Determine whether each of the following is a solution of $x + 7 \leq 3$.
   a. -4 **b.** 0 **c.** $-\frac{17}{4}$ **d.** -3.9

8. Determine whether each of the following is a solution of $-4x < -12$.
   a. 3 **b.** 0 **c.** $\frac{7}{3}$ **d.** π

Write and solve an inequality that models each situation.

9. You plan to buy a bicycle that will cost at least $180. You have saved $38 and your parents have given you $50.
   a. Write an inequality to find how much more money m you need to save.
   b. Solve your inequality.

10. Your local garden shop has plants on sale for $1.50 each. You are planning a vegetable garden. You have $20 to spend on tomato plants.
   a. Write an inequality to find the greatest number of plants p you can buy.
   b. How many plants can you buy?

Read the exercise below and the description of how Gina found Kia's mistake. Check your understanding with the exercise at the bottom of the page.

77. a. Error Analysis Kia solved $-15q \leq 135$ by adding 15 to each side of the inequality. What mistake did she make?

b. Kia's solution was $q \leq 150$. She checked her work by substituting 150 for q in the original inequality. Why didn't her check let her know that she had made a mistake?

c. Open-Ended Find a number that satisfies Kia's solution but does not satisfy the original inequality.

What Gina Thinks

The problem says Kia added 15 to each side of the inequality. Since q is being multiplied by -15, she should have divided both sides by -15.

I'll substitute 150 in the original inequality. Kia's check didn't let her know she was wrong because 150 makes the inequality true. Any positive number times -15 is negative, so for a positive number q, $-15q$ is less than 135.

Now, I need to find a number that satisfies Kia's solution but not the original inequality. First I'll solve the original inequality. The solution is $q \geq -9$. So I need a number that is less than 150, and is not greater than or equal to -9. I'll use a number less than -9. Let $q = -10$.

Yes, -10 works!

I'll write my answer as a sentence.

What Gina Writes

a. Kia's mistake was adding 15 to both sides. She should have divided both sides by -15.

b. Let $q = 150$.
$$-15q \leq 135$$
$$-15(150) \leq 135$$
$$-2250 \leq 135 \text{ True}$$

Kia's check didn't let her know she had made a mistake because her solution made the inequality true.

c. $-15q \leq 135$
$$q \geq \frac{135}{-15}$$
$$q \geq -9$$

Let $q = -10$

Kia's: $q \leq 150 \Rightarrow -10 \leq 150$ True

Original: $-15q \leq 135 \Rightarrow 150 \leq 135$ False

-10 satisfies Kia's solution but not the original inequality.

EXERCISE

a. To solve the inequality $-\frac{1}{2}k \geq -5$, Danny multiplied both sides by the reciprocal of $-\frac{1}{2}$. His solution was $k \geq 10$. What mistake did he make?

b. Danny checked his solution, but his check did not let him know that he had made an error. What number could he have substituted?

c. Find a number that satisfies the original inequality but not Danny's solution.

3-4

Solving Multi-Step Inequalities

Lesson Preview

What You'll Learn

OBJECTIVE 1
To solve multi-step inequalities with variables on one side

OBJECTIVE 2
To solve multi-step inequalities with variables on both sides

. . . And Why

To find the measurements of a banner, as in Example 2

✔ Check Skills You'll Need

(For help, go to Lessons 2-2 and 2-3.)

Solve each equation, if possible. If the equation is an identity or if it has no solution, write *identity* or *no solution*.

1. $3(c + 4) = 6$

2. $3t + 6 = 3(t - 2)$

3. $5p + 9 = 2p - 1$

4. $7n + 4 - 5n = 2(n + 2)$

5. $\frac{1}{2}k - \frac{2}{3} + k = \frac{7}{6}$

6. $2t - 32 = 5t + 1$

Find the missing dimension of each rectangle.

7. perimeter = 110 cm

15 cm

ℓ

8. perimeter = 78 in.

w

26 in.

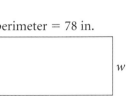 Interactive lesson includes instant self-check, tutorials, and activities.

OBJECTIVE

1 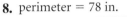 Solving Inequalities With Variables on One Side

Sometimes you need more than one step to solve an equation. The same is true when you solve inequalities. Just as with equations, you undo addition and subtraction first. Then undo multiplication and division.

1 EXAMPLE Using More Than One Step

Solve $7 + 6a > 19$. Check the solution.

$7 + 6a - 7 > 19 - 7$ **Subtract 7 from each side.**

$6a > 12$ **Simplify.**

$\frac{6a}{6} > \frac{12}{6}$ **Divide each side by 6.**

$a > 2$ **Simplify.**

Check $7 + 6a = 19$ **Check the computation.**

$7 + 6(2) \stackrel{?}{=} 19$ **Substitute 2 for *a*.**

$19 = 19$ ✓

$7 + 6a > 19$ **Check the direction of the inequality.**

$7 + 6(3) > 19$ **Substitute 3 for *a*.**

$25 > 19$ ✓

✔ Check Understanding **1** Solve each inequality. Check your solution.

a. $-3x - 4 \leq 14$

b. $5 < 7 - 2t$

c. $-8 < 5n - 23$

d. $5k + 12 \leq 2$

You can adapt familiar formulas like the formula for the perimeter of a rectangle to write inequalities. You determine which inequality symbol to use from the real-world situation.

2 EXAMPLE **Real-World Problem Solving**

Geometry The school band needs a banner to carry in a parade. The banner committee decides that the length of the banner should be 18 feet. A committee member drew the diagram at the left to help understand the problem. What are the possible widths of the banner if they can use no more than 48 feet of trim?

Relate Since the border goes around the edges of a rectangular banner, you can adapt the perimeter formula $P = 2\ell + 2w$.

twice the length	plus	twice the width	can be no more than	the length of trim

Write $2(18)$ $+$ $2w$ $\leq$ 48

$$2(18) + 2w \leq 48$$
$$36 + 2w \leq 48 \qquad \textbf{Simplify 2(18).}$$
$$36 + 2w - 36 \leq 48 - 36 \qquad \textbf{Subtract 36 from each side.}$$
$$2w \leq 12 \qquad \textbf{Simplify.}$$
$$\frac{2w}{2} \leq \frac{12}{2} \qquad \textbf{Divide each side by 2.}$$
$$w \leq 6 \qquad \textbf{Simplify.}$$

The banner's width must be 6 feet or less.

Check Is the solution reasonable? The trim is 48 feet long, so the greatest possible perimeter is 48 ft. For a length of 18 feet and a width of 6 feet, the perimeter is $2(18 + 6) = 2(24) = 48$, or 48 feet. So the width can be at most 6 feet. The answer is correct.

✓ **Check Understanding** ❷ To make a second banner, the committee decided to make the length 12 feet. They have 40 feet of a second type of trim. Write and solve an inequality to find the possible widths of the second banner.

Sometimes solving an inequality involves using the Distributive Property.

3 EXAMPLE **Using the Distributive Property**

Solve $2(t + 2) - 3t \geq -1$.

$$2t + 4 - 3t \geq -1 \qquad \textbf{Use the Distributive Property.}$$
$$-t + 4 \geq -1 \qquad \textbf{Combine like terms.}$$
$$-t + 4 - 4 \geq -1 - 4 \qquad \textbf{Subtract 4 from each side.}$$
$$-t \geq -5 \qquad \textbf{Simplify.}$$
$$\frac{-t}{-1} \leq \frac{-5}{-1} \qquad \textbf{Divide each side by } -1. \textbf{ Reverse the inequality symbol.}$$
$$t \leq 5 \qquad \textbf{Simplify.}$$

✓ **Check Understanding** ❸ Solve each inequality. Check your solution.
   a. $4p + 2(p + 7) < 8$ **b.** $15 \leq 5 - 2(4m + 7)$ **c.** $8 > 3(5 - b) + 2$

Solving Inequalities With Variables on Both Sides

Many inequalities have variables on both sides of the inequality symbol. You need to gather the variable terms on one side of the inequality and the constant terms on the other side.

4 EXAMPLE Gathering Variables on One Side of an Inequality

Solve $6z - 15 < 4z + 11$.

$6z - 15 - 4z < 4z + 11 - 4z$	To gather variables on the left, subtract **4z** from each side.
$2z - 15 < 11$	Combine like terms.
$2z - 15 + 15 < 11 + 15$	To gather the constants on the right, add **15** to each side.
$2z < 26$	Simplify.
$\frac{2z}{2} < \frac{26}{2}$	Divide each side by 2.
$z < 13$	Simplify.

✓ Check Understanding **4** Solve $3b + 12 > 27 - 2b$. Check your solution.

5 EXAMPLE Multi-Step Inequalities

Solve $-3(4 - m) \geq 4(2m + 1)$.

$-12 + 3m \geq 8m + 4$	Use the Distributive Property.
$-12 + 3m - 8m \geq 8m + 4 - 8m$	Subtract **8m** from each side.
$-12 - 5m \geq 4$	Combine like terms.
$-12 - 5m + 12 \geq 4 + 12$	Add **12** to each side.
$-5m \geq 16$	Simplify.
$\frac{-5m}{-5} \leq \frac{16}{-5}$	Divide each side by −5. Reverse the inequality symbol.
$m \leq -3\frac{1}{5}$	Simplify.

✓ Check Understanding **5** Solve $-6(x - 4) \geq 7(2x - 3)$. Check your solution.

EXERCISES

For more practice, see *Extra Practice*.

Practice and Problem Solving

A Practice by Example

Solve each inequality. Check your solution.

Example 1
(page 153)

1. $4d + 7 \leq 23$ **2.** $5m - 3 > -18$ **3.** $-4x - 2 < 8$

4. $5 - 3n \geq -4$ **5.** $8 \leq -12 + 5q$ **6.** $5 \leq 11 + 3h$

7. $-7 \leq 5 - 4a$ **8.** $10 > 29 - 3b$ **9.** $5 - 9c > -13$

Example 2
(page 154)

Write and solve an inequality.

10. On a trip from Virginia to Florida, the Sampson family wants to travel at least 420 miles in 8 hours of driving. What must be their average rate of speed?

11. Geometry The perimeter of an isosceles triangle is at most 27 cm. One side is 8 cm long. Find the possible lengths of the two congruent sides.

Example 3
(page 154)

12. You want to solve an inequality containing the expression $-3(2x - 3)$. The next line in your solution would rewrite this expression as __?__ .

Solve each inequality.

13. $2(j - 4) \geq -6$ **14.** $-(6b - 2) > 0$ **15.** $-2(h + 2) < -14$

16. $-3 \leq 3(5x - 16)$ **17.** $25 > -(4y + 7)$ **18.** $4(w - 2) \leq 10$

19. $-3(c + 4) - 2 > 7$ **20.** $-2(r - 3) + 7 \geq 8$ **21.** $16 \leq 4 - 3(n - 13)$

Example 4
(page 155)

22. $3w + 2 < 2w + 5$ **23.** $3t + 7 \geq 5t + 9$ **24.** $4d + 7 \geq 1 + 5d$

25. $5 - 2n \leq 3 - n$ **26.** $2k - 3 \leq 5k + 9$ **27.** $3s + 16 > 6 + 4s$

28. $6p - 1 > 3p + 8$ **29.** $3x + 2 > -4x + 16$ **30.** $2 - 3m < 4 + 5m$

31. $4d + 5 < -4d - 3$ **32.** $4 - 5y \geq 8 - y$ **33.** $2k + 6 \leq 4 + 5k$

Example 5
(page 155)

34. $-3(v - 3) \geq 5 - 4v$ **35.** $3q + 6 \leq -5(q + 2)$ **36.** $3(2 + r) \geq 15 - 2r$

37. $9 + x < 7 - 2(x - 3)$ **38.** $2(m - 8) < -8 + 3m$ **39.** $2v - 4 \leq 2(3v - 6)$

B Apply Your Skills

Tell what you must do to the first inequality in order to get the second.

40. $8 - 4s > 16; -4s > 8$ **41.** $\frac{2}{3}g + 7 \geq 9; \frac{2}{3}g \geq 2$

42. $2y - 5 > 9 + y; y > 14$ **43.** $-8 > \frac{z}{-5} - 2; 30 < z$

44. $4j + 5 \geq 23 + 3j; j \geq 18$ **45.** $2(q - 3) < 9 - 3q; q < 3$

46. a. Solve $5t + 4 \leq 8t - 5$ by gathering the variable terms on the left side and the constant terms on the right side of the inequality.
b. Solve $5t + 4 \leq 8t - 5$ by gathering the constant terms on the left side and the variable terms on the right side of the inequality.
c. Compare the results of parts (a) and (b).

Write and solve an inequality for each of the following statements.

Sample Four times the sum of x and 10 is less than 20.
$$4(x + 10) < 20$$
$$x + 10 < 5 \qquad \text{Divide each side by 4.}$$
$$x < -5 \qquad \text{Subtract 10 from each side.}$$

47. Six minus the sum of r and 3 is less than 15.

48. One half the difference of t and six is less than or equal to four.

49. Three times the quantity z plus 2 is greater than 12.

50. Writing Suppose a friend is having difficulty solving $2.5(p - 4) > 3(p + 2)$. Explain how to solve the inequality, showing all necessary steps and identifying the properties you would use.

51. a. Mental Math Like equations, some inequalities are true for all values of the variable, and some inequalities are not true for any values of the variable. Determine whether each inequality is *always* true or *never* true.
i. $4s + 6 \geq 6 + 4s$ **ii.** $3r + 5 > 3r - 2$ **iii.** $4(n + 1) < 4n - 3$
b. Critical Thinking How can you tell whether an inequality is always true or never true without solving?

Need Help?

Inequalities or equations that are always true are called *identities*. (See p. 98)

Real-World Connection

Normal blood pressure for teens is about 110/70.

52. **Expenses** The sophomore class is planning a picnic. The cost of a permit to use a city park is $250. To pay for the permit, there is a fee of $.75 for each sophomore and $1.25 for each guest who is not a sophomore. Two hundred sophomores plan to attend. Write and solve an inequality to find how many guests must attend for the sophomores to pay for the permit.

53. **Health Care** Systolic blood pressure is the higher number in a blood pressure reading. It is measured as your heart muscle contracts. The formula $P \le \frac{1}{2}a + 110$ gives the normal systolic blood pressure P based on age a.
   a. At age 20, does 120 represent a maximum or a minimum normal systolic pressure?
   b. Find the normal systolic blood pressure for a 50-year-old person.

Match each inequality with its graph below.

54. $-2x - 2 > 4$ 55. $2 - 2x > 4$ 56. $2x + 2 > 4$

57. $2x + 2 > 4x$ 58. $2x - 2 > 4$ 59. $-2(x - 2) > 4$

A.
   $-5\ -4\ -3\ -2\ -1\ \ 0\ \ 1\ \ 2\ \ 3$

B.
   $-5\ -4\ -3\ -2\ -1\ \ 0\ \ 1\ \ 2\ \ 3$

C.
   $-5\ -4\ -3\ -2\ -1\ \ 0\ \ 1\ \ 2\ \ 3$

D.
   $-3\ -2\ -1\ \ 0\ \ 1\ \ 2\ \ 3\ \ 4\ \ 5$

E.
   $-5\ -4\ -3\ -2\ -1\ \ 0\ \ 1\ \ 2\ \ 3$

F.
   $-3\ -2\ -1\ \ 0\ \ 1\ \ 2\ \ 3\ \ 4\ \ 5$

60. **Open-Ended** Write two different inequalities that you can solve by adding 5 and multiplying by -3. Solve each inequality.

Solve each inequality.

61. $\frac{4}{3}r - 3 < r + \frac{2}{3} - \frac{1}{3}r$

62. $4 - 2m \le 5 - m + 1$

63. $-2(0.5 - 4s) \ge -3(4 - 3.5s)$

64. $\frac{1}{2}n - \frac{1}{8} \ge \frac{3}{4} + \frac{5}{6}n$

65. $-(8 - s) < 0$

66. $3.8 - k \le 5.2 - 2k$

67. $10 > 3(2n - 1) - 5(4n + 3)$

68. $3(3r + 1) - (r + 4) \le 13$

69. $2(3x + 7) > 4(7 - 2x)$

70. $4(a - 2) - 6a \le -9$

71. $4(3m - 1) \ge 2(m + 3)$

72. $17 - (4k - 2) \ge 2(k + 3)$

73. $2n - 3(n + 3) \le 14$

74. $5x - \frac{1}{2}(3x + 8) \le -4 + 3x$

75. $5a - 2(a - 15) < 10$

76. $5c + 4(c - 1) \ge 2 + 5(2 + c)$

77. **Business** Mandela is starting a part-time word-processing business out of his home. He plans to charge $15 per hour. The table at the right shows his expected monthly business expenses. Write and solve an inequality to find the number of hours he must work in a month to make a profit of at least $600.

Expense	Cost
Equipment rental	$490
Materials	$45
Business phone	$65

78. **Commission** Joleen is a sales associate in a clothing store. Each week she earns $250 plus a commission equal to 3% of her sales. This week her goal is to earn no less than $460. Write and solve an inequality to find the dollar amount of the sales she must have to reach her goal.

Error Analysis Find and correct the mistake in each of the following.

79.

$$3x + 3 \leq -2x + 5$$
$$3x \leq -2x + 2$$
$$x \leq 2$$

80.

$$4(n + 2) > 3n + 1$$
$$4n + 2 > 3n + 1$$
$$4n > 3n - 1$$
$$n > -1$$

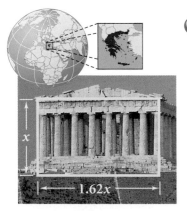

Real-World Connection

The Parthenon, an ancient Greek temple, has dimensions that form a golden rectangle.

C Challenge

81. a. Solve $ax + b > c$ for x, where a is positive.
b. Reasoning Solve $ax + b > c$ for x, where a is negative.

82. Geometry The base of a triangle is 10 in. Its height is $(x + 4)$ in. Its area is no more than 56 in.² What are the possible integer values of x?

83. Architecture The rectangle shown on the building at the left is a golden rectangle. Artists often use the golden rectangle because they consider it to be pleasing to the eye. The ratio of two sides of a golden rectangle is approximately 1 : 1.62. Suppose you are making a picture frame in the shape of a golden rectangle. You have a 46-in. length of wood to use for a frame. What are the dimensions of the largest frame you can make? Round to the nearest tenth of an inch.

84. Critical Thinking Find a value of a such that the number line below shows all the solutions of $ax + 4 \leq -12$.

$$\leftarrow\!\!+\!\!\!+\!\!\!+\!\!\!+\!\!\!+\!\!\!+\!\!\!+\!\!\!+\!\!\!+\!\!\!+\!\!\!\bullet\!\!\rightarrow$$
$$-1\ \ 0\ \ 1\ \ 2\ \ 3\ \ 4\ \ 5\ \ 6\ \ 7\ \ 8\ \ 9$$

85. Earning You can earn money by handing out flyers in the afternoon for $6.50 an hour and by typing a newsletter in the evening for $8 an hour. You have 20 hours available to work. What are the greatest number of hours you can spend handing out flyers and still make at least $145?

86. Freight Handling The freight elevator of a building can safely carry a load of at most 4000 lb. A worker needs to move supplies in 50-lb boxes from the loading dock to the fourth floor of the building. The worker weighs 160 lb. The cart she uses weighs 95 lb.
a. What is the greatest number of boxes she can move in one trip?
b. The worker must deliver 310 boxes to the fourth floor. How many trips must she make?

Standardized Test Prep

Multiple Choice

87. The Science Club hopes to collect at least 200 kg of aluminum cans for recycling this semester (21 weeks). The graph at the right shows the first week's results.

Let x represent the average mass of cans required per week for the remainder of the semester. Which inequality would you use to find x?

A. $x \geq \frac{200}{21}$ **B.** $x \geq \frac{(200 - 8)}{21}$

C. $x \geq \frac{(200 - 8)}{20}$ **D.** $x > \left(\frac{200}{20}\right) - 8$

Aluminum Cans Collected in Week 1

88. Solve $2x - 8 > 4x + 2$.

   F. $x < -5$ **G.** $x > -5$ **H.** $x < 5$ **I.** $x > 5$

89. Solve $-5n + 16 \le -7n$.

   A. $n \le -8$ **B.** $n \ge -8$ **C.** $n \le 8$ **D.** $n \ge 8$

90. Great Gifts pays its supplier \$65 for each box of 12 bells. The owner wants to determine the least amount x he can charge his customers per bell in order to make at least a 50% profit per box. Which inequality should he use?

   F. $12x \ge 1.50(65)$ **G.** $65x \le 1.50(12)$

   H. $0.50(12x) \ge 65$ **I.** $0.50(12x) \le 65$

Short Response

91. Maxwell orders at least 30 bottles of flea shampoo per month for his pet-grooming business. His supplier charges \$3 per quart bottle plus a \$25 handling fee per order. A competing supplier offers a similar product for \$4 per quart bottle plus a \$5 handling fee per order. The salesman for the competitor shows Maxwell that 10 bottles from his company would cost only \$45 compared to \$55 from Maxwell's current supplier.

Which supplier would you advise Maxwell to use? Explain or show work to support your advice to Maxwell.

Take It to the NET
Online lesson quiz at
www.PHSchool.com
.... Web Code: aea-0304

Mixed Review

Lesson 3-3

Solve each inequality.

92. $-9m \ge 36$ **93.** $-24 \le 3y$ **94.** $\frac{x}{3} > -4$ **95.** $-\frac{t}{3} \le 1$

96. $\frac{2}{3}b < 18$ **97.** $42 > -\frac{3}{7}w$ **98.** $56 < 42p$ **99.** $0.5d \ge 3.5$

Lesson 2-5

100. Your family leaves your town traveling at an average rate of 45 mi/h. Two hours later, your neighbor leaves your town along the same road at an average rate of 60 mi/h. How many hours will it take your neighbor to overtake you?

Lesson 1-6

Simplify each expression.

101. -4^2 **102.** $(-4)^2$ **103.** $(-2)^3(-3)$ **104.** -2^4

Algebra at Work

•••••••••••••••••••••• Marketing Director

Marketing directors rely on equations and inequalities to predict the actions their companies must take to stay competitive. For example, the marketing director of a manufacturing company determines how much the cost of raw materials can increase before the company must raise the price of its finished goods or services. The director also predicts the effect of price changes on the quantity of goods and services sold by his company.

Take It to the NET For more information about a career in marketing, go to **www.PHSchool.com**.
.... Web Code: aeb-2031

When you solve inequalities, the possible values for the variable make up the *replacement set*. Real numbers or integers can be replacement sets. The notation {3, 4, 5} indicates that 3, 4, and 5 is a replacement set. Your solution depends on the replacement set for the variable.

EXAMPLE

a. Solve $-5 < 2k$.

$$-5 < 2k$$

$$\frac{-5}{2} < \frac{2k}{2} \quad \text{Divide by 2.}$$

$$-2\tfrac{1}{2} < k \quad \text{Simplify.}$$

b. Graph the solutions for each replacement set.

i. the real numbers

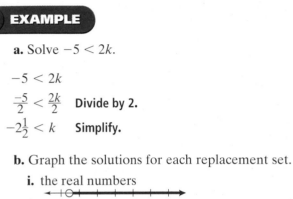

ii. the integers

iii. {−5, −3, −2, 0, 3}

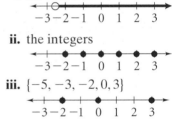

EXERCISES

Graph each inequality for the given replacement set.

1. $9v + 6 \le 18$, for {−4, −2, 0, 2, 4}

2. $2n + 6 < 12$; integers

3. $-3(d - 1) \le 4.5$; positive integers

4. $-2 < 2(c + 5)$; negative integers

5. $-4 \le q + 1$; negative real numbers

6. $4 < 2 - 2m$; for {−2, −1, 0, 1, 2}

Write an inequality that represents each situation. Identify each replacement set. Solve and graph the solution on a number line.

7. Geometry The length of a rectangle is 20 cm. For a perimeter of at most 48 cm, what is the width of the rectangle?

8. Grades Your grades on three tests are 85, 80, and 75. You will take one more 20-question test. Each question is worth 5 points. Your goal is to have a test average of at least 83. What grades on the fourth test will give you the average that you want?

3-5

Compound Inequalities

Lesson Preview

What You'll Learn

OBJECTIVE 1
To solve and graph inequalities containing *and*

OBJECTIVE 2
To solve and graph inequalities containing *or*

...And Why

To solve a problem involving the chemistry of a swimming pool, as in Example 3

✔ Check Skills You'll Need

(For help, go to Lessons 1-1 and 3-1.)

Graph each pair of inequalities on one number line.

1. $c < 8; c \geq 10$ **2.** $t \geq -2; t \leq -5$ **3.** $m \leq 7; m > 12$

Use the given value of the variable to evaluate each expression.

4. $3n - 6; 4$ **5.** $7 - 2b; 5$

6. $\dfrac{12 + 13 + y}{3}; 17$ **7.** $\dfrac{2d - 3}{5}; 9$

New Vocabulary
• compound inequality

OBJECTIVE

1   Solving Compound Inequalities Containing *And*

iTEXT Interactive lesson includes instant self-check, tutorials, and activities.

Two inequalities that are joined by the word *and* or the word *or* form a **compound inequality.**

You can write the compound inequality $x \geq -5$ and $x \leq 7$ as $-5 \leq x \leq 7$.

$$x \geq -5$$
$$x \leq 7$$
$$-6 \quad -5 \quad -4 \quad -3 \quad -2 \quad -1 \quad 0 \quad 1 \quad 2 \quad 3 \quad 4 \quad 5 \quad 6 \quad 7 \quad 8$$
$$-5 \leq x \leq 7$$

 Reading Math

The word *inclusive* is related to the word *included.*

The graph above shows that a solution of $-5 \leq x \leq 7$ is in the overlap of the solutions of the inequality $x \geq -5$ and the inequality $x \leq 7$.

You can read $-5 \leq x \leq 7$ as "*x* is greater than or equal to -5 and less than or equal to 7." Another way to read it is "*x* is between -5 and 7, inclusive."

1 EXAMPLE   Writing a Compound Inequality

Write a compound inequality that represents each situation. Graph the solutions.

a. all real numbers that are at least -2 and at most 4

$n \geq -2$ and $n \leq 4$

$-2 \leq n \leq 4$

$$-3 \quad -2 \quad -1 \quad 0 \quad 1 \quad 2 \quad 3 \quad 4 \quad 5$$

b. Today's temperatures will be above 32°F, but not as high as 40°F.

$32 < t$ and $t < 40$

$32 < t < 40$

$$30 \quad 31 \quad 32 \quad 33 \quad 34 \quad 35 \quad 36 \quad 37 \quad 38 \quad 39 \quad 40 \quad 41 \quad 42$$

✔ Check Understanding ❶ Write a compound inequality that represents each situation. Graph your solution.
a. all real numbers greater than -2 but less than 9
b. The books were priced between $3.50 and $6.00, inclusive.

A solution of a compound inequality joined by *and* is any number that makes both inequalities true. One way you can solve a compound inequality is by writing two inequalities.

2 EXAMPLE   Solving a Compound Inequality Containing *And*

Solve $-4 < r - 5 \le -1$. Graph your solution.

Write the compound inequality as two inequalities joined by *and*.

$$
\begin{array}{ccc}
-4 < r - 5 & \text{and} & r - 5 \le -1 \\
-4 + 5 < r - 5 + 5 & & r - 5 + 5 \le -1 + 5 \quad \textbf{Solve each inequality.} \\
1 < r & \text{and} & r \le 4 \qquad\qquad \textbf{Simplify.}
\end{array}
$$

$$1 < r \le 4$$

<-----+----+----+----+----+----+----⊕----+----+----●----+----->
$\;\; -5 \; -4 \; -3 \; -2 \; -1 \;\; 0 \;\; 1 \;\; 2 \;\; 3 \;\; 4 \;\; 5$

✔ **Check Understanding** ② Solve each inequality. Graph your solution.
   a. $-6 \le 3x < 15$ **b.** $-3 < 2x - 1 < 7$ **c.** $7 < -3n + 1 \le 13$

You could also solve an inequality like $-4 < r - 5 \le -1$ by working on all three parts of the inequality at the same time. You work to get the variable alone between the inequality symbols.

3 EXAMPLE   Real-World 🌐 Problem Solving

Chemistry The acidity of the water in a swimming pool is considered normal if the average of three pH readings is between 7.2 and 7.8, inclusive. The first two readings for a swimming pool are 7.4 and 7.9. What possible values for the third reading p will make the average pH normal?

Relate	7.2	is less than or equal to	the average	which is less than or equal to	7.8
Write	7.2	$\le$	$\dfrac{7.4 + 7.9 + p}{3}$	$\le$	7.8

$$7.2 \le \frac{7.4 + 7.9 + p}{3} \le 7.8$$

$$3(7.2) \le 3\left(\frac{7.4 + 7.9 + p}{3}\right) \le 3(7.8) \qquad \textbf{Multiply by 3.}$$

$$21.6 \le 15.3 + p \le 23.4 \qquad \textbf{Simplify.}$$

$$21.6 - 15.3 \le 15.3 + p - 15.3 \le 23.4 - 15.3 \qquad \textbf{Subtract 15.3.}$$

$$6.3 \le p \le 8.1 \qquad \textbf{Simplify.}$$

The value for the third reading must be between 6.3 and 8.1, inclusive.

Real-World 🌐 Connection

The lifeguard is checking the pH of swimming pool water. The pH of a substance is a measure of how acidic or basic it is. pH is measured on a scale from 1 to 14. Pure water is neutral, with a pH of 7.

✔ **Check Understanding** ③ **a.** Suppose the first two readings for the acidity of water in a swimming pool are 7.0 and 7.9. What possible values for the third reading will make the average pH normal?
   b. **Critical Thinking** If two readings are 8.0 and 8.4, what possible values for the third reading will make the average pH normal? Are these third readings likely? Explain.

A solution of a compound inequality joined by *or* is any number that makes either inequality true.

4 **EXAMPLE** **Writing Compound Inequalities**

Write a compound inequality that represents each situation. Graph the solution.

a. all real numbers that are less than -3 or greater than 7

$x < -3$ or $x > 7$

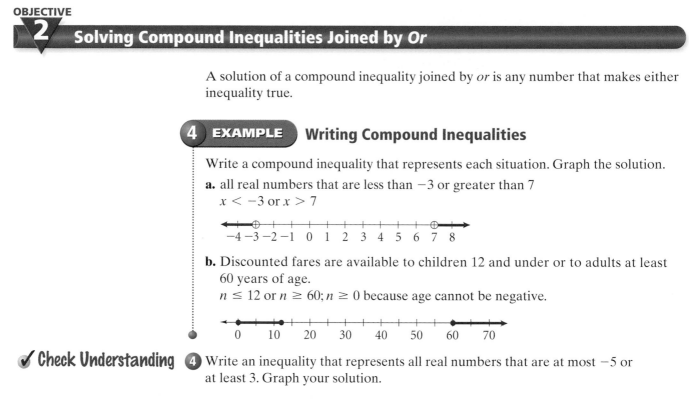

b. Discounted fares are available to children 12 and under or to adults at least 60 years of age.

$n \leq 12$ or $n \geq 60$; $n \geq 0$ because age cannot be negative.

✓**Check Understanding** **4** Write an inequality that represents all real numbers that are at most -5 or at least 3. Graph your solution.

For a compound inequality joined by *or*, you must solve each of the two inequalities separately.

?
Need Help?
Remember to reverse the inequality symbol when you multiply or divide by a negative number.

5 **EXAMPLE** **Solving a Compound Inequality Containing *Or***

Solve the compound inequality $4v + 3 < -5$ or $-2v + 7 < 1$. Graph the solution.

$$4v + 3 < -5 \qquad \text{or} \qquad -2v + 7 < 1$$
$$4v + 3 - 3 < -5 - 3 \qquad\qquad -2v + 7 - 7 < 1 - 7$$
$$4v < -8 \qquad\qquad\qquad -2v < -6$$
$$\frac{4v}{4} < \frac{-8}{4} \qquad\qquad\qquad \frac{-2v}{-2} > \frac{-6}{-2}$$
$$v < -2 \qquad \text{or} \qquad v > 3$$

✓**Check Understanding** **5** Solve the compound inequality $-2x + 7 > 3$ or $3x - 4 \geq 5$. Graph your solution.

EXERCISES

For more practice, see *Extra Practice*.

Practice and Problem Solving

A **Practice by Example**

Example 1
(page 161)

Write a compound inequality that represents each situation. Graph your solution.

1. all real numbers that are between -4 and 6

2. all real numbers that are at least 2 and at most 9

3. The circumference of a baseball is between 23 cm and 23.5 cm.

4. Tropical Storm The wind speeds of a tropical storm are at least 40 mi/h but no more than 74 mi/h.

Solve each compound inequality. Graph your solution.

5. $-3 < j + 2 < 7$ **6.** $3 \leq w + 2 \leq 7$ **7.** $2 < 3n - 4 \leq 14$

8. $7 \leq 3 - 2p < 11$ **9.** $-2 < -3x + 7 < 4$ **10.** $1.5 < w + 3 \leq 6.5$

11. $-16 < -3x + 8 < -7$ **12.** $-1 < 4m + 7 \leq 11$ **13.** $-9 < -2s - 1 \leq -7$

14. $-\frac{1}{2} < \frac{1}{4}t - \frac{3}{4} < \frac{1}{8}$ **15.** $3 \geq 4r - 5 \geq -1$ **16.** $3.2 \geq 2r + 0.2 > -3.8$

17. $12 \leq \frac{14 + 17 + a}{3} \leq 16$ **18.** $\frac{1}{2} < \frac{3x - 1}{4} < 5$ **19.** $-2 \leq \frac{5 - x}{3} \leq 2$

Example 4
(page 163)

For each situation write and graph an inequality.

20. all real numbers n that are at most -3 or at least 5

21. all real numbers x that are less than 3 or greater than 7

22. all real numbers h less than 1 or greater than 3

23. all real numbers b less than 100 or greater than 300

Example 5
(page 163)

Solve each compound inequality. Graph your solution.

24. $3b - 1 < -7$ or $4b + 1 > 9$ **25.** $4 + k > 3$ or $6k < -30$

26. $3c + 4 \geq 13$ or $6c - 1 < 11$ **27.** $6 - a < 1$ or $3a \leq 12$

28. $7 - 3c \geq 1$ or $5c + 2 \geq 17$ **29.** $5y + 7 \leq -3$ or $3y - 2 \geq 13$

30. $2d + 5 \leq -1$ or $-2d + 5 \leq 5$ **31.** $5z - 3 > 7$ or $4z - 6 < -10$

32. $x - 5 \geq 0$ or $x + 1 < -2$ **33.** $-3n < -9$ or $-2n > 10$

B **Apply Your Skills**

Write a compound inequality that each graph could represent.

34.

35.

36.

37.

Solve each compound inequality.

38. $3q - 2 > 10$ or $3q - 2 \leq -10$ **39.** $3 - 2h > 17$ or $5h - 3 > 17$

40. $1 \leq 0.25t \leq 3.5$ **41.** $25r < 400$ or $100 < 4r$

42. $-20 \leq 3t - 2 < 1$ **43.** $\frac{3x + 1}{4} - 4 > 3$ or $\frac{3 - 2x}{5} > 3$

44. Physical Science The force exerted on a spring is proportional to the distance the spring stretches from its relaxed position. Suppose you stretch a spring distance d in inches by applying force F in pounds. For a certain spring, $\frac{d}{F} = 0.8$. You apply forces between 25 and 40 pounds, inclusive. Write a compound inequality describing the stretch of the spring.

at rest

$\leftarrow d$ in. $\rightarrow$

45. Reasoning Describe the solutions of $3x - 8 < 7$ or $2x - 9 > 1$.

46. Writing Explain the difference between the words *and* and *or* in a compound inequality.

Geometry The sum of the lengths of any two sides of a triangle is greater than the length of the third side. The lengths of two sides of a triangle are given. Find the range of values for the possible lengths of the third side.

Sample 3 cm, 7 cm

Write inequalities for x as the longest side and for 7 cm as the longest side. The length 3 cm cannot be the longest side.

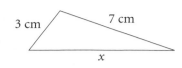

$x + 3 > 7$ and $3 + 7 > x$

$\qquad x > 4$ and $10 > x$ **Solve each inequality.**

$\qquad 4 < x < 10$

The length of the third side is greater than 4 cm and less than 10 cm.

47. 2.5 in., 5 in. **48.** 12 ft, 18 ft **49.** 28 mm, 21 mm **50.** 5 m, 16 m

Meteorology The graph below shows the average monthly high and low temperatures for Detroit, Michigan, and Charlotte, North Carolina.

51. Write a compound inequality for Charlotte's average temperature in June.

52. Write a compound inequality for Detroit's average temperature in January.

53. Write a compound inequality for the yearly temperature range for each city.

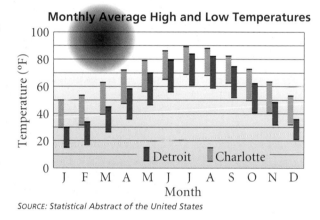

SOURCE: Statistical Abstract of the United States

54. Open-Ended Describe a real-life situation that you could represent with the inequality $-2 < x < 8$.

Challenge

55. Nursing In nursing school, students learn temperature ranges for bath water. Tepid water is approximately 80°F to 93°F, warm water is approximately 94°F to 98°F, and hot water is approximately 110°F to 115°F. Model these ranges on one number line. Label each interval.

Write a compound inequality that each graph could represent.

56.

−4 −2 0 2 4

57.

−2 0 2 4

58. Pulse Rates When you exercise, your pulse rate rises. Recommended pulse rates vary with age and physical condition. For vigorous exercise, such as jogging, the inequality $0.7(220 - a) \le R \le 0.85(220 - a)$ gives a target range for pulse rate R (in beats per minute), based on age a (in years).
 a. What is the target range for pulse rates for a person 35 years old? Round to the nearest whole number.
 b. Your cousin's target pulse rate is in the range between 140 and 170 beats per minute. What is your cousin's age?

59. Find three consecutive even integers whose sum is between 48 and 60.

60. Find three consecutive even integers such that one half of their sum is between 15 and 21.

Real-World Connection

To estimate your pulse rate, count the number of beats you feel in 15 seconds at a pressure point. Multiply this number by 4.

Multiple Choice

61. An emergency vehicle responding to a 911 call for a heart attack victim traveled 5 miles to the patient's home and then delivered him to the hospital 10 miles away. Which graph below represents the possible distances the emergency vehicle was from the hospital when the call was received?

A.
```
<-+--+--+--●--+--●--+--+--+--+->
  0  2  4  6  8  10 12 14 16 18
```

B.
```
<-+--+--+--●--+--+--+--+--●--+->
  0  2  4  6  8  10 12 14 16 18
```

C.
```
<-+--●--+--+--●--+--+--+--+--+->
  0  2  4  6  8  10 12 14 16 18
```

D.
```
<-+--●--+--+--+--+--●--+--+--+->
  0  2  4  6  8  10 12 14 16 18
```

62. Which value below is a solution of neither $-3x - 7 \geq 8$ nor $-2x - 11 \leq -31$?

   F. –6   **G.** 0   **H.** 10   **I.** 16

Short Response

Take It to the NET
Online lesson quiz at
www.PHSchool.com
Web Code: aea-0305

63. The County Water Department charges a monthly administration fee of $10.40 plus $.0059 for each gallon g of water used, up to 7,500 gallons. Find the minimum and maximum water consumption (in gallons) for customers whose monthly charge is at least $35 but no more than $50. Express amounts to the nearest gallon. Show your work.

Mixed Review

Lesson 3-4

Solve each inequality.

64. $5 < 6b + 3$ **65.** $12n \leq 3n + 27$ **66.** $2 + 4r \geq 5(r - 1)$

Lesson 2-4

Solve. If the equation is an identity or if it has no solution, write *identity* or *no solution*.

67. $x - 3 = 5x + 1$ **68.** $4(w + 3) = 10w$ **69.** $8p - 4 = 4(2p - 1)$

Checkpoint Quiz 2   Lessons 3-4 through 3-5

Instant self-check quiz online and on CD-ROM

Solve each inequality. Graph the solution.

1. $8d + 2 < 5d - 7$ **2.** $2n + 1 \geq -3$ **3.** $-1 \leq 4m + 7 \leq 11$

4. $5s - 3 + 1 < 8$ **5.** $5(3p - 2) > 50$ **6.** $3 - x \geq 7$ or $2x - 3 > 5$

Write an inequality that represents each situation.

7. A cat weighs less than 8 pounds.

8. We expect today's temperature to be between 65°F and 75°F, inclusive.

9. Geometry The length of each side of a rectangular picture frame needs to be 15 in. You have only one 48 in. piece of wood to use for this frame. Write and solve an inequality that describes the possible widths for this frame.

10. Solve $-2x + 7 \leq 45$.

3-6 Absolute Value Equations and Inequalities

Lesson Preview

What You'll Learn

OBJECTIVE 1 To solve equations that involve absolute value

OBJECTIVE 2 To solve inequalities that involve absolute value

... And Why

To find a range of acceptable measurements for parts of an engine, as in Example 4

✓ Check Skills You'll Need
(For help, go to Lessons 1-3 and 1-4.)

Simplify.

1. $|15|$ 2. $|-3|$ 3. $|18 - 12|$

4. $-|-7|$ 5. $|12 - (-12)|$ 6. $|-10 + 8|$

Complete each statement with $<$, $=$, or $>$.

7. $|3 - 7|$ ■ 4   8. $|-5| + 2$ ■ 6   9. $|7| - 1$ ■ 8

10. $\left|6 - 2\frac{1}{4}\right|$ ■ $3\frac{5}{8}$ 11. $\left|-4\frac{2}{3}\right| + 2\frac{1}{3}$ ■ $2\frac{1}{2}$ 12. $\left|-3\frac{1}{8} - 4\frac{1}{2}\right|$ ■ $7\frac{5}{8}$

OBJECTIVE

1 Solving Absolute Value Equations

iTEXT Interactive lesson includes instant self-check, tutorials, and activities.

Recall that the absolute value of a number is its distance from zero on a number line. Since absolute value represents distance, it can never be negative.

The graph of $|x| = 3$ is below.

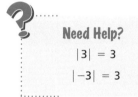

Need Help?

$|3| = 3$

$|-3| = 3$

3 units   3 units

−5 −4 −3 −2 −1   0   1   2   3   4   5

Find the numbers that are 3 units from 0.

The two solutions of the equation $|x| = 3$ are -3 and 3.

You can use the properties of equality to solve an absolute value equation.

1 EXAMPLE   Solving an Absolute Value Equation

Solve $|x| + 5 = 11$.

$|x| + 5 - 5 = 11 - 5$ **Subtract 5 from each side.**

$|x| = 6$ **Simplify.**

$x = 6$ or $x = -6$ **Definition of absolute value.**

Check $|x| + 5 = 11$

$|6| + 5 \stackrel{?}{=} 11$ ← Substitute 6 and −6 for x. → $|-6| + 5 \stackrel{?}{=} 11$

$6 + 5 = 11$ ✓ $6 + 5 = 11$ ✓

✓ Check Understanding

1 Solve each equation. Check your solution.

a. $|t| - 2 = -1$ **b.** $3|n| = 15$ **c.** $4 = 3|w| - 2$

d. Critical Thinking Is there a solution of $2|n| = -15$? Explain.

Some absolute value equations such as $|2p + 5| = 11$ have variable expressions within the absolute value symbols. The expression inside the absolute value symbols can be either positive or negative.

Key Concepts

Rule	Solving Absolute Value Equations

To solve an equation in the form $|A| = b$, where A represents a variable expression and $b > 0$, solve $A = b$ and $A = -b$.

2 EXAMPLE Solving an Absolute Value Equation

Solve $|2p + 5| = 11$.

$2p + 5 = 11$	← Write two equations. →	$2p + 5 = -11$
$2p + 5 - 5 = 11 - 5$	← Subtract 5 from each side. →	$2p + 5 - 5 = -11 - 5$
$2p = 6$		$2p = -16$
$\dfrac{2p}{2} = \dfrac{6}{2}$	← Divide each side by 2. →	$\dfrac{2p}{2} = \dfrac{-16}{2}$
$p = 3$		$p = -8$

● The value of p is 3 or -8.

✓ Check Understanding ❷ Solve each equation. Check your solution.

a. $|c - 2| = 6$ **b.** $-5.5 = |t + 2|$ **c.** $|7d| = 14$

2 Solving Absolute Value Inequalities

You can write absolute value inequalities as compound inequalities.

The graphs below show two absolute value inequalities.

$|n - 1| < 3$ $|n - 1| > 3$

$|n - 1| < 3$ represents all numbers whose distance from 1 is less than 3 units. So $-3 < n - 1 < 3$.

$|n - 1| > 3$ represents all numbers whose distance from 1 is greater than 3 units. So $n - 1 < -3$ or $n - 1 > 3$.

Key Concepts

Rule	Solving Absolute Value Inequalities

To solve an inequality in the form $|A| < b$, where A is a variable expression and $b > 0$, solve $-b < A < b$.

To solve an inequality in the form $|A| > b$, where A is a variable expression and $b > 0$, solve $A < -b$ or $A > b$.

Similar rules are true for $|A| \leq b$ or $|A| \geq b$.

3 EXAMPLE   Solving an Absolute Value Inequality

Solve $|v - 3| \geq 4$. Graph the solutions.

$v - 3 \leq -4$	or	$v - 3 \geq 4$	**Write a compound inequality.**
$v - 3 + 3 \leq -4 + 3$		$v - 3 + 3 \geq 4 + 3$	**Add 3.**
$v \leq -1$	or	$v \geq 7$	**Simplify.**

$$\leftarrow\!+\!\!-\!\!\bullet\!\!-\!\!+\!\!-\!\!+\!\!-\!\!+\!\!-\!\!+\!\!-\!\!+\!\!-\!\!+\!\!-\!\!\bullet\!\!-\!\!+\!\!\rightarrow$$
$$-2\ -1\quad 0\quad 1\quad 2\quad 3\quad 4\quad 5\quad 6\quad 7\quad 8$$

✓ **Check Understanding** ③ **a.** Solve and graph $|w + 2| > 5$.
  b. Critical Thinking What are the solutions of $|w + 2| > -5$?

To maintain quality, a manufacturer sets limits for how much an item can vary from its specifications. You can use an absolute value equation to model a quality-control situation.

4 EXAMPLE   Real-World  Problem Solving

Manufacturing The ideal diameter of a piston for one type of car engine is 90.000 mm. The actual diameter can vary from the ideal by at most 0.008 mm. Find the range of acceptable diameters for the piston.

Relate   difference between actual and ideal   is at most   0.008 mm

Define Let d = actual diameter in millimeters of the cylindrical part.

Write $|d - 90.000|$ $\leq$ 0.008 mm

$|d - 90.000| \leq 0.008$			
$-0.008 \leq$	$d - 90.000$	≤ 0.008	**Write a compound inequality.**
$-0.008 + 90.000 \leq d - 90.000 + 90.000 \leq 0.008 + 90.000$			**Add 90.000.**
$89.992 \leq$	d	≤ 90.008	**Simplify.**

The actual diameter must be between 89.992 mm and 90.008 mm, inclusive.

✓ **Check Understanding** ④ The ideal weight of one type of model airplane engine is 33.86 ounces. The actual weight may vary from the ideal by at most 0.05 ounce. Find the range of acceptable weights for this engine.

Real-World  Connection

Careers A quality-control inspector inspects products to maintain quality. For engines produced on an assembly line, an inspector selects engines at random to check quality of materials and manufacturing.

EXERCISES

For more practice, see *Extra Practice*.

Practice and Problem Solving

Ⓐ **Practice by Example**

Example 1
(page 167)

Solve each equation. If there is no solution, write *no solution*.

1. $|b| = 2$ **2.** $4 = |y|$ **3.** $|w| = \frac{1}{2}$

4. $|n| + 2 = 8$ **5.** $7 = |s| + 4$ **6.** $|x| - 10 = -3$

7. $4|d| = 20$ **8.** $-3|m| = -6$ **9.** $|y| + 3 = 3$

10. $12 = -4|k|$ **11.** $2|z| - 5 = 1$ **12.** $16 = 5|p| - 4$

Example 2
(page 168)

Solve each equation. If there is no solution, write *no solution*.

13. $|r - 8| = 5$

14. $|c + 2| = 6$

15. $2 = |g + 1|$

16. $3 = |m + 2|$

17. $|v - 2| = 7$

18. $-3|y - 3| = 9$

19. $2|d + 3| = 8$

20. $-2|7d| = -14$

21. $1.2|5p| = 3.6$

Example 3
(page 169)

22. Complete each statement with *less than* or *greater than*.

    a. For $|x| < 5$, the graph includes all points whose distance is __?__ 5 units from 0.

    b. For $|x| > 5$, the graph includes all points whose distance is __?__ 5 units from 0.

Solve each inequality. Graph your solution.

23. $|k| > 2.5$

24. $|w| < 2$

25. $|x + 3| < 5$

26. $|n + 8| \geq 3$

27. $|y - 2| \leq 1$

28. $|p - 4| \leq 3$

29. $|2c - 5| < 9$

30. $|2y - 3| \geq 7$

31. $|3t + 1| > 8$

32. $|4x + 1| > 11$

33. $|5t - 4| \geq 16$

34. $|3 - r| < 5$

Example 4
(page 169)

35. Manufacturing The ideal diameter of a gear for a certain type of clock is 12.24 mm. An actual diameter can vary by 0.06 mm. Find the range of acceptable diameters.

36. Manufacturing The ideal width of a certain conveyor belt for a manufacturing plant is 50 in. An actual conveyor belt can vary from the ideal by at most $\frac{7}{32}$ in. Find the acceptable widths for this conveyor belt.

B **Apply Your Skills**

Solve each equation or inequality.

37. $|2d| + 3 = 21$

38. $|-3n| - 2 = 7$

39. $|p| - \frac{2}{3} = \frac{5}{6}$

40. $|t| + 2.7 = 4.5$

41. $4|k + 1| = 16$

42. $-2|c - 4| = -8$

43. $|3d| \geq 6$

44. $|n| - 3 > 7$

45. $9 < |c + 7|$

46. $\frac{|v|}{-3} = -4.2$

47. $|6.5x| < 39$

48. $4|n| = 32$

49. $\left|\frac{1}{2}a\right| + 1 = 5$

50. $|a| + \frac{1}{2} = 3\frac{1}{2}$

51. $4 - 3|m + 2| > -14$

Write an absolute value inequality that represents each situation.

52. all numbers less than 3 units from 0

53. all numbers greater than 7.5 units from 0

54. all numbers more than 2 units from 6

55. all numbers at least 3 units from –1

56. Manufacturing A pasta manufacturer makes 16-ounce boxes of macaroni. The manufacturer knows that not every box weighs exactly 16 ounces. The allowable difference is 0.05 ounce. Write and solve an absolute value inequality that represents this situation.

57. Elections In a poll for the upcoming mayoral election, 42% of likely voters said they planned to vote for Lucy Jones. This poll has a margin of error of $\pm$ 3 percentage points. Use the inequality $|v - 42| \leq 3$ to find the least and greatest percent of voters v likely to vote for Lucy Jones according to this poll.

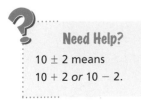

Need Help?

10 ± 2 means

$10 + 2$ *or* $10 - 2$.

58. Quality Control A box of one brand of crackers should weigh 454 g. The quality-control inspector randomly selects boxes to weigh. The inspector sends back any box that is not within 5 g of the ideal weight.
 a. Write an absolute value inequality for this situation.
 b. What is the range of allowable weights for a box of crackers?

59. Gears Acceptable diameters for one type of gear are from 6.25 mm to 6.29 mm. Write an absolute value inequality for the acceptable diameters for the gear.

60. Writing Explain why the absolute value inequality $|2c - 5| + 9 < 4$ has no solution.

61. Open-Ended Write an absolute value equation using the numbers $5, 3, -12$. Then solve your equation.

Write an absolute value equation that has the given values as solutions.

Sample $8, 2$

$|x - 5| = 3$ Since 8 and 2 are both 3 units from 5, write $|x - 5| = 3$.

62. $2, 6$	**63.** $-2, 6$	**64.** $-3, 9$	**65.** $9, 16$
66. $-1, 7$	**67.** $3, 8$	**68.** $-15, -3$	**69.** $2, 10$

70. Banking The ideal weight of a nickel is 0.176 ounce. To check that there are 40 nickels in a roll, a bank weighs the roll and allows for an error of 0.015 ounce in the total weight.
 a. What is the range of acceptable weights if the wrapper weighs 0.05 ounce?
 b. Critical Thinking For any given roll of nickels, can you be certain that all the coins are acceptable? Explain.

71. a. Meteorology A meteorologist reported that the previous day's temperatures varied 14 degrees from the normal temperature of 25°F. What were the maximum and minimum temperatures possible on the previous day?
 b. Write an absolute value equation for the temperature.

Challenge

Solve each equation. Check your solution.

72. $|x + 4| = 3x$ **73.** $|4x - 5| = 2x + 1$ **74.** $\frac{4}{3}|2x + 3| = 4x$

Replace the ■ with ≤, ≥, or =.

75. $|a + b|$ ■ $|a| + |b|$ **76.** $|a - b|$ ■ $|a| - |b|$

77. $|ab|$ ■ $|a| \cdot |b|$ **78.** $\left|\frac{a}{b}\right|$ ■ $\frac{|a|}{|b|}, b \neq 0$

Write an absolute value inequality that each graph could represent.

79. ◄—+—⊕—+—+—+—⊕—+—+—►
      -6 -4 -2 0 2 4 6

80. ◄—+—+—+—●—+—+—+—●—►
      -6 -4 -2 0 2 4 6

Multiple Choice

81. Which compound inequality has the same meaning as $|x + 4| < 8$?
  A. $-12 < x < 4$ **B.** $-12 > x > 4$
  C. $x < -12$ or $x > 4$ **D.** $x > -12$ or $x < 4$

82. Which of the following values is a solution of $|2 - x| < 4$?
  F. -2 **G.** -1 **H.** 6   **I.** 7

83. The ideal diameter of a metal rod for a lamp is 1.25 inches with an allowable error of at most 0.005 inch. Which rod below would not be suitable?
  A. a rod with diameter 1.249 inches
  B. a rod with diameter 1.251 inches
  C. a rod with diameter 1.253 inches
  D. a rod with diameter 1.355 inches

84. A delivery driver receives a bonus if he delivers pizza to a customer in 30 minutes plus or minus 5 minutes. Which inequality or equation represents the driver's allotted time to receive a bonus?

  F. $|x - 30| < 5$ **G.** $|x - 30| > 5$

  H. $|x - 30| = 5$ **I.** $|x - 30| \leq 5$

85. Water is in a liquid state if its temperature t, in degrees Fahrenheit, satisfies the inequality $|t - 122| < 90$. Which graph represents the temperatures described by this inequality?

86. A bicycling club is planning a trip. The graphs below show the number of miles three people want to cycle per day.

Take It to the NET
Online lesson quiz at
www.PHSchool.com
Web Code: aea-0306

  a. Draw a graph showing a trip length that would be acceptable to all three bikers.
  b. Explain how your graph relates to the graphs above.

Mixed Review

Lesson 3-5

Write a compound inequality to model each situation.

87. Elevation in North America is between the highest elevation of 20,320 ft above sea level at Mount McKinley, Alaska, and the lowest elevation of 282 ft below sea level at Death Valley, California.

88. Normal body temperature t is within 0.6 degrees of 36.6°C.

Lesson 2-3

Solve each equation.

89. $3t + 4t = -21$ **90.** $9(-2n + 3) = -27$ **91.** $k + 5 - 4k = -10$

92. $5x + 3 - 2x = -21$ **93.** $5.4m - 2.3 = -0.5$ **94.** $3(y - 4) = 9$

Lesson 1-3

Write each group of numbers from least to greatest.

95. $3, -2, 0, -2.5, \pi$ **96.** $\frac{15}{2}, -1.5, -\frac{4}{3}, 7, -2$

97. $0.001, 0.01, 0.009, 0.011$ **98.** $-\pi, 2\pi, -2.5, -3, 3$

Algebraic Reasoning

You can use the properties you have studied along with the four properties below to prove algebraic relationships.

Reflexive, Symmetric, and Transitive Properties of Equality

For every real number a, b, and c:

Reflexive Property: $\quad a = a$ **Example:** $5x = 5x$

Symmetric Property: If $a = b$, then $b = a$.   **Example:** If $15 = 3t$, then $3t = 15$.

Transitive Property: If $a = b$ and $b = c$,   **Example:** If $d = 3y$ and $3y = 6$, then $a = c$.   then $d = 6$.

Transitive Property of Inequality

For all real numbers a, b, and c,   **Example:** If $8x < 7$ and $7 < y^2$, then if $a < b$ and $b < c$, then $a < c$. $8x < y^2$.

EXAMPLE

Prove each statement for all real numbers a, b, and c.

a. If $a = b$, then $ac = bc$.

$a = b$	Given
$ac = ac$	Reflexive Property
$ac = bc$	Substitute b for a.

b. If $c < 0$ and $a < b$, then $c < b - a$.

$c < 0$	Given
$a < b$	Given
$a - a < b - a$	Subtraction Property of Inequality
$a + (-a) < b - a$	Definition of subtraction
$0 < b - a$	Inverse Property of Addition
$c < b - a$	Transitive Property of Inequality

EXERCISES

Name the property that each exercise illustrates.

1. If $3.8 = z$, then $z = 3.8$.   **2.** If $x = \frac{1}{2}y$ and $\frac{1}{2}y = -2$, then $x = -2$.   **3.** $-r = -r$

4. If $k < m^2$ and $m^2 < 4$, then $k < 4$.   **5.** If $x = w^2$, then $w^2 = x$.

Supply the missing reasons to prove each statement.

6. $(a + b) + (-a) = b$

$(a + b) + (-a) = (b + a) + (-a)$	?
$= b + [a + (-a)]$	?
$= b + 0$	?
$= b$	?
$(a + b) + (-a) = b$	?

7. If $a < b$ and $c < d$, then $a + c < b + d$.

$a < b$	Given
$a + c < b + c$	?
$c < d$	Given
$b + c < b + d$	?
$a + c < b + d$	?

Writing Extended Responses

An extended-response question is usually worth a maximum of 4 points in this textbook. It sometimes has multiple parts. To get full credit, you need to answer each part and show all your work or justify your reasoning.

EXAMPLE

The Theatre Club needs to raise at least $440 to cover the cost of its children's play. The ticket prices are $14 for an adult and $2 for a child. The club expects that three times as many children as adults will attend the play. Write and solve an inequality to find how many adults and children have to buy tickets in order for the club to cover its costs.

Three responses are below with the points each received.

4 points	3 points	1 point
x = number of adults $3x$ = number of children $14(x) + 2(3x) \geq 440$ $14x + 6x \geq 440$ $20x \geq 440$ $x \geq 22$ $3x \geq 66$ At least 22 adults and 66 children must attend the play.	x = number of adults $14(x) + 2(3x) \geq 440$ $14x + 5x \geq 440$ $19x \geq 440$ $x \geq 23.2$ At least 24 adults and $3(24) = 72$ children must attend the play.	x = number of adults $x + 3x \geq 440$ $4x \geq 440$ $x \geq 110$

The 4-point response shows the work and gives a written answer to the problem. Note that it begins by identifying the variable before writing the inequality.

The 3-point response contains a computational error, but the student completed both parts.

The 1-point response shows an incorrect inequality, and it does not give the number of children who must attend to cover costs.

EXERCISES

Use the Example above to answer each question.

1. Read the 3-point response. What error did the student make?

2. Write a 2-point response that begins by defining variables.

3. **Error Analysis** Why is the inequality in the 1-point response incorrect?

Chapter Review

Vocabulary

compound inequalities (p. 161)　　　equivalent inequalities (p. 140)　　　solution of an inequality (p. 134)

Reading Math
Understanding
Vocabulary

Write the letter of the choice that correctly completes each sentence.

1. A solution of an inequality is any number that makes the inequality __?__.
   A. complete　　　　　　　　　　　　B. reverse direction
   C. true　　　　　　　　　　　　　　D. false

2. An inequality is equivalent to another inequality if the two inequalities have __?__.
   A. the same number of terms　　　　B. the same graphs
   C. real-number solutions　　　　　　D. no solutions

Take It to the NET
Online vocabulary quiz
at www.PHSchool.com
Web Code: aej-0351

3. Compound inequalities are joined by __?__.
   A. either the word *and* or the word *or*　　B. the word *or*
   C. the word *and*　　　　　　　　　　　　　D. equations

4. Write the expression "absolute value of *x*" as __?__.
   A. $[x]$　　　　　　B. $-x$　　　　　　C. $|x|$　　　　　　D. $a = x$

5. A number's distance from 0 on a number line is the number's __?__.
   A. solution of an inequality　　　　B. compound form
   C. equivalent form　　　　　　　　D. absolute value

Skills and Concepts

3-1 Objectives

▼ To identify solutions of inequalities (p. 134)

▼ To graph and write inequalities (p. 135)

A **solution of an inequality** is any number that makes the inequality true. A graph can indicate all the solutions of an inequality. On the graph, a closed dot indicates that the number is a solution. An open dot indicates that the number is *not* a solution.

Graph each inequality.

　　6. $x > 3$　　　　　　**7.** $m \le -5$　　　　　　**8.** $10 \ge p$　　　　　　**9.** $r < 2.5$

Write an inequality for each graph.

10.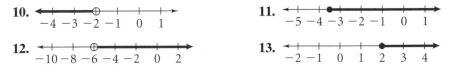

11.

12.

13.

Define a variable and write an inequality to model each situation.

14. At least 600 people attended a school play.

15. An elevator can carry at most 15 people.

16. The temperature was less than 32°F.

3-2 and 3-3 Objectives

▼ To use addition to solve inequalities (p. 140)

▼ To use subtraction to solve inequalities (p. 141)

▼ To use multiplication to solve inequalities (p. 146)

▼ To use division to solve inequalities (p. 148)

To solve inequalities, you may need to find a simpler, equivalent inequality. **Equivalent inequalities** have the same solution. You can add, subtract, multiply, or divide both sides of an inequality by the same number to find a simpler equivalent inequality. Multiplying or dividing by a negative number causes the direction of the inequality symbol to be *reversed*.

Properties of Inequality

For all real numbers a, b, and c:

- If $a > b$, then $a + c > b + c$ and $a - c > b - c$.
- If $a < b$, then $a + c < b + c$ and $a - c < b - c$.
- If $a > b$ and $c > 0$, then $ac > bc$ and $\frac{a}{c} > \frac{b}{c}$.
- If $a < b$ and $c > 0$, then $ac < bc$ and $\frac{a}{c} < \frac{b}{c}$.
- If $a > b$ and $c < 0$, then $ac < bc$ and $\frac{a}{c} < \frac{b}{c}$.
- If $a < b$ and $c < 0$, then $ac > bc$ and $\frac{a}{c} > \frac{b}{c}$.

These properties are also true for inequalities involving $\leq$ and $\geq$.

Solve each inequality. Graph and check the solution.

17. $h + 3 > 2$ **18.** $t - 4 < -9$ **19.** $8m \geq -24$ **20.** $-6w \leq 12$

21. $q + 0.5 > -2$ **22.** $y - 8 > -22$ **23.** $-\frac{3}{5}n \geq -9$ **24.** $\frac{5}{8}d \geq \frac{5}{2}$

25. $0 \leq 2 + t$ **26.** $0 < 4c$ **27.** $-0.3 \geq u - 2.8$ **28.** $3 > -\frac{1}{3}p$

29. Weekly Budget You have an allowance of $12.00. You buy a discount movie ticket that costs at least $3.50 and popcorn that costs $2.75. Write and solve an inequality to find how much you have for other spending.

30. Jobs Suppose you earn $7.25 per hour working part-time as a florist. Write and solve an inequality to find how many full hours you must work to earn at least $200.

3-4 Objectives

▼ To solve multi-step inequalities with variables on one side (p. 153)

▼ To solve multi-step inequalities with variables on both sides (p. 155)

When you solve equations, sometimes you need to use more than one step. The same is true for inequalities. Many inequalities have variables on both sides of the inequality symbol. You need to gather the variable terms on one side of the inequality and the constant terms on the other side.

Solve each inequality. Check your solution.

31. $3n + 5 > -1$ **32.** $4k - 1 \leq -3$ **33.** $\frac{5}{8}b < 25$

34. $6(c - 1) \leq -18$ **35.** $3m > 5m + 12$ **36.** $t - 4t < -9$

37. $0.5x - 2 \geq -4x + 7$ **38.** $-\frac{6}{7}y - 6 \geq 42$ **39.** $4 + \frac{x}{2} > 2x$

40. Commission Trenton sells electronic supplies. Each week he earns $190 plus a commission equal to 4% of his sales. This week his goal is to earn no less than $500. Write and solve an inequality to find the amount of sales he must have to reach his goal.

3-5 Objectives

▼ To solve and graph inequalities containing *and* (p. 161)

▼ To solve and graph inequalities containing *or* (p. 163)

Two inequalities that are joined by the word *and* or the word *or* are called **compound inequalities.** A solution of a compound inequality joined by *and* makes both inequalities true. A solution of a compound inequality joined by *or* makes either inequality true. A number sentence with two inequality symbols, such as $a < x < b$ represents the compound inequality $a < x$ and $x < b$.

Graph each compound inequality.

41. $x > -3$ and $x < 2$

42. $m < -2$ or $m \geq 1$

43. $-3 \leq k < 4$

Solve each compound inequality and graph the solutions.

44. $-3 \leq z - 1 < 3$

45. $-2 \leq d + \frac{1}{2} < 4\frac{1}{2}$

46. $0 < -8b \leq 12$

47. $2t \leq -4$ or $7t \geq 49$

48. $-1 \leq a - 3 < 2$

49. $-2 \leq 3a - 8 < 4$

50. Climate In Miami, Florida, July's average high temperature is 89°F. July's average low temperature is 75°F. Write a compound inequality to represent Miami's average temperature in July.

3-6 Objectives

▼ To solve equations that involve absolute value (p. 167)

▼ To solve inequalities that involve absolute value (p. 168)

Recall that the absolute value of a number is its distance from 0 on a number line. Since absolute value represents distance, it can never be negative.

Solving Absolute Value Equations and Inequalities

- To solve an equation in the form $|A| = b$, where A represents a variable expression and $b > 0$, solve the equations $A = b$ or $A = -b$.
- To solve an inequality in the form $|A| < b$, where A represents a variable expression and $b > 0$, solve $-b < A < b$.
- To solve an inequality in the form $|A| > b$, where A represents a variable expression and $b > 0$, solve $A < -b$ or $A > b$.

Similar rules are true for $|A| \leq b$ and $|A| \geq b$.

Write an absolute value inequality that represents each set of numbers.

51. all numbers n that are more than 3 units from -2

52. all numbers n that are within 5 units of 12

Solve each equation or inequality.

53. $|y| = 5$

54. $|n + 2| \geq 4$

55. $|-5x| \leq 15$

56. $\left|\frac{1}{2}m\right| < 4.8$

57. $|2x - 7| - 1 > 0$

58. $|p + 3| = 9.5$

59. $|k - 8| = 0$

60. $|3x + 5| > -2$

61. $|6 - b| = -1$

62. $4|k + 5| > 8$

63. $4 + |r + 2| = 7$

64. $-2 + |3.6z| \geq -1.1$

65. Manufacturing The ideal diameter of a steel reinforcement rod is 2.8 cm. The actual diameter may vary from the ideal by at most 0.06 cm. Find the range of acceptable diameters for this steel rod.

66. Manufacturing The ideal length of a certain nail is 20 mm. The actual length can vary from the ideal by at most 0.4 mm. Find the range of acceptable lengths of the nail.

Chapter Test

Take It to the NET
Online chapter test at
www.PHSchool.com
Web Code: aea-0352

Determine whether each number is a solution of the given inequality.

1. $4z + 7 \geq 15$ **a.** -2 **b.** 2 **c.** 5

2. $-2g + 3 > 5$ **a.** -3 **b.** -1 **c.** 4

Define a variable and write an inequality to model each situation.

3. A student can take at most 7 classes.

4. The school track team needs at least 5 runners to compete at Saturday's meet.

5. Elephants can drink up to 40 gallons of water at a time.

6. Your cousin's early-morning paper route has more than 32 homes.

Write an inequality for each graph.

7.
8.
9.
10.

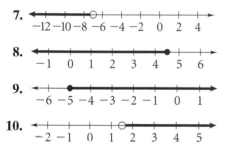

Solve each inequality. Graph the solution.

11. $z + 7 \leq 9$ **12.** $-16 \geq 4y$

13. $-\frac{1}{3}x < 2$ **14.** $8 - u > 4$

15. $-5 + 4t \leq 3$ **16.** $5w \geq -6w + 11$

17. $-\frac{7}{2}m < 14$ **18.** $6y - 7 < -2y + 13$

19. $|x - 5| \geq 3$ **20.** $|2h + 1| < 5$

21. $9 \leq 6 - b < 12$ **22.** $-10 < 4q < 12$

23. $4 + 3n \geq 1$ or $-5n > 25$

24. $10k < 75$ and $4 - k \leq 0$

Solve each inequality. Check your solution.

25. $3(d - 1) > -4$ **26.** $5(-2 + b) < 3b + 2$

27. $3(m + 3) + 4 \leq 15$ **28.** $0.5(x + 3) - 2.1 \geq -1$

Write a compound inequality that each graph could represent.

29.
30.

Solve each equation. Check your solution.

31. $|4k - 2| = 11$ **32.** $23 = |n + 10|$

33. $|3c + 1| - 4 = 13$ **34.** $4|5 - t| = 20$

35. Writing Explain why the solution to $ax - 1 < 3$ is not $x < \frac{4}{a}$. Use solutions of the inequality with different values of a to support your explanation.

36. Open-Ended Write an absolute value inequality that has 3 and -5 as two of its solutions.

37. Community Service The chart below shows the number of cans of food collected by a club during the first four weeks of a food drive.

Food Drive

Week	Number of Cans
1	702
2	470
3	492
4	547

The goal is to collect at least 3000 cans in 5 weeks. Write and solve an inequality to find how many cans should be collected during Week 5 to meet or exceed the goal.

38. Safe Load A freight elevator can safely hold no more than 2000 pounds. An elevator operator must take 55-pound boxes to a storage area. If he weighs 165 pounds, how many boxes can he safely move at one time?

39. Manufacturing A manufacturer is cutting plastic sheets to make rectangles that are 11.125 in. by 7.625 in. Each rectangle's length and width must be within 0.005 in. of the desired size. Write and solve inequalities to find the acceptable range for the length ℓ and for the width w.

Standardized Test Prep

Reading Comprehension Read the passage below. Then answer the questions on the basis of what is *stated* or *implied* in the passage.

Geometry of Earth Long before Columbus, a Greek scholar named Eratosthenes (274–194 B.C.) calculated the circumference of Earth by making some simple observations about shadows at noon and applying some insights from geometry.

The size of Earth has been estimated and measured many times since then. The French Academy of Sciences tried to make an accurate measurement in the late 1700s in order to create a new unit of measure, the meter. They proposed to define the meter as one ten-millionth of the distance from the North Pole to the equator.

Today we can measure Earth's circumference very accurately using data from satellites and making calculations on computers. The circumference at the equator is 24,901.55 miles. Earth is not a perfect sphere, however, because its rotation causes it to bulge a little at the equator. So the circumference from pole to pole is a bit smaller, about 24,859.82 miles.

---

1. How many centuries before the French Academy of Sciences measured the circumference of Earth did Eratosthenes live?
   A. 22 centuries   B. 20 centuries
   C. 18 centuries   D. 16 centuries

2. How much greater is the circumference of Earth at the equator than the circumference at the poles?
   F. about 20 miles
   G. about 40 miles
   H. about 80 miles
   I. about 200 miles

3. Earth is divided into 24 time zones. About how wide is each time zone at the equator?
   A. 1031 miles
   B. 1036 miles
   C. 1038 miles
   D. 1042 miles

4. Which is the best estimate of the diameter of Earth measured from pole to pole?
   F. 3960 miles
   G. 4530 miles
   H. 6300 miles
   I. 7920 miles

5. A geostationary satellite moves in an orbit 22,300 miles above the equator. The satellite moves at a rate such that it stays at the same point above Earth as Earth rotates on its axis. What is the approximate speed of the satellite?
   A. 700 miles per hour
   B. 7000 miles per hour
   C. 10,000 miles per hour
   D. 14,000 miles per hour

6. a. One mile is equal to about 1610 meters. Write an equation expressing this relationship. Use the equation to calculate the approximate circumference of Earth from pole to pole in meters.
   b. Is the meter unit of measure you found close to the Academy of Sciences' original definition? Explain.

7. a. As Earth rotates, the line separating night from day moves west across Earth's surface. How fast is this line moving in miles per minute at the equator? Show your work.
   b. Does the day-night dividing line move more quickly or more slowly across your state than it does at the equator? Explain.

Where You've Been

- In Chapter 1 you used the distributive property to simplify variable expressions.

- In Chapter 2 you used the properties of equality to solve equations.

- In Chapter 3 you built on this knowledge to solve inequalities and absolute value equations.

Diagnosing Readiness

(For help, go to the Lesson in green.)

Multiplying and Dividing Fractions (Skills Handbook page 727)

Multiply or divide. Write your answers in simplest form.

1. $\frac{2}{3} \cdot \frac{3}{5}$ **2.** $4\frac{1}{2} \cdot \frac{1}{8}$ **3.** $2\frac{2}{5} \div \frac{3}{4}$ **4.** $8 \div \frac{8}{3}$

Fractions, Decimals, and Percents (Skills Handbook page 728)

Write each number as a percent.

5. 0.75   **6.** $\frac{5}{8}$ **7.** 12.5   **8.** 0.002   **9.** $\frac{105}{150}$

Writing Expressions (Lessons 1-1 and 1-2)

Write an expression for each phrase.

10. a number n less 22

11. A number p increased by 40

12. 20 times a number m

13. 17 more than a number z

Using the Distributive Property (Lesson 1-7)

Simplify each expression.

14. $3(2 - n)$ **15.** $0.4(t + 5)$ **16.** $-8(x - 1)$

17. $25(a + 8)$ **18.** $-2.5(4 - c)$ **19.** $-(b + 12)$

Solving One-Step Equations (Lesson 2-1)

Solve each equation. Check your solution.

20. $\frac{t}{3} = 8$ **21.** $\frac{2}{5}w = -4$ **22.** $7x = \frac{42}{5}$ **23.** $\frac{4}{9}y = \frac{13}{3}$

24. $-2k = \frac{5}{2}$ **25.** $20y = -2$ **26.** $\frac{w}{2} = \frac{1}{3}$ **27.** $\frac{11}{3}x = 5$

Solving and Applying Proportions

Key Vocabulary

Where You're Going

- In this chapter, you will find ratios and rates to model real-world situations.

- You will use proportions to measure objects indirectly.

- You will solve problems that involve discounts, taxes, and interest.

 Real-World Snapshots Applying what you learn, you will use ratios and probability to do activities related to baseball, on pages 232–233.

Ratio and Proportion

Lesson Preview

What You'll Learn

OBJECTIVE 1 To find ratios and rates

OBJECTIVE 2 To solve proportions

... And Why

To use proportions for finding time, as in Example 5

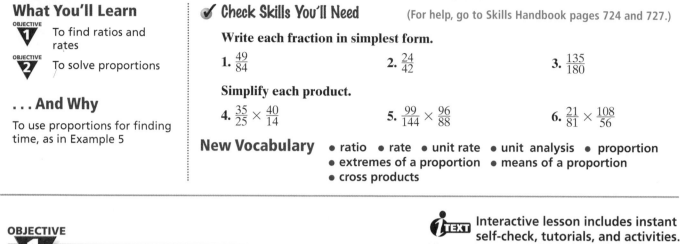

✓ Check Skills You'll Need
(For help, go to Skills Handbook pages 724 and 727.)

Write each fraction in simplest form.

1. $\frac{49}{84}$ **2.** $\frac{24}{42}$ **3.** $\frac{135}{180}$

Simplify each product.

4. $\frac{35}{25} \times \frac{40}{14}$ **5.** $\frac{99}{144} \times \frac{96}{88}$ **6.** $\frac{21}{81} \times \frac{108}{56}$

New Vocabulary
- ratio • rate • unit rate • unit analysis • proportion
- extremes of a proportion • means of a proportion
- cross products

OBJECTIVE 1

Ratios and Rates

iTEXT Interactive lesson includes instant self-check, tutorials, and activities.

A **ratio** is a comparison of two numbers by division. The ratio of a to b is $a:b$ or $\frac{a}{b}$, where $b \neq 0$. If a and b represent quantities measured in different units, then the ratio of a to b is a **rate**. A **unit rate** is a rate with a denominator of 1. An example of a unit rate is $\frac{40\ miles}{1\ hour}$. You can write this rate as 40 miles per hour or 40 mi/h.

Price of Apple Juice

Price	Volume
$ .72	16 oz
$1.20	32 oz
$1.60	64 oz

1 EXAMPLE Using Unit Rates

Comparison Shopping The table at the left gives prices for different sizes of the same brand of apple juice. Find the unit rate (cost per ounce) for the 16-oz size.

$$\text{cost} \longrightarrow \frac{\$.72}{16\ oz} = \$.045/oz \quad \textbf{Divide the numerator and denominator by 16.}$$

The unit rate is 4.5¢/oz.

✓ Check Understanding

1 **a.** Find the unit rates for the other two sizes.

b. Which of the three sizes has the lowest cost per ounce?

To change one unit of measure to another, you can use rates that equal 1. Since 60 min = 1 h, both $\frac{60\ min}{1\ h}$ and $\frac{1\ h}{60\ min}$ equal 1. You can use $\frac{60\ min}{1\ h}$ as a *conversion factor* to change hours into minutes. For example,

$$7\ h = \frac{7\ \cancel{h}}{1} \cdot \frac{60\ min}{1\ \cancel{h}} = 420\ min \quad \textbf{Divide the common unit, which is hours (h). The result is minutes.}$$

When converting from one unit to another, as in hours to minutes or minutes to hours, you must decide which conversion factor will produce the appropriate unit. This process is called **unit analysis,** or *dimensional analysis*.

2 EXAMPLE Converting Rates

Speed of Cheetah A cheetah ran 300 feet in 2.92 seconds. What was the cheetah's speed in miles per hour?

You need to convert feet to miles and seconds to hours.

$$\frac{300 \text{ ft}}{2.92 \text{ s}} \cdot \frac{1 \text{ mi}}{5280 \text{ ft}} \cdot \frac{60 \text{ s}}{1 \text{ min}} \cdot \frac{60 \text{ min}}{1 \text{ h}}$$ Use appropriate conversion factors.

$$= \frac{300 \text{ ft}}{2.92 \text{ s}} \cdot \frac{1 \text{ mi}}{5280 \text{ ft}} \cdot \frac{60 \text{ s}}{1 \text{ min}} \cdot \frac{60 \text{ min}}{1 \text{ h}}$$ Divide the common units.

$$\approx 70 \text{ mi/h}$$ Simplify.

The cheetah's speed was about 70 mi/h.

✔ **Check Understanding** **2** A sloth travels 0.15 miles per hour. Convert this speed to feet per minute.

OBJECTIVE

2 Solving Proportions

A **proportion** is an equation that states that two ratios are equal.

$$\frac{a}{b} = \frac{c}{d} \quad \text{for } b \neq 0 \text{ and } d \neq 0$$

You read this proportion as "a is to b as c is to d." For this proportion a and d are the **extremes of the proportion,** and b and c are the **means of the proportion.** Another way you may see this proportion written is $a : b = c : d$.

You can use the Multiplication Property of Equality to solve a proportion for a variable.

3 EXAMPLE Using the Multiplication Property of Equality

Solve $\frac{t}{9} = \frac{5}{6}$.

$$\frac{t}{9} \cdot 18 = \frac{5}{6} \cdot 18$$ Multiply each side by the least common multiple of 9 and 6, which is 18.

$$2t = 15$$ Simplify.

$$\frac{2t}{2} = \frac{15}{2}$$ Divide each side by 2.

$$t = 7.5$$ Simplify.

✔ **Check Understanding** **3** Solve each proportion.

a. $\frac{x}{8} = \frac{5}{6}$ **b.** $\frac{y}{12} = \frac{4}{7}$ **c.** $\frac{18}{50} = \frac{m}{15}$

You can use the Multiplication Property of Equality to prove an important property of proportions.

$$\text{If } \frac{a}{b} = \frac{c}{d},$$

$$\text{then } \frac{a}{b} \cdot bd = \frac{c}{d} \cdot bd$$ Multiplication Property of Equality

$$\frac{ab^1d}{1b} = \frac{cbd^1}{1d}$$ Divide the common factors.

$$\text{and } ad = cb$$ Simplify.

$$\text{or } ad = bc$$ Commutative Property of Multiplication

The products ad and bc are the **cross products** of the proportion $\frac{a}{b} = \frac{c}{d}$.

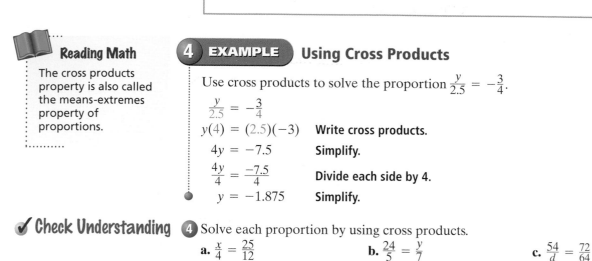

Property	Cross Products of a Proportion

If $\frac{a}{b} = \frac{c}{d}$, then $ad = bc$.

Example $\frac{2}{3} = \frac{8}{12}$, so $2 \cdot 12 = 3 \cdot 8$.

Reading Math

The cross products property is also called the means-extremes property of proportions.

4 EXAMPLE Using Cross Products

Use cross products to solve the proportion $\frac{y}{2.5} = -\frac{3}{4}$.

$\frac{y}{2.5} = -\frac{3}{4}$

$y(4) = (2.5)(-3)$ **Write cross products.**

$4y = -7.5$ **Simplify.**

$\frac{4y}{4} = \frac{-7.5}{4}$ **Divide each side by 4.**

$y = -1.875$ **Simplify.**

✓ Check Understanding **4** Solve each proportion by using cross products.

a. $\frac{x}{4} = \frac{25}{12}$ **b.** $\frac{24}{5} = \frac{y}{7}$ **c.** $\frac{54}{d} = \frac{72}{64}$

You can use proportions to solve real-world problems. To write a correct proportion, form rates on each side that compare units in the same way such as $\frac{\text{kilometers}}{\text{hour}} = \frac{\text{kilometers}}{\text{hour}}$.

5 EXAMPLE Real-World 🌐 Problem Solving

Cycling In 2001, Lance Armstrong won the Tour de France, completing the 3454-km course in about 86.3 hours. Traveling at his average speed, how long would it take him to ride 185 km? Round the answer to the nearest tenth.

Define Let t = time needed to ride 185 km.

Relate | Tour de France average speed | equals | 185-km trip average speed |

Write $\begin{array}{c} \text{kilometers} \rightarrow \\ \text{hours} \longrightarrow \end{array}$ $\frac{3454}{86.3}$ $=$ $\frac{185}{t}$ $\begin{array}{l} \leftarrow \text{kilometers} \\ \longleftarrow \text{hours} \end{array}$

$\frac{3454}{86.3} = \frac{185}{t}$

$3454t = 86.3(185)$ **Write cross products.**

$t = \frac{(86.3)(185)}{(3454)}$ **Divide each side by 3454.**

$t \approx 4.6$ **Simplify. Round to the nearest tenth.**

Traveling at his average speed, it would take Lance approximately 4.6 hours to cycle 185 km.

Real-World 🌐 Connection

Lance Armstrong has won the 21-day Tour de France several times.

✓ Check Understanding **5** Suppose you walk 2 miles in 35 minutes.
   a. Write a proportion to find how far you would walk in an hour if you were to continue at the same rate.
   b. Solve the proportion.

In Example 6, the ratios that form the proportion have variable expressions with more than one term. To solve for the variable, you will use cross products and the Distributive Property.

6 EXAMPLE **Solving Multi-Step Proportions**

Solve the proportion $\frac{x + 4}{5} = \frac{x - 2}{7}$

$$\frac{x + 4}{5} = \frac{x - 2}{7}$$

$(x + 4)(7) = 5(x - 2)$ Write cross products.

$7x + 28 = 5x - 10$ Use the Distributive Property.

$2x + 28 = -10$ Subtract 5x from each side.

$2x = -38$ Subtract 28 from each side.

$x = -19$ Divide each side by 2.

✓ **Check Understanding** **6** Solve each proportion.

a. $\frac{x + 2}{14} = \frac{x}{10}$

b. $\frac{y - 15}{y + 4} = \frac{35}{7}$

c. $\frac{3}{w + 6} = \frac{5}{w - 4}$

d. $\frac{d - 7}{4} = \frac{2d + 1}{3}$

EXERCISES

For more practice, see *Extra Practice*.

Practice and Problem Solving

A **Practice by Example**

Example 1
(page 182)

Find each unit rate.

1. $57 for 6 hours

2. $\frac{\$2}{5 \text{ lb}}$

3. $\frac{524 \text{ cars}}{4 \text{ weeks}}$

4. $\frac{600 \text{ calories}}{1.5 \text{ h}}$

5. A 10-ounce bottle of shampoo costs $2.40. What is the cost per ounce?

6. A 12-ounce bottle of juice costs $1.08. What is the cost per ounce?

Example 2
(page 183)

Choose A or B for the correct conversion factor for each situation.

7. quarts to gallons

   A. $\frac{1 \text{ gal}}{4 \text{ qt}}$ **B.** $\frac{4 \text{ qt}}{1 \text{ gal}}$

8. ounces to pounds

   A. $\frac{1 \text{ lb}}{16 \text{ oz}}$ **B.** $\frac{16 \text{ oz}}{1 \text{ lb}}$

9. inches to yards

   A. $\frac{36 \text{ in.}}{1 \text{ yd}}$ **B.** $\frac{1 \text{ yd}}{36 \text{ in.}}$

10. miles to feet

   A. $\frac{5280 \text{ ft}}{1 \text{ mi}}$ **B.** $\frac{1 \text{ mi}}{5280 \text{ ft}}$

Complete each statement.

11. 8 h = ■ min

12. 120 cm = ■ m

13. 3 h = ■ s

Examples 3, 4
(pages 183, 184)

Solve each proportion.

14. $\frac{5}{6} = \frac{c}{9}$

15. $\frac{3}{8} = \frac{x}{30}$

16. $\frac{2}{8} = \frac{n}{20}$

17. $\frac{7}{5} = \frac{k}{18}$

18. $\frac{3}{4} = \frac{x}{10}$

19. $\frac{4}{6} = \frac{m}{9}$

20. $\frac{8}{d} = -\frac{12}{30}$

21. $\frac{5}{9} = \frac{8}{w}$

22. $\frac{2}{14} = \frac{m}{63}$

23. $-\frac{8}{11} = \frac{12}{v}$

24. $\frac{4}{9} = \frac{b}{15}$

25. $\frac{3}{k} = -\frac{20}{35}$

26. $\frac{q}{42} = \frac{15}{7}$

27. $\frac{6}{8} = \frac{21}{x}$

28. $\frac{7}{n} = \frac{35}{88}$

29. $\frac{20}{18} = \frac{75}{w}$

Example 5
(page 184)

30. A canary's heart beats 200 times in 12 seconds. Use a proportion to find how many times its heart beats in 42 seconds.

31. Suppose you traveled 66 kilometers in 1.25 hours. Moving at the same speed, how many kilometers would you cover in 2 hours?

Example 6
(page 185)

Solve each proportion.

32. $\frac{x + 3}{4} = \frac{7}{8}$

33. $\frac{a - 6}{5} = \frac{7}{12}$

34. $\frac{8}{9} = \frac{w - 2}{6}$

35. $\frac{1}{c + 5} = \frac{2}{3}$

36. $\frac{8}{b + 10} = \frac{4}{2b - 7}$

37. $\frac{k + 5}{10} = \frac{k - 12}{9}$

B Apply Your Skills

Complete each statement.

38. $2/lb = ■ ¢/oz

39. $3/lb = ■ ¢/oz

40. 4¢/day = $ ■/yr

41. 5¢/day = $ ■/yr

42. 5 cm/min = ■ m/week

43. 1 qt/min = ■ gal/week

Express each rate in miles per hour.

44. 1 mi in 3 min

45. 1 mi in 4 min

46. 1 mi in 300 s

47. 10,560 ft in 2 h

48. 21,120 ft in 4 h

49. 270 ft in 10.8 min

50. You are riding your bicycle. It takes you 21 min to go 5 mi. If you continue traveling at the same rate, how long will it take you to go 12 mi?

51. Hair Human hair grows at a rate of about 0.35 mm per day. How much does it grow in 30 days?

52. Record Speed According to the *Guinness Book of World Records*, the peregrine falcon has a record diving speed of 168 miles per hour. Write this speed in feet per second.

Solve each proportion.

53. $\frac{m + 12}{9m} = \frac{5}{9}$

54. $\frac{p}{20} = \frac{p - 4}{5}$

55. $\frac{n + 12}{4} = \frac{n}{16}$

56. $\frac{29}{24} = \frac{b + 24}{b}$

57. $\frac{w}{15} = \frac{w - 9}{12}$

58. $\frac{9}{3t - 6} = \frac{6}{0.2t + 4}$

59. $\frac{n + 2}{25} = \frac{n - 4}{35}$

60. $\frac{q - 11}{q + 13} = \frac{2}{3}$

61. $\frac{18 + d}{14 - d} = \frac{3}{7}$

Data Analysis Below are the survey results of 60 students out of 1250 students in a school. These results are representative of the school population. Use the table for Exercises 62–64.

Question	Number Answering Yes
Do you work on weekends?	31
Do you spend 2 or more hours per night on homework?	36
Do you buy lunch in the school cafeteria?	48

62. Predict the number of students in the school who work on weekends.

63. Predict the number of students in the school who spend 2 or more hours per night on homework.

64. Predict the number of students in the school who buy lunch in the school cafeteria.

Real-World Connection

Enrollment in grades 9 through 12 has risen over 19% since 1990.

Need Help?
5,280 ft = 1 mi

65. Writing Write an explanation telling an absent classmate how to use cross products to solve a proportion. Include an example.

66. Gasoline Cost Your car averages 34 miles per gallon on the highway. If gas costs $1.79 per gallon, how much does it cost in dollars per mile to drive your car on the highway?

67. Demographics Population density is a unit rate describing the number of individuals per unit of area. An example of population density is 5 people per square mile. Use the diagram below. Find the population densities of Mongolia, Bangladesh, and the United States. Round your answers to the nearest integer.

MONGOLIA
Population: 2,651,000
Land area: 604,000 mi^2

UNITED STATES
Population: 275,562,000
Land area: 3,536,000 mi^2

BANGLADESH
Population: 129,194,000
Land area: 52,000 mi^2

68. Open-Ended Estimate your walking rate in feet per second. Write this rate in miles per hour.

69. a. Solve the proportions $\frac{x-1}{x} = \frac{6}{7}$ and $\frac{x-2}{x} = \frac{6}{7}$.

   b. Based on your answers to part (a), predict the answer for $\frac{x-3}{x} = \frac{6}{7}$.

   c. Check your answer for $\frac{x-3}{x} = \frac{6}{7}$.

   d. Critical Thinking For the ratio $\frac{x-a}{x} = \frac{6}{7}$, describe the relationship between a and x.

70. Bonnie and Tim do some yardwork for their neighbor. The ratio comparing the amount of time each one works is $7:4$. The neighbor pays them $88. If Bonnie worked more, how much should each of them receive?

71. Engineering Transformers use coils of wire to increase or decrease voltage. The following proportion relates the number of turns of wire in the coils to the voltages. (*Note:* Each semi-circle in the diagram represents a turn of wire.)

primary coil | secondary coil $\dfrac{\text{primary turns}}{\text{secondary turns}} = \dfrac{\text{primary voltage}}{\text{secondary voltage}}$

Suppose the primary-coil voltage is 120 volts. Use the proportion $\frac{5}{2} = \frac{120}{v}$ to find the secondary-coil voltage.

C Challenge

72. Find y if $\frac{12}{72} = \frac{x}{24}$ and $\frac{x}{36} = \frac{y}{81}$.

Solve each proportion.

73. $\frac{x^2-3}{5x+2} = \frac{x}{5}$

74. $\frac{w^3+7}{w} = \frac{9w^2+7}{9}$

75. $\frac{m^2-8}{3m} = \frac{4m+1}{12}$

76. Sports Long-distance runners usually refer to their speed in terms of pace, a rate measured in minutes per mile rounded to the nearest hundredth.

   a. Naoko Takahashi of Japan won the gold medal in the marathon at the 2000 Olympic games. She set an Olympic record, completing the 26.2-mile race in $2:23:14$ (2 hours, 23 minutes, 14 seconds). Find her pace.

   b. Tegla Loroupe of Kenya set the women's world record at the 1999 Berlin marathon. Her time was $2:20:43$. Find her pace.

Multiple Choice

77. Which ratio is greater than $\frac{3}{4}$?

    A. $\frac{25}{35}$ **B.** $\frac{27}{36}$ **C.** $\frac{18}{25}$ **D.** $\frac{32}{42}$

78. To the nearest tenth of a cent, what is the unit cost of a 28-ounce bottle of dish detergent that is on sale for $2.50?

    F. 8¢/ounce   **G.** 8.9¢/ounce   **H.** 11¢/ounce   **I.** 11.2¢/ounce

79. Trey works in a neighbor's yard from 8:00 A.M. to noon, cutting the lawn and trimming shrubs. After taking an hour off for lunch, he rakes the yard and sweeps the steps and walkways. He finishes at 3:00 P.M. Trey earned $24 for the work he did. Which unit rate indicates his hourly wage?

    A. $12 in 3 hours   **B.** $6/hour

    C. $4/hour   **D.** $3/hour

80. Most mammals breathe about once every 4 heartbeats. A large dog's heart beats about 180 times in one minute. Which unit rate represents the number of times this dog breathes in 1 minute?

    F. $\frac{40 \text{ breaths}}{\text{minute}}$ **G.** $\frac{45 \text{ breaths}}{\text{minute}}$ **H.** $\frac{180 \text{ breaths}}{4 \text{ minutes}}$ **I.** $\frac{720 \text{ breaths}}{\text{minute}}$

Short Response

Take It to the NET
Online lesson quiz at
www.PHSchool.com
Web Code: aea-0401

81. Many trees have concentric rings that can be counted to determine the tree's age. Each ring represents one year's growth. If a maple tree with a diameter of 12 inches has 32 rings, write a proportion to find the number of rings in a maple tree that has a diameter of 20 inches. Estimate the age of a maple tree with a 20-inch diameter. Show your work.

Mixed Review

Lessons 3-5, 3-6

Graph each inequality on a number line. Use positive integers as a replacement set. If there are no solutions, write *no solutions*.

82. $|r| > 1$ **83.** $|t - 9| > 2$

84. $-7 \leq k \leq 3$ **85.** $-3 < 2g + 1 < 7$

86. $e > 7$ or $e < -4$ **87.** $|8(b + 5)| < 16$

Define a variable and write an inequality to model each situation.

88. You are no more than 72 inches tall.

89. At least 235 students attended the school dance.

90. The car can travel up to 344 miles on a full tank of gas.

91. A dog weighs more than 20 pounds.

Graph each inequality from the given word descriptions.

92. g is at least 4   **93.** p is positive   **94.** v is no more than -2

Lesson 2-1

Solve and check each equation.

95. $15x = 90$ **96.** $34 = \frac{t}{4}$ **97.** $-35 = 7h$

98. $4.3 - b = 9.8$ **99.** $-\frac{3}{5}c = 54$ **100.** $v + 7\frac{1}{6} = \frac{2}{3}$

Proportions and Similar Figures

Lesson Preview

What You'll Learn

OBJECTIVE 1 To find missing measures of similar figures

OBJECTIVE 2 To use similar figures when measuring indirectly

. . . And Why

To apply proportions when finding distances represented on maps, as in Example 3

✓ **Check Skills You'll Need** (For help, go to the Skills Handbook and Lesson 4-1.)

Simplify each ratio.

1. $\frac{36}{42}$ 2. $\frac{81}{108}$ 3. $\frac{26}{52}$

Solve each proportion.

4. $\frac{x}{12} = \frac{7}{30}$ 5. $\frac{y}{12} = \frac{8}{45}$ 6. $\frac{w}{15} = \frac{12}{27}$

7. $\frac{9}{a} = \frac{81}{10}$ 8. $\frac{25}{75} = \frac{z}{30}$ 9. $\frac{n}{9} = \frac{n+1}{24}$

New Vocabulary • similar figures • scale drawing • scale

---

iTEXT Interactive lesson includes instant self-check, tutorials, and activities.

OBJECTIVE

1 Similar Figures

Real-World Connection

The triangles in the quilt are the same shape, so they are *similar*.

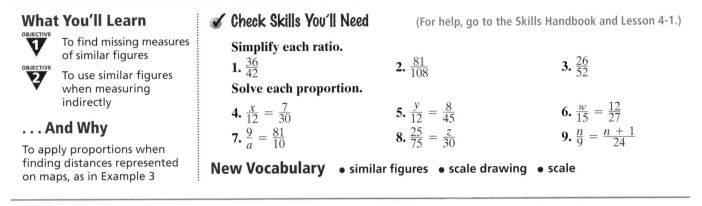

Investigation: Proportions in Triangles

The figure below shows $\triangle ACB$ and $\triangle DCE$.

1. Measure *AB*, *CA*, *CB*, *CD*, *CE*, and *DE* using a metric ruler.

2. Find each ratio.
   a. $\frac{DE}{AB}$ b. $\frac{CE}{CB}$ c. $\frac{CD}{CA}$

3. Tell whether each statement is true.
   a. $\frac{DE}{AB} = \frac{CE}{CB}$ b. $\frac{CD}{CA} = \frac{CE}{CB}$ c. $\frac{AB}{DE} = \frac{CA}{CD}$

4. Using the lengths you have measured, write two ratios that equal $\frac{CB}{CE}$.

In the diagram below, $\triangle ABC$ and $\triangle FGH$ are similar. **Similar figures** have the same shape but not necessarily the same size. The symbol $\sim$ means "is similar to".

In similar triangles, corresponding angles are congruent and corresponding sides are in proportion. The order of the letters indicates the corresponding angles. If $\triangle ABC \sim \triangle FGH$, then the following is true.

Need Help?

Congruent angles have equal measures. The symbol $\cong$ means "is congruent to."

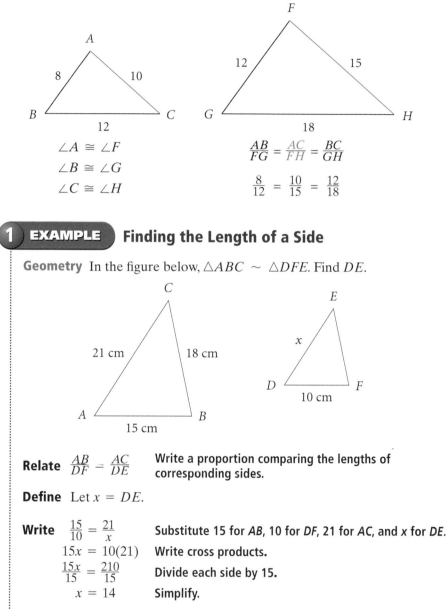

$$\angle A \cong \angle F$$
$$\angle B \cong \angle G$$
$$\angle C \cong \angle H$$

$$\frac{AB}{FG} = \frac{AC}{FH} = \frac{BC}{GH}$$

$$\frac{8}{12} = \frac{10}{15} = \frac{12}{18}$$

1 EXAMPLE Finding the Length of a Side

Geometry In the figure below, $\triangle ABC \sim \triangle DFE$. Find DE.

Relate $\dfrac{AB}{DF} = \dfrac{AC}{DE}$ Write a proportion comparing the lengths of corresponding sides.

Define Let $x = DE$.

Write $\dfrac{15}{10} = \dfrac{21}{x}$ Substitute 15 for *AB*, 10 for *DF*, 21 for *AC*, and *x* for *DE*.

      $15x = 10(21)$ Write cross products.

      $\dfrac{15x}{15} = \dfrac{210}{15}$ Divide each side by 15.

      $x = 14$ Simplify.

● *DE* is 14 cm.

✓ **Check Understanding** ❶ In the figure below, $\triangle FGH \sim \triangle KLM$. Find *LM*.

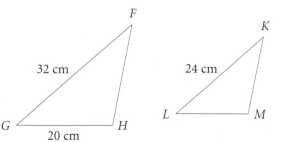

You can use proportions to find the dimensions of objects that are difficult to measure directly.

2 EXAMPLE **Applying Similarity**

Indirect Measurement A tree casts a shadow 7.5 ft long. A woman 5 ft tall casts a shadow 3 ft long. The triangle shown for the tree and its shadow is similar to the triangle shown for the woman and her shadow. How tall is the tree?

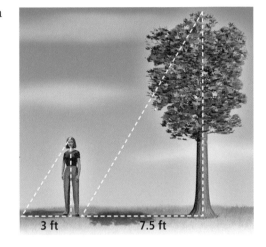
3 ft   7.5 ft

$\dfrac{3}{7.5} = \dfrac{5}{x}$ Corresponding sides of similar figures are in proportion.

$3x = 7.5 \cdot 5$ Write cross products.

$3x = 37.5$ Simplify.

$x = 12.5$ Divide each side by 3.

● The tree is 12.5 ft tall.

✓**Check Understanding** **2** **a.** A tree casts a 26-ft shadow. A boy standing nearby casts a 12-ft shadow. His height is 4.5 ft. How tall is the tree?
   b. A house casts a 56-ft shadow. A girl standing nearby casts a 7.2-ft shadow. Her height is 5.4 ft. What is the height of the house?

A **scale drawing** is an enlarged or reduced drawing that is similar to an actual object or place. Floor plans, blueprints, and maps are all examples of scale drawings. The ratio of a distance in the drawing to the corresponding actual distance is the **scale** of the drawing.

3 EXAMPLE **Finding Distances on Maps**

The scale of the map at the left is 1 inch : 10 miles. Approximately how far is it from Valkaria to Wabasso?

Map distance = 1.75 in.   Measure the map distance.

$\begin{array}{l} \text{map} \rightarrow \\ \text{actual} \rightarrow \end{array} \quad \dfrac{1}{10} = \dfrac{1.75}{d} \quad \begin{array}{l} \leftarrow \text{map} \\ \leftarrow \text{actual} \end{array}$ Write a proportion.

$1 \cdot d = 10 \cdot 1.75$ Write cross products.

$d = 17.5$ Simplify.

● Wabasso is about 17.5 mi from Valkaria.

✓**Check Understanding** **3** **a.** On the map above, measure the map distance from Grant to Gifford. Find the actual distance.
   b. **Critical Thinking** If another map showed the distance from Valkaria to Wabasso but had a scale of 1 inch : 5 miles, what would the map distance be between the two locations?

EXERCISES

For more practice, see *Extra Practice*.

Practice and Problem Solving

A **Practice by Example**

Example 1
(page 190)

The figures in each pair are similar. Identify the corresponding sides and angles.

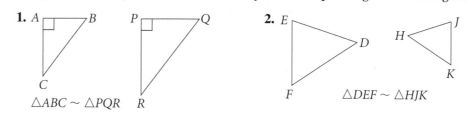

1.
$\triangle ABC \sim \triangle PQR$

2.
$\triangle DEF \sim \triangle HJK$

The figures in each pair are similar. Find the missing length.

3.
5 ft
8 ft
x
5 ft

4.
20 cm
18 cm
y
12 cm

5.
120 in.
18 in.
12 in.
x

6.
15 m
k
21 m
56 m

7.
x
24 cm
27 cm
32 cm

8.
k
6 ft
6 ft
5 ft

Example 2
(page 191)

The child in the figure is 3 ft tall.

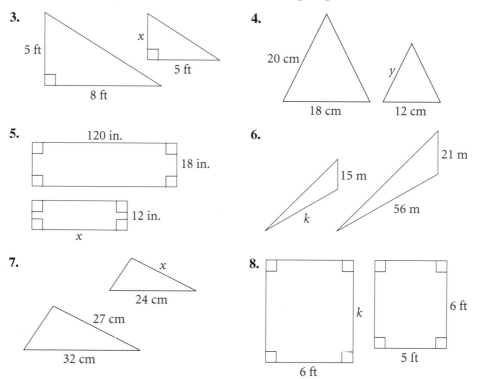

60 in.   8 ft

9. How tall is the tree?

10. The cat casts an 18-in. shadow. How tall is the cat?

Example 3
(page 191)

The scale of a map is 1 in. : 17.5 mi. Find the actual distance corresponding to each map distance.

11. 5 in.   **12.** 8.3 in.   **13.** 18.6 in.   **14.** 20 in.

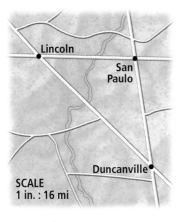

SCALE
1 in. : 16 mi

15. a. Use a ruler and the map at the left. Find the distance from each town to the others.
   b. A student lives halfway between Lincoln and San Paulo and takes the shortest route to school in Duncanville. How far does the student travel each day to school?

16. The actual distance between two towns is 28 km. Suppose you measure the distance on your map and find that it is 3.5 cm. What is the scale of your map?

Using each of the following scales, find the dimensions in a blueprint of an 8 ft-by-12 ft room.

17. 1 in. : 2 ft   **18.** 1 in. : 3 ft   **19.** 1 in. : 4 ft   **20.** 1 in. : 2.5 ft

B **Apply Your Skills**

21. Two rectangles are similar. The first is 4 in. wide and 15 in. long. The second is 9 in. wide. Find the length of the second rectangle.

22. Architecture A blueprint scale is 1 in. : 9 ft. On the plan, the room measures 2.5 in. by 3 in. What are the actual dimensions of the room?

23. Error Analysis The two figures are similar. Robert uses the proportion $\frac{GH}{PQ} = \frac{GK}{RQ}$ to find RQ.
   a. What is Robert's error?
   b. What proportion should he have used?

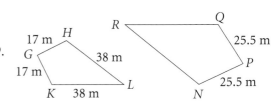

Architecture **A 2-in. length in the scale drawing represents an actual length of 24 ft.**

24. What is the scale of the drawing?

25. What are the actual dimensions of the kitchen?

26. Find the actual width of the doorways that lead into the kitchen and the dining room.

27. Find the actual area of the dining room.

28. Can a table 7 ft long and 4 ft wide fit into the narrower section of the dining room? Explain your answer.

29. Two rectangles are similar. One is 5 cm by 12 cm. The longer side of the second rectangle is 8 cm greater than twice its shorter side. Find its length and width.

30. Geometry Rectangle $ABCD$ is similar to rectangle $KLMN$.
   a. What is the width w of rectangle $KLMN$?
   b. What is the perimeter of each rectangle?
   c. Is the ratio of the perimeters of the rectangles (small : large) equal to the ratio of corresponding sides? Explain.
   d. What is the area of each rectangle?
   e. Critical Thinking Find the ratio of the areas (small : large). Explain how the ratio of the areas is related to the ratio of the corresponding sides.

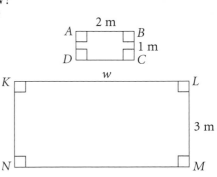

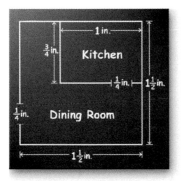

31. Open-Ended Give some examples of similar figures found in everyday life.

32. a. Writing Are the two cubes similar? Explain your answer.

b. Explain how the ratio of volumes (small : large) is related to the ratio of their sides (small : large).

c. If the ratio of the sides of the two cubes is 3 : 1, what is the ratio of their volumes?

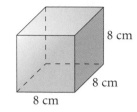

Problem Solving Hint

For Exercise 33, drawing a diagram can help you understand the problem.

33. Geometry The perimeter of a triangle with sides a, b, and c is 24 cm. Side a is 2 cm longer than side b. The ratio of the lengths of sides b and c is 3 : 5. What are the lengths of the three sides of the triangle?

Challenge

34. The state of Alabama is about 335 mi long and 210 mi wide. What scale would you use to draw a map of Alabama on an $8\frac{1}{2}$ in.-by-11 in. paper to make the map as large as possible?

35. Astronomy You can block out the moon by holding a coin up at a distance from your eye that is 110 times the diameter of the coin. Using similar figures, $\frac{\text{coin diameter}}{\text{moon diameter}} = \frac{\text{coin distance}}{\text{moon distance}}$. The moon is roughly 3640 kilometers in diameter. How far away is it?

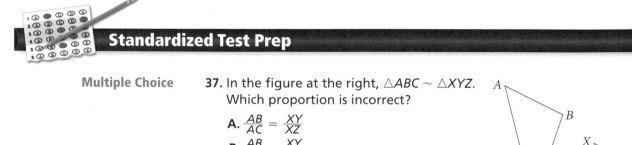

Not drawn to scale.

36. Geometry In the figure at the right, $\triangle ABC \sim \triangle ADE$.

a. Substitute values from the diagram into the following proportion. $\frac{AD}{AB} = \frac{DE}{BC}$ (*Hint:* $AB = AD + DB$.)

b. Solve the proportion for x.

c. Find the length of AB.

d. What is the area of $\triangle ABC$?

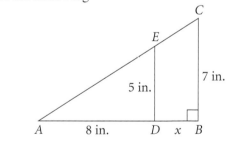

Standardized Test Prep

Multiple Choice

37. In the figure at the right, $\triangle ABC \sim \triangle XYZ$. Which proportion is incorrect?

A. $\frac{AB}{AC} = \frac{XY}{XZ}$

B. $\frac{AB}{BC} = \frac{XY}{XZ}$

C. $\frac{BC}{AC} = \frac{YZ}{XZ}$

D. $\frac{AC}{XZ} = \frac{BC}{YZ}$

38. A map of Kentucky is drawn with a scale of 1 cm : 11 km. The map distance between Louisville and Bowling Green is 14.5 cm. Which is the best estimate of the actual distance?

  F. 1.3 km   **G.** 14 km   **H.** 100 km   **I.** 160 km

Short Response

39. You can paint a 6 ft-by-5 ft rectangular wall using 0.5 gallon of paint. How many gallons of paint will you need to cover a 10 ft-by-12 ft wall? Show your work.

Extended Response

40. Leonardo da Vinci's famous painting the Mona Lisa measures 77.5 cm by 55 cm.
  a. Explain how you know that a 16 cm-by-12 cm reproduction postcard is NOT similar to the original painting.
  b. What dimensions would make a postcard similar to the original painting? Approximate to the nearest tenth. Show your work or explain how you found your answer.

····· **Take It to the NET**
: Online lesson quiz at
: **www.PHSchool.com**
········· Web Code: aea-0402

Mixed Review

Lesson 4-1

Solve each proportion.

41. $\frac{x}{2} = \frac{9}{4}$ **42.** $\frac{5}{n} = \frac{3}{10}$ **43.** $\frac{-8}{m} = \frac{7}{20}$ **44.** $\frac{12}{30} = \frac{16}{v}$

Lesson 3-3

Solve.

45. $5b < -20$ **46.** $\frac{4}{7}x \geq 4$ **47.** $-3m > 12$ **48.** $-\frac{2}{3}h < 1$

✓ Checkpoint Quiz 1   Lessons 4-1 through 4-2

iTEXT Instant self-check quiz online and on CD-ROM

1. Complete the statement 2 days = ▉ minutes.

2. Write $48 for 8 hours as a unit rate.

Solve each proportion.

3. $\frac{x}{6} = \frac{7}{4}$ **4.** $\frac{8}{k} = -\frac{12}{30}$ **5.** $\frac{3}{5} = \frac{y+1}{9}$

6. You are riding your bicycle. It takes you 12 min to go 2.5 mi. If you continue traveling at the same rate, how long will it take you to go 7 mi?

The figures in each pair are similar. Find the missing length.

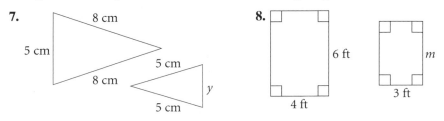

9. A 3.5-ft child casts a 60-in. shadow. She is standing next to a telephone pole that casts a 50-ft shadow. How tall is the telephone pole?

10. The scale of a map is 3 in. : 20 mi. Find the actual distance if the map distance between two towns is 5.5 in.

Modeling Percents

You can use a model to show relationships involving percents. The model at the right shows 60% of 80.

You can write this proportion for the model.

$$\text{part} \rightarrow \quad \frac{60}{100} = \frac{n}{80}$$
$$\text{whole} \rightarrow$$

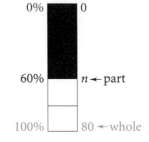

EXAMPLE

a. What percent of 50 is 35?

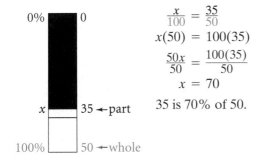

$\frac{x}{100} = \frac{35}{50}$ **Write a proportion.**

$x(50) = 100(35)$ **Write cross products.**

$\frac{50x}{50} = \frac{100(35)}{50}$ **Divide each side by 50.**

$x = 70$ **Simplify.**

35 is 70% of 50.

b. 75 is 60% of what number?

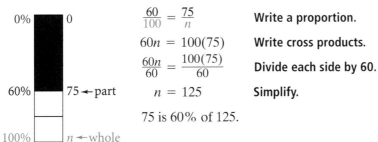

$\frac{60}{100} = \frac{75}{n}$ **Write a proportion.**

$60n = 100(75)$ **Write cross products.**

$\frac{60n}{60} = \frac{100(75)}{60}$ **Divide each side by 60.**

$n = 125$ **Simplify.**

75 is 60% of 125.

EXERCISES

Write and solve a proportion.

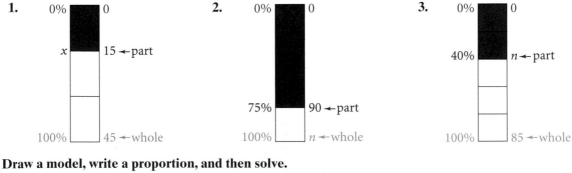

Draw a model, write a proportion, and then solve.

4. What percent of 36 is 27?   **5.** What percent of 60 is 15?   **6.** 40 is 80% of what number?

7. 8 is 20% of what number?   **8.** 13 is 25% of what number?   **9.** What percent of 63 is 42?

Proportions and Percent Equations

Lesson Preview

What You'll Learn

OBJECTIVE 1
To use proportions when solving percent problems

OBJECTIVE 2
To write and solve percent equations

... And Why

To calculate the total water supply of the United States, as in Example 3

✔ Check Skills You'll Need
(For help, go to Skills Handbook pages 727 and 728.)

Find each product.

1. $0.6 \cdot 9$ **2.** $3.8 \cdot 6.8$ **3.** $\frac{23}{60} \cdot \frac{20}{46}$ **4.** $\frac{17}{135} \cdot \frac{5}{34}$

Write each fraction as a decimal and as a percent.

5. $\frac{7}{10}$ **6.** $\frac{23}{100}$ **7.** $\frac{2}{5}$ **8.** $\frac{13}{20}$

9. $\frac{35}{40}$ **10.** $\frac{7}{16}$ **11.** $\frac{4}{25}$ **12.** $\frac{170}{200}$

OBJECTIVE

TEXT Interactive lesson includes instant self-check, tutorials, and activities.

1 Applying Proportions to Percent Problems

Need Help?

For help with percent see Skills Handbook p. 728.

Recall that a percent is a ratio that compares a number to 100. For example, $23\% = \frac{23}{100}$. You can solve a percent problem by writing and solving a proportion.

$$\text{percent} \left\{ \frac{n}{100} = \frac{\text{part}}{\text{whole}} \right.$$

1 EXAMPLE   Finding the Percent

What percent of 80 is 18?

$$\text{percent} \left\{ \frac{n}{100} = \frac{18}{80} \right. \quad \begin{array}{l} \longleftarrow \text{ part} \\ \longleftarrow \text{ whole} \end{array}$$

$$80n = 1800 \quad \textbf{Find the cross products.}$$

$$n = 22.5 \quad \textbf{Divide each side by 80.}$$

22.5% of 80 is 18.

✔ Check Understanding ① What percent of 40 is 30?

You can use a proportion to find the part or the whole in a percent problem.

2 EXAMPLE   Finding the Part

Find 75% of 320.

$$\frac{75}{100} = \frac{a}{320} \quad \begin{array}{l} \longleftarrow \text{ part} \\ \longleftarrow \text{ whole} \end{array}$$

$$24{,}000 = 100a \quad \textbf{Find the cross products.}$$

$$240 = a \quad \textbf{Divide each side by 100.}$$

75% of 320 is 240.

✔ Check Understanding ② Find 30% of 40.

3 EXAMPLE Finding the Whole

Water Supply According to the United States Geological Survey, surface water accounts for 77.6% of our country's total water supply. The surface water supply is about 264.4 billion gallons per day. Find the total water supply.

Relate 77.6% of total water supply is 264.4 billion gallons per day.

Define Let w = the total water supply.

Write $\dfrac{77.6}{100} = \dfrac{264.4}{w}$ ⟵ part
⟵ whole

$77.6w = 26{,}440$ **Find cross products.**

$w \approx 340.7$ **Divide each side by 77.6.**

● The total water supply is about 340.7 billion gallons per day.

Real-World Connection

One million gallons of water would fill a 267 ft × 50 ft ×10 ft swimming pool.

✓ **Check Understanding** ③ Carlos worked 31.5 hours at a hospital as a volunteer. This represents 87.5% of his school's requirement for community service. How many hours does his school require for community service?

🦴 **Key Concepts**

Summary	Percents and Proportions	
Finding the Percent	**Finding the Part**	**Finding the Whole**
What percent of 45 is 10?	What is 16% of 261?	71% of what number is 87?
$\dfrac{n}{100} = \dfrac{10}{45}$ ⟵ part ⟵ whole	$\dfrac{16}{100} = \dfrac{w}{261}$ ⟵ part ⟵ whole	$\dfrac{71}{100} = \dfrac{87}{v}$ ⟵ part ⟵ whole

The summary above illustrates the "three cases of percent": finding the percent, finding the part, and finding the whole.

OBJECTIVE

2 Percent Equations

You can also solve a percent problem by translating the words into an equation.

4 EXAMPLE Using a Percent Equation

What percent of 170 is 68?

Relate What percent of 170 is 68?

Define Let k = the decimal form of the percent.

Write k · 170 = 68

$170k = 68$

$k = 0.4$ **Divide each side by 170.**

$k = 40\%$ **Write the decimal as a percent.**

● 40% of 170 is 68.

✓ **Check Understanding** ④ Write and solve a percent equation for each problem.
a. What is 85% of 320? **b.** 393 is 60% of what number?

Remember that percents can be greater than 100% and less than 1%.

5 EXAMPLE **Percents Greater Than 100% and Less Than 1%**

a. What percent of 90 is 135?

$$n \qquad \cdot 90 = 135$$

$90n = 135$ **Write an equation.**

$n = 1.5$ **Divide each side by 90.**

150% of 90 is 135.

b. What is 0.48% of 250?

$$n = 0.0048 \cdot 250 \qquad \textbf{Write an equation. 0.48\% = 0.0048}$$

$$= 1.2 \qquad\qquad\quad \textbf{Simplify.}$$

1.2 is 0.48% of 250.

✓ Check Understanding   **5** Find each number or percent.
  a. 105 is 125% of what number?   **b.** What percent of 320 is 1.6?
  c. 640 is what percent of 32?   **d.** 0.13% of what number is 3900?

You can estimate some percents using fractions. You can use estimation to help check your calculations or in using mental math in real-world situations. For example, if you wanted to find 26.1% of a number, you could multiply $\frac{1}{4}$ times the number to estimate the answer. The table below gives the fraction equivalents of percents you should know.

Percents and Fractional Equivalents

Percent	5%	10%	20%	25%
Fraction	$\frac{1}{20}$	$\frac{1}{10}$	$\frac{1}{5}$	$\frac{1}{4}$
Percent	33.$\overline{3}$%	40%	50%	60%
Fraction	$\frac{1}{3}$	$\frac{2}{5}$	$\frac{1}{2}$	$\frac{3}{5}$
Percent	66.$\overline{6}$%	75%	80%	90%
Fraction	$\frac{2}{3}$	$\frac{3}{4}$	$\frac{4}{5}$	$\frac{9}{10}$

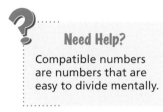

Need Help?

Compatible numbers are numbers that are easy to divide mentally.

6 EXAMPLE **Using Estimation**

Estimate the number that is 32% of 241.

$32\% \approx \frac{1}{3}$ $\frac{1}{3} = 33\frac{1}{3}\%$**. So $\frac{1}{3}$ is a good approximation of 32%.**

$241 \approx 240$ **240 and 3 are compatible numbers.**

$\frac{1}{3} \cdot 240 = 80$

80 is approximately 32% of 241.

✓ Check Understanding   **6** Use fractions to estimate each answer.
  a. 49% of 280 is what number?   **b.** What is 65% of 334?
  c. What is 74.2% of 44?   **d.** 11% of 521 is what number?

7 EXAMPLE Real-World Problem Solving

Agriculture In 1997, the total production of milk in the United States was 156 billion pounds. The midwestern states of Michigan, Minnesota, Iowa, Wisconsin, and Illinois produced 25.2% of this total. Estimate the amount of milk produced in these five midwestern states.

Relate What   is   25.2%   of   156?

Define Let n = the unknown number.

Write n $\approx$ $\frac{1}{4}$ ·   156   Use $\frac{1}{4}$ to estimate 25.2%.

$n = \frac{1}{4} \cdot 156$
$n = 39$ **Simplify.**

● The five midwestern states produced about 39 billion pounds of milk in 1997.

Real-World Connection

U.S. per capita consumption of milk is about 24 gallons per year. One gallon of milk weighs about 8.6 lb.

✓ **Check Understanding** **7 Sales** A store advertises sneakers on sale for 33% off. The original price of sneakers is $56.
a. Estimate the amount the sneakers have been marked down.
b. Estimate the sale price of the sneakers.

EXERCISES

For more practice, see *Extra Practice*.

Practice and Problem Solving

A Practice by Example

Example 1
(page 197)

Solve each problem using a proportion.

1. What percent of 40 is 20?   **2.** What percent of 80 is 20?

3. 15 is what percent of 45?   **4.** What percent of 50 is 10?

5. What percent of 24 is 6?   **6.** 18 is what percent of 90?

Example 2
(page 197)

7. What is 40% of 20?   **8.** What is 80% of 20?

9. 30% of 70 is what number?   **10.** What is 40% of 70?

11. 8% of 125 is what number?   **12.** 16% of 125 is what number?

Example 3
(page 198)

Write a proportion and solve to find the whole.

13. 20 is 40% of what number?   **14.** 20 is 80% of what number?

15. 15% of what number is 24?   **16.** 20% of what number is 48?

17. 60% of what number is 42?   **18.** 42 is 30% of what number?

19. Teresa worked 18 hours at a day-care center as a volunteer. This represents 60% of her school's requirement for community service. How many hours of community service does her school require?

Example 4
(page 198)

Write an equation and solve.

20. 50 is 25% of what number?   **21.** 25 is 50% of what number?

22. 96 is what percent of 150?   **23.** 45 is what percent of 60?

24. What is 5% of 300?   **25.** What is 5% of 200?

Example 5
(page 199)

Solve each percent problem.

26. What is 150% of 14?

27. 28 is what percent of 14?

28. 18 is 450% of what number?

29. 75 is what percent of 25?

30. What is 0.6% of 70?

31. 2.1 is what percent of 700?

Estimate each answer.

32. What is 51% of 400?

33. 24.8% of 400 is what number?

34. 67.18% of 33 is what number?

35. What is 74% of 201?

36. 9.8% of 680 is what number?

37. What is 39% of 80.3?

38. The freshman class of Mann High School has 1218 students. The graduation rate for the school is 82% of the freshman class. Estimate the number of students who will graduate.

B **Apply Your Skills**

Write a proportion or an equation and find each answer.

39. 3 is 75% of what number?

40. What percent of 75 is 300?

41. What is 0.2% of 900?

42. 1.8 is 2% of what number?

43. 988 is what percent of 1000?

44. 140% of 84 is what number?

Critical Thinking Use estimation to decide which number is closer to the exact answer. Explain your reasoning.

45. 51.3% of 122; 60 or 62

46. 23.9% of 84; 20 or 22

47. 9.79% of 740; 73 or 75

48. 76.02% of 240; 175 or 185

49. Sales Tax Jane, who lives in Florida, plans to buy a car that costs $13,500. Her friend Julie lives in Georgia. She also plans to buy a car for $13,500. How much more will Jane pay in sales tax?

50. Sales Suppose you work in an electronics store and earn a 6% commission on every item you sell. How much do you earn if you sell a $545 sound system?

51. Sales Juan earns a 5.5% commission on his bicycle sales. In September, he earned $214.28 in commissions. What were his sales for the month?

52. Writing Estimate a 15% tip for a restaurant bill of $8.25. Explain your method.

53. Finance The formula for simple interest is $I = prt$, where I is the interest, p is the principal, r is the interest rate per year, and t is the time in years.
   a. You invest $550 for three years. Find the amount of simple interest you earn with an annual interest rate of 4.5%.
   b. Suppose you invested $900 for two years. You earned $67.50 in simple interest. What was the annual rate of interest?
   c. You invest $812 with an annual interest rate of 6.5%. You earned $316.68 in simple interest. How many years was the money invested?

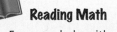

Reading Math

For more help with exercise 53b, go to page 203.

Finance Use the formula for simple interest, $I = prt$. Find each missing value.

54. $I = \blacksquare$, $p = \$340$, $r = 6\%$, $t = 3$ yr

55. $I = \$312.50$, $p = \blacksquare$, $r = 5\%$, $t = 5$ yr

56. $I = \$392$, $p = \$1400$, $r = \blacksquare$, $t = 4$ yr

57. $I = \$1540$, $p = \$22,000$, $r = 3.5\%$, $t = \blacksquare$

58. Open-Ended What percent of your time do you spend sleeping? Describe the method you used to find this percent.

Challenge

59. Since percent is a ratio that compares a number to 100, $a\% = \frac{a}{100} = 0.01a$.
  a. What is $n\%$ of $\frac{6}{n}, n \neq 0$?   **b.** $2k$ is $k\%$ of what, $k \neq 0$?
  c. What percent of $0.75x$ is $3x$, $x \neq 0$?

60. Comparing Costs At a store in Canada, Phillipe saw a CD he wanted to buy. It cost 16.99 Canadian dollars plus 15% sales tax. At the time, one Canadian dollar was approximately equal to 0.66 U.S. dollars. In the United States, Phillipe can buy the same CD for 13.99 U.S. dollars plus 6% tax. Is the CD less expensive in Canada? Explain.

Standardized Test Prep

Reading Comprehension

Read the passage below before doing Exercises 61 and 62.

LUIS CORTES WINS LOCAL ELECTION

MIDDLETOWN, NOVEMBER 7
In local elections yesterday, Luis Cortes was elected mayor with 43% of the vote. His main opponent, Tom Morris, received 40% of the vote. The remaining 17% of the vote was split among three other candidates. Election officials noted that 62% of the registered voters took part in the election.

Gridded Response

61. If there were 43,931 registered voters in Middletown, how many people actually voted?

62. How many people actually voted for Cortes?

63. The U.S. Postal Service handles 170 billion pieces of mail each year. If this is 40% of the world's total, how many pieces, in billions, are mailed each year in the world?

64. Pete chose a shirt from a sale rack. The ink on the price tag had smeared, and he couldn't read what the percent discount was. The original price was $35.00. When the clerk rang up the sale, the price before tax was $22.75. What percent was taken off the original price of the shirt?

65. There were 580 students in ninth grade last year. If this year's ninth-grade class has 15% more students, how many ninth-graders are there this year?

Take It to the NET
Online lesson quiz at
www.PHSchool.com
Web Code: aea-0403

66. Jessie plants sunflowers in $\frac{2}{5}$ of her garden area and daisies in 40% of her garden area. What percent is still available for planting?

Mixed Review

Lesson 4-2

The scale of a map is 3 in. : 40 mi. Find the actual distance for each map distance.

67. 1 in.   **68.** 4.5 in.   **69.** $6\frac{3}{4}$ in.   **70.** 8 in.

Lesson 3-3

Solve each inequality. Check your solutions. Graph each solution.

71. $5b < -20$ **72.** $\frac{4}{7}x \geq 4$ **73.** $-\frac{2}{3}h < 14$ **74.** $3.4 < -10.2p$

Read the exercise below and the explanation of how to interpret the formula. Check your understanding with the exercise at the bottom of the page.

Finance The formula for simple interest is $I = prt$, where I is the interest, p is the principal, r is the interest rate per year, and t is the time in years.

53b. Suppose you invested $900 for two years. You earned $67.50 in simple interest. What was the annual rate of interest?

Formulas represent mathematical relationships among quantities. When you're using formulas to solve problems, it's helpful to consider a few questions: What do the symbols mean? What does the formula mean? What information do I have?

What do the symbols mean?

Each symbol, or "variable," used in the formula represents one of the quantities. The quantities below are highlighted in colored boxes to help you see how the words relate to the variables. A different color is used for each variable.

I	$=$	p	$\times$	r	$\times$	t
simple Interest	$=$	principal amount	$\times$	interest rate (per year) in decimal form	$\times$	time (in years)

Another place to look for help is the Glossary. For simple interest, see page 779.

What does the formula mean?

Once you know what the variables represent, write the formula in your own words.

interest you earn on your money	$=$	amount of money you deposit in bank	$\times$	interest rate your money will earn	$\times$	number of years you leave money in bank

What information do I have?

Read the problem to identify the information given and the missing information.

The principal p is $900. The interest earned I is $67.50. The time t is 2 years. You have to find the annual rate of interest r. Substitute these values into the formula and solve for r.

$$I = p \times r \times t$$
$$67.5 = 900 \times r \times 2$$
$$67.5 = 1800\,r$$
$$0.0375 = r$$

The annual rate of interest was 3.75%.

Remember: Rate is a percent. Multiply your solution by 100 and write a percent sign.

EXERCISE

You earned $110.25 in simple interest on money that you invested over three years. The interest rate was 5.25%. How much money did you invest?

Percent of Change

Lesson Preview

What You'll Learn

OBJECTIVE
1 To find percent of change

OBJECTIVE
2 To find percent error

... And Why

To use percent of change in a real-world situation involving farming, as in Example 2

✓ Check Skills You'll Need

(For help, go to Lesson 4-3.)

Write an equation for each problem and solve.

1. What is 20% of 20?

2. 8 is what percent of 20?

3. 18 is 90% of what number?

4. 27 is 90% of what number?

Estimate each answer.

5. 67.3% of 24

6. 65% of 48

New Vocabulary

- percent of change
- percent of increase
- percent of decrease
- greatest possible error
- percent error

OBJECTIVE
1 Percent of Change

iTEXT Interactive lesson includes instant self-check, tutorials, and activities.

Suppose the price of a $20 sweatshirt increases by $2. You can express the increase as a percent.

$$\text{increase in price} \longrightarrow \frac{2}{20} = \frac{1}{10} = 10\%$$
$$\text{original price} \longrightarrow$$

There was 10% increase in the price. This is an example of percent of change. **Percent of change** is the ratio $\frac{\text{amount of change}}{\text{original amount}}$ expressed as a percent. When a value increases from its original amount, it is the **percent of increase**. When a value decreases from its original amount, it is the **percent of decrease**.

1 EXAMPLE Finding Percent of Change

The price of a sweater decreased from $29.99 to $24.49. Find the percent of decrease.

$$\text{percent of decrease} = \frac{\text{amount of change}}{\text{original amount}}$$

$$= \frac{29.99 - 24.49}{29.99} \quad \text{Subtract to find the amount of change.}$$
$$\text{Substitute the original amount.}$$

$$= \frac{5.50}{29.99} \quad \text{Simplify the numerator.}$$

$$\approx 0.18 \text{ or } 18\% \quad \text{Write as a decimal and then as a percent.}$$

The price of the sweater decreased by about 18%.

✓ Check Understanding

1 **a.** Find the percent of change if the price of a CD increases from $12.99 to $13.99. Round to the nearest percent.

b. Find the percent of change if the CD is on sale, and its price decreases from $13.99 to $12.99. Round to the nearest percent.

2 EXAMPLE **Real-World** **Problem Solving**

Farming In 1990, there were 1330 registered alpacas in the United States. By the summer of 2000, there were 29,856. What was the percent of increase in registered alpacas?

$$\text{percent of increase} = \frac{\text{amount of change}}{\text{original amount}}$$

$$= \frac{29{,}856 - 1330}{1330} \qquad \textbf{Substitute.}$$

$$= \frac{28{,}526}{1330} \qquad \textbf{Simplify the numerator.}$$

$$\approx 21.448 \text{ or } 2145\% \qquad \textbf{Write as a decimal and then as a percent.}$$

● The number of registered alpacas increased by nearly 2145%.

Real-World **Connection**

Alpacas produce 5 to 8 pounds of fleece per year, which sells for $32 to $128 per pound.

✓ **Check Understanding** ❷ The number of alpaca owners increased from 146 in 1991 to 2919 in 2000. Find the percent of increase. Round to the nearest percent.

OBJECTIVE

2 Percent Error

Think about the last time you used a ruler. You probably measured to the nearest inch, half-inch, centimeter, or millimeter. Because no measurement is exact, you always measure to the nearest "something." The **greatest possible error** in a measurement is one half of that measuring unit.

3 EXAMPLE **Finding the Greatest Possible Error**

You use a beam balance to find the mass of a rock sample for a science lab. You read the scale as 3.8 g. What is your greatest possible error?

The rock's mass was measured to the nearest 0.1 g, so the greatest possible error is one half of 0.1 g, or 0.05 g.

✓ **Check Understanding** ❸ You measure a picture for the yearbook and record its height as 9 cm. What is your greatest possible error?

4 EXAMPLE **Finding Maximum and Minimum Areas**

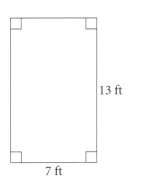

You measure a room and make the diagram shown at the left. Use the greatest possible error to find the maximum and minimum possible areas.

Both measurements were made to the nearest whole foot, so the greatest possible error is 0.5 ft. The length could be as little as 12.5 ft or as great as 13.5 ft. The width could be as little as 6.5 ft or as great as 7.5 ft. Find the minimum and maximum areas.

Minimum Area	**Maximum Area**
12.5 ft × 6.5 ft = 81.25 ft²	13.5 ft × 7.5 ft = 101.25 ft²

● The minimum area is 81.25 ft², and the maximum area is 101.25 ft².

✓ **Check Understanding** ❹ You measure a wall of your room as 8 ft high and 12 ft wide. Find the minimum and maximum possible areas of the wall.

Percent error is another useful way to think of the error in a measurement. It is the ratio of the greatest possible error and the measurement.

$$\textbf{percent error} = \frac{\text{greatest possible error}}{\text{measurement}}$$

5 EXAMPLE Finding Percent Error

Suppose you measure a CD and record its diameter as 12.1 cm. Find the percent error in your measurement.

Since the measurement is to the nearest 0.1 cm, the greatest possible error is 0.05 cm.

percent error $= \dfrac{\text{greatest possible error}}{\text{measurement}}$	Use the percent error formula.
$= \dfrac{0.05}{12.1}$	Substitute.
≈ 0.0041322314	Divide.
$\approx 0.4\%$	Round and write as a percent.

● The percent error is about 0.4%.

✔ **Check Understanding** **5** **a.** You measure the length of a table as 168 inches. Find the percent error in this measurement.
b. You measure the length of a table as 168.0 inches. Find the percent error in this measurement.

6 EXAMPLE Finding Percent Error in Calculating Volume

10.9 cm

6.8 cm

1.6 cm

The diagram at the left shows the dimensions of a cassette case. Find the percent error in calculating its volume.

The measurements are to the nearest 0.1 cm. The greatest possible error is 0.05 cm.

as measured	maximum value	minimum value
$V = \ell \cdot w \cdot h$	$V = \ell \cdot w \cdot h$	$V = \ell \cdot w \cdot h$
$= 6.8 \cdot 1.6 \cdot 10.9$	$= 6.85 \cdot 1.65 \cdot 10.95$	$= 6.75 \cdot 1.55 \cdot 10.85$
$\approx 118.59 \text{ cm}^3$	$\approx 123.76 \text{ cm}^3$	$\approx 113.52 \text{ cm}^3$

Possible Error:	maximum $-$ measured	measured $-$ minimum
	$123.76 - 118.59 = 5.17$	$118.59 - 113.52 = 5.07$

Use the difference that shows the greatest possible error to find the percent error.

percent error $= \dfrac{\text{greatest possible error}}{\text{measurement}}$	Use the percent error formula.
$= \dfrac{123.76 - 118.59}{118.59}$	Substitute.
$= \dfrac{5.17}{118.59}$	Simplify the numerator.
≈ 0.0435955814	Write as a decimal.
$\approx 4\%$	Round and write as a percent.

● The percent error is about 4%.

✔ **Check Understanding** **6** Suppose you measured your math book and recorded the dimensions as 1 in. $\times$ 9 in. $\times$ 10 in. Find the percent error in calculating its volume.

EXERCISES

For more practice, see *Extra Practice*.

Practice and Problem Solving

A **Practice by Example**

Example 1
(page 204)

Find each percent of change. Describe the percent of change as an increase or decrease. If necessary, round to the nearest tenth.

1. $2 to $3   **2.** $3 to $2   **3.** 4 ft to 5 ft   **4.** 5 ft to 4 ft

5. 9 m to 12 m   **6.** 12 cm to 9 cm   **7.** 12 in. to 15 in.   **8.** 15 lb to 18 lb

9. 4.5 cm to 8.3 cm **10.** $38 to $65   **11.** $12.20 to $4.80   **12.** 125 lb to 143 lb

Example 2
(page 205)

13. Physical Therapy Physical therapists measure strength on a dynamometer, which uses a unit called a foot-pound. Suppose you increase the strength in your elbow joint from 90 foot-pounds to 125 foot-pounds. Find the percent of increase to the nearest percent.

14. Environment From 1999 to 2000, the number of days of unhealthy air quality in Charlotte, North Carolina, dropped from 5 to 2. Find the percent of decrease in the number of days of unhealthy air.

Example 3
(page 205)

Find the greatest possible error for each measurement.

15. 14 ft   **16.** 3.5 cm   **17.** 56.38 g   **18.** 17 in.

Example 4
(page 205)

Find the minimum and maximum possible areas for rectangles with the following measured areas.

19. 4 cm × 6 cm   **20.** 7 mi × 8 mi   **21.** 6 in. × 9 in.

22. 12 km × 5 km   **23.** 18 in. × 15 in.   **24.** 23 km × 14 km

Example 5
(page 206)

Find the percent error of each measurement.

25. 2 cm   **26.** 0.2 cm   **27.** 4 cm   **28.** 0.4 cm

Example 6
(page 206)

29. The table below shows the measured dimensions of the prism and the maximum and minimum possible values based on the greatest possible error.

Dimensions	ℓ	w	h
Measured	8	3	2
Maximum	8.5	3.5	2.5
Minimum	7.5	2.5	1.5

a. Find the measured volume.   **b.** Find the maximum volume.
c. Find the minimum volume.   **d.** Find the greatest possible error.
e. What is the percent error? Round to the nearest percent.

B **Apply Your Skills**

Find each percent of change. Describe the percent of change as an increase or decrease. Round to the nearest percent.

30. 26 to 20   **31.** $4.95 to $3.87   **32.** 21 in. to 54 in.

33. 2 ft to $5\frac{1}{2}$ ft   **34.** $24,000 to $25,000   **35.** 18 to $17\frac{1}{2}$

36. 8.99 to 3.99   **37.** 132 lb to 120 lb   **38.** $42.69 to $49.95

39. Sports In the 1988 Olympics, Florence Griffith-Joyner of the United States won the women's 100-meter run in 10.54 seconds. In 2000, Marion Jones, also of the United States, won with a time of 10.75 seconds. Find the percent of change in the winning times. Round to the nearest percent.

40. Meteorology In 1999, the National Oceanographic and Atmospheric Administration reported a total of 16 Atlantic cyclones. In 2000, there were 19 Atlantic cyclones. Find the percent of change in the number of cyclones from 1999 to 2000. Round to the nearest percent.

41. If you want accuracy of 0.5 mm, what measuring unit should you use?

42. Critical Thinking An item costs $64. The price is increased by $10, then reduced by $10. Is the percent of increase equal to the percent of decrease? Explain your answer.

43. Critical Thinking An item costs $64. The price is increased by 10%, then reduced by 10%. Is the final price equal to the original price? Explain.

44. Open-Ended Write a word problem involving percent of change. Include your solution.

Find the minimum and maximum possible areas for rectangles with the following measured dimensions. Round to the nearest tenth.

45. 4.1 cm × 6.1 cm   **46.** 7.0 mi × 8.4 mi   **47.** 6.01 in. × 9.02 in.

48. Sales Suppose that you are selling sweatshirts for a class fund-raiser. The wholesaler charges you $8 for each sweatshirt.
  a. You charge $16 for each sweatshirt. Find the percent of increase.
  b. Generalize your answer to part (a). Doubling a price is the same as a ___?___ percent of increase.
  c. After the fund-raiser is over, you reduce the price on the remaining sweatshirts to $8. Find the percent of decrease.
  d. Generalize your answer to part (c). Cutting a price in half is the same as a ___?___ percent of decrease.

Find the percent error in calculating the volume of each rectangular prism. Round to the nearest percent.

49.

12 in.

17 in.

15 in.

50.

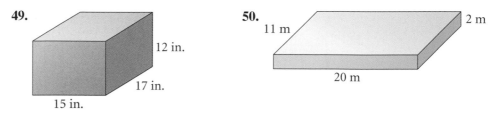

2 m

11 m

20 m

51. Writing Explain how to find the percent error when calculating the area of a rectangle.

52. Error Analysis Jorge found the percent of change from $15 to $10 to be 50%. What error did he make?

Real-World Connection

Atlantic cyclones can be tropical depressions, tropical storms, or hurricanes.

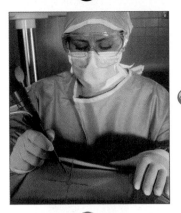

C Challenge

Real-World 🌐 **Connection**

Careers Students who want to become physicians must take calculus, physics, biology, and chemistry before going to medical school.

53. Suppose you measure two cubes. The smaller one measures 18 cm on each side. The larger one measures 45 cm on each side.
  a. Find the percent error of the volume of each cube. Round to the nearest percent.
  b. Critical Thinking Explain why using the same measuring unit did not yield the same percent error for the two cubes.

54. Data Analysis A reporter states, "From 1980 to 1996, the number of female physicians more than tripled." A second reporter states, "From 1980 to 1996, the number of female physicians increased about 205%." Can both reports be correct? Explain.

Year	U.S. Female Physicians
1980	48,700
1990	96,100
1996	148,300

55. a. The sides of a 12 cm × 12 cm square are all increased in length by 10%. Find the percent of increase in the area.
  b. The sides of a 14 cm × 14 cm square are all increased in length by 10%. Find the percent of increase in the area.
  c. Predict the percent of increase in the area if the sides of a 16 cm × 16 cm square are all increased by 10%. Explain your prediction and check.

Standardized Test Prep

Multiple Choice

56. Which percent of change best reflects a price increase from $32 to $36?
  A. 4%   **B.** 8%   **C.** 12%   **D.** 89%

57. A carpenter measured a rectangle as 5 in. by 8 in. Which number is the maximum possible area?
  F. 33.75 in.^{2} **G.** 38.25 in.^{2} **H.** 40 in.^{2} **I.** 46.75 in.^{2}

58. A student records the measured length of an object as 24.7 cm. What is the greatest possible error in this measurement?
  A. 0.05 cm   **B.** 0.2 cm   **C.** 0.5 cm   **D.** 1.0 cm

Short Response

Take It to the NET
Online lesson quiz at
www.PHSchool.com
.... Web Code: aea-0404

59. A softball diamond is a 60 ft-by-60 ft square. The base lines of a baseball diamond are 50% longer than those of a softball diamond. What is the percent of increase from a softball diamond to a baseball diamond of the trip around all four bases? What is the percent of increase in the area from a softball diamond to a baseball diamond?

Mixed Review

Lesson 4-3

Write a proportion or an equation for each problem and solve. Round to the nearest tenth or to the nearest percent.

60. 5 is what percent of 67?

61. What percent of 15 is 13?

62. 79 is 44% of what number?

63. 96 is what percent of 32?

64. What is 0.2% of 834?

65. 266% of 14 is what?

Lesson 3-4

Solve each inequality.

66. $5 - 7n > 4 + 8n$ **67.** $8(q - 9) \le 12q - 4$ **68.** $4x + 17 - 2x \ge -15x$

Understanding Probability

When you toss a number cube, there are a variety of possible results. You can find the probabilities of these results by first listing all the possible results.

1. List all the possible results of tossing a number cube like those at the right.

2. How many possible results are there?

3. List all the possible results that are divisible by 3.

4. Use the ratio below to find the probability of tossing a number divisible by 3.

number of possible results that are divisible by 3
———————————————————————
total number of possible results

The table at the right shows all the possible results of tossing a red and blue number cube.

5. How many results are there?

6. **a.** List the results that have a sum of 1.
   b. What is the probability of a sum of 1?

7. **a.** List the results that have a sum of 4.
   b. What is the probability of a sum of 4?

8. **a.** List the results that have a sum of 11.
   b. What is the probability of a sum of 11?

9. Find another sum that has the same probability of occurring as 11.

10. **Reasoning** Are the sums 2–12 equally likely? Explain.

11. Are the probabilities of getting an even sum or an odd sum equal?

Sample Space for Two Number Cubes

(1, 1)	(1, 2)	(1, 3)	(1, 4)	(1, 5)	(1, 6)
(2, 1)	(2, 2)	(2, 3)	(2, 4)	(2, 5)	(2, 6)
(3, 1)	(3, 2)	(3, 3)	(3, 4)	(3, 5)	(3, 6)
(4, 1)	(4, 2)	(4, 3)	(4, 4)	(4, 5)	(4, 6)
(5, 1)	(5, 2)	(5, 3)	(5, 4)	(5, 5)	(5, 6)
(6, 1)	(6, 2)	(6, 3)	(6, 4)	(6, 5)	(6, 6)

The photo at the right shows two regular tetrahedrons. Assume you are tossing a pair of regular tetrahedrons with the numbers 1 through 4 printed on the faces, like those at the right. The same number appears at the bottom of each face, and this number is the result of the toss.

12. Construct a table that shows all the possible results..

13. How many results are there?

14. **a.** List the results that have a sum of 4.
    b. What is the probability of a sum of 4?

15. **Critical Thinking** Is the probability of a sum of 4 with two regular tetrahedrons the same as the probability of a sum of 4 with two cubes? Explain.

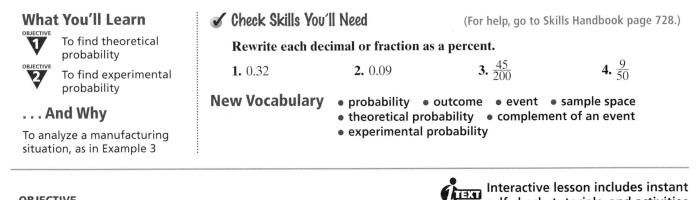

4-5 Applying Ratios to Probability

Lesson Preview

What You'll Learn

OBJECTIVE 1 To find theoretical probability

OBJECTIVE 2 To find experimental probability

. . . And Why

To analyze a manufacturing situation, as in Example 3

✔ **Check Skills You'll Need**   (For help, go to Skills Handbook page 728.)

Rewrite each decimal or fraction as a percent.

1. 0.32   **2.** 0.09   **3.** $\frac{45}{200}$ **4.** $\frac{9}{50}$

New Vocabulary • probability • outcome • event • sample space
• theoretical probability • complement of an event
• experimental probability

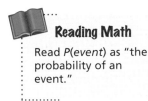

> 🕮 **Reading Math**
>
> Read *P(event)* as "the probability of an event."

OBJECTIVE 1 Theoretical Probability

🅣 TEXT Interactive lesson includes instant self-check, tutorials, and activities.

The **probability** of an event, or *P*(event), tells you how likely it is that something will occur. An **outcome** is the result of a single trial, like one roll of a number cube. An **event** is any outcome or group of outcomes. The **sample space** is all of the possible outcomes.

Here is how these terms apply to finding the probability of rolling an even number on a number cube.

event	sample space	favorable outcome
↓	↓	↓
rolling an even number	1, 2, 3, 4, 5, 6	2, 4, 6

The possible outcomes of rolling a fair number cube are *equally likely* to occur. When all possible outcomes are equally likely, you can find the theoretical probability of an event using the following formula.

theoretical probability $P(\text{event}) = \dfrac{\text{number of favorable outcomes}}{\text{number of possible outcomes}}$

$$P(\text{rolling an even number}) = \frac{3}{6} = \frac{1}{2}$$

You can write the probability of an event as a fraction, a decimal, or a percent. The probability of an event ranges from 0 to 1.

Probability

← less likely   more likely →

0	0.5	1
impossible event	**equally likely and unlikely**	**certain event**
rolling a 7 on a number cube	getting a head when flipping a coin	rolling a number less than 7 on a number cube

1 EXAMPLE Finding Theoretical Probability

A bowl contains 12 slips of paper, each with a different name of a month. Find the theoretical probability that a slip selected at random from the bowl has a name of a month that starts with the letter J.

$$P(\text{event}) = \frac{\text{number of favorable outcomes}}{\text{number of possible outcomes}}$$

$$= \frac{3}{12} \qquad \textbf{There are 3 months out of 12 that begin with the letter J:}$$
$$\textbf{January, June, and July.}$$

$$= \frac{1}{4} \qquad \textbf{Simplify.}$$

The probability of picking a month that begins with the letter J is $\frac{1}{4}$.

✔ Check Understanding 1 Suppose you write the names of days of the week on identical pieces of paper. Find the theoretical probability of picking a piece of paper at random that has the name of a day that starts with the letter T.

The **complement of an event** consists of all the outcomes not in the event.

possible outcomes for rolling a number cube	outcomes for rolling an even number	complement of rolling an even number
↓	↓	↓
1, 2, 3, 4, 5, 6	2, 4, 6	1, 3, 5

The sum of the probabilities of an event and its complement is 1.

$$P(\text{event}) + P(\text{not event}) = 1$$

or

$$P(\text{not event}) = 1 - P(\text{event})$$

2 EXAMPLE Finding the Complement of an Event

Games On a popular television game show, a contestant must choose one of five envelopes. One envelope contains the grand prize, a car. Find the probability of not choosing the car.

$$P(\text{car}) = \frac{\text{number of favorable outcomes}}{\text{number of possible outcomes}} = \frac{1}{5}$$

$$P(\text{not choosing the car}) = 1 - P(\text{car}) \qquad \textbf{Use the complement formula.}$$

$$= 1 - \frac{1}{5} = \frac{4}{5} \qquad \textbf{Simplify.}$$

The probability of not choosing the car is $\frac{4}{5}$.

✔ Check Understanding 2 **Critical Thinking** In Example 2, what happens to $P(\text{not choosing the car})$ as the number of envelopes increases?

OBJECTIVE 2 Experimental Probability

Probability based on data collected from repeated trials is experimental probability. You can find the experimental probability of an event using this formula.

experimental probability $\quad P(\text{event}) = \dfrac{\text{number of times an event occurs}}{\text{number of times the experiment is done}}$

Real-World Connection

More than 100,000 skateboards are manufactured each month.

3 EXAMPLE Finding Experimental Probability

Quality Control After receiving complaints, a skateboard manufacturer inspected 1000 skateboards at random. The manufacturer found no defects in 992 skateboards. What is the probability that a skateboard selected at random had no defects? Write the probability as a percent.

$$P(\text{no defects}) = \frac{\text{number of times an event occurs}}{\text{number of times the experiment is done}}$$

$= \frac{992}{1000}$ **Substitute.**

$= 0.992$ **Simplify.**

$= 99.2\%$ **Write as a percent.**

● The probability that a skateboard has no defects is 99.2%.

✓ Check Understanding ③ The manufacturer decides to inspect 2500 skateboards. There are 2450 skateboards that have no defects. Find the probability that a skateboard selected at random has no defects.

You can use experimental probability to make a prediction. Predictions are not exact, so round your results.

4 EXAMPLE Using Experimental Probability

Quality Control The same manufacturer has 8976 skateboards in its warehouse. If the probability that a skateboard has no defect is 99.2%, predict how many skateboards are likely to have no defect.

number with no defects = $P(\text{no defects}) \cdot$ number of skateboards

$= 0.992 \times 8976$ **Substitute. Use 0.992 for 99.2%.**

$= 8904.192$ **Simplify.**

● Approximately 8900 boards are likely to have no defect.

✓ Check Understanding ④ A manufacturer inspects 700 light bulbs. She finds that the probability that a light bulb works is 99.6%. There are 35,400 light bulbs in the warehouse. Predict how many light bulbs are likely to work.

How does the experimental probability of flipping a fair coin compare to the theoretical probability? Below are the results of flipping a coin 10, 100, and 1000 times.

number of times a coin is flipped	10	100	1000
number of times the coin is heads	7	58	498
experimental probability of heads	$\frac{7}{10}$	$\frac{58}{100}$	$\frac{498}{1000}$

The table above shows that the more times the coin is flipped, the closer the experimental probability comes to the theoretical probability, $\frac{1}{2}$. In general, as the amount of data you use to find an experimental probability increases, the closer the experimental probability will be to the theoretical probability. This is called the *Law of Large Numbers.*

EXERCISES

For more practice, see *Extra Practice*.

Practice and Problem Solving

A **Practice by Example**

Example 1
(page 212)

Example 2
(page 212)

Examples 3, 4
(page 213)

For Exercises 1–13, use the spinner at the right. Find the theoretical probability of landing on the given section(s) of the spinner.

1. P(purple) **2.** P(green) **3.** P(5)

4. P(even) **5.** P(purple or white) **6.** P(8)

7. P(greater than 4) **8.** P(even or odd) **9.** P(1 or 6)

10. P(not white) **11.** P(not 2) **12.** P(not purple) **13.** P(not 8)

14. Suppose the probability that you will be picked for a committee at school is 20%. What is the probability that you will not be picked?

The results of a survey of 100 randomly selected students at a 2000-student high school are below. Find the experimental probability that a student selected at random makes the given response.

15. P(community college)

16. P(4-year college)

17. P(trade school)

18. P(not trade school)

19. P(trade school or community college)

20. P(community or 4-year college)

Plans for After Graduation

Response	Number of Respondents
Go to community college	24
Go to 4-year college	43
Take a year off before college	12
Go to trade school	15
Do not plan to go to college	6

21. A forest contains about 500 trees. You randomly pick 67 trees and find that 27 of them are oaks.
a. What is the experimental probability that a tree in the forest is an oak?
b. Predict how many oak trees there are in the forest.

22. Suppose 12 out of 30 families on your street have a cat or a dog as a pet.
a. What is the experimental probability that a randomly selected family in your neighborhood will have a cat or a dog as a pet?
b. Based on P(cat or dog) from part (a), predict how many cat- or dog-owning families you can expect among 57 families in your neighborhood.

B **Apply Your Skills**

Suppose you roll a number cube. Find each probability.

23. P(5) **24.** P(7) **25.** P(3 or 4) **26.** P(not 5)

Suppose you select a 3-digit number at random from the set of all positive 3-digit numbers. Find each probability. (*Hint:* First find how many positive 3-digit numbers there are.)

27. P(odd number) **28.** P(number less than 900)

29. P(243 or 244) **30.** P(number less than 100)

31. P(number is a multiple of 30) **32.** P(number less than 500)

Real-World Connection

About 10,700 people celebrate their sixteenth birthday each day.

33. **Birthdays** Each day in the United States, about 753,000 people have a birthday. Use the information at the left to find the probability that someone celebrating a birthday today will turn 16. Round to the nearest percent.

34. **Land Area** The United States has a land area of about 3,536,278 mi². Illinois has a land area of about 57,918 mi². What is the probability that a location in the United States chosen at random is in Illinois?

35. **Open-Ended** Suppose your teacher chooses a student at random from your algebra class.
    a. What is the probability that you are selected?
    b. What is the probability that a boy is not selected?
    c. How did you find your answer to part (b)? Describe another way to find the probability that a boy is not selected.

36. **Data Analysis** The population of the United States is about 275,400,000. Use the pie graph at the right to answer the following questions. Round to the nearest percent.
    a. What is the probability of selecting at random a person whose age is between 10 and 19?
    b. What is the probability of selecting at random a person whose age is between 40 and 49?

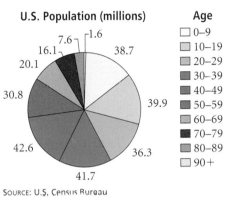

U.S. Population (millions)

SOURCE: U.S. Census Bureau

37. **Radio** A disc jockey makes music selections for a radio program. For his first selection, he can choose from eight alternative rock songs, three hip-hop dance mixes, five country-western ballads, and four rhythm-and-blues songs. Assume that all selections have equal chances of being chosen.
    a. What is the probability that he does not choose a ballad?
    b. What is the probability that he chooses a rock song?
    c. What is the probability that he chooses a hip-hop dance mix?

38. **Writing** Explain the difference between theoretical probability and experimental probability.

Geometry Use the diagram at the right. Assume that all angles are right angles. If you choose a point inside the figure, what is the probability that it will be in each shaded region?

39. P(red)   40. P(purple)

41. P(yellow or white)   42. P(not purple)

For Exercises 43 and 44, use the spinner at the left. Use the formula below to find the odds in favor of an event.

$$\text{odds in favor} = \frac{\text{number of favorable outcomes}}{\text{number of unfavorable outcomes}}$$

43. Find the odds in favor of the spinner stopping on green.

44. Find the odds in favor of the spinner not stopping on white.

45. **Critical Thinking** Explain how you can use odds to find probability. Include an example.

Difference Between Winning and Losing Super Bowl Scores

0	1 4 5 7 7
1	0 0 2 3 4 5 7 7 9
2	2 3 9
3	2 6
4	5

Key: 1|0 means 10 points

46. Find the probability that the winning team won by less than 10 points.

47. Find the probability that the winning team won by 10 to 15 points.

48. Find the probability that the winning team won by more than 20 points.

Real-World Connection

The greatest total score of both teams in a Super Bowl was 75, in 1994.

49. Data Collection Roll a pair of number cubes and record the product of the results. Repeat 30 times.
  a. Use your data to find the following experimental probabilities: $P(5), P(6), P(12), P(36)$.
  b. Make a chart to find the sample space for the product of two cubes.
  c. Find the theoretical probabilities for $P(5), P(6), P(12), P(36)$.
  d. Are your experimental probabilities exactly the same as the theoretical probabilities?
  e. Suppose you roll the number cubes 1000 times. Would you expect the experimental probabilities and the theoretical probabilities to be about the same? Explain.

Standardized Test Prep

Multiple Choice

50. Suppose you roll a number cube with the numbers 1–6 on it. Which has the same probability as $P(1 \text{ or prime})$?
  A. $P(\text{factor of } 6)$
  B. $P(1 \text{ or } 2)$
  C. $P(\text{less than } 3)$
  D. $P(\text{not odd})$

51. Of 150 widgets inspected, 142 passed inspection. Out of 2855 widgets, about how many would you predict would fail an inspection?
  F. 140   **G.** 150   **H.** 2700   **I.** 2850

52. There are 28 right-handed students in a class of 31. What is the probability that a student chosen at random will be left-handed?
  A. $\frac{31}{28}$ **B.** $\frac{28}{31}$ **C.** $\frac{3}{28}$ **D.** $\frac{3}{31}$

Extended Response

53. A "Bag-of-Beads" for crafts contains five different colors of beads. The company that makes them claims that each bag contains the same number of each color.
  a. If this claim is true, what is the theoretical probability of picking a red bead at random?
  b. Rosheeda purchased a bag to test the company's claim. She recorded the number of each color. Based on the results in the table to the right, what is the experimental probability of picking a red bead out of the bag?
  c. How does the experimental probability compare with the theoretical probability in Rosheeda's experiment? Explain why her results do or do not support the company's claim.

Color	Number
red	55
blue	53
green	64
yellow	47
purple	61

Short Response

Take It to the NET
Online lesson quiz at
www.PHSchool.com
.... Web Code: aea-0405

54. An inspector for an office-supply company checked a batch of 350 staplers. He found that 18 of them were defective. What is the experimental probability of getting a defective stapler in this batch? Production must be stopped when the percent of defective staplers exceeds 4%. Should the inspector stop production? Explain.

Mixed Review

Lesson 4-4   **Find each percent of change. Describe each percent of change as an increase or decrease.**

55. 8 ft to 10 ft   **56.** 4 m to 6 m   **57.** 25 in. to 35 in.

58. $22 to $11   **59.** 16 cm to 12 cm   **60.** 80 ft to 70 ft

Lesson 3-5   **Solve the following compound inequalities. Graph the solutions.**

61. $-3 \le t \le 4$ **62.** $8 < b + 3 < 10$

63. $7h < 14$ or $4h > 20$ **64.** $5 < 7 - 2w \le 11$

65. $1 - 3x > -5$ or $-x \le -4$ **66.** $-2 \le 4k - 6 \le 6$

Lesson 2-7   **Find the mean, median, and mode of each set of numbers.**

67. 3 4 5 5 8 12   **68.** 1 8 9 11 22 35 35

Make a stem-and-leaf plot for each set of data.

69. 34 37 39 41 49 65 71   **70.** 12 14 16 23 27 47 68 79

✓ Checkpoint Quiz 2   Lessons 4-3 through 4-5

iTEXT Instant self-check quiz online and on CD-ROM

Solve each percent problem.

1. What is 60% of 200?   **2.** 4 is what percent of 5?

3. 18 is 75% of what number?   **4.** What is 175% of 40?

Find the percent of increase or decrease.

5. $20 to $25   **6.** $20 to $30

7. What are the minimum and maximum possible areas for a rectangle that you measure as 3 ft by 5 ft?

8. Suppose you measure the length of a pencil as 5 in. What is the percent error in this measurement?

9. Suppose you write the days of the week on identical pieces of paper. You mix them in a bowl and choose one at random. What is the probability that the day you select will have the letter *e* in it?

10. A manufacturer inspects 100 bicycles at random. She finds that 98 of them have no defects. There are 2400 bicycles in the warehouse. Predict how many bicycles are likely to be free of defects.

Technology

Conducting a Simulation

FOR USE WITH LESSON 4-5

A *simulation* is a model of a real-life situation. One way to do a simulation is to use random numbers generated by a graphing calculator or a computer program.

On a graphing calculator, the command randInt generates random integers. To create a list of random integers, press MATH ◄ 5. You will see randInt(. After the parenthesis, press 0 ▸ 99, and press ENTER repeatedly to create 1- and 2-digit random numbers.

Take It to the NET
Graphing Calculator procedures online at **www.PHSchool.com**
Web Code: aee-2115

1 EXAMPLE

According to the American Red Cross, 40% of the people in the United States have type A blood. Find the probability that the next two people who donate blood have type A blood.

To simulate this problem, use 2-digit numbers to represent groups of 2 people. Use your calculator to generate 40 random numbers.

Define how the simulation will be done.

Since 40% of people have type A blood, let 40%, or 4 out of 10 digits, represent people in this group. Using numbers from the random number table, let 0, 1, 2, 3 represent people with type A blood. Let 4, 5, 6, 7, 8, 9 represent people who do not have type A blood.

25	71	47	46
66	13	63	36
01	59	27	07
83	25	72	24
73	52	59	81
14	09	40	64
81	72	02	38
21	09	92	10
93	34	36	45
53	18	23	75

Interpret the simulation

The six numbers in red represent "these two people have type A blood." Each of the other groups has at least one person with a different blood type.

P(next two people have type A blood) =

$$\frac{\text{number of times an event happens}}{\text{number of times the experiment is done}} = \frac{6}{40} = 0.15 = 15\%$$

The probability that the next two people will have type A blood is about 15%.

EXERCISES

1. For this simulation, could you use 4, 5, 6, and 7 to represent donors who have type A blood? Explain.

2. Blood Types In the United States, about 50% of people have type O blood. Use the random number table above to find the probability that the next two donors have type O blood.

3. a. Use a graphing calculator to find another set of 40 random numbers. Use these random numbers to answer Exercise 2 again.
   b. Are the results exactly the same as in Exercise 2?
   c. Suppose you were to do this experiment with 400 random numbers. Which set of results would be more reliable, one with 40 random numbers or one with 400? Explain.

Probability of Compound Events

Lesson Preview

What You'll Learn

OBJECTIVE 1 To find the probability of independent events

OBJECTIVE 2 To find the probability of dependent events

. . . And Why

To use probability in a game, as in Example 2

✓ Check Skills You'll Need

(For help, go to Lesson 4-5.)

Find each probability for one roll of a number cube.

1. $P(\text{multiple of 3})$

2. $P(\text{greater than 4})$

3. $P(\text{greater than 5})$

4. $P(\text{greater than 6})$

Simplify.

5. $\frac{2}{14} \cdot \frac{7}{6}$

6. $\frac{15}{24} \cdot \frac{12}{30}$

7. $\frac{6}{55} \cdot \frac{44}{3}$

New Vocabulary • independent events • dependent events

OBJECTIVE

1 Finding the Probability of Independent Events

iTEXT Interactive lesson includes instant self-check, tutorials, and activities.

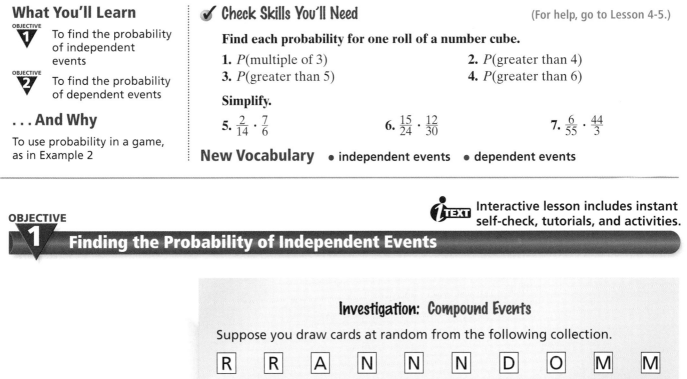

Investigation: Compound Events

Suppose you draw cards at random from the following collection.

R R A N N N D O M M

1. You draw an R card and replace it. What is the probability that the next card you draw will be an R card?

2. You draw an R card and do *not* replace it. What is the probability that the next card you draw will be an R card?

3. Copy and complete each table.

Probability With Replacement		Probability Without Replacement	
First Card	Second Card Matches	First Card	Second Card Matches
$P(\text{R}) = \blacksquare$	$P(\text{R}) = \blacksquare$	$P(\text{R}) = \blacksquare$	$P(\text{R}) = \blacksquare$
$P(\text{A}) = \blacksquare$	$P(\text{A}) = \blacksquare$	$P(\text{A}) = \blacksquare$	$P(\text{A}) = \blacksquare$
$P(\text{N}) = \blacksquare$	$P(\text{N}) = \blacksquare$	$P(\text{N}) = \blacksquare$	$P(\text{N}) = \blacksquare$
$P(\text{D}) = \blacksquare$	$P(\text{D}) = \blacksquare$	$P(\text{D}) = \blacksquare$	$P(\text{D}) = \blacksquare$
$P(\text{O}) = \blacksquare$	$P(\text{O}) = \blacksquare$	$P(\text{O}) = \blacksquare$	$P(\text{O}) = \blacksquare$
$P(\text{M}) = \blacksquare$	$P(\text{M}) = \blacksquare$	$P(\text{M}) = \blacksquare$	$P(\text{M}) = \blacksquare$

4. For each letter, the probability of drawing the first card is the same with replacement and without replacement. Explain why the probability of drawing the second card is not the same.

The diagram at the right shows the results of randomly choosing a checker, putting it back, and choosing again. The probability of getting a red on either pick is $\frac{1}{2}$. The first pick, or first event, does not affect the second event. The events are independent.

Independent events are events that do not influence one another.

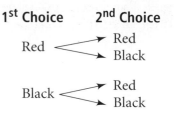

1st Choice   2nd Choice

Red <— Red, Black

Black <— Red, Black

Key Concepts

Rule	Probability of Two Independent Events

If A and B are independent events,

$$P(A \text{ and } B) = P(A) \cdot P(B).$$

1 EXAMPLE **Independent Events**

Suppose you roll a red number cube and a blue number cube. What is the probability that you will roll a 3 on the red cube and an even number on the blue cube?

$P(\text{red } 3) = \frac{1}{6}$ **There is one way to get a 3 out of six numbers.**

$P(\text{blue even}) = \frac{3}{6} = \frac{1}{2}$ **There are three even numbers out of six numbers.**

$P(\text{red 3 and blue even}) = P(\text{red 3}) \cdot P(\text{blue even})$

$= \frac{1}{6} \cdot \frac{1}{2}$ **Substitute.**

$= \frac{1}{12}$ **Simplify.**

The probability that you will roll a 3 on the red number cube and an even number on the blue cube is $\frac{1}{12}$.

✓ Check Understanding **1** Suppose you roll a red number cube and a blue number cube. What is the probability that you will roll a 5 on the red cube and a 1 or 2 on the blue cube?

2 EXAMPLE **Selecting With Replacement**

Games In a word game, you choose a tile from a bag containing the letter tiles shown. You *replace* the first tile in the bag and then choose again. What is the probability that you will choose an A and then an E?

Since you replace the first tile, the events are independent.

$P(A) = \frac{4}{15}$ **There are 4 *A*'s in the 15 tiles.**

$P(E) = \frac{3}{15}$ **There are 3 *E*'s in the 15 tiles.**

$P(A \text{ and } E) = P(A) \cdot P(E)$

$= \frac{4}{15} \cdot \frac{3}{15}$ **Multiply.**

$= \frac{12}{225} = \frac{4}{75}$

The probability that you will choose an A and then an E is $\frac{4}{75}$.

✓ Check Understanding **2** Find the probability of picking a U and then an I after replacing the first tile.

When you select one tile from a bag of 15 tiles and you do *not* replace it, there are only 14 tiles when you make your second selection. These events are dependent.

Dependent events are events that influence each other. The occurrence of one event affects the probability of a second event.

Key Concepts

Rule	Probability of Two Dependent Events

If A and B are dependent events,

$P(A$ then $B) = P(A) \cdot P(B$ after $A)$.

3 EXAMPLE Selecting Without Replacement

Games Suppose you choose a tile from the letter tiles shown in Example 2. Without replacing the tile, you select a second tile. What is the probability that you will choose an A and then an E?

$P(A) = \frac{4}{15}$ **There are 4 A's in the 15 tiles.**

$P(E$ after $A) = \frac{3}{14}$ **There are 3 E's in the 14 remaining tiles.**

$P(A$ then $E) = P(A) \cdot P(E$ after $A)$

$= \frac{4}{15} \cdot \frac{3}{14}$ **Multiply.**

$= \frac{12}{210} = \frac{2}{35}$

● The probability that you will choose an A and then an E is $\frac{2}{35}$.

✓ Check Understanding   **3** Find the probability that you will choose a U and then an O without replacing the first tile.

4 EXAMPLE Real-World 🌐 Problem Solving

Selecting Representatives Suppose a teacher must select 2 high school students to represent their school at a conference. The teacher randomly picks names from a hat that contains the names of 3 freshmen, 2 sophomores, 4 juniors, and 4 seniors. What is the probability that a sophomore and then a freshman are chosen?

$P(\text{sophomore}) = \frac{2}{13}$ **There are 2 sophomores among 13 students.**

$P(\text{freshman after sophomore}) = \frac{3}{12}$ **There are 3 freshmen among the 12 remaining students.**

$P(\text{sophomore then freshman}) = P(\text{sophomore}) \cdot P(\text{freshman after sophomore})$

$= \frac{2}{13} \cdot \frac{3}{12}$ **Substitute.**

$= \frac{1}{26}$ **Simplify.**

● The probability that the teacher chooses a sophomore and then a freshman is $\frac{1}{26}$.

✓ Check Understanding   **4 a.** What is the probability that the teacher chooses a sophomore and then a junior?
   b. What is the probability that the teacher chooses a junior and then a sophomore?
   c. Critical Thinking Does the probability of choosing without replacement change if the order of the events is reversed? Explain.

EXERCISES

For more practice, see *Extra Practice*.

Practice and Problem Solving

A Practice by Example

Example 1
(page 220)

You roll a blue number cube and a green number cube. Find each probability.

1. *P*(blue 1 and green 1)

2. *P*(blue 1 and green 1 or 2)

3. *P*(blue 1 or 2 and green 1)

4. *P*(blue 1 or 2 and green 1 or 2)

5. *P*(blue even and green even)

6. *P*(blue and green both less than 6)

7. *P*(blue and green less than 7)

8. *P*(blue 6 and green 7)

Example 2
(page 220)

Suppose you choose a tile from a bag containing 2 A's, 3 B's, and 4 C's. You *replace* the first tile in the bag and then choose again. Find each probability.

9. *P*(A and A)

10. *P*(A and B)

11. *P*(B and B)

12. *P*(C and C)

13. *P*(B and C)

14. *P*(C and B)

Example 3
(page 221)

You select a card at random from those below. Without replacing the card, you choose a second card. Find each probability. Consider Y to be a vowel.

$$\boxed{P}\ \boxed{R}\ \boxed{O}\ \boxed{B}\ \boxed{A}\ \boxed{B}\ \boxed{I}\ \boxed{L}\ \boxed{I}\ \boxed{T}\ \boxed{Y}$$

15. *P*(vowel then vowel)

16. *P*(consonant then consonant)

17. *P*(*I* then *I*)

18. *P*(consonant then vowel)

19. *P*(*A* then *A*)

20. *P*(letter then letter)

Example 4
(page 221)

21. Four girls and three boys volunteer to represent their class at a school assembly. The teacher selects one name and then another from a bag containing the seven students' names. What is the probability that both representatives will be girls?

22. A refrigerator contains 11 drinks: 5 lemon drinks, 3 apple drinks, and 3 orange drinks. Abby is first in line for drinks. Telly is second. What is the probability that Abby will get a lemon drink and Telly will get an orange drink, if they are given drinks at random?

B Apply Your Skills

You pick two marbles from the bag at the left. You pick the second one without replacing the first one. Find each probability.

23. *P*(red then blue)

24. *P*(two blues)

25. *P*(blue then green)

26. *P*(two reds)

27. *P*(green then yellow)

28. *P*(two greens)

Are the two events dependent or independent? Explain.

29. Toss a penny and a nickel.

30. Pick a name from a hat. Without replacement, pick a different name.

31. Pick a ball from a basket of both yellow and pink balls. Return the ball and pick again.

32. Writing Use your own words to explain the difference between independent and dependent events. Give an example of each.

222 Chapter 4 Solving and Applying Proportions

Real-World Connection

There are roughly 430 million acres of cropland in the United States, about the same area as Texas, Arizona, California, and New Mexico combined.

33. a. Agriculture An acre of land in Indiana is chosen at random. What is the probability that it is cropland?

b. An acre of land is chosen at random from each of the three states listed. What is the probability that all three acres will be cropland?

Percent of Cropland	
Alabama	8%
Florida	7%
Indiana	58%

34. Open-Ended Find the number of left-handed students in your class. Suppose your teacher randomly picks two students to work on a problem at the board.

a. Find the probability that they are both left-handed.
b. Find the probability that they are both right-handed.
c. Find the probability that the first student is right-handed and the second student is left-handed.

35. Quality Control The probability that a new spark plug is defective is 0.06. You need two new spark plugs for a motorcycle. What is the probability that both spark plugs you buy are defective?

You have three $1 bills, two $5 bills, and a $20 bill in your pocket. You choose two bills without looking. Find each probability.

36. P($5 then $1) with replacing

37. P($1 then $20) without replacing

38. P($20 then $1) with replacing

39. P($1 then $1) without replacing

40. P($5 then $20) without replacing

41. P($20 then $5) with replacing

42. A class has 12 girls and 10 boys. A hat contains the names of all the students in the class. To select representatives of the class to attend a meeting, the teacher draws two names from the hat without replacing the first name.

a. Find P(two girls).
b. Find P(two boys).
c. Find P(boy then girl).
d. Find P(girl then boy).
e. Predict the sum of the probabilities in parts (a)–(d). Check to see that the sum agrees with your prediction.

Challenge

43. a. You take a five-question multiple-choice quiz. You guess on all of the questions, selecting one of five answers randomly each time. What is the probability you will get a perfect score?

b. What is the probability that you would get a perfect score if there were six questions on the quiz?

c. Find the ratio of P(perfect score on five-question quiz) to P(perfect score on six-question quiz).

44. Suppose you roll a red number cube and a yellow number cube.

a. Find P(red 1 and yellow 1).
b. Find P(red 2 and yellow 2).
c. Find the probability of rolling any matching pair of numbers. (*Hint:* Add the probabilities of each of the six matches.)

Problem Solving Hint

For Exercise 45, making an organized list can help you understand the problem.

45. A two-digit number is formed by randomly selecting from the digits 1, 2, 3, and 5 without replacement.

a. How many different two-digit numbers can be formed?
b. What is the probability that a two-digit number contains a 2 or a 5?
c. What is the probability that a two-digit number is prime?

Multiple Choice

46. You roll a pair of number cubes. What is the probability of getting even numbers on both cubes?

A. 1   **B.** $\frac{1}{2}$ **C.** $\frac{1}{4}$ **D.** $\frac{1}{6}$

47. You take a three-question true or false quiz. You guess on all the questions. What is the probability that you will get a perfect score?

F. $\frac{1}{8}$ **G.** $\frac{3}{8}$ **H.** $\frac{1}{2}$ **I.** $\frac{3}{2}$

Take It to the NET
Online lesson quiz at
www.PHSchool.com
Web Code: aea-0406

48. A standard domino set has 28 dominoes. Seven of these are called "doubles" since they have the same number on both ends or are blank on both ends. The first and second player each take a domino at random. What is the probability that they will both draw a double?

A. $\frac{1}{16}$ **B.** $\frac{1}{18}$ **C.** $\frac{3}{56}$ **D.** $\frac{13}{756}$

Short Response

49. You have a bag containing 3 green marbles, 4 red marbles, and 2 yellow marbles. You select 2 marbles randomly, without replacement. How does the probability that they will both be green compare to the probability that they will both be red? Show your work.

Mixed Review

Lesson 4-5

Suppose you select a two-digit number at random from 10 to 30 (including 10 and 30). Find each probability.

50. P(number is even)   **51.** P(number is a multiple of 6)

52. P(number is prime)   **53.** P(number is less than 18)

Lesson 3-6

Solve each equation or inequality. If there is no solution, explain why.

54. $|6g| + 7 = 31$ **55.** $|-p + 2| = 0$ **56.** $|4a| > -3$

57. $|5 - y| - 2 < -9$ **58.** $|8w| + 9 < -7$ **59.** $16 < |26 - t| + 7$

Algebra at Work

.... Cartographer

A cartographer, or mapmaker, makes measurements of the area being mapped. The cartographer uses these dimensions to create the scale of the map, showing the ratio of map distance to actual distance. Knowing the scale of a map means that you can use a proportion to calculate any distance on the map.

Take It to the NET For more information about a career in cartography, go to **www.PHSchool.com**.
Web Code: aeb-2031

Sampling

Suppose you want to gather data about the kinds of music teenagers in the United States prefer. It would not be possible to survey all 40 million teenagers in the United States. You could select a sample of teenagers and study their preferences. A *population* is a group of objects, plants, animals, or people. A *sample* is part of a population.

To gather data that reflect characteristics of the population, you need a random sample. When a *random sample* is being chosen, all members of a population have equal chances of being selected.

1 EXAMPLE Choosing a Random Sample

You want to find out how many videos or DVDs students at your school rent in a month. State whether each survey plan describes a good sample.

a. Interview every tenth teenager you see at a mall.

This sample will probably include students who do not go to your school. It is not a good sample because it is not taken from the population you want to study.

b. Interview every third student from your school that you see in a video store.

Teenagers in a video store are likely to be renting a video or DVD. This is not a good sample because it is not random.

c. Interview every tenth student leaving a school assembly.

This is a good sample. It is selected at random from the population you want to study.

EXERCISES

For Exercises 1 and 2, state whether each plan describes a good sample. Explain.

1. You want to know how often teens get haircuts. You plan to survey customers in a barbershop or salon.

2. You want to know about peoples' favorite foods. You plan to survey every fifth person leaving the post office.

3. You survey every tenth person leaving a sporting goods store. Of those surveyed, 83% support the mayor's proposal for bike paths. You are writing an article for the school newspaper. Do you report that there is overwhelming support for the mayor's proposal? Explain why or why not.

4. **Critical Thinking** You review the results of survey questions given to two random samples of registered voters in your city. Why are the results not the same?

	Yes	No
Do you think that reckless skateboarders should be restricted in public playgrounds?	72%	28%
Do you think that skateboarders should be banned from public places?	42%	58%

Making Quantitative Comparisons

A Quantitative Comparison question asks you to determine the relationship between two quantities. Your answer is either A, B, C, or D.

- You pick A if the quantity in Column A is greater.
- You pick B if the quantity in Column B is greater.
- You pick C if the two quantities are always equal.
- You pick D if the relationship cannot be determined from the information given. If neither A nor B nor C is *always* true, then pick D.

Here are two strategies for answering quantitative comparison questions.

1 EXAMPLE   Rewriting the Quantities

Column A	Column B
$\frac{1}{3}$	33%

Quantities are easier to compare if they have the same form. Rewrite $\frac{1}{3}$ as the decimal 0.3333 . . . and compare it to 33% or 0.33. Since $\frac{1}{3} > 33\%$, the answer is A.

2 EXAMPLE   Evaluating a Variable

Column A	Column B
x^2	x^4

Substitute numbers for the variable. When you evaluate the variable, remember to include negative numbers as well as fractions. When $x = 2$, the quantity in column B is greater. However, when $x = \frac{1}{2}$, the quantity in column A is greater. The relationship cannot be determined because the value of x determines which quantity is greater. The answer is D.

EXERCISES

Refer to the Examples to answer each question.

1. Compare the quantities in Example 1 by writing the quantities as fractions with a common denominator.

2. If values of x in Example 2 are between -1 and 0, which quantity in Example 2 is greater?

3. Explain why an answer can never be D if the quantities in both boxes are numbers.

4. Answer the following Quantitative Comparison question using A, B, C, or D as described above.

Column A	Column B
the value of x in the equation $x - 5 = 3x + 7$	the value of n in the equation $4n - 3 = 2(2n + 2) - 7$

Chapter Review

Vocabulary

complement of an event (p. 212)
cross products (p. 183)
dependent events (p. 221)
event (p. 211)
experimental probability (p. 212)
extremes of a proportion (p. 183)
greatest possible error (p. 205)
independent events (p. 220)

means of a proportion (p. 183)
outcome (p. 211)
percent error (p. 206)
percent of change (p. 204)
percent of decrease (p. 204)
percent of increase (p. 204)
probability (p. 211)
proportion (p. 183)
rate (p. 182)

ratio (p. 182)
sample space (p. 211)
scale (p. 191)
scale drawing (p. 191)
similar figures (p. 190)
theoretical probability (p. 211)
unit analysis (p. 182)
unit rate (p. 182)

Reading Math
Understanding
Vocabulary

Choose the correct term to complete each sentence.

1. To change one unit of measure to another you can use a (*proportion, rate*) that is equal to 1.

2. You can use (*cross products, unit analysis*) to solve a proportion that involves one variable.

3. The ratio $\frac{\text{amount of change}}{\text{original amount}}$ is used to find (*percent of change, probability*).

4. The (*greatest possible error, percent error*) in a measurement is one half of the measuring unit.

5. The result of a single trial, such as one toss of a coin, is (*an outcome, a sample space*).

6. (*Theoretical probability, Complement of an event*) is all the outcomes not in an event.

7. You select a card, replace it, then select another card. The events are (*dependent, independent*).

8. The (*probability, sample space*) for rolling a number cube is 1, 2, 3, 4, 5, and 6.

9. If you drive 210 miles in 3 hours, your (*scale, unit rate*) of travel is 70 miles per hour.

10. Last year, Taylor earned $4.50 per hour baby-sitting. This year she earns $5.25 per hour. The (*percent of decrease, percent of increase*) is about 17%.

Take It to the NET
Online vocabulary quiz
at **www.PHSchool.com**
Web Code: aej-0451

Skills and Concepts

4-1 Objectives

▼ To find ratios and rates (p.182)

▼ To solve proportions (p.183)

A **ratio** is a comparison of two numbers by division. A **rate** is a ratio that compares quantities measured in different units. A **unit rate** is a rate with a denominator of 1.

A **proportion** is a statement that two ratios are equal. You can solve a proportion that involves one variable by finding the **cross products.**

Write in miles per hour. Round to the nearest hundredth.

11. 2.5 mi/min

12. 300 ft/min

13. 4 in./s

Solve each proportion.

14. $\frac{4}{12} = \frac{c}{6}$

15. $\frac{t}{5} = \frac{23}{50}$

16. $\frac{-9}{m} = \frac{3}{2}$

17. $\frac{x}{8} = \frac{x-5}{6}$

18. $\frac{12}{r} = \frac{4}{0.5r-1}$

19. $\frac{d-2}{d+9} = \frac{3}{14}$

4-2 Objectives

▼ To find missing measures of similar figures (p. 189)

▼ To use similar figures when measuring indirectly (p. 191)

Similar figures have the same shape but not necessarily the same size. If two figures are **similar,** then corresponding angles are congruent, and corresponding sides are in proportion.

A scale drawing is an enlarged or reduced drawing of an object. The ratio of the length of the drawing to the actual length of the object is the **scale** of the drawing. You can use proportions to solve problems involving scale drawings. A map is an example of a scale drawing.

In the figure at the right, $\triangle DEF \sim \triangle QRS$.

20. Find RS.

21. Find QR.

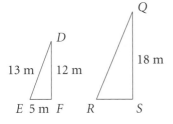

22. Hobbies A certain model airplane is $\frac{1}{48}$ of the airplane's actual size. The length of the model airplane's wing is $\frac{3}{4}$ ft. How long is the airplane's wing?

4-3 Objectives

▼ To use proportions when solving percent problems (p. 197)

▼ To write and solve percent equations (p. 198)

Below is a summary of how to solve problems involving percents by using proportions and by writing equations.

Finding the Percent	**Finding the Part**	**Finding the Whole**
What percent of 45 is 10?	What is 16% of 261?	71% of what number is 87?
$\frac{n}{100} = \frac{10}{45}$ ← **part** ← **whole**	$\frac{16}{100} = \frac{n}{261}$ ← **part** ← **whole**	$\frac{71}{100} = \frac{87}{n}$ ← **part** ← **whole**
$n \cdot 45 = 10$	$n = 0.16 \cdot 261$	$0.71n = 87$

Solve each percent problem.

23. What is 15% of 86?

24. 1.8 is 72% of what number?

25. What percent of 5 is 40?

26. 4% of what number is 34?

27. In one high school, 30 of the school's 800 students work on the school paper. What percent of the students work on the paper?

28. Finance You invest $2000 in a bank account. Find the amount of simple interest you earn in two years for an annual interest rate of 5.5%. Use the formula for simple interest $I = p \cdot r \cdot t$, where I is the interest, p is the principal, r is the annual interest rate, and t is the time in years.

4-4 Objectives

▼ To find percent of change (p. 204)

▼ To find percent error (p. 205)

The **percent of change** $= \frac{\text{amount of change}}{\text{original amount}}$. If a value increases from its original amount, the percent of change is the **percent of increase.** If a value decreases from its original amount, the percent of change is the **percent of decrease.**

The greatest possible error in a measurement is one half of the measuring unit. The percent error is $\frac{\text{greatest possible error}}{\text{measurement}}$.

For Exercises 29–31, find each percent of change. Where necessary, round to the nearest percent. Describe the percent of change as a percent of increase or percent of decrease.

29. $75,000 to $85,000   **30.** 20 feet to 15 feet   **31.** 60 hours to 40 hours

32. Open-Ended Describe a situation that involves a percent of increase that is more than 100%.

33. Suppose you measure a box. Its dimensions are 32 in. × 28 in. × 25 in. Find the percent error in calculating its volume. Round to the nearest tenth of a percent.

4-5 Objectives

▼ To find theoretical probability (p. 211)

▼ To find experimental probability (p. 212)

The **probability** of an event, or P(event), tells you how likely it is that something will occur. An **outcome** is the result of a single trial. An **event** is any outcome or group of outcomes. The **sample space** is all of the possible outcomes.

theoretical probability $P(\text{event}) = \dfrac{\text{number of favorable outcomes}}{\text{number of possible outcomes}}$

experimental probability $P(\text{event}) = \dfrac{\text{number of times an event occurs}}{\text{number of times the experiment is done}}$

Find each probability for one roll of a number cube.

34. $P(\text{number} \geq 7)$ **35.** $P(\text{not } 5)$ **36.** $P(2 \text{ or } 6)$ **37.** $P(3)$

38. Suppose you toss a coin 4 times.
   a. What is the probability that you toss exactly 3 heads?
   b. Explain what $P(\text{not } 3 \text{ heads})$ means.

39. Science An astronomer calculates that the probability that a visible meteor shower will occur in May is $\frac{3}{14}$. What is the probability that a visible meteor shower will not occur in May?

4-6 Objectives

▼ To find the probability of independent events (p. 219)

▼ To find the probability of dependent events (p. 221)

Independent events do not affect one another. When the outcome of one event affects the outcome of a second event, the events are **dependent events.**

For independent events A and B: For dependent events A and B:

$P(A \text{ and } B) = P(A) \cdot P(B)$. $P(A \text{ and } B) = P(A) \cdot P(B \text{ after } A)$.

For Exercises 40 and 41, suppose you choose two numbers from a box containing the numbers 1–10. State whether the two events are independent or dependent. Then find each probability.

40. $P(6 \text{ and an even number})$ without replacing the card

41. $P(1 \text{ and an odd number})$ with replacing the card

42. Writing Explain what the word *dependent* means in probability and what it means in everyday language.

Are the two events dependent or independent? Explain.

43. Roll a red and a blue number cube.

44. Randomly select a green sock and then another green sock to wear to school.

Chapter Test

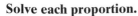
...... **Take It to the NET**
Online chapter test at
www.PHSchool.com
.... Web Code: aea-0452

Solve each proportion.

1. $\frac{3}{4} = \frac{c}{20}$

2. $\frac{8}{15} = \frac{4}{w}$

3. $\frac{w}{6} = \frac{6}{15}$

4. $\frac{5}{t} = \frac{25}{100}$

Solve an equation to answer each question.

5. What is 16% of 250?

6. 8 is what percent of 12.5?

7. 19 is 95% of what?

8. The ratio of the length of a side of one square to that of another square is 3:4. A side of the smaller square is 9 cm. Find the length of a side of the larger square.

9. Finance You invest $500 for three years and receive $60 in simple interest. What is the annual interest rate? Use the formula for simple interest $I = p \cdot r \cdot t$, where I is the interest, p is the principal, r is the annual interest rate, and t is the time in years.

10. Suppose a person contributes 6% of her salary to her retirement account. She works 20 hours per week at $6.50 per hour. Find her weekly contribution.

Calculate the percent of change. If necessary, round to the nearest tenth. Describe each as a percent of increase or a percent of decrease.

11. $4.50/h to $5/h

12. 60 km/h to 45 km/h

13. 150 lb to 135 lb

14. $18 to $24

15. Survey A random survey of 60 students showed that 36 students used calculators for computation. What is the probability that a student chosen at random used a calculator for computation?

16. A softball player made a hit 34 times in the last 170 times at bat. Find the probability that the softball player will get a hit the next time at bat.

Complete each statement.

17. 14¢/oz = $■ /lb

18. 7 gal/wk = ■ qt/h

19. 35 mi/h = ■ ft/min

20. 120 ft/day = ■ in./min

21. A scale on a map is 1 in.:25 mi. You measure 6.5 inches. How many miles is the actual distance?

22. A boy 5 ft tall casts a shadow 8 ft long. He stands next to a monument that has a shadow 20 ft long. How tall is the monument?

23. Suppose you have a bag containing 3 red, 4 blue, 5 white, and 2 black marbles. One marble is selected at random. Find the theoretical probability of choosing each of the following.
a. P(not white)
b. P(red or blue)
c. P(orange)

24. Comparison Shopping A bouquet of 12 carnations costs $6.99, while a bouquet of 8 carnations costs $4.99. Which is the better buy?

25. Open-Ended Write and solve a probability problem involving dependent events.

26. The game Monopoly™ was introduced in 1935. The table shows how much some amounts in the game should have increased to have kept up with inflation.

Category	Money Values	
	in 1935	in 2000
Total money in game	$15,140	$188,203
Amount each player starts the game with	$1500	$18,646
Park Place rent with no houses	$35	$435
Money collected when passing GO	$200	$2486

a. Estimate the percent of inflation from 1935 to 2000 by finding the percent of increase in any one of the dollar amounts.
b. Writing Describe the steps you used to calculate your answer to part (a).

27. You have 8 red checkers and 8 black checkers in a bag. You choose two checkers. Find each probability.
a. P(red and red) with replacing
b. P(red and black) without replacing
c. P(black and red) with replacing

Standardized Test Prep

Multiple Choice

For Exercises 1–10, choose the correct letter.

1. Tamara's teacher allows students to decide whether to use the mean, median, or mode for their test averages. Tamara will receive the highest average if she uses the mean. Which set of test scores are Tamara's?
   A. 95, 82, 76, 95, 96
   B. 79, 80, 91, 83, 80
   C. 65, 84, 75, 74, 65
   D. 100, 87, 94, 94, 81

2. A store owner has a bicycle priced at $100. She raises the price 10%. During a sale, she then lowers the price 10%. What is the new price of the bicycle?
   F. $101
   G. $100
   H. $99
   I. $98

3. A bag contains 10 red marbles and 20 white marbles. You draw a marble, keep it, and draw another. What is the probability of drawing two red marbles?
   A. $\frac{1}{10}$
   B. $\frac{3}{29}$
   C. $\frac{1}{9}$
   D. $\frac{1}{3}$

4. Which equation does NOT have the same solution as $\frac{7}{y} = \frac{31}{36}$?
   F. $\frac{7}{31} = \frac{y}{36}$
   G. $7 \cdot 36 = 31y$
   H. $\frac{y}{36} = \frac{7}{31}$
   I. $\frac{36}{31} = \frac{7}{y}$

5. The number of subscribers to a magazine fell from 210,000 to 190,000. Find the approximate percent of decrease.
   A. 5%
   B. 10%
   C. 20%
   D. 90%

6. Find the value of n if $3n - 5 = 7$.
   F. 6
   G. 5
   H. 4
   I. 3

7. The sum of four consecutive integers is 190. What is the third integer?
   A. 45
   B. 46
   C. 47
   D. 48

8. Evaluate $\frac{4a^2}{2b - 3}$ for $a = 3$ and $b = 6$.
   F. 3
   G. 4
   H. 6
   I. 16

9. Which ordered pair is graphed below?
   A. $(-2, 3)$
   B. $(-3, 2)$
   C. $(-2, -3)$
   D. $(-3, -2)$

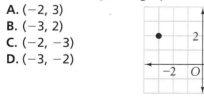

10. Which are solutions of $3(x - 4) \leq 18$ and $2(x - 1) \geq 6$?
    I. 9   II. 12   III. 15
    F. I only
    G. II only
    H. I and III
    I. II and III

Quantitative Comparison

Compare the boxed quantity in Column A with the boxed quantity in Column B. Choose the best answer.

   A. The quantity in Column A is greater.
   B. The quantity in Column B is greater.
   C. The two quantities are equal.
   D. The relationship cannot be determined from the information given.

Column A	Column B
11. $-x - 1$	$x + 1$

A number cube is rolled.

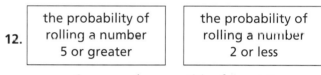

Column A	Column B
12. the probability of rolling a number 5 or greater	the probability of rolling a number 2 or less

Compare the quantities for $x \neq 0$.

Column A	Column B
13. $-|x|$	$|-x|$

Gridded Response

Find each answer.

14. A CD player that normally costs $225 would cost an employee $180. What is the percent of the employee's discount?

15. Solve $\frac{3}{5}(2m - 3) = -6$.

Short Response

Show your work.

16. **Art** In 1996, an exhibit in Washington, D.C., showed 21 paintings by Jan Vermeer. This is about $\frac{3}{5}$ of his known paintings. About how many of his paintings are known to exist?

17. Suppose you earn $80 a week at your summer job. Your employer offers you a $20 raise or a 20% raise. Which should you take? Explain why.

A Swing of the Bat

Applying Probability One of the most difficult athletic feats is also the one attempted most often in the United States—hitting a baseball with a baseball bat. A good batting average is .280 or better, which means that the batter gets a hit at least 28% of the time. The last major-league player with a season batting average above .400 was Ted Williams of the Boston Red Sox, who hit .406 in 1941. How do real batting averages compare with the probability of getting a hit?

Borders Cracks the Barrier
In 1997, Ila Borders, a left-handed pitcher with the St. Paul Saints, became the first woman to start and win a professional baseball game since the 1940s.

Activity 1

Materials: baseball bat, tape measure or ruler, pencil and paper

Suppose you are standing at the plate, ready to swing at a ball. Use the assumptions below.

- Every pitch will be in the strike zone.
- The timing of your swing will be correct so that the ball and bat are over the plate at the same time.

a. Use the given information to estimate the area of your strike zone.

b. Measure the bat and estimate the area that passes through the strike zone.

c. Use your answers to parts (a) and (b) to estimate the probability of making contact with the ball during a given swing.

Activity 2

a. Use your estimate from Activity 1 to calculate the probability of missing the ball during a given swing.

b. Use your answer to part (a) to estimate the probability of missing the ball three times in a row, or striking out.

c. Use your answer to part (b) to calculate the probability of not striking out.

KEY
- strikes ● balls ■ strike zone

Chin music; brushback

High inside strike

At the letters

Up and away ●

High and tight

Right down the pipe; down the middle; right down Broadway

Outside

Inside

Caught the corner

Down and away ●

At the knees

Down and in ●

The Strike Zone

Vertically, the strike zone extends from the hollow just below the batter's knee cap to a point midway between the top of the batter's belt and top of the batter's shoulders.

Horizontally, the strike zone is the width of home plate, which is 17 in., plus twice the diameter of the ball, or 5.8 in.

Power Hitter

The bat bends from the power of Mark McGwire's swing during the 1992 All-Star Game.

Activity 3

a. Having the bat make contact with the ball doesn't always mean that you get a hit. Estimate the percentage of contacts with the ball that result in a hit, either through interviewing baseball players in your school or by researching baseball statistics.

b. Use your answer to part (a) and your results from Activity 2 to estimate the batting average you could expect to have if you kept your eyes closed.

Anatomy of a Hit

Begin with your feet about shoulders-width apart. As you swing the bat, your hips turn and your hands follow your hips. As the bat makes contact with the ball, snap your wrists and watch the ball soar.

Heavy Hitter

Ted Williams of the Boston Red Sox watches the ball sail over the crowd.

Take It to the NET
For more information about baseball, go to **www.PHSchool.com**.
Web Code: aee-0453

233

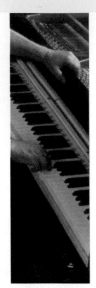

Where You've Been

● In Chapter 1, you learned to represent relationships using variables, and you reviewed graphing points on a coordinate plane.

● In Chapter 2, you learned the methods for solving equations in one variable. In Chapter 3, you applied those methods to solving inequalities and in Chapter 4, to solving proportions.

Instant self-check online and on CD-ROM

Diagnosing Readiness

(For help, go to the Lesson in green.)

Writing Equations (Lesson 1-1)

Define a variable and write an equation to model each situation.

1. The total price is the number of pens times $.59.

2. The tower is 200 feet taller than the house.

3. What is the perimeter of an equilateral triangle?

Evaluating Expressions (Lesson 1-2)

Evaluate each expression.

4. $3x - 2y$, for $x = -1$ and $y = 2$

5. $-w^2 + 3w$, for $w = -3$

6. $\frac{3 + k}{k}$, for $k = 3$

7. $h - (h^2 - 1) \div 2$, for $h = -1$

Graphing on the Coordinate Plane (Lesson 1-9)

Graph the points on the same coordinate plane.

8. $(3, -3)$

9. $(0, -5)$

10. $(-2, 2)$

11. $(-2, 0)$

Solving Absolute Value Equations (Lesson 3-6)

Solve each equation. If there is no solution, write *no solution*.

12. $|r + 2| = 2$

13. $-3|d - 5| = -6$

14. $-3.2 = |8p|$

Using Cross Products (Lesson 4-1)

Solve the following proportions.

15. $\frac{4}{w} = \frac{5}{8}$

16. $\frac{c}{2.2} = \frac{3}{11}$

17. $\frac{4}{0.5} = \frac{36}{p}$

18. $-\frac{29}{2} = \frac{d}{4}$

Graphs and Functions

Key Vocabulary

- arithmetic sequence (p. 269)
- common difference (p. 269)
- conjecture (p. 268)
- constant of variation (p. 262)
- dependent variable (p. 248)
- direct variation (p. 262)
- domain (p. 241)
- function (p. 242)
- function notation (p. 243)
- function rule (p. 243)
- independent variable (p. 248)
- inductive reasoning (p. 268)
- range (p. 241)
- relation (p. 241)
- sequence (p. 269)
- term (p. 269)
- vertical-line test (p. 242)

Where You're Going

- In this chapter, you will move from the specific case of equations in one variable to the study of functions in two variables.

- You will learn about function rules, and model data using equations, tables, and graphs.

- You will learn how to use inductive reasoning for recognizing number patterns called sequences.

 Real-World Connection Applying what you learn, you will solve a problem using sequences to describe a pattern relating the frequencies of musical notes, on page 271.

Relating Graphs to Events

Lesson Preview

What You'll Learn

OBJECTIVE

1 To interpret, sketch, and analyze graphs from situations

. . . And Why

To use a sketch in showing a plane's altitude during a flight, as in Example 2

✓ **Check Skills You'll Need**

(For help, go to Lesson 1-9.)

Use the graph at the right.

Name the point with the given coordinates.

1. $(4, -2)$ **2.** $(4, 3)$

3. $(2, -4)$ **4.** $(-2, 1)$

Name the coordinates of each given point.

5. B **6.** F **7.** G

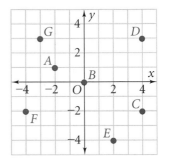

OBJECTIVE

1 Interpreting, Sketching, and Analyzing Graphs

You can use an equation, an inequality, or a proportion to make a statement about a variable. You can use a graph to show the relationship between two variables. For example, you can use a graph to show how a quantity changes over time.

1 EXAMPLE Interpreting Graphs

Commute One student walks and takes a bus to get from school to home each day. The graph at the right shows the student's commute by relating the time the student spends commuting and the distance he travels.

Describe what the graph shows by labeling each part.

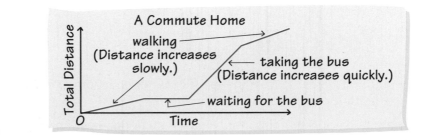

✓ **Check Understanding** **1** The graph at the right shows a trip from home to school and back. The trip involves walking and getting a ride from a neighbor. Copy the graph and label each section.

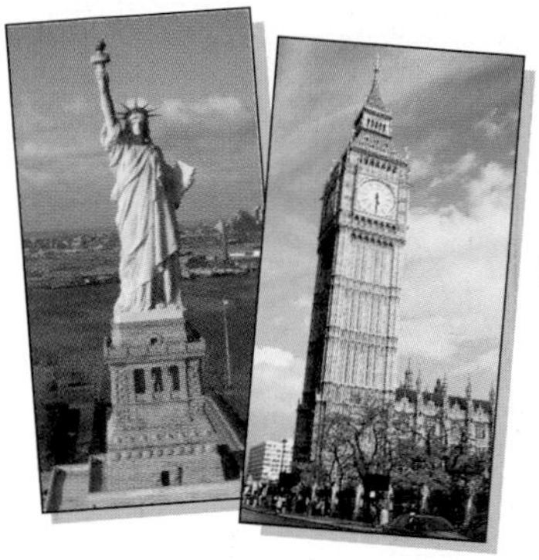

Real-World Connection

The Statue of Liberty, in New York harbor, is 151 ft from base to torch. The clock tower, which is part of the Houses of Parliament in London, is 320 ft tall.

In Example 1, distance, which is on the vertical axis, depends on time, which is on the horizontal axis. When one quantity depends on another, show the dependent quantity on the vertical axis.

2 EXAMPLE Sketching a Graph

Travel A plane is flying from New York to London. Sketch a graph of the plane's altitude during the flight. Label each section.

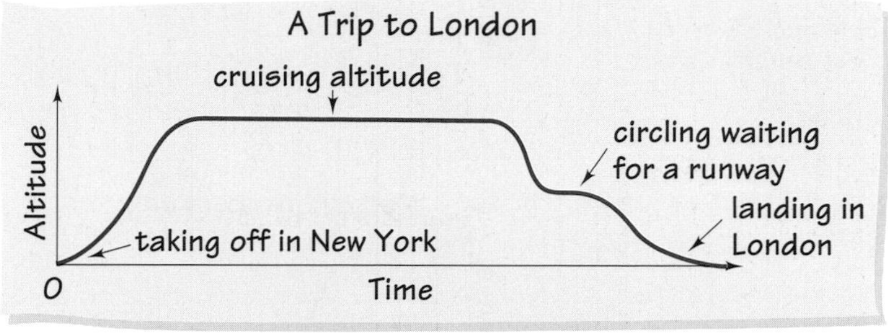

✓ Check Understanding 2 Sketch a graph of the distance from a child's feet to the ground as the child jumps rope. Label each section.

Most of the graphs in this lesson do not have numbers along the axes. You can analyze a graph based on the shape of the graph alone.

3 EXAMPLE Analyzing Graphs

A car travels at a steady speed. Which graph could you use to show the speed of the car, and which could you use to show the distance it has traveled? Explain.

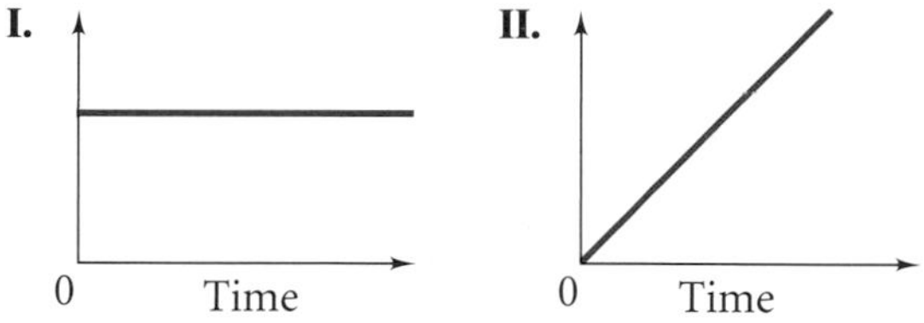

Graph I indicates a quantity that does not change with time. You could use it to indicate a car going at a steady speed. Graph II shows an increase over time. You could use it to indicate the distance a car travels at a steady speed over a given amount of time.

✓ Check Understanding 3 Suppose you pour water into each container below at a steady rate. Match each container with the graph that shows the change in the height of the liquid in the container over time. Explain your choices.

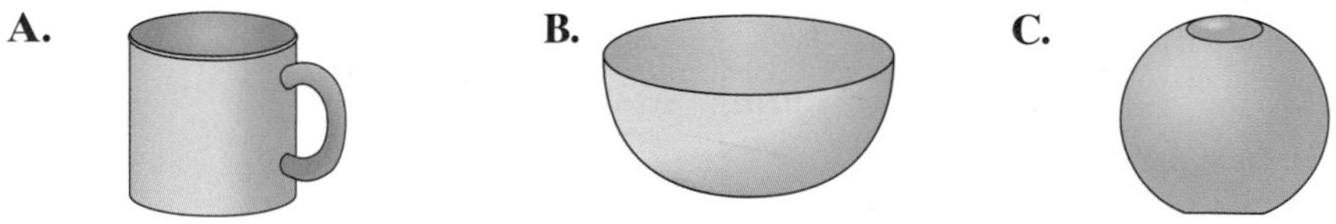

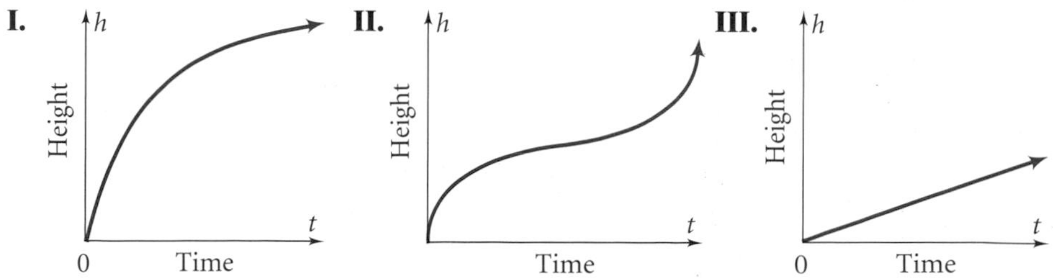

EXERCISES

For more practice, see *Extra Practice*.

Practice and Problem Solving

A **Practice by Example**

Example 1
(page 236)

Copy each graph. Label each section of the graph.

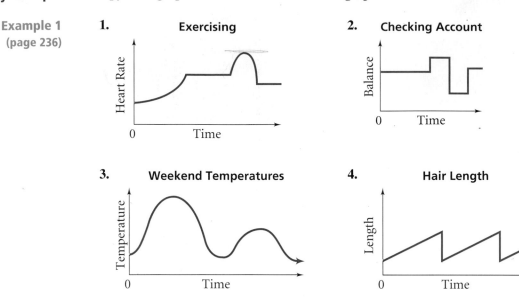

1. Exercising
2. Checking Account
3. Weekend Temperatures
4. Hair Length

Example 2
(page 237)

Sketch a graph of each situation. Label each section.

5. hours of daylight over the course of one year

6. your distance from the ground as you ride a Ferris wheel for five minutes

7. your pulse rate as you watch a scary movie

8. your walking speed during five minutes between classes

Example 3
(page 237)

9. **Cooking** You turn on your oven to bake a casserole. Which graph best represents the oven temperature over time? Explain your choice.

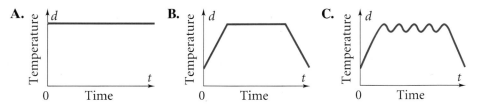

A.
B.
C.

B **Apply Your Skills**

10. **Weather** The graph shows the barometric pressure in Pittsburgh, Pennsylvania, during a blizzard. Describe what happened to the pressure during the storm.

Blizzard of 1993

7 A.M.   7 P.M.   7 A.M.
Time

SOURCE: Purdue Weather Processor

11. Sketch graphs of each situation. Are the graphs the same? Explain.
   a. Your speed as you travel from the bottom of a ski slope to the top.
   b. Your speed as you travel from the top of a ski slope to the bottom.

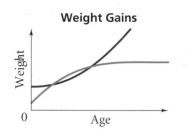

Weight Gains

Weight

0   Age

12. The graph at the left shows the weight of a baby and the weight of a puppy for their first two years.
   a. Which curve represents the puppy's weight? The baby's weight?
   b. Writing Describe the growth patterns of the baby and the puppy.

13. You pour juice into a pitcher like the one shown in the photographs below. You pour the juice at a constant rate. Make a sketch to show the height of juice in the pitcher as you fill it.

14. Error Analysis The graph at the right shows a person's speed over the course of a bike ride. Your friend said that this graph describes a person bicycling up and then down a hill. Explain your friend's error.

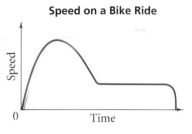

Speed on a Bike Ride

Speed

0   Time

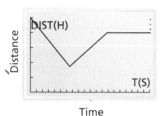

DIST(H)

Distance

T(S)

Time

15. A student used a graphing calculator, a data collector, and a motion detector to make the graph at the left, which shows a classmate's distance from the motion detector.
   a. Copy the graph and label each section.
   b. During which section was the student walking toward the motion detector?
   c. During which section(s) was the student walking at a constant speed?

16. Which graph better represents a person's change in height from birth to age 80? Explain your choice.

A.

h

Height

0   Age a

B.

h

Height

0   Age a

17. a. Open-Ended Sketch a graph of the daily high temperature over the course of one year for your town.
   b. Critical Thinking How would your graph be different if you lived at the equator?

C **Challenge**

Use the graph at the right for Exercises 18–21.

18. How much does it cost to park for 2 hours?

19. How much does it cost to park for 121 minutes?

20. Suppose your mother pays $6 for parking. About how long was her car parked in the garage?

21. Vocabulary This graph is a *step graph*. Does this name make sense? Explain.

Parking Garage Costs

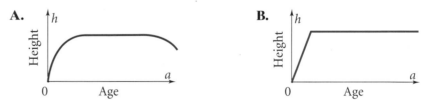

Cost (dollars)

14
12
9
6
3

0   2   4   6   8   10
Time (hours)

22. In-Line Skating **a.** Describe what the graph at the right shows about a student's in-line skating experience. **b.** Label each section.

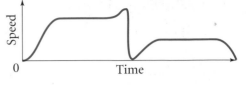

In-Line Skating After School

Multiple Choice

The graph at the right shows the distance Molly was from home throughout Tuesday. She spent about six hours at school, one hour at a friend's house, and about 30 minutes waiting for a bus. She also walked and rode the bus part of the day. Use the graph for Exercises 23–24.

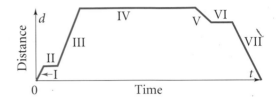

23. What section most likely represents walking to the bus stop?
   A. I   **B.** II   **C.** IV   **D.** V

24. What section most likely represents spending time at a friend's house?
   F. II   **G.** IV   **H.** VI   **I.** VII

Short Response

25. An hourglass has two compartments that hold sand. The graph at the right shows the height of the sand in the bottom container as it fills. Which hourglass does the graph represent? Explain your choice.

    I   II   III   IV

Take It to the NET
Online lesson quiz at
www.PHSchool.com
Web Code: aea-0501

Lesson 4-6   **You roll a red number cube and a blue number cube. Find each probability.**

26. $P(\text{red } 1 \text{ and blue } 6)$ **27.** $P(\text{red } 3 \text{ and blue } 5)$ **28.** $P(\text{red} > 4 \text{ and blue } 5)$

29. $P(\text{red odd and blue } 3)$ **30.** $P(\text{red and blue even})$ **31.** $P(\text{red and blue equal})$

Lesson 3-4   **Solve each inequality.**

32. $5x + 2 < 37$ **33.** $x + 4 > 2x - 4$ **34.** $8x + 4 - 3x \geq 3x$

35. $7 > -4x - 9$ **36.** $7(x + 1) \leq 6(x - 1)$ **37.** $-2 + 5x < 8 - 10x$

Lesson 2-1   **Solve each equation.**

38. $4t = 44$ **39.** $x - 8 = 9$ **40.** $\frac{d}{3} = 15$ **41.** $-9 = m + 6$

42. $y + 18 = 2$ **43.** $\frac{k}{7} = 42$ **44.** $1.2q = 7.2$ **45.** $g + 22 = 25$

46. $-1 = p - 8$ **47.** $3x = 123$ **48.** $b - 78 = 101$ **49.** $2c = \frac{1}{2}$

5-2

Relations and Functions

Lesson Preview

What You'll Learn

OBJECTIVE 1 To identify relations and functions

OBJECTIVE 2 To evaluate functions

. . . And Why

To determine whether a relation is a function, as in Examples 2 and 3

✓ Check Skills You'll Need

(For help, go to Lessons 1-9 and 1-2.)

Graph each point on a coordinate plane.

1. $(2, -4)$ **2.** $(0, 3)$ **3.** $(-1, -2)$ **4.** $(-3, 0)$

Evaluate each expression.

5. $3a - 2$ for $a = -5$ **6.** $\dfrac{x + 3}{-6}$ for $x = 3$ **7.** $3x^2$ for $x = 6$

New Vocabulary   • relation   • domain   • range   • function   • vertical-line test   • function rule   • function notation

---

OBJECTIVE 1

ⓘTEXT Interactive lesson includes instant self-check, tutorials, and activities.

Identifying Relations and Functions

A **relation** is a set of ordered pairs. The (age, height) ordered pairs below form a relation.

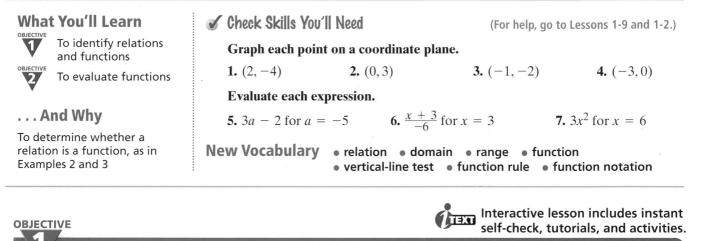

Giraffes

Age (years)	Height (meters)
18	4.25
20	4.40
21	5.25
14	5.00
18	4.85

age height
↓   ↓
(18, 4.25)
(20, 4.40)
(21, 5.25)
(14, 5.00)
(18, 4.85)

The **domain** of a relation is the set of first coordinates of the ordered pairs. The **range** is the set of second coordinates.

1 EXAMPLE   Finding Domain and Range

Real-World 🌐 Connection

Adult giraffes have heights from 4.25 m to 5.5 m, or about 14 ft to 18 ft.

Find the domain and range of the ordered pairs listed for the giraffe data above.

domain: {14, 18, 20, 21}   **List the values in order. Do not repeat values.**
range: {4.25, 4.40, 4.85, 5.00, 5.25}

✓ Check Understanding   **1** Find the domain and range of the relation represented by the data in the table.

Domain	Range
4	3
−2	1
−1	3
4	−2
−1	1

Definition	**Function**

A **function** is a relation that assigns exactly one value in the range to each value in the domain.

One way you can tell whether a relation is a function is to analyze the graph of the relation using the **vertical-line test.** If any vertical line passes through more than one point of the graph, the relation is not a function.

2 EXAMPLE **Using the Vertical-Line Test**

Determine whether the relation $\{(3, 0), (-2, 1), (0, -1), (-3, 2), (3, 2)\}$ is a function.

Step 1 Graph the ordered pairs on a coordinate plane.

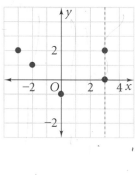

Step 2 Pass a pencil across the graph as shown.

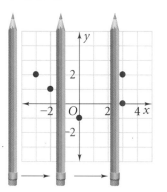

A vertical line would pass through both $(3, 0)$ and $(3, 2)$, so the relation is not a function.

✓ **Check Understanding** **2** Use the vertical-line test to determine whether each relation is a function.
  a. $\{(4, -2), (1, 2), (0, 1), (-2, 2)\}$ **b.** $\{(0, 2), (1, -1), (-1, 4), (0, -3), (2, 1)\}$

Another way you can tell whether a relation is a function is by making a *mapping diagram.* List the domain values and the range values in order. Draw arrows from the domain values to their range values.

3 EXAMPLE **Using a Mapping Diagram**

Determine whether each relation is a function.
  a. $\{(11, -2), (12, -1), (13, -2), (20, 7)\}$ **b.** $\{(-2, -1), (-1, 0), (6, 3), (-2, 1)\}$

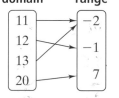

There is no value in the domain that corresponds to more than one value of the range.

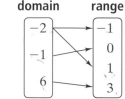

The domain value corresponds to two range values, -1 and 1.

Need Help?

In a mapping diagram, functions have no more than one arrow starting from each value of the domain.

The relation is a function.

The relation is not a function.

✓ **Check Understanding** **3** Use a mapping diagram to determine whether each relation is a function.
  a. $\{(3, -2), (8, 1), (9, 2), (3, 3), (-4, 0)\}$ **b.** $\{(6.5, 0), (7, -1), (6, 2), (2, 6), (5, -1)\}$

2 Evaluating Functions

A **function rule** is an equation that describes a function. You can think of a function rule as an input-output machine.

Words and Notations Used With a Function

Domain	Range
input	output
x	$f(x)$
x	y

The domain is the set of input values.

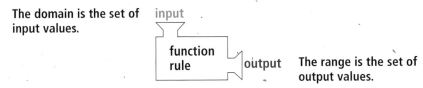

The range is the set of output values.

If you know the input values, you can use a function rule to find the output values. The output values depend on the input values.

$$y = 3x + 4$$

output   input

input values for x

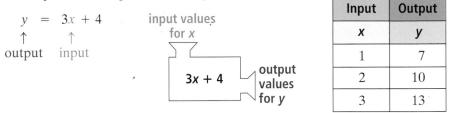

output values for y

Input	Output
x	y
1	7
2	10
3	13

Another way to write the function $y = 3x + 4$ is $f(x) = 3x + 4$. A function is in **function notation** when you use $f(x)$ to indicate the outputs. You read $f(x)$ as "f of x" or "f is a function of x." The notations $g(x)$ and $h(x)$ also indicate functions of x.

4 EXAMPLE Evaluating a Function Rule

Reading Math

You can think of the notation $f(6)$ as "Replace n with 6 to find the value of $f(6)$."

a. Evaluate $f(n) = -3n - 10$ for $n = 6$.   **b.** Evaluate $y = -2x^2 + 7$ for $x = -4$.

$f(n) = -3n - 10$

$f(6) = -3(6) - 10$ **Substitute 6 for n.**

$f(6) = -18 - 10$ **Simplify.**

$f(6) = -28$

$y = -2x^2 + 7$

$y = -2(-4)^2 + 7$ **Substitute -4 for x.**

$y = -2(16) + 7$ **Simplify the power.**

$y = -32 + 7$ **Simplify.**

$y = -25$

✓ **Check Understanding** 4 Evaluate each function rule for $x = 2.1$.

a. $y = 2x + 1$ **b.** $f(x) = x^2 - 4$ **c.** $g(x) = -x + 2$

You can use a function rule and a given domain to find the range of the function. After computing the range values, write the values in order from least to greatest.

5 EXAMPLE Finding the Range

Evaluate the function rule $f(a) = -3a + 5$ to find the range of the function for the domain $\{-3, 1, 4\}$.

$f(a) = -3a + 5$

$f(-3) = -3(-3) + 5$

$f(-3) = 14$

$f(a) = -3a + 5$

$f(1) = -3(1) + 5$

$f(1) = 2$

$f(a) = -3a + 5$

$f(4) = -3(4) + 5$

$f(4) = -7$

The range is $\{-7, 2, 14\}$.

✓ **Check Understanding** 5 Find the range of each function for the domain $\{-2, 0, 5\}$.

a. $f(x) = x - 6$ **b.** $y = -4x$ **c.** $g(t) = t^2 + 1$

EXERCISES

For more practice, see *Extra Practice*.

Practice and Problem Solving

A **Practice by Example**

Example 1
(page 241)

Find the domain and range of each relation.

1. $\{(4, 6), (6, 7), (4, 3), (5, 19), (5, 7)\}$ **2.** $\{(-3, 5), (-2, 8), (0, 7), (4, 22), (0, 5)\}$

3. $\{(2, -3), (-2, 3), (2, 3), (-2, -3), (3, -2)\}$ **4.** $\{(1, 0), (1, 5), (1, -7), (1, 6.1), (1, 10)\}$

5. $\{(1.2, 4), (-3.1, -5.2), (8.4, 0), (-3.1, 0)\}$ **6.** $\{\left(\frac{1}{2}, -1\right), \left(-\frac{2}{3}, -1\right), \left(4, \frac{3}{5}\right), (5, 0)\}$

Example 2
(page 242)

Use the vertical-line test to determine whether each relation is a function.

7. $\{(2, 5), (3, -5), (4, 5), (5, -5)\}$ **8.** $\{(5, 0), (0, 5), (5, 1), (1, 5)\}$

9. $\{(3, -1), (-2, 3), (-1, -5), (3, 2)\}$ **10.** $\{(-2, 9), (3, 9), (-0.5, 9), (4, 9)\}$

Example 3
(page 242)

Use a mapping diagram to determine whether each relation is a function.

11. $\{(3, 7), (3, 8), (3, -2), (3, 4), (3, 1)\}$ **12.** $\{(6, -7), (5, -8), (1, 4), (5, 5)\}$

13. $\{(0.04, 0.2), (0.2, 1), (1, 5), (5, 25)\}$ **14.** $\{(4, 2), (1, 1), (0, 0), (1, -1), (4, -2)\}$

Example 4
(page 243)

Evaluate each function rule for $x = -3$.

15. $y = x + 7$ **16.** $y = 11x - 1$ **17.** $f(x) = x^2$ **18.** $f(x) = -4x$

19. $f(x) = 15 - x$ **20.** $y = 3x + 2$ **21.** $y = \frac{1}{4}x$ **22.** $f(x) = -x + 2$

Example 5
(page 243)

Find the range of the function rule $y = 5x - 2$ for each domain.

23. $\{0.5, 11\}$ **24.** $\{-1.2, 0, 4\}$ **25.** $\{-5, -1, 0, 2, 10\}$ **26.** $\left\{-\frac{1}{2}, \frac{1}{4}, \frac{2}{5}\right\}$

B **Apply Your Skills**

Determine whether each relation is a function. If the relation is a function, state the domain and range.

27.

x	y
1	-3
6	-2
9	-1
1	3

28.

x	y
0	2
3	1
3	-1
5	3

29.

x	y
-4	-4
-1	-4
0	-4
3	-4

30. Iguanas Use the data in the table at the left. Is an iguana's length a function of its age? Explain.

31. Error Analysis A student thinks that the relation $\{(2, 1), (3, -2), (4, 5), (5, -2)\}$ is not a function because two values in the domain have the same range value. What is the student's error?

32. a. Profit A store bought a case of disposable cameras for $300. The store's profit p on the cameras is a function of the number c of cameras sold. Find the range of the function $p = 6c - 300$ when the domain is $\{0, 15, 50, 62\}$.

     b. Critical Thinking In this situation, what do the domain and range represent?

33. Open-Ended Create a data table for a relation that is *not* a function. Describe what your data might represent.

Iguanas

Age (years)	Length (inches)
2	30
4	37
3	31
5	45
4	40

Find the range of each function for the domain {−1, 0.5, 3.7}.

34. $f(x) = 4x + 1$ **35.** $g(x) = -4x + 1$ **36.** $y = |x| - 1$ **37.** $s(t) = t^2 - 1$

Use the vertical-line test to determine whether each graph is the graph of a function.

38.
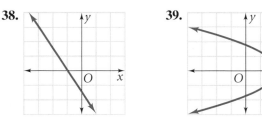

39.

40.

41. Telephone Bill The cost of a long-distance telephone call c is a function of the time spent talking t in minutes. The rule $c(t) = 0.09t$ describes the function for one service provider. At the right, a student has calculated how much a 2-hour phone call would cost.

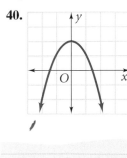

$c = 0.09 \times 2$

$= 0.18$

$\$.18$ for 2 hours

a. **Writing** Why does the student's answer seem unreasonable?

b. **Error Analysis** What mistake(s) did the student make?

c. How much would it cost to make a 2-hour phone call?

d. **Critical Thinking** What set of numbers is reasonable for the domain values? For the range values?

Real-World Connection

A telecommunications device for the deaf (TDD) includes a keyboard and a visual display of the conversation. This lets a hearing-impaired person use a telephone.

42. Physics Light travels about 186,000 miles per second. The rule $d = 186{,}000t$ describes the relationship between distance d in miles and time t in seconds.

a. How far does light travel in 20 seconds?

b. How far does light travel in 1 minute?

C Challenge

Use the functions $f(x) = 2x$ and $g(x) = x^2 + 1$ to find the value of each expression.

43. $f(3) + g(4)$ **44.** $g(3) + f(4)$ **45.** $f(5) - 2g(1)$ **46.** $f(g(3))$

47. Critical Thinking Can the graph of a function be a horizontal line? A vertical line? Explain why or why not.

48. The function $y = [x]$ is called the *greatest-integer function*. $[x]$ is the greatest integer less than or equal to x. For example, $[2.99] = 2$ and $[-2.3] = -3$.

a. Evaluate the function for $0.5, -0.1, -1.99,$ and -5.2.

b. The domain of $y = [x]$ is all real numbers. What is the range of $y = [x]$?

Standardized Test Prep

Gridded Response

49. Evaluate the function rule $f(x) = 7x$ for $x = 0.75$.

50. Evaluate the function rule $f(x) = 9 - 0.2x$ for $x = 1.5$.

51. What is the greatest value in the range of $y = x^2 - 7$ for the domain {−2, 0, 1}?

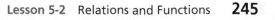

52. What is the greatest value in the domain of the function $f(x) = 3x - 5$ for the range $\{-2, 0, 4\}$?

Short Response **53.** Determine whether the data below are a function. Show your work.

Mount Rushmore Temperatures (°F)

At Base of Mountain	At Top of Mountain
80	72
65	58
93	84
98	91
74	69

Take It to the NET
Online lesson quiz at
www.PHSchool.com
Web Code: aea-0502

Mixed Review

Lesson 5-1 **54.** The graph shows distance from home as a family drives to the mountains for a vacation. Copy the graph. Label each section of the graph.

A Trip to the Mountains

Distance Traveled vs *Time*

Lesson 4-2 **The scale of a map is 1 in. : 15 mi. Find the actual distance corresponding to each map distance.**

55. 2 in. **56.** 1.5 in. **57.** 0.5 in.

58. 3.25 in. **59.** 5.5 in. **60.** 7.25 in.

Lesson 2-7 **Find the mean, median, mode, and range.**

61. 34 33 35 33 32 35 34 32 **62.** 1 −2 0 −1 1 −2 2 0 1 −2

63. 4 5 3 7 1 12 6 9 5 **64.** 15 13 19 20 9 13 15 13

65. −4 −8 −7 −7 −4 −7 −1 −9 **66.** 43 45 51 42 48 48 43 52

✓ Checkpoint Quiz 1   Lessons 5-1 through 5-2

TEXT Instant self-check quiz online and on CD-ROM

Sketch a graph of each situation. Label each section.

1. the height of a plant that grows at a steady rate

2. the temperature in a classroom after the heater is turned on

3. a child's height above the ground while on a swing

4. Is the graph at the right the graph of a function? Explain.

Evaluate each function rule for $x = 0.6$.

5. $f(x) = -4x$ **6.** $g(x) = x + 1.53$

7. $y = 2 - 0.5x$ **8.** $y = 3x^2$

9. $f(x) = 34 - x$ **10.** $g(x) = -3 + 2x$

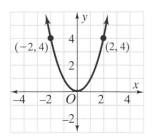

Function Rules, Tables, and Graphs

Lesson Preview

What You'll Learn

OBJECTIVE

1 To model functions using rules, tables, and graphs

...And Why

To find the cost of making CDs, as in Example 2

✓ Check Skills You'll Need

(For help, go to Lesson 5-2.)

Graph the data in each table.

1.

x	y
−3	−7
−1	−1
0	2
2	8

2.

x	y
−3	4
−2	0
0	−2
2	4

3.

x	y
−4	−3
0	−2
2	−1.5
4	−1

New Vocabulary • independent variable • dependent variable

---

iTEXT Interactive lesson includes instant self-check, tutorials, and activities.

OBJECTIVE

1 Modeling Functions

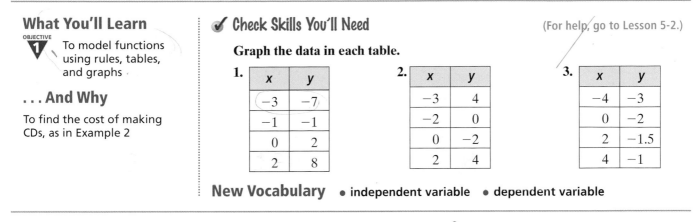

Investigation: Functions

1 in. $1\frac{1}{2}$ in.   2 in.

1. Copy and complete the table for squares.

Side length (in.)	Perimeter (in.)	Area (in.²)
1	4	1
$1\frac{1}{2}$	6	$2\frac{1}{4}$
2	▨	▨
$2\frac{1}{2}$	▨	▨
3	▨	▨

2. a. Make a graph of side length ℓ and perimeter p for ordered pairs (ℓ, p).
   b. Make a graph of side length ℓ and area A for ordered pairs (ℓ, A).

3. For which of the two graphs could you join the points to form a line?

4. Write two rules, one for finding the perimeter of a square with side length ℓ, and one for finding the area A of a square.

You can model functions using rules, tables, and graphs. A function rule shows how the variables are related. A table identifies specific input and output values of the function. A graph gives a visual picture of the function.

The inputs are values of the **independent variable.** The outputs are the corresponding values of the **dependent variable.**

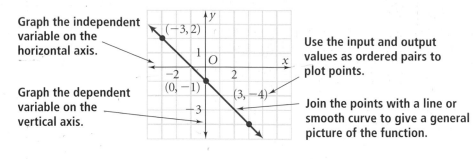

Graph the independent variable on the horizontal axis.

Graph the dependent variable on the vertical axis.

(−3, 2)

(0, −1)

(3, −4)

Use the input and output values as ordered pairs to plot points.

Join the points with a line or smooth curve to give a general picture of the function.

1 EXAMPLE **Three Views of a Function**

Model the function rule $y = \frac{1}{2}x + 3$ using a table of values and a graph.

Step 1 Choose input values for x. Evaluate to find y.

Step 2 Plot points for the ordered pairs.
Step 3 Join the points to form a line.

x	$y = \frac{1}{2}x + 3$	(x, y)
−4	$y = \frac{1}{2}(-4) + 3 = 1$	$(-4, 1)$
0	$y = \frac{1}{2}(0) + 3 = 3$	$(0, 3)$
2	$y = \frac{1}{2}(2) + 3 = 4$	$(2, 4)$

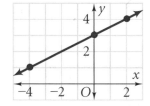

✔ **Check Understanding** ❶ Model the rule $f(x) = 3x + 4$ with a table of values and a graph.

When you draw a graph for a real-world situation, choose appropriate intervals for the units on the axes. Be sure the intervals are equal. Also, if the data are positive numbers, use only the first quadrant.

2 EXAMPLE **Real-World** 🌐 **Problem Solving**

Recording Costs Suppose your group recorded a CD. Now you want to copy and sell it. One company charges $250 for making a master CD and designing the art for the cover. There is also a cost of $3 to burn each CD. The total cost $P(c)$ depends on the number of CDs c burned. Use the function rule $P(c) = 250 + 3c$ to make a table of values and a graph.

c	$P(c) = 250 + 3c$	$(c, P(c))$
100	$250 + 3(100) = 550$	$(100, 550)$
200	$250 + 3(200) = 850$	$(200, 850)$
300	$250 + 3(300) = 1150$	$(300, 1150)$
500	$250 + 3(500) = 1750$	$(500, 1750)$

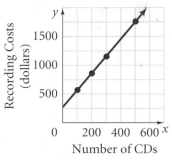

Recording Costs (dollars)
Number of CDs

Real-World 🌐 **Connection**

Careers Recording engineers record singers and instruments separately. The sounds are mixed later to achieve the desired effect.

✔ **Check Understanding** ❷ **a.** Another company charges $300 for making a master and designing the art. It charges $2.50 for burning each CD. Use the function rule $P(c) = 300 + 2.5c$. Make a table of values and a graph.

b. Critical Thinking Compare your graph from part (a) to the graph in Example 2. For what number of CDs is the studio in the Example less expensive?

Some functions have graphs that are not straight lines. You can graph a function as long as you know its rule. After you have graphed the ordered pairs that you have calculated from a rule, join the points with a smooth line or curve.

3 EXAMPLE Graphing Functions

a. Graph the function $y = |x| + 1$.

Make a table of values.

x	$y = |x| + 1$	(x, y)
-3	$|-3| + 1 = 4$	$(-3, 4)$
-1	$|-1| + 1 = 2$	$(-1, 2)$
0	$|0| + 1 = 1$	$(0, 1)$
1	$|1| + 1 = 2$	$(1, 2)$
3	$|3| + 1 = 4$	$(3, 4)$

Then graph the data.

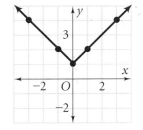

b. Graph the function $f(x) = x^2 + 1$.

Make a table of values.

x	$f(x) = x^2 + 1$	$(x, f(x))$
-2	$4 + 1 = 5$	$(-2, 5)$
-1	$1 + 1 = 2$	$(-1, 2)$
0	$0 + 1 = 1$	$(0, 1)$
1	$1 + 1 = 2$	$(1, 2)$
2	$4 + 1 = 5$	$(2, 5)$

Then graph the data.

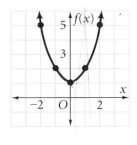

✓ **Check Understanding** **3** Make a table of values and graph each function.
a. $f(x) = |x| - 1$ **b.** $y = x^2 - 1$

EXERCISES

For more practice, see *Extra Practice*.

Practice and Problem Solving

A Practice by Example

Example 1
(page 248)

Match each graph with its rule.

1. $f(x) = 2x$ **2.** $f(x) = \frac{1}{2}x$ **3.** $f(x) = x + 2$

A. 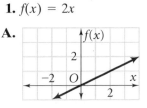   **B.** 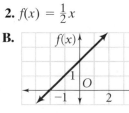   **C.**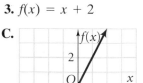

Model each rule with a table of values and a graph.

4. $f(x) = -3x$ **5.** $f(x) = -3x + 1$ **6.** $f(x) = -3x - 2$

7. $y = 2x - 7$ **8.** $f(x) = 8 - x$ **9.** $y = 5 + 4x$

10. $f(x) = \frac{1}{4}x$ **11.** $y = 4x$ **12.** $y = x + 4$

Example 2
(page 248)

13. Earnings Juan charges $3.50 per hour for baby-sitting.
    a. Write a rule to describe how the amount of money M earned is a function of the number of hours h spent baby-sitting.
    b. Make a table of values.
    c. Graph the values and join the points with a line.
    d. Estimation Use the graph to estimate how long it will take Juan to earn $30.

14. Geometry The figure at the right is a regular pentagon. The function $P(\ell) = 5\ell$ describes the perimeter of a regular pentagon with side length ℓ.
    a. Make a table of values for $\ell = 1, 2, 3,$ and 4.
    b. Graph the function.

Regular pentagon

Example 3
(page 249)

Graph each function.

15. $y = |x|$

16. $y = |x| + 2$

17. $y = x^2$

18. $f(x) = x^2 - 1$

19. $f(x) = |x| + 3$

20. $y = x^2 + 3$

21. $y = |x| - 4$

22. $f(x) = -x^2 - 1$

23. $f(x) = -x^2 + 2$

B **Apply Your Skills**

24. a. Make a table for the perimeters of the rectangles formed by each set of blue tiles.
    b. The perimeter $P(t)$ is a function of the number of tiles t. Write a rule for the data in your table and graph the function.

Fig. 1 Fig. 2 Fig. 3 Fig. 4

25. Writing Describe the steps you would use to graph the function rule $f(x) = 3x - 2$.

Graph each function.

26. $f(x) = \frac{3}{4}x + 7$

27. $y = x^2 - 4x + 4$

28. $y = |2x|$

29. $y = x + \frac{1}{2}$

30. $f(x) = 7 - 5x$

31. $f(x) = \left|\frac{1}{2}x\right|$

32. $f(x) = \left|\frac{1}{2}x\right| + 1$

33. $y = 1 - x^2$

34. $f(x) = -5x^2$

35. $y = 2x - 3$

36. $y = \left|\frac{1}{3}x\right|$

37. $f(x) = -|x + 2|$

38. Conserving Water The equation $w = 6m$ models the gallons of water w used by a standard shower head for a shower that takes m minutes. The function $w = 3m$ models the water-saving shower head.
    a. Suppose you take a 6-minute shower using a water-saving shower head. How much water do you save compared to an average shower with a standard shower head?
    b. Graph both functions on the same coordinate plane.
    c. Open-Ended How much water did you use during your last shower?
    d. How did you find your answer?

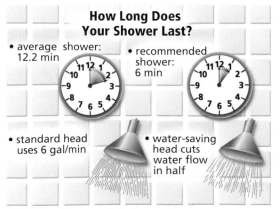

How Long Does Your Shower Last?
- average shower: 12.2 min
- recommended shower: 6 min
- standard head uses 6 gal/min
- water-saving head cuts water flow in half

SOURCE: Opinion Research Corp.

39. a. Language Arts Copy and complete the analogy: "Input value is to output value as independent variable is to _?_."
    b. Write an analogy using *input*, *output*, *domain*, and *range*.

40. a. Geometry The function $A(\ell) = \frac{1}{2}\ell^2$ describes the area of an isosceles right triangle with leg ℓ. Make a table of values for $\ell = 1, 2, 3,$ and 4.
  b. Graph the function.

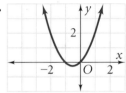

Isosceles right triangle

41. Calling Costs For one calling plan, the cost $C(a)$ of a call from Sacramento, California, to Salt Lake City, Utah, is a function of the number of additional minutes a after the first minute. The rule $C(a) = 0.27 + 0.11(a - 1)$ models the cost.
  a. How much will a 5-minute call cost?
  b. How many minutes can you talk for $1.50?

42. a. Graph $y = |x|$ and $y = -|x|$ on the same coordinate plane.
  b. The graph of $y = -|x|$ is the reflection of the graph of $y = |x|$. Over which axis is the graph of $y = |x|$ reflected?
  c. Write an equation of the reflection of the graph of $y = |x| + 1$ over the same axis.

43. Which is the graph of the function $f(x) = \frac{1}{2}x^2 + x$?

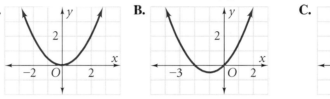

Need Help?

To review reflections, see Skills Handbook page 733.

Challenge

44. a. Graph each function on the same coordinate plane.
  i. $f(x) = |x| + 2$ **ii.** $f(x) = |x| + 4$ **iii.** $f(x) = |x| - 3$
  b. Critical Thinking In the function $y = |x| + b$, how does changing the value of b change the graph of the function?

45. a. Graph each function on the same coordinate plane.
  i. $f(x) = |2x|$ **ii.** $f(x) = |0.5x|$ **iii.** $f(x) = |3x|$
  b. Critical Thinking In the function $y = |ax|$, how does changing the value of a change the graph of the function?

46. The function $s(x)$, sometimes called the signum function, is defined as

$$s(x) = \begin{cases} 1 \text{ if } x > 0 \\ 0 \text{ if } x = 0 \\ -1 \text{ if } x < 0 \end{cases}$$

For example, $s(17) = 1, s(0) = 0,$ and $s(-32) = -1$.
  a. Evaluate $s(3.77), s(0.003), s(-1.5),$ and $s(-2300)$.
  b. The domain of the function is all real numbers. What is the range?
  c. Make a table of values and graph the function.
  d. Make a Conjecture Do you think $s(a + b) = s(a) + s(b)$? First, test some values of a and b. If your answer is *yes*, justify your answer. If your answer is *no*, give a counterexample.

Standardized Test Prep

Multiple Choice

47. Suppose you hire an electrician to install several electrical outlets in your home. The electrician charges $68 for materials plus $40 per hour (or fraction of an hour). How much will the electrician charge you if the job takes $2\frac{1}{4}$ hours?
  A. $148   **B.** $158   **C.** $188   **D.** $208

48. Which is the graph of the function rule $f(x) = \frac{1}{2}x - 2$?

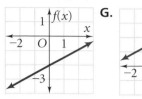 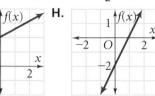 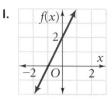

49. Which function is modeled by the table at the right?
  A. $f(x) = x - 2$ **B.** $f(x) = 2x + 1$
  C. $f(x) = -x + 1$ **D.** $f(x) = \frac{1}{2}x - 1$

x	f(x)
-3	-5
0	1
2	5
3	7

50. Which points are on the graph of the function rule $f(x) = 10 - 4x$?
  F. $(18, -2), (10, 0), (2, 2)$
  G. $(-18, 2), (-10, 0), (-2, -2)$
  H. $(2, -18), (0, -10), (-2, -2)$
  I. $(-2, 18), (0, 10), (2, 2)$

Take It to the NET

Online lesson quiz at
www.PHSchool.com
Web Code: aea-0503

Short Response

51. Graph the equations $y = x + 3$, $y = x^2 + 3$, and $y = |x| + 3$ on the same coordinate plane. Describe the similarities and differences in the graphs.

Extended Response

52. a. Make a table of values for the function rule $f(x) = |x + 1| - 2$.
  b. Graph $f(x) = |x + 1| - 2$.

Mixed Review

Lesson 5-2

Find the range of each function for the domain $\{-2, 0, 3.5\}$.

53. $f(x) = 3x + 1$ **54.** $g(x) = 3x - 5$ **55.** $f(s) = -3s + 4$

56. $g(v) = |v| - 5$ **57.** $h(n) = 12 - n$ **58.** $g(w) = 5(w - 2)$

59. $p(n) = 6n + 1$ **60.** $f(x) = 0.5x - 8$ **61.** $k(n) = -11n + 9$

Lesson 3-6

Solve each equation. If there is no solution, explain.

62. $|x| + 7 = 11$ **63.** $9 = 10 + |b|$ **64.** $5|t| = 18$

65. $-2|k| = -14$ **66.** $20 = 4|c| - 8$ **67.** $3 = |z - 1|$

68. $|r + 11| = 4$ **69.** $|m - 0.5| = 1$ **70.** $3|w + 4| = 9$

Lesson 4-2

The scale of a map is 1 cm : 16 km. Find the actual distance corresponding to each map distance.

71. 3 cm   **72.** 2.5 cm   **73.** 6.3 cm   **74.** 8.5 cm   **75.** 10.2 cm

76. Architecture The Lyndon Johnson Presidential Library has a model of the Oval Office in the White House. The model in the Johnson Library is $\frac{7}{8}$ the size of the original. Write and solve a proportion to find each dimension in the Johnson Library given the following actual Oval Office dimensions.
  a. greatest width: 29 ft
  b. greatest length: 35 ft 10 in.
  c. height: 18 ft 6 in.

Function Rules, Tables, and Graphs

You can use a graphing calculator to explore the relationship among a function rule, a table, and a graph. When you use the table feature, the calculator computes the values for y based on the values of x that you enter.

Take It to the NET
Graphing Calculator procedures online at **www.PHSchool.com**
Web Code: aee-2104

1 EXAMPLE

For the function $y = -2x + 5$, find the range when the domain is $\{-12, 2, 0, 3, 8\}$.

Access the **TBLSET** feature. Use the arrow key to shade the **Ask** to the right of **Indpnt**.

Press **ENTER**.

TABLE SETUP
Tbl Start=0
▲Tbl=5
Indpnt: Auto **Ask**
Depend: **Auto** Ask

Press **Y=** . Enter the function. Access the **TABLE** feature. Enter values for x.

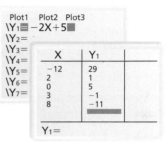

The range is $\{29, 1, 5, -1, -11\}$.

To graph an equation, use the **GRAPH** feature. You can use the **TRACE** feature to find x- and y- values. If you graph and trace the equation in Example 1, you will see that the x- and y- values are generally given as 8-digit numbers. To see values for x that are given in tenths, press **ZOOM** 4 and then **TRACE** .

2 EXAMPLE

Graph $y = -0.5x - 2$. Where does the graph cross each axis?

Press **Y=** . Enter the function rule. Then press **GRAPH** .

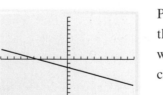

Press **ZOOM** 4 and then **TRACE** to find where the graph crosses the axes.

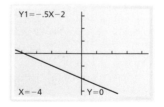

The graph crosses the y-axis at -2 and the x-axis at -4.

EXERCISES

Find the range of each function for the given domain.

1. $y = 3x + 6; \{-5, 0, 3, 7\}$

2. $y = 0.4x - 5.1; \{-2.1, 1.35, 5.7\}$

Determine where each graph crosses the y-axis and the x-axis.

3. $y = -2x + 3$

4. $y = -0.25x - 1$

5. $y = 1.2x + 2.16$

6. Open-Ended Graph $y = -0.2x + 6$. Using the **WINDOW** screen, experiment with values for Xmin, Xmax, Ymin, and Ymax until you can see the graph crossing both axes. What values did you use for Xmin, Xmax, Ymin, and Ymax?

Writing a Function Rule

Lesson Preview

What You'll Learn

OBJECTIVE
1 To write a function rule given a table or a real-world situation

...And Why

To write a function rule for finding profit, as in Example 3

✓ Check Skills You'll Need

(For help, go to Lesson 5-3.)

Model each rule with a table of values.

1. $f(x) = 5x - 1$
2. $y = -3x + 4$
3. $g(t) = 0.2t - 7$
4. $y = 4x + 1$
5. $f(x) = 6 - x$
6. $c(d) = d + 0.9$

Evaluate each function rule for $n = 2$.

7. $A(n) = 2n - 1$
8. $f(n) = -3 + n - 1$
9. $g(n) = 6 - n$

OBJECTIVE
1 **Writing Function Rules**

🅘**TEXT** Interactive lesson includes instant self-check, tutorials, and activities.

You can write a rule for a function by analyzing a table of values. Look for a pattern relating the independent and dependent variables.

1 EXAMPLE **Writing a Rule from a Table**

Write a function rule for each table.

a.

x	f(x)
1	5
2	6
3	7
4	8

Ask yourself, "What can I do to 1 to get 5, to 2 to get 6, . . . ?"

You add 4 to each x-value to get the $f(x)$ value.

Relate	$f(x)$	equals	x	plus	4
Write	$f(x)$	=	x	+	4

A rule for the function is $f(x) = x + 4$.

b.

x	y
1	1
3	9
6	36
9	81

Ask yourself, "What can I do to 3 to get 9, to 6 to get 36, . . . ?"

You multiply each x-value times itself to get the $f(x)$ value.

Relate	y	equals	x times itself
Write	y	=	x^2

A rule for the function is $y = x^2$.

✓ Check Understanding

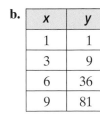 **1** Write a function rule for each table.

a.

x	f(x)
1	−1
2	0
3	1
4	2

b.

x	y
1	2
2	4
3	6
4	8

c.

x	y
1	3
2	4
3	5
4	6

Real-World 🌐 **Connection**

The Museum of Science in Boston, Massachusetts, has an exhibit called The Walk Through Computer™ 2000.

2 EXAMPLE **Real-World** 🌐 **Problem Solving**

Scale Model The exhibit at the left is a scale model of a desktop computer. It is about 20 times the size of a normal-sized desktop computer.

a. Write a function rule to describe this relationship.

Relate larger is 20 times normal

Define Let n = length of normal-sized computer.

Let $L(n)$ = length of larger size shown in museum exhibit.

Write $L(n)$ = 20 · n

The function rule $L(n) = 20n$ describes the relationship between the size of the computer in the exhibit and a normal-sized computer.

b. A space bar on a normal-sized computer is $4\frac{3}{8}$ in long. About how long is the space bar in the exhibit?

$L(n) = 20 \cdot n$
$L(n) = 20 \cdot 4\frac{3}{8}$ Substitute $4\frac{3}{8}$ for *n*.
$L(n) = 87\frac{1}{2}$ Simplify.

The space bar in the exhibit is about $87\frac{1}{2}$ in. long.

✓ **Check Understanding** **2 a. Carpentry** A carpenter buys finishing nails by the pound. Each pound of nails costs $1.19. Write a function rule to describe this relationship.
b. How much do 12 lb of finishing nails cost?

When you write a function, the dependent variable is defined in terms of the independent variable. In Example 3 below, profit depends on the number of lawns mowed, so profit is a function of the number of lawns mowed.

3 EXAMPLE **Real-World** 🌐 **Problem Solving**

Earnings Suppose you borrow money from a relative to buy a lawn mower that costs $245. You charge $18 to mow a lawn. Write a rule to describe your profit as a function of the number of lawns mowed.

Relate total profit is $18 times lawns mowed minus cost of mower

Define Let n = number of lawns mowed.

Let $P(n)$ = total profit.

Write $P(n)$ = 18 · n — 245

The function rule $P(n) = 18n - 245$ describes your profit as a function of the number of lawns mowed.

✓ **Check Understanding** **3 Earnings** Suppose you buy a word-processing software package for $199. You charge $15 per hour for word processing. Write a rule to describe your profit as a function of the number of hours you work.

EXERCISES

For more practice, see *Extra Practice*.

Practice and Problem Solving

 Practice by Example

Example 1
(page 254)

Match each table with its rule.

1. $y = 4x$ **2.** $y = x - 4$ **3.** $y = -4 - x$

A.

x	y
−2	−6
−1	−5
0	−4
1	−3

B.

x	y
−1	−4
−2	−8
−3	−12
−4	−16

C.

x	y
−1	−3
0	−4
1	−5
2	−6

Write a function rule for each table.

4.

x	f(x)
1	3
2	6
3	9
4	12

5.

x	f(x)
1	0.5
2	1.5
3	2.5
4	3.5

6.

x	f(x)
1	0.5
2	1
3	1.5
4	2

7.

x	f(x)
1	−3
2	−6
3	−9
4	−12

8.

x	y
−2	−8
−1	−4
0	0
1	4

9.

x	y
−8	64
−4	16
0	0
4	16
8	64

Example 2
(page 255)

Write a function rule for each situation.

10. the total cost $t(c)$ of c ounces of cinnamon if each ounce costs $.79

11. the total distance $d(n)$ traveled after n hours at a constant speed of 45 miles per hour

12. the height $f(h)$ of an object in feet when you know the height h in inches

13. a worker's earnings $e(n)$ for n hours when the worker's hourly wage is $6.37

14. the area $A(n)$ of a square when you know the length n of a side

15. the volume $V(n)$ of a cube when you know the length n of a side

16. the area $A(r)$ of a circle with radius r

Example 3
(page 255)

17. Food Costs At a supermarket salad bar, the price of a salad depends on its weight. Salad costs $.19 per ounce.
  a. Write a rule to describe the function.
  b. How much would an 8-ounce salad cost?

18. Postage In 2002, the price of mailing a letter was $.34 for the first ounce or part of an ounce and $.21 for each ounce or part of an ounce after the first ounce.
  a. Write a rule to describe the function.
  b. How much did it cost to mail a 4-ounce letter?

Apply Your Skills   **Write a function rule for each table.**

19.

Distance (km)	Distance (m)
0.5	500
1.0	1000
1.5	1500
2.0	2000

20.

Inches	Centimeters
1	2.54
2	5.08
3	7.62
4	10.16

Math in the Media **Use the advertisement at the left for Exercises 21–22.**

21. a. Write a rule to find the total cost $C(a)$ for all the books a person buys through Book Express. Let a represent the number of additional books bought (after the first 6 books).
   b. Suppose a person buys 9 books in all. Find the total cost.
   c. Evaluate the function for $a = 6$. What does the output represent?

22. A bookstore sells the same books for an average price of $6 each.
   a. Write a function rule to model the total cost $C(b)$ of books bought at the bookstore. Let b represent the number of books bought.
   b. Evaluate your function for $b = 12$. What does the output represent?
   c. You plan to buy 12 books. What is your average cost per book as a member of Book Express?
   d. Is it less expensive to buy 12 books through the club or at the bookstore? Explain.

BOOK **EXPRESS!**

Get your first
6
books for
$1.00

Buy additional books at our regular low Club price of $10.00 per book. To become a Book Express member, just buy 2 additional books within the first year. You may resign your membership at any time.

23. Writing What advantage(s) can you see of having a function rule instead of a table of values for a function?

24. Water Usage Use the function in the table at the right.
   a. Identify the dependent and independent variables.
   b. Write a rule to describe the function.
   c. How many gallons of water would you use for 7 loads of laundry?
   d. Critical Thinking In one month, you used 442 gallons of water for laundry. How many loads did you wash?

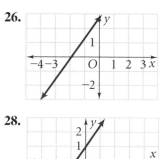

Water Used for Laundry	
1 load	34 gallons
2 loads	68 gallons
3 loads	102 gallons
4 loads	136 gallons

Make a table of values for each graph. Use the table to write a function rule.

25.

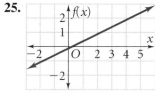

26.

27.

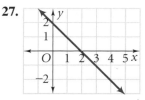

28.

29. Open-Ended Write a function rule that models a real-world situation. Evaluate your function for an input value and explain what the output represents.

30. Tipping You go out to dinner and decide to leave a 15% tip for the server.
 a. The bill for your meal is b. Write an expression for the amount of the tip in terms of b.
 b. The total cost $c(b)$ of your meal is the original bill plus the tip. Write a function rule to model this situation.
 c. Suppose the original bill is $18. Find the cost of your meal with a 15% tip.

C **Challenge**   Write a function rule for each table.

31.

x	f(x)
1	1
2	8
3	27
4	64

32.

x	f(x)
−1	1
−2	8
−3	27
−4	64

33.

x	f(x)
−1	0
−2	7
−3	26
−4	63

34. Truck Rental A truck rental company charges $44 per day for renting a medium-sized truck. There is also a charge of $.38 per mile.
 a. Write a function rule $c(m)$ to model the cost of renting a truck for a day and driving m miles.
 b. Evaluate your function rule for $m = 70$ and $m = 120$.
 c. You return the truck to the rental company and pay $58.44 (excluding tax). How far did you drive?
 d. Suppose you need to rent a truck for two days. You plan to drive 150 miles each day. How much will this cost?

Real-World Connection

Pickling preserves vegetables by inhibiting the growth of bacteria. Pickling requires salt and acids, such as vinegar.

35. Making Pickles The table at the right shows the relationship between the amount of pickling salt added to a gallon of water and the brine concentration, which is the percent of salt by weight.
 a. Write a function rule to describe the relationship between salt volume and brine concentration.
 b. Write a function rule to describe the relationship between salt weight and brine concentration.

Brine Strength

Salt Volume (cup)	Salt Weight (oz)	Brine Concentration (percent salt)
$\frac{1}{3}$	3.3	2.31
$\frac{1}{2}$	4.95	3.465
$\frac{2}{3}$	6.6	4.62
$\frac{3}{4}$	7.425	5.1975
1	9.9	6.93

Standardized Test Prep

Multiple Choice

36. What is the function rule for the total cost $T(b)$ of b books, if each book costs $11.95?
 A. $T(b) = 11.95b$ **B.** $T(b) = b + 11.95$
 C. $T(b) = 11.95 - b$ **D.** $T(b) = b - 11.95$

37. What is the function rule for the amount of change $C(x)$ you receive from a $50 bill if you buy x pounds of dog food at $1.60 a pound?
 F. $C(x) = 1.6x - 50$ **G.** $C(x) = 50x - 1.6$
 H. $C(x) = 50 - 1.6x$ **I.** $C(x) = 160 - 50x$

38. What is the function rule for the table at the right?

A. $f(x) = x - 5$
B. $f(x) = -5x - 4$
C. $f(x) = 5x - 1$
D. $f(x) = -5x + 1$

x	f(x)
0	1
1	-4
2	-9
3	-14
4	-19

Quantitative Comparison

Compare the boxed quantity in Column A with the boxed quantity in Column B. Choose the best answer.

A. The quantity in Column A is greater.
B. The quantity in Column B is greater.
C. The two quantities are equal.
D. The relationship cannot be determined from the information given.

Column A	Column B
39. $f(3)$ when $f(x) = 4x - 12$	$f(0)$ when $f(x) = x + 1$
40. $f(-3)$ when $f(x) = x^2 - 4$	$f(-2)$ when $f(x) = -2x + 1$

Short Response

Take It to the NET
Online lesson quiz at
www.PHSchool.com
Web Code: aea-0504

41. The recommended dosage D in milligrams of a certain medicine depends on a person's body mass w in kilograms. The function rule $D = 0.1w^2 + 5w$ describes the relationship of the dosage to body mass. Evaluate the function for a person who has a mass of 60 kilograms. Show your work.

Mixed Review

Lesson 5-3

Model each rule with a table of values and a graph.

42. $f(x) = x - 3$ **43.** $y = 5 - x$ **44.** $g(x) = -x + 3$

45. $f(x) = 2x - 3$ **46.** $y = |2x| - 3$ **47.** $y = 2x^2 - 3$

Lesson 4-4

Find each percent of change. Describe the percent of change as an increase or decrease. Round to the nearest percent.

48. 12 cm to 14 cm   **49.** 98 oz to 100 oz   **50.** 65 ml to 60 ml

51. 6 ft to 1 ft   **52.** 1.4 m to 1.8 m   **53.** $1\frac{1}{2}$ in. to $\frac{7}{8}$ in.

Lesson 4-1

54. Measurement The figure at the right shows how much juice you can get from some fruits.

a. What is the minimum number of oranges needed to make a cup of orange juice? What is the maximum number of oranges needed? (*Hint:* 16 tablespoons = 1 cup)

b. Suppose you buy a bag of 6 lemons and a bag of 5 limes. What is the most juice you can expect to get from these bags of fruit?

How Much Juice in an Average Fruit?

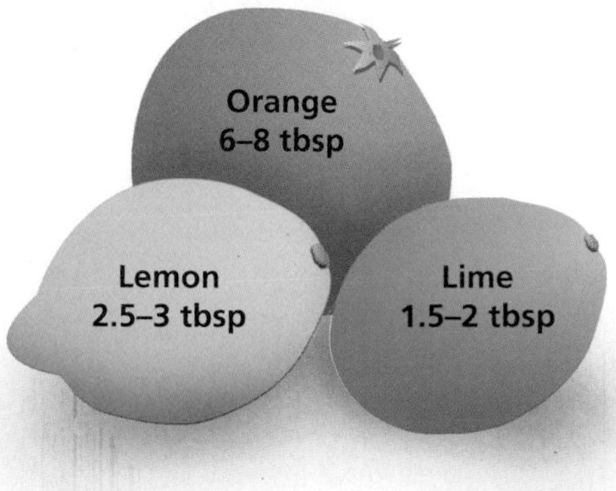

Orange
6–8 tbsp

Lemon
2.5–3 tbsp

Lime
1.5–2 tbsp

The problem below will help you recognize patterns in numerical data. These data describe the coordinates of points on the graph of a line. Read and solve the problem as you follow along. Check your understanding with the exercise at the bottom of the page.

Make a table of values for the graph. Use the table to write a function rule.

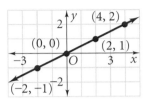

To create a table from a graph, identify the coordinates of points on the graph. For each point, list the x-value in the left column, and the corresponding $f(x)$-value (or y-value) in the right column.

x	f(x)
−2 +1	−1
0 +0	0
2 −1	1
4 −2	2

+2 ... +1
+2 ... +1
+2 ... +1

- Look for patterns between x-values and their corresponding y-values.

- Look for patterns between consecutive x-values and between consecutive y-values

To write a function rule from a table, you need to find a pattern among the data. You can ask yourself,

What do I need to do to x to get $f(x)$?

Make a guess using one pair of data points. Then try your guess with another pair to see if it works. The numbers in red in the table show that the difference between x and $f(x)$ values are not the same. So you cannot add the same number to an x value to get the corresponding $f(x)$ value.

As you go down the table, you can see that as x-values increase by 2, the corresponding y-values increase by 1. Notice that if you multiply −2 by $\frac{1}{2}$ you get −1, and (−2, −1) is an (x, y) pair in the table. Using mental math, you can see that $\frac{1}{2}$ times any x-value gives the corresponding y-value.

$f(x)$ equals x multiplied by $\frac{1}{2}$. Relate.

$f(x) = \frac{1}{2}x$ Write.

EXERCISE

Make a table of values for the graph. Use the table to write a function rule.

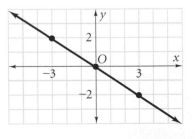

5-5

Direct Variation

Lesson Preview

What You'll Learn

OBJECTIVE 1
To write an equation of a direct variation

OBJECTIVE 2
To use ratios and proportions with direct variations

...And Why

To write a direct variation relating to weather, as in Example 3

✔ Check Skills You'll Need

(For help, go to Lessons 2-6 and 4-1.)

Solve each equation for the given variable.

1. $nq = m; q$ **2.** $d = rt; r$ **3.** $ax + by = 0; y$

Solve each proportion.

4. $\frac{5}{8} = \frac{x}{12}$ **5.** $\frac{4}{9} = \frac{n}{45}$ **6.** $\frac{25}{15} = \frac{y}{3}$

7. $\frac{7}{n} = \frac{35}{50}$ **8.** $\frac{8}{d} = \frac{20}{36}$ **9.** $\frac{14}{18} = \frac{63}{n}$

New Vocabulary • direct variation • constant of variation

OBJECTIVE

1 Writing the Equation of a Direct Variation

** i TEXT** Interactive lesson includes instant self-check, tutorials, and activities.

Investigation: Direct Variation

As you watch a movie, 24 individual pictures, or frames, flash on the screen each second. Here are three ways you can model the relationship between the number of frames $f(s)$ and the number of seconds s.

Table

s number of seconds	$f(s)$ number of frames
1	24
2	48
3	72
4	96
5	120

Graph

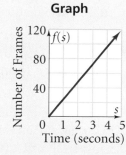

Function Rule

$f(s) = 24s$

1. As the number of seconds doubles, what happens to the number of frames?

2. Find the ratio $\frac{\text{number of frames}}{\text{number of seconds}}$ for each pair of data in the table.

3. For every increase of 1 second on the horizontal axis of the graph, what is the increase on the vertical axis?

4. What do you notice about your answers to Questions 2 and 3 and the coefficient of s in the function rule?

5. **a.** What number of frames corresponds to $s = 0$?
   b. What is the ordered pair on the graph for the seconds and number of frames when $s = 0$?

When a film is projected the number of frames doubles as the number of seconds doubles. The number of frames is proportional to the number of seconds; that is, the number of frames varies directly with the number of seconds.

Key Concepts

Definition	Direct Variation

A function in the form $y = kx$, where $k \neq 0$, is a **direct variation.** The **constant of variation** k is the coefficient of x. The variables y and x are said to vary directly with each other.

Reading Math

Constant means *remaining the same*. Constant of variation means changing at the *same* rate.

For $y = kx$, y is a function of x. If $x = 0$, then $y = 0$, so the graph of a direct variation is a line that passes through $(0, 0)$. To tell whether an equation represents a direct variation, solve for y. If the equation can be written in the form $y = kx$, it represents a direct variation.

1 EXAMPLE Is an Equation a Direct Variation?

Is each equation a direct variation? If it is, find the constant of variation.

a. $5x + 2y = 0$

$2y = -5x$ **Subtract 5x from each side.**

$y = -\frac{5}{2}x$ **Divide each side by 2.**

The equation has the form $y = kx$, so the equation is a direct variation. The constant of variation is $-\frac{5}{2}$.

b. $5x + 2y = 9$

$2y = 9 - 5x$ **Subtract 5x from each side.**

$y = \frac{9}{2} - \frac{5}{2}x$ **Divide each side by 2.**

The equation cannot be written in the form $y = kx$. It is not a direct variation.

✔ **Check Understanding** ❶ Is each equation a direct variation? If it is, find the constant of variation.
  a. $7y = 2x$ **b.** $3y + 4x = 8$ **c.** $y - 7.5x = 0$

To write an equation for a direct variation, you first find the constant of variation k using a point other than the origin that lies on the graph of the equation. Then use the value of k to write an equation.

2 EXAMPLE Writing an Equation Given a Point

Write an equation of the direct variation that includes the point $(4, -3)$.

$y = kx$ **Start with the function form of a direct variation.**

$-3 = k(4)$ **Substitute 4 for x and −3 for y.**

$-\frac{3}{4} = k$ **Divide each side by 4 to solve for k.**

$y = -\frac{3}{4}x$ **Write an equation. Substitute $-\frac{3}{4}$ for k in $y = kx$.**

An equation of the direct variation is $y = -\frac{3}{4}x$.

✔ **Check Understanding** ❷ Write an equation of the direct variation that includes the point $(-3, -6)$.

You can use a direct variation to describe a real-world situation in which the dependent variable varies directly with the independent variable.

3 EXAMPLE Real-World 🌐 Problem Solving

Weather Your distance from lightning varies directly with the time it takes you to hear thunder. If you hear thunder 10 seconds after you see lightning, you are about 2 miles from the lightning. Write an equation for the relationship between time and distance.

Relate The distance varies directly with the time. When $x = 10$, $y = 2$.

Define Let $x =$ the number of seconds between your seeing lightning and your hearing thunder.

Let $y =$ your distance in miles from the lightning.

Write
$y = kx$ Use the general form of a direct variation.

$2 = k(10)$ Substitute 10 for *x* and 2 for *y*.

$\frac{1}{5} = k$ Divide each side by 10 to solve for *k*.

$y = \frac{1}{5}x$ Write an equation. Substitute $\frac{1}{5}$ for *k* in $y = kx$.

The equation $y = \frac{1}{5}x$ relates the time x in seconds it takes you to hear the thunder to the distance y in miles you are from the lightning.

Real-World 🌐 Connection

The total energy released by a single flash of lightning could power an ordinary light bulb for a few months.

✓ **Check Understanding** ❸ A recipe for a dozen corn muffins calls for 1 cup of flour. The number of muffins varies directly with the amount of flour you use. Write a direct variation for the relationship between the number of cups of flour and the number of muffins.

OBJECTIVE

2 Ratios, Proportions, and Direct Variations

You can rewrite a direct variation $y = kx$ as $\frac{y}{x} = k$. When two sets of data vary directly, the ratio $\frac{y}{x}$ is the constant of variation. It is the same for each data pair.

4 EXAMPLE Direct Variations and Tables

For each table, use the ratio $\frac{y}{x}$ to tell whether y varies directly with x. If it does, write an equation for the direct variation.

a.

x	y	$\frac{y}{x}$
-3	2.25	$\frac{2.25}{-3} = -0.75$
1	-0.75	$\frac{-0.75}{1} = -0.75$
4	-3	$\frac{-3}{4} = -0.75$
6	-4.5	$\frac{-4.5}{6} = -0.75$

Yes, the constant of variation is -0.75. The equation is $y = -0.75x$.

b.

x	y	$\frac{y}{x}$
2	-1	$\frac{-1}{2} = -0.5$
4	1	$\frac{1}{4} = 0.25$
6	3	$\frac{3}{6} = 0.5$
9	4.5	$\frac{4.5}{9} = 0.5$

No, the ratio $\frac{y}{x}$ is not the same for all pairs of data.

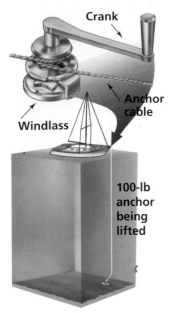

Crank

Anchor cable

Windlass

100-lb anchor being lifted

A windlass is a winch turned by a crank. It is used in a water well and to raise an anchor on a boat.

✓ Check Understanding **4** For the data in each table, tell whether y varies directly with x. If it does, write an equation for the direct variation.

a.

x	y
-2	3.2
1	2.4
4	1.6

b.

x	y
4	6
8	12
10	15

In a direct variation, the ratio $\frac{y}{x}$ is the same for all pairs of data where $x \neq 0$. So the proportion $\frac{y_1}{x_1} = \frac{y_2}{x_2}$ is true for the ordered pairs (x_1, y_1) and (x_2, y_2), where neither x_1 nor x_2 are zero.

5 **EXAMPLE** **Real-World** **Problem Solving**

Physics The force you must apply to lift an object varies directly with the object's weight. You would need to apply 0.625 lb of force to a windlass to lift a 28-lb weight. How much force would you need to lift 100 lb?

Relate A force of 0.625 lb lifts 28 lb. What force lifts 100 lb?

Define Let $n =$ the force you need to lift 100 lb.

Write $\dfrac{\text{force}_1}{\text{weight}_1} = \dfrac{\text{force}_2}{\text{weight}_2}$ Use a proportion.

$\dfrac{0.625}{28} = \dfrac{n}{100}$ Substitute 0.625 for force$_1$, 28 for weight$_1$, and 100 for weight$_2$.

$0.625(100) = 28n$ Use cross products.

$n \approx 2.2$ Solve for n.

● You need about 2.2 lb of force to lift 100 lb.

✓ Check Understanding **5** **Physics** Suppose a second windlass requires 0.5 lb of force to lift an object that weighs 32 lb. How much force would you need to lift 160 lb?

EXERCISES

For more practice, see *Extra Practice*.

Practice and Problem Solving

A **Practice by Example**

Example 1
(page 262)

Is each equation a direct variation? If it is, find the constant of variation.

1. $2y = 5x + 1$

2. $8x + 9y = 10$

3. $-12x = 6y$

4. $y + 8 = -x$

5. $5x - 6y = 0$

6. $-4 + 7x + 4 = 3y$

7. $-x = 10y$

8. $0.7x - 1.4y = 0$

9. $\frac{1}{2}x + \frac{1}{3}y = 0$

Example 2
(page 262)

Write an equation of the direct variation that includes the given point.

10. $(1, 5)$

11. $(5, 1)$

12. $(-8, 10)$

13. $(-5, -9)$

14. $(-2, 3)$

15. $(-6, 1)$

16. $(3, -4)$

17. $(6, -8)$

18. $(-6, 8)$

19. $(-5, -10)$

20. $(12, -8)$

21. $(35, 7)$

Example 3
(page 263)

Define the variables. Then write a direct variation to model each relationship.

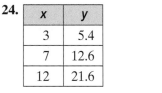

22. Geometry The perimeter of a regular octagon varies directly with the length of one side of the octagon.

23. Earnings When you have a job that pays an hourly wage, the amount you earn varies directly with the number of hours you work. Suppose you earn $7.10/hour working at the library.

Example 4
(page 263)

For the data in each table, tell whether y varies directly with x. If it does, write an equation for the direct variation.

24.

x	y
3	5.4
7	12.6
12	21.6

25.

x	y
−2	1
3	6
8	11

26.

x	y
−6	9
1	−1.5
8	−12

Example 5
(page 264)

27. Physics The maximum weight you can lift with a lever varies directly with the amount of force you apply. Suppose you can lift a 50-lb weight by applying 20 lb of force to a certain lever.
  a. What is the ratio of weight to force for the lever?
  b. Write a proportion and find the force you need to lift a friend weighing 130 lb.

28. Bicycling A bicyclist traveled at a constant speed during a timed practice period. Write a proportion to find the distance the cyclist traveled in 30 min.

A Bicyclist's Practices

Elapsed Time	Distance
10 min	3 mi
25 min	7.5 mi

B Apply Your Skills

Write an equation of the direct variation that includes the given point.

29. $\left(3, \frac{1}{2}\right)$ **30.** $\left(\frac{1}{4}, -5\right)$ **31.** $\left(\frac{-5}{6}, \frac{6}{5}\right)$ **32.** $(1.2, 7.2)$

33. $(0.5, 4.5)$ **34.** $\left(-2, \frac{1}{16}\right)$ **35.** $(5.2, -1.5)$ **36.** $\left(-\frac{8}{3}, -\frac{9}{8}\right)$

37. a. Writing How can you tell whether two sets of data vary directly?
  b. How can you tell if a line is the graph of a direct variation?

Critical Thinking Is each statement true or false? Explain.

38. The graph of a direct variation may pass through $(-2, 4)$.

39. The graph of a direct variation may pass through $(0, 3)$.

40. If you triple an x-value of a direct variation, the y-value also triples.

Graph the direct variation that includes the given point. Write an equation of the line.

41. $(2, 5)$ **42.** $(-2, 5)$ **43.** $(2, -5)$ **44.** $(-2, -5)$

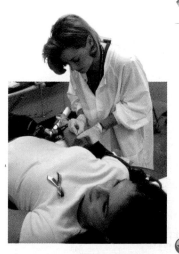

Real-World Connection

You must be at least 17 years old and weigh at least 110 pounds to give blood.

45. Biology The amount of blood in a person's body varies directly with body weight. A person who weighs 160 lb has about 5 qt of blood.
  a. Find the constant of variation.
  b. Write an equation relating quarts of blood to weight.
  c. Open-Ended Estimate the number of quarts of blood in your body.

🌐 **46. Electricity** Ohm's Law $V = I \times R$ relates the voltage, current, and resistance of a circuit. V is the voltage measured in volts. I is the current measured in amperes. R is the resistance measured in ohms.

    a. Find the voltage of a circuit that has a current of 24 amperes and resistance of 2 ohms.

    b. Find the resistance of a circuit that has a current of 24 amperes and a voltage of 18 volts.

C Challenge

The ordered pairs in each exercise are for the same direct variation. Find each missing value.

47. $(3, 4)$ and $(9, y)$ **48.** $(-1, 2)$ and $(4, y)$ **49.** $(-5, 3)$ and $(x, -4.8)$

50. $(1, y)$ and $\left(\frac{3}{2}, -9\right)$ **51.** $(2, 5)$ and $(x, 12.5)$ **52.** $(-2, 5)$ and $(x, -5)$

Problem Solving Hint

For Exercise 53, start with the relationship of miles and gallons: $\frac{m}{g} = 24$.

🌐 **53. Gas Mileage** A car gets 24 miles per gallon. The number of gallons g of gas used varies directly with the number of miles m traveled.

    a. Suppose the price of gas is \$1.83 per gallon. Write a function relating the cost c for g gallons of gas. Is this a direct variation?

    b. Write a direct variation relating the cost of gas to the miles traveled.

Standardized Test Prep

Multiple Choice

54. Which equation is a direct variation?

    A. $y = -0.7x$ **B.** $y = \frac{21}{x}$ **C.** $y - x = 4$ **D.** $y = 3x + 2$

55. A direct variation includes the point $(-8, 2)$. Which is an equation of the direct variation?

    F. $-8y = x + 2$ **G.** $2y = -8x$ **H.** $y = \frac{x}{-4}$ **I.** $y = -4x$

Quantitative Comparison

Compare the boxed quantity in Column A with the boxed quantity in Column B. Choose the best answer.

    A. The quantity in Column A is greater.

    B. The quantity in Column B is greater.

    C. The two quantities are equal.

    D. The relationship cannot be determined from the information given.

Use this statement for Exercises 56–58.

A direct variation includes the point $(5, -4)$.

	Column A	Column B
56.	constant of variation of the equation	y-value, when $x = 3$
57.	y-value, when $x = 5$	y-value, when $x = -5$
58.	y-value, when $x = 0$	0

💻 **Take It to the NET**

Online lesson quiz at **www.PHSchool.com**

Web Code: aea-0505

Short Response

59. Write an equation of the direct variation that includes the point $(-1, -4)$. Show your work.

Lesson 5-4

Write a function rule for each table.

60.

Number of People	Total Bill
1	$3.00
2	$6.00
3	$9.00
4	$12.00

61.

Amount Earned	Amount Spent
$15	$5
$30	$10
$45	$15
$60	$20

62.

Number of Days	Supplies Remaining
0	12 lb
2	10 lb
4	8 lb
6	6 lb

63.

Weight on Earth (lb)	Weight on Moon (lb)
96	16
123	20.5
144	24
171	28.5

Lessons 3-2, 3-3

Solve each inequality.

64. $r + 6 > -12$ **65.** $5 + c \le 3.2$ **66.** $7m < -21$ **67.** $a - 4.5 \ge 12.1$

68. $\frac{n}{4} < -20$ **69.** $3t \ge 9.12$ **70.** $\frac{v}{-5} \le \frac{1}{2}$ **71.** $b + 4\frac{2}{3} > 5\frac{1}{6}$

Lesson 1-6 🌐 **72. Shipping** For the ships that pass through the Panama Canal, the average toll is $45,000 per ship. The canal authority earned about $700 million in the ycar 2000. About how many ships passed through the canal that year? Round to the nearest hundred.

✓ Checkpoint Quiz 2   Lessons 5-3 through 5-5

TEXT Instant self-check quiz online and on CD-ROM

Model each rule with a table of values and a graph. If the rule describes a direct variation, state the constant of variation.

1. $y = 4x + 1$ **2.** $y = \frac{1}{2}x$ **3.** $f(x) = -3x$ **4.** $y = -3x + 2$

Write a function rule for each situation.

5. the total cost $t(p)$ of p pounds of potatoes at $.79 per pound

6. the total distance $d(n)$ traveled in n hours at a constant speed of 60 mi/h

Write an equation for the direct variation that includes the given point.

7. $(7, -2)$ **8.** $(-3, -6)$ **9.** $(-4, -5)$

 10. a. Bicycling The distance a wheel moves forward varies directly with the number of rotations. Suppose the distance d the wheel moves is 56 ft when the number of rotations n is 8. Find the constant of variation and write a direct variation equation to model this situation.

b. Use the direct variation you wrote for part (a) to find the distance the wheel moves in 20 rotations.

Describing Number Patterns

Lesson Preview

What You'll Learn

OBJECTIVE 1
To use inductive reasoning in continuing number patterns

OBJECTIVE 2
To write rules for arithmetic sequences

...And Why

To predict the next numbers in a pattern, as in Example 1

✓ Check Skills You'll Need

(For help, go to Lesson 1-2 and 1-5.)

Evaluate each expression for $x = 2, 3, 4$.

1. $9 + 3(x - 1)$ **2.** $8 + 7(x - 1)$ **3.** $0.4 - 3(x - 1)$

Subtract.

4. $8 - (-6)$ **5.** $-7 - 10$ **6.** $1.5 - 3.4$

New Vocabulary
- inductive reasoning • conjecture • sequence • term
- arithmetic sequence • common difference

OBJECTIVE
1

Inductive Reasoning and Number Patterns

ⓘTEXT Interactive lesson includes instant self-check, tutorials, and activities.

Suppose you are in a city and notice that the first three streets you pass are 10th Street, 11th Street, and 12th Street. You would probably conclude that the next street would be 13th Street. You would be basing your conclusion on inductive reasoning.

Inductive reasoning is making conclusions based on patterns you observe. A conclusion you reach by inductive reasoning is a **conjecture.**

1 EXAMPLE Extending Number Patterns

Use inductive reasoning to describe each pattern. Then find the next two numbers in each pattern.

a. 2,   5,   8,   11
     $+3$ $+3$ $+3$

The pattern is "add 3 to the previous term." To find the next two numbers, you add 3 to each previous term: $11 + 3 = 14$ and $14 + 3 = 17$.

b. 2,   4,   8,   16
     $\times 2$ $\times 2$ $\times 2$

The pattern is "multiply the previous term by 2." To find the next two numbers, you multiply each previous term by 2: $16 \times 2 = 32$ and $32 \times 2 = 64$.

c. $1, 4, 9, 16, \ldots$

The pattern is "square consecutive integers": $1^2, 2^2, 3^2, 4^2$. To find the next two numbers, square the next two consecutive integers: $5^2 = 25$ and $6^2 = 36$.

Reading Math

You read "..." at the end of a sequence as "and so on."

✓ **Check Understanding** **①** Use inductive reasoning to describe each pattern. Then find the next two numbers in each pattern.

     a. $3, 9, 27, 81, \ldots$ **b.** $9, 15, 21, 27, \ldots$ **c.** $2, -4, 8, -16, \ldots$

A number pattern is also called a **sequence.** Each number in a sequence is a **term** of the sequence.

One kind of number sequence is an arithmetic sequence. You form an **arithmetic sequence** by adding a fixed number to each previous term. This fixed number is the **common difference.**

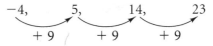

$$-4, \quad 5, \quad 14, \quad 23$$
$$+9 \quad +9 \quad +9$$

2 EXAMPLE Finding the Common Difference

Find the common difference of each arithmetic sequence.

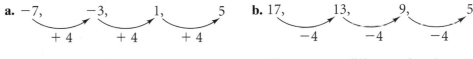

a. $-7, \quad -3, \quad 1, \quad 5$
$\quad +4 \quad +4 \quad +4$

b. $17, \quad 13, \quad 9, \quad 5$
$\quad -4 \quad -4 \quad -4$

The common difference is 4.   The common difference is -4.

Check Understanding **2** Find the common difference of each sequence.
a. $11, 23, 35, 47, \ldots$ **b.** $8, 3, -2, -7, \ldots$

Consider the sequence $7, 11, 15, 19, \ldots$ Think of each term as the output of a function. Think of the term number as the input.

term number   1   2   3   4   ← input

term   ⑦   11   15   19   ← output

You can use the common difference of the terms of an arithmetic sequence to write a function rule for the sequence. For the sequence $7, 11, 15, 19, \ldots$, the common difference is 4.

Let $n =$ the term number in the sequence.

Let $A(n) =$ the value of the nth term of the sequence.

$A(1) = 7$

$A(2) = 7 + 4 = 7 + 1 \cdot 4$ **4 is the common difference.**

$A(3) = 7 + 4 + 4 = 7 + 2 \cdot 4$ **Note that the number in red is one less**

$A(4) = 7 + 4 + 4 + 4 = 7 + 3 \cdot 4$ **than the term number, which is in blue.**

$A(n) = 7 + 4 + 4 + 4 + \ldots + 4 = 7 + (n - 1)4$

For an arithmetic sequence, you can use the first term, the term number, and the common difference to find the value of any given term.

Key Concepts

Rule	Arithmetic Sequence
$A(n) = a + (n - 1)d$	
nth first term common	
term term number difference	

3 EXAMPLE Finding Terms of a Sequence

Find the first, fifth, and tenth terms of the sequence that has the rule
$A(n) = 12 + (n - 1)(-2)$.

first term: $A(1) = 12$

fifth term: $A(5) = 12 + (5 - 1)(-2) = 12 + 4(-2) = 4$

tenth term: $A(10) = 12 + (10 - 1)(-2) = 12 + 9(-2) = -6$

✓ **Check Understanding** ③ Find the first, sixth, and twelfth terms of each sequence.
   a. $A(n) = -5 + (n - 1)(3)$ **b.** $A(n) = 6.3 + (n - 1)(5)$

EXERCISES

For more practice, see *Extra Practice*.

Practice and Problem Solving

Ⓐ **Practice by Example**

Example 1
(page 268)

Use inductive reasoning to describe each pattern. Then find the next two numbers in each pattern.

1. $4, 6, 8, 10, \ldots$ **2.** $4, 6, 9, 13\frac{1}{2}, \ldots$ **3.** $4, 6, 9, 13, \ldots$

4. $3, 3.04, 3.08, 3.12, \ldots$ **5.** $3, 3.3, 3.63, 3.993, \ldots$ **6.** $3, 1, -1, -3, \ldots$

7. $1.1, 2.2, 3.3, 4.4, \ldots$ **8.** $0.001, 0.01, 0.1, 1, \ldots$ **9.** $2, 8, 32, 128, \ldots$

10. $1, \frac{1}{4}, \frac{1}{9}, \frac{1}{16}, \ldots$ **11.** $9, -5, -19, -33, \ldots$ **12.** $1.5, 7.5, 37.5, 187.5, \ldots$

Example 2
(page 269)

Find the common difference of each arithmetic sequence.

13. $-5, -2, 1, 4, \ldots$ **14.** $-6, -10, -14, -18, \ldots$ **15.** $18, 7, -4, -15, \ldots$

16. $8, 21, 34, 47, \ldots$ **17.** $\frac{1}{2}, \frac{1}{3}, \frac{1}{6}, 0, \ldots$ **18.** $0.7, 1.5, 2.3, 3.1, \ldots$

19. $8, 6, 4, 2, \ldots$ **20.** $10, 22, 34, 46, \ldots$ **21.** $-9, -4, 1, 6, \ldots$

Example 3
(page 270)

Find the second, fifth, and ninth terms of each sequence.

22. $A(n) = 2 + (n - 1)(3)$ **23.** $A(n) = -9 + (n - 1)(6)$

24. $A(n) = -7 + (n - 1)(4)$ **25.** $A(n) = 8 + (n - 1)(9)$

26. $A(n) = 0.5 + (n - 1)(3)$ **27.** $A(n) = -5 + (n - 1)(7)$

28. $A(n) = 9 + (n - 1)(-6)$ **29.** $A(n) = -2.1 + (n - 1)(-5)$

30. $A(n) = 65 + (n - 1)(-7)$ **31.** $A(n) = 21 + (n - 1)(-4)$

32. $A(n) = -5 + (n - 1)(-3)$ **33.** $A(n) = 0.2 + (n - 1)(-1)$

Ⓑ **Apply Your Skills**

Find the next two terms in each sequence.

34. $20, 14, 8, 2, \ldots$ **35.** $2, 2\frac{1}{4}, 2\frac{1}{2}, 2\frac{3}{4}, 3, \ldots$ **36.** $2, 5, 10, 17, \ldots$

37. $12, 4, 1\frac{1}{3}, \frac{4}{9}, \ldots$ **38.** $0, 3, 8, 15, 24, \ldots$ **39.** $-5, 4, 13, 22, \ldots$

40. $40, 20, 10, 5, \ldots$ **41.** $7, 7\frac{1}{4}, 7\frac{1}{2}, 7\frac{3}{4}, \ldots$ **42.** $12, -4, \frac{4}{3}, -\frac{4}{9}, \ldots$

43. a. Writing Explain the difference between inductive and deductive reasoning.
   b. Open-Ended Give an example of inductive reasoning and of deductive reasoning.

44. Transportation Buses on your route run every 7 minutes from 6:30 A.M. to 10:00 A.M. You get to the bus stop at 7:56 A.M. How long will you have to wait for a bus?

45. Open-Ended Write a function rule for a sequence that has −30 as the eighth term.

For Exercises 46 and 47, write the first five terms in each sequence. Explain what the fifth term means in the context of the situation.

46. A baby's birth weight is 7 lb 4 oz. The baby gains 5 oz each week.

47. The balance of a car loan starts at $4,500 and decreases $150 each month.

48. Use the sequence $1, 2, 4, \ldots$
   a. Find the difference between consecutive terms in the sequence. Use inductive reasoning to make a conjecture about the next term in the sequence.
   b. Find the quotient of consecutive terms in the sequence. Use inductive reasoning to make a conjecture about the next term in the sequence.
   c. Critical Thinking Explain why having more than three terms in a sequence can help you make a conjecture that is more likely to be correct.

Real-World 🌐 **Connection**

About 15% of all trips on mass transit are students going to or from school.

Is each given sequence arithmetic? Justify your answer.

49. $0.3, 3, 30, 300, \ldots$ **50.** $-3, -7, -11, -15, \ldots$ **51.** $1, 8, 27, 64, \ldots$

52. $2, 4, 8, 16, 32, \ldots$ **53.** $46, 31, 16, 1, \ldots$ **54.** $0.2, -0.6, -1.4, -2.2, \ldots$

55. The first five rows of Pascal's Triangle are at the right.
   a. Predict the numbers in the sixth row.
   b. Find the sum of the numbers in each of the first five rows. Predict the sum of the numbers in the sixth row.

```
            1
          1   1
        1   2   1
      1   3   3   1
    1   4   6   4   1
```

Find the second, fourth, and eighth terms of each sequence.

56. $A(n) = 11 + (n - 1)\left(\frac{1}{3}\right)$ **57.** $A(n) = 9 + (n - 1)(-4.5)$

58. $A(n) = -2 + (n - 2)(-1.6)$ **59.** $A(n) = \frac{1}{5} + (n - 1)\left(\frac{4}{5}\right)$

60. a. Complete the table at the right for an arithmetic sequence.
   b. Graph the ordered pairs (term number, term) on a coordinate plane.
   c. What do you notice about the points on your graph?

x	y
1	5
2	8
3	■
4	■

🌐 **61. Music** There are 52 white keys on a piano. The frequency produced when a key is struck is the number of vibrations per second the key's string makes.
   ✏ **a. Reasoning** Is this relation a function? Explain.
   ✏ **b. Writing** Describe the pattern in the relation.

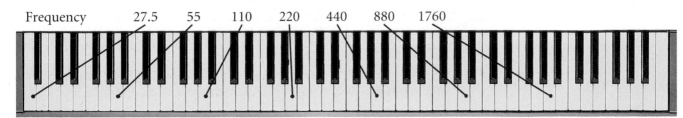

Frequency   27.5   55   110   220   440   880   1760

62. Number Theory The Fibonacci sequence is $1, 1, 2, 3, 5, 8, 13, \ldots$ After the first two numbers, each number is the sum of the two previous numbers.
  a. What is the next term of the sequence?
  b. What is the eleventh term of the sequence?
  c. Open-Ended Choose two other numbers to start a Fibonacci-like sequence. Write the first seven terms of your sequence.

Need Help?

Recursive formulas can include operations other than addition.

A *recursive formula* relates a new term of a sequence to the previous term of the sequence. Describe each of the sequences using a recursive formula.

Sample $3, 7, 11, 15, \ldots$

$$\text{value of new term} = \text{value of previous term} + 4$$

63. $12, 18, 24, 30, \ldots$

64. $12, 18, 27, 40.5, \ldots$

65. $54, 51.5, 49, 46.5, \ldots$

66. $1.1, 5.1, 9.1, 13.1, \ldots$

67. $98, 14, 2, \frac{2}{7}, \ldots$

68. $-8, 20, -50, 125, \ldots$

○C Challenge

Find the common difference of each sequence. Then find the next term.

69. $4, x + 4, 2x + 4, 3x + 4, \ldots$

70. $a + b + c, 4a + 3b + c, 7a + 5b + c, \ldots$

71. Use the sequence $10, 4, -2, -8, \ldots$
  a. What is the first term of the sequence?
  b. What is the common difference of the sequence?
  c. Write a function rule $A(n)$ for the sequence.

72. a. Draw the next figure in the pattern.

  b. Reasoning What is the color of the 20th figure? Explain.
  c. How many sides does the 28th figure have? Explain.

73. Use the arithmetic sequence $-5, 1, 7, 13, \ldots$
  a. What is the first term?
  b. What is the common difference?
  c. Use your answers from parts (a) and (b) to write a rule for the sequence.

Standardized Test Prep

Multiple Choice

74. What is the seventh term of the sequence 24, 12, 6, 3, . . . ?
  A. 0   **B.** 0.25   **C.** 0.375   **D.** 1.5

75. What is the common difference of the arithmetic sequence 9, −1, −11, −21, . . . ?
  F. −10   **G.** −9   **H.** 9   **I.** 10

76. What is the common difference of the arithmetic sequence $\frac{1}{5}, \frac{6}{5}, \frac{11}{5}, \frac{16}{5}, \ldots$?
  A. 1   **B.** $1\frac{1}{5}$ **C.** $\frac{21}{5}$ **D.** 5

77. What is the seventh term of the sequence $A(n) = -9 + (n - 1)0.5$?
  F. −7   **G.** −6.5   **H.** −6   **I.** −5.5

78. What is the first term of the sequence $A(n) = (n - 1)(-3)$?

A. -3 **B.** -2 **C.** 0 **D.** 1

79. What is the next term in the sequence $x - 4, x - 2, x, x + 2, \ldots$?

F. $2x$ **G.** $x + 3$ **H.** $x + 4$ **I.** $2x + 2$

Short Response **80.** Explain how to find the seventh term of the sequence $24, 21, 18, 15, \ldots$

Extended Response **81.** Marta started to work at a company in the year 2001. Her yearly salary was $26,500. At the beginning of the next year she received a $2,880 raise. Assume that she receives the same raise each year.
 a. Write a function $f(n)$ to find Marta's salary n years after 2001.
 b. Find Marta's salary in 2008. Show your work.

Take It to the NET
Online lesson quiz at
www.PHSchool.com
Web Code: aea-0506

Mixed Review

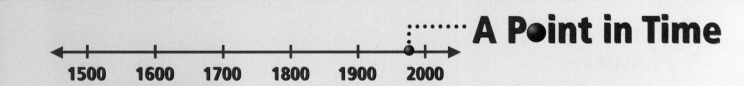

Lesson 5-5 Write an equation of the direct variation that includes the given point.

82. $(4, -5)$ **83.** $(0.5, 12)$ **84.** $(-1, 14)$ **85.** $(10, 1.4)$

86. $(1.1, -3.1)$ **87.** $(11, -3.1)$ **88.** $(2, -3)$ **89.** $\left(\frac{1}{2}, \frac{1}{3}\right)$

Lesson 5-2 Find the range of each function for the domain $\{-2, 1, 5\}$.

90. $f(x) = -4x$ **91.** $g(x) = 1 - 4x$ **92.** $y = 3x + 4$

93. $y = 2|x|$ **94.** $h(x) = |2x|$ **95.** $f(x) = \frac{3}{4}x - 5$

Lesson 4-3 **96. Time Zones** In 2001, people in some counties of Indiana did not set clocks forward in the spring to use daylight saving time. There are 92 counties in the state. Of those, 77 counties used eastern time without daylight saving. Five counties used eastern time with daylight saving. Ten counties were on central time with daylight saving.
 a. About what percent of Indiana's counties did *not* use daylight saving time?
 b. About what percent of the counties used central time?

A P•int in Time

1500   1600   1700   1800   1900   2000

In 1971, Romana Acosta Bañuelos became the first Mexican American woman to hold the office of United States Treasurer. Before her appointment to this post by President Nixon, she founded and managed her own multimillion-dollar food enterprise and established the Pan American National Bank of East Los Angeles. As a highly successful businesswoman, she had to work on a daily basis with interest rates, balance sheets, investments, and other activities required in the corporate world.

Take It to the NET For more information about the office of United States Treasurer, go to **www.PHSchool.com**.
Web Code: aee-2032

Using a Variable

You can solve many problems by using a variable to represent an unknown quantity. Try to let the variable be the quantity that you are looking for. Then use the variable to write an equation or inequality.

1 EXAMPLE

A brand of cereal comes in two sizes. The 12-oz size costs $4.35. At that rate, how much should the 20-oz box cost?

The problem is asking for the cost of a 20-oz box. Let the variable x be the cost of the 20-oz box. Write and solve a proportion to answer the question.

$\dfrac{12}{20} = \dfrac{4.35}{x}$ **Write a proportion.**

$12x = 20(4.35)$ **Find the cross products.**

$12x = 87.00$ **Simplify.**

$x = 7.25$ **Divide each side by 12.**

● The 20-oz box should cost about $7.25.

2 EXAMPLE

One house painter charges an initial fee of $25, plus $15 per hour. A second painter charges $25 per hour. Find out how many hours a job takes for the charge of the second painter to be the same as the charge of the first painter.

Let h = number of hours each painter must work for the charges to be the same. Then write an equation that expresses the charges for each painter.

First painter   Second painter

$25 + 15h \quad = \quad 25h$

$25 = 10h$ **Subtract 15h from each side.**

$2.5 = h$ **Divide each side by 10.**

● The charges are the same when both painters have worked 2.5 hours.

EXERCISES

1. Another way to solve the problem in Example 2 is to try values and test them until you find the correct answer. What is the advantage of using a variable?

2. The pressure of water varies directly with the depth. At 98 meters, the pressure is 10.21 atmospheres.
   a. Let x be the depth where the pressure is 5 atmospheres. Use this variable to write and solve an equation to find that depth.
   b. Let x be the pressure at a depth of 150 meters. Use this variable to write and solve an equation to find the pressure.

Chapter Review

Vocabulary

arithmetic sequence (p. 269)
common difference (p. 269)
conjecture (p. 268)
constant of variation (p. 262)
dependent variable (p. 248)
direct variation (p. 262)

domain (p. 241)
function (p. 242)
function notation (p. 243)
function rule (p. 243)
independent variable (p. 248)
inductive reasoning (p. 268)

range (p. 241)
relation (p. 241)
sequence (p. 269)
term (p. 269)
vertical-line test (p. 242)

Reading Math
Understanding
Vocabulary

Match the vocabulary term in the column on the left with the most specific description in the column on the right.

1. direct variation

2. inductive reasoning

3. independent variable

4. function

5. range

6. sequence

7. conjecture

A. x-coordinate

B. y-coordinate

C. a function that can be expressed in the form $y = kx$, where $k \neq 0$

D. drawing conclusions based on observed patterns

E. a relation with exactly one value of the dependent variable for each value of the independent variable

F. a conclusion based on inductive reasoning

G. a number pattern

Skills and Concepts

5-1 Objective

▼ To interpret, sketch, and analyze graphs from situations (p. 236)

A graph shows a visual representation of the relationship between two sets of data.

Describe a situation for each graph.

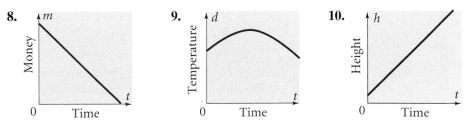

8. Money vs. Time

9. Temperature vs. Time

10. Height vs. Time

Sketch a graph of each situation. Label each section.

11. the height of a sunflower over a summer

12. the number of customers in a restaurant each hour of one day

13. the number of vehicles that enter a school parking lot during one day

14. the number of bags of peanuts sold during a 2-hour baseball game

5-2 Objectives

▼ To identify relations and functions (p. 241)

▼ To evaluate functions (p. 243)

A **relation** is a set of ordered pairs. The **domain** of a relation is the set of first coordinates of the ordered pairs. The **range** is the set of second coordinates.

A **function** is a relation that assigns exactly one value in the range to each value in the domain. A **function rule** is an equation that describes a function. A function is in **function notation** when it uses $f(x)$ for the outputs.

Find the range of each function when the domain is $\{-4, 0, 1, 5\}$.

15. $y = 4x - 7$ **16.** $m = 0.5n + 3$ **17.** $p = q^2 + 1$ **18.** $w = 5 - 3z$

Determine whether each relation is a function.

19.

x	y
0	1
1	2
2	3
1	4

20.

x	y
0	-2
2	0
-2	-4
4	2

21.

x	y
2	-3
-1	-3
0	-3
5	-3

22. Use the vertical-line test to determine if the graph at the right is a function.

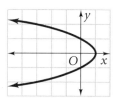

23. Writing When is a relation also a function?

5-3 and 5-4 Objectives

▼ To model functions using rules, tables, and graphs (p. 247)

▼ To write a function rule given a table or a real-world situation (p. 254)

When you graph data, put the **independent variable** on the horizontal axis and the **dependent variable** on the vertical axis. The dependent variable depends on the independent variable. You can model functions using rules, tables, and graphs.

Model each rule with a table of values and a graph.

24. $f(x) = x^2 - 3$ **25.** $f(x) = -\frac{1}{2}x - 3$ **26.** $y = |x| - 7$ **27.** $y = 2x + 1$

Write a function rule for each table of values.

28.

x	f(x)
2	3
4	5
6	7
8	9

29.

x	f(x)
-3	3
0	0
3	-3
6	-6

30.

x	f(x)
3.0	6.5
3.5	7.0
4.0	7.5
4.5	8.0

31. Weather The table at the right compares inches of snow to the corresponding amounts of rain. Write a function rule that models the data.

Precipitation

Snow (in.)	Rain (in.)
3	0.3
5	0.5
10	1.0
7.5	0.75

32. Campaign Advertising Brad wants to buy plain balloons and personalize them with his name to promote his campaign for class president. Each plain balloon costs $.07. Personalizing costs an initial setup fee of $27.00 plus $.13 for each plain balloon that is imprinted. Write a function rule to show the total cost of Brad's personalized campaign balloons.

5-5 Objectives

▼ To write the equation of a direct variation (p. 261)

▼ To use ratios and proportions with direct variations (p. 263)

A function is a **direct variation** if it has the form $y = kx$, where $k \neq 0$. The coefficient k is the **constant of variation**.

Is each equation a direct variation? If it is, find the constant of variation.

33. $f(x) = -3x$ **34.** $y = x - 3$ **35.** $y = 2x + 5$ **36.** $y = \frac{2}{5}x$

Write an equation of the direct variation that includes the given point.

37. $(5, 1)$ **38.** $(-2, -2)$ **39.** $(1, 2)$ **40.** $(-2, 6)$

For the data in each table, tell whether y varies directly with x. If it does, write an equation for the direct variation.

41.

x	y
−7	14
−5	10
−3	6
−1	2

42.

x	y
−6	−2
−3	−1
3	2
6	1

43.

x	y
24	4
18	3
−12	−2
−6	−1

44. Biology The number of kilograms of water w in a human body varies directly with the total body mass b. A person with a mass of 75 kg contains 54 kg of water. How many kilograms of water are there in a person with a mass of 95 kg?

45. Science The weight V of an object on Venus varies directly with its weight E on Earth. A person weighing 120 lb on Earth would weigh 106 lb on Venus. How much would a person weighing 150 lb on Earth weigh on Venus?

5-6 Objectives

▼ To use inductive reasoning in continuing number patterns (p. 268)

▼ To write rules for arithmetic sequences (p. 269)

Inductive reasoning is the process of making conclusions or **conjectures** based on patterns you observe. A number pattern is called a **sequence,** and each number in the sequence is a **term.**

An **arithmetic sequence** is formed by adding a fixed number, the **common difference,** to each previous term.

Use inductive reasoning to describe each pattern. Then find the next three numbers in each pattern.

46. $99, 90, 81, 72, \ldots$ **47.** $5, 8, 11, 14, \ldots$ **48.** $12, 23, 34, 45, \ldots$

Find the common difference in each arithmetic sequence. Then find the next three terms.

49. $9, 8\frac{1}{2}, 8, 7\frac{1}{2}, \ldots$ **50.** $6, 4, 2, 0, -2, \ldots$ **51.** $1, 14, 27, 40, \ldots$

Find the third, eighth, and tenth terms of each sequence.

52. $A(n) = -1 + (n - 1)\,2$ **53.** $A(n) = 4 + (n - 1)\,3$

54. $A(n) = 1.5 + (n - 1)\,1.5$ **55.** $A(n) = 4 + (n - 1)(-3)$

Determine whether each sequence is arithmetic. If it is, find the next three terms.

56. $14, 21, 28, 35, \ldots$ **57.** $16, -8, 4, -2, \ldots$

Chapter
5

Chapter Test

····· Take It to the NET
Online chapter test at
www.PHSchool.com
········· Web Code: aea-0552

Sketch a graph of each situation. Label each section.

1. the speed of a bicycle during an afternoon ride

2. the amount of milk in your container over one lunch period

Determine whether each relation is a function. If the relation is a function, state the domain and range.

3.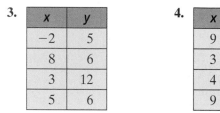

x	y
−2	5
8	6
3	12
5	6

4.

x	y
9	6
3	8
4	9.5
9	2

5. **Writing** Explain how to use the vertical-line test to determine whether a graph is a graph of a function.

Find the range of each function when the domain is {−3, −1.5, 0, 1, 4}.

6. $r = 4t^2 + 5$

7. $m = -3n - 2$

Model each rule with a table of values and a graph.

8. $f(x) = 1.5x - 3$

9. $f(x) = -x^2 + 4$

Write a function rule to describe each statement.

10. the cost in dollars of printing dollar bills when it costs 3.8¢ to print a dollar bill

11. the amount of money you earn mowing lawns at $15 per lawn

12. the profit you make selling flowers at $1.50 each when each flower costs you $.80

Write a function rule for each table of values.

13.

x	y
0	1
1	3
2	5
−3	−5

14.

x	f(x)
0	0
1	−4.5
−1	4.5
2	−9

15. **Open-Ended** Describe a situation that could be modeled by the equation $y = 5x$.

16. **Purchasing** The price of turkey depends on its weight. Suppose turkeys sell for $.59 per lb.
   a. Write a rule to describe the function.
   b. What is the price of a 14-lb turkey?
   c. If you had $10 to buy a turkey, how big a turkey could you buy?

Write an equation of the direct variation that includes the given point.

17. $(2, 2)$ 18. $(-8, -4)$ 19. $(3, -1)$ 20. $(-5, 3)$

Determine whether each of the following graphs shows a direct variation. Write an equation for each direct variation.

21. 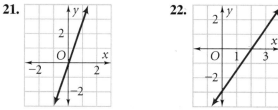   22.

Find the constant of variation for each direct variation.

23. $10y = 13x$ 24. $f(x) = 4.5x$ 25. $x + y = 0$

26. **Plumbing** The total amount of water dripping from a leaky faucet varies directly with time. If water drips at the rate of 5 mL/min, how much water drips in 30 min?

Find the common difference for each arithmetic sequence. Then find the next three terms.

27. $-55, -50, -45, -40, \ldots$ 28. $1.7, 2.7, 3.7, 4.7, \ldots$

Find the fifth term of each arithmetic sequence.

29. $A(n) = 2 + (n - 1)(-2.5)$

30. $A(n) = -9 + (n - 1)\,3$

Is each sequence arithmetic? Justify your answer.

31. $128, 64, 32, 16, \ldots$ 32. $3, 3.25, 3.5, 3.75, \ldots$

33. Write a function rule for the cost of catfish shown in the table below.

Weight (lb)	1	2	3	4	5
Cost (dollars)	3	6	9	12	15

Standardized Test Prep

Reading Comprehension Read the passage below. Then answer the questions on the basis of what is *stated* or *implied* in the passage.

Train Math Amtrak's Acela regional train has taken more than an hour off the old five-hour train trip from Boston to New York City. The faster Acela Express makes the 231-mile run in about 3.5 hours. The Express goes from New York to Washington, D.C., in about 2.75 hours.

A train's speed depends on how secure the track is and how well banked the curves are. On the best stretches, the Express can go as fast as 150 miles an hour.

For the New York–Washington, D.C., run, Amtrak carries 70% of the passengers traveling by either train or air. For the Boston–New York run, Amtrak carries only 30% of the passengers. The average number of riders that Amtrak carries in one month on the Boston–New York run is 100,404. The average number of riders in a month on the New York–Washington, D.C., run is 771,900. Amtrak hopes the new, faster train will increase ridership between Boston and New York.

---

1. Which is closest to the average speed for the old five-hour Boston–New York run?
   A. 30 miles per hour
   B. 40 miles per hour
   C. 80 miles per hour
   D. 1000 miles per hour

2. How much longer was the old five-hour Boston–New York run than the same trip on the Acela Express?
   F. 0.75 hour
   G. 1.5 hours
   H. 2.25 hours
   I. 2.5 hours

3. Which is closest to the average speed of the Boston–New York run for the Acela Express?
   A. 57 miles per hour
   B. 70 miles per hour
   C. 85 miles per hour
   D. 114 miles per hour

4. What is the percent of change between the Acela and Acela Express Boston–New York trip times?
   F. 12.5%   G. 20%
   H. 30%   I. 70%

5. If the Acela Express could make the entire trip from Boston to New York at 150 miles an hour, how long would it take?
   A. 1 hour
   B. $1\frac{1}{2}$ hours
   C. $2\frac{1}{5}$ hours
   D. 3 hours

6. If you took the Acela Express train from Boston to Washington, D.C., what portion of your travel time would be spent on the part of the trip between Boston and New York?
   F. $\frac{11}{14}$ G. $\frac{14}{25}$
   H. $\frac{14}{11}$ I. $\frac{25}{14}$

7. Providence, Rhode Island, is on the Boston–New York run. It is about 180 miles from New York City. If the Acela travels at a constant speed, what portion of its Boston–New York run is spent on the Boston–Providence section?

8. If the number of passengers on the Boston–New York run doubled, would the percent of passengers on the Boston–New York run also double? Justify your answer.

Where You've Been

● In Chapter 1, you used integers to graph points in the coordinate plane.

● In Chapters 2, 3, and 4, you solved multi-step problems, including equations, inequalities, and proportions, and applied this skill to solving a formula for a given variable.

● In Chapter 5, you graphed functions by making a table of values.

Diagnosing Readiness

i**TEXT** Instant self-check online and on CD-ROM

(For help, go to the Lesson in green.)

Adding and Subtracting Real Numbers (Lessons 1-4 and 1-5)

Simplify each expression.

1. $-5 + 7$ **2.** $2 - (-3)$ **3.** $-\frac{3}{4} + \frac{5}{6}$ **4.** $11 + (-4)$ **5.** $|1 - 8|$

Analyzing Data Using Scatter Plots (Lesson 1-9)

Make a scatter plot of the data below.

6. **Average Life Span of American Currency**

Value of Currency ($)	1	5	10	20	50	100
Time (years)	1.5	1.25	1.5	2	5	8.5

Solving Equations (Lesson 2-4)

Solve each equation. Check your solution.

7. $3x + 4x = 8 - x$ **8.** $12 - 3d = d$ **9.** $6x - 8 = 7 + x$

Transforming Equations (Lesson 2-6)

Solve each equation for y.

10. $2y - x = 4$ **11.** $3x = y + 2$ **12.** $-2y - 2x = 4$

Graphing Functions (Lesson 5-3)

Make a table of values and graph each function.

13. $y = -\frac{2}{3}x$ **14.** $y = 2x + 1$ **15.** $y = x - 5$

Linear Equations and Their Graphs

Where You're Going

- In this chapter, you will learn how to write linear equations and recognize their different forms.

- By working with the rate of change, you will understand how the slope of a line can be interpreted in real-world situations.

- You will determine whether the graphs of two linear equations are parallel or perpendicular.

 Real-World Snapshots Applying what you learn, you will do activities involving pyramids, on pages 336–337.

Key Vocabulary

- absolute value equation (p. 325)
- correlation coefficient (p. 319)
- line of best fit (p. 319)
- linear equation (p. 291)
- negative reciprocal (p. 312)
- parallel lines (p. 311)
- perpendicular lines (p. 312)
- point-slope form (p. 304)
- rate of change (p. 282)
- slope (p. 284)
- slope-intercept form (p. 292)
- standard form (p. 298)
- translation (p. 325)
- x-intercept (p. 298)
- y-intercept (p. 291)

Rate of Change and Slope

Lesson Preview

What You'll Learn

OBJECTIVE 1
To find rates of change from tables and graphs

OBJECTIVE 2
To find slope

...And Why

To find the rate of change of an airplane's altitude, as in Example 2

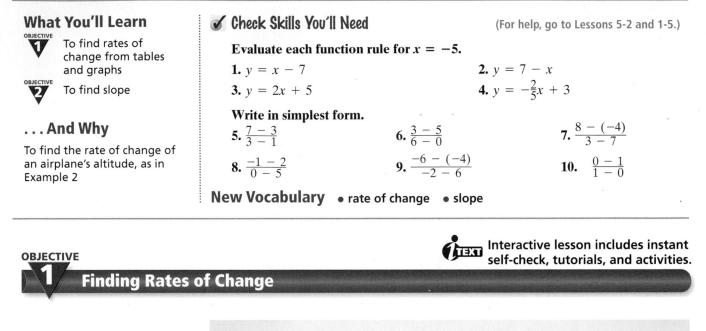

✔ Check Skills You'll Need

(For help, go to Lessons 5-2 and 1-5.)

Evaluate each function rule for $x = -5$.

1. $y = x - 7$ **2.** $y = 7 - x$

3. $y = 2x + 5$ **4.** $y = -\frac{2}{5}x + 3$

Write in simplest form.

5. $\dfrac{7 - 3}{3 - 1}$ **6.** $\dfrac{3 - 5}{6 - 0}$ **7.** $\dfrac{8 - (-4)}{3 - 7}$

8. $\dfrac{-1 - 2}{0 - 5}$ **9.** $\dfrac{-6 - (-4)}{-2 - 6}$ **10.** $\dfrac{0 - 1}{1 - 0}$

New Vocabulary • rate of change • slope

---

i TEXT Interactive lesson includes instant self-check, tutorials, and activities.

OBJECTIVE 1 Finding Rates of Change

Investigation: Exploring Rate of Change

The diagram at the right shows the side view of a ski lift.

1. What is the vertical change from *A* to *B*? From *B* to *C*? From *C* to *D*?

2. What is the horizontal change from *A* to *B*? From *B* to *C*? From *C* to *D*?

3. Find the ratio of the vertical change to the horizontal change for each section of the ski lift.

4. Which section is the steepest? Explain.

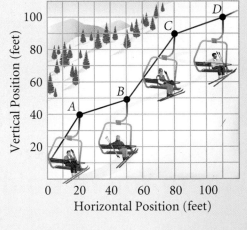

? **Need Help?**

A rate is a comparison of two quantities measured in different units.

In the graph above, $\overline{AB}$ and $\overline{BC}$ have different rates of change.

Rate of change allows you to see the relationship between two quantities that are changing. If one quantity depends on the other, then the following is true.

$$\text{rate of change} = \frac{\text{change in the dependent variable}}{\text{change in the independent variable}}$$

Cost of Renting a Computer	
Number of Days	Rental Charge
1	$60
2	$75
3	$90
4	$105
5	$120

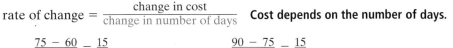

1 EXAMPLE   Finding Rate of Change Using a Table

Business For the data at the left, is the rate of change for each pair of consecutive days the same? What does the rate of change represent?

$$\text{rate of change} = \frac{\text{change in cost}}{\text{change in number of days}} \quad \textbf{Cost depends on the number of days.}$$

$$\frac{75 - 60}{2 - 1} = \frac{15}{1} \qquad\qquad \frac{90 - 75}{3 - 2} = \frac{15}{1}$$

$$\frac{105 - 90}{4 - 3} = \frac{15}{1} \qquad\qquad \frac{120 - 105}{5 - 4} = \frac{15}{1}$$

The rate of change for each consecutive pair of days is $\frac{15}{1}$. The rate of change is the same for all the data. It costs $15 for each day a computer is rented after the first day.

✓ Check Understanding **1 a.** Find the rate of change using Days 5 and 2.

b. Critical Thinking Does finding the rate of change for just one pair of days mean that the rate of change is the same for all the data? Explain.

The graphs of all the ordered pairs (number of days, cost) in Example 1 lie on a line as shown at the right. So, the data are linear.

You can use a graph to find a rate of change. Recall that the independent variable is plotted on the horizontal axis and the dependent variable is plotted on the vertical axis.

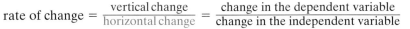

$$\text{rate of change} = \frac{\text{vertical change}}{\text{horizontal change}} = \frac{\text{change in the dependent variable}}{\text{change in the independent variable}}$$

2 EXAMPLE   Finding Rate of Change Using a Graph

Airplane Altitude The graph shows the altitude of an airplane as it comes in for a landing. Find the rate of change. Explain what this rate of change means.

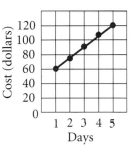

$$\begin{array}{ll} \text{rate of} \\ \text{change} \end{array} = \frac{\text{vertical change}}{\text{horizontal change}} \quad \begin{array}{l} \leftarrow \textbf{change in altitude} \\ \leftarrow \textbf{change in time} \end{array}$$

$$= \frac{1000 - 0}{60 - 180} \quad \textbf{Use two points.}$$

$$= \frac{1000}{-120} \quad \begin{array}{l}\textbf{Divide the vertical change} \\ \textbf{by the horizontal change.}\end{array}$$

$$= -8\tfrac{1}{3} \quad \textbf{Simplify.}$$

The rate of change is $-8\tfrac{1}{3}$. The airplane descends $8\tfrac{1}{3}$ feet each second.

✓ Check Understanding **2** Find the rate of change of the data in the graph.

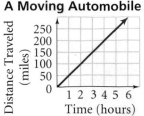

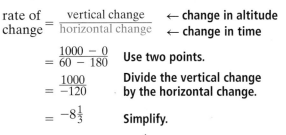

Some roads are steeper than others. A steeper road has a greater rate of change.

Real-World  Connection

The grade of a road is the ratio of rise to run expressed as a percent. For example, a road with 100% grade is at a 45° angle with level ground.

The slope of a line is its rate of change.

$$\text{slope} = \frac{\text{vertical change}}{\text{horizontal change}} = \frac{\text{rise}}{\text{run}}$$

3 EXAMPLE **Finding Slope Using a Graph**

Find the slope of each line.

a.

right 5 units

up 2 units

(4, 3)

(−1, 1)

$$\text{slope} = \frac{\text{rise}}{\text{run}}$$

$$= \frac{3 - 1}{4 - (-1)}$$

$$= \frac{2}{5}$$

The slope of the line is $\frac{2}{5}$.

b.

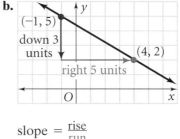

(−1, 5)

down 3 units

(4, 2)

right 5 units

$$\text{slope} = \frac{\text{rise}}{\text{run}}$$

$$= \frac{2 - 5}{4 - (-1)}$$

$$= \frac{-3}{5} = -\frac{3}{5}$$

The slope of the line is $-\frac{3}{5}$.

✓ **Check Understanding** **3** Find the slope of each line.

a.

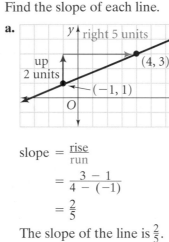

(3, 4)

(−2, 1)

b.

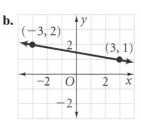

(−3, 2)

(3, 1)

Reading Math

You read the coordinates (x_1, y_1) as "x sub 1, y sub 1."

You can use any two points on a line to find its slope. You use subscripts to distinguish between two points. In the diagram, (x_1, y_1) are the coordinates of P, and (x_2, y_2) are the coordinates of Q. To find the slope of $\overleftrightarrow{PQ}$, you can use the following formula.

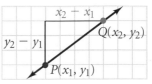

$x_2 - x_1$

$Q(x_2, y_2)$

$y_2 - y_1$

$P(x_1, y_1)$

Key Concepts

Formula	Slope
$\text{slope} = \dfrac{\text{rise}}{\text{run}} = \dfrac{y_2 - y_1}{x_2 - x_1}$, where $x_2 - x_1 \neq 0$	

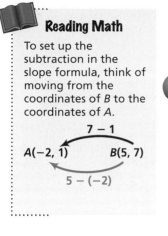

Keep in mind that the x-coordinate you use first in the denominator must belong to the same ordered pair as the y-coordinate you use first in the numerator.

4 EXAMPLE **Finding Slope Using Points**

Find the slope of the line through $A(-2, 1)$ and $B(5, 7)$.

$$\text{slope} = \frac{y_2 - y_1}{x_2 - x_1}$$

$$= \frac{7 - 1}{5 - (-2)} \qquad \text{Substitute (5, 7) for } (x_2, y_2) \text{ and } (-2, 1) \text{ for } (x_1, y_1).$$

$$= \frac{6}{7} \qquad \text{Simplify.}$$

The slope of $\overleftrightarrow{AB}$ is $\frac{6}{7}$.

✓ **Check Understanding** **4** Find the slope of the line through each pair of points.
    a. $C(2, 5)$ and $D(4, 7)$ **b.** $P(-1, 4)$ and $Q(3, -2)$ **c.** $M(a, b)$ and $N(c, d)$

You can also analyze the graphs of horizontal and vertical lines. The next example shows why the slope of a horizontal line is 0, and the slope of a vertical line is undefined.

5 EXAMPLE **Horizontal and Vertical Lines**

Find the slope of each line.

a.
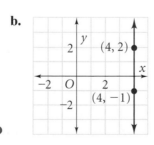

$$\text{slope} = \frac{y_2 - y_1}{x_2 - x_1}$$

$$= \frac{2 - 2}{4 - 1} \qquad \text{Substitute (4, 2) for } (x_2, y_2) \text{ and (1, 2) for } (x_1, y_1).$$

$$= \frac{0}{3} \qquad \text{Simplify.}$$

$$= 0$$

The slope of the horizontal line is 0.

b.

$$\text{slope} = \frac{y_2 - y_1}{x_2 - x_1}$$

$$= \frac{2 - (-1)}{4 - 4} \qquad \text{Substitute (4, 2) for } (x_2, y_2) \text{ and (4, −1) for } (x_1, y_1).$$

$$= \frac{3}{0} \qquad \text{Simplify.}$$

Division by zero is undefined. So, the slope of the vertical line is undefined.

✓ **Check Understanding** **5** Find the slope of each line.

    a.   **b.**

The following summarizes what you have learned about slope.

Summary	Slopes of Lines

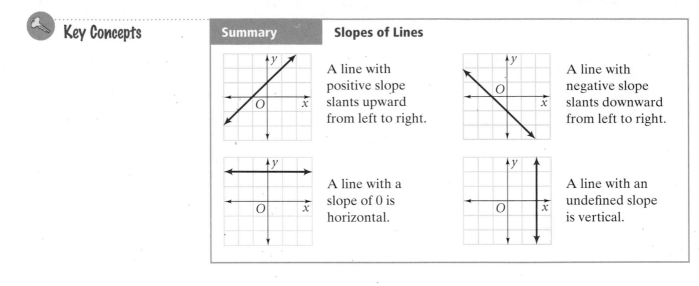

A line with positive slope slants upward from left to right.

A line with negative slope slants downward from left to right.

A line with a slope of 0 is horizontal.

A line with an undefined slope is vertical.

EXERCISES

For more practice, see *Extra Practice*.

Practice and Problem Solving

Ⓐ Practice by Example

Examples 1, 2
(page 283)

The rate of change is constant in each table and graph. Find the rate of change. Explain what the rate of change means for each situation.

1.

Time (hours)	Temperature (°F)
1	−2
4	7
7	16
10	25
13	34

2.

People	Cost (dollars)
2	7.90
3	11.85
4	15.80
5	19.75
6	23.70

3. A Tank of Gas

4. Emissions: Generating Electricity for TV Use

5. Descent of a Skydiver

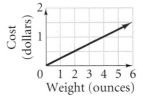

6. Price of Oregano

Real-World 🌎 Connection

A jump from 11,000 feet gives a skydiver about 60 seconds of free fall at more than 100 mi/h.

Example 3
(page 284)

Find the slope of each line.

7.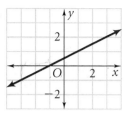

8.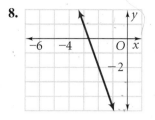

9.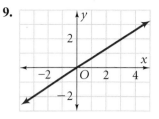

Example 4
(page 285)

Find the slope of the line that passes through each pair of points.

10. $(3, 2), (5, 6)$

11. $(5, 6), (3, 2)$

12. $(4, 8), (8, 11)$

13. $(-4, 4), (2, -5)$

14. $(-2, 1), (1, -2)$

15. $(-3, 1), (3, -5)$

16. $(-8, 0), (1, 5)$

17. $(0, 0), (3, 5)$

18. $(-4, -5), (-9, 1)$

19. $(5, 0), (0, 2)$

20. $(-7, 1), (7, 8)$

21. $(0, -1), (1, -6)$

Example 5
(page 285)

State whether the slope is zero or undefined.

22.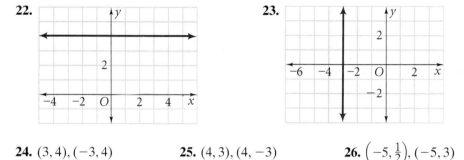

23.

24. $(3, 4), (-3, 4)$

25. $(4, 3), (4, -3)$

26. $\left(-5, \frac{1}{2}\right), (-5, 3)$

B **Apply Your Skills**

Find the rate of change for each situation.

27. A baby is 18 in. long at birth and 27 in. long at ten months.

28. The cost of group museum tickets is $48 for four people and $78 for ten people.

29. You drive 30 mi in one hour and 120 mi in four hours.

Find the slope of the line passing through each pair of points.

30. $(-7, 1), (7, 8)$

31. $\left(4, 1\frac{2}{3}\right), \left(-2, \frac{2}{3}\right)$

32. $(0, 3.5), (-4, 2.5)$

33. $\left(\frac{1}{2}, 8\right), (1, -2)$

34. $\left(-5, \frac{1}{2}\right), (-5, 3)$

35. $(0.5, 6.25), (3, -1.25)$

Through the given point, draw the line with the given slope.

36. $K(3, 5)$
slope -2

37. $M(5, 2)$
slope $-\frac{1}{2}$

38. $Q(-2, 3)$
slope $\frac{3}{5}$

39. $R(2, -3)$
slope $-\frac{4}{3}$

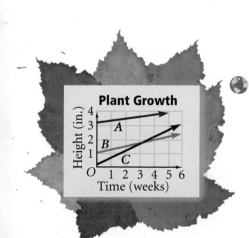

40. a. Biology Which line in the graph at the left is the steepest?
  b. During the 6-week period, which plant had the greatest rate of change? The least rate of change? How do you know?

41. a. Find the slope of the line through $A(4, -3)$ and $B(1, -5)$ using A for (x_2, y_2) and B for (x_1, y_1).
  b. Find the slope of the line in part (a) using B for (x_2, y_2) and A for (x_1, y_1).
  c. Critical Thinking Explain why it does not matter which point you use for (x_2, y_2) and which point you use for (x_1, y_1) when you calculate a slope.

42. Construction An extension ladder has a label that says, "Do not place base of ladder less than 5 ft from the vertical surface." What is the greatest slope possible if the ladder can safely extend to reach a height of 12 ft? Of 18 ft?

43. Writing If two points on a line have positive coordinates, is the slope necessarily positive? Explain.

Geometry Find the slope of the sides of each figure.

44.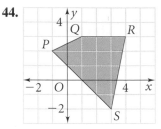

45.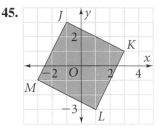

Need Help?

For help with direct variation and the constant of variation see p. 262.

46. a. Graph the direct variation $y = -\frac{2}{3}x$.
  b. What is the constant of variation?
  c. What is the slope?
  d. What is the relationship between the constant of variation and the slope?

47. a. Open-Ended Name two points on a line with a slope of $\frac{3}{4}$.
  b. Name two points on a line with a slope of $-\frac{1}{2}$.

Each pair of points lies on a line with the given slope. Find *x* or *y*.

48. $(2, 4), (x, 8);$ slope $= -2$

49. $(2, 4), (x, 8);$ slope $= -\frac{1}{2}$.

50. $(4, 3), (x, 7);$ slope $= 2$

51. $(x, 3), (2, 8);$ slope $= -\frac{5}{2}$

52. $(-4, y), (2, 4y);$ slope $= 6$

53. $(3, 5), (x, 2);$ undefined slope

Reasoning In Exercises 54–60, tell whether each statement is *true* or *false*. If false, give a counterexample.

54. A rate of change must be either positive or zero.

55. All horizontal lines have the same slope.

56. A line with slope 1 always passes through the origin.

57. Two lines may have the same slope.

58. The slope of a line that passes through Quadrant III must be negative.

59. A line with slope 0 never passes through point $(0, 0)$.

60. Two points with the same *x*-coordinate are always on the same vertical line.

61. Business The graph shows how much it costs to rent carousel equipment.
  a. Estimate the slope of the line. What does that number mean?
  b. Customers pay $2 for a ride. What is the average number of customers needed to cover the rental costs?

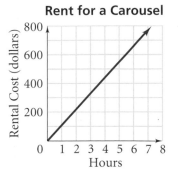

Rent for a Carousel

62. Error Analysis A friend says the slope of a line passing through $(1, 7)$ and $(3, 9)$ is equal to the ratio $\frac{1 - 3}{7 - 9}$. What is your friend's error?

Real-World Connection

On a carousel, the outer horses cover more distance than the inner horses, giving them a faster speed.

Find the slope of the line passing through each pair of points.

63. $(a, -b), (-a, -b)$ **64.** $(-m, n), (3m, -n)$ **65.** $(2a, b), (c, 2d)$

Do the points in each set lie on the same line? Explain your answer.

66. $A(1, 3), B(4, 2), C(-2, 4)$ **67.** $G(3, 5), H(-1, 3), I(7, 7)$

68. $D(-2, 3), E(0, -1), F(2, 1)$ **69.** $P(4, 2), Q(-3, 2), R(2, 5)$

70. $G(1, -2), H(-1, -5), I(5, 4)$ **71.** $S(-3, 4), T(0, 2), X(-3, 0)$

Standardized Test Prep

Multiple Choice

72. A line has slope $\frac{4}{3}$. Through which two points could this line pass?
- **A.** (24, 19), (8, 10)
- **B.** (10, 8), (16, 0)
- **C.** (28, 10), (22, 2)
- **D.** (4, 20), (0, 17)

73. A horizontal line passes through (5, 22). Which other point does the line contain?
- **F.** (5, 2)   **G.** (0, 22)   **H.** (22, 5)   **I.** (0, 5)

Short Response

74. The steepness, or grade, of a road is expressed as a percent. If a road rises 3 feet for every 24 horizontal feet, what is the slope of the road? What percent grade is this? Show your work.

Quantitative Comparison

Compare the quantity in Column A with the quantity in Column B. Choose the best answer.
- **A.** The quantity in Column A is greater.
- **B.** The quantity in Column B is greater.
- **C.** The two quantities are equal.
- **D.** The relationship cannot be determined from the information given.

Take It to the NET
Online lesson quiz at
www.PHSchool.com
Web Code: aea-0601

	Column A	Column B
75.	the slope of the line through the points $(-3, 4)$ and $(-2, 5)$	the slope of the line through the points $(3, 4)$ and $(2, 5)$

Mixed Review

Lesson 5-6

Write a function rule for each situation.

76. the total cost of renting a movie for n days if it costs \$3.50/day

77. the total profit if supplies and wages cost \$232, and each item q sells for \$4.95

Lesson 4-5

Find each probability based on one roll of a number cube.

78. $P(10)$ **79.** $P(\text{even number})$ **80.** $P(3 \text{ or } 5)$ **81.** $P(\text{integer})$

Lesson 2-3

Solve.

82. $x + 3 + 2x = -6$ **83.** $3(2t + 5) = -9$ **84.** $9 = y + 2(4y - 5)$

85. $4n - 7(n - 9) = 42$ **86.** $2(7 - q) - 4 = 0$ **87.** $\frac{2}{5}(p + 10) = 0$

Investigating $y = mx + b$

FOR USE WITH LESSON 6-2

You can use a graphing calculator to explore the graph of an equation in the form $y = mx + b$. For this Investigation, use a standard screen by pressing **ZOOM** 6.

1. Graph these equations on the same screen. Then complete each statement.

$$y = x + 1 \qquad y = 2x + 1 \qquad y = \tfrac{1}{2}x + 1$$

   a. The graph of __?__ is closest to the y-axis.
   b. The graph of __?__ is closest to the x-axis.

2. Match each equation with the best choice for its graph.
   A. $y = \tfrac{1}{5}x - 1$ **B.** $y = 5x - 1$ **C.** $y = x - 1$

   I.   **II.**   **III.**

   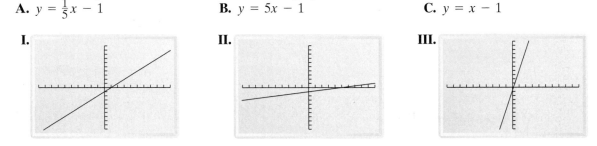

3. How does changing m affect the graph of an equation in the form $y = mx + b$?

4. Graph these equations on the same screen.

$$y = 2x + 1 \qquad y = -2x + 1$$

   How does the sign of m affect the graph of an equation?

5. Graph these equations on the same screen.

$$y = 2x + 1 \qquad y = 2x - 2 \qquad y = 2x + 2$$

   Where does the graph of each equation cross the y-axis? (*Hint:* Use the **ZOOM** feature to better see the points of intersection.)

6. Match each equation with the best choice for its graph.
   A. $y = \tfrac{1}{2}x - 5$ **B.** $y = \tfrac{1}{2}x$ **C.** $y = \tfrac{1}{2}x + 3$

   I.   **II.**   **III.**

   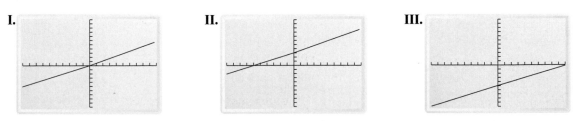

7. How does changing the value of b affect the graph of an equation in the form $y = mx + b$?

8. You can change the appearance of a graph by changing its scale in the **WINDOW** screen. Describe how the graph of $y = 2x + 1$ changes from its appearance on a standard screen using the following values for Xmin, Xmax, Ymin, and Ymax.

   a. Xmin = –5 Ymin = –10
       Xmax = 5 Ymax = 10

   b. Xmin = –10 Ymin = –5
       Xmax = 10 Ymax = 5

Slope-Intercept Form

Lesson Preview

What You'll Learn

OBJECTIVE 1 To write equations in slope-intercept form

OBJECTIVE 2 To graph linear equations

. . . And Why

To use a graph for relating total earnings to sales, as in Example 5

✓ Check Skills You'll Need

(For help, go to Lessons 1-6 and 2-6.)

Evaluate each expression.

1. $6a + 3$ for $a = 2$

2. $-2x - 5$ for $x = 3$

3. $\frac{1}{4}x + 2$ for $x = 16$

4. $0.2x + 2$ for $x = 15$

Solve each equation for y.

5. $y - 5 = 4x$

6. $y + 2x = 7$

7. $2y + 6 = -8x$

New Vocabulary • linear equation • y-intercept • slope-intercept form

---

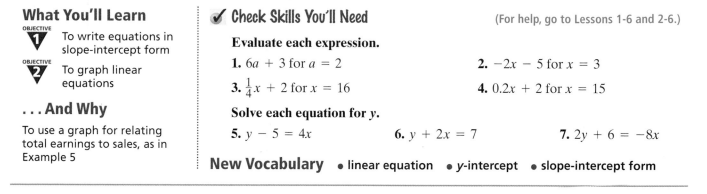

TEXT Interactive lesson includes instant self-check, tutorials, and activities.

OBJECTIVE

1 Writing Linear Equations

An equation whose graph is a line is a **linear equation.** Since a function rule is an equation, a function can also be linear. Here are some examples of linear equations.

$$y = 2x + 5 \qquad\qquad f(x) = \frac{3x}{5} + 4$$

Not all equations are linear. Here are some examples of equations that are not linear.

$$y = x^2 \qquad\qquad f(x) = 2x^3 + x + 1$$

Real-World 🌐 Connection

The skateboarder performs a rail slide on a bar that has slope $-\frac{3}{8}$.

The **y-intercept** is the y-coordinate of the point where a line crosses the y-axis. The line shown at the right crosses the y-axis at $(0, 4)$. The y-intercept is 4. The slope of the line is $-\frac{3}{8}$.

If you know the slope of a line and its y-intercept, you can write the equation of the line. The letter m refers to the *slope*.

$\dfrac{y_2 - y_1}{x_2 - x_1} = m$ **Start with the slope formula.**

$\dfrac{y - 4}{x - 0} = -\dfrac{3}{8}$ **Substitute $(0, 4)$ for (x_1, y_1), (x, y) for (x_2, y_2), and $-\frac{3}{8}$ for m.**

$\dfrac{y - 4}{x} = -\dfrac{3}{8}$ **Simplify $x - 0$.**

$y - 4 = -\dfrac{3}{8}x$ **Multiply each side by x.**

$y = -\dfrac{3}{8}x + 4$ **Add 4 to each side.**

     ↑   ↑

   slope y-intercept

The slope and y-intercept appear in the equation!

Key Concepts

Definition	Slope-Intercept Form of a Linear Equation

The **slope-intercept form** of a linear equation is $y = mx + b$.

$$\uparrow \qquad \uparrow$$
$$\text{slope} \quad y\text{-intercept}$$

---

1 EXAMPLE Identifying Slope and *y*-Intercept

What are the slope and *y*-intercept of $y = 3x - 5$?

$y = mx + b$ **Use the slope-intercept form.**

$y = 3x + (-5)$ **Think of $y = 3x - 5$ as $y = 3x + (-5)$.**

● The slope is 3; the *y*-intercept is −5.

✔ **Check Understanding** ❶ Find the slope and *y*-intercept of each equation.

   a. $y = -2x + 1$ **b.** $y = \frac{7}{6}x - \frac{3}{4}$ **c.** $y = -\frac{4}{5}x$

You can write an equation of a line when you know its slope and *y*-intercept.

---

2 EXAMPLE Writing an Equation

Write an equation of the line with slope $\frac{3}{8}$ and *y*-intercept 6.

$y = mx + b$ **Use the slope-intercept form.**

$y = \frac{3}{8}x + 6$ **Substitute $\frac{3}{8}$ for *m* and 6 for *b*.**

✔ **Check Understanding** ❷ Write an equation of a line with slope −3 and *y*-intercept 4.

You can write an equation from a graph. Use two points to find the slope. Then use the slope and the *y*-intercept to write the equation.

---

3 EXAMPLE Writing an Equation From a Graph

Write the equation of the line.

Step 1 Find the slope. Two points on the line are $(0, 2)$ and $(4, -1)$.

$$\text{slope} = \frac{-1 - 2}{4 - 0}$$
$$= -\frac{3}{4}$$

Step 2 Write an equation in slope-intercept form. The *y*-intercept is 2.

$y = mx + b$

$y = -\frac{3}{4}x + 2$ **Substitute $-\frac{3}{4}$ for *m* and 2 for *b*.**

✔ **Check Understanding** ❸ Write the equation of the line.

Each point on the graph of an equation is an ordered pair that makes the equation true. The graph of a linear equation is a line that indicates all the solutions of the equation. You can use the slope and y-intercept to graph a line.

4 **EXAMPLE** **Graphing Equations**

Graph $y = 3x - 1$.

Step 1
The y-intercept is -1.
So plot a point at
$(0, -1)$.

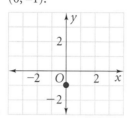

Step 2
The slope is 3, or $\frac{3}{1}$.
Use the slope to plot
a second point.

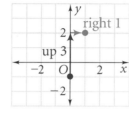

right 1
up 3

Step 3
Draw a line through
the two points.

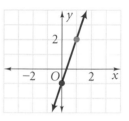

✓ **Check Understanding** **4** Graph $y = \frac{3}{2}x - 2$.

When you graph equations for real-world situations, use scales on the x- and y-axes that are reasonable for the situation. Recall that you can avoid having a large blank space in a graph by using a zigzag line to show a break in a scale.

5 **EXAMPLE** **Real-World** **Problem Solving**

Commission The base pay of a water-delivery person is $210 per week. He also earns 20% commission on any sale he makes. The equation $t = 210 + 0.2s$ relates total earnings t to sales s. Graph the equation.

Step 1 Identify the slope and y-intercept.

$t = 210 + 0.2s$

$t = 0.2s + 210$ **Rewrite the equation in slope-intercept form.**

↑   ↑
slope y-intercept

Step 2 Plot two points. First plot $(0, 210)$, the y-intercept. Then use the slope to plot a second point.

The slope is 0.2, which equals $\frac{2}{10}$, or $\frac{20}{100}$. Plot a second point 20 units above and 100 units to the right of the y-intercept.

Step 3 Draw a line through the points.

Real-World **Connection**

Between 1990 and 1999, the sales of bottled water in the United States increased 107.6%, which means that sales more than doubled.

Weekly Earnings for a Water-Delivery Person

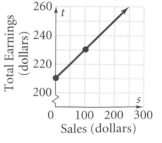

✓ **Check Understanding** **5** Suppose the base pay of the delivery person is $150, and his commission on each sale is 30%. The equation relating his total earnings t to sales s is $t = 150 + 0.3s$. Graph the equation.

EXERCISES

For more practice, see *Extra Practice*.

Practice and Problem Solving

A Practice by Example

Example 1
(page 292)

Find the slope and *y*-intercept of each equation.

1. $y = -2x + 1$ **2.** $y = -\frac{1}{2}x + 2$ **3.** $y = x - \frac{5}{4}$

4. $y = 5x + 8$ **5.** $y = \frac{2}{3}x + 1$ **6.** $y = -4x$

7. $y = -x - 7$ **8.** $y = -0.7x - 9$ **9.** $y = -\frac{3}{4}x - 5$

Example 2
(page 292)

Write an equation of a line with the given slope and *y*-intercept.

10. $m = \frac{2}{9}, b = 3$ **11.** $m = 3, b = \frac{2}{9}$ **12.** $m = \frac{9}{2}, b = 3$

13. $m = 0, b = 1$ **14.** $m = -1, b = -6$ **15.** $m = -\frac{2}{3}, b = 5$

16. $m = 0.3, b = 4$ **17.** $m = 0.4, b = 0.6$ **18.** $m = -7, b = \frac{1}{3}$

19. $m = -\frac{1}{5}, b = -\frac{2}{5}$ **20.** $m = -\frac{1}{4}, b = \frac{5}{4}$ **21.** $m = \frac{8}{3}, b = \frac{2}{3}$

Example 3
(page 292)

Write the slope-intercept form of the equation for each line.

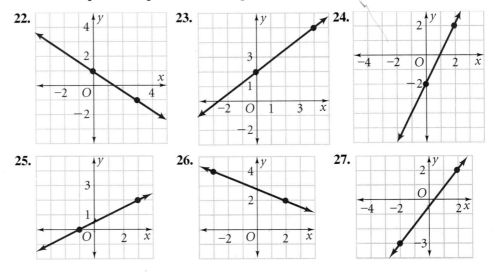

Example 4
(page 293)

Use the slope and *y*-intercept to graph each equation.

28. $y = \frac{1}{2}x + 4$ **29.** $y = \frac{2}{3}x - 1$ **30.** $y = -5x + 2$ **31.** $y = 2x + 5$

32. $y = x + 4$ **33.** $y = -x + 2$ **34.** $y = 4x - 3$ **35.** $y = -\frac{3}{2}x$

36. $y = \frac{2}{5}x - 3$ **37.** $y = -\frac{2}{3}x + 2$ **38.** $y = -\frac{4}{5}x + 4$ **39.** $y = -0.5x + 2$

Example 5
(page 293)

40. Retail Sales A music store is offering a coupon promotion on its CDs. The regular price for CDs is \$14. With the coupon, customers are given \$4 off the total purchase. The equation $t = 14c - 4$, where c is the number of CDs and t is the total cost of the purchase, models this situation.
a. Graph the equation.
b. Find the total cost for a sale of 6 CDs.

B Apply Your Skills

Find the slope and *y*-intercept of each equation.

41. $y - 2 = -3x$ **42.** $y + \frac{1}{2}x = 0$ **43.** $y - 9x = \frac{1}{2}$

44. $y = 3x - 9$ **45.** $2y - 6 = 3x$ **46.** $-2y = 6(5 - 3x)$

47. $y - d = cx$ **48.** $y = (2 - a)x + a$ **49.** $2y + 4n = -6x$

Use the slope and *y*-intercept to graph each equation.

50. $y = 7 - 3x$

51. $2y + 4x = 0$

52. $3y + 6 = -2x$

53. $y + 2 = 5x - 4$

54. $4x + 3y = 2x - 1$

55. $-2(3x - 4) + y = 0$

56. Error Analysis Fred drew the graph at the right for the equation $y = -2x + 1$. What error did he make?

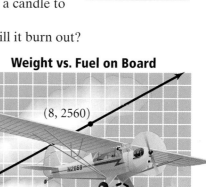

57. a. A candle begins burning at time $t = 0$. Its original height is 12 in. After 30 min the height of the candle is 8 in. Draw a graph showing the change in the height of the candle.

b. Write an equation that relates the height of a candle to the time it has been burning.

c. How many minutes after the candle is lit will it burn out?

58. Airplane Fuel The graph shows the relationship between the number of gallons of fuel in the tank of an airplane and the weight of the airplane. The equation $y = 6x + 2512$, where x is the number of gallons of fuel and y is the weight of the airplane, models this situation.

a. What does the slope represent?

b. Use the equation to predict the weight of the plane when the tank contains 25 gallons of fuel.

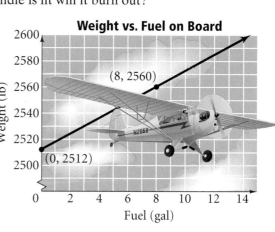

Weight vs. Fuel on Board

(8, 2560)

(0, 2512)

Real-World Connection

Careers Airport ground crews direct airplanes to and from their gates.

Is the ordered pair on the graph of the given equation?

59. $(-3, 4); y = -2x + 1$

60. $(-6, 5); y = -\frac{1}{2}x + 2$

61. $(0, -1); y = x - \frac{5}{4}$

Match the equation with its graph. Each mark on the scale indicates one unit.

62. $y = x + 5$

63. $y = -\frac{5}{2}x + 5$

64. $y = -\frac{1}{2}x + 5$

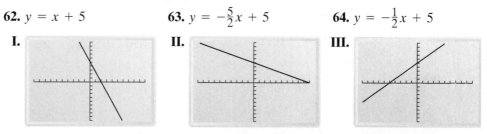

I.

II.

III.

65. a. Math in the Media Write an equation relating the data in the cartoon.

b. How many dog years are 12 human years?

Mother Goose and Grimm

66. **Pet Care** When the Bryants leave town for a vacation, they put their dog Tyco in a kennel. The kennel charges $15 for a first-day flea bath and $5 per day. The equation $t = 15 + 5d$ relates the total charge t to the number of days d.
    a. Rewrite the equation in slope-intercept form.
    b. Graph the equation.
    c. Explain why the line you graph should lie only in Quadrant I.

67. **Writing** Explain the steps you would use to graph $y = \frac{3}{4}x + 5$.

68. **Critical Thinking** Which graphed line has the greater slope? Explain.

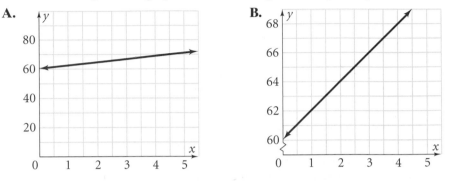

Given two points on a line, write the equation of the line in slope-intercept form.

69. $(3, 5), (5, 9)$

70. $(5, -13), (2, -1)$

71. $(-4, 10), (6, 5)$

72. $(8, 7), (-12, 2)$

73. $(-7, 4), (11, -14)$

74. $(-1, -9), (2, 0)$

75. **Graphing Calculator** Suppose you want to graph the equation $y = \frac{5}{4}x - 3$. Enter each key sequence and display the graph.
    a. [Y=] 5 [÷] 4 [X,T,θ,n] [−] 3
    b. [Y=] [(] 5 [÷] 4 [)] [X,T,θ,n] [−] 3
    c. Which equation gives you the graph of $y = \frac{5}{4}x - 3$? Explain.

76. a. What is the slope of each line?
    b. What is the y-intercept of each line?
    c. **Geometry** The lines in the graph are parallel. What appears to be true about the slopes of parallel lines?

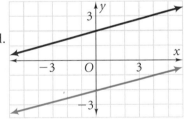

77. **Open-Ended** Write a linear equation. Identify the slope and y-intercept. Then graph your equation.

C **Challenge**

Find the value of a such that the graph of the equation has the given slope.

78. $y = 2ax + 4; m = -1$

79. $y = -\frac{1}{2}ax - 5; m = \frac{5}{2}$

80. $y = \frac{3}{4}ax + 3; m = \frac{9}{16}$

81. a. **Geometry** Graph these equations on the same grid.
    $$y = 3 \qquad y = -3 \qquad x = 2 \qquad x = -2$$
    b. Which geometric figure did you draw? Justify your answer.
    c. Draw a diagonal of the figure. What is the equation of this line? Explain.

82. **Recreation** A group of mountain climbers begin an expedition with 265 lb of food. They plan to eat a total of 15 lb of food per day.
    a. Write an equation in slope-intercept form relating the remaining food supply r to the number of days d.
    b. Graph your equation.
    c. The group plans to eat the last of their food the day their expedition ends. Use your graph to find how many days they expect the expedition to last.

Multiple Choice

83. Which equation has the same y-intercept as $y = 4x - 3$?

A. $y - 3 = x$ **B.** $y = 8x + 3$ **C.** $3 - y = 4x$ **D.** $y = -3 + 8x$

84. Which of the following is the equation of the line that has the same slope as $y = -\frac{3}{2}x + 2$ and the same y-intercept as $y = 3x - 2$?

F. $y - 2 = -\frac{3}{2}x$ **G.** $-\frac{3}{2}x = y + 2$

H. $y + 2 = -\frac{3}{2}$ **I.** $-\frac{3}{2}x = y + 3$

85. A software company started with 2 employees. In 6 months, the company had 7 employees. The number of employees increased at a steady rate. Which equation models the relationship between the number of employees n and the number of months m since the company started?

A. $n = \frac{5}{6}m + 2$ **B.** $m = 2n + \frac{5}{6}$

C. $n = \frac{6}{5}m + 2$ **D.** $m = \frac{5}{6}n + 2$

Take It to the NET
Online lesson quiz at
www.PHSchool.com
Web Code: aea-0602

Short Response

86. A line passes through the points (0, 3) and (1, 5). Graph this line and find an equation for the line in slope-intercept form. Show your work.

Mixed Review

Lesson 6-1

Find the slope of the line that passes through each pair of points.

87. $(-2, 8), (5, -1)$ **88.** $(0, 0), (-6, 5)$ **89.** $(4, 6), (2, -3)$ **90.** $(1, 2), (2, 1)$

Lesson 4-3

91. The greeting card industry sells over 6 billion cards annually. Women purchase 80% of all greeting cards sold. How many cards do women purchase annually?

A Point in Time

1500   1600   1700   1800   1900   2000

On August 30, 1984, Astronaut Judith A. Resnik became the second American woman in space, on the shuttle *Discovery*'s first voyage. Resnik was an electrical engineer with a Ph.D. from the University of Maryland. Prior to her mission, she helped to design and develop a remote manipulator system. This required skill in writing linear equations. Her job during *Discovery*'s six-day voyage was to manipulate a robotic arm and to extend and retract the shuttle's solar power array. Resnik died tragically in the *Challenger* disaster in 1986.

Take It to the NET For more information about astronauts, go to **www.PHSchool.com**.
Web Code: aee-2032

Standard Form

Lesson Preview

What You'll Learn

OBJECTIVE 1 To graph equations using intercepts

OBJECTIVE 2 To write equations in standard form

. . . And Why

To use an equation to model a real-world situation that involves exercise, as in Example 5

✓ Check Skills You'll Need

(For help, go to Lessons 2-3 and 2-6.)

Solve each equation for y.

1. $3x + y = 5$ **2.** $y - 2x = 10$ **3.** $x - y = 6$

4. $20x + 4y = 8$ **5.** $9y + 3x = 1$ **6.** $5y - 2x = 4$

Clear each equation of decimals.

7. $6.25x + 8.5 = 7.75$ **8.** $0.4 = 0.2x - 5$ **9.** $0.9 - 0.222x = 1$

New Vocabulary

• standard form of a linear equation   • x-intercept

---

iTEXT Interactive lesson includes instant self-check, tutorials, and activities.

OBJECTIVE 1 Graphing Equations Using Intercepts

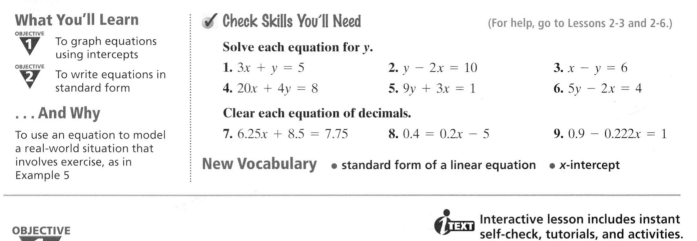

Investigation: Intercepts

1. Make a table of values for the equation $3y - 2x = 12$.

2. Use the table of values to graph $3y - 2x = 12$.

3. What is the y-intercept?

4. What is the value of x when the line crosses the x-axis?

5. In the equation $3y - 2x = 12$, what is the value of y when $x = 0$? What is the value of x when $y = 0$?

6. Using your answers to 3, 4, and 5, explain how you can make a graph of $3y - 2x = 12$ without making a table.

The slope-intercept form is just one form of a linear equation. Another form is standard form, which is useful in making quick graphs.

Key Concepts

Definition	Standard Form of a Linear Equation

The **standard form of a linear equation** is $Ax + By = C$, where A, B, and C are real numbers, and A and B are not both zero.

You can use the x- and y-intercepts to make a graph. The **x-intercept** is the x-coordinate of the point where a line crosses the x-axis. To graph a linear equation in standard form, you can find the x-intercept by substituting 0 for y and solving for x. Similarly, to find the y-intercept, substitute 0 for x and solve for y.

1 EXAMPLE Finding *x*- and *y*-Intercepts

Find the *x*- and *y*-intercept of $3x + 4y = 8$.

Step 1 To find the *x*-intercept, substitute 0 for *y* and solve for *x*.

$$3x + 4y = 8$$
$$3x + 4(0) = 8$$
$$3x = 8$$
$$x = \frac{8}{3}$$

The *x*-intercept is $\frac{8}{3}$.

Step 2 To find the *y*-intercept, substitute 0 for *x* and solve for *y*.

$$3x + 4y = 8$$
$$3(0) + 4y = 8$$
$$4y = 8$$
$$y = 2$$

The *y*-intercept is 2.

✓ **Check Understanding** ① Find the *x*- and *y*-intercepts of $4x - 9y = -12$.

If the *x*- and *y*-intercepts are integers, you can use them to make a quick graph.

2 EXAMPLE Graphing Lines Using Intercepts

Graph $2x + 3y = 12$ using intercepts.

Step 1 Find the intercepts.

$$2x + 3y = 12$$
$$2x + 3(0) = 12 \quad \textbf{Substitute 0 for } y.$$
$$2x = 12 \quad \textbf{Solve for } x.$$
$$x = 6$$

$$2(0) + 3y = 12 \quad \textbf{Substitute 0 for } x.$$
$$3y = 12 \quad \textbf{Solve for } y.$$
$$y = 4$$

Step 2 Plot $(0, 4)$ and $(6, 0)$. Draw a line through the points.

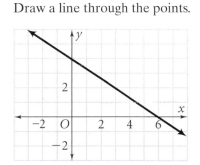

✓ **Check Understanding** ② Graph $5x + 2y = -10$ using the *x*- and *y*-intercepts.

In the standard form of an equation $Ax + By = C$, either *A* or *B*, but not both, *may* be zero. If *A* or *B* is zero, the line is either horizontal or vertical.

Need Help?
The slope of a horizontal line is 0, and the slope of a vertical line is undefined.

3 EXAMPLE Graphing Horizontal and Vertical Lines

a. Graph $y = -3$.

$0x + 1y = -3$ ← Write in standard form. →
For all values of *x*, $y = -3$.

b. Graph $x = 2$.

$1x + 0y = 2$
For all values of *y*, $x = 2$.

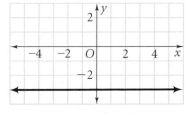

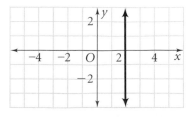

✓ **Check Understanding** ③ Graph each equation.
  a. $y = 5$ **b.** $y = 0$ **c.** $x = -4$ **d.** $x = 0$

You can change an equation from slope-intercept form to standard form. If the equation contains fractions or decimals, multiply to write the equation using integers.

4 EXAMPLE Transforming to Standard Form

Write $y = \frac{3}{4}x + 2$ in standard form using integers.

$$y = \frac{3}{4}x + 2$$

$$4y = 4\left(\frac{3}{4}x + 2\right)$$ Multiply each side by 4.

$$4y = 3x + 8$$ Use the Distributive Property.

$$-3x + 4y = 8$$ Subtract 3x from each side.

The standard form of $y = \frac{3}{4}x + 2$ is $-3x + 4y = 8$.

✓ **Check Understanding** ➍ Write $y = -\frac{2}{5}x + 1$ in standard form using integers.

You can write equations for real-world situations using standard form.

5 EXAMPLE Real-World 🌐 Problem Solving

Data Analysis Write an equation in standard form to find the minutes someone who weighs 150 lb would need to bicycle and swim laps in order to burn 300 calories. Use the data below.

Activity by a 150-lb Person	Calories Burned per Minute
Bicycling	10
Bowling	4
Hiking	7
Running 5.2 mi/h	11
Swimming, laps	12
Walking 3.5 mi/h	5

Real-World 🌐 Connection

Doctors recommend 30 minutes of exercise each day.

Define Let x = the minutes spent bicycling.

Let y = the minutes spent swimming laps.

Relate 10 · minutes bicycling   plus   12 · minutes swimming laps   equals   300 calories

Write $10x$ + $12y$ =   300

The equation in standard form is $10x + 12y = 300$.

✓ **Check Understanding** ➎ **Data Analysis** Write an equation in standard form to find the minutes someone who weighs 150 lb would need to bowl and walk to burn 250 calories.

EXERCISES

For more practice, see *Extra Practice*.

Practice and Problem Solving

A **Practice by Example**

Example 1
(page 299)

Find the *x*- and *y*-intercepts of each equation.

1. $x + 2y = 18$
2. $3x - y = 9$
3. $-5x + y = 30$

4. $-6x + 3y = -9$
5. $4x + 12y = -18$
6. $9x - 6y = -72$

7. $-2x - 3y = -12$
8. $7x - 2y = 4$
9. $-8x + 10y = 40$

Example 2
(page 299)

Match each equation with its graph.

10. $2x - 5y = 10$
11. $-2x + 5y = 10$
12. $2x + 5y = 10$

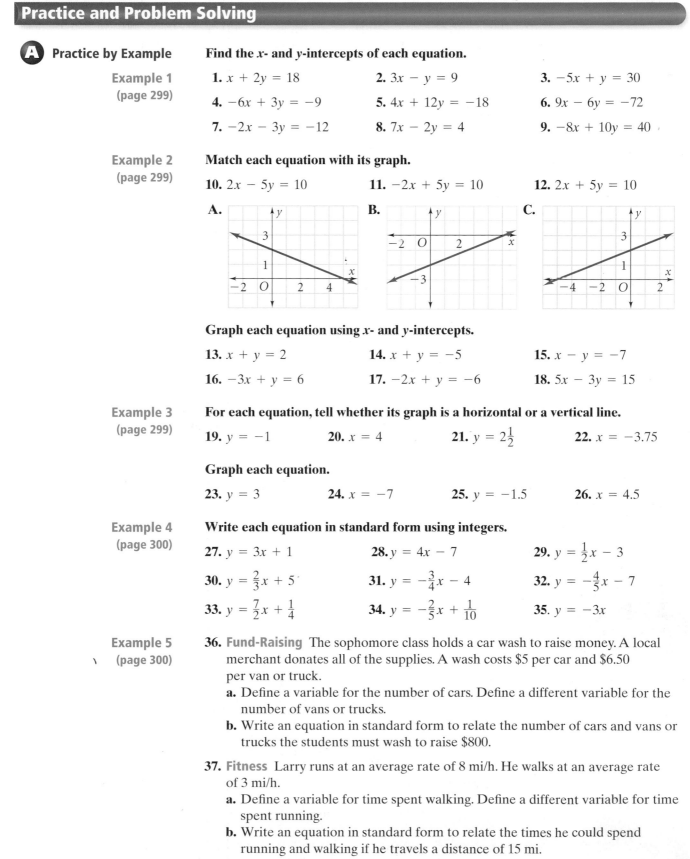

Graph each equation using *x*- and *y*-intercepts.

13. $x + y = 2$
14. $x + y = -5$
15. $x - y = -7$

16. $-3x + y = 6$
17. $-2x + y = -6$
18. $5x - 3y = 15$

Example 3
(page 299)

For each equation, tell whether its graph is a horizontal or a vertical line.

19. $y = -1$
20. $x = 4$
21. $y = 2\frac{1}{2}$
22. $x = -3.75$

Graph each equation.

23. $y = 3$
24. $x = -7$
25. $y = -1.5$
26. $x = 4.5$

Example 4
(page 300)

Write each equation in standard form using integers.

27. $y = 3x + 1$
28. $y = 4x - 7$
29. $y = \frac{1}{2}x - 3$

30. $y = \frac{2}{3}x + 5$
31. $y = -\frac{3}{4}x - 4$
32. $y = -\frac{4}{5}x - 7$

33. $y = \frac{7}{2}x + \frac{1}{4}$
34. $y = -\frac{2}{5}x + \frac{1}{10}$
35. $y = -3x$

Example 5
(page 300)

36. Fund-Raising The sophomore class holds a car wash to raise money. A local merchant donates all of the supplies. A wash costs $5 per car and $6.50 per van or truck.
   a. Define a variable for the number of cars. Define a different variable for the number of vans or trucks.
   b. Write an equation in standard form to relate the number of cars and vans or trucks the students must wash to raise $800.

37. Fitness Larry runs at an average rate of 8 mi/h. He walks at an average rate of 3 mi/h.
   a. Define a variable for time spent walking. Define a different variable for time spent running.
   b. Write an equation in standard form to relate the times he could spend running and walking if he travels a distance of 15 mi.

Graph each equation.

38. $-3x + 2y = -6$ **39.** $x + y = 1$ **40.** $2x - 3y = 18$

41. $y - x = -4$ **42.** $y = 2x + 5$ **43.** $y = -3x - 1$

44. $2 - y = x - 6$ **45.** $9 + y = 8 - x$ **46.** $6x = y$

Real-World 🌐 Connection

A peanut contains about 0.24 gram of protein.

47. Nutrition Suppose you are preparing a snack mix. You want the total protein from peanuts and granola to equal 28 grams. Peanuts have 7 grams of protein per ounce, and granola has 3 grams of protein per ounce.
  a. Write an equation for the protein content of your mix.
  b. Graph your equation. Use your graph to find how many ounces of granola you should use if you use 1 ounce of peanuts.

48. You are sent to the store to buy sliced meat for a party. You are told to get roast beef and turkey, and you are given $30. Roast beef is $4.29/lb and turkey is $3.99/lb. Write an equation in standard form to relate the pounds of each kind of meat you could buy at the store with $30.

Graphing Calculator Write each equation in slope-intercept form. Then use a graphing calculator to graph each equation. Make a sketch of the graph. Include the x- and y-intercepts.

49. $8x - 10y = -100$ **50.** $-6x + 7y = 21$ **51.** $12x + 15y = -45$

52. $-5x + 9y = -15$ **53.** $16x + 11y = -88$ **54.** $3x - 27y = 18$

55. Writing Two of the forms of a linear equation are slope-intercept form and standard form. Explain when each is the more useful.

56. Critical Thinking The definition of standard form states that A and B can't both be zero. Explain why.

57. Error Analysis A student says that the equation $3x + 2y = 6$ is a standard form of the equation $y = \frac{3}{2}x + 3$. What is the student's error?

Write an equation for each line on the graph.

58. a **59.** b **60.** c **61.** d

62. a. Fund-Raising Suppose your school is having a talent show to raise money for new music supplies. You estimate that 200 students and 150 adults will attend. You estimate $200 in expenses. Write an equation to find what ticket prices you should set to raise $1000.
  b. Open-Ended Graph your equation. Choose three possible prices you could set for students' and adults' tickets. Which is the best choice? Explain.

C Challenge

63. Write an equation of a line that has the same slope as the line $3x - 5y = 7$ and the same y-intercept as the line $2y - 9x = 8$.

64. Geometry Graph each of the four lines below on the same graph. What figure do the four lines form?
  $-2x + 3y = 10$ $3x + 2y = -2$ $-2x + 3y = -3$ $3x + 2y = 11$

65. a. Graph $2x + 3y = 6$ and $2x + 3y = 18$.
  b. What is the slope of each line?
  c. Compare the x-intercepts of the two lines. How are they related? How are the y-intercepts related?

Multiple Choice

66. Which of the following is the standard form of $y = -\frac{2}{3}x + 6$ written using integers?

   A. $\frac{2}{3}x + y = 6$ **B.** $-6 = -\frac{2}{3}x - y$ **C.** $2x + 3y = 18$ **D.** $-2x - 3y = 18$

67. Which is the slope of $Ax + By = C$?

   F. $-\frac{B}{A}$ **G.** $\frac{C}{A}$ **H.** $-\frac{A}{B}$ **I.** $\frac{C}{B}$

Short Response

68. A basket with 4 apples weighs 2 pounds. The same basket with 12 apples weighs 4 pounds. Write an equation in slope-intercept form for the weight y in terms of the number of apples x. Write an equation in standard form with integer coefficients that shows the relationship of the weight y and the number of apples x.

Extended Response

69. A tire dealer sells Supreme tires for $48 each and Prestige tires for $56 each. During one week, the sales for both tires totaled $2008.
  a. Write an equation that you can use to determine the possible combinations of Supreme tires x and Prestige tires y sold.
  b. Graph your equation on a coordinate plane.
  c. Use your graph to list 3 possible combinations of Supreme and Prestige tires sold.

Take It to the NET
Online lesson quiz at
www.PHSchool.com
······· Web Code: aea-0603

Mixed Review

Lesson 6-2

Determine whether the ordered pair is a solution of the equation.

70. $(2, -3); y = -x - 1$ **71.** $(6, -1); y = 2x - 15$ **72.** $(-5, -7); y = -3x - 8$

Lesson 4-6

Find each probability for rolling a number cube.

73. $P(\text{rolling a 2, then a 4})$ **74.** $P(\text{rolling a 5, then an even number})$

Lesson 4-1

Solve each proportion.

75. $\frac{a}{5} = \frac{12}{15}$ **76.** $\frac{2}{8} = \frac{w}{9}$ **77.** $\frac{x+2}{4} = \frac{3}{8}$ **78.** $\frac{14}{4m} = \frac{16}{5m+9}$

Checkpoint Quiz 1   **Lessons 6-1 through 6-3**

TEXT Instant self-check quiz online and on CD-ROM

Find the slope of the line passing through each pair of points.

1. $(-1, 3), (6, -2)$ **2.** $(4, 5), (0, 2)$ **3.** $(-2, -3), (-1, -7)$ **4.** $(4, -4), (-5, 5)$

5. Credit Cards In 1990, people charged $534 billion on the two most-used types of credit cards. In 1994, people charged $1.021 trillion on these same two types of credit cards. What was the rate of change?

Graph each equation.

6. $y = 4x - 1$ **7.** $y = -\frac{2}{5}x + 6$ **8.** $5x + 3y = -30$ **9.** $2x - 7y = 15$

10. Writing How are the graphs of $y = 3x + 5$, $y = \frac{2}{3}x + 5$, and $y = \frac{3}{5}x + 5$ alike? How are they different?

6-4 Point-Slope Form and Writing Linear Equations

Lesson Preview

What You'll Learn

OBJECTIVE 1 To graph and write linear equations using point-slope form

OBJECTIVE 2 To write a linear equation using data

. . . And Why

To write an equation relating altitude and the boiling point of water, as in Example 5

Find the rate of change of the data in each table.

1.

x	y
2	4
5	-2
8	-8
11	-14

2.

x	y
-3	-5
-1	-4
1	-3
3	-2

3.

x	y
10	4
7.5	-1
5	-6
2.5	-11

Simplify each expression.

4. $-3(x - 5)$

5. $5(x + 2)$

6. $-\frac{4}{9}(x - 6)$

New Vocabulary
• point-slope form

OBJECTIVE 1 Using Point-Slope Form

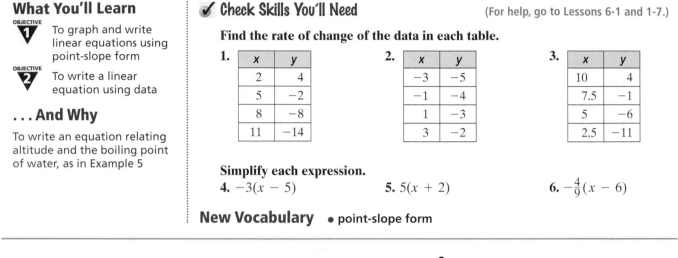

Interactive lesson includes instant self-check, tutorials, and activities.

Suppose you know that a line passes through the point $(3, 4)$ with slope 2. You can quickly write an equation of the line using the x- and y-coordinates of the point and using the slope.

$$y - 4 = 2(x - 3)$$

y-coordinate   slope x-coordinate

You can use the definition of slope to verify that $y - 4 = 2(x - 3)$ is the equation of the line through the point $(3, 4)$ with slope 2.

$\dfrac{y_2 - y_1}{x_2 - x_1} = m$ **Use the definition of slope.**

$\dfrac{y - 4}{x - 3} = 2$ **Substitute (3, 4) for (x_1, y_1), (x, y) for (x_2, y_2), and 2 for m.**

$\dfrac{y - 4}{x - 3}(x - 3) = 2(x - 3)$ **Multiply each side by $x - 3$.**

$y - 4 = 2(x - 3)$ **Simplify the left side of the equation.**

The equation $y - 4 = 2(x - 3)$ is in point-slope form.

🔑 Key Concepts

Definition	Point-Slope Form of a Linear Equation

The **point-slope form** of the equation of a nonvertical line that passes through the point (x_1, y_1) with slope m is

$$y - y_1 = m(x - x_1)$$

1 EXAMPLE Graphing Using Point-Slope Form

Graph the equation $y - 5 = \frac{1}{2}(x - 2)$.

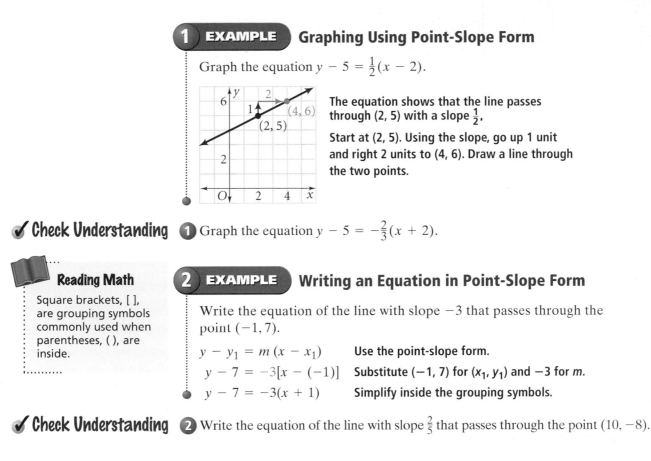

The equation shows that the line passes through (2, 5) with a slope $\frac{1}{2}$.

Start at (2, 5). Using the slope, go up 1 unit and right 2 units to (4, 6). Draw a line through the two points.

✓ **Check Understanding** ❶ Graph the equation $y - 5 = -\frac{2}{3}(x + 2)$.

Reading Math

Square brackets, [ ], are grouping symbols commonly used when parentheses, ( ), are inside.

2 EXAMPLE Writing an Equation in Point-Slope Form

Write the equation of the line with slope -3 that passes through the point $(-1, 7)$.

$y - y_1 = m(x - x_1)$	Use the point-slope form.
$y - 7 = -3[x - (-1)]$	Substitute $(-1, 7)$ for (x_1, y_1) and -3 for m.
$y - 7 = -3(x + 1)$	Simplify inside the grouping symbols.

✓ **Check Understanding** ❷ Write the equation of the line with slope $\frac{2}{5}$ that passes through the point $(10, -8)$.

If you know two points on a line, first use them to find the slope. Then you can write an equation using either point.

3 EXAMPLE Using Two Points to Write an Equation

Write equations for the line in point-slope form and in slope-intercept form.

Step 1 Find the slope.
$$\frac{y_2 - y_1}{x_2 - x_1} = m$$
$$\frac{-5 - 3}{-1 - 2} = \frac{8}{3}$$

The slope is $\frac{8}{3}$.

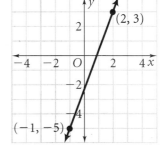

Need Help?

For help with slope-intercept form see p. 292.

Step 2 Use either point to write the equation in point-slope form. Use (2, 3).
$$y - y_1 = m(x - x_1)$$
$$y - 3 = \frac{8}{3}(x - 2)$$

Step 3 Rewrite the equation from Step 2 in slope-intercept form.
$$y - 3 = \frac{8}{3}(x - 2)$$
$$y - 3 = \frac{8}{3}x - 5\frac{1}{3}$$
$$y = \frac{8}{3}x - 2\frac{1}{3}$$

✓ **Check Understanding** ❸ **a.** Write an equation for the line in Example 3 in point-slope form using the point $(-1, -5)$.
  b. Write the equation you found in part (a) in slope-intercept form.
  c. What is true about the equation you wrote in part (b) and the equation in Step 3 of Example 3?

You can write a linear equation to model data in tables. Two sets of data have a linear relationship if the rate of change between consecutive pairs of data is the same. For data that have a linear relationship, the rate of change is the slope.

4 EXAMPLE Writing an Equation Using a Table

Is the relationship shown by the data linear? If so, model the data with an equation.

Step 1 Find the rate of change for consecutive ordered pairs.

x	y
−1	4
3	6
5	7
11	10

$4 \quad 2 \quad \frac{2}{4} = \frac{1}{2}$

$2 \quad 1 \quad \frac{1}{2} = \frac{1}{2}$

$6 \quad 3 \quad \frac{3}{6} = \frac{1}{2}$

Step 2 Use the slope and a point to write an equation.

$$y - y_1 = m(x - x_1)$$

Substitute (5, 7) for (x_1, y_1) and $\frac{1}{2}$ for m.

$$y - 7 = \frac{1}{2}(x - 5)$$

✓ **Check Understanding** ④ Is the relationship shown by the data at the right linear? If so, model the data with an equation.

x	y
−11	−7
−1	−3
4	−1
19	5

5 EXAMPLE Real-World 🌐 Problem Solving

Is the relationship shown by the data linear? If so, model the data with an equation.

Boiling Point of Water

Altitude (1000 ft)	Temperature (°F)
8	197.6
4.5	203.9
3	206.6
2.5	207.5

$-3.5 \quad 6.3$

$-1.5 \quad 2.7$

$-0.5 \quad 0.9$

Step 1 Find the rates of change for consecutive ordered pairs.

$$\frac{6.3}{-3.5} = -1.8 \qquad \frac{2.7}{-1.5} = -1.8 \qquad \frac{0.9}{-0.5} = -1.8$$

The relationship is linear. The rate of change is −1.8 degrees Fahrenheit per 1000 ft of altitude.

Step 2 Use the slope and a point to write an equation.

$$y - y_1 = m(x - x_1) \qquad \text{Use the point-slope form.}$$

$$y - 206.6 = -1.8(x - 3) \qquad \text{Substitute (3, 206.6) for } (x_1, y_1) \text{ and } -1.8 \text{ for } m.$$

The equation $y - 206.6 = -1.8(x - 3)$ relates altitude in thousands of feet x to the boiling point temperature in degrees Fahrenheit.

Real-World 🌐 Connection

At 5280 feet above sea level it takes 17 minutes to hard-boil an egg. This is more than 40% longer than it takes the same egg to cook at sea level.

5 Is the relationship shown by the data in the table linear? If it is, model the data with an equation.

Working Outdoors

Temperature	Calories Burned per Day
68°F	3030
62°F	3130
56°F	3230
50°F	3330

In Example 5 you could rewrite $y - 206.6 = -1.8(x - 3)$ as $y = -1.8x + 212$. This form gives you useful information about the y-intercept. For instance, 212°F is the boiling point of water at sea level.

Here are the three forms of linear equations you have studied..

Key Concepts

Reading Math

For more help with the three forms of a linear equation, see page 310.

Summary	**Linear Equations**	
Slope-Intercept Form	**Standard Form**	**Point-Slope Form**
$y = mx + b$	$Ax + By = C$	$(y - y_1) = m(x - x_1)$
m is the slope and b is the y-intercept.	A and B are not both 0.	(x_1, y_1) lies on the graph of the equation, and m is the slope.
Examples		
$y = -\frac{2}{3}x + \frac{5}{3}$	$2x + 3y = 5$	$y - 1 = -\frac{2}{3}(x - 1)$

EXERCISES

For more practice, see *Extra Practice*.

Practice and Problem Solving

A **Practice by Example**

Example 1
(page 305)

Graph each equation.

1. $y - 2 = (x - 3)$ **2.** $y - 2 = 2(x - 3)$ **3.** $y - 2 = -\frac{3}{2}(x - 3)$

4. $y + 5 = -(x - 2)$ **5.** $y + 1 = \frac{2}{3}(x + 4)$ **6.** $y - 1 = -3(x + 2)$

7. $y + 3 = -2(x - 1)$ **8.** $y - 4 = (x - 5)$ **9.** $y - 2 = 3(x + 2)$

Example 2
(page 305)

Write an equation in point-slope form for the line through the given point with the given slope.

10. $(3, -4); m = 6$ **11.** $(4, 2); m = -\frac{5}{3}$ **12.** $(0, 2); m = \frac{4}{5}$

13. $(-2, -7); m = -\frac{3}{2}$ **14.** $(4, 0); m = 1$ **15.** $(5, -8); m = -3$

16. $(-5, 2); m = 0$ **17.** $(1, -8); m = -\frac{1}{5}$ **18.** $(-6, 1); m = \frac{2}{3}$

Example 3
(page 305)

A line passes through the given points. Write an equation for the line in point-slope form. Then rewrite the equation in slope-intercept form.

19. $(-1, 0), (1, 2)$ **20.** $(3, 5), (0, 0)$ **21.** $(4, -2), (9, -8)$

22. $(6, -4), (-3, 5)$ **23.** $(-1, -5), (-7, -6)$ **24.** $(-3, -4), (3, -2)$

25. $(2, 7), (1, -4)$ **26.** $(-2, 6), (5, 1)$ **27.** $(3, -8), (-2, 5)$

28. $\left(1, \frac{1}{2}\right), (3, 2)$ **29.** $\left(\frac{1}{2}, 2\right), \left(-\frac{3}{2}, 4\right)$ **30.** $(0.2, 1.1), (7, 3)$

Example 4
(page 306)

Is the relationship shown by the data linear? If so, model the data with an equation.

31.

x	y
−4	9
2	−3
5	−9
9	−17

32.

x	y
−10	−5
−2	19
5	40
11	58

33.

x	y
3	1
6	4
9	13
15	49

Example 5
(page 306)

34.

Speed Over Posted Speed (mi/h)	Fine ($)
10	75
12	95
15	125
19	165

35.

Volume (gal)	Weight (lb)
0	0
2	16
4	33
6	50

B **Apply Your Skills**

Write an equation of each line in point-slope form.

36. 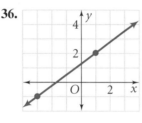   **37.** 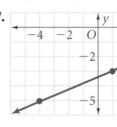   **38.**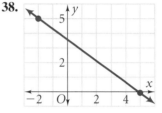

Write one equation of the line through the given points in point-slope form and one in standard form using integers.

39. $(1, 4), (−1, 1)$

40. $(6, −3), (−2, −3)$

41. $(0, 0), (−1, −2)$

42. $(0, 2), (−4, 2)$

43. $(−6, 6), (3, 3)$

44. $(2, 3), (−1, 5)$

45. $(5, −3), (3, 4)$

46. $(2, 2), (−1, 7)$

47. $(−7, 1), (5, −1)$

48. $(−8, 4), (−4, −2)$

49. $(2, 4), (−3, −6)$

50. $(5, 3), (4, 5)$

51. $(0, 1), (−3, 0)$

52. $(−2, 4), (0, −5)$

53. $(6, 2), (1, −1)$

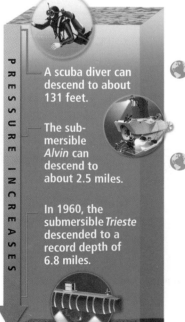

54. Science At the surface of the ocean, pressure is 1 atmosphere. At 66 ft below sea level, the pressure is 3 atmospheres. The relationship of pressure and depth is linear.
  a. Write an equation for the data.
  b. Predict the pressure at 100 ft below sea level.

55. Environment Worldwide carbon monoxide emissions are decreasing about 2.6 million metric tons each year. In 1991, carbon monoxide emissions were 79 million metric tons. Use a linear equation to model the relationship between carbon monoxide emissions and time. Let $x = 91$ correspond to 1991.

56. a. Open-Ended Write an equation in point-slope form that contains the point $(−4, −6)$. Explain your steps.
  b. How many equations could you write in part(a)? Explain.

57. Critical Thinking How would the graph of $y − 12 = 8(x − 2)$ change if all of the subtraction signs were changed to addition signs?

58. Reasoning Is $y − 5 = 2(x − 1)$ an equation of a line through $(4, 11)$? Explain.

59. Open-Ended Write an equation in each of the following forms.
   a. slope-intercept form
   b. standard form
   c. point-slope form

 60. Science Use the scatter plot.
   a. Write an equation to model the data.
   b. What is the speed of sound at 15°C?
   c. Predict the speed of sound at 60°C.

Effect of Air Temperature on Speed of Sound

 **Challenge**

Write an equation in slope-intercept form of each line described below.

61. The line contains the point $(-3, -5)$ and has the same slope as $y + 2 = 7(x + 3)$.

62. The line contains the point $(1, 3)$ and has the same y-intercept as $y - 5 = 2(x - 1)$.

63. The line contains the point $(2, -2)$ and has the same x-intercept as $y + 9 = 3(x - 4)$.

64. The table shows data that you can model using a linear function.
   a. Find the value of y when $x = 6$.
   b. Find the value of y when $x = 120$.
   c. Find the value of x when $y = 11$.
   d. Find the value of x when $y = 50$.

x	y
4	14
8	15.5
12	17
16	18.5

Standardized Test Prep

Gridded Response

65. What is the slope of the graph of $y - 8 = \frac{1}{2}(x + 2)$?

66. Find the y-intercept of the line $y + 3 = 4(x + 3)$.

67. What is the x-intercept of the line $y = 3x - 7$?

68. When $y - 1 = -\frac{4}{5}(x - 3)$ is written in standard form using positive integers, what is the coefficient of x?

69. When $y = -\frac{5}{2}x + \frac{2}{3}$ is written in standard form using positive integers, what is the coefficient of y?

Take It to the NET
Online lesson quiz at
www.PHSchool.com
Web Code: aea-0604

Mixed Review

Lesson 6-3

Graph each line.

70. $6x + 7y = 14$ **71.** $-2x + 9y = -9$ **72.** $5x - 4y = 24$

73. $3x - 8y = 4$ **74.** $5x + 18y = 6$ **75.** $-7x + 4y = -21$

Lesson 5-5

Find the common difference of each sequence. Then write the next two terms.

76. $-12, -7, -2, \ldots$ **77.** $\frac{1}{2}, \frac{5}{6}, \frac{7}{6}, \ldots$ **78.** $2.45, 2.52, 2.59, \ldots$

79. $-3.2, -3.25, -3.3, \ldots$ **80.** $18, 35, 52, \ldots$ **81.** $-7, -3, 1, \ldots$

There are three forms of a linear equation that you have studied in this chapter:
- slope-intercept form
- standard form
- point-slope form

To understand and remember these forms, it may help you to connect the English words with their specialized meanings in mathematics.

English words often have specialized meanings in mathematics. Usually you can relate your understanding of a word to its mathematical meaning.

Word	English Meaning	Mathematical Meaning
Slope	An inclined surface (for example, the upward slope of a hill)	The rate of change that gives the steepness of a line $$\text{slope} = \frac{\text{vertical change}}{\text{horizontal change}} = \frac{\text{rise}}{\text{run}}$$
Intercept	To cut off from a path (for example, to intercept a football)	The values of the points at which x-axis or y-axis intersect (or cut) a line
Standard	Generally accepted	A general form for an equation
Point	A dot or speck (noun)	A fixed location on a coordinate plane. Every point has a unique x-value and y-value.

Slope-intercept form, standard form, and point-slope form all have their advantages.
- Knowing the slope and y-intercept makes an equation in slope-intercept form easy to graph.
- An equation in point-slope form is also easy to graph.
- You can model many real-world situations using the standard form. Also, it is easy to find the x- and y-intercepts of an equation in this form.

When you write an equation in each of these forms, think about what the values mean.

slope-intercept form
$y = 3x - 1$

The graph of this equation has y-intercept -1 and slope 3.

standard form
$5x - y = 100$

The graph of this equation intersects the y-axis at -100 and intersects the x-axis at 20.

point-slope form
$y - 2 = 3(x - 5)$

The graph of this equation passes through the point (5, 2), and its slope is 3.

EXERCISE

a. Find the slope and y-intercept of the graph of $y = 2x + 5$.
b. Find the x- and y-intercepts of the graph of $50x + 25y = 100$.
c. Find a point and the slope on the graph of $y - 4 = 2(x + 3)$.

Parallel and Perpendicular Lines

Lesson Preview

What You'll Learn

OBJECTIVE 1 To determine whether lines are parallel

OBJECTIVE 2 To determine whether lines are perpendicular

...And Why

To use parallel and perpendicular lines to plan a bike path, as in Example 4

✓ **Check Skills You'll Need** (For help, go to Lessons 1-6 and 6-2.)

What is the reciprocal of each fraction?

1. $\frac{1}{2}$ **2.** $\frac{4}{3}$ **3.** $-\frac{2}{5}$ **4.** $-\frac{7}{5}$

What are the slope and y-intercept of each equation?

5. $y = \frac{5}{3}x + 4$ **6.** $y = \frac{5}{3}x - 8$ **7.** $y = 6x$ **8.** $y = 6x + 2$

New Vocabulary • parallel lines • perpendicular lines • negative reciprocal

---

OBJECTIVE 1   **Parallel Lines**

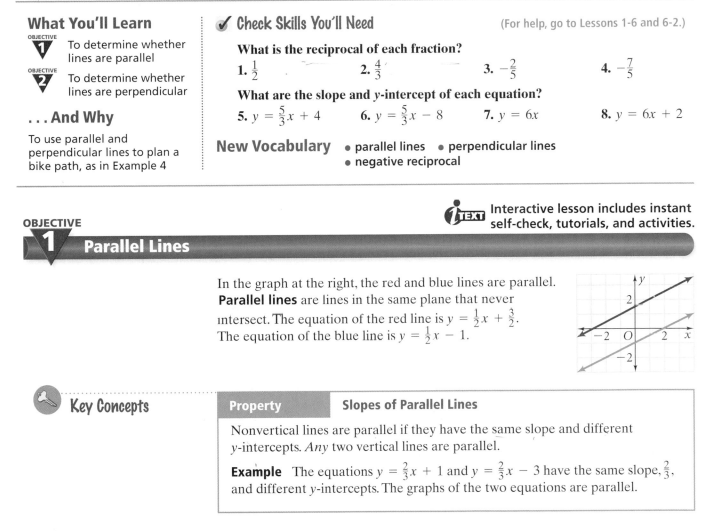

🄸 TEXT **Interactive lesson includes instant self-check, tutorials, and activities.**

In the graph at the right, the red and blue lines are parallel. **Parallel lines** are lines in the same plane that never intersect. The equation of the red line is $y = \frac{1}{2}x + \frac{3}{2}$. The equation of the blue line is $y = \frac{1}{2}x - 1$.

🗝 **Key Concepts**

Property   **Slopes of Parallel Lines**

Nonvertical lines are parallel if they have the same slope and different y-intercepts. *Any* two vertical lines are parallel.

Example The equations $y = \frac{2}{3}x + 1$ and $y = \frac{2}{3}x - 3$ have the same slope, $\frac{2}{3}$, and different y-intercepts. The graphs of the two equations are parallel.

You can use slope-intercept form to determine whether the lines are parallel.

1 EXAMPLE   **Determining Whether Lines Are Parallel**

Are the graphs of $y = -\frac{1}{3}x + 5$ and $2x + 6y = 12$ parallel? Explain.

Write $2x + 6y = 12$ in slope-intercept form. Then compare with $y = -\frac{1}{3}x + 5$.

$6y = -2x + 12$ **Subtract 2x from each side.**

$\frac{6y}{6} = \frac{-2x + 12}{6}$ **Divide each side by 6.**

$y = -\frac{1}{3}x + 2$ **Simplify.**

The lines are parallel. The equations have the same slope, $-\frac{1}{3}$, and different y-intercepts.

Real-World 🌐 Connection

The lanes for competitive swimming are parallel.

✓ **Check Understanding** **1** Are the graphs of $-6x + 8y = -24$ and $y = \frac{3}{4}x - 7$ parallel? Explain.

You can use the fact that the slopes of parallel lines are the same to write the equation of a line parallel to a given line. To write the equation, you use the slope of the given line and the point-slope form of a linear equation.

2 EXAMPLE **Writing Equations of Parallel Lines**

Write an equation for the line that contains $(5, 1)$ and is parallel to $y = \frac{3}{5}x - 4$.

Step 1 Identify the slope of the given line.

$$y = \frac{3}{5}x - 4$$
$$\uparrow$$
$$\text{slope}$$

Step 2 Write the equation of the line through $(5, 1)$ using slope-intercept form.

$y - y_1 = m(x - x_1)$ **point-slope form**

$y - 1 = \frac{3}{5}(x - 5)$ **Substitute (5, 1) for (x_1, y_1) and $\frac{3}{5}$ for m.**

$y - 1 = \frac{3}{5}x - \frac{3}{5}(5)$ **Use the Distributive Property.**

$y - 1 = \frac{3}{5}x - 3$ **Simplify.**

$y = \frac{3}{5}x - 2$ **Add 1 to each side.**

✔ **Check Understanding** ② Write an equation for the line that contains $(2, -6)$ and is parallel to $y = 3x + 9$.

OBJECTIVE

2 Perpendicular Lines

The lines at the right are perpendicular. **Perpendicular lines** are lines that intersect to form right angles. The equation of the red line is $y = -\frac{1}{4}x - 1$. The equation of the blue line is $y = 4x + 2$.

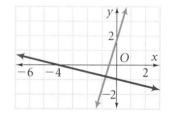

🔑 **Key Concepts**

Property	**Slopes of Perpendicular Lines**

Two lines are perpendicular if the product of their slopes is -1. A vertical and a horizontal line are also perpendicular.

Example   The slope of $y = -\frac{1}{4}x - 1$ is $-\frac{1}{4}$. The slope of $y = 4x + 2$ is 4. Since $-\frac{1}{4} \cdot 4 = -1$, the graphs of the two equations are perpendicular.

The product of two numbers is -1 if one number is the **negative reciprocal** of the other. Here is how to find the negative reciprocal of a number.

Start with   Find its   Write the
a fraction: $-\frac{3}{5}$.   →   reciprocal: $-\frac{5}{3}$.   →   negative reciprocal: $\frac{5}{3}$.

Since $-\frac{3}{5} \cdot \frac{5}{3} = -1$, $\frac{5}{3}$ is the negative reciprocal of $-\frac{3}{5}$.

Start with   Find its   Write its
an integer: 4.   →   reciprocal: $\frac{1}{4}$.   →   negative reciprocal: $-\frac{1}{4}$.

Since $4\left(-\frac{1}{4}\right) = -1$, $-\frac{1}{4}$ is the negative reciprocal of 4.

You can use the negative reciprocal of the slope of a given line to write an equation of a line perpendicular to that line.

3 EXAMPLE Writing Equations for Perpendicular Lines

Find an equation of the line that contains $(0, -2)$ and is perpendicular to $y = 5x + 3$.

Step 1 Identify the slope of the given line.

$$y = 5x + 3$$
$$\uparrow$$
$$\text{slope}$$

Step 2 Find the negative reciprocal of the slope.

The negative reciprocal of 5 is $-\frac{1}{5}$.

Step 3 Use the slope-intercept form to write an equation.

$$y = mx + b$$
$$y = -\frac{1}{5}x + (-2) \qquad \text{Substitute } -\frac{1}{5} \text{ for } m, \text{ and } -2 \text{ for } b.$$
$$y = -\frac{1}{5}x - 2 \qquad \text{Simplify.}$$

● The equation is $y = -\frac{1}{5}x - 2$.

✓ **Check Understanding** **3** Write an equation of the line that contains $(1, 8)$ and is perpendicular to $y = \frac{3}{4}x + 1$.

You can use equations of parallel and perpendicular lines to solve some real-world problems.

4 EXAMPLE Real-World 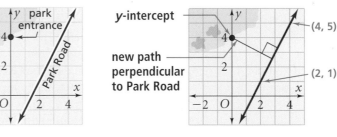 Problem Solving

Urban Planning A bike path for a new city park will connect the park entrance to Park Road. The path will be perpendicular to Park Road. Write an equation for the line representing the bike path.

Step 1 Find the slope m of Park Road.

$$m = \frac{y_2 - y_1}{x_2 - x_1} = \frac{5 - 1}{4 - 2} = \frac{4}{2} = 2 \qquad \text{Points (2, 1) and (4, 5) are on Park Road.}$$

Step 2 Find the negative reciprocal of the slope.

The negative reciprocal of 2 is $-\frac{1}{2}$. So the slope of the bike path is $-\frac{1}{2}$. The y-intercept is 4.

● The equation for the bike path is $y = -\frac{1}{2}x + 4$.

✓ **Check Understanding** **4** A second bike path is planned. It will be parallel to Park Road and will also contain the park entrance. Write an equation for the line representing this bike path.

EXERCISES

For more practice, see *Extra Practice*.

Practice and Problem Solving

A Practice by Example

Example 1
(page 311)

Find the slope of a line parallel to the graph of each equation.

1. $y = \frac{1}{2}x + 2.3$ **2.** $y = -\frac{2}{3}x - 1$ **3.** $y = x$

4. $y = 6$ **5.** $3x + 4y = 12$ **6.** $7x - y = 5$

Are the graphs of the lines in each pair parallel? Explain.

7. $y = 4x + 12$ **8.** $y = -\frac{3}{2}x + 2$ **9.** $y = \frac{1}{3}x + 3$
      $-4x + 3y = 21$ $3x + 2y = 8$ $x - 3y = 6$

10. $y = -\frac{1}{2}x + \frac{3}{2}$ **11.** $y = -3x$ **12.** $y = \frac{3}{4}x - 2$
      $5x - 10y = 15$ $21x + 7y = 14$ $-3x + 4y = 8$

Example 2
(page 312)

Write an equation for the line that is parallel to the given line and that passes through the given point.

13. $y = 6x - 2; (0,0)$ **14.** $y = -3x; (3,0)$ **15.** $y = -2x + 3; (-3,5)$

16. $y = -\frac{7}{2}x + 6; (-4,-6)$ **17.** $y = 0.5x - 8; (8,-5)$ **18.** $y = -\frac{2}{3}x + 12; (5,-3)$

Example 3
(page 313)

Find the slope of a line perpendicular to the graph of each equation.

19. $y = 2x$ **20.** $y = -3x$ **21.** $y = \frac{7}{5}x - 2$

22. $y = -\frac{x}{5} - 7$ **23.** $2x + 3y = 5$ **24.** $y = -8$

Write an equation for the line that is perpendicular to the given line and that passes through the given point.

25. $y = 2x + 7; (0,0)$ **26.** $y = x - 3; (4,6)$

27. $y = -\frac{1}{3}x + 2; (4,2)$ **28.** $3x + 5y = 7; (-1,2)$

29. $-10x + 8y = 3; (15,12)$ **30.** $4x - 2y = 9; (8,-2)$

Example 4
(page 313)

31. Maps A city's civil engineer is planning a new parking garage and a new street. The new street will go from the entrance of the parking garage to Handel St. It will be perpendicular to Handel St. What is the equation of the line representing the new street?

B Apply Your Skills

Tell whether the lines for each pair of equations are *parallel, perpendicular,* or *neither.*

32. $y = 4x + \frac{3}{4}, y = -\frac{1}{4}x + 4$ **33.** $y = \frac{2}{3}x - 6, y = \frac{2}{3}x + 6$

34. $y = -x + 5, y = x + 5$ **35.** $y = 5x, y = -5x + 7$

36. $y = \frac{x}{3} - 4, y = \frac{1}{3}x + 2$ **37.** $x = 2, y = 9$

38. $2x + y = 2, 2x + y = 5$ **39.** $3x - 5y = 3, -5x + 3y = 8$

40. $4x - 3y = 36, 3x + 4y = 20$ **41.** $2x - 5y = 15, 2x + 5y = 10$

42. Critical Thinking Explain how you can tell that the graphs of $7x - 3y = 5$ and $7x - 3y = 8$ are parallel without finding their slopes.

314 Chapter 6 Linear Equations and Their Graphs

Real-World 🌐 **Connection**

A skier's fastest speed occurs when the skis are parallel.

Find the equation for each line.

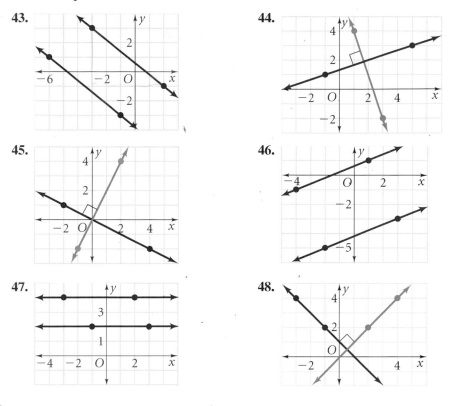

43.

44.

45.

46.

47.

48.

🌐 **Maps** Use the map below for Exercises 49–51.

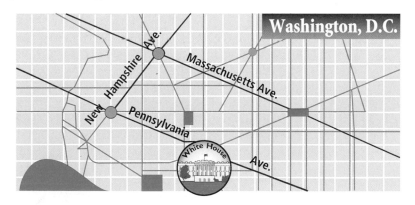

Washington, D.C.

New Hampshire Ave.

Massachusetts Ave.

Pennsylvania

White House

Ave.

49. What is the slope of New Hampshire Avenue?

50. Show that the ts of Pennsylvania Avenue and Massachusetts Avenue near New Hampshir enue are parallel.

51. Show that New H hire Avenue is not perpendicular to Pennsylvania Avenue.

52. a. The graphs of $y = x$ and $y = -x$ are shown on the standard screen at the right. The product of the slopes is -1. Explain why the lines do not appear to be perpendicular.

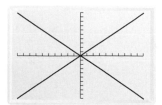

   b. Graphing Calculator Graph $y = x$ and $y = -x$ on a graphing calculator. In the **ZOOM** feature, choose the square screen. What do you notice?

53. Open-Ended Write an equation for a line parallel to the graph of $4x - y = 1$.

54. Are the graphs of $2x + 7y = 6$ and $7y = 2x + 6$ parallel? Explain.

55. Are the graphs of $8x + 3y = 6$ and $8x - 3y = 6$ perpendicular? Explain.

56. Writing Are all horizontal lines parallel? Explain.

Tell whether each statement is *true* or *false*. Explain your choice.

57. Two lines with positive slopes can be perpendicular.

58. Two lines with positive slopes can be parallel.

59. The graphs of two different direct variations can be parallel.

....
Problem Solving Hint

For Exercises 57–59, sketch a graph to help you understand the statement in each exercise.
....

Geometry A quadrilateral with both pairs of opposite sides parallel is a parallelogram. Use slopes to determine whether each figure is a parallelogram.

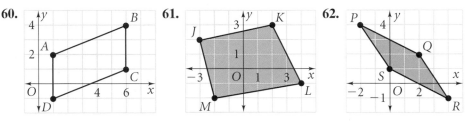

60. **61.** **62.**

Geometry A quadrilateral with four right angles is a rectangle. Use slopes to determine whether each figure is a rectangle.

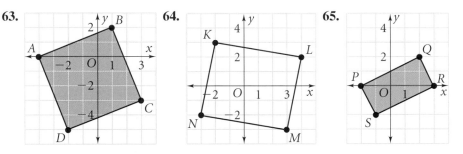

63. **64.** **65.**

Challenge

66. Geometry A quadrilateral with two pairs of parallel sides and with diagonals that are perpendicular is a rhombus. Quadrilateral $ABCD$ has vertices $A(-2, 2)$, $B(1, 6)$, $C(6, 6)$, and $D(3, 2)$. Show that $ABCD$ is a rhombus.

67. Geometry A triangle with two sides that are perpendicular to each other is a right triangle. Triangle PQR has vertices $P(3, 3)$, $Q(2, -2)$, and $R(0, 1)$. Determine whether PQR is a right triangle. Explain.

Tell whether the lines in each pair are *parallel, perpendicular,* or *neither.*

68. $ax - by = c; \; -ax + by = d$ **69.** $ax + by = c; \; bx - ay = d$

Assume the two lines are perpendicular. Find an equation for each line.

70.   **71.**

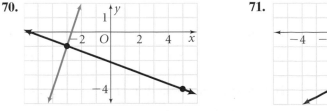
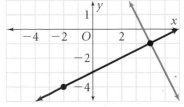

72. For what value of k are the graphs of $3x + 12y = 8$ and $6y = kx - 5$ parallel? Perpendicular?

Multiple Choice

73. Which equation has as its graph a line perpendicular to a line with a slope of $\frac{2}{3}$?

A. $y = \frac{2}{3}x + 5$ **B.** $y = \frac{3}{2}x - 1$ **C.** $y = 3x - 2$ **D.** $3x + 2y = 8$

74. Which equation has as its graph a line parallel to the graph of $-2x - 4y = 3$?

F. $y = -\frac{1}{2}x + 5$ **G.** $y = 2x - 6$ **H.** $y = -2x + 4$ **I.** $y = \frac{1}{2}x - 2$

75. A parallelogram has vertices $A(0, 2)$, $B(2, -1)$, $C(6, 3)$, and $D(p, q)$. Which of the following ordered pairs has possible values for (p, q)?

A. $(0, 6)$ **B.** $(6, 1)$ **C.** $(4, 6)$ **D.** $(6, 4)$

Short Response

76. Suppose the line through points $(x, 6)$ and $(1, 2)$ is parallel to the graph of $2x + y = 3$. Find the value of x. Show your work.

Quantitative Comparison

Compare the equation in Column A with the equation in Column B. Choose the best answer.

  A. The quantity in Column A is greater.
  B. The quantity in Column B is greater.
  C. The two quantities are equal.
  D. The relationship cannot be determined from the information given.

	Column A	Column B
77.	the slope of $y = -5x - 1$	the slope of $10x + 2y = -2$
78.	the product of the slopes of $y = -\frac{4}{3}x + 5$ and $3x + 4y = 12$	-1
79.	the slope of $6y = 3x + 10$	2

Take It to the NET
Online lesson quiz at
www.PHSchool.com
····· Web Code: aea-0605

Mixed Review

Lesson 6-4

Write an equation for the line through the given point with the given slope.

80. $(0, 4); m = 3$ **81.** $(-2, 0); m = -4$

82. $(5, -3); m = \frac{3}{4}$ **83.** $(-1, -9); m = -\frac{2}{3}$

84. $(-6, 4); m = -\frac{3}{5}$ **85.** $(7, 11); m = \frac{1}{2}$

Lesson 5-6

Find the third, fifth, and seventh term in the sequence that has each given rule.

86. $A(n) = 2n + 1$ **87.** $A(n) = 3 - 4n$

Lesson 5-2

Determine whether each relation is a function.

88. $\{(1, 1), (2, 2), (3, 3)\}$ **89.** $\{(1, 3), (2, 5), (3, 5)\}$

90. $\{(5, 1), (5, 2), (4, 3)\}$ **91.** $\{(1, 3), (2, 2), (3, 1)\}$

Scatter Plots and Equations of Lines

Lesson Preview

What You'll Learn

OBJECTIVE 1 To write an equation for a trend line and use it to make predictions

OBJECTIVE 2 To write the equation for a line of best fit and use it to make predictions

. . . And Why

To use a trend line to make a prediction, as in Example 1

✓ Check Skills You'll Need

(For help, go to Lesson 1-9.)

Use the data in each table to draw a scatter plot.

1.

x	y
1	2
2	−3
3	8
4	9
5	−25

2.

x	y
1	21
2	15
3	12
4	9
5	7

New Vocabulary
• line of best fit • correlation coefficient

Interactive lesson includes instant self-check, tutorials, and activities.

OBJECTIVE 1

Writing an Equation for a Trend Line

In Chapter 1 you used scatter plots to determine how two sets of data are related. You can now write an equation for a trend line.

1 EXAMPLE Trend Line

Birds Make a scatter plot of the data at the left. Draw a trend line and write its equation. Use the equation to predict the wingspan of a hawk that is 28 in. long.

Length and Wingspan of Hawks

Type of Hawk	Length (in.)	Wing-span (in.)
Cooper's	21	36
Crane	21	41
Gray	18	38
Harris's	24	46
Roadside	16	31
Broad-winged	19	39
Short-tailed	17	35
Swanson's	19	46

SOURCE: *Birds of North America*

Step 1 Make a scatter plot and draw a trend line. Estimate two points on the line.

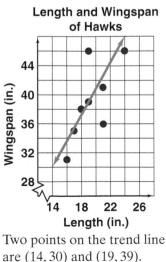

Length and Wingspan of Hawks

Two points on the trend line are (14, 30) and (19, 39).

Step 2 Write an equation of the trend line.

$$m = \frac{y_2 - y_1}{x_2 - x_1} = \frac{39 - 30}{19 - 14} = \frac{9}{5}$$

$y - y_1 = m(x - x_1)$ Use point-slope form.

$y - 30 = \frac{9}{5}(x - 14)$ Substitute $\frac{9}{5}$ for m and (14, 30) for (x_1, y_1).

Step 3 Predict the wingspan of a hawk that is 28 in. long.

$y - 30 = \frac{9}{5}(28 - 14)$ Substitute 28 for x.

$y - 30 = \frac{9}{5}(14)$ Simplify within the parentheses.

$y - 30 = 25.2$ Multiply.

$y = 55.2$ Add 30 to each side.

The wingspan of a hawk 28 in. long is about 55.2 in.

✓ Check Understanding **1** Graph the data below and draw a trend line. Find an equation for the trend line. Estimate the number of calories in a fast-food that has 14g of fat.

Calories and Fat in Selected Fast-Food Meals

Fat (g)	6	7	10	19	20	27	36
Calories	276	260	220	388	430	550	633

2 Writing an Equation for a Line of Best Fit

The trend line that shows the relationship between two sets of data most accurately is called the **line of best fit.** A graphing calculator computes the equation of a line of best fit using a method called linear regression.

The graphing calculator also gives you the **correlation coefficient** r, which tells you how closely the equation models the data.

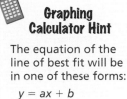

Graphing Calculator Hint

The equation of the line of best fit will be in one of these forms:

$y = ax + b$
↑   ↑
slope y-intercept

$y = a + bx$
↑   ↑
y-intercept slope

$$-1 \qquad 0 \qquad 1$$

negative correlation   no correlation   positive correlation

When the data points cluster around a line, there is a strong correlation between the line and the data. So the nearer r is to 1 or -1, the more closely the data cluster around the line of best fit. In later chapters, you will learn how to find non-linear models which may better describe some data.

2 EXAMPLE Line of Best Fit

Recreation Use a graphing calculator to find the equation of the line of best fit for the data at the right. What is the correlation coefficient?

Take It to the NET
Graphing Calculator procedures online at
www.PHSchool.com
Web Code: aee-2122

Step 1 Use the **EDIT** feature of the
[STAT] screen on your graphing calculator.
Let 93 correspond to 1993. Enter the data for years and then the data for costs.

Step 2 Use the **CALC** feature in the
[STAT] screen. Find the equation for the line of best fit.

```
LinReg
 y = ax+b
 a = 32.33333333  ←———— slope
 b = −2671.666667 ←———— y-intercept
 r² = .9929145373
 r = .9964509708  ←———— correlation
                        coefficient
```

Recreation Expenditures

Year	Dollars (billions)
1993	340
1994	369
1995	402
1996	430
1997	457
1998	489
1999	527
2000	574

SOURCE: *Statistical Abstract of the United States.* Go to **www.PHSchool.com** for a data update. Web Code: aeg-2041

The equation for the line of best fit is $y = 32.33x - 2671.67$ for values of a and b rounded to the nearest hundredth. The correlation coefficient is 0.9964509708.

② Find the equation of the line of best fit. Let 91 correspond to 1991. What is the correlation coefficient?

Yearly Box Office Gross for Movies (billions)

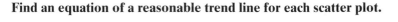

1991	1992	1993	1994	1995	1996	1997	1998	1999
$4.8	$4.9	$5.2	$5.4	$5.5	$6.0	$6.4	$7.0	$7.4

EXERCISES

For more practice, see *Extra Practice*.

Practice and Problem Solving

A Practice by Example

Example 1
(page 318)

Find an equation of a reasonable trend line for each scatter plot.

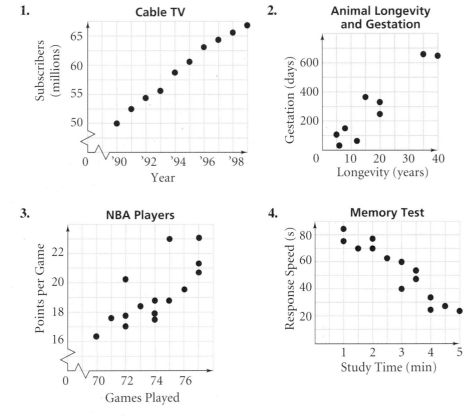

1. Cable TV

2. Animal Longevity and Gestation

3. NBA Players

4. Memory Test

5. Graph the data in the table below for the attendance and revenue at theme parks. Find an equation for the trend line of the data.

Attendance and Revenue at U.S. Theme Parks

Year	1991	1992	1993	1994	1995	1996	1997	1998	1999
Attendance (millions)	260	267	275	267	280	290	300	300	309
Revenue (billions of dollars)	6.1	6.5	6.8	7.0	7.4	7.9	8.4	8.7	9.1

SOURCE: International Association of Amusement Parks and Attractions.
Go to **www.PHSchool.com** for a data update.
Web Code: aeg-2041

Example 2
(page 319)

🖩 **Graphing Calculator** Use a graphing calculator to find the equation of the line of best fit for the data. Find the value of the correlation coefficient *r*.

6. Graph the data for the average July temperature and the annual precipitation of the cities in the table below. Find an equation for the line of best fit of the data. Estimate the average rainfall for a city with average July temperature of 75° F.

Precipitation and Temperature in Selected Eastern Cities

City	Average July Temperature (°F)	Average Annual Precipitation (in.)
New York	76.4	42.82
Baltimore	76.8	41.84
Atlanta	78.6	48.61
Jacksonville	81.3	52.76
Washington, D.C.	78.9	39.00
Boston	73.5	43.81
Miami	82.5	57.55

SOURCE: Time *Almanac*

7. ### Average Temperatures in Northern Latitudes

Latitude (° N)	0	10	20	30	40	50	60	70	80
Temp. (°F)	79.2	80.1	77.5	68.7	57.4	42.4	30.0	12.7	1.0

8. ### Retail Department Store Sales (billions of dollars)

Year	1980	1985	1990	1994	1995	1996	1997	1998
Sales	86	126	166	217	231	245	261	279

SOURCE: *Statistical Abstract of the United States.*
Go to **www.PHSchool.com** for an update.
Web Code: aeg-2041

Real-World 🌐 Connection

The 500-meter men's speed skating race has been an Olympic event since 1924.

9. ### Olympic 500-Meter Men's Gold Medal Speed Skating Times

Year	1980	1984	1988	1992	1994	1998
Time (seconds)	422	432	404	420	395	382

SOURCE: International Skating Union

10. ### Average Male Lung Power

Respiration (breaths/min)	50	30	25	20	18	16	14
Heart Rate (beats/min)	200	150	140	130	120	110	100

SOURCE: Encyclopedia Britannica

11. ### Wind Chill Temperature for 15 mi/h Wind

Air Temp. (°F)	35	30	25	20	15	10	5	0
Wind-Chill Temp. (°F)	16	9	2	−5	−11	−18	−25	−31

12. Geometry Students measured the diameters and circumferences of the tops of a variety of cylinders. Below is the data that they collected.

Cylinder Tops

Diameter (cm)	3	3	5	6	8	8	9.5	10	10	12
Circumference (cm)	9.3	9.5	16	18.8	25	25.6	29.5	31.5	30.9	39.5

a. Graph the data. **b.** Find the equation of a trend line.
c. What does the slope of the equation mean?
d. Find the diameter of a cylinder with a circumference of 45 cm.

Population Growth

1790

1860

Today

■ More than 2 persons per square mile

13. Population Use the data at the right.
a. Graph the data for the male and female populations of the United States.
b. Find the equation of a trend line.
c. Use your equation to predict the number of females if the number of males were to increase to 138,476,000.
d. Critical Thinking Would it be reasonable to predict the population in 2025 from these data? Explain.

14. a. Open-Ended Make a table of data for a linear function. Use a graphing calculator to find the equation of the line of best fit.
b. What is the correlation coefficient for your linear data?

15. Writing What kind of trend line do you think data for the following comparison would be likely to show? Explain.
temperature and the number of students absent from school

Estimated Population of the United States (thousands)

Year	Male	Female
1991	122,956	129,197
1992	124,424	130,606
1993	125,788	131,995
1994	127,049	133,278
1995	128,294	134,510
1996	129,504	135,724
1997	130,783	137,001
1998	132,030	138,218
1999	133,277	139,414
2000	138,054	143,368

Source: U.S. Census Bureau. Go to **www.PHSchool.com** for a data update. Web Code: aeg-2041

16. Graphing Calculator A school collected data on math and science grades of nine randomly selected students.

Student	1	2	3	4	5	6	7	8	9
Math	76	89	84	79	94	71	79	91	84
Science	82	94	89	89	94	84	68	89	84

a. Use a graphing calculator to find the equation of the line of best fit for the data.
b. Critical Thinking Should the equation for the line of best fit be used to predict grades? Explain.

17. Graphing Calculator Use a graphing calculator to find the equation of the line of best fit for the data below. Predict sales of greeting cards in the year 2010.

Greeting Card Sales

Year	1989	1990	1991	1992	1993	1994	1995	1996	1997	1998
Sales (billions)	$4.2	$4.6	$5.0	$5.3	$5.6	$5.9	$6.3	$6.8	$7.3	$7.5

Source: Greeting Card Association

18. a. Data Collection Find two sets of data that you could display in a scatter plot, such as the number of boys and girls in each class in your school, or the population and the number of airports in some states. Then graph the data.
  b. Find the equation of a trend line.
  c. Use the equation to predict another value that could be on your scatter plot.
  d. What is the correlation coefficient?

19. Another way you can find a line of best fit is the *median-median method*. The graph below shows how this method works. The points in red indicate the original data.

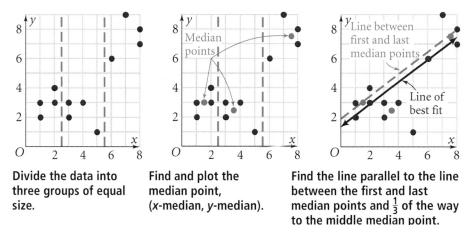

Divide the data into three groups of equal size.

Find and plot the median point, (x-median, y-median).

Find the line parallel to the line between the first and last median points and $\frac{1}{3}$ of the way to the middle median point.

  a. Estimate two coordinates on the purple line in the graph at the right above. Find the equation of the line of best fit.
  b. Graphing Calculator You can use a graphing calculator to find the line of best fit with the median-median method. Below are the coordinates of the points graphed in red. Use the **EDIT** feature of the STAT screen on your graphing calculator. Use the **Med-Med** feature to find a line of best fit.
    $(1, 2), (1, 3), (2, 3), (2, 4), (3, 2), (3, 3), (4, 3), (5, 1), (6, 6), (7, 9), (8, 8), (8, 7)$

C Challenge

20. a. Make a scatter plot of the data below. Then find the equation of the line of best fit.

Car Stopping Distances

Speed (mi/h)	10	15	20	25	30	35	40	45
Stopping Distances (ft)	27	44	63	85	109	136	164	196

  b. Use your equation to predict the stopping distance at 90 mi/h.
  c. Critical Thinking The actual stopping distance at 90 mi/h is close to 584 ft. Why do you think this is not close to your prediction?

Standardized Test Prep

Multiple Choice

21. A horizontal line passes through (5, −2). Which other point does it also pass through?
    A. (5, 2)   **B.** (−5, −2)   **C.** (−5, 2)   **D.** (5, 0)

22. Which of the following equations contains the ordered pairs (−3, 4) and (1, −4)?
    F. $x + 2y = 8$ **G.** $2x − y = 4$ **H.** $2x + y = −2$ **I.** $x − 2y = −6$

23. The table right shows the number of elderly in the United States from 1960 through 2000.
  a. Graph the data and draw a trend line.
  b. Write an equation for the trend line you drew.
  c. Predict the elderly population in the United States in 2005. Show your work.

U.S. Elderly Population

Year	Elderly (millions)
1960	16.560
1970	19.980
1980	25.550
1990	31.235
2000	34.709

SOURCE: *Statistical Abstract of the United States.*
Go to **www.PHSchool.com** for a data update.
Web Code: aeg-2041

Take It to the NET
Online lesson quiz at
www.PHSchool.com
Web Code: aea-0606

Mixed Review

Lesson 6-5 **Write the equation for the line that is parallel to the given line and that passes through the given point.**

24. $y = 5x + 1; (2, -3)$ **25.** $y = -x - 9; (0, 5)$ **26.** $2x + 3y = 9; (-1, 4)$

27. $y = -\frac{1}{2}x; (3, -4)$ **28.** $y = -2x + 3 \, (-2, -1)$ **29.** $y = \frac{2}{3}x + 7; (-1, 2)$

Lesson 3-4 **Solve each inequality.**

30. $1 + 5x + 1 > x + 9$ **31.** $7x + 3 < 2x + 28$ **32.** $4x + 4 > 2 + 2x$

33. $4x + 3 \leq 2x - 7$ **34.** $-x + 5 < 3x - 1$ **35.** $2x > 7x - 3 - 4x$

Checkpoint Quiz 2   Lessons 6-4 through 6-6

TEXT Instant self-check quiz online and on CD-ROM

Write an equation for the line through the given point with the given slope.

1. $(3, 4); m = -\frac{1}{4}$ **2.** $(0, -3); m = 18$ **3.** $(-7, -5); m = 0$

4. Write an equation for the line through the points $(2, -6)$ and $(-1, -4)$.

Write an equation of the line that is parallel to the given line and that passes through the given point.

5. $x + y = 3; (5, 4)$ **6.** $3x + 2y = 1; (-2, 6)$

Write an equation of a line that is perpendicular to the given line and that passes through the given point.

7. $y = -4x + 2; (0, 2)$ **8.** $y = \frac{2}{3}x + 6; (-6, 2)$

9. Find the equation for a trend line for the data at the right.

x	1	2	3	4	5	6	7
y	7	12	19	20	28	33	40

10. Graphing Calculator Use a graphing calculator to find the equation for the line of best fit for the data at the right.

x	1	2	3	4	5	6	7
y	54	52	45	40	33	27	18

Graphing Absolute Value Equations

Lesson Preview

What You'll Learn

OBJECTIVE 1 To translate the graph of an absolute value equation

...And Why

To graph an absolute value equation quickly, as in Examples 2 and 4

✓ Check Skills You'll Need

(For help, go to Lessons 1-5 and 5-3.)

Simplify each expression.

1. $|2 - 7|$ **2.** $|7 - 12|$ **3.** $|38 - 56|$ **4.** $|-24 + 12|$

Model each rule using a table of values.

5. $y = 6 - x$ **6.** $y = |x| + 1$ **7.** $y = |x + 1|$

New Vocabulary • absolute value equation • translation

OBJECTIVE

1 Translating Graphs of Absolute Value Equations

? Need Help?

The absolute value of a number is its distance from 0 on a number line.

A V-shaped graph that points upward or downward is the graph of an **absolute value equation.** In Lesson 5-3, you graphed absolute value equations by making tables of values.

In this lesson you will graph by translating the graph of $y = |x|$. A **translation** is a shift of a graph horizontally, vertically, or both. The result is a graph of the same shape and size, but in a different position.

1 EXAMPLE **Vertical Translations**

Below are the graphs of $y = |x|$ and $y = |x| + 2$. Describe how the graphs are the same and how they are different.

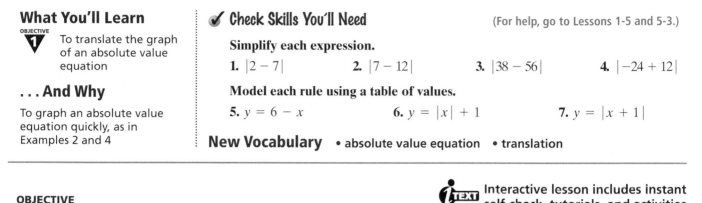

The graphs are the same shape. The y-intercept of the first graph is 0. The y-intercept of the second graph is 2.

✓ Check Understanding

1 Describe how each graph below is like $y = |x|$ and how it is different.

a.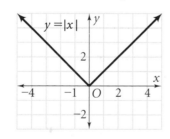

$y = |x| + 3$

b.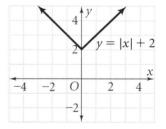

$y = |x| - 3$

The graph of $y = |x| + k$ is a translation of $y = |x|$. Let k be a positive number. Then $y = |x| + k$ translates the graph of $y = |x|$ up k units, while $y = |x| - k$ translates the graph of $y = |x|$ down k units.

2 EXAMPLE Graphing a Vertical Translation

Graph $y = |x| - 1$.

Start with the graph of $y = |x|$.
Translate the graph *down* 1 unit.

✓**Check Understanding** **2** Graph each function by translating $y = |x|$.
a. $y = |x| + 4$ b. $y = |x| - 5$

You can write an equation to describe a vertical translation.

3 EXAMPLE Writing an Absolute Value Equation

Write an equation for each translation of $y = |x|$.
a. 8 units down   b. 6 units up
   The equation is $y = |x| - 8$.   The equation is $y = |x| + 6$.

✓**Check Understanding** **3** For each translation of $y = |x|$, write an equation.
a. 2 units up   b. 5 units down

The following tables of values and graphs show what happens when you graph $y = |x - 3|$ and $y = |x + 3|$.

x	$y = |x|$	$y = |x - 3|$
-3	$|-3| = 3$	$|-3 - 3| = 6$
-2	$|-2| = 2$	$|-2 - 3| = 5$
-1	$|-1| = 1$	$|-1 - 3| = 4$
0	$|0| = 0$	$|0 - 3| = 3$
1	$|1| = 1$	$|1 - 3| = 2$
2	$|2| = 2$	$|2 - 3| = 1$
3	$|3| = 3$	$|3 - 3| = 0$

x	$y = |x|$	$y = |x + 3|$
-3	$|-3| = 3$	$|-3 + 3| = 0$
-2	$|-2| = 2$	$|-2 + 3| = 1$
-1	$|-1| = 1$	$|-1 + 3| = 2$
0	$|0| = 0$	$|0 + 3| = 3$
1	$|1| = 1$	$|1 + 3| = 4$
2	$|2| = 2$	$|2 + 3| = 5$
3	$|3| = 3$	$|3 + 3| = 6$

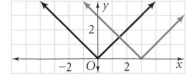

For the graph of $y = |x - 3|$,
$y = |x|$ is translated 3 units to the right.

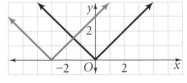

For the graph of $y = |x + 3|$,
$y = |x|$ is translated 3 units to the left.

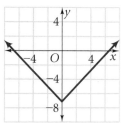

Moving this chess piece is a horizontal and vertical translation.

So for a positive number h, $y = |x + h|$ translates the graph of $y = |x|$ by h units to the left, and $y = |x - h|$ translates the graph of $y = |x|$ by h units to the right.

4 EXAMPLE **Graphing a Horizontal Translation**

Graph each equation by translating $y = |x|$.
a. $y = |x + 2|$ **b.** $y = |x - 2|$

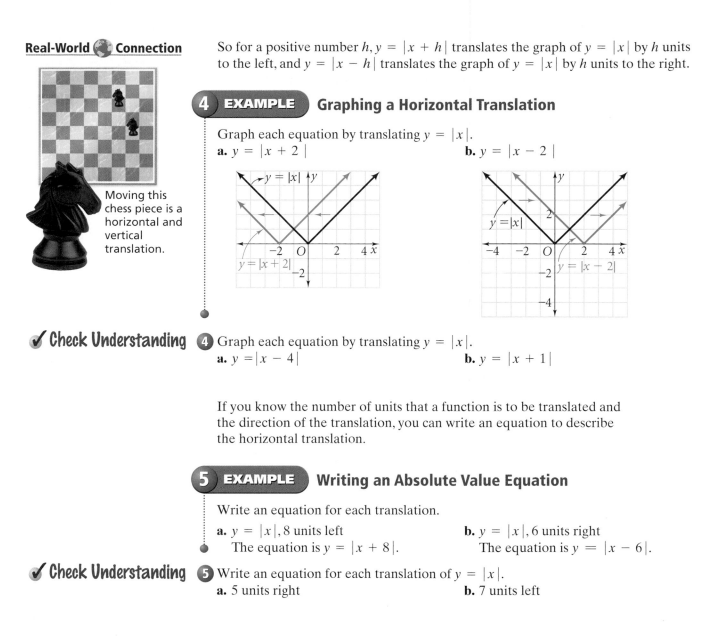

✓ Check Understanding ④ Graph each equation by translating $y = |x|$.
a. $y = |x - 4|$ **b.** $y = |x + 1|$

If you know the number of units that a function is to be translated and the direction of the translation, you can write an equation to describe the horizontal translation.

5 EXAMPLE **Writing an Absolute Value Equation**

Write an equation for each translation.
a. $y = |x|$, 8 units left   **b.** $y = |x|$, 6 units right
   The equation is $y = |x + 8|$.   The equation is $y = |x - 6|$.

✓ Check Understanding ⑤ Write an equation for each translation of $y = |x|$.
a. 5 units right   **b.** 7 units left

EXERCISES

For more practice, see *Extra Practice*.

Practice and Problem Solving

Ⓐ Practice by Example

Example 1
(page 325)

Describe how each graph is like the graph of $y = |x|$ and how it is different.

1.   **2.**   **3.**

Example 2
(page 326)

Graph each function by translating $y = |x|$.

4. $y = |x| + 2$ **5.** $y = |x| - 4$ ◄ **6.** $y = |x| + 8$

7. $y = |x| + 1$ **8.** $y = |x| - 6$ **9.** $y = |x| - 2.5$

Example 3
(page 326)

Write an equation for each translation of $y = |x|$.

10. 9 units up   **11.** 6 units down   **12.** 0.25 units up

13. $\frac{5}{2}$ units up   **14.** 5.90 units up   **15.** 1 unit down

Example 4
(page 327)

Graph each function by translating $y = |x|$.

16. $y = |x - 3|$ **17.** $y = |x + 3|$ **18.** $y = |x - 1|$

19. $y = |x + 5|$ **20.** $y = |x - 7|$ **21.** $y = |x + 2.5|$

Example 5
(page 327)

Write an equation for each translation of $y = |x|$.

22. left 9 units   **23.** right 9 units   **24.** right $\frac{5}{2}$ units

25. left $\frac{3}{2}$ units   **26.** left 0.5 unit   **27.** right 8.2 units

B **Apply Your Skills**

At the right is the graph of $y = -|x|$.
Graph each function by translating $y = -|x|$.

28. $y = -|x| + 3$ **29.** $y = -|x| - 3$

30. $y = -|x + 3|$ **31.** $y = -|x - 3|$

Problem Solving Hint

For Exercises 28–31, you can check your work by substituting ordered pairs from the graph into the corresponding equation.

Write an equation for each translation of $y = -|x|$.

32. 2 units up   **33.** 2.25 units left

34. $\frac{3}{2}$ units down   **35.** 4 units right

36. The graph at the right shows a translation of
$y = |x|$ where there is both a vertical and a
horizontal change. Which equation below is an
equation for this graph?
  A. $y = |x + 2| - 1$ **B.** $y = |x - 2| + 1$
  C. $y = |x - 2| - 1$ **D.** $y = |x + 2| + 1$

Graph each translation of $y = |x|$.

Sample For $y = |x + 3| - 2$, the 3 indicates the
translation of the graph 3 units left. The 2 indicates
the translation of the graph 2 units down.

37. $y = |x - 1| + 2$ **38.** $y = |x + 2| - 1$

39. $y = |x - 3| - 4$ **40.** $y = |x + 3| + 4$

41. a. Graph $y = |x - 2| + 3$. (*Hint:* Read the sample
above for Exercises 37–40.)
  b. The vertex of an absolute value function is the point at which the function
changes direction. What is the vertex of $y = |x - 2| + 3$?
  c. What relationship do you see between the vertex and the equation?
  d. Writing Explain how you would graph any equation of the form
$y = |x - a| + b$.

C **Challenge**

42. a. Graph $y = |2x|$ by making a table of values.
  b. Translate $y = |2x|$ to graph $y = |2x| + 3$.
  c. Translate $y = |2x|$ to graph $y = |2(x - 1)|$.
  d. Translate $y = |2x|$ to graph $y = |2(x - 1)| + 3$.

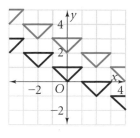

43. Programming A computer programmer is plotting the triangles at the left. The pattern extends infinitely in both directions. She will use two equations for each triangle: some translation of $y = |x|$ and $y = c$ (c is a constant).

    a. What equations will the programmer use to plot the red triangle with vertices at $(0, 0), (-1, 1)$, and $(1, 1)$?

    b. What are the least and greatest values in the domain for the equations the programmer would use to plot the triangle with vertices $(0, 0), (-1, 1)$ and $(1, 1)$?

    c. What linear equation can the programmer use to find the lowest vertex on each red triangle? Each blue triangle?

Multiple Choice

44. Which equation translates $y = |x|$ 8 units to the left?

    A. $y = |x| + 8$ **B.** $y = |x + 8|$ **C.** $y = |x| - 8$ **D.** $y = |x - 8|$

45. What is the lowest point of the graph of $y = |x - 9|$?

    F. $(0, -9)$ **G.** $(-9, 0)$ **H.** $(9, 0)$ **I.** $(0, 9)$

46. What point do the graphs of $y = |x - 3|$ and $y = |x + 5|$ have in common?

    A. $(-1, 4)$ **B.** $(1, 4)$ **C.** $(4, 1)$ **D.** $(4, -1)$

47. The graph of which equation contains the point $(3, 5)$?

    F. $y = |x + 3| + 5$ **G.** $y = |x - 3| + 5$

    H. $y = |x + 3| - 5$ **I.** $y = |x - 3| - 5$

Extended Response

48. a. Graph the equation $y = |x| - 4$ on a coordinate plane.

    b. Graph the equation $y = |x| + 4$ on the same coordinate plane.

    c. Describe the relationship of the ordered pairs in the graphs of $y = |x| - 4$ to the graph of $y = |x| + 4$.

Take It to the NET

Online lesson quiz at
www.PHSchool.com

Web Code: aea-0607

Mixed Review

Lesson 6-6

Graphing Calculator **The data below follow a linear pattern. Write an equation for a trend line or use a graphing calculator to find the equation of the line of best fit.**

49.

Year	Sales
1988	$27,000
1989	$32,000
1990	$37,000
1991	$42,000
1992	$47,000
1993	$52,000
1994	$57,000

50.

Year	Sales
1990	$47,000
1991	$51,000
1992	$55,000
1993	$59,000
1994	$63,000
1995	$67,000
1996	$71,000

Lesson 1-4

Add the matrices.

51. $\begin{bmatrix} 5 & 3 \\ 1 & 2 \end{bmatrix} + \begin{bmatrix} 7 & 2 \\ 1 & 4 \end{bmatrix}$ **52.** $\begin{bmatrix} -3 & 2 \\ -7 & 4 \end{bmatrix} + \begin{bmatrix} 7 & -1 \\ 8 & 0 \end{bmatrix}$ **53.** $\begin{bmatrix} -5.6 & 9.8 \\ -4.2 & 3.2 \end{bmatrix} + \begin{bmatrix} 8.1 & 4.2 \\ 2.2 & 7.5 \end{bmatrix}$

Drawing a Diagram

For some problems, it may help to draw a diagram of the given information if one is not provided.

1 EXAMPLE

The points R, S, and T lie on a line in order such that the length of $\overline{ST}$ is twice the length of $\overline{RS}$. The length of $\overline{RT}$ is 5 cm more than the length of $\overline{ST}$. Find the length of $\overline{RS}$ and $\overline{ST}$.

Draw $\overline{RST}$. Since $\overline{ST}$ is twice as long as $\overline{RS}$, let $RS = x$ and $ST = 2x$. Since the length of $\overline{RT}$ is 5 cm more than the length of $\overline{ST}$, let $RT = 5 + 2x$.

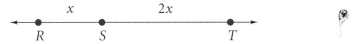

You can see from your diagram that $2x + x = 5 + 2x$. Solve this equation, and you find that $x = 5$. The length of $\overline{RS}$ is 5 cm and the length of $\overline{ST}$ is 10 cm.

2 EXAMPLE

The points $A(-8, 1)$, $B(-2, 7)$ and $C(4, -11)$ form a right triangle. Which two segments form the right angle of the triangle?

Two lines form a right angle if the product of their slopes is -1.

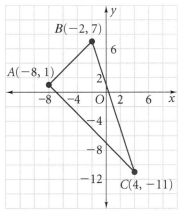

When you draw a diagram, you can see that the right angle cannot be at point C. You need to see if the product of the slopes of $\overline{AC}$ and $\overline{AB}$ or of $\overline{BC}$ and $\overline{AB}$ is -1. The slope of $\overline{AB}$ is 1, and the slope of $\overline{AC}$ is -1. Therefore $\overline{AB}$ and $\overline{AC}$ form the right angle.

EXERCISES

Draw a diagram to solve each exercise.

1. The points $L(4, 0)$, $M(10, 0)$, and $N(7, 5)$ form $\triangle LMN$. What is the sum of the slopes of the three sides of the triangle?

2. Three towns A, B, and C lie on a straight road in that order. The distance from B to C is 6 miles more than twice the distance from A to B. The distance from A to C is 2 miles more than four times the distance from A to B. What is the distance from A to B?

3. $P(1, 3)$ and $R(5, 5)$ are the endpoints of a diagonal of the rectangle $PQRS$. Which sides of the rectangle are parallel to the x-axis? To the y-axis? What is the perimeter of the rectangle?

Chapter 6

Chapter Review

Vocabulary

absolute value equation (p. 325)	perpendicular lines (p. 312)	standard form of a
correlation coefficient (p. 319)	point-slope form (p. 304)	linear equation (p. 298)
line of best fit (p. 319)	rate of change (p. 282)	translation (p. 325)
linear equation (p. 291)	slope (p. 284)	x-intercept (p. 298)
negative reciprocal (p. 312)	slope-intercept form (p. 292)	y-intercept (p. 291)
parallel lines (p. 311)		

Reading Math
Understanding
Vocabulary

Take It to the NET
Online vocabulary quiz
at www.PHSchool.com
   Web Code: aej-0651

Choose the vocabulary term that correctly completes the sentence.

1. Two lines are ___?___ if the product of their slopes is -1.

2. Two lines in the same plane that never intersect are ___?___ .

3. A(n) ___?___ shifts a graph horizontally, vertically, or both.

4. The ratio of the vertical change to the horizontal change is called the ___?___ .

5. The y-coordinate of the point at which the graph of a line crosses the vertical axis is called the ___?___ .

Skills and Concepts

6-1 Objectives

▼ To find rates of change from tables and graphs (p. 282)

▼ To find slope (p. 284)

Rate of change allows you to look at how two quantities change relative to each other.

$$\text{rate of change} = \frac{\text{change in the dependent variable}}{\text{change in the independent variable}}$$

Slope is the ratio of the vertical change to the horizontal change.

$$\text{slope} = \frac{\text{vertical change}}{\text{horizontal change}} = \frac{\text{rise}}{\text{run}}$$

Find the rate of change for each situation.

6. A kitten grows from 5 oz at birth to 3 lb 5 oz at 6 months. (*Hint:* 1 lb = 16 oz)

7. A plant measures 0.5 in. at the end of Week 1 and 14 in. at the end of Week 5.

Find each rate of change. Explain what *rate of change* means in each situation.

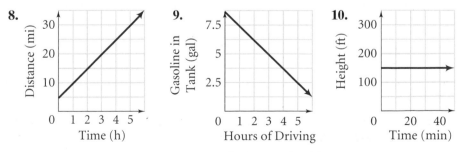

Find the slope of the line that passes through each pair of points.

11. $(3, -2)$ and $(-5, -4)$ **12.** $(4.5, -1)$ and $(4.5, 2.6)$ **13.** $(2, 5)$ and $(-5, -2)$

The graph of a **linear equation** is a line. The **x-intercept** of a line is the
x-coordinate of the point where the line crosses the x-axis, and the **y-intercept** is
the y-coordinate of the point where the line crosses the y-axis. Following are three
forms of linear equations.

- **slope-intercept form:** $y = mx + b$ where m is the slope and b is the y-intercept
- **standard form:** $Ax + By = C$, where A, B, and C are real numbers, and A and B are not both zero
- **point-slope form:** $y - y_1 = m(x - x_1)$, which passes through the point (x_1, y_1) with slope m

Write an equation of a line with the given slope and y-intercept. Then graph the equation.

14. $m = 0, b = -3$ **15.** $m = -7, b = \frac{1}{2}$ **16.** $m = \frac{2}{5}, b = 0$

Write the slope-intercept form of the equation for each line.

17. 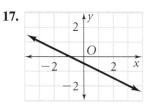   **18.**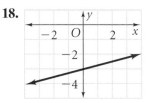

Find the x- and y-intercepts. Then graph each equation.

19. $5x + 2y = 10$ **20.** $6.5x - 4y = 52$ **21.** $x + 3y = -1$

Use point-slope form to write an equation of a line that passes through the point $(1, -2)$ with slope m.

22. $m = 2$ **23.** $m = \frac{3}{4}$ **24.** $m = -3$ **25.** $m = 0$

Use the point-slope form to write an equation of a line through the given points.

26. $(4, 3), (-2, 1)$ **27.** $(5, -4), (0, 2)$ **28.** $(-1, 0), (-3, -1)$

29. Earnings A job at a retail store pays \$75 each week plus 25% commission on total weekly sales.
   a. Write an equation for the total weekly pay p for total weekly sales s.
   b. Use p as the vertical axis and s as the horizontal axis. Graph your equation.
   c. What is the total weekly pay if total weekly sales are \$800?
   d. What is the p intercept? What does it mean in this situation?

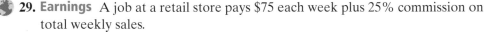

Parallel lines are lines in the same plane that never intersect. Nonvertical lines are
parallel if they have the same slope. Two lines are **perpendicular lines** if they
intersect to form right angles. For perpendicular lines that are not horizontal and
vertical, the product of their slopes is -1.

Write an equation for each of the following conditions.

30. parallel to $y = 5x - 2$, through $(2, -1)$

31. perpendicular to $y = -3x + 7$, through $(3, 5)$

32. parallel to $y = 9x$, through $(0, -5)$

33. perpendicular to $y = 8x - 1$, through $(4, 10)$

You can find an equation to model the relationship between two sets of data in a scatter plot by sketching a trend line and using two points on the line to write an equation.

The **line of best fit** of a scatter plot is the most accurate trend line for the data. You can find the equation of a line of best fit using a graphing calculator. The **correlation coefficient** tells how well the equation of the line of best fit models the data.

Years	Pounds
1970	33.8
1975	32.9
1980	40.8
1985	45.5
1990	56.3
1995	62.9
2000	68.4

34. Graphing Calculator The table shows the average consumption of poultry in the United States in pounds per person from 1970 to 2000.
  a. Find the equation of a trend line or use a graphing calculator to find the equation of the line of best fit.
  b. Use your equation to **predict** how much poultry the average person will eat in 2010.

SOURCE: U.S. Department of Agriculture. Go to **www.PHSchool.com** for a data update. Web Code: aeg-2041

The graph of an **absolute value equation** is a V-shaped graph that points upward or downward.

A **translation** shifts a graph either vertically, horizontally, or both. It results in a graph of the same shape and size in a different position.

Graph each equation by translating $y = |x|$.

35. $y = |x - 2|$

36. $y = |x| - 3$

Match each equation with one of the graphs below.

37. $y = |x| + 2$ **38.** $y = |x + 2|$ **39.** $y = -|x + 2|$ **40.** $y = -2|x|$

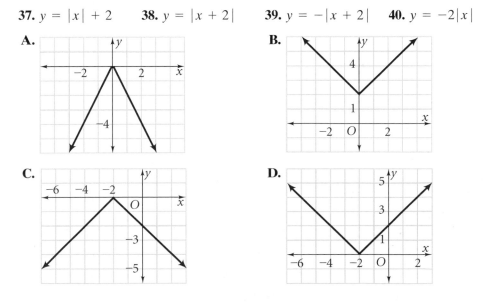

A.

B.

C.

D.

Chapter

6

Chapter Test

Take It to the NET

Online chapter test at
www.PHSchool.com
Web Code: aea-0625

Tell whether each statement is *true* or *false*. Explain.

1. A rate of change must be positive.

2. The rate of change for a vertical line is 0.

Find the slope of the line that passes through each pair of points.

3. $(4, 3), (3, 8)$

4. $(-2, 1), (6, -1)$

Graph each equation.

5. $x - 4y = 8$

6. $2x + 4y = -4$

7. $y = \frac{1}{3}x + 2$

8. $y - 1 = -3(x - 3)$

Write each equation in slope-intercept form.

9. $-7y = 8x - 3$

10. $x - 3y = -18$

11. $5x + 4y = 100$

12. $9x = 2y + 13$

Find the *x*- and *y*-intercepts of each line.

13. $3x + 4y = -24$

14. $-6x + 2y = -8$

15. $-5x + 10y = 60$

16. $x + y = 1$

Write an equation in point-slope form for the line with the given slope and through the given point.

17. slope $= \frac{8}{3}, (-2, -7)$

18. slope $= 3, (4, -8)$

19. slope $= \frac{-1}{2}, (0, 3)$

20. slope $= -5, (9, 0)$

Write an equation in point-slope form for the line through the given points.

21. $(4, 9), (-2, -6)$

22. $(-1, 0), (3, 10)$

23. $(5, -8), (-9, -8)$

24. $(0, 7), (1, 5)$

25. Which of the following lines is *not* perpendicular to $y = -2.5x + 13$?
   A. $y = 0.4x - 7$
   B. $-2x + 5y = 8$
   C. $y = \frac{2}{5}x + 4$
   D. $2y = 5x + 1.5$

Write an equation in slope-intercept form for a line that passes through the given point and is parallel to the given line.

26. $y = 5x; (2, -1)$

27. $y = 5; (-3, 6)$

Write an equation in slope-intercept form for a line that passes through the given point and that is perpendicular to the given line.

28. $y = -2x; (4, 0)$

29. $x = -7; (0, 2)$

30. Open-Ended Write the equation of a line parallel to $y = 0.5x - 10$.

31. You start a pet-washing service. You spend $30 on supplies. You plan to charge $5 to wash each pet.
   a. Write an equation to relate your income y to the number of pets x you wash.
   b. Graph the equation. What are the x- and y-intercepts?

Write an equation for each translation of $y = |x|$.

32. 2 units down

33. right $\frac{3}{4}$ unit

Graph each function by translating $y = |x|$.

34. $y = |x - 4|$

35. $y = |x| + 2$

Use the data below for Exercises 36 and 37.

**Local Governments in the United States
(thousands)**

Year	Municipalities	School Districts
1967	18.0	21.8
1972	18.5	15.8
1977	18.9	15.2
1982	19.1	14.9
1987	19.2	14.7
1992	19.3	14.4
1997	19.4	13.7

Source: *Statistical Abstract of the United States.*
Go to **www.PHSchool.com** for a data update.
Web Code: aeg-2041

36. a. Graphing Calculator Find an equation of a trend line or the line of best fit for the number of municipalities and the year.
   b. Predict the number of municipalities in 2010.

37. a. Graphing Calculator Find the equation of a trend line or the line of best fit for the number of school districts and the year.
   b. Predict the number of school districts in the year 2010.

Standardized Test Prep

Multiple Choice

For Exercises 1–9, choose the correct letter.

1. Suppose you earn $74.25 for working 9 hours. How much will you earn for working 15 hours?
   A. $120
   B. $123.75
   C. $124.50
   D. $127.25

2. Which is *not* a solution of $5x - 4 < 12$?
   F. -2 G. 0 H. 3 I. 4

3. A line perpendicular to $y = 3x - 2$ passes through the point $(0, 6)$. Which other point lies on the line?
   A. $(9, 3)$
   B. $(-9, 3)$
   C. $(9, -3)$
   D. $(-9, -3)$

4. If a, b, and c are three consecutive positive integers, which of the following is true?
   I. $a + c < 2b$ II. $a + b < c$
   III. $a + c > 2b$ IV. $h + c > a$
   F. I only
   G. IV only
   H. I and II
   I. III and IV

5. A scatter plot shows a positive correlation. Which of the following could be an equation of the line of best fit?
   A. $y = -5x + 1$
   B. $2x + 3y = 6$
   C. $x = 16$
   D. $y = 2x - 1$

6. Which of the following is the solution of $6(4x - 3) = -54$?
   F. -3 G. -1.5 H. 1.5 I. 3

7. Find $f(-2)$ when $f(x) = -3x + 4$.
   A. -10 B. -2 C. 2 D. 10

8. Mariko runs 800 ft in one minute. What is her approximate speed in miles per hour? (*Hint:* 5280 ft = 1 mi)
   F. 6 G. 8 H. 9 I. 12

9. Which of the following formulas correctly represent(s) the perimeter of the rectangle?
   I. $p = c + c + d + d$
   II. $p = cd$
   III. $p = 2c + 2d$

   A. I and III
   B. II and III
   C. I only
   D. II only

Quantitative Comparison

Compare the boxed quantity in Column A with the boxed quantity in Column B. Choose the best answer.

A. The quantity in Column A is greater.
B. The quantity in Column B is greater.
C. The two quantities are equal.
D. The relationship cannot be determined from the information given.

Column A	Column B
10.	the y-intercept of the graph of $6y - 5x = 2$	the y-intercept of the graph of $x + 9y = 2$
11.	the slope of the line through $(2, -5)$ and $(-3, 1)$	the slope of the graph of $15y + 12x = 5$

Gridded Response

Find each answer.

12. A car rental company charges $19.95 per day plus $.15 per mile. Calculate the cost in dollars to travel 250 miles over a 2-day period.

13. The ratio of crocus bulbs to tulip bulbs at a nursery is 5 to 2. The nursery has 175 crocus bulbs. How many crocus and tulip bulbs does the nursery have altogether?

14. A train moving at a constant speed travels 260 miles in 5 hours. At this rate, how many miles does the train travel in 9 hours?

Short Response

Show all of your work.

15. Write an equation in slope-intercept form of the line through $(2, -1)$ and $(3, 4)$.

16. Write an equation in slope-intercept form of the line through $(2, -3)$ that is perpendicular to the line $y = \frac{2}{5}x - \frac{7}{8}$.

17. Solve $-3 \leq 2x + 1 < 7$. Graph the solutions.

Mathematically Inclined

Measuring Force Although there are more than 80 pyramids in Egypt, the most famous are the three at Giza, near Cairo. Archaeologists think that the ancient Egyptians used ramps, either similar to the one below, or in a spiral around the perimeter of the pyramid, to lift the stone blocks into place. Moving heavy objects up a ramp requires a certain amount of effort, or force. The heavier the object, the more force is required.

Made of mud bricks, the ramp grew in height as layers were added to the pyramid.

Stone blocks were dragged on sleds with wooden rollers underneath.

Solidly Built

The Great Pyramid, around the Pharaoh's Chamber, is almost entirely solid. It contains more than 2,300,000 blocks, or 90 million ft^3 of stone. The same volume of brick and stone would build 40 Empire State Buildings.

Activity

Materials: paper and pencil, yardstick, wooden board at least 30 in. long, toy truck with a rubber band attached to the front axle

a. Raise one end of the plank to a height of 10 in. Hold the rubber band and pull the truck up the ramp. When your hand reaches the top, stop pulling, keeping the rubber band stretched. Hold the truck still while your partner records the height of the ramp (x) and the length of the rubber band (y).

b. **Data Collection** Raise the end of the ramp in 2-in. increments. Repeat part (a) until you have at least 10 (x, y) pairs of data. Record your data.

c. Graph your data and draw a line of best fit. Determine the equation of the line.

d. **Writing** The variable y represents the force required to move the toy truck. How does the height of the plank affect the force required?

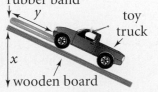

rubber band
y
toy truck
x
wooden board

The Pharaoh's Chamber lies almost in the center of the pyramid.

The tip of the pyramid may have been encased in gold to make it shine like the sun.

Some of the Tura limestone facing is left near the summit.

Each face of the Great Pyramid rises at an angle of 51.5°.

Incredible Accuracy

The difference between the longest and shortest sides of the base of the Great Pyramid is only 7.9 in.

Ancient Tools

This ancient cord on a peg is probably one of a pair used to mark the foundations of a building.

The Pyramid Lives On

A glass pyramid covers the entrance to the Louvre Museum in Paris, France. Its sides rise at the same angle as the sides of the Great Pyramid.

 Take It to the NET
For more information about pyramids, go to **www.PHSchool.com**.
Web Code: aee-0653

Where You've Been

- In Chapter 2, you solved multi-step equations, employing the Distributive Property and the properties of equality.

- In Chapter 3, you graphed one-variable inequalities and interpreted their solutions.

- In Chapters 5 and 6, you graphed linear equations and used them to model real-world situations.

Diagnosing Readiness

(For help, go to the Lesson in green.)

Instant self-check online and on CD-ROM

Solving Equations (Lesson 2-4)

Solve each equation. If the equation is an identity, write *identity*. If it has no solution, write *no solution*.

1. $3(2 - 2x) = -6(x - 1)$
2. $3m + 1 = -m + 5$
3. $4x - 1 = 3(x + 1) + x$
4. $\frac{1}{2}(6x - 4) = 4 + x$
5. $5x = 2 - (x - 7)$
6. $x + 5 = x - 5$

Solving for a Variable (Lesson 2-6)

Solve for y in terms of x.

7. $3x - 2y = -2$
8. $10 = x + 5y$
9. $2y = -2x - 8$

Writing Compound Inequalities (Lesson 3-5)

Write an inequality that represents each situation. Graph the solutions.

10. all real numbers that are between -10 and 3

11. Discounts are given to children under 12 and seniors over 60.

Writing a Function Rule (Lesson 5-4)

12. For every $35 ticket, the box office charges a fee of $4.50.
   a. Write a function rule that relates the total cost $C(t)$ to t, the number of tickets.
   b. What is the total cost for 3 tickets?
   c. How many tickets were purchased if the total cost was $237?

Graphing Linear Equations (Lessons 6-2, 6-3, and 6-4)

Graph each line.

13. $2x + 4y = -8$
14. $y = -\frac{2}{3}x + 3$
15. $2x = y - 4$

Systems of Equations and Inequalities

Key Vocabulary

Where You're Going

- In this chapter, you will extend your ability to solve equations to include solving a system of two equations with two variables.

- You will learn methods of solving a linear system, including graphing, substitution, and elimination, and how to determine which method is best for a given situation.

 Real-World Connection Applying what you learn about linear systems, you will solve a problem involving ultralight aircraft on page 367.

Solving Systems by Graphing

Lesson Preview

What You'll Learn

OBJECTIVE 1 To solve systems by graphing

OBJECTIVE 2 To analyze special types of systems

. . . And Why

To use graphs to compare growth of plants, as in Example 2

✓ Check Skills You'll Need

(For help, go to Lessons 2-4 and 6-2.)

Solve each equation.

1. $2n + 3 = 5n - 2$　　　**2.** $8 - 4z = 2z - 13$　　　**3.** $8q - 12 = 3q + 23$

Graph each pair of equations on the same coordinate plane.

4. $y = 3x - 6$　　　　　　　　　　　　**5.** $y = 6x + 1$
　　$y = -x + 2$　　　　　　　　　　　　　$y = 6x - 4$

6. $y = 2x - 5$　　　　　　　　　　　　**7.** $y = x + 5$
　　$6x - 3y = 15$　　　　　　　　　　　　$y = -3x + 5$

New Vocabulary

- system of linear equations
- solution of a system of linear equations
- no solution
- infinitely many solutions

OBJECTIVE 1

Solving Systems by Graphing

Interactive lesson includes instant self-check, tutorials, and activities.

Two or more linear equations together form a **system of linear equations.** One way to solve a system of linear equations is by graphing each equation. Look for any point common to all the lines. Any ordered pair in a system that makes *all* the equations true is a **solution of the system of linear equations.**

1 EXAMPLE Solving a System of Equations

Solve by graphing.　$y = 2x - 3$
　　　　　　　　　　$y = x - 1$

Graph both equations on the same coordinate plane.

$y = 2x - 3$　　**The slope is 2. The y-intercept is −3.**
$y = x - 1$　　　**The slope is 1. The y-intercept is −1.**

Find the point of intersection.

The lines intersect at $(2, 1)$, so $(2, 1)$ is the solution of the system.

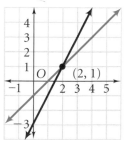

Check　See if $(2, 1)$ makes both equations true.

$y = 2x - 3$　　　　　　　　　　　　　　$y = x - 1$
$1 \stackrel{?}{=} 2(2) - 3$　　←Substitute (2, 1)→　$1 \stackrel{?}{=} 2 - 1$
　　　　　　　　　　for (x, y).
$1 \stackrel{?}{=} 4 - 3$　　　　　　　　　　　　$1 = 1$ ✓
$1 = 1$ ✓

> **? Need Help?**
>
> The slope-intercept form of a linear equation is
>
> $y = mx + b$, where m = slope and b = y-intercept.

✓ Check Understanding

1 Solve by graphing. Check your solution.

a. $y = x + 5$　　　　　　　　　**b.** $y = -\frac{1}{2}x + 2$
　　$y = -4x$　　　　　　　　　　　　$y = -3x - 3$

2 EXAMPLE   Real-World 🌎 Problem Solving

Plant Growth Suppose you are testing two fertilizers on bamboo plants A and B, which are growing under identical conditions. Plant A is 6 cm tall and growing at a rate of 4 cm/day. Plant B is 10 cm tall and growing at a rate of 2 cm/day. After how many days will the bamboo plants be the same height? What will their height be?

Define Let d = number of days.
Let $H(d)$ = the height of the plant after d days.

Relate plant height   is   initial height   plus   daily growth

Write   Plant A: $H(d)$ =   6   + $4d$
Plant B: $H(d)$ =   10   + $2d$

Method 1 Using paper and pencil

$H(d) = 4d + 6$ **The slope is 4. The intercept on the vertical axis is 6.**
$H(d) = 2d + 10$ **The slope is 2. The intercept on the vertical axis is 10.**

Graph the equations.

$H(d) = 4d + 6$
$H(d) = 2d + 10$

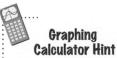

The lines intersect at (2, 14). After 2 days, both plants will be 14 cm tall.

Method 2 Using a graphing calculator

First rewrite the equations using x and y.

$H(d) = 4d + 6$ → $y = 4x + 6$
$H(d) = 2d + 10$ → $y = 2x + 10$

Then graph the equations using a graphing calculator.

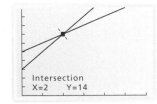

WINDOW FORMAT
Xmin=0
Xmax=6
Xscl=1
Ymin=0
Ymax=20
Yscl=2█

Y₁◻4X+6
Y₂◻2X+10
Y₃=
Y₄=
Y₅=
Y₆=
Y₇=
Y₈=

Intersection
X=2   Y=14

Set an appropriate range.   **Then graph the equations.**   **Use CALC to find the coordinates of the intersection point.**

The lines intersect at (2, 14). After 2 days, both plants will be 14 cm tall.

✓ **Check Understanding** ② You are testing two fertilizers on bamboo plants C and D. Plant C is 5 cm tall and growing at a rate of 2 cm/day. Plant D is 11 cm tall and growing at a rate of 1 cm/day. After how many days will the bamboo plants be the same height? What will their heights be?

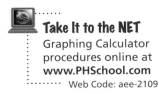

Real-World 🌎 Connection

Under ideal conditions, some bamboo shoots can grow 2 feet per day.

Graphing Calculator Hint

You can also use the **TABLE** feature to find the intersection point. The ZOOM and TRACE keys will only estimate the point of intersection.

Take It to the NET
Graphing Calculator procedures online at **www.PHSchool.com**
Web Code: aee-2109

Analyzing Special Types of Systems

When two lines are parallel, there are no points of intersection. So a system of linear equations has **no solution** when the graphs of the equations are parallel.

3 EXAMPLE Systems With No Solution

Solve by graphing. $y = -2x + 1$
$y = -2x - 1$

Graph both equations on the same coordinate plane.

$y = -2x + 1$ **The slope is −2. The y-intercept is 1.**
$y = -2x - 1$ **The slope is −2. The y-intercept is −1.**

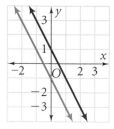

● The lines are parallel. There is no solution.

✓ Check Understanding   **3 Critical Thinking** Without graphing, how can you tell if a system has no solution? Give an example.

A system of linear equations has **infinitely many solutions** when the graphs of the equations are the same line. The coordinates of the points on the common line are all solutions of the system.

Reading Math

Infinitely many solutions is another way of saying that there are an infinite number of solutions of a system.

4 EXAMPLE Systems With Infinitely Many Solutions

Solve by graphing. $2x + 4y = 8$
$y = -\frac{1}{2}x + 2$

Graph both equations on the same coordinate plane.

$2x + 4y = 8$ **The y-intercept is 2. The x-intercept is 4.**
$y = -\frac{1}{2}x + 2$ **The slope is −$\frac{1}{2}$. The y-intercept is 2.**

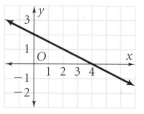

● The graphs are the same line. The solutions are an infinite number of ordered pairs (x, y) such that $y = -\frac{1}{2}x + 2$.

✓ Check Understanding   **4 Solve by graphing.** $y = \frac{1}{5}x + 9$
$5y = x + 45$

Key Concepts

Summary	Numbers of Solutions of Systems of Linear Equations

different slopes	same slope different y-intercepts	same slope same y-intercept
The lines intersect so there is one solution.	The lines are parallel so there are no solutions.	The lines are the same so there are infinitely many solutions.

EXERCISES

For more practice, see *Extra Practice*.

Practice and Problem Solving

A Practice by Example

Example 1
(page 340)

Is $(-1, 5)$ a solution of each system? Explain.

1. $x + y = 4$
   $x = -1$

2. $y = -x + 4$
   $y = -\frac{1}{5}x$

3. $y = 5$
   $x = y - 6$

4. $y = 2x + 7$
   $y = x + 6$

Solve by graphing. Check your solution.

5. $y = x + 2$
   $y = -2x + 2$

6. $y = x$
   $y = 5x$

7. $y = 1$
   $y = x$

8. $y = x + 4$
   $y = 4x + 1$

9. $y = -\frac{1}{3}x + 1$
   $y = \frac{1}{3}x - 3$

10. $y = \frac{1}{2}x + 1$
   $y = -3x + 8$

11. $3x + 4y = 12$
   $2x + 4y = 8$

12. $y = \frac{1}{2}x + 2$
   $y = -x + 5$

Example 2
(page 341)

13. Suppose you have $20 in your bank account. You start saving $5 each week. Your friend has $5 in his account and is saving $10 each week. Assume that neither you nor your friend makes any withdrawals.
   a. After how many weeks will you and your friend have the same amount of money in your accounts?
   b. How much money will each of you have?

14. Suppose you have $55 in your bank account. You start saving $10 each week. Your friend has $20 in her account and is saving $15 each week. When will you and your friend have the same amount of money in your accounts?

Examples 3, 4
(page 342)

Graph each system. Tell whether the system has *no solution* or *infinitely many solutions*.

15. $y = -2x + 1$
   $y = -2x - 3$

16. $x + 2y = 10$
   $2x + 4y = 10$

17. $y = 3x + 4$
   $-12x + 4y = 16$

18. $y = 2x + 6$
   $4x - 2y = 8$

B Apply Your Skills

Without graphing, decide whether each system has *one solution, no solution,* or *infinitely many solutions*. Explain.

19. $y = 2x$
   $y = 2x - 5$

20. $x + y = 4$
   $2x + 2y = 8$

21. $y = -3x + 1$
   $y = 3x + 7$

22. $3x - 5y = 0$
   $y = \frac{3}{5}x$

23. Which graphing calculator screen shows the solution of the system below?
   $y = -5x + 4$
   $y = \frac{3}{4}x - 3$

A.

B.

24. **Communications** A communications company offers a variety of calling card options. Card A has a 30¢ connection fee and then costs 2¢ per minute. Card B has a 10¢ connection fee and then costs 6¢ per minute. Find the length of the call that would cost the same with both cards.

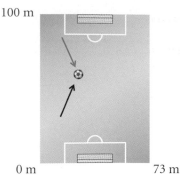

100 m

0 m   73 m

25. Soccer Jim and Tony are on opposing teams in a soccer match. They are running after the same ball. Jim's path is the line $y = 3x$. Tony's path is the line $y = -2x + 100$. Solve by graphing to find the coordinates of the ball.

Open-Ended **Write a system of two linear equations with the given characteristics.**

26. One solution; perpendicular lines

27. No solution; one equation is $y = 2x + 5$.

28. Infinitely many solutions; one equation has a y-intercept of 3.

Solve by graphing. Check your solution.

29. $y = 4x + 12$ **30.** $y = 3x - 5$ **31.** $y = x + 18$ **32.** $y = 4x + 80$
      $y = -2x + 24$ $y = 2x + 10$ $y = -\frac{1}{2}x + 36$ $y = \frac{1}{2}x + 10$

33. Below is a retelling of one of Aesop's fables. Read it and use the story to answer the questions below.

One day, the tortoise challenged the hare to a race. The hare laughed while bragging about how fast a runner he was. On the day of the race, the hare was so confident that he took a nap during the race. When he awoke, he ran as hard as he could, but he could not beat the slow-but-sure tortoise across the finish line.

a. The graph at the right shows the race of the tortoise and the hare. Which label should be on each axis?

b. Writing Which color indicates the tortoise? Which indicates the hare? Explain your answers.

c. What does the point of intersection mean?

Graphing Calculator **Find the solution of each system. If necessary, round answers to the nearest tenth.**

34. $y = 1.5x + 2$ **35.** $y = -\frac{7}{3}x + \frac{16}{3}$ **36.** $y = 0.2x + 3.5$ **37.** $y = 3.2x + 4.5$
     $y = 2.5x + 14$ $y = \frac{4}{3}x + \frac{38}{3}$ $y = 0.4x + 9.5$ $y = -8.7x - 6.1$

38. Use the spreadsheet to find the solution of the following system.

$y = -4x + 11$
$y = 3x - 3$

	A	B	C
1	x	$y = -4x + 11$	$y = 3x - 3$
2	−1	15	−6
3	0	11	−3
4	1	7	0
5	2	3	3
6	3	−1	6

39. Recording Music Suppose you and your friends form a band. You want to record a demo. Studio A rents for $100 plus $50/hour. Studio B rents for $50 plus $75/hour.

a. Solve the system by graphing.

b. Explain what the solution of the system means in terms of renting a studio.

C **Challenge**

40. a. Critical Thinking For what values of w and v does the system have exactly one solution?
$$y = -5x + w$$
$$y = -5x + v$$

  b. For what values of w and v does the system have no solution?

  c. For what values of w and v does the system have infinitely many solutions?

41. a. If $g \geq h$, the system at the right has no solution *always, sometimes,* or *never?*
$$y = gx + 3$$
$$y = hx + 7$$

  b. If $g \leq h$, the system has infinitely many solutions *always, sometimes,* or *never?*

42. The slope of the line joining point P to the origin is $\frac{2}{9}$. The slope of the line joining point P to $(-4, 3)$ is 1. Find the coordinates of point P.

Standardized Test Prep

Multiple Choice

43. Which ordered pair is the solution of the system?
$$6x - 6y = 2$$
$$3x + 9y = -7$$
  A. $\left(\frac{2}{3}, -\frac{1}{3}\right)$ **B.** $\left(\frac{1}{3}, \frac{2}{3}\right)$
  C. $\left(-\frac{2}{3}, \frac{1}{3}\right)$ **D.** $\left(-\frac{1}{3}, -\frac{2}{3}\right)$

44. Which value of b will make the graphs of $y = 2x + 3$ and $y = 2.5x + b$ intersect at (2, 7)?
  F. 2   **G.** 3   **H.** 5   **I.** 7

Short Response

45. The first equation in a system of two equations is $x - 2y = 10$. The graph of the second equation does not intersect the first.
  a. Write a possible second equation for the system.
  b. Explain your answer to part (a).

Extended Response

46. The advertisements at the right are for two jobs you are considering.
  a. Write a system of equations that relates the amount of sales x to the money y earned in a week at each job.
  b. How much would you need to sell in a week at each job to earn the same amount of money at both?
  c. After talking with salespeople, you estimate weekly sales of about $600 at either job. At which job would you earn more money?

Sales Position
Salesperson Wanted
Knowledge of Cellular Phones
On-Site Sales
$150/week + 20% commission

CAREER OPPORTUNITY
Sell Stereo Equipment in
National Electronics Retail Chain!
$200/week + 10% commission

Mixed Review

Lesson 6-7

Graph each equation and describe its translation from $y = |x|$.

47. $y = |x| + 2$ **48.** $y = |x + 3|$ **49.** $y = |x - 2| + 5$

Lesson 4-4

Find each percent of change. Describe the percent of change as an increase or decrease.

50. 4 cm to 5 cm   **51.** 12 in. to 8 in.   **52.** $20 to $24   **53.** 10 ft to 25 ft

54. $9 to $6   **55.** 12 cm to 15 cm   **56.** 50 m to 55 m   **57.** $48 to $42

Solving Systems Using Algebra Tiles

You can model and solve some linear systems using algebra tiles.

Solve the following system.
$$2x + y = 5$$
$$y = x - 1$$

Model the value of y, which is $x - 1$.

To model the equation $2x + y = 5$, substitute the value of y, which is $x - 1$.

$$2x + y = 5$$
$$2x + x - 1 = 5$$
$$3x - 1 = 5$$

Using the Addition Property of Equality, add 1 to each side. Simplify the model by removing the zero pair.

$$3x - 1 + 1 = 5 + 1$$
$$3x = 6$$

Divide each side into three identical groups.

$$\frac{3x}{3} = \frac{6}{3}$$

Solve for x.

$$x = 2$$

To find y, substitute the value of x into the equation $y = x - 1$.

$$y = x - 1$$
$$= 2 - 1$$
$$= 1$$

The solution of the system is $(2, 1)$.

EXERCISES

Model and solve each system.

1. $y = x + 1$
   $2x + y = 10$

2. $x + 4y = 1$
   $x = y - 4$

3. $y = 2x - 1$
   $y = x + 5$

4. $x = 3y + 2$
   $2x = y + 9$

5. $x - 4y = 2$
   $x = y + 1$

6. $y = x + 3$
   $y = 2x + 6$

7. Open-Ended Let the equation $y = x + 2$ be part of a system. Write the second equation of the system such that the system could be solved using algebra tiles.

7-2

Solving Systems Using Substitution

Lesson Preview

What You'll Learn

OBJECTIVE
1 To solve systems using substitution

...And Why

To solve problems involving transportation, as in Example 3

✓ Check Skills You'll Need

(For help, go to Lessons 2-4 and 7-1.)

Solve each equation.

1. $m - 6 = 4m + 8$ **2.** $4n = 9 - 2n$ **3.** $\frac{1}{3}t + 5 = 10$

For each system, is the ordered pair a solution of both equations?

4. $(5, 1)$ $y = -x + 4$
            $y = x - 6$

5. $(2, 2.4)$ $4x + 5y = 20$
                $2x + 6y = 10$

New Vocabulary
• substitution method

OBJECTIVE
1   **Using Substitution**

iTEXT Interactive lesson includes instant self-check, tutorials, and activities.

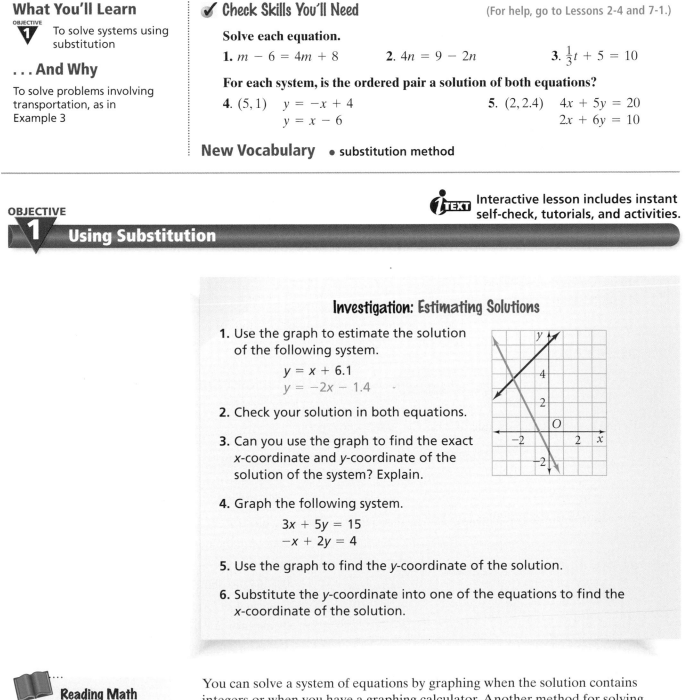

Investigation: Estimating Solutions

1. Use the graph to estimate the solution of the following system.

     $y = x + 6.1$
     $y = -2x - 1.4$

2. Check your solution in both equations.

3. Can you use the graph to find the exact x-coordinate and y-coordinate of the solution of the system? Explain.

4. Graph the following system.

     $3x + 5y = 15$
     $-x + 2y = 4$

5. Use the graph to find the y-coordinate of the solution.

6. Substitute the y-coordinate into one of the equations to find the x-coordinate of the solution.

Reading Math

Substitution means one value or expression is used in place of another.

You can solve a system of equations by graphing when the solution contains integers or when you have a graphing calculator. Another method for solving systems of equations is the **substitution method.** By replacing one variable with an equivalent expression containing the other variable, you can create a one-variable equation that you can solve using methods shown in chapter 2.

1 EXAMPLE Using Substitution

Solve using substitution. $y = -4x + 8$
$y = x + 7$

Step 1 Write an equation containing only one variable, and solve it.

$y = -4x + 8$	**Start with one equation.**
$x + 7 = -4x + 8$	**Substitute $x + 7$ for y.**
$5x + 7 = 8$	**Add $4x$ to each side.**
$5x = 1$	**Subtract 7 from each side.**
$x = 0.2$	**Divide each side by 5.**

Step 2 Solve for the other variable in either equation.

$y = 0.2 + 7$	**Substitute 0.2 for x in $y = x + 7$.**
$y = 7.2$	**Simplify.**

Since $x = 0.2$ and $y = 7.2$, the solution is $(0.2, 7.2)$.

Check $7.2 \stackrel{?}{=} -4(0.2) + 8$ Since $y = x + 7$ was used in step 2, see if $(0.2, 7.2)$ solves $y = -4x + 8$.

$7.2 = 7.2$ ✓   **Simplify.**

✓**Check Understanding** ❶ Solve using substitution. Check your solution. $y = 2x$
$7x - y = 15$

To use the substitution method, you must have an equation that has already been solved for one of the variables. Solving for a variable that has a coefficient of 1 or −1 is a good place to start.

2 EXAMPLE Using Substitution and the Distributive Property

Solve using the substitution method. $3y + 2x = 4$
$-6x + y = -7$

Step 1 Solve the second equation for y because it has a coefficient of 1.

$-6x + y = -7$

$y = 6x - 7$	**Add $6x$ to each side.**

Step 2 Write an equation containing only one variable and solve.

$3y + 2x = 4$	**Start with the other equation.**
$3(6x - 7) + 2x = 4$	**Substitute $6x - 7$ for y. Use parentheses.**
$18x - 21 + 2x = 4$	**Use the Distributive Property.**
$20x = 25$	**Combine like terms and add 21 to each side.**
$x = 1.25$	**Divide each side by 20.**

Step 3 Solve for the other variable in either equation.

$-6(1.25) + y = -7$	**Substitute 1.25 for x in $-6x + y = -7$.**
$-7.5 + y = -7$	**Simplify.**
$y = 0.5$	**Add 7.5 to each side.**

Since $x = 1.25$ and $y = 0.5$, the solution is $(1.25, 0.5)$.

✓**Check Understanding** ❷ Solve using substitution. Check your solution. $6y + 8x = 28$
$3 = 2x - y$

You can use substitution to solve systems that model real-world situations.

3 **EXAMPLE** Real-World  Problem Solving

Transportation Your school committee is planning an after-school trip by 193 people to a competition at another school. There are eight drivers available and two types of vehicles, school buses and minivans. The school buses seat 51 people each, and the minivans seat 8 people each. How many buses and minivans will be needed?

Let b = number of school buses.
Let m = number of minivans.

drivers $b + m = 8$
people $51b + 8m = 193$

Solve using the substitution method.

Step 1 Write an equation containing only one variable.

$b + m = 8$ **Solve the first equation for m.**
$m = -b + 8$

Step 2 Write and solve an equation containing the variable b.

$51b + 8(-b + 8) = 193$ **Substitute −b + 8 for m in the second equation.**
$51b - 8b + 64 = 193$ **Solve for b.**
$43b + 64 = 193$
$43b = 129$
$b = 3$

Step 3 Solve for m in either equation.

$(3) + m = 8$ **Substitute 3 for b in b + m = 8.**
$m = 5$

Three school buses and five minivans will be needed to transport 193 people.

Check Is the answer correct? Three buses, each transporting 51 people, carry $3(51)$, or 153, people. Five minivans, each transporting 8 people, carry $5(8)$, or 40, people. The total number of people transported by buses and minivans is $153 + 40$, or 193. The answer is correct.

✓ **Check Understanding** **3** **Geometry** A rectangle is 4 times longer than it is wide. The perimeter of the rectangle is 30 cm. Find the dimensions of the rectangle.

Real-World  Connection

According to the U.S. Department of Transportation, every year about 440,000 public school buses transport 24 million students to and from school.

EXERCISES

For more practice, see *Extra Practice.*

Practice and Problem Solving

A **Practice by Example**

Example 1
(page 348)

Mental Math **Match each system with its solution at the right.**

1. $y = x + 1$
   $y = 2x - 1$

2. $y = \frac{1}{2}x + 4$
   $2y + 2x = 2$

A. $(3, 2)$

B. $(3, 3)$

3. $2y = x + 3$
   $x = y$

4. $x - y = 1$
   $x = \frac{1}{2}y + 2$

C. $(-2, 3)$

D. $(2, 3)$

Solve each system using substitution. Check your solution.

5. $y = 4x - 8$
$y = 2x + 10$

6. $C(n) = -3n - 6$
$C(n) = n - 4$

7. $m = 5p + 8$
$m = -10p + 3$

8. $y = -4x + 12\frac{1}{2}$
$y = \frac{1}{4}x + 4$

9. $h = 6g - 4$
$h = -2g + 28$

10. $a = \frac{2}{5}b - 3$
$a = 2b - 18$

Example 2
(page 348)

11. $y = x - 2$
$2x + 2y = 4$

12. $c = 3d - 27$
$4d + 10c = 120$

13. $3x - 6y = 30$
$y = -6x + 34$

14. $m = 4n + 11$
$-6n + 8m = 36$

15. $7x - 8y = 112$
$y = -2x + 9$

16. $t = 0.2s + 10$
$4s + 5t = 35$

Example 3
(page 349)

17. **Geometry** The length of a rectangle is 5 cm more than twice the width. The perimeter of the rectangle is 34 cm. Find the dimensions of the rectangle.

18. Suppose you have $28.00 in your bank account and start saving $18.25 every week. Your friend has $161.00 in his account and is withdrawing $15 every week. When will your account balances be the same?

B **Apply Your Skills**

Solve each system by substitution. Check your solution.

19. $a - 1.2b = -3$
$0.2b + 0.6a = 12$

20. $0.5x + 0.25y = 36$
$y + 18 = 16x$

21. $y = 0.8x + 7.2$
$20x + 32y = 48$

For Exercises 22–24, define variables and write a system of equations for each situation. Solve using substitution.

22. **Renting Videos** Suppose you want to join a video store. Big Video offers a special discount card that costs $9.99 for one year. With the discount card, each video rental costs $2.49. A discount card from Main Street Video costs $20.49 for one year. With the Main Street Video discount card, each video rental costs $1.79. After how many video rentals is the cost the same?

23. **Agriculture** A farmer grows only sunflowers and flax on his 240-acre farm. This year he wants to plant 80 more acres of sunflowers than of flax. How many acres of each crop does the farmer need to plant?

24. **Buying a Car** Suppose you are thinking about buying one of two cars. Car A will cost $17,655. You can expect to pay an average of $1230 per year for fuel, maintenance, and repairs. Car B will cost about $15,900. Fuel, maintenance, and repairs for it will average about $1425 per year. After how many years are the total costs for the cars the same?

Real-World Connection

Sunflower seeds are sold as snacks and as bird food, and they are a source of cooking oil.

Estimation Graph each system to estimate the solution. Then use substitution to find the exact solution of the system.

25. $y = 2x$
$y = -6x + 4$

26. $y = \frac{1}{2}x + 4$
$y = -4x - 5$

27. $x + y = 0$
$5x + 2y = -3$

28. $y = 2x + 3$
$y = 0.5x - 2$

29. $y = -x + 4$
$y = 2x + 6$

30. $y = 0.7x + 3$
$y = -1.5x - 7$

31. **a.** You have 28 coins that are all nickels and dimes. The value of the coins is $2.05. Define variables and write a system of equations for this situation.
    b. **Writing** Explain the steps necessary to solve the system in part (a).
    c. Solve the system.

32. **Open-Ended** Write a system of linear equations with exactly one solution. Use substitution to solve your system.

33. a. Solve the system below using substitution.

$$y = 0.5x + 4$$
$$-x + 2y = 8$$

b. Solve the system by graphing.

c. Critical Thinking Make a general statement about the solutions you get when solving by graphing and the results you get when solving by substitution.

34. a. Solve the system below using substitution.

$$6x - 2y = 10$$
$$y = 3x + 1$$

b. Solve by graphing.

c. Critical Thinking Make a general statement about the solutions you get when solving by graphing and the results you get when solving by substitution.

Solve each system using substitution.

35. $y = 2x$
$6x - y = 8$

36. $y = 3x + 1$
$x = 3y + 1$

37. $x - 3y = 14$
$x - 2 = 0$

38. $2x + 2y = 5$
$y = \frac{1}{4}x$

39. $4x + y = -2$
$-2x - 3y = 1$

40. $3x + 5y = 2$
$x + 4y = -4$

C **Challenge**

For Exercises 41–43, suppose you are solving a system of linear equations and get the given result. How many solutions must the system have?

41. a true statement, such as $2 = 2$

42. a false statement, such as $10 = 1$

43. a statement such as $x = 4$

44. There are 1170 students in a school. The ratio of girls to boys is 23 : 22. The system below describes relationships between the number of girls and the number of boys.

$$g + b = 1170 \qquad \frac{g}{b} = \frac{23}{22}$$

a. Solve the proportion for g.

b. Solve the system.

c. How many more girls are there than boys?

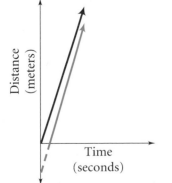

45. Sprinting The graph at the left represents the start of a 100-meter race between Joetta and Gail. The red line and blue line represent Joetta's and Gail's time and distance. Joetta averages 8.8 m/s. Gail averages 9 m/s but started 0.2 s after Joetta. At time 0.2, Gail's distance is 0 m. You can use point-slope form to write an equation that relates Gail's time t to her distance d.

$$y - y_1 = m(x - x_1)$$
$$d - 0 = 9(t - 0.2)$$
$$d = 9t - 1.8$$

Since Joetta started at $t = 0$, the equation $d = 8.8t$ relates her time and distance.

a. Solve the system using substitution.

b. Will Gail overtake Joetta before the finish line?

46. Use substitution to solve the following system.

$$t + r + s = 20$$
$$r = t + 3$$
$$t + 5r + 10s = 129$$

Gridded Response

47. Find the value of the y-coordinate of the solution to the given system.

$5x + 5y = 179$
$x = 5y - 143$

48. Find the value of the y-coordinate of the solution to the given system.

$y = 9x + 3480$
$y = 81x - 7104$

Take It to the NET
Online lesson quiz at
www.PHSchool.com
Web Code: aea-0702

49. Tina has $220 in her account. Cliff has $100 in his account. Starting in July, Tina adds $25 to her account on the first of each month, while Cliff adds $35 to his. How many dollars will they have in their accounts when the amounts are the same?

Short Response

50. Is $(-2, -7)$ the solution of the following system? Justify your answer.
$7y - 4x = 29$
$x = y - 5$

Mixed Review

Lesson 7-1   **Solve each system by graphing.**

51. $y = x - 2$
$y = \frac{1}{2}x + 4$

52. $y = -2x + 5$
$y = -x + 3$

53. $y = \frac{3}{4}x - 1$
$y = \frac{1}{4}x + 1$

Lesson 5-3   **Graph each function.**

54. $y = 3x - 2$

55. $f(x) = x + 1$

56. $f(x) = -2x$

57. $y = |x| + 5$

58. $y = -2|x|$

59. $y = |x + 3| - 1$

Checkpoint Quiz 1   Lessons 7-1 through 7-2

TEXT Instant self-check quiz online and on CD-ROM

Solve each system by graphing.

1. $y = 3x - 4$
$y = -2x + 1$

2. $y = \frac{4}{3}x - 2$
$y = \frac{2}{3}x$

3. $y = \frac{1}{4}x - 1$
$y = -2x - 10$

Solve each system using substitution.

4. $y = 3x - 14$
$y = x - 10$

5. $y = 2x + 5$
$y = 6x + 1$

6. $x = y + 7$
$y = 8 + 2x$

7. $3x + 4y = 12$
$y = -2x + 10$

8. $4x + 9y = 24$
$y = -\frac{1}{3}x + 2$

In Exercises 9 and 10, write and solve a system of equations for each situation.

9. A rectangle is 3 times longer than it is wide. The perimeter is 44 cm. Find the dimensions of the rectangle.

10. A farmer grows only pumpkins and corn on her 420-acre farm. This year she wants to plant 250 more acres of corn than of pumpkins. How many acres of each crop does the farmer need to plant?

7-3

Solving Systems Using Elimination

Lesson Preview

What You'll Learn

OBJECTIVE 1 To solve systems by adding or subtracting

OBJECTIVE 2 To multiply first when solving systems

...And Why

To analyze a ticket-sales situation, as in Example 2

✓ **Check Skills You'll Need** (For help, go to Lesson 7-2.)

Solve each system using substitution.

1. $y = 4x - 3$
$y = 2x + 13$

2. $y + 5x = 4$
$y = 7x - 20$

3. $y = -2x + 2$
$3x - 17 = 2y$

New Vocabulary • elimination method

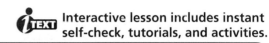

OBJECTIVE 1 Adding or Subtracting to Solve Systems

Interactive lesson includes instant self-check, tutorials, and activities.

Need Help?

Addition Property of Equality:
If $a = b$,
then $a + c = b + c$.

Subtraction Property of Equality:
If $a = b$,
then $a - c = b - c$.

The Addition and Subtraction Properties of Equality can be extended to state,

If $a = b$ and $c = d$, then $a + c = b + d$.   If $a = b$ and $c = d$, then $a - c = b - d$.

You can use the Addition and Subtraction Properties of Equality to solve a system by the **elimination method.** You can add or subtract equations to eliminate a variable.

1 EXAMPLE Adding Equations

Solve by elimination. $5x - 6y = -32$
$3x + 6y = 48$

Step 1 Eliminate y because the sum of the coefficients of y is zero.

$5x - 6y = -32$

$\underline{3x + 6y =\ \ \ 48}$

$8x + 0\ \ =\ \ \ 16$ **Addition Property of Equality**

$x\ =\ \ \ 2$ **Solve for x.**

Step 2 Solve for the eliminated variable y using either of the original equations.

$3x + 6y = 48$ **Choose the second equation.**

$3(2) + 6y = 48$ **Substitute 2 for x.**

$6 + 6y = 48$ **Simplify. Then solve for y.**

$y = \ \ 7$

Since $x = 2$ and $y = 7$, the solution is $(2, 7)$.

Check $5(2) - 6(7) \stackrel{?}{=} -32$ **See if (2, 7) solves $5x - 6y = -32$.**

$10 - 42 \stackrel{?}{=} -32$

$-32 = -32$ ✓

✓ **Check Understanding** **1** Solve by elimination. $6x - 3y = 3$
$-6x + 5y = 3$

2 EXAMPLE **Real-World 🌐 Problem Solving**

Ticket Sales Suppose your community center sells a total of 292 tickets for a basketball game. An adult ticket costs $3. A student ticket costs $1. The sponsors collect $470 in ticket sales. Write and solve a system to find the number of each type of ticket sold.

Define Let a = number of adult tickets.
Let s = number of student tickets.

Relate total number of tickets   total amount of sales
Write $a + s = 292$ $3a + 1s = 470$

Solve by elimination.

Step 1 Eliminate s because the difference of the coefficients of s is zero.

$$a + s = \quad 292$$
$$\underline{3a + s = \quad 470}$$
$$-2a + 0 = -178 \qquad \text{Subtraction Property of Equality}$$
$$a = \quad\; 89 \qquad \text{Solve for } a.$$

Step 2 Solve for the eliminated variable using either of the original equations.

$$a + s = 292 \qquad \text{Choose the first equation.}$$
$$89 + s = 292 \qquad \text{Substitute 89 for } a.$$
$$s = 203 \qquad \text{Solve for } s.$$

There were 89 adult tickets sold and 203 student tickets sold.

Check Is the solution reasonable? The total number of tickets is $89 + 203$, or 292. The total sales is $3(89)$, or 267, plus $1(203)$, or 203, which is 470. The solution is correct.

✓ Check Understanding **2** Your class sells a total of 64 tickets to a play. A student ticket costs $1, and an adult ticket costs $2.50. Your class collects $109 in total ticket sales. How many adult tickets did you sell? How many student tickets did you sell?

OBJECTIVE
2
Multiplying First to Solve Systems

From examples 1 and 2 you can see that to eliminate a variable its coefficients must have a sum or difference of zero. Sometimes you may need to multiply one or both of the equations by a nonzero number first.

3 EXAMPLE **Multiplying One Equation**

Solve by the elimination method. $2x + 5y = -22$
                                     $10x + 3y = 22$

Step 1 Eliminate one variable.

Start with the given system.	To prepare for eliminating x, multiply the first equation by 5.	Subtract the equations to eliminate x.
$2x + 5y = -22 \;\rightarrow$	$5(2x + 5y = -22) \quad\rightarrow$	$10x + 25y = -110$
$10x + 3y = \;\; 22 \;\rightarrow$	$\underline{10x + 3y = \quad 22} \quad\rightarrow$	$\underline{10x + \;\; 3y = \quad\; 22}$
		$0 \; + 22y = -132$

Step 2 Solve for y.

$$22y = -132$$
$$y = -6$$

Step 3 Solve for the eliminated variable using either of the original equations.

$$2x + 5y = -22 \quad \textbf{Choose the first equation.}$$
$$2x + 5(-6) = -22 \quad \textbf{Substitute } -6 \textbf{ for } y.$$
$$2x - 30 = -22 \quad \textbf{Solve for } x.$$
$$2x = 8$$
$$x = 4$$

● The solution is $(4, -6)$.

✓ **Check Understanding** ❸ Solve by elimination. $\quad -2x + 15y = -32$
$$7x - 5y = 17$$

To solve problems that arise from real-world situations, you can also use the elimination method.

❹ EXAMPLE **Real-World 🌐 Problem Solving**

Sales Suppose your class sells gift wrap for $4 per package and greeting cards for $10 per package. Your class sells 205 packages in all and receives a total of $1084. Find the number of packages of gift wrap and the number of packages of greeting cards sold.

Define Let w = number of packages of gift wrap sold.
Let c = number of packages of greeting cards sold.

Relate total number of packages   total amount of sales

Write $w + c = 205$ $4w + 10c = 1084$

Step 1 Eliminate one variable.

Start with the given system.	To prepare for eliminating w, multiply the first equation by 4.	Subtract the equations to eliminate w.
$w + c = 205 \quad \rightarrow$	$4(w + c = 205)$	$\rightarrow \quad 4w + 4c = 820$
$4w + 10c = 1084 \quad \rightarrow$	$\underline{4w + 10c = 1084}$	$\rightarrow \quad \underline{4w + 10c = 1084}$
		$0 - 6c = -264$

Step 2 Solve for c.

$$-6c = -264$$
$$c = 44$$

Step 3 Solve for the eliminated variable using either of the original equations.

$$w + c = 205 \quad \textbf{Use the first equation.}$$
$$w + 44 = 205 \quad \textbf{Substitute 44 for } c.$$
$$w = 161 \quad \textbf{Solve for } w.$$

● The class sold 161 packages of gift wrap and 44 packages of greeting cards.

✓ **Check Understanding** ❹ Suppose your younger brother's elementary school class sells a different brand of gift wrap, which costs $2 per package, and cards, which cost $5 per package. His class sells 220 packages in all and earns a total of $695. Find the number of each type of package sold.

To eliminate a variable, you may need to multiply both equations in a system by a nonzero number. Multiply each equation by values such that when you write equivalent equations, you can then add or subtract to eliminate a variable.

5 EXAMPLE **Multiplying Both Equations**

Solve by elimination. $4x + 2y = 14$
$7x - 3y = -8$

Step 1 Eliminate one variable.

Need Help?

To eliminate y find the least common multiple (LCM) of $2y$ and $3y$, which is $6y$. (See Skills Handbook p. 721.)

Start with the given system.	To prepare for eliminating y, multiply one equation by 3 and the other equation by 2.	Add the equations to eliminate y.
$4x + 2y = 14$ →	$3(4x + 2y = 14)$ →	$12x + 6y = 42$
$7x - 3y = -8$ →	$2(7x - 3y = -8)$ →	$14x - 6y = -16$
		$26x + 0 = 26$

Step 2 Solve for x.
$$26x = 26$$
$$x = 1$$

Step 3 Solve for the eliminated variable y using either of the original equations.
$$4x + 2y = 14 \quad \text{Use the first equation.}$$
$$4(1) + 2y = 14 \quad \text{Substitute 1 for } x.$$
$$2y = 10$$
$$y = 5$$

● The solution is $(1, 5)$.

✓ Check Understanding **5** Solve by elimination. $15x + 3y = 9$
$10x + 7y = -4$

When you solve systems using elimination, plan a strategy. A flowchart like the one below can help you to decide how to eliminate a variable.

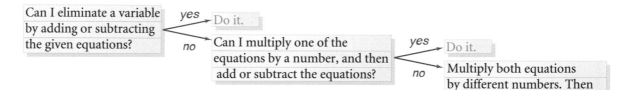

Can I eliminate a variable by adding or subtracting the given equations? — **yes** → Do it.

no → Can I multiply one of the equations by a number, and then add or subtract the equations? — **yes** → Do it.

no → Multiply both equations by different numbers. Then add or subtract the equations.

EXERCISES

For more practice, see *Extra Practice*.

Practice and Problem Solving

A **Practice by Example**

Example 1
(page 353)

Solve by elimination.

1. $2x + 5y = 17$
$6x - 5y = -9$

2. $7x + 2y = 10$
$-7x + y = -16$

3. $2x - 3y = 61$
$2x + y = -7$

4. $8x + 11y = 20$
$5x - 11y = -59$

5. $2x + 18y = -9$
$4x + 18y = -27$

6. $20x + 3y = 20$
$-20x + 5y = 60$

Example 2
(page 354)

7. The sum of two numbers is 20. Their difference is 4.
   a. Write a system of equations that describes this situation.
   b. Solve by elimination to find the two numbers.

8. Ticket Sales Your school sold 456 tickets for a high school play. An adult ticket cost $3.50. A student ticket cost $1. Total ticket sales equaled $1131. Let a equal the number of adult tickets sold, and let s equal the number of student tickets sold.
   a. Write a system of equations that relates the number of adult and student tickets sold to the total number of tickets sold and to the total ticket sales.
   b. Solve by elimination to find the number of each type of ticket sold.

Example 3
(page 354)

Solve by elimination.

9. $3x - 10y = -25$
$4x + 40y = 20$

10. $7x + 15y = 32$
$x - 3y = 20$

11. $x - 8y = 18$
$-16x + 16y = -8$

12. $24x + 2y = 52$
$6x - 3y = -36$

13. $88x - 5y = 39$
$-8x + 3y = -1$

14. $2x + 4y = 8$
$5x + y = -7$

Example 4
(page 355)

15. Sales A photo studio that takes school pictures offers several different packages. Let w equal the cost of a wallet-sized portrait, and let ℓ equal the cost of an 8×10 portrait.

Basic Package
30 wallet-sized photos
1 8″ x 10″ portrait
$17.65

Deluxe Package
20 wallet-sized photos
3 8″ x 10″ portraits
$25.65

a. Write a system of equations that relates the cost of wallet-sized portraits and 8×10 portraits to the cost of the basic and deluxe packages.
b. Find the cost of each type of portrait.

16. Two groups of students order burritos and tacos at a local restaurant. One order of 3 burritos and 4 tacos costs $11.33. The other order of 9 burritos and 5 tacos costs $23.56.
   a. Write a system of equations that describes this situation.
   b. Solve by elimination to find the cost of a burrito and the cost of a taco.

Example 5
(page 356)

Solve by elimination.

17. $3x + 2y = -9$
$-10x + 5y = -5$

18. $4x + 5y = 15$
$6x - 4y = 11$

19. $3x - 2y = 10$
$2x + 3y = -2$

20. $-2x + 5y = 20$
$3x - 7y = -26$

21. $10x + 8y = 2$
$8x + 6y = 1$

22. $9x + 5y = 34$
$8x - 2y = -2$

B **Apply Your Skills**

Solve each system using any method. Tell why you chose the method you used.

23. $y = 2x$
$y = x - 1$

24. $7x + 8y = 25$
$9x + 10y = 35$

25. $x = 12y - 14$
$3y + 2x = 26$

26. $-20x + 7y = 137$
$4x + 5y = 43$

27. $5y = x$
$2x - 3y = 7$

28. $y = x + 2$
$y = -2x + 3$

One weekend for
$195
One week for
$650
(per person, double occupancy)

Beach
Bay
Hotel

29. Vacation A weekend at the Beach Bay Hotel in Florida includes 2 nights and 4 meals. A week includes 7 nights and 10 meals. Let n = the cost of 1 night and m = the cost of 1 meal. Find the cost of 1 night and the cost of 1 meal.

30. a. Business A company sells brass and steel machine parts. One shipment contains 3 brass and 10 steel parts and costs $48. A second shipment contains 7 brass and 4 steel parts and costs $54. Find the cost of each type of machine part.

   b. How much would a shipment containing 10 brass and 13 steel machine parts cost?

31. Error Analysis Beth is solving a system by elimination. Her work is shown below. What error did she make?

$$4x - 6y = 1 \longrightarrow 20x - 30y = 5$$
$$3x + 5y = -8 \longrightarrow 18x + 30y = -8$$

32. Open-Ended Write a system of equations that can be solved by elimination. Solve your system.

Solve by elimination.

33. $\frac{1}{2}x + y = -1$
$16x - \frac{1}{2}y = 163$

34. $\frac{1}{4}x - 6y = -70$
$5x + \frac{3}{4}y = 49$

35. $-0.2x + 4y = -1$
$x + 0.5y = -15.5$

36. $y = 0.5x + 2$
$1.5x + y = 42$

37. $\frac{1}{4}x + \frac{33}{2} = y$
$y - 12 = -2x$

38. $\frac{2}{3}x - y = 70$
$\frac{1}{3}x - \frac{2}{3}y = 43$

39. Critical Thinking Find a value of n such that the x-value of the solution of the system at right is 4.
$5x - 10y = 50$
$nx + 10y = 6$

 40. Writing Explain how to solve a system using elimination. Give examples of when you use addition, subtraction, and multiplication.

41. Electricity Two batteries produce a total voltage of 4.5 volts ($B_1 + B_2 = 4.5$). The difference in their voltages is 1.5 volts ($B_1 - B_2 = 1.5$). Find the voltages of the two batteries.

C Challenge

Solve by elimination.

42. $\frac{6}{x} - \frac{4}{y} = -4$
$\frac{3}{x} + \frac{8}{y} = 3$

43. $ax + y = c$
$ax + by = c$

44. $x + y + z = 41$
$x - y + z = 15$
$3x - z = 4$

45. Music Suppose your band wants to sell CDs and cassette tapes of your music. You use a production company that offers two different production packages.

	CDs	Tapes	Mastering	Artwork	Total Cost
Package #1	300	400	✓	✓	$2080
Package #2	500	600	✓	✓	$3120

Both companies charge $100 to master your original recording and $240 to create cover artwork. Find the average production cost of each CD and cassette tape.

......
Problem Solving Hint

For Exercise 45, simplify each equation before solving by elimination.
......

46. Jewelry A ring is made out of gold and copper. Gold has a density of 19.3 g/cm³. Copper has a density of 9 g/cm³. Mass m, density d, and volume v are related by the formula $m = dv$. The ring has a volume of 8.4 cm³, and a mass of 104.44 g.

Let a = volume of gold.　　　mass of gold = $dv = 19.3a$
Let c = volume of copper.　　mass of copper = $dv = 9c$

a. Solve the following system by elimination to find out how many grams of gold are in the ring.

$$a + c = 8.4$$
$$19.3a + 9c = 104.44$$

b. What is the percent of gold by mass?

Standardized Test Prep

Multiple Choice

47. Which of the following systems does NOT have the same solution as the system at the right?

$$7x - 4y = 5$$
$$6x + 7y = -11$$

A. $49x - 28y = 35$
$24x + 28y = -44$

B. $42x - 24y = 30$
$42x + 49y = -77$

C. $-14x + 8y = -10$
$12x + 14y = -22$

D. $21x + 12y = 15$
$-24x - 28y = 44$

Take It to the NET
Online lesson quiz at
www.PHSchool.com
Web Code: aea-0703

48. Use the solution of the system below to find $x - y$.
$$4x - 2y = 11$$
$$3x - 4y = -6$$

F. 11.3　　　**G.** 0.1　　　**H.** −0.1　　　**I.** −11.3

Short Response

49. Solve the following system by elimination. Show your work.
$$y - x = 13$$
$$7y + x = 11$$

Extended Response

50. A trapezoid is formed by lines with the following equations.
$$2x + 4y = 16 \qquad x = 4 \qquad x = 0 \qquad y = 0$$
Find the area of the trapezoid.

Mixed Review

Lesson 7-2

Solve using substitution. Give the solutions in alphabetical order.

51. $y = 4x + 2$
$y = 6x - 10$

52. $p = q - 5$
$3p + q = 1$

53. $w + a = 4$
$w + 2a = 13$

Lesson 4-6

You have a bag with two red marbles, three blue marbles, and five green marbles. You choose a marble at random. Without replacing the marble, you choose a second marble. Find each probability.

54. P(red then green)　　**55.** P(two greens)　　**56.** P(blue then red)

Lesson 2-1

Solve and check each solution.

57. $c - 4 = 67$　　**58.** $t + 27 = 9$　　**59.** $n - 12 = -56$

60. $-9 + k = 13$　　**61.** $x - 82 = 1$　　**62.** $17 + b = 11$

Matrices and Solving Systems

In Chapter 1, you learned how to add and subtract two matrices. You can also multiply matrices. You multiply the elements in a row of the first matrix by the corresponding elements in a column of the second matrix. Then you add the products.

3 elements in a row → $\begin{bmatrix} 2 & 5 & -3 \\ 3 & 1 & 6 \end{bmatrix} \begin{bmatrix} 7 \\ 2 \\ 1 \end{bmatrix} = \begin{bmatrix} 2 \cdot 7 + 5 \cdot 2 + (-3 \cdot 1) \\ 3 \cdot 7 + 1 \cdot 2 + \quad 6 \cdot 1 \end{bmatrix} = \begin{bmatrix} 21 \\ 29 \end{bmatrix}$

↑
3 elements in a column

The second matrix can have more than one column.

$$\begin{bmatrix} 2 & 5 & -3 \\ 3 & 1 & 6 \end{bmatrix} \begin{bmatrix} 7 & 3 \\ 2 & 9 \\ 1 & 2 \end{bmatrix} = \begin{bmatrix} 2 \cdot 7 + 5 \cdot 2 + (-3 \cdot 1) & 2 \cdot 3 + 5 \cdot 9 + (-3 \cdot 2) \\ 3 \cdot 7 + 1 \cdot 2 + \quad 6 \cdot 1 & 3 \cdot 3 + 1 \cdot 9 + \quad 6 \cdot 2 \end{bmatrix} = \begin{bmatrix} 21 & 45 \\ 29 & 30 \end{bmatrix}$$

first row and first column **first row and second column**

second row and first column **second row and second column**

You can use a graphing calculator to multiply matrices. To enter matrices, you must know their dimensions. A matrix with two rows and three columns is a 2×3 matrix.

1 EXAMPLE

Use a graphing calculator to find $A \times B$ for

$$A = \begin{bmatrix} 2 & 5 & -3 \\ 3 & 1 & 6 \end{bmatrix} \qquad B = \begin{bmatrix} 7 & 3 \\ 2 & 9 \\ 1 & 2 \end{bmatrix}$$

Step 1 Use the **MATRX** feature. Edit the dimensions and enter the values of the elements. You have to quit the first matrix screen before using the **MATRX** feature to enter the second matrix.

Matrix A Matrix B

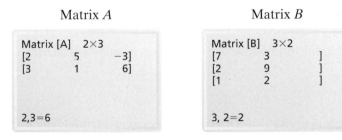

```
Matrix [A]   2×3
[2        5        -3]
[3        1         6]



2,3=6
```

```
Matrix [B]   3×2
[7        3        ]
[2        9        ]
[1        2        ]


3, 2=2
```

Step 2 Use the **NAMES** list on the matrix screen. Select [A]. Then use the name list on the matrix screen to select [B]. Press ENTER. The product matrix will appear on the main screen.

```
[A] [B]
              [[21    45]
               [29    30]]

```

You can use matrices to solve systems of equations. Start with equations in standard form.

System of Equations

$$2x + 6y = 80$$
$$4x + 5y = -1$$

Matrices for the System

$$\underbrace{\begin{bmatrix} 2 & 6 \\ 4 & 5 \end{bmatrix}}_{A} \cdot \underbrace{\begin{bmatrix} x \\ y \end{bmatrix}}_{X} = \underbrace{\begin{bmatrix} 80 \\ -1 \end{bmatrix}}_{B}$$

A is the matrix for the coefficients of the variables, X is a matrix for the variables, and B is a matrix for the constants. To solve the system you must use the inverse of A, which is A^{-1}. The product $A^{-1} \times B$ gives you X.

2 EXAMPLE

Solve the system at the right by using matrix multiplication.

$$2x + 6y = 80$$
$$4x + 5y = -1$$

$A = \begin{bmatrix} 2 & 6 \\ 4 & 5 \end{bmatrix}$ and $B = \begin{bmatrix} 80 \\ -1 \end{bmatrix}$

Step 1

Use the matrix feature. Edit the dimensions and enter the values of the elements for each matrix.

Step 2

Use the matrix feature. Select [A]. Then press $\boxed{x^{-1}}$. $[A]^{-1}$ will appear on the main screen.

Step 3

Use the matrix feature. Select [B]. Then press $\boxed{\text{ENTER}}$.

The values of matrix X will appear as shown at the right.

$\begin{matrix} [[-29] \\ [23]] \end{matrix}$ corresponds to $\begin{bmatrix} x \\ y \end{bmatrix}$, so $x = -29$ and $y = 23$.

● The solution of the system is $(-29, 23)$.

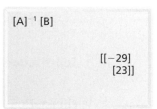

[A]⁻¹[B]

[[−29]
  [23]]

EXERCISES

Find each product.

1. $[4 \quad 2 \quad 9]\begin{bmatrix} 3 \\ 1 \\ 7 \end{bmatrix}$

2. $\begin{bmatrix} 12 & 10 \\ 8 & -11 \end{bmatrix}\begin{bmatrix} 0 & 4 \\ 9 & -1 \end{bmatrix}$

3. $\begin{bmatrix} 44 & -12 \\ 27 & 35 \\ 25 & -16 \end{bmatrix}\begin{bmatrix} 21 & -41 \\ 25 & 17 \end{bmatrix}$

4. The table at the near right shows the number of three sizes of widgets made at a manufacturing plant on Monday and Tuesday. The table at the far right shows the production costs of each widget. Write each table as a matrix. Then multiply to find the total production cost each day.

Number of Widgets

Day	Size A	Size B	Size C
Monday	212	318	175
Tuesday	185	292	221

Cost of Widgets

Cost A	$.96
Cost B	$1.23
Cost C	$1.51

Solve each system using matrix multiplication.

5. $1x + 8y = 16$
$9x + 12y = 66$

6. $29x + 7y = 1012$
$8x - 25y = 737$

7. $76x + 18y = 86$
$189x + 47y = 132$

Applications of Linear Systems

Lesson Preview

What You'll Learn

OBJECTIVE 1 To write systems of linear equations

... And Why

To find average wind speed during an airplane flight, as in Example 3

✓ **Check Skills You'll Need** (For help, go to Lesson 2-5.)

1. Two trains run on parallel tracks. The first train leaves a city $\frac{1}{2}$ hour before the second train. The first train travels at 55 mi/h. The second train travels at 65 mi/h. How long does it take for the second train to pass the first train?

2. Carl drives to the beach at an average speed of 50 mi/h. He returns home on the same road at an average speed of 55 mi/h. The trip home takes 30 min less. What is the distance from his home to the beach?

iText Interactive lesson includes instant self-check, tutorials, and activities.

OBJECTIVE

1 Writing Systems of Linear Equations

Below is a summary of the methods you have used to solve systems of equations. You must choose a method before you solve a word problem.

 Key Concepts

Summary	Methods for Solving Systems of Linear Equations
Graphing	Use graphing for solving systems that are easily graphed. If the point of intersection does not have integers for coordinates, find the exact solution by using one of the methods below or by using a graphing calculator.
Substitution	Use substitution for solving systems when one variable has a coefficient of 1 or -1.
Elimination	Use elimination for solving any system.

Real-World Connection

The melting point of copper is 1083°C.

1 EXAMPLE **Real-World 🌐 Problem Solving**

Metallurgy A metalworker has some ingots of metal alloy that are 20% copper and others that are 60% copper. How many kilograms of each type of ingot should the metalworker combine to create 80 kg of a 52% copper alloy?

Define Let g = the mass of the 20% alloy.
Let h = the mass of the 60% alloy.

Relate mass of alloys   mass of copper

Write $g + h = 80$ $0.2g + 0.6h = 0.52(80)$

Solve using substitution.

Step 1 Choose one of the equations and solve for a variable.

$g + h = 80$ **Solve for g.**

$g = 80 - h$ **Subtract h from each side.**

Step 2 Find h.

$$0.2g + 0.6h = 0.52(80)$$
$$0.2(80 - h) + 0.6h = 0.52(80) \qquad \textbf{Substitute 80 } - \textbf{ } h \textbf{ for } g\textbf{. Use parentheses.}$$
$$16 - 0.2h + 0.6h = 0.52(80) \qquad \textbf{Use the Distributive Property.}$$
$$16 + 0.4h = 41.6 \qquad \textbf{Simplify. Then solve for } h.$$
$$0.4h = 25.6$$
$$h = 64$$

Step 3 Find g. Substitute 64 for h in either equation.

$$g = 80 - 64$$
$$g = 16$$

To make 80 kg of 52% copper alloy, you need 16 kg of 20% copper alloy and 64 kg of 60% copper alloy.

✓ Check Understanding ❶ Suppose you combine ingots of 25% copper alloy and 50% copper alloy to create 40 kg of 45% copper alloy. How many kilograms of each do you need?

Reading Math

In business, the point at which income equals expenses is called the break-even point.

When starting a business, people want to know the *break-even point*, the point at which their income equals their expenses. The graph at the right shows the break-even point for one business.

☐ Lose money ☐ Make money

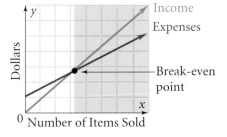

Notice that the values of y on the red line represent dollars spent on expenses, and the values of y on the blue line represent dollars received as income. So y is used to represent both expenses and income.

❷ EXAMPLE   Finding a Break-Even Point

Publishing Suppose a model airplane club publishes a newsletter. Expenses are $.90 for printing and mailing each copy, plus $600 total for research and writing. The price of the newsletter is $1.50 per copy. How many copies of the newsletter must the club sell to break even?

Define Let x = the number of copies.
Let y = the amount of dollars of expenses or income.

Relate Expenses are printing costs   Income is price
plus research and writing.   times copies sold.

Write $y = 0.9x + 600$ $y = 1.5x$

Choose a method to solve this system. Use substitution since it is easy to substitute for y with these equations.

$$y = 0.9x + 600 \qquad \textbf{Start with one equation.}$$
$$1.5x = 0.9x + 600 \qquad \textbf{Substitute 1.5} x \textbf{ for } y.$$
$$0.6x = 600 \qquad \textbf{Solve for } x.$$
$$x = 1000$$

To break even, the model airplane club must sell 1000 copies.

2 Suppose an antique car club publishes a newsletter. Expenses are $.35 for printing and mailing each copy, plus $770 total for research and writing. The price of the newsletter is $.55 per copy. How many copies of the newsletter must the club sell to break even?

Need Help?

rate × time = distance

In Chapter 6, you modeled rate-time-distance problems using one variable. You can also model rate-time-distance problems using two variables. The steady west-to-east winds across the United States act as tail winds for planes traveling from west to east. The tail winds increase a plane's groundspeed. For planes traveling east to west, the head winds decrease a plane's groundspeed.

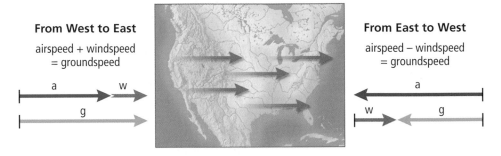

From West to East

airspeed + windspeed
= groundspeed

From East to West

airspeed − windspeed
= groundspeed

3 EXAMPLE **Real-World 🌎 Problem Solving**

Travel Suppose you fly from Miami, Florida, to San Francisco, California. It takes 6.5 hours to fly 2600 miles against a head wind. At the same time, your friend flies from San Francisco to Miami. Her plane travels at the same average airspeed, but her flight only takes 5.2 hours. Find the average airspeed of the planes. Find the average wind speed.

Define Let A = the airspeed. Let W = the wind speed.

Relate with tail wind   with head wind
(rate)(time) = distance   (rate)(time) = distance
$(A + W)$(time) = distance. $(A - W)$(time) = distance.

Write $(A + W)5.2 = 2600$ $(A - W)6.5 = 2600$

Step 1 Divide to get the variables of each equation with coefficients of 1 or −1.
$(A + W)5.2 = 2600 \rightarrow A + W = 500$ **Divide each side by 5.2.**
$(A - W)6.5 = 2600 \rightarrow A - W = 400$ **Divide each side by 6.5.**

Step 2 Eliminate W.
$A + W = 500$
$\underline{A - W = 400}$ **Add the equations to eliminate _W_.**
$2A + 0 = 900$

Step 3 Solve for A.
$A = 450$ **Divide each side by 2.**

Step 4 Solve for W using either of the original equations.
$A + W = 500$ **Use the first equation.**
$450 + W = 500$ **Substitute 450 for _A_.**
$W = 50$ **Solve for _W_.**

● The average airspeed of the planes is 450 mi/h. The average wind speed is 50 mi/h.

✓ **Check Understanding** ❸ A plane takes about 6 hours to fly 2400 miles from New York City to Seattle, Washington. At the same time, your friend flies from Seattle to New York City. His plane travels with the same average airspeed, but his flight takes 5 hours. Find the average airspeed of the planes. Find the average wind speed.

EXERCISES

For more practice, see *Extra Practice*.

Practice and Problem Solving

Ⓐ **Practice by Example**

1. Tyrel and Dalia bought some pens and pencils. Tyrel bought 4 pens and 5 pencils, which cost him $6.71. Dalia bought 5 pens and 3 pencils, which cost her $7.12. Let *a* equal the price of a pen. Let *b* equal the price of a pencil.
   a. Write an equation that relates the number of pens and pencils Tyrel bought to the amount he paid for them.
   b. Write an equation that relates the number of pens and pencils Dalia bought to the amount she paid for them.
   c. Solve the system you wrote for parts (a) and (b) to find the price of a pen and the price of a pencil.

Example 1
(page 362)

2. Suppose you have just enough money, in coins, to pay for a loaf of bread priced at $1.95. You have 12 coins, all quarter and dimes. Let *q* equal the number of quarters and *d* equal the number of dimes. Which system models the given information?
   A. $q + d = 12$ **B.** $25q + 10d = 195$
       $q + d = 1.95$ $q + 12 = d$
   C. $10q + 25d = 12$ **D.** $q + d = 12$
       $q + d = 1.95$ $25q + 10d = 195$

3. Suppose you want to combine two types of fruit drink to create 24 kilograms of a drink that will be 5% sugar by weight. Fruit drink A is 4% sugar by weight, and fruit drink B is 8% sugar by weight.
   a. Copy and complete the table below.

	Fruit Drink A 4% Sugar	Fruit Drink B 8% Sugar	Mixed Fruit Drink 5% Sugar
Fruit Drink (kg)	■	■	■
Sugar (kg)	■	■	■

   b. Write a system of equations that relates the amounts of fruit drink A and fruit drink B to the total amount of drink needed and to the total amount of sugar needed.
   c. Solve the system to find how much of each type of fruit drink you need to use.

4. You have $22 in your bank account and deposit $11.50 each week. At the same time your cousin has $218 but is withdrawing $13 each week.
   a. When will your accounts have the same balance?
   b. How much money will each of you have after 12 weeks?

Example 2
(page 363)

5. Business Suppose you invest $10,410 in equipment to manufacture a new board game. Each game costs $2.65 to manufacture and sells for $20. How many games must you make and sell before your business breaks even?

6. Business Several students decide to start a T-shirt company. After initial expenses of $280, they purchase each T-shirt wholesale for $3.99. They sell each T-shirt for $10.99. How many must they sell to break even?

Example 3
(page 364)

7. Travel A family is canoeing downstream (with the current). Their speed relative to the banks of the river averages 2.75 mi/h. During the return trip, they paddle upstream (against the current), averaging 1.5 mi/h relative to the riverbank.
 a. Write an equation for the rate of the canoe downstream.
 b. Write an equation for the rate of the canoe upstream.
 c. Solve the system to find the family's paddling speed in still water.
 d. Find the speed of the current of the river.

8. Travel John flies from Atlanta, Georgia, to San Francisco, California. It takes 5.6 hours to travel 2100 miles against the head wind. At the same time Debby flies from San Francisco to Atlanta. Her plane travels with the same average airspeed but, with a tail wind, her flight takes only 4.8 hours.
 a. Write a system of equations that relates time, airspeed, and wind speed to distance for each traveler.
 b. Solve the system to find the airspeed.
 c. Find the wind speed.

B Apply Your Skills

Open-Ended **Without solving, what method would you choose to solve each system: *graphing*, *substitution*, or *elimination*? Explain your reasoning.**

9. $4s - 3t = 8$
  $t = -2s - 1$

10. $y = 3x - 1$
  $y = 4x$

11. $3m - 4n = 1$
  $3m - 2n = -1$

12. $y = -2x$
  $y = -\frac{1}{2}x + 3$

13. $2x - y = 4$
  $x + 3y = 16$

14. $u = 4v$
  $3u - 2v = 7$

15. Chemistry A piece of glass with an initial temperature of 99°C is cooled at a rate of 3.5 degrees Celsius per minute (°C/min). At the same time, a piece of copper with an initial temperature of 0°C is heated at a rate of 2.5°C/min. Let m = the number of minutes, and t = the temperature in degrees Celsius after m minutes.
 a. Write a system of equations that relates the temperature t of each material to the time m. Solve the system.
 b. Writing Explain what the solution means in this situation.

16. Geometry The perimeter of the rectangle is 34 cm. The perimeter of the triangle is 30 cm. Find the values of m and n.

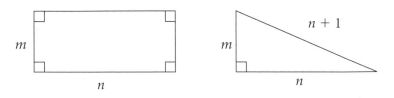

Real-World Connection

Glass can be drawn into optical fibers 16 km long. One fiber can carry 20 times as many phone calls as 500 copper wires.

17. Open-Ended Write a problem for the total of two types of coins. Then solve the problem.

18. Sales A garden supply store sells two types of lawn mowers. Total sales of mowers for the year were $8379.70. The total number of mowers sold was 30. The small mower costs $249.99. The large mower costs $329.99. Find the number sold of each type of mower.

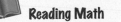

Reading Math

For help reading and solving Exercise 18, see page 369.

19. Aviation Suppose you are flying an ultralight aircraft like the one pictured at the left. You fly to a nearby town, 18 miles away. With a tail wind, the trip takes $\frac{1}{3}$ hour. Your return flight with a head wind takes $\frac{3}{5}$ hour.
a. Find the average airspeed of the ultralight aircraft.
b. Find the average wind speed.

Real-World Connection

Ultralight aircraft like the one pictured above can weigh less than 400 lb.

20. Suppose the ratio of girls to boys in your school is 19 : 17. There are 1908 students altogether.
a. Solve the proportion $\frac{g}{b} = \frac{19}{17}$ for g.
b. Write and solve the system of equations to find the total number of boys b and girls g.

21. Consumer Decisions Suppose you are trying to decide whether to buy ski equipment. Typically, it costs you $60 a day to rent ski equipment and buy a lift ticket. You can buy ski equipment for about $400. A lift ticket alone costs $35 for one day.
a. Find the break-even point.
b. **Critical Thinking** If you expect to ski five days a year, should you buy the ski equipment? Explain.

22. Geometry Find the values of x and y.

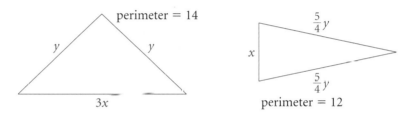

Challenge

23. You can represent the value of any two-digit number with the expression $10a + b$, where a is the tens' place digit and b is the ones' place digit. If a is 5 and b is 7, then the value of the number is $10(5) + 7$, or 57.
Use a system of equations to find the two-digit number described below.

• The ones' place digit is one more than twice the tens' place digit.
• The value of the number is two more than five times the ones' place digit.

24. Sales An artist sells original hand-painted greeting cards. He makes $2.50 profit on a small card and $4.00 profit on a large card. He generally sells 5 large cards for every 2 small cards. He wants a profit of $10,000 from large and small cards this year.
a. Find the quantity of each card the artist needs to sell to reach his goal.
b. The artist can create a card every 12 minutes. How many hours will he need to make enough to reach his profit target if he sells them all?
c. What is the artist's hourly rate of pay?

Standardized Test Prep

Multiple Choice

25. Which system describes the following situation: The sum of two numbers is 20. The difference between three times the larger and twice the smaller is 40.
A. $x + y = 20$
$3x + 2y = 40$

B. $x - y = 20$
$3x - 2y = 40$

C. $x + y = 20$
$3x - 2y = 40$

D. $x - y = 20$
$3x + 2y = 40$

26. The federal tax on a $12,000 salary was 8 times the state tax. If the combined taxes were $2700, find the state's share of taxes.
    F. $400   G. $150
    H. $300   I. $350

27. Which system describes the following situation? Craig has 80¢ in nickels n and dimes d. He has four more nickels than dimes.
    A. $d + n = 4$ B. $n - d = 4$
       $10d + 5n = 80$ $10d + 5n = 80$
    C. $d - n = 4$ D. $d + n = 4$
       $10d + 5n = 80$ $10d - 5n = 80$

Short Response

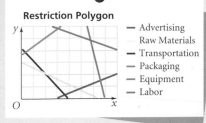

Take It to the NET
Online lesson quiz at
www.PHSchool.com
Web Code: aea-0704

28. A large group of students wants to go to the movies. If the students take 3 vans and 1 car, they can transport 22 people. If they take 2 vans and 4 cars, they can transport 28 people. Write and solve a system of equations to find the number of people that can be transported in a van. Show your work.

Mixed Review

Lesson 7-3   **Solve by elimination.**

29. $2x + 5y = 13$ 30. $4x + 2y = -10$ 31. $7x + 6y = 30$
    $3x - 5y = 7$ $-2x + 3y = 33$ $9x - 8y = 15$

Lesson 6-1   **Find the slope of the line that passes through each pair of points.**

32. $(2, 4), (6, 10)$ 33. $(-3, 1), (10, 14)$ 34. $(8, -11), (5, -12)$

35. $(1.2, 7), (4.6, 0.2)$ 36. $\left(5, -\frac{1}{2}\right), \left(-6, 3\frac{1}{2}\right)$ 37. $(8, 0), (8, 5)$

Lesson 3-5   **Solve each inequality and graph the solutions.**

38. $6 < y < 10$ 39. $-8 < n \le 3$ 40. $2 < k + 1 < 7$

41. $4 \le 4p \le 16$ 42. $-13 < 3c + 2 \le 17$ 43. $21 > 5w - 4 > 1$

Algebra at Work

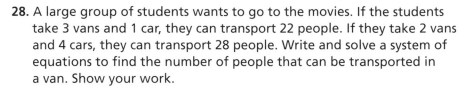

Businessperson

Some of the goals of a business are to minimize costs and maximize profits. People in business use systems of linear inequalities to analyze data in order to achieve these goals.

The illustration lists some of the variables involved in operating a small manufacturing company. To solve a problem, a businessperson must identify the variables and restrictions, and then search for the best of many possible solutions.

Restriction Polygon
— Advertising
— Raw Materials
— Transportation
— Packaging
— Equipment
— Labor

Take It to the NET For more information about a career in business, go to **www.PHSchool.com**.
Web Code: aeb-2031

Read the exercise below and then follow along with what Bill thinks and writes. Check your understanding by solving the exercise at the bottom of the page.

A garden supply store sells two types of lawn mowers. Total sales of mowers for the year were $8379.70. The total number of mowers sold was 30. The small mowers cost $249.99. The large mowers cost $329.99. Find the number of each type of mower sold.

What Bill Thinks

I'll read the problem and write down the important information.

Where should I start? Well, it's always helpful to write sentences based on the information I'm given. Total sales include the sales for both the small mowers and the large mowers.

Total number of mowers is the number of small mowers *plus* the number of large mowers.

Now I'll define some variables. The problem asks for the number of small mowers and the number of large mowers. I'll use 2 variables.

Now I can write 2 equations.

Since the first equation has large numbers, it's probably easier to rewrite the second equation and substitute into the first equation. I'll then solve for *w* and *s*.

I'll write my answer in a sentence.

What Bill Writes

Total sales = $8379.70
Total number of mowers = 30
Small mowers cost $249.99.
Large mowers cost $329.99.

Total sales = sales from small mowers + sales from large mowers

Total number of mowers = number of small mowers + number of large mowers

Number of small mowers = s
Number of large mowers = w

Total sales: $8379.70 = 249.99s + 329.99w$
Total number: $30 = s + w$

$s = 30 - w$
$8379.70 = (249.99)(30 - w) + 329.99w$
$8379.70 = 7499.70 + 80w$
$880 = 80w$
$11 = w; s = 30 - 11 = 19$

The store sold 19 small mowers and 11 large mowers.

EXERCISE

A nursery sells small apple trees for $19.99 and large apple trees for $35.99. Total sales for the year were $1907.27. The total number of apple trees sold was 73. Find the number of each type of apple tree sold.

Linear Inequalities

Lesson Preview

What You'll Learn

OBJECTIVE 1 To graph linear inequalities

OBJECTIVE 2 To write and use linear inequalities when modeling real-world situations

. . . And Why

To analyze possible purchases within a budget, as in Example 3

✓ **Check Skills You'll Need** (For help, go to Lessons 3-1 and 6-2.)

Describe each statement as *always*, *sometimes*, or *never* true.

1. $-3 > -2$ **2.** $8 \leq 8$ **3.** $4n \geq n$

Write each equation in slope-intercept form.

4. $2x - 3y = 9$ **5.** $y + 3x = 6$ **6.** $4y - 3x = 1$

New Vocabulary • linear inequality • solutions of an inequality

---

OBJECTIVE

1 **Graphing Linear Inequalities**

iTEXT Interactive lesson includes instant self-check, tutorials, and activities.

Investigation: Graphing Inequalities

1. Graph $y = x + 4$ on a coordinate plane.

2. Test three points that lie above the graph of $y = x + 4$. Substitute the coordinates of each of the points for (x, y) in the inequality $y > x + 4$. If the results are true statements, mark the points on your graph.

3. Test three points that lie below the graph of $y = x + 4$. Substitute the coordinates of each of the points for (x, y) in the inequality $y > x + 4$. If the results are true statements, mark the points on your graph.

4. Critical Thinking To graph $y > x + 4$, would you choose points above or below $y = x + 4$?

5. Determine whether you would graph points above or below the graph of $y = x - 2$ to graph the inequality $y < x - 2$.

Just as you have used inequalities to describe graphs on a number line, you can use inequalities to describe regions of a coordinate plane.

? Need Help?

To review graphing inequalities in one variable see p. 135.

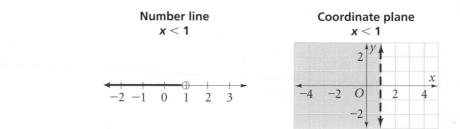

Number line
$x < 1$

Coordinate plane
$x < 1$

A **linear inequality** describes a region of the coordinate plane that has a boundary line. The **solutions of an inequality** are the coordinates of the points that make the inequality true.

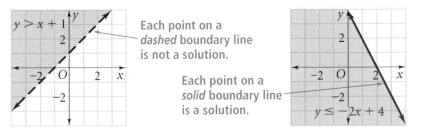

Each point on a *dashed* boundary line is not a solution.

Each point on a *solid* boundary line is a solution.

As you can see in the graphs above, you can tell from an inequality whether to shade above or below the boundary line. For an inequality written in the form of $y <$ or $y \leq$, shade below the boundary line. For an inequality written in the form of $y >$ or $y \geq$, shade above the boundary line.

1 EXAMPLE Graphing an Inequality

Graph $y < 2x + 3$.

First graph the boundary line $y = 2x + 3$.

The coordinates of points on the boundary line do not make the inequality true. So, use a dashed line.

Shade below the boundary line.

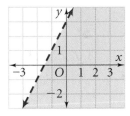

Check The point $(0, 0)$ is in the region of the graph of the inequality. See if $(0, 0)$ satisfies the inequality.

$y < 2x + 3$

$0 < 2(0) + 3$ **Substitute (0, 0) for (x, y).**

$0 < 3$ ✓

✓ **Check Understanding** ❶ Graph $y \geq 3x - 1$.

In order to tell whether you shade above or below a boundary line, you may need to write the inequality in slope-intercept form.

2 EXAMPLE Rewriting to Graph an Inequality

Graph $3x - 5y \leq 10$.

Solve $3x - 5y \leq 10$ for y.

$3x - 5y \leq 10$

$\qquad -5y \leq -3x + 10$ **Subtract 3x from each side.**

$\qquad y \geq \frac{3}{5}x - 2$ **Divide each side by −5. Reverse the inequality symbol.**

Graph $y = \frac{3}{5}x - 2$.

The coordinates of points on the boundary line make the inequality true. So, use a solid line.

Since $y \geq \frac{3}{5}x - 2$, shade above the boundary line.

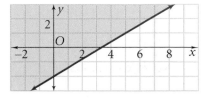

> **Need Help?**
>
> Multiplying or dividing an inequality by a negative number reverses the order of the inequality.

✓ **Check Understanding** ❷ Graph $6x + 8y \geq 12$.

Many situations are modeled by inequalities that have a boundary line of the form $Ax + By = C$. You can use the intercepts to graph the boundary line of the inequality. Choose a test point such as $(0, 0)$ to determine whether the solutions are above or below the boundary line.

3 **EXAMPLE** <u>Real-World</u> **Problem Solving**

Budget Suppose your budget for a party allows you to spend no more than $12 on peanuts and cashews. Peanuts cost $2/lb and cashews cost $4/lb. Find three possible combinations of peanuts and cashews you can buy.

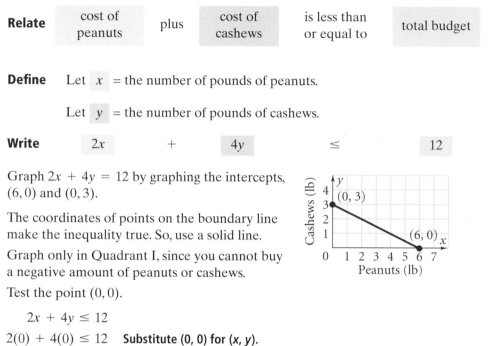

| **Relate** | cost of peanuts | plus | cost of cashews | is less than or equal to | total budget |

Define Let x = the number of pounds of peanuts.

Let y = the number of pounds of cashews.

Write $2x$ $+$ $4y$ $\leq$ 12

Graph $2x + 4y = 12$ by graphing the intercepts, $(6, 0)$ and $(0, 3)$.

The coordinates of points on the boundary line make the inequality true. So, use a solid line.

Graph only in Quadrant I, since you cannot buy a negative amount of peanuts or cashews.

Test the point $(0, 0)$.

$2x + 4y \leq 12$

$2(0) + 4(0) \leq 12$ **Substitute (0, 0) for (x, y).**

$0 \leq 12$ **Since the inequality is true, (0, 0) is a solution.**

Shade the region containing $(0, 0)$. The graph below shows all the possible solutions of the problem.

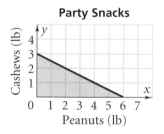

Party Snacks

Since the boundary line is included in the graph, the intercepts are also solutions of the inequality. The solution $(2, 2)$ means that if you buy 2 lb of peanuts, you can buy 2 lb of cashews. Three solutions are $(2, 2)$, $(3, 1)$, and $(1, 2)$.

Real-World Connection

One ounce of peanuts has 9 g of protein. One ounce of cashews has 5.4 g of protein.

✔ **Check Understanding** **3** **Cooking** Suppose you plan to spend no more than $24 on meat for a cookout. At your local market, hamburger costs $3.00/lb and chicken wings cost $2.40/lb. Find three possible combinations of hamburger and chicken you can buy.

For more practice, see *Extra Practice*.

Practice and Problem Solving

 Practice by Example

Example 1
(page 371)

Determine whether point *P* is a solution of the linear inequality.

1. $y \leq -2x + 1; P(2, 2)$ **2.** $x < 2; P(1, 0)$ **3.** $y \geq 3x - 2; P(0, 0)$

4. $y > x - 1; P(0, 1)$ **5.** $y \geq -\frac{2}{5}x + 4; P(0, 0)$ **6.** $y > \frac{5}{3}x - 4; P(0, 1)$

Choose the linear inequality that describes each graph.

7.

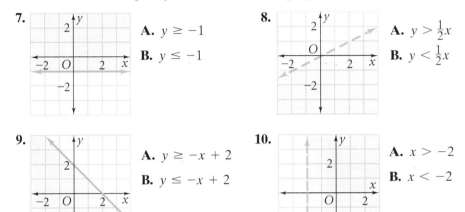

A. $y \geq -1$

B. $y \leq -1$

8.

A. $y > \frac{1}{2}x$

B. $y < \frac{1}{2}x$

9.

A. $y \geq -x + 2$

B. $y \leq -x + 2$

10.

A. $x > -2$

B. $x < -2$

Graph each linear inequality.

11. $y \leq \frac{1}{4}x - 1$ **12.** $y \geq \frac{1}{4}x - 1$ **13.** $y < -4x - 1$ **14.** $y \geq 4x - 1$

15. $y < 5x - 5$ **16.** $y \leq \frac{2}{5}x - 3$ **17.** $y \leq -3x$ **18.** $y \geq -\frac{1}{2}x$

Example 2
(page 371)

Write each linear inequality in slope-intercept form. Then graph the inequality.

19. $2x - 3y \geq 7$ **20.** $5x - 3y \leq 6$ **21.** $4x - 6y \geq 16$ **22.** $-4y - 6x > 8$

Example 3
(page 372)

23. Budget Suppose you are shopping for crepe paper to decorate the school gym for a dance. Gold crepe paper costs $5 per roll, and blue crepe paper costs $3 per roll. Your budget allows you to spend at most $48 for crepe paper. How many rolls of gold and blue crepe paper can you buy without exceeding your budget?

Let x = the number of rolls of blue crepe paper.
Let y = the number of rolls of gold crepe paper.

a. Write a linear inequality that describes the situation.
b. Graph the linear inequality.
c. Write three possible solutions to the problem.
d. Critical Thinking The point $(-2, 5)$ is a solution of the inequality. Is it a solution of the problem? Explain.

Real-World 🌐 **Connection**

The American Academy of Orthopaedic Surgeons suggest that a backpack's weight should not be more than 20% of a student's body weight.

24. Manufacturing A company makes nylon and canvas backpacks, as shown at the left. The profit on a nylon backpack is $3 and the profit on a canvas backpack is $10. How many backpacks must the company sell to make a profit of more than $250?

a. Write a linear inequality that describes the situation.
b. Graph the linear inequality.
c. Write three possible solutions to the problem.
d. Critical Thinking Which values are reasonable for the domain and for the range? Explain.

Graph each linear inequality.

25. $y \leq \frac{2}{5}x + 2$ **26.** $y \geq -\frac{2}{5}x + 2$ **27.** $4x - 5y \leq 10$ **28.** $4x + 5y \leq 10$

29. $4y < 6x + 2$ **30.** $2x + 3y \leq 6$ **31.** $4x - 4y \leq 8$ **32.** $y - 2x < 2$

33. Writing Explain how you can tell from a linear inequality whether you will shade above or below the graph of the boundary line.

Write the inequality shown in each graph.

34. **35.** **36.**

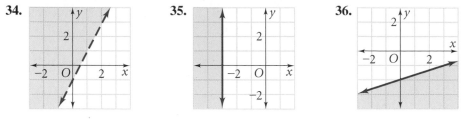

Real-World Connection

In 2000, there were about 12,900 licensed radio stations in the United States.

37. Budget Suppose you work at a local radio station. You are in charge of a $180 budget for new tapes and CDs. Record companies will give you 21 promotional (free) CDs. You can buy tapes for $8 and CDs for $12.

　Let $x =$ the number of CDs you buy.
　Let $y =$ the number of tapes you buy.

　a. Write an inequality that shows the number of tapes and CDs you can buy.
　b. Graph the inequality.
　c. Is $(8, 9)$ a solution of the inequality? Explain what the solution means.
　d. If you buy only tapes and you buy as many as possible, how many new recordings will the station get?

Write the linear inequality described. Then graph the inequality.

38. x is positive.　　　　　　　　　　　**39.** y is negative.

40. y is not negative.　　　　　　　　　**41.** x is less than y.

42. Error Analysis Jan's graph of the inequality $4x + 6y > 12$ is shown below. What is wrong with the graph?

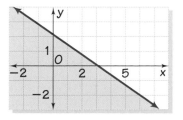

43. Critical Thinking Write an inequality that describes the entire part of the coordinate plane *not* included in the solution of $y \geq x + 2$.

44. Probability Suppose you play a carnival game. You toss one blue and one red number cube. If the number on the blue cube is greater than the number on the red cube, you win a prize. The graph at the left shows all the possible outcomes of tossing the cubes.

　a. Copy and shade the graph to show the winning outcomes.
　b. Write an inequality that describes the shaded region.
　c. What is the probability that you will win a prize?

Comparing Cubes

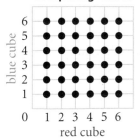

45. Geometry You want to fence a rectangular area of your yard for a garden. You plan to use no more than 50 ft of fencing.
  a. Write and graph a linear inequality that describes this situation.
  b. Open-Ended What are two possible sizes for a square garden?
  c. Can you make the garden 12 ft by 15 ft? Justify your answer.

C Challenge

For Exercises 46–47, write the inequality that has the solution described.

46. The points $(0, -3)$ and $(8, 5)$ lie on the boundary line, but neither point is a solution. The point $(1, 1)$ is not a solution.

47. The points $(7, 12)$ and $(-3, -8)$ lie on the boundary line, and each point is a solution. The point $(1, 1)$ is also a solution.

48. a. Open-Ended Write and graph an inequality in the form $Ax + By > C$, where $A, B,$ and C are all positive.
  b. Write and graph an inequality in the form $Ax + By < C$, where $A, B,$ and C are all positive.
  c. Reasoning Both inequalities are in standard form. Make a conjecture about the inequality symbol and the region shaded.
  d. Would your conjecture in part (c) be different if B were negative?

49. a. Is the point $(4, 5)$ a solution of the inequality $y > x - 1$?
  b. Is the point $(4, 5)$ a solution of the inequality $y < 3x$?
  c. Find one other point that is a solution of both inequalities.
  d. Draw a graph that shows all the points that are solutions of both inequalities.

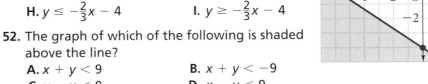

Standardized Test Prep

Multiple Choice

50. Which of the following is true of the graph of $y \geq -x + 1$?
  A. The line is solid, and the shading is above the line.
  B. The line is dashed, and the shading is above the line.
  C. The line is solid, and the shading is below the line.
  D. The line is dashed, and the shading is below the line.

51. Which linear inequality describes the graph at the right?
  F. $y < -\frac{2}{3}x - 4$ **G.** $y > -\frac{2}{3}x - 4$
  H. $y \leq -\frac{2}{3}x - 4$ **I.** $y \geq -\frac{2}{3}x - 4$

52. The graph of which of the following is shaded above the line?
  A. $x + y < 9$ **B.** $x + y < -9$
  C. $y - x < 9$ **D.** $x - y < 9$

53. Which inequality below models the following situation?

You want to spend less than $20 on asparagus and bananas. Asparagus is $3.00 per pound and bananas are $.50 per pound. Let a represent the weight of the asparagus and b represent the weight of the bananas.

  F. $3a + 0.5b < 20$ **G.** $3a + 0.5b > 20$
  H. $3a + 0.5b \leq 20$ **I.** $3a + 0.5b \geq 20$

Take It to the NET
Online lesson quiz at
www.PHSchool.com
········ Web Code: aea-0705

Short Response

54. Explain how to graph $y \leq 3x - 4$. Then graph the inequality.

Lesson 7-4   **For Exercises 55–56, define the variables and write a system of equations for each situation. Solve by any method.**

🌎 **55. Business** Suppose you invest $12,000 in equipment to manufacture a new board game. Each game costs $2.50 to manufacture and sells for $18. How many games must you make and sell for your business to break even?

56. Suppose you are canoeing along a river with a steady current. Your average speed upstream is 2.5 mi/h. On the return trip you paddle with the current, and your average speed is 4 mi/h. Find the average speed of the current and your average speed if you were paddling in still water.

Lesson 5-6   **Find the common difference of each arithmetic sequence.**

57. $-8, -3, 2, \ldots$ **58.** $4, 11, 18, \ldots$ **59.** $13, 24, 35, \ldots$ **60.** $11, 5, -1, \ldots$

Find the second and fourth terms of each sequence.

61. $A(n) = 3 + (n - 1)(5)$ **62.** $A(n) = -9 + (n - 1)(2.3)$

Lesson 4-1   **Solve each proportion.**

63. $\frac{3}{4} = \frac{m}{16}$ **64.** $\frac{6}{7} = \frac{24}{8}$ **65.** $\frac{4}{w} = \frac{8}{22}$ **66.** $\frac{9}{10} = \frac{15}{a}$

67. $\frac{x + 1}{3} = \frac{2}{9}$ **68.** $\frac{n - 2}{5} = \frac{6}{15}$ **69.** $\frac{8}{r + 1} = \frac{4}{7}$ **70.** $\frac{9}{x + 3} = \frac{18}{19}$

✓ **Checkpoint Quiz 2**   **Lessons 7-3 through 7-5**

iTEXT Instant self-check quiz online and on CD-ROM

For Exercises 1–5, solve each system using elimination.

1. $2x + 5y = 2$
   $3x - 5y = 53$

2. $-8x - 3y = 69$
   $8x + 7y = -65$

3. $4x + 2y = 34$
   $10x - 4y = -5$

4. $11x - 13y = 89$
   $-11x + 13y = 107$

5. $3x + 6y = 42$
   $-7x + 8y = -109$

6. You have a total of 21 coins, all nickels and dimes. The total value is $1.70. Write and solve a system of equations to find the number of dimes d and the number of nickels n that you have.

🌎 **7. Business** Suppose you start an ice cream business. You buy a freezer for $200. It costs you $.35 to make each single-scoop ice cream cone. You sell each cone for $1.20. Write and solve a system of equations to find the break-even point for your business.

8. To go to a campsite 12 miles away, you paddle a canoe against the current of a river for 4 hours. During your return trip you paddle with the current, and you travel the same distance in 3 hours. Write and solve a system of equations to find your paddling speed in still water. Find the speed of the current of the river.

Graph each inequality.

9. $y \geq 2x - 4$ **10.** $3x + 4y < 18$

Systems of Linear Inequalities

Lesson Preview

What You'll Learn

OBJECTIVE 1
To solve systems of linear inequalities by graphing

OBJECTIVE 2
To model real-world situations using systems of linear inequalities

. . . And Why

To find the possible dimensions for a zoo habitat, as in Example 3

✓ Check Skills You'll Need

(For help, go to Lessons 7-1 and 7-5.)

Solve each system by graphing.

1. $y = 3x - 6$
$y = -x + 2$

2. $y = -\frac{1}{2}x + 4$
$y = -\frac{1}{2}x + 3$

3. $x + y = 4$
$2x - y = 8$

Graph each inequality.

4. $y > 5$

5. $y \leq \frac{2}{3}x - 1$

6. $4x - 8y \geq 4$

New Vocabulary

• system of linear inequalities
• solution of a system of linear inequalities

OBJECTIVE 1

TEXT Interactive lesson includes instant self-check, tutorials, and activities.

Solving Systems of Linear Inequalities by Graphing

Two or more linear inequalities together form a **system of linear inequalities.** The system below describes the lavender-shaded region of the graph. Notice that there are two boundary lines.

System of Linear Inequalities

$x \geq 3$
$y < -2$

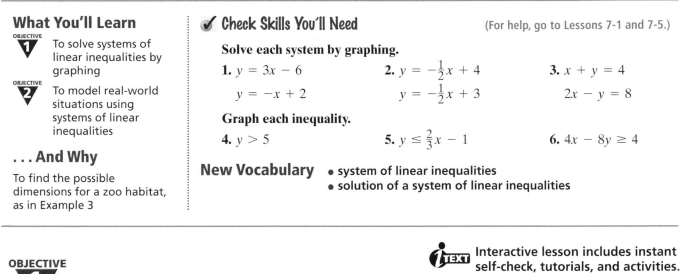

You can describe all the points of a quadrant with a system of linear inequalities.

$x < 0$
$y > 0$

$x > 0$
$y > 0$

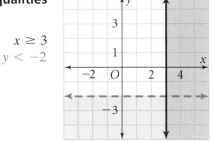

$x < 0$
$y < 0$

$x > 0$
$y < 0$

A **solution of a system of linear inequalities** makes each inequality in the system true. The graph of a system shows all of its solutions.

1 EXAMPLE Graphing a System of Inequalities

Solve by graphing.　$y > 2x - 5$
$3x + 4y < 12$

Graph $y > 2x - 5$ and $3x + 4y < 12$.

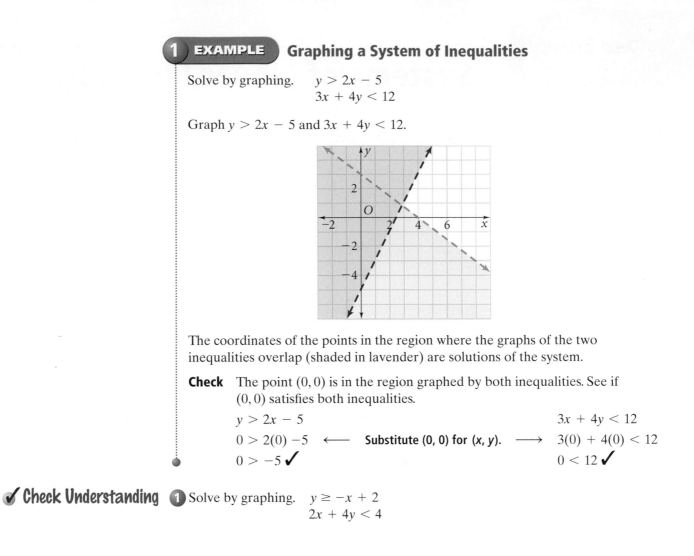

The coordinates of the points in the region where the graphs of the two inequalities overlap (shaded in lavender) are solutions of the system.

Check　The point $(0, 0)$ is in the region graphed by both inequalities. See if $(0, 0)$ satisfies both inequalities.

$y > 2x - 5$ 　　　　　　　　　　　　　　　　　 $3x + 4y < 12$

$0 > 2(0) - 5$　$\longleftarrow$　**Substitute (0, 0) for (x, y).**　$\longrightarrow$　$3(0) + 4(0) < 12$

$0 > -5$ ✓ 　　　　　　　　　　　　　　　　　　 $0 < 12$ ✓

✓ **Check Understanding**　**1** Solve by graphing.　$y \geq -x + 2$
$2x + 4y < 4$

You can combine your knowledge of linear equations with your knowledge of inequalities to describe a graph using a system of inequalities.

2 EXAMPLE Writing a System of Inequalities From a Graph

Write a system of inequalities from each shaded region below.

red region

boundary: $y = x - 2$

The region lies above the boundary line, so the inequality is $y > x - 2$.

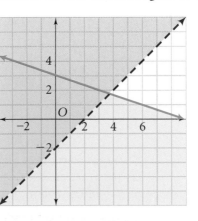

blue region

boundary: $y = -\frac{1}{3}x + 3$

The region includes the boundary line and the points lying below the boundary line, so the inequality is $y \leq -\frac{1}{3}x + 3$.

system for the lavender region:　$y > x - 2$
$y \leq -\frac{1}{3}x + 3$

✓ **Check Understanding** ② Write a system of inequalities for the lavender region in each of the following graphs.

a.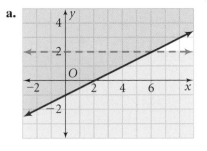

b.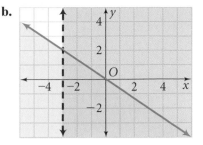

2 Writing and Using Systems of Linear Inequalities

You can model some real-world situations by graphing linear inequalities. When you graph real-world situations, you often need to plan how you will scale each axis. Use the values for the x- and y-intercepts to determine your scale.

③ **EXAMPLE** Real-World 🌎 Problem Solving

Animal Habitat A zoo keeper wants to fence a rectangular habitat for goats. The length of the habitat should be at least 80 ft, and the distance around it should be no more than 310 ft. What are the possible dimensions of the habitat?

Relate | the length | is at least | 80 ft | | the perimeter | is no more than | 310 ft |

Define Let x = width of the habitat.
Let y = length of the habitat.

Write | y | $\geq$ | 80 | | $2x + 2y$ | $\leq$ | 310 |

Solve by graphing. $y \geq 80$
$2x + 2y \leq 310$.

Real-World 🌎 Connection

Careers A zoologist studies individual animals and the processes that sustain an animal within its group and its environment. To adapt an animal to a zoo habitat, a zoologist must research ways to help an animal adapt to a restricted environment.

$y \geq 80$
$m = 0$
$b = 80$

Shade above
$y = 80$.

Size of Goat Pen

$2x + 2y \leq 310$

Graph the intercepts
$(155, 0)$ and $(0, 155)$.

Test $(0, 0)$.
$2(0) + 2(0) \leq 310$
$0 \leq 310$

Shade below
$2x + 2y = 310$.

The solutions are the coordinates of the points that lie in the region shaded lavender and on the parts of the lines $y = 80$ and $2x + 2y = 310$ that border the lavender region.

✓ **Check Understanding** ③ Suppose you want to fence a rectangular garden plot. You want the length of the garden to be at least 50 ft and the perimeter to be no more than 140 ft. Solve by graphing to show all of the possible dimensions of the garden.

Some real-world situations have a domain and range that include only integers. In such cases, the solutions will be some, but not all, of the points in the region included in the graphs of both inequalities.

4 EXAMPLE Real-World 🌐 Problem Solving

Mailing Packages Suppose you need $2.40 in postage to mail a package to a friend. You have 9 stamps, some 20¢ and some 34¢. How many of each do you need to mail the package?

Relate | the number of 20¢ and 34¢ stamps | is less than or equal to | 9 | | the value of 20¢ and 34¢ stamps | is at least | 240¢ |

Define Let a = the number of 20¢ stamps.
Let b = the number of 34¢ stamps.

Write $a + b$ $\leq$ 9 $20a + 34b$ $\geq$ 240

Solve by graphing.
$a + b \leq 9$
$20a + 34b \geq 240$

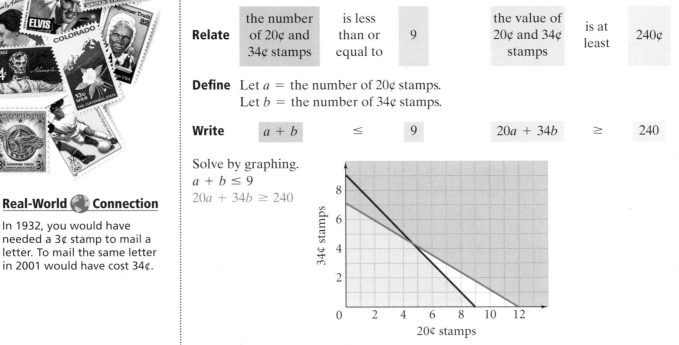

34¢ stamps (vertical axis)
20¢ stamps (horizontal axis)

The solutions are all of the coordinates of points that are nonnegative integers lying in the region shaded lavender and on its boundary lines.

✓ **Check Understanding**   **4**   **a.** Give two solutions from the graph in Example 4.
b. Does either solution give you the exact postage needed to mail the package?
c. Critical Thinking Why are the solutions to the problem only nonnegative integers?

EXERCISES

For more practice, see *Extra Practice*.

Practice and Problem Solving

A **Practice by Example**

Example 1
(page 378)

Is the given ordered pair a solution of the system?

1. $(1, 19)$
$y \leq 7x - 13$
$y > 3x + 6$

2. $(4, 10)$
$9x - y \geq 23$
$5x + 0.2y \geq 20$

3. $(-2, 40)$
$y > -13x + 29$
$y \leq 9x + 11$

Solve each system by graphing.

4. $y < 2x + 4$
$-3x - 2y \geq 6$

5. $y < 2x + 4$
$2x - y \leq 4$

6. $y > 2x + 4$
$2x - y \leq 4$

7. $y > \frac{1}{4}x$
$y \leq -x + 4$

8. $y < 2x - 3$
$y > 5$

9. $y \leq -\frac{1}{3}x + 7$
$y \geq -x + 1$

10. $x + 2y \le 10$
    $x + 2y \ge 9$

11. $y \ge -x + 5$
    $y \le 3x - 4$

12. $y \le 0.75x - 2$
    $y > 0.75x - 3$

13. $8x + 4y \ge 10$
    $3x - 6y > 12$

14. $2x - \frac{1}{4}y < 1$
    $4x + 8y > 4$

15. $6x - 5y < 15$
    $x + 2y \ge 7$

Example 2
(page 378)

Write a system of inequalities for each graph.

16.

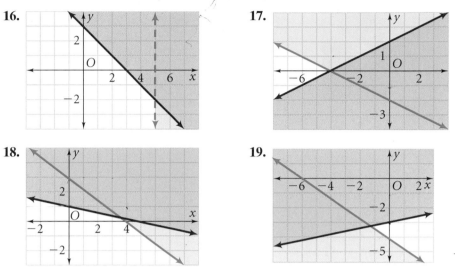

17.

18.

19.

Example 3
(page 379)

20. Budget Suppose you buy flour and cornmeal in bulk to make flour tortillas and corn tortillas. Flour costs $1.50/lb. Cornmeal costs $2.50/lb. You want to spend less than $9.50 on flour and cornmeal, and you need at least 4 lb altogether.
  a. Write a system of inequalities that describes this situation.
  b. Graph the system to show all possible solutions.

21. Suppose you want to fence a rectangular area for your dog. You will use the house as one of the four sides. Since the house is 40 ft wide, the length ℓ needs to be no more than 40 ft. You plan to use at least 150 ft of fencing. Graph the following system to find possible dimensions for the rectangle.

$$\ell \le 40$$
$$\ell + 2w \ge 150$$

Example 4
(page 380)

22. Suppose you receive a $50 gift certificate to the Cityside Music and Books store. All CDs at the store cost $9.99, and all books cost $5.99. You want to buy some books and at least one CD.
  a. Write a system of inequalities for x books and y CDs that describes this situation.
  b. Graph the system to show all possible solutions.
  c. What purchase does the ordered pair $(2, 6)$ represent? Is it a solution to your system? Explain.
  d. Find a solution in which you spend almost all of the gift certificate.

Perch $4.00/lb

Salmon $3.00/lb

23. Business A seafood restaurant owner orders perch and salmon. He wants to buy at least 50 pounds of fish but cannot spend more than $180. Write and graph a system of inequalities to show the possible combinations of perch and salmon he could buy.

24. Earnings Suppose you have a job in an ice cream shop that pays $6 per hour. You also have a babysitting job that pays $4 per hour. You want to earn at least $60 per week but would like to work no more than 12 hours per week.
 a. Graph and write a system of linear inequalities that describes this situation.
 b. Give three possible solutions to the system.

Write a system of inequalities for each of the following graphs.

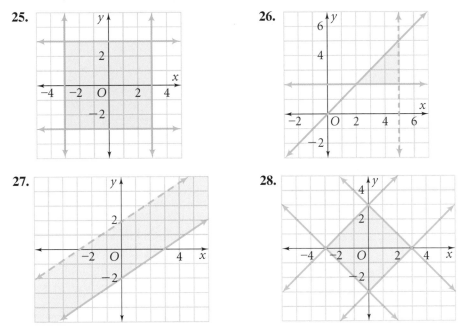

25.

26.

27.

28.

29. Open-Ended Write a system of four inequalities that describes a rectangle. Graph the system.

30. Geometry The following system of inequalities describes a right isosceles triangle.
 a. Find m.
 b. Find the area of the triangle.

$x > 0$
$y > 0$
$y < mx + 4$

Geometry The solution region of each system of linear inequalities below forms a figure. (a) Describe the shape. (b) Find the vertices. (c) Find the area.

31. $y \geq \frac{1}{2}x + 1$ **32.** $x \geq 1$ **33.** $x \geq 0$ **34.** $x \geq 2$
$\quad y \leq 2$ $\qquad x \leq 5$ $\qquad x \leq 2$ $\qquad y \geq -3$
$\quad x \geq -4$ $\qquad y \geq -1$ $\qquad y \geq -4$ $\qquad x + y \leq 4$
$\qquad\qquad\quad y \leq 3$ $\qquad y \leq -x + 2$

35. a. Business A clothing store has a going-out-of-business sale. They are selling pants for $10.99 and shirts for $4.99. You can spend as much as $45 and want to buy at least one pair of pants. Write and graph a system of inequalities that describes this situation.
 b. Suppose you need to buy at least three pairs of pants. From your graph, find all the ordered pairs that are possible solutions.

36. a. Graph each inequality. $y > 4x + 1$
$y < 4x - 2$

b. Writing Will the boundary lines $y = 4x + 1$ and $y = 4x - 2$ ever intersect? Explain.

c. Will the shaded regions you drew in part (a) overlap?

d. Does the system of inequalities have any solutions?

37. a. Graph the system of inequalities. $y > 3x - 5$
$y < 3x + 4$

b. Will the boundary lines $y = 3x - 5$ and $y = 3x + 4$ ever intersect? Explain.

c. Describe the shape of the overlapping region.

Open-Ended **Write a system of linear inequalities with the given characteristics.**

38. $(0, 0)$ is a solution.

39. Solutions are only in Quadrant II.

40. There is no solution.

41. $(3, 7)$ is not a solution.

42. Solutions are only in Quadrant IV.

C **Challenge** **43. Business** A jeweler plans to produce a ring made of silver and gold. The price of gold is approximately \$10/g. The price of silver is approximately \$.15/g. She considers the following in deciding how much gold and silver to use in the ring.

- The total mass must be more than 10 g but less than 20 g.
- The ring must contain at least 3 g of gold.
- The total cost of the gold and silver must be less than \$60.

Let s = the mass of silver in grams and d = the mass of gold in grams.
a. Write and graph the four inequalities that describe this situation.
b. For one solution (s, d), find the mass of the ring and the cost of the gold and silver.

44. Solve $|y| \geq x$. (*Hint*: Write two inequalities; then graph them.)

Write a system of linear inequalities with the given characteristics.

45. $(2, 5)$ and $(5, 2)$ are not solutions; $(5, 5)$ is a solution.

46. $(-3, 2)$ and $(3, 2)$ are not solutions; $(-2, 6)$ is a solution.

47. Sports During part of the baseball season, a player had 120 hits in 305 at-bats. The ratio $\frac{120}{305}$ gave him a .393 batting average. (Batting averages are rounded to the nearest thousandth.) The inequality $\frac{120 + h}{305 + a} \geq .400$ gives the number of hits h needed during his next at-bats a to reach at least a .400 average. The inequality $h \leq a$ indicates the player cannot have more hits than at-bats.
a. Solve $\frac{120 + h}{305 + a} \geq .400$ for h.
b. Graph the system.
c. What does a solution mean in terms of the original problem?

48. Business A drum maker sells two sizes of frame drums like the ones at the left. A 14-in. drum sells for \$180 and an 18-in. drum sells for \$240. He is trying to decide how many drums to build and considers the following:

- He wants to produce and sell at least \$2700 worth of drums.
- He has materials to make no more than 17 drums.
- He plans to make more 14-in. drums than 18-in. drums.
- He wants to make at least four 18-in. drums.

a. Write and graph the four inequalities that describe this situation.
b. Give one possible solution to the system.

Multiple Choice

49. Which point is a solution of the following system? $y > x$
$$y < 3x - 4$$

  I. (1, 2)   **II.** (3, 4)   **III.** (3, 9)

  A. I only   **B.** I and II   **C.** I and III   **D.** II only

50. There are at most 12 bicycles and tricycles in a school playground. There are at least 17 wheels altogether. Let b equal the number of bicycles and t equal the number of tricycles. Which system describes this situation?

  F. $b + t < 12$ **G.** $b + t \leq 12$
     $2b + 3t \geq 17$ $2b + 3t \geq 17$

  H. $b + t \leq 12$ **I.** $b + t \leq 12$
     $2b + 3t > 17$ $2b + 3t \leq 17$

Short Response

51. Describe the solution to the following system. $3x + 4y \geq 12$
$$3x + 4y \leq 12$$

Extended Response

52. Suppose you and your friends are going out for pizza.
  a. Write a system of equations for the cost of a large pizza at each restaurant, based on the information at the right.
  b. Solve the system. Interpret your results.
  c. Where will you go for pizza? Explain your reasons.

Tony's Pizza	Maria's Pizza
Large cheese $7	Large cheese $8
Each topping $.75	Each topping $.50

Take It to the NET
Online lesson quiz at
www.PHSchool.com
Web Code: aea-0706

Mixed Review

Lesson 7-5

Graph each linear inequality.

53. $y > x - 5$ **54.** $y \leq -2x + 4$ **55.** $y > -3$

56. $y + x \leq 7$ **57.** $3y - x \geq 6$ **58.** $4y + 2x < 8$

Find the slope of a line parallel to the graph of each equation.

59. $5x - 2y = 8$ **60.** $y - 17 = -3x$ **61.** $0.5y - 10 + 4x = 0$

Lesson 6-5

Find the slope of a line perpendicular to the graph of each equation.

62. $y = 4x$ **63.** $y = 5x - 7$ **64.** $y = \frac{3}{8}x + 19$

65. $y = -\frac{9}{10}x - 3$ **66.** $6y + 13x = 22$ **67.** $-4x - 15y = 74$

Lesson 5-4

Write a function rule for each table.

68.

x	$f(x)$
1	7
2	14
3	21
4	28
5	35

69.

x	$f(x)$
1	7
2	8
3	9
4	10
5	11

70.

x	$f(x)$
-2	4
-1	1
0	0
1	1
2	4

Technology # Graphing Linear Inequalities

FOR USE WITH LESSON 7-6

You can use a graphing calculator to show the solutions of an incquality or a system of inequalities. The symbol before each Y in the **Y=** window indicates the graph style. You can use the graph style to shade above or below a line. The standard style, indicated by \, shows only the line.

Take It to the NET
Graphing Calculator procedures online at **www.PHSchool.com**
Web Code: aee-2108

To change the graph style, select \ and press **ENTER** to rotate through the seven styles available. You can use ◥ to shade above the line and ◣ to shade below the line.

← to graph above the line $y = 2x - 1$
← to graph below the line $y = 3x + 4$

The graphing calculator does not make a distinction between a boundary line that is dotted ($y < 2x - 1$) and a boundary line that is solid ($y \le 2x - 1$). You must decide whether a boundary line should be solid or dotted when you sketch the inequality.

1 EXAMPLE

Graph $y > -4x + 1$.

- Enter the equation for the boundary line $y = -4x + 1$.
- Select ◥ to shade above the boundary line.

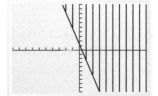

2 EXAMPLE

Graph the system: $y < -x + 4$
$\qquad\qquad\qquad y > 2x + 3$

Enter the equation of the first boundary line as Y_1.
Enter the equation of the second boundary line as Y_2.

- Select ◣ to shade below $y = -x + 4$.
- Select ◥ to shade above $y = 2x + 3$.

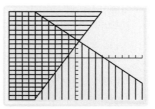

EXERCISES

Use a graphing calculator to graph each inequality. Sketch your graph.

1. $y < x$ **2.** $y > 2x - 3$ **3.** $y \ge -x + 3$ **4.** $y \le 5$

Use a graphing calculator to graph each system of inequalities. Sketch your graph.

5. $y \ge -1$ **6.** $y \ge 0.5x - 2$ **7.** $y < x$ **8.** $y \ge -4x + 6$
   $y \ge 2x$ $y \le x + 2$ $y \ge 1$ $y \ge -2x + 5$

In multiple correct answer questions, you have to determine the truth or falsehood of a number of statements. As you test each statement, mark it as true or false. Then choose the option with all those that are true.

1 EXAMPLE

Which system(s) of inequalities represent(s) the shaded region below?

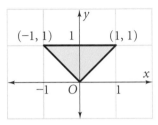

I. $y \geq x$
$y \geq -x$
$y \leq 1$

II. $x + y \geq 0$
$x - y \geq 0$
$y \leq 1$

III. $y \geq |x|$
$y \leq 1$

A. I only
C. I and II only
B. I and III only
D. I, II, and III

Method 1 Graph each system in I, II, and III to see which systems match the shaded region. The graph of the systems in I and III match the shaded region. Statements I and III are true; the correct answer is B.

Method 2 Choose a point, such as $(0, 0.5)$, inside the given shaded region. Test each of the three statements with the values $x = 0$ and $y = 0.5$. When $x = 0$ and $y = 0.5$, all the inequalities in I are true. The second inequality in II is $x - y = 0 - 0.5 \geq 0$, which is false. All the inequalities in III are true. Statements I and III are true; the correct answer is B.

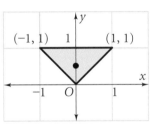

When you use Method 2, you should choose more than one point to test each system. This is because the point you choose may show a system to be true when it is really false. For example, if you choose to test the point $(1, 1)$, all the inequalities in II will be true, so you might think that II is true.

EXERCISES

1. Choose another point in the shaded region and test each of the three statements with the coordinates to determine which are true.

2. Writing The point $(0, 0)$ is in the shaded region. Test each of the three statements with its coordinates to determine which are true. Explain why this point is not a good choice with which to answer this question.

3. Louis is selling lemonade for $.25 per cup. He bought the lemonade mix for $8.40 and the cups for $.05 each. Which statement(s) must be true?
  I. His break-even point is 42 cups.
  II. When he sells 20 cups, his income will be $13.40.
  III. His income is greater than his expenses when he sells 20 cups.
A. I and II only
C. I only
B. I and III only
D. III only

Chapter 7

Chapter Review

Vocabulary

elimination method (p. 353)
infinitely many solutions (p. 342)
linear inequality (p. 371)
no solution (p. 342)

solution of a system of linear
  equations (p. 340)
solution of a system of linear
  inequalities (p. 377)

solutions of an inequality (p. 371)
substitution method (p. 347)
system of linear equations (p. 340)
system of linear inequalities (p. 377)

Reading Math
Understanding
Vocabulary

Take It to the NET
Online vocabulary quiz
at **www.PHSchool.com**
Web Code: aej-0751

Choose the vocabulary term that correctly completes each sentence.

1. _____?_____ is a method for solving a system of linear equations in which you multiply one or both equations by a nonzero number to get a variable term with coefficients that have a sum or difference of zero.

2. Any ordered pair that makes all equations in a system of equations true is a(n)_____?_____.

3. A(n)_____?_____ is formed by two or more linear inequalities.

4. Each point whose coordinates make an inequality true is a(n)_____?_____.

5. _____?_____ is a method for solving a system of linear equations in which at least one equation must first be solved for a single variable.

Skills and Concepts

7-1 Objectives

▼ To solve systems by graphing (p. 340)

▼ To analyze special types of systems (p. 342)

Two or more linear equations form a **system of linear equations.** You can solve a system of linear equations by graphing. The point where all the lines intersect is the **solution of the system.**

6. Which graph shows the solution of the following system? $y = x - 1$
   $y = -x + 3$

   A.   **B.**

7. Is $(2, 5)$ a solution of the following system? Explain. $y = 2x + 1$
   $2x - y = 8$

8. How many solutions does the following system have? Explain. $y = -\frac{1}{2}x + 2$
   $3x + 6y = 12$

9. **Critical Thinking** What kinds of systems would be hard to solve by graphing?

Solve each system by graphing.

10. $y = 3x - 1$
    $y = -x + 3$

11. $x - y = -3$
    $3x + y = -1$

12. $-x + 2y = -2$
    $y = \frac{1}{2}x + 3$

13. $y = -2x + 1$
    $y = 2x - 3$

Chapter 7   Chapter Review   **387**

You can also solve a system of linear equations using the **substitution method.** By replacing one variable with an equivalent expression containing the other variable, you create a one-variable equation to solve.

Solve each system using substitution.

14. $y = 3x + 11$
$y = -2x + 1$

15. $4x - y = -12$
$-6x + 5y = -3$

16. $8x = -2y - 10$
$2x = 4y$

17. $y = 5x - 8$
$5y = 2x + 6$

18. Writing Explain how you determine if a system has no solution or infinitely many solutions when you solve a system using substitution.

19. There are 24 questions on a test. Each question is worth either 4 points or 5 points. The total is 100 points.
  a. Write a system of equations to find the number of each type of question.
  b. Solve the system by substitution.
  c. How many questions of each type are on the test?

You can solve a system of linear equations using the **elimination method.** You add or subtract the equations to eliminate one variable. You can multiply one or both of the equations by a nonzero number before adding or subtracting.

Solve each system using elimination. Check your solution.

20. $y = -3x + 5$
$y = -4x - 1$

21. $2x - 3y = 5$
$x + 2y = -1$

22. $x + y = 10$
$x - y = 2$

23. $x + 4y = 12$
$2x - 3y = 6$

24. Farming A farmer raises chickens and cows. There are 34 animals in all. The farmer counts 110 legs on these animals. Write a system of equations to find the number of each type of animal. Solve the system by elimination. How many of each animal does the farmer have?

You can use systems of linear equations to solve word problems. First, define variables. Then model the situation with a system of linear equations.

25. A furniture finish consists of turpentine and linseed oil. It contains twice as much turpentine as linseed oil. If you plan to make 16 fluid ounces of furniture finish, how much turpentine do you need?

26. Geometry The difference between the measures of two complementary angles is 36°. Find both angle measures. (*Hint*: Two angles are complementary if the sum of their measures is 90°.)

27. Geometry The perimeter of a rectangle is 114 feet. Its length is three more than twice its width. Find the dimensions of the rectangle.

28. Supplies Marcella and Rupert bought some party supplies. Marcella bought 3 packages of balloons and 4 packages of favors for $14.63. Rupert bought 2 packages of balloons and 5 packages of favors for $16.03. Find the price of a package of balloons.

29. An airplane flew for 6 hours with a 22-km/h tail wind. The return flight against the same wind took 8 hours. Find the speed of the plane in still air.

7-5 Objectives

▼ To graph linear inequalities (p. 370)

▼ To use linear inequalities when modeling real-world situations (p. 372)

A **linear inequality** describes a region of the coordinate plane. The **solutions of the inequality** are the coordinates of the points that make the inequality true.

Graph each linear inequality.

30. $y < -3x + 8$ **31.** $y \geq 2x - 1$ **32.** $y \leq 0.5x + 6$ **33.** $y > -\frac{1}{4}x - 2$

Write the linear inequality shown in each graph.

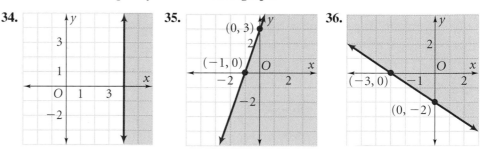

34.   **35.**   **36.**

7-6 Objectives

▼ To solve systems of linear inequalities by graphing (p. 377)

▼ To model real-world situations using systems of linear inequalities (p. 379)

Two or more linear inequalities form a **system of linear inequalities.** To find the **solution of a system of linear inequalities,** graph each linear inequality. The solution region is where all the inequalities are true.

Solve each system of linear inequalities by graphing.

37. $y \geq -4x + 1$ **38.** $x - y < 10$ **39.** $y \leq x - 3$ **40.** $y < 5x$
    $y \leq \frac{5}{2}x - \frac{9}{2}$ $x + y \leq 8$ $y > x - 7$ $y \geq 0$

Write the system of inequalities shown in each graph.

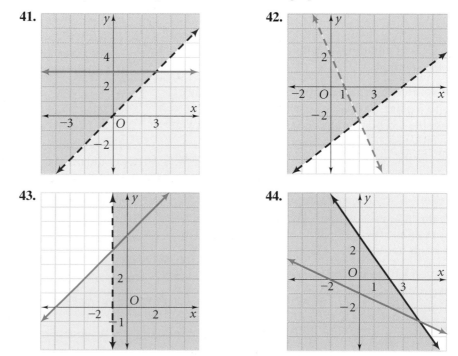

41.   **42.**

43.   **44.**

45. Open-Ended Write a system of linear inequalities for which the solution region is a pentagon.

Chapter 7

Chapter Test

Take It to the NET
Online chapter test at
www.PHSchool.com
Web Code: aea-0752

Solve each system by graphing.

1. $y = 3x - 7$
$y = -x + 1$

2. $4x + 3y = 12$
$2x - 5y = -20$

Critical Thinking Suppose you try to solve systems of linear equations using substitution and get the results below. How many solutions does each system have?

3. $x = 8$

4. $5 = y$

5. $-7 = 4$

6. $x = -1$

7. $2 = y$

8. $9 = 9$

Solve each system using substitution.

9. $y = 4x - 7$
$y = 2x + 9$

10. $y = -2x - 1$
$y = 3x - 16$

11. $8x + 2y = -2$
$y = -5x + 1$

12. $y + 6 = 2x$
$4x - 10y = 4$

Solve each system using elimination.

13. $4x + y = 8$
$-3x - y = 0$

14. $2x + 5y = 20$
$3x - 10y = 37$

15. $x + y = 10$
$-x - 2y = -14$

16. $3x + 2y = -19$
$x - 12y = 19$

Write a system of equations to model each situation. Solve by any method.

17. Cable Service Your local cable television company offers two plans: basic service with one movie channel for $35 per month or basic service with two movie channels for $45 per month. What is the charge for the basic service and the charge for each movie channel?

18. Education A writing workshop enrolls novelists and poets in a ratio of 5 to 3. There are 24 people at the workshop. How many novelists are there? How many poets are there?

19. You have 15 coins in your pocket that are either quarters or nickels. They total $2.75. How many of each coin do you have?

20. Writing Compare solving a system of linear equations with solving a system of linear inequalities. What are the similarities? What are the differences?

21. Which point is *not* a solution of $y < 3x - 1$?
A. $(2, -4)$ **B.** $(5, 7)$ **C.** $(0, -1)$ **D.** $(-2, -9)$

Solve each system by graphing.

22. $y > 4x - 1$
$y \le -x + 4$

23. $y \ge 3x + 5$
$y > x - 2$

24. $x > -3$
$-3x + y \ge 6$

25. $2x - y \le 2$
$y \ge 4$

26. Open-Ended Write a system of two linear equations. Solve by any method.

27. Garage Sale Leo held a garage sale. He priced all the items at a dime or a quarter. His sales totaled less than $5.
a. Write a linear inequality that describes the situation. Graph the linear inequality.
b. What is the maximum possible number of items that could have been sold for a dime?
c. What is the maximum possible number of items that could have been sold for a quarter?

28. Gardening Mrs. Paulson bought chicken wire to enclose a rectangular garden. She is restricted to a width of no more than 30 ft. She would like to use at most 180 ft of chicken wire.
a. Write a system of linear inequalities that describes this situation.
b. Graph the system to show all possible solutions.

29. A chemist needs to mix a solution containing 30% insecticide with a solution containing 50% insecticide to make 200 L of a solution that is 42% insecticide. How much of each solution should she use?
a. Complete the table below.

	30% Insecticide	50% Insecticide	42% Insecticide
Liters of Solution	▪	▪	▪
Liters of Insecticide	▪	▪	▪

b. Write a system of equations that describes the situation. Solve the system.

Standardized Test Prep

Reading Comprehension Read the passage below. Then answer the questions on the basis of what is *stated* or *implied* in the passage.

> **Music to Our Ears** The way in which the music industry delivers music has changed dramatically since 1985. In that year, according to industry sources, there were 22.6 million CDs shipped. By 1990, the number of CDs shipped increased to 286.5 million. In 1999, shipments swelled to 938.9 million CDs, an increase of over 4000% from the number in 1985.
>
> From 1985 to 1999, cassette shipments decreased from 339.1 million cassettes to 123.6 million, and record album shipments went from 167.0 million albums to 2.9 million. Clearly, CDs have replaced both cassettes and record albums as listeners' favorites.

1. What was the total number of CDs, cassettes, and record albums shipped in 1985?
   - **A.** 22.6 million
   - **B.** 528.7 million
   - **C.** 1065.4 million
   - **D.** 1445 million

2. Which graph correctly illustrates data in the article above?

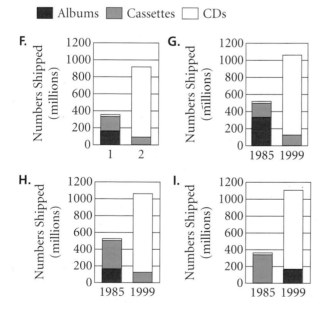

3. Which equation could you use to find the percent of change in the number of cassettes shipped from 1985 to 1999?
   - **A.** $\dfrac{339.1 + 123.6}{123.6}$
   - **B.** $\dfrac{339.1 - 123.6}{123.6}$
   - **C.** $\dfrac{339.1 + 123.6}{339.1}$
   - **D.** $\dfrac{339.1 - 123.6}{339.1}$

4. Suppose a linear equation models record album shipments from 1985 to 1999. What is a correct interpretation of the slope of the model?
   - **F.** about 12 million fewer shipped each year
   - **G.** 164.1 million fewer shipped in all
   - **H.** about 12 million more shipped each year
   - **I.** 164.1 million more shipped in all

5. Which of the following statements is true?
   - **A.** There is a positive correlation between the numbers of CDs and record albums shipped.
   - **B.** There is a negative correlation between the numbers of CDs and record albums shipped.
   - **C.** There is a positive correlation between the numbers of cassettes and CDs shipped.
   - **D.** There is a negative correlation between the numbers of cassettes and record albums shipped.

6. Use percent of change to describe the change in the number of cassettes shipped between 1985 and 1999.

7. According to the article, the increase in CD shipments from 1985 to 1999 was over 4000%. Do you agree? Explain.

8. Write a linear equation to model the number of CDs shipped from 1985 to 1999. Use the equation to predict the number of CDs shipped in 2010.

9. Do you agree with the main conclusion stated in the article? Explain.

Where You've Been

● In Chapter 1 you learned how to use the order of operations to simplify expressions containing exponents.

● In Chapter 5 you studied number patterns and learned to recognize an arithmetic sequence. You also wrote equations for function rules.

● In Chapter 6 you found a line of best fit for a set of data.

Instant self-check online and on CD-ROM

Diagnosing Readiness   (For help, go to the Lesson in green.)

Converting Fractions to Decimals (Skills Handbook page 725)

Write as a decimal.

1. $\frac{7}{10}$ **2.** $6\frac{2}{5}$ **3.** $\frac{8}{1000}$ **4.** $\frac{7}{2}$ **5.** $\frac{3}{11}$

Using the Order of Operations (Lesson 1-2)

Simplify each expression.

6. $(9 \div 3 + 4)^2$ **7.** $5 + (0.3)^3$ **8.** $3 - (1.5)^2$ **9.** $64 \div 2^4$

Evaluating Expressions (Lessons 1-4 to 1-6)

Evaluate each expression for $a = -2$ and $b = 5$.

10. $(ab)^2$ **11.** $(a - b)^2$ **12.** $a^3 + b^2$ **13.** $b - (3a)^2$

Calculating Simple Interest (Lesson 4-3)

Use the formula for simple interest, $I = Prt$. Find each missing value.

14. $I = \blacksquare, p = \$1000, r = 3\%, t = 4$ yr   **15.** $I = \$672, p = \blacksquare, r = 7\%, t = 12$ yr

Understanding Domain and Range (Lesson 5-2)

Find the range of each function with domain $\{-2, 0, 3.5\}$.

16. $f(x) = -2x^2$ **17.** $g(x) = 10 - x^3$ **18.** $y = 5x - 1$

Finding Terms of a Sequence (Lesson 5-6)

Find the next two terms of each sequence.

19. $1, 3, 5, 7, \ldots$ **20.** $-1, 0, 2, 5, 9, \ldots$ **21.** $7, 13, 19, 25, \ldots$

Exponents and Exponential Functions

Key Vocabulary

- common ratio (p. 424)
- compound interest (p. 438)
- decay factor (p. 440)
- exponential decay (p. 440)
- exponential function (p. 430)
- exponential growth (p. 437)
- geometric sequence (p. 424)
- growth factor (p. 437)
- interest period (p. 438)
- scientific notation (p. 400)

Where You're Going

- In this chapter you will extend your knowledge about exponents to include zero and negative exponents.

- You will learn the properties of exponents, and how exponents are used to write a geometric sequence.

- By making a table of values, you will graph exponential functions.

Real-World Snapshots Applying what you learn, you will use functions and graphs to do activities related to animals, on pages 452–453.

Zero and Negative Exponents

Lesson Preview

What You'll Learn

OBJECTIVE 1 To simplify expressions with zero and negative exponents

OBJECTIVE 2 To evaluate exponential expressions

. . . And Why

To find the size of a population, as in Example 4

✓ Check Skills You'll Need

(For help, go to Lessons 1-2 and 1-6.)

Simplify each expression.

1. 2^3

2. $\frac{1}{4^2}$

3. $4^2 \div 2^2$

4. $(-3)^3$

5. -3^3

6. $6^2 \div 12$

Evaluate each expression for $a = 2$, $b = -1$, and $c = 0.5$.

7. $\frac{a}{2a}$

8. $\frac{bc}{c}$

9. $\frac{ab}{bc}$

OBJECTIVE 1

Zero and Negative Exponents

iTEXT Interactive lesson includes instant self-check, tutorials, and activities.

Investigation: Exponents

1. a. Copy the table below. Replace each blank with the value of the power in simplest form.

2^x	5^x	10^x
$2^4 = \blacksquare$	$5^4 = \blacksquare$	$10^4 = \blacksquare$
$2^3 = \blacksquare$	$5^3 = \blacksquare$	$10^3 = \blacksquare$
$2^2 = \blacksquare$	$5^2 = \blacksquare$	$10^2 = \blacksquare$

b. Look at the values that you used to replace the blanks. What pattern do you see as you go down each column?

2. Copy the table below. Use the pattern you described in Question 1 to complete the table.

2^x	5^x	10^x
$2^1 = \blacksquare$	$5^1 = \blacksquare$	$10^1 = \blacksquare$
$2^0 = \blacksquare$	$5^0 = \blacksquare$	$10^0 = \blacksquare$
$2^{-1} = \blacksquare$	$5^{-1} = \blacksquare$	$10^{-1} = \blacksquare$
$2^{-2} = \blacksquare$	$5^{-2} = \blacksquare$	$10^{-2} = \blacksquare$

3. Critical Thinking What pattern do you notice in the row with 0 as an exponent?

4. Copy and complete each expression.

a. $2^{-1} = \frac{1}{2^\blacksquare}$

b. $2^{-2} = \frac{1}{2^\blacksquare}$

c. $2^{-3} = \frac{1}{2^\blacksquare}$

Consider 3^3, 3^2, and 3^1. Decreasing the exponent by one is the same as dividing by 3. Continuing the pattern, 3^0 equals 1 and 3^{-1} equals $\frac{1}{3}$.

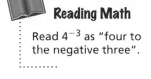 **Key Concepts**

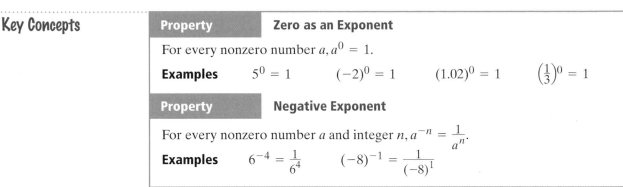

Property	**Zero as an Exponent**

For every nonzero number a, $a^0 = 1$.

Examples $5^0 = 1$ $(-2)^0 = 1$ $(1.02)^0 = 1$ $\left(\frac{1}{3}\right)^0 = 1$

Property	**Negative Exponent**

For every nonzero number a and integer n, $a^{-n} = \frac{1}{a^n}$.

Examples $6^{-4} = \frac{1}{6^4}$ $(-8)^{-1} = \frac{1}{(-8)^1}$

Why can't you use 0 as a base? By the first property, $3^0 = 1$, $2^0 = 1$, and $1^0 = 1$, which implies $0^0 = 1$. However, the pattern $0^3 = 0$, $0^2 = 0$, and $0^1 = 0$ implies $0^0 = 0$. Since both 1 and 0 cannot be the answer, 0^0 is undefined. In the second property, using 0 as a base results in division by zero, which you know is undefined.

Reading Math

Read 4^{-3} as "four to the negative three".

1 EXAMPLE **Simplifying a Power**

Simplify.

a. $4^{-3} = \frac{1}{4^3}$ Use the definition of negative exponent.

$= \frac{1}{64}$ Simplify.

b. $(-1.23)^0 = 1$ Use the definition of zero as an exponent.

✔ **Check Understanding** **1** Simplify each expression.

a. 3^{-4} **b.** $(-7)^0$ **c.** $(-4)^{-3}$ **d.** 7^{-1} **e.** -3^{-2}

An algebraic expression is in simplest form when it is written with only positive exponents. If the expression is a fraction in simplest form, the only common factor of the numerator and denominator is 1.

2 EXAMPLE **Simplifying an Exponential Expression**

Simplify each expression.

a. $4yx^{-3} = 4y\left(\frac{1}{x^3}\right)$ Use the definition of negative exponent.

$= \frac{4y}{x^3}$ Simplify.

b. $\frac{1}{w^{-4}} = 1 \div w^{-4}$ Rewrite using a division symbol.

$= 1 \div \frac{1}{w^4}$ Use the definition of negative exponent.

$= 1 \cdot w^4$ Multiply by the reciprocal of $\frac{1}{w^4}$, which is w^4.

$= w^4$ Identity Property of Multiplication

✔ **Check Understanding** **2** Simplify each expression.

a. $11m^{-5}$ **b.** $7s^{-4}t^2$ **c.** $\frac{2}{a^{-3}}$ **d.** $\frac{n^{-5}}{v^2}$

Evaluating Exponential Expressions

When you evaluate an exponential expression, you can write the expression with positive exponents before substituting values.

3 EXAMPLE Evaluating an Exponential Expression

Evaluate $3m^2t^{-2}$ for $m = 2$ and $t = -3$.

Method 1 Write with positive exponents first.

$$3m^2t^{-2} = \frac{3m^2}{t^2} \qquad \text{Use the definition of negative exponent.}$$

$$= \frac{3(2)^2}{(-3)^2} \qquad \text{Substitute 2 for } m \text{ and } -3 \text{ for } t.$$

$$= \frac{12}{9} = 1\frac{1}{3} \qquad \text{Simplify.}$$

Method 2 Substitute first.

$$3m^2t^{-2} = 3(2)^2(-3)^{-2} \qquad \text{Substitute 2 for } m \text{ and } -3 \text{ for } t.$$

$$= \frac{3(2)^2}{(-3)^2} \qquad \text{Use the definition of negative exponent.}$$

$$= \frac{12}{9} = 1\frac{1}{3} \qquad \text{Simplify.}$$

✔ **Check Understanding** **3** Evaluate each expression for $n = -2$ and $w = 5$.

a. $n^{-3}w^0$ **b.** $\dfrac{n^{-1}}{w^2}$ **c.** $\dfrac{w^0}{n^4}$ **d.** $\dfrac{1}{nw^{-2}}$

You can also evaluate exponential expressions that model real-world situations.

4 EXAMPLE Real-World 🌐 Problem Solving

Population Growth A biologist is studying green peach aphids, like the one shown at the left. In the lab, the population doubles every week. The expression $1000 \cdot 2^w$ models an initial population of 1000 insects after w weeks of growth.

a. Evaluate the expression for $w = 0$. Then describe what the value of the expression represents in the situation.

$$1000 \cdot 2^w = 1000 \cdot 2^0 \quad \text{Substitute 0 for } w.$$

$$= 1000 \cdot 1 \quad \text{Simplify.}$$

$$= 1000$$

The value of the expression represents the initial population of insects. This makes sense because when $w = 0$, no time has passed.

b. Evaluate the expression for $w = -3$. Then describe what the value of the expression represents in the situation.

$$1000 \cdot 2^w = 1000 \cdot 2^{-3} \quad \text{Substitute } -3 \text{ for } w.$$

$$= 1000 \cdot \frac{1}{8} \quad \text{Simplify.}$$

$$= 125$$

There were 125 aphids 3 weeks before the present population of 1000 insects.

Real-World 🌐 Connection

During the months of June and July, green peach aphids in a field of potato plants can double in population every three days.

✔ **Check Understanding** **4** A sample of bacteria triples each month. The expression $5400 \cdot 3^m$ models a population of 5400 bacteria after m months of growth. Evaluate the expression for $m = -2$ and $m = 0$. Describe what each value of the expression represents in the situation.

EXERCISES

For more practice, see *Extra Practice*.

Practice and Problem Solving

A **Practice by Example**

Example 1
(page 395)

Simplify each expression.

1. $-(2.57)^0$ **2.** 4^{-2} **3.** $(-5)^{-2}$ **4.** -5^{-2}

5. $(-4)^{-2}$ **6.** -3^{-4} **7.** 2^{-6} **8.** -12^{-1}

9. $\frac{1}{2^0}$ **10.** 78^{-1} **11.** $(-4)^{-3}$ **12.** -4^{-3}

Example 2
(page 395)

Copy and complete each equation.

13. $4n^{\blacksquare} = \frac{4}{n^2}$ **14.** $\frac{x^{\blacksquare}}{2y^{\blacksquare}} = \frac{1}{2x^{-3}y^4}$ **15.** $\frac{a^{\blacksquare}}{3b^{\blacksquare}} = \frac{b^3}{3}$ **16.** $3xy^{\blacksquare} = \frac{3x}{y^5}$

Simplify each expression.

17. $3ab^0$ **18.** $5x^{-4}$ **19.** $\frac{1}{x^{-7}}$ **20.** $\frac{1}{c^{-1}}$

21. $\frac{5^{-2}}{p}$ **22.** $a^{-4}c^0$ **23.** $\frac{3x^{-2}}{y}$ **24.** $\frac{7ab^{-2}}{3w}$

25. $x^{-5}y^{-7}$ **26.** $x^{-5}y^7$ **27.** $\frac{8}{2c^{-3}}$ **28.** $\frac{7s}{5t^{-3}}$

29. $\frac{6a^{-1}c^{-3}}{d^0}$ **30.** $2^{-3}x^2z^{-7}$ **31.** $9^0y^7t^{-11}$ **32.** $\frac{7s^0t^{-5}}{2^{-1}m^2}$

Example 3
(page 396)

Evaluate each expression for $r = -3$ and $s = 5$.

33. s^{-2} **34.** r^{-2} **35.** $-r^{-2}$ **36.** s^0

37. $3s^{-2}$ **38.** $(2s)^{-2}$ **39.** $r^{-4}s^2$ **40.** $\frac{1}{r^{-4}s^2}$

41. s^2r^{-3} **42.** r^0s^{-2} **43.** $5r^3s^{-1}$ **44.** $2^{-4}r^3s^{-2}$

Example 4
(page 396)

45. a. Suppose your allowance doubles every week. This week you receive $2.56. How much will your allowance be three weeks from now? How much was your allowance three weeks ago?

    b. Critical Thinking From a parent's point of view, is doubling your allowance each week a good plan? Explain.

B **Apply Your Skills**

Mental Math Is the value of each expression *positive* or *negative*?

46. -2^2 **47.** $(-2)^2$ **48.** 2^{-2} **49.** $(-2)^3$ **50.** $(-2)^{-3}$

Write each number as a power of 10 using negative exponents.

51. $\frac{1}{10}$ **52.** $\frac{1}{100}$ **53.** $\frac{1}{1000}$ **54.** $\frac{1}{10,000}$ **55.** $\frac{1}{100,000}$

Write each expression as a decimal.

56. 10^{-3} **57.** 10^{-6} **58.** $7 \cdot 10^{-1}$ **59.** $3 \cdot 10^{-2}$ **60.** $5 \cdot 10^{-4}$

61. a. Patterns Complete the pattern using powers of 5.

$$\frac{1}{5^2} = \blacksquare \qquad \frac{1}{5^1} = \blacksquare \qquad \frac{1}{5^0} = \blacksquare \qquad \frac{1}{5^{-1}} = \blacksquare \qquad \frac{1}{5^{-2}} = \blacksquare$$

    b. Write $\frac{1}{5^{-4}}$ using a positive exponent.

    c. Rewrite $\frac{1}{a^{-n}}$ so that the power of a is in the numerator.

62. Writing Explain why the value of -3^0 is negative but the value of $(-3)^0$ is positive.

Simplify each expression.

63. $45 \cdot (0.5)^0$ **64.** $54 \cdot 3^{-2}$ **65.** $\dfrac{5^{-2}}{10^{-3}}$ **66.** $\dfrac{4^{-1}}{9^0}$ **67.** $\dfrac{(-3)^{-4}}{-3}$

Evaluate each expression for $a = 3$, $b = 2$, and $c = -4$.

68. c^b **69.** $a^{-b}b$ **70.** b^{-a} **71.** b^c **72.** $c^{-a}b^{ab}$

73. Copy and complete the table below.

a	4	▪	▪	$\dfrac{7}{8}$	▪
a^{-1}	▪	3	$\dfrac{1}{6}$	▪	0.5

74. a. Critical Thinking Simplify $a^n \cdot a^{-n}$.
  b. What is the mathematical relationship of a^n and a^{-n}? Justify your answer.

75. Which expressions equal $\frac{1}{4}$?
  A. 4^{-1} **B.** 2^{-2} **C.** -4^1 **D.** $\dfrac{1}{2^2}$ **E.** 1^4 **F.** -2^{-2}

76. Open-Ended Choose a fraction to use as a value for the variable a. Find the values of a^{-1}, a^2, and a^{-2}.

77. Critical Thinking Are $3x^{-2}$ and $3x^2$ reciprocals? Explain.

78. Error Analysis A student simplified an expression as shown at the right. What error did the student make?

$$\frac{x^n}{a^{-n}b^0} = \frac{a^n x^n}{b^0}$$
$$= \frac{a^n x^n}{0} \text{ undefined}$$

79. Probability Suppose your history teacher gives a multiple-choice quiz. There are four questions, each with five answer choices. The probability p of guessing the answer to a question correctly is $\frac{1}{5}$. The probability q of guessing the answer to each question incorrectly is $\frac{4}{5}$.
  a. The table has expressions to find the probability of correctly guessing a certain number of answers on this quiz. Copy and complete the table.

Multiple-Choice Quiz

Number Correct	Expression	Probability
0	$p^0 q^4$	$\left(\frac{1}{5}\right)^0 \left(\frac{4}{5}\right)^4 = 0.4096$
1	$4p^1 q^3$	▪
2	$6p^2 q^2$	▪
3	$4p^3 q^1$	▪
4	$p^4 q^0$	▪

  b. Which number of correct answers is most likely?

80. Communication Suppose you are the only person in your class who knows a certain story. After a minute you tell a classmate. Every minute after that, every student who knows the story tells another student (sometimes the person being told already will have heard it). In a class of 30 students, the expression $\dfrac{30}{1 + 29 \cdot 2^{-t}}$ predicts the approximate number of people who will have heard the story after t minutes. About how many students will have heard your story after 2 min? After 5 min? After 10 min?

Simplify each expression.

81. $2^3(5^0 - 6m^2)$

82. $(-5)^2 - (0.5)^{-2}$

83. $\frac{6}{m^2} + \frac{5m^{-2}}{3^{-3}}$

84. $(0.8)^{-3} + 19^0 - 2^{-6}$

85. $\frac{2r^{-5}y^3}{n^2} \div \frac{r^2y^5}{2n}$

86. $2^{-1} - \frac{1}{3^{-2}} + 5\left(\frac{1}{2^2}\right)$

87. For what values of n is $n^{-3} = \left(\frac{1}{n}\right)^5$?

Standardized Test Prep

Gridded Response

88. Evaluate the expression xy^{-1} for $x = 2$ and $y = 3$.

89. Simplify $\frac{3^{-2}b^2}{a^0b^2}$.

90. Evaluate the expression $(4cd)^{-2}$ for $c = 2$ and $d = 1$.

91. Simplify $-6(-6)^{-1}$.

92. Write $26 \cdot 10^{-2}$ as a decimal.

93. Write $0.2584 \cdot 10^3$ as a decimal.

Take It to the NET
Online lesson quiz at
www.PHSchool.com
Web Code: aea-0801

Mixed Review

Lesson 7-6

Solve each system by graphing.

94. $y > 3x + 4$
$y \le -3x + 1$

95. $y \le -2x + 1$
$y < 2x - 1$

96. $y \ge 0.5x$
$y \le x + 2$

Lesson 6-6

97. Hat Sales Use the data in the table at the right.
  a. Make a scatter plot of the data. Use 87 for 1987.
  b. Draw a trend line.
  c. Write an equation for the trend line.
  d. Use your trend line to predict the retail sales of women's hats in 2005.

Estimated Women's Retail Hat Sales

Year	Sales (millions of dollars)
1987	300
1988	345
1989	397
1990	457
1991	510
1992	587
1993	664
1994	700
1995	770
1996	792
1997	830
1998	872
1999	915

Source: Headwear Information Bureau

Lesson 6-2

Write an equation of the line with the given slope and y-intercept.

98. $m = -1, b = 4$

99. $m = 5, b = -2$

100. $m = \frac{2}{5}, b = -3$

101. $m = -\frac{3}{11}, b = -17$

102. $m = \frac{5}{9}, b = \frac{1}{3}$

103. $m = 1.25, b = -3.79$

Scientific Notation

Lesson Preview

What You'll Learn

OBJECTIVE 1 To write numbers in scientific and standard notation

OBJECTIVE 2 To use scientific notation

. . . And Why

To order planets based on their masses, as in Example 4

✓ Check Skills You'll Need

(For help, go to Lesson 8-1.)

Simplify each expression.

1. $6 \cdot 10^4$ **2.** $7 \cdot 10^{-2}$ **3.** $8.2 \cdot 10^5$

4. $3 \cdot 10^{-3}$ **5.** $3.4 \cdot 10^1$ **6.** $5.24 \cdot 10^2$

7. Simplify $3 \times 10^2 + 6 \times 10^1 + 7 \times 10^0 + 8 \times 10^{-1}$.

New Vocabulary

• scientific notation

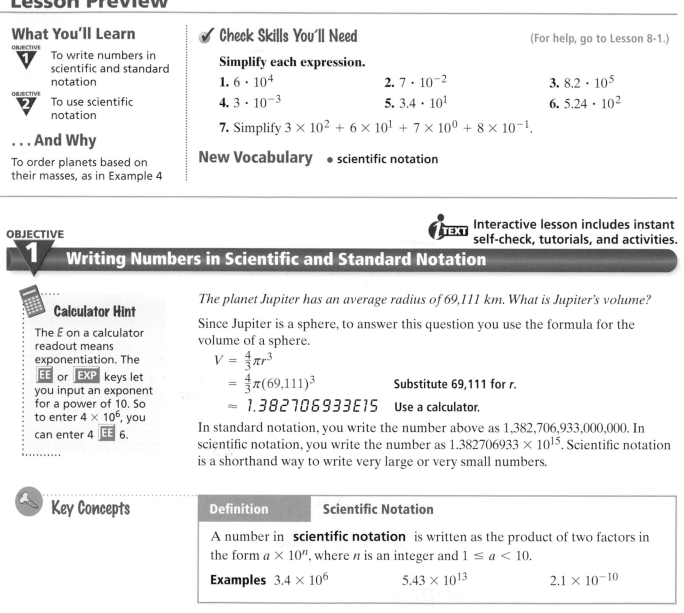

🔬 Interactive lesson includes instant self-check, tutorials, and activities.

OBJECTIVE

1 Writing Numbers in Scientific and Standard Notation

Calculator Hint

The E on a calculator readout means exponentiation. The EE or EXP keys let you input an exponent for a power of 10. So to enter 4×10^6, you can enter 4 EE 6.

The planet Jupiter has an average radius of 69,111 km. What is Jupiter's volume?

Since Jupiter is a sphere, to answer this question you use the formula for the volume of a sphere.

$$V = \frac{4}{3}\pi r^3$$
$$= \frac{4}{3}\pi (69{,}111)^3 \qquad \textbf{Substitute 69,111 for } r.$$
$$\approx \textit{1.382706933E15} \qquad \textbf{Use a calculator.}$$

In standard notation, you write the number above as 1,382,706,933,000,000. In scientific notation, you write the number as $1.382706933 \times 10^{15}$. Scientific notation is a shorthand way to write very large or very small numbers.

🔑 Key Concepts

Definition	Scientific Notation

A number in **scientific notation** is written as the product of two factors in the form $a \times 10^n$, where n is an integer and $1 \le a < 10$.

Examples 3.4×10^6 5.43×10^{13} 2.1×10^{-10}

---

1 EXAMPLE   Recognizing Scientific Notation

Is each number written in scientific notation? If not, explain.

a. 56.29×10^{12} No; 56.29 is greater than 10.

b. 0.84×10^{-3} No; 0.84 is less than 1.

c. 6.11×10^5 yes

✓ Check Understanding ① Is each number written in scientific notation? If not, explain.

a. 3.42×10^{-7} **b.** 52×10^4 **c.** 0.04×10^{-5}

In scientific notation, you use positive exponents to write a number greater than 1. You use negative exponents to write a number between 0 and 1.

2 EXAMPLE Writing a Number in Scientific Notation

Write each number in scientific notation.

a. 56,900,000

$56{,}900{,}000 = 5.69 \times 10^7$ Move the decimal point 7 places to the left and use 7 as an exponent. Drop the zeros after the 9.

b. 0.00985

$0.00985 = 9.85 \times 10^{-3}$ Move the decimal point 3 places to the right and use -3 as an exponent. Drop the zeros before the 9.

✓ **Check Understanding** ② Write each number in scientific notation.
   a. 267,000   **b.** 46,205,000   **c.** 0.0000325   **d.** 0.000000009
   e. Critical Thinking You express 1 billion as 10^9. Explain why you express 436 billion as 4.36×10^{11}.

3 EXAMPLE Writing a Number in Standard Notation

Physical Science Write each number in standard notation.

a. temperature at the sun's core: 1.55×10^6 kelvins

$1.55 \times 10^6 = 1.550000$ A positive exponent indicates a number greater than 10. Move the decimal point 6 places to the right.

$= 1{,}550{,}000$

b. lowest temperature recorded in a lab: 2×10^{-11} kelvin

$2 \times 10^{-11} = 000000000002.$ A negative exponent indicates a number between 0 and 1. Move the decimal point 11 places to the left.

$= 0.00000000002$

✓ **Check Understanding** ③ Write each number in standard notation.
   a. 3.2×10^{12} **b.** 5.07×10^4 **c.** 5.6×10^{-4} **d.** 8.3×10^{-2}

OBJECTIVE

2 Using Scientific Notation

Masses of Planets (kilograms)

Jupiter 3.7×10^{27}
Uranus 8.7×10^{25}
Neptune 1.0×10^{26}
Saturn 5.7×10^{26}

You can compare and order numbers in scientific notation. First compare the powers of 10, and then compare the decimals.

4 EXAMPLE Real-World Problem Solving

Astronomy List the planets in order from least to greatest mass.

Order the powers of 10. Arrange the decimals with the same power of 10 in order.

8.7×10^{25}	1.0×10^{26}	5.7×10^{26}	3.7×10^{27}
Uranus	Neptune	Saturn	Jupiter

From least to greatest mass, the order of the planets is Uranus, Neptune, Saturn, and Jupiter.

✓ **Check Understanding** ④ The following masses of parts of an atom are measured in grams. Order the parts of an atom from least to greatest mass.

neutron: 1.6749×10^{-24}, electron: 9.1096×10^{-28}, proton: 1.6726×10^{-24}

You can write numbers like 815×10^5 and 0.078×10^{-2} in scientific notation.

$$815 \times 10^5 = 81,500,000 = 8.15 \times 10^7 \qquad 0.078 \times 10^{-2} = 0.00078 = 7.8 \times 10^{-4}$$

The examples above show this pattern: When you move a decimal n places left, the exponent of 10 increases by n; when you move a decimal point n places right, the exponent of 10 decreases by n.

5 EXAMPLE Using Scientific Notation to Order Numbers

Order 0.052×10^7, 5.12×10^5, 53.2×10, and 534 from least to greatest.

Write each number in scientific notation.

$$0.052 \times 10^7 \quad 5.12 \times 10^5 \quad 53.2 \times 10 \quad 534$$
$$\downarrow \qquad\qquad \downarrow \qquad\qquad \downarrow \qquad\qquad \downarrow$$
$$5.2 \times 10^5 \quad 5.12 \times 10^5 \quad 5.32 \times 10^2 \quad 5.34 \times 10^2$$

Order the powers of 10. Arrange the decimals with the same power of 10 in order.

$$5.32 \times 10^2 \quad 5.34 \times 10^2 \quad 5.12 \times 10^5 \quad 5.2 \times 10^5$$

Write the original numbers in order.

$$53.2 \times 10 \quad 534 \quad 5.12 \times 10^5 \quad 0.052 \times 10^7$$

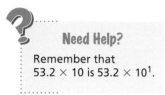

Need Help?

Remember that
53.2×10 is 53.2×10^1.

✓ **Check Understanding** ⑤ Order 60.2×10^{-5}, 63×10^4, 0.067×10^3, and 61×10^{-2} from least to greatest.

You can multiply a number that is in scientific notation by another number. If the product is less than one or greater than 10, rewrite the product in scientific notation.

6 EXAMPLE Multiplying a Number in Scientific Notation

Simplify. Write each answer using scientific notation.

a. $7(4 \times 10^5) = (7 \cdot 4) \times 10^5$ Use the Associative Property of Multiplication.

$$= 28 \times 10^5$$ Simplify inside the parentheses.

$$= 2.8 \times 10^6$$ Write the product in scientific notation.

b. $0.5(1.2 \times 10^{-3}) = (0.5 \cdot 1.2) \times 10^{-3}$ Use the Associative Property of Multiplication.

$$= 0.6 \times 10^{-3}$$ Simplify inside the parentheses.

$$= 6 \times 10^{-4}$$ Write the product in scientific notation.

✓ **Check Understanding** ⑥ Simplify. Write each answer using scientific notation.
     a. $2.5(6 \times 10^3)$ **b.** $0.4(2 \times 10^{-9})$

EXERCISES

For more practice, see *Extra Practice*.

Practice and Problem Solving

Example 1
(page 400)

A   **Practice by Example**

Is each number written in scientific notation? If not, explain.

1. 55×10^4 **2.** 3.2×10^5 **3.** 0.9×10^{-2}

4. 7.3×10^{-5} **5.** 1.12×10^1 **6.** 46×10^7

Example 2 (page 401)	**Write each number in scientific notation.**

7. 9,040,000,000   **8.** 0.02   **9.** 9.3 million   **10.** 21,700

11. 0.00325   **12.** 8,003,000   **13.** 0.00092   **14.** 0.0156

Example 3 (page 401)	**Write each number in standard notation.**

15. 5×10^2 **16.** 5×10^{-2} **17.** 2.04×10^3 **18.** 7.2×10^5

19. 8.97×10^{-1} **20.** 1.3×10^0 **21.** 2.74×10^{-5} **22.** 4.8×10^{-3}

Examples 4, 5 (pages 401, 402)	**Order the numbers in each list from least to greatest.**

23. $10^5, 10^{-3}, 10^0, 10^{-1}, 10^1$

24. $9 \times 10^{-7}, 8 \times 10^{-8}, 7 \times 10^{-6}, 6 \times 10^{-10}$

25. $50.1 \times 10^{-3}, 4.8 \times 10^{-1}, 0.52 \times 10^{-3}, 56 \times 10^{-2}$

26. $0.53 \times 10^7, 5300 \times 10^{-1}, 5.3 \times 10^5, 530 \times 10^8$

27. Measuring instruments may have different degrees of precision. Instrument A is precise to 10^{-2} cm, Instrument B is precise to 5×10^{-2} cm, and Instrument C is precise to 8×10^{-3} cm. Order the instruments from most precise (least possible error) to least precise (greatest possible error).

Example 6 (page 402)	**Simplify. Write each answer using scientific notation.**

28. $8(7 \times 10^{-3})$ **29.** $8(3 \times 10^{14})$ **30.** $0.2(3 \times 10^2)$

31. $6(5.3 \times 10^{-4})$ **32.** $0.3(8.2 \times 10^{-3})$ **33.** $0.5(6.8 \times 10^5)$

B **Apply Your Skills**

For Exercises 34–39, find the missing value.

Selected Masses (kilograms)

		Standard Notation	Scientific Notation
34.	Elephant	■	5.4×10^3
35.	Adult human	70	■
36.	Dog	10	■
37.	Golf ball	0.046	■
38.	Paper clip	■	5×10^{-4}
39.	Oxygen atom	0.000000000000000000000000003	■

Real-World **Connection**

Elephant calves weigh from 100 to 145 kilograms.

40. Critical Thinking Is the number 10^5 in scientific notation? Explain.

41. Writing Explain how to write 48 million and 48 millionths in scientific notation.

42. Health Care In 2005, the population in the United States will be about 2.87×10^8. Spending for health care will be about $5745 per person. About how much will the United States spend on health care in 2005? Use scientific notation.

43. Computers A computer can perform 4.66×10^8 instructions per second. How many instructions is that per minute? Per hour? Use scientific notation.

44. Open-Ended If you were writing a report about the national debt, would you use scientific notation or standard notation to express the debt amount? Explain why.

45. Math in the Media Use the cartoon below.

FOX TROT by Bill Amend

a. Write 500 trillion in scientific notation.

b. Since the 10-second length of the movie is off by a factor of 500 trillion, what time span does the movie actually represent?

C Challenge **46. World Population** The world population in 2025 may reach 7.84×10^9 persons. This is about 3 times the world population in 1950. What was the world population in 1950?

47. Astronomy Use a calculator to find the volume of each planet with the given radius.

a. Mercury: 2439 km   **b.** Earth: 6378 km   **c.** Saturn: 60,268 km

48. Write $\frac{1}{300}$ using scientific notation.

Standardized Test Prep

Multiple Choice

49. Simplify $90(1.2 \times 10^{-5})$. Write the answer in scientific notation.
A. 1.08×10^{-7} **B.** 108.0×10^{-5} **C.** 108.0×10^{-3} **D.** 1.08×10^{-3}

50. Which answer has the states in the table at the right ordered from least to greatest projected population?
 F. New York, Florida, Virginia, Vermont
 G. Vermont, Virginia, New York, Florida
 H. Vermont, Virginia, Florida, New York
 I. Florida, New York, Virginia, Vermont

Projected Population in 2025

State	Population
Florida	2.07×10^7
Virginia	8.47×10^6
Vermont	6.78×10^5
New York	1.98×10^7

51. Which equals 275 million?
A. 275×10^5 **B.** 2.75×10^6
C. 2.75×10^8 **D.** 275×10^9

Short Response

52. A microscope set on 1000X makes an object appear 1000 times its actual size. If a bacterium is 8×10^{-4} millimeters in diameter, how large will it appear under this microscope? Use scientific notation. Show your work.

Mixed Review

Lesson 8-1   **Simplify each expression.**

53. $4(1.8)^0$ **54.** $12 \cdot 2^{-2}$ **55.** $6 \cdot 3^{-2}$ **56.** $\frac{4^3}{7^2}$ **57.** $\frac{3^{-2}}{9^0}$

Lesson 7-5   **Graph each linear inequality.**

58. $y < -\frac{1}{4}x + 2$ **59.** $y \geq \frac{2}{3}x$ **60.** $y < 3x - 4$

8-3

Multiplication Properties of Exponents

Lesson Preview

What You'll Learn

OBJECTIVE 1 To multiply powers

OBJECTIVE 2 To work with scientific notation

. . . And Why

To find the number of red blood cells in the human body, as in Example 5

✓ Check Skills You'll Need

(For help, go to Lesson 1-6.)

Rewrite each expression using exponents.

1. $t \cdot t \cdot t \cdot t \cdot t \cdot t \cdot t$

2. $(6 - m)(6 - m)(6 - m)$

3. $(r + 5)(r + 5)(r + 5)(r + 5)(r + 5)$

4. $5 \cdot 5 \cdot 5 \cdot s \cdot s \cdot s$

Simplify.

5. -5^4

6. $(-5)^4$

7. $(-5)^0$

8. $(-5)^{-4}$

OBJECTIVE

1 | **Multiplying Powers**

🔑 **Interactive lesson includes instant self-check, tutorials, and activities.**

You can write a power as a product of powers with the same base. Think of the power as the product of factors.

$$8^6 = \underbrace{8 \cdot 8 \cdot 8 \cdot 8}_{8^4} \cdot \underbrace{8 \cdot 8}_{8^2} \qquad 8^6 = \underbrace{8 \cdot 8 \cdot 8}_{8^3} \cdot \underbrace{8 \cdot 8 \cdot 8}_{8^3}$$

The work above shows that $8^6 = 8^4 \cdot 8^2$ and $8^6 = 8^3 \cdot 8^3$. Notice the pattern in the exponents. The sums $4 + 2$ and $3 + 3$ both equal 6, the exponent of 8^6.

🔑 **Key Concepts**

Property	**Multiplying Powers With the Same Base**

For every nonzero number a and integers m and n, $a^m \cdot a^n = a^{m + n}$.

Examples $3^5 \cdot 3^4 = 3^{5 + 4} = 3^9$ $h^2 \cdot h^9 = h^{2 + 9} = h^{11}$

1 EXAMPLE **Multiplying Powers**

Rewrite each expression using each base only once.

a. $11^4 \cdot 11^3 = 11^{4 + 3}$ Add exponents of powers with the same base.

     $= 11^7$ Simplify the sum of the exponents.

b. $2^5 \cdot 2^2 \cdot 2^{-1} = 2^{5 + 2 - 1}$ Think of $5 + 2 - 1$ as $5 + 2 + (-1)$ so you can add the exponents.

     $= 2^6$ Simplify the sum of the exponents.

c. $5^{-2} \cdot 5^2 = 5^{-2 + 2}$ Add exponents of powers with the same base.

     $= 5^0$ Simplify the sum of the exponents.

     $= 1$ Use the definition of zero as an exponent.

✓ **Check Understanding** **1** Rewrite each expression using each base only once.

     a. $5^3 \cdot 5^6$ **b.** $2^4 \cdot 2^{-3}$ **c.** $7^{-3} \cdot 7^2 \cdot 7^6$

2 EXAMPLE Multiplying Powers in an Algebraic Expression

Need Help?

Remember that $x = x^1$.

Simplify each expression.

a. $x \cdot x^2 \cdot x^4 = x^{1 + 2 + 4}$ **Add exponents of powers with the same base.**

         $= x^7$ **Simplify.**

b. $2n^5 \cdot 3n^{-2} = (2 \cdot 3)(n^5 \cdot n^{-2})$ **Commutative Property of Multiplication**

         $= 6(n^{5 + (-2)})$ **Add exponents of powers with the same base.**

         $= 6n^3$ **Simplify.**

✓ **Check Understanding**   2 Simplify each expression.

    a. $a \cdot a^5$ **b.** $n^2 \cdot n^3 \cdot 7n$ **c.** $6y^2 \cdot 3y^3 \cdot 2y^{-4}$

When variable factors have more than one base, be careful to combine only those powers with the same base.

3 EXAMPLE Multiplying Powers in an Algebraic Expression

Simplify each expression.

a. $c^4 \cdot d^{-3} \cdot c^2 = c^4 \cdot c^2 \cdot d^{-3}$ **Commutative Property of Multiplication**

         $= c^{4 + 2} \cdot d^{-3}$ **Add exponents of powers with the same base.**

         $= \dfrac{c^6}{d^3}$ **Simplify.**

b. $5x \cdot 2y^4 \cdot 3x^8 = (5 \cdot 2 \cdot 3)(x \cdot x^8)(y^4)$ **Commutative and Associative Properties of Multiplication**

         $= 30(x^1 \cdot x^8)(y^4)$ **Multiply the coefficients. Write x as x^1.**

         $= 30(x^{1 + 8})(y^4)$ **Add exponents of powers with the same base.**

         $= 30x^9y^4$ **Simplify.**

✓ **Check Understanding**   3 Simplify each expression.

    a. $a \cdot b \cdot a^5$ **b.** $2y^3 \cdot 7x^2 \cdot 2y^4$ **c.** $m^2 \cdot n^{-2} \cdot 7m$

OBJECTIVE

2   Working With Scientific Notation

In Lesson 8-2, you wrote numbers in scientific notation using patterns to move decimal points. You can now use the property for multiplying powers with the same base to write numbers and to multiply numbers in scientific notation.

4 EXAMPLE Multiplying Numbers in Scientific Notation

Simplify $(7 \times 10^2)(4 \times 10^5)$. Write the answer in scientific notation.

$(7 \times 10^2)(4 \times 10^5) = (7 \cdot 4)(10^2 \cdot 10^5)$ **Commutative and Associative Properties of Multiplication**

         $= 28 \times 10^7$ **Simplify.**

         $= 2.8 \times 10^1 \cdot 10^7$ **Write 28 in scientific notation.**

         $= 2.8 \times 10^{1 + 7}$ **Add exponents of powers with the same base.**

         $= 2.8 \times 10^8$ **Simplify the sum of the exponents.**

✓ **Check Understanding**   4 Simplify each expression. Write each answer in scientific notation.

    a. $(2.5 \times 10^8)(6 \times 10^3)$ **b.** $(1.5 \times 10^{-2})(3 \times 10^4)$ **c.** $(9 \times 10^{-6})(7 \times 10^{-9})$

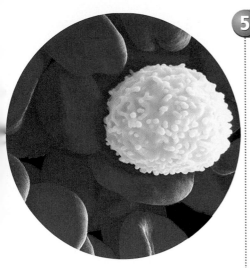

EXAMPLE Real-World 🌐 Problem Solving

Biology A human body contains about 3.2×10^4 μL (microliters) of blood for each pound of body weight. Each microliter of blood contains about 5×10^6 red blood cells. Find the approximate number of red blood cells in the body of a 125-lb person.

red blood cells = pounds $\cdot$ $\dfrac{\text{microliters}}{\text{pound}}$ $\cdot$ $\dfrac{\text{cells}}{\text{microliter}}$ **Use dimensional analysis.**

$\quad = 125 \text{ lb} \cdot (3.2 \times 10^4) \dfrac{\mu L}{\text{lb}} \cdot (5 \times 10^6) \dfrac{\text{cells}}{\mu L}$ **Substitute.**

$\quad = (125 \cdot 3.2 \cdot 5) \times (10^4 \cdot 10^6)$ **Commutative and Associative Properties of Multiplication**

$\quad = (2000) \times (10^{4\,+\,6})$ **Simplify.**

$\quad = 2000 \times 10^{10}$ **Add exponents.**

$\quad = 2 \times 10^3 \cdot 10^{10}$ **Write 2000 in scientific notation.**

$\quad = 2 \times 10^{13}$ **Add the exponents.**

There are about 2×10^{13} red blood cells in a 125-lb person.

Real-World 🌐 Connection

The blood cells shown in the photo above are magnified 5×10^3 times their actual size.

✔ **Check Understanding** ⑤ About how many red blood cells are in the body of a 160-lb soccer player?

EXERCISES

For more practice, see *Extra Practice*.

Practice and Problem Solving

Ⓐ **Practice by Example**

Example 1
(page 405)

Rewrite each expression using each base only once.

1. $2^6 \cdot 2^4$ **2.** $5^{-13} \cdot 10^5$ **3.** $10^{-6} \cdot 10^5 \cdot 10^1$

4. $(0.99)^3 \cdot (0.99)^0$ **5.** $6^6 \cdot 6^{-2} \cdot 6^5$ **6.** $(1.025)^2(1.025)^{-2}$

Example 2
(page 406)

Simplify each expression.

7. $c^{-2}c^7$ **8.** $3r \cdot r^4$ **9.** $5t^{-2} \cdot 2t^{-5}$

10. $(7x^5)(8x)$ **11.** $3x^2 \cdot x^2$ **12.** $(-2.4n^4)(2n^{-1})$

13. $b^{-2} \cdot b^4 \cdot b$ **14.** $(-2m^3)(3.5m^{-3})$ **15.** $(15a^3)(-3a)$

Example 3
(page 406)

16. $(x^5y^2)(x^{-6}y)$ **17.** $(5x^5)(3y^6)(3x^2)$ **18.** $(4c^4)(ac^3)(3a^5c)$

19. $x^6 \cdot y^2 \cdot x^4$ **20.** $a^6b^3 \cdot a^2b^{-2}$ **21.** $-m^2 \cdot 4r^3 \cdot 12r^{-4} \cdot 5m$

Example 4
(page 406)

Simplify each expression. Write each answer in scientific notation.

22. $(2 \times 10^3)(3 \times 10^2)$ **23.** $(2 \times 10^6)(3 \times 10^3)$ **24.** $(4 \times 10^6) \cdot 10^{-3}$

25. $(1 \times 10^3)(3.4 \times 10^{-8})$ **26.** $(8 \times 10^{-5})(7 \times 10^{-3})$ **27.** $(5 \times 10^7)(3 \times 10^{14})$

Example 5
(page 407)

Write each answer in scientific notation.

28. Astronomy The distance light travels in one year (one light-year) is about 5.88×10^{12} miles. The closest star to Earth (other than the sun) is Alpha Centauri, which is 4.35 light-years from Earth. About how many miles from Earth is Alpha Centauri?

Write each answer in scientific notation.

29. **Geology** Earth's crust contains approximately 120 trillion metric tons of gold. One metric ton of gold is worth about $9 million. What is the approximate value of the gold in Earth's crust?

30. **Astronomy** Light travels through space at a constant speed of about 3×10^5 km/s. Sunlight reflecting from the moon takes about 1.28×10^0 s to reach Earth. Find the distance from the moon to Earth.

B **Apply Your Skills**

Complete each equation.

31. $5^2 \cdot 5^{\blacksquare} = 5^{11}$

32. $5^7 \cdot 5^{\blacksquare} = 5^3$

33. $2^{\blacksquare} \cdot 2^4 = 2^1$

34. $c^{-5} \cdot c^{\blacksquare} = c^6$

35. $m^{\blacksquare} \cdot m^{-4} = m^{-9}$

36. $a \cdot a \cdot a^3 = a^{\blacksquare}$

37. $a^{\blacksquare} \cdot a^4 = 1$

38. $a^{12} \cdot a^{\blacksquare} = a^{12}$

39. $x^3 y^{\blacksquare} \cdot x^{\blacksquare} = y^2$

Geometry **Find the area of each figure.**

40.
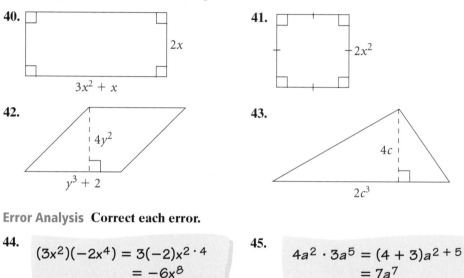
$2x$

$3x^2 + x$

41.
$2x^2$

42.
$4y^2$

$y^3 + 2$

43.
$4c$

$2c^3$

Error Analysis **Correct each error.**

44.
$(3x^2)(-2x^4) = 3(-2)x^{2 \cdot 4}$
$= -6x^8$

45.
$4a^2 \cdot 3a^5 = (4 + 3)a^{2 + 5}$
$= 7a^7$

46.
$x^6 \cdot x \cdot x^3 = x^{6 + 3}$
$= x^9$

47.
$3^4 \cdot 2^2 = 6^{4 + 2}$

Simplify each expression. Write each answer in scientific notation.

48. $(9 \times 10^7)(3 \times 10^{-16})$

49. $(8 \times 10^{-3})(0.1 \times 10^9)$

50. $(0.7 \times 10^{-12})(0.3 \times 10^8)$

51. $(0.4 \times 10^0)(3 \times 10^{-4})$

52. $(0.2 \times 10^5)(4 \times 10^{-12})$

53. $(0.5 \times 10^{13})(0.3 \times 10^{-4})$

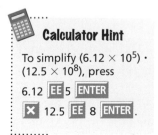

Calculator Hint

To simplify $(6.12 \times 10^5) \cdot (12.5 \times 10^8)$, press

6.12 [EE] 5 [ENTER]

[×] 12.5 [EE] 8 [ENTER].

54. **Chemistry** The term *mole* can be used in chemistry to refer to 6.02×10^{23} atoms of a substance. The mass of a single hydrogen atom is approximately 1.67×10^{-24} gram. What is the mass of 1 mole of hydrogen atoms?

55. a. **Open-Ended** Write y^8 as a product of two powers with the same base in four different ways. Use only positive exponents.
    b. Write y^8 as a product of two powers with the same base in four different ways using negative or zero exponents in each.
    c. **Reasoning** How many ways are there to write y^8 as the product of two powers? Explain your reasoning.

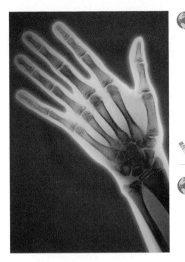

56. Medicine Medical X-rays, with a wavelength of about 10^{-10} meter, can penetrate your skin.
   a. Ultraviolet rays, which cause sunburn by penetrating only the top layers of skin, have a wavelength about 1000 times the wavelength of an X-ray. Find the wavelength of ultraviolet rays.
   b. Critical Thinking The wavelengths of visible light are between 4×10^{-7} meters and 7.5×10^{-7} meters. Are these wavelengths longer or shorter than those of ultraviolet rays? Explain.

57. Writing Explain why $x^3 \cdot y^5$ cannot be written with fewer bases.

58. Technology A CD-ROM stores about 650 megabytes (6.5×10^8 bytes) of information along a spiral track. Each byte uses about 9 micrometers (9×10^{-6} m) of space along the track. Find the length of the track.

Real-World Connection

X-rays are absorbed more by dense objects such as bones, and less by soft tissue. So bones show up as darker than soft tissues.

Use a calculator. Simplify each expression. Write each answer in scientific notation.

59. $(6.12 \times 10^5)(12.5 \times 10^8)$
60. $(1.98 \times 10^{-3})(2.04 \times 10^{11})$
61. $(9.55 \times 10^7)(7.371 \times 10^{-15})$
62. $(6.934 \times 10^{-9})(2.579 \times 10^{-4})$

63. Measurement There are about 3.35×10^{25} molecules in a liter of water. Pine Lake, in New York, has about 2×10^8 liters of water. About how many molecules of water are in Pine Lake?

64. Measurement About 8.4×10^{11} drops of water flow over Niagara Falls each minute. Each drop of water contains about 1.7×10^{21} molecules of water. About how many molecules of water flow over the falls each minute?

Simplify each expression.

65. $\dfrac{1}{x^2 \cdot x^{-5}}$
66. $\dfrac{1}{a^3 \cdot a^{-2}}$
67. $\dfrac{5}{c \cdot c^{-4}}$
68. $2a^2(3a + 5)$
69. $8m^3(m^2 + 7)$
70. $-4x^3(2x^2 - 9x)$

C Challenge

Simplify.

71. $3^x \cdot 3^{2 - x} \cdot 3^2$
72. $2^n \cdot 2^{n + 2} \cdot 2$
73. $3^x \cdot 2^y \cdot 3^2 \cdot 2^x$
74. $(a + b)^2(a + b)^{-3}$
75. $(t + 3)^7(t + 3)^{-5}$
76. $5^{x + 1} \cdot 5^{1 - x}$

77. a. Geometry Find the volume of a rectangular prism with length 1.3×10^{-3} km, width 1.5×10^{-3} km, and height 9.4×10^{-4} km. Write your answer in scientific notation.
   b. What is the volume of the prism in cubic meters?

78. Science An illustrator plans to draw a diagram of a protozoan for a science book. A protozoan is 1.1×10^{-4} meters long. The illustrator wants the diagram to be 7.7 centimeters long. The diagram will be how many times greater than the protozoan in size?

Standardized Test Prep

Multiple Choice

79. Simplify $(2x^2y^3)(4xy^{-2})$.
   A. $6x^3y^5$
   B. $6x^2y^6$
   C. $8x^2y$
   D. $8x^3y$

80. In the 2000 Olympics, the winning time for the women's 100-meter race was 1.79×10^{-1} min. Which is another way of expressing this time in minutes?
   F. 0.179
   G. 17.9
   H. 179×10^1
   I. 179×10^{-2}

Compare the boxed quantity in Column A with the boxed quantity in Column B. Choose the best answer.

A. The quantity in Column A is greater.
B. The quantity in Column B is greater.
C. The two quantities are equal.
D. The relationship cannot be determined from the given information.

	Column A	Column B
81.	$\left(3.84 \times 10^{-2}\right)\left(3.84 \times 10^{2}\right)$	$\frac{1}{12} \cdot (12)$
82.	the slope of $y = -\frac{1}{3}x + 7$	$3^5 \cdot 3^2 \cdot 3^{-9}$

Short Response

83. Approximately 4.7×10^7 disposable diapers are thrown away each day in the United States. About how many are thrown away in one year? Write your answer in scientific notation. Show your work.

Extended Response

84. Sophie's Desserts packages its cheesecake in boxes with square bottoms, as shown below. Answer each of the following, showing all of your work.

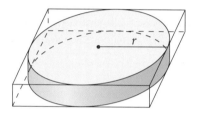

a. Write an expression for the area of the bottom of the box.
b. If the cheesecake has a radius of 5 in., what is the area of the bottom of the box?
c. The area of the bottom of a second box is 144 in.^{2}. What is the diameter of the largest cheesecake the box can hold?

Take It to the NET

Online lesson quiz at
www.PHSchool.com
Web Code: aea-0803

Mixed Review

Lesson 8-2

Write each number in scientific notation.

85. 1,280,000 **86.** 0.0035 **87.** 0.00009 **88.** 6.2 million

Write each number in standard form.

89. 8.76×10^8 **90.** 1.052×10^{-3} **91.** 9.1×10^{11} **92.** 2.9×10^{-4}

Lesson 7-6

Solve each system by graphing.

93. $y < 3x + 2$
$2x + y \geq 4$

94. $y < x + 6$
$x - 3y \leq 6$

95. $y > x + 4$
$x + 2y \leq 6$

Lesson 5-6

Find the third, seventh, and tenth terms of each sequence.

96. $A(n) = 10 + (n - 1)(4)$ **97.** $A(n) = -5 + (n - 1)(2)$

98. $A(n) = 12 + (n - 1)(-4)$ **99.** $A(n) = 1.2 + (n - 1)(-4)$

8-4 More Multiplication Properties of Exponents

Lesson Preview

What You'll Learn

OBJECTIVE 1
To raise a power to a power

OBJECTIVE 2
To raise a product to a power

...And Why

To find the resting energy of an object, as in Example 5

✔ Check Skills You'll Need

(For help, go to Lesson 8-3.)

Rewrite each expression using each base only once.

1. $3^2 \cdot 3^2 \cdot 3^2$
2. $2^3 \cdot 2^3 \cdot 2^3 \cdot 2^3$
3. $5^7 \cdot 5^7 \cdot 5^7 \cdot 5^7$
4. $7 \cdot 7 \cdot 7$

Simplify.

5. $x^3 \cdot x^3$
6. $a^2 \cdot a^2 \cdot a^2$
7. $y^{-2} \cdot y^{-2} \cdot y^{-2}$
8. $n^{-3} \cdot n^{-3}$

---

iTEXT Interactive lesson includes instant self-check, tutorials, and activities.

OBJECTIVE

1 Raising a Power to a Power

Investigation: Powers of Powers

You can use what you learned in the previous lesson to find a shortcut for simplifying expressions with powers. Copy and complete each statement.

1. $(3^6)^2 = 3^6 \cdot 3^6 = 3^{\blacksquare + \blacksquare} = 3^{6 \cdot \blacksquare} = 3^{\blacksquare}$

2. $(5^4)^3 = 5^4 \cdot 5^4 \cdot 5^4 = 5^{\blacksquare + \blacksquare + \blacksquare} = 5^{4 \cdot \blacksquare} = 5^{\blacksquare}$

3. $(2^7)^4 = 2^7 \cdot 2^7 \cdot 2^7 \cdot 2^7 = 2^{\blacksquare + \blacksquare + \blacksquare + \blacksquare} = 2^{7 \cdot \blacksquare} = 2^{\blacksquare}$

4. $(a^3)^2 = a^3 \cdot a^3 = a^{\blacksquare + \blacksquare} = a^{3 \cdot \blacksquare} = a^{\blacksquare}$

5. $(g^4)^3 = g^4 \cdot g^4 \cdot g^4 = g^{\blacksquare + \blacksquare + \blacksquare} = g^{4 \cdot \blacksquare} = g^{\blacksquare}$

6. $(c^3)^4 = c^3 \cdot c^3 \cdot c^3 \cdot c^3 = c^{\blacksquare + \blacksquare + \blacksquare + \blacksquare} = c^{3 \cdot \blacksquare} = c^{\blacksquare}$

7. a. **Make a Conjecture** What pattern do you see in your answers to Questions 1−6?
   b. Use your pattern to simplify $(8^6)^3$.

Raising a power to a power is the same as raising the base to the product of the exponents.

🔑 **Key Concepts**

Property	Raising a Power to a Power

For every nonzero number a and integers m and n, $(a^m)^n = a^{mn}$.

Examples $(5^4)^2 = 5^{4 \cdot 2} = 5^8$ $\qquad$ $(n^2)^5 = n^{2 \cdot 5} = n^{10}$

1 EXAMPLE Simplifying a Power Raised to a Power

Simplify $(x^3)^6$.

$(x^3)^6 = x^{3 \cdot 6}$ **Multiply exponents when raising a power to a power.**

$= x^{18}$ **Simplify.**

✓ **Check Understanding** **1** Simplify $(a^4)^7$ and $(a^{-4})^7$.

Be sure to use the order of operations. Simplify expressions in parentheses that are being raised to a power before multiplying by expressions outside the parentheses.

2 EXAMPLE Simplifying an Expression With Powers

Simplify $c^5(c^3)^{-2}$.

$c^5(c^3)^{-2} = c^5 \cdot c^{3 \cdot (-2)}$ **Multiply exponents in $(c^3)^{-2}$.**

$= c^5 \cdot c^{-6}$ **Simplify.**

$= c^{5 + (-6)}$ **Add exponents when multiplying powers with the same base.**

$= c^{-1}$ **Simplify.**

$= \dfrac{1}{c}$ **Write using only positive exponents.**

✓ **Check Understanding** **2** Simplify each expression.

  a. $(n^4)^3 \cdot n^5$ **b.** $t^2(t^7)^{-2}$ **c.** $(a^4)^2 \cdot (a^2)^5$

OBJECTIVE

2 Raising a Product to a Power

You can use repeated multiplication to simplify expressions like $(5y)^3$.

$(5y)^3 = 5y \cdot 5y \cdot 5y$

$= 5 \cdot 5 \cdot 5 \cdot y \cdot y \cdot y$

$= 5^3 y^3$

$= 125y^3$

Notice that $(5y)^3 = 5^3 y^3$. This illustrates another property of exponents.

🔑 **Key Concepts**

Property	**Raising a Product to a Power**

For every nonzero number a and b and integer n, $(ab)^n = a^n b^n$.

Example $(3x)^4 = 3^4 x^4 = 81x^4$

3 EXAMPLE Simplifying a Product Raised to a Power

Simplify $(2x^2)^4$.

$(2x^2)^4 = 2^4(x^2)^4$ **Raise each factor to the 4th power.**

$= 2^4 x^8$ **Multiply exponents of a power raised to a power.**

$= 16x^8$ **Simplify.**

✓ **Check Understanding** **3** Simplify each expression.

  a. $(2z)^4$ **b.** $(4g^5)^{-2}$ **c.** $(3t^0)^4$

Some expressions have more than one power raised to a power.

4 EXAMPLE Simplifying a Product Raised to a Power

Simplify $(x^{-2})^2(3xy^2)^4$.

$$(x^{-2})^2(3xy^2)^4 = (x^{-2})^2 \cdot 3^4 x^4 (y^2)^4$$ Raise the three factors to the 4th power.

$$= x^{-4} \cdot 3^4 x^4 y^8$$ Multiply the exponents of a power raised to a power.

$$= 3^4 \cdot x^{-4} \cdot x^4 \cdot y^8$$ Use the Commutative Property of Multiplication.

$$= 3^4 x^0 y^8$$ Add exponents of powers with the same base.

$$= 81 y^8$$ Simplify.

✔ **Check Understanding** **4** Simplify each expression.
   a. $(c^2)^3 (3c^5)^4$
   b. $(2a^3)^5(3ab^2)^3$
   c. $(6mn)^3(5m^{-3})^2$

You can use the property of raising a product to a power to solve problems involving scientific notation. For an expression like $(3 \times 10^8)^2$, raise both 3 and 10^8 to the second power.

5 EXAMPLE Real-World 🌐 Problem Solving

Physical Science All objects, even resting ones, contain energy. A raisin has a mass of 10^{-3} kg. The expression $10^{-3} \cdot (3 \times 10^8)^2$ describes the amount of resting energy in joules the raisin contains. Simplify the expression.

$$10^{-3} \cdot (3 \times 10^8)^2 = 10^{-3} \cdot 3^2 \cdot (10^8)^2$$ Raise each factor within parentheses to the second power.

$$= 10^{-3} \cdot 3^2 \cdot 10^{16}$$ Simplify $(10^8)^2$.

$$= 3^2 \cdot 10^{-3} \cdot 10^{16}$$ Use the Commutative Property of Multiplication.

$$= 3^2 \cdot 10^{-3 + 16}$$ Add exponents of powers with the same base.

$$= 9 \times 10^{13}$$ Simplify. Write in scientific notation.

Real-World 🌐 Connection

Albert Einstein is famous for discovering the relationship $E = mc^2$, where E is energy (in joules), m is mass (in kg), and c is the speed of light (about 3×10^8 meters per second).

✔ **Check Understanding** **5** **Energy** An hour of television use consumes 1.45×10^{-1} kWh (kilowatt-hour) of electricity. Each kilowatt-hour of electric use is equivalent to 3.6×10^6 joules of energy.
   a. Simplify the expression $(1.45 \times 10^{-1})(3.6 \times 10^6)$ to find how many joules a television uses in 1 hour.
   b. **Critical Thinking** Suppose you could release the resting energy in a raisin. About how many hours of television use could be powered by that energy?

EXERCISES

For more practice, see *Extra Practice*.

Practice and Problem Solving

A   **Practice by Example**

Examples 1, 2
(page 412)

Simplify each expression.

1. $(c^5)^2$
   2. $(c^2)^5$
   3. $(n^8)^4$
   4. $(q^{10})^{10}$

5. $(c^5)^3 c^4$
   6. $(d^3)^5(d^3)^0$
   7. $(t^2)^{-2}(t^2)^{-5}$
   8. $(x^3)^{-1}(x^2)^5$

Example 3
(page 412)

Simplify each expression.

9. $(5y)^4$ **10.** $(4m)^5$ **11.** $(7a)^2$ **12.** $(12g^4)^{-1}$

13. $(6y^2)^2$ **14.** $(3n^6)^4$ **15.** $(2y^4)^{-3}$ **16.** $(2p^6)^0$

Example 4
(page 413)

17. $(x^2)^5(x^3)^2$ **18.** $(2xy)^3x^2$ **19.** $(mg^4)^{-1}(mg^4)$

20. $(c^{-2})^3c^{-12}$ **21.** $(3b^{-2})^2(a^2b^4)^3$ **22.** $(2a^2c^4)^{-5}(c^{-1}a^7)^6$

Example 5
(page 413)

Simplify. Write each answer in scientific notation.

23. $(4 \times 10^5)^2$ **24.** $(3 \times 10^5)^2$ **25.** $(2 \times 10^{-10})^3$ **26.** $(2 \times 10^{-3})^3$

27. $(7 \times 10^4)^2$ **28.** $(6 \times 10^{12})^2$ **29.** $(4 \times 10^8)^{-2}$ **30.** $(3.5 \times 10^{-4})^3$

31. Geometry The length of one side of a cube is 9.5×10^{-4} m. What is the volume of the cube?

B **Apply Your Skills**

Complete each equation.

32. $(x^2)^{\blacksquare} = x^6$ **33.** $(m^{\blacksquare})^3 = m^{-12}$ **34.** $(b^2)^{\blacksquare} = b^8$

35. $(y^{-4})^{\blacksquare} = y^{12}$ **36.** $(n^9)^{\blacksquare} = 1$ **37.** $7(c^1)^{\blacksquare} = 7c^8$

38. $(5x^{\blacksquare})^2 = 25x^{-4}$ **39.** $(3x^3y^{\blacksquare})^3 = 27x^9$ **40.** $(m^2n^3)^{\blacksquare} = \dfrac{1}{m^6n^9}$

41. Error Analysis One student simplified $x^5 + x^5$ to x^{10}. A second student simplified $x^5 + x^5$ to $2x^5$. Which student is correct? Explain.

Simplify each expression.

42. $(4.1)^5 \cdot (4.1)^{-5}$ **43.** $3^2(3x)^3$ **44.** $(b^5)^3b^2$

45. $(-5x)^2 + 5x^2$ **46.** $(2x^{-3})^2 \cdot (0.2x)^2$ **47.** $(-2a^2b)^3(ab)^3$

48. $(3^7)^2 \cdot (3^{-4})^3$ **49.** $(10^3)^4(4.3 \times 10^{-8})$ **50.** $(4xy^2)^4(-y)^{-3}$

51. a. Geometry Write an expression for the surface area of each cube.
    b. How many times greater than the surface area of the small cube is the surface area of the large cube?
    c. Write an expression for the volume of each cube.
    d. How many times greater than the volume of the small cube is the volume of the large cube?

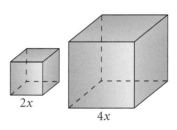

$2x$

$4x$

Write each expression with only one exponent. Use parentheses.

52. $m^4 \cdot n^4$ **53.** $(a^5)(b^5)(a^0)$ **54.** $49x^2y^2z^2$ **55.** $\dfrac{12x^2}{3y^2}$

56. Open-Ended Choose a value of n for the expression a^n. Express the power you wrote as a product of the form $(a^c)^d$ in four different ways.

57. Measurement Write each answer as a power of 10.
    a. How many cubic centimeters are in a cubic meter?
    b. How many cubic millimeters are in a cubic meter?
    c. How many cubic meters are in a cubic kilometer?
    d. How many cubic millimeters are in a cubic kilometer?

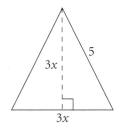

58. Computers Write each answer as a power of 2.
  a. Computer capacity is often measured in bits and bytes. A bit is the smallest unit, a 1 or 0 in the computer's memory. A byte is 2^3 bits. A megabyte (MB) is 2^{20} bytes. How many bits are in a megabyte?
  b. A gigabyte (GB) is 2^{10} megabytes. How many bytes are there in a gigabyte? How many bits are there in a gigabyte?

59. a. Geography Earth has a radius of about 6.4×10^6 m. Approximate the surface area of Earth using the formula for the surface area of a sphere, $S = 4\pi r^2$.
  b. Earth's surface is about 70% water, almost all of it in oceans. About how many square meters of Earth's surface are covered with water? .
  c. The oceans have an average depth of 3795 m. Estimate the volume of water on Earth.

60. Which expression or expressions do *not* equal 64?
  A. $2^5 \cdot 2$ **B.** 2^6 **C.** $2^2 \cdot 2^3$ **D.** $(2^3)^2$ **E.** $(2^2)(2^2)^2$

61. Writing Explain how you know when to add the exponents of powers and when to multiply the exponents.

Challenge

Solve each equation.

Sample $\quad 25^3 = 5^x$
$\qquad\quad (5^2)^3 = 5^x \quad$ Write 25 as a power of 5.
$\qquad\qquad 5^6 = 5^x \quad$ Simplify $(5^2)^3$.
$\qquad\qquad\quad 6 = x \quad$ Since the bases are the same, the exponents must be equal.

62. $5^6 = 25^x$ **63.** $8^2 = 2^x$ **64.** $3^x = 27^4$

65. $4^x = 2^6$ **66.** $3^{2x} = 9^4$ **67.** $2^x = \frac{1}{32}$

68. Critical Thinking Simplify $(x^3)^4$ and x^{3^4}. Are the expressions equivalent?

Standardized Test Prep

Multiple Choice

69. Which expression could you use for the area of the triangle at the right?
  A. $3x$
  B. $4.5x^2$
  C. $9x^2$
  D. $22.5x^2$

70. Evaluate $3a^2$ for $a = 5.1 \times 10^{-5}$.
  F. 1.53×10^{-10} **G.** 7.803×10^{-10}
  H. 1.53×10^{-9} **I.** 7.803×10^{-9}

71. If 7^{-2} is raised to the power of 3, which of the following describes the result?
  A. a number less than -7 **B.** a number between -1 and 0
  C. a number between 0 and 1   **D.** a number greater than 1

72. Which expression does NOT equal $25n^{12}$?
  F. $(5n^6)^2$ **G.** $(5n^3)(5n^9)$ **H.** $25(n^3)^9$ **I.** $5^2(n^2)^6$

Short Response

73. Does $(x^2 + 3y)^2$ equal $x^4 + 9y^2$? Substitute values for x and y to justify your answer.

Take It to the NET
Online lesson quiz at
www.PHSchool.com
Web Code: aea-0804

Lesson 8-3 Simplify each expression.

74. $bc^{-6} \cdot b$ **75.** $(a^2 b^3)(a^6)$ **76.** $9m^3(6m^2 n^4)$ **77.** $2t(-2t^4)$

Lesson 7-2 Solve each system using substitution.

78. $y = 3x + 5$ **79.** $y = 0.5x - 1$ **80.** $y = 5x - 9$ **81.** $y = x + 4$
     $y = -4x + 12$ $y = 0.2x + 0.4$ $y = 3x + 5$ $y = -5$

Lesson 6-1 Find the slope of the line that passes through each pair of points.

82. $(0, 3), (4, 0)$ **83.** $(2, -5), (3, 1)$ **84.** $(-3, 6), (1, 0)$ **85.** $(0, 0), (11, -9)$

✓ Checkpoint Quiz 1   Lessons 8-1 through 8-4

iTEXT Instant self-check quiz online and on CD-ROM

Simplify each expression.

1. $5^{-1}(3^{-2})$ **2.** $(r^{-5})^{-4}$ **3.** $(2x^5)(3x^{12})$ **4.** $\dfrac{mn^{-4}}{p^0 q^{-2}}$

5. $a^2 b^0(a^{-3})$ **6.** $(3^2)^{-1}(4m^2)^3$ **7.** $(2m^3)(3m^6)$ **8.** $(3t^2)^3(2t^0)^{-3}$

9. A certain bacteria population doubles in size every day. Suppose a sample starts with 500 bacteria. The expression $500 \cdot 2^x$ models the number of bacteria in the sample after x days. Evaluate the expression for $x = 0, 2, 5$.

10. Astronomy The diameter of Mars is about 6800 km.
   a. Write this number in scientific notation.
   b. Approximate the surface area of Mars using the formula for the surface area of a sphere, $S = 4\pi r^2$. Write your answer in scientific notation.
   c. Write your answer from part (b) in standard form.

Algebra at Work

•••••••••••••••••••••Dr. Jewel Plummer Cobb

Dr. Jewel Plummer Cobb was born in 1924 and obtained her master's and doctor's degrees in cell physiology from New York University. Dr. Cobb has concentrated on the study of normal and malignant skin cells and has published nearly 50 books, articles, and reports. Because the number of cancer cells grows exponentially, cell biologists often write cancer cell data in scientific notation.

Take It to the NET For more information about a career in cancer research, go to **www.PHSchool.com**.
Web Code: aeb-2031

Division Properties of Exponents

Lesson Preview

What You'll Learn

OBJECTIVE 1 To divide powers with the same base

OBJECTIVE 2 To raise a quotient to a power

...And Why

To find the amount of paper recycled per person in the United States, as in Example 2

✓ Check Skills You'll Need

(For help, go to Skills Handbook page 724.)

Write each fraction in simplest form.

1. $\frac{5}{20}$
2. $\frac{125}{25}$
3. $\frac{60}{100}$
4. $\frac{124}{4}$
5. $\frac{6}{15}$
6. $\frac{8}{30}$
7. $\frac{10}{35}$
8. $\frac{18}{63}$
9. $\frac{5xy}{15x}$
10. $\frac{6y^2}{3x}$
11. $\frac{3ac}{12a}$
12. $\frac{24m}{6mn^2}$

OBJECTIVE

1 **Dividing Powers With the Same Base**

> **i TEXT** Interactive lesson includes instant self-check, tutorials, and activities.

You can use repeated multiplication to simplify fractions. Expand the numerator and the denominator using repeated multiplication. Then cancel like terms.

$$\frac{5^6}{5^2} = \frac{\cancel{5} \cdot \cancel{5} \cdot 5 \cdot 5 \cdot 5 \cdot 5}{\cancel{5} \cdot \cancel{5}} = 5^4$$

This illustrates the following property of exponents.

🔑 **Key Concepts**

Property	**Dividing Powers With the Same Base**

For every nonzero number a and integers m and n, $\dfrac{a^m}{a^n} = a^{m-n}$.

Example $\dfrac{3^7}{3^3} = 3^{7-3} = 3^4$

Since division by zero is undefined, assume that no variable is equal to zero.

1 **EXAMPLE** **Simplifying an Algebraic Expression**

Simplify each expression.

a. $\dfrac{a^6}{a^{14}} = a^{6-14}$ Subtract exponents when dividing powers with the same base.

$= a^{-8}$ Simplify the exponents.

$= \dfrac{1}{a^8}$ Rewrite using positive exponents.

b. $\dfrac{c^{-1}d^3}{c^5d^{-4}} = c^{-1-5}d^{3-(-4)}$ Subtract exponents when dividing powers with the same base.

$= c^{-6}d^7$ Simplify.

$= \dfrac{d^7}{c^6}$ Rewrite using positive exponents.

1 Simplify each expression.

a. $\dfrac{b^4}{b^9}$ **b.** $\dfrac{z^{10}}{z^5}$ **c.** $\dfrac{a^2b}{a^4b^3}$ **d.** $\dfrac{m^{-1}n^2}{m^3n}$ **e.** $\dfrac{x^2y^{-1}z^4}{xy^4z^{-3}}$

When you divide numbers that are in scientific notation, you can use the property of dividing powers with the same base. In real-world situations, decide whether to write the result in standard or scientific notation.

2 **EXAMPLE** **Real-World** 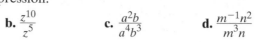 **Problem Solving**

Recycling In 1998, the total amount of wastepaper and cardboard recycled in the United States was 35 million tons. The population of the United States in 1998 was 270.5 million. On average, how much paper did each person recycle?

$\dfrac{35 \text{ million tons}}{270.5 \text{ million people}} = \dfrac{3.5 \times 10^7 \text{ tons}}{2.705 \times 10^8 \text{ people}}$ **Write in scientific notation.**

$\quad\quad = \dfrac{3.5}{2.705} \times 10^{7-8}$ **Subtract exponents when dividing powers with the same base.**

$\quad\quad = \dfrac{3.5}{2.705} \times 10^{-1}$ **Simplify the exponent.**

$\quad\quad \approx 1.3 \times 10^{-1}$ **Divide. Round to the nearest tenth.**

$\quad\quad = 0.13$ **Write in standard notation.**

● There was about 0.13 ton of waste paper recycled per person in 1998.

Real-World 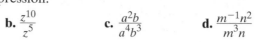 **Connection**

Worldwide, about 43% of the paper that is discarded is recovered for recycling.

✓ **Check Understanding** **2** Find each quotient. Write each answer in scientific notation.

a. $\dfrac{2 \times 10^3}{8 \times 10^8}$ **b.** $\dfrac{7.5 \times 10^{12}}{2.5 \times 10^{-4}}$ **c.** $\dfrac{4.2 \times 10^5}{12.6 \times 10^2}$

d. In 1998 the total amount of glass recycled in the United States was 3.2 million tons. The population of the United States in 1998 was 270.5 million people. On average, about how many tons of glass were recycled per person?

OBJECTIVE

2 **Raising a Quotient to a Power**

You can use repeated multiplication to simplify the expression $\left(\dfrac{x}{y}\right)^3$.

$\left(\dfrac{x}{y}\right)^3 = \dfrac{x}{y} \cdot \dfrac{x}{y} \cdot \dfrac{x}{y}$

$\quad\quad = \dfrac{x \cdot x \cdot x}{y \cdot y \cdot y}$

$\quad\quad = \dfrac{x^3}{y^3}$

This illustrates another property of exponents.

Key Concepts

Property	**Raising a Quotient to a Power**

For every nonzero number a and b and integer n, $\left(\dfrac{a}{b}\right)^n = \dfrac{a^n}{b^n}$.

Example $\left(\dfrac{4}{5}\right)^3 = \dfrac{4^3}{5^3} = \dfrac{64}{125}$

Raising a Quotient to a Power

Simplify $\left(\frac{4}{x^2}\right)^3$.

$$\left(\frac{4}{x^2}\right)^3 = \frac{4^3}{(x^2)^3}$$ Raise the numerator and the denominator to the third power.

$$= \frac{4^3}{x^6}$$ Multiply the exponents in the denominator.

$$= \frac{64}{x^6}$$ Simplify.

✓ **Check Understanding** **3** Simplify each expression.

a. $\left(\frac{3}{x^2}\right)^2$ **b.** $\left(\frac{x}{y^2}\right)^3$ **c.** $\left(\frac{t^7}{2^3}\right)^2$

You can use what you know about exponents to write an expression in the form $\left(\frac{a}{b}\right)^{-n}$ using positive exponents.

$$\left(\frac{a}{b}\right)^{-n} = \frac{1}{\left(\frac{a}{b}\right)^n}$$ Use the definition of negative exponent.

$$= \frac{1}{\frac{a^n}{b^n}}$$ Raise the quotient to a power.

$$= \frac{1}{\frac{a^n}{b^n}} \cdot \frac{b^n}{b^n}$$ Use the Identity Property of Multiplication to multiply by $\frac{b^n}{b^n}$.

$$= \frac{b^n}{a^n}$$ Simplify.

$$= \left(\frac{b}{a}\right)^n$$ Write the quotient using one exponent.

So, $\left(\frac{a}{b}\right)^{-n} = \left(\frac{b}{a}\right)^n$.

4 **EXAMPLE** **Simplifying an Exponential Expression**

Simplify each expression.

a. $\left(\frac{3}{5}\right)^{-2} = \left(\frac{5}{3}\right)^2$ Rewrite using the reciprocal of $\frac{3}{5}$.

$$= \frac{5^2}{3^2}$$ Raise the numerator and denominator to the second power.

$$= \frac{25}{9} \text{ or } 2\frac{7}{9}$$ Simplify.

b. $\left(-\frac{2x}{y}\right)^{-4} = \left(-\frac{y}{2x}\right)^4$ Rewrite using the reciprocal of $-\frac{2x}{y}$.

$$= \left(\frac{-y}{2x}\right)^4$$ Write the fraction with a negative numerator.

$$= \frac{(-y)^4}{(2x)^4}$$ Raise the numerator and denominator to the fourth power.

$$= \frac{y^4}{16x^4}$$ Simplify.

✓ **Check Understanding** **4** Simplify each expression.

a. $\left(\frac{3}{4}\right)^{-3}$ **b.** $\left(\frac{-1}{2}\right)^{-5}$ **c.** $\left(\frac{2r}{s}\right)^{-1}$ **d.** $\left(\frac{7a}{m}\right)^{-2}$

EXERCISES

For more practice, see *Extra Practice*.

Practice and Problem Solving

A **Practice by Example**

Example 1
(page 417)

Copy and complete each equation.

1. $\dfrac{5^9}{5^2} = 5^{\blacksquare}$

2. $\dfrac{2^4}{2^3} = 2^{\blacksquare}$

3. $\dfrac{3^2}{3^5} = 3^{\blacksquare}$

4. $\dfrac{5^2 5^3}{5^3 5^2} = 5^{\blacksquare}$

Simplify each expression.

5. $\dfrac{2^5}{2^7}$

6. $\dfrac{2^7}{2^5}$

7. $\dfrac{c^{12}}{c^{15}}$

8. $\dfrac{m^{-2}}{m^{-5}}$

9. $\dfrac{3s^{-9}}{6s^{-11}}$

10. $\dfrac{x^{13}y^2}{x^{13}y}$

11. $\dfrac{c^2 d^{-3}}{c^3 d^{-1}}$

12. $\dfrac{3^2 m^3 t^6}{3^5 m^7 t^{-5}}$

Example 2
(page 418)

Simplify each quotient. Write each answer in scientific notation.

13. $\dfrac{6.5 \times 10^{15}}{1.3 \times 10^8}$

14. $\dfrac{2.7 \times 10^{-8}}{9 \times 10^{-4}}$

15. $\dfrac{4.2 \times 10^8}{7 \times 10^5}$

16. $\dfrac{8.4 \times 10^{-5}}{2 \times 10^{-8}}$

17. $\dfrac{4.65 \times 10^{-4}}{3.1 \times 10^2}$

18. $\dfrac{3.5 \times 10^6}{5 \times 10^8}$

19. Television In 2000, people in the United States over age 2 watched television a total of 386 billion hours. The population of the United States over age 2 was about 265 million people.
   a. Write each number in scientific notation.
   b. Find the average number of hours of TV viewing per person older than age 2 for 2000.
   c. On average, how many hours per day did each person older than age 2 watch television in 2000?

20. Computers The speed of computers is measured in number of calculations per picosecond. There are 3.6×10^{15} picoseconds per hour. What fraction of a second is a picosecond?

Example 3
(page 419)

Simplify each expression.

21. $\left(\dfrac{3}{5}\right)^2$

22. $\left(\dfrac{1}{x}\right)^3$

23. $\left(\dfrac{2x}{y}\right)^5$

24. $\left(\dfrac{3a}{2b}\right)^4$

25. $\left(\dfrac{2^2}{5}\right)^3$

26. $\left(\dfrac{3^3}{3^4}\right)^2$

27. $\left(\dfrac{6}{n^6}\right)^2$

28. $\left(\dfrac{2p}{5}\right)^3$

Example 4
(page 419)

29. $\left(\dfrac{2}{3}\right)^{-1}$

30. $\left(\dfrac{2}{3}\right)^{-2}$

31. $\left(-\dfrac{2}{3}\right)^{-2}$

32. $\left(-\dfrac{2}{3}\right)^{-3}$

33. $\left(\dfrac{3x^4}{15}\right)^2$

34. $\left(\dfrac{4n}{2n^2}\right)^3$

35. $\left(\dfrac{c^5}{c^9}\right)^3$

36. $\left(\dfrac{3b^2}{5}\right)^0$

B **Apply Your Skills**

Explain why each expression is *not* in simplest form.

37. $5^3 m^3$

38. $x^5 y^{-2}$

39. $(2c)^4$

40. $x^0 y$

41. $\dfrac{d^7}{d}$

Simplify each expression.

42. $\dfrac{3^2 \cdot 5^0}{2^3}$

43. $\left(\dfrac{2m^5}{m^2}\right)^{-4}$

44. $\dfrac{5x^3}{(5x)^3}$

45. $\dfrac{(2a^7)(3a^2)}{6a^3}$

46. $\left(\dfrac{7t^3}{21t}\right)^3$

47. $\left(\dfrac{n^4 n}{n^{-2}}\right)^{-4}$

48. $\left(\dfrac{2k^3}{3k^{-2}}\right)^{-2}$

49. $\dfrac{7^9 \cdot (10)^2}{7^7}$

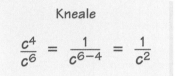

50. Telecommunications In 2000, there were 97.4 million households with telephones. The people in these households made 544 billion local calls and 97 billion long distance calls.
  a. Write each number in scientific notation.
  b. What was the average number of local calls placed per household? Round to the nearest whole number.
  c. What was the average number of long distance calls placed per household? Round to the nearest whole number.

1920's

1950's

51. a. Writing While simplifying the expression $\frac{c^4}{c^6}$, Kneale said, "I've found a property of exponents that's not in my algebra book!" Write an explanation of why Kneale's method works.
  b. Open-Ended Apply Kneale's method to an example you create.

> Kneale
>
> $$\frac{c^4}{c^6} = \frac{1}{c^{6-4}} = \frac{1}{c^2}$$

Today

Simplify each expression.

52. $\left(\dfrac{2ab^6}{a^3b}\right)^{-2}$

53. $\dfrac{a^3b^2c^{-4}}{a^{-2}b^5c^{-9}}$

54. $\dfrac{\left(\frac{1}{3}\right)^{-3}}{\left(\frac{1}{6}\right)^{-2}}$

55. $\dfrac{0.2^2 \cdot 0.2^3}{0.2^6}$

56. $\left(\dfrac{p^{-2}q^4r}{p^3q^5}\right)^5$

57. $\left(\dfrac{(-3)^2}{(-2)^{-4}}\right)^2$

58. $\left(\dfrac{(3x)^2y}{x^2y^4}\right)^{-2}$

59. $\dfrac{(5a^2)(6b^3)}{(2a^3)(25b^{-2})}$

60. a. Census The 2000 census counted approximately 281 million people in the United States. About 65,000 of those were centenarians, which means their ages are 100 or greater. Centenarians are about what percent of the population?
  b. About what percent of the population does not include people who are centenarians?

61. Critical Thinking Lena and Jared used different methods to simplify $\left(\dfrac{b^7}{b^3}\right)^2$. Why are both methods correct?

> Lena
>
> $$\left(\frac{b^7}{b^3}\right)^2 = \frac{b^{14}}{b^6}$$
> $$= b^8$$

> Jared
>
> $$\left(\frac{b^7}{b^3}\right)^2 = (b^4)^2$$
> $$= b^8$$

62. a. Finance In 1990, The United States government owed $3.23 trillion to its creditors. The population of the United States was 248.7 million people. How much did the government owe per person in 1990? Round to the nearest dollar.
  b. In 1999 the debt had grown to $5.66 trillion, with a population of 273 million. How much did the government owe per person? Round to the nearest dollar.
  c. What was the percent of increase in the average amount owed per person from 1990 to 1999?

63. a. Error Analysis What error did the student make in simplifying the expression at the right?
  b. What is the correct answer?

> $$5^4 \div 5 = \frac{5^4}{5}$$
> $$= 1^4$$
> $$= 1$$

Write each expression with only one exponent. You may need to use parentheses.

64. $\dfrac{3^5}{5^5}$ **65.** $\dfrac{m^7}{n^7}$ **66.** $\dfrac{d^8}{d^5}$ **67.** $\dfrac{10^7 \cdot 10^0}{10^{-3}}$

68. $\dfrac{27x^3}{8y^3}$ **69.** $\dfrac{4m^2}{169m^4}$ **70.** $\dfrac{49m^2}{25n^2}$ **71.** $\dfrac{125c^7}{216c^4}$

72. Medicine If you donate blood regularly, the American Red Cross recommends a 56-day waiting period between donations. One pint of blood contains about 2.4×10^{12} red blood cells. Your body normally produces about 2×10^6 red blood cells per second.
   a. At its normal rate, in how many seconds will your body replace the red blood cells lost by giving one pint of blood?
   b. Convert your answer from part (a) to days.

73. a. Open Ended Write three numbers in scientific notation.
   b. Divide each number by 2.
   c. Critical Thinking Is the power of 10 divided by 2 when you divide a number in scientific notation by 2? Explain.

Which property or properties of exponents would you use to simplify each expression?

74. 2^{-3} **75.** $\dfrac{2^2}{2^5}$ **76.** $\left(\dfrac{1}{2}\right)^3$ **77.** $\dfrac{1}{2^{-4}2^7}$ **78.** $\dfrac{(2^4)^3}{2^{15}}$

C Challenge **Simplify each expression.**

79. $n^{x+2} \div n^x$ **80.** $n^{5x} \div n^x$ **81.** $\left(\dfrac{x^m}{x^{m-2}}\right)^2$ **82.** $\dfrac{\left(\dfrac{n^5}{n^4}\right)}{n^3}$

83. Astronomy The ratio of a planet's maximum to minimum distance from the sun is related to how circular its orbit is.
   a. Copy and complete the table below. Round decimals to the nearest hundredth.
   b. Reasoning How can you use the ratio maximum : minimum to determine whether a planet's orbit is close to circular?
   c. Which planet has the least circular orbit? The most circular orbit?

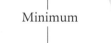

Minimum

Maximum

Distance From the Sun (kilometers)

Planet	Maximum	Minimum	Maximum : Minimum
Mercury	6.97×10^7	4.59×10^7	$\blacksquare : \blacksquare = \dfrac{6.97 \times 10^7}{4.59 \times 10^7} = \dfrac{6.97}{4.59} \approx 1.52$
Venus	1.089×10^8	1.075×10^8	$1.089 \times 10^8 : \blacksquare \approx \blacksquare$
Earth	1.521×10^8	1.471×10^8	$\blacksquare : 1.471 \times 10^8 \approx \blacksquare$
Mars	2.491×10^8	2.067×10^8	$\blacksquare : \blacksquare \approx \blacksquare$
Jupiter	8.157×10^8	7.409×10^8	$\blacksquare : \blacksquare \approx \blacksquare$
Saturn	1.507×10^9	1.347×10^9	$\blacksquare : \blacksquare \approx \blacksquare$
Uranus	3.004×10^9	2.735×10^9	$\blacksquare : \blacksquare \approx \blacksquare$
Neptune	4.537×10^9	4.457×10^9	$\blacksquare : \blacksquare \approx \blacksquare$
Pluto	7.375×10^9	4.425×10^9	$\blacksquare : \blacksquare \approx \blacksquare$

Multiple Choice

84. Simplify the expression $\frac{(-6)^5}{6^5}$.

    A. -6^5 **B.** -1 **C.** 1 **D.** 6^7

85. Evaluate $\frac{-5x^3y^5}{15x^{-7}y^5z^{-2}}$ for $x = -1$, $y = 5$, and $z = 3$.

    F. -9 **G.** -3 **H.** -1 **I.** 0

86. Which point on the number line below could be the graph of 2^n if n is a negative integer?

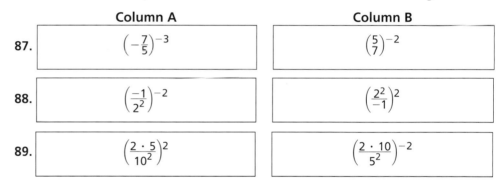

    A. W **B.** X **C.** Y **D.** Z

Quantitative Comparison

Compare the boxed quantity in Column A with the boxed quantity in Column B. Choose the best answer.

    A. The quantity in Column A is greater.
    B. The quantity in Column B is greater.
    C. The two quantities are equal.
    D. The relationship cannot be determined from the information given.

Column A	Column B
87. $\left(-\frac{7}{5}\right)^{-3}$	$\left(\frac{5}{7}\right)^{-2}$
88. $\left(\frac{-1}{2^2}\right)^{-2}$	$\left(\frac{2^2}{-1}\right)^2$
89. $\left(\frac{2 \cdot 5}{10^2}\right)^2$	$\left(\frac{2 \cdot 10}{5^2}\right)^{-2}$

Extended Response

Take It to the NET
Online lesson quiz at
www.PHSchool.com
Web Code: aea-0805

90. At its closest, Saturn is about 743,000,000 miles from Earth. A deep-space probe travels from Earth to Saturn at an average speed of 25,000 miles per hour. Assume that the probe can go straight from Earth to Saturn. How many hours will it take the probe to get from Earth to Saturn? About how many years will it take? Show your work.

Mixed Review

Lesson 8-4

Simplify each expression.

91. $(3y^2)^3$ **92.** $(2m^{-7})^3$ **93.** $(r^2t^{-5})^{-4}$ **94.** $2(3s^{-2})^{-3}$

95. $(2^3c^2)^{-1}$ **96.** $(-3)^2(-r^3)^2$ **97.** $(7^0n^{-3})^2(n^5)^2$ **98.** $(7^2y^{12})^0$

Lesson 7-1

Solve each system by graphing.

99. $y = 3x$ **100.** $y = 2x + 1$ **101.** $y = 5$ **102.** $y = 7$
        $y = -2x$ $y = x - 3$ $x = 3$ $y = 8$

Lesson 6-7

103. Graph $y = |x|$ and its translation $y = |x| + 3$.

Geometric Sequences

Lesson Preview

What You'll Learn

OBJECTIVE 1 To form geometric sequences

OBJECTIVE 2 To use formulas when describing geometric sequences

. . . And Why

To find the height of a ball after a number of bounces, as in Example 5

✓ Check Skills You'll Need

(For help, go to Lesson 5-6.)

Find the common difference of each sequence.

1. $1, 3, 5, 7, \ldots$ **2.** $19, 17, 15, 13, \ldots$

3. $1.3, 0.1, -1.1, -2.3, \ldots$ **4.** $18, 21.5, 25, 28.5, \ldots$

Use inductive reasoning to find the next two numbers in each pattern.

5. $2, 4, 8, 16, \ldots$ **6.** $4, 12, 36, \ldots$

7. $0.2, 0.4, 0.8, 1.6, \ldots$ **8.** $200, 100, 50, 25, \ldots$

New Vocabulary • geometric sequence • common ratio

---

i TEXT Interactive lesson includes instant self-check, tutorials, and activities.

OBJECTIVE 1 Geometric Sequences

Recall that a number pattern is also called a sequence, and each number in a sequence is a term of the sequence.

Reading Math

When you write a ratio of one term to the previous term in a geometric sequence, the ratios are equal. Thus the name is *common ratio*.

In Chapter 5 you studied arithmetic sequences, where you found each new term by adding the same amount to each previous term. Another kind of number sequence is a geometric sequence. You form a **geometric sequence** by multiplying a term in the sequence by a fixed number to find the next term. The fixed number is the **common ratio.**

$$\text{Term} \quad 2, \quad 10, \quad 50, \quad 250$$
$$\text{Common Ratio} \quad \times 5 \quad \times 5 \quad \times 5$$

1 EXAMPLE Finding the Common Ratio

Find the common ratio of each sequence.

a. $3, 12, 48, 192, \ldots$

$$3, \quad 12, \quad 48, \quad 192$$
$$\times 4 \quad \times 4 \quad \times 4$$

The common ratio is 4.

b. $80, 20, 5, \frac{5}{4}, \ldots$

$$80, \quad 20, \quad 5, \quad \frac{5}{4}$$
$$\times \frac{1}{4} \quad \times \frac{1}{4} \quad \times \frac{1}{4}$$

The common ratio is $\frac{1}{4}$.

✓ **Check Understanding** ❶ Find the common ratio of each sequence.

a. $750, 150, 30, 6, \ldots$ **b.** $-3, -6, -12, -24, \ldots$ **c.** $4, 6, 9, 13.5, \ldots$

2 EXAMPLE Finding the Next Terms in a Sequence

Find the next three terms of the sequence $2, -6, 18, -54, \ldots$

$$
\begin{array}{cccc}
2, & -6, & 18, & -54 \\
& \times(-3) & \times(-3) & \times(-3)
\end{array}
$$

The common ratio is -3. The next three terms are $-54(-3) = 162$, $162(-3) = -486$, and $-486(-3) = 1458$.

✔ **Check Understanding** ❷ Find the next three terms of each sequence.

a. $1, 3, 9, 27, \ldots$ **b.** $120, -60, 30, -15, \ldots$ **c.** $1.1, 2.2, 4.4, 8.8, \ldots$

You can find the common difference or common ratio to determine whether a sequence is arithmetic or geometric. If there is no common difference or common ratio, the sequence is neither arithmetic nor geometric.

3 EXAMPLE Arithmetic or Geometric Sequence

Determine whether each sequence is arithmetic or geometric.

a. $-7, -5, -3, -1, \ldots$

$$
\begin{array}{cccc}
-7, & -5, & -3, & -1 \\
& +2 & +2 & +2
\end{array}
$$

The sequence has a common difference. The sequence is arithmetic.

b. $56, 28, 14, 7, \ldots$

$$
\begin{array}{cccc}
56, & 28, & 14, & 7 \\
& \times\frac{1}{2} & \times\frac{1}{2} & \times\frac{1}{2}
\end{array}
$$

The sequence has a common ratio. The sequence is geometric.

✔ **Check Understanding** ❸ Determine whether each sequence is arithmetic or geometric.

a. $2, 4, 6, 8, \ldots$ **b.** $2, 4, 8, 16, \ldots$ **c.** $1, 3, 5, 7, \ldots$

OBJECTIVE

2 Using a Formula

You can use the common ratio of a geometric sequence to write a function rule for the sequence. Consider the sequence $2, 6, 18, 54, \ldots$ Its common ratio is 3.

Let $n = $ the term number in a sequence.

Let $A(n) = $ the value of the nth term of the sequence.

$A(1) = 2$

$A(2) = 2 \cdot 3 = 2 \cdot 3^1$

$A(3) = 2 \cdot 3 \cdot 3 = 2 \cdot 3^2$

Note that each exponent is one less than its term number.

$A(4) = 2 \cdot 3 \cdot 3 \cdot 3 = 2 \cdot 3^3$

$\vdots$

$A(n) = 2 \cdot 3 \cdot 3 \cdot 3 \cdot 3 \ldots \cdot 3 = 2 \cdot 3^{n-1}$

In general, you can write a function rule using the first term, the term number, and the common ratio. For the sequence above, the rule is $A(n) = 2 \cdot 3^{n-1}$.

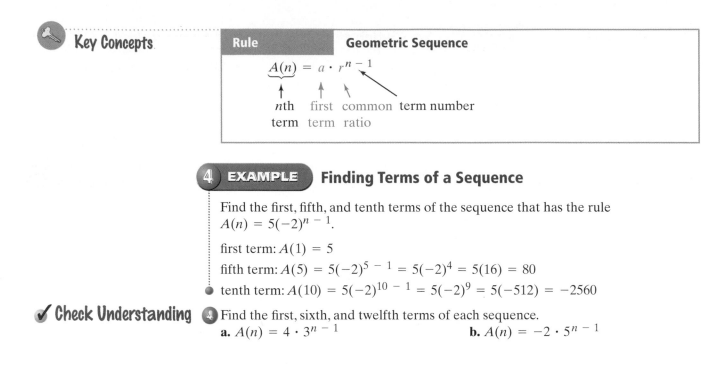

Rule	Geometric Sequence

$$A(n) = a \cdot r^{n-1}$$

nth term   first term   common ratio   term number

---

4 EXAMPLE   **Finding Terms of a Sequence**

Find the first, fifth, and tenth terms of the sequence that has the rule $A(n) = 5(-2)^{n-1}$.

first term: $A(1) = 5$

fifth term: $A(5) = 5(-2)^{5-1} = 5(-2)^4 = 5(16) = 80$

tenth term: $A(10) = 5(-2)^{10-1} = 5(-2)^9 = 5(-512) = -2560$

✓ Check Understanding   **4** Find the first, sixth, and twelfth terms of each sequence.

  a. $A(n) = 4 \cdot 3^{n-1}$ **b.** $A(n) = -2 \cdot 5^{n-1}$

You can write and evaluate a rule for a geometric sequence that models a real-world situation.

5 EXAMPLE   **Real-World 🌐 Problem Solving**

Sports You drop a rubber ball from a height of 1 meter and it bounces back to lower and lower heights. Each curved path has 80% the height of the previous path. Write a rule for the height of each successive path. What height will the ball reach at the top of the fifth path?

Draw a diagram to help understand the problem.

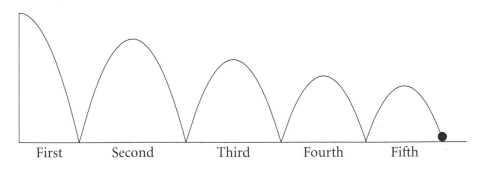

First   Second   Third   Fourth   Fifth

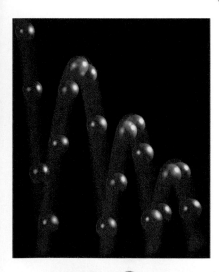

Real-World 🌐 Connection

Strobe-light photography is often used to highlight details of the motion of objects.

The height of the first path is 100 cm. So the height is 100 cm for the first term, with $n = 1$. The height of the fifth path is given by the term $n = 5$. The common ratio is 80%, or 0.8.

A rule for the sequence is $A(n) = 100 \cdot 0.8^{n-1}$.

$A(n) = 100 \cdot 0.8^{n-1}$ **Use the sequence to find the height of the fifth path.**

$A(5) = 100 \cdot 0.8^{5-1}$ **Substitute 5 for n.**

$\quad\;\; = 100 \cdot 0.8^4$ **Simplify exponents.**

$\quad\;\; = 100 \cdot 0.4096$ **Evaluate powers.**

$\quad\;\; = 40.96$ **Simplify.**

The height of the fourth bounce will be 40.96 cm.

5 Basketball You drop a basketball from a height of 2 meters. Each curved path has 56% of the height of the previous path. Using the height in centimeters, write a rule for the sequence. What height will the basketball reach at the top of the fourth path (when $n = 4$)? Round to the nearest tenth of a centimeter.

EXERCISES

For more practice, see *Extra Practice*.

Practice and Problem Solving

A **Practice by Example**

Find the common ratio of each sequence.

Example 1
(page 424)

1. $2, 8, 32, 128, \ldots$ **2.** $-3, -12, -48, -192, \ldots$ **3.** $70, 7, 0.7, 0.07, \ldots$

4. $8, 20, 50, 125, \ldots$ **5.** $-80, 20, -5, 1.25, \ldots$ **6.** $0.45, 0.9, 1.8, 3.6, \ldots$

Example 2
(page 425)

Find the next three terms of each sequence.

7. $2.5, 5, 10, 20, \ldots$ **8.** $3, 6, 12, 24, \ldots$ **9.** $4, 6, 9, 13.5, \ldots$

10. $-8, 4, -2, 1, \ldots$ **11.** $225, 45, 9, 1.8 \ldots$ **12.** $-3, 6, -12, 24, \ldots$

Example 3
(page 425)

Determine whether each sequence is *arithmetic* or *geometric*.

13. $2, 14, 98, 686, \ldots$ **14.** $12, 8, 4, 0, \ldots$ **15.** $9, -36, 144, -576, \ldots$

16. $-5, -10, -15, -20, \ldots$ **17.** $0.6, 1.3, 2, 2.7, \ldots$ **18.** $9, 12, 16, 21\frac{1}{3}, \ldots$

Example 4
(page 426)

Find the first, fourth, and eighth terms of each sequence.

19. $A(n) = 5 \cdot 3^{n-1}$ **20.** $A(n) = -5 \cdot 3^{n-1}$ **21.** $A(n) = 5 \cdot (-3)^{n-1}$

22. $A(n) = 0.5 \cdot 3^{n-1}$ **23.** $A(n) = -2 \cdot 5^{n-1}$ **24.** $A(n) = -1.1 \cdot (-4)^{n-1}$

Example 5
(page 426)

Write a rule and find the given term in each geometric sequence described below.

25. What is the fifth term when the first term is 6 and the common ratio is 0.5?

26. What is the tenth term when the first term is -6 and the common ratio is 2?

27. What is the fourth term when the first term is 7 and the common ratio is 1.1?

28. What is the seventh term when the first term is 1 and the common ratio is -4?

29. You drop a handball from a height of 1 meter. Each curved path has 64% of the height of the previous path.
 a. Write a rule for the sequence using centimeters. The initial height is when $n = 1$.
 b. What height will the ball reach at the top of the sixth path?

B **Apply Your Skills**

Find the next three terms of each sequence. Then write a rule for each sequence.

30. $216, 72, 24, 8, \ldots$ **31.** $625, 125, 25, 5, \ldots$

32. $0.1, 0.9, 8.1, 72.9, \ldots$ **33.** $16, -8, 4, -2, \ldots$

Problem Solving Hint

For Exercises 30 and 31, making a list of the terms of a sequence, and their factors, can help you write a rule.

34. Open-Ended Write four terms of a geometric sequence. Then write a rule for your sequence.

35. Writing How can you determine whether a sequence is arithmetic or geometric?

36. Paper Folding You can fold a sheet of paper in half, making 2 rectangles. If you fold the paper in half again, you divide the paper into 4 rectangles. Suppose you were to keep folding the paper and making more rectangles.

a. Copy and complete the table at the right.
b. Write a rule to model this situation.
c. Suppose you could continue to fold the paper. How many rectangles would would there be if you could fold the paper 10 times?

Number of Folds	Number of Rectangles
0	1
1	2
2	4
3	■
4	■
5	■

Determine whether each sequence is *arithmetic*, *geometric*, or *neither*. Find the next three terms of each sequence.

37. $11, 9, 7, 5, \ldots$

38. $7, 6, 4, 1, \ldots$

39. $18, 9, 4.5, 2.25, \ldots$

40. $12, 14, 16, 18, \ldots$

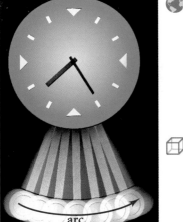

41. Physics On the first swing, a pendulum swings through an arc of length 36 centimeters. On each successive swing, the length of the arc is 90% of the length of the previous swing.

a. Write a rule to model this situation.
b. **Critical Thinking** What value of n would you use to find the length of the arc on the sixth swing? Explain.
c. Find the length of the arc on the sixth swing, to the nearest tenth of a centimeter.

42. a. Geometry What fraction of each figure is shaded?
b. Rewrite each fraction from part (a) in the form $2^■$.
c. Write a rule that relates the figure number n to the shaded rectangle r.
d. What portion of the square would be shaded in Figure 10?

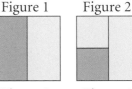

Figure 1 Figure 2

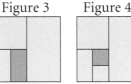

Figure 3 Figure 4

43. Reasoning Can zero be a term of a geometric sequence that has terms that are not zero? Explain.

C **Challenge** **44. Fractal Geometry** The figures below show the first four steps in making Sierpinski's Triangle.

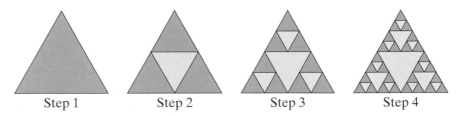

Step 1   Step 2   Step 3   Step 4

a. **Patterns** What fraction of each step is shaded?
b. Use your answer from part (a) to write a rule that relates the step number n to the fraction r of the figure that is shaded.
c. What fraction of Step 6 would be shaded?
d. **Patterns** What fraction of each step is *not* shaded?
e. Write a rule that relates the step number n to the fraction r of the figure that is *not* shaded.
f. What fraction of Step 8 would *not* be shaded?

Find each common ratio. Then find the next three terms in each sequence.

45. $x, x^2, x^3, x^4, \ldots$ **46.** $\frac{1}{3}, x, 3x^2, 9x^3, \ldots$ **47.** $xy, x^2y^3, x^3y^5, x^4y^7, \ldots$

48. $\frac{2}{b^2}, \frac{2a}{b}, 2a^2, 2a^3b, \ldots$ **49.** $2 \times 10^7, 1.2 \times 10^6, 7.2 \times 10^4, 4.32 \times 10^3, \ldots$

50. What term is 512 in the geometric sequence with the first term 2 and the common ratio 4?

51. Which set of numbers continues the pattern 27, 9, 3, 1, ... ?

A. $-3, -9, -27$ **B.** $-\frac{1}{3}, -\frac{1}{6}, -\frac{1}{9}$

C. $\frac{1}{3}, \frac{1}{6}, \frac{1}{9}$ **D.** $\frac{1}{3}, \frac{1}{9}, \frac{1}{27}$

52. Charlie is stacking cans at a grocery store. The picture shows the first four tiers. How many cans are there in 6 rows?

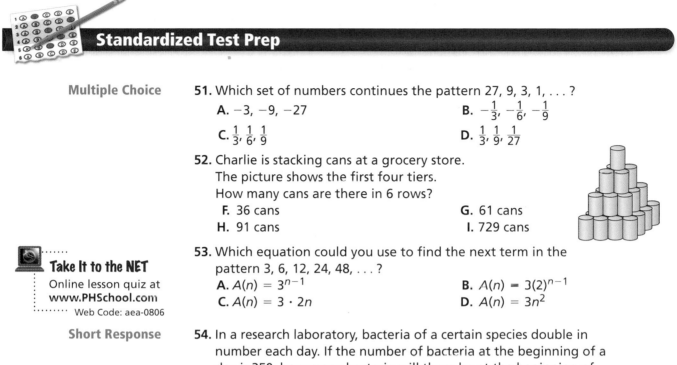

  F. 36 cans   **G.** 61 cans
  H. 91 cans   **I.** 729 cans

53. Which equation could you use to find the next term in the pattern 3, 6, 12, 24, 48, ... ?

  A. $A(n) = 3^{n-1}$ **B.** $A(n) = 3(2)^{n-1}$
  C. $A(n) = 3 \cdot 2n$ **D.** $A(n) = 3n^2$

Short Response

54. In a research laboratory, bacteria of a certain species double in number each day. If the number of bacteria at the beginning of a day is 350, how many bacteria will there be at the beginning of the 5th day? Show your work.

Mixed Review

Lesson 8-5

Simplify each expression.

55. $\left(\frac{a^2}{a^3}\right)^{-4}$ **56.** $\left(\frac{1}{2}\right)^{-4}$ **57.** $\left(\frac{x^2z}{z^{-3}}\right)^{-5}$ **58.** $\left(\frac{m^{-3}}{n^4}\right)^0$

59. $\left(\frac{8}{9}\right)^{-2}$ **60.** $\left(\frac{m^4}{m^2}\right)^{-7}$ **61.** $\left(\frac{pq^0}{p^4}\right)^5$ **62.** $\left(\frac{c^2d^{-2}}{d^3}\right)^{-1}$

63. Write 0.002467 in scientific notation.

Lesson 8-2

64. Water Conservation The Folsom Dam in California holds 1 million acre-feet of water in a reservoir. An acre-foot of water is the amount of water that covers an acre to the depth of one foot, or 326,000 gal. How many gallons are in the reservoir? Write your answer in scientific notation.

Lesson 5-5

Write an equation of the direct variation that includes the given point.

65. $(3, 8)$ **66.** $(-5, 2)$ **67.** $(6, -7)$ **68.** $(-3, -5)$

69. $(4, 7)$ **70.** $(-16, 4)$ **71.** $(9, 5)$ **72.** $(4, -2)$

Exponential Functions

Lesson Preview

What You'll Learn

OBJECTIVE 1
To evaluate exponential functions

OBJECTIVE 2
To graph exponential functions

...And Why

To use an exponential model for a population of rabbits, as in Example 2

✓ Check Skills You'll Need

(For help, go to Lessons 6-2 and 8-1.)

Graph each function.

1. $y = 3x$ **2.** $y = 4x$ **3.** $y = -2x$

Simplify each expression.

4. 3^2 **5.** 5^{-3} **6.** $2 \cdot 3^4$

7. $2 \cdot 3^{-2}$ **8.** $3 \cdot 2^{-1}$ **9.** $10 \cdot 3^2$

New Vocabulary
• exponential function

OBJECTIVE

1   Evaluating Exponential Functions

🔲 Interactive lesson includes instant self-check, tutorials, and activities.

The rules you wrote in Lesson 8-6 to describe geometric sequences, such as $A(n) = 3 \cdot 4^{n-1}$, are examples of exponential functions.

🔑 **Key Concepts**

Definition	**Exponential Function**

An **exponential function** is a function in the form $y = a \cdot b^x$, where a is a nonzero constant, b is greater than 0 and not equal to 1, and x is a real number.

Examples $y = 0.5 \cdot 2^x$ $f(x) = -2 \cdot 0.5^x$

You can evaluate an exponential function for given values of the domain to find the corresponding values of the range.

1 EXAMPLE   Evaluating an Exponential Function

❓ Need Help?

You can review domain and range in Lesson 5-2.

Evaluate each exponential function.

a. $y = 5^x$ for $x = 2, 3, 4$

x	5^x	y
2	$5^2 =\ \ 25$	25
3	$5^3 = 125$	125
4	$5^4 = 625$	625

b. $t(n) = 4 \cdot 3^n$ for the domain $\{-3, 6\}$

n	$4 \cdot 3^n$	$t(n)$
-3	$4 \cdot 3^{-3} = 4 \cdot \frac{1}{27} = \frac{4}{27}$	$\frac{4}{27}$
6	$4 \cdot 3^6 = 4 \cdot 729 = 2916$	2916

✓ **Check Understanding**   **1** Evaluate each exponential function for the domain $\{-2, 0, 3\}$.

    a. $y = 4^x$ **b.** $f(x) = 10 \cdot 5^x$ **c.** $g(x) = -2 \cdot 3^x$

You can evaluate exponential functions to solve real-world problems.

2 EXAMPLE **Real-World Problem Solving**

Biology Suppose 20 rabbits are taken to an island. The rabbit population then triples every half year. The function $f(x) = 20 \cdot 3^x$, where x is the number of half-year periods, models this situation. How many rabbits would there be after 2 years?

$$f(x) = 20 \cdot 3^x$$
$$= 20 \cdot 3^4 \quad \text{In 2 years, there are 4 half years. Evaluate the function for } x = 4.$$
$$= 20 \cdot 81 \quad \text{Simplify powers.}$$
$$= 1620 \quad \text{Simplify.}$$

After two years, there would be 1620 rabbits.

Real-World Connection

Rabbits were brought to Australia in 1860. Their numbers increased exponentially.

✓ **Check Understanding** ② Suppose 10 animals are taken to an island, and then the population of these animals quadruples every year. Use the function $f(x) = 10 \cdot 4^x$. How many animals would there be after 6 years?

OBJECTIVE

2 Graphing Exponential Functions

Here are two graphs that show what exponential functions generally look like.

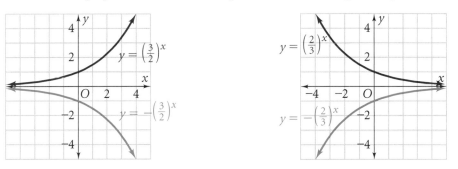

To graph an exponential function, make a table of values. Plot the points. Then join the points to form a smooth curve.

3 EXAMPLE **Graphs of Exponential Functions**

Graph $y = 3 \cdot 2^x$.

x	$3 \cdot 2^x$	(x, y)
-2	$3 \cdot 2^{-2} = \frac{3}{2^2} = \frac{3}{4}$	$\left(-2, \frac{3}{4}\right)$
-1	$3 \cdot 2^{-1} = \frac{3}{2^1} = 1\frac{1}{2}$	$\left(-1, 1\frac{1}{2}\right)$
0	$3 \cdot 2^0 = 3 \cdot 1 = 3$	$(0, 3)$
1	$3 \cdot 2^1 = 3 \cdot 2 = 6$	$(1, 6)$
2	$3 \cdot 2^2 = 3 \cdot 4 = 12$	$(2, 12)$

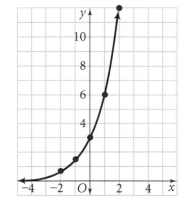

✓ **Check Understanding** ③ Graph each exponential function.
  a. $y = 0.5 \cdot 2^x$ **b.** $y = -0.5 \cdot 2^x$ **c.** $y = 2 \cdot (0.5)^x$

You can graph exponential functions to model real-world situations.

4 EXAMPLE <u>Real-World</u> 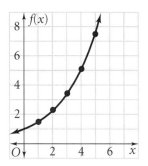 **Problem Solving**

Photocopying Many photocopiers allow you to choose how large you want an image to be. The function $f(x) = 1.5^x$ models the new size of an image being copied over and over at 150%, where x is the number of enlargements. Graph the function.

x	1.5^x	$(x, f(x))$
1	$1.5^1 = 1.5$	$(1, 1.5)$
2	$1.5^2 = 2.25 \approx 2.3$	$(2, 2.3)$
3	$1.5^3 = 3.375 \approx 3.4$	$(3, 3.4)$
4	$1.5^4 = 5.0625 \approx 5.1$	$(4, 5.1)$
5	$1.5^5 = 7.59375 \approx 7.6$	$(5, 7.6)$

✓**Check Understanding** **4** **a.** You can also make images that are smaller than the original on a photocopier. The function $y = 0.9^x$ models the new size of an image being copied over and over at 90%. Graph the function.

b. Critical Thinking In both models, what does $f(0)$ represent?

EXERCISES

For more practice, see *Extra Practice*.

Practice and Problem Solving

A **Practice by Example**

Example 1
(page 430)

Evaluate each function rule for the given value.

1. $f(x) = 6^x$ for $x = 3$

2. $g(t) = 2 \cdot 3^t$ for $t = -2$

3. $y = 20 \cdot (0.5)^x$ for $x = 3$

4. $h(w) = 0.5 \cdot 4^w$ for $w = 3$

5. $y = 50 \cdot (0.3)^x$ for $x = 2$

6. $f(x) = 1.8 \cdot 2^x$ for $x = 6$

7. $y = 100 \cdot \left(\frac{1}{2}\right)^x$ for $x = -4$

8. $y = 9 \cdot \left(\frac{5}{2}\right)^x$ for $x = -3$

Example 2
(page 431)

9. Finance Suppose an investment of $10,000 doubles in value every 13 years. How much is the investment worth after 52 years? After 65 years?

10. Finance Suppose an investment of $500 doubles in value every 15 years. How much is the investment worth after 30 years? After 45 years?

11. Finance Suppose an investment of $2000 doubles in value every 8 years. How much is the investment worth after 24 years? After 32 years?

Example 3
(page 431)

Match each table with the function that models the data.

12. $y = 3x$ 　　　　　　 **13.** $y = x^3$ 　　　　　　 **14.** $y = 3^x$

A.

x	y
1	3
2	6
3	9
4	12

B.

x	y
1	3
2	9
3	27
4	81

C.

x	y
1	1
2	8
3	27
4	64

Match each function rule with the graph of the function.

15. $y = 2^x$ **16.** $y = -(2^x)$ **17.** $y = \left(\frac{1}{2}\right)^x$ **18.** $y = -\left(\frac{1}{2}\right)^x$

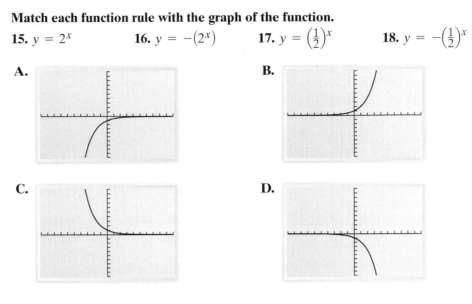

A.

B.

C.

D.

Graph each function.

19. $y = 10 \cdot 2^x$ **20.** $y = 0.1 \cdot 2^x$ **21.** $y = \frac{1}{4} \cdot 2^x$ **22.** $y = 4^x$

Example 4
(page 432)

23. Photocopying Suppose you are photocopying an image, reducing it to 85% its original size. The function $y = 0.85^x$ models the size of an image after x number of times it is reduced. Graph the function.

24. Science A population of 100 insects triples in size every month. The function $y = 100 \cdot 3^x$ models the population after x months. Graph the function.

B **Apply Your Skills**

Evaluate each function for the domain $\{-2, -1, 0, 1, 2, 3\}$. As the values of the domain increase, do the values of the range *increase* or *decrease*?

25. $f(x) = 5^x$ **26.** $y = 2.5^x$ **27.** $h(x) = 0.1^x$ **28.** $f(x) = 5 \cdot 4^x$

29. $y = 0.5^x$ **30.** $y = \left(\frac{2}{3}\right)^x$ **31.** $g(x) = 4 \cdot 10^x$ **32.** $y = 100 \cdot 0.3^x$

33. a. Open-Ended Write an exponential function for which values of y increase as values of x increase.
 b. Write an exponential function for which values of y decrease as values of x increase.

34. Biology A certain species of bacteria in a laboratory culture begins with 75 cells and doubles in number every 20 min.
 a. Copy, complete, and extend the table to find when there will be more than 5,000 bacteria cells.

Time (min)	Number of 20-min Time Periods	Pattern	Number of Bacteria Cells
Initial	0	75	75
20	1	75 · 2	$75 \cdot 2^{\blacksquare} = \blacksquare$
40	▓	75 · 2 · 2	$75 \cdot 2^{\blacksquare} = \blacksquare$
60	▓	▓	$75 \cdot 2^{\blacksquare} = \blacksquare$
▓	▓	▓	▓

 b. Write a function rule to model the situation.

35. a. Graph $y = 2^x$, $y = 4^x$, and $y = (0.25)^x$.
  b. What point is on each graph?
  c. Does the graph of an exponential function intersect the x-axis? Explain.
  d. **Critical Thinking** How does the graph of an exponential function change as the base increases or decreases?

36. Ecology In 50 days, a water hyacinth can generate 1000 offspring (the number of plants is multiplied by 1000).
  a. How many hyacinth plants could there be after 150 days?
  b. How many hyacinth plants could there be after 200 days?

37. a. Make a table of values for the domain $\{1, 2, 3, 4, 5\}$ of the function $y = (-2)^x$.
  b. What pattern do you see in the outputs?
  c. **Critical Thinking** Is $y = (-2)^x$ an exponential function? Justify your answer.

Which function is greater at the given value?

38. $y = 5^x$ or $y = x^5$ at $x = 3$ **39.** $f(t) = 10 \cdot 2^t$ or $f(t) = 200 \cdot t^2$ at $t = 7$

40. $y = 3^x$ or $y = x^3$ at $x = 4$ **41.** $f(x) = 2^x$ or $f(x) = 100x^2$ at $x = 10$

42. Writing Analyze the range of the function $f(x) = 500 \cdot 1^x$ using the domain $\{1, 2, 3, 4, 5\}$. Explain why the definition of *exponential function* includes the restriction that $b \neq 1$.

43. a. Graphing Calculator Graph the functions $y = x^2$ and $y = 2^x$.
  b. What happens to the graphs between $x = 1$ and $x = 3$?
  c. **Critical Thinking** How do you think the graph of $y = 6^x$ would compare to the graphs of $y = x^2$ and $y = 2^x$?

Challenge   **Solve each equation.**

44. $3^x = 9$ **45.** $3^x = \frac{1}{27}$ **46.** $2^x = 64$

47. $3 \cdot 2^x = 24$ **48.** $2 \cdot 3^x = 162$ **49.** $5 \cdot 2^x - 152 = 8$

50. Suppose $(0, 4)$ and $(2, 36)$ are on the graph of an exponential function.
  a. Use $(0, 4)$ in the general form of an exponential function $y = a \cdot b^x$ to find the value of the constant a.
  b. Use your answer from part (a) along with $(2, 36)$ to find the value of the constant b.
  c. Write a rule for the function.
  d. Evaluate the function for $x = -2$ and $x = 4$.

Standardized Test Prep

Multiple Choice

51. For the function $y = -3^x$, what is the value of y when $x = -2$?
  A. -9 **B.** $-\frac{1}{9}$ **C.** $\frac{1}{9}$ **D.** 9

52. Which function contains the points $(1, 3)$ and $(3, 6.75)$?
  F. $y = 1.675x + 1.325$ **G.** $y = 2 \cdot 1.5^x$
  H. $y = 1.5 \cdot 2^x$ **I.** $y = 1.325x + 1.675$

53. Which function has the same y-intercept as $y = 2^x$?
  A. $y = x + 1$ **B.** $y = 2x$ **C.** $y = x$ **D.** $y = 2(x + 1)$

Take It to the NET
Online lesson quiz at
www.PHSchool.com
.... Web Code: aea-0807

Short Response

54. A population of 6000 doubles in size every 10 years. Which equation relates the size of the population y to the number of 10-year periods x?

   F. $y = 6000 \cdot 10^x$ **G.** $y = 10 \cdot 2^x$

   H. $y = 6000 \cdot 2^x$ **I.** $y = 2 \cdot 100^x$

55. Between what two integer values of x do the graphs of $y = 20(0.5)^x$ and $y = 0.5 \cdot 4^x$ intersect? Show your work.

Mixed Review

Lesson 8-6

Find each common ratio. Then find the next three terms in each sequence.

56. $2, 10, 50, 250, \ldots$ **57.** $7, -21, 63, -189, \ldots$

58. $-0.2, -0.4, -0.8, -1.6, \ldots$ **59.** $27, -9, 3, -1, \ldots$

60. $450, 45, 4.5, 0.45, \ldots$ **61.** $7168, 1792, 448, 112, \ldots$

Lesson 6-5

Write an equation for the line that passes through the given point and is parallel to the given line.

62. $y = 5x + 1; (0, 0)$ **63.** $y = 3x - 2; (0, 1)$

64. $y = -2x + 5; (4, 0)$ **65.** $y = 0.4x + 5; (2, -3)$

✓ Checkpoint Quiz 2   Lessons 8-5 through 8-7

iTEXT Instant self-check quiz online and on CD-ROM

Simplify each expression.

1. $\left(\dfrac{3^2}{3^{-1}}\right)^4$ **2.** $\left(\dfrac{x^2}{y^3}\right)^{-5}$ **3.** $\left(\dfrac{10m^{-3}}{25n^{-6}}\right)^2$ **4.** $\left(\dfrac{6^2 t^{-3}}{6^2 r^0 t^2}\right)^2$

Determine whether each sequence is *arithmetic* or *geometric*.

5. $22, 11, 5.5, 2.75, \ldots$ **6.** $5, 10, 20, 40, 80, \ldots$ **7.** $5, 10, 15, 20, 25, \ldots$

8. Use the sequence $-100, 20, -4, \ldots$
   a. What is the first term?
   b. What is the common ratio?
   c. Write a rule for the sequence.
   d. Use your rule to find the fifth and seventh terms in the sequence.

9. Physics On the first swing, a pendulum swings through an arc of length 40 cm. On each successive swing, the length of the arc is 85% of the length of the previous swing.
   a. Write a rule to model this situation.
   b. Find the length of the arc on the fifth swing. Round your answer to the nearest millimeter.

10. Commuting Refer to the information at the left.
   a. Write the number of vehicles that crossed the George Washington Bridge in scientific notation.
   b. The Port Authority collected about $249 million in tolls from this bridge. Write this number in scientific notation.
   c. What was the average toll per vehicle?

Real-World Connection

About 108 million vehicles crossed the George Washington Bridge between New York and New Jersey in 2000.

Fitting Exponential Curves to Data

In Chapter 6 you learned how to find a line of best fit for a set of data. You can model some data better using an exponential function. To graph an exponential function, you may need to adjust your viewing window. Use your data to choose appropriate Xmax and Ymax values.

Take It to the NET
Graphing Calculator procedures online at **www.PHSchool.com**
Web Code: aee-2122

EXAMPLE

The table at the right shows the predicted number of customers downloading music files. Use a graphing calculator to find the best-fitting exponential function for the data. Then graph the function.

Digital Download

Year	Customers (millions)
2000	0.4
2001	1.0
2002	2.2
2003	4.4

Step 1 Use your calculator's STAT feature. Enter the data. Let 2000 correspond to $x = 0$.

Step 2 To get the equation of the best-fitting exponential function, press STAT ▶ 0 ENTER .

```
ExpReg
 y=a*b^x
 a=.4236368467
 b=2.221570366
 r²=.9960912309
 r=.9980437019
```

Step 3 To view the graph of the function press Y= CLEAR VARS 5 ▶ ▶ 1 GRAPH .

Xmin=0   Ymin=0
Xmax=6   Ymax=6

EXERCISES

Use a graphing calculator to find the exponential function that fits each set of data. Then (a) write a function for the data rounding decimals to the nearest hundredth, (b) sketch a graph of the function, and (c) use your answer from part (a) to predict the value of the function in the year 2010.

1. Shipment of Record Singles Let 1990 correspond to $x = 0$.

Year	1990	1994	1995	1996	1997	1998	1999
Record Singles (millions)	27.6	11.7	10.2	10.1	7.5	5.4	5.3

2. U.S. Energy Consumption Let 1990 correspond to $x = 0$.

Year	1990	1992	1993	1994	1995	1996	1997	1998
Btu (quadrillions)	84.3	85.5	87.3	89.2	90.9	93.9	94.3	94.6

3. U.S. Homes Heated by Coal Let 1950 correspond to $x = 0$.

Year	1950	1960	1970	1980	1991	1997
Percent of Homes	34.6	12.2	2.9	0.6	0.3	0.2

8-8

Exponential Growth and Decay

Lesson Preview

What You'll Learn

OBJECTIVE 1 To model exponential growth

OBJECTIVE 2 To model exponential decay

. . . And Why

To find the balance of a bank account, as in Examples 2 and 3

✓ Check Skills You'll Need

(For help, go to Lesson 4-3.)

Use the formula $I = prt$ to find the interest for principal p, interest rate r, and time t in years.

1. principal: $1000; interest rate: 5%; time: 2 years

2. principal: $360; interest rate: 6%; time: 3 years

3. principal: $2500; interest rate: 4.5%; time: 2 years

4. principal: $1680; interest rate: 5.25%; time: 4 years

5. principal: $1350; interest rate: 4.8%; time: 5 years

New Vocabulary • exponential growth • growth factor • compound interest • interest period • exponential decay • decay factor

---

OBJECTIVE 1

 Interactive lesson includes instant self-check, tutorials, and activities.

Exponential Growth

Real-World Connection

In 2000, Florida's population was about 16 million. Roughly 23% of the population was under the age of 18.

In 1990, Florida's population was about 13 million. Since 1990, the state's population has grown about 1.7% each year. This means that Florida's population is growing exponentially.

To find Florida's population in 1991, multiply the 1990 population by 1.7% and add this to the 1990 population. So the population in 1991 is (1.7% + 100%) of the 1990 population, or 101.7% of the 1990 population. Here is a function that models Florida's population since 1990.

population in millions
↓
$$y = 13.0(1.017)^x \quad \leftarrow \text{number of years since 1990}$$
↑
101.7% as a decimal

The following is a general rule for modeling exponential growth.

Key Concepts

Rule	Exponential Growth

Exponential growth can be modeled with the function $y = a \cdot b^x$ for $a > 0$ and $b > 1$.

starting amount (when $x = 0$)
↓
$y = a \cdot b^x \quad \leftarrow \text{exponent}$
↑
The base, which is greater than 1, is the **growth factor.**

1 EXAMPLE Modeling Exponential Growth

Medical Care Since 1985, the daily cost of patient care in community hospitals in the United States has increased about 8.1% per year. In 1985, such hospital costs were an average of $460 per day.

a. Write an equation to model the cost of hospital care.

  Relate $y = a \cdot b^x$ Use an exponential function.

  Define Let $x =$ the number of years since 1985.
      Let $y =$ the cost of community hospital care at various times.
      Let $a =$ the initial cost in 1985, $460.
      Let $b =$ the growth factor, which is $100\% + 8.1\% = 108.1\% = 1.081$.

  Write $y = 460 \cdot 1.081^x$

Calculator Hint

To evaluate
$460 \cdot 1081^{15}$, press

460 ✖ 1.081 ⋀

15 ENTER .

b. Use your equation to find the approximate cost per day in 2000.

  $y = 460 \cdot 1.081^x$

  $y = 460 \cdot 1.081^{15}$ **2000 is 15 years after 1985, so substitute 15 for *x*.**

  ≈ 1480 **Use a calculator. Round to the nearest dollar.**

  The average cost per day in 2000 was about $1480.

✓ **Check Understanding** **1** **a.** Suppose your community has 4512 students this year. The student population is growing 2.5% each year. Write an equation to model the student population.
  b. What will the student population be in 3 years?

When a bank pays interest on both the principal *and* the interest an account has already earned, the bank is paying **compound interest.** An **interest period** is the length of time over which interest is calculated.

2 EXAMPLE Compound Interest

BANK 1

Deposit **$1500**

Interest compounded
annually **6.5%**

Balance after 18 years
$4659.98

Savings Suppose your parents deposited $1500 in an account paying 6.5% interest compounded annually (once a year) when you were born. Find the account balance after 18 years.

  Relate $y = a \cdot b^x$ Use an exponential function.

  Define Let $x =$ the number of interest periods.
      Let $y =$ the balance.
      Let $a =$ the initial deposit, $1500.
      Let $b = 100\% + 6.5\% = 106.5\% = 1.065$.

  Write $y = 1500 \cdot 1.065^x$

      $= 1500 \cdot 1.065^{18}$ **Once a year for 18 years is 18 interest periods.**
                       Substitute 18 for *x*.

      ≈ 4659.98 **Use a calculator. Round to the nearest cent.**

  The balance after 18 years will be $4659.98.

✓ **Check Understanding** **2** **a.** Suppose the interest rate on the account in Example 2 was 8%. How much would be in the account after 18 years?
  b. Another formula for compound interest is $B = p(1 + r)^x$, where B is the balance, p is the principal, and r is the interest rate in decimal form. Use this formula to find the balance in the account in part (a).
  c. **Critical Thinking** Explain why the two formulas for finding compound interest are actually the same.

When interest is compounded quarterly (four times per year), you divide the interest rate by 4, the number of interest periods per year. To find the number of payment periods, you multiply the number of years by the number of interest periods per year.

Annual Interest Rate of 8%

Compounded	Periods per Year	Interest Rate per Period
annually	1	8% every year
semi-annually	2	$\frac{8\%}{2} = 4\%$ every 6 months
quarterly	4	$\frac{8\%}{4} = 2\%$ every 3 months
monthly	12	$\frac{8\%}{12} = 0.\overline{6}\%$ every month

3 EXAMPLE Compound Interest

Savings Suppose the account in Example 2 paid interest compounded quarterly instead of annually. Find the account balance after 18 years.

BANK 2

Deposit **$1500**

Interest compounded quarterly **6.5%**

Balance after 18 years **$4787.75**

Relate $y = a \cdot b^x$ Use an exponential function.

Define Let $x =$ the number of interest periods.
Let $y =$ the balance.
Let $a =$ the initial deposit, $1500.

Let $b = 100\% + \frac{6.5\%}{4}$ **There are 4 interest periods in 1 year, so divide the interest into 4 parts.**

$= 1 + 0.01625 = 1.01625$

Write $y = 1500 \cdot 1.01625^x$

$= 1500 \cdot 1.01625^{72}$ **Four interest periods a year for 18 years is 72 interest periods. Substitute 72 for x.**

≈ 4787.75 **Use a calculator. Round to the nearest cent.**

The balance after 18 years will be $4787.75.

✓ **Check Understanding** **3** **a.** Suppose the account in Example 3 paid interest compounded monthly. How much money would be in the account after 18 years?
b. You deposit $200 into an account earning 5%, compounded monthly. How much will be in the account after 1 year? After 2 years? After 5 years?

OBJECTIVE

2 Exponential Decay

The graphs at the right show exponential growth and exponential decay. For exponential growth, as x increases, y increases exponentially. For exponential decay, as x increases, y decreases exponentially.

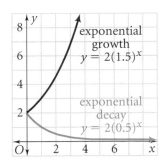

exponential growth
$y = 2(1.5)^x$

exponential decay
$y = 2(0.5)^x$

A real-world example of exponential decay is radioactive decay, in which radioactive elements break down by releasing particles and energy.

4 **EXAMPLE** **Real-World** 🌐 **Problem Solving**

Reading Math

Marie Curie (1867–1934) received Nobel prizes in physics and chemistry for her pioneering work with radioactive elements. The curie (a unit of radioactivity) is named for Marie Curie.

Medicine The half-life of a radioactive substance is the length of time it takes for one half of the substance to decay into another substance. To treat some forms of cancer, doctors use radioactive iodine. The half-life of iodine-131 is 8 days. A patient receives a 12-mCi (millicuries, a measure of radiation) treatment. How much iodine-131 is left in the patient 16 days later?

In 16 days, there are two 8-day half-lives.

After one half-life, there are 6 mCi left in the patient.

After two half-lives, there are 3 mCi left in the patient.

✓ **Check Understanding** **4** **a.** How many half-lives of iodine-131 occur in 32 days?

b. Suppose you start with a 50-mCi sample of iodine-131. How much iodine-131 is left after one half-life? After two half-lives?

c. **Chemistry** Cesium-137 has a half-life of 30 years. Suppose a lab stored a 30-mCi sample in 1973. How much of the sample will be left in 2003? In 2063?

The function $y = a \cdot b^x$ can model exponential decay as well as exponential growth.

🔑 **Key Concepts**

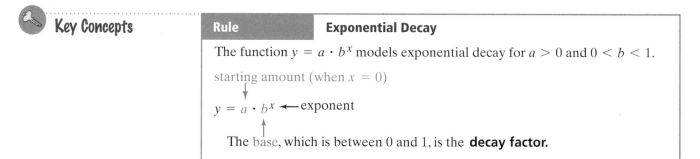

Rule **Exponential Decay**

The function $y = a \cdot b^x$ models exponential decay for $a > 0$ and $0 < b < 1$.

starting amount (when $x = 0$)

$y = a \cdot b^x$ ⟵ exponent

The base, which is between 0 and 1, is the **decay factor.**

When a number is decreased by 5%, the result is 95% of the original number. So when you find the decay factor, think 100% minus the percent a number is decreasing.

5 **EXAMPLE** **Modeling Exponential Decay**

Milk Consumption Since 1980, the number of gallons of whole milk each person in the United States drinks each year has decreased 4.1% each year. In 1980, each person drank an average of 16.5 gallons of whole milk per year.

a. Write an equation to model the gallons of whole milk drunk per person.

Relate $y = a \cdot b^x$ **Use an exponential function.**

Define Let x = the number of years since 1980.
Let y = the consumption of whole milk, in gallons.
Let $a = 16.5$, the initial number of gallons in 1980.
Let b = the decay factor, which is $100\% - 4.1\% = 95.9\% = 0.959$.

Write $y = 16.5 \cdot 0.959^x$

Real-World 🌐 **Connection**

One cup of milk contains 300 mg of calcium. The body absorbs about 32% of the calcium in milk.

b. Use your equation to find the approximate consumption per person of whole milk in 2000.

$y = 16.5 \cdot 0.959^x$

$y = 16.5 \cdot 0.959^{20}$ **2000 is 20 years after 1980, so substitute 20 for x.**

≈ 7.1 **Use a calculator. Round to the nearest tenth of a gallon.**

The average annual consumption of whole milk in 2000 was about 7 gal/person.

✔ **Check Understanding** ⑤ **Statistics** In 1990, the population of Washington, D.C., was about 604,000 people. Since then the population has decreased about 1.8% per year.
a. What is the initial number of people?
b. What is the decay factor?
c. Write an equation to model the population of Washington, D.C., since 1990.
d. Suppose the current trend in population change continues. Predict the population of Washington, D.C., in 2010.

EXERCISES

For more practice, see *Extra Practice*.

Practice and Problem Solving

Ⓐ Practice by Example

Example 1
(page 438)

Identify the initial amount a and the growth factor b in each exponential function.

1. $g(x) = 20 \cdot 2^x$ **2.** $y = 200 \cdot 1.0875^x$ **3.** $y = 10,000 \cdot 1.01^x$ **4.** $f(t) = 1.5^t$

5. Suppose the population of a city is 50,000 and is growing 3% each year.
a. The initial amount a is ▇.
b. The growth factor b is 100% + 3%, which is 1 + ▇ = ▇.
c. To find the population after one year, you multiply 50,000 · ▇.
d. Complete the equation $y = ▇ \cdot ▇^{▇}$ to find the population after x years.
e. Use your equation to predict the population after 25 years.

Examples 2, 3
(pages 438, 439)

Each percent is an annual interest rate. In the formula $y = a \cdot b^x$, what value would you use for b?

6. 4%   **7.** 5%   **8.** 3.7%   **9.** 8.75%   **10.** 0.5%

Assume each interest rate below is an annual interest rate. Find the interest rate for an account that is compounded quarterly and monthly.

11. 3%   **12.** 4%   **13.** 4.5%   **14.** 7.6%   **15.** 6.25%

Find the balance in each account.

16. $4000 principal earning 6% compounded annually, after 5 years

17. $12,000 principal earning 4.8% compounded annually, after 7 years

18. $500 principal earning 4% compounded quarterly, after 6 years

19. $20,000 deposit earning 3.5% compounded quarterly, after 10 years

Example 4
(page 440)

20. Chemistry The half-life of iodine-124 is 4 days. A technician measures a 40-mCi sample of iodine-124.
a. How many half-lives of iodine-124 occur in 16 days?
b. How much iodine-124 is in the sample 16 days after the technician measures the original sample?

21. Chemistry The half-life of carbon-11 is 20 min. A sample of carbon-11 has 25 mCi.
a. How many half-lives of carbon-11 occur in 1 hour?
b. How much carbon-11 is in the sample 1 hour after the original sample is measured?

Example 5
(page 440)

Identify the decay factor in each function.

22. $y = 5 \cdot 0.5^x$

23. $f(x) = 10 \cdot 0.1^x$

24. $g(x) = 100 \cdot \left(\frac{2}{3}\right)^x$

25. $y = 0.1 \cdot 0.9^x$

Identify each function as *exponential growth* or *exponential decay*.

26. $y = 0.68 \cdot 2^x$ **27.** $y = 2 \cdot 0.68^x$ **28.** $y = 68 \cdot 2^x$ **29.** $y = 68 \cdot 0.2^x$

30. Cars The value of a new car decreases exponentially. Suppose your mother buys a new car for $22,000. The value of the car decreases by 20% each year.
a. What is the initial price of the car? The decay factor?
b. Write an equation to model the value of the car x years after she buys it.
c. Find the value of the car after 6 years.

B **Apply Your Skills**   **Write an exponential function to model each situation. Find each amount after the specified time.**

31. A population of 130,000 grows 1% per year for 9 years.

32. A population of 3,000,000 decreases 1.5% annually for 10 years.

33. A $2400 principal earns 7% compounded annually for 10 years.

34. A $2400 principal earns 7% compounded monthly for 10 years.

35. Education Since 1985, the average annual cost y (in dollars) for tuition and fees at public two-year colleges in the United States has increased about 6.5% per year. In 1985, tuition and fees were an average of $584 per year.
a. Write an equation to model the cost of two-year colleges. Predict the average annual cost for 2005.
b. **Open-Ended** Predict the average annual cost for the year you plan to graduate from high school.

Tell whether each graph shows a *linear function*, an *exponential function*, or *neither*. Justify your reasoning.

36.
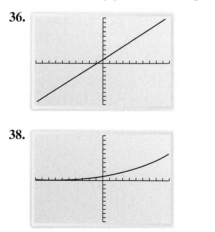

37.
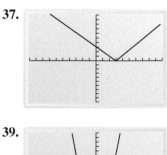

38.

39.
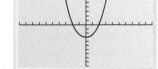

Graph the function represented in each table. Then tell whether the table represents a _linear function_ or an _exponential function_.

40.

x	y
1	20
2	40
3	60
4	80

41.

x	y
1	3
2	9
3	27
4	81

42.

x	y
1	3
2	9
3	15
4	21

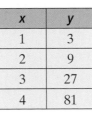

43. Writing Would you rather have $500 in an account paying 6% interest compounded quarterly or $600 in an account paying 5% compounded annually? Summarize your reasoning.

Reading Math

For help with Exercise 46 go to page 445.

Real-World 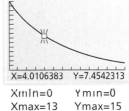 **Connection**

Careers A medical researcher may use equipment such as a scanning electron microscope.

How many half-lives occur in each period of time?

44. 2 days (1 half-life = 8 h)

45. 300 years (1 half-life = 75 yr)

46. Medicine The function $y = 15 \cdot 0.84^x$ models the amount y of a 15-mg dose of antibiotic remaining in the bloodstream after x hours.
  a. Estimation Use the graphing calculator screen to estimate the half-life of this antibiotic in the bloodstream.
  b. Use your estimate to predict the fraction of the dose that will remain in the bloodstream after 8 hours.
  c. Verify your prediction by using the function to find the amount of antibiotic remaining after 8 hours.

Antibiotic Decay in the Bloodstream

X=4.0106383   Y=7.4542313
Xmin=0   Ymin=0
Xmax=13   Ymax=15

47. Population Growth Since 1990, the population of Virginia has grown at an average annual rate of about 1%. In 1990, the population was about 6,284,000.
  a. Write an equation to model the population growth in Virginia since 1990.
  b. Suppose this rate of growth continues. Predict Virginia's population in 2010.

By which percent would you multiply a number to decrease it by the given amount?

48. 6%   **49.** 12%   **50.** 3.5%   **51.** 53.9%

52. a. Estimation Use the graph at the right. Estimate the half-life of cesium-134.
  b. Suppose a scientist had 800 mCi of cesium-134 in a sample. After how many years would the sample have 200 mCi of cesium-134?

Cesium-134 Decay

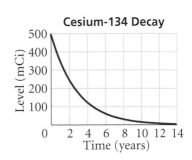

C Challenge

53. Credit Card Balances Suppose you charge $250 for a new suit. If you do not pay the whole amount the first month, you are charged 1.8% monthly interest on your account balance. Suppose you can make a $30 payment each month.
  a. What is your balance after your first payment?
  b. How much interest are you charged after your first payment?
  c. What is your balance just before you make your second payment?
  d. What is your balance after your second payment?
  e. How many months will it take for you to pay off the entire bill?
  f. How much interest will you have paid in all?

54. Data Collection Complete the table at the right using any ball. The height 0 is the starting height. Record the maximum height after the first, second, and third bounce.
   a. Graph your data.
   b. Write an exponential decay function that models your data.

Bounce	Height (centimeters)
0	■
1	■
2	■
3	■

55. On January 1, 2000, Chessville had a population of 40,000 people. Its population increases 7% each year. On the same day, Checkersville had a population of 60,000 people. Its population decreases 4% each year. During what year will the population of Chessville exceed that of Checkersville?

Standardized Test Prep

Multiple Choice

56. For which function will values of y decrease as values of x increase?
   A. $y = 12.5(1.325)^x$　　　　　　**B.** $y = 300(1.06)^x$
   C. $y = 5000(0.98)^x$　　　　　　**D.** $y = 1.02^x$

57. Suppose you deposit $1000 in an account earning 6% interest. You make no further deposits to the account and interest is compounded semi-annually. What is the balance after 5 years?
   F. $538.62　　　**G.** $1006.00　　　**H.** $1343.92　　　**I.** $1790.85

Reading Comprehension

58. Read the passage below and answer the following problem.

Manhattan, Then and Now

In 1626, the Dutch landed on the island we now call Manhattan. They bought the island for $24 worth of merchandise. Today

Manhattan is one of the most expensive places in the world to live. Rent for a one-bedroom apartment averages $2000 a month.

Suppose $24 had been invested in 1626 in an account paying 4.5% interest compounded annually. Which amount is closest to the balance in 2000?
   A. $339 million　　　**B.** $89 million　　　**C.** $9400　　　**D.** $8900

Short Response

Take It to the NET
Online lesson quiz at
www.PHSchool.com
Web Code: aea-0808

59. Which is greater, the amount in an account that pays 5% interest compounded quarterly for 5 years or the amount in an account that pays 5.5% compounded annually for 5 years? Assume the accounts start with the same amount. Show your work.

Mixed Review

Lesson 8-7　　**Graph each function.**

60. $y = 2 \cdot 10^x$　　　　**61.** $f(x) = 100 \cdot 0.9^x$　　　　**62.** $g(x) = \frac{1}{10} \cdot 0.1^x$

Lesson 8-3　　**63. Geography** In 2000, about 1.4×10^4 ships passed through the Panama Canal. About 5.2×10^7 gallons of water flow out of the canal with each ship. About how many gallons of water flowed out of the canal with ships in 2000? Write your answer in scientific notation.

Read the exercise below, and then learn how to use a graphing calculator to solve it. Check your understanding by solving the exercise at the bottom of the page.

Medicine The function $y = 15 \cdot 0.84^x$ models the amount y of a 15-mg dose of antibiotic remaining in the bloodstream after x hours.

a. Estimation Use the graphing calculator screen to estimate the half-life of this antibiotic in the bloodstream.

b. Use your estimate to predict the fraction of the dose that will remain in the bloodstream after 8 hours.

c. Verify your prediction by using the function to find the amount of antibiotic remaining after 8 hours.

Antibiotic Decay in the Bloodstream

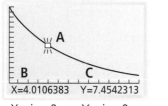

X=4.0106383 Y=7.4542313

D
Xmin=0
Xmax=13

E
Ymin=0
Ymax=15

To solve this problem, use the graphing calculator screen shown at the left. Parts of this screen are explained below.

A — The point shown on the screen is a point (x, y) on the graph.

B and C — These are the x-coordinates and y-coordinates of the highlighted point. The coordinates of the point are $(4.0106383, 7.4542313)$.

D and E — These give the domain and range for the x- and y-axes. The screen displays the graph for x-values from 0 to 13 and y-values from 0 to 15.

a. *Half-life* is the time required for the body to eliminate half of the initial dose. How do the coordinates $(4.0106383, 7.4542313)$ relate to the half-life of the antibiotic? At time $x = 0$, the amount in the bloodstream is $y = 15$. When $y = \frac{15}{2} = 7.5$, the corresponding value of x represents the half-life. When $y \approx 7.5$, $x \approx 4$, so the half-life is about 4 hours.

b. If 7.5 mg remain after 4 hours, then $\frac{7.5}{2} = 3.75$ mg will remain after 8 hours.

c. $y = 15 \cdot 0.84^x$

$y = 15 \cdot 0.84^8$ **Substitute 8 for x.**

$y \approx 3.72$ **Use a calculator.**

The amount of antibiotic remaining after 8 hours will be about 3.72 mg.

EXERCISE

Memory Suppose the function $y = 40 \cdot 0.75^x$ models the number y of foreign-language words recalled from a list of 40 words after x weeks (without additional practice or study).

a. Estimation Use the graphing calculator to estimate the number of vocabulary words recalled after 5 weeks.

b. Verify your prediction by using the function to find the number of vocabulary words recalled after 5 weeks.

Testing Multiple Choices

One advantage of multiple-choice tests is that the correct answer is among the choices. A strategy is to work backward by taking answers and testing them in the original problem.

1 EXAMPLE

Find the value of x if $x, x + 2$, and $4x$ are three consecutive terms of a geometric sequence.

A. 0   **B.** 1   **C.** 2   **D.** 3

The ratios of consecutive terms of a geometric sequence are the same. So $\frac{x + 2}{x}$ must equal $\frac{4x}{x + 2}$. Find the number for which this is true by substituting each answer choice for x.

Let $x = 0$. The sequence $0, 2, 0$ is not a geometric sequence because $\frac{2}{0} \neq \frac{0}{2}$. So A is not correct.

Let $x = 1$. The sequence $1, 3, 4$ is not a geometric sequence because $\frac{3}{1} \neq \frac{4}{3}$. So B is not correct.

Let $x = 2$. The sequence $2, 4, 8$ is a geometric sequence because $\frac{4}{2} = \frac{8}{4}$. The correct answer is C.

● You do not need to try choice D.

2 EXAMPLE

Find the value of x if $2x^{-3} = \frac{1}{4}$.

F. 1   **G.** 2   **H.** 3   **I.** 4

Solve by substituting each answer choice into the original equation.

Let $x = 1$. ⟶ $2(1)^{-3} = 2(1) = 2$. ⟶ $2 \neq \frac{1}{4}$.   F is not the answer.

Let $x = 2$. ⟶ $2(2)^{-3} = 2\left(\frac{1}{8}\right) = \frac{2}{8}$ ⟶ $\frac{1}{4} = \frac{1}{4}$.   G is the answer.

● You do not have to test answer choices H and I.

EXERCISES

Solve each of the following by working backward.

1. Find the value of x if $x - 2, x$, and $x + 3$ are three consecutive terms of a geometric sequence.
      A. 4   **B.** 6   **C.** 8   **D.** 10

2. Find the value of x if $x^{-1} + x^{-2} = 0$.
      F. -2 **G.** -1 **H.** 1   **I.** 2

3. The area of a square is 1.21×10^{-4}. What is its perimeter?
      A. 0.00044   **B.** 0.0044   **C.** 0.044   **D.** 0.44

4. Find the value of x if $x, 3x + 1$, and $6x - 1$ are three consecutive terms of an arithmetic sequence.
      F. -3 **G.** -1 **H.** 1   **I.** 3

Chapter Review

Vocabulary

common ratio (p. 424)
compound interest (p. 438)
decay factor (p. 440)
exponential decay (p. 440)

exponential function (p. 430)
exponential growth (p. 437)
geometric sequence (p. 424)
growth factor (p. 437)

interest period (p. 438)
scientific notation (p. 400)

Reading Math
Understanding
Vocabulary

Take It to the NET
Online vocabulary quiz
at **www.PHSchool.com**
Web Code: aej-0851

Choose the correct term to complete each sentence.

1. The function $y = a \cdot b^x$ models __?__ for $a > 0$ and $b > 1$.

2. For the function $y = a \cdot b^x$, where $a > 0$ and $b > 1$, b is the __?__.

3. __?__ is a shorthand way to write very large and very small numbers.

4. The function rule $y = a \cdot b^x$ models __?__ for $a > 0$ and $0 < b < 1$.

5. For the function $y = a \cdot b^x$, where $a > 0$ and $0 < b < 1$, b is the __?__.

6. __?__ is calculated using both the principal and the interest that an account has already earned.

7. Each term of a geometric sequence is found by multiplying the previous term by a fixed number called the __?__.

8. The length of time over which interest is calculated is the __?__.

9. When a sequence has a common ratio, it is a(n) __?__.

10. The rule $y = 7^x$ is a(n) __?__.

Skills and Concepts

8-1 Objectives

▼ To simplify expressions with zero and negative exponents (p. 394)

▼ To evaluate exponential expressions (p. 396)

You can use zero and negative numbers as exponents. For every nonzero number a, $a^0 = 1$. For every nonzero number a and any integer n, $a^{-n} = \frac{1}{a^n}$.

Simplify each expression.

11. $b^{-4}c^0d^6$

12. $\frac{x^{-2}}{y^{-8}}$

13. $7k^{-8}h^3$

14. $\frac{1}{p^2q^{-4}r^0}$

15. $\left(\frac{2}{5}\right)^{-4}$

16. $(-2)^{-3}$

17. -2^{-3}

18. $7^{-2}y^{-4}$

19. $\frac{9w^{-4}}{x^{-2}y^7}$

Evaluate each expression for $p = 2$, $q = -3$, and $r = 0$.

20. p^2q^2

21. $(-p)^2q^{-2}$

22. p^qq^p

23. p^rq^r

24. $-p^2q^3$

25. Which expression has the greatest value for $a = 4$, $b = -3$, and $c = 0$?

   A. a^b　　**B.** b^c　　**C.** $\frac{1}{b^{-a}}$　　**D.** $\frac{a^c}{b^c}$　　**E.** $\frac{c}{a^{-b}}$

26. **Critical Thinking** Is $(-3b)^4 = -12b^4$? Explain why or why not.

8-2 Objectives

▼ To write numbers in scientific and standard notation (p. 400)

▼ To use scientific notation (p. 401)

You can use **scientific notation** to express very large or very small numbers. A number is in scientific notation if it is in the form $a \times 10^n$, where $1 \leq a < 10$, and n is an integer.

Is each number written in scientific notation? If not, explain.

27. 950×10^5 **28.** 72.35×10^8 **29.** 1.6×10^{-6} **30.** 0.84×10^{-5}

31. The space probe Voyager 2 traveled 2,793,000 miles. Write the number of miles in scientific notation.

32. There are 189 million passenger cars and trucks in use in the United States. Write the number of passenger cars and trucks using scientific notation.

8-3 and 8-4 Objectives

▼ To multiply powers (p. 405)

▼ To work with scientific notation (p. 406)

▼ To raise a power to a power (p. 411)

▼ To raise a product to a power (p. 412)

To multiply powers with the same base, add the exponents.

$$a^m \cdot a^n = a^{m+n}$$

To raise a power to a power, multiply the exponents.

$$(a^m)^n = a^{mn}$$

To raise a product to a power, raise each factor in the product to the power.

$$(ab)^n = a^n b^n$$

Simplify each expression.

33. $2d^2d^3$ **34.** $(q^3r)^4$ **35.** $(5c^{-4})(-4m^2c^8)$

36. $(1.34^2)^5(1.34)^{-8}$ **37.** $(12x^2y^{-2})^5(4xy^{-3})^{-8}$ **38.** $(-2r^{-4})^2(-3r^2z^8)^{-1}$

39. Estimation Each square inch of your body has about 6.5×10^2 pores. Suppose the back of your hand has an area of about 0.12×10^2 in.^{2}. About how many pores are on the back of your hand?

40. Open-Ended Write and solve a problem that involves multiplying exponents.

8-5 Objectives

▼ To divide powers with the same base (p. 417)

▼ To raise a quotient to a power (p. 418)

To divide powers with the same base, subtract the exponents.

$$\frac{a^m}{a^n} = a^{m-n}$$

To raise a quotient to a power, raise the dividend and the divisor to the power.

$$\left(\frac{a}{b}\right)^n = \frac{a^n}{b^n}$$

Simplify each expression.

41. $\frac{w^2}{w^5}$ **42.** $(8^3) \cdot 8^{-5}$ **43.** $\left(\frac{21x^3}{3x}\right)$ **44.** $\left(\frac{n^5}{v^3}\right)^7$ **45.** $\frac{e^{-6}c^3}{e^5}$

Simplify each quotient. Give your answer in scientific notation.

46. $\frac{4.2 \times 10^8}{2.1 \times 10^{11}}$ **47.** $\frac{3.1 \times 10^4}{12.4 \times 10^2}$ **48.** $\frac{4.5 \times 10^3}{9 \times 10^7}$ **49.** $\frac{5.1 \times 10^5}{1.7 \times 10^2}$

50. Writing List the steps that you would use to simplify $\left(\frac{5a^8}{10a^6}\right)^{-3}$.

You find each term of a **geometric sequence** by multiplying the previous term by a fixed number called the common ratio.

Find the common ratio in each geometric sequence.

51. $750, 75, 7.5, 0.75, \ldots$ **52.** $0.04, 0.12, 0.36, 1.08, \ldots$ **53.** $20, -10, 5, -\frac{5}{2}, \ldots$

Determine whether each sequence is *arithmetic*, *geometric*, or *neither*. Find the next three terms.

54. $1600, 400, 100, 25, \ldots$ **55.** $-40, -39, -37, -34, \ldots$ **56.** $14, 21, 28, 35, \ldots$

You can use exponents to show repeated multiplication. An **exponential function** involves repeated multiplication of an initial amount by the same positive number.

Evaluate each function for the given values.

57. $f(x) = 3 \cdot 2^x$ for the domain $\{1, 2, 3, 4\}$

58. $y = 10 \cdot (0.75)^x$ for the domain $\{1, 2, 3\}$

59. a. One kind of bacteria in a laboratory culture triples in number every 30 minutes. Suppose a culture is started with 30 bacteria cells. How many bacteria will there be after 2 hours?
   b. After how many minutes will there be more than 20,000 bacteria cells?

The general form of an exponential function is $y = a \cdot b^x$.

When $b > 1$, the function increases, and the function shows **exponential growth.** The base of the exponent, b, is called the **growth factor.** An example of exponential growth is **compound interest**.

When $0 < b < 1$, the function decreases, and the function shows **exponential decay.** Then the base of the exponent b is called the **decay factor.** An example of exponential decay is the half-life model.

Identify the initial amount a and the growth or decay factor b in each exponential function.

60. $y = 100 \cdot 1.025^x$ **61.** $y = 32 \cdot 0.75^x$ **62.** $y = 0.4 \cdot 2^x$

Identify each function as *exponential growth* or *exponential decay*. Then identify the growth or decay factor.

63. $y = 5.2 \cdot 3^x$ **64.** $y = 0.15 \cdot \left(\frac{3}{2}\right)^x$ **65.** $y = 7 \cdot 0.32^x$ **66.** $y = 1.3 \cdot \left(\frac{1}{4}\right)^x$

Graph each function.

67. $f(x) = 2.5^x$ **68.** $y = 0.5 \cdot (0.5)^x$ **69.** $f(x) = \left(\frac{1}{2}\right) \cdot 3^x$ **70.** $y = 0.1^x$

71. The function $y = 25 \cdot 0.80^x$ models the amount y of a 25-mg dose of medicine remaining in the bloodstream after x hours. How many milligrams of medicine remain in the bloodstream after 5 hours?

Chapter 8

Chapter Test

Take It to the NET
Online chapter test at
www.PHSchool.com
Web Code: aea-0852

Simplify each expression.

1. $\dfrac{r^3 t^{-7}}{t^5}$

2. $\left(\dfrac{a^3}{m}\right)^{-4}$

3. $\dfrac{t^{-8} m^2}{m^{-3}}$

4. $c^3 v^9 c^{-1} c^0$

5. $h^2 k^{-5} d^3 k^2$

6. $9 y^4 j^2 y^{-9}$

7. $(w^2 k^0 p^{-5})^{-7}$

8. $2 y^{-9} h^2 (2 y^0 h^{-4})^{-6}$

9. $(1.2)^5 (1.2)^{-2}$

10. $(-3 q^{-1})^3 q^2$

11. If $n = -3$, which expression has the least value?

    A. $n^2 n^0$ **B.** n^n

    C. $n^8 n^{-5}$ **D.** $-n^n n^{-4}$

Write each number in scientific notation.

12. **History** There were 44,909,000 votes cast for Bill Clinton in the 1992 presidential election.

13. **Pets** More than 450,000 households in the United States have reptiles as pets.

Is each number written in scientific notation? If not, explain.

14. 76×10^{-9}

15. 7.3×10^5

16. $4.05 \times 10 \times 10^{-8}$

17. 32.5×10^{13}

18. **a. Astronomy** The speed of light in a vacuum is about 186,300 mi/s. Use scientific notation to express how far light travels in one hour.

    b. At its farthest, Saturn is about 1.03×10^9 mi from Earth. About how many hours does it take for light to travel from Earth to Saturn?

19. Use the sequence $-32, 16, -8, 4, \ldots$

    a. What is the common ratio?

    b. What are the next three terms?

    c. Write a rule for the sequence.

    d. What is the ninth term of the sequence?

20. You drop a ball from a height of 12 ft. Each path has $\frac{3}{5}$ the height of the previous path.

    a. Write a rule for the sequence. The initial height is given by the term $n = 1$.

    b. What height will the ball reach at the top of the fourth path ($n = 4$)?

21. Find the fifth term of the sequence $A(n) = -3(-2)^{n + 1}$.

Evaluate each function for $x = 1, 2,$ and 3.

22. $y = 3 \cdot 5^x$

23. $f(x) = \frac{1}{2} \cdot 4^x$

24. $f(x) = 4(0.95)^x$

25. $g(x) = 5\left(\frac{3}{4}\right)^x$

Graph each function.

26. $y = \frac{1}{2} \cdot 2^x$ 27. $y = 2 \cdot \left(\frac{1}{2}\right)^x$ 28. $f(x) = 3^x$

29. **Open-Ended** Write and solve a problem involving exponential decay.

30. **Writing** Explain when the function $y = a \cdot b^x$ shows exponential growth and when it shows exponential decay.

31. **Banking** A customer deposits \$1000 in a savings account that pays 4% interest compounded quarterly. How much money will the customer have in the account after 2 years? After 5 years?

32. The function $y = 1.3 \cdot (1.07)^x$ models a city's annual electrical consumption for x years since 1985, where y is kilowatt-hours.

    a. Determine whether the function models exponential growth or decay, and find the growth or decay factor.

    b. According to the model, what will be the annual electrical usage in 2010?

    c. According to the model, what was the annual electrical usage in 1975?

    d. What value of x should you substitute to find the value of y now? Use this value for x to find y.

33. **Automobiles** Suppose a new car is worth \$20,000. You can use the function $y = 20{,}000(0.85)^x$ to estimate the car's value after x years.

    a. What is the decay factor? What does it mean?

    b. Estimate the car's value after one year.

    c. Estimate the car's value after four years.

34. The function $y = 10 \cdot 1.08^x$ models the cost of annual tuition (in thousands of dollars) at a local college x years after 1997.

    a. What is the annual percent increase?

    b. How much was tuition in 1997? In 2000?

    c. How much will the tuition be the year you plan to graduate from high school?

Standardized Test Prep

Multiple Choice

For Exercises 1–10, choose the correct letter.

1. If a is positive and b is negative, which of the following is negative?
   - **A.** $a + |b|$
   - **B.** $a|b|$
   - **C.** $|a|b$
   - **D.** $|a| - b$

2. The scores on your first five algebra tests are 88, 78, 81, 83, and 90. What score must you get on your next test to raise the mean to 85?
   - **F.** 90
   - **G.** 87
   - **H.** 86
   - **I.** 85

3. Which value of x is NOT a solution to the inequality $5 - 6x < -x + 2$?
   - **A.** -1
   - **B.** 1
   - **C.** 3
   - **D.** 5

4. You earn a commission of 6% on your first $500 of sales and 10% on all sales above $500. If you earn $130 in commission, what are your total sales?
   - **F.** $800
   - **G.** $1000
   - **H.** $1300
   - **I.** $1500

5. Find the solution of the system of equations.
   $$\frac{1}{3}x - y = 4$$
   $$x + 3y = 0$$
   - **A.** $(9, -1)$
   - **B.** $(-6, 2)$
   - **C.** $(6, -2)$
   - **D.** $(-9, 1)$

6. You flip a coin and roll a number cube. What is the probability of getting a head and a multiple of three?
   - **F.** $\frac{1}{12}$
   - **G.** $\frac{1}{6}$
   - **H.** $\frac{1}{4}$
   - **I.** $\frac{3}{2}$

7. Which number has the least value?
   - **A.** 2.8×10^{-5}
   - **B.** 5.3×10^{-4}
   - **C.** 8.3×10^{-7}
   - **D.** 1.6×10^{-8}

8. Potassium-42 has a half-life of 12.5 h. How many half-lives are in 75 h?
   - **F.** 6
   - **G.** 8
   - **H.** 25
   - **I.** 150

9. Simplify $-3a^8 \cdot cb^{-3} \cdot b^{12} \cdot 9c^5$.
   - **A.** $6a^9b^5c^6$
   - **B.** $-27a^8b^9c^6$
   - **C.** $-27a^8b^{15}c^6$
   - **D.** $-3abc$

10. Which statement is true for every solution of the following system?
    $$y > x + 4$$
    $$y + x > 4$$
    - **F.** $x \leq -3$
    - **G.** $y < 5$
    - **H.** $x > 4$
    - **I.** $y > 4$

Quantitative Comparison

Compare the boxed quantity in Column A with the boxed quantity in Column B. Choose the best answer.

- **A.** The quantity in Column A is greater.
- **B.** The quantity in Column B is greater.
- **C.** The two quantities are equal.
- **D.** The relationship cannot be determined from the information given.

Column A	Column B
11. the growth factor of an exponential function	the decay factor of an exponential function

$$\begin{bmatrix} 6 & 1 \\ 0 & x \end{bmatrix} + \begin{bmatrix} 1 & y \\ -5 & 3 \end{bmatrix} = \begin{bmatrix} 7 & 9 \\ -5 & 6 \end{bmatrix}$$

Column A	Column B
12. x	y

Gridded Response

13. A cafeteria charges $.21/oz for frozen yogurt. How many dollars would a 9-oz serving cost?

14. For a spinner numbered from 1 to 6, the outcomes are equally likely. What is the probability of getting an odd number?

Short Response

Show all work.

15. On April 1, 2000, the day of the 2000 national census, the population of the United States was 281,421,906 people. This was a 13.2% increase from the 1990 census. What was the 1990 population of the United States?

16. Graph the inequality $|x - 2| \leq 9$ on a number line.

Extended Response

17. The slopes of four different lines are $\frac{3}{5}$, $-\frac{10}{6}$, $-\frac{5}{3}$, and $\frac{9}{15}$. Do these lines determine a rectangle? Explain why or why not.

How Fast Can You Run?

Applying Linear Equations Animals run to escape predators and to chase prey. The display below compares animals as if they were able to sprint along at their top velocities or speeds for a whole hour. Linear equations and graphs are good tools for describing and comparing motion at constant velocities.

Instant Records

A stopwatch is a watch used to time races. It can be started and stopped quickly for accurate timing.

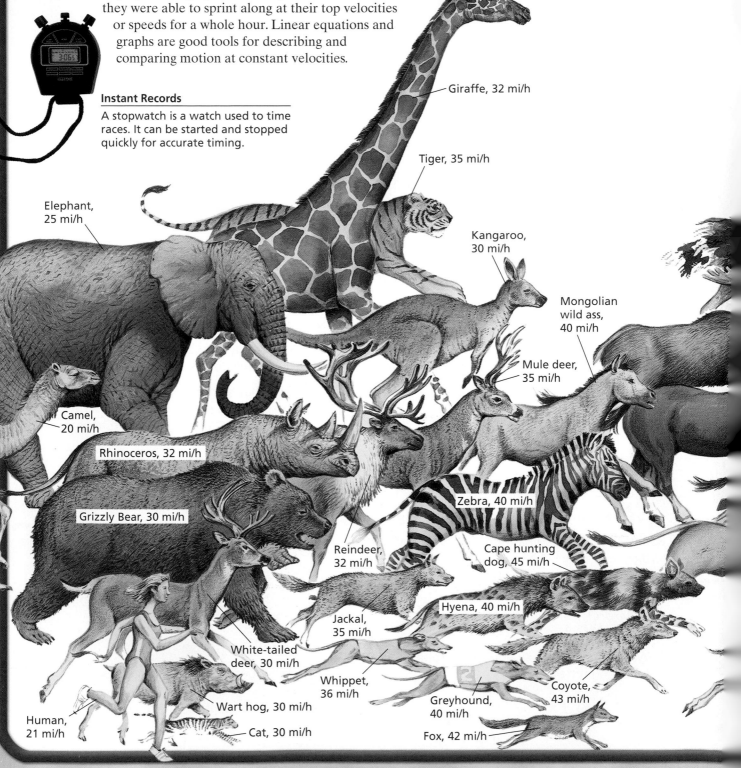

Giraffe, 32 mi/h

Tiger, 35 mi/h

Kangaroo, 30 mi/h

Mongolian wild ass, 40 mi/h

Mule deer, 35 mi/h

Elephant, 25 mi/h

Camel, 20 mi/h

Rhinoceros, 32 mi/h

Grizzly Bear, 30 mi/h

Zebra, 40 mi/h

Reindeer, 32 mi/h

Cape hunting dog, 45 mi/h

Hyena, 40 mi/h

Jackal, 35 mi/h

White-tailed deer, 30 mi/h

Whippet, 36 mi/h

Coyote, 43 mi/h

Greyhound, 40 mi/h

Wart hog, 30 mi/h

Human, 21 mi/h

Cat, 30 mi/h

Fox, 42 mi/h

Car Racing

Formula 1 cars compete at speeds as high as 200 mi/h. The speed limit on most U.S. highways and interstates is 65 mi/h.

Activity 1

Materials: graph paper, pencil

a. Suppose two animals are in a race. Choose the two animals and calculate the speed of each animal in yards per second.

b. Decide how much of a head start (in yards) the faster animal offers the slower animal. For each animal, write an equation relating distance from the starting line to time.

c. Graph the two equations on the same coordinate plane.

d. How long will it take the faster animal to overtake the slower animal? How many yards from the starting line are the animals when the faster animal overtakes the slower animal?

e. Reduce the head start by half and repeat parts (c) and (d).

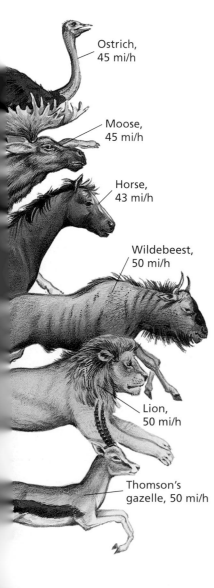

Ostrich, 45 mi/h

Moose, 45 mi/h

Horse, 43 mi/h

Wildebeest, 50 mi/h

Lion, 50 mi/h

Thomson's gazelle, 50 mi/h

Activity 2

a. Choose a third animal. Calculate its speed in yards per second. Compare its speed with the speed of the two animals you chose in Activity 1.

b. Decide which two animals should get head starts and how much of a head start each should get. Write three equations relating distance from the starting line to time.

c. Graph all three equations on the same coordinate plane.

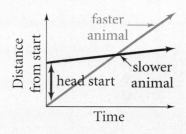

Cheetah, 70 mi/h

 Take It to the NET For more information about speeds, go to **www.PHSchool.com**.
Web Code: aee-0853

Where You've Been

● In Chapter 1, you learned how to use variables and applied the Distributive Property to variable expressions.

● In Chapter 2, you combined like terms to solve equations.

● In Chapter 8, you simplified variable expressions with exponents by using the multiplication and division properties of exponents.

Instant self-check online and on CD-ROM

Diagnosing Readiness   (For help, go to the Lesson in green.)

Finding Factors of Composite Numbers (Skills Handbook page 720)

List all the factors of each number.

1. 12   **2.** 56   **3.** 31   **4.** 27

5. 110   **6.** 65   **7.** 50   **8.** 200

9. 11   **10.** 42   **11.** 66   **12.** 73

Simplifying Expressions (Lesson 1-7)

Simplify each expression.

13. $2x^2 - x + x^2 - 3x$

14. $-b + 2 + 3b + 4$

15. $-5y - y^2 + 4y^2 - 6y$

16. $(3w - 2w^2 + 4w - 2w^2)\frac{1}{6}$

17. $-8(z + 2) + 5(3z - 10)$

18. $2(x + 4x^2 - 2x - 2x^2)$

19. $12t - 5t^2 - 2t - t^2$

20. $p - 3 - (p^2 - 3) - 3p$

Multiplying Expressions With Exponents (Lessons 8-3 and 8-4)

Simplify each expression.

21. $(7w)^2$ **22.** $(-5n^2)(-5n)$ **23.** $(3z^2)^2$ **24.** $(2t^3)(5t^4)$

25. $(4y^3)^2$ **26.** $(-9ab)^2$ **27.** $4(x^2)^2$ **28.** $(-6p^4)^2$

Dividing Expressions With Exponents (Lesson 8-5)

Simplify each expression.

29. $\dfrac{x^5y^8}{x^3y^4}$ **30.** $\dfrac{(3c)^2}{(3c)}$ **31.** $\dfrac{-5t}{(10t^3)(2t)}$ **32.** $\dfrac{(3a)(4a^3)}{6a^2}$

Polynomials and Factoring

Key Vocabulary

- binomial (p. 457)
- degree of a monomial (p. 457)
- degree of a polynomial (p. 457)
- factor by grouping (p. 496)
- monomial (p. 456)
- perfect-square trinomial (p. 490)
- polynomial (p. 457)
- standard form of a polynomial (p. 457)
- trinomial (p. 457)

Where You're Going

- In this chapter, you will categorize polynomials by their degree and number of terms.

- You will learn to add, subtract, and multiply polynomials.

Real-World Connection Applying what you learn, you will multiply binomials to model combinations of inherited color genes, on page 475.

Adding and Subtracting Polynomials

Lesson Preview

What You'll Learn

OBJECTIVE 1
To describe polynomials

OBJECTIVE 2
To add and subtract polynomials

. . . And Why

To combine and simplify polynomials, as in Example 4

✔ Check Skills You'll Need

(For help, go to Lesson 1-7.)

Simplify each expression.

1. $6t + 13t$
2. $5g + 34g$
3. $7k - 15k$
4. $2b - 6 + 9b$
5. $4n^2 - 7n^2$
6. $8x^2 - x^2$

New Vocabulary

- monomial
- degree of a monomial
- polynomial
- standard form of a polynomial
- degree of a polynomial
- binomial
- trinomial

OBJECTIVE

1 Describing Polynomials

> 🄸 TEXT Interactive lesson includes instant self-check, tutorials, and activities.

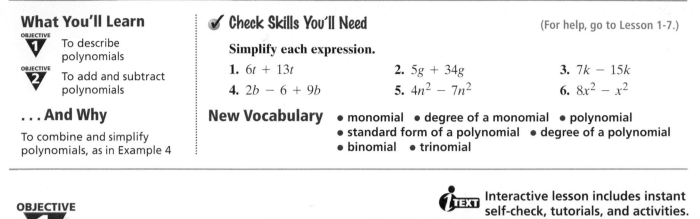

Investigation: Using Polynomials

Business Suppose you work at a pet store. The spreadsheet below shows the details of several customers' orders.

	A	B	C	D	E	F
1	Customer	Seed	Cuttlebone	Millet	G. Paper	Perches
2	Davis			✔		
3	Brooks	✔	✔			
4	Casic	✔		✔		
5	Martino	✔			✔	✔

The following variables represent the number of each item ordered.

s = bags of birdseed m = bags of millet
c = packages of cuttlebone g = packages of gravel paper
p = packages of perches

1. Which expression represents the cost of Casic's order?
A. $27.99(s + m)$ **B.** $3.99s + 24m$ **C.** $27.99sm$

2. Write expressions to represent each of the other customers' orders.

3. Martino buys 10 bags of birdseed, 4 packages of gravel paper, and 2 packages of perches. What is the total cost of his order?

Rocky's Friends Bird Supplies

bird seed (5 lb) $3.99
cuttlebone (2 ct) $2.00
spray millet (5 lb) $24.00
gravel paper (1 pkg) $2.29
perches (2 ct) $1.89

A **monomial** is an expression that is a number, a variable, or a product of a number and one or more variables. Each of the following is a monomial.

$$12 \qquad\qquad y \qquad\qquad -5x^2y \qquad\qquad \frac{c}{3}$$

The fraction $\frac{c}{3}$ is a monomial, but the expression $\frac{c}{x}$ is *not* a monomial because there is a variable in the denominator.

The **degree of a monomial** is the sum of the exponents of its variables. For a nonzero constant, the degree is 0. Zero has no degree.

1 EXAMPLE **Degree of a Monomial**

Find the degree of each monomial.

a. $\frac{2}{3}x$ Degree: 1 $\frac{2}{3}x = \frac{2}{3}x^1$. The exponent is 1.

b. $7x^2y^3$ Degree: 5   The exponents are 2 and 3. Their sum is 5.

c. -4 Degree: 0   The degree of a nonzero constant is 0.

✓ **Check Understanding** ① **Critical Thinking** What is the degree of $9x^0$? Explain.

A **polynomial** is a monomial or the sum or difference of two or more monomials.

$$3x^4 + 5x^2 - 7x + 1$$
$$\uparrow \quad\quad \uparrow \quad\quad \uparrow \quad\quad \uparrow$$
$$\text{degree} \rightarrow \quad 4 \quad\quad 2 \quad\quad 1 \quad\quad 0$$

The polynomial shown above is in standard form. **Standard form of a polynomial** means that the degrees of its monomial terms decrease from left to right. The **degree of a polynomial** in one variable is the same as the degree of the monomial with the greatest exponent. The degree of $3x^4 + 5x^2 - 7x + 1$ is 4.

After you simplify a polynomial by combining like terms, you can name the polynomial based on its degree or the number of monomials it contains.

Polynomial	Degree	Name Using Degree	Number of Terms	Name Using Number of Terms
$7x + 4$	1	linear	2	**binomial**
$3x^2 + 2x + 1$	2	quadratic	3	**trinomial**
$4x^3$	3	cubic	1	monomial
$9x^4 + 11x$	4	fourth degree	2	binomial
5	0	constant	1	monomial

2 EXAMPLE **Classifying Polynomials**

Write each polynomial in standard form. Then name each polynomial based on its degree and the number of its terms.

a. $5 - 2x$

   $-2x + 5$ **Place terms in order.**

   linear binomial

b. $3x^4 - 4 + 2x^2 + 5x^4$

   $3x^4 + 5x^4 + 2x^2 - 4$ **Place terms in order.**

   $8x^4 + 2x^2 - 4$ **Combine like terms.**

   fourth degree trinomial

✓ **Check Understanding** ② Write each polynomial in standard form. Then name each polynomial based on its degree and the number of its terms.

a. $6x^2 + 7 - 9x^4$ **b.** $3y - 4 - y^3$ **c.** $8 + 7v - 11v$

You can add polynomials by adding like terms.

3 **EXAMPLE** **Adding Polynomials**

Simplify $(4x^2 + 6x + 7) + (2x^2 - 9x + 1)$.

Method 1 Add vertically.

Line up like terms. Then add the coefficients.

$$\begin{array}{r} 4x^2 + 6x + 7 \\ + \; 2x^2 - 9x + 1 \\ \hline 6x^2 - 3x + 8 \end{array}$$

Method 2 Add horizontally.

Group like terms. Then add the coefficients.

$$(4x^2 + 6x + 7) + (2x^2 - 9x + 1) = (4x^2 + 2x^2) + (6x - 9x) + (7 + 1)$$
$$= 6x^2 - 3x + 8$$

✓ **Check Understanding** **3** Simplify each sum.
a. $(12m^2 + 4) + (8m^2 + 5)$ **b.** $(t^2 - 6) + (3t^2 + 11)$
c. $(9w^3 + 8w^2) + (7w^3 + 4)$ **d.** $(2p^3 + 6p^2 + 10p) + (9p^3 + 11p^2 + 3p)$

In Chapter 1, you learned that subtraction means to add the opposite. So when you subtract a polynomial, change each of the terms to its opposite. Then add the coefficients.

4 **EXAMPLE** **Subtracting Polynomials**

Simplify $(2x^3 + 5x^2 - 3x) - (x^3 - 8x^2 + 11)$.

Method 1 Subtract vertically.

$$\begin{array}{r} 2x^3 + 5x^2 - 3x \\ - \; (x^3 - 8x^2 \quad\;\; + 11) \end{array}$$ Line up like terms.

$$\begin{array}{r} 2x^3 + 5x^2 - 3x \\ -x^3 + 8x^2 \quad\;\; - 11 \\ \hline x^3 + 13x^2 - 3x - 11 \end{array}$$ Then add the opposite of each term in the polynomial being subtracted.

Method 2 Subtract horizontally.

$$(2x^3 + 5x^2 - 3x) - (x^3 - 8x^2 + 11)$$
$$= 2x^3 + 5x^2 - 3x - x^3 + 8x^2 - 11$$ Write the opposite of each term in the polynomial being subtracted.
$$= (2x^3 - x^3) + (5x^2 + 8x^2) - 3x - 11$$ Group like terms.
$$= x^3 + 13x^2 - 3x - 11$$ Simplify.

✓ **Check Understanding** **4** Simplify each difference.
a. $(v^3 + 6v^2 - v) - (9v^3 - 7v^2 + 3v)$ **b.** $(30d^3 - 29d^2 - 3d) - (2d^3 + d^2)$
c. $(4x^2 + 5x + 1) - (6x^2 + x + 8)$

EXERCISES

For more practice, see *Extra Practice*.

Practice and Problem Solving

A Practice by Example

Example 1
(page 457)

Find the degree of each monomial.

1. $4x$ **2.** $7c^3$ **3.** -16 **4.** $6y^2w^8$

5. $8ab^3$ **6.** 6 **7.** $-9x^4$ **8.** 11

Example 2
(page 457)

Name each expression based on its degree and number of terms.

9. $5x^2 - 2x + 3$ **10.** $\frac{3}{4}z + 5$ **11.** $7a^3 + 4a - 12$

12. $\frac{3}{x} + 5$ **13.** -15 **14.** $w^2 + 2$

Write each polynomial in standard form. Then name each polynomial based on its degree and number of terms.

15. $4x - 3x^2$ **16.** $4x + 9$ **17.** $c^2 - 2 + 4c$

18. $9z^2 - 11z^2 + 5z - 5$ **19.** $y - 7y^3 + 15y^8$ **20.** $-10 + 4q^4 - 8q + 3q^2$

Example 3
(page 458)

Simplify each sum.

21. $\begin{array}{r} 5m^2 + 9 \\ + 3m^2 + 6 \\ \hline \end{array}$ **22.** $\begin{array}{r} 3k - 8 \\ + 7k + 12 \\ \hline \end{array}$ **23.** $\begin{array}{r} w^2 + w - 4 \\ + 7w^2 - 4w + 8 \\ \hline \end{array}$

24. $(8x^2 + 1) + (12x^2 + 6)$ **25.** $(g^4 + 4g) + (9g^4 + 7g)$

26. $(a^2 + a + 1) + (5a^2 - 8a + 20)$ **27.** $(7y^3 - 3y^2 + 4y) + (8y^4 + 3y^2)$

Example 4
(page 458)

Simplify each difference.

28. $\begin{array}{r} 6c - 5 \\ - (4c + 9) \\ \hline \end{array}$ **29.** $\begin{array}{r} 2b + 6 \\ -(b + 5) \\ \hline \end{array}$ **30.** $\begin{array}{r} 7h^2 + 4h - 8 \\ - (3h^2 - 2h + 10) \\ \hline \end{array}$

31. $(17n^4 + 2n^3) - (10n^4 + n^3)$ **32.** $(24x^5 + 12x) - (9x^5 + 11x)$

33. $(6w^2 - 3w + 1) - (w^2 + w - 9)$ **34.** $(-5x^4 + x^2) - (x^3 + 8x^2 - x)$

B Apply Your Skills

Simplify. Write each answer in standard form.

35. $(7y^2 - 3y + 4y) + (8y^2 + 3y^2 + 4y)$ **36.** $(2x^3 - 5x^2 - 1) - (8x^3 + 3 - 8x^2)$

37. $(-7z^3 + 3z - 1) - (-6z^2 + z + 4)$ **38.** $(7a^3 - a + 3a^2) + (8a^2 - 3a - 4)$

Geometry Find the perimeter of each figure.

39.

$9c - 10$

$5c + 2$

40.

$9x$

$5x + 1$

$8x - 2$

$17x - 6$

Need Help?

Recall that the perimeter of a figure is the sum of all the sides of the figure.

41. Error Analysis Kwan's work is shown below. What mistake did he make?

$$(5x^2 - 3x + 1) - (2x^2 - 4x - 2) = 5x^2 - 3x + 1 - 2x^2 - 4x - 2$$
$$= 5x^2 - 2x^2 - 3x - 4x + 1 - 2$$
$$= 3x^2 - 7x - 1$$

42. a. Writing Write the definition of each word. Use a dictionary if necessary.

    monogram   binocular   tricuspid   polyglot

b. Open-Ended Find other words that begin with *mono*, *bi*, *tri*, or *poly*.

c. Do these prefixes have meanings similar to those in mathematics?

Simplify. Write each answer in standard form.

43. $(x^3 + 3x) + (12x - x^4)$

44. $(6g - 7g^8) - (4g + 2g^3 + 11g^2)$

45. $(2h^4 - 5h^9) - (-8h^5 + h^{10})$

46. $(-4t^4 - 9t + 6) + (13t + 5t^4)$

47. $(8b - 6b^7 + 3b^8) + (2b^7 - 5b^9)$

48. $(11 + k^3 - 6k^4) - (k^2 - k^4)$

Geometry **Find each missing length.**

49. Perimeter $= 25x + 8$

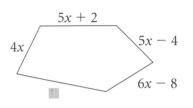

5x + 2

4x

5x − 4

6x − 8

50. Perimeter $= 23a - 7$

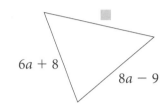

6a + 8

8a − 9

51. Critical Thinking Is it possible to write a binomial with degree 0? Explain.

Challenge

52. a. Write the equations for line P and line Q. Use slope-intercept form.

b. Use the expressions on the right side of each equation to write a function for the vertical distance $D(x)$ between points on lines P and Q with the same x-value.

c. For what value of x does $D(x)$ equal zero?

d. Critical Thinking How does the x-value in part (c) relate to the graph?

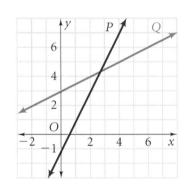

Simplify each expression.

53. $(ab^2 + ba^3) + (4a^3b - ab^2 - 5ab)$

54. $(9pq^6 - 11p^4q) - (-5pq^6 + p^4q^4)$

55. Graduation You can model the number of men and women in the United States who enrolled in college within a year of graduating from high school with the linear equations shown below. Let t equal the year of enrollment, with $t = 0$ corresponding to 1990. Let $m(t)$ equal the number of men in thousands, and let $w(t)$ equal the number of women in thousands.

$$m(t) = 35.4t + 1146.8 \qquad \text{men enrolled in college}$$

$$w(t) = 21.6t + 1185.5 \qquad \text{women enrolled in college}$$

a. Add the expressions on the right side of each equation to model the total number of recent high school graduates $p(t)$ who enrolled in college between 1990 and 1998.

b. Use the equation you created in part (a) to find the number of high school graduates who enrolled in college in 1995.

c. Critical Thinking If you had subtracted the expressions on the right side of each equation above, what information would the resulting expression model?

Real-World **Connection**

There were about 12 million students enrolled in college in 1980, 13.8 million in 1990, and 15 million in 2000.

Multiple Choice

56. Which expression represents the sum of an odd integer n and the next three odd integers?

A. $n + 6$ **B.** $n + 12$ **C.** $4n + 6$ **D.** $4n + 12$

57. Simplify $(8x^2 + 3) + (7x^2 + 10)$.

F. $x^2 - 7$ **G.** $15x^2 + 13$ **H.** $15x^4 + 13$ **I.** $56x^4 + 30$

Quantitative Comparison

Compare the boxed quantity in Column A with the boxed quantity in Column B. Choose the best answer.

A. The quantity in Column A is greater.
B. The quantity in Column B is greater.
C. The two quantities are equal.
D. The relationship cannot be determined from the information given.

	Column A	Column B
58.	sum of the coefficients of $3a^4 - 2a^3 + a + 8$	sum of the coefficients of $3a^7 - 6a + 9$
59.	sum of the exponents of $11a^5 - 5a^3 - 3$	sum of the exponents of $10a^4 + 4a^3 + 5a + 6$
60.	value of $4a^2 - 9a + 7$ for $a = 2$	value of $-a^2 + 12a + 8$ for $a = 2$
61.	$(2k - 6) + (3k + 1)$	$(k^2 + 4k) - (k^2 - k + 5)$

Take It to the NET
Online lesson quiz at
www.PHSchool.com
Web Code: aea-0901

Short Response

62. Simplify $(9x^3 - 4x^2 + 1) - (x^2 + 2)$. Show your work.

Mixed Review

Lesson 8-8

Identify the growth factor in each function.

63. $y = 6 \cdot 2^x$ **64.** $y = 0.6 \cdot 1.4^x$ **65.** $y = 2 \cdot 5^x$ **66.** $y = 0.3 \cdot 5^x$

Identify each function as *exponential growth* or *exponential decay*.

67. $y = 10 \cdot 3^x$ **68.** $y = 1.8 \cdot 0.4^x$ **69.** $y = 0.3 \cdot 7^x$ **70.** $y = 0.3 \cdot 0.5^x$

Lesson 8-3

Simplify each expression.

71. $7^8 \cdot 7^{10}$ **72.** $2^6 \cdot 2^{-7}$ **73.** $(4x^2)(9x^3)$ **74.** $(3ab)(a^2b)$

75. $(-5t^2)(6t^{-9})$ **76.** $(-3)^6 \cdot (-3)^{-4}$ **77.** $(6h^2)(-2h^8)$ **78.** $(2q^5)(5q^2)$

Lesson 6-7

Write an equation for each translation of $y = |x|$.

79. 5 units up   **80.** right 6 units   **81.** 12 units down   **82.** 7 units up

83. left 10 units   **84.** left 0.4 units   **85.** 5.2 units up   **86.** 2.3 units down

Multiplying and Factoring

Lesson Preview

What You'll Learn

OBJECTIVE
1 To multiply a polynomial by a monomial

OBJECTIVE
2 To factor a monomial from a polynomial

. . . And Why

To factor a monomial out of a polynomial, as in Example 3

✔ Check Skills You'll Need

(For help, go to Lesson 1-7.)

Multiply.

1. $3(302)$ **2.** $41(7)$ **3.** $9(504)$

Simplify each expression.

4. $4(6 + 5x)$ **5.** $-8(2y + 1)$ **6.** $(5v - 1)5$

7. $7(p - 2)$ **8.** $(6 - x)9$ **9.** $-2(4q - 1)$

---

iTEXT Interactive lesson includes instant self-check, tutorials, and activities.

OBJECTIVE

1 Distributing a Monomial

In Chapter 1 you used the Distributive Property to multiply a number by a sum or difference.

$$5(a + 3) = 5a + 15 \quad (x - 2)(3) = 3x - 6 \quad -2(2y + 7) = -4y - 14$$

You can also use the Distributive Property or an area model to multiply polynomials. The diagram shows the product of $2x$ and $(3x + 1)$.

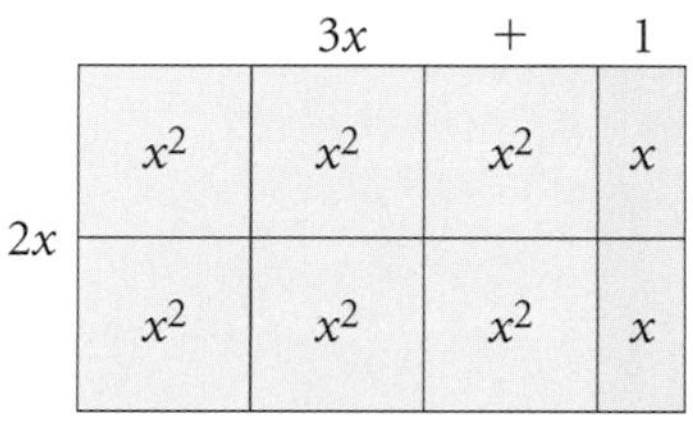

The same product is found below using the Distributive Property.

	$3x$	$+$	1
	x^2	x^2 x^2	x
$2x$	x^2	x^2 x^2	x

$$2x(3x + 1) = 2x(3x) + 2x(1)$$
$$= 6x^2 + 2x$$

You can use the Distributive Property for multiplying powers with the same base when multiplying by a monomial.

1 EXAMPLE   Multiplying a Monomial and a Trinomial

Need Help?

Multiplying powers with the same base:
$3^5 \cdot 3^4 = 3^{5+4} = 3^9$

Simplify $-4y^2(5y^4 - 3y^2 + 2)$.

$-4y^2(5y^4 - 3y^2 + 2)$

$= -4y^2(5y^4) - 4y^2(-3y^2) - 4y^2(2)$ **Use the Distributive Property.**

$= -20y^{2+4} + 12y^{2+2} - 8y^2$ **Multiply the coefficients and add the exponents of powers with the same base.**

$= -20y^6 + 12y^4 - 8y^2$ **Simplify.**

✔ Check Understanding **1** Simplify each product.

a. $4b(5b^2 + b + 6)$ **b.** $-7h(3h^2 - 8h - 1)$ **c.** $2x(x^2 - 6x + 5)$

Factoring a Monomial From a Polynomial

Factoring a polynomial reverses the multiplication process. To factor a monomial from a polynomial, first find the greatest common factor (GCF) of its terms.

Need Help?

The greatest common factor (GCF) is the greatest factor that divides evenly into each term of an expression. See Skills Handbook page 721.

2 EXAMPLE **Finding the Greatest Common Factor**

Find the GCF of the terms of $4x^3 + 12x^2 - 8x$.

List the prime factors of each term. Identify the factors common to all terms.

$4x^3 = 2 \cdot 2 \cdot x \cdot x \cdot x$

$12x^2 = 2 \cdot 2 \cdot 3 \cdot x \cdot x$

$8x = 2 \cdot 2 \cdot 2 \cdot x$

The GCF is $2 \cdot 2 \cdot x$ or $4x$.

✓ **Check Understanding** **2** Find the GCF of the terms of each polynomial.
  a. $5v^5 + 10v^3$ **b.** $3t^2 - 18$ **c.** $4b^3 - 2b^2 - 6b$

To factor a polynomial completely, you must factor until there are no common factors other than 1.

3 EXAMPLE **Factoring Out a Monomial**

Factor $3x^3 - 12x^2 + 15x$.

Step 1 Find the GCF.

$3x^3 = 3 \cdot x \cdot x \cdot x$

$12x^2 = 2 \cdot 2 \cdot 3 \cdot x \cdot x$

$15x = 3 \cdot 5 \cdot x$

Step 2 Factor out the GCF.

$3x^3 - 12x^2 + 15x$

$= 3x(x^2) + 3x(-4x) + 3x(5)$

$= 3x(x^2 - 4x + 5)$

The GCF is $3 \cdot x$ or $3x$.

✓ **Check Understanding** **3** Use the GCF to factor each polynomial.
  a. $8x^2 - 12x$ **b.** $5d^3 + 10d$ **c.** $6m^3 - 12m^2 - 24m$

EXERCISES

For more practice, see *Extra Practice*.

Practice and Problem Solving

A Practice by Example

Example 1
(page 462)

Simplify each product.

1. $8m(m + 6)$ **2.** $(x + 10)3x$ **3.** $9k(7k + 4)$

4. $-5a(a - 1)$ **5.** $2x^2(9 + x)$ **6.** $-p^2(p - 11)$

7. $2x(6x^3 - x^2 + 5x)$ **8.** $4y^2(9y^3 + 8y^2 - 11)$ **9.** $-5c^3(9c^2 - 8c - 5)$

10. $-7q^2(6q^5 - 2q - 7)$ **11.** $-3g^7(g^4 - 6g^2 + 5)$ **12.** $-4x^6(10x^3 + 3x^2 - 7)$

Example 2
(page 463)

Find the GCF of the terms of each polynomial.

13. $15w + 21$ **14.** $6a^2 - 8a$ **15.** $36v + 24$

16. $x^3 + 7x^2 - 5x$ **17.** $5b^3 + 15b - 30$ **18.** $9x^3 - 6x^2 + 12x$

Example 3
(page 463)

Factor each polynomial.

19. $6x - 4$

20. $v^2 + 4v$

21. $10x^3 - 25x^2 + 20$

22. $2t^2 - 10t^4$

23. $15n^3 - 3n^2 + 12n$

24. $6p^6 + 24p^5 + 18p^3$

25. Error Analysis Kevin said that $-2x(4x - 3) = -8x^2 - 6x$. Karla said that $-2x(4x - 3) = -8x^2 + 6x$. Who is correct? Explain.

26. Open-Ended Write a polynomial that has a common factor in each term. Factor your polynomial.

Simplify. Write in standard form.

27. $-3a(4a^2 - 5a + 9)$

28. $-7p^2(-2p^3 + 5p)$

29. $12c(-5c^2 + 3c - 4)$

30. $y(y + 3) - 5y(y - 2)$

31. $x^2(x + 1) - x(x^2 - 1)$

32. $4t(3t^2 - 4t) - t(7t)$

33. Building Models Suppose you are building a model of the square castle shown at the left. The moat of the model castle is made of blue paper.
   a. Find the area of the moat using the diagram with the photo.
   b. Write your answer in factored form.

Factor each polynomial.

34. $9m^{12} - 36m^7 + 81m^5$

35. $24x^3 - 96x^2 + 48x$

36. $16n^3 + 48n^2 - 80n$

37. $5x^4 + 4x^3 + 3x^2$

38. $13ab^3 + 39a^2b^4$

39. $7g^2k^3 - 35g^5k^2$

40. Critical Thinking The GCF of two numbers p and q is 5. What is the GCF of p^2 and q^2? Explain your answer.

41. a. Factor $n^2 - n$.
   b. Writing Suppose n is an integer. Is $n^2 - n$ *always, sometimes,* or *never* even? Justify your answer.

42. A triangular number is a number you can represent with a triangular arrangement of objects. A triangular number can also be written as a product of two factors, as in the table.
   a. Find the values of $a, b, c,$ and d, and then write an expression in factored form for the nth triangular number.

	1	2	3	4
Triangular Number	1	3	6	10
Factored Form	$\frac{a}{2}(a + 1)$	$\frac{b}{2}(b + 1)$	$\frac{c}{2}(c + 1)$	$\frac{d}{2}(d + 1)$

   b. Use the expression you wrote to find the 100th triangular number.

43. a. Geometry How many sides does the polygon have? How many of its diagonals come from one vertex?
   b. Suppose a polygon has n sides. How many diagonals will it have from one vertex?
   c. The number of diagonals from all the vertices is $\frac{n}{2}(n - 3)$. Multiply the two factors.
   d. For a polygon with 8 sides, what is the total number of diagonals that can be drawn from the vertices?

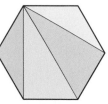

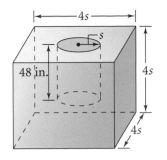

44. Manufacturing The diagram shows a cube of metal with a cylinder cut out of it. The formula for the volume of a cylinder is $V = \pi r^2 h$, where r is the radius and h is the height.

  a. Write a formula for the volume of the cube in terms of s.
  b. Write a formula for the volume of the cylinder in terms of s.
  c. Write a formula in terms of s for the volume V of the metal left after the cylinder has been removed.
  d. Factor your formula from part (c).
  e. Find V in cubic inches for $s = 15$ in.

Standardized Test Prep

Multiple Choice

45. $x(6x^2 - 4x - 2)$ equals which of the following expressions?
  A. $6x^3 - 4x - 2$
  B. $6x^3 - 4x^2 - 2x$
  C. $6x^3 - 4x^2 - 2$
  D. $7x^3 - 5x^2 - 3x$

46. Simplify $(p^2 - 3) - (5 - p + 2p^2) - (4p + 5 - 2p^2)$. What is the coefficient of p^2?
  F. 1
  G. 2
  H. 4
  I. 5

47. Let $\boxed{n}$ represent the number of different pairs of integers whose product is n. For example, -1×10, -2×5, $1 \times (-10)$, and $2 \times (-5)$ give -10. So $\boxed{-10} = 4$. What does $\boxed{-24}$ equal?
  A. 4
  B. 6
  C. 8
  D. 10

48. Which of the following represents an odd number for any integer n?
  F. $n + 1$
  G. $2n + 1$
  H. $3n$
  I. $3n + 1$

Take It to the NET
Online lesson quiz at
www.PHSchool.com
Web Code: aea-0902

49. Factor $6g^8 - 3g^4 + 9g^2$ completely.
  A. $g^2(6g^4 - 3g^2 + 9)$
  B. $3g^2(2g^6 - g^2 + 3)$
  C. $g^2(6g^6 - 3g^2 + 9g)$
  D. $3g^2(2g^6 - g^2 + 3g)$

Short Response

50. How do you know if you've factored out the GCF of a polynomial? Illustrate your explanation by using the GCF to factor $10x^4 + 6x^3 + 2x^2$.

Mixed Review

Lesson 9-1

Simplify. Write each answer in standard form.

51. $(x^2 + 3) - (4x^2 - 7)$
52. $(m^3 + 8m + 6) + (-5m^2 + 4m)$

53. $(g^2 + 6g - 2) + (4g^2 - 7g + 2)$
54. $(3r^2 - 8r + 7) - (2r^2 + 8r - 9)$

55. $(t^4 - t^3 + 1) + (t^3 + 5t^2 - 10)$
56. $(3b^3 - b^2) - (5b^2 + 12)$

Lesson 8-1

Simplify each expression.

57. 5^{-1}
58. 5^{-2}
59. $(-2)^{-3}$
60. 8^0

61. $n^{-3}m^2$
62. $3w^{-5}$
63. $\dfrac{4}{c^{-3}}$
64. $\dfrac{ab^{-8}}{c^5}$

Lesson 7-3

Solve by elimination.

65. $7x + 6y = 33$
    $2x - 6y = -6$
66. $8x + 4y = 28$
    $3x - 2y = 21$
67. $4x + 2y = 16$
    $11x - 3y = -7$

Using Models to Multiply

FOR USE WITH LESSON 9-3

You can use algebra tiles to multiply two binomials.

1 EXAMPLE Multiplying Binomials

Find the product $(2x + 1)(x + 5)$.

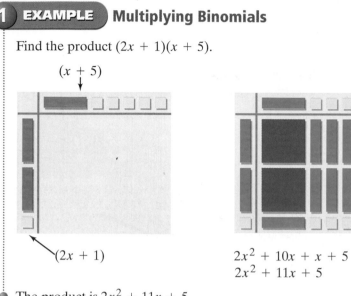

$(x + 5)$

$(2x + 1)$

$2x^2 + 10x + x + 5$
$2x^2 + 11x + 5$ **Add coefficients of like terms.**

● The product is $2x^2 + 11x + 5$.

You can also model products that involve subtraction. Red tiles indicate negative variables and negative numbers.

2 EXAMPLE Multiplying With Negative Tiles

Find the product $(x - 2)(3x + 1)$.

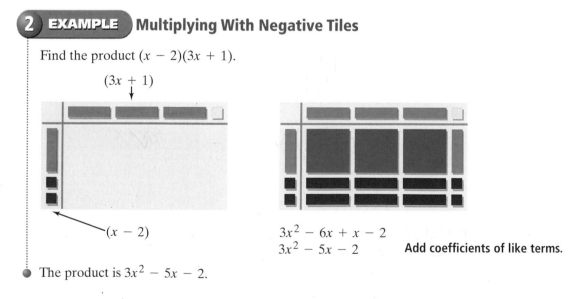

$(3x + 1)$

$(x - 2)$

$3x^2 - 6x + x - 2$
$3x^2 - 5x - 2$ **Add coefficients of like terms.**

● The product is $3x^2 - 5x - 2$.

EXERCISES

Use algebra tiles to find each product.

1. $(x + 1)(x + 6)$

2. $(x + 1)(x - 2)$

3. $(x + 1)(4x - 1)$

4. $(x + 4)(2x + 1)$

5. $(x - 3)(3x + 5)$

6. $(2x + 3)(3x + 5)$

9-3

Multiplying Binomials

Lesson Preview

What You'll Learn

OBJECTIVE 1 To multiply binomials using FOIL

OBJECTIVE 2 To multiply trinomials by binomials

. . . And Why

To find the area of a geometric figure, as in Example 3

✓ **Check Skills You'll Need** (For help, go to Lesson 9-2.)

Find each product.

1. $4r(r - 1)$ **2.** $6h(h^2 + 8h - 3)$ **3.** $y^2(2y^3 - 7)$

Simplify. Write each answer in standard form.

4. $(x^3 + 3x^2 + x) + (5x^2 + x + 1)$ **5.** $(3t^3 - 6t + 8) + (5t^3 + 7t - 2)$

6. $w(w + 1) + 4w(w - 7)$ **7.** $6b(b - 2) - b(8b + 3)$

8. $m(4m^2 - 6) + 3m^2(m + 9)$ **9.** $3d^2(d^3 - 6) - d^3(2d^2 + 4)$

---

iTEXT Interactive lesson includes instant self-check, tutorials, and activities.

OBJECTIVE

1 Multiplying Two Binomials

You can use an area model to multiply two binomials. The diagram below shows $(2x + 3)(x + 4)$.

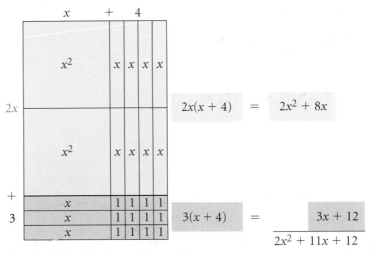

$2x(x + 4) = 2x^2 + 8x$

$3(x + 4) = \underline{3x + 12}$

$2x^2 + 11x + 12$

You can also use the Distributive Property to find the product of two binomials.

1 EXAMPLE Using the Distributive Property

Simplify $(2x + 3)(x + 4)$.

$(2x + 3)(x + 4) = 2x(x + 4) + 3(x + 4)$ **Distribute x + 4.**

$= 2x^2 + 8x + 3x + 12$ **Now distribute 2x and 3.**

$= 2x^2 + 11x + 12$ **Simplify.**

✓ **Check Understanding** **1** Simplify each product.

a. $(6h - 7)(2h + 3)$ **b.** $(5m + 2)(8m - 1)$ **c.** $(9a - 8)(7a + 4)$

One way to organize multiplying two binomials is to use FOIL, which stands for "First, Outer, Inner, Last." The term *FOIL* is a memory device for applying the Distributive Property to the product of two binomials.

2 EXAMPLE **Multiplying Using FOIL**

Simplify $(3x - 5)(2x + 7)$.

	First	Outer	Inner	Last
	$= (3x)(2x)$	$+ (3x)(7)$	$- (5)(2x)$	$- (5)(7)$

$(3x - 5)(2x + 7)$ $= 6x^2 + 21x - 10x - 35$

$= 6x^2 + 11x - 35$

● The product is $6x^2 + 11x - 35$.

✔ **Check Understanding** ② Simplify each product using FOIL.
 a. $(3x + 4)(2x + 5)$ **b.** $(3x - 4)(2x + 5)$
 c. $(3x + 4)(2x - 5)$ **d.** $(3x - 4)(2x - 5)$

You can use FOIL to find the area of some geometric figures.

3 EXAMPLE **Applying Multiplication of Polynomials**

Geometry Find the area of the shaded region. Simplify.

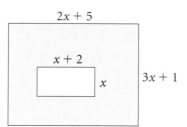

area of outer rectangle $= (3x + 1)(2x + 5)$
area of hole $= x(x + 2)$
area of shaded region

$\quad = \quad$ area of outer rectangle $-$ area of hole

$\quad = \quad (3x + 1)(2x + 5) \quad - \quad x(x + 2)$ **Substitute.**

$\quad = 6x^2 + 15x + 2x + 5 \quad - \quad x^2 - 2x$ **Use FOIL to simplify $(3x + 1)(2x + 5)$ and the Distributive Property to simplify $-x(x + 2)$.**

$\quad = 6x^2 - x^2 + 15x + 2x - 2x + 5$ **Group like terms.**

● $\quad = 5x^2 + 15x + 5$ **Simplify.**

✔ **Check Understanding** ③ Find the area of each shaded region. Simplify.

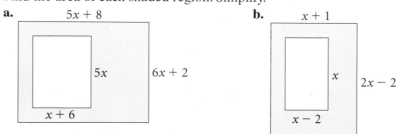

2 Multiplying a Trinomial and a Binomial

FOIL works when you multiply two binomials, but it is not helpful when multiplying a trinomial and a binomial. You can use the vertical method or the horizontal method to distribute each term in such factors.

4 EXAMPLE Multiplying a Trinomial and a Binomial

Simplify the product $(4x^2 + x - 6)(2x - 3)$.

Method 1 Multiply using the vertical method.

$$
\begin{array}{r}
4x^2 + x - 6 \\
2x - 3 \\
\hline
-12x^2 - 3x + 18 \\
8x^3 + 2x^2 - 12x \\
\hline
8x^3 - 10x^2 - 15x + 18
\end{array}
$$

Multiply by -3.
Multiply by $2x$.
Add like terms.

Method 2 Multiply using the horizontal method.

$$(2x - 3)(4x^2 + x - 6)$$

$= 2x(4x^2) + 2x(x) + 2x(-6) - 3(4x^2) - 3(x) - 3(-6)$

$= 8x^3 + 2x^2 - 12x - 12x^2 - 3x + 18$

$= 8x^3 - 10x^2 - 15x + 18$ **Add like terms.**

● The product is $8x^3 - 10x^2 - 15x + 18$.

Problem Solving Hint

For Check Understanding 4, drawing arrows between terms can help you identify all six products.

✔ **Check Understanding** 4 Simplify $(6n - 8)(2n^2 + n + 7)$ using both methods shown in Example 4.

EXERCISES

For more practice, see *Extra Practice.*

Practice and Problem Solving

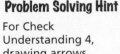 **Practice by Example**

Example 1
(page 467)

Copy and fill in each blank.

1. $(5a + 2)(6a - 1) = \blacksquare a^2 + 7a - 2$ **2.** $(3c - 7)(2c - 5) = 6c^2 - 29c + \blacksquare$

3. $(z - 4)(2z + 1) = 2z^2 - \blacksquare z - 4$ **4.** $(2x + 9)(x + 2) = 2x^2 + \blacksquare x + 18$

Simplify each product using the Distributive Property.

5. $(x + 2)(x + 5)$ **6.** $(h + 3)(h + 4)$ **7.** $(k + 7)(k - 6)$

8. $(a - 8)(a - 9)$ **9.** $(2x - 1)(x + 2)$ **10.** $(2y + 5)(y - 3)$

Example 2
(page 468)

Simplify each product using FOIL.

11. $(r + 6)(r - 4)$ **12.** $(y + 4)(5y - 8)$ **13.** $(x + 6)(x - 7)$

14. $(m - 6)(m - 9)$ **15.** $(4b - 2)(b + 3)$ **16.** $(8w + 2)(w + 5)$

17. $(x - 7)(x + 9)$ **18.** $(a + 11)(a + 5)$ **19.** $(p - 1)(p + 10)$

Example 3
(page 468)

Geometry Find the area of each shaded region. Simplify.

20.

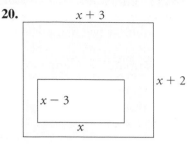

21.

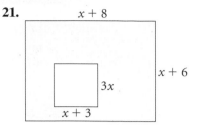

Example 4
(page 469)

Simplify. Use the vertical method.

22. $(x + 9)(x^2 - 4x + 1)$ **23.** $(a - 4)(a^2 - 2a + 1)$

24. $(g - 3)(2g^2 + 3g + 3)$ **25.** $(k + 8)(3k^2 - 5k + 7)$

Simplify. Use the horizontal method.

26. $(x^2 + 2x + 1)(9x - 3)$ **27.** $(t^2 - 6t + 3)(2t - 5)$

28. $(7p^2 + 5p - 1)(8p + 9)$ **29.** $(12w^2 - w - 1)(4w - 2)$

B **Apply Your Skills**

Simplify each product. Write in standard form.

30. $(p - 7)(p + 8)$ **31.** $(-7 + p)(8 + p)$ **32.** $(p^2 - 7)(p + 8)$

33. $(5c - 9)(5c + 1)$ **34.** $(n^2 + 3)(n + 11)$ **35.** $(3k^2 + 2)(k + 5k^2)$

36. $(6h - 1)(4h^2 + h + 3)$ **37.** $(9y^2 + 2)(y^2 - y - 1)$ **38.** $(8q - 4)(6q^2 + q + 1)$

39. Construction You are planning a rectangular garden. Its length is twice its width. You want a walkway 2 ft wide around the garden.
  a. Write an expression for the area of the garden and walk.
  b. Write an expression for the area of the walk only.
  c. You have enough gravel to cover 76 ft^2 and want to use it all on the walk. How big should you make the garden?

40. Open-Ended Write a binomial and a trinomial. Find their product.

41. Writing Which method do you prefer for multiplying a binomial and a trinomial? Explain.

Geometry Write an expression for the area of each shaded region. Write your answer in simplest form.

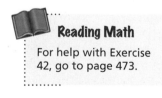

Reading Math

For help with Exercise 42, go to page 473.

42.

43.

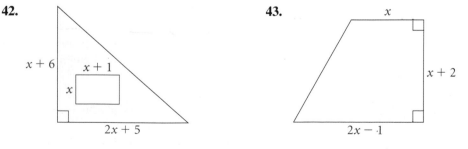

44. a. Simplify each pair of products.
  i. $(x + 1)(x + 1)$ **ii.** $(x + 1)(x + 2)$ **iii.** $(x + 1)(x + 3)$
       $11 \cdot 11$ $11 \cdot 12$ $11 \cdot 13$

  b. Critical Thinking What are the similarities between the two answers in each pair of products?

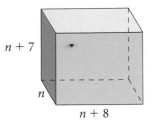

45. Geometry Use the formula $V = \ell wh$ to write a polynomial in standard form for the volume of the box.

46. If n represents an even number, write an expression that represents the product of the next two even numbers. Simplify.

$n + 7$

n

$n + 8$

 Challenge

For Exercises 47–49, each expression represents the side length of a cube. Write an expression in standard form for the surface area of each cube.

47. $x + 3$ **48.** $4t + 1$ **49.** $2w^2 + 7$

50. a. Vegetable Consumption Multiply the expressions on the right side of each equation to create a model for the total number of pounds of fresh vegetables $V(t)$ consumed in a year in the United States.

$C(t) = 2.7t + 165$ the U.S. annual per capita consumption of fresh vegetables, in pounds, from 1990 to 1997

$P(t) = 2.6t + 248$ the U.S. population, in millions, from 1990 to 1997

  b. Evaluate the equation you found in part (a) with $t = 5$ to find the total vegetable consumption for 1995. ($t = 0$ corresponds to the year 1990.)

51. Financial Planning Suppose you deposit $2000 for college in a savings account that has an annual interest rate r. At the end of three years, the value of your account will be $2000(1 + r)^3$ dollars.

  a. Rewrite the expression $2000(1 + r)^3$ by finding the product $2000(1 + r)(1 + r)(1 + r)$. Write your answer in standard form.

  b. Find the amount of money in the account if the interest rate is 3%.

For Exercises 52–54, each expression represents the radius of a circle. Write an expression in standard form for the area of each circle.

52. $g + 2$ **53.** $4k + 5$ **54.** $3x + 1$

For Exercises 55–58, find each product using lattice multiplication, which is explained below.

Lattice multiplication probably originated in India in the twelfth century. It came into use in Italy in the fourteenth century.

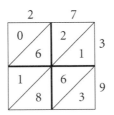

This example shows $27 \cdot 39$. Each number is treated as a binomial. The four products are placed in the small, diagonally split squares. The product of 2 and 3, shown in red, is 6. The first square shows 0/6, which indicates 6. The product of 7 and 3 is 21. The second square shows 2/1.

The products are totaled diagonally. For the diagonal shaded blue, the tens place of the sum $1 + 6 + 8$ is carried into the diagonal above and added into that diagonal: $1 + (2 + 6 + 1)$. The product 1053 appears down the left side of the lattice and across the bottom.

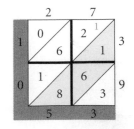

55. $14 \cdot 72$ **56.** $53 \cdot 87$

57. $91 \cdot 64$ **58.** $38 \cdot 64$

Real-World **Connection**

In 2000, the U.S. consumption of fresh tomatoes was 17.8 lb per person.

Multiple Choice

59. $(n - 1)(n - 4)$ is equivalent to which expression?

   A. $n^2 - 5n + 4$ **B.** $n^2 - 3n + 4$

   C. $n^2 + 3n + 4$ **D.** $n^2 - 5n - 5$

60. $(8k - 3)(k^2 - k + 1)$ is equivalent to which expression?

   F. $8k^3 + 11k^2 - 11k - 3$ **G.** $9k^3 - 8k^2 + 8k - 2$

   H. $8k^3 - 11k^2 + 11k - 3$ **I.** $9k^3 - 3k^2 + 3k - 3$

61. Which of the following products is always odd for integer values of n?

   A. $(n + 1)(n + 1)$ **B.** $(2n - 1)(2n + 1)$

   C. $(2n - 1)(n + 1)$ **D.** $(2n + 1)(n - 1)$

Short Response

62. Explain how to find the product of $(4v - 1)(2v^2 + v + 1)$, and simplify.

Extended Response

63. Find the area of the shaded region. Show your work.

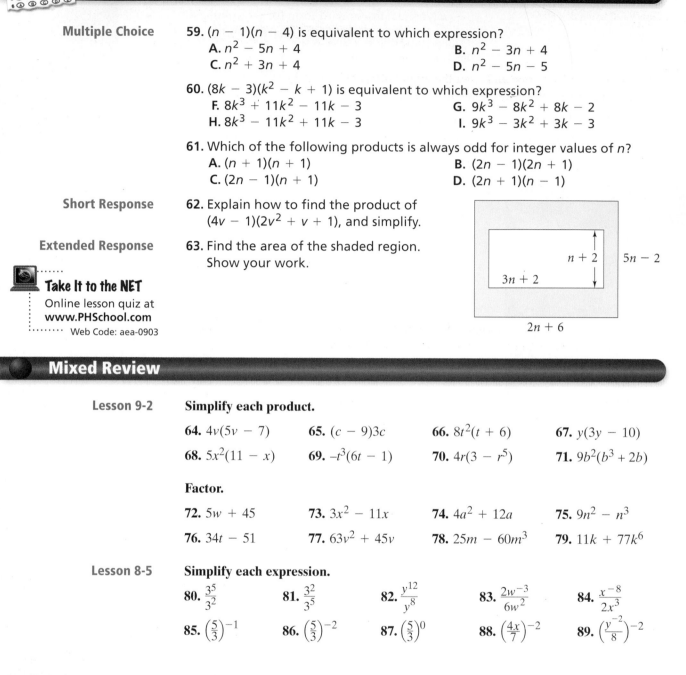

(dimensions shown: $n + 2$, $5n - 2$, $3n + 2$, $2n + 6$)

Take It to the NET
Online lesson quiz at
www.PHSchool.com
Web Code: aea-0903

Mixed Review

Lesson 9-2

Simplify each product.

64. $4v(5v - 7)$ **65.** $(c - 9)3c$ **66.** $8t^2(t + 6)$ **67.** $y(3y - 10)$

68. $5x^2(11 - x)$ **69.** $-t^3(6t - 1)$ **70.** $4r(3 - r^5)$ **71.** $9b^2(b^3 + 2b)$

Factor.

72. $5w + 45$ **73.** $3x^2 - 11x$ **74.** $4a^2 + 12a$ **75.** $9n^2 - n^3$

76. $34t - 51$ **77.** $63v^2 + 45v$ **78.** $25m - 60m^3$ **79.** $11k + 77k^6$

Lesson 8-5

Simplify each expression.

80. $\dfrac{3^5}{3^2}$ **81.** $\dfrac{3^2}{3^5}$ **82.** $\dfrac{y^{12}}{y^8}$ **83.** $\dfrac{2w^{-3}}{6w^2}$ **84.** $\dfrac{x^{-8}}{2x^3}$

85. $\left(\dfrac{5}{3}\right)^{-1}$ **86.** $\left(\dfrac{5}{3}\right)^{-2}$ **87.** $\left(\dfrac{5}{3}\right)^{0}$ **88.** $\left(\dfrac{4x}{7}\right)^{-2}$ **89.** $\left(\dfrac{y^{-2}}{8}\right)^{-2}$

✓ Checkpoint Quiz 1   Lessons 9-1 through 9-3

TEXT Instant self-check quiz online and on CD-ROM

Simplify each expression.

1. $(4x^2 + x + 3) + (5x^2 + 9x - 2)$ **2.** $(7b^2 - 5b + 3) - (b^2 + 8b - 6)$

3. $3w(12w - 1) - 8w$ **4.** $6k(4k + k^2) + 9k(2k - 6k^2)$

5. $(x + 3)(x - 5)$ **6.** $(2n^3 - 5)(6n^2 + n)$ **7.** $(g^2 + 4)(4g^2 + 8g - 9)$

Factor each polynomial.

8. $12y^2 - 10$ **9.** $5t^6 + 25t^3 - 10t$ **10.** $18v^4 + 27v^3 + 36v^2$

Read the exercise below and then the explanation of how to interpret the diagram. Check your understanding by solving the problem at the bottom of the page.

Geometry Write an expression for the area of the shaded region. Write your answer in simplest form.

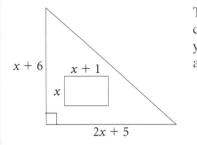

To solve this problem, you must refer to the diagram. It contains the rest of the information you need. To find this information, ask yourself a few questions.

What do I see?

There are two figures—a right triangle and a rectangle inside it. The rectangle is *not* shaded. There are also some variable expressions.

What do the variable expressions tell me?

The expressions represent the dimensions of the figures.

Triangle: The length of the base is $2x + 5$.
The height is $x + 6$.

Rectangle: The length is x.
The width is $x + 1$.

Now you can solve the problem.

area of shaded region   = area of triangle − area of the rectangle

$$= \frac{1}{2}(\text{base})(\text{height}) - (\text{length})(\text{width})$$

$$= \frac{1}{2}(2x + 5)(x + 6) - x(x + 1)$$ **Use values in the diagram to substitute.**

$$= \frac{1}{2}(2x^2 + 5x + 12x + 30) - (x^2 + x)$$ **Simplify $(x + 6)(2x + 5)$ and $(x + 1)(x)$.**

$$= x^2 + \frac{17}{2}x + 15 - x^2 - x$$ **Use the Distributive Property.**

$$= 7.5x + 15$$ **Simplify.**

EXERCISE

Geometry Write an expression for the area of the colored region. Write your answer in simplest form.

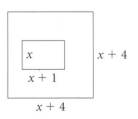

9-4

Multiplying Special Cases

Lesson Preview

What You'll Learn

OBJECTIVE 1 To find the square of a binomial

OBJECTIVE 2 To find the difference of squares

...And Why

To find the probability of a Labrador retriever inheriting dark fur, as in Example 2

✓ Check Skills You'll Need

(For help, go to Lessons 8-4 and 9-3.)

Simplify.

1. $(7x)^2$ **2.** $(3v)^2$ **3.** $(-4c)^2$ **4.** $(5g^3)^2$

Use FOIL to find each product.

5. $(j + 5)(j + 7)$ **6.** $(2b - 6)(3b - 8)$

7. $(4y + 1)(5y - 2)$ **8.** $(x + 3)(x - 4)$

9. $(8c^2 + 2)(c^2 - 10)$ **10.** $(6y^2 - 3)(9y^2 + 1)$

OBJECTIVE

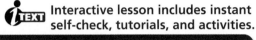

1   **Finding the Square of a Binomial**

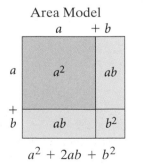 **Interactive lesson includes instant self-check, tutorials, and activities.**

Investigation: Exploring Special Products

1. Find each product.

Row 1: $(x + 8)(x + 8)$ $(y + 5)(y + 5)$ $(2p + 3)(2p + 3)$

Row 2: $(d - 3)(d - 3)$ $(t - 1)(t - 1)$ $(9r - 2)(9r - 2)$

Row 3: $(x + 4)(x - 4)$ $(k + 9)(k - 9)$ $(3c + 7)(3c - 7)$

2. Describe the pattern or patterns you found in each row.

3. Based on the patterns you found, predict each product.

    $(p + 6)(p + 6)$ $(v - 5)(v - 5)$ $(x + 8)(x - 8)$

4. Use FOIL to find each product in Question 2. Were your predictions correct?

You can write the expression $(a + b)^2$ as $(a + b)(a + b)$. You can find $(a + b)^2$ using the methods you learned in Lesson 9-3.

Area Model   FOIL

$$\begin{array}{c|c|c}
 & a & +\ b \\
\hline
a & a^2 & ab \\
\hline
+\ b & ab & b^2 \\
\end{array}$$

$a^2 + 2ab + b^2$

$(a + b)(a + b)$
$= a^2 + ab + ba + b^2$ **Use FOIL.**
$= a^2 + 2ab + b^2$ **Simplify.**

The expressions $(a - b)^2$ and $(a + b)^2$ are squares of binomials. To square a binomial, you can use FOIL or the following rule.

Key Concepts

Rule	The Square of a Binomial

$(a + b)^2 = a^2 + 2ab + b^2$

$(a - b)^2 = a^2 - 2ab + b^2$

The square of a binomial is the square of the first term plus twice the product of the two terms plus the square of the last term.

1 EXAMPLE Squaring a Binomial

a. Find $(x + 7)^2$.

$(x + 7)^2 = x^2 + 2x(7) + 7^2$ **Square the binomial.**

$\qquad\quad = x^2 + 14x + 49$ **Simplify.**

b. Find $(4k - 3)^2$.

$(4k - 3)^2 = (4k)^2 - 2(4k)(3) + 3^2$ **Square the binomial.**

$\qquad\qquad = 16k^2 - 24k + 9$ **Simplify.**

✓ **Check Understanding** ❶ Find each square.

a. $(t + 6)^2$ **b.** $(5y + 1)^2$ **c.** $(7m - 2p)^2$ **d.** $(9c - 8)^2$

You can square binomials to find probabilities that apply to real-world situations.

2 EXAMPLE Real-World Problem Solving

Among Labrador retrievers, the dark-fur gene D is dominant, and the yellow-fur gene Y is recessive. This means that a dog with at least one dominant gene (DD or DY) will have dark fur. A dog with two recessive genes (YY) will have yellow fur.

The Punnett square at the right models the possible combinations of color genes that parents who carry both genes can pass on to their offspring. Since YY is $\frac{1}{4}$ of the outcomes, the probability that a puppy has yellow fur is $\frac{1}{4}$.

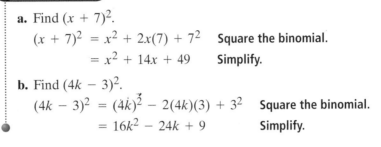

	D	Y
D	DD	DY
Y	DY	YY

You can model the probabilities found in the Punnett square with the expression $\left(\frac{1}{2}D + \frac{1}{2}Y\right)^2$. Show that this product gives the same result as the Punnett square.

$\left(\frac{1}{2}D + \frac{1}{2}Y\right)^2 = \left(\frac{1}{2}D\right)^2 + 2\left(\frac{1}{2}D\right)\left(\frac{1}{2}Y\right) + \left(\frac{1}{2}Y\right)^2$ **Square the binomial.**

$\qquad\qquad\qquad = \frac{1}{4}D^2 + \frac{1}{2}DY + \frac{1}{4}Y^2$ **Simplify.**

The expressions $\frac{1}{4}D^2$ and $\frac{1}{4}Y^2$ indicate that the probability offspring will have either two dominant genes or two recessive genes is $\frac{1}{4}$. The expression $\frac{1}{2}DY$ indicates that there is $\frac{1}{2}$ chance that the offspring will inherit both genes. These are the same probabilities shown in the Punnett square.

Real-World ● **Connection**

The color of a Labrador retriever is determined by a pair of genes. The offspring inherits a single gene at random from each of its parents.

✔ Check Understanding **2 Games** When you play a game with two number cubes, you can find probabilities by squaring a binomial. Let A represent rolling 1 or 2 and B represent rolling 3, 4, 5, or 6. The probability of A is $\frac{1}{3}$, and the probability of B is $\frac{2}{3}$.

a. Find $\left(\frac{1}{3}A + \frac{2}{3}B\right)^2$.

b. What is the probability that both number cubes you roll show 1 or 2?

c. What is the probability that one number cube shows a 1 or 2 and the other shows 3, 4, 5, or 6?

d. What is the probability that both number cubes show 3, 4, 5, or 6?

Using mental math, you can square a binomial to find the square of a number.

3 EXAMPLE **Mental Math**

a. Find 51^2 using mental math.

$51^2 = (50 + 1)^2$

$= 50^2 + 2(50 \cdot 1) + 1^2$ ⟵ Square the binomial. ⟶ $= 50^2 - 2(50 \cdot 1) + 1^2$

$= 2500 + 100 + 1 = 2601$ ⟵ Simplify. ⟶ $= 2500 - 100 + 1 = 2401$

b. Find 49^2 using mental math.

$49^2 = (50 - 1)^2$

✔ Check Understanding **3** Find each square using mental math.
a. 31^2 **b.** 29^2 **c.** 98^2 **d.** 203^2

OBJECTIVE

2 Difference of Squares

The product of the sum and difference of the same two terms also produces a pattern.

$$(a + b)(a - b) = a^2 - ab + ba - b^2$$
$$= a^2 - b^2$$

Notice that the sum $-ab$ and ba is 0, leaving $a^2 - b^2$. This product is called the difference of squares.

Key Concepts

Rule	The Difference of Squares
$(a + b)(a - b) = a^2 - b^2$	

The product of the sum and difference of the same two terms is the difference of their squares.

Need Help?

When you raise a power to a power, multiply the exponents.
$(t^3)^2 = t^6$

4 EXAMPLE **Finding the Difference of Squares**

Find $(t^3 - 6)(t^3 + 6)$.

$(t^3 - 6)(t^3 + 6) = (t^3)^2 - (6)^2$ **Find the difference of squares.**
$= t^6 - 36$ **Simplify.**

✔ Check Understanding **4** Find each product.
a. $(d + 11)(d - 11)$ **b.** $(c^2 + 8)(c^2 - 8)$ **c.** $(9v^3 + w^4)(9v^3 - w^4)$

You can use the difference of squares to calculate products using mental math.

5 EXAMPLE Mental Math

Find $82 \cdot 78$.

$82 \cdot 78 = (80 + 2)(80 - 2)$ **Express each factor using 80 and 2.**

$\qquad = 80^2 - 2^2$ **Find the difference of squares.**

$\qquad = 6400 - 4 = 6396$ **Simplify.**

✓ **Check Understanding**   **5** Find each product.

   a. $18 \cdot 22$ **b.** $19 \cdot 21$ **c.** $59 \cdot 61$ **d.** $87 \cdot 93$

EXERCISES

For more practice, see *Extra Practice*.

Practice and Problem Solving

Ⓐ Practice by Example

Examples 1, 2
(page 475)

Find each square.

1. $(c + 1)^2$ **2.** $(x + 4)^2$ **3.** $(2v + 11)^2$ **4.** $(3m + 7)^2$

5. $(w - 12)^2$ **6.** $(b - 5)^2$ **7.** $(6x - 8)^2$ **8.** $(9j - 2)^2$

9. Games Suppose you play a game with two spinners like the one shown at the right. Let C represent spinning an even number. Let D represent spinning an odd number. The probability of C is $\frac{1}{4}$. The probability of D is $\frac{3}{4}$.

   a. Simplify $\left(\frac{1}{4}C + \frac{3}{4}D\right)^2$.

   b. Find $P(C \text{ and } C)$.

   c. How does the answer in part (b) relate to the polynomial in part (a)?

Example 3
(page 476)

Mental Math **Find each square.**

10. 61^2 **11.** 99^2 **12.** 48^2 **13.** 302^2 **14.** 499^2

Example 4
(page 476)

Find each product.

15. $(x + 4)(x - 4)$ **16.** $(a + 8)(a - 8)$ **17.** $(d + 7)(d - 7)$

18. $(h + 15)(h - 15)$ **19.** $(y + 12)(y - 12)$ **20.** $(k + 5)(k - 5)$

Example 5
(page 477)

Mental Math **Find each product.**

21. $31 \cdot 29$ **22.** $89 \cdot 91$ **23.** $52 \cdot 48$ **24.** $197 \cdot 203$ **25.** $299 \cdot 301$

Ⓑ Apply Your Skills   **Geometry** Find the area of each shaded region. Write your answers in standard form.

26.

27.

Find each square.

28. $(x + 3y)^2$ **29.** $(5p - q)^2$ **30.** $(6m + n)^2$ **31.** $(x - 7y)^2$

32. $(4k + 7j)^2$ **33.** $(2y - 9x)^2$ **34.** $(3w + 10t)^2$ **35.** $(6a + 11b)^2$

36. $(5p - 6q)^2$ **37.** $(6h - 8p)^2$ **38.** $(y^5 - 9x^4)^2$ **39.** $(8k + 4h)^2$

40. Biology The coat color of shorthorn cattle is determined by two genes, Red R and White W. RR produces red, WW produces white, and RW produces a third type of coat color called roan.

	R	W
R	RR	RW
W	RW	WW

a. Model the Punnett square with the square of a binomial.
b. If both parents have RW, what is the probability the offspring will also be RW?
c. Write an expression to model a situation where one parent is RW while the other is RR.
d. What is the probability that the offspring of the parents in step (c) will have a white coat?

Real-World **Connection**

The cow in the photo shows a typical roan coat.

41. a. Copy and complete the table.
b. Describe any patterns you see.
c. Writing How does the difference of squares account for the pattern in the table?

$4^2 = 16$	$3 \cdot 5 = 15$
$5^2 = \blacksquare$	$4 \cdot 6 = 24$
$6^2 = \blacksquare$	$5 \cdot 7 = \blacksquare$
$7^2 = \blacksquare$	$6 \cdot 8 = \blacksquare$

42. Open-Ended Give a counterexample to show that $(x + y)^2 = x^2 + y^2$ is false.

43. Critical Thinking Does $\left(3\frac{1}{2}\right)^2 = 9\frac{1}{4}$? Explain.

Find each product.

44. $(3y + 5w)(3y - 5w)$ **45.** $(p + 9q)(p - 9q)$ **46.** $(2d + 7g)(2d - 7g)$

47. $(7b - 8c)(7b + 8c)$ **48.** $(g + 7h)(g - 7h)$ **49.** $(g^3 + 7h^2)(g^3 - 7h^2)$

50. $(2a^2 + b)(2a^2 - b)$ **51.** $(11x - y^3)(11x + y^3)$ **52.** $(4k - 3h^2)(4k + 3h^2)$

Challenge

53. Find the general formula for $(a + b + c)^2$.

54. Games Suppose you play a game by tossing 3 coins. You can find the probabilities by simplifying $\left(\frac{1}{2}H + \frac{1}{2}T\right)^3$.
a. Simplify the expression.
b. Use the answer you found in part (a) to find the probability of getting a head and two tails $\left(HT^2\right)$.

55. Number Theory You can use factoring to show that the sum of two multiples of 3 is also a multiple of 3.

> If m and n are integers, then $3n$ and $3m$ are multiples of three.
> $3m + 3n = 3(m + n)$
> Since $(m + n)$ is an integer, $3(m + n)$ is a multiple of three.

a. Show that if a number is one more than a multiple of 3, then its square is also one more than a multiple of 3.
b. Reasoning If a number is two more than a multiple of 3, is its square also two more than a multiple of 3? Explain.

56. The formula $V = \frac{4}{3}\pi r^3$ gives the volume of a sphere. Find the formula for the volume of a sphere that has a radius 3 more than r. Write your answer in standard form.

57. The area of the shaded region in the diagram is $9^2 - 2^2$.

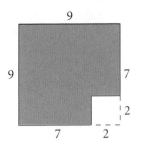

  a. Copy the figure. Make a single cut across the shaded region and reassemble it to show that $9^2 - 2^2 = (9 - 2)(9 + 2)$.

  b. Draw your reassembled figure. Include its dimensions.

Multiple Choice

58. Which value of a makes $(9x - 1)^2 = ax^2 - 18x + 1$ true?

  A. 9   **B.** 18   **C.** 64   **D.** 81

59. Which value of n makes $(b^7 + 2)^2 = b^n + 4b^7 + 4$ true?

  F. 14   **G.** 28   **H.** 42   **I.** 49

Quantitative Comparison

Compare the boxed quantity in Column A with the boxed quantity in Column B. Choose the best answer.

  A. The quantity in Column A is greater.

  B. The quantity in Column B is greater.

  C. The two quantities are equal.

  D. The relationship cannot be determined from the information given.

	Column A	Column B
60.	coefficient of a^2 in the product $(3a - 10)(3a + 10)$	coefficient of b^2 in the product $(9b - 10)(b - 10)$
61.	coefficient of a in the product $(4a - 6)(5a + 1)$	coefficient of b in the product $(8b - 7)(3b + 9)$
62.	constant term in the product $(7a + 3)(8a + 2)$	constant term in the product $(12b - 1)(b - 6)$

Take It to the NET

Online lesson quiz at www.PHSchool.com

.... Web Code: aea-0904

Short Response

63. Explain how to compute the xy term of the product $(3x - 4y)^2$.

Lesson 9-3

Find each product.

64. $(k + 7)(k - 9)$ **65.** $(2x - 11)(x - 6)$ **66.** $(5p + 4)(3p - 1)$

67. $(3y + 1)(y + 1)$ **68.** $(4h - 2)(6h + 1)$ **69.** $(9b + 7)(8b + 2)$

70. $(2w^2 + 5)(w + 8)$ **71.** $(r - 7)(r^2 + 3r - 9)$ **72.** $(5m^2 - 2)(6m^3 + 4m)$

Lesson 8-2

Write each number in scientific notation.

73. 8713   **74.** 0.031   **75.** 68,952   **76.** 1.2 million

77. 11   **78.** 523   **79.** 6 billion   **80.** 0.72

Using Models to Factor

You can sometimes write a trinomial as the product of two binomial factors. You can use algebra tiles to find the factors by arranging all of the tiles to form a rectangle. The lengths of the sides of the rectangle are the factors of the trinomial.

EXAMPLE

Write $2x^2 + 7x + 6$ as the product of two binomial factors.

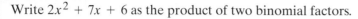
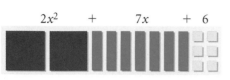

$$2x^2 \quad + \quad 7x \quad + \; 6$$

Model of polynomial

Use the tiles to form a rectangle.

First try:

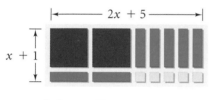

Second try:

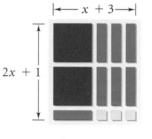

Third try:

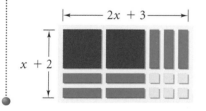

Correct! No tiles are left over.
$2x^2 + 7x + 6 = (2x + 3)(x + 2)$

EXERCISES

Use tiles to find binomial factors of each trinomial.

1. $x^2 + 8x + 15$ **2.** $x^2 + 4x + 4$ **3.** $x^2 + 8x + 7$

4. $2x^2 + 7x + 3$ **5.** $4x^2 + 12x + 5$ **6.** $6x^2 + 7x + 2$

7. Critical Thinking Explain why the trinomial $x^2 + 3x + 5$ cannot be represented as a rectangle using algebra tiles.

8. Critical Thinking Complete $2x^2 + \blacksquare x + 6$ with three different integers so that each trinomial has two binomial factors. Write each trinomial as the product of binomial factors.

Factoring Trinomials of the Type $x^2 + bx + c$

Lesson Preview

What You'll Learn

OBJECTIVE
1 To factor trinomials

. . . And Why

To factor trinomials like $h^2 - 4hk - 77k^2$, as in Example 4

✔ **Check Skills You'll Need** (For help, go to the Skills Handbook p.720)

List all of the factors of each number.

1. 24   **2.** 12   **3.** 54   **4.** 15

5. 36   **6.** 56   **7.** 64   **8.** 96

OBJECTIVE

1 Factoring Trinomials

iTEXT Interactive lesson includes instant self-check, tutorials, and activities.

In earlier courses, you learned how to find the factors of whole numbers like 15. Since $3 \times 5 = 15$, 3 and 5 are factors of 15. You can also find the factors of some trinomials. Consider the product below.

$$(x + 3)(x + 5) = x^2 + 5x + 3x + 3 \cdot 5$$
$$(5 + 3)x$$
$$= x^2 + 8x + 15$$

Notice that the coefficient of the middle term $8x$ is the sum of 3 and 5. Also the constant term 15 is the product of 3 and 5. To factor a trinomial of the form $x^2 + bx + c$, you must find two numbers that have a sum of b and a product of c.

The next example shows how to use a table to list the factors of the constant term c and how to add the factors until the sum is the middle term b.

1 EXAMPLE Factoring $x^2 + bx + c$

Factor $x^2 + 7x + 12$.

Find the factors of 12. Identify the pair that has a sum of 7.

Factors of 12	Sum of Factors
1 and 12	13
2 and 6	8
3 and 4	7 ✓

$x^2 + 7x + 12 = (x + 3)(x + 4)$.

Check $x^2 + 7x + 12 \stackrel{?}{=} (x + 3)(x + 4)$
$$= x^2 + 4x + 3x + 12$$
$$= x^2 + 7x + 12 ✓$$

✔ **Check Understanding** **1** Factor each expression. Check your answer.
     a. $g^2 + 7g + 10$ **b.** $v^2 + 21v + 20$ **c.** $a^2 + 13a + 30$

Some factorable trinomials have a negative middle term and a positive constant term. If the middle term is negative, you need to inspect the negative factors of c to find the factors of the trinomial.

2 EXAMPLE **Factoring $x^2 - bx + c$**

Factor $d^2 - 17d + 42$.

Since the middle term is negative, find the negative factors of 42. Identify the pair that has a sum of -17.

Factors of 42	Sum of Factors
-1 and -42	-43
-2 and -21	-23
-3 and -14	-17 ✓

$d^2 - 17d + 42 = (d - 3)(d - 14)$

✓ **Check Understanding** **2** Factor each expression.
a. $k^2 - 10k + 25$ **b.** $x^2 - 11x + 18$ **c.** $q^2 - 15q + 36$

When you factor trinomials with a negative constant, you will need to inspect pairs of positive and negative factors of c.

3 EXAMPLE **Factoring Trinomials With a Negative c**

a. Factor $m^2 + 6m - 27$.

Identify the pair of factors of -27 that has a sum of 6.

Factors of -27	Sum of Factors
1 and -27	-26
27 and -1	26
3 and -9	-6
9 and -3	6 ✓

$m^2 + 6m - 27 = (m - 3)(m + 9)$

b. Factor $p^2 - 3p - 18$.

Identify the pair of factors of -18 that has a sum of -3.

Factors of -18	Sum of Factors
1 and -18	-17
18 and -1	17
-6 and 3	-3 ✓

$p^2 - 3p - 18 = (p + 3)(p - 6)$

✓ **Check Understanding** **3** Factor each expression.
a. $m^2 + 8m - 20$ **b.** $p^2 - 3p - 40$ **c.** $y^2 - y - 56$

You can also factor some trinomials that have more than one variable. Consider the product $(p + 10q)(p + 4q)$.

$$(p + 10q)(p + 4q) = p^2 + 4pq + 10pq + 10q \cdot 4q$$
$$(4 + 10)pq$$
$$= p^2 + 14pq + 40q^2$$

You can see that the first term is the square of the first variable, the middle term includes both variables, and the last term includes the square of the second variable.

4 EXAMPLE **Factoring Trinomials With Two Variables**

Factor $h^2 - 4hk - 77k^2$.

Find the factors of -77. Identify the pair that has a sum of -4.

Factors of -77	Sum of Factors
1 and -77	-76
77 and -1	76
7 and -11	-4 ✓

$h^2 - 4hk - 77k^2 = (h + 7k)(h - 11k)$

✓ **Check Understanding** **4** Factor each expression.
a. $x^2 + 11xy + 24y^2$ **b.** $v^2 + 2vw - 48w^2$ **c.** $m^2 - 17mn - 60n^2$

EXERCISES

For more practice, see *Extra Practice*.

Practice and Problem Solving

A **Practice by Example**

Examples 1, 2
(pages 481, 482)

Complete.

1. $t^2 + 7t + 10 = (t + 2)(t + \blacksquare)$ **2.** $y^2 - 13y + 36 = (y - 4)(y - \blacksquare)$

3. $x^2 - 8x + 7 = (x - 1)(x - \blacksquare)$ **4.** $x^2 + 9x + 18 = (x + 3)(x + \blacksquare)$

Factor each expression. Check your answer.

5. $r^2 + 4r + 3$ **6.** $n^2 - 3n + 2$ **7.** $k^2 + 5k + 6$

8. $y^2 + 6y + 8$ **9.** $x^2 - 2x + 1$ **10.** $p^2 + 19p + 18$

11. $k^2 - 16k + 28$ **12.** $w^2 + 6w + 5$ **13.** $m^2 - 9m + 8$

14. $d^2 + 21d + 38$ **15.** $t^2 - 13t + 42$ **16.** $q^2 - 18q + 45$

Example 3
(page 482)

Complete.

17. $m^2 + 3m - 10 = (m - 2)(m + \blacksquare)$ **18.** $v^2 - 2v - 24 = (v + 4)(v - \blacksquare)$

19. $k^2 - 8k - 9 = (k + 1)(k - \blacksquare)$ **20.** $q^2 + 3q - 18 = (q - 3)(q + \blacksquare)$

Factor each expression.

21. $x^2 + 3x - 4$ **22.** $q^2 - 2q - 8$ **23.** $y^2 + y - 20$

24. $h^2 + 16h - 17$ **25.** $x^2 - 14x - 32$ **26.** $d^2 + 6d - 40$

27. $m^2 - 13m - 30$ **28.** $p^2 + 3p - 54$ **29.** $p^2 - 15p - 54$

Example 4
(page 483)

Choose the correct factoring for each expression.

30. $p^2 + 10pq + 9q^2$ **A.** $(p + 9q)(p + q)$ **B.** $(p + 9)(p + q^2)$

31. $m^2 + 4mn + 3n^2$ **A.** $(m + n)(3m + n)$ **B.** $(m + 3n)(m + n)$

32. $x^2 + 8xy + 15y^2$ **A.** $(x + 15y^2)(x + 1)$ **B.** $(x + 5y)(x + 3y)$

Factor each expression.

33. $t^2 + 7tv - 18v^2$ **34.** $x^2 + 12xy + 35y^2$ **35.** $p^2 - 10pq + 16q^2$

36. $m^2 - 3mn - 54n^2$ **37.** $h^2 + 18hj + 17j^2$ **38.** $x^2 - 10xy - 39y^2$

Open-Ended Find three different values to complete each expression so that it can be factored into the product of two binomials. Show each factorization.

39. $x^2 - 3x - \blacksquare$ **40.** $x^2 + x - \blacksquare$ **41.** $x^2 + \blacksquare x + 12$

42. Writing Suppose you can factor $x^2 + bx + c$ into the product of two binomials.
  a. Explain what you know about the factors if $c > 0$.
  b. Explain what you know about the factors if $c < 0$.

ⓑ Apply Your Skills

Factor each expression.

43. $k^2 + 10k + 16$ **44.** $m^2 + 10m - 24$ **45.** $n^2 + 10n - 56$

46. $g^2 + 20g + 96$ **47.** $x^2 + 8x - 65$ **48.** $t^2 + 28t + 75$

49. $x^2 - 11x - 42$ **50.** $k^2 + 23k + 42$ **51.** $m^2 + 14m - 51$

52. $x^2 + 29xy + 100y^2$ **53.** $t^2 - 10t - 75$ **54.** $d^2 - 19de + 48e^2$

Write the standard form for each of the polynomials modeled below. Then factor each expression.

55.
56.

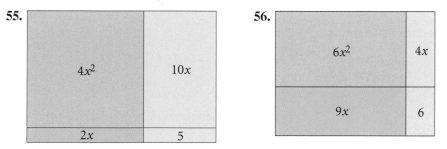

57. Critical Thinking Let $x^2 - 12x - 28 = (x + a)(x + b)$.
  a. What do you know about the signs of a and b?
  b. Suppose $|a| > |b|$. Which number, a or b, is a negative integer? Explain.

58. Critical Thinking Let $x^2 + 12x - 28 = (x + a)(x + b)$.
  a. What do you know about the signs of a and b?
  b. Suppose $|a| > |b|$. Which number, a or b, is a negative integer? Explain.

ⓒ Challenge

Factor each trinomial.

Sample $n^6 + n^3 - 56 = n^{3+3} + n^3 - 56$
$$= (n^3 + 8)(n^3 - 7)$$

59. $x^{12} + 12x^6 + 35$ **60.** $t^8 + 5t^4 - 24$ **61.** $r^6 - 21r^3 + 80$

62. $m^{10} + 18m^5 + 17$ **63.** $x^{12} - 19x^6 - 120$ **64.** $p^6 + 14p^3 - 72$

Multiple Choice

65. Which of the following is NOT a factor of 72?
A. 12   B. 16   C. 18   D. 24

66. Which value of b would make the expression $x^2 + bx - 36$ factorable?
F. 5   G. 4   H. 3   I. 2

67. Which value of c would NOT make $x^2 + 10x + c$ factorable?
A. 25   B. 24   C. 21   D. 18

68. Which of the following products is represented by the area model?
F. $(x + 1)(x + 18)$
G. $(x + 3)(x + 6)$
H. $(x - 1)(x - 18)$
I. $(x + 2)(x + 9)$

x^2	$9x$
$2x$	18

69. Which of the following shows the factors of $g^2 + 18g + 72$?
A. $(g + 6)(g + 12)$ B. $(g + 18)(g + 72)$
C. $(g - 6)(g - 12)$ D. $(g - 18)(g - 72)$

70. Which of the following shows the factors of $n^2 - 15g + 50$?
F. $(n - 5)(n - 10)$ G. $(n + 5)(n - 10)$
H. $(n - 15)(n + 50)$ I. $(n + 15)(n - 50)$

Take It to the NET
Online lesson quiz at
www.PHSchool.com
·········· Web Code: aea-0905

Short Response

71. Explain how to factor the trinomial $x^2 - 18x - 40$ and state the factors.

Mixed Review

Lesson 9-4

Simplify each product.

72. $(x + 4)(x + 4)$ **73.** $(w - 6)(w - 6)$ **74.** $(r - 5)(r + 5)$

75. $(2q + 7)(2q + 7)$ **76.** $(8v - 2)(8v + 2)$ **77.** $(3a - 9)(3a - 9)$

78. $(3a - 5)(3a + 5)$ **79.** $(6t + 9)(6t + 9)$ **80.** $(2x + 8y)(2x - 8y)$

Lesson 7-4

81. You start with $40 in your bank account and deposit $18 each week. At the same time, your friend starts with $220 but withdraws $12 each week. When will your accounts have the same balance?

82. The sum of the two numbers is 42. The smaller number is 63 less than twice the larger number. Find both numbers.

83. Sales A department store sells two types of DVD players. Total sales of players for the year were $16,918.71. The total number of players sold was 129. The basic model costs $119.99. The deluxe model costs $149.99.
a. Find the number sold of each type of player.
b. What were the sales for the basic player?

Lesson 7-1

Solve each system by graphing.

84. $y = -2x - 1$
$y = 2x + 3$

85. $y = x + 4$
$y = 0.5x + 5$

86. $2x + 4y = 12$
$x - y = 3$

Factoring Trinomials of the Type $ax^2 + bx + c$

Lesson Preview

What You'll Learn

OBJECTIVE 1
To factor trinomials of the type $ax^2 + bx + c$

...And Why

To factor trinomials in order to solve equations in Chapter 10

✓ Check Skills You'll Need

(For help, go to Lessons 9-2 and 9-5.)

Find the GCF of the terms of each polynomial.

1. $12x^2 + 6x$ **2.** $28m^2 - 35m + 14$ **3.** $4v^3 + 36v^2 + 10$

Factor each expression.

4. $x^2 + 5x + 4$ **5.** $y^2 - 3y - 28$ **6.** $t^2 - 11t + 30$

---

iTEXT Interactive lesson includes instant self-check, tutorials, and activities.

OBJECTIVE

1 Factoring $ax^2 + bx + c$

To understand how to factor $ax^2 + bx + c$, where a is a positive integer greater than 1, consider the following product simplified using FOIL.

$$\begin{array}{cccccc} & F & O & I & L \\ (2x + 3)(5x + 4) = & 10x^2 & + & 8x & + & 15x & + & 12 & = 10x^2 + 23x + 12 \end{array}$$

To go from $ax^2 + bx + c$ to its factors, look for binomials that have the following characteristics:

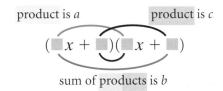

product is a ⌢ product is c

$$(\blacksquare x + \blacksquare)(\blacksquare x + \blacksquare)$$

sum of products is b

If c is positive and b is positive, the two factors of c are positive. If c is positive and b is negative, the two factors of c are negative.

1 EXAMPLE c Is Positive

Factor $6n^2 + 23n + 7$.

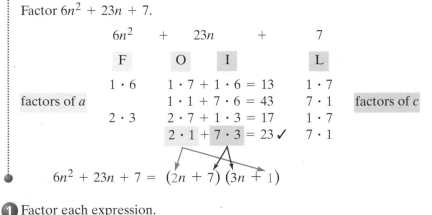

$$6n^2 + 23n + 7$$

	F	O I	L	
	$1 \cdot 6$	$1 \cdot 7 + 1 \cdot 6 = 13$	$1 \cdot 7$	
factors of a		$1 \cdot 1 + 7 \cdot 6 = 43$	$7 \cdot 1$	factors of c
	$2 \cdot 3$	$2 \cdot 7 + 1 \cdot 3 = 17$	$1 \cdot 7$	
		$2 \cdot 1 + 7 \cdot 3 = 23$ ✓	$7 \cdot 1$	

$$6n^2 + 23n + 7 = (2n + 7)(3n + 1)$$

✓ Check Understanding ❶ Factor each expression.

a. $2y^2 + 5y + 2$ **b.** $6n^2 - 23n + 7$ **c.** $2y^2 - 5y + 2$

In the next example, c is negative. In this case, you need to consider combinations that equal -8, like $(-8)(1)$. You must also consider $(-1)(8)$.

2 EXAMPLE *c* **Is Negative**

Factor $7x^2 - 26x - 8$.

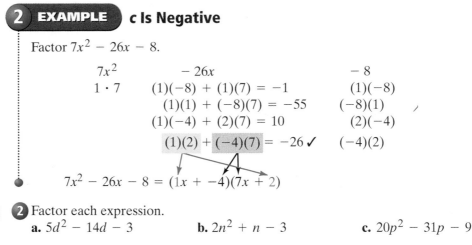

$$\begin{array}{ccc} 7x^2 & -26x & -8 \\ 1 \cdot 7 & (1)(-8) + (1)(7) = -1 & (1)(-8) \\ & (1)(1) + (-8)(7) = -55 & (-8)(1) \\ & (1)(-4) + (2)(7) = 10 & (2)(-4) \\ & (1)(2) + (-4)(7) = -26 \checkmark & (-4)(2) \end{array}$$

$$7x^2 - 26x - 8 = (1x + -4)(7x + 2)$$

✓ **Check Understanding** **2** Factor each expression.

a. $5d^2 - 14d - 3$ **b.** $2n^2 + n - 3$ **c.** $20p^2 - 31p - 9$

Some polynomials can be factored repeatedly. Continue the process of factoring until there are no common factors other than 1. If a trinomial has a common monomial factor, factor it out before trying to find binomial factors.

3 EXAMPLE **Factoring Out a Monomial First**

Factor $20x^2 + 80x + 35$ completely.

$20x^2 + 80x + 35 = 5(4x^2 + 16x + 7)$ **Factor out the GCF.**

Factor $4x^2 + 16x + 7$.

$$\begin{array}{ccc} 4x^2 & 16x & 7 \\ 1 \cdot 4 & 1 \cdot 7 + 1 \cdot 4 = 11 & 1 \cdot 7 \\ & 1 \cdot 1 + 7 \cdot 4 = 29 & 7 \cdot 1 \\ 2 \cdot 2 & 2 \cdot 7 + 1 \cdot 2 = 16 \checkmark & 1 \cdot 7 \end{array}$$

$$4x^2 + 16x + 7 = (2x + 1)(2x + 7)$$

$20x^2 + 80x + 35 = 5(2x + 1)(2x + 7)$ **Include the GCF in your final answer.**

✓ **Check Understanding** **3** Factor each expression.

a. $2v^2 - 12v + 10$ **b.** $4y^2 + 14y + 6$ **c.** $18k^2 - 12k - 6$

EXERCISES

For more practice, see *Extra Practice*.

Practice and Problem Solving

A **Practice by Example**

Example 1
(page 486)

Factor each expression.

1. $2n^2 + 15n + 7$ **2.** $7d^2 + 50d + 7$ **3.** $11w^2 - 14w + 3$

4. $3x^2 - 17x + 10$ **5.** $6t^2 + 25t + 11$ **6.** $3d^2 - 17d + 20$

7. $16m^2 + 26m + 9$ **8.** $15p^2 - 26p + 11$ **9.** $8y^2 + 30y + 13$

10. $2y^2 + 35y + 17$ **11.** $7x^2 - 30x + 27$ **12.** $8x^2 + 18x + 9$

Example 2 (page 487)	**Factor each expression.**		

13. $2t^2 - t - 3$ **14.** $8y^2 - 10y - 3$ **15.** $2q^2 - 11q - 21$

16. $7x^2 - 20x - 3$ **17.** $13p^2 + 8p - 5$ **18.** $5k^2 - 2k - 7$

19. $10w^2 + 11w - 8$ **20.** $12d^2 - d - 20$ **21.** $14n^2 + 23n - 15$

Example 3 (page 487)

22. $24m^2 - 32m + 8$ **23.** $21v^2 - 70v + 49$ **24.** $6t^2 + 26t + 24$

25. $25x^2 - 10x - 15$ **26.** $11p^2 + 77p + 66$ **27.** $24v^2 + 10v - 6$

B **Apply Your Skills**

Open-Ended Find three different values that complete each expression so that the trinomial can be factored into the product of two binomials. Factor your trinomials.

28. $4g^2 + \blacksquare g + 10$ **29.** $15m^2 + \blacksquare m - 24$ **30.** $35g^2 + \blacksquare g - 16$

31. a. Write each area as a product of two binomials.

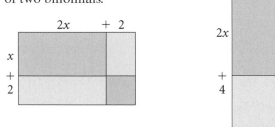

   b. Are the products equal?

   c. Critical Thinking Explain how the two products you found in part (a) can equal the same trinomial.

 32. Writing Explain how you would factor the expression $50x^2 - 90x + 16$.

Factor each expression.

33. $54p^2 + 87p + 28$ **34.** $66r^2 + 57r + 12$ **35.** $14x^2 - 53x + 14$

36. $28m^2 + 28m - 56$ **37.** $21h^2 + 72h - 48$ **38.** $55n^2 - 52n + 12$

39. $36y^2 + 114y - 20$ **40.** $63w^2 - 89w + 30$ **41.** $99q^2 - 92q + 9$

C **Challenge**

42. Critical Thinking If a and c in $ax^2 + bx + c$ are prime numbers, and the trinomial is factorable, how many positive values are possible for b?

43. Open-Ended Write three different factorable trinomials that are of the form $\blacksquare x^2 - 12x + \blacksquare$. Factor your trinomials.

Factor each expression.

44. $56x^3 + 43x^2 + 5x$ **45.** $49p^2 + 63pq - 36q^2$ **46.** $108g^2h - 162gh + 54h$

47. The graph of the function $y = x^2 + 5x + 6$ is shown at the right.
   a. What are the x-intercepts?
   b. Factor $x^2 + 5x + 6$.
   c. Critical Thinking Describe the relationship between the binomial factors you found in part (b) and the x-intercepts.

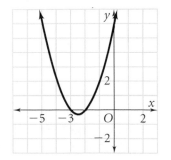

Multiple Choice

48. Which of the following expressions does NOT equal $12n^2 + 32n - 140$?

A. $4(n + 5)(3n - 7)$ **B.** $(4n + 20)(3n - 7)$

C. $(2n + 10)(6n - 14)$ **D.** $(n + 5)(12n - 7)$

49. Which value would make the expression $8p^2 + \blacksquare p + 11$ factorable?

F. 24   **G.** 46   **H.** 48   **I.** 52

50. Which binomial is one of the factors of $13x^2 + 32x - 21$?

A. $13x + 3$ **B.** $13x + 7$ **C.** $13x + 21$ **D.** $13x - 7$

51. A rectangle has dimensions that are the binomial factors of $3x^2 + 22x + 24$. Which of the following expressions describes the perimeter of the rectangle?

F. $4x + 10$ **G.** $4x + 25$ **H.** $8x + 20$ **I.** $8x + 50$

52. The table at the right shows the atomic masses, rounded to the nearest whole number, for the first five elements. Which of the following values is the median of the data?

Element	Atomic Mass
Hydrogen	1
Helium	4
Lithium	7
Beryllium	9
Boron	11

A. 5.5   **B.** 6

C. 6.4   **D.** 7

Take It to the NET

Online lesson quiz at
www.PHSchool.com
Web Code: aea-0906

Short Response

53. What are the factors of $3x^2 + 40x - 75$? Show your work.

Mixed Review

Lesson 9-5

Factor each expression.

54. $y^2 + 8y + 7$ **55.** $t^2 - 7t + 12$ **56.** $p^2 - p - 20$

57. $m^2 - 15m + 36$ **58.** $k^2 + 16k - 36$ **59.** $g^2 + 17g + 72$

60. $h^2 - 13h - 48$ **61.** $x^2 - 13x - 30$ **62.** $d^2 - 18d + 56$

Lesson 9-4

Mental Math Find each square.

63. 89^2 **64.** 401^2 **65.** 903^2 **66.** 197^2

Mental Math Find each product.

67. $39 \cdot 41$ **68.** $38 \cdot 42$ **69.** $198 \cdot 202$ **70.** $73 \cdot 67$

Evaluate each exponential function for the domain $\{-3, 0, 2\}$.

71. $f(x) = 4 \cdot 2^x$ **72.** $h(x) = -3 \cdot 3^x$ **73.** $k(x) = \frac{1}{3} \cdot 3^x$

74. $g(x) = 5 \cdot \left(\frac{1}{10}\right)^x$ **75.** $g(x) = \frac{1}{10} \cdot 5^x$ **76.** $h(x) = 8 \cdot (0.2)^x$

Lesson 8-7

Graph each function.

77. $y = 3 \cdot 2^x$ **78.** $y = -3 \cdot 2^x$ **79.** $y = \frac{1}{2} \cdot 2^x$ **80.** $y = \frac{1}{3} \cdot 3^x$

Factoring Special Cases

Lesson Preview

What You'll Learn

OBJECTIVE 1
To factor perfect-square trinomials

OBJECTIVE 2
To factor the difference of squares

. . . And Why

To find the length of a side of a square, as In Example 2

✓ Check Skills You'll Need

(For help, go to Lessons 8-4 and 9-4.)

Simplify each expression.

1. $(3x)^2$ **2.** $(5y)^2$ **3.** $(15h^2)^2$ **4.** $(2ab^2)^2$

Simplify each product.

5. $(c - 6)(c + 6)$ **6.** $(p - 11)(p - 11)$ **7.** $(4d + 7)(4d + 7)$

New Vocabulary • perfect-square trinomial

OBJECTIVE 1

> **TEXT** Interactive lesson includes instant self-check, tutorials, and activities.

Factoring Perfect-Square Trinomials

Investigation: Perfect-Square Trinomials

1. Factor each trinomial.

$x^2 + 6x + 9$ $x^2 + 10x + 9$ $m^2 + 15m + 36$

$m^2 + 12m + 36$ $k^2 + 26k + 25$ $k^2 + 10k + 25$

2. a. Which trinomials have pairs of binomial factors that are identical?
   b. Describe the relationship between the middle and last terms of the trinomials that have identical pairs of factors.

In Lesson 9-4 you found the square of a binomial.

$$(a + b)^2 = (a + b)(a + b) = a^2 + 2ab + b^2 \text{ and}$$
$$(a - b)^2 = (a - b)(a - b) = a^2 - 2ab + b^2$$

Any trinomial of the form $a^2 + 2ab + b^2$ or $a^2 - 2ab + b^2$ is a **perfect-square trinomial.** You can factor a perfect-square trinomial into identical binomial factors.

Key Concepts

Rule	Perfect-Square Trinomials

For every real number a and b:

$a^2 + 2ab + b^2 = (a + b)(a + b) = (a + b)^2$

$a^2 - 2ab + b^2 = (a - b)(a - b) = (a - b)^2$

Examples $x^2 + 10x + 25 = (x + 5)(x + 5) = (x + 5)^2$

             $x^2 - 10x + 25 = (x - 5)(x - 5) = (x - 5)^2$

You can factor a perfect-square trinomial using the method shown in the previous lesson. Or you can recognize a perfect-square trinomial and then factor it quickly. Here is how to recognize a perfect-square trinomial.

- The first and the last terms can both be written as the product of two identical factors.

- The middle term is twice the product of one factor from the first term and one factor from the last term.

Consider the following trinomials.

$$4x^2 \quad + \quad 12x \quad + \quad 9$$
$$2x \cdot 2x \qquad\qquad\qquad 3 \cdot 3$$
$$2(2x \cdot 3) = 12x$$

This is a perfect-square trinomial. In factored form the trinomial is $(2x + 3)(2x + 3)$, or $(2x + 3)^2$.

$$4x^2 \quad + \quad 20x \quad + \quad 9$$
$$2x \cdot 2x \qquad\qquad\qquad 3 \cdot 3$$
$$2(2x \cdot 3) \neq 20x$$

This is not a perfect-square trinomial. Factor by listing factors, as shown in Lesson 9-6.

When you factor a perfect-square trinomial, it may help to write the first and last terms as the products of identical factors.

1 EXAMPLE Factoring a Perfect-Square Trinomial With $a = 1$

Factor $x^2 - 8x + 16$.

$$x^2 - 8x + 16 = x \cdot x - 8x + 4 \cdot 4 \qquad \textbf{Rewrite first and last terms.}$$
$$= x \cdot x - 2(x \cdot 4) + 4 \cdot 4 \qquad \textbf{Does the middle term equal } 2ab? \ 8x = 2(x \cdot 4)$$
$$= (x - 4)^2 \qquad \textbf{Write the factors as the square of a binomial.}$$

✓ **Check Understanding** ❶ Factor each expression.
  a. $x^2 + 8x + 16$
  b. $n^2 + 16n + 64$
  c. $n^2 - 16n + 64$

When you write the identical factors of the first and last terms, you can write them as square terms. Notice in Example 2, $9g^2$ is written as $(3g)^2$ and 4 is written as 2^2.

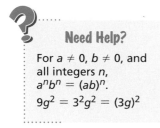

Need Help?

For $a \neq 0$, $b \neq 0$, and all integers n,
$a^n b^n = (ab)^n$.
$9g^2 = 3^2 g^2 = (3g)^2$

2 EXAMPLE Factoring a Perfect-Square Trinomial with $a \neq 1$

Geometry The area of the square shown at the right is $(9g^2 + 12g + 4)$ cm^2. Find the length of a side.

$$9g^2 + 12g + 4 = (3g)^2 + 12g + 2^2 \qquad \textbf{Rewrite } 9g^2 \textbf{ as } (3g)^2 \textbf{ and 4 as } 2^2.$$
$$= (3g)^2 + 2(3g)(2) + 2^2 \qquad \textbf{Does the middle term equal } 2ab? \ 12g = 2(3g)(2) \checkmark$$
$$= (3g + 2)^2 \qquad \textbf{Write the factors as the square of a binomial.}$$

The side of the square has length of $(3g + 2)$ cm.

✓ **Check Understanding** ❷ Factor each expression.
  a. $9g^2 - 12g + 4$
  b. $4t^2 + 36t + 81$
  c. $4t^2 - 36t + 81$

2   Factoring the Difference of Squares

Recall from Lesson 9-4 that $(a + b)(a - b) = a^2 - b^2$. So you can factor a difference of two squares as $(a + b)(a - b)$.

Key Concepts

Rule	Difference of Two Squares

For every real number a and b:

$$a^2 - b^2 = (a + b)(a - b)$$

Examples $x^2 - 81 = (x + 9)(x - 9)$
$16x^2 - 49 = (4x + 7)(4x - 7)$

3 EXAMPLE   The Difference of Two Squares for $a = 1$

Factor $x^2 - 64$.
$$x^2 - 64 = x^2 - 8^2 \qquad \textbf{Rewrite 64 as } 8^2.$$
$$= (x + 8)(x - 8) \quad \textbf{Factor.}$$

Check   Use FOIL to multiply.
$$(x + 8)(x - 8)$$
$$x^2 - 8x + 8x - 64$$
$$x^2 - 64 \checkmark$$

✓ **Check Understanding** **3** Factor each expression. Check your answer.
  a. $x^2 - 36$ **b.** $m^2 - 100$ **c.** $p^2 - 49$

4 EXAMPLE   The Difference of Two Squares for $a \neq 1$

Factor $4x^2 - 121$.
$$4x^2 - 121 = (2x)^2 - (11)^2 \qquad \textbf{Rewrite } 4x^2 \textbf{ as } (2x)^2 \textbf{ and 121 as } 11^2.$$
$$= (2x + 11)(2x - 11) \quad \textbf{Factor.}$$

✓ **Check Understanding** **4** Factor each expression.
  a. $9v^2 - 4$ **b.** $25x^2 - 64$ **c.** $4w^2 - 49$

Some binomials that do not appear to be the difference of squares may have the form $n(a^2 - b^2)$ after a GCF is factored out.

5 EXAMPLE   Factoring Out a Common Factor

Factor $10x^2 - 40$.
$$10x^2 - 40 = 10(x^2 - 4) \qquad \textbf{Factor out the GCF of 10.}$$
$$= 10(x - 2)(x + 2) \quad \textbf{Factor } (x^2 - 4).$$

✓ **Check Understanding** **5** Factor each expression.
  a. $8y^2 - 50$ **b.** $3c^2 - 75$ **c.** $28k^2 - 7$

EXERCISES

For more practice, see *Extra Practice*.

Practice and Problem Solving

A **Practice by Example**

Example 1
(page 491)

Factor each expression.

1. $c^2 + 10c + 25$ **2.** $x^2 - 2x + 1$ **3.** $h^2 + 12h + 36$

4. $m^2 - 24m + 144$ **5.** $k^2 - 16k + 64$ **6.** $t^2 - 14t + 49$

Example 2
(page 491)

Find the side length of each square.

7.

$4m^2 + 20m + 25$

8.

$49d^2 + 28d + 4$

9.

$25g^2 - 40g + 16$

Factor each expression. Check your answer.

10. $25g^2 - 30g + 9$ **11.** $64r^2 - 144r + 81$ **12.** $100v^2 - 220v + 121$

Example 3
(page 492)

13. $x^2 - 4$ **14.** $y^2 - 81$ **15.** $k^2 - 196$

16. $r^2 - 144$ **17.** $h^2 - 100$ **18.** $m^2 - 225$

19. $w^2 - 256$ **20.** $x^2 - 400$ **21.** $y^2 - 900$

Example 4
(page 492)

22. $25q^2 - 9$ **23.** $49y^2 - 4$ **24.** $9c^2 - 64$

25. $4m^2 - 81$ **26.** $16k^2 - 49$ **27.** $144p^2 - 1$

28. $81v^2 - 100$ **29.** $400n^2 - 121$ **30.** $25w^2 - 196$

Example 5
(page 492)

31. $3m^2 - 12$ **32.** $5k^2 - 245$ **33.** $3x^2 + 48x + 192$

34. $2t^2 - 36t + 162$ **35.** $6r^3 - 150r$ **36.** $7h^2 - 56h + 112$

B **Apply Your Skills**

37. Writing Summarize the procedure for factoring a perfect-square trinomial. Give at least two examples.

38. Error Analysis Suppose a classmate factored the binomial at the right. What error did your classmate make?

$$4x^2 - 121 = (4x - 11)(4x - 11)$$
$$= (4x - 11)^2$$

Mental Math **Find a pair of factors for each number by using the difference of two squares.**

Sample $143 = 144 - 1$ Write 143 as the difference of two squares.

$\quad\quad\quad\quad = 12^2 - 1^2$ Rewrite 144 as 12^2 and 1 as 1^2.

$\quad\quad\quad\quad = (12 - 1)(12 + 1)$ Factor.

$\quad\quad\quad\quad = (11)(13)$ Simplify.

39. 99   **40.** 91   **41.** 75   **42.** 117   **43.** 224

44. a. Open-Ended Write an expression that is a perfect-square trinomial.
   b. Explain how you know your trinomial is a perfect-square trinomial.

Factor each expression.

45. $100v^2 - 25w^2$

46. $16p^2 - 48pq + 36q^2$

47. $28c^2 + 140cd + 175d^2$

48. $\frac{1}{4}m^2 - \frac{1}{9}$

49. $x^2 + x + \frac{1}{4}$

50. $64g^2 - 192gh + 144h^2$

51. $\frac{1}{4}p^2 - 2p + 4$

52. $\frac{1}{9}n^2 - \frac{1}{25}$

53. $\frac{1}{25}k^2 + \frac{6}{5}k + 9$

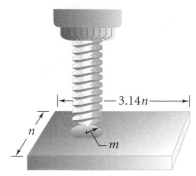

54. a. Geometry Write an expression in terms of n and m for the area of the top of the solid region being drilled at the right. Use 3.14 for π. Factor your expression.
  b. Find the area of the solid region if $n = 10$ in. and $m = 3$ in.

55. a. Factor $4x^2 - 100$ by removing the common monomial factor and then factoring the remaining expression as the difference of squares.
  b. Factor $4x^2 - 100$ as the difference of squares, and then remove the common monomial factors.
  c. Critical Thinking Why can $4x^2 - 100$ be factored in two different ways?
  d. Can you factor $3x^2 - 75$ in the two ways you factored $4x^2 - 100$ in parts (a) and (b)? Explain your answer.

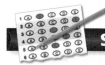 **Challenge**

Factor each expression.

56. $64r^6 - 144r^3 + 81$

57. $p^6 + 40p^3q + 400q^2$

58. $36m^4 + 84m^2 + 49$

59. $81p^{10} + 198p^5 + 121$

60. $108m^6 - 147$

61. $x^{20} - 4x^{10}y^5 + 4y^{10}$

62. $256g^4 - 100h^6$

63. $45x^4 - 60x^2y + 20y^2$

64. $37g^8 - 37h^8$

65. a. The expression $(t - 3)^2 - 16$ is a difference of two squares. Identify a and b.
  b. Factor $(t - 3)^2 - 16$ and simplify.

66. The binomial $16 - 81n^4$ can be factored twice as the difference of squares.
  a. Factor $16 - 81n^4$ completely.
  b. Critical Thinking What characteristics do 16 and $81n^4$ share that make this possible?
  c. Open-Ended Write a binomial that can be factored twice as the difference of squares.

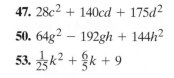

Standardized Test Prep

Gridded Response

67. The area of the square shown at the right is $4x^2 + 28x + 49$. What is the sum of a and b?

68. For what value of p would $(x + p)(x + p)$ be the factors of $x^2 - 24x + 144$?

69. For what value of k are the factors of $x^2 - kx + 225$ the same?

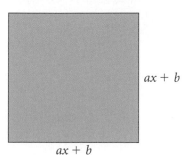

70. The diagram shows two squares. The area of the region shaded green is $4x^2 + 16x + 16$. The area of the region shaded purple is $5x^2 + 14x + 9$. What is the value of b?

71. For what value of a does $144x^4 - 121 = (ax^2 + 11)(ax^2 - 11)$?

72. The expression $81x^2 - 36$ can factored as $9(ax + b)(ax - b)$. What is the mean of a and b?

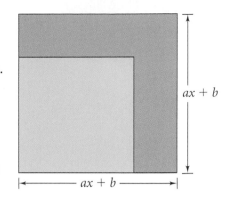

$ax + b$

$ax + b$

Take It to the NET
Online lesson quiz at
www.PHSchool.com
Web Code: aea-0907

Mixed Review

Lesson 9-6

Factor each expression.

73. $2d^2 + 11d + 5$

74. $2x^2 - 11x + 12$

75. $4t^2 + 16t + 7$

76. $5w^2 - 44w - 9$

77. $6t^2 + 19t + 8$

78. $21m^2 - 20m - 9$

79. $14x^2 - 11x - 9$

80. $4y^2 + 32y + 55$

81. $12k^2 - 5k - 2$

Lesson 8-6

Find the next three terms of each sequence. Then write a rule for each sequence.

82. $3, 12, 48, 192, \ldots$

83. $-3, 5, 13, 21, \ldots$

84. $25, 16, 7, -2, \ldots$

85. $200, 20, 2, 0.2, \ldots$

86. $-2, 4, -8, 16, \ldots$

87. $0.1, 0.6, 3.6, 21.6, \ldots$

88. $10, 4, \frac{8}{5}, \frac{16}{25}, \ldots$

89. $\frac{1}{2}, 2, 3\frac{1}{2}, 5, \ldots$

90. $\frac{1}{32}, \frac{1}{8}, \frac{1}{2}, 2, \ldots$

Lesson 6-6

91. A teacher is comparing time her students spent studying, in hours, with their grades on a math test.

a. Graphing Calculator Use a graphing calculator to find the equation of the line of best fit.

b. What test score would you predict for a student who studied 2.5 hours?

c. What test score would you predict for a student who studied 1.25 hours?

Student	Time Studying	Grade
1	1	82
2	2	92
3	1.5	80
4	2	88
5	1	70
6	3	97
7	0.5	70

✓ Checkpoint Quiz 2   Lessons 9-4 through 9-7

iTEXT Instant self-check quiz online and on CD-ROM

Simplify each expression.

1. $(k - 7)^2$

2. $(5t + 9)^2$

3. $(h - 11)(h - 11)$

Factor each expression.

4. $v^2 + 20v + 100$

5. $p^2 - 6p - 40$

6. $k^2 - 17k + 60$

7. $2x^2 + 13x + 11$

8. $10m^2 + 19m + 7$

9. $3w^2 - 6w - 24$

10. $9t^2 - 25$

9-8

Factoring by Grouping

Lesson Preview

What You'll Learn

OBJECTIVE
1 To factor polynomials with four terms

OBJECTIVE
2 To factor trinomials by grouping

. . . And Why

To find expressions for the dimensions of a rectangular prism, as in Example 4

✓ **Check Skills You'll Need**   (For help, go to Lessons 9-2 and 9-3.)

Find the GCF of the terms of each polynomial.

1. $6y^2 + 12y - 4$ **2.** $9r^3 + 15r^2 + 21r$

3. $30h^3 - 25h^2 - 40h$ **4.** $16m^3 - 12m^2 - 36m$

Find each product.

5. $(v + 3)(v^2 + 5)$ **6.** $(2q^2 - 4)(q - 5)$

7. $(2t - 5)(3t + 4)$ **8.** $(4x - 1)(x^2 + 2x + 3)$

New Vocabulary   • factor by grouping

OBJECTIVE
1

 Interactive lesson includes instant self-check, tutorials, and activities.

Factoring Polynomials With Four Terms

You can use the Distributive Property to **factor by grouping** if two groups of terms have the same factor.

$$\underbrace{y^3 + 3y^2}_{} \ + \ \underbrace{4y + 12}_{}$$

$$\underbrace{y^2(y + 3)}_{} \ + \ \underbrace{4(y + 3)}_{}$$

$$(y^2 + 4)(y + 3)$$

These factors are the same, so factor again.

To factor by grouping, look for a common binomial factor of two pairs of terms.

1 EXAMPLE   **Factoring a Four-Term Polynomial**

Factor $4n^3 + 8n^2 - 5n - 10$.

$4n^3 + 8n^2 - 5n - 10 = 4n^2(n + 2) - 5(n + 2)$ Factor the GCF from each group of two terms.

$\qquad\qquad\qquad\qquad = (4n^2 - 5)(n + 2)$ Factor out $(n + 2)$.

Check $4n^3 + 8n^2 - 5n - 10 \overset{?}{=} (4n^2 - 5)(n + 2)$

$\qquad\qquad\qquad\qquad = 4n^3 + 8n^2 - 5n - 10$ ✓   Use FOIL.

✓ **Check Understanding**   **1** Factor each expression. Check your answer.

a. $5t^4 + 20t^3 + 6t + 24$ **b.** $2w^3 + w^2 - 14w - 7$

Before you factor by grouping, you may need to factor the GCF of all the terms of a polynomial. Remember, a polynomial is not completely factored until there are no common factors other than 1.

Factoring Completely

Factor $12p^4 + 10p^3 - 36p^2 - 30p$.

$$12p^4 + 10p^3 - 36p^2 - 30p = 2p(6p^3 + 5p^2 - 18p - 15) \qquad \text{Factor out the GCF, } 2p.$$
$$= 2p[(p^2(6p + 5) - 3(6p + 5)] \qquad \text{Factor by grouping.}$$
$$= 2p(p^2 - 3)(6p + 5) \qquad \text{Factor again.}$$

✓ **Check Understanding** ② Factor $45m^4 - 9m^3 + 30m^2 - 6m$.

OBJECTIVE

2 | **Factoring Trinomials by Grouping**

You can also factor by grouping to find the factors of a trinomial of the form $ax^2 + bx + c$. You may want to use this method when you cannot quickly factor a trinomial using the method you learned in Lesson 9-6.

You can use these steps to factor a trinomial such as $48x^2 + 46x + 5$.

Step 1 Find the product ac.

$48 \cdot 5 = 240$

Step 2 Find the two factors of ac that have sum b.

Factors	→	Sum		Factors	→	Sum
$1 \cdot 240$	→	$1 + 240 = 241$		$4 \cdot 60$	→	$4 + 60 = 64$
$2 \cdot 120$	→	$2 + 120 = 122$		$5 \cdot 48$	→	$5 + 48 = 53$
$3 \cdot 80$	→	$3 + 80 = 83$		$6 \cdot 40$	→	$6 + 40 = 46$ ✓

Step 3 Rewrite the trinomial using the sum.

$$48x^2 + 46x + 5 = 48x^2 + (6 + 40)x + 5$$
$$= 48x^2 + 6x + 40x + 5$$

Step 4 Factor by grouping.

$$48x^2 + 6x + 40x + 5$$
$$6x(8x + 1) + 5(8x + 1)$$
$$(6x + 5)(8x + 1)$$

Problem Solving Hint

Use mental math to determine where to start. -10, 60 and -20, 30 are two pairs of factors of 600 that have sums 50 and 10. Since 25 is between 50 and 10, the negative factor must be between -10 and -20.

As you look for factors of the product ac that have a sum b, you do not have to list all the possible factors. Use mental math to eliminate those factors that give sums too great or too small to be reasonable choices.

3 EXAMPLE **Factoring a Trinomial by Grouping**

Factor $24q^2 + 25q - 25$.

Step 1 $24(-25) = -600$ Find the product ac.

Step 2 Factors → Sum

$(-12)(50) \rightarrow -12 + 50 = 38$ Find two factors of ac that have sum b.
$(-15)(40) \rightarrow -15 + 40 = 25$ ✓   Use mental math to determine a good place to start.

Step 3 $24q^2 - 15q + 40q - 25$ Rewrite the trinomial.

Step 4 $3q(8q - 5) + 5(8q - 5)$ Factor by grouping.
$(3q + 5)(8q - 5)$ Factor again.

3 Factor each trinomial by grouping.

a. $63d^2 + 44d + 5$ **b.** $11k^2 + 49k + 20$ **c.** $4y^2 + 33y - 70$

Given a polynomial expression for the volume of a rectangular prism, you can sometimes factor to find possible expressions for the length, width, and height.

4 **EXAMPLE** **Finding the Dimensions of a Rectangular Prism**

Geometry The volume (ℓwh) of the rectangular prism at the right is $80x^3 + 224x^2 + 60x$. Factor to find possible expressions for the length, width, and height of the prism.

Factor $80x^3 + 224x^2 + 60x$.

Step 1 $4x(20x^2 + 56x + 15)$ Factor out the GCF, $4x$.

Step 2 $20 \cdot 15 = 300$ Find the product ac.

Step 3 Factors $\rightarrow$ Sum

$\begin{array}{rll} 5 \cdot 60 & \rightarrow \quad 5 + 60 & = 65 \\ 10 \cdot 30 & \rightarrow \quad 10 + 30 & = 40 \\ 15 \cdot 20 & \rightarrow \quad 15 + 20 & = 35 \\ 6 \cdot 50 & \rightarrow \quad 6 + 50 & = 56 \checkmark \end{array}$

Find two factors of ac that have sum b. Use mental math to determine a good place to start.

Step 4 $4x(20x^2 + 50x + 6x + 15)$ Rewrite the trinomial.

Step 5 $4x[10x(2x + 5) + 3(2x + 5)]$ Factor by grouping.

$4x(10x + 3)(2x + 5)$ Factor again.

● The possible dimensions of the prism are $4x$, $(10x + 3)$, and $(2x + 5)$.

✓ **Check Understanding** **4** Find expressions for the possible dimensions of each rectangular prism.

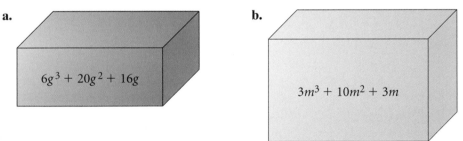

a. $6g^3 + 20g^2 + 16g$

b. $3m^3 + 10m^2 + 3m$

Here is a summary of what to remember as you factor polynomials.

🔧 **Key Concepts**

Summary	Factoring Polynomials

1. Factor out the greatest common factor (GCF).
2. If the polynomial has two terms or three terms, look for a difference of two squares, a product of two squares, or a pair of binomial factors.
3. If there are four or more terms, group terms and factor to find common binomial factors.
4. As a final check, make sure there are no common factors other than 1.

EXERCISES

For more practice, see *Extra Practice*.

Practice and Problem Solving

A **Practice by Example**

Example 1
(page 496)

Find the GCF of the first two terms and the GCF of the last two terms for each polynomial.

1. $2m^3 + 6m^2 + 3m + 9$

2. $10p^3 - 25p^2 + 4p - 10$

3. $2z^3 + 12z^2 - 5z - 30$

4. $6n^3 + 3n^2 + 2n + 1$

Factor each expression.

5. $6n^3 + 8n^2 + 3n + 4$

6. $14t^3 + 21t^2 + 16t + 24$

7. $27t^3 + 45t^2 - 3t - 5$

8. $13y^3 - 8y^2 + 13y - 8$

9. $45x^3 + 20x^2 + 9x + 4$

10. $10w^3 + 16w^2 - 15w - 24$

Example 2
(page 497)

Factor completely.

11. $12v^3 - 32v^2 + 6v - 16$

12. $7q^4 - 4q^3 + 28q^2 - 16q$

13. $20m^3 - 18m^2 + 40m - 36$

14. $6x^4 + 4x^3 - 6x^2 - 4x$

15. $12y^3 - 20y^2 + 30y - 50$

16. $9c^3 - 12c^2 + 18c - 24$

Example 3
(page 497)

Factor by grouping.

17. $12p^2 + 16p + 5$

18. $16t^2 + 24t + 9$

19. $18n^2 + 57n - 10$

20. $9w^2 - 27w + 20$

21. $24m^2 + 8m - 2$

22. $36v^2 - 9v - 7$

23. $6x^2 + 11x - 10$

24. $20v^2 - 41v + 9$

25. $63q^2 - 52q - 20$

Example 4
(page 498)

Find expressions for the possible dimensions of each rectangular prism.

26.

$3m^3 + 7m^2 + 2m$

27.

$5k^3 + 30k^2 + 40k$

B **Apply Your Skills**

Factor completely.

28. $7h^3 - 35h^2 - 42h$

29. $60t^3 - 200t^2 - 66t + 220$

30. $8d^3 + 16d^2 + 24d + 48$

31. $12x^2 - 4xy - 56y^2$

32. $54r^3 - 45r^2 + 9r$

33. $150k^3 + 350k^2 + 180k + 420$

34. a. Factor $(28x^3 - 7x^2) + (36x - 9)$.

b. Factor $(28x^3 + 36x) + (-7x^2 - 9)$.

c. Critical Thinking Why can you factor the same polynomial using different pairs of terms?

Write each expression in standard form and factor.

35. $-8w + 49w^2 + 14w^3 - 28$

36. $2m^3 + 16 - m - 32m^2$

37. $-6 + 44t^3 - 4t^2 + 66t$

38. $2 - 50x - x^2 + 25x^3$

39. Geometry The polynomial shown at the right represents the volume of the rectangular prism. Factor the polynomial to find possible expressions for the length, width, and height of the prism.

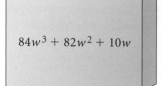
$84w^3 + 82w^2 + 10w$

40. Open-Ended Write a four-term polynomial that can be factored by grouping. Factor your polynomial.

41. Writing Describe how to factor the expression $10x^3 - 15x^2 + 2x - 3$ by grouping.

C Challenge

Factor by grouping.

42. $30m^5 + 24m^3n - 35m^2n^2 - 28n^3$ **43.** $x^2p + x^2q^5 + yp + yq^5$

44. $h^3 + 11h^2 - 4h - 44$ **45.** $w^6 - w^4 - 9w^2 + 9$

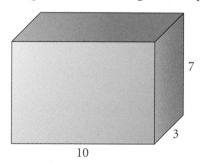

46. Geometry The polynomial $2\pi x^3 + 12\pi x^2 + 18\pi x$ represents the volume of a cylinder. The formula for the volume of a cylinder is $V = \pi r^2 h$.
a. Factor $2\pi x^3 + 12\pi x^2 + 18\pi x$.
b. Based on your answer to part (a), write an expression for a possible radius of the cylinder.

The number 63 can be written as $2^5 + 2^4 + 2^3 + 2^2 + 2^1 + 2^0$. For exercises 47 and 48, factor each expression by grouping. Then simplify the powers of 2 to write 63 as the product of two numbers.

47. $(2^5 + 2^4 + 2^3) + (2^2 + 2^1 + 2^0)$

48. $(2^5 + 2^4) + (2^3 + 2^2) + (2^1 + 2^0)$

49. a. Open-Ended For the rectangular prism below, let $x = 3$. Write linear expressions for the length, width, and height of the prism.

7

3

10

b. Using your answers from part (a), write a polynomial that represents the volume of the prism.

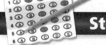

Standardized Test Prep

Multiple Choice

50. Which of the following expressions is a factor of $27x^4 + 15x^3 + 63x + 35$?
A. $3x + 7$ **B.** $3x^2 + 7$ **C.** $3x^3 + 7$ **D.** $3x^4 + 7$

51. Which of the following expressions equals the sum of the factors of $6q^3 - 5q^2 + 24q - 20$?
F. $7q^3 - 1$ **G.** $6q^3 - 1$ **H.** $q^2 + 6q - 1$ **I.** $q^2 + 6q + 1$

Short Response

52. Factor $9a^4 - 54a^3 - 2a + 12$ completely. Show your work.

53. The volume of the rectangular prism is $96x^3 + 48x^2 + 6x$. Find an expression that could describe the perimeter of one of the prism's square faces. Show your work.

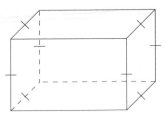

Mixed Review

Lesson 9-7

Factor each expression.

54. $k^2 + 14k + 49$ **55.** $r^2 + 6r + 9$ **56.** $y^2 - 16y + 64$

57. $2t^2 + 12t + 18$ **58.** $m^2 - 64$ **59.** $4g^2 + 40g + 100$

60. $4d^2 - 25$ **61.** $5n^2 - 45$ **62.** $25q^2 + 40q + 16$

Lesson 8-4

Simplify each expression.

63. $(b^2)^2$ **64.** $x^4 \cdot x^{-2}$ **65.** $(t^3)^5$ **66.** $(c^5d)^7$

67. $(2y)^3$ **68.** $(9m)^0$ **69.** $(x^3)(x^7)^{-2}$ **70.** $(3w^2v^3)^4$

Simplify . Write each answer in scientific notation.

71. $(2 \times 10^5)^4$ **72.** $(3 \times 10^6)^2$ **73.** $(7 \times 10^{-6})^2$ **74.** $(2 \times 10^7)^5$

75. $(5.3 \times 10^2)^2$ **76.** $(8.1 \times 10^{-3})^2$ **77.** $(1.9 \times 10^8)^3$ **78.** $(4 \times 10^{-3})^{-2}$

Lesson 7-2

Solve each system using substitution.

79. $y = -7x + 12$
$\quad\;\; y = 3x + 2$

80. $y = -3x + 4$
$\quad\;\; y = -5x + 12$

81. $10x + 2y = 15$
$\quad\;\;\; y = -4x + 7$

82. $x + y = -28$
$\quad\; y = -2x - 26$

83. $8x + 2y = 50$
$\quad\; y = -4x + 25$

84. $y = x - 5$
$\quad\; 11x - 6y = 65$

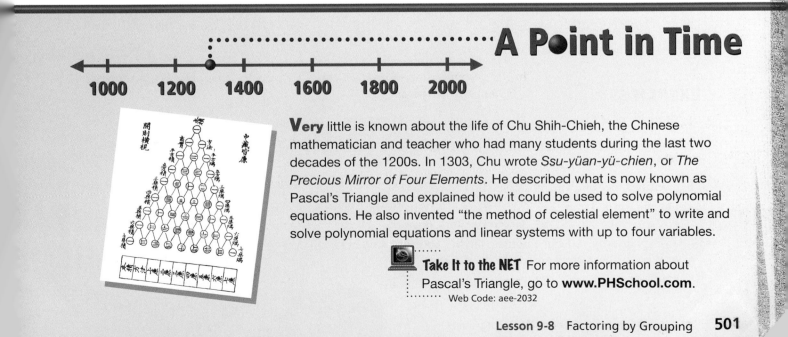

A Point in Time

1000 1200 1400 1600 1800 2000

Very little is known about the life of Chu Shih-Chieh, the Chinese mathematician and teacher who had many students during the last two decades of the 1200s. In 1303, Chu wrote *Ssu-yüan-yü-chien*, or *The Precious Mirror of Four Elements*. He described what is now known as Pascal's Triangle and explained how it could be used to solve polynomial equations. He also invented "the method of celestial element" to write and solve polynomial equations and linear systems with up to four variables.

Eliminating Answers

Before you do all the work involved in solving a multiple-choice problem, you usually can eliminate some answer choices. This can save you time in arriving at the answer to the problem, or in making an "educated" guess if you do not actually know how to find the answer.

1 EXAMPLE

One factor of $x^3 + x^2 + x - 3$ is $x - 1$. What is the other factor?

A. $x^2 + 2x - 3$ **B.** $x^2 + 2x + 3$ **C.** $x^3 + 2x + 3$ **D.** $x^2 - 2x + 3$

Look at the degrees of the polynomials. The original polynomial has degree 3 and the given factor has degree 1. The answer must have degree $3 - 1 = 2$. Since answer choice C has degree 3, you can eliminate choice C.

Look at the constant terms of the polynomials. The constant term of the original polynomial is -3. Since the constant term of the factor is -1, the other constant term must be 3 for the product of the two factors to be -3. The constant term of answer choice A is -3, so you can eliminate choice A.

● The correct answer is either B or D.

2 EXAMPLE

$(3x + 5)(x - 2) = \blacksquare$

A. $3x^2 - 2x - 10$ **B.** $3x^2 - 5x - 2$ **C.** $3x^2 + 2x - 10$ **D.** $3x^2 - x - 10$

Substitute a number. The original polynomial has $x - 2$ as a factor. If you let x equal 2, then the polynomial will equal 0. The correct answer will have to equal 0 when x is 2.

Choice A: $3(2)^2 - 2(2) - 10 = 3(4) - 4 - 10 = 12 - 4 - 10 = -2.$ You can eliminate A.

Choice B: $3(2)^2 - 5(2) - 2 = 3(4) - 10 - 2 = 12 - 10 - 2 = 0.$ B is a possible answer.

Choice C: $3(2)^2 + 2(2) - 10 = 3(4) + 4 - 10 = 12 + 4 - 10 = 6.$ You can eliminate C.

Choice D: $3(2)^2 - 2 - 10 = 3(4) - 2 - 10 = 12 - 2 - 10 = 0.$ D is a possible answer.

● The correct answer is either B or D.

EXERCISES

1. Multiply $x - 1$ by choices B and D in Example 1 to find the correct answer.

2. Look at the constant terms in choices B and D in Example 2, and explain why you can eliminate choice B.

3. Consider the following multiple-choice problem.

One factor of $3x^3 + 2x^2 + x - 6$ is $x - 1$. What is the other factor?
F. $3x^2 - 5x - 6$ **G.** $3x^2 + 5x + 6$ **H.** $3x^3 + x^2 - 3$ **I.** $3x^2 - 5x + 6$

a. Explain why you can eliminate answer choices F and H.
b. What is the correct answer to the problem?

Chapter Review

Vocabulary

binomial (p. 457)
degree of a monomial (p. 457)
degree of a polynomial (p. 457)

factor by grouping (p. 496)
monomial (p. 456)
perfect-square trinomial (p. 490)

polynomial (p. 457)
standard form of a polynomial (p. 457)
trinomial (p. 457)

Reading Math
Understanding
Vocabulary

Take It to the NET
Online vocabulary quiz
at **www.PHSchool.com**
Web Code: aej-0951

Match the vocabulary term in the column on the left with the most accurate description in the column on the right.

1. binomial

2. degree of a monomial

3. monomial

4. perfect-square trinomial

5. standard form of a polynomial

A. a polynomial with two terms

B. a polynomial in which the terms decrease in degree from left to right and there are no like terms

C. a polynomial with two identical binomial factors

D. the sum of the exponents of the variables

E. an expression that is a number, a variable, or a product of a number and one or more variables

Skills and Concepts

9-1 Objectives

▼ To describe polynomials (p. 456)

▼ To add and subtract polynomials (p. 458)

The degree of a term with one variable is the exponent of the variable. A **polynomial** is one monomial or the sum or difference of two or more monomials. The **degree of a polynomial** is the same as the degree of the term with the highest degree. A polynomial can be named by its degree or by the number of its terms. You can simplify polynomials by adding the coefficients of like terms.

Write each polynomial in standard form. Then name each polynomial based on its degree and number of terms.

6. $5y + 2 - 6y^2 + 3y$

7. $1 + 9h^2$

8. $k^3 + 3k^5 + k - k^3$

9. $6t^3 + 9 + 8t + 7t^2 - 6t^3$

10. x^2y^2

11. $5 + x^2 + x^3$

12. **Open-Ended** Write a polynomial using the variable z. What is the degree of your polynomial?

Simplify. Write each answer in standard form.

13. $(-4b^5 + 3b^3 - b + 10) + (3b^5 - b^3 + b - 4)$

14. $(3g^4 + 5g^2 + 5) + (5g^4 - 10g^2 + 11g)$

15. $(3x^3 + 8x^2 + 2x + 9) - (-4x^3 + 5x - 3)$

16. $(2t^3 - 4t^2 + 9t - 7) - (t^3 + t^2 - 3t + 1)$

17. $(6y^2 + 3y + 5) - (2y^2 + 1)$

18. $(7w^5 - 7w^3 + 3w) - (5w^4 - w^2 + 3)$

You can multiply a monomial and a polynomial using the Distributive Property. You can factor a polynomial by finding the greatest common factor (GCF) of the terms of the polynomial.

Simplify each product. Write in standard form.

19. $8x(2 - 5x)$　　　**20.** $5g(3g + 7g^2 - 9)$　　**21.** $8t^2(3t - 4 - 5t^2)$

22. $5m(3m + m^2)$　　**23.** $-2w^2(4w - 10 + 3w^2)$　**24.** $b(10 + 5b - 3b^2)$

Find the GCF of the terms of each polynomial. Then factor the polynomial.

25. $9x^4 + 12x^3 + 6x$　　**26.** $4t^5 - 12t^3 + 8t^2$　　**27.** $40n^5 + 70n^4 - 30n^3$

28. $2k^4 + 4k^3 - 6k - 8$　**29.** $3d^2 - 6d$　　　**30.** $10m^4 - 12m^3 + 4m^2$

31. $10v - 5$　　　　**32.** $12w^3 + 8w^2 + 20w$　**33.** $18d^5 + 6d^4 + 9d^3$

34. Critical Thinking The GCF of two numbers x and y is 3. Can you predict the GCF of $4x$ and $4y$? Explain your answer.

35. Critical Thinking Amanda says the GCF of $8m^2n$ and $4mn$ is 4. Kris says the GCF is $4n$. Kim says the GCF is $4mn$. Which student is correct? Explain your answer.

You can use tiles or the Distributive Property to multiply polynomials. You can use the FOIL method (First, Outer, Inner, Last) to multiply two binomials.

Simplify each product. Write in standard form.

36. $(x + 3)(x + 5)$　　**37.** $(5v + 2)(3v - 7)$　　**38.** $(2b + 5)(3b - 2)$

39. $(k - 1)(-k + 4)$　　**40.** $(p + 2)(p^2 + p + 1)$　　**41.** $(4a - 1)(a - 5)$

42. $(y - 4)(y^2 - 5y - 2)$　**43.** $(3x + 4)(x + 2)$　　**44.** $(-2h^2 + h - 1)(h - 5)$

45. $(q - 4)(q - 4)$　　**46.** $(2k^3 + 5)^2$　　　**47.** $(8 - 3t^2)(8 + 3t^2)$

48. $(2m^2 + 5)(2m^2 - 5)$　**49.** $(w - 4)(w + 4)$　　**50.** $(4g^2 - 5h^4)(4g^2 + 5h^4)$

51. Geometry A rectangle has dimensions $2x + 1$ and $x + 4$. Write an expression for the area of the rectangle as a product and as a polynomial in standard form.

52. Error Analysis Suppose a classmate claims that the difference between $(x^2 - y^2)$ and $(x - y)^2$ must be 0. Is your classmate correct? Explain your answer.

Some quadratic trinomials are the product of two binomial factors. You can factor trinomials using tiles or by using FOIL. Factor any common monomial factors first.

Factor each expression.

53. $x^2 + 3x + 2$　　**54.** $y^2 - 9y + 14$　　**55.** $x^2 - 2x - 15$

56. $2w^2 - w - 3$　　**57.** $b^2 - 7b + 12$　　**58.** $2t^2 + 3t - 2$

59. $x^2 + 5x - 6$　　**60.** $6x^2 + 10x + 4$　　**61.** $21x^2 - 22x - 8$

62. $3x^2 + x - 2$　　**63.** $15y^2 + 16y + 1$　　**64.** $15y^2 - 16y + 1$

9-7 Objectives

▼ To factor perfect-square trinomials (p. 490)

▼ To factor the difference of squares (p. 492)

When you factor a **perfect-square trinomial,** the two binomial factors are the same.

$$a^2 + 2ab + b^2 = (a + b)(a + b) = (a + b)^2 \text{ and}$$
$$a^2 - 2ab + b^2 = (a - b)(a - b) = (a - b)^2$$

When you factor the difference of squares of two terms, the two binomial factors are the sum and the difference of the two terms.

$$a^2 - b^2 = (a + b)(a - b)$$

Factor each expression.

65. $q^2 + 2q + 1$

66. $b^2 - 16$

67. $x^2 - 4x + 4$

68. $4t^2 - 121$

69. $4d^2 - 20d + 25$

70. $9c^2 + 6c + 1$

71. $9k^2 - 25$

72. $x^2 + 6x + 9$

73. $24y^2 - 6$

74. Geometry Find the length of a side of the square with an area of $\frac{1}{4}d^2 + d + 1$.

75. Critical Thinking Suppose you are using tiles to factor a quadratic trinomial. What do you know about the factors of the trinomial if the tiles form a square?

76. The area of a rectangle is $25u^2 + 65u + 36$. If the dimensions of the rectangle are factors of $25u^2 + 65u + 36$, could the rectangle be a square? Explain.

9-8 Objectives

▼ To factor polynomials with four terms (p. 496)

▼ To factor trinomials by grouping (p. 497)

To factor a polynomial, first see if you can factor out the GCF. If the polynomial has four or more terms, you can group the terms and look for a common binomial factor. Then you can use the Distributive Property to factor the polynomial. If you do not quickly recognize the binomial factors of a polynomial of the form $ax^2 + bx + c$, grouping the terms may help you factor the polynomial.

Find the GCF of the first two terms and the GCF of the last two terms for each polynomial.

77. $16x^3 + 12x^2 - 8x - 6$

78. $9k^3 + 15k^2 - 6k - 10$

79. $72y^3 + 24y^2 - 12y - 4$

80. $20n^4 - 10n^3 + 14n - 7$

Factor completely.

81. $6x^3 + 3x^2 + 8x + 4$

82. $20y^4 - 45y^2$

83. $9g^2 + 15g - 6$

84. $6c^2 - 5cd + d^2$

85. $11k^2 + 23k + 2$

86. $3u^2 + 21u + 18$

87. $15p^2 + 14p + 3$

88. $3u^2 - 21u + 18$

89. $15h^3 + 11h^2 - 45h - 33$

90. $30x^3 + 42x^2 - 5x - 7$

91. $12s^4t + 20s^3t - 8s^2t$

92. $2x^3 + 7x^2 + 4x + 14$

93. Geometry The volume of the rectangular prism is $6p^3 + 38p^2 + 40p$. Find expressions for the possible dimensions of the prism.

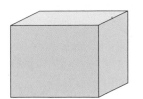

Chapter 9

Chapter Test

 Take It to the NET
Online chapter test at
www.PHSchool.com
Web Code: aea-0952

Write each polynomial in standard form. Then name each polynomial based on its degree and number of terms.

1. $y^2 + 2y + 5 - 3y^2 - 5y$

2. $4 - 5v - 12v - 6v^2 - 4 - 2v^3$

3. $-4x^4 + x^2 - 10 + 12x^4 - 7x^2$

4. $3k^5 + 4k^2 - 6k^5 - 5k^2$

Simplify. Write each answer in standard form.

5. $(4x^2 + 2x + 5) + (7x^2 - 5x + 2)$

6. $(9a^2 - 4 - 5a) - (12a - 6a^2 + 3)$

7. $(-4m^2 + m - 10) + (3m + 12 - 7m^2)$

8. $(3c - 4c^2 + c^3) - (5c^2 + 8c^3 - 6c)$

9. **Open-Ended** Write a trinomial with a degree of 6.

10. Write the standard form for the polynomial modeled at the right. Then factor the expression.

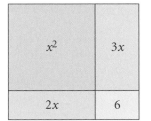

Simplify each product. Write in standard form.

11. $8b(3b + 7 - b^2)$

12. $-t(5t^2 + t)$

13. $3q(4 - q + 3q^3)$

14. $2c(c^5 + 4c^3)$

15. $(x + 6)(x + 1)$

16. $(d + 4)(d - 3)$

17. $(2h - 1)(h - 4)$

18. $(2m + 5)(3m - 7)$

19. $(p + 2)(2p^2 - 5p + 4)$

20. $(a - 4)(6a^2 + 10a - 3)$

21. $(3x + 5)(7x^2 - 2x + 1)$

Find the GCF of the terms of each polynomial.

22. $21x^4 + 18x^2 + 36x^3$

23. $3t^2 - 5t - 2t^4$

24. $-3a^{10} + 9a^5 + 6a^{15}$

25. $9m^3 - 7m^4 + 8m^2$

26. **Writing** Explain how to use the Distributive Property to multiply polynomials. Include an example.

Write an expression for each situation as a product. Then write each expression in standard form.

27. A plot of land has width x meters. The length of the plot of land is 5 meters more than 3 times its width. What is the area of the land?

28. The height of a box is 2 in. less than its width w. The length of the box is 3 in. more than 4 times its width. What is the volume of the box in terms of w?

Geometry Write an expression for the area of each shaded region. Write your answer in simplest form.

29.

30.

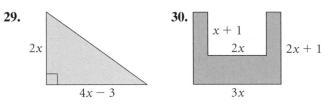

Factor each expression.

31. $w^2 - 5w - 14$

32. $g^2 + 10g + 25$

33. $9k^2 + 24k + 16$

34. $n^2 - 100$

35. $y^2 - 4y + 4$

36. $4x^2 - 49$

37. $4p^2 + 164p + 81$

38. $13c^2 - 52$

Write the missing value in each perfect-square trinomial.

39. $x^2 + \blacksquare x + 49$

40. $\blacksquare t^2 + 12t + 9$

41. $9x^2 - 30x + \blacksquare$

42. $4w^2 - \blacksquare w + 81$

Find the GCF of the first two terms and the GCF of the last two terms for each polynomial.

43. $6x^4 + 9x^3 - 8x + 12$

44. $16n^3 + 20n^2 - 4n - 5$

Factor completely.

45. $12n^3 + 15n^2 + 4n + 5$

46. $4x^2 - 10x + 6$

47. $x^3 - 5x^2 + 5x - 25$

48. $6r^3 - 9r^2 - 4r + 6$

49. $12y^3 + 28y^2 - 3y - 7$

50. $3n^3 - 4n^2 - 6n + 8$

51. **Open-Ended** Find three different values to complete the expression $x^2 + \blacksquare x + 30$ so that it can be factored into the product of two binomials. Show each factorization.

Standardized Test Prep

Reading Comprehension Read the passage below, and then answer the questions on the basis of what is *stated* or *implied* in the passage.

Saving for College For years, college costs have risen steadily. Although general inflation in our economy averages 3.0% to 3.5%, the rate of increase in college costs is about 5% a year. While many prospective students expect to benefit from financial aid, they also must prepare to pay some portion of the costs themselves.

To help with these preparations, Congress has authorized special college-saver plans, called "529 Plans" because they are described in section 529 of the Internal Revenue Code. The plans allow the gains (interest from savings accounts or dividends from stocks) on college savings to grow without incurring federal income tax when the money is withdrawn for college expenses.

If college savings are invested in stocks, you could expect an average increase of about 10.5% each year. This has been the historical rate of growth for stocks in the United States. Of course, it is impossible to predict what the growth will be in any particular year. But if you start saving for college early, with 5 or more years for your money to grow, you can expect good returns.

1. Suppose that total freshman year costs are $20,000. About what will the total costs be for senior year, assuming average increases?
   A. $20,000.00
   B. $23,000.00
   C. $23,152.50
   D. $24,310.13

2. Which expression represents college costs over time? Let t = the time in years and c = the starting cost in dollars.
   F. $c \cdot 0.05^t$
   G. $c \cdot 1.05^t$
   H. $t \cdot 1.05^c$
   I. $c \cdot 2^{5\%}$

3. Which equation represents the average value of stock investments over time? Let t = the time in years, x = the amount of the initial investment in dollars, and V = the value of the investment in dollars.
   A. $V = x \cdot 0.05^t$
   B. $V = x \cdot 1.105^t$
   C. $V = x \cdot 10.5^t$
   D. $V = x \cdot 210.5\%$

4. Suppose you have a scholarship that will pay 75% of your college costs each year. Total freshman year costs are $20,000. To prepare for your senior year costs, you invest $4,870 in bonds paying 4% a year at the beginning of your freshman year.

   Which answer gives the best estimates of the investment value and of your college costs at the beginning of your senior year?
   F. investment $5478, costs $5788
   G. investment $6571, costs $6500
   H. investment $5800, costs $23,000
   I. investment $5454, costs $5788

5. a. Suppose your grandparents put $1000 for your college costs in a savings account earning 6% interest compounded annually. In 10 years, how much money would be in the savings account?
   b. Suppose your grandparents did not know about the 529 plan. If you had to pay a 23% tax on the interest the account earned, how much would you have to pay?

Where You've Been

- In Chapter 5, you learned about functions and their graphs.

- In Chapter 8, you discovered that not all functions are linear as you explored exponential functions and fit data to them.

- In Chapter 9, you learned to factor trinomials of the form $ax^2 + bx + c$.

Diagnosing Readiness

$\mathbf{\hat{1}}$**TEXT** Instant self-check online and on CD-ROM

(For help, go to the Lesson in green.)

Evaluating Expressions (Lesson 1-6)

Evaluate each expression for $a = -1$, $b = 3$, and $c = -2$.

1. $2a - b^2 + c$

2. $\frac{c^2 - ab}{2a}$

3. $bc - 3a^2$

4. $\frac{b^2 - 4ac}{2a}$

5. $5a + 2b(c - 1)$

6. $c^2 + 2ab - 1$

Evaluating Function Rules (Lesson 5-2)

Evaluate each function rule for $x = -6$.

7. $f(x) = -3x^2$

8. $y = x^2 - 10$

9. $h(x) = x^2 + 6x$

10. $y = (x - 1)^2$

11. $y = 5 - 2x^2$

12. $y = (1 + x)^2$

13. $g(x) = \frac{2}{3}x^2$

14. $y = (2x)^2$

Graphing Functions (Lesson 5-3)

Graph each function.

15. $y = x$

16. $y = -x^2$

17. $y = |x|$

Multiplying Binomials (Lesson 9-3)

Simplify each product using FOIL.

18. $(x + 2)(x - 3)$

19. $(2y + 1)(2y + 3)$

20. $(3x - 7)(x + 4)$

Factoring (Lessons 9-5 and 9-6)

Factor each expression.

21. $4x^2 + 4x + 1$

22. $5x^2 + 32x - 21$

23. $8x^2 - 10x + 3$

24. $m^2 - 7m - 18$

25. $12y^2 + 8y - 15$

26. $x^2 - 18x + 81$

Quadratic Equations and Functions

Where You're Going

- In this chapter, you will examine quadratic graphs and their equations.

- You will solve quadratic equations by various techniques such as factoring, finding square roots, completing the square, and applying the quadratic formula.

- You will determine an appropriate linear, quadratic, or exponential model for real-world data.

Real-World Snapshots Applying what you learn, you will do activities involving space station design, on pages 574–575.

Key Vocabulary

Exploring Quadratic Graphs

Lesson Preview

What You'll Learn

OBJECTIVE 1
To graph quadratic functions of the form $y = ax^2$

OBJECTIVE 2
To graph quadratic functions of the form $y = ax^2 + c$

...And Why

To model a problem involving gravity, as in Example 5

✓ Check Skills You'll Need

(For help, go to Lessons 1-2 and 5-3.)

Evaluate each expression for $h = 3$, $k = 2$, and $j = -4$.

1. hkj **2.** kh^2 **3.** hk^2 **4.** $kj^2 + h$

Graph each equation.

5. $y = 2x - 1$ **6.** $y = |x|$ **7.** $y = x^2 + 2$

New Vocabulary

- quadratic function
- standard form of a quadratic function
- parabola
- axis of symmetry
- vertex
- minimum
- maximum

OBJECTIVE 1

Graphing $y = ax^2$

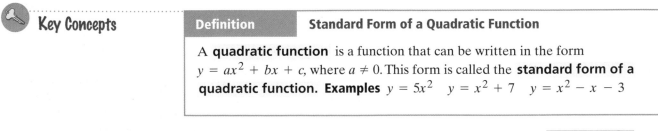

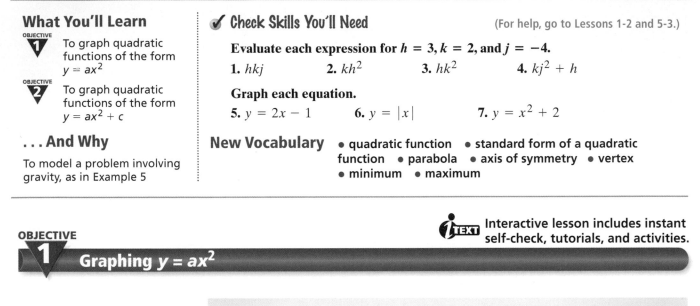

🖥 Interactive lesson includes instant self-check, tutorials, and activities.

Investigation: Plotting Quadratic Curves

1. Graph the equations $y = x^2$ and $y = 3x^2$ on the same coordinate plane.

2. **a.** Describe how the graphs are alike.
   b. Describe how the graphs are different.

3. Predict how the graph of $y = \frac{1}{3}x^2$ will be similar to and different from the graph of $y = x^2$.

4. Graph $y = \frac{1}{3}x^2$. Were your predictions correct? Explain.

The functions shown above are quadratic functions.

🔑 **Key Concepts**

Definition	**Standard Form of a Quadratic Function**

A **quadratic function** is a function that can be written in the form $y = ax^2 + bx + c$, where $a \neq 0$. This form is called the **standard form of a quadratic function.** **Examples** $y = 5x^2$ $y = x^2 + 7$ $y = x^2 - x - 3$

The graph of a quadratic function is a U-shaped curve called a **parabola.** The graph of $y = x^2$, shown at the right, is a parabola.

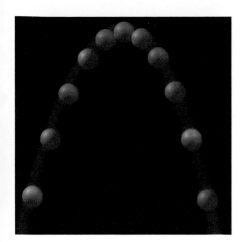

You can fold a parabola so that the two sides match exactly. This property is called *symmetry*. The fold or line that divides the parabola into two matching halves is called the **axis of symmetry.**

The highest or lowest point of a parabola is its **vertex,** which is on the axis of symmetry.

If $a > 0$ in $y = ax^2 + bx + c$ If $a < 0$ in $y = ax^2 + bx + c$

$\downarrow$ $\downarrow$

the parabola opens upward.   the parabola opens downward.

$\downarrow$ $\downarrow$

The vertex is the **minimum** point   The vertex is the **maximum** point
or lowest point of the parabola.   or highest point of the parabola.

1 EXAMPLE   Identifying a Vertex

Identify the vertex of each graph. Tell whether it is a minimum or maximum.

a. 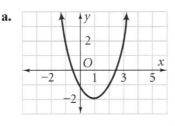   **b.**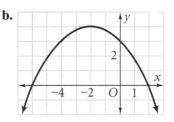

The vertex is $(1, -2)$. It is a minimum.   The vertex is $(-2, 4)$. It is a maximum.

✓ Check Understanding **1** Identify the vertex of each graph. Tell whether it is a minimum or maximum.

a. 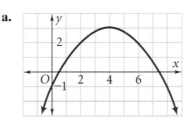   **b.**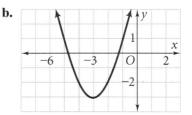

You can use the fact that a parabola is symmetric to graph it quickly. First find the coordinates of the vertex and several points on either side of the vertex. Then reflect the points across the axis of symmetry. For functions of the form $y = ax^2$, the vertex is at the origin.

2 EXAMPLE   Graphing $y = ax^2$

Make a table of values and graph the quadratic function $y = \frac{1}{2}x^2$.

x	$y = \frac{1}{2}x^2$	(x, y)
0	$\frac{1}{2}(0)^2 = 0$	$(0, 0)$
2	$\frac{1}{2}(2)^2 = 2$	$(2, 2)$
4	$\frac{1}{2}(4)^2 = 8$	$(4, 8)$

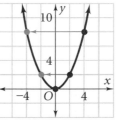

Find the corresponding points on the other side of the axis of symmetry.

✓ Check Understanding **2** Make a table of values and graph the quadratic function $f(x) = -2x^2$.

The value of a, the coefficient of the x^2 term in a quadratic function, affects the width of a parabola as well as the direction in which it opens.

3 EXAMPLE Comparing Widths of Parabolas

Use the graphs below. Order the quadratic functions $f(x) = -4x^2$, $f(x) = \frac{1}{4}x^2$, and $f(x) = x^2$ from widest to narrowest graph.

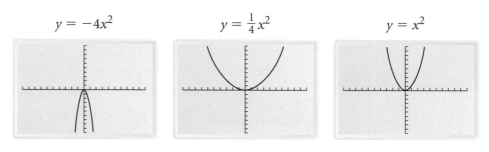

$$y = -4x^2 \qquad\qquad y = \frac{1}{4}x^2 \qquad\qquad y = x^2$$

Of the three graphs, $f(x) = \frac{1}{4}x^2$ is the widest and $f(x) = -4x^2$ is the narrowest. So, the order from widest to narrowest is $f(x) = \frac{1}{4}x^2$, $f(x) = x^2$, and $f(x) = -4x^2$.

✔ **Check Understanding** ❸ Order the quadratic functions $y = x^2$, $y = \frac{1}{2}x^2$, and $y = -2x^2$ from widest to narrowest graph.

As you can see in Example 3, for $|m| < |n|$, the graph of $y = mx^2$ is wider than the graph of $y = nx^2$.

OBJECTIVE

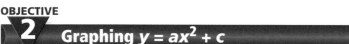

2 Graphing $y = ax^2 + c$

The value of c, the constant term in a quadratic function, translates the graph up or down.

The y-axis is the axis of symmetry for functions in the form $y = ax^2 + c$.

4 EXAMPLE Graphing $y = ax^2 + c$

Graph the quadratic functions $y = 2x^2$ and $y = 2x^2 + 3$. Compare the graphs.

Problem Solving Hint

You can use symmetry of the parabola to check calculated (x, y) coordinates or points on the graph.

x	$y = 2x^2$	$y = 2x^2 + 3$
-2	8	11
-1	2	5
0	0	3
-1	2	5
-2	8	11

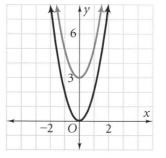

The graph of $y = 2x^2 + 3$ has the same shape as the graph of $y = 2x^2$, but it is shifted up 3 units.

✔ **Check Understanding** ❹ **a.** Graph $y = x^2$ and $y = x^2 - 4$. Compare the graphs.
b. Critical Thinking Describe what positive and negative values of c do to the position of the vertex.

You can model the height of an object moving under the influence of gravity using a quadratic function. As an object falls, its speed continues to increase. Ignoring air resistance, you can find the approximate height of a falling object using the function $h = -16t^2 + c$. The height h is in feet, the time t is in seconds, and the initial height of the object c is in feet.

5 EXAMPLE Real-World Problem Solving

Nature Suppose you see an eagle flying over a canyon. The eagle is 30 ft above the level of the canyon's edge when it drops a stick from its claws. The force of gravity causes the stick to fall toward Earth. The function $h = -16t^2 + 30$ gives the height of the stick h in feet after t seconds. Graph this quadratic function.

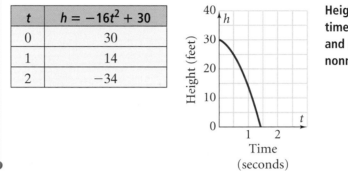

t	$h = -16t^2 + 30$
0	30
1	14
2	-34

Height h is dependent on time t. Graph t on the x-axis and h on the y-axis. Use nonnegative values for t.

✓ **Check Understanding** **5 a.** Suppose a squirrel is in a tree 24 ft above the ground. She drops an acorn. The function $h = -16t^2 + 24$ gives the height of the acorn in feet after t seconds. Graph this function.
  b. Critical Thinking In Example 5, why is the domain nonnegative values of t?

EXERCISES

For more practice, see *Extra Practice*.

Practice and Problem Solving

A Practice by Example

Example 1
(page 511)

Identify the vertex of each graph. Tell whether it is a minimum or maximum.

1.
2.
3.

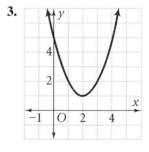

Example 2
(page 511)

Graph each function.

4. $y = -4x^2$ **5.** $f(x) = 1.5x^2$ **6.** $y = \frac{2}{3}x^2$

7. $f(x) = -\frac{1}{2}x^2$ **8.** $y = -\frac{1}{3}x^2$ **9.** $f(x) = 3x^2$

Example 3
(page 512)

Order each group of quadratic functions from widest to narrowest graph.

10. $y = 3x^2, y = \frac{1}{2}x^2, y = 4x^2$ **11.** $f(x) = 5x^2, f(x) = \frac{1}{3}x^2, f(x) = x^2$

12. $y = -\frac{1}{2}x^2, y = 5x^2, y = -\frac{1}{4}x^2$ **13.** $f(x) = -2x^2, f(x) = -\frac{2}{3}x^2, f(x) = -4x^2$

Example 4
(page 512)

Graph each function.

14. $f(x) = x^2 + 2$ **15.** $y = x^2 - 3$ **16.** $y = \frac{1}{2}x^2 + 4$

17. $f(x) = -x^2 - 1$ **18.** $y = -2x^2 + 2$ **19.** $f(x) = 4x^2 - 7$

Example 5
(page 513)

20. A gull drops a clam shell onto some rocks from a height of 50 ft. The function $h = -16t^2 + 50$ gives the shell's approximate height h in feet after t seconds. Graph the function.

B **Apply Your Skills**

Match each graph with its function.

A. $f(x) = x^2 - 1$ **B.** $f(x) = x^2 + 4$ **C.** $f(x) = -x^2 + 2$

D. $f(x) = 3x^2 - 5$ **E.** $f(x) = -3x^2 + 8$ **F.** $f(x) = -0.2x^2 + 5$

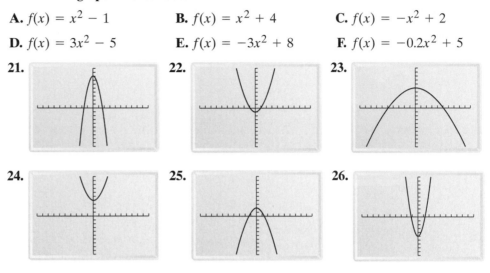

21.   **22.**   **23.**

24.   **25.**   **26.**

Writing Without graphing, describe how each graph differs from the graph of $y = x^2$.

27. $y = 2x^2$ **28.** $y = -x^2$ **29.** $y = 1.5x^2$ **30.** $y = \frac{1}{2}x^2$

Graph each function.

31. $y = -\frac{1}{4}x^2 + 3$ **32.** $f(x) = -1.5x^2 + 5$ **33.** $y = 3x^2 - 6$

Trace each parabola on a sheet of paper and draw its axis of symmetry.

34. 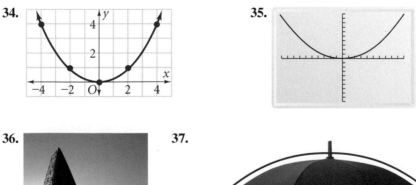   **35.**

36.    **37.**

38. A bungee jumper dives from a platform. The function $h = -16t^2 + 200$ gives her approximate height h in feet after t seconds.
  a. Graph the function. Graph t on the x-axis and h on the y-axis.
  b. What will the jumper's height be after 1 second?
  c. What will the jumper's height be after 3 seconds?

39. Geometry Suppose that a pizza must fit into a box with a base that is 12 in. long and 12 in. wide. You can use the quadratic function $A = \pi r^2$ to find the area of a pizza in terms of its radius.
  a. What values of r make sense for the function?
  b. What values of A make sense for the function?
  c. Graph the function. Round values of A to the nearest tenth.

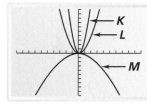

Three graphs are shown below. For Exercises 40–43, identify the graph(s) that fit each description.

40. $a > 0$ **41.** $a < 0$

42. $|a|$ has the greatest value.

43. $|a|$ has the least value.

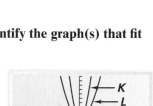

44. Open-Ended Give an example of a quadratic function for each description.
  a. Its graph opens upward and its vertex is at the origin.
  b. Its graph has the same shape as the graph in part (a), but the graph opens downward.
  c. Its graph is wider than the graph of the function in part (a).

45. Gravity Suppose a person is riding in a hot-air balloon, 144 feet above the ground. He drops an apple. The height of the apple above the ground is given by the formula $h = -16t^2 + 144$, where h is height in feet and t is time in seconds.
  a. Graph the function.
  b. How far has the apple fallen from time $t = 0$ to $t = 1$?
  c. Critical Thinking Does the apple fall as far from time $t = 1$ to $t = 2$ as it does from time $t = 0$ to $t = 1$? Explain.

C Challenge

46. Critical Thinking Complete each statement. Assume $a \neq 0$.
  a. The graph of $y = ax^2 + c$ intersects the x-axis in two places when __?__.
  b. The graph of $y = ax^2 + c$ does not intersect the x-axis when __?__.

47. Landscaping The plan for a 20 ft-by-12 ft patio has a square garden in the middle of it. If each side of the garden is x ft, the function $y = 240 - x^2$ gives the area of the patio in square feet.
  a. Graph the function.
  b. What values make sense for the domain? Explain.
  c. What is the range of the function? Explain.
  d. Use the graph to estimate the side length of the garden if the area of the patio is 200 ft^2.

48. Consider the graphs of $y = ax^2$ and $y = (ax)^2$. Assume $a \neq 0$.
  a. For what values of a will both graphs lie in the same quadrants?
  b. For what values of a will the graph of $y = ax^2$ be wider than the graph of $y = (ax)^2$?

49. Architecture An architect wants to design an archway with the following requirements.

- The archway is 6 ft wide and has vertical sides 7 ft high.
- The top of the archway is modeled by the function $y = -\frac{1}{3}x^2 + 10$.

a. Sketch the archway by drawing vertical lines 7 units high at $x = -3$ and $x = 3$ and graphing the portion of the quadratic function that lies between $x = -3$ and $x = 3$.

b. The plan for the archway is then changed so that the top is modeled by the function $y = -0.5x^2 + 11.5$. Make a revised sketch of the archway.

Standardized Test Prep

Multiple Choice

50. Which of the following equations has a graph that is narrower than the graph of $y = 2x^2 + 3$?
A. $y = 2x^2 - 3$ **B.** $y = -3x^2 + 2$
C. $y = 0.5x^2 + 3$ **D.** $y = -0.5x^2 - 2$

51. Which of the following equations has a graph that crosses the y-axis at a point lower than the graph of $y = -2x^2 - 1$?
F. $y = -3x^2 - 1$ **G.** $y = 3x^2 - 3$
H. $y = -3x^2 + 1$ **I.** $y = -3x^2 + 3$

52. The graph of $y = 4x^2 + 3$ does NOT pass through which of the following points?
A. $(0, 3)$ **B.** $(1, 7)$ **C.** $(-1, 7)$ **D.** $(3, 27)$

Extended Response

Take It to the NET
Online lesson quiz at
www.PHSchool.com
Web Code: aea-1001

53. A construction worker drops a tool from the top of a building that is 200 ft high. The height of the tool above the ground can be modeled by $h = -16t^2 + 200$, where h is height in feet and t is time in seconds.
a. Make a table and graph this function.
b. Use your graph to estimate the amount of time it takes for the tool to hit the ground. Round to the nearest tenth of a second.

Mixed Review

Lesson 9-8

Factor each expression.

54. $x^3 - 4x^2 + 2x - 8$ **55.** $15a^3 - 18a^2 - 10a + 12$

56. $7b^3 + 14b^2 + b + 2$ **57.** $y^3 + 3y^2 - 4y - 12$

58. $2n^3 - 2n^2 - 24n$ **59.** $30m^3 + 51m^2 + 9m$

Lesson 9-2

Simplify each expression.

60. $5x(3x - 4)$ **61.** $(n - 7)9n$ **62.** $-2t^2(6t - 11)$

63. $4m^2(3m^4 - m^3 + 5)$ **64.** $-5y(3y^5 + 2y^3 - 4)$ **65.** $3c^3(-4c^2 + 7c - 8)$

66. Business The City Council invites your art club to sell helium balloons during a citywide celebration. The rental of the helium tank is $27.00 for the day. Each balloon costs $.20. If the balloons sell for $2.00 each, how many will your art club have to sell to break even?

10-2

Quadratic Functions

Lesson Preview

What You'll Learn

OBJECTIVE 1
To graph quadratic functions of the form $y = ax^2 + bx + c$

OBJECTIVE 2
To graph quadratic inequalities

. . . And Why

To model height of fireworks, as in Example 2

✓ **Check Skills You'll Need** (For help, go to Lessons 1-6 and 10-1.)

Evaluate the expression $\frac{-b}{2a}$ for the following values of a and b.

1. $a = -6, b = 4$
2. $a = 15, b = 20$
3. $a = -8, b = -56$
4. $a = -9, b = 108$

Graph each function.

5. $y = x^2$
6. $y = -x^2 + 2$
7. $y = \frac{1}{2}x^2 - 1$

OBJECTIVE

1

iTEXT Interactive lesson includes instant self-check, tutorials, and activities.

Graphing $y = ax^2 + bx + c$

In Lesson 10-1, you investigated the graphs of $y = ax^2$ and $y = ax^2 + c$. In the quadratic function $y = ax^2 + bx + c$, the value of b affects the position of the axis of symmetry.

Consider the graphs of the following functions.

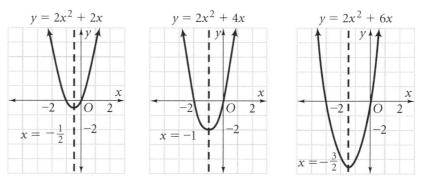

$$y = 2x^2 + 2x \qquad y = 2x^2 + 4x \qquad y = 2x^2 + 6x$$

$$x = -\frac{1}{2} \qquad x = -1 \qquad x = -\frac{3}{2}$$

Notice that all three graphs have the same y-intercept. This is because in all three equations $c = 0$. The axis of symmetry changes with each change in the b value. The equation of the axis of symmetry is related to the ratio $\frac{b}{a}$.

equation: $\quad y = 2x^2 + 2x \qquad\qquad y = 2x^2 + 4x \qquad\qquad y = 2x^2 + 6x$

$\frac{b}{a}$: $\qquad\quad \frac{2}{2} = 1 \qquad\qquad\qquad \frac{4}{2} = 2 \qquad\qquad\qquad \frac{6}{2} = 3$

axis of symmetry: $\quad x = -\frac{1}{2} \qquad\qquad x = -1, \text{or} -\frac{2}{2} \qquad\qquad x = -\frac{3}{2}$

The equation of the axis of symmetry is $x = -\frac{1}{2}\left(\frac{b}{a}\right)$, or $\frac{-b}{2a}$.

Key Concepts

Property	**Graph of a Quadratic Function**

The graph of $y = ax^2 + bx + c$, where $a \neq 0$, has the line $x = \frac{-b}{2a}$ as its axis of symmetry. The x-coordinate of the vertex is $\frac{-b}{2a}$.

When you substitute $x = 0$ into the equation $y = ax^2 + bx + c$, $y = c$. So the y-intercept of a quadratic function is the value of c. You can use the axis of symmetry and the y-intercept to help you graph a quadratic function.

1 EXAMPLE Graphing $y = ax^2 + bx + c$

Graph the function $y = -3x^2 + 6x + 5$.

Step 1 Find the equation of the axis of symmetry and the coordinates of the vertex.

$x = \dfrac{-b}{2a} = \dfrac{-6}{2(-3)} = 1$ **Find the equation of the axis of symmetry.**

The axis of symmetry is $x = 1$.

$y = -3x^2 + 6x + 5$

$y = -3(1)^2 + 6(1) + 5$ **To find the y-coordinate of the vertex, substitute 1 for x.**

$ = 8$

The vertex is $(1, 8)$.

Step 2 Find two other points on the graph.

Use the y-intercept.

For $x = 0$, $y = 5$, so one point is $(0, 5)$.

Choose a value for x on the same side of the vertex as the y-intercept.
Let $x = -1$.

$y = -3(-1)^2 + 6(-1) + 5$ **Find the y-coordinate for $x = -1$.**

$ = -4$

For $x = -1$, $y = -4$, so another point is $(-1, -4)$.

Step 3 Reflect $(0, 5)$ and $(-1, -4)$ across the axis of symmetry to get two more points. Then draw the parabola.

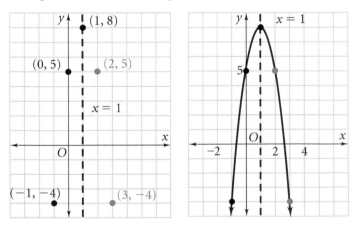

✓ **Check Understanding** ➊ Graph $f(x) = x^2 - 6x + 9$. Label the axis of symmetry and the vertex.

You saw in the previous lesson that the formula $h = -16t^2 + c$ describes the height above the ground of an object falling from an initial height c, at time t. If an object is given an initial upward velocity v and continues with no additional force of its own, the formula $h = -16t^2 + vt + c$ describes its approximate height above the ground.

2 EXAMPLE Real-World Problem Solving

Fireworks In professional fireworks displays, aerial fireworks carry "stars" upward, ignite them, and project them into the air.

Suppose a particular star is projected from an aerial firework at a starting height of 520 ft with an initial upward velocity of 72 ft/s. How long will it take for the star to reach its maximum height? How far above the ground will it be?

The equation $h = -16t^2 + 72t + 520$ gives the star's height h in feet at time t in seconds. Since the coefficient of t^2 is negative, the curve opens downward, and the vertex is the maximum point.

Step 1 Find the t-coordinate of the vertex.

$$\frac{-b}{2a} = \frac{-(72)}{2(-16)} = 2.25$$

After 2.25 seconds, the star will be at its greatest height.

Step 2 Find the h-coordinate of the vertex.

$h = -16(2.25)^2 + 72(2.25) + 520$ **Substitute 2.25 for t.**

$h = 601$ **Simplify using a calculator.**

The maximum height of the star will be 601 ft.

✓ **Check Understanding**   **2** A ball is thrown into the air with an initial upward velocity of 48 ft/s. Its height h in feet after t seconds is given by the function $h = -16t^2 + 48t + 4$.
a. In how many seconds will the ball reach its maximum height?
b. What is the ball's maximum height?

OBJECTIVE

2 Graphing Quadratic Inequalities

Graphing a quadratic inequality is similar to graphing a linear inequality. The curve is dashed if the inequality involves < or >. The curve is solid if the inequality involves ≤ or ≥.

3 EXAMPLE Graphing Quadratic Inequalities

Graph the quadratic inequality $y \leq x^2 - 3x - 4$.

Graph the boundary curve, $y = x^2 - 3x - 4$. Use a solid line because the solution of the inequality $y \leq x^2 - 3x - 4$ includes the boundary. Shade below the curve.

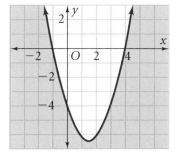

✓ **Check Understanding**   **3** Graph each quadratic inequality.
a. $y \leq x^2 + 2x - 5$
b. $y > x^2 + x + 1$

Practice and Problem Solving

A **Practice by Example**

Example 1
(page 518)

Find the equation of the axis of symmetry and the coordinates of the vertex of the graph of each function.

1. $y = 2x^2 + 4$

2. $f(x) = 2x^2 + 4x - 5$

3. $y = x^2 - 8x - 9$

4. $y = 3x^2 - 9x + 5$

Match each graph with its function.

A. $y = x^2 - 6x$ **B.** $y = x^2 + 6x$ **C.** $y = -x^2 - 6x$

D. $y = -x^2 + 6x$ **E.** $y = -x^2 + 6$ **F.** $y = x^2 - 6$

5.
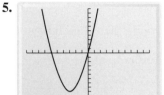

6.
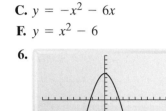

7.
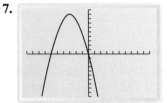

8.
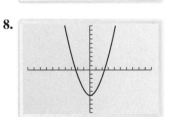

9.

10.
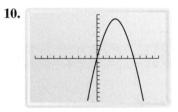

Graph each function. Label the axis of symmetry and the vertex.

11. $f(x) = x^2 + 4x + 3$

12. $y = 2x^2 - 6x$

13. $y = -x^2 + 4x - 4$

14. $y = 2x^2 + 3x + 1$

Example 2
(page 519)

15. Gardening Suppose you have 80 ft of fence to enclose a rectangular garden. The function $A = 40x - x^2$ gives you the area of the garden in square feet where x is the width in feet.

a. What width gives you the maximum gardening area?

b. What is the maximum area?

16. A ball is thrown into the air with an upward velocity of 40 ft/s. Its height h in feet after t seconds is given by the function $h = -16t^2 + 40t + 6$.

a. In how many seconds does the ball reach its maximum height?

b. What is the ball's maximum height?

Example 3
(page 519)

Graph each quadratic inequality.

17. $y > x^2$

18. $f(x) < -x^2$

19. $y \leq x^2 + 3$

20. $y < -x^2 + 4$

21. $y \geq -2x^2 + 6$

22. $f(x) > -x^2 + 4x - 4$

Graph each function. Label the axis of symmetry and the vertex.

23. $y = x^2 - 9x + 3$ **24.** $f(x) = -x^2 - 4x - 6$ **25.** $f(x) = x^2 - 2x + 1$

26. $y = 2x^2 + x - 3$ **27.** $y = x^2 + 3x + 2$ **28.** $y = -x^2 + 8x - 5$

29. $y = \frac{1}{2}x^2 + 2x + 1$ **30.** $y = \frac{1}{4}x^2 + 2x + 1$ **31.** $y = -\frac{1}{4}x^2 + 2x - 3$

Open-Ended For Exercises 32–34, give an example of a quadratic function for each description.

32. Its axis of symmetry is to the right of the y-axis.

33. Its graph opens downward and has its vertex at $(0, 0)$.

34. Its graph lies entirely above the x-axis.

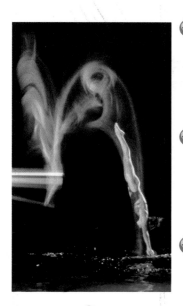

35. Diving An athlete dives from the 3-meter springboard. Her altitude y, at horizontal distance x, can be approximated by the function $y = -2.2x^2 + 5.3x + 4$. Both the altitude and distance are in meters.
   a. How far has she traveled horizontally when she reaches her maximum altitude? Round to the nearest tenth of a meter.
   b. What is her maximum altitude? Round to the nearest tenth of a meter.

36. Road Construction An archway over a road is cut out of rock. Its shape is modeled by the quadratic function $y = -0.1x^2 + 12$ for $y \geq 0$.
   a. Write an inequality that describes the opening of the archway.
   b. Graph the inequality.
   c. Critical Thinking Can a camper 6 ft wide and 7 ft high fit under the arch without crossing the median line? Explain.

37. Business A small company markets a new toy. The function $S = -64p^2 + 1600p$ predicts, in dollars, the total sales S as a function of the price p of the toy.
   a. What price will produce the highest total sales?
   b. What is the maximum total sales predicted?

Real-World 🌐 **Connection**

After turning a somersault, the diver followed a parabolic path.

Estimation For each of the graphs below, estimate the area enclosed by the parabola, the x-axis, and the vertical lines $x = 1$ and $x = 7$. Follow the instructions below.

- Count the number of whole grid squares in the region.
- If half a square or more is included in the region, count it as one.
- If less than half a square is included in the region, do *not* count it.
- Add the counted squares to estimate the area.

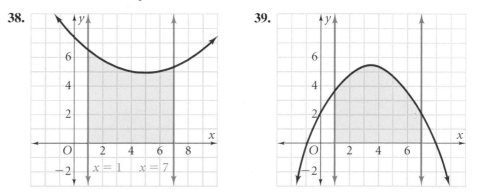

38.

39.

40. Critical Thinking Why is it important to consider the coefficient of the squared term when solving a real-world maximum or minimum problem?

41. Writing Explain how changing the values of a, b, and c in a quadratic function affects the graph of the function.

42. Pets Suppose you have 26 ft of fence and want to build a rectangular enclosure for rabbits. You want to make an enclosure with the greatest possible area.
  a. Write an expression for the width of the rectangle in terms of the length.
  b. Write an equation for the area of the rectangle in terms of the length.
  c. Find the vertex of the parabola described by the equation in part (b).
  d. Which dimensions give the rectangle the greatest area?

C   **Challenge**

43. Sports Suppose a volleyball player serves from 1 m behind the back line. If no other player touches the ball, it will land in bounds. The equation $h = -4.9t^2 + 3.82t + 1.7$ gives the ball's height h in meters in terms of time t in seconds.

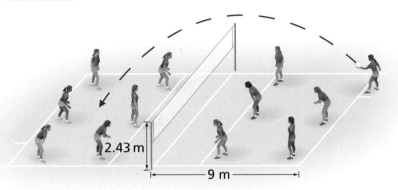

2.43 m
9 m

  a. When will the ball be at its highest point? Round to the nearest tenth of a second.
  b. The ball will reach the net at $t = 0.6$ s. Will it clear the net? Explain.

44. Architecture An architect designs a monument for a new park. The solution of the following system of inequalities describes the shape of the monument. Make a graph of the monument.

$$y \geq -x^2 + 6 \qquad\qquad y \leq -\frac{1}{2}x^2 + 8 \qquad\qquad y \geq 0$$

45. Sports Suppose a tennis player hits a ball over the net. The ball leaves his racket 0.5 m above the ground. The equation $h = -4.9t^2 + 3.8t + 0.5$ gives the ball's height h in meters at time t in seconds.
  a. When will the ball be at the highest point in its path? Round to the nearest tenth of a second.
  b. Critical Thinking If you double the answer from part (a), will you find the amount of time the ball is in the air before it hits the court? Explain.

Real-World **Connection**

A standard tennis court is 78 ft long and 36 ft wide.

46. The parabola shown at the right is of the form $y = x^2 + bx + c$.
  a. Use the graph to find the y-intercept.
  b. Find the equation of the axis of symmetry.
  c. Use the vertex formula $x = \frac{-b}{2a}$ to find b.
  d. Write the equation of the parabola.
  e. Test one point using the equation from part (d).
  f. Critical Thinking Would this method work if the value of a were not known? Explain.

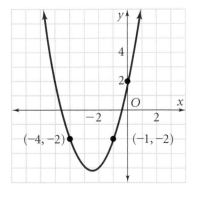

$(-4, -2)$ $(-1, -2)$

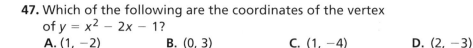
Multiple Choice

47. Which of the following are the coordinates of the vertex of $y = x^2 - 2x - 1$?

A. $(1, -2)$ B. $(0, 3)$ C. $(1, -4)$ D. $(2, -3)$

48. Which of the following parabolas has the greatest *b*-value?

F. $y = -x^2 - 2x$ G. $y = -x^2 - 3x$

H. $y = -x^2 + 2x$ I. $y = -x^2 + 3x$

49. Which of the following is the graph of $y = 0.5x^2 - 2x + 1$?

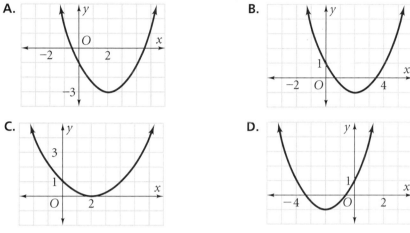

Take It to the NET
Online lesson quiz at
www.PHSchool.com
Web Code: aea-1002

Short Response

50. An arrow is shot into the air. It follows a path given by the equation $y = -0.009x^2 + 0.3x + 4.5$, where *x* and *y* are in feet. Find its maximum height. Show your work.

Mixed Review

Lesson 10-1

Match each graph with its function.

A. $y = \frac{1}{8}x^2 + 2$ B. $y = \frac{1}{2}x^2 + 2$ C. $y = -x^2 - 2$

D. $y = x^2 + 2$ E. $y = -x^2 + 2$ F. $y = -\frac{1}{2}x^2 - 2$

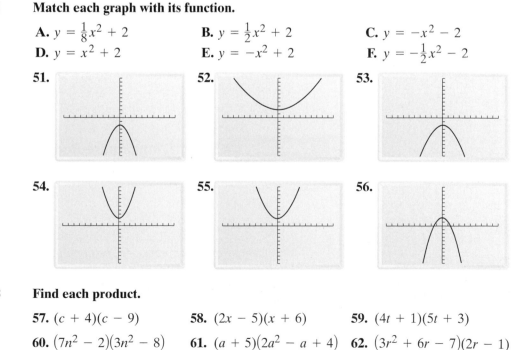

51.   **52.**   **53.**

54.   **55.**   **56.**

Lesson 9-3

Find each product.

57. $(c + 4)(c - 9)$ **58.** $(2x - 5)(x + 6)$ **59.** $(4t + 1)(5t + 3)$

60. $(7n^2 - 2)(3n^2 - 8)$ **61.** $(a + 5)(2a^2 - a + 4)$ **62.** $(3r^2 + 6r - 7)(2r - 1)$

Finding and Estimating Square Roots

Lesson Preview

What You'll Learn

OBJECTIVE 1 To find square roots

OBJECTIVE 2 To estimate and use square roots

. . . And Why

To apply square roots in a real-world situation involving construction, as in Example 5

✓ Check Skills You'll Need

(For help, go to Lessons 1-2 and 8-5.)

Simplify each expression.

1. 11^2 **2.** $(-12)^2$ **3.** $-(12)^2$ **4.** 1.5^2

5. 0.6^2 **6.** $\left(\frac{1}{2}\right)^2$ **7.** $\left(-\frac{2}{3}\right)^2$ **8.** $\left(\frac{4}{5}\right)^2$

New Vocabulary • square root • principal square root • negative square root • radicand • perfect squares

---

OBJECTIVE

1 **Finding Square Roots**

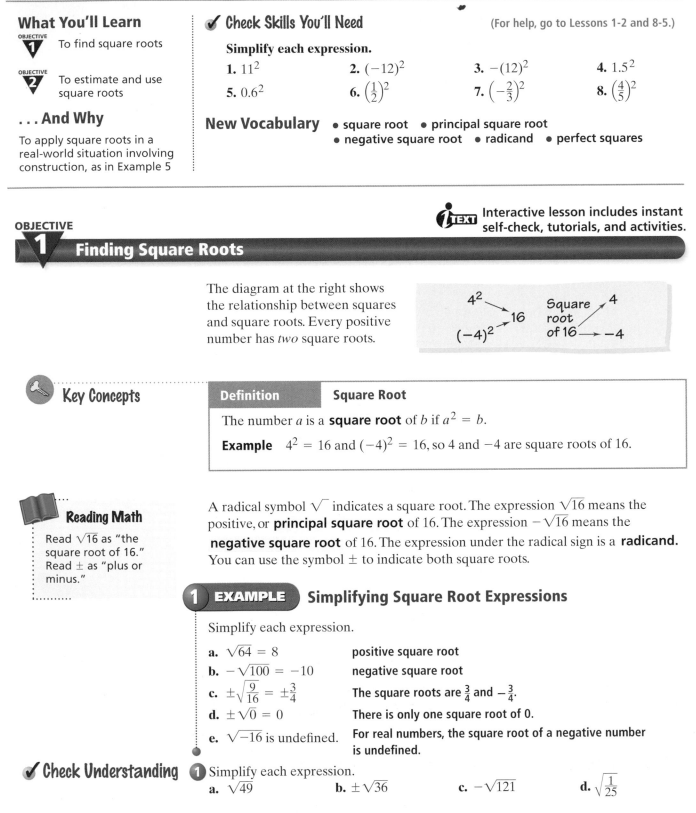

> 🔘 Interactive lesson includes instant self-check, tutorials, and activities.

The diagram at the right shows the relationship between squares and square roots. Every positive number has *two* square roots.

$$4^2 \longrightarrow 16 \qquad \text{Square root} \longrightarrow 4$$
$$(-4)^2 \longrightarrow 16 \qquad \text{of } 16 \longrightarrow -4$$

🔑 Key Concepts

Definition	**Square Root**

The number a is a **square root** of b if $a^2 = b$.

Example $4^2 = 16$ and $(-4)^2 = 16$, so 4 and -4 are square roots of 16.

📖 Reading Math

Read $\sqrt{16}$ as "the square root of 16." Read $\pm$ as "plus or minus."

A radical symbol $\sqrt{}$ indicates a square root. The expression $\sqrt{16}$ means the positive, or **principal square root** of 16. The expression $-\sqrt{16}$ means the **negative square root** of 16. The expression under the radical sign is a **radicand**. You can use the symbol $\pm$ to indicate both square roots.

1 EXAMPLE Simplifying Square Root Expressions

Simplify each expression.

a. $\sqrt{64} = 8$ positive square root

b. $-\sqrt{100} = -10$ negative square root

c. $\pm\sqrt{\frac{9}{16}} = \pm\frac{3}{4}$ The square roots are $\frac{3}{4}$ and $-\frac{3}{4}$.

d. $\pm\sqrt{0} = 0$ There is only one square root of 0.

e. $\sqrt{-16}$ is undefined.   For real numbers, the square root of a negative number is undefined.

✓ Check Understanding

1 Simplify each expression.

a. $\sqrt{49}$ **b.** $\pm\sqrt{36}$ **c.** $-\sqrt{121}$ **d.** $\sqrt{\frac{1}{25}}$

Some square roots are rational numbers and some are irrational numbers.

Rational: $\sqrt{100} = 10$ $\pm\sqrt{0.36} = \pm0.6$ $\sqrt{\frac{16}{121}} = \frac{4}{11}$

Irrational: $\sqrt{10} \approx 3.16227766$ $\sqrt{\frac{1}{7}} \approx 0.377964473$

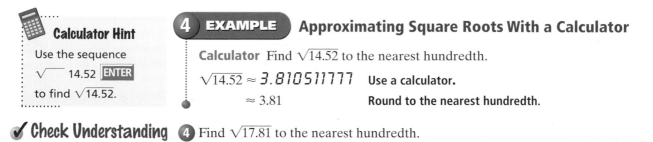

Need Help?

In decimal form a *rational* number terminates or repeats. In decimal form an *irrational* number continues without repeating.

2 EXAMPLE Rational and Irrational Square Roots

Tell whether each expression is *rational* or *irrational*.

a. $\pm\sqrt{81} = \pm9$ rational

b. $-\sqrt{1.44} = -1.2$ rational

c. $-\sqrt{5} \approx -2.23606797$ irrational

d. $\sqrt{\frac{4}{9}} = \frac{2}{3}$ rational

e. $\sqrt{\frac{1}{3}} \approx 0.57735026$ irrational

✓ **Check Understanding** ② Tell whether each expression is *rational* or *irrational*.

a. $\sqrt{8}$ **b.** $\pm\sqrt{225}$ **c.** $-\sqrt{75}$ **d.** $\sqrt{\frac{1}{4}}$

OBJECTIVE

2 Estimating and Using Square Roots

The squares of integers are called **perfect squares.**

consecutive integers:	1	2	3	4	5	6
	↓	↓	↓	↓	↓	↓
consecutive perfect squares:	1	4	9	16	25	36

You can estimate square roots by using perfect squares.

3 EXAMPLE Estimating Square Roots

Estimation Between what two consecutive integers is $\sqrt{14.52}$?

$\sqrt{9} < \sqrt{14.52} < \sqrt{16}$ **14.52 is between the two consecutive perfect squares 9 and 16.**

↓   ↓   ↓

$3 < \sqrt{14.52} < 4$ **The square roots of 9 and 16 are 3 and 4, respectively.**

$\sqrt{14.52}$ is between 3 and 4.

✓ **Check Understanding** ③ Between what two consecutive integers is $-\sqrt{105}$?

You can find the approximate value of a square root using a calculator.

Calculator Hint

Use the sequence

$\sqrt{}$ 14.52 [ENTER]

to find $\sqrt{14.52}$.

4 EXAMPLE Approximating Square Roots With a Calculator

Calculator Find $\sqrt{14.52}$ to the nearest hundredth.

$\sqrt{14.52} \approx 3.810511777$ **Use a calculator.**

     ≈ 3.81 **Round to the nearest hundredth.**

✓ **Check Understanding** ④ Find $\sqrt{17.81}$ to the nearest hundredth.

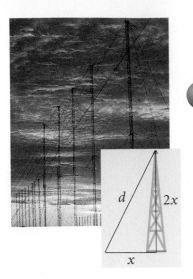

Many real-world formulas involve square roots.

5 EXAMPLE **Real-World Problem Solving**

Construction The formula $d = \sqrt{x^2 + (2x)^2}$ gives the length d of each wire for the tower at the left. Find the length of the wire if $x = 12$ ft.

$d = \sqrt{x^2 + (2x)^2}$

$d = \sqrt{12^2 + (2 \cdot 12)^2}$ **Substitute 12 for x.**

$d = \sqrt{144 + 576}$ **Simplify.**

$d = \sqrt{720}$

$d \approx 26.8$ **Use a calculator. Round to the nearest tenth.**

The wire is about 26.8 ft long.

✓ **Check Understanding** ⑤ Suppose the tower is 140 ft tall. How long is the supporting wire? Round to the nearest tenth of a foot.

EXERCISES

For more practice, see *Extra Practice*.

Practice and Problem Solving

Ⓐ Practice by Example

Example 1
(page 524)

Simplify each expression.

1. $\sqrt{169}$ **2.** $\sqrt{400}$ **3.** $\sqrt{\frac{1}{9}}$ **4.** $\sqrt{900}$

5. $\sqrt{0.25}$ **6.** $\sqrt{\frac{36}{49}}$ **7.** $-\sqrt{1.21}$ **8.** $\sqrt{1.96}$

9. $\sqrt{0.36}$ **10.** $-\sqrt{144}$ **11.** $\sqrt{\frac{25}{16}}$ **12.** $\pm\sqrt{0.01}$

Example 2
(page 525)

Tell whether each expression is *rational* or *irrational*.

13. $\sqrt{37}$ **14.** $-\sqrt{0.04}$ **15.** $\pm\sqrt{\frac{1}{5}}$ **16.** $-\sqrt{\frac{16}{121}}$

Example 3
(page 525)

Between what two consecutive integers is each square root?

17. $\sqrt{35}$ **18.** $\sqrt{27}$ **19.** $-\sqrt{130}$ **20.** $\sqrt{170}$

Example 4
(page 525)

Use a calculator to find each square root to the nearest hundredth.

21. $\sqrt{12}$ **22.** $-\sqrt{203}$ **23.** $\sqrt{11,550}$ **24.** $-\sqrt{150}$

Example 5
(page 526)

25. Sports The elasticity coefficient e of a ball relates the height r of its rebound to the height h from which it is dropped. You can use the function $e = \sqrt{\frac{r}{h}}$ to find the elasticity coefficient. What is the elasticity coefficient of a tennis ball that rebounds 3 ft after it is dropped from a height of 3.5 ft? Round to the nearest hundredth.

Ⓑ Apply Your Skills

Find the square root(s) of each number.

26. 400   **27.** 0   **28.** 625   **29.** $\frac{9}{49}$

30. 1.69   **31.** $\frac{1}{81}$ **32.** 729   **33.** 2.25

34. 256   **35.** 0.01   **36.** $\frac{64}{121}$ **37.** 40804

38. Critical Thinking What number other than 0 is its own square root?

39. Space The formula

$$d = \sqrt{12{,}800h + h^2}$$

gives the distance d in kilometers to the horizon from a satellite h kilometers above Earth.

a. Find the distance to the horizon from a satellite 4200 km above Earth. Round to the nearest kilometer.

b. Find the distance to the horizon from a satellite 3600 km above Earth. Round to the nearest kilometer.

Find the value of each expression. If necessary, round to the nearest hundredth.

40. $\sqrt{441}$

41. $-\sqrt{\dfrac{4}{25}}$

42. $\sqrt{2}$

43. $\sqrt{1.6}$

44. $-\sqrt{30}$

45. $-\sqrt{1089}$

46. $-\sqrt{0.64}$

47. $\sqrt{41}$

48. $\sqrt{75}$

49. Writing Explain the difference between $-\sqrt{1}$ and $\sqrt{1}$.

50. Open-Ended Find two integers a and b between 1 and 20 such that $a^2 + b^2$ is a perfect square.

51. In the cartoon, to what number is the golfer referring?

Challenge **52. Physics** If you drop an object, the time t in seconds that it takes to fall d feet is given by the formula $t = \sqrt{\dfrac{d}{16}}$.

a. Find the time it takes an object to fall 400 ft.

b. Find the time it takes an object to fall 1600 ft.

c. Critical Thinking In part (b), the object falls four times as far as in part (a). Does it take four times as long to fall? Explain.

Critical Thinking For Exercises 53–58, tell whether each statement is *true* or *false*. If the statement is false, give a counterexample.

53. Every nonnegative number has two square roots.

54. The square root of a positive number is always less than the number.

55. The square root of an even perfect square is always an even number.

56. If a number is the product of two perfect squares, it has a rational square root.

57. $\sqrt{p} + \sqrt{q} = \sqrt{p + q}$

58. If $\sqrt{p}$ and $\sqrt{q}$ are both irrational, then $\sqrt{pq}$ is always an irrational number.

Problem Solving Hint

For Exercise 54, use positive values less than 1, equal to 1, and greater than 1 to help you solve the problem.

59. a. What is the total area of the large square shown at the right?
   b. What is the area of each shaded triangle?
   c. What is the area of the shaded square?
   d. What is the length of the diagonal of each 1×1 square?

Gridded Response

60. Find the value of $\sqrt{1.69}$.

61. Simplify the following expression. $\sqrt{4^2 + 3^2 + 11}$

62. Find the value of $\sqrt{\frac{4}{81}}$.

63. Round $\sqrt{80}$ to the nearest whole number.

64. The formula $\ell = \sqrt{\frac{A}{6}}$ relates the surface area A of a cube to the length of its edge ℓ. A cube has a surface area of 726 cm². How many centimeters is the length of the edge?

65. Find the area of the shaded region.

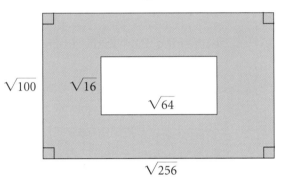

Take It to the NET
Online lesson quiz at
www.PHSchool.com
····· Web Code: aea-1003

Lesson 10-2

Graph each function. Label the axis of symmetry and the vertex.

66. $y = x^2 + 4x + 3$ **67.** $y = x^2 + 2$

68. $y = 2x^2 - 8x - 5$ **69.** $y = -x^2 + 6x - 1$

70. $y = 6x^2 - 12x + 1$ **71.** $y = -3x^2 + 18x$

Lesson 9-4

Simplify each expression.

72. $(d + 9)(d - 9)$ **73.** $(3t - 5)(3t + 5)$ **74.** $85 \cdot 95$

75. $(x + 13)^2$ **76.** $(4y - 7)^2$ **77.** 101^2

78. 902^2 **79.** $(6k - 7)(6k + 7)$ **80.** $(12b - 7)^2$

Lesson 8-1

Evaluate each expression for $x = 3$, $y = -2$, and $z = 6$.

81. $x^{-2}y^{-1}z^2$ **82.** $\dfrac{y^{-2}}{x^{-3}z^2}$ **83.** $\dfrac{x^0y^{-3}}{z^{-1}}$

84. $\dfrac{x^2y^{-1}}{z^{-3}}$ **85.** $x^{-1}y^{-2}z^0$ **86.** $x^2y^{-4}z^2$

Solving Quadratic Equations

Lesson Preview

What You'll Learn

OBJECTIVE 1
To solve quadratic equations by graphing

OBJECTIVE 2
To solve quadratic equations using square roots

. . . And Why

To use square roots in a real-world situation involving city planning, as in Example 3

✓ Check Skills You'll Need

(For help, go to Lesson 10-3.)

Simplify each expression.

1. $\sqrt{36}$ **2.** $-\sqrt{81}$ **3.** $\pm\sqrt{121}$

4. $\sqrt{1.44}$ **5.** $\sqrt{0.25}$ **6.** $\pm\sqrt{1.21}$

7. $\sqrt{\frac{1}{4}}$ **8.** $\pm\sqrt{\frac{1}{9}}$ **9.** $\sqrt{\frac{49}{100}}$

New Vocabulary

• quadratic equation   • standard form of a quadratic equation

---

OBJECTIVE

1 **Solving Quadratic Equations by Graphing**

iTEXT Interactive lesson includes instant self-check, tutorials, and activities.

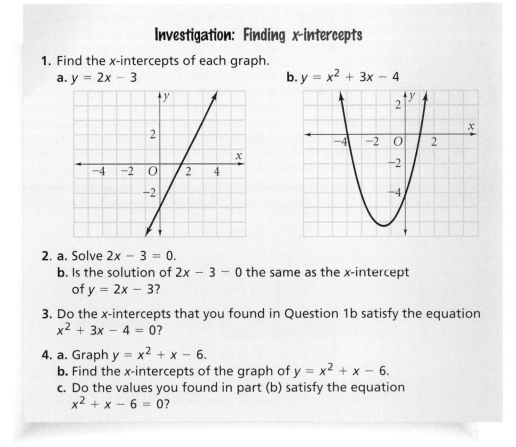

Investigation: Finding x-intercepts

1. Find the x-intercepts of each graph.

    a. $y = 2x - 3$ **b.** $y = x^2 + 3x - 4$

2. **a.** Solve $2x - 3 = 0$.
    b. Is the solution of $2x - 3 = 0$ the same as the x-intercept of $y = 2x - 3$?

3. Do the x-intercepts that you found in Question 1b satisfy the equation $x^2 + 3x - 4 = 0$?

4. **a.** Graph $y = x^2 + x - 6$.
    b. Find the x-intercepts of the graph of $y = x^2 + x - 6$.
    c. Do the values you found in part (b) satisfy the equation $x^2 + x - 6 = 0$?

The equation $x^2 + 3x - 4 = 0$ is called a quadratic equation, and its related quadratic function is $y = x^2 + 3x - 4$. The solutions of a quadratic equation and the x-intercepts of its related quadratic function are the same.

Definition	Standard Form of a Quadratic Equation

A **quadratic equation** is an equation that can be written in the form $ax^2 + bx + c = 0$, where $a \neq 0$. This form is called the **standard form of a quadratic equation.**

A quadratic equation can have two, one, or no real-number solutions. In a future course you will learn about solutions of quadratic equations that are not real numbers. In this course *solutions* refers to real-number solutions.

You can solve some quadratic equations by graphing their related functions.

1 EXAMPLE Solving by Graphing

Solve each equation by graphing the related function.

a. $x^2 - 4 = 0$
Graph $y = x^2 - 4$.

b. $x^2 = 0$
Graph $y = x^2$.

c. $x^2 + 4 = 0$
Graph $y = x^2 + 4$.

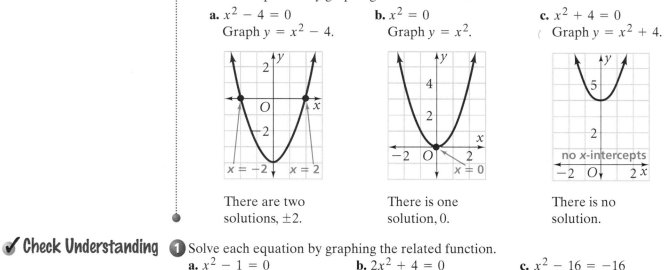

There are two solutions, ± 2.

There is one solution, 0.

There is no solution.

✓ **Check Understanding** ❶ Solve each equation by graphing the related function.
a. $x^2 - 1 = 0$ **b.** $2x^2 + 4 = 0$ **c.** $x^2 - 16 = -16$

OBJECTIVE

2 Solving Quadratic Equations Using Square Roots

You can solve equations of the form $x^2 = a$ by finding the square roots of each side. Since $6^2 = 36$ and $(-6)^2 = 36$ are both true statements, 6 and -6 are both solutions to the equation $x^2 = 36$. We write the solution to $x^2 = 36$ as $\pm\sqrt{36}$ or ± 6.

2 EXAMPLE Using Square Roots

Solve $2x^2 - 98 = 0$.

$2x^2 - 98 + 98 = 0 + 98$ **Add 98 to each side.**

$2x^2 = 98$

$x^2 = 49$ **Divide each side by 2.**

$x = \pm\sqrt{49}$ **Find the square roots.**

$x = \pm 7$ **Simplify.**

✓ **Check Understanding** ❷ Solve each equation.
a. $t^2 - 25 = 0$ **b.** $3n^2 + 12 = 12$ **c.** $2g^2 + 32 = 0$

You can solve real-world problems by finding square roots. In many cases, the negative solution of a quadratic equation will not be a reasonable solution to the original problem.

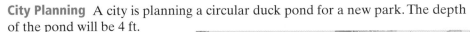

3 EXAMPLE **Real-World Problem Solving**

City Planning A city is planning a circular duck pond for a new park. The depth of the pond will be 4 ft. Because of water resources, the maximum volume will be 20,000 ft^3. Find the radius of the pond. Use the equation $V = \pi r^2 h$, where V is the volume, r is the radius, and h is the depth.

$$V = \pi r^2 h$$

$20{,}000 = \pi r^2(4)$ **Substitute 20,000 for V and 4 for h.**

$\dfrac{20{,}000}{(\pi \cdot 4)} = r^2$ **Put in calculator-ready form.**

$\sqrt{\dfrac{20{,}000}{(\pi \cdot 4)}} = r$ **Find the principal square root.**

$39.89422804 \approx r$ **Use a calculator.**

● The pond will have a radius of about 39.9 ft.

Real-World Connection

Ponds and fountains enhance the quality of life in cities around the world.

✓ **Check Understanding** ❸ A city is planning a circular fountain. The depth of the fountain will be 3 ft. The maximum volume will be 1800 ft^3. Find the radius of the fountain.

EXERCISES

For more practice, see *Extra Practice.*

Practice and Problem Solving

Ⓐ Practice by Example

Example 1
(page 530)

Solve each equation by graphing the related function. If the equation has no solution, write *no solution*.

1. $x^2 - 9 = 0$ **2.** $x^2 + 5 = 0$ **3.** $4x^2 = 0$

4. $2x^2 - 8 = 0$ **5.** $x^2 + 16 = 0$ **6.** $\frac{1}{3}x^2 - 3 = 0$

7. $\frac{1}{2}x^2 + 1 = 0$ **8.** $x^2 + 7 = 7$ **9.** $\frac{1}{4}x^2 - 1 = 0$

Example 2
(page 530)

Solve each equation by finding square roots. If the equation has no solution, write *no solution*.

10. $k^2 = 49$ **11.** $b^2 = 441$ **12.** $m^2 - 225 = 0$

13. $c^2 + 25 = 25$ **14.** $x^2 - 9 = -16$ **15.** $4r^2 = 25$

16. $64p^2 = 4$ **17.** $6w^2 - 24 = 0$ **18.** $27 - y^2 = 0$

Example 3
(page 531)

Model each problem with a quadratic equation. Then solve. If necessary, round to the nearest tenth.

19. Find the side of a square with an area of 256 m^2.

20. Find the side of a square with an area of 90 ft^2.

21. Find the radius of a circle with an area of 80 cm^2.

B **Apply Your Skills** 22. **Geometry** Suppose a map company wants to produce a globe with a surface area of 450 in.². Use the formula $A = 4\pi r^2$, where A is the surface area and r is the radius of the sphere.
 a. What should the radius be? Round to the nearest tenth of an inch.
 b. Critical Thinking Why is the principal square root the only root that makes sense in this situation?

Mental Math **Tell the number of solutions each equation has.**

23. $y^2 = -36$ **24.** $a^2 - 12 = 6$ **25.** $n^2 - 15 = -15$

26. **Framing** Find dimensions for the square picture at the right that would make the area of the picture equal to 75% of the total area enclosed by the frame. Round to the nearest tenth of an inch.

27. Suppose you have a can of paint that will cover 400 ft².
 a. Find the radius of the largest circle you can paint. Round to the nearest tenth of a foot. (*Hint:* Use the formula $A = \pi r^2$.)
 b. Suppose you have two cans of paint, which will cover a total of 800 ft². Find the radius of the largest circle you can paint. Round to the nearest tenth of a foot.
 c. Critical Thinking Does the radius of the circle double when the amount of paint doubles? Explain.

Solve each equation by finding square roots. If the equation has no solution, write *no solution.* **If the value is irrational, round to the nearest tenth.**

28. $1.2q^2 - 7 = -34$ **29.** $49t^2 - 16 = -7$ **30.** $3d^2 - \frac{1}{12} = 0$
31. $\frac{1}{2}x^2 - 4 = 0$ **32.** $7h^2 + 0.12 = 1.24$ **33.** $-\frac{1}{4}x^2 + 3 = 0$

34. **Physics** The equation $d = \frac{1}{2}at^2$ gives the distance d an object starting at rest travels given acceleration a and time t.
 Suppose a ball rolls down the ramp shown at the right with acceleration $a = 2$ ft/s². Find the time it will take to roll from the top of the ramp to the bottom. Round to the nearest tenth of a second.

35. Find a value for c such that the equation $x^2 - c = 0$ has 11 and -11 as solutions.

36. **a. Critical Thinking** For what values of n will $x^2 = n$ have two solutions?
 b. For what value of n will $x^2 = n$ have exactly one solution?
 c. For what values of n will $x^2 = n$ have no solution?

37. **Error Analysis** Michael's work is shown at the right. Explain the error that he made.

$$x^2 + 25 = 0$$
$$x^2 = 25$$
$$x = \pm 5$$

38. **a.** Solve $x^2 - 4 = 0$ and $2x^2 - 8 = 0$ by graphing their related functions.
 b. Critical Thinking Why does it make sense that the graphs have the same x-intercepts?

BIKE CLUB

39. **Design** Suppose your class wants to design a T-shirt logo similar to the one shown at the left. You want the shaded region to have an area of 80 in.^{2}.
   a. Write expressions for the area of the square and of the circle.
   b. Write an equation for the area of the shaded region.
   c. Solve the equation to find the radius of the circle and the side of the square. Round to the nearest tenth of an inch.

40. **Open-Ended** Write and solve equations in the form $ax^2 + c = 0$ for each of the following.
   a. The equation has no solutions.
   b. The equation has one solution.
   c. The equation has two solutions.

Geometry Find the value of h for each triangle. If necessary, round to the nearest tenth.

41.

20 ft^2

h

h

42.

h

120 cm^2

$2h$

C **Challenge** 43. **Physics** The time t a pendulum takes to make a complete swing back and forth depends on the length of the pendulum. The formula $\ell = \frac{2.45t^2}{\pi^2}$ relates the length of a pendulum ℓ in meters to the time t in seconds.
   a. Find the length of the pendulum if $t = 1$ s. Round to the nearest tenth.
   b. Find t if $\ell = 1.6$ m. Round to the nearest tenth.
   c. Find t if $\ell = 2.2$ m. Round to the nearest tenth.
   d. **Writing** You can adjust a clock that has a pendulum by making the pendulum longer or shorter. If a clock is running slowly, would you lengthen or shorten the pendulum to make the clock run faster? Explain.

44. a. Solve the equation $(x + 7)^2 = 0$.
   b. Find the vertex of the related function $y = (x + 7)^2$.
   c. **Open-Ended** Choose a value for h and repeat parts (a) and (b) using $(x + h)^2 = 0$ and $y = (x + h)^2$.
   d. Where would you expect to find the vertex of $y = (x - 4)^2$? Explain.

45. **Geometry** The trapezoid has an area of 1960 cm^2. Use the formula $A = \frac{1}{2}h(b_1 + b_2)$ to find the value of y.

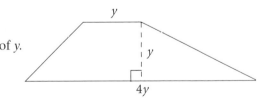

y

y

$4y$

Standardized Test Prep

Multiple Choice 46. Which of the following shows all of the real solutions of $3x^2 - 48 = 0$?
   A. 4   **B.** -4, 4   **C.** -16, 16   **D.** no solution

47. For which of the following values of c does $5x^2 + c = 10$ have no real solutions?
   F. 1   **G.** 5   **H.** 9   **I.** 12

48. The x-intercepts of the graph at the right are solutions to which equation?
  A. $-0.25x^2 = 4$ **B.** $-0.25x^2 + 4 = 0$
  C. $-0.5x^2 + 2 = 0$ **D.** $-4x^2 + 1 = 0$

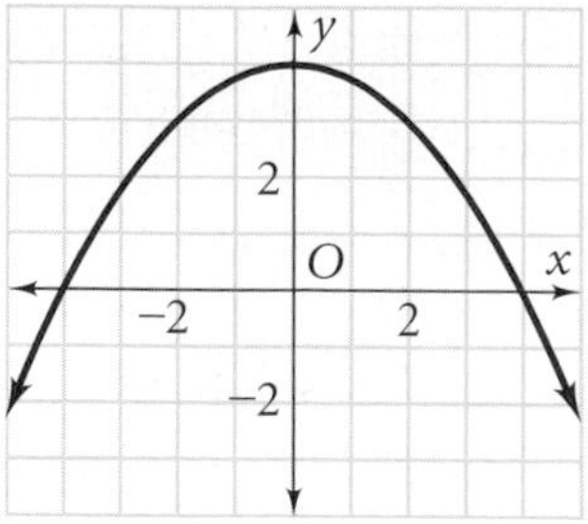

Short Response

49. Make a table for the function $y = 3x^2 - 7$. Graph the function. Estimate the value of the x-intercepts.

Extended Response

50. The surface area of a cube is 96 ft^2.
  a. Find the length of each edge. Show your work.
  b. If you double the length of each edge, what happens to the surface area of the cube? Show your work.

Take It to the NET
Online lesson quiz at
www.PHSchool.com
Web Code: aea-1004

Mixed Review

Lesson 10-3

Simplify each expression.

51. $\sqrt{9}$ **52.** $-\sqrt{169}$ **53.** $\sqrt{1600}$ **54.** $\sqrt{225}$

55. $\sqrt{0.04}$ **56.** $-\sqrt{2.56}$ **57.** $\sqrt{\dfrac{25}{64}}$ **58.** $\sqrt{\dfrac{49}{81}}$

Lesson 9-5

Factor each expression.

59. $x^2 + 5x + 4$ **60.** $y^2 - 15y + 26$ **61.** $a^2 + 3a - 10$

62. $z^2 - 6z - 72$ **63.** $c^2 - 14cd + 24d^2$ **64.** $t^2 + tu - 2u^2$

Lesson 8-2

Write each number in scientific notation.

65. 3,613,500   **66.** 0.0000348   **67.** -8.12

Write each number in standard notation.

68. 3.1×10^4 **69.** 7.01×10^5 **70.** 6.2×10^{-4}

✓ Checkpoint Quiz 1   Lessons 10-1 through 10-4

TEXT Instant self-check quiz online and on CD-ROM

Graph each function. Label the axis of symmetry and the vertex.

1. $y = x^2 - 4$ **2.** $y = 8x^2 - 2x$ **3.** $f(x) = x^2 + 5x - 6$

4. A ball is thrown up in the air. Its height h in feet after t seconds is given by the function $h = -16t^2 + 24t + 6$.
  a. When does the ball reach its maximum height?
  b. What is the ball's maximum height?

Simplify each expression.

5. $\sqrt{100}$ **6.** $\pm\sqrt{0.36}$ **7.** $-\sqrt{4}$

Solve each equation.

8. $t^2 - 64 = 0$ **9.** $6m^2 - 150 = 0$

10. Solve $3x^2 - 27 = 0$ by graphing the related function.

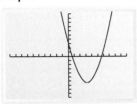

Technology

Finding Roots

The solutions of a quadratic equation are the *x*-intercepts of the related quadratic function. The solutions of a quadratic equation and the related *x*-intercepts are often called *roots* of the equation or *zeros* of the function.

Take It to the NET
Graphing Calculator procedures online at **www.PHSchool.com**
Web Code: aea-2110

EXAMPLE

Use a graphing calculator to solve $x^2 - 6x + 3 = 0$.

Step 1

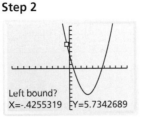

Enter $y = x^2 - 6x + 3$. Use the **CALC** feature. Select 2:ZERO. The calculator will plot the graph.

Step 2

Left bound?
X=-.4255319 Y=5.7342689

Move the cursor to the left of the first *x*-intercept. Press ENTER to set the left bound.

Step 3

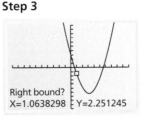

Right bound?
X=1.0638298 Y=2.251245

Move the cursor slightly to the right of the intercept. Press ENTER to set the right bound.

Step 4

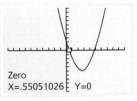

Zero
X=.55051026 Y=0

Press ENTER to display the first root, which is about 0.55.

Repeating the steps near the second intercept, you find that the second root is about 5.45. So the solutions are about 0.55 and 5.45.

Suppose you cannot see both of the *x*-intercepts on your graph. You can find the values of *y* that are close to zero by using the **TABLE** feature. You can use the **TBLSET** feature to control how the table behaves. Set ΔTbl to 0.5. Set **Indpnt:** and **Depend:** to **Auto**. The calculator screen at the right shows part of the table for $y = 2x^2 - 48x + 285$.

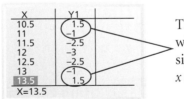

X	Y1
10.5	1.5
11	−1
11.5	−2.5
12	−3
12.5	−2.5
13	−1
13.5	1.5
X=13.5	

The graph crosses the *x*-axis when the values for *y* change signs. So the range of values of *x* should include 10.5 and 13.5.

EXERCISES

1. Find the *x*-intercepts of $y = 2x^2 - 48x + 285$. First use the WINDOW feature. Change **Xmin** to 10 and **Xmax** to 14.

Use a graphing calculator to solve each equation.

2. $x^2 - 6x - 16 = 0$

3. $2x^2 + x - 6 = 0$

4. $\frac{1}{3}x^2 + 8x - 3 = 0$

5. $x^2 - 18x + 5 = 0$

6. $0.25x^2 - 8x - 45 = 0$

7. $0.5x^2 + 3x - 36 = 0$

8. **Geometry** A rectangle has a length of *x* and a width of $2x + 3$. It has an area of 200 cm².
   a. Write an equation using the dimensions and the area.
   b. Graph the related function using a graphing calculator.
   c. Find the dimensions of the rectangle. Round to the nearest hundredth.

Factoring to Solve Quadratic Equations

Lesson Preview

What You'll Learn

OBJECTIVE

1 To solve quadratic equations by factoring

...And Why

To find the dimensions of a box, as in Example 4

✓ Check Skills You'll Need

(For help, go to Lessons 2-2 and 9-6.)

Solve and check each equation.

1. $6 + 4n = 2$
2. $\frac{a}{8} - 9 = 4$
3. $7q + 16 = -3$

Factor each expression.

4. $2c^2 + 29c + 14$
5. $3p^2 + 32p + 20$
6. $4x^2 - 21x - 18$

New Vocabulary • Zero-Product Property

OBJECTIVE

🄸TEXT Interactive lesson includes instant self-check, tutorials, and activities.

1 Solving Quadratic Equations

In the previous lesson, you solved quadratic equations by finding square roots. This method works if $b = 0$. You can solve some quadratic equations when $b \neq 0$ by using the Zero-Product Property.

🔑 **Key Concepts**

Property	**Zero-Product Property**

For every real number a and b, if $ab = 0$, then $a = 0$ or $b = 0$.

Example If $(x + 3)(x + 2) = 0$, then $x + 3 = 0$ or $x + 2 = 0$.

1 EXAMPLE Using the Zero-Product Property

Solve $(x + 5)(2x - 6) = 0$.

$(x + 5)(2x - 6) = 0$

$x + 5 = 0$ or $2x - 6 = 0$ **Use the Zero-Product Property.**

$2x = 6$ **Solve for x.**

$x = -5$ or $x = 3$

Check Substitute -5 for x.   Substitute 3 for x.

$(x + 5)(2x - 6) = 0$ $(x + 5)(2x - 6) = 0$

$(-5 + 5)[2(-5) - 6] \stackrel{?}{=} 0$ $(3 + 5)[2(3) - 6] \stackrel{?}{=} 0$

$(0)(-16) = 0 ✓$ $(8)(0) = 0 ✓$

✓ **Check Understanding** **1** Solve each equation.

a. $(x + 7)(x - 4) = 0$
b. $(3y - 5)(y - 2) = 0$
c. $(6k + 9)(4k - 11) = 0$

You can also use the Zero-Product Property to solve equations of the form $ax^2 + bx + c = 0$ if the quadratic expression $ax^2 + bx + c$ can be factored.

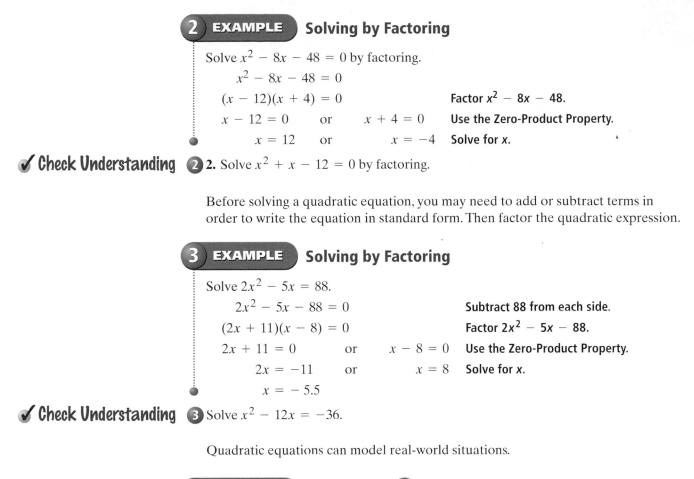

2 EXAMPLE Solving by Factoring

Solve $x^2 - 8x - 48 = 0$ by factoring.

$x^2 - 8x - 48 = 0$

$(x - 12)(x + 4) = 0$ — Factor $x^2 - 8x - 48$.

$x - 12 = 0$ or $x + 4 = 0$ — Use the Zero-Product Property.

$x = 12$ or $x = -4$ — Solve for x.

✓ **Check Understanding** 2 **2.** Solve $x^2 + x - 12 = 0$ by factoring.

Before solving a quadratic equation, you may need to add or subtract terms in order to write the equation in standard form. Then factor the quadratic expression.

3 EXAMPLE Solving by Factoring

Solve $2x^2 - 5x = 88$.

$2x^2 - 5x - 88 = 0$ — Subtract 88 from each side.

$(2x + 11)(x - 8) = 0$ — Factor $2x^2 - 5x - 88$.

$2x + 11 = 0$ or $x - 8 = 0$ — Use the Zero-Product Property.

$2x = -11$ or $x = 8$ — Solve for x.

$x = -5.5$

✓ **Check Understanding** 3 Solve $x^2 - 12x = -36$.

Quadratic equations can model real-world situations.

4 EXAMPLE Real-World 🌐 Problem Solving

Manufacturing The diagram shows a pattern for an open-top box. The total area of the sheet of material used to manufacture the box is 288 in.² The height of the box is 3 in. Therefore, 3-in. × 3-in. squares are cut from each corner. Find the dimensions of the box.

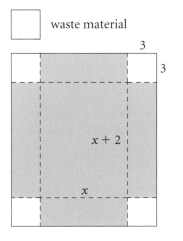

waste material

3

3

$x + 2$

x

Define Let x = width of a side of the box.
Then the width of the material = $x + 3 + 3 = x + 6$.
The length of the material = $x + 2 + 3 + 3 = x + 8$.

Relate length × width = area of the sheet

Write $(x + 8)(x + 6) = 288$

$(x + 8)(x + 6) = 288$

$x^2 + 14x + 48 = 288$ — Find the product $(x + 8)(x + 6)$.

$x^2 + 14x - 240 = 0$ — Subtract 288 from each side.

$(x + 24)(x - 10) = 0$ — Factor $x^2 + 14x - 240$.

$x + 24 = 0$ or $x - 10 = 0$ — Use the Zero-Product Property.

$x = -24$ or $x = 10$ — Solve for x.

The only reasonable solution is 10. So the dimensions of the box are 10 in. × 12 in. × 3 in.

✓ **Check Understanding** 4 Suppose that a box has a base with a width of x, a length of $x + 1$, and a height of 2 in. It is cut from a rectangular sheet of material with an area of 182 in.² Find the dimensions of the box.

EXERCISES

For more practice, see *Extra Practice*.

Practice and Problem Solving

A **Practice by Example**

Example 1
(page 536)

Use the Zero-Product Property to solve each equation.

1. $(x - 3)(x - 7) = 0$ **2.** $(x + 4)(2x - 9) = 0$ **3.** $t(t + 1) = 0$

4. $-3n(2n - 5) = 0$ **5.** $(7x + 2)(5x + 4) = 0$ **6.** $(4a - 7)(3a + 8) = 0$

Example 2
(page 537)

Solve by factoring.

7. $b^2 + 3b - 4 = 0$ **8.** $m^2 - 5m - 14 = 0$ **9.** $w^2 - 8w = 0$

10. $x^2 - 16x + 55 = 0$ **11.** $k^2 - 3k - 10 = 0$ **12.** $n^2 + n - 12 = 0$

Example 3
(page 537)

13. $x^2 + 8x = -15$ **14.** $t^2 - 3t = 28$ **15.** $n^2 = 6n$

16. $2c^2 - 7c = -5$ **17.** $3q^2 + 16q = -5$ **18.** $4y^2 = 25$

19. $5q^2 + 18q = 8$ **20.** $2z^2 - 10z = -12$ **21.** $12 = 2x^2 + 5x$

Example 4
(page 537)

22. Geometry The sides of a square are all increased by 3 cm. The area of the new square is 64 cm^2. Find the length of a side of the original square.

23. Geometry A rectangular box has volume 280 in.^{3}. Its dimensions are 4 in. $\times$ $(n + 2)$ in. $\times$ $(n + 5)$ in. Find n. Use the formula $V = \ell wh$.

24. Construction You are building a rectangular wading pool. You want the area of the bottom to be 90 ft^2. You want the length of the pool to be 3 ft longer than twice its width. What will the dimensions of the pool be?

25. Sailing Suppose the area of the sail shown in the photo at the left is 110 ft^2. Find the dimensions of the sail.

26. The product of two consecutive numbers is 14 less than 10 times the smaller number. Find each number.

2x + 2

x

B **Apply Your Skills**

Write each equation in standard form. Then solve.

27. $2q^2 + 22q = -60$ **28.** $4 = -5n + 6n^2$

29. $6y^2 + 12y + 13 = 2y^2 + 4$ **30.** $3a^2 + 4a = 2a^2 - 2a - 9$

31. $3t^2 + 8t = t^2 - 3t - 12$ **32.** $4x^2 + 20 = 10x + 3x^2 - 4$

33. $2k^2 - 3 + 12k = k + 60$ **34.** $15y^2 + 45y - 9 = 4y - 5y^2$

35. Manufacturing The length of an open box is 2 in. greater than its width. The box was made from an 80 in.^{2} rectangular sheet of material. The height of the box is 1 in. Therefore 1-in. $\times$ 1-in. squares are cut from each corner. What were the dimensions of the original sheet of material? (*Hint:* Draw a diagram.)

36. Baseball Suppose you throw a baseball into the air with an initial upward velocity of 29 ft/s and an initial height of 6 ft. The formula $h = -16t^2 + 29t + 6$ gives the ball's height h in feet at time t in seconds.
   a. The ball's height h is 0 when it is on the ground. Find the number of seconds that pass before the ball lands by solving $0 = -16t^2 + 29t + 6$.
   b. Graphing Calculator Graph the related function for the equation in part (a). Use your graph to estimate how high the ball is tossed.

37. Writing Summarize the procedure for solving a quadratic equation by factoring. Include an example.

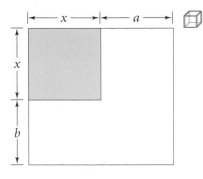

38. Geometry In the diagram at the left, x is a positive integer, and a and b are integers. List several possible values for x, a, and b such that the large rectangle has an area of 56 square units.

39. Open-Ended Write and solve a quadratic equation using the Zero-Product Property.

40. a. Solve $x^2 = x$ and $x^2 = -x$ by factoring.
    b. What number is a solution to both equations?

Solve each cubic equation.

Sample $x^3 + 7x^2 + 12x = 0$

$\qquad x(x^2 + 7x + 12) = 0$ **Factor out the GCF.**

$\qquad x(x + 3)(x + 4) = 0$ **Factor the quadratic trinomial.**

$x = 0 \quad \text{or} \quad x + 3 = 0 \quad \text{or} \quad x + 4 = 0$ **Use the Zero-Product Property.**

$x = 0 \quad \text{or} \quad \qquad x = -3 \quad \text{or} \qquad \quad x = -4$ **Solve for x.**

41. $x^3 - 10x^2 + 24x = 0$ **42.** $x^3 - 5x^2 + 4x = 0$ **43.** $3x^3 - 9x^2 = 0$

44. $x^3 + 3x^2 - 70x = 0$ **45.** $3x^3 - 30x^2 + 27x = 0$ **46.** $2x^3 = -2x^2 + 40x$

C **Challenge** **47. Construction** You are building a rectangular patio with two rectangular openings for gardens. You have 124 one-foot-square paving stones. Using the diagram below, what value of x would allow you to use all of the stones?

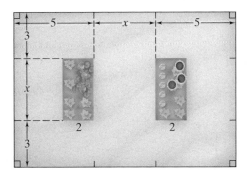

48. Find an equation that has the given numbers as solutions. For example, 4 and -3 are solutions to $x^2 - x - 12 = 0$.

    a. $-5, 8$ **b.** $3, -2$ **c.** $\frac{1}{2}, -10$ **d.** $\frac{2}{3}, -\frac{5}{7}$

Factor the expression on the left side of each equation by grouping. Then solve.

49. $x^3 + 5x^2 - x - 5 = 0$ **50.** $x^3 + x^2 - 4x - 4 = 0$

Standardized Test Prep

Multiple Choice

51. What are the solutions of $(x - 7)(2x + 8) = 0$?
    A. 7, 8   **B.** 7, 4   **C.** 7, -8 **D.** 7, -4

52. Which of the following is the sum of the solutions of $4x^2 - 35x - 9 = 0$?
    F. -8 **G.** 8   **H.** 8.75   **I.** 9.25

53. Which of the following is NOT a solution of $(n)(2n - 5)(10n + 3) = 0$?
    A. -3 **B.** -0.3 **C.** 0   **D.** 2.5

Compare the boxed quantity in Column A with the boxed quantity in Column B. Choose the best answer.

A. The quantity in Column A is greater.
B. The quantity in Column B is greater.
C. The two quantities are equal.
D. The relationship cannot be determined from the information given.

	Column A	Column B
54.	the number of real-number solutions of $3x^2 = 11$	the number of real-number solutions of $5y^2 - 12 = 0$
55.	twice the square of a number n	the square of twice a number n

Take It to the NET
Online lesson quiz at
www.PHSchool.com
Web Code: aea-1005

Short Response   **56.** Find the solutions of the equation $3x^2 + 20x + 1 = 8$. Show your work.

Mixed Review

Lesson 10-4   **Geometry Model each situation with a quadratic equation. Then solve. Round answers to the nearest tenth.**

57. Find the side of a square with an area of 320 ft^2.

58. Find the radius of a circle with an area of 38 ft^2.

Lesson 9-6   **Factor each expression.**

59. $2x^2 + 13x + 15$ **60.** $3y^2 - 10y + 3$ **61.** $4t^2 + 5t - 6$

62. $6n^2 + 7n - 3$ **63.** $15a^3 - 50a^2 - 40a$ **64.** $-18b^3 + 42b^2 - 20b$

A Point in Time

1500   1600   1700   1800   1900   2000

In 1923, Juan de la Cierva (1895–1936) designed the first successful autogyro, a rotor-based aircraft. The autogyro had rotating blades to give the aircraft lift, a propeller for forward thrust, and short, stubby wings for balance. Autogyros needed only short runways for takeoff and could descend almost vertically.

By hinging the rotor blades at the hub, de la Cierva allowed each blade to respond to aerodynamic forces. This was a significant contribution in the development of the modern helicopter.

De la Cierva's work on problems of lift and gravity, like the work of aeronautical engineers of today, involved quadratic functions.

Take It to the NET For more information about autogyros, go to **www.PHSchool.com**.
Web Code: aee-2032

Completing the Square

Lesson Preview

What You'll Learn

OBJECTIVE
1 To solve quadratic equations by completing the square

... And Why

To solve real-world problems involving carpentry, as in Example 4

OBJECTIVE

1 **Solving by Completing the Square**

TEXT **Interactive lesson includes instant self-check, tutorials, and activities.**

In previous lessons, you solved quadratic equations by finding square roots and by factoring. These methods work in some cases. A third method, completing the square, works with every quadratic equation. Completing the square turns every quadratic equation into the form $m^2 = n$. You can model completing the square of a quadratic expression using algebra tiles.

The algebra tiles at the right represent the expression $x^2 + 8x$.

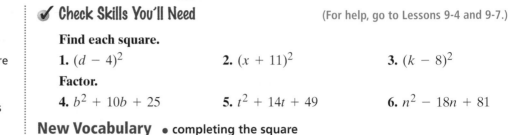

Here is the same expression rearranged to form part of a square. Notice that the x-tiles have been split evenly into two groups of four.

You can complete the square by adding 4^2, or 16, single tiles. The completed square is $x^2 + 8x + 16$ or $(x + 4)^2$.

To explore this method algebraically, consider the equation below. In a perfect square trinomial, with $a = 1$, c must be the square of half of b.

$$(x + 4)^2 = x^2 + 2(4)x + 4^2$$
$$= x^2 + 8x + 16$$
$$\downarrow \qquad \uparrow$$
$$\frac{8}{2} = 4 \rightarrow 4^2$$

You can change an expression like $x^2 + bx$ into a perfect square trinomial by adding $\left(\frac{b}{2}\right)^2$ to $x^2 + bx$. This process is called **completing the square.** The process is the same whether b is positive or negative.

1 EXAMPLE Finding *n* to Complete the Square

Find the value of *n* such that $x^2 - 12x + n$ is a perfect square trinomial.

The value of *b* in the expression $x^2 - 12x + n$ is -12. The term to add to $x^2 - 12x$ is $\left(-\frac{12}{2}\right)^2$ or 36. So $n = 36$.

✓ **Check Understanding** **1** Find the value of *n* such that $x^2 + 22x + n$ is a perfect square trinomial.

The simplest equations in which to complete the square have the form $x^2 + bx = c$.

2 EXAMPLE Solving $x^2 + bx = c$

Solve the equation $x^2 + 9x = 136$.

Step 1 Write the left side of $x^2 + 9x = 136$ as a perfect square.

$$x^2 + 9x = 136$$
$$x^2 + 9x + \left(\frac{9}{2}\right)^2 = 136 + \left(\frac{9}{2}\right)^2 \qquad \text{Add } \left(\frac{9}{2}\right)^2, \text{ or } \frac{81}{4}, \text{ to each side of the equation.}$$
$$\left(x + \frac{9}{2}\right)^2 = \frac{544}{4} + \frac{81}{4} \qquad \begin{array}{l}\text{Write } x^2 + 9x + \left(\frac{9}{2}\right)^2 \text{ as a square.} \\ \text{Rewrite 136 as a fraction with denominator 4.}\end{array}$$
$$\left(x + \frac{9}{2}\right)^2 = \frac{625}{4} \qquad \text{Simplify the right side of the equation.}$$

Step 2 Solve the equation.

$$\left(x + \frac{9}{2}\right) = \pm\sqrt{\frac{625}{4}} \qquad \text{Find the square root of each side.}$$
$$x + \frac{9}{2} = \pm\frac{25}{2} \qquad \text{Simplify.}$$
$$x + \frac{9}{2} = \frac{25}{2} \quad \text{or} \quad x + \frac{9}{2} = -\frac{25}{2} \qquad \text{Write as two equations.}$$
$$x = 8 \quad \text{or} \qquad x = -17 \qquad \begin{array}{l}\text{Solve for } x \text{ by subtracting } \frac{9}{2} \text{ from each} \\ \text{side of the equations and simplifying.}\end{array}$$

✓ **Check Understanding** **2** Solve the equation $m^2 - 6m = 247$.

To solve an equation in the form $x^2 + bx + c = 0$, first subtract the constant term *c* from each side of the equation.

3 EXAMPLE Solving $x^2 + bx + c = 0$

Solve $x^2 - 20x + 32 = 0$.

Step 1 Rewrite the equation in the form $x^2 + bx = c$ and complete the square.

$$x^2 - 20x + 32 = 0$$
$$x^2 - 20x = -32 \qquad \text{Subtract 32 from each side.}$$
$$x^2 - 20x + 100 = -32 + 100 \qquad \begin{array}{l}\text{Add } \left(-\frac{20}{2}\right)^2, \text{ or 100, to each side} \\ \text{of the equation.}\end{array}$$
$$(x - 10)^2 = 68 \qquad \text{Write } x^2 - 20x + 100 \text{ as a square.}$$

Step 2 Solve the equation.

$$(x - 10) = \pm\sqrt{68} \qquad \text{Find the square root of each side.}$$
$$x - 10 \approx \pm 8.25 \qquad \text{Use a calculator to find } \sqrt{68}.$$
$$x - 10 \approx 8.25 \qquad \text{or} \quad x - 10 \approx -8.25 \qquad \text{Write as two equations.}$$
$$x \approx 8.25 + 10 \quad \text{or} \qquad x \approx -8.25 + 10 \qquad \text{Add 10 to each side.}$$
$$x \approx 18.25 \qquad \text{or} \qquad x \approx 1.75 \qquad \text{Simplify.}$$

✓ **Check Understanding** ③ Solve each equation. Round to the nearest hundredth.
　　a. $x^2 + 5x + 3 = 0$　　　　　　　　**b.** $x^2 - 14x + 16 = 0$

The method of completing the square works when $a = 1$. To solve an equation like $3x^2 + 6x - 9 = 0$, you need to divide each side by 3 before completing the square.

$$3x^2 + 6x - 9 = 0 \quad \rightarrow \quad \frac{3x^2 + 6x - 9}{3} = \frac{0}{3} \quad \rightarrow \quad x^2 + 2x - 3 = 0$$

④ **EXAMPLE**　**Real-World　Problem Solving**

Carpentry Suppose a woodworker wants to build a tabletop like the one shown at the right. If the surface area is 26 ft^2, what is the value of x?

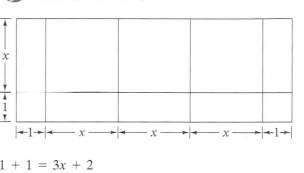

Define　width $= x + 1$
　　　　length $= x + x + x + 1 + 1 = 3x + 2$

Relate　length $\times$ width $=$ area

Write　$(3x + 2)(x + 1) = 26$
　　　　$3x^2 + 5x + 2 = 26$

Step 1　Rewrite the equation in the form $x^2 + bx = c$.

　$3x^2 + 5x + 2 = 26$
　$3x^2 + 5x = 24$　　　**Subtract 2 from each side.**
　$x^2 + \frac{5}{3}x = 8$　　　**Divide each side by 3.**

Step 2　Complete the square.

$x^2 + \frac{5}{3}x + \frac{25}{36} = 8 + \frac{25}{36}$　　**Add $\left(\frac{5}{6}\right)^2$, or $\frac{25}{36}$, to each side.**

$\left(x + \frac{5}{6}\right)^2 = \frac{288}{36} + \frac{25}{36}$　　**Write $x^2 + \frac{5}{3}x + \frac{25}{36}$ as a square. Rewrite 8 as a fraction with denominator 36.**

$\left(x + \frac{5}{6}\right)^2 = \frac{313}{36}$　　**Simplify.**

Step 3　Solve the equation.

$\left(x + \frac{5}{6}\right) = \pm\sqrt{\frac{313}{36}}$　　**Take the square root of each side.**

$x + \frac{5}{6} \approx \pm 2.95$　　**Use a calculator. $\sqrt{\frac{313}{36}} \approx 2.95$**

$x + \frac{5}{6} \approx 2.95$　　or　$x + \frac{5}{6} \approx -2.95$　　**Write as two equations.**

$x \approx 2.95 - \frac{5}{6}$　or　$x \approx -2.95 - \frac{5}{6}$　　**Subtract $\frac{5}{6}$ from each side.**

$x \approx 2.95 - 0.83$　or　$x \approx -2.95 - 0.83$　　**$\frac{5}{6} \approx 0.83$, so substitute 0.83 for $\frac{5}{6}$.**

$x \approx 2.12$　　　or　　$x \approx -3.78$　　**Use the positive answer for this problem.**

● The value of x is about 2.12 ft.

✓ **Check Understanding** ④ Solve each equation. Round to the nearest hundredth.
　　a. $4a^2 - 8a = 24$　　　　　　　　**b.** $5n^2 - 3n - 15 = 10$

EXERCISES

For more practice, see *Extra Practice*.

Practice and Problem Solving

A **Practice by Example**

Example 1
(page 542)

Find the value of n such that each expression is a perfect square trinomial.

1. $k^2 + 14k + n$ **2.** $m^2 - 8m + n$ **3.** $y^2 - 40y + n$

4. $p^2 - 6p + n$ **5.** $v^2 + 24v + n$ **6.** $w^2 - 36w + n$

Example 2
(page 542)

Solve each equation by completing the square. If necessary, round to the nearest hundredth.

7. $r^2 + 8r = 48$ **8.** $x^2 - 10x = 40$ **9.** $q^2 + 22q = -85$

10. $m^2 + 6m = 9$ **11.** $r^2 + 20r = 261$ **12.** $g^2 - 2g = 323$

Example 3
(page 542)

13. $r^2 - 2r - 35 = 0$ **14.** $x^2 + 10x + 17 = 0$ **15.** $p^2 - 12p + 11 = 0$

16. $w^2 + 3w - 5 = 0$ **17.** $m^2 + m - 28 = 0$ **18.** $a^2 + 9a - 682 = 0$

Example 4
(page 543)

What term do you need to add to each side to complete the square?

19. $2k^2 + 4k = 10$ **20.** $3x^2 + 12x = 24$ **21.** $5t^2 + 9t = 15$

Solve each equation by completing the square. If necessary, round to the nearest hundredth.

22. $4y^2 + 8y - 36 = 0$ **23.** $3q^2 - 12q = 15$ **24.** $2x^2 - 10x - 20 = 8$

25. a. Write an expression for the total area of the model below.

b. The total area is 28 square units. Write an equation to find x.
c. Solve by completing the square.

B **Apply Your Skills**

Solve each equation. If necessary, round to the nearest hundredth. If there is no solution, write *no solution*.

26. $b^2 + 4b + 1 = 0$ **27.** $c^2 + 7c = -12$ **28.** $h^2 + 6h - 40 = 0$

29. $y^2 - 8y = -12$ **30.** $4m^2 - 40m + 56 = 0$ **31.** $k^2 + 4k + 11 = -10$

32. $2x^2 - 15x + 6 = 41$ **33.** $3d^2 - 24d = 3$ **34.** $x^2 + 9x + 20 = 0$

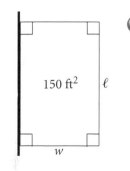

35. Gardening Suppose you want to enclose a rectangular garden plot against a house using fencing on three sides, as shown at the left. Assume you have 50 ft of fencing material and want to create a garden with an area of 150 ft².
a. Let w = the width. Write an expression for the length of the plot.
b. Write and solve an equation for the area of the plot. Round to the nearest tenth of a foot.
c. What dimensions should the garden have?
d. Critical Thinking Find the area of the garden by using the dimensions you found in part (b). Does the area equal 150 ft²? Explain.

36. Error Analysis A classmate was completing the square to solve $4x^2 + 10x = 0$. For her first step she wrote $4x^2 + 10x + 25 = 25$. What was her error?

37. Writing Explain to a classmate how to solve $x^2 + 30x - 1 = 0$ by completing the square.

38. Open-Ended Write a quadratic equation and solve it by completing the square. Show your work.

Use each graph to estimate the values of x for which $f(x) = 5$. Write and solve an equation to find the values of x such that $f(x) = 5$. Round to the nearest hundredth.

39. $f(x) = x^2 - 4x - 1$

40. $f(x) = -\frac{1}{2}x^2 + 4x + 1$

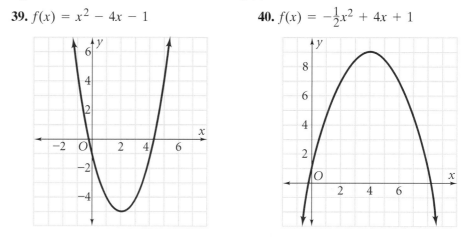

41. Geometry A rectangle has a length of x. Its width is 3 feet longer than twice the length. Find the dimensions if its area is 80 ft². Round to the nearest tenth of a foot.

C Challenge **42. Geometry** Suppose the prism shown at the right has the same surface area as an 8-in. cube.

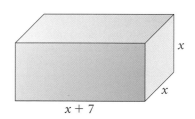

  a. Write an expression for the surface area of the prism shown at the right.
  b. Write an equation that relates the surface area of the prism to the surface area of the 8-in. cube.
  c. Solve the equation you wrote in part (b) to find the dimensions of the prism.

43. Design Suppose you want to design a patio like the one shown below.

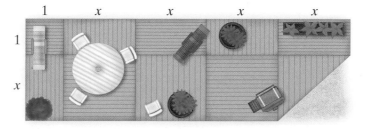

  a. Write an expression for the total area.
  b. If you want the total area to be 200 ft², what is the value of x?
  c. If you rounded the value of x to the nearest integer, what would the total area be?

44. **a.** Solve the equation $x^2 - 6x + 4 = 0$, but leave your answers in the form $p \pm \sqrt{q}$.
b. Use the vertex formula $x = \frac{-b}{2a}$ to find the coordinates of the vertex of $y = x^2 - 6x + 4$.
c. **Critical Thinking** Explain the relationship between your answers in part (a) and part (b).

Standardized Test Prep

Multiple Choice

45. Which values of b will make the expression $x^2 + bx + 100$ a perfect square trinomial?
A. $-10, 10$ B. $-20, 20$ C. $-25, 25$ D. $-50, 50$

46. Which of the following expressions is NOT a perfect square trinomial?
F. $t^2 - 14t + 49$ G. $9b^2 + 66b + 121$
H. $4m^2 - 24m + 36$ I. $81k^2 - 120k + 100$

47. Which of the following is closest to a solution of the equation $x^2 + 6x - 11 = 0$?
A. -3 B. -1 C. 0 D. 2

Short Response

48. The area of the figure at the right is 200 cm^2. Find the value of x. Round to the nearest hundredth. Show your work.

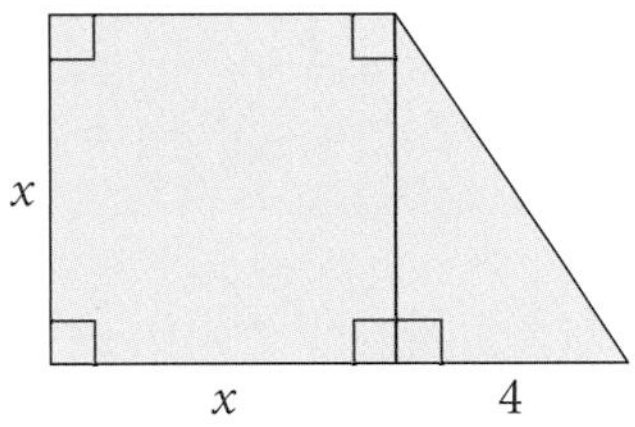

Extended Response

49. Kevin's office cubicle measures 8 ft by 12 ft.
a. Write an equation to find the amount x that should be added to the current length and width to double the area.
b. Solve the equation. Show your work.
c. What will the new dimensions be?

Take It to the NET
Online lesson quiz at **www.PHSchool.com**
Web Code: aea-1006

Mixed Review

Lesson 10-5 **Solve each equation.**

50. $x^2 - 4x - 21 = 0$ **51.** $n^2 + 11n + 30 = 0$ **52.** $t^2 - 5t = 0$

53. $9v^2 - 64 = 0$ **54.** $4c^2 + 12c = -9$ **55.** $12w^2 = 28w + 5$

Lesson 9-7 **Factor each expression.**

56. $x^2 + 4x + 4$ **57.** $t^2 - 22t + 121$ **58.** $b^2 - 25$

59. $16c^2 + 24c + 9$ **60.** $49s^2 - 169$ **61.** $8m^3 - 18m$

62. $25m^2 + 120m + 144$ **63.** $400k^2 - 9$ **64.** $256g^2 - 121$

Lesson 8-4 **Simplify.**

65. $(r^3)^4$ **66.** $p(p^2)^6$ **67.** $-y^3(y^{-1})^2$

68. $(m^5)^{-8}$ **69.** $-w^7(w^8)^{-1}$ **70.** $t^8(t^{-7})^{-3}$

10-7

Using the Quadratic Formula

Lesson Preview

What You'll Learn

OBJECTIVE
▼ 1 To use the quadratic formula when solving quadratic equations

OBJECTIVE
▼ 2 To choose an appropriate method for solving a quadratic equation

... And Why

To investigate real-world situations involving sports, as in Example 3

✓ **Check Skills You'll Need** (For help, go to Lesson 10-6.)

Find the value of c to complete the square for each expression.

1. $x^2 + 6x + c$ **2.** $x^2 + 7x + c$ **3.** $x^2 - 9x + c$

Solve each equation by completing the square.

4. $x^2 - 10x + 24 = 0$ **5.** $x^2 + 16x - 36 = 0$

6. $3x^2 + 12x - 15 = 0$ **7.** $2x^2 - 2x - 112 = 0$

New Vocabulary • quadratic formula

OBJECTIVE

1 Using the Quadratic Formula

i **TEXT** Interactive lesson includes instant self-check, tutorials, and activities.

Real-World 🌐 Connection

The path of a golf ball can be modeled with a quadratic function.

In Lesson 10-6, you solved quadratic equations by completing the square. If you complete the square of the general equation $ax^2 + bx + c = 0$, you can derive the **quadratic formula,** which will solve any quadratic equation.

Step 1 Write $ax^2 + bx + c = 0$ so the coefficient of x^2 is 1.

$$ax^2 + bx + c = 0$$
$$x^2 + \frac{b}{a}x + \frac{c}{a} = 0 \quad \text{Divide each side by } a.$$

Step 2 Complete the square.

$$x^2 + \frac{b}{a}x = -\frac{c}{a} \quad \text{Subtract } \tfrac{c}{a} \text{ from each side.}$$

$$x^2 + \frac{b}{a}x + \left(\frac{b}{2a}\right)^2 = -\frac{c}{a} + \left(\frac{b}{2a}\right)^2 \quad \text{Add } \left(\tfrac{b}{2a}\right)^2 \text{ to each side.}$$

$$\left(x + \frac{b}{2a}\right)^2 = -\frac{c}{a} + \left(\frac{b}{2a}\right)^2 \quad \text{Write the trinomial as a perfect square.}$$

$$= -\frac{4ac}{4a^2} + \frac{b^2}{4a^2} \quad \text{Multiply } -\tfrac{c}{a} \text{ by } \tfrac{4a}{4a} \text{ to get like denominators, and simplify } \left(\tfrac{b}{2a}\right)^2.$$

$$= \frac{b^2 - 4ac}{4a^2} \quad \text{Simplify the right side.}$$

Step 3 Solve the equation.

$$\sqrt{\left(x + \frac{b}{2a}\right)^2} = \sqrt{\frac{b^2 - 4ac}{4a^2}} \quad \text{Take the square root of each side.}$$

$$x + \frac{b}{2a} = \pm \frac{\sqrt{b^2 - 4ac}}{2a} \quad \text{Simplify the right side. } \frac{1}{\sqrt{4a^2}} = \pm\frac{1}{2a}$$

$$x = -\frac{b}{2a} \pm \frac{\sqrt{b^2 - 4ac}}{2a} \quad \text{Subtract } \tfrac{b}{2a} \text{ from each side.}$$

$$x = \frac{-b \pm \sqrt{b^2 - 4ac}}{2a} \quad \text{Simplify.}$$

Rule **Quadratic Formula**

If $ax^2 + bx + c = 0$, and $a \neq 0$, then
$$x = \frac{-b \pm \sqrt{b^2 - 4ac}}{2a}$$

Be sure to write a quadratic equation in standard form before using the quadratic formula.

1 EXAMPLE **Using the Quadratic Formula**

Reading Math

For more help with Example 1, see p. 553.

Solve $x^2 + 6 = 5x$.

$x^2 - 5x + 6 = 0$ — Subtract 5x from each side and write in standard form.

$x = \dfrac{-b \pm \sqrt{b^2 - 4ac}}{2a}$ — Use the quadratic formula.

$x = \dfrac{-(-5) \pm \sqrt{(-5)^2 - (4)(1)(6)}}{2(1)}$ — The coefficient of x is 1. Substitute 1 for a, −5 for b, and 6 for c.

$x = \dfrac{5 \pm \sqrt{1}}{2}$ — Simplify −(−5) and the radicand.

$x = \dfrac{5 + 1}{2}$ or $x = \dfrac{5 - 1}{2}$ — Write as two equations.

$x = 3$ or $x = 2$ — Simplify.

Check Substitute 3 for x.

$(3)^2 + 6 \stackrel{?}{=} 5(3)$

$9 + 6 \stackrel{?}{=} 15$

$15 = 15$ ✓

Substitute 2 for x.

$(2)^2 + 6 \stackrel{?}{=} 5(2)$

$4 + 6 \stackrel{?}{=} 10$

$10 = 10$ ✓

✓ **Check Understanding** ❶ Use the quadratic formula to solve each equation.
a. $x^2 - 2x - 8 = 0$ **b.** $x^2 - 4x = 117$

Need Help?

The radicand is the quantity inside the radical symbol. The radicand of $\sqrt{b^2 - 4ac}$ is $b^2 - 4ac$.

When the radicand in the quadratic formula is not a perfect square, you can use a calculator to approximate the solutions of an equation.

2 EXAMPLE **Finding Approximate Solutions**

Solve $2x^2 + 4x - 7 = 0$. Round the solutions to the nearest hundredth.

$x = \dfrac{-b \pm \sqrt{b^2 - 4ac}}{2a}$ — Use the quadratic formula.

$x = \dfrac{-4 \pm \sqrt{4^2 - (4)(2)(-7)}}{2(2)}$ — Substitute 2 for a, 4 for b, and −7 for c.

$x = \dfrac{-4 \pm \sqrt{72}}{4}$

$x = \dfrac{-4 + \sqrt{72}}{4}$ or $x = \dfrac{-4 - \sqrt{72}}{4}$ — Write as two equations.

$x \approx \dfrac{-4 + 8.49}{4}$ or $x \approx \dfrac{-4 - 8.49}{4}$ — Use a calculator. $\sqrt{72} \approx 8.49$

$x \approx 1.12$ or $x \approx -3.12$ — Simplify. Round to the nearest hundredth.

✓ **Check Understanding** ❷ Solve each equation. Round to the nearest hundredth.
a. $-3x^2 + 5x - 2 = 0$ **b.** $7x^2 - 2x - 8 = 0$

You can use the quadratic formula to solve real-world problems. You must decide whether a solution makes sense in the real-world situation. For example, a negative value for time would not be a reasonable solution in most situations.

3 EXAMPLE   Real-World 🌐 Problem Solving

Sports Suppose a football player kicks a ball and gives it an initial upward velocity of 47 ft/s. The starting height of the football is 3 ft. If no one catches the football, how long will it be in the air?

Step 1 Use the vertical motion formula.

$$h = -16t^2 + vt + c$$ The initial upward velocity is v, and the starting height is c.

$$0 = -16t^2 + 47t + 3$$ Substitute 0 for h, 47 for v, and 3 for c.

Step 2 Use the quadratic formula.

$$x = \frac{-b \pm \sqrt{b^2 - 4ac}}{2a}$$

$$t = \frac{-(47) \pm \sqrt{(47)^2 - (4)(-16)(3)}}{2(-16)}$$ Substitute -16 for a, 47 for b, 3 for c, and t for x.

$$t = \frac{-47 \pm \sqrt{2209 + 192}}{-32}$$ Simplify.

$$t = \frac{-47 \pm \sqrt{2401}}{-32}$$

$$t = \frac{-47 + 49}{-32} \quad \text{or} \quad t = \frac{-47 - 49}{-32}$$ Write as two equations.

$$t \approx -0.06 \quad \text{or} \quad t - 3$$ Simplify. Use the positive answer because it is the only reasonable answer in this situation.

● The football will be in the air for 3 seconds.

✓ **Check Understanding** ③ A football player kicks a ball with an initial upward velocity of 38.4 ft/s from a starting height of 3.5 ft.
   a. Substitute the values into the vertical motion formula. Let $h = 0$.
   b. Solve. If no one catches the ball, how long will it be in the air? Round to the nearest tenth of a second.

OBJECTIVE

2 Choosing an Appropriate Method

There are many methods for solving a quadratic equation. You can always use the quadratic formula, but sometimes another method may be easier.

Method	When to Use
Graphing	Use if you have a graphing calculator handy.
Square Roots	Use if the equation has no x term.
Factoring	Use if you can factor the equation easily.
Completing the Square	Use if the x^2 term is 1, but you cannot factor the equation easily.
Quadratic Formula	Use if the equation cannot be factored easily or at all.

4 EXAMPLE   Choosing an Appropriate Method

Which method(s) would you choose to solve each equation? Justify your reasoning.

a. $2x^2 - 6 = 0$ Square roots; there is no x term.

b. $6x^2 + 13x - 17 = 0$ Quadratic formula; the equation cannot be factored easily.

c. $x^2 + 2x - 15 = 0$ Factoring; the equation is easily factorable.

d. $16x^2 - 96x + 45 = 0$ Quadratic formula; the equation cannot be factored easily, and the numbers are large.

e. $x^2 - 7x + 4 = 0$ Quadratic formula, completing the square, or graphing; the coefficient of the x^2 term is 1, but the equation is not factorable.

✓ **Check Understanding** **4** Which method(s) would you choose to solve each equation? Justify your reasoning.
a. $13x^2 - 5x + 21 = 0$ **b.** $x^2 - x - 30 = 0$ **c.** $144x^2 = 25$

EXERCISES

For more practice, see *Extra Practice*.

Practice and Problem Solving

Ⓐ Practice by Example

Example 1
(page 548)

Use the quadratic formula to solve each equation. If necessary, round answers to the nearest hundredth.

1. $2x^2 + 5x + 3 = 0$ **2.** $5x^2 + 16x - 84 = 0$ **3.** $4x^2 - 12x + 9 = 0$

4. $3x^2 + 47x = -30$ **5.** $12x^2 - 77x - 20 = 0$ **6.** $3x^2 + 39x + 108 = 0$

7. $3x^2 + 40x - 128 = 0$ **8.** $2x^2 - 9x - 221 = 0$ **9.** $5x^2 - 68x = 192$

Example 2
(page 548)

10. $5x^2 + 13x - 1 = 0$ **11.** $2x^2 - 24x + 33 = 0$ **12.** $7x^2 + 100x - 4 = 0$

13. $8x^2 - 3x - 7 = 0$ **14.** $6x^2 + 5x - 40 = 0$ **15.** $3x^2 - 11x - 2 = 0$

Example 3
(page 549)

For Exercises 16 and 17, use the vertical motion formula $h = -16t^2 + vt + c$.

16. A child tosses a ball upward with a starting velocity of 10 ft/s from a height of 3 ft.
   a. Substitute the values into the vertical motion formula. Let $h = 0$.
   b. Solve. If it is not caught, how long will the ball be in the air? Round to the nearest tenth of a second.

17. A soccer ball is kicked with a starting upward velocity of 50 ft/s from a starting height of 3.5 ft.
   a. Substitute the values into the vertical motion formula. Let $h = 0$.
   b. Solve. If no one touches the ball, how long will the ball be in the air? Round to the nearest tenth of a second.

Example 4
(page 550)

Which method(s) would you choose to solve each equation? Justify your reasoning.

18. $x^2 + 2x - 13 = 0$ **19.** $4x^2 - 81 = 0$ **20.** $9x^2 - 31x = 51$

21. $3x^2 - 5x + 9 = 0$ **22.** $x^2 + 4x - 60 = 0$ **23.** $-4x^2 + 3x + 2 = 0$

Use any method you choose to solve each equation. If necessary, round to the nearest hundredth.

24. $2t^2 = 72$ **25.** $3x^2 + 2x - 4 = 0$ **26.** $5b^2 - 10 = 0$

27. $3x^2 + 4x = 10$ **28.** $m^2 - 4m = -4$ **29.** $13n^2 - 117 = 0$

30. $3s^2 - 4s = 2$ **31.** $5b^2 - 2b - 7 = 0$ **32.** $15x^2 - 12x - 48 = 0$

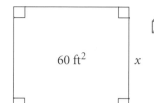

60 ft^2 x

$x + 1$

33. Geometry Suppose you want to make a rectangle like the one shown at the left.
 a. Estimate each dimension of the rectangle to the nearest integer.
 b. Write a quadratic equation and use the quadratic formula to find each dimension to the nearest hundredth.

34. Vertical Motion Suppose you throw a ball upward with a starting velocity of 30 ft/s. The ball is 6 ft high when it leaves your hand. After how many seconds will it hit the ground? Use the vertical motion formula $h = -16t^2 + vt + c$.

35. Writing Compare the way you solve the linear equation $mx + b = 0$ with the way you solve the quadratic equation $ax^2 + bx + c = 0$.

Geometry Find the base and height of each triangle below. If necessary, round to the nearest hundredth.

36.

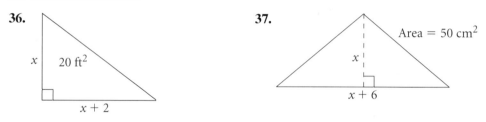

x 20 ft^2

$x + 2$

37.

Area = 50 cm^2

x

$x + 6$

38. Open-Ended Write a problem in which you find the area of a rectangle that you can solve using a quadratic equation. Draw a diagram and solve.

39. Critical Thinking How you can tell from the quadratic formula that a quadratic equation has one solution? Explain.

40. Vertical Motion Refer to the cartoon. Suppose the man's starting upward velocity v is 5 ft/s. Use $0 = -16t^2 + vt + c$, where c is the starting height. Find the number of seconds t before he hits the water.

C Challenge

Real-World Connection

Careers Demographers use mathematics to help describe trends in populations.

41. Population The function below models the United States population P in millions since 1900, where t is the number of years after 1900.

$P = 0.0089t^2 + 1.1149t + 78.4491$

 a. Use the function to estimate the United States population the year you graduate from high school.
 b. Estimate the United States population in 2025.
 c. Use the function to predict the year in which the population will reach 300 million.

42. Critical Thinking The two solutions of any quadratic equation are

$$\frac{-b + \sqrt{b^2 - 4ac}}{2a} \text{ and } \frac{-b - \sqrt{b^2 - 4ac}}{2a}.$$

 a. Find a formula for the sum of the solutions.
 b. One solution of $2x^2 + 3x - 104 = 0$ is -8. Use the formula you found in part (a) to find the second solution.

Standardized Test Prep

Reading Comprehension

The Gateway to the West

The Gateway Arch in St. Louis, Missouri, was completed in 1965. The arch spans 630 feet at its base and is 630 feet tall. More than 5100 tons of steel and 38,100 tons of concrete were used in its construction.

43. Use the data in the article above to answer the following questions.

 a. How many pounds of concrete were used in the construction of the Gateway Arch? Write your answer in scientific notation.

 b. How many more tons of concrete than steel were used? Write your answer in scientific notation.

 c. Suppose that a cleaner at the top of the Gateway Arch drops a cleaning brush. Use the vertical motion formula $h = -16t^2 + vt + c$. The starting upward velocity v is 0 and c is the starting height. How many seconds will the brush take to hit the ground?

Take It to the NET
Online lesson quiz at
www.PHSchool.com
Web Code: aea-1007

Multiple Choice

44. The expression $\dfrac{9 \pm \sqrt{(-9)^2 - 4(5)(-7)}}{2(5)}$ gives the solutions to which of the following equations?

 A. $-9x^2 + 5x = -7$ **B.** $5x^2 + 7x = 9$
 C. $5x^2 - 9x = -7$ **D.** $5x^2 - 9x = 7$

45. The graph of $y = 15x^2 - 59x - 112$ crosses the x-axis closest to which of the following x-values?

 F. -1 **G.** 0 **H.** 3 **I.** 6

Short Response

46. Find the solutions to the equation $6x^2 - 40 = 11x$. Round to the nearest tenth.

Mixed Review

Lesson 10-6

Solve each equation by completing the square. If necessary, round to the nearest hundredth.

47. $d^2 - 10d + 13 = 0$ **48.** $z^2 + 3z = -2$ **49.** $3x^2 + 18x - 1 = 0$

Lesson 9-8

Factor by grouping.

50. $2c^2 + 11c + 15$ **51.** $3z^2 + 10z - 8$ **52.** $5n^2 - 33n - 14$

53. $12v^2 + 32v - 35$ **54.** $6x^2 - 13x + 5$ **55.** $15t^2 + 19t + 6$

Read the example below and the explanation about how to use the quadratic formula.

EXAMPLE

Solve $x^2 + 6 = 5x$.

To use the quadratic formula, you must know the following.

$a \rightarrow$ the coefficient of the squared term, which is the term with a power of 2

$b \rightarrow$ the coefficient of the term with a power of 1

$c \rightarrow$ the value of the constant

To determine the values of a, b, and c, write the equation in standard form $ax^2 + bx + c = 0$.

So, for $x^2 + 6 = 5x$, subtract $5x$ from both sides and write in standard form.

$$x^2 \qquad -5x \qquad +6 = 0$$

↑	↑	↑
Coefficient of x^2 is 1.	**Coefficient of x is −5.**	**Constant is 6.**

Use these values in the quadratic formula. Be careful when substituting negative values that you do not "lose" a negative sign.

$$x = \frac{-b \pm \sqrt{b^2 - 4ac}}{2a}$$

$$x = \frac{-(-5) \pm \sqrt{(-5)^2 - 4 \cdot 1 \cdot 6}}{2(1)}$$

Substitute 1 for a, −5 for b, and 6 for c.

$$x = \frac{5 \pm \sqrt{25 - 24}}{2}$$

Simplify using as many steps as you need to keep the signs of the numbers organized.

$$x = \frac{5 \pm 1}{2}$$

$$x = \frac{5 + 1}{2} \qquad \text{or} \qquad x = \frac{5 - 1}{2} \qquad \textbf{5 ± 1 means 5 + 1 or 5 − 1.}$$

$$x = \frac{6}{2} \qquad \text{or} \qquad x = \frac{4}{2}$$

$$x = 3 \qquad \text{or} \qquad x = 2$$

EXERCISE

Use the equation $4x^2 - 8x = 45$.

a. Write the equation in standard form.

b. Identify a, b, and c.

c. Use the quadratic formula to solve the equation.

10-8

Using the Discriminant

Lesson Preview

What You'll Learn

OBJECTIVE
1 To find the number of solutions of a quadratic equation

... And Why

To solve physics problems, as in Example 2

✓ **Check Skills You'll Need**   (For help, go to Lessons 1-6 and 10-7.)

Evaluate $b^2 - 4ac$ for the given values of a, b, and c.

1. $a = 3, b = 4, c = 8$ **2.** $a = -2, b = 0, c = 9$ **3.** $a = 11, b = -5, c = 7$

Solve using the quadratic formula. If necessary, round to the nearest hundredth.

4. $3x^2 - 7x + 1 = 0$ **5.** $4x^2 + x - 1 = 0$ **6.** $x^2 - 12x + 35 = 0$

New Vocabulary   • discriminant

OBJECTIVE

1   **Number of Real Solutions of a Quadratic Equation**

iTEXT **Interactive lesson includes instant self-check, tutorials, and activities.**

Quadratic equations can have two, one, or no solutions. You can determine how many solutions a quadratic equation has, before you solve it, by using the discriminant. The **discriminant** is the expression under the radical in the quadratic formula.

$$x = \frac{-b \pm \sqrt{b^2 - 4ac}}{2a} \quad \longleftarrow \quad \text{the discriminant}$$

Consider the graphs of the functions below and the discriminant of each related equation.

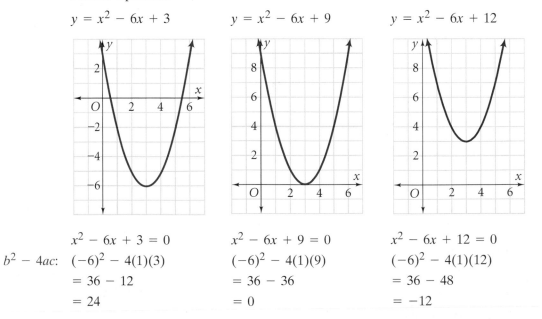

$y = x^2 - 6x + 3$	$y = x^2 - 6x + 9$	$y = x^2 - 6x + 12$

$b^2 - 4ac$:

$x^2 - 6x + 3 = 0$	$x^2 - 6x + 9 = 0$	$x^2 - 6x + 12 = 0$
$(-6)^2 - 4(1)(3)$	$(-6)^2 - 4(1)(9)$	$(-6)^2 - 4(1)(12)$
$= 36 - 12$	$= 36 - 36$	$= 36 - 48$
$= 24$	$= 0$	$= -12$

The relationship you see between the graphs and discriminants above is true for all cases. If the discriminant is positive, there are two solutions. If the discriminant is zero, there is one solution. If the discriminant is negative, there are no solutions.

This graph shows the three cases together.

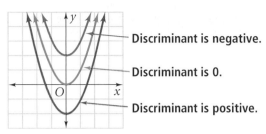

— Discriminant is negative.

— Discriminant is 0.

— Discriminant is positive.

Key Concepts

Property	Property of the Discriminant

For the quadratic equation $ax^2 + bx + c = 0$, where $a \neq 0$, you can use the value of the discriminant to determine the number of solutions.

If $b^2 - 4ac > 0$, there are two solutions.

If $b^2 - 4ac = 0$, there is one solution.

If $b^2 - 4ac < 0$, there are no solutions.

1 EXAMPLE **Using the Discriminant**

Find the number of solutions of $3x^2 - 5x = 1$.

$3x^2 - 5x - 1 = 0$ **Write in standard form.**

$b^2 - 4ac = (-5)^2 - (4)(3)(-1)$ **Evaluate the discriminant. Substitute for a, b, and c.**

$= 25 - (-12)$ **Use the order of operations.**

$= 37$ **Simplify.**

● Since $37 > 0$, the equation has two solutions.

✓ Check Understanding ① Find the number of solutions for each equation.

a. $x^2 = 2x - 3$ **b.** $3x^2 - 4x = 7$ **c.** $5x^2 + 8 = 2x$

2 EXAMPLE **Real-World** **Problem Solving**

Physics A construction worker on the ground tosses an apple to a fellow worker who is 20 ft above the ground. The starting height of the apple is 5 ft. Its initial upward velocity is 30 ft/s. Will the apple reach the second worker?

$h = -16t^2 + vt + c$ **Use the vertical motion formula.**

$20 = -16t^2 + 30t + 5$ **Substitute 20 for h, 30 for v, and 5 for c.**

$0 = -16t^2 + 30t - 15$ **Write in standard form.**

$b^2 - 4ac = (30)^2 - 4(-16)(-15)$ **Evaluate the discriminant.**

$= 900 - 960$ **Use the order of operations.**

$= -60$ **Simplify.**

● The discriminant is negative. The apple will not reach the second worker.

✓ Check Understanding ② Suppose the same construction worker tosses an apple with an initial upward velocity of 32 ft/s. Will the apple reach the second worker?

For more practice, see *Extra Practice.*

Practice and Problem Solving

 Practice by Example

Example 1
(page 555)

For which discriminant is each graph possible?

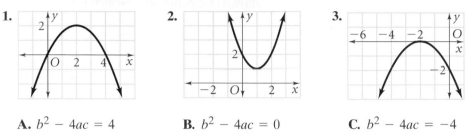

1.

2.

3.

A. $b^2 - 4ac = 4$

B. $b^2 - 4ac = 0$

C. $b^2 - 4ac = -4$

Mental Math Find the number of solutions of each equation.

4. $x^2 - 3x + 4 = 0$

5. $x^2 - 6x + 9 = 0$

6. $x^2 + 4x - 2 = 0$

7. $x^2 - 1 = 0$

8. $x^2 - 2x - 3 = 0$

9. $x^2 + x = 0$

10. $2x^2 - 3x + 4 = 0$

11. $0 = x^2 - 6x + 5$

12. $x^2 - 7x + 6 = 0$

13. $x^2 + 2x + 1 = 0$

14. $0 = 2x^2 + 4x - 3$

15. $0 = x^2 + 2x + 9$

Example 2
(page 555)

16. Home Improvements The Reeves family's garden is 18 ft long and 15 ft wide. They want to decrease the length by x feet and increase the width by the same amount. The equation $A = (18 - x)(15 + x)$ models the new area of the garden. What value of x, if any, will give a new area of 280 ft^2?

17. Business An apartment rental agency uses the formula $I = 5400 + 300n - 50n^2$ to find its monthly income I based on renting n apartments. Will the agency's monthly income ever be $7000? Explain.

18. Physics Suppose the equation $h = -16t^2 + 35t$ models the altitude a football will reach t seconds after it is kicked. Is the given altitude possible?
   a. $h = 16$ ft   **b.** $h = 20$ ft   **c.** $h = 30$ ft   **d.** $h = 35$ ft

B **Apply Your Skills**

Find the number of x-intercepts of the related function of each equation.

19. $2x^2 + 4x = -15$

20. $4x^2 + 5x = -2$

21. $x^2 - 8x = -12$

22. $\frac{1}{2}x^2 + 4x = 7$

23. $0.25x^2 - 1.2x + 3.2 = 0$

24. $5x^2 = 3.5 + 4.7x$

25. Business A software company is producing a new computer application. The equation $S = p(54 - 0.75p)$ relates price p in dollars to total sales S in thousands of dollars.
   a. Write the equation in standard form.
   b. Use the discriminant to determine if it is possible for the company to earn $1,000,000 in sales.
   c. According to the model, what price would generate the greatest sales?
   d. Critical Thinking Total sales S decrease as p increases beyond the value in part (c). Why does this make sense in the given situation? Explain.

26. Open-Ended For the equation $x^2 + 4x + k = 0$, find all values of k such that the equation has the given number of solutions.
   a. none   **b.** one   **c.** two

27. You can use a spreadsheet like the one at the right to find the discriminant for each value of b shown in column A.

	A	B	C
1	b	x^2 + bx + 1 = 0	x^2 + bx + 2 = 0
2	−3		
3	−2		
4	−1		
5	0		
6	1		
7	2		
8	3		

a. What spreadsheet formula would you use to find the value in cell B2? What value would you use for cell C2?

b. Describe the integer values of b for which $x^2 + bx + 1 = 0$ has no solutions.

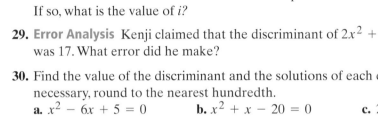

28. Electrical Engineering The function $P = 3i^2 - 2i + 450$ models the power P in an electric circuit with a current i. Can the power in this circuit ever be zero? If so, what is the value of i?

29. Error Analysis Kenji claimed that the discriminant of $2x^2 + 5x - 1 = 0$ was 17. What error did he make?

30. Find the value of the discriminant and the solutions of each equation. If necessary, round to the nearest hundredth.
a. $x^2 - 6x + 5 = 0$
b. $x^2 + x - 20 = 0$
c. $2x^2 - 7x - 3 = 0$
d. **Reasoning** When the discriminant is a perfect square, are the solutions rational or irrational? Explain.

Real-World Connection

Careers An electrical engineer designs circuits that are used in a wide variety of devices.

Does the graph of each function cross the x-axis? If so, find the x-intercepts.

31. $y = x^2 - 2x + 5$ **32.** $y = 2x^2 - 4x + 3$ **33.** $y = 4x^2 + x - 5$

34. $y = -3x^2 - x + 2$ **35.** $y = x^2 - 5x + 7$ **36.** $y = 2x^2 - 3x - 5$

37. Writing How can you use the discriminant to write an equation that has two solutions?

Challenge

Reasoning For each condition given, tell whether $ax^2 + bx + c = 0$ will have two solutions *sometimes*, *always*, or *never*.

38. $b^2 < 4ac$ **39.** $b^2 = 0$ **40.** $ac < 0$

41. Critical Thinking The graph of a quadratic equation includes the points $(2, -1)$ and $(3, 2)$. How many solutions does the equation have? Explain.

42. Critical Thinking The discriminant of $0 = 2x^2 + 6x + 7$ is -20. The discriminant of $0 = 2x^2 + 8x + 10$ is -16. Without graphing, determine which related function has a vertex closer to the x-axis. Explain.

Standardized Test Prep

Multiple Choice

43. Which of the following is equal to $b^2 - 4ac$, if $a = 1$, $b = 7$, and $c = -4$?
A. −111 B. 33 C. 65 D. 113

44. Which of the following equations has NO real-number solutions?
F. $3x^2 - 5x + 1 = 0$ G. $3x^2 - 5x + 4 = 0$
H. $-3x^2 - 11x + 4 = 0$ I. $-2x^2 - 3x + 1 = 0$

Compare the boxed quantity in Column A with the boxed quantity in Column B. Choose the best answer.

A. The quantity in Column A is greater.
B. The quantity in Column B is greater.
C. The two quantities are equal.
D. The relationship cannot be determined from the information given.

	Column A	Column B
45.	the number of real-number solutions of $35 = 20x^2 - 15x + 47$	the number of real-number solutions of $15x + 7 = 0$
46.	the number of real-number solutions of $ax^2 + 5x - 3 = 0$	the number of real-number solutions of $5x^2 + bx - 3 = 0$
47.	the discriminant of $4x^2 - x = 6$	the discriminant of $4x^2 + 6 = x$

Take It to the NET
Online lesson quiz at
www.PHSchool.com
······· Web Code: aea-1008

Short Response

48. A rectangle has a perimeter of 50 cm. Is it possible for it to have an area of 136 cm²? If so, what are the dimensions? Show your work.

Mixed Review

Lesson 10-7

Use the quadratic formula to solve each equation. If necessary, round to the nearest hundredth.

49. $4x^2 + 4x - 3 = 0$ **50.** $x^2 + 2x - 7 = 0$ **51.** $6x^2 - 2x - 1 = 0$

52. $x^2 + x = 5$ **53.** $3x^2 - 8x + 1 = 0$ **54.** $2x^2 - 7x = -6$

Lesson 8-8

Find the balance in each account.

55. $1000 principal earning 3% compounded quarterly; after 3 years

56. $200 principal earning 4.5% compounded quarterly; after 10 years

57. $5000 principal earning 5% annual interest compounded monthly; after 4 years

Lesson 8-6

Determine whether each sequence is *arithmetic* or *geometric*.

58. $5, 9, 13, \ldots$ **59.** $-11, -16, -21, \ldots$ **60.** $10, 20, 40, \ldots$ **61.** $3, 6, 9, \ldots$

✓ Checkpoint Quiz 2   Lessons 10-5 through 10-8

TEXT Instant self-check quiz online and on CD-ROM

Solve each equation. If necessary, round to the nearest tenth. If there is no solution, write *no solution*.

1. $(x + 3)(x - 7) = 0$ **2.** $x^2 + 12x + 27 = 0$ **3.** $x^2 - 5x = 50$

4. $x^2 + 2x - 1 = 0$ **5.** $x^2 - 5x - 4 = 0$ **6.** $x^2 - 8x - 33 = 0$

7. $4x^2 - x - 3 = 0$ **8.** $4x^2 - x + 3 = 0$ **9.** $2x^2 - 3x + 1 = 0$

10. Use the discriminant to determine the number of solutions of the equation $4x^2 - 3x + 5 = 0$.

Lesson Preview

What You'll Learn

OBJECTIVE

▼ To choose a linear, quadratic, or exponential model for data

. . . And Why

To model changes in an animal population, as in Example 3

✓ **Check Skills You'll Need**   (For help, go to Lessons 6-2, 8-7, and 10-1.)

Graph each function.

1. $y = 3x - 1$ **2.** $y = \frac{1}{4}x + 2$

3. $y = 2^x$ **4.** $y = \left(\frac{1}{3}\right)^x$

5. $y = x^2 + 5$ **6.** $y = 2x^2 - 1$

OBJECTIVE

1 Choosing a Linear, Quadratic, or Exponential Model

🄸**TEXT** Interactive lesson includes instant self-check, tutorials, and activities.

You can use the linear, exponential, or quadratic functions you have studied to model some sets of data. Recall the general appearance of each type of function.

🔑 **Key Concepts**

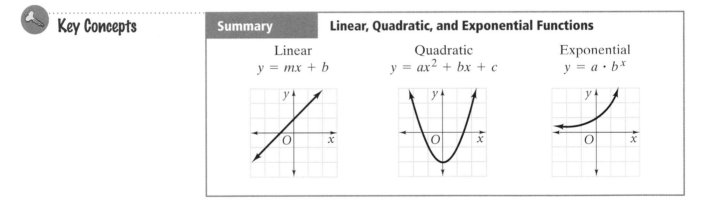

Summary   **Linear, Quadratic, and Exponential Functions**

Linear	Quadratic	Exponential
$y = mx + b$	$y = ax^2 + bx + c$	$y = a \cdot b^x$

You may be able to use the graph of data points to determine a model for the data.

1 EXAMPLE Choosing a Model by Graphing

Graph each set of points. Which model is most appropriate for each set?

a. $(-3, 6), (-2, 2), (0, -2),$
$(3, 6), (1, -1), (2, 2)$

b. $(-2, 5), (0, 3),$
$(1, 2.5), (2, 2)$

c. $(-2, 4), (-1, 2),$
$(1, -2), (2, -4)$

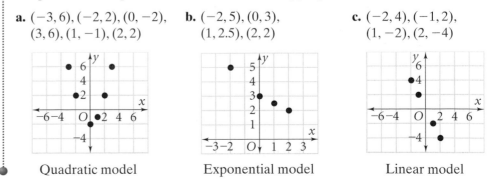

Quadratic model   Exponential model   Linear model

① Graph each set of points. Which model is most appropriate for each set?
a. $(-1.5, -2), (0, 2), (1, 4), (2, 6)$ **b.** $(-1, 1), (0, 0), (1, 1), (2, 4)$
c. $(-1, 0.5), (0, 1), (1, 2), (2, 4)$

You can also analyze data numerically to find the best model.

In Lesson 5-6, you learned that the terms of an arithmetic sequence have a common difference. You can model an arithmetic sequence with a linear function.

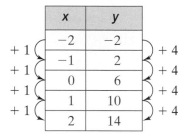

The y-coordinates have a common difference of 4. A linear model fits the data.

In Lesson 8-6, you learned that the terms of a geometric sequence have a common ratio. You can model a geometric sequence with an exponential function.

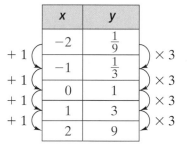

The y-coordinates have a common ratio of 3. An exponential model fits the data.

Data from quadratic functions show a different pattern. For linear data, the first differences are the same. For quadratic data, the second differences are the same. If data have a common second difference, then you can model them with a quadratic function.

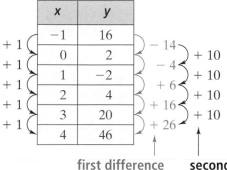

first difference   **second difference**

The y-coordinates have a common second difference of 10. A quadratic model fits the data.

2 EXAMPLE Modeling Data

x	y
−1	20
0	8
1	3.2
2	1.28
3	0.512

a. Which kind of function best models the data at the left? Write an equation to model the data.

Step 1 Graph the data.

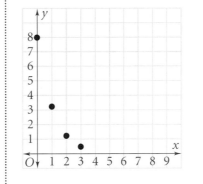

Step 2 The data appear to suggest an exponential model. Test for a common ratio.

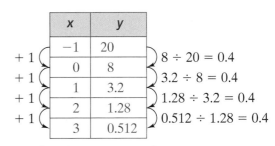

There is a common ratio, 0.4.

Step 3 Write an exponential model.

Relate $y = a \cdot b^x$

Define Let a = the initial value, 8.
Let b = the decay factor, 0.4.

Write $y = 8 \cdot 0.4^x$

Step 4 Test two points other than $(0, 8)$.

$y = 8 \cdot 0.4^1$ $y = 8 \cdot 0.4^3$
$y = 8 \cdot 0.4$ $y = 8 \cdot 0.064$
$y = 3.2$ $y = 0.512$

$(1, 3.2)$ and $(3, 0.512)$ are both data points.

The equation $y = 8 \cdot 0.4^x$ models the data.

x	y
0	0
1	0.3
2	1.2
3	2.7
4	4.8

b. Which kind of function best models the data at the left? Write an equation to model the data.

Step 1 Graph the data.

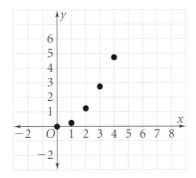

Step 2 The data appear to be quadratic. Test for a common second difference.

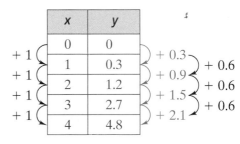

There is a common second difference, 0.6.

Step 3 Write a quadratic model.

$y = ax^2$

$1.2 = a(2)^2$ **Use a point other than (0, 0) to find a.**

$1.2 = 4a$ **Simplify.**

$0.3 = a$ **Divide each side by 4.**

$y = 0.3x^2$ **Write a quadratic function.**

Step 4 Test two points other than $(2, 1.2)$ and $(0, 0)$.

$y = 0.3(3)^2$ $y = 0.3(4)^2$
$y = 0.3 \cdot 9$ $y = 0.3 \cdot 16$
$y = 2.7$ $y = 4.8$

$(3, 2.7)$ and $(4, 4.8)$ are both data points.

The equation $y = 0.3x^2$ models the data.

2 Which kind of function best models the data in each table? Write an equation to model the data.

a.

x	y
0	4
1	4.4
2	4.84
3	5.324
4	5.8564

b.

x	y
0	$\frac{1}{2}$
1	1
2	$1\frac{1}{2}$
3	2

c.

x	y
0	0
1	−0.5
2	−2
3	−4.5
4	−8

While real-world data seldom fall exactly into linear, exponential, or quadratic patterns, you can find a best-possible model.

3 EXAMPLE **Real-World 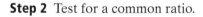 Problem Solving**

Zoology Suppose you are studying frogs that live in a nearby wetland area. The data at the right were collected by a local conservation organization. They indicate the number of frogs estimated to be living in the wetland area over a five-year period. Determine which kind of function best models the data. Write an equation to model the data.

Year	Estimated Population
0	120
1	101
2	86
3	72
4	60

Step 1 Graph the data to decide which model is most appropriate.

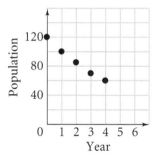

The graph curves, and it does not look quadratic. It may be exponential.

Step 2 Test for a common ratio.

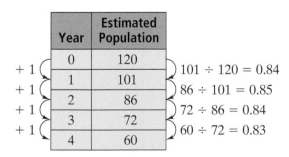

The common ratio is roughly 0.84.

The population of frogs is roughly 0.84 times its value the previous year.

Step 3 Write an exponential model.

Relate $y = a \cdot b^x$

Define Let a = the initial value, 120.
Let b = the decay factor, 0.84.

Write $y = 120 \cdot 0.84^x$

Real-World 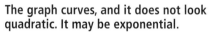 Connection

Frog populations around the world have been declining over the past 20 years.

Step 4 Test two points other than $(0, 120)$.

$$y = 120 \cdot 0.84^3 \qquad\qquad y = 120 \cdot 0.84^4$$
$$y \approx 71 \qquad\qquad\qquad y \approx 60$$

The point $(3, 71)$ is close to the data point $(3, 72)$. The predicted value $(4, 60)$ matches the corresponding data point. The equation $y = 120 \cdot 0.84^x$ models the data.

✓ **Check Understanding** ❸ The profits of a small company are shown in the table at the right. Let $x = 0$ correspond to the year 2000.
  a. Determine which kind of function best models the data.
  b. Write an equation to model the data.

Year	Profit (dollars)
0	0
1	5,000
2	20,000
3	44,000
4	79,000

EXERCISES

For more practice, see *Extra Practice*.

Practice and Problem Solving

Ⓐ **Practice by Example**

Example 1
(page 559)

Graph each set of points. Which model is most appropriate for each set?

1. $(-2, -3), (-1, 0), (0, 1), (1, 0), (2, -3)$ **2.** $(-2, -8), (0, -4), (3, 2), (5, 6)$

3. $(-3, 6), (-1, 0), (0, -1), (1, -1.5)$ **4.** $(-2, 5), (-1, -1), (0, -3), (1, -1), (2, 5)$

5. $\left(2, -5\frac{8}{9}\right), \left(-1, -5\frac{2}{3}\right), (0, -5), (2, 3)$ **6.** $(-3, 8), (-1, 6), (0, 5), (2, 3), (3, 2)$

Example 2
(page 561)

Which kind of function best models the data in each table? Write an equation to model the data.

7.

x	y
0	0
1	1.5
2	6
3	13.5
4	24

8.

x	y
0	−5
1	−3
2	−1
3	1
4	3

9.

x	y
0	0
1	2.8
2	11.2
3	25.2
4	44.8

10.

x	y
0	1
1	1.2
2	1.44
3	1.728
4	2.0736

11.

x	y
0	5
1	2
2	0.8
3	0.32
4	0.128

12.

x	y
0	2
1	1.5
2	1
3	0.5
4	0

Example 3
(page 562)

13. The table at the right shows the end-of-the-month balance in a checking account.
  a. Graph the data. Does the graph suggest a linear, exponential, or quadratic model?
  b. Find the differences of consecutive terms. Are they roughly the same?
  c. Estimate a common difference based on your answer to part (b).
  d. Write an equation to model the data.

Month	Balance (dollars)
1	58
2	123
3	187
4	251

Age (years)	Value (dollars)
0	16,500
1	14,500
2	12,750
3	11,200
4	9900

14. Car Value The value of a car over several years is shown in the table at the left.
  a. Determine which model is most appropriate for the data.
  b. Write an equation to model the data.

15. Physics Your class collected the data in the table at the right by rolling a ball down a ramp. The ramp had the same angle throughout.
  a. Find the differences of consecutive terms.
  b. Find the second differences.
  c. Write an equation to model the data. Let t be the time in seconds and d be the distance in centimeters.
  d. Based on your equation, how far would the ball have rolled down the ramp in 2.5 seconds?

Time (seconds)	Distance (centimeters)
0	0
1	41
2	164
3	370

Apply Your Skills

16. The table below shows the population of a small town. Let $t = 0$ correspond to the year 2020.
  a. Graph the data. Does the graph suggest a linear, exponential, or quadratic model?
  b. What is the difference in years?
  c. Find the differences of consecutive terms. Divide by the difference in years to find possible common differences.
  d. Write a linear equation to model the data based on your answer to part (c).

Year	Population
0	5100
5	5700
10	6300
15	6900

Year	Population (millions)
0	4457
5	4855
10	5284
15	5691
20	6080

Sources: U. S. Census Bureau.
Go to **www.PHSchool.com** for a data update.

Web Code: aeg-2041

17. Population The table at the left shows the world population in millions from 1980 to 2000. The year $t = 0$ corresponds to 1980.
  a. What is the difference in years?
  b. Find the differences of consecutive terms. Divide by the difference in years to find possible common differences.
  c. Find the average of the common differences you found in part (b).
  d. Write a linear equation to model the data based on your answer to part (c).
  e. Use your equation to predict the world population in 2010.

18. Writing Explain in writing to a classmate how to decide whether a linear, exponential, or quadratic function is the most appropriate equation to model a set of data.

Use LinReg, ExpReg, or QuadReg to find an equation to model the data. The greatest value of r^2 indicates the best model for the data.

19.
x	y
0	1.7
1	1.4
2	4.7
3	7.9

20.
x	y
0	2.0
1	1.5
2	1.2
3	0.9

21.
x	y
0	2.8
1	1.4
2	2.7
3	9.8

22.
x	y
−1	4.3
0	5.1
1	4.3
2	2.2
3	1.3

23.
x	y
−1	4.6
0	3.5
1	2.4
2	1.3
3	0.2

24.
x	y
−1	0.04
0	0.10
1	0.26
2	0.68
3	1.76

25. a. Make a table of five points using consecutive x-values for each function. Find the common second difference.
    i. $f(x) = x^2 - 3$ **ii.** $f(x) = 3x^2$ **iii.** $f(x) = 4x^2 - 5x$

b. What is the relationship between the common second difference and the coefficient of x^2?

c. Critical Thinking Explain how you could use this relationship to help you model data if the function were not given.

26. Open-Ended Write a set of data you could model with a quadratic function.

27. Physics A group of students dropped ping-pong balls and found the distance the balls traveled, given a certain amount of time. The diagram below shows their results.

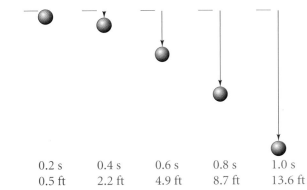

a. Determine which model is most appropriate for the data.

b. Write an equation to model the data. If necessary, round to the nearest tenth.

c. Use your equation to predict the distance a ping-pong ball would fall in 2 s.

0.2 s	0.4 s	0.6 s	0.8 s	1.0 s
0.5 ft	2.2 ft	4.9 ft	8.7 ft	13.6 ft

Challenge

28. Data Collection Complete the chart at the right for your town.

a. Use ExpReg or QuadReg to find an equation to model the data.

b. Use the equation you found in part (a) to predict the current population of your town.

c. Use the equation you found in part (a) to predict the population of your town in 2010.

Year	Population (thousands)
1970	■
1980	■
1990	■
2000	■

29. Data Analysis There are times when data show trends but not consistent ratios or differences. The data in the table below show the total U.S. retail auto sales for the years 1980 through 2000. The value $t = 0$ corresponds to the year 1980.

a. Find the ratios of consecutive entries in the sales columns. Round to the nearest hundredth.

b. Find the differences of consecutive entries in the sales columns.

c. Find the second differences of consecutive entries in the sales column.

d. Which ratio is the most inconsistent? Explain.

e. Critical Thinking If sales data increase every year, can a second difference be negative? Explain.

f. Graph the data. Draw a curve to show the trend.

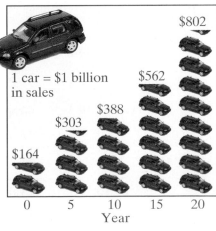

United States Retail Auto Sales

1 car = $1 billion in sales

$802

$562

$388

$303

$164

0   5   10   15   20
Year

Multiple Choice

30. Which equation best models the data in the table at the right?
    A. $y = 4x$
    B. $y = 2x + 2$
    C. $y = 2^x$
    D. $y = 2x^2$

x	y
0	2
1	4
2	6
3	8
4	10

31. Which of the following sets of data is best described by an exponential model?
    F. $(-1, 16)$, $\left(-\frac{1}{2}, 4\right)$, $(0, 2)$, $\left(\frac{1}{2}, -2\right)$, $(1, 4)$
    G. $(1, -7)$, $(2, -4)$, $(3, -1)$, $(4, 2)$, $(5, 5)$
    H. $(1, 1)$, $(3, 3)$, $(0, 0.5)$, $(5, 8)$, $(7, 14)$
    I. $(-2, -4)$, $(-1, 3)$, $(0, 8)$, $(1, 14)$, $(2, 12)$

Short Response

32. The population of a town was 33,500 in 2000. The population is increasing by about 1.4% each year. Write an equation that will predict the population n years after 2000. Let 2000 correspond to $n = 0$. Predict the town's population in 2010.

Extended Response

33. Suppose you put marbles into a cup hanging from an elastic band (spring). You measure the distance d from the floor in centimeters as the number n of marbles is increased.

n	0	1	2	3	4	5
d	43.5	41	38.5	36	33.5	31

a. Which type of model best fits this data set?
b. Write an equation for the data.
c. Suppose the pattern shown above continues. Find the least number of marbles you need to make the cup rest on the floor.

Take It to the NET
Online lesson quiz at
www.PHSchool.com
Web Code: aea-1009

Mixed Review

Lesson 10-8

Find the number of x-intercepts of each function.

34. $y = -x^2$

35. $y = x^2 + 3x + 4$

36. $y = 4x^2 - 10x + 3$

Lesson 10-1

Graph each function.

37. $y = -2x^2$

38. $f(x) = \frac{1}{4}x^2$

39. $f(x) = x^2 + 4$

40. $y = -x^2 - 2$

41. $y = 3x^2 + 1$

42. $y = -\frac{1}{2}x^2 + 1$

Lesson 8-7

Evaluate each function rule for the given value.

43. $y = 2^x$ for $x = -3$

44. $f(x) = -2^x$ for $x = 5$

45. $g(t) = 2 \cdot 3^t$ for $t = -3$

46. $f(t) = 10 \cdot 5^t$ for $t = 2$

47. $y = \left(\frac{1}{2}\right)^t$ for $t = -4$

48. $y = 9 \cdot \left(\frac{3}{2}\right)^x$ for $x = 3$

Cubic Functions

FOR USE WITH LESSON 10-9

In this chapter you learned about quadratic functions. You can also construct and explore functions in which the highest power is greater than two. Functions of the form $y = ax^3 + bx^2 + cx + d$, where $a \neq 0$, are called cubic functions.

EXAMPLE

Make a table of values and graph $y = x^3$ and $y = \frac{1}{3}x^3$.

$$y = x^3 \qquad\qquad\qquad y = \frac{1}{3}x^3$$

x	$y = x^3$	$y = \frac{1}{3}x^3$
-2	-8	$-2\frac{2}{3}$
-1	-1	$-\frac{1}{3}$
0	0	0
1	1	$\frac{1}{3}$
2	8	$2\frac{2}{3}$

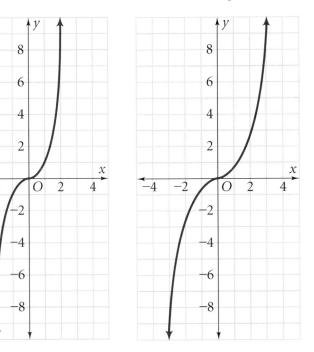

EXERCISES

1. **Critical Thinking** Describe the similarities and differences in the graphs in the Example.

2. **a.** Graph each of the following functions.
   i. $y = -x^3$ **ii.** $y = 2x^3$ **iii.** $y = -\frac{1}{4}x^3$
   b. Describe the similarities and differences in the graphs in part (a).

3. **Critical Thinking** Does a play the same role in cubic functions of the form $y = ax^3$ as it does in quadratic functions? Explain.

4. **a.** Do cubic graphs of the form $y = ax^3$ have an axis of symmetry?
   b. **Critical Thinking** Do cubic graphs have any form of symmetry? Explain.

5. The volume V of a sphere with radius r is given by the function $V = \frac{4}{3}\pi r^3$.
   a. Graph $V = \frac{4}{3}\pi r^3$ from $r = 0$ to $r = 2$.
   b. Use the graph to estimate the radius of a sphere with a volume of 10 ft^3.

Choosing "Cannot Be Determined"

Some multiple-choice questions do not contain enough information. One of the answer choices will then be "Cannot be determined." In such cases, you will not be able to find a specific answer. However, just because the answer choice "Cannot be determined" appears, do not assume that you cannot answer the question; the choice may have been put there as a distraction.

1 EXAMPLE

How many real solutions does the equation $x^2 + bx + 4 = 0$ have if $b > 0$?

   A. None   **B.** One   **C.** Two   **D.** Cannot be determined

Calculate the discriminant and see if it is negative, zero, or positive when $b > 0$.

The discriminant is $b^2 - 4ac = b^2 - 4(1)(4) = b^2 - 16$. This expression is zero when $b = \pm 4$, and positive when $b < -4$ or $b > 4$. Since the value of the discriminant depends on the value of b, you cannot determine how many real solutions the equation has. The correct answer is D.

2 EXAMPLE

A parabola passes through the points $(2, 8)$, $(6, 2)$, and $(8, 8)$. What is the x-coordinate of its vertex?

   A. 4   **B.** 5   **C.** 7   **D.** Cannot be determined

The x-coordinate of the vertex of $y = ax^2 + bx + c$ is $-\frac{b}{2a}$. However, you don't have an equation for the parabola, so you can't use the formula. You might think that the answer is D.

Graph the points and you will notice that $(2, 8)$ and $(8, 8)$ have the same y value, so they are symmetrically placed about the axis of symmetry. The axis of symmetry will be $x = \frac{2 + 8}{2} = 5$. Since the x-coordinate of the vertex is on the axis of symmetry, the correct answer is B. Choice D is a distraction; it was put there in case you thought that the problem could not be done.

EXERCISES

1. Use the question below to answer parts a–c.
   How many real solutions does the equation $x^2 + 4x - n^2 = 0$ have?
      A. None   **B.** One   **C.** Two   **D.** Cannot be determined

   a. What is the discriminant of the equation?
   b. Explain why the discriminant is always positive for all values of n.
   c. What is the correct answer to the question?

2. If $x \neq 0$ and $y \neq 0$, and $x^2 + 2xy + y^2 = 0$, which of the following could be the ratio of x to y?
      A. $1 : 1$ **B.** $2 : 1$ **C.** $-1 : 1$ **D.** Cannot be determined

Chapter Review

Vocabulary

axis of symmetry (p. 511)	perfect squares (p. 525)	standard form of a quadratic function (p. 510)
completing the square (p. 541)	principal square root (p. 524)	standard form of a quadratic equation (p. 530)
discriminant (p. 554)	quadratic equation (p. 530)	
maximum (p. 511)	quadratic formula (p. 547)	vertex (p. 511)
minimum (p. 511)	quadratic function (p. 510)	Zero-Product Property (p. 536)
negative square root (p. 524)	radicand (p. 524)	
parabola (p. 510)	square root (p. 524)	

Reading Math
Understanding
Vocabulary

Take It to the NET
Online vocabulary quiz
at www.PHSchool.com
Web Code: aej-1051

Choose the term that correctly completes each sentence.

1. The U-shaped graph of a quadratic function is a (*parabola, perfect square*).

2. If the quadratic expression $ax^2 + bx + c$ *cannot* be factored, one good way to solve the equation $ax^2 + bx + c = 0$ is to use (*completing the square, the Zero-Product Property*).

3. If $a^2 = b$ and $a > 0$, then a is the (*negative square root, principal square root*) of b.

4. The (*radicand, vertex*) of a parabola is the point at which the parabola intersects the axis of symmetry.

5. The (*discriminant, axis of symmetry*) can be used to determine the number of solutions of a quadratic equation.

Skills and Concepts

10-1 and 10-2 Objectives

▼ To graph quadratic functions of the form $y = ax^2$ (p. 510)

▼ To graph quadratic functions of the form $y = ax^2 + c$ (p. 512)

▼ To graph quadratic functions of the form $y = ax^2 + bx + c$ (p. 517)

▼ To graph quadratic inequalities (p. 519)

A function of the form $y = ax^2 + bx + c$, where $a \neq 0$, is a **quadratic function.** The shape of its graph is a **parabola.** The **axis of symmetry** of a parabola divides it into two congruent halves. The **vertex** of a parabola is the point at which the parabola intersects the axis of symmetry. The axis of symmetry is the line with the equation $x = \frac{-b}{2a}$. The x-coordinate of the vertex of the parabola is $\frac{-b}{2a}$.

The value of a in a quadratic function $y = ax^2 + bx + c$ determines the width of the parabola and whether it opens upward or downward. The value of c is the y-intercept of the graph. Changing the value of c shifts the parabola up or down.

When the parabola opens downward, the y-coordinate of the vertex is a **maximum** point of the function. When the parabola opens upward, the y-coordinate of the vertex is a **minimum** point of the function.

Open-Ended Give an example of a quadratic function for each description.

6. Its graph opens downward.

7. Its vertex is at the origin.

8. Its graph opens upward.

9. Its graph is wider than $y = x^2$.

Graph each function.

10. $y = \frac{2}{3}x^2$

11. $y = -x^2 + 1$

12. $y = x^2 - 4$

13. $y = 5x^2 + 8$

State whether each function has a *maximum* or *minimum* point.

14. $y = 4x^2 + 1$ **15.** $y = -3x^2 - 7$ **16.** $y = \frac{1}{2}x^2 + 9$ **17.** $y = -x^2 + 6$

Graph each function. Label the axis of symmetry and the vertex.

18. $y = -\frac{1}{2}x^2 + 4x + 1$ **19.** $y = -2x^2 - 3x + 10$ **20.** $y = x^2 + 6x - 2$

Graph each quadratic inequality.

21. $y \le 3x^2 + x - 5$ **22.** $y > 3x^2 + x - 5$ **23.** $y \ge -x^2 - x - 8$

10-3 Objectives

▼ To find square roots (p. 524)

▼ To estimate and use square roots (p. 525)

If $a^2 = b$, then a is the **square root** of b. The positive or **principal square root** of b is indicated by $\sqrt{b}$. The **negative square root** is indicated by $-\sqrt{b}$. The squares of integers are called **perfect squares.**

Tell whether each expression is *rational* or *irrational*. Then find the value of each expression. If necessary, round to the nearest hundredth.

24. $\sqrt{86}$ **25.** $-\sqrt{121}$ **26.** $\pm\sqrt{\frac{1}{2}}$ **27.** $\sqrt{2.55}$ **28.** $-\sqrt{\frac{4}{25}}$

29. $-\sqrt{47}$ **30.** $\sqrt{0.36}$ **31.** $\sqrt{140}$ **32.** $-\sqrt{1}$ **33.** $\sqrt{196}$

10-4, 10-5, and 10-6 Objectives

▼ To solve quadratic equations by graphing (p. 529)

▼ To solve quadratic equations using square roots (p. 530)

▼ To solve quadratic equations by factoring (p. 536)

▼ To solve quadratic equations by completing the square (p. 541)

The **standard form of a quadratic equation** is $ax^2 + bx + c = 0$, where $a \ne 0$. Quadratic equations can have two, one, or no solutions. You can solve some quadratic equations by graphing the related function and finding the x-intercepts. If the quadratic expression $ax^2 + bx + c$ can be factored, you can use the **Zero-Product Property** to find the solutions of the equation $ax^2 + bx + c = 0$. This property states that for all real numbers a and b, if $ab = 0$, then $a = 0$ or $b = 0$.

You can solve any quadratic equation by writing it in the form $x^2 + bx = -c$, **completing the square,** and finding the square roots of each side of the equation.

Solve each equation. If the equation has no solution, write *no solution*.

34. $6(x^2 - 2) = 12$ **35.** $-5m^2 = -125$

36. $9(w^2 + 1) = 9$ **37.** $3r^2 + 27 = 0$

Write each equation in standard form. Then solve by factoring.

38. $x^2 + 7x + 12 = 0$ **39.** $5x^2 - 10x = 0$ **40.** $2x^2 - 9x = x^2 - 20$

41. $2x^2 + 5x = 3$ **42.** $3x^2 - 5x = -3x^2 + 6$ **43.** $x^2 - 5x + 4 = 0$

Solve each equation by completing the square. If necessary, round to the nearest hundredth.

44. $x^2 + 6x - 5 = 0$ **45.** $x^2 = 3x - 1$ **46.** $2x^2 + 7x = -6$

47. Geometry The area of a circle is given by the formula $A = \pi r^2$. Find the radius of a circle with area 16 in.^{2}. Round to the nearest tenth of an inch.

48. Gardening Alice is planning a rectangular garden. Its length is 3 ft less than twice its width. Its area is 170 ft^2. Find the dimensions of the garden.

10-7 and 10-8 Objectives

▼ To use the quadratic formula when solving quadratic equations (p. 547)

▼ To choose an appropriate method for solving a quadratic equation (p. 549)

▼ To find the number of solutions of a quadratic equation (p. 554)

You can solve the quadratic equation $ax^2 + bx + c = 0$ when $a \neq 0$ by using the **quadratic formula** $x = \frac{-b \pm \sqrt{b^2 - 4ac}}{2a}$. When a quadratic equation is in the form $ax^2 + bx + c = 0 \ (a \neq 0)$, the **discriminant** is $b^2 - 4ac$.

If $b^2 - 4ac > 0$, there are two solutions.
If $b^2 - 4ac = 0$, there is one solution.
If $b^2 - 4ac < 0$, there is no solution.

Find the number of solutions of each equation.

49. $x^2 - 10 = 3$　　　　　　　**50.** $3x^2 = 27$

51. $x^2 + 3 = 2x$　　　　　　　**52.** $x^2 + 10x = -25$

Solve each equation using the quadratic formula. Round to the nearest hundredth.

53. $4x^2 + 3x - 8 = 0$　　　　　**54.** $2x^2 - 7x = -3$

55. $-x^2 + 8x + 4 = 5$　　　　　**56.** $9x^2 - 270 = 0$

Writing Solve each equation. Explain why you chose the method you used.

57. $5x^2 - 10 = x^2 + 90$　　　　**58.** $9x^2 + 30x - 29 = 0$

59. $2x^2 - 9x = x^2 - 20$　　　　**60.** $x^2 - 6x + 9 = 0$

61. $x^2 + 3x - 225 = 3x$　　　　**62.** $x^2 + 8x = 4$

63. Geometry A square pool has side length p. The border of the pool is 1 ft wide. The combined area of the border and the pool is 400 ft^2. Find the length and the area of the pool.

64. Vertical Motion Suppose you throw a ball in the air. The ball is 6 ft high when it leaves your hand. Use the equation $0 = -16t^2 + 20t + 6$ to find the number of seconds t that the ball is in the air.

10-9 Objectives

▼ To choose a linear, quadratic, or exponential model for data (p. 559)

Graphing data points or analyzing data numerically can help you find the best model. Linear data have a common difference. Exponential data have a common ratio. Quadratic data have a common second difference.

Graph each set of points. Which model is most appropriate for each set?

65. $(-3, 0), (1, 4), (-1, 6), (2, 0)$　　**66.** $(0, 5), (1, 3), (3, -1), (-1, 7)$

67. $(0, 6), (5, 2), (1, 4), (8, 1.5), (2, 3)$　　**68.** $(1, 4), (4, 2), (2, 3), (5, 3.5), (6, 5)$

Write an equation to model the data.

69.

x	y
−1	2.5
0	5
1	10
2	20
3	40

70.

x	y
−1	−5
0	−2
1	1
2	4
3	7

71.

x	y
−3	4
−2	1
−1	0
0	1
1	4

72.

x	y
0	0.5
1	5
2	50
3	500
4	5000

Chapter 10

Chapter Test

Take It to the NET
Online chapter test at
www.PHSchool.com
Web Code: aea-1052

Match each graph with its function.

   A. $y = 3x^2$ **B.** $y = -3x^2 + 1$

   C. $y = -2x^2$ **D.** $y = x^2 - 3$

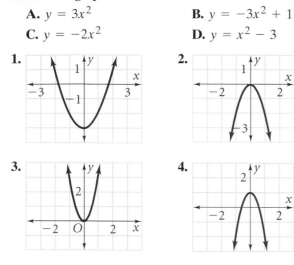

1.

2.

3.

4.

Find the equation of the axis of symmetry and the coordinates of the vertex of the graph of each function. Is the vertex a maximum or a minimum?

5. $y = 3x^2 - 7$ **6.** $y = x^2 - 3x + 2$

7. $y = -2x^2 + 10x - 1$ **8.** $y = \frac{1}{2}x^2 + 6x$

Graph each function.

9. $y = x^2 - 4$ **10.** $y = -x^2 + 1$

11. $y = 5x^2$ **12.** $y = \frac{1}{2}x^2 + 3x$

13. $y = x^2 - 3x + 5$ **14.** $y = 2x^2 - 5$

15. Writing Explain what you can determine about the shape of a parabola from its equation alone.

Find the number of x-intercepts of each function.

16. $y = 5x^2$ **17.** $y = 3x^2 + 10$

18. $y = -2x^2 + x + 7$ **19.** $y = x^2 - 4x$

Graph each inequality.

20. $y \le 2x^2 - 1$ **21.** $y > \frac{1}{2}x^2$

Find the principal square root of each number.

22. 1.44 **23.** 1600 **24.** $\frac{4}{9}$ **25.** 0.04

Between what two consecutive integers is each square root?

26. $\sqrt{28}$ **27.** $\sqrt{136}$ **28.** $\sqrt{332}$ **29.** $-\sqrt{8.99}$

Find the number of solutions of each equation.

30. $x^2 + 4x = -4$ **31.** $x^2 + 8 = 0$

32. $2x^2 + x = 0$ **33.** $3x^2 - 9x = -5$

34. The equation $kx^2 - 10x + 25 = 0$ has one solution. Find the value of k.

Solve each equation. If necessary, round to the nearest hundredth.

35. $2x^2 = 50$ **36.** $-3x^2 + 7x = -10$

37. $x^2 + 6x + 9 = 25$ **38.** $-x^2 - x + 2 = 0$

39. $x^2 + 4x = 1$ **40.** $12x^2 + 16x - 28 = 0$

41. Open-Ended Write an equation of a parabola that has two x-intercepts and a maximum value. Include a graph of your parabola.

Model each problem with a quadratic equation. Then solve.

42. Geometry The volume V of a cylinder is given by the formula $V = \pi r^2 h$, where r is the radius of the cylinder and h is the height. A cylinder with height 10 ft has volume 140 ft^3. To the nearest tenth of a foot, what is the radius of the cylinder?

43. Landscaping The area of a rectangular patio is 800 ft^2. The patio's length is twice its width. Find the dimensions of the patio.

Identify each graph as *linear*, *quadratic*, or *exponential*. Write an equation that models the data shown in each graph.

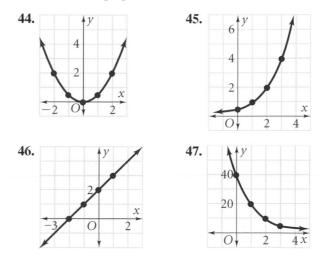

44.

45.

46.

47.

Standardized Test Prep

Multiple Choice

For Exercises 1–9, choose the correct letter.

1. Choose the best approximation of the solutions of $3x^2 - 5x + 1 = 0$.
   A. 2 and −3   B. 1.5 and 1.75
   C. −3 and 2   D. 1.5 and 0.25

2. Which is the equation of the axis of symmetry of the graph of $y = 5x^2 - 2x + 3$?
   F. $x = \frac{1}{5}$ G. $x = -\frac{1}{5}$
   H. $y = \frac{1}{5}$ I. $y = -\frac{1}{5}$

3. Between which two consecutive integers is $\sqrt{52}$?
   A. 5 and 6   B. 6 and 7
   C. 7 and 8   D. 8 and 9

4. A line perpendicular to $y = 3x - 2$ passes through the point (0, 6). Which other point lies on the line?
   F. (9, 3)   G. (−9, 3)
   H. (−9, −3)   I. (9, −3)

5. What is the probability of *not* rolling a 1 or 2 on a number cube?
   A. $\frac{1}{6}$ B. $\frac{1}{3}$ C. $\frac{1}{2}$ D. $\frac{2}{3}$

6. What is the value of the discriminant of $0 = 3x^2 - 4x - 3$?
   F. −20   G. 4   H. 25   I. 52

7. What is the standard form of the product $(3x - 1)(5x + 3)$?
   A. $15x^2 + 2x - 3$
   B. $15x^2 + 2x + 3$
   C. $15x^2 - 4x - 3$
   D. $15x^2 + 4x - 3$

8. If $x^2 + 4x + 4 = 49$, then which statement is true?
   I. $x = 5$ II. $x = -9$
   III. $x = \sqrt{47}$ IV. $x = -\sqrt{47}$
   F. I only   G. III only
   H. III and IV   I. I and II

9. How many solutions are there for the following system?
   $$y = x - 3$$
   $$6y - x = 24$$
   A. 0   B. 1   C. 2   D. 3

Quantitative Comparison

Compare the boxed quantity in Column A with the boxed quantity in Column B. Choose the best answer.

A. The quantity in Column A is greater.
B. The quantity in Column B is greater.
C. The two quantities are equal.
D. The relationship cannot be determined from the information given.

Column A	Column B

10. For the system of equations
    $$x + y = 5$$
    $$2y - x = 4$$

2	x

11. $x^2 + x - 20 = 0$

the value of the discriminant of the equation	the sum of the solutions of the equation

Gridded Response

12. Find the slope of the line that passes through (−1, 3) and (4, 6).

13. A new company employed 12 people. Two years later, it employed a total of 20 people. What was the percent of increase rounded to the nearest percent?

Short Response

14. **Geometry** The length of a rectangle is 6 m less than twice its width. The area of the rectangle is 140 m². Find the dimensions of the rectangle. Show your work.

15. Describe the shape of the graph for each type of function: linear, quadratic, and absolute value.

16. Simplify $9a + 3b - 3 - 4a + 7 - 8b$. Show your work.

Extended Response

17. Graph $y = 4x^2 - 3x$. Show the vertex, axis of symmetry, and x-intercepts of the equation.

Real-World Snapshots

Weight No More

Applying Circles If you traveled in space, you could stay in a weightless environment like the astronauts who inhabit the International Space Station, or you could stay on the circumference of a rotating space station that simulates the feeling of weight you have on Earth. You can calculate the gravitational pull necessary to keep you grounded in space.

Satellite Capture
One of the main uses of the space station is the repair of damaged satellites.

Modular Construction

An important feature of the space station is its modular construction. Each pressurized section is built of similar units, so that if one fails, a similar one can take its place.

Spaceplane cockpit controls

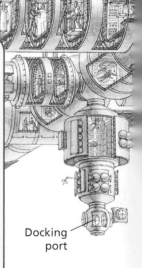

Docking port

How It Works

As the space station rotates, your body wants to move in a straight line. The outside rim of the space station pushes on the bottoms of your feet to keep you moving in a circular path. If the size and rotational speed of the space station are chosen carefully, this push, called the centripetal force, can make you feel the same "weight" that you experience on Earth.

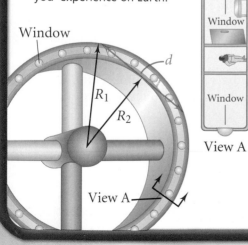

Window

R_1
R_2

View A

h

Window

Window

View A

Activity 1

The figures at the left show a diagram of a circular space station and a cross section of the space station.

a. Select R_1 and R_2 so that the height h of the living space, the difference between the two, is a value that makes sense for humans.

b. The station's curvature limits how far inhabitants can see as they walk. In the diagram, d is a measure of the viewing distance. Use the formula $d = 2\sqrt{(R_2)^2 - (R_1)^2}$. Calculate d for your values of R_1 and R_2.

c. If the viewing distance is too short, inhabitants may feel claustrophobic. Keep the height of the living space the same, but adjust your values of R_1 and R_2 so that d is at least 80 ft. Limit the diameter of the space station to 300 ft or less.

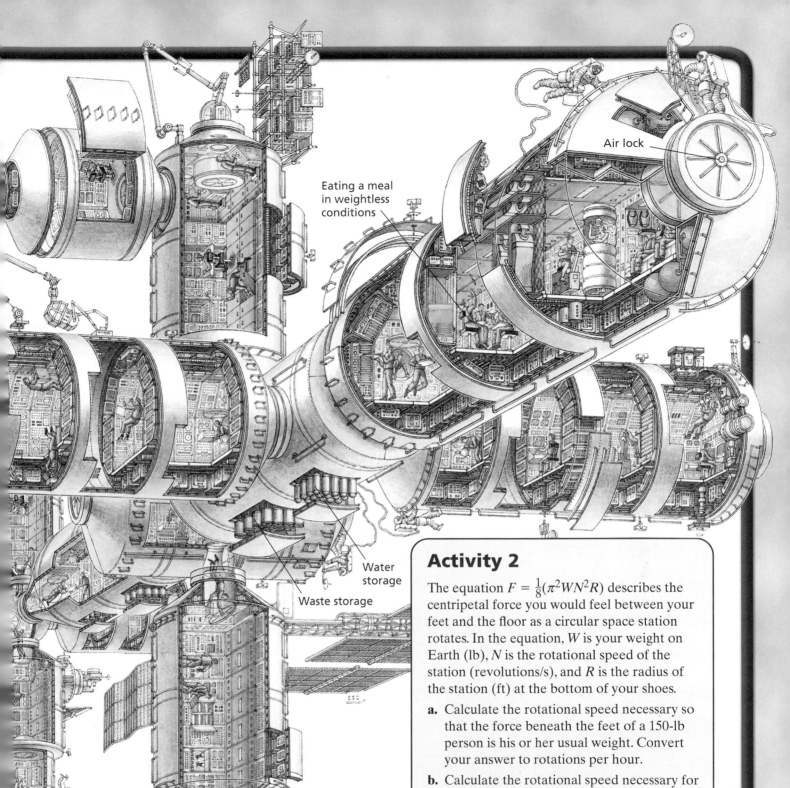

Eating a meal in weightless conditions

Air lock

Water storage

Waste storage

Activity 2

The equation $F = \frac{1}{8}(\pi^2 W N^2 R)$ describes the centripetal force you would feel between your feet and the floor as a circular space station rotates. In the equation, W is your weight on Earth (lb), N is the rotational speed of the station (revolutions/s), and R is the radius of the station (ft) at the bottom of your shoes.

a. Calculate the rotational speed necessary so that the force beneath the feet of a 150-lb person is his or her usual weight. Convert your answer to rotations per hour.

b. Calculate the rotational speed necessary for a 20-lb dog to experience its usual weight. Convert your answer to rotations per hour.

c. Writing Compare your answers from parts (a) and (b). What do you notice?

Which Way Is Up?

To give astronauts a sense of standing upright, each module has a "floor," two "walls," and a "ceiling." Lights are always in the ceiling, and frequently needed supplies and controls are in the walls.

Take It to the NET For more information about weightlessness, go to **www.PHSchool.com**.
Web Code: aee-1053

Where You've Been

- In Chapter 4, you learned about ratios and how to solve a proportion for a given variable.

- In Chapter 8, you learned to simplify expressions containing exponents.

- In Chapter 10, you learned about square roots and evaluated the discriminants of quadratic equations to determine the number of solutions.

Diagnosing Readiness

iTEXT Instant self-check online and on CD-ROM

(For help, go to the Lesson in green.)

Calculating the Mean (Lesson 2-7)

Find the mean of each set of data.

1. $1, 4, 2, 5, 3, 2$ **2.** $40, 55, 60, 52$ **3.** $1.6, 2.1, 1.8, 1.8$

4. $-4, 2, 0, -1$ **5.** $214, 198, 202$ **6.** $3, 2, 2, 3, 4, 4$

Solving Proportions (Lesson 4-1)

Solve each proportion.

7. $\frac{8}{x} = \frac{24}{9}$ **8.** $\frac{k-4}{27} = \frac{1}{3}$ **9.** $\frac{5}{6} = \frac{25}{c}$

10. $\frac{42}{x+8} = \frac{7}{2}$ **11.** $\frac{9}{13} = \frac{y}{65}$ **12.** $\frac{6}{x-5} = \frac{1}{2}$

13. $\frac{3n-1}{14} = \frac{4}{7}$ **14.** $\frac{4}{33} = \frac{8}{w}$ **15.** $\frac{y-1}{5} = \frac{y+3}{7}$

Finding Square Roots (Lesson 10-3)

Simplify each expression.

16. $\sqrt{4}$ **17.** $\sqrt{225}$ **18.** $\sqrt{\frac{9}{25}}$ **19.** $-\sqrt{0.0036}$

Simplify each expression. Round to the nearest hundredth.

20. $\sqrt{40}$ **21.** $\sqrt{84}$ **22.** $\sqrt{104}$ **23.** $\sqrt{3.2}$

Using the Discriminant (Lesson 10-8)

Find the number of real solutions of each equation.

24. $x^2 + 6x + 1 = 0$ **25.** $x^2 - 5x - 6 = 0$ **26.** $x^2 - 2x + 9 = 0$

27. $4x^2 - 4x = -1$ **28.** $6x^2 + 5x - 2 = -3$ **29.** $(2x - 5)^2 = 121$

Radical Expressions and Equations

WORLD SOLAR CHALLENGE

Key Vocabulary

- angle of depression (p. 624)
- angle of elevation (p. 623)
- conjugates (p. 601)
- converse (p. 586)
- cosine (p. 621)
- distance formula (p. 591)
- extraneous solution (p. 609)
- hypotenuse (p. 584)
- hypothesis (p. 586)
- leg (p. 584)
- midpoint formula (p. 593)
- Pythagorean Theorem (p. 584)
- radical equation (p. 607)
- radical expression (p. 578)
- rationalize (p. 581)
- sine (p. 621)
- square root function (p. 614)
- tangent (p. 621)
- trigonometric ratios (p. 621)

Where You're Going

- In this chapter, you will simplify expressions containing radicals.

- You will use the Pythagorean Theorem to find the lengths of sides of right triangles.

- You will solve radical equations.

 Real-World Connection Trigonometry is used in real-world situations to find distances that cannot be measured directly.

Simplifying Radicals

Lesson Preview

What You'll Learn

OBJECTIVE 1 To simplify radicals involving products

OBJECTIVE 2 To simplify radicals involving quotients

. . . And Why

To find the distance to the horizon, as in Example 4

✓ **Check Skills You'll Need** (For help, go to Lessons 8-3 and 10-3.)

Complete each equation.

1. $a^3 = a^2 \cdot a^{\blacksquare}$ **2.** $b^7 = b^6 \cdot b^{\blacksquare}$ **3.** $c^6 = c^3 \cdot c^{\blacksquare}$ **4.** $d^8 = d^4 \cdot d^{\blacksquare}$

Find the value of each expression.

5. $\sqrt{4}$ **6.** $\sqrt{169}$ **7.** $\sqrt{25}$ **8.** $\sqrt{49}$

New Vocabulary • radical expression • rationalize

OBJECTIVE

1 **Simplifying Radical Expressions Involving Products**

Interactive lesson includes instant self-check, tutorials, and activities.

Radical expressions like $2\sqrt{3}$ and $\sqrt{x+3}$ contain a radical. You read $\sqrt{x+3}$ as "the square root of the quantity x plus three." You can simplify a radical expression by removing perfect-square factors from the radicand. Recall that a radicand is the quantity or expression under the radical sign.

Key Concepts

Property	Multiplication Property of Square Roots
For every number $a \geq 0$ and $b \geq 0$, $\sqrt{ab} = \sqrt{a} \cdot \sqrt{b}$.	
Example $\sqrt{54} = \sqrt{9} \cdot \sqrt{6} = 3 \cdot \sqrt{6} = 3\sqrt{6}$	

You can use the Multiplication Property of Square Roots to simplify radical expressions by rewriting the radicand as a product of the perfect-square factors times the remaining factors.

1 EXAMPLE **Removing Perfect-Square Factors**

Simplify $\sqrt{192}$.

$\sqrt{192} = \sqrt{64 \cdot 3}$ **64 is a perfect square and a factor of 192.**

$= \sqrt{64} \cdot \sqrt{3}$ **Use the Multiplication Property of Square Roots.**

$= 8\sqrt{3}$ **Simplify $\sqrt{64}$.**

✓ **Check Understanding** **1** Simplify each radical expression.

a. $\sqrt{50}$ **b.** $-5\sqrt{300}$ **c.** $\sqrt{18}$

You can simplify radical expressions that contain variables. A variable with a nonzero, even exponent is a perfect square. Variables with odd exponents (other than 1 and -1) are the product of a perfect square and the variable. For example, $n^3 = n^2 \cdot n$, so $\sqrt{n^3} = \sqrt{n^2 \cdot n}$. Assume that all variables of all radicands represent nonnegative numbers..

2 EXAMPLE Removing Variable Factors

Simplify $\sqrt{45a^5}$.

$$\sqrt{45a^5} = \sqrt{9a^4 \cdot 5a} \qquad \text{$9a^4$ is a perfect square and a factor of $45a^5$.}$$
$$= \sqrt{9a^4} \cdot \sqrt{5a} \qquad \text{Use the Multiplication Property of Square Roots.}$$
$$= 3a^2 \sqrt{5a} \qquad \text{Simplify $\sqrt{9a^4}$.}$$

✓ **Check Understanding** ② Simplify each radical expression.

a. $\sqrt{27n^2}$ **b.** $-a\sqrt{60a^7}$ **c.** $\sqrt{x^2y^5}$

You can use the Multiplication Property of Square Roots to write $\sqrt{a} \cdot \sqrt{b} = \sqrt{ab}$. Sometimes the product of two radicals has a perfect-square factor.

3 EXAMPLE Multiplying Two Radicals

Simplify each radical expression.

a.
$$\sqrt{8} \cdot \sqrt{12} = \sqrt{8 \cdot 12} \qquad \text{Use the Multiplication Property of Square Roots.}$$
$$= \sqrt{96} \qquad \text{Simplify under the radical.}$$
$$= \sqrt{16 \cdot 6} \qquad \text{16 is a perfect square and a factor of 96.}$$
$$= \sqrt{16} \cdot \sqrt{6} \qquad \text{Use the Multiplication Property of Square Roots.}$$
$$- 4\sqrt{6} \qquad \text{Simplify $\sqrt{16}$.}$$

Problem Solving Hint

Another method of simplifying is using prime factors.

$$\sqrt{8} \cdot \sqrt{12}$$
$$= \sqrt{2 \cdot 2 \cdot 2 \cdot 2 \cdot 2 \cdot 3}$$
$$= \sqrt{2^2 \cdot 2^2 \cdot 2 \cdot 3}$$
$$= 2 \cdot 2\sqrt{6}$$
$$= 4\sqrt{6}$$

b.
$$3\sqrt{2b} \cdot 4\sqrt{10b} = 12\sqrt{20b^2} \qquad \text{Multiply the whole numbers and use the Multiplication Property of Square Roots.}$$
$$= 12\sqrt{4b^2 \cdot 5} \qquad \text{$4b^2$ is a perfect square and a factor of $20b^2$.}$$
$$= 12\sqrt{4b^2} \cdot \sqrt{5} \qquad \text{Use the Multiplication Property of Square Roots.}$$
$$= 12 \cdot 2b\sqrt{5} \qquad \text{Simplify $\sqrt{4b^2}$.}$$
$$= 24b\sqrt{5} \qquad \text{Simplify.}$$

✓ **Check Understanding** ③ Simplify each radical expression.

a. $\sqrt{13} \cdot \sqrt{52}$ **b.** $5\sqrt{3c} \cdot \sqrt{6c}$ **c.** $2\sqrt{5a^2} \cdot 6\sqrt{10a^3}$

When you use radical expressions to solve real-world problems, you may need to use a calculator to find an approximate value of the radical expression.

4 EXAMPLE Real-World 🌐 Problem Solving

500 ft

Sightseeing You can use the formula $d = \sqrt{1.5h}$ to estimate the distance d in miles to a horizon when h is the height of the viewer's eyes above the ground in feet. Estimate the distance a visitor at the Washington Monument can see to the horizon from the observation windows. Round your answer to the nearest mile.

$$d = \sqrt{1.5h}$$
$$= \sqrt{1.5 \cdot 500} \qquad \text{Substitute 500 for h.}$$
$$= \sqrt{750} \qquad \text{Multiply.}$$
$$\approx 27 \qquad \text{Use a calculator.}$$

The distance a visitor can see is about 27 miles.

✓ **Check Understanding** ④ Suppose you are looking out a second floor window 25 ft above the ground. Find the distance you can see to the horizon. Round your answer to the nearest mile.

2 Simplifying Radical Expressions Involving Quotients

You can use the Division Property of Square Roots to simplify expressions.

🔑 **Key Concepts**

Property	**Division Property of Square Roots**

For every number $a \geq 0$ and $b > 0$, $\sqrt{\dfrac{a}{b}} = \dfrac{\sqrt{a}}{\sqrt{b}}$.

Example $\sqrt{\dfrac{16}{25}} = \dfrac{\sqrt{16}}{\sqrt{25}} = \dfrac{4}{5}$

When the denominator of the radicand is a perfect square, it is easier to simplify the numerator and denominator separately.

5 EXAMPLE Simplifying Fractions Within Radicals

📖 **Reading Math**

Read $\dfrac{\sqrt{2}}{3}$ as "the square root of 2 over 3," and $\sqrt{\dfrac{2}{3}}$ as "the square root of two thirds."

Simplify each radical expression.

a. $\sqrt{\dfrac{11}{49}} = \dfrac{\sqrt{11}}{\sqrt{49}}$ Use the Division Property of Square Roots.

$= \dfrac{\sqrt{11}}{7}$ Simplify $\sqrt{49}$.

b. $\sqrt{\dfrac{25}{b^4}} = \dfrac{\sqrt{25}}{\sqrt{b^4}}$ Use the Division Property of Square Roots.

$= \dfrac{5}{b^2}$ Simplify $\sqrt{25}$ and $\sqrt{b^4}$.

✓ **Check Understanding** ❺ Simplify each radical expression.

a. $\sqrt{\dfrac{144}{9}}$ **b.** $\sqrt{\dfrac{25p^3}{q^2}}$ **c.** $\sqrt{\dfrac{75}{16t^2}}$

When the denominator of the radicand is not a perfect square, it may be easier to divide first and then simplify the radical expression.

6 EXAMPLE Simplifying Radicals by Dividing

Simplify each radical expression.

a. $\sqrt{\dfrac{88}{11}} = \sqrt{8}$ Divide.

$= \sqrt{4 \cdot 2}$ 4 is a perfect square and a factor of 8.

$= \sqrt{4} \cdot \sqrt{2}$ Use the Multiplication Property of Square Roots.

$= 2\sqrt{2}$ Simplify $\sqrt{4}$.

b. $\sqrt{\dfrac{12a^3}{27a}} = \sqrt{\dfrac{4a^2}{9}}$ Divide the numerator and denominator by 3a.

$= \dfrac{\sqrt{4a^2}}{\sqrt{9}}$ Use the Division Property of Square Roots.

$= \dfrac{\sqrt{4} \cdot \sqrt{a^2}}{\sqrt{9}}$ Use the Multiplication Property of Square Roots.

$= \dfrac{2a}{3}$ Simplify $\sqrt{4}$, $\sqrt{a^2}$ and $\sqrt{9}$.

✓ **Check Understanding** ❻ Simplify each radical expression.

a. $\sqrt{\dfrac{90}{5}}$ **b.** $\sqrt{\dfrac{48}{75}}$ **c.** $\sqrt{\dfrac{27x^3}{3x}}$

A radicand in the denominator of a radical expression may not be a perfect square. To simplify, you may need to **rationalize** the denominator. To do this, you multiply the numerator and the denominator by the same radical expression. You choose a radical expression that will make the denominator a perfect square.

Need Help?

Multiplying by $\frac{\sqrt{5}}{\sqrt{5}}$ is the same as multiplying by 1.

Multiplying by $\frac{\sqrt{5}}{\sqrt{5}}$ changes the appearance of a radical expression but not its value.

7 EXAMPLE **Rationalizing a Denominator**

Simplify by rationalizing the denominator.

a. $\frac{2}{\sqrt{5}} = \frac{2}{\sqrt{5}} \cdot \frac{\sqrt{5}}{\sqrt{5}}$ Multiply by $\frac{\sqrt{5}}{\sqrt{5}}$ to make the denominator a perfect square.

$= \frac{2\sqrt{5}}{\sqrt{25}}$ Use the Multiplication Property of Square Roots.

$= \frac{2\sqrt{5}}{5}$ Simplify $\sqrt{25}$.

b. $\frac{\sqrt{7}}{\sqrt{8n}} = \frac{\sqrt{7}}{\sqrt{8n}} \cdot \frac{\sqrt{2n}}{\sqrt{2n}}$ Multiply by $\frac{\sqrt{2n}}{\sqrt{2n}}$ to make the denominator a perfect square.

$= \frac{\sqrt{14n}}{\sqrt{16n^2}}$ Use the Multiplication Property of Square Roots.

$= \frac{\sqrt{14n}}{4n}$ Simplify $\sqrt{16n^2}$.

✔ **Check Understanding** **7** Simplify by rationalizing the denominator.

a. $\frac{3}{\sqrt{3}}$ b. $\frac{\sqrt{5}}{\sqrt{18t}}$ c. $\sqrt{\frac{7m}{10}}$

The summary below can help you determine whether a radical expression is in simplest radical form.

🔑 **Key Concepts**

Summary	Simplest Radical Form

A radical expression is in simplest radical form when all three statements are true.
- The radicand has no perfect-square factors other than 1.
- The radicand has no fractions.
- The denominator of a fraction has no radical.

EXERCISES

For more practice, see *Extra Practice.*

Practice and Problem Solving

A **Practice by Example**

Simplify each radical expression.

Examples 1, 2
(pages 578, 579)

1. $\sqrt{200}$ 2. $\sqrt{98}$ 3. $\sqrt{75}$ 4. $-\sqrt{80}$

5. $-3\sqrt{120}$ 6. $5\sqrt{320}$ 7. $\sqrt{28n^2}$ 8. $\sqrt{108b^4}$

9. $3\sqrt{12x^2}$ 10. $\sqrt{4n^3}$ 11. $\sqrt{20a^5}$ 12. $-\sqrt{48b^4}$

Example 3
(page 579)

13. $\sqrt{10} \cdot \sqrt{40}$ 14. $3\sqrt{6} \cdot \sqrt{6}$ 15. $\sqrt{22} \cdot \sqrt{11}$ 16. $2\sqrt{18} \cdot 7\sqrt{6}$

17. $\sqrt{7} \cdot \sqrt{21}$ 18. $-3\sqrt{20} \cdot \sqrt{15}$ 19. $\sqrt{3n} \cdot \sqrt{24n}$ 20. $2\sqrt{7t} \cdot \sqrt{14t}$

21. $\sqrt{3x} \cdot \sqrt{51x^3}$ 22. $5\sqrt{8t} \cdot \sqrt{32t^5}$ 23. $\sqrt{2a^2} \cdot \sqrt{9a^4}$ 24. $-2\sqrt{6a^3} \cdot \sqrt{3a}$

Example 4
(page 579)

For Exercises 25–27, use the formula $d = \sqrt{1.5h}$ to approximate distance d in miles to a horizon when h is the height in feet of the viewer's eyes above the ground. **Round your answer to the nearest mile.**

25. Find the distance you can see to the horizon from a height of 6 feet.

26. Find the distance you can see to the horizon from a height of 100 feet.

27. Find the distance you can see to the horizon from a height of 200 feet.

Example 5
(page 580)

Simplify each radical expression.

28. $\sqrt{\dfrac{21}{49}}$　　　**29.** $3\sqrt{\dfrac{3}{4}}$　　　**30.** $\sqrt{\dfrac{625}{100}}$　　　**31.** $\sqrt{\dfrac{120}{121}}$

32. $\sqrt{\dfrac{5}{9a^2}}$　　　**33.** $\sqrt{\dfrac{7}{16c^2}}$　　　**34.** $\sqrt{\dfrac{75a}{49}}$　　　**35.** $\sqrt{\dfrac{8n^3}{81}}$

Example 6
(page 580)

36. $\sqrt{\dfrac{15}{5}}$　　　**37.** $\sqrt{\dfrac{54}{24}}$　　　**38.** $\sqrt{\dfrac{60}{5}}$　　　**39.** $-\sqrt{\dfrac{160}{8}}$

40. $\sqrt{\dfrac{140x^3}{5x}}$　　**41.** $\sqrt{\dfrac{3s^3}{27s}}$　　**42.** $\sqrt{\dfrac{30a^5}{40a}}$　　**43.** $\sqrt{\dfrac{63y}{7y^3}}$

Example 7
(page 581)

Simplify each radical expression by rationalizing the denominator.

44. $\dfrac{3}{\sqrt{2}}$　　　**45.** $\dfrac{5}{\sqrt{5}}$　　　**46.** $\dfrac{\sqrt{3}}{\sqrt{7x}}$　　　**47.** $\dfrac{2\sqrt{2}}{\sqrt{5n}}$

48. $\dfrac{9}{\sqrt{8}}$　　　**49.** $\dfrac{12}{\sqrt{12}}$　　　**50.** $\dfrac{3\sqrt{2}}{\sqrt{9b}}$　　　**51.** $\dfrac{5\sqrt{11}}{\sqrt{20y}}$

B　**Apply Your Skills**

Writing **Explain why each radical expression is or is not in simplest radical form.**

52. $\dfrac{13}{\sqrt{4}}$　　　**53.** $\dfrac{3}{\sqrt{3}}$　　　**54.** $4\sqrt{3}$　　　**55.** $5\sqrt{30}$

56. Suppose a and b are positive integers.
　a. Verify that if $a = 18$ and $b = 10$, then $\sqrt{a} \cdot \sqrt{b} = 6\sqrt{5}$.
　b. Open-Ended Find two other pairs of positive integers a and b such that $\sqrt{a} \cdot \sqrt{b} = 6\sqrt{5}$.

Simplify each radical expression.

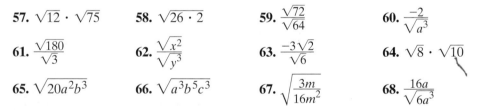

57. $\sqrt{12} \cdot \sqrt{75}$　　**58.** $\sqrt{26 \cdot 2}$　　**59.** $\dfrac{\sqrt{72}}{\sqrt{64}}$　　**60.** $\dfrac{-2}{\sqrt{a^3}}$

61. $\dfrac{\sqrt{180}}{\sqrt{3}}$　　**62.** $\dfrac{\sqrt{x^2}}{\sqrt{y^3}}$　　**63.** $\dfrac{-3\sqrt{2}}{\sqrt{6}}$　　**64.** $\sqrt{8} \cdot \sqrt{10}$

65. $\sqrt{20a^2b^3}$　　**66.** $\sqrt{a^3b^5c^3}$　　**67.** $\sqrt{\dfrac{3m}{16m^2}}$　　**68.** $\dfrac{16a}{\sqrt{6a^3}}$

Solve each equation. Leave your answer in simplest radical form.

69. $x^2 + 6x - 9 = 0$　　　**70.** $n^2 - 2n + 1 = 5$　　　**71.** $3y^2 - 4y - 2 = 0$

72. a. Show work to verify that $\sqrt{50}$ equals $5\sqrt{2}$.
　b. Writing Explain why $5\sqrt{2}$ is in simplest radical form.

73. Open-Ended What are three numbers whose square roots can be written in the form $a\sqrt{3}$ for some value of a?

74. Newspaper Layout A square picture on the front page of a newspaper occupies an area of 24 in.^{2}.
　a. Find the length of each side in simplest radical form.
　b. Calculate the length of each side to the nearest hundredth of an inch.

C Challenge

Simplify each radical expression.

75. $\sqrt{24} \cdot \sqrt{2x} \cdot \sqrt{3x}$ **76.** $2b(\sqrt{5b})^2$ **77.** $\sqrt{45a^7} \cdot \sqrt{20a}$

78. Physics The time that a pendulum of a grandfather clock takes to swing back and forth one cycle is the period of the pendulum. The formula for finding the period T in seconds is $T = 2\pi\sqrt{\frac{L}{32}}$, where L is the length of the pendulum in feet. Find the period of a pendulum that is 8 feet long. Write your answer in terms of π.

Standardized Test Prep

Multiple Choice

79. Simplify $\sqrt{80}$.
    A. $10\sqrt{8}$ **B.** $8\sqrt{10}$ **C.** $4\sqrt{5}$ **D.** 40

80. Simplify $5\sqrt{3x^2} \cdot \sqrt{6x}$.
    F. $15x\sqrt{2x}$ **G.** $5x\sqrt{18x}$ **H.** $3x\sqrt{10x}$ **I.** $6x\sqrt{5x}$

81. Which of the following equals $\frac{2}{3}$?
    A. $\sqrt{\frac{9}{25}}$ **B.** $\sqrt{\frac{20}{45}}$ **C.** $2\sqrt{\frac{4}{27}}$ **D.** $\sqrt{\frac{6}{9}}$

82. Which of the following equals $1.5\sqrt{0.038}$?
    F. $150\sqrt{3.8}$ **G.** $15\sqrt{3.8}$ **H.** $15\sqrt{0.38}$ **I.** $15\sqrt{0.00038}$

Take It to the NET
Online lesson quiz at
www.PHSchool.com
Web Code: aea-1101

Short Response

83. A square window occupies an area of 96 ft². What is the length of each side of the window in simplest radical form? Show your work.

Mixed Review

Lesson 10-9

Which kind of function best models the data in each table? Write an equation to model the data.

84.

x	y
−1	0.2
0	0
1	0.2
2	0.8
3	1.8
4	3.2

85.

x	y
−1	1.6
0	4
1	10
2	25
3	62.5
4	156.25

86.

x	y
−1	11.2
0	7
1	2.8
2	−1.4
3	−5.6
4	−9.8

Lesson 10-2

Graph each function. Label the axis of symmetry and the vertex.

87. $f(x) = x^2 + 8x - 4$ **88.** $y = x^2 - 10x + 7$ **89.** $y = 3x^2 + 12x - 5$

Lesson 9-1

Simplify. Write each answer in standard form.

90. $(n^2 + 5n - 1) + (2n^2 + 6)$ **91.** $(4v^2 + 8v - 2) - (v^2 + 9v + 7)$

92. $(5t^3 - 14t) + (8t^2 - 11)$ **93.** $(2b^2 - 12b - 8) - (5b^2 + 11b + 13)$

The Pythagorean Theorem

Lesson Preview

What You'll Learn

OBJECTIVE 1
To solve problems using the Pythagorean Theorem

OBJECTIVE 2
To identify right triangles

. . . And Why

To calculate heights indirectly, as in Example 2

✓ Check Skills You'll Need

(For help, go to Lesson 10-4.)

Simplify each expression.

1. $5^2 + 6^2$　　　**2.** $9^2 - 4^2$　　　**3.** $(3t)^2 + (4t)^2$

Solve each equation.

4. $c^2 = 36$　　　**5.** $24 + b^2 = 49$　　　**6.** $a^2 + 16 = 65$

7. $12 + b^2 = 32$　　**8.** $80 = c^2$　　　**9.** $100 = a^2 + 52$

New Vocabulary

- hypotenuse　• leg　• Pythagorean Theorem
- conditional　• hypothesis　• conclusion　• converse

---

iTEXT Interactive lesson includes instant self-check, tutorials, and activities.

OBJECTIVE 1

Solving Problems Using the Pythagorean Theorem

Investigation: The Pythagorean Theorem

1. The values in the chart represent the sides of a right triangle. Copy and complete the chart.

a	b	c	a^2	b^2	$a^2 + b^2$	c^2
3	4	5	▨	▨	▨	▨
5	12	13	▨	▨	▨	▨
$\frac{3}{5}$	$\frac{4}{5}$	1	▨	▨	▨	▨
0.9	1.2	1.5	▨	▨	▨	▨

2. Compare the value of $a^2 + b^2$ for each row in the table to the value of c^2.

3. Complete the following statement: For a right triangle, the square of the longest side __?__ the sum of the squares of the other two sides.

Reading Math

The Pythagorean Theorem is named after Pythagoras, a Greek philosopher and mathematician who taught about 530 B.C.

In a right triangle, the side opposite the right angle is the **hypotenuse.** It is the longest side. Each of the sides forming the right angle is a **leg.**

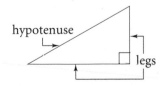

The **Pythagorean Theorem** describes the relationship of the lengths of the sides of a right triangle.

Theorem	The Pythagorean Theorem

In any right triangle, the sum of the squares of the lengths of the legs is equal to the square of the length of the hypotenuse.

$$a^2 + b^2 = c^2$$

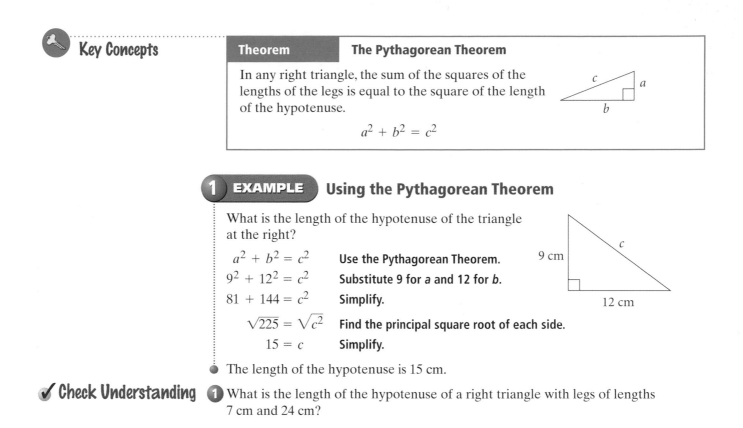

1 EXAMPLE Using the Pythagorean Theorem

What is the length of the hypotenuse of the triangle at the right?

$a^2 + b^2 = c^2$ **Use the Pythagorean Theorem.**

$9^2 + 12^2 = c^2$ **Substitute 9 for *a* and 12 for *b*.**

$81 + 144 = c^2$ **Simplify.**

$\sqrt{225} = \sqrt{c^2}$ **Find the principal square root of each side.**

$15 = c$ **Simplify.**

● The length of the hypotenuse is 15 cm.

✔ **Check Understanding** ❶ What is the length of the hypotenuse of a right triangle with legs of lengths 7 cm and 24 cm?

You can also use the Pythagorean Theorem to find the length of a leg of a right triangle when you know the lengths of the hypotenuse and the other leg.

2 EXAMPLE Real-World Problem Solving

Fire Rescue A fire truck parks beside a building such that the base of the ladder is 16 ft from the building. The fire truck extends its ladder 30 ft as shown at the left. How high is the top of the ladder above the ground?

Define Let b = height (in feet) of the ladder from a point 10 ft above the ground.

Relate The triangle formed is a right triangle. Use the Pythagorean Theorem.

Write $a^2 + b^2 = c^2$

$16^2 + b^2 = 30^2$ **Substitute.**

$256 + b^2 = 900$ **Simplify.**

$b^2 = 644$ **Subtract 256 from each side.**

$\sqrt{b^2} = \sqrt{644}$ **Find the principal square root of each side.**

$b \approx 25.4$ **Use a calculator and round to the nearest tenth.**

The height to the top of the ladder is 10 feet higher than 25.4 ft, so it is about 35.4 ft from the ground.

✔ **Check Understanding** ❷ Use the figure at the right. About how many miles is it from downtown to the harbor? Round to the nearest tenth of a mile.

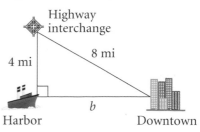

An *if-then* statement like "If an animal is a horse, then it has four legs" is called a **conditional.** Every conditional has two parts. The part following *if* is the **hypothesis,** and the part following *then* is the **conclusion.**

The **converse** of a conditional switches the hypothesis and the conclusion. Somtimes converses of conditionals are not true. For example, "If an animal has four legs, then the animal is a horse" is not a true statement.

You can rewrite the Pythagorean Theorem as an *if-then* statement, "If a triangle is a right triangle with legs of lengths a and b and hypotenuse of length c, then $a^2 + b^2 = c^2$." The Pythagorean Theorem has a converse that is always true.

Key Concepts

Property	**The Converse of the Pythagorean Theorem**

If a triangle has sides of lengths a, b, and c, and $a^2 + b^2 = c^2$, then the triangle is a right triangle with hypotenuse of length c.

You can use the converse of the Pythagorean Theorem to determine whether a triangle is a right triangle. Since the Pythagorean Theorem and its converse are always true, you can also determine whether a triangle is *not* a right triangle.

3 **EXAMPLE** **Using the Converse of the Pythagorean Theorem**

Determine whether the given lengths can be sides of a right triangle.

a. 5 in., 12 in., and 13 in.

$5^2 + 12^2 \stackrel{?}{=} 13^2$

$25 + 144 \stackrel{?}{=} 169$

$\qquad 169 = 169$ ✓

The triangle is a right triangle.

Determine whether $a^2 + b^2 = c^2$, where c is the longest side.

b. 7 m, 9 m, and 12 m

$7^2 + 9^2 \stackrel{?}{=} 12^2$

$49 + 81 \stackrel{?}{=} 144$

$\qquad 130 \neq 144$

The triangle is not a right triangle.

✓ Check Understanding **3** A triangle has sides of lengths 10 m, 24 m, and 26 m. Is the triangle a right triangle?

You can use the converse of the Pythagorean Theorem to solve a physics problem involving force.

4 **EXAMPLE** **Real-World 🌐 Problem Solving**

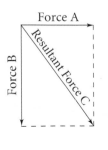

Force A

Resultant Force C

Force B

Physics If two forces pull at right angles to each other, the resultant force is represented as the diagonal of a rectangle, as shown at the left. The diagonal forms a right triangle with two of the perpendicular sides of the rectangle. For a 30-lb force and a 40-lb force, the resultant force is 50 lb. Are the forces pulling at right angles to each other?

$30^2 + 40^2 \stackrel{?}{=} 50^2$ *Determine whether $a^2 + b^2 = c^2$, where c is the greatest force.*

$900 + 1600 \stackrel{?}{=} 2500$

$\qquad 2500 = 2500$ ✓

Yes, the 30-lb and 40-lb forces are pulling at right angles to each other.

✓ **Check Understanding** ④ For a 70-lb force and a 60-lb force, the resultant force is 100 lb. Are the forces pulling at right angles to each other?

EXERCISES

For more practice, see *Extra Practice.*

Practice and Problem Solving

Ⓐ Practice by Example

Example 1
(page 585)

Use the triangle at the right. Find the length of the missing side. If necessary, round to the nearest tenth.

1. $a = 6, b = 8$

2. $a = 15, b = 20$

3. $a = 8, b = 15$

4. $a = 10, b = 24$

5. $a = 1.5, b = 2$

6. $a = \frac{3}{5}, b = \frac{4}{5}$

Example 2
(page 585)

7. $a = 3, c = 5$

8. $b = 12, c = 13$

9. $a = 9, c = 15$

10. $b = 7, c = 10$

11. $a = 5, c = 9$

12. $a = 0.8, c = 1$

13. Packaging Use the diagram at the right. Find the width w that the box needs to be for the fishing rod to fit flat inside of it.

14. A 16-ft ladder is placed 4 ft from the base of a building. How high on the building will the ladder reach?

15. A pigeon leaves its nest in New York City and flies 5 km due east. The pigeon then flies 3 km due north. How far is the pigeon from its nest?

Example 3
(page 586)

Determine whether the given lengths can be sides of a right triangle.

16. 9 ft, 12 ft, 15 ft

17. 1 in., 2 in., 3 in.

18. 2 m, 4 m, 5 m

19. 16 cm, 30 cm, 34 cm

20. 4 m, 4 m, 8 m

21. 10 in., 24 in., 26 in.

Example 4
(page 586)

Physics Determine whether the forces in each pair are pulling at right angles to each other.

22. 45 lb, 24 lb, resultant force 51 lb

23. 3.5 lb, 6.2 lb, resultant force 9.1 lb

24. 20 lb, 10 lb, resultant force 30 lb

25. 1.25 lb, 3 lb, resultant force 3.25 lb

Ⓑ Apply Your Skills

For the values given, a and b are legs of a right triangle, and c is the hypotenuse. Find the length of the missing side of each right triangle. If necessary, round to the nearest tenth.

26. $a = 1.2, b = 0.9$

27. $a = \frac{1}{5}, c = \frac{1}{3}$

28. $a = \sqrt{5}, c = \sqrt{14}$

29. $a = \sqrt{7}, b = \sqrt{29}$

30. $a = 2.4, b = 1.0$

31. $a = 2\frac{1}{2}, b = 6\frac{1}{2}$

🌐 **32. Sailing** The diagram at the left shows a sailboat.
   a. Use the Pythagorean Theorem to find the height of the sail in simplest radical form.
   b. Use the result of part (a) and the formula for the area of a triangle to find the area of the sail. Round to the nearest tenth.

Determine whether the given lengths can be sides of a right triangle.

33. $1, \sqrt{3}, 2$ **34.** $\sqrt{2}, \sqrt{2}, 4$ **35.** $\sqrt{6.2}, \sqrt{2.8}, 3$ **36.** $\frac{3}{4}, 1, 1\frac{1}{4}$

37. Manufacturing What is the diameter of the smallest circular opening through which the rectangular rod shown at the right will fit? Round to the nearest tenth.

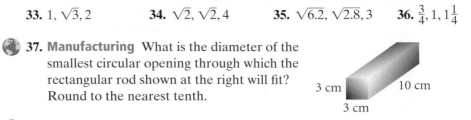

3 cm   3 cm   10 cm

38. Physics Two utility vehicles at a 90° angle to each other try to pull a third vehicle out of the snow. If one utility vehicle exerts a force of 600 lb, and the other exerts a force of 800 lb, what is the resulting force on the vehicle stuck in the snow?

Find the missing length to the nearest tenth.

39.

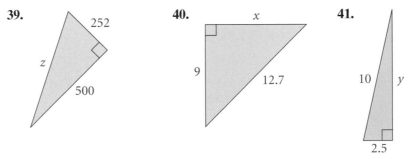

252
z
500

40.

x
9
12.7

41.

10
y
2.5

42. You know that two sides of a right triangle measure 10 in. and 8 in.
   a. Writing Explain why this is not enough information to be sure of finding the length of the third side.
   b. Give two possible values for the length of the third side.

43. Any set of three positive integers that satisfies the relationship $a^2 + b^2 = c^2$ is called a *Pythagorean triple*.
   a. Verify that the numbers 6, 8, and 10 form a Pythagorean triple.
   b. Copy the table at the right. Complete the table so that the values in each row form a Pythagorean triple.
   c. Open-Ended Find a Pythagorean triple that does not appear in the table.

a	b	c
3	4	▪
5	▪	13
▪	24	25
9	40	▪

44. Solar Power Solar cars use panels built out of photovoltaic cells, which convert sunlight into electricity. Consider a car like the one shown. Not counting the driver's "bubble," the panels form a rectangle.
   a. The length of the rectangle is 13 ft and the diagonal is 14.7 ft. Find the width. Round to the nearest tenth of a foot.
   b. Find the area of the rectangle.
   c. The panels produce a maximum power of about 11 watts/ft². Find the maximum power produced by the panels on the car. Round to the nearest watt.

45. Construction A carpenter braces an 8 ft × 10 ft wall by nailing a board diagonally across the wall. How long is the bracing board?

46. a. Open-Ended Find a right triangle that has legs with irrational length and a hypotenuse with a rational length.
   b. Use a calculator to find the area of your triangle. Round to the nearest tenth.

Real-World Connection

This solar-powered car only weighs 110 lb. It can reach a top speed of 80 mi/h.

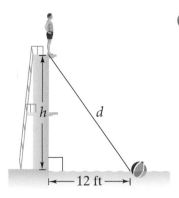

47. Diving Suppose you are standing at the top of a diving platform h feet tall. Looking down, you see a ball on the water 12 feet from the bottom of the diving platform as in the diagram at the left.
   a. Find the distance d to the ball if $h = 6$ feet.
   b. Find the distance d to the ball if $h = 12$ feet.
   c. Suppose you know the distance d to the ball is 16 feet. About how tall is the diving platform?
   d. Critical Thinking Could the distance d to the ball be 7 feet? Explain.

State the hypothesis and the conclusion of each conditional. Then write the converse. Tell whether the converse is true or false.

48. If an integer has 2 as a factor, then the integer is even.

49. If a figure is a square, then the figure is a rectangle.

50. If you are in Brazil, then you are south of the equator.

51. If an angle is a right angle, then its measure is 90°.

52. Geometry The yellow, green, and blue figures at the right are squares. Use the Pythagorean Theorem to find the area of the blue square.

53. Geometry The diagonal of a square measures $6\sqrt{2}$ in. Find the length of the side of the square.

Challenge

Use the Pythagorean Theorem to find s. Express s as a radical expression in simplest form.

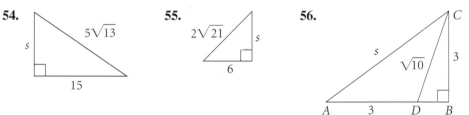

54.

$5\sqrt{13}$
s
15

55.

$2\sqrt{21}$
s
6

56.

C
s
$\sqrt{10}$
3
A 3 D B

57. Geometry The lengths of the sides of a right triangle are three consecutive integers. Write and solve an equation to find the three integers.

58. a. Critical Thinking The vertex of the right angle of a right triangle is at the origin of coordinate axes. The length of the horizontal side is 5 units. The length of the vertical side is 7 units. The triangle is located in Quadrant II. Sketch the graph.
   b. Find the length of the hypotenuse in simplified radical form.

59. On graph paper, draw a right triangle like the one at the right. Then draw the square by drawing four right triangles as shown.
   a. Find the area of the larger square. Write your answer as a trinomial.
   b. Find the area for the smaller square. Write your answer as a monomial.
   c. Find the area of each triangle in terms of a and b.
   d. The area of the larger square equals the sum of the area of the smaller square and the areas of the four triangles. Write this equation and simplify.
   e. What do you notice about the equation you wrote for part (d)?

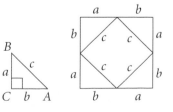

Multiple Choice

60. Find the approximate length of the hypotenuse of a right triangle with leg lengths 8.4 cm and 7.6 cm.
  A. 4.00 cm   **B.** 5.66 cm   **C.** 7.99 cm   **D.** 11.33 cm

61. Find the length of the leg of a right triangle with one leg length $2\sqrt{3}$ and hypotenuse length $3\sqrt{3}$.
  F. $\sqrt{3}$ **G.** $\sqrt{14}$ **H.** $\sqrt{15}$ **I.** $\sqrt{39}$

Quantitative Comparison

Compare the boxed quantity in Column A with the boxed quantity in Column B. Choose the best answer.
  A. The quantity in Column A is greater.
  B. The quantity in Column B is greater.
  C. The two quantities are equal.
  D. The relationship cannot be determined from the information given.

For Exercises 62–64, a and b represent the lengths of the legs and c represents the length of the hypotenuse of a right triangle.

	Column A	**Column B**
62.	b if $a = 9$ and $c = 10$	c if $a = 9$ and $b = 10$
63.	c if $a = 15$ and $b = 11$	c if $a = 11$ and $b = 15$
64.	a if $b = 10$ and $c = 22$	a if $b = 12$ and $c = 20$

Take It to the NET
Online lesson quiz at
www.PHSchool.com
 Web Code: aea-1102

Short Response

65. The sides of a triangular garden are 8 ft, 17 ft, and 15 ft. Is the garden in the shape of a right triangle? Justify your answer.

Mixed Review

Lesson 11-1

Simplify each radical expression.

66. $\sqrt{8} \cdot \sqrt{6}$ **67.** $\dfrac{\sqrt{12}}{\sqrt{18}}$ **68.** $\sqrt{5 \cdot 10}$

69. $\sqrt{40b^5}$ **70.** $\dfrac{\sqrt{2x^2}}{\sqrt{4x^6}}$ **71.** $\sqrt{\dfrac{24v}{v^8}}$

Lesson 10-3

Between which two consecutive integers is each square root?

72. $\sqrt{11}$ **73.** $\sqrt{80}$ **74.** $-\sqrt{51}$ **75.** $\sqrt{125}$

Tell whether each expression is rational or irrational.

76. $-\sqrt{1.44}$ **77.** $\sqrt{130}$ **78.** $\sqrt{\dfrac{2}{3}}$ **79.** $\sqrt{\dfrac{1}{36}}$

Lesson 9-2

Simplify each product.

80. $x(8x - 4)$ **81.** $(4a + 5)3a$ **82.** $6t^2(3t - 1)$

83. $2p^3(13 - 5p)$ **84.** $5b(3b^2 + b - 9)$ **85.** $-7v(v^3 - 6v + 1)$

11-3

The Distance and Midpoint Formulas

Lesson Preview

What You'll Learn

OBJECTIVE 1
To find the distance between two points on a coordinate plane

OBJECTIVE 2
To find the coordinates of the midpoint of a line segment

. . . And Why

To solve problems involving geometric figures, as in Examples 2 and 4

✓ Check Skills You'll Need

(For help, go to Lessons 11-2 and 2-7.)

Find the length of the hypotenuse with the given leg lengths. If necessary, round to the nearest tenth.

1. $a = 3, b = 4$ **2.** $a = 2, b = 5$

3. $a = 3, b = 8$ **4.** $a = 7, b = 5$

For each set of values, find the mean.

5. $x_1 = 6, x_2 = 14$ **6.** $y_1 = -4, y_2 = 8$

7. $x_1 = -5, x_2 = -7$ **8.** $y_1 = -10, y_2 = -3$

New Vocabulary • distance formula • midpoint • midpoint formula

---

OBJECTIVE

1

Finding the Distance Between Two Points

ⓘTEXT Interactive lesson includes instant self-check, tutorials, and activities.

In the diagram at the left, $\overline{AB}$ is a horizontal line segment. You can find its length by subtracting the x-coordinate of A from the x-coordinate of B. The length of $\overline{AB}$ is $5 - 1 = 4$.

Similarly, you can find the length of $\overline{CD}$ by subtracting the y-coordinate of C from the y-coordinate of D. The length of $\overline{CD}$ is $3 - (-2) = 5$.

For any two points $P(x_1, y_1)$ and $Q(x_2, y_2)$ not on a horizontal or vertical line, you can graph the points and form a right triangle as shown at the right. You can then use the Pythagorean Theorem to find the distance between the points.

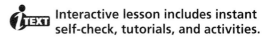

Need Help?

PQ is the distance between points P and Q and the length of $\overline{PQ}$.

$(PQ)^2 = (PR)^2 + (RQ)^2$ **Use the Pythagorean Theorem.**

$(PQ)^2 = (x_2 - x_1)^2 + (y_2 - y_1)^2$ **Substitute.**

$\sqrt{(PQ)^2} = \sqrt{(x_2 - x_1)^2 + (y_2 - y_1)^2}$ **Find the principal square root of each side.**

$PQ = \sqrt{(x_2 - x_1)^2 + (y_2 - y_1)^2}$

The equation above is known as the distance formula.

Key Concepts

Theorem	The Distance Formula

The distance d between any two points (x_1, y_1) and (x_2, y_2) is

$d = \sqrt{(x_2 - x_1)^2 + (y_2 - y_1)^2}.$

You find an *exact* distance by substituting values in the formula and simplifying the radical expressions. You find an *approximate* distance by using a calculator to estimate when a radical expression is not a perfect square.

1 EXAMPLE Using the Distance Formula

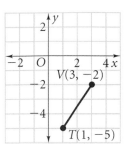

Find the distance between $T(1, -5)$ and $V(3, -2)$.

$d = \sqrt{(x_2 - x_1)^2 + (y_2 - y_1)^2}$ **Use the distance formula.**

$d = \sqrt{(3 - 1)^2 + [-2 - (-5)]^2}$ **Substitute $(3, -2)$ for (x_2, y_2) and $(1, -5)$ for (x_1, y_1).**

$d = \sqrt{(2)^2 + (3)^2}$ **Simplify within parentheses.**

$d = \sqrt{13}$ **Simplify to find the exact distance.**

$d \approx 3.6$ **Use a calculator. Round to the nearest tenth.**

● The distance between T and V is about 3.6 units.

✔ **Check Understanding** ❶ Find the distance between $M(-2, 1)$ and $N(-5, 4)$. Round to the nearest tenth.

You can use the distance formula to find the lengths of the sides of a geometric figure drawn on a coordinate plane. When adding values that are square roots, use a calculator to add before you round the answer.

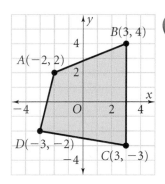

2 EXAMPLE Finding Lengths of Sides

Find the exact lengths of each side of quadrilateral $ABCD$. Then find the perimeter to the nearest tenth.

$AB = \sqrt{[3 - (-2)]^2 + (4 - 2)^2}$ $BC = 4 - (-3) = 7$

$\quad = \sqrt{5^2 + 2^2}$

$\quad = \sqrt{25 + 4}$

$\quad = \sqrt{29}$

$CD = \sqrt{(-3 - 3)^2 + [-2 - (-3)]^2}$ $AD = \sqrt{[-3 - (-2)]^2 + (-2 - 2)^2}$

$\quad = \sqrt{(-6)^2 + 1^2}$ $\quad = \sqrt{(-1)^2 + (-4)^2}$

$\quad = \sqrt{36 + 1}$ $\quad = \sqrt{1 + 16}$

$\quad = \sqrt{37}$ $\quad = \sqrt{17}$

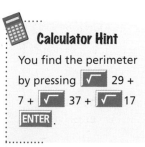

Calculator Hint

You find the perimeter by pressing $\sqrt{}$ 29 + 7 + $\sqrt{}$ 37 + $\sqrt{}$ 17 ENTER.

● The perimeter $= \sqrt{29} + 7 + \sqrt{37} + \sqrt{17} \approx 22.6$ units.

✔ **Check Understanding** ❷ **a.** Find the perimeter of triangle RST below.

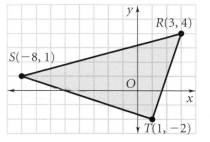

b. Critical Thinking Verify that this triangle is a right triangle.

2 Finding the Midpoint of a Line Segment

The **midpoint** of $\overline{AB}$ is the point M that divides the segment into two equal segments, such that $AM = MB$.

Key Concepts

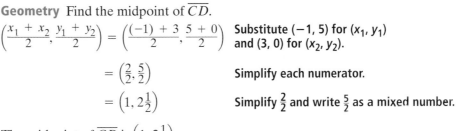

Rule The Midpoint Formula

The midpoint M of a line segment with endpoints $A(x_1, y_1)$ and $B(x_2, y_2)$ is

$$\left(\frac{x_1 + x_2}{2}, \frac{y_1 + y_2}{2}\right).$$

3 EXAMPLE Using the Midpoint Formula

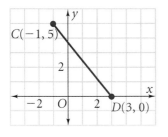

Geometry Find the midpoint of $\overline{CD}$.

$$\left(\frac{x_1 + x_2}{2}, \frac{y_1 + y_2}{2}\right) = \left(\frac{(-1) + 3}{2}, \frac{5 + 0}{2}\right) \quad \text{Substitute } (-1, 5) \text{ for } (x_1, y_1) \text{ and } (3, 0) \text{ for } (x_2, y_2).$$

$$= \left(\frac{2}{2}, \frac{5}{2}\right) \quad \text{Simplify each numerator.}$$

$$= \left(1, 2\tfrac{1}{2}\right) \quad \text{Simplify } \tfrac{2}{2} \text{ and write } \tfrac{5}{2} \text{ as a mixed number.}$$

The midpoint of $\overline{CD}$ is $\left(1, 2\tfrac{1}{2}\right)$.

✓**Check Understanding** **3** Find the midpoint of $\overline{PQ}$.

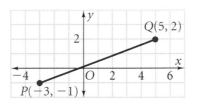

If you know the coordinates of the endpoints of a diameter of a circle, you can use the midpoint formula to find the coordinates of the center of the circle.

4 EXAMPLE Finding the Center of a Circle

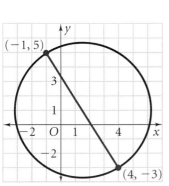

Geometry A circle is drawn on a coordinate plane as shown at the left. The endpoints of a diameter are $(-1, 5)$ and $(4, -3)$. What is the center of the circle?

The center of the circle is the midpoint of a diameter.

$$\left(\frac{x_1 + x_2}{2}, \frac{y_1 + y_2}{2}\right) = \left(\frac{-1 + 4}{2}, \frac{5 + (-3)}{2}\right) \quad \text{Substitute } (-1, 5) \text{ for } (x_1, y_1) \text{ and } (4, -3) \text{ for } (x_2, y_2).$$

$$= \left(\frac{3}{2}, \frac{2}{2}\right) = \left(1\tfrac{1}{2}, 1\right)$$

The coordinates of the center of the circle are $\left(1\tfrac{1}{2}, 1\right)$.

✓**Check Understanding** **4** $\overline{AB}$ is a diameter of a circle. The coordinates of A are $(-4, 7)$ and the coordinates of B are $(-8, -2)$. Find the center of the circle.

EXERCISES

For more practice, see *Extra Practice*.

Practice and Problem Solving

A **Practice by Example**

Example 1
(page 592)

Find the distance between each pair of points. If necessary, round to the nearest tenth.

1. $(7, -3), (-8, -3)$ **2.** $(-2, 7), (-2, -7)$ **3.** $(0, 0), (6, -8)$

4. $(-4, -4), (4, 4)$ **5.** $(9, 10), (11, 12)$ **6.** $(3, -2), (-1, 5)$

Example 2
(page 592)

Geometry **Find the perimeter of each figure. Round to the nearest tenth.**

7.

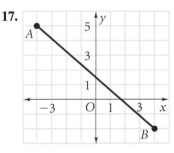

8.

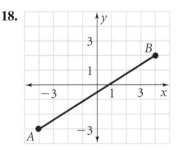

Example 3
(page 593)

Find the midpoint of each segment with the given endpoints.

9. $A(2, 5)$ and $B(0, 7)$ **10.** $X(-3, 14)$ and $Y(1, 10)$

11. $M(4, 1)$ and $N(-4, -1)$ **12.** $R(5, 3)$ and $S(-9, 3)$

13. $C(12, -2)$ and $D(-2, -9)$ **14.** $P(0, 6)$ and $Q(-5, -8)$

Example 4
(page 593)

15. $\overline{PQ}$ is a diameter of a circle. The coordinates of P are $(-1, 8)$ and the coordinates of Q are $(-7, 0)$. Find the center of the circle.

16. $\overline{RS}$ is a diameter of a circle. The coordinates of R are $(5, -11)$ and the coordinates of S are $(12, -7)$. Find the center of the circle.

B **Apply Your Skills**

Find *AB*. Round to the nearest tenth.

17.

18.

Find the lengths of the sides of a triangle with the given vertices. If necessary, round to the nearest tenth.

19. $A(2, 2), B(6, 3), C(5, 6)$ **20.** $D(-1, -7), E(-2, -1), F(-5, -3)$

21. $R(-2, 2), S(1, 1), T(-3, -3)$ **22.** $M(-1, -5), N(4, -4), P(2, -1)$

23. $J(3, 5), K(3, 9), L(5, 8)$ **24.** $T(-1, 4), U(6, 7), V(2, -9)$

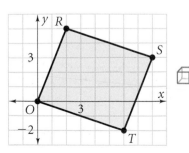

25. Geometry A quadrilateral is a parallelogram if a pair of its opposite sides are congruent and parallel.
   a. For the figure at the left, find the lengths of $\overline{OR}$ and $\overline{ST}$.
   b. Find the slope of $\overline{OR}$ and $\overline{ST}$.
   c. Is $ORST$ a parallelogram?

Real-World 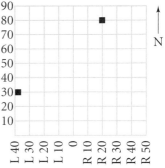 **Connection**

Careers Archaeologists log and tag objects they find, noting the location of the find using a coordinate system.

26. Archaeology In an archaeological excavation, a grid resembling the grid at the right is used to identify the location of artifacts. On the grid, 80R30 means 80 ft north and 30 ft east. In a coordinate plane, this location corresponds to the ordered pair (30, 80).
  a. Rewrite 80R20 and 30L40 as ordered pairs.
  b. Find the distance between the two locations.
  c. Find the midpoint between the two locations.

27. Writing Summarize the distance formula and the midpoint formula. Use examples to show the use of each formula.

28. a. Open-Ended Suppose the distance between two points on a coordinate plane is between 10 and 13 units. Find two points A and B not directly above or across from each other that meet this requirement.
  b. Plot your points on graph paper.
  c. Verify that your points satisfy the requirement by finding AB.

29. a. Graph Mr. Tanaka's and Ms. Elisa's locations on a coordinate grid with the substation as the origin.

I am 4 mi south and 3 mi west of the substation.

Copy that. I am 3 mi north and 3 mi east of the substation. I will meet you halfway between our locations.

Ms. Elisa   Mr. Tanaka

  b. What are the coordinates of the point where they will meet?
  c. Describe their meeting place in miles north or south and east or west of the substation.

30. Hiking The Gato and Wilson families are staying at a campground. The Gatos leave camp and hike 2 km west and 5 km south. The Wilsons leave camp and hike 1 km east and 4 km north. How far apart are the families?

31. a. Flight Two news helicopters are flying at the same altitude on their way to a political rally. Helicopter A is 20 mi due west of the rally. Helicopter B is 15 mi south and 15 mi east of the rally. How far apart are they?
  b. How far from the rally is each helicopter?
  c. Both helicopters are flying at an average of 80 mi/h. How many minutes will it take each of them to arrive at the scene?

32. Geometry A quadrilateral is a rhombus if all four sides are congruent. Quadrilateral $PQRS$ has vertices $P(6, 5)$, $Q(2, 2)$, $R(6, -1)$, and $S(10, 2)$. Is $PQRS$ a rhombus?

33. a. Find the midpoint of the line segment with endpoints $P(-24, -7)$ and $Q(-30, -3)$. Identify the midpoint as R.
  b. Reasoning Verify that $PR = RQ$.

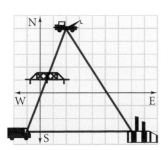

34. a. Transportation On the grid at the left, each unit represents one mile. A van breaks down on its way to a factory. The driver calls a garage for a tow truck. There is a bridge halfway between the garage and the van. How far is the bridge from the van?
  b. The van is towed to the factory and then to the garage. How many miles did the truck tow the van?

35. a. Geometry Quadrilateral $ABCD$ is a trapezoid. Find the midpoints of $\overline{AB}$ and $\overline{CD}$. Label the midpoints M and N.
   b. Compare the average of the lengths of $\overline{BC}$ and $\overline{AD}$ to the length of $\overline{MN}$.

36. $\overline{EF}$ is a diameter of a circle. The coordinates of E are $(x - 3, y + 2)$ and the coordinates of F are $(x + 3, y - 2)$. Find the center of the circle.

37. Critical Thinking If the midpoint of a line segment is at the origin, what must be true about the coordinates of the endpoints of the segment?

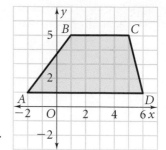

© Challenge

38. a. What is the distance of the point $(3, 4)$ from the origin?
   b. Find seven other points that are the same distance from the origin.
   c. Graph $(3, 4)$ and the seven points you named in part (b). What figure do these points suggest?

39. Use the steps that follow to find the distance between the parallel lines ℓ and m as graphed at the right.
   a. An equation for line ℓ is $y = \frac{3}{4}x + 1$. An equation for line m is $y = \frac{3}{4}x - \frac{11}{4}$. Write an equation for line n, which is perpendicular to line ℓ at point B.
   b. Use the equations of lines m and n to find their point of intersection.
   c. Find the distance between points B and C.

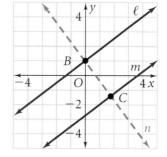

40. Is the point $(-2, 3)$ the center of a circle that passes through $(-6, 0)$, $(1, -1)$, and $(-5, 7)$? Verify your answer.

Standardized Test Prep

Gridded Response

41. Find the distance between $(-5, 10)$ and $(8, -4)$. Round to the nearest tenth.

42. Find the x-coordinate of the midpoint of the segment with endpoints at $(12, 0)$ and $(-2, -6)$.

43. Find the perimeter of the triangle with vertices at $(4.5, 0.5)$, $(-1.5, -2.5)$, and $(-4.5, 3.5)$. Round to the nearest tenth.

44. $\overline{AB}$ is the diameter of a circle. The coordinates of A are $(17, -1)$ and the coordinates of B are $(10, -9)$. What is the y-coordinate of the center of the circle?

45. The distance between two points with coordinates $(3, -1)$ and $(x, 4)$ is 5. What is the value of x?

46. The midpoint of the segment with endpoints at $(-1, y)$ and $(7, 16)$ is $(3, 4)$. What is the value of y?

47. One hiker is 4 mi west and 3 mi north of the campground. Another is 6 mi east and 3 mi south of the campground. How many miles apart are the hikers? Round to the nearest tenth.

Lesson 11-2

For the values given, *a* and *b* are legs of a right triangle, and *c* is the hypotenuse. Find the length of the missing side of each right triangle. If necessary, round to the nearest tenth.

48. $a = 2, b = 11$

49. $a = 8, c = 13$

50. $a = 10, b = 24$

51. $a = \sqrt{15}, c = \sqrt{27}$

52. $a = 5, c = \sqrt{89}$

53. $a = 0.9, b = 4$

Lesson 10-4

Solve each equation by finding square roots. If the equation has no solution, write *no solution*.

54. $t^2 - 196 = 0$

55. $3k^2 = 300$

56. $5y^2 + 1 = 0$

57. $8m^2 - 9 = 191$

58. $16q^2 + 9 = 4$

59. $9b^2 + 1 = 5$

Lesson 9-3

Find each product.

60. $(k + 3)(k + 8)$

61. $(v - 5)(v + 7)$

62. $(2p + 1)(p - 9)$

63. $(8w^2 + 11)(w^2 + 1)$

64. $(7t - 2)(t^2 + t + 1)$

65. $(6c + 3)(c^2 - 5c + 8)$

✓ **Checkpoint Quiz 1**   **Lessons 11-1 through 11-3**

📱 **TEXT** Instant self-check quiz online and on CD-ROM

Simplify each radical expression.

1. $\sqrt{8} \cdot \sqrt{20}$ **2.** $\sqrt{45} \cdot \sqrt{3}$ **3.** $\sqrt{\frac{12}{27}}$ **4.** $\frac{5}{\sqrt{2x^3}}$

Find each missing length. If necessary, round to the nearest tenth.

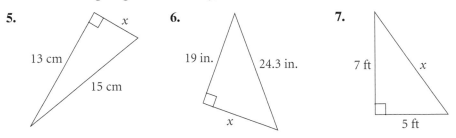

5. 13 cm, 15 cm, *x*

6. 19 in., 24.3 in., *x*

7. 7 ft, 5 ft, *x*

Determine whether the given lengths can be sides of a right triangle.

8. 9 in., 12 in., 15 in.

9. 2 m, 4 m, 5 m

10. a. Find the midpoint of the segment shown at the right.
     b. Then find the length of the segment to the nearest tenth.

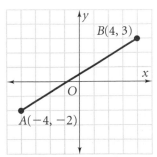

Special Right Triangles

Some right triangles have special properties. Consider the isosceles right triangle at the right. It is called a 45°-45°-90° triangle.

$c^2 = a^2 + b^2$	**Use the Pythagorean Theorem.**
$c^2 = x^2 + x^2$	**Substitute x for b and for a.**
$c^2 = 2x^2$	**Simplify.**
$\sqrt{c^2} = \sqrt{2x^2}$	**Find the principal square root of each side.**
$c = \sqrt{2} \cdot \sqrt{x^2}$	**Use the Multiplication Property of Square Roots.**
$c = \sqrt{2} \cdot x$, or $x\sqrt{2}$	**Simplify.**

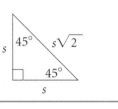

Theorem	45°-45°-90° Triangle Theorem

In a 45°-45°-90° triangle, the length of the hypotenuse is the length of the leg times $\sqrt{2}$.

$$\text{hypotenuse} = \text{leg} \cdot \sqrt{2}$$

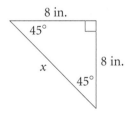

1 EXAMPLE **Finding Lengths in a 45°-45°-90° Triangle**

Find the length of the hypotenuse in the triangle at the right.

$\text{hypotenuse} = \text{leg} \cdot \sqrt{2}$	
$x = 8 \cdot \sqrt{2}$	**The length of either leg is 8 in.**
≈ 11.3	**Round to the nearest tenth.**

● The length of the hypotenuse is about 11.3 in.

EXERCISES

Find the hypotenuse of each 45°-45°-90° triangle. Round to the nearest tenth.

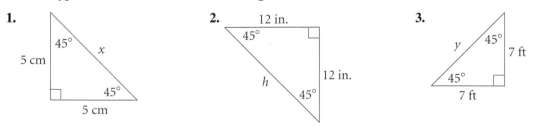

1.

5 cm, 45°, x, 45°, 5 cm

2.

12 in., 45°, h, 12 in., 45°

3.

y, 45°, 7 ft, 45°, 7 ft

4. A baseball diamond is a square. The distance from any base to the next base is 90 ft. How far is it from home plate to second base? (*Hint:* Draw a diagram.)

5. The hypotenuse of a 45°-45°-90° triangle is 40.2 ft long. How long is each leg? Round to the nearest tenth.

6. Open-Ended Draw and label a 45°-45°-90° triangle in which the leg length is irrational and the hypotenuse length is rational.

Another special right triangle is the 30°-60°-90° triangle. You can form two congruent 30°-60°-90° triangles by bisecting an angle of an equilateral triangle. As the diagram at the right shows, the length of the hypotenuse is twice the length of the shorter leg. You can use the Pythagorean Theorem to find the length of the longer leg b shown in the diagram at the right below.

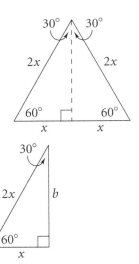

$(2x)^2 = x^2 + b^2$ Use the Pythagorean Theorem.

$4x^2 = x^2 + b^2$ Simplify.

$3x^2 = b^2$ Subtract x^2 from each side.

$\sqrt{3x^2} = \sqrt{b^2}$ Find the principal square root of each side.

$\sqrt{3} \cdot \sqrt{x^2} = b$ Use the Multiplication Property of Square Roots.

$b = \sqrt{3} \cdot x$ Simplify.

The length of the longer leg is $\sqrt{3} \cdot x$, or $x\sqrt{3}$.

Theorem	**30°-60°-90° Triangle Theorem**

In a 30°-60°-90° triangle, the length of the hypotenuse is twice the length of the shorter leg. The length of the longer leg is $\sqrt{3}$ times the length of the shorter leg.

hypotenuse = 2 · shorter leg

longer leg = $\sqrt{3}$ · shorter leg

---

2 EXAMPLE **Finding Lengths in a 30°-60°-90° Triangle**

Find the missing lengths in the triangle at the right.

hypotenuse = 2 · shorter leg

$x = 2 \cdot 9$ The length of the shorter leg is 9.

$x = 18$ Simplify.

longer leg = $\sqrt{3}$ · shorter leg

$y = 9 \cdot \sqrt{3}$ The length of the shorter leg is 9.

$y \approx 15.6$ Simplify. Round to the nearest tenth.

The length of the hypotenuse is 18 ft, and the length of the longer leg is about 15.6 ft.

EXERCISES

Find the missing lengths in each triangle. Round to the nearest tenth.

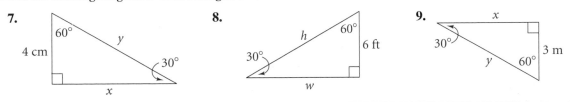

7.

8.

9.

Operations With Radical Expressions

Lesson Preview

What You'll Learn

OBJECTIVE 1 To simplify sums and differences

OBJECTIVE 2 To simplify products and quotients

. . . And Why

To find the width of a painting, as in Example 6

✓ **Check Skills You'll Need** (For help, go to Lesson 11-1.)

Simplify each radical expression.

1. $\sqrt{52}$ **2.** $\sqrt{200}$ **3.** $4\sqrt{54}$ **4.** $\sqrt{125x^2}$

Rationalize each denominator.

5. $\dfrac{\sqrt{3}}{\sqrt{11}}$ **6.** $\dfrac{\sqrt{5}}{\sqrt{8}}$ **7.** $\dfrac{\sqrt{15}}{\sqrt{2x}}$

New Vocabulary • like radicals • unlike radicals • conjugates

---

OBJECTIVE

1 **Simplifying Sums and Differences**

Interactive lesson includes instant self-check, tutorials, and activities.

For radical expressions, **like radicals** have the same radicand. **Unlike radicals** do not have the same radicand. For example, $4\sqrt{7}$ and $-12\sqrt{7}$ are like radicals, but $3\sqrt{11}$ and $2\sqrt{5}$ are unlike radicals. To simplify sums and differences, you use the Distributive Property to combine like radicals.

1 EXAMPLE **Combining Like Radicals**

Simplify $\sqrt{2} + 3\sqrt{2}$.

$\sqrt{2} + 3\sqrt{2} = 1\sqrt{2} + 3\sqrt{2}$ **Both terms contain $\sqrt{2}$.**

$\phantom{\sqrt{2} + 3\sqrt{2}} = (1 + 3)\sqrt{2}$ **Use the Distributive Property to combine like radicals.**

$\phantom{\sqrt{2} + 3\sqrt{2}} = 4\sqrt{2}$ **Simplify.**

✓ **Check Understanding** **1** Simplify each expression.

a. $-3\sqrt{5} - 4\sqrt{5}$ **b.** $\sqrt{10} - 5\sqrt{10}$

You may need to simplify a radical expression to determine if you have like radicals.

Need Help?

Multiplication Property of Square Roots:

$\sqrt{ab} = \sqrt{a} \cdot \sqrt{b}$ and $\sqrt{a} \cdot \sqrt{b} = \sqrt{ab}$

2 EXAMPLE **Simplifying to Combine Like Radicals**

Simplify $7\sqrt{3} - \sqrt{12}$.

$7\sqrt{3} - \sqrt{12} = 7\sqrt{3} - \sqrt{4 \cdot 3}$ **4 is a perfect square and a factor of 12.**

$\phantom{7\sqrt{3} - \sqrt{12}} = 7\sqrt{3} - \sqrt{4} \cdot \sqrt{3}$ **Use the Multiplication Property of Square Roots.**

$\phantom{7\sqrt{3} - \sqrt{12}} = 7\sqrt{3} - 2\sqrt{3}$ **Simplify $\sqrt{4}$.**

$\phantom{7\sqrt{3} - \sqrt{12}} = (7 - 2)\sqrt{3}$ **Use the Distributive Property to combine like radicals.**

$\phantom{7\sqrt{3} - \sqrt{12}} = 5\sqrt{3}$ **Simplify.**

✓ **Check Understanding** **2** Simplify each expression.

a. $3\sqrt{20} + 2\sqrt{5}$ **b.** $3\sqrt{3} - 2\sqrt{27}$

When simplifying a radical expression like $\sqrt{3}\left(\sqrt{6}+7\right)$, use the Distributive Property to multiply $\sqrt{3}$ times $\left(\sqrt{6}+7\right)$.

3 **EXAMPLE** **Using the Distributive Property**

Simplify $\sqrt{3}(\sqrt{6}+7)$.

$$\sqrt{3}(\sqrt{6}+7) = \sqrt{18} + 7\sqrt{3} \qquad \text{Use the Distributive Property.}$$
$$= \sqrt{9} \cdot \sqrt{2} + 7\sqrt{3} \qquad \text{Use the Multiplication Property of Square Roots.}$$
$$= 3\sqrt{2} + 7\sqrt{3} \qquad \text{Simplify.}$$

✓**Check Understanding** **3** Simplify each radical expression.
  a. $\sqrt{5}(2+\sqrt{10})$ **b.** $\sqrt{2x}(\sqrt{6x}-11)$ **c.** $\sqrt{5a}(\sqrt{5a}+3)$

If both radical expressions have two terms, you can multiply the same way you find the product of two binomials, by using FOIL.

4 **EXAMPLE** **Simplifying Using FOIL**

Simplify $\left(\sqrt{5}-2\sqrt{15}\right)\left(\sqrt{5}+\sqrt{15}\right)$.

$$\left(\sqrt{5}-2\sqrt{15}\right)\left(\sqrt{5}+\sqrt{15}\right)$$
$$= \sqrt{25} + \sqrt{75} - 2\sqrt{75} - 2\sqrt{225} \qquad \text{Use FOIL.}$$
$$= 5 - \sqrt{75} - 2(15) \qquad \text{Combine like radicals and simplify } \sqrt{25} \text{ and } \sqrt{225}.$$
$$= 5 - \sqrt{25 \cdot 3} - 30 \qquad \text{25 is a perfect square factor of 75.}$$
$$= 5 - \sqrt{25} \cdot \sqrt{3} - 30 \qquad \text{Use the Multiplication Property of Square Roots.}$$
$$= 5 - 5\sqrt{3} - 30 \qquad \text{Simplify } \sqrt{25}.$$
$$= -25 - 5\sqrt{3} \qquad \text{Simplify.}$$

✓**Check Understanding** **4** Simplify each radical expression.
  a. $\left(2\sqrt{6}+3\sqrt{3}\right)\left(\sqrt{6}-5\sqrt{3}\right)$ **b.** $\left(\sqrt{7}+4\right)^2$

Conjugates are the sum and the difference of the same two terms. The radical expressions $\sqrt{5}+\sqrt{2}$ and $\sqrt{5}-\sqrt{2}$ are conjugates. The product of two conjugates results in a difference of two squares.

$$\left(\sqrt{5}+\sqrt{2}\right)\left(\sqrt{5}-\sqrt{2}\right) = \left(\sqrt{5}\right)^2 - \left(\sqrt{2}\right)^2$$
$$= 5 - 2$$
$$= 3$$

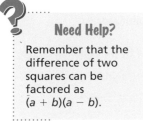

Need Help?

Remember that the difference of two squares can be factored as $(a+b)(a-b)$.

Notice that the product of these conjugates has no radical.

You recall that a simplified radical expression has no radical in the denominator. When a denominator contains a sum or a difference including radical expressions, you can rationalize the denominator by multiplying the numerator and the denominator by the conjugate of the denominator. For example, to simplify a radical expression like $\dfrac{6}{\sqrt{5}-\sqrt{2}}$, you multiply by $\dfrac{\sqrt{5}+\sqrt{2}}{\sqrt{5}+\sqrt{2}}$.

5 EXAMPLE Rationalizing a Denominator Using Conjugates

Simplify $\dfrac{6}{\sqrt{5} - \sqrt{2}}$.

$$\dfrac{6}{\sqrt{5} - \sqrt{2}} = \dfrac{6}{\sqrt{5} - \sqrt{2}} \cdot \dfrac{\sqrt{5} + \sqrt{2}}{\sqrt{5} + \sqrt{2}}$$
Multiply the numerator and the denominator by the conjugate of the denominator.

$$= \dfrac{6(\sqrt{5} + \sqrt{2})}{5 - 2}$$
Multiply in the denominator.

$$= \dfrac{6(\sqrt{5} + \sqrt{2})}{3}$$
Simplify the denominator.

$$= 2(\sqrt{5} + \sqrt{2})$$
Divide 6 and 3 by the common factor 3.

$$= 2\sqrt{5} + 2\sqrt{2}$$
Simplify the expression.

✓ **Check Understanding** ⑤ Simplify each expression.

a. $\dfrac{4}{\sqrt{7} + \sqrt{5}}$ **b.** $\dfrac{-4}{\sqrt{10} + \sqrt{8}}$ **c.** $\dfrac{-5}{\sqrt{11} - \sqrt{3}}$

You can solve a ratio involving radical expressions.

6 EXAMPLE Real-World Problem Solving

Art The ratio length : width of this painting by Mondrian is approximately equal to the *golden ratio* $(1 + \sqrt{5}) : 2$. The length of the painting is 81 inches. Find the width of the painting in simplest radical form. Then find the approximate width to the nearest inch.

Define $81 = $ length of painting
            $x = $ width of painting

Relate $(1 + \sqrt{5}) : 2 = $ length : width

Write $\dfrac{1 + \sqrt{5}}{2} = \dfrac{81}{x}$

$$x(1 + \sqrt{5}) = 162$$
Cross multiply.

$$\dfrac{x(1 + \sqrt{5})}{(1 + \sqrt{5})} = \dfrac{162}{(1 + \sqrt{5})}$$
Divide both sides by $(1 + \sqrt{5})$.

$$x = \dfrac{162}{(1 + \sqrt{5})} \cdot \dfrac{(1 - \sqrt{5})}{(1 - \sqrt{5})}$$
Multiply the numerator and the denominator by the conjugate of the denominator.

$$x = \dfrac{162(1 - \sqrt{5})}{1 - 5}$$
Multiply in the denominator.

$$x = \dfrac{162(1 - \sqrt{5})}{-4}$$
Simplify the denominator.

$$x = \dfrac{-81(1 - \sqrt{5})}{2}$$
Divide 162 and −4 by the common factor −2.

$$x = 50.06075309$$
Use a calculator.

$$x \approx 50$$

The exact width of the painting is $\dfrac{-81(1 - \sqrt{5})}{2}$ inches. The approximate width of the painting is 50 inches.

✓ **Check Understanding** ⑥ Another painting has a length : width ratio approximately equal to the golden ratio $(1 + \sqrt{5}) : 2$. Find the length of a painting if the width is 34 inches.

Real-World Connection

Mondrian painted straight lines at right angles because he felt this to be the angle of complete equilibrium.

EXERCISES

For more practice, see *Extra Practice*.

Practice and Problem Solving

A **Practice by Example**

Example 1
(page 600)

Simplify each expression.

1. $-3\sqrt{6} + 8\sqrt{6}$

2. $16\sqrt{10} + 2\sqrt{10}$

3. $\sqrt{5} - 3\sqrt{5}$

4. $6\sqrt{7} - 4\sqrt{7}$

5. $15\sqrt{2} - \sqrt{2}$

6. $-5\sqrt{3} - 3\sqrt{3}$

Example 2
(page 600)

Tell whether each pair of expressions can be simplified to like radicals.

7. $\sqrt{2}, \sqrt{32}$

8. $\sqrt{3}, \sqrt{75}$

9. $\sqrt{5}, \sqrt{50}$

Simplify each expression.

10. $\sqrt{18} + \sqrt{2}$

11. $2\sqrt{12} - 7\sqrt{3}$

12. $\sqrt{8} + 2\sqrt{2}$

13. $4\sqrt{5} - 2\sqrt{45}$

14. $3\sqrt{7} - \sqrt{28}$

15. $-4\sqrt{10} + 6\sqrt{40}$

Example 3
(page 601)

16. $\sqrt{2}(\sqrt{8} - 4)$

17. $\sqrt{3}(\sqrt{27} + 1)$

18. $2\sqrt{3}(\sqrt{3} - 1)$

19. $\sqrt{3}(\sqrt{15} + 2)$

20. $\sqrt{2}(3 + 3\sqrt{2})$

21. $\sqrt{6}(\sqrt{6} - 5)$

Example 4
(page 601)

22. $(3\sqrt{2} + \sqrt{3})(\sqrt{2} - 5\sqrt{3})$

23. $(2\sqrt{5} - \sqrt{6})(4\sqrt{5} - 3\sqrt{6})$

24. $(\sqrt{7} - 2)^2$

25. $(2\sqrt{10} + \sqrt{3})^2$

26. $(2\sqrt{11} + 5)(\sqrt{11} + 2)$

27. $(4 - \sqrt{13})(9 + \sqrt{13})$

Example 5
(page 602)

28. $\dfrac{8}{\sqrt{7} - \sqrt{3}}$

29. $\dfrac{-12}{\sqrt{8} - \sqrt{2}}$

30. $\dfrac{48}{\sqrt{6} - \sqrt{18}}$

31. $\dfrac{3}{\sqrt{10} - \sqrt{5}}$

32. $\dfrac{-40}{\sqrt{11} - \sqrt{3}}$

33. $\dfrac{9}{\sqrt{12} - \sqrt{11}}$

Example 6
(page 602)

Find an exact solution for each equation. Find the approximate solution to the nearest tenth.

34. $\dfrac{5\sqrt{2}}{\sqrt{2} - 1} = \dfrac{x}{\sqrt{2}}$

35. $\dfrac{3}{1 + \sqrt{5}} = \dfrac{1 - \sqrt{5}}{x}$

36. $\dfrac{\sqrt{2} - 1}{\sqrt{2} + 1} = \dfrac{x}{2}$

37. The ratio of the length to the width of a painting is $(1 + \sqrt{5}) : 2$. The length is 12 ft. What is the width?

B **Apply Your Skills**

Simplify each expression.

38. $\sqrt{40} + \sqrt{90}$

39. $3\sqrt{2}(2 + \sqrt{6})$

40. $\sqrt{12} + 4\sqrt{75} - \sqrt{36}$

41. $(\sqrt{3} + \sqrt{5})^2$

42. $\dfrac{\sqrt{13} + \sqrt{10}}{\sqrt{13} - \sqrt{5}}$

43. $(\sqrt{7} + \sqrt{8})(\sqrt{7} + \sqrt{8})$

44. $2\sqrt{2}(-2\sqrt{32} + \sqrt{8})$

45. $4\sqrt{50} - 7\sqrt{18}$

46. $\dfrac{2\sqrt{12} + 3\sqrt{6}}{\sqrt{9} - \sqrt{6}}$

47. Chemistry The ratio of the rates of diffusion of two gases is given by the formula $\dfrac{r_1}{r_2} = \dfrac{\sqrt{m_1}}{\sqrt{m_2}}$, where m_1 and m_2 are the masses of the molecules of the gases. Find $\dfrac{r_1}{r_2}$ if $m_1 = 12$ units and $m_2 = 30$ units.

Geometry Find the exact perimeter of each figure below.

48.

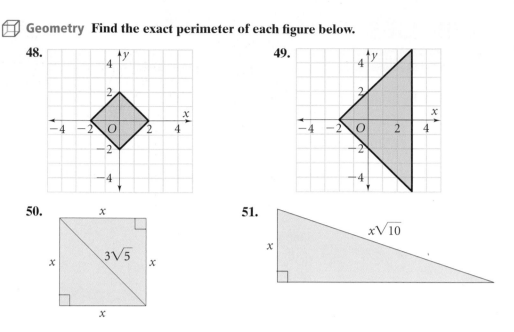

49.

50.

A square with diagonal $3\sqrt{5}$, with side x on each side and right angle marks at top-right and bottom-left corners.

51.

A right triangle with vertical side x, hypotenuse $x\sqrt{10}$, and right angle at bottom-left.

52. Open-Ended Make up three sums that are less than or equal to 50. Use the square roots of 2, 3, 5, or 7, and the whole numbers less than 10. For example, $8\sqrt{5} + 9\sqrt{7} \le 50$.

53. Error Analysis When simplifying $\sqrt{24} + \sqrt{48}$, a student wrote $3\sqrt{24} = 6\sqrt{6}$.
  a. What error did the student make?
  b. Simplify $\sqrt{24} + \sqrt{48}$ correctly.

54. You can make a box kite like the one at the right in the shape of a rectangular solid. The opening at each end of the kite is a square.
  a. Suppose the sides of the square are 2 ft long. How long are the diagonal struts used for bracing?
  b. Suppose each side of the square has length s. Find the length of the diagonal struts in terms of s. Write your answer in simplest form.

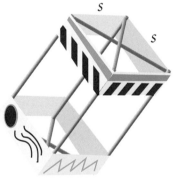

Investments For Exercises 55–57, the formula $r = \sqrt{\frac{A}{P}} - 1$ gives the interest rate r that will allow principal P to grow into amount A in two years, if the interest is compounded annually. Use the formula to find the interest rate you would need to meet each goal.

55. Suppose you have $500 to deposit into an account. Your goal is to have $595 in that account at the end of the second year.

56. Suppose you have $550 to deposit into an account. Your goal is to have $700 in that account at the end of two years.

57. Suppose you have $600 to deposit into an account. Your goal is to have $800 in that account at the end of two years.

58. a. Suppose n is an even number. Simplify $\sqrt{x^n}$.
  b. Suppose n is an odd number greater than 1. Simplify $\sqrt{x^n}$.

59. Critical Thinking Simplify $\frac{a\sqrt{b}}{b\sqrt{a}}$.

60. Find the value of the numerical expression for Professor Hinkle's age in the cartoon.

61. Writing Explain why $\sqrt{3} + \sqrt{6}$ cannot be simplified.

62. a. Copy and complete the table.

a	b	$\sqrt{a}$	$\sqrt{b}$	$\sqrt{a} + \sqrt{b}$	$\sqrt{a+b}$
1	0	▧	▧	▧	▧
16	1	▧	▧	▧	▧
25	9	▧	▧	▧	▧
64	36	▧	▧	▧	▧
100	81	▧	▧	▧	▧

b. Does $\sqrt{a} + \sqrt{b}$ always equal $\sqrt{a+b}$? Explain.

63. Error Analysis Explain the error in the work below.

$$\sqrt{41} = \sqrt{16+25} = \sqrt{16} + \sqrt{25} = 4 + 5 = 9$$

C Challenge

Simplify each expression.

64. $\sqrt{18} + \dfrac{3}{\sqrt{2}}$

65. $\dfrac{\sqrt{28}}{3} + \dfrac{3}{\sqrt{7}}$

66. $\sqrt{\dfrac{3}{5}} + \sqrt{\dfrac{5}{3}}$

67. $\dfrac{\sqrt{27} + \sqrt{48} - \sqrt{75}}{\sqrt{3}}$

68. $\sqrt{288} + \sqrt{50} - \sqrt{98}$

69. $\left(\sqrt{2} + \sqrt{32}\right)\left(\sqrt{2} + \sqrt{8} + \sqrt{32}\right)$

70. $\dfrac{\sqrt{5} + \sqrt{10} - \sqrt{15}}{\sqrt{10} - \sqrt{5}}$

71. Find the length of each hypotenuse. Write your answers in simplified radical form.

a.

$\sqrt{10} - \sqrt{2}$

$\sqrt{10} + \sqrt{2}$

b.

$\sqrt{20} - \sqrt{6}$

$\sqrt{20} + \sqrt{6}$

c. If the length of the legs of a right triangle are $\sqrt{p} + \sqrt{q}$ and $\sqrt{p} - \sqrt{q}$, write an expression for the length of the hypotenuse.

Standardized Test Prep

Multiple Choice

72. Simplify $4\sqrt{75} + \sqrt{27}$.

    A. $12\sqrt{3}$ **B.** $23\sqrt{3}$ **C.** $4\sqrt{102}$ **D.** $5\sqrt{102}$

Take It to the NET
Online lesson quiz at
www.PHSchool.com
Web Code: aea-1104

Short Response

Extended Response

73. Which radical expression is NOT equal to $5\sqrt{2}$?

    F. $\sqrt{8} + \sqrt{18}$ **G.** $\sqrt{98} - \sqrt{8}$

    H. $-\sqrt{32} + \sqrt{162}$ **I.** $\sqrt{48} + \sqrt{2}$

74. Simplify $(3\sqrt{5} - \sqrt{2})(\sqrt{5} + 5\sqrt{2})$. Show your work.

75. Explain the steps needed to simplify $\dfrac{5}{\sqrt{7} + \sqrt{21}}$.

Mixed Review

Lesson 11-3

Find the distance between the points in each pair. If necessary, round to the nearest tenth.

76. $(2, 6), (8, 13)$ **77.** $(-1, 7), (5, 10)$ **78.** $(-6, 2), (20, -1)$

Find the midpoint of each segment with the given endpoints.

79. $A(4, -1)$ and $B(2, 11)$ **80.** $H(-5, 6)$ and $K(1, 7)$

Lesson 10-5

Solve each equation by factoring.

81. $5t^2 - 35t = 0$ **82.** $p^2 - 7p - 18 = 0$ **83.** $k^2 + 12k + 27 = 0$

84. $y^2 - 2y = 24$ **85.** $m^2 + 30 = -17m$ **86.** $2a^2 = -7a - 3$

Lesson 9-4

Find each product.

87. $(b + 11)(b + 11)$ **88.** $(2p + 7)(2p + 7)$ **89.** $(5g - 7)(5g + 7)$

90. $(3x + 1)(3x - 1)$ **91.** $\left(\frac{1}{3}k - 9\right)\left(\frac{1}{3}k + 9\right)$ **92.** $(d - 1.1)(d - 1.1)$

Algebra at Work

• Auto Mechanic

Auto mechanics work to see that car engines get the most out of every gallon of gasoline. Formulas used by mechanics often involve radicals. For example, a car gets its power when gas and air in each cylinder are compressed and ignited by a spark plug. An engine's efficiency e is given by the formula $e = \frac{c - \sqrt{c}}{c}$, where c is the compression ratio.

Because of the complexity of such formulas and of modern high-performance engines, today's auto mechanic must be a highly trained and educated professional who understands algebra, graph reading, and the operation of computerized equipment.

Take It to the NET For more information about a career as an auto mechanic, go to **www.PHSchool.com**.
Web Code: aeb-2031

11-5

Solving Radical Equations

Lesson Preview

What You'll Learn

OBJECTIVE 1 To solve equations containing radicals

OBJECTIVE 2 To identify extraneous solutions

. . . And Why

To design an amusement park ride, as in Example 2

✓ **Check Skills You'll Need** (For help, go to Lesson 10-3.)

Evaluate each expression for the given value.

1. $\sqrt{x} - 3$ for $x = 16$ **2.** $\sqrt{x + 7}$ for $x = 9$ **3.** $2\sqrt{x + 3}$ for $x = 1$

Simplify each expression.

4. $(\sqrt{3})^2$ **5.** $(\sqrt{x + 1})^2$ **6.** $(\sqrt{2x - 5})^2$

New Vocabulary • radical equation • extraneous solution

OBJECTIVE

🅘**TEXT** Interactive lesson includes instant self-check, tutorials, and activities.

1 Solving Radical Equations

❓ Need Help?

For every real number a and b, if $a = b$, then $a^2 = b^2$.

A **radical equation** is an equation that has a variable in a radicand. You can often solve a radical equation by getting the radical by itself on one side of the equation. Then you square both sides. Remember that the expression under a radical must be nonnegative.

$$\text{When } x \geq 0, (\sqrt{x})^2 = x.$$

1 EXAMPLE **Solving by Isolating the Radical**

Solve each equation. Check your solution.

a. $\sqrt{x} - 3 = 4$

$\qquad \sqrt{x} = 7$ **Get the radical on the left side of the equation.**

$\qquad (\sqrt{x})^2 = 7^2$ **Square both sides.**

$\qquad x = 49$

Check $\sqrt{x} - 3 = 4$

$\qquad \sqrt{49} - 3 \stackrel{?}{=} 4$ **Substitute 49 for x.**

$\qquad 7 - 3 = 4$ ✓

b. $\sqrt{x - 3} = 4$

$\qquad (\sqrt{x - 3})^2 = 4^2$ **Square both sides.**

$\qquad x - 3 = 16$ **Solve for x.**

$\qquad x = 19$

Check $\sqrt{x - 3} = 4$

$\qquad \sqrt{19 - 3} \stackrel{?}{=} 4$ **Substitute 19 for x.**

$\qquad \sqrt{16} = 4$ ✓

✓ **Check Understanding** ➊ Solve each equation. Check your solution.

a. $\sqrt{x} + 7 = 12$ **b.** $\sqrt{a} - 4 = 5$ **c.** $\sqrt{c - 2} = 6$

For an equation like $2\sqrt{x} = 8$, you could square both sides first, or you could divide by 2 to get $\sqrt{x}$ alone on one side of the equation.

2 EXAMPLE Real-World  Problem Solving

Designing a Ride On a roller coaster ride, your speed in a loop depends on the height of the hill you have just come down and the radius of the loop in feet. The equation $v = 8\sqrt{h - 2r}$ gives the velocity v in feet per second of a car at the top of the loop.

Suppose the loop has a radius of 18 ft. You want the car to have a velocity of 30 ft/s at the top of the loop. How high should the hill be?

Solve $v = 8\sqrt{h - 2r}$ for h when $v = 30$ and $r = 18$.

$30 = 8\sqrt{h - 2(18)}$ **Substitute 30 for v and 18 for r.**

$\dfrac{30}{8} = \dfrac{8\sqrt{h - 2(18)}}{8}$ **Divide each side by 8 to isolate the radical.**

$3.75 = \sqrt{h - 36}$ **Simplify.**

$(3.75)^2 = (\sqrt{h - 36})^2$ **Square both sides.**

$14.0625 = h - 36$

$50.0625 = h$

The hill should be about 50 ft high.

Real-World Connection

When the roller coaster cars are upside down, the riders and the cars fall at the same rate and stay together.

✓ **Check Understanding** **2 a.** Find the height of the hill when the velocity at the top of the loop is 35 ft/s, and the radius of the loop is 24 ft.

b. Critical Thinking Would you expect the velocity of the car to increase as the radius of the loop increases? Explain.

You can square both sides of an equation to solve an equation involving radical expressions.

3 EXAMPLE Solving With Radical Expressions on Both Sides

Solve $\sqrt{3n - 2} = \sqrt{n + 6}$.

$(\sqrt{3n - 2})^2 = (\sqrt{n + 6})^2$ **Square both sides.**

$3n - 2 = n + 6$ **Simplify.**

$3n = n + 8$ **Add 2 to each side.**

$2n = 8$ **Subtract n from each side.**

$n = 4$ **Divide each side by 2.**

Check $\sqrt{3n - 2} = \sqrt{n + 6}$

$\sqrt{3(4) - 2} \overset{?}{=} \sqrt{4 + 6}$ **Substitute 4 for n.**

$\sqrt{10} = \sqrt{10}$ ✓

The solution is 4.

✓ **Check Understanding** **3** Solve $\sqrt{3t + 4} = \sqrt{5t - 6}$. Check your answer.

2 Solving Equations With Extraneous Solutions

When you solve an equation by squaring each side, you create a new equation. This new equation may have solutions that do not solve the original equation.

Original equation	Square of each side	New equation	Solutions of new equation
$x = 2$ $\longrightarrow$	$(x)^2 = (2)^2$ $\longrightarrow$	$x^2 = 4$ $\longrightarrow$	$2, -2$

In the example above, -2 does not satisfy the original equation. It is an extraneous solution. An **extraneous solution** is a solution that does not satisfy the original equation. Be sure to check all solutions in the original equation to determine whether a solution is extraneous.

4 EXAMPLE Identifying Extraneous Solutions

Solve $x = \sqrt{x + 6}$.

$$(x)^2 = (\sqrt{x + 6})^2 \qquad \text{Square both sides.}$$
$$x^2 = x + 6 \qquad \text{Simplify.}$$
$$x^2 - x - 6 = 0 \qquad \text{Subtract } x \text{ and 6 from both sides.}$$
$$(x - 3)(x + 2) = 0 \qquad \text{Solve the quadratic equation by factoring.}$$
$$(x - 3) = 0 \quad \text{or} \quad (x + 2) = 0 \qquad \text{Use the Zero-Product Property.}$$
$$x = 3 \quad \text{or} \qquad x = -2 \quad \text{Solve for } x.$$

Check $\qquad\qquad x = \sqrt{x + 6}$

$$3 \overset{?}{=} \sqrt{3 + 6} \qquad\qquad -2 \overset{?}{=} \sqrt{-2 + 6} \qquad \text{Substitute 3 and 2 for } x.$$
$$3 = 3 ✓ \qquad\qquad\qquad -2 \neq 2$$

● The solution to the original equation is 3. The value -2 is an extraneous solution.

Problem Solving Hint

For Check Understanding 4b, you can use any method to solve a quadratic equation: graphing, factoring, or the quadratic formula.

✓ **Check Understanding** **4** **a.** **Critical Thinking** How could you determine that -2 was not a solution of $x = \sqrt{x + 6}$ without going through all the steps of the check?
b. Solve $y = \sqrt{y + 2}$. Check your solutions.

It is possible that the only solution you get after squaring both sides of an equation is extraneous. In that case, the original equation has no solution.

5 EXAMPLE No Solution

Solve $\sqrt{2x} + 6 = 4$.
$$\sqrt{2x} = -2$$
$$(\sqrt{2x})^2 = (-2)^2 \qquad \text{Square both sides.}$$
$$2x = 4$$
$$x = 2$$

Check $\quad \sqrt{2x} + 6 = 4$
$$\sqrt{2(2)} + 6 \overset{?}{=} 4 \qquad \text{Substitute 2 for } x.$$
$$\sqrt{4} + 6 \overset{?}{=} 4$$
$$2 + 6 \neq 4 \qquad x = 2 \text{ does not solve the original equation.}$$

● $\sqrt{2x} + 6 = 4$ has no solution.

✓ **Check Understanding** **5** Solve $8 - \sqrt{2n} = 20$. Check your solution.

EXERCISES

For more practice, see *Extra Practice*.

Practice and Problem Solving

A **Practice by Example**

Example 1
(page 607)

Solve each radical equation. Check your solution.

1. $\sqrt{x} + 3 = 5$

2. $\sqrt{t} + 2 = 9$

3. $\sqrt{s} - 1 = 5$

4. $\sqrt{n + 7} = 12$

5. $\sqrt{a - 6} = 3$

6. $\sqrt{z} - 7 = -3$

Example 2
(page 608)

7. Distance The time t in seconds it takes an object to fall d feet is given by $t = \sqrt{\frac{d}{16}}$. Find the distance an object falls after 6 seconds.

8. Power The current of an electrical circuit I in amps is related to the power P in watts and the resistance R in ohms by the formula $I = \sqrt{\frac{P}{R}}$. Find the power (to the nearest watt) when the current is 8 amps and the resistance is 9.4 ohms.

Example 3
(page 608)

Solve each radical equation. Check your solution.

9. $\sqrt{3x + 1} = \sqrt{5x - 8}$

10. $\sqrt{2y} = \sqrt{9 - y}$

11. $\sqrt{7v - 4} = \sqrt{5v + 10}$

12. $\sqrt{s + 10} = \sqrt{6 - s}$

13. $\sqrt{n + 5} = \sqrt{5n - 11}$

14. $\sqrt{3m + 1} = \sqrt{7m - 9}$

Examples 4, 5
(page 609)

Tell which solutions, if any, are extraneous for each equation.

15. $-z = \sqrt{-z + 6}; z = -3, z = 2$

16. $\sqrt{12 - n} = n; n = -4, n = 3$

17. $y = \sqrt{2y}; y = 0, y = 2$

18. $2a = \sqrt{4a + 3}; a = \frac{3}{2}, a = -\frac{1}{2}$

19. $x = \sqrt{28 - 3x}; x = 4, x = -7$

20. $-t = \sqrt{-6t - 5}; t = -5, t = -1$

Solve each radical equation. Check your solution. If there is no solution, write *no solution*.

21. $x = \sqrt{2x + 3}$

22. $n = \sqrt{4n + 5}$

23. $\sqrt{3b} = -3$

24. $2y = \sqrt{5y + 6}$

25. $-2\sqrt{2r + 5} = 6$

26. $\sqrt{d + 12} = d$

27. $\sqrt{z + 5} = 2z$

28. $2t = \sqrt{5t - 1}$

B **Apply Your Skills**

29. Geometry In the right triangle $\triangle ABC$, the altitude $\overline{CD}$ is at a right angle to the hypotenuse. You can use $CD = \sqrt{(AD)(DB)}$ to find missing lengths.
  a. Find AD if $CD = 10$ and $DB = 4$.
  b. Find DB if $AD = 20$ and $CD = 15$.

30. Packaging The volume V in cubic units for a cylindrical can is given by the formula $V = \pi r^2 h$, where r is the radius of the can and h is the height. The volume of the can is 98 in.^{3}, and the height of the can is 5 in. Find the radius of the can.

31. Writing Explain what is meant by an extraneous solution.

32. Open-Ended Write two radical equations that have 3 for a solution.

33. The formula $t = \sqrt{\frac{n}{16}}$ gives the time t in seconds for an object that is initially at rest to fall n feet. Find the distance an object falls in the first 10 seconds.

Solve each radical equation. Check your solution. If there is no solution, write *no solution*.

34. $\sqrt{5x + 10} = 5$

35. $-6 - \sqrt{3y} = -3$

36. $\sqrt{7p + 5} = \sqrt{p - 3}$

37. $a = \sqrt{7a - 6}$

38. $\sqrt{y + 12} = 3\sqrt{y}$

39. $\sqrt{x - 10} = 1$

40. $\frac{x}{2} = \sqrt{3x}$

41. $\frac{c}{3} = \sqrt{c - 2}$

42. $7 = \sqrt{x + 5}$

43. $3 - \sqrt{4a + 1} = 12$

44. a. The equation $v = 8\sqrt{h - 2r}$ gives the velocity v in feet per second of a car at the top of the loop of a roller coaster. Find the radius of the loop when the hill is 150 ft high and the velocity of the car is 30 ft/s.
  b. Find the approximate speed in mi/h for 30 ft/s. (*Hint:* 1 mi = 5280 ft)
  c. Critical Thinking Would you expect the velocity of the car to increase or decrease as the radius of the loop increases? As the height of the hill decreases?
  d. Explain your reasoning in your answer for part (c).

45. a. Graphing Calculator Graph the equations $y = \sqrt{2x + 1}$ and $y = \sqrt{3x - 5}$.
  b. What is the solution to the system of equations?
  c. Solve $\sqrt{2x + 1} = \sqrt{3x - 5}$. Compare this solution with your answer to part (b).

Reading Math

For help reading and solving exercise 46, go to page 613.

46. Packaging The diagram at the right shows a piece of cardboard that makes a box when sections of it are folded and taped. The ends of the box are x inches by x inches and the body of the box is 10 inches long.
  a. Write an equation for the volume V of the box.
  b. Solve the equation in part (a) for x.
  c. Find the integer values of x that would give the box a volume between 40 in.^{3} and 490 in.^{3}, inclusive.

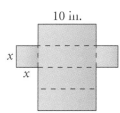

10 in.

47. a. Solve $x^2 - 3 = 4$.
  b. Solve $\sqrt{x} - 3 = 4$.
  c. How are solving part (a) and solving part (b) alike? How are they different?

Challenge

Solve each radical equation. Check your solution. If there is no solution, write *no solution*.

48. $\sqrt{x^2 - 6x} = 4$

49. $\sqrt{2x^2 + 8x} = x$

50. $\sqrt{x^2 + 4x + 5} = x$

51. $x + 3 = \sqrt{x^2 - 4x - 1}$

52. Writing Explain how you would solve the equation $\sqrt{2x} + \sqrt{x + 2} = 0$.

53. Critical Thinking Explain the difference between squaring $\sqrt{x - 1}$ and squaring $\sqrt{x} - 1$.

54. Physics The equation $T = \sqrt{\frac{2\pi^2 r}{F}}$ gives the time T in seconds it takes a satellite with mass 0.5 kilograms to complete one orbit of radius r meters. The force F in newtons pulls the body toward the center of the orbit.
  a. It takes 2 seconds for an object to make one revolution with a force of 10 newtons. Find the radius of the orbit.
  b. Find the radius of the orbit if the force is 160 newtons and $T = 2$.

Real-World ⊕ Connection

In the yo-yo trick called "Around the World," the yo-yo is a satellite circling a person's hand.

Multiple Choice

55. What is the solution of $k = \sqrt{5k + 6}$?

   A. 6, -1 **B.** -6, 1   **C.** 6   **D.** -1

56. What is the solution of $\sqrt{2x + 1} = \sqrt{3x - 5}$?

   F. -1 **G.** 6   **H.** $\frac{4}{5}$, 6   **I.** no solution

57. Which radical equation has no solution?

   A. $-\sqrt{x} = -25x$ **B.** $\sqrt{3x + 1} = -10$

   C. $-3\sqrt{3x} = -5$ **D.** $\frac{x}{2} = \sqrt{x - 1}$

Quantitative Comparison

Compare the boxed quantity in Column A with the boxed quantity in Column B. Choose the best answer.

  A. The quantity in Column A is greater.

  B. The quantity in Column B is greater.

  C. The two quantities are equal.

  D. The relationship cannot be determined from the information given.

	Column A	Column B
58.	the solution of $\sqrt{2n - 4} = 6$	the solution of $\sqrt{9 - 2m} = 7$
59.	0	the solution of $8 - 3\sqrt{y} = 2$
60.	the solution of $\frac{2\sqrt{3x - 9}}{3} = 4$	the solution of $\frac{16}{\sqrt{a + 1}} = 4$

Take It to the NET

Online lesson quiz at
www.PHSchool.com
Web Code: aea-1105

Short Response

61. Solve $\sqrt{15 - 5x} = \sqrt{4x - 3}$. Show your work.

Mixed Review

Lesson 11-4

Simplify each expression.

62. $\sqrt{20} + \sqrt{45}$ **63.** $\sqrt{3}(\sqrt{6} + 4)$

64. $\sqrt{72} - \sqrt{50}$ **65.** $\sqrt{2}(2\sqrt{8} + 4\sqrt{18})$

66. $\frac{8}{\sqrt{5} + \sqrt{3}}$ **67.** $\sqrt{12}(7\sqrt{6} + \sqrt{24})$

Lesson 10-6

Solve by completing the square. If necessary, round to the nearest tenth.

68. $w^2 + 2w - 11 = 0$ **69.** $k^2 - 8k = 3$

70. $d^2 + 5d + 1 = 0$ **71.** $2a^2 + 20a = 16$

72. $\frac{1}{5}x^2 + 2x = 4$ **73.** $6g^2 - 9g - 30 = 0$

Lesson 9-5

Factor each expression.

74. $x^2 + 10x - 24$ **75.** $m^2 - 14m + 13$

76. $b^2 + 16b - 36$ **77.** $2p^2 + 15p + 7$

78. $3d^2 + 12d - 15$ **79.** $4v^2 - 25v + 25$

Read the problem below, and then follow along with what Lily thinks as she solves the problem. Check your understanding by solving the exercise at the bottom of the page.

Packaging The diagram at the right shows a piece of cardboard that makes a box when sections of it are folded and taped. The ends of the box are x inches by x inches and the box is 10 inches long.

a. Write an equation for the volume V of the box.

b. Solve the equation in part (a) for x.

c. Find the integer values of x that give the box a volume between 40 in.^{3} and 490 in.^{3}, inclusive.

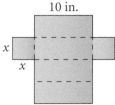

What Lily Thinks   ## What Lily Writes

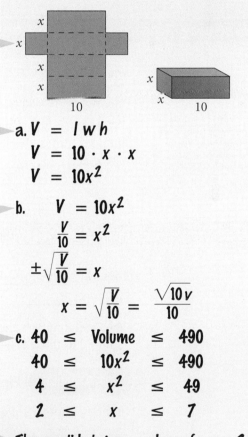

What will this box look like? I'll draw a sketch.

Okay, I can see now that the box has length 10 in., width x in., and height x in. I can substitute these into the formula for the volume of a rectangular prism.

a. $V = l\,w\,h$

$V = 10 \cdot x \cdot x$

$V = 10x^2$

Part (b) asks me to solve the equation for x. Since x is a dimension of the box, it can't be negative. So the solution is the positive square root only.

b. $V = 10x^2$

$\dfrac{V}{10} = x^2$

$\pm\sqrt{\dfrac{V}{10}} = x$

$x = \sqrt{\dfrac{V}{10}} = \dfrac{\sqrt{10v}}{10}$

Part (c) asks me to write a sentence showing that the volume is between 40 in.^{3} and 490 in.^{3}. Oh, I can write an inequality! Then I can solve for x.

c. $40 \le$ Volume ≤ 490

$40 \le 10x^2 \le 490$

$4 \le x^2 \le 49$

$2 \le x \le 7$

Wait! The problem asks for *integer values* only.

The possible integer values of x are 2, 3, 4, 5, 6, and 7.

EXERCISE

Geometry Each edge of a cube has length e.

a. Write an equation for the surface area, S, of the cube in terms of e.

b. Find the integer values of e that will give the cube a surface area between 726 cm^2 and 1176 cm^2, inclusive.

11-6

Graphing Square Root Functions

Lesson Preview

What You'll Learn

OBJECTIVE 1
To graph square root functions

OBJECTIVE 2
To translate graphs of square root functions

...And Why

To solve problems involving police work, as in Example 2

✓ Check Skills You'll Need

(For help, go to Lessons 10-1 and 10-3.)

Graph each pair of quadratic functions on the same graph.

1. $y = x^2, y = x^2 + 3$

2. $y = x^2, y = x^2 - 4$

Evaluate each expression for the given value of x.

3. $\sqrt{x}$ for $x = 4$

4. $\sqrt{x + 7} - 3$ for $x = 2$

5. $3\sqrt{x} + 2$ for $x = 9$

New Vocabulary
• square root function

OBJECTIVE

1

Graphing Square Root Functions

🔁 **TEXT** Interactive lesson includes instant self-check, tutorials, and activities.

? Need Help?

For the function $y = \sqrt{x}$, the domain is all nonnegative values of x. The range is all the corresponding values of y.

A **square root function** is a function that contains the independent variable in the radicand. The function $y = \sqrt{x}$ is the simplest square root function. For x-values that are not perfect squares, you can approximate the y-values to the nearest tenth.

You can graph a square root function by plotting points. Plot the least value in the domain and several other points. Then join the points using a curve.

x	y
0	0
1	1
2	1.4
4	2
6	2.4
9	3

For real numbers, the value of the radicand cannot be negative. So the domain is limited to those values of x that make the radicand greater than or equal to 0.

1 EXAMPLE Finding the Domain of a Square Root Function

Find the domain of each function.

a. $y = \sqrt{x + 3}$

$x + 3 \geq 0$ ←Make the radicand ≥ 0.→

$x \geq -3$

The domain is the set of all numbers greater than or equal to -3.

b. $y = 3\sqrt{2x - 8}$

$2x - 8 \geq 0$

$2x \geq 8$

$x \geq 4$

The domain is the set of all numbers greater than or equal to 4.

✓ **Check Understanding** **1** Find the domain of $y = \sqrt{x - 7}$.

2 **EXAMPLE** Real-World 🌐 Problem Solving

Measurement For good weather conditions, police can use the formula $r = 2\sqrt{5L}$ to find the approximate speed r of a car that leaves a skid mark of length L in feet. Graph the function.

Length of Skid Mark (ft)	Speed (mi/h)
0	0
10	14.1
20	20
30	24.5
40	28.3

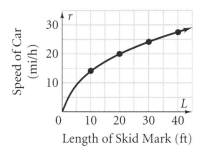

✓ **Check Understanding** 2 **a.** Copy and extend the graph in Example 2 for skid mark lengths from 60 ft to 100 ft.
b. Critical Thinking How long is the skid mark when a car's speed before putting on the brakes is 85 mi/h?

OBJECTIVE

2 **Translating Graphs of Square Root Functions**

For any positive number k, $y = \sqrt{x} + k$ translates the graph of $y = \sqrt{x}$ up k units, while $y = \sqrt{x} - k$ translates the graph of $y = \sqrt{x}$ down k units.

3 **EXAMPLE** Graphing a Vertical Translation

Graph $y = \sqrt{x} + 3$ by translating the graph of $y = \sqrt{x}$.

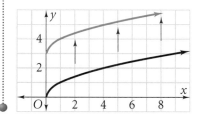

For the graph of $y = \sqrt{x} + 3$, the graph of $y = \sqrt{x}$ is shifted 3 units up.

✓ **Check Understanding** 3 Graph $f(x) = \sqrt{x} - 4$ by translating the graph of $f(x) = \sqrt{x}$.

For any positive number h, $y = \sqrt{x + h}$ translates the graph of $y = \sqrt{x}$ to the left h units, while $y = \sqrt{x - h}$ translates the graph of $y = \sqrt{x}$ to the right h units.

4 **EXAMPLE** Graphing a Horizontal Translation

Graph $f(x) = \sqrt{x + 4}$ by translating the graph of $f(x) = \sqrt{x}$.

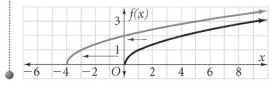

For the graph of $f(x) = \sqrt{x + 4}$, the graph of $f(x) = \sqrt{x}$ is shifted 4 units to the left.

✓ **Check Understanding** 4 Graph $f(x) = \sqrt{x - 3}$ by translating the graph of $f(x) = \sqrt{x}$.

EXERCISES

For more practice, see *Extra Practice*.

Practice and Problem Solving

Ⓐ Practice by Example

Example 1
(page 614)

Find the domain of each function.

1. $y = \sqrt{x - 2}$
2. $f(x) = \sqrt{4x - 3}$
3. $y = \sqrt{1.5x}$
4. $f(x) = \sqrt{7 + x}$
5. $y = \sqrt{x + 3} - 1$
6. $f(x) = \sqrt{x - 5} + 1$
7. $f(x) = \sqrt{3x + 5}$
8. $f(x) = \sqrt{2 + x}$
9. $f(x) = \sqrt{6x - 8} + 1$

Example 2
(page 615)

Make a table of values and graph each function.

10. $y = \sqrt{2x}$
11. $f(x) = 2\sqrt{x}$
12. $y = \sqrt{4x - 8}$
13. $y = \sqrt{3x}$
14. $f(x) = 3\sqrt{x}$
15. $y = -3\sqrt{x}$

16. **Physics** You can use the function $v = \sqrt{64h}$ to find the velocity v of an object, ignoring air resistance, after it has fallen h feet. Make a table of values and graph the function.

Examples 3, 4
(page 615)

Match each graph with its function.

17. $y = \sqrt{x + 4}$
18. $y = \sqrt{x - 2}$
19. $y = \sqrt{x} + 4$
20. $y = \sqrt{x} - 2$

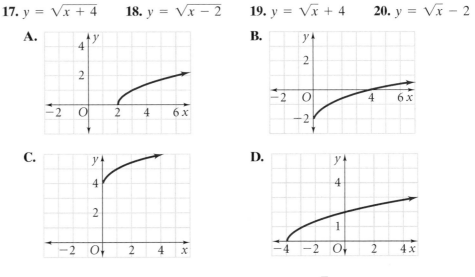

Graph each function by translating the graph of $y = \sqrt{x}$.

21. $y = \sqrt{x} + 5$
22. $y = \sqrt{x} - 5$
23. $y = \sqrt{x} - 3$
24. $y = \sqrt{x} + 2$
25. $f(x) = \sqrt{x - 2}$
26. $f(x) = \sqrt{x - 4}$
27. $y = \sqrt{x} + 1$
28. $y = \sqrt{x + 1}$
29. $y = \sqrt{x - 1}$

Ⓑ Apply Your Skills

30. What are the domain and the range of the function $y = \sqrt{2x - 8}$?

31. What are the domain and the range of the function $y = \sqrt{8 - 2x}$?

32. **Writing** Explain how to find the domain of a square root function. Include an example.

33. **Open-Ended** Give an example of a square root function in each form. Choose $n \neq 0$.
    a. $y = \sqrt{x} + n$
    b. $y = \sqrt{x + n}$
    c. $y = n\sqrt{x}$
    d. Graph each function in parts (a)–(c).

Writing Describe how to translate the graph of $y = \sqrt{x}$ to obtain the graph of each function.

34. $y = \sqrt{x} + 8$
35. $f(x) = \sqrt{x} - 10$
36. $f(x) = \sqrt{x} + 12$
37. $y = \sqrt{x - 9}$

Make a table of values and graph each function.

38. $y = \sqrt{x} - 2.5$
39. $f(x) = 4\sqrt{x}$
40. $y = \sqrt{x} + 6$
41. $y = \sqrt{0.5x}$
42. $y = \sqrt{x - 2} + 3$
43. $f(x) = \sqrt{x + 2} - 4$
44. $y = \sqrt{2x} + 3$
45. $y = \sqrt{2x + 6} + 1$
46. $y = \sqrt{3x - 3} - 2$

Match each graph with its function.

47. $y = \sqrt{x + 1} - 3$
48. $y = \sqrt{x - 1} + 3$
49. $y = \sqrt{x - 3} - 1$
50. $y = \sqrt{x + 3} + 1$

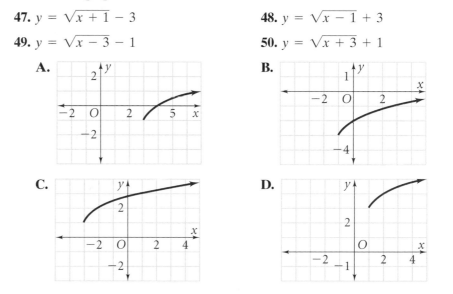

A.

B.

C.

D.

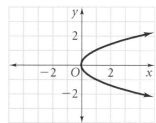

Real-World Connection

Careers There are more than 300,000 paid firefighters in the United States, with thousands more volunteer firefighters.

51. Firefighting When firefighters are trying to put out a fire, the rate at which they can spray water on the fire depends on the nozzle pressure. You can find the flow rate f in gallons per minute (gal/min) using the function $f = 120\sqrt{p}$, where p is the nozzle pressure in pounds per square inch (lb/in.²).
   a. What is the domain of the function?
   b. Graph the function.
   c. Use the graph to estimate the pressure when the flow rate is 800 gal/min.

52. The graph of $x = y^2$ is shown at the right.
   a. Is this the graph of a function?
   b. How does $x = y^2$ relate to the square root function $y = \sqrt{x}$?
   c. Critical Thinking What is a function for the part of the graph that is shown in Quadrant IV?

53. Without graphing, determine which graph rises more steeply, $y = \sqrt{3x}$ or $y = 3\sqrt{x}$. Explain your answer.

Determine whether each statement is true or false. If it is false, explain why.

54. If $\sqrt{x} = 9$, then $x = 3$.

55. The expression $3 + 4\sqrt{x}$ is equivalent to $7\sqrt{x}$.

56. For $\sqrt{x + 5} = 12, x = 139$.

57. $\sqrt{x + 5} = 2$ has no solution.

Real-World 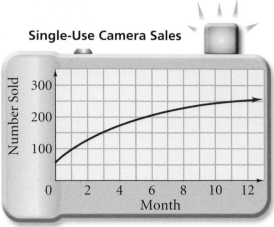 **Connection**

Single-use cameras were introduced in 1986. By 1992, manufacturers had redesigned the cameras so that their parts could be reused or recycled.

58. Business Last year a store had an advertising campaign. The graph shows the sales for single-use cameras. The function $n = 27\sqrt{5t} + 53$ models the sales volume n for the cameras as a function of time t, the number of months after the start of the advertising campaign.

Single-Use Camera Sales

a. Evaluate the function to find how many disposable cameras the store sold in the seventh month.

b. Solve an equation to find the month in which the number of single-use cameras sold was about 175.

C Challenge

59. a. Graph $y = \sqrt{x^2} + 5$.
b. Write a function for the graph you drew that does not require a radical.

60. Explain how you can translate $y = \sqrt{x}$ to graph $y = \sqrt{x - 2} + 3$.

61. a. Graph each function.
  i. $y = \sqrt{4x}$ **ii.** $y = \sqrt{5x}$ **iii.** $y = \sqrt{6x}$ **iv.** $y = \sqrt{-6x}$
b. Critical Thinking Describe how the graph of $y = \sqrt{nx}$ changes as the value of n varies.

62. Data Collection Roll a ball down a ramp which is at least 6 ft long. Record the time the ball takes to roll several different distances down the ramp, up to its full length.
a. Graph your data with time as a function of distance (d, t).
b. Describe your graph. Explain why it is *not* linear.

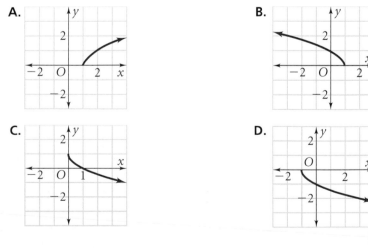

Standardized Test Prep

Multiple Choice

63. Which of the following is the graph of $y = \sqrt{1 - x}$?

A.

B.

C.

D.

64. What is the least possible value for x for the graph of $y = \sqrt{2x - 44} + 3$?
   F. 3   **G.** 19   **H.** 22   **I.** 25

65. What is the greatest possible value of y for the graph of $y = -\sqrt{5x - 10}$?

    A. -10 **B.** -2 **C.** 0 **D.** 2

66. If $x = -2$, which function has the least value?

    F. $y = \sqrt{7 - x}$ **G.** $y = \sqrt{7 + x}$

    H. $y = \sqrt{-x} - 7$ **I.** $y = \sqrt{-x} + 7$

67. If $a = \sqrt{24}$, and $\dfrac{a}{b} = \dfrac{\sqrt{6}}{c}$, then what does $\dfrac{c}{b}$ equal?

    A. $\dfrac{1}{4}$ **B.** $\dfrac{1}{2}$ **C.** 2 **D.** 4

68. In which quadrant(s) is the graph of $y = \sqrt{x} + 7$?

    F. I, II, and III   **G.** I and IV   **H.** I   **I.** I and II

Take It to the NET
Online lesson quiz at
www.PHSchool.com
Web Code: aea-1106

Short Response

69. Graph $y = \sqrt{x - 6}$.

Mixed Review

Lesson 11-5

Solve each equation. Check your solutions.

70. $\sqrt{x} + 7 = 11$ **71.** $\sqrt{c + 1} = \sqrt{2c - 6}$

72. $\sqrt{x} - 4 = 9$ **73.** $13 = 5\sqrt{m - 8}$

74. $\sqrt{k + 3} + 12 = 6$ **75.** $\sqrt{5h - 2} = \sqrt{2h}$

Lesson 10-7

Use the quadratic formula to solve each equation.

76. $2x^2 + 4x - 7 = 0$ **77.** $x^2 - 8x - 23 = 0$

78. $5x^2 - x + 11 = 0$ **79.** $9x^2 + 6x - 10 = 0$

80. $1.2x^2 + x + 6 = 0$ **81.** $9x^2 + 13x - 7 = 0$

Lesson 9-6

Factor completely.

82. $2x^2 - 7x - 4$ **83.** $3x^2 + x - 10$

84. $4x^2 + 20x + 9$ **85.** $2x^2 - 10x - 48$

86. $4x^2 - 4x - 60$ **87.** $x^3 - 12x^2 - 13x$

✓ Checkpoint Quiz 2   Lessons 11-4 through 11-6

TEXT Instant self-check quiz online and on CD-ROM

Simplify each expression.

1. $-10\sqrt{7} + 2\sqrt{7}$ **2.** $\sqrt{16} - 5\sqrt{2}$

3. $2\sqrt{5} + 3\sqrt{25}$ **4.** $\sqrt{6}(\sqrt{12} - \sqrt{3})$

5. $(\sqrt{3} + \sqrt{2})^2$ **6.** $\dfrac{\sqrt{8} - \sqrt{27}}{\sqrt{6} - \sqrt{5}}$

Solve each equation.

7. $4 - \sqrt{m} = -12$ **8.** $\sqrt{t + 5} = \sqrt{2t - 3}$ **9.** $r = \sqrt{4r + 5}$

10. Writing Describe how to translate the graph of $y = \sqrt{x}$ in order to graph $y = \sqrt{x} + 2$. Then graph the function.

Rational Exponents

You can have roots other than square roots. The third root of a number x is written as $\sqrt[3]{x}$. For example, $\sqrt[3]{8} = 2$ because $2^3 = 8$. You can also express roots using exponents. The expression $a^{\frac{1}{n}}$ is defined as $\sqrt[n]{a}$. An example is $9^{\frac{1}{2}} = \sqrt[2]{9} = 3$.

Rational exponents follow the same rules as integer exponents, so $9^{\frac{1}{2}} \cdot 9^{\frac{1}{2}} = 9^{\left(\frac{1}{2} + \frac{1}{2}\right)} = 9^1 = 9$, just as $\sqrt{9} \cdot \sqrt{9} = 9$.

1 EXAMPLE

Simplify $16^{\frac{1}{4}}$.

$$16^{\frac{1}{4}} = 2 \qquad 16 = 2 \cdot 2 \cdot 2 \cdot 2, \text{ so } \sqrt[4]{16} = 2$$

An exponent can be any rational number. You can simplify rational exponents using the property of raising a power to a power, $a^{mn} = (a^m)^n$.

2 EXAMPLE

Simplify $8^{\frac{2}{3}}$.

a.

$$8^{\frac{2}{3}} = 8^{\frac{1}{3} \cdot 2} \qquad \longleftarrow \text{ Write } \tfrac{2}{3} \text{ as a product of 2 and } \tfrac{1}{3}. \longrightarrow \qquad \textbf{b. } 8^{\frac{2}{3}} = 8^{2 \cdot \frac{1}{3}}$$

$$= \left(8^{\frac{1}{3}}\right)^2 \qquad \longleftarrow \text{ Use the property of raising a power to a power. } \longrightarrow \qquad = \left(8^2\right)^{\frac{1}{3}}$$

$$= (2)^2 \qquad \longleftarrow \text{ Simplify within the parentheses. } \longrightarrow \qquad = (64)^{\frac{1}{3}}$$

$$= 4 \qquad \longleftarrow \text{ Simplify. } \longrightarrow \qquad = 4$$

3 EXAMPLE

Simplify $\left(x^{\frac{3}{4}}\right)^5 \left(y^{\frac{1}{2}}\right) y^{\frac{2}{5}}$.

$$\left(x^{\frac{3}{4}}\right)^5 \left(y^{\frac{1}{2}}\right) y^{\frac{2}{5}} = \left(x^{\frac{15}{4}}\right)\left(y^{\frac{1}{2}} \cdot y^{\frac{2}{5}}\right) \qquad \text{Multiply exponents in } \left(\boldsymbol{x^{\frac{3}{4}}}\right)^{\boldsymbol{5}}.$$

$$= x^{\frac{15}{4}}\left(y^{\frac{1}{2} + \frac{2}{5}}\right) \qquad \text{Add exponents of powers with the same base.}$$

$$= x^{\frac{15}{4}} y^{\frac{9}{10}} \qquad \text{Simplify fractions. } \tfrac{1}{2} + \tfrac{2}{5} = \tfrac{9}{10}. \text{ Leave } \tfrac{15}{4} \text{ as an improper fraction.}$$

EXERCISES

Simplify each expression.

1. $100^{\frac{1}{2}}$ **2.** $25^{\frac{1}{2}}$ **3.** $8^{\frac{1}{3}}$ **4.** $\left(49^{\frac{1}{2}}\right)^3$

5. $\left(8^{\frac{1}{3}}\right)^2$ **6.** $8^{\frac{4}{3}}$ **7.** $25^{\frac{3}{2}}$ **8.** $64^{\frac{4}{3}}$

9. $\left(x^{\frac{1}{3}}\right)^6$ **10.** $\left(b^{\frac{1}{4}}\right)^4$ **11.** $\left(m^{\frac{2}{5}}\right)^{\frac{5}{3}}$ **12.** $\left(m^{\frac{2}{5}}\right)\left(m^{\frac{3}{5}}\right)$

13. $\left(a^{\frac{1}{3}}\right)\left(a^{\frac{5}{6}}\right)$ **14.** $\left(k^{\frac{1}{2}}\right)\left(k^{\frac{1}{4}}\right)^3$ **15.** $(36y^7)^{\frac{3}{2}}$ **16.** $(81c^8)^{\frac{3}{4}}$

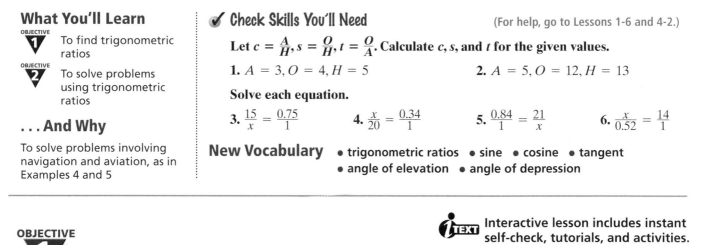

Trigonometric Ratios

11-7

Lesson Preview

What You'll Learn

OBJECTIVE 1
To find trigonometric ratios

OBJECTIVE 2
To solve problems using trigonometric ratios

. . . And Why

To solve problems involving navigation and aviation, as in Examples 4 and 5

✔ **Check Skills You'll Need**   (For help, go to Lessons 1-6 and 4-2.)

Let $c = \frac{A}{H}, s = \frac{O}{H}, t = \frac{O}{A}$. Calculate c, s, and t for the given values.

1. $A = 3, O = 4, H = 5$ **2.** $A = 5, O = 12, H = 13$

Solve each equation.

3. $\frac{15}{x} = \frac{0.75}{1}$ **4.** $\frac{x}{20} = \frac{0.34}{1}$ **5.** $\frac{0.84}{1} = \frac{21}{x}$ **6.** $\frac{x}{0.52} = \frac{14}{1}$

New Vocabulary • trigonometric ratios • sine • cosine • tangent
                    • angle of elevation • angle of depression

---

OBJECTIVE

1 Finding Trigonometric Ratios

Interactive lesson includes instant self-check, tutorials, and activities.

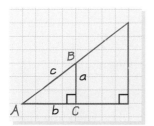

Investigation: Trigonometric Ratios

1. On graph paper, draw a right triangle like the one at the left. Extend sides $\overline{AB}$ and $\overline{AC}$ to form a second triangle similar to the first.

2. **a.** Copy the table at the right. Measure and record the lengths of the legs of each triangle.

Triangle	a	b	c	$\frac{a}{b}$	$\frac{a}{c}$	$\frac{b}{c}$
First	■	■	■	■	■	■
Second	■	■	■	■	■	■

   b. Calculate c, the length of each hypotenuse.

   c. Calculate and record the ratios $\frac{a}{b}$, $\frac{a}{c}$, and $\frac{b}{c}$ for each triangle.

3. How do corresponding ratios in the two triangles compare?

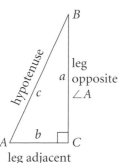

Ratios of the sides of a right triangle are called **trigonometric ratios.** In $\triangle ABC$, at the left, you see the relationships between an angle and the legs of a triangle. The same letter indicates the lengths of the sides of the triangle and the angle opposite that side.

You can use these relationships to express trigonometric ratios.

sine of $\angle A = \dfrac{\text{length of leg opposite } \angle A}{\text{length of hypotenuse}}$ or $\sin A = \dfrac{a}{c} = \dfrac{\text{opposite leg}}{\text{hypotenuse}}$

cosine of $\angle A = \dfrac{\text{length of leg adjacent to } \angle A}{\text{length of hypotenuse}}$ or $\cos A = \dfrac{b}{c} = \dfrac{\text{adjacent leg}}{\text{hypotenuse}}$

tangent of $\angle A = \dfrac{\text{length of leg opposite } \angle A}{\text{length of leg adjacent to } \angle A}$ or $\tan A = \dfrac{a}{b} = \dfrac{\text{opposite leg}}{\text{adjacent leg}}$

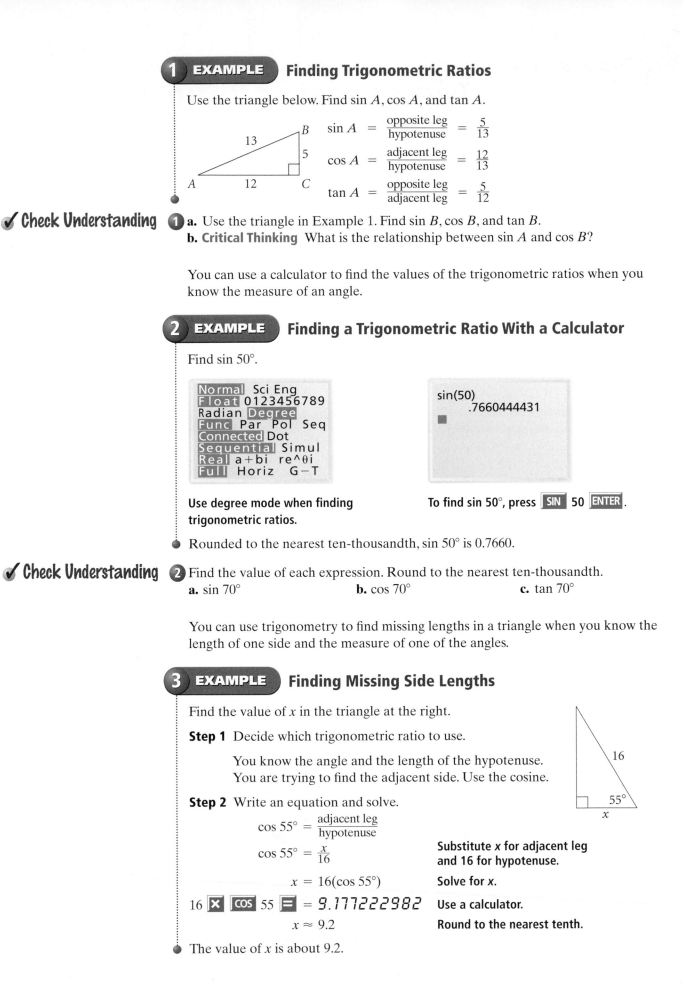

1 EXAMPLE **Finding Trigonometric Ratios**

Use the triangle below. Find sin A, cos A, and tan A.

$$\sin A = \frac{\text{opposite leg}}{\text{hypotenuse}} = \frac{5}{13}$$

$$\cos A = \frac{\text{adjacent leg}}{\text{hypotenuse}} = \frac{12}{13}$$

$$\tan A = \frac{\text{opposite leg}}{\text{adjacent leg}} = \frac{5}{12}$$

✓ Check Understanding **1** **a.** Use the triangle in Example 1. Find sin B, cos B, and tan B.

b. **Critical Thinking** What is the relationship between sin A and cos B?

You can use a calculator to find the values of the trigonometric ratios when you know the measure of an angle.

2 EXAMPLE **Finding a Trigonometric Ratio With a Calculator**

Find sin 50°.

Normal Sci Eng
Float 0123456789
Radian Degree
Func Par Pol Seq
Connected Dot
Sequential Simul
Real a+bi re^θi
Full Horiz G-T

sin(50)
                    .7660444431

Use degree mode when finding trigonometric ratios.

To find sin 50°, press SIN 50 ENTER.

Rounded to the nearest ten-thousandth, sin 50° is 0.7660.

✓ Check Understanding **2** Find the value of each expression. Round to the nearest ten-thousandth.

a. sin 70°   **b.** cos 70°   **c.** tan 70°

You can use trigonometry to find missing lengths in a triangle when you know the length of one side and the measure of one of the angles.

3 EXAMPLE **Finding Missing Side Lengths**

Find the value of x in the triangle at the right.

Step 1 Decide which trigonometric ratio to use.

You know the angle and the length of the hypotenuse. You are trying to find the adjacent side. Use the cosine.

Step 2 Write an equation and solve.

$$\cos 55° = \frac{\text{adjacent leg}}{\text{hypotenuse}}$$

$$\cos 55° = \frac{x}{16}$$ Substitute x for adjacent leg and 16 for hypotenuse.

$$x = 16(\cos 55°)$$ Solve for x.

16 × COS 55 = *9.177222982*   Use a calculator.

$$x \approx 9.2$$ Round to the nearest tenth.

The value of x is about 9.2.

✓ Check Understanding ③ Find the value of x in each triangle. Round to the nearest tenth.

a.

b.

$42°$

x

5

OBJECTIVE

2 Solving Problems Using Trigonometric Ratios

You can use trigonometric ratios to measure distances indirectly when you know an angle of elevation. An **angle of elevation** is an angle from the horizontal up to a line of sight.

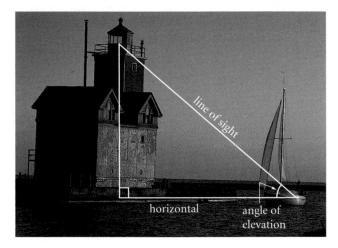

line of sight

horizontal   angle of
elevation

4 EXAMPLE Using Angle of Elevation

Navigation Suppose the angle of elevation from a rowboat to the light of a lighthouse is 35°. You know that the lighthouse is 96 ft tall. How far from the lighthouse is the rowboat? Round your answer to the nearest foot.

Draw a diagram.

Define Let x = the distance from the boat to the lighthouse.

Relate You know the angle of elevation and the opposite leg. You are trying to find the adjacent leg. Use the tangent.

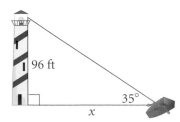

96 ft

35°

x

Write $\tan A = \dfrac{\text{opposite leg}}{\text{adjacent leg}}$

$\tan 35° = \dfrac{96}{x}$ Substitute for the angle and the legs.

$x(\tan 35°) = 96$ Multiply each side by x.

$x = \dfrac{96}{\tan 35}$ Divide each side by tan 35°.

$x \approx 137.1022086$ Use a calculator.

$x \approx 137$ Round to the nearest unit.

● The rowboat is about 137 ft from the lighthouse.

Lesson 11-7 Trigonometric Ratios **623**

✔ **Check Understanding** ④ The angle of elevation from a point on the ground 300 ft from a tower is 42°. How tall is the tower?

An **angle of depression** is an angle from the horizontal down to a line of sight. In the picture below, a ranger is looking down from the tower to the distant fire.

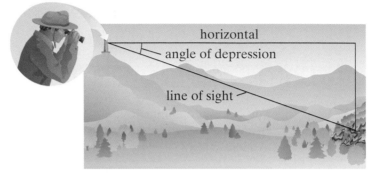

When you solve real-world problems involving trigonometry, you frequently have to round your answers. Round your answers to the measurements used in the problem. If the problem has measurements to the nearest foot, round your answer to the nearest foot. If the problem has measurements to the nearest 10,000 feet, round your answer to the nearest 10,000 feet.

⑤ EXAMPLE Using Angle of Depression

Aviation A pilot is flying a plane 20,000 ft above the ground. The pilot begins a 2° descent to an airport runway. How far is the airplane from the start of the runway (in ground distance)?

Draw a diagram.

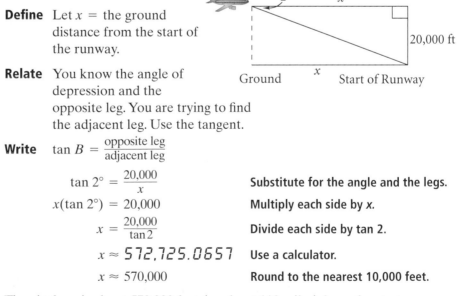

Define Let x = the ground distance from the start of the runway.

Relate You know the angle of depression and the opposite leg. You are trying to find the adjacent leg. Use the tangent.

Write $\tan B = \dfrac{\text{opposite leg}}{\text{adjacent leg}}$

$\tan 2° = \dfrac{20{,}000}{x}$ **Substitute for the angle and the legs.**

$x(\tan 2°) = 20{,}000$ **Multiply each side by x.**

$x = \dfrac{20{,}000}{\tan 2}$ **Divide each side by tan 2.**

$x \approx 572{,}725.0657$ **Use a calculator.**

$x \approx 570{,}000$ **Round to the nearest 10,000 feet.**

The airplane is about 570,000 feet (or about 110 miles) from the start of the runway.

✔ **Check Understanding** ⑤ Suppose the pilot in Example 5 is flying at an altitude of 26,000 ft when the airplane begins a 2° descent. How far is the airplane from the start of the runway?

EXERCISES

For more practice, see *Extra Practice*.

Practice and Problem Solving

A **Practice by Example**

Example 1
(page 622)

Use △ *RST* at the right. Find the value of each expression.

1. sin *R*   **2.** cos *R*   **3.** tan *R*

4. sin *S*   **5.** cos *S*   **6.** tan *S*

Example 2
(page 622)

Find the value of each expression. Round to the nearest ten-thousandth.

7. sin 32°   **8.** cos 55°   **9.** tan 52°   **10.** sin 85°   **11.** cos 15°

Example 3
(page 622)

Find the value of *x* to the nearest tenth.

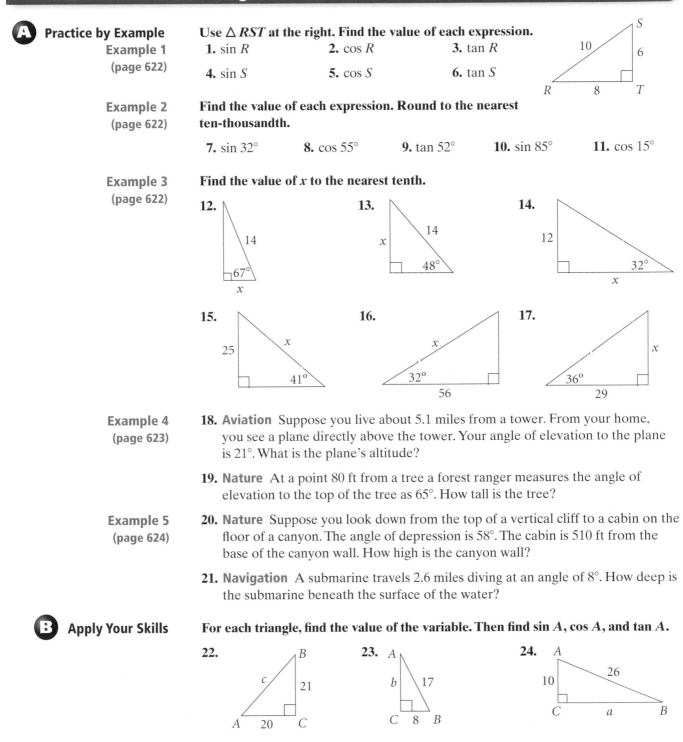

12.   **13.**   **14.**

15.   **16.**   **17.**

Example 4
(page 623)

18. Aviation Suppose you live about 5.1 miles from a tower. From your home, you see a plane directly above the tower. Your angle of elevation to the plane is 21°. What is the plane's altitude?

19. Nature At a point 80 ft from a tree a forest ranger measures the angle of elevation to the top of the tree as 65°. How tall is the tree?

Example 5
(page 624)

20. Nature Suppose you look down from the top of a vertical cliff to a cabin on the floor of a canyon. The angle of depression is 58°. The cabin is 510 ft from the base of the canyon wall. How high is the canyon wall?

21. Navigation A submarine travels 2.6 miles diving at an angle of 8°. How deep is the submarine beneath the surface of the water?

B **Apply Your Skills**

For each triangle, find the value of the variable. Then find sin *A*, cos *A*, and tan *A*.

22.   **23.**   **24.**

Suppose △ *ABC* has right angle *C*. Find the measures of the other sides to the nearest whole number.

25. *m*∠*A* = 40°, *BC* = 5   **26.** *m*∠*A* = 32°, *AB* = 42

27. *m*∠*B* = 71°, *AC* = 17   **28.** *m*∠*B* = 5°, *BC* = 50

Lesson 11-7 Trigonometric Ratios   **625**

29. Hobbies Suppose you are flying a kite. The kite string is 60 m long, and the angle of elevation of the string is 65° from your hand. Your hand is 1 m above the ground. How high above the ground is the kite?

30. Engineering To support a pole, a cable is drawn tightly between the pole and the ground. The cable is 4.1 m from the base of the pole, and the angle of elevation from the bottom of the cable to the top of the pole is 47°. How tall is the pole?

31. a. Aviation A pilot is flying a plane at an altitude of 30,000 ft. The pilot begins a 1° descent to an airport runway. How far is the airplane from the start of the runway (in ground distance)?
b. What is your answer to part (a) in miles?

32. Nature The length of a tree's shadow is 15 m. The angle of elevation of the sun is 38°. What is the height of the tree?

33. A 7-meter ladder rests against the side of a house. The angle of elevation of the ladder is 75°. How high is the top of the ladder?

Find the value of the variable in each figure to the nearest tenth.

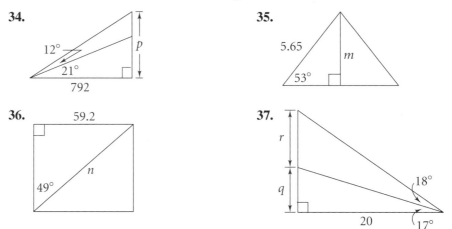

34.
12°
21°
792
p

35.
5.65
53°
m

36.
59.2
49°
n

37.
r
q
20
18°
17°

38. Recreation Use the Ferris wheel photo at the left.
a. Find the height at the top of the Ferris wheel.
b. If the hub or center of the wheel is about 91 feet off the ground, what is the radius of the wheel?

39. Nature Suppose you are lying on the ground looking up at a California redwood tree. Your angle of elevation to the top of the tree is 42°. You are 280 ft from the base of the tree.
a. How tall is the tree?
b. How far would a bird have to fly to get from the top of the tree to your location?

40. Open-Ended Draw a right triangle. Measure one acute angle and one leg. Use a trigonometric ratio to find the length of the other leg.

41. A person is in a lighthouse 225 ft above sea level. She sees a ship in the harbor. The angle of depression from her position to the ship is 48°. How far is the ship from shore?

42. An air-traffic controller is in a 78-meter-high tower and sees a plane, which is 7500 meters away (in ground distance), at an angle of elevation of 38°. What is the altitude of the plane?

Challenge

43. An architect is designing an access ramp. The angle of the ramp with the ground will be 5°. The top of the ramp will be 5 ft above the ground. How long will the ramp be?

44. At a certain point in a large, level park, the angle of elevation to the top of an office building is 30°. If you move 400 ft closer to the building, the angle of elevation is 45°. To the nearest 10 feet, how tall is the building?

45. A line passes through the origin and forms an angle of 14° with the *x*-axis. Find the slope of the line. Round to the nearest hundreth.

46. An airplane flies at an altitude of 12 km.
   a. If the pilot wants the angle of descent to be 3°, how far from the airport must he start descending?
   b. Assume the pilot begins his descent at the distance you found in part (a). If he uses an angle of descent of 2°, what will his altitude be as the plane passes over the airport?

Standardized Test Prep

Multiple Choice

47. Find the value of *x* to the nearest tenth.
   A. 7.2   **B.** 9.1
   C. 10.9   **D.** 11.9

48. △*KLM* is a right triangle with a right angle at *M*. Which of the given statements is false?

   F. $\sin K = \frac{LM}{KL}$ **G.** $\cos K = \frac{KL}{KM}$ **H.** $\tan K = \frac{LM}{KM}$ **I.** $\cos L = \frac{LM}{KL}$

Short Response

49. Using the triangle at the right, find sin *A*, cos *A*, and tan *A*.

Extended Response

50. A fox is at the edge of a cliff 850 ft above the base of the cliff. He sees a mouse in a canyon. The angle of depression from his position to the mouse is 56°. Draw and label a diagram for the situation. Then write and solve a trigonometric equation that will determine how far the mouse is from the base of the cliff. Round to the nearest foot.

Mixed Review

Lesson 11-6   **Graph each function.**

51. $y = \sqrt{5x}$ **52.** $y = \sqrt{x + 3}$ **53.** $y = \sqrt{x - 7}$

Lesson 10-8   **Find the number of real solutions of each equation.**

54. $2x^2 - x - 4 = 0$ **55.** $7x^2 + x + 20 = 0$ **56.** $9x^2 + 6x + 1 = 0$

Lesson 9-7   **Factor each expression.**

57. $n^2 - 400$ **58.** $x^2 - 30x + 225$ **59.** $100p^2 - 49$

60. $\frac{1}{16}d^2 - \frac{9}{4}$ **61.** $98w^2 - 128$ **62.** $x^2 + 26x + 169$

Using Estimation

Using estimation may help you find answers, check an answer, or eliminate one or more answer choices.

EXAMPLE

The length of the hypotenuse of a right triangle is 9 cm and the length of one leg is 4 cm. Which is closest to the length of the other leg?

A. 7.7 cm **B.** 7.8 cm **C.** 8.1 cm **D.** 9.8 cm

First, use the Pythagorean Theorem to find the length of the other leg in radical form. Then use estimation to see which answer choice is closest to it.

$a^2 + b^2 = c^2$ **Use the Pythagorean Theorem.**

$4^2 + b^2 = 9^2$ **Substitute 4 for *a* and 9 for *c*.**

$16 + b^2 = 81$ **Simplify.**

$b^2 = 65$ **Subtract 16 from each side.**

$b = \sqrt{65}$ **Take the square root of each side.**

A good estimate for $\sqrt{65}$ is 8, since $\sqrt{65}$ is close to $\sqrt{64}$. You can now eliminate answer choices A, B, and D, which are not as close to 8 as C.
- C is the correct answer.

EXERCISES

1. The lengths of the two legs of a right triangle are 8 ft and 9 ft. Which is closest to the length of the hypotenuse?

   A. 4.1 ft   **B.** 8.5 ft   **C.** 9.3 ft   **D.** 12.0 ft

2. Which is the best estimate of the area of the figure below?

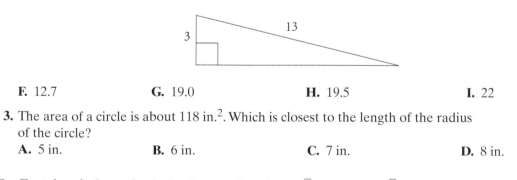

   F. 12.7   **G.** 19.0   **H.** 19.5   **I.** 22

3. The area of a circle is about 118 in.^{2}. Which is closest to the length of the radius of the circle?

   A. 5 in.   **B.** 6 in.   **C.** 7 in.   **D.** 8 in.

For Exercises 4–6, use the decimal approximations $\sqrt{2} \approx 1.4$ and $\sqrt{3} \approx 1.7$.

4. Error Analysis Bill multiplied $(\sqrt{3} + 3)(\sqrt{3} - 1)$ and got the answer $3 - 3 = 0$. Use estimation to show that his answer is wrong.

5. Find an estimate for $\sqrt{8}$ using the estimate for $\sqrt{2}$.

6. Find an estimate for $\sqrt{12}$ using the estimate for $\sqrt{3}$.

Chapter Review

Vocabulary

angle of depression (p. 624)	extraneous solution (p. 609)	radical equation (p. 607)
angle of elevation (p. 623)	hypotenuse (p. 584)	radical expression (p. 578)
conclusion (p. 586)	hypothesis (p. 586)	rationalize (p. 581)
conditional (p. 586)	leg (p. 584)	sine (p. 621)
conjugates (p. 601)	like radicals (p. 600)	square root function (p. 614)
converse (p. 586)	midpoint (p. 593)	tangent (p. 621)
cosine (p. 621)	midpoint formula (p. 593)	trigonometric ratios (p. 621)
distance formula (p. 591)	Pythagorean Theorem (p. 584)	unlike radicals (p. 600)

Reading Math
Understanding
Vocabulary

Choose the vocabulary term that correctly completes each sentence.

1. Two radical expressions that are the sum and the difference of the same two terms are ___?___.

2. The two sides of a right triangle that form the right angle are the ___?___.

3. One method of simplifying a radical expression is to ___?___ the denominator.

4. A(n) ___?___ is a value that satisfies the new equation but not the original equation.

5. Radicals with the same radicand are ___?___.

6. The ___?___ states that in a right triangle with sides $a, b,$ and $c,$ in which the longest side is $c, a^2 + b^2 = c^2$.

7. In a right triangle, the ___?___ is the trigonometric ratio of the length of the leg opposite an angle to the length of the hypotenuse of the triangle.

8. A horizontal and the line of sight to an object above the horizontal form a(n) ___?___.

Take It to the NET
Online vocabulary quiz
at **www.PHSchool.com**
Web Code: aej-1151

9. The expression $\sqrt{(x_2 - x_1)^2 + (y_2 - y_1)^2}$ is part of the ___?___, which determines the length of the line from point (x_1, y_1) to point (x_2, y_2).

10. The coordinates $\left(\dfrac{x_1 + x_2}{2}, \dfrac{y_1 + y_2}{2}\right)$ identify the ___?___ between points (x_1, y_1) and (x_2, y_2).

Skills and Concepts

11-1 Objectives

▼ To simplify radicals involving products (p. 578)

▼ To simplify radicals involving quotients (p. 580)

You can simplify some radical expressions by using products or quotients. The Multiplication Property of Square Roots states that for $a \geq 0$ and $b \geq 0,$ $\sqrt{ab} = \sqrt{a} \cdot \sqrt{b}.$ The Division Property of Square Roots states that for $a \geq 0$ and $b > 0, \sqrt{\dfrac{a}{b}} = \dfrac{\sqrt{a}}{\sqrt{b}}.$

Simplify each radical expression.

11. $\sqrt{32} \cdot \sqrt{144}$ 12. $\sqrt{\dfrac{84}{121}}$ 13. $\sqrt{96c^3} \cdot \sqrt{25c}$ 14. $\dfrac{10}{\sqrt{13}}$

15. A rectangle is 7 times as long as it is wide. Its area is 1400 cm². Find the dimensions of the rectangle in simplest radical form.

11-2 Objectives

▼ To solve problems using the Pythagorean Theorem (p. 584)

▼ To identify right triangles (p. 586)

For a right triangle with **legs** a and b and **hypotenuse** c, the **Pythagorean Theorem** states that $a^2 + b^2 = c^2$. The converse of the Pythagorean Theorem states that if a triangle has sides of lengths a, b, and c, and if $a^2 + b^2 = c^2$, then it is a right triangle with hypotenuse of length c.

Find the length of the hypotenuse with the given leg lengths. If necessary, round to the nearest tenth.

16. $a = 3, b = 5$ **17.** $a = 11, b = 14$ **18.** $a = 7, b = 13$ **19.** $a = 4, b = 9$

Determine whether the given lengths can be sides of a right triangle.

20. $XY = 16, YZ = 34, XZ = 30$ **21.** $XY = 2.5, YZ = 2.4, XZ = 0.7$

22. Baseball The bases on a playground baseball diamond form a square, 60 ft on a side. How far would a catcher standing on home plate need to throw the ball to get a runner out at second base?

11-3 Objectives

▼ To find the distance between two points on a coordinate plane (p. 591)

▼ To find the coordinates of the midpoint of a line segment (p. 593)

The **distance formula** $d = \sqrt{(x_2 - x_1)^2 + (y_2 - y_1)^2}$ gives the distance between two points (x_1, x_2) and (y_1, y_2). The **midpoint formula** $M = \left(\frac{x_1 + x_2}{2}, \frac{y_1 + y_2}{2}\right)$ gives the coordinates of their midpoint.

Find the distance between the points in each pair. If necessary, round to the nearest tenth.

23. $A(4, 0), B(1, 4)$ **24.** $C(-2, -3), D(-4, 5)$ **25.** $P(-3, 2), Q(6, -4)$

26. Open-Ended Draw a square on a coordinate plane. Find the length of the diagonal of the square you drew.

Find the midpoint of the segment with the given endpoints.

27. $A(3, 7), B(-2, 4)$ **28.** $A\left(4\frac{3}{4}, -2\right), B\left(6\frac{1}{4}, 10\frac{1}{2}\right)$

11-4 and 11-5 Objectives

▼ To simplify sums and differences (p. 600)

▼ To simplify products and quotients (p. 601)

▼ To solve equations containing radicals (p. 607)

▼ To identify extraneous solutions (p. 609)

You can use the Distributive Property to simplify expressions with sums and differences of radicals. First, simplify the radicals and check for **like radicals.** When a denominator contains a sum or a difference including radical expressions, you can **rationalize** the denominator by multiplying the numerator and the denominator by the **conjugate** of the denominator.

A **radical equation** has a variable in the radicand. Sometimes you can solve such an equation by squaring both sides. You may also square both sides of the equation when each side is a square root. Squaring both sides of a radical equation may produce an **extraneous solution.** It is not a solution of the original equation.

Simplify each radical expression.

29. $6\sqrt{7} - 2\sqrt{28}$ **30.** $5(\sqrt{20} + \sqrt{80})$ **31.** $\sqrt{54} - 2\sqrt{6}$

32. $\sqrt{125} - 3\sqrt{5}$ **33.** $\sqrt{10}(\sqrt{10} - \sqrt{20})$ **34.** $(\sqrt{2} + \sqrt{7})(3\sqrt{2} - \sqrt{7})$

35. $(\sqrt{5} + 4\sqrt{3})^2$ **36.** $\sqrt{28} + 5\sqrt{63}$ **37.** $\frac{3}{\sqrt{6} - \sqrt{3}}$

Solve each radical equation.

38. $\sqrt{x + 7} = 3$

39. $\sqrt{x} + 3\sqrt{x} = 16$

40. $\sqrt{x + 7} = \sqrt{2x - 1}$

41. $\sqrt{x} - 5 = 4$

Tell which of the given solutions is extraneous for each equation.

42. $\sqrt{4x} = x - 3$; $x = 1, x = 9$

43. $\sqrt{d - 3} = 5 - d$; $d = 4, d = 7$

44. A rectangle has a width of $2\sqrt{5}$ cm and an area of 50 cm². Find the length of the rectangle.

45. The volume V of a cylinder is given by $V = \pi r^2 h$, where r is the radius of a cylinder and h is its height. If the volume of the cylinder is 54 in.³, and its height is 2 in., what is its radius to the nearest 0.01 in.?

11-6 Objectives

▼ To graph square root functions (p. 614)

▼ To translate graphs of square root functions (p. 615)

The simplest square root function is $y = \sqrt{x}$. The graphs of $y = \sqrt{x} + k$ and $y = \sqrt{x} - k$ are vertical translations of $y = \sqrt{x}$. The graphs of $y = \sqrt{x - h}$ and $y = \sqrt{x + h}$ are horizontal translations of $y = \sqrt{x}$.

Make a table of values and graph each function.

46. $y = \sqrt{\dfrac{x}{2}}$

47. $y = \dfrac{\sqrt{x}}{2}$

48. $y = \sqrt{2x}$

49. $y = 1 + \sqrt{x}$

Find the domain of each function. Then graph each function by translating the graph of $y = \sqrt{x}$.

50. $y = \sqrt{x} + 5$

51. $y = \sqrt{x} - 2$

52. $y = \sqrt{x + 1}$

53. $f(x) = 2\sqrt{x}$

11-7 Objectives

▼ To find trigonometric ratios (p. 621)

▼ To solve problems using trigonometric ratios (p. 623)

Trigonometric ratios are triangle measurement ratios. For a right triangle of a given shape, the ratios do not change no matter how large or small the triangle is. Three trigonometric ratios—**sine** (sin), **cosine** (cos), and **tangent** (tan)—are shown below.

sine of $\angle A = \dfrac{\text{length of leg opposite } \angle A}{\text{length of hypotenuse}}$

cosine of $\angle A = \dfrac{\text{length of leg adjacent to } \angle A}{\text{length of hypotenuse}}$

tangent of $\angle A = \dfrac{\text{length of leg opposite } \angle A}{\text{length of leg adjacent to } \angle A}$

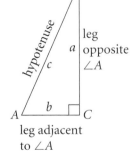

You can use trigonometric ratios to measure distances indirectly. You can use an angle of elevation or angle of depression to measure heights indirectly.

Suppose $\triangle ABC$ has right angle C. Find the measures of the other sides to the nearest whole number.

54. $AB = 12, m\angle A = 34°$

55. $BC = 9, m\angle B = 72°$

56. $AC = 8, m\angle B = 52°$

57. $AB = 25, m\angle A = 12°$

58. During a violent thunderstorm, a tree near John's house was broken by the wind. The top part of the tree was bent so that it touched the ground 21 ft from the base of the tree. If the broken top part of the tree made a 48° angle with the ground, how tall was the tree before the storm?

Chapter

11

Chapter Test

Take It to the NET
Online chapter test at
www.PHSchool.com
Web Code: aea-1152

Determine whether the given lengths can be sides of a right triangle.

1. $6, 8, 10$

2. $6, 7, 9$

3. $4, 5, 11$

4. $10, 24, 26$

5. The length of each leg of an isosceles right triangle is 40.9 cm. Find the length of the hypotenuse to the nearest tenth.

Find AB. Round to the nearest tenth.

6. $A(1, -2), B(5, 7)$

7. $A(3.1, 5), B(7.2, 4.6)$

8. $A(4, 7), B(-11, -6)$

9. $A(0, -5), B(3, 2)$

Find the midpoint of the segment with the given endpoints.

10. $A(4, 9), B(1, -5)$

11. $P(-2, -7), Q(3, 0)$

12. $D(3, -10), E(-4, 6)$

13. $K\left(0, 8\frac{1}{2}\right), L\left(-1, 1\frac{1}{2}\right)$

Find the measure of each side to the nearest tenth.

14. AB

15. AC

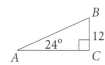

16. A wire is stretched from the top of a 3-ft pole to the top of an 8-ft fence. If the pole and fence are 12 ft apart, how long is the wire?

17. One house is 12 mi east of a school. Another house is 9 mi north of the school. How far apart are the houses?

Simplify each radical expression.

18. $\sqrt{\frac{128}{64}}$

19. $\sqrt{\frac{27}{75}}$

20. $\sqrt{48}$

21. $\sqrt{12} \cdot \sqrt{8}$

22. $3\sqrt{32} + 5\sqrt{2}$

23. $2\sqrt{27} + 5\sqrt{3}$

24. $7\sqrt{125} - 3\sqrt{175}$

25. $\sqrt{128} - \sqrt{192}$

26. $\frac{15}{\sqrt{3}}$

27. $\frac{8}{\sqrt{10} + \sqrt{6}}$

28. **Open-Ended** Write an expression involving addition of two like radicals. Simplify the sum.

29. Which expression shows $\sqrt{24x^2y^3}$ written in simplest radical form?

A. $2xy\sqrt{12xy^2}$

B. $2xy\sqrt{6y}$

C. $xy\sqrt{24y}$

D. $4xy\sqrt{3y}$

Solve each radical equation.

30. $3\sqrt{x} + 2\sqrt{x} = 10$

31. $8 = \sqrt{5x - 1}$

32. $5\sqrt{x} = \sqrt{15x + 60}$

33. $\sqrt{x} = \sqrt{2x - 7}$

34. $3\sqrt{x + 3} = 2\sqrt{x + 9}$

35. $\sqrt{3x} = x - 5$

36. A rectangle is 5 times as long as it is wide. The area of the rectangle is 100 ft². How wide is the rectangle? Express your answer in simplest radical form.

Find the domain of each function. Graph the function.

37. $y = 3\sqrt{x}$

38. $y = \sqrt{x} + 4$

39. $y = \sqrt{x - 4}$

40. $y = \sqrt{x + 9}$

41. The hypotenuse of a right triangle is 26 cm. The length of one leg is 10 cm. Find the length of the other leg.

42. **Writing** Explain how to graph $y = \sqrt{x} - 3$ by translating the graph of $y = \sqrt{x}$.

43. **Geometry** The formula for the volume V of a cylinder with height h and radius r is $V = \pi r^2 h$. Solve for r in terms of V and h.

44. From ground level you can see a satellite dish on the roof of a building 60 ft high. The angle of elevation is 62°. How far away from you is the building?

Find the values for $\triangle RST$.

45. RT

46. ST

47. $\tan T$

48. $\sin T$

49. **Geometry** In $\triangle ABC$, $\angle C$ is a right angle, $AB = 7$, and $m\angle B = 28°$. What are the lengths of $\overline{BC}$ and $\overline{AC}$ to the nearest tenth?

50. Ken has a 20-ft ladder to use for washing windows. When leaned against a building, the ladder forms an angle of 75° with the ground. How far from the side of the building is the base of the ladder?

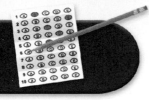

Standardized Test Prep

Reading Comprehension Read the passage below and then answer the questions on the basis of what is *stated* or *implied* in the passage.

Pricing Products Carlos and Anna have created a new electronic game that they think will be a big hit. But they can't decide how much to sell it for. They have manufactured 2500 to start out, at a cost to them of $18 for each game, but they doubt they can sell all of them right away.

They have completed a market study. By interviewing potential buyers, they have learned that if they set a price of $40, they should be able to sell 1000 games during the first six months. They have also discovered that for every $5 they increase the price they will lose 50 sales.

Carlos and Anna realize that the data are important. They need help in determining the price that will maximize their sales revenue, which is the amount of total sales.

---

1. What is the total cost to Carlos and Anna for manufacturing 2500 electronic games?
   A. $36,000   B. $45,000
   C. $50,000   D. $60,000

2. At a selling price of $40 each, how much revenue does the market research indicate they could expect in the first six months?
   F. $100,000   G. $55,000
   H. $40,000   I. $22,000

3. Suppose Carlos and Anna raise the price to $45. From their market analysis, how many sales and how much revenue can they expect?
   A. 1050, $57,750
   B. 1050, $47,250
   C. 1000, $45,000
   D. 950, $42,750

4. Their accountant tells them that they can use the function $r = 40,000 + 3000n - 250n^2$ to find the price for the game that will produce the greatest revenue r. The variable n is the number of times they increase the price $5. What type of function is this?
   F. linear
   G. quadratic
   H. exponential
   I. absolute value

5. The accountant found the function in Exercise 4 by writing functions for the price p and the number of sales s, given the number of times n the price is increased. Which functions did he use?
   A. $s = 1000 - 5n, p = 40 - 5n$
   B. $s = 1000 + 50n, p = 40 - 5n$
   C. $s = 1000 - 50n, p = 40n$
   D. $s = 1000 - 50n, p = 40 + 5n$

6. Carlos and Anna want to find the maximum of the function $r = 40,000 + 3000n - 250n^2$, where r is the revenue and n is the number of times the price is increased.
   a. How many times can they increase the price to obtain the maximum?
   b. What is the maximum revenue possible using this model?
   c. What would be the number of sales?
   d. Based on this information, what price should Carlos and Anna set for the electronic game?

7. Suppose the market analysis also indicated that with each $5 decrease in price, Carlos and Anna could expect an increase of 50 sales. Would you suggest they decrease the price to increase the sales? Explain.

Where You've Been

- In Chapter 4, you used ratios to express probability.

- In Chapter 5, you learned to model some situations with a direct variation.

- In Chapter 8, you used the properties of exponents to simplify expressions containing exponents that are zero or negative.

- In Chapters 10 and 11, you solved quadratic and radical equations and checked for extraneous solutions.

Diagnosing Readiness   (For help, go to the Lesson in green.)

Adding and Subtracting Fractions (Skills Handbook page 726)

Add or subtract. Write each answer in simplest form.

1. $\frac{2}{3} + \frac{1}{2}$ 　　　 **2.** $\frac{3}{13} + \frac{6}{13}$ 　　　 **3.** $\frac{16}{25} + \frac{3}{10}$ 　　　 **4.** $\frac{5}{9} - \frac{5}{36}$

Finding Probabilities (Lesson 4-6)

You have three $1 bills and two $5 bills in your pocket. You choose two bills without looking. Find each probability.

5. P(two $1 bills) 　　　　　　　 **6.** P(two $5 bills)

7. P(two bills of the same kind) 　　　 **8.** P(two different kinds of bills)

Simplifying Expressions (Lesson 8-5)

Simplify each expression.

9. $\frac{6w^3x^2}{2wx}$ 　　　 **10.** $\frac{81r^{10}s^6}{(3r^2s)^4}$ 　　　 **11.** $\frac{(5k^5)(2k^3)}{(2k^2)^2}$

Solving Radical Equations (Lesson 11-5)

Solve each radical equation. If there is no solution, write *no solution*.

12. $\sqrt{x} - 4 = 6$ 　　　 **13.** $\sqrt{3x} + 5 = 2$ 　　　 **14.** $2x = \sqrt{3x + 1}$

Finding the Domain (Lesson 11-6)

Find the domain of each function.

15. $f(x) = 5 - \sqrt{x}$ 　　　 **16.** $y = -2 + \sqrt{3x}$ 　　　 **17.** $y = \sqrt{10 - 3x}$

Rational Expressions and Functions

Key Vocabulary

- asymptote (p. 644)
- combination (p. 686)
- constant of variation (p. 637)
- inverse variation (p. 637)
- multiplication counting principle (p. 680)
- permutation (p. 681)
- rational equation (p. 672)
- rational expression (p. 652)
- rational function (p. 644)

Where You're Going

- In this chapter, you will study inverse variation and learn to distinguish between direct and inverse variation.

- You will graph and solve equations involving rational expressions, utilizing your knowledge of polynomials and domains.

- You will use permutations and combinations to find the number of outcomes of real-world situations.

 Real-World Snapshots Applying what you learn, you will solve inverse variation equations for vibrating strings in order to construct a guitar "neck," on pages 700–701.

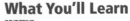

Inverse Variation

Lesson Preview

What You'll Learn

OBJECTIVE
1 To solve inverse variations

OBJECTIVE
2 To compare direct and inverse variation

... And Why

To balance weights on a fulcrum, as in Example 3

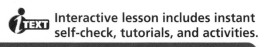

✓ Check Skills You'll Need

(For help, go to Lesson 5-5.)

Suppose y varies directly with x. Find each constant of variation.

1. $y = 5x$ **2.** $y = -7x$ **3.** $3y = x$ **4.** $0.25y = x$

Write an equation of the direct variation that includes the given point.

5. $(2, 4)$ **6.** $(3, 1.5)$ **7.** $(-4, 1)$ **8.** $(-5, -2)$

New Vocabulary   • inverse variation   • constant of variation

---

OBJECTIVE

1   **Solving Inverse Variations**

🅸TEXT Interactive lesson includes instant self-check, tutorials, and activities.

Real-World 🌐 Connection

With volunteer labor, Habitat for Humanity helped build over 115,000 homes for families around the world in its first 25 years.

SOURCE: *Habitat for Humanity*

Investigation: Inverse Variation

Suppose you are part of a volunteer crew constructing affordable housing. Building a house requires a total of 160 workdays. For example, a crew of 20 people can complete a house in 8 days.

1. How long should it take a crew of 40 people?

2. Copy and complete the table.

Crew size (x)	Construction Days (y)	Total Workdays
2	80	160
5	▨	160
8	▨	▨
▨	16	▨
20	8	160
40	▨	▨

3. Graph the (x, y) data in the table above.

4. Describe what happens to construction time as the crew size increases.

In the table, the total number of workdays remains the same. The number of construction days decreases as the number of people on the crew increases. The relationship of construction days and crew size is an inverse variation.

Definition	Inverse Variation

An equation in the form $xy = k$ or $y = \frac{k}{x}$, where $k \neq 0$, is an **inverse variation**.

The **constant of variation** is k.

Inverse variations have graphs with the same general shape. You can see from the graph at the right how the constant of variation k affects the graph of $xy = k$.

If you know the values of x and y for one point on the graph of an inverse variation, you can use the point to find the constant of variation k and the equation of the inverse variation.

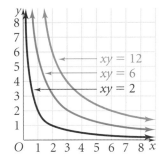

$$xy = 12$$
$$xy = 6$$
$$xy = 2$$

Reading Math

There are several ways to describe an inverse variation:

- y varies inversely with x.
- y varies inversely as x.
- y is inversely proportional to x.

1 EXAMPLE **Writing an Equation Given a Point**

Suppose y varies inversely with x and $y = 7$ when $x = 5$. Write an equation for the inverse variation.

$\begin{aligned} xy &= k & \text{Use the general form of an inverse variation.} \\ 5(7) &= k & \text{Substitute 5 for } x \text{ and 7 for } y. \\ 35 &= k & \text{Multiply to solve for } k. \\ xy &= 35 & \text{Write an equation. Substitute 35 for } k \text{ in } xy = k. \end{aligned}$

The equation of the inverse variation is $xy = 35$, or $y = \frac{35}{x}$.

✓ **Check Understanding** ❶ Suppose y varies inversely with x and $y = 9$ when $x = 2$. Write an equation for the inverse variation.

Suppose (x_1, y_1) and (x_2, y_2) are two ordered pairs of an inverse variation. Each ordered pair of an inverse variation has the same product k, that is $x_1 \cdot y_1 = k$ and $x_2 \cdot y_2 = k$. So $x_1 \cdot y_1 = x_2 \cdot y_2$.

2 EXAMPLE **Finding the Missing Coordinate**

The points $(3, 8)$ and $(2, y)$ are two points on the graph of an inverse variation. Find the missing value.

$\begin{aligned} x_1 \cdot y_1 &= x_2 \cdot y_2 & \text{Use the equation } x_1 \cdot y_1 = x_2 \cdot y_2 \text{ since you know coordinates but} \\ & & \text{not the constant of variation.} \\ 3(8) &= 2(y_2) & \text{Substitute 3 for } x_1, \text{ 8 for } y_1, \text{ and 2 for } x_2. \\ 24 &= 2(y_2) & \text{Simplify.} \\ 12 &= y_2 & \text{Solve for } y_2. \end{aligned}$

The missing value is 12. The point $(2, 12)$ is on the graph of the inverse variation that includes the point $(3, 8)$.

✓ **Check Understanding** ❷ Each pair of points is on the graph of an inverse variation. Find the missing value.
  a. $(3, y)$ and $(5, 9)$ **b.** $(75, 0.2)$ and $(x, 3)$

③ EXAMPLE   **Real-World 🌐 Problem Solving**

Physics The weight needed to balance a lever varies inversely with the distance from the fulcrum to the weight. Where should Julio, who weighs 150 lb, sit to balance the lever?

Relate   A weight of 120 lb is 6 ft from the fulcrum. A weight of 150 lb is x ft from the fulcrum.
Weight and distance vary inversely.

Real-World 🌐 Connection

A fulcrum is the point at which a lever pivots. Students can use levers in science labs to investigate physical properties.

Define   Let $weight_1 = 120$ lb.
Let $weight_2 = 150$ lb.
Let $distance_1 = 6$ ft.
Let $distance_2 = x$ ft.

Write $weight_1 \cdot distance_1 = weight_2 \cdot distance_2$

$120 \quad \cdot \quad 6 \quad = \quad 150 \quad \cdot \quad x$ **Substitute.**

$720 = 150x$ **Simplify.**

$\dfrac{720}{150} = x$ **Solve for x.**

$4.8 = x$ **Simplify.**

Julio should sit 4.8 feet from the fulcrum to balance the lever.

✔ Check Understanding   **③ a. Physics** A 100-lb weight is placed 4 ft from a fulcrum. How far from the fulcrum should a 75-lb weight be placed to balance the lever?
b. An 80-lb weight is placed 9 ft from a fulcrum. What weight should you put 6 ft from the fulcrum to balance the lever?

OBJECTIVE

2   **Comparing Direct and Inverse Variation**

Recall that a direct variation is an equation in the form $y = kx$. This summary will help you recognize and use direct and inverse variations.

🔑 **Key Concepts**

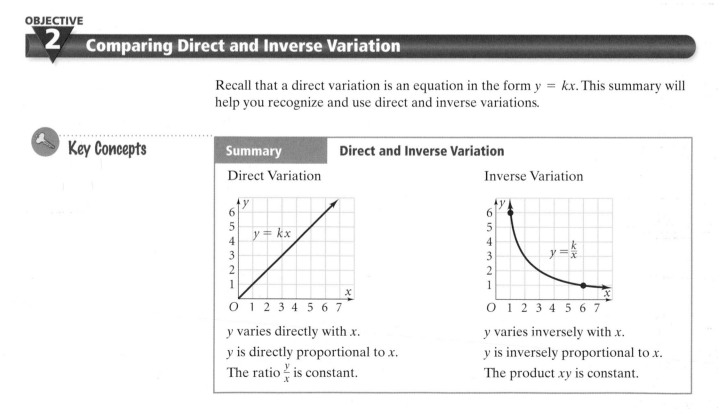

Summary	**Direct and Inverse Variation**

Direct Variation

y varies directly with x.
y is directly proportional to x.
The ratio $\frac{y}{x}$ is constant.

Inverse Variation

y varies inversely with x.
y is inversely proportional to x.
The product xy is constant.

4 EXAMPLE Determining Direct or Inverse Variation

Do the data in each table represent a *direct variation* or an *inverse variation*? For each table, write an equation to model the data.

a.

x	y
2	5
4	10
10	25

The values of y seem to vary directly with the values of x. Check each ratio $\frac{y}{x}$.

$$\frac{y}{x} \to \frac{5}{2} = 2.5 \qquad \frac{10}{4} = 2.5 \qquad \frac{25}{10} = 2.5$$

The ratio $\frac{y}{x}$ is the same for all pairs of data. So this is a direct variation, and $k = 2.5$.

The equation is $y = 2.5x$.

b.

x	y
5	20
10	10
25	4

The values of y seem to vary inversely with the values of x. Check each product xy.

xy: $5(20) = 100 \qquad 10(10) = 100 \qquad 25(4) = 100$

The product xy is the same for all pairs of data. So this is an inverse variation, and $k = 100$.

The equation is $xy = 100$.

✓ **Check Understanding** **4** Determine whether the data in each table represent a direct variation or an inverse variation. Write an equation to model the data in each table.

a.

x	y
3	12
6	6
9	4

b.

x	y
3	12
5	20
8	32

Many real-world situations involve variation. You can look for a constant ratio or a constant product to determine whether the relationship is a direct variation or an inverse variation.

5 EXAMPLE Real-World 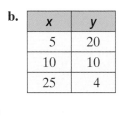 Problem Solving

Explain whether each situation represents a direct variation or an inverse variation.

a. Carpooling The cost of $20 worth of gasoline is split among several people.

The cost per person times the number of people equals the total cost of the gasoline. Since the total cost is a constant product of $20, this is an inverse variation.

b. School Supplies You buy several markers for 70¢ each.

The cost per marker times the number of markers equals the total cost of the markers. Since the ratio $\frac{\text{cost}}{\text{marker}}$ is constant at 70¢ each, this is a direct variation.

✓ **Check Understanding** **5** Explain whether each situation represents a direct variation or an inverse variation.
a. You are in a discount store. All sweaters are on sale for $15 each.
b. You walk 5 miles each day. Your speed and time vary from day to day.

EXERCISES

For more practice, see *Extra Practice*.

Practice and Problem Solving

A Practice by Example

Suppose y varies inversely with x. Write an equation for the inverse variation.

Example 1
(page 637)

1. $y = 6$ when $x = 3$ **2.** $y = 1$ when $x = 2$ **3.** $y = 7$ when $x = 8$

4. $y = 3$ when $x = 0.5$ **5.** $y = 10$ when $x = 2.4$ **6.** $y = 3.5$ when $x = 2.2$

7. $y = 6$ when $x = \frac{1}{3}$ **8.** $y = \frac{1}{16}$ when $x = 8$ **9.** $y = \frac{1}{10}$ when $x = \frac{3}{5}$

Example 2
(page 637)

Each pair of points is on the graph of an inverse variation. Find the missing value.

10. $(6, 12)$ and $(9, y)$ **11.** $(3, 5)$ and $(1, n)$ **12.** $(x, 11)$ and $(1, 66)$

13. $(x, 55)$ and $(5, 77)$ **14.** $(9.4, b)$ and $(6, 4.7)$ **15.** $(50, 13)$ and $(t, 5)$

16. $(4, 3.6)$ and $(1.2, g)$ **17.** $(24, 1.6)$ and $(c, 0.4)$ **18.** $(500, 25)$ and $(4, n)$

19. $\left(\frac{1}{2}, 24\right)$ and $(6, y)$ **20.** $\left(x, \frac{1}{2}\right)$ and $\left(\frac{1}{3}, \frac{1}{4}\right)$ **21.** $\left(\frac{1}{2}, 5\right)$ and $\left(b, \frac{1}{8}\right)$

Example 3
(page 638)

22. Travel Suppose you take $2\frac{1}{2}$ h to drive from your house to the lake at 48 mi/h. How long will your return trip take at 40 mi/h?

23. Bicycling Suppose a camper took 2 h to ride around a reservoir at 10 mi/h at the beginning of the summer. By the end of the summer, she can ride around the reservoir in $1\frac{1}{2}$ h. What is her rate at the end of the summer?

Example 4
(page 639)

Do the data in each table represent a direct variation or an inverse variation? Write an equation to model the data in each table.

24.

x	y
2	1
5	2.5
8	4

25.

x	y
4	15
6	10
10	6

26.

x	y
3	24
9	8
12	6

Example 5
(page 639)

Explain whether each situation represents a direct variation or an inverse variation.

27. You buy some chicken for $1.79/lb.

28. An 8-slice pizza is shared equally by a group of friends.

29. You find the length and width of several rectangles. Each has an area of 24 square units.

B Apply Your Skills

Find the constant of variation k for each inverse variation. Then write an equation for the inverse variation.

30. $y = 8$ when $x = 4$ **31.** $r = 3.3$ when $t = \frac{1}{3}$ **32.** $x = \frac{1}{2}$ when $y = 5$

33. $a = 25$ when $b = 0.04$ **34.** $p = 10.4$ when $q = 1.5$ **35.** $x = 5$ when $y = 75$

Geometry Does each formula represent a direct or an inverse variation? Explain.

36. the perimeter of an equilateral triangle: $P = 3s$

37. the time t to travel 150 mi at r mi/h: $t = \frac{150}{r}$

38. the circumference of a circle with radius r: $C = 2\pi r$

39. Surveying Each of two rectangular building lots is one quarter acre in size. One lot measures 99 ft by 110 ft. The other lot is 90 ft wide. What is the second lot's length?

40. Construction Suppose 4 people can paint a house if they work 3 days each. How long would it take a crew of 5 people to paint the house?

Do the data in each table represent a direct or an inverse variation? Write an equation to model the data. Then complete the table.

41.

x	y
10	4
20	■
8	3.2

42.

x	y
0.4	28
1.2	84
■	63

43.

x	y
1.6	30
4.8	10
■	96

44. Math in the Media According to the First Law of Air Travel, for each situation below, will the distance to your gate be *greater* or *less* for this trip than for your last trip?
 a. You have more luggage.
 b. You have less time to make your flight.
 c. You have less luggage.

45. a. Earnings Suppose you want to earn $80. How long will it take you if you are paid $5/h; $8/h; $10/h; $20/h?
 b. What are the two variable quantities in part (a)?
 c. Write an equation to represent this situation.

46. Open-Ended Write and graph a direct variation and an inverse variation that have the same constant of variation.

CLOSE TO HOME by John McPherson

GATE 31-Y
3.4 MILES

The First Law of Air Travel
The distance to your connecting gate is directly proportional to the amount of luggage you are carrying and inversely proportional to the amount of time you have.

47. Physics Boyle's Law states that volume V varies inversely with pressure P for any gas at a constant temperature in an enclosed space. Suppose a gas at constant temperature occupies 15.3 liters at a pressure of 40 millimeters of mercury. What is the volume of the gas when the pressure is 60 millimeters of mercury?

48. Critical Thinking The graphs of p and q represent a direct variation and an inverse variation. Write an equation for each graph.

49. Writing Explain how the variable y changes in each situation.
 a. y varies directly with x. The value of x is doubled.
 b. y varies inversely with x. The value of x is doubled.

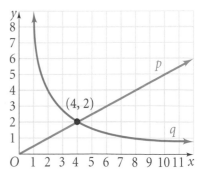

C Challenge   **50. Physics** The intensity of a sound s varies inversely with the square of the distance d from the sound. This can be modeled by the equation $sd^2 = k$. If you move half the distance closer to the source of a sound, by what factor will the intensity of the sound increase? Explain your reasoning.

51. Write an equation to model each situation.
a. y varies inversely with the fourth power of x.
b. y varies inversely with the fourth power of x and directly with z.

Standardized Test Prep

Multiple Choice

52. Suppose y varies inversely with x and $x = 12$ when $y = 3$. What is the equation of the inverse variation?
A. $\frac{y}{x} = 36$ **B.** $y = \frac{12}{3}$ **C.** $y = \frac{36}{x}$ **D.** $12 = \frac{3}{y}$

53. The volume V of a gas varies inversely with the pressure P. When the volume is 75 in.^{3}, the pressure is 30 lb/in.^{2}. Which equation models this relationship?
F. $VP = 2250$ **G.** $V = \frac{P}{75}$ **H.** $V = \frac{75}{P}$ **I.** $V = \frac{P}{2250}$

Short Response

54. Use the table at the right. Find a value such that the y-values vary directly with the x-values. Then find a value such that the y-values vary inversely with the x-values. Show your work.

x	y
5	10
8	▪

Extended Response

55. You are traveling to visit your best friend who moved 100 miles away.
a. Copy and complete the table below to find the time the trip takes at different speeds.
b. Describe the relationship of the variables.
c. How long would the round trip take if you could travel at 80 mi/h?

Distance (d)	100	100	100	100
Speed (r)	30	40	50	60
Time (t)	▪	▪	▪	▪

Take It to the NET
Online lesson quiz at
www.PHSchool.com
····· Web Code: aea-1201

Mixed Review

Lesson 11-7   Use △FGH to evaluate each expression.

56. $\sin F$ **57.** $\sin G$ **58.** $\cos F$

59. $\cos G$ **60.** $\tan F$ **61.** $\tan G$

Lesson 11-3   Find the distance between the points in each pair. Round to the nearest tenth.

62. $(5, 2)$ and $(4, 7)$ **63.** $(-2, 9)$ and $(6, 0)$ **64.** $(4, 8)$ and $(-4, -1)$

65. $(8, 10)$ and $(1, 2)$ **66.** $(-3, -5)$ and $(-2, -7)$ **67.** $(1.5, 1)$ and $(2, 3.5)$

Lesson 9-6   Factor each expression.

68. $3a^2 + 11a - 4$ **69.** $15x^2 + 41x + 14$ **70.** $2y^2 + 13y - 24$

642   Chapter 12 Rational Expressions and Functions

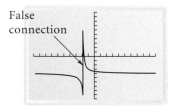

Technology

Graphing Rational Functions

 **For Use With Lesson 12-2**

Functions like $y = \frac{1}{x}$, $y = \frac{1}{x+2}$, and $y = \frac{1}{x} - 4$ are rational functions. When you use a graphing calculator to graph a rational function, sometimes false connections appear on the screen. When this happens, you need to make adjustments to see the true shape of the graph.

Graph the function $y = \frac{1}{x+2} - 4$. You can enter this as $y = 1 \div (x + 2) - 4$. The graph of the function may look like the graph at the right on your screen. The highest point and lowest point on the graph that appear on the screen are not supposed to connect. If you use the trace feature on the calculator, no point on the graph lies on this connecting line. So this is a false connection.

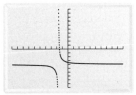

False connection

Here's how you can graph a rational function and avoid false connections.

Step 1 Press the MODE key. Then scroll down and right to highlight the word **Dot**. Then press ENTER.

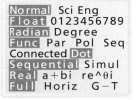

Step 2 Graph again. Now the false connection is gone!

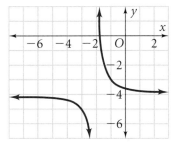

Step 3 Use the TRACE key or TABLE key to find points on the graph. Sketch the graph.

EXERCISES

Use a graphing calculator to graph each function. Then sketch the graph.

1. $y = \frac{4}{x}$

2. $y = \frac{-2}{x}$

3. $y = \frac{1}{x+3}$

4. $y = \frac{1}{x-4}$

5. $y = \frac{1}{x} + 3$

6. $y = \frac{1}{x} - 4$

7. $y = \frac{1}{x-2} - 3$

8. $y = \frac{4}{x+1} - 3$

9. $y = \frac{-4}{x+1} - 3$

10. a. Graph $y = \frac{1}{x}$, $y = \frac{1}{x-3}$, and $y = \frac{1}{x+4}$.

   b. Make a Conjecture How does adding or subtracting a number in the denominator translate the graph?

11. a. Graph $y = \frac{1}{x}$, $y = \frac{1}{x} - 3$, and $y = \frac{1}{x} + 4$.

   b. Make a Conjecture How does adding or subtracting a number to the expression translate the graph?

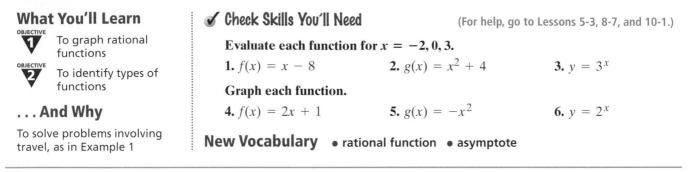

12-2

Graphing Rational Functions

Lesson Preview

What You'll Learn

OBJECTIVE
1 To graph rational functions

OBJECTIVE
2 To identify types of functions

. . . And Why

To solve problems involving travel, as in Example 1

✓ **Check Skills You'll Need**   (For help, go to Lessons 5-3, 8-7, and 10-1.)

Evaluate each function for $x = -2, 0, 3$.

1. $f(x) = x - 8$ **2.** $g(x) = x^2 + 4$ **3.** $y = 3^x$

Graph each function.

4. $f(x) = 2x + 1$ **5.** $g(x) = -x^2$ **6.** $y = 2^x$

New Vocabulary   • rational function   • asymptote

OBJECTIVE
1   **Graphing Rational Functions**

iTEXT Interactive lesson includes instant self-check, tutorials, and activities.

You can write the inverse variation $xy = 3$ as $y = \frac{3}{x}$. This is a rational function. In simplest form, a **rational function** has a polynomial of at least degree 1 in the denominator.

1 **EXAMPLE**   **Graphing a Rational Function**

Travel On any trip, the time you travel in a car varies inversely with your average speed. The function $t = \frac{60}{r}$ models the time it will take you to travel 60 miles at different rates of speed. Graph this function.

Step 1 Make a table of values.

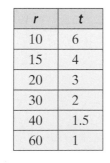

r	t
10	6
15	4
20	3
30	2
40	1.5
60	1

Step 2 Plot the points.

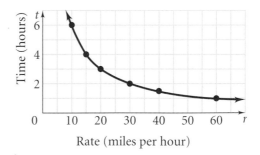

Rate (miles per hour)

✓ **Check Understanding**   **1** **a.** The function $t = \frac{40}{r}$ models the time it will take you to travel 40 miles at different rates of speed. Graph this function.

b. Critical Thinking Why is it reasonable in this situation to graph the function in Quadrant I only?

As you can see in the graph in Example 1, the graph approaches both axes but does not cross either axis. A line is an **asymptote** of a graph if the graph of the function gets closer to the line as x or y gets larger in absolute value. In the graph in Example 1, the horizontal and vertical axes are asymptotes.

The graphs of many rational functions are related to each other. Look at the graphs of the functions below.

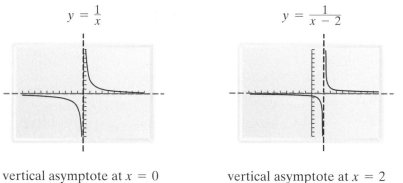

$$y = \frac{1}{x}$$
$$y = \frac{1}{x - 2}$$

vertical asymptote at $x = 0$

horizontal asymptote at $y = 0$

vertical asymptote at $x = 2$

horizontal asymptote at $y = 0$

The graphs are identical in shape, but the second graph is translated two units to the right.

When the numerator and denominator of a rational function have no common factors other than 1, there is a vertical asymptote at the x-value that makes the denominator equal zero. This is because division by zero is undefined. The domain of a function does not include that x-value where there is a vertical asymptote.

2 EXAMPLE   Using a Vertical Asymptote

Identify the vertical asymptote of $y = \frac{4}{x + 3}$. Then graph the function.

Step 1 Find the vertical asymptote.

$x + 3 = 0$ The numerator and denominator have no common factors. Find any value(s) where the denominator equals zero.

$x = -3$ This is the equation of the vertical asymptote.

Step 2 Make a table of values. Use values of x near -3, the asymptote.

Step 3 Graph the function.

Use a dashed line for the asymptote $x = -3$.

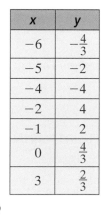

x	y
−6	$-\frac{4}{3}$
−5	−2
−4	−4
−2	4
−1	2
0	$\frac{4}{3}$
3	$\frac{2}{3}$

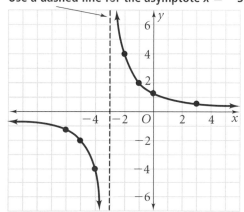

✓ **Check Understanding** ② Identify the vertical asymptote of each function. Then graph the function.

a. $f(x) = \frac{1}{x + 2}$

b. $h(x) = \frac{2}{x - 3}$

You can also see how to shift the graph of a rational function vertically.

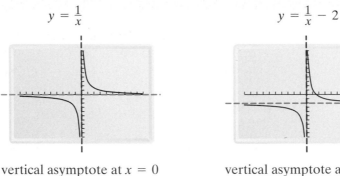

$$y = \frac{1}{x}$$

$$y = \frac{1}{x} - 2$$

vertical asymptote at $x = 0$

horizontal asymptote at $y = 0$

vertical asymptote at $x = 0$

horizontal asymptote at $y = -2$

The graphs are identical in shape, but the second graph is translated two units down.

3 EXAMPLE   Using Vertical and Horizontal Asymptotes

Identify the asymptotes of $y = \frac{4}{x + 3} + 2$. Then graph the function.

Step 1 From the form of the function, you can see that there is a vertical asymptote at $x = -3$ and a horizontal asymptote at $y = 2$. Sketch the asymptotes.

Step 2 Make a table of values using values of x near -3.

Step 3 Graph the function.

x	y
−7	1
−6	$\frac{2}{3}$
−5	0
−4	−2
−2	6
−1	4
1	3
3	$\frac{8}{3}$

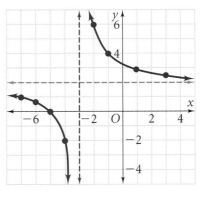

✔ Check Understanding **3** Identify the asymptotes of each function. Then graph the function.

a. $f(x) = \frac{1}{x + 2} - 3$

b. $y = \frac{1}{x - 4} + 1$

Key Concepts

Summary   Graphs of Rational Functions

The graph of a rational function in the form $y = \frac{a}{x - b} + c$ has a vertical asymptote at $x = b$ and a horizontal asymptote at $y = c$. The graph is a translation of $y = \frac{a}{x}$, b units right or left (for b positive or negative) and c units up or down (for c positive or negative).

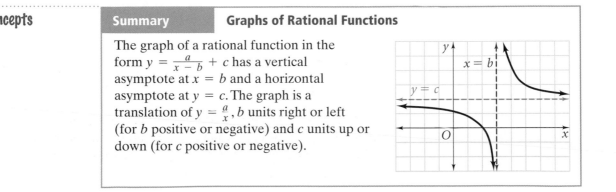

You can think of graphs of functions with similar features as families of functions. You have studied six families of functions this year. Their properties and graphs are shown in this summary.

Key Concepts

Summary	Families of Functions

Linear function
$y = mx + b$

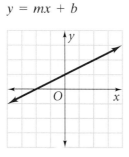

slope $= m$
y-intercept $= b$
The greatest exponent is 1.

Absolute value function
$y = |x - a| + b$

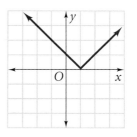

shift $y = |x|$ horizontally a units
shift $y = |x|$ vertically b units
vertex at (a, b)
The greatest exponent is 1.

Quadratic function
$y = ax^2 + bx + c$

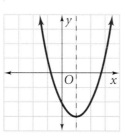

parabola with axis of
symmetry at $x = -\frac{b}{2a}$
The greatest exponent is 2.

Exponential function
$y = ab^x$

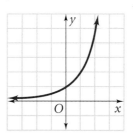

growth for $b > 1$
decay for $0 < b < 1$
The variable is the exponent.

Radical function
$y = \sqrt{x - b} + c$

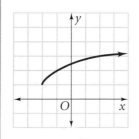

shift $y = \sqrt{x}$ horizontally b units
shift $y = \sqrt{x}$ vertically c units
The variable is under the radical.

Rational function
$y = \frac{a}{x - b} + c$

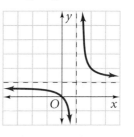

vertical asymptote at $x = b$
horizontal asymptote at $y = c$
The variable is in the denominator.

4 EXAMPLE **Identifying Functions**

Describe the graph of each function.

a. $y = 5^x$ The graph is of exponential growth.

b. $y = 5x$ The graph is a line with slope 5 and y-intercept 0.

c. $y = \frac{x}{5}$ The graph is a line with slope $\frac{1}{5}$ and y-intercept 0.

d. $y = \frac{5}{x}$ The graph is a rational function with vertical asymptote at $x = 0$ and horizontal asymptote at $y = 0$.

e. $y = 5x^2$ The graph is a parabola with an axis of symmetry at $x = 0$.

f. $y = \sqrt{x - 5}$ The graph is the radical function $y = \sqrt{x}$ shifted right 5 units.

g. $y = |x - 5|$ The graph is an absolute value function with a vertex at $(5, 0)$.

✓ **Check Understanding** **4** Describe the graph of each function.

a. $g(x) = |x + 4|$ **b.** $f(x) = 8 \cdot 2^x$ **c.** $h(x) = \frac{2}{x + 1}$

EXERCISES

For more practice, see *Extra Practice*.

Practice and Problem Solving

A **Practice by Example**

Example 1
(page 644)

Graph each function.

1. $y = \frac{3}{x}$ **2.** $y = \frac{4}{x}$ **3.** $f(x) = \frac{5}{x}$ **4.** $h(x) = \frac{6}{x}$

5. The function $t = \frac{24}{r}$ models the time it will take you to travel 24 miles at different rates of speed. Graph this function.

Example 2
(page 645)

What value of x makes the denominator of each function equal zero?

6. $f(x) = \frac{3}{x}$ **7.** $y = \frac{1}{x - 2}$ **8.** $y = \frac{x}{x + 2}$ **9.** $h(x) = \frac{3}{2x - 4}$

Identify the asymptotes of each graph.

10.

11.

12.

13.

Identify the vertical asymptote of each function. Then graph the function.

14. $g(x) = \frac{10}{x}$ **15.** $f(x) = \frac{12}{x}$ **16.** $y = \frac{1}{x + 1}$

17. $f(x) = \frac{1}{x - 5}$ **18.** $g(x) = \frac{4}{x + 4}$ **19.** $y = \frac{2}{x + 4}$

Example 3
(page 646)

Identify the asymptotes of each function. Then graph the function.

20. $y = \frac{1}{x} - 5$

21. $y = \frac{1}{x} + 5$

22. $y = \frac{1}{x} - 6$

23. $h(x) = \frac{2}{x+1} + 4$

24. $f(x) = \frac{1}{x-3} - 5$

25. $h(x) = \frac{1}{x-1} - 2$

Example 4
(page 648)

Describe the graph of each function.

26. $y = 4x + 1$

27. $h(x) = |x - 4|$

28. $y = 0.4^x$

29. $f(x) = \frac{x}{4}$

30. $y = \frac{4}{x} + 1$

31. $h(x) = \sqrt{x - 4} + 1$

32. $g(x) = x^2 - 4$

33. $f(x) = \frac{4}{x+4} - 1$

34. $g(x) = 4x^2 + 2x + 1$

B **Apply Your Skills**

Describe how the graphs of each function are translations of the graph of $f(x) = \frac{7}{x}$.

35. $g(x) = \frac{7}{x+1}$

36. $y = \frac{7}{x-3}$

37. $y = \frac{7}{x} - 15$

38. $f(x) = \frac{7}{x+12}$

39. $g(x) = \frac{7}{x} + 12$

40. $h(x) = \frac{7}{x+3}$

41. $g(x) = \frac{7}{x} - 2$

42. $y = \frac{7}{x+3} - 2$

Identify the asymptotes of each function. Then graph the function.

43. $f(x) = \frac{-1}{x}$

44. $y = \frac{-4}{x}$

45. $g(x) = \frac{-2}{x+4}$

46. $y = \frac{-1}{x} + 1$

47. $y = \frac{1}{x+1} + 4$

48. $g(x) = \frac{1}{x+1} - 3$

49. $f(x) = \frac{1}{x-1} + 3$

50. $g(x) = \frac{2}{x+5} + 1$

51. $h(x) = \frac{-4}{x-3} - 2$

52. Open-Ended Write two rational functions whose graphs are identical except that one has been shifted vertically 3 units.

53. Light In the formula $I = \frac{445}{x^2}$, I is the intensity of light in lumens at a distance x feet from a light bulb with 445 watts. What is the intensity of light 5 ft from the light bulb? 15 ft from the light bulb?

54. a. Graph $y = \frac{1}{x}$ and $y = \frac{1}{x^2}$.
  b. What are the vertical and horizontal asymptotes of the graph of each function?
  c. What is the range of $y = \frac{1}{x}$? Of $y = \frac{1}{x^2}$?

55. Physics As radio signals move away from a transmitter, they become weaker. The function $s = \frac{1600}{d^2}$ relates the strength s of a signal at a distance d miles from a transmitter.
  a. Graphing Calculator Graph the function. For what distances is $s \le 1$?
  b. Find the signal strength at 10 mi, 1 mi, and 0.1 mi.
  c. Critical Thinking Suppose you drive by the transmitter for one radio station while your car radio is tuned to a second station. The signal from the transmitter can interfere and come through your radio. Use your results from part (b) to explain why.

Real-World  **Connection**

Careers Photographers use high-intensity lights to get dramatic photos.

56. Writing Describe the similarities and differences between the graphs of $y = \frac{3}{x}$ and $y = \frac{-3}{x}$.

C **Challenge**

Graph each function. Include a dashed line for each asymptote.

57. $g(x) = \frac{x}{x-1}$

58. $y = \frac{1}{(x-1)^2}$

59. $y = \frac{2}{(x-2)(x+2)}$

60. $y = \frac{1}{x^2 - 2x}$

61. Use the graph at the right. It is a translation of the graph of $y = \frac{1}{x}$.
 a. What are the asymptotes of the graph?
 b. Reasoning Write a function rule for the graph.

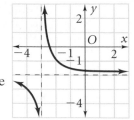

62. Graph $f(x) = \frac{(x + 2)(x + 1)}{x + 2}$ and $g(x) = x + 1$. Are the graphs the same? Explain.

Multiple Choice

63. Which describes the graph of the function $y = \frac{3}{x} + 2$?
 A. a line with slope 3 and y-intercept 2
 B. a line with slope $\frac{1}{3}$ and y-intercept 2
 C. a rational function with asymptotes at $x = 0$ and $y = 2$
 D. a rational function with asymptotes at $x = -3$ and $y = -2$

64. The graph of $y = \frac{2}{x}$ is translated down 3 units. What is the equation of the new graph?
 F. $y = \frac{2}{x + 3}$
 G. $y = \frac{2}{x - 3}$
 H. $y = \frac{2}{x} + 3$
 I. $y = \frac{2}{x} - 3$

Quantitative Comparison

Compare the quantity in Column A with the quantity in Column B. Choose the best answer.
 A. The quantity in Column A is greater.
 B. The quantity in Column B is greater.
 C. The two quantities are equal.
 D. The relationship cannot be determined from the information given.

Column A	Column B

65.

the value of x for which $y = \frac{3}{x - 2} + 1$ is undefined	the value of x for which $y = \frac{3}{x + 2} + 1$ is undefined

66.

the value of x for which $y = \frac{1}{x - 1} + 2$ is undefined	the value of x for which $y = \frac{1}{x + 1} + 2$ is undefined

Short Response

67. a. Describe how the graph of $g(x) = \frac{4}{x - 1} + 5$ is a translation of $f(x) = \frac{4}{x}$.
 b. What are the asymptotes of $g(x) = \frac{4}{x - 1} + 5$?

Mixed Review

Lesson 12-1

Write the equation of an inverse variation that includes the given point.

68. $(3, 7)$ **69.** $(8, 2)$ **70.** $(4, 5.5)$ **71.** $(6.2, 3.4)$

Lesson 10-8

Find the number of real solutions of each equation.

72. $x^2 + x + 1 = 0$ **73.** $x^2 + 2x + 1 = 0$ **74.** $x^2 - 8x = 7$

Lesson 9-8

Factor completely.

75. $3d^2 - 108$ **76.** $2m^2 - 14m - 120$ **77.** $t^3 - t^2 + 3t - 3$

Determining Limits

Use the graph at the right to answer Questions 1–3.

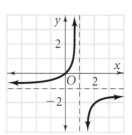

1. In Quadrant I, as x increases, y gets closer and closer to _?_.

2. In Quadrant III, as x decreases, y gets closer and closer to _?_.

3. What happens to y as x gets very close to 1 from the right? From the left?

You can think of an asymptote as showing the *limit* of a rational function as $|x|$ or $|y|$ increases. In the graph above, the limit of y as $|x|$ increases is -1, and the limit of x as $|y|$ increases is 1.

4. Use the graph at the right.

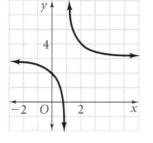

   a. What is the limit as x increases?
   b. What is the limit as y increases?
   c. What is the limit as x decreases?
   d. What is the limit as y decreases?

Find the limits as $|x|$ increases for each graph.

5.

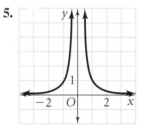

6.

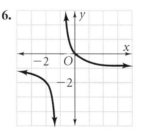

7.

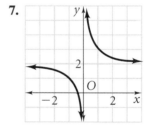

8. a. Graph the linear function $y = 3x + 2$.
   b. Does this function have a limit as $|x|$ increases? Explain.

9. a. Copy and extend the table at the right for the first 7 terms of the sequence.
   b. Use each term number as an x-value and the term value as its y-value. Graph the points.
   c. What is the limit of the sequence?

Term Number	Term
1	4
2	$3\frac{1}{2}$
3	$3\frac{1}{4}$

10. a. Graph the exponential functions $y = 0.4^x$, $y = 0.5^x$, and $y = 0.5^x - 4$. Describe any limits as x increases.
   b. **Make a Conjecture** Describe the limits of exponential decay functions.

11. a. Graph the functions $y = \frac{1}{x^2}$ and $y = \frac{1}{x^2 + 1}$.
   b. Describe the limits of each function.

Simplifying Rational Expressions

Lesson Preview

What You'll Learn

OBJECTIVE

1 To simplify rational expressions

...And Why

To find the baking time for bread, as in Example 4

✓ **Check Skills You'll Need** (For help, go to Skills Handbook page 724 and Lesson 9-5)

Write each fraction in simplest form.

1. $\frac{8}{2}$ **2.** $-\frac{15}{24}$ **3.** $\frac{25}{35}$

Factor each quadratic expression.

4. $x^2 + x - 12$ **5.** $x^2 + 6x + 8$ **6.** $x^2 - 2x - 15$

7. $x^2 + 8x + 16$ **8.** $x^2 - x - 12$ **9.** $x^2 - 7x + 12$

New Vocabulary • rational expression

OBJECTIVE

1 Interactive lesson includes instant self-check, tutorials, and activities.

Simplifying Rational Expressions

Fractions like $\frac{5}{9}$, $\frac{7}{12}$, and $\frac{1}{2}$ are rational numbers. A ratio of two polynomials is a **rational expression.** Here are some examples of rational expressions.

$$\frac{1}{x} \qquad \frac{x+2}{x-3} \qquad \frac{x^2-5}{x^2-10x+25}$$

Of course, the value of the expression in the denominator cannot be zero, since division by zero is undefined. For the rest of this chapter, assume that the values of the variables that make the denominator zero are excluded from the domain.

Like rational numbers, a rational expression is in simplest form if the numerator and denominator have no common factors except 1. For example, $\frac{z+5}{10z}$ is in simplest form since neither 10 nor z is a factor of $z+5$.

1 EXAMPLE Simplifying a Rational Expression

Simplify $\frac{6x+12}{x+2}$.

$$\frac{6x+12}{x+2} = \frac{6(x+2)}{x+2}$$ Factor the numerator. The denominator cannot be factored.

$$= \frac{6\cancel{(x+2)}^{\,1}}{\cancel{x+2}_{1}}$$ Divide out the common factor $x+2$.

$$= 6$$ Simplify.

✓ **Check Understanding** **1** Simplify each expression.

a. $\frac{15b}{25b^2}$ **b.** $\frac{12c^2}{3c+6}$ **c.** $\frac{4m-2}{2m-1}$ **d.** $\frac{20+4t}{t+5}$

Recall that you learned to factor quadratic expressions in Lessons 9-5 and 9-6. You may need to factor a quadratic expression to simplify a rational expression.

② EXAMPLE Simplifying a Rational Expression

Simplify $\dfrac{2x - 12}{x^2 - 7x + 6}$.

$\dfrac{2x - 12}{x^2 - 7x + 6} = \dfrac{2(x - 6)}{(x - 6)(x - 1)}$ **Factor the numerator and the denominator.**

$= \dfrac{2\cancel{(x - 6)}^1}{1\cancel{(x - 6)}(x - 1)}$ **Divide out the common factor $x - 6$.**

$= \dfrac{2}{x - 1}$ **Simplify.**

✓ **Check Understanding** ② Simplify each expression.

a. $\dfrac{3x + 12}{x^2 - x - 20}$ **b.** $\dfrac{2z - 2}{z^2 - 4z + 3}$ **c.** $\dfrac{8a + 16}{2a^2 + 5a + 2}$ **d.** $\dfrac{c^2 - c - 6}{c^2 + 5c + 6}$

The numerator and denominator of $\dfrac{x - 3}{3 - x}$ are opposites. To simplify the expression, you can factor -1 from $3 - x$ to get $-1(-3 + x)$, which you can rewrite as $-1(x - 3)$. Then simplify $\dfrac{x - 3}{-1(x - 3)}$.

③ EXAMPLE Recognizing Opposite Factors

Simplify $\dfrac{5x - 15}{9 - x^2}$.

$\dfrac{5x - 15}{9 - x^2} = \dfrac{5(x - 3)}{(3 - x)(3 + x)}$ **Factor the numerator and the denominator.**

$= \dfrac{5(x - 3)}{-1(x - 3)(3 + x)}$ **Factor -1 from $3 - x$.**

$= \dfrac{5\cancel{(x - 3)}^1}{-1_1\cancel{(x - 3)}(x + 3)}$ **Divide out the common factor $x - 3$.**

$= -\dfrac{5}{x + 3}$ **Simplify.**

✓ **Check Understanding** ③ Simplify each expression.

a. $\dfrac{x - 4}{4 - x}$ **b.** $\dfrac{8 - m}{m^2 - 64}$ **c.** $\dfrac{8 - 4r}{r^2 + 2r - 8}$ **d.** $\dfrac{2c^2 - 2}{3 - 3c^2}$

You can use a rational expression to model some real-world situations.

④ EXAMPLE Evaluating a Rational Expression

Baking The baking time for bread depends, in part, on its size and shape. A good approximation for the baking time, in minutes, of a cylindrical loaf is $\dfrac{60 \cdot \text{volume}}{\text{surface area}}$, or $\dfrac{30rh}{r + h}$, where the radius r and the length h of the baked loaf are in inches. Find the baking time for a loaf that is 5 inches long and has a radius of 4 inches. Round your answer to the nearest minute.

$\dfrac{30rh}{r + h} = \dfrac{30(4)(5)}{4 + 5}$ **Substitute 4 for r and 5 for h.**

$= \dfrac{600}{9}$ **Simplify.**

≈ 67 **Round to the nearest whole number.**

The baking time is approximately 67 minutes.

Real-World 🌐 Connection

For a given volume of dough, the greater the surface area is, the shorter the baking time.

④ **a.** Find the baking time for a loaf that is 4 inches long and has a radius of 3 inches. Round your answer to the nearest minute.

b. Critical Thinking The ratio $\frac{60 \cdot \text{volume}}{\text{surface area}}$ for a cylinder is $\frac{60\pi r^2 h}{2\pi r^2 + 2\pi rh}$. Simplify this expression to show that it is the same as the expression evaluated in Example 4.

EXERCISES

For more practice, see *Extra Practice*.

Practice and Problem Solving

Ⓐ **Practice by Example**

Simplify each expression.

Example 1
(page 652)

1. $\frac{6a + 9}{12}$

2. $\frac{4x^3}{28x^4}$

3. $\frac{2m - 5}{6m - 15}$

4. $\frac{2p - 24}{4p - 48}$

5. $\frac{3x^2 - 9x}{x - 3}$

6. $\frac{3x + 6}{3x^2}$

Example 2
(page 653)

7. $\frac{2x^2 + 2x}{3x^2 + 3x}$

8. $\frac{2b - 8}{b^2 - 16}$

9. $\frac{m + 6}{m^2 - m - 42}$

10. $\frac{w^2 + 7w}{w^2 - 49}$

11. $\frac{a^2 + 2a + 1}{5a + 5}$

12. $\frac{m^2 + 7m + 12}{m^2 + 6m + 8}$

13. $\frac{c^2 - 6c + 8}{c^2 + c - 6}$

14. $\frac{b^2 + 8b + 15}{b + 5}$

15. $\frac{m + 4}{m^2 + 2m - 8}$

Example 3
(page 653)

16. $\frac{5 - 4n}{4n - 5}$

17. $\frac{12 - 4t}{t^2 - 2t - 3}$

18. $\frac{4m - 8}{4 - 2m}$

19. $\frac{m - 2}{4 - 2m}$

20. $\frac{v - 5}{25 - v^2}$

21. $\frac{4 - w}{w^2 - 8w + 16}$

Example 4
(page 653)

Baking Use the expression $\frac{30rh}{r + h}$ to estimate the baking time in minutes for each type of bread. Round your answer to the nearest minute.

22. baguette: $r = 1.25$ in., $h = 26$ in.

23. pita: $r = 3.5$ in., $h = 0.5$ in.

24. biscuit: $r = 1$ in., $h = 0.75$ in.

Ⓑ **Apply Your Skills**

Simplify each expression.

25. $\frac{2r^2 + 9r - 5}{r^2 + 10r + 25}$

26. $\frac{7z^2 + 23z + 6}{z^2 + 2z - 3}$

27. $\frac{5t^2 + 6t - 8}{3t^2 + 5t - 2}$

28. $\frac{32a^3}{16a^2 - 8a}$

29. $\frac{3z^2 + 12z}{z^4}$

30. $\frac{2s^2 + s}{s^3}$

31. $\frac{4a^2 - 8a - 5}{15 - a - 2a^2}$

32. $\frac{16 + 16m + 3m^2}{m^2 - 3m - 28}$

33. $\frac{10c + c^2 - 3c^3}{5c^2 - 6c - 8}$

34. Open-Ended Write an expression that has 2 and −3 excluded from the domain.

 35. a. Construction To keep heating costs down for a structure, architects want the ratio of surface area to volume as small as possible. Find an expression for the ratio of the surface area to volume for each shape.

    i. square prism   **ii.** cylinder

b. Find the ratio for each figure when $b = 12$ ft, $h = 18$ ft, and $r = 6$ ft.

36. Error Analysis Explain what error the student made in simplifying the rational expression at the right.

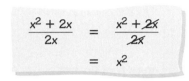

$$\frac{x^2 + 2x}{2x} = \frac{x^2 + \cancel{2x}}{\cancel{2x}}$$
$$= x^2$$

37. Writing Explain why $\frac{x^2 - 9}{x + 3}$ is not the same as $x - 3$.

Probability **If a point is selected at random from a figure and is equally likely to be any point in the figure, then the probability that the point is in a shaded part of the figure is** $\frac{\text{area of shaded part}}{\text{area of whole figure}}$. **Find the probability that a point will be in the shaded part of each figure.**

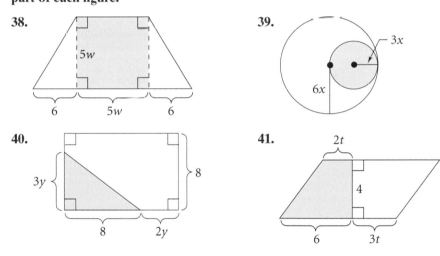

38.

39.

40.

41.

Challenge   **Simplify each expression.**

42. $\dfrac{m^2 - n^2}{m^2 + 11mn + 10n^2}$ **43.** $\dfrac{a^2 - 5ab + 6b^2}{a^2 + 2ab - 8b^2}$ **44.** $\dfrac{36v^2 - 49w^2}{18v^2 + 9vw - 14w^2}$

Reasoning **Determine whether each statement is *sometimes*, *always*, or *never* true for real numbers a and b.**

45. $\dfrac{2b}{b} = 2$ **46.** $\dfrac{ab^3}{b^4} = ab$ **47.** $\dfrac{a^2 + 6a - 5}{2a + 2} = \dfrac{a + 5}{2}$

Standardized Test Prep

Multiple Choice   **48.** Which expression simplifies to -1?

     A. $\dfrac{x + 1}{x - 1}$ **B.** $\dfrac{r + 3}{3 - r}$ **C.** $\dfrac{n - 2}{2 - n}$ **D.** $\dfrac{4 - p}{4 + p}$

49. Simplify $\dfrac{y^2 + 8y - 9}{y^2 - 81}$.

F. $\dfrac{8y}{9}$ **G.** $\dfrac{y + 9}{y + 81}$ **H.** $\dfrac{1}{9}$ **I.** $\dfrac{y - 1}{y - 9}$

50. Which expression is in simplest form?

A. $\dfrac{t + 1}{t^2 - 1}$ **B.** $\dfrac{2n - 1}{n^2 + 4}$ **C.** $\dfrac{c - 7}{7 - c}$ **D.** $\dfrac{2r - 4}{8 + 6r}$

Quantitative Comparison

Compare the quantity in Column A with the quantity in Column B. Choose the best answer.

A. The quantity in Column A is greater.
B. The quantity in Column B is greater.
C. The two quantities are equal.
D. The relationship cannot be determined from the information given.

Take It to the NET
Online lesson quiz at
www.PHSchool.com
Web Code: aea-1203

	Column A	Column B
51.	$\dfrac{-5(x + 5)}{x + 1}$	$-10x \cdot \dfrac{2x}{4x^2}$
52.	$\dfrac{4}{8 - 2b}, \; b \ne 4$	$\dfrac{2}{4 - b}, \; b \ne 4$

Short Response

53. A student simplified $\dfrac{x - 5}{4x - 20}$ to 4. What error did the student make? Show how to simplify the expression correctly.

Mixed Review

Lesson 12-2 **Identify the asymptotes of each function. Then graph the function.**

54. $h(x) = \dfrac{8}{x} + 2$ **55.** $f(x) = \dfrac{8}{x - 4}$ **56.** $g(x) = \dfrac{8}{x} - 4$

Lesson 11-1 **Simplify each radical expression.**

57. $\sqrt{20} \cdot \sqrt{10}$ **58.** $\sqrt{a^4 b^7 c^8}$ **59.** $\dfrac{\sqrt{80}}{\sqrt{10}}$ **60.** $\sqrt{\dfrac{2m}{25m^5}}$

Lesson 10-1 **Order each group of quadratic functions from widest to narrowest graph.**

61. $y = x^2, y = 3x^2, y = -2x^2$ **62.** $y = \frac{1}{3}x^2, y = \frac{1}{4}x^2, y = \frac{2}{5}x^2$

63. $y = 2x^2, y = 0.5x^2, y = -4x^2$ **64.** $y = -x^2, y = 2.3x^2, y = -3.8x^2$

Checkpoint Quiz 1 Lessons 12-1 through 12-3

TEXT Instant self-check
quiz online and
on CD-ROM

Each pair of points is on the graph of an inverse variation. Find the missing value.

1. $(9, 2)$ and $(x, 6)$ **2.** $(8.2, -3)$ and $(12.3, y)$ **3.** $(0.5, 7.2)$ and $(0.9, y)$

Identify the asymptotes of each function. Then graph the function.

4. $y = \dfrac{5}{x}$ **5.** $f(x) = \dfrac{8}{x - 4}$ **6.** $y = \dfrac{1}{x} + 4$

Simplify each expression.

7. $\dfrac{6x^2 - 24}{x + 2}$ **8.** $\dfrac{3c + 9}{3c - 9}$ **9.** $\dfrac{k - 2}{k^2 + 2k - 8}$

10. Open-Ended Write an expression that is not defined when the variable equals 3.

Multiplying and Dividing Rational Expressions

Lesson Preview

What You'll Learn

OBJECTIVE 1 To multiply rational expressions

OBJECTIVE 2 To divide rational expressions

...And Why

To find loan payments, as in Exercises 38–40

✔ Check Skills You'll Need

(For help, go to Lessons 8-3 and 9-6.)

Simplify each expression.

1. $r^2 \cdot r^8$ **2.** $b^3 \cdot b^4$ **3.** $c^7 \div c^2$

4. $3x^4 \cdot 2x^5$ **5.** $5n^2 \cdot n^2$ **6.** $15a^3(-3a^2)$

Factor each polynomial.

7. $2c^2 + 15c + 7$ **8.** $15t^2 - 26t + 11$ **9.** $2q^2 + 11q + 5$

Interactive lesson includes instant self-check, tutorials, and activities.

OBJECTIVE

1 Multiplying Rational Expressions

Multiplying rational expressions is similar to multiplying rational numbers. If $a, b, c,$ and d represent polynomials (with $b \neq 0$ and $d \neq 0$), then $\frac{a}{b} \cdot \frac{c}{d} = \frac{ac}{bd}$.

Need Help?

Remember that the value of the expression in the denominator cannot be zero.

1 EXAMPLE   Multiplying Rational Expressions

Multiply.

a. $\dfrac{3}{x} \cdot \dfrac{4}{x^2}$

$\dfrac{3}{x} \cdot \dfrac{4}{x^2} = \dfrac{12}{x^3}$ **Multiply the numerators and multiply the denominators.**

b. $\dfrac{x}{x+4} \cdot \dfrac{x-3}{x-2}$

$\dfrac{x}{x+4} \cdot \dfrac{x-3}{x-2} = \dfrac{x(x-3)}{(x+4)(x-2)}$ **Multiply the numerators and multiply the denominators. Leave the answer in factored form.**

✔ Check Understanding   **1** Multiply.

a. $\dfrac{6}{a^2} \cdot \dfrac{-2}{a^3}$ **b.** $\dfrac{x-5}{x+3} \cdot \dfrac{x-7}{x}$

As with rational numbers, the product $\frac{ac}{bd}$ may not be in simplest form. Look for factors common to the numerator and the denominator to divide out.

2 EXAMPLE   Using Factoring

Multiply $\dfrac{2x+1}{3}$ and $\dfrac{6x}{4x^2-1}$.

$\dfrac{2x+1}{3} \cdot \dfrac{6x}{4x^2-1} = \dfrac{2x+1}{3} \cdot \dfrac{6x}{(2x+1)(2x-1)}$ **Factor the denominator.**

$= \dfrac{2x+1^1}{1^3} \cdot \dfrac{6^2x}{1(2x+1)(2x-1)}$ **Divide out the common factors 3 and $(2x+1)$.**

$= \dfrac{2x}{2x-1}$ **Simplify.**

✔ Check Understanding   **2** Multiply $\dfrac{x-2}{8x}$ and $\dfrac{-8x-16}{x^2-4}$.

You can also multiply a rational expression by a polynomial. Leave the product in factored form.

3 EXAMPLE **Multiplying a Rational Expression by a Polynomial**

Multiply $\frac{3s + 2}{2s + 4}$ and $s^2 + 5s + 6$.

$$\frac{3s + 2}{2s + 4} \cdot (s^2 + 5s + 6) = \frac{3s + 2}{2(s + 2)} \cdot \frac{(s + 2)(s + 3)}{1} \qquad \text{Factor.}$$

$$= \frac{3s + 2}{2_1(s + 2)} \cdot \frac{(s + 2)^1(s + 3)}{1} \qquad \begin{array}{l}\textbf{Divide out the common factor}\\ \textbf{\textit{s} + 2.}\end{array}$$

$$= \frac{(3s + 2)(s + 3)}{2} \qquad \text{Leave in factored form.}$$

✓ **Check Understanding** **3** Multiply.

a. $\frac{3}{c} \cdot (c^3 - c)$
b. $\frac{2v}{v + 3} \cdot (v^2 - 2v - 15)$
c. $(m - 1) \cdot \frac{4m + 8}{m^2 - 1}$

OBJECTIVE

2 **Dividing Rational Expressions**

Recall that $\frac{a}{b} \div \frac{c}{d} = \frac{a}{b} \cdot \frac{d}{c}$, where $b \neq 0, c \neq 0$, and $d \neq 0$.

When you divide rational expressions that can be factored, first rewrite the expression using the reciprocal before dividing out common factors.

Reading Math

The vinculum or fraction bar is a grouping symbol.

4 EXAMPLE **Dividing Rational Expressions**

Divide $\frac{a^2 + 7a + 10}{a - 6}$ by $\frac{a + 5}{a^2 - 36}$.

$$\frac{a^2 + 7a + 10}{a - 6} \div \frac{a + 5}{a^2 - 36} = \frac{a^2 + 7a + 10}{a - 6} \cdot \frac{a^2 - 36}{a + 5} \qquad \begin{array}{l}\textbf{Multiply by }\frac{a^2 - 36}{a + 5}\textbf{,}\\ \textbf{the reciprocal of }\frac{a + 5}{a^2 - 36}\textbf{.}\end{array}$$

$$= \frac{(a + 2)(a + 5)}{(a - 6)} \cdot \frac{(a - 6)(a + 6)}{a + 5} \qquad \textbf{Factor.}$$

$$= \frac{(a + 2)(a + 5)^1}{1(a - 6)} \cdot \frac{(a - 6)^1(a + 6)}{1 a + 5} \qquad \begin{array}{l}\textbf{Divide out the common factors}\\ \textbf{\textit{a} + 5 and \textit{a} - 6.}\end{array}$$

$$= (a + 2)(a + 6) \qquad \textbf{Leave in factored form.}$$

✓ **Check Understanding** **4** Divide.

a. $\frac{a - 2}{ab} \div \frac{a - 2}{a}$
b. $\frac{5m + 10}{2m - 20} \div \frac{7m + 14}{14m - 20}$
c. $\frac{6n^2 - 5n - 6}{2n^2 - n - 3} \div \frac{2n - 3}{n + 1}$

The reciprocal of a polynomial such as $5x^2 + 5x$ is $\frac{1}{5x^2 + 5x}$.

5 EXAMPLE **Dividing a Rational Expression by a Polynomial**

Divide $\frac{x^2 + 3x + 2}{4x}$ by $(5x^2 + 5x)$.

$$\frac{x^2 + 3x + 2}{4x} \div \frac{5x^2 + 5x}{1} = \frac{x^2 + 3x + 2}{4x} \cdot \frac{1}{5x^2 + 5x} \qquad \begin{array}{l}\textbf{Multiply by the reciprocal}\\ \textbf{of }5x^2 + 5x\textbf{.}\end{array}$$

$$= \frac{(x + 1)(x + 2)}{4x} \cdot \frac{1}{5x(x + 1)} \qquad \textbf{Factor.}$$

$$= \frac{(x + 1)^1(x + 2)}{4x} \cdot \frac{1}{5x_1(x + 1)} \qquad \begin{array}{l}\textbf{Divide out the common}\\ \textbf{factor \textit{x} + 1.}\end{array}$$

$$= \frac{x + 2}{20x^2} \qquad \textbf{Simplify.}$$

✓ **Check Understanding** ⑤ Divide.

a. $\frac{3x^3}{2} \div \left(-15x^5\right)$ **b.** $\frac{y+3}{y+2} \div (y+2)$ **c.** $\frac{z^2 + 2z - 15}{z^2 + 9z + 20} \div (z - 3)$

EXERCISES

For more practice, see *Extra Practice*.

Practice and Problem Solving

Ⓐ Practice by Example

Multiply.

Example 1
(page 657)

1. $\frac{7}{3} \cdot \frac{5x}{12}$ **2.** $\frac{3}{t} \cdot \frac{4}{t}$ **3.** $\frac{5}{3a^2} \cdot \frac{8}{a^3}$

4. $\frac{m-2}{m+2} \cdot \frac{m}{m-1}$ **5.** $\frac{2x}{x+1} \cdot \frac{x-1}{3}$ **6.** $\frac{6x^2}{5} \cdot \frac{2}{x+1}$

Example 2
(page 657)

7. $\frac{4c}{2c+2} \cdot \frac{c+1}{c-1}$ **8.** $\frac{5x^3}{x^2} \cdot \frac{3x^4}{6x}$ **9.** $\frac{3t}{t-2} \cdot \frac{3t-6}{t^2}$

10. $\frac{m-2}{3m+9} \cdot \frac{2m+6}{2m-4}$ **11.** $\frac{x-5}{4x+6} \cdot \frac{6x+9}{3x-15}$ **12.** $\frac{4x+1}{5x+10} \cdot \frac{30x+60}{2x-2}$

Example 3
(page 658)

13. $\frac{4t+4}{t-3} \cdot \left(t^2 - t - 6\right)$ **14.** $\frac{2m+1}{3m-6} \cdot \left(9m^2 - 36\right)$ **15.** $\left(x^2 - 1\right) \cdot \frac{x-2}{3x+3}$

Example 4
(page 658)

Find the reciprocal of each expression.

16. $\frac{2}{x+1}$ **17.** $\frac{-6d^2}{2d-5}$ **18.** $c^2 - 1$ **19.** $s + 4$

Divide.

20. $\frac{x-1}{x+4} \div \frac{x+3}{x+4}$ **21.** $\frac{3t+12}{5t} \div \frac{t+4}{10t}$ **22.** $\frac{y-4}{10} \div \frac{4-y}{5}$

23. $\frac{x-3}{6} \div \frac{3-x}{2}$ **24.** $\frac{x^2+6x+8}{x^2+x-2} \div \frac{x+4}{2x+4}$ **25.** $\frac{2n^2-5n-3}{4n^2-12n-7} \div \frac{4n+5}{2n-7}$

Example 5
(page 658)

26. $\frac{3x+9}{x} \div (x+3)$ **27.** $\frac{11k+121}{7k-15} \div (k+11)$ **28.** $\frac{x^2+10x-11}{x^2+12x+11} \div (x-1)$

Ⓑ Apply Your Skills

Multiply or divide.

29. $\frac{t^2+5t+6}{t-3} \cdot \frac{t^2-2t-3}{t^2+3t+2}$ **30.** $\frac{c^2+3c+2}{c^2-4c+3} \div \frac{c+2}{c-3}$

31. $\frac{7t^2-28t}{2t^2-5t-12} \cdot \frac{6t^2-t-15}{49t^3}$ **32.** $\frac{5x^2+10x-15}{5-6x+x^2} \div \frac{2x^2+7x+3}{4x^2-8x-5}$

33. $\frac{x^2+x-6}{x^2-x-6} \div \frac{x^2+5x+6}{x^2+4x+4}$ **34.** $\left(\frac{x^2-25}{x^2-4x}\right)\left(\frac{x^2+x-20}{x^2+10x+25}\right)$

35. Error Analysis In the work shown at the right, what error did the student make in dividing the rational expressions?

36. Open-Ended Write two rational expressions. Find the product.

37. Critical Thinking For what values of x is the expression $\frac{2x^2-5x-12}{6x} \div \frac{-3x-12}{x^2-16}$ undefined?

$$\frac{3a}{a+2} \div \frac{(a+2)^2}{a-4} = \frac{3a}{\cancel{a+2}} \div \frac{\cancel{(a+2)^2}}{a-4}$$

$$= 3a \div \frac{a+2}{a-4}$$

$$= 3a \cdot \frac{a-4}{a+2}$$

$$= \frac{3a(a-4)}{a+2}$$

Lesson 12-4 Multiplying and Dividing Rational Expressions   **659**

Loan Payments The formula below gives the monthly payment m on a loan when you know the amount borrowed A, the annual rate of interest r, and the number of months of the loan n. Use this formula and a calculator for Exercises 38–40.

$$m = \frac{A\left(\frac{r}{12}\right)\left(1 + \frac{r}{12}\right)^n}{\left(1 + \frac{r}{12}\right)^n - 1}$$

38. What is the monthly payment on a loan of $1500 at 8% annual interest for 18 months?

39. What is the monthly payment on a loan of $3000 at 6% annual interest for 24 months?

40. Suppose your parents want to buy the house shown at the left. They have $15,000 for a down payment. Their mortgage will have an annual interest rate of 6%. The loan is to be repaid over a 30-year period.
  a. How much will your parents have to borrow?
  b. How many monthly payments will there be?
  c. What will the monthly payment be?
  d. How much will it cost your parents to repay this mortgage over the 30-year period?

http://www.rileyrealty.com
Riley Realty
518 Main Street
$115,000
Homes
Business
Contact
Links
FOR SALE

Geometry Find the volume of each rectangular solid.

41.

42.

43.

44.

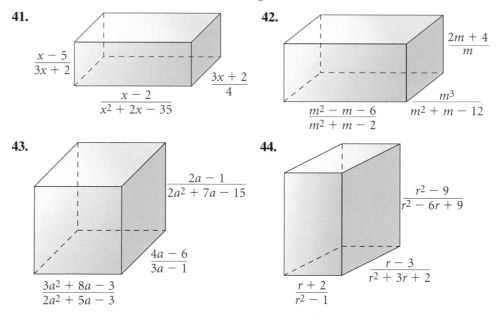

45. Writing Robin's first step in finding the product $\frac{2}{w} \cdot w^5$ was to rewrite the expression as $\frac{2}{w} \cdot \frac{w^5}{1}$. Why do you think Robin did this?

46. Probability If a point is selected at random from a figure and is equally likely to be any point in the figure, then the probability that the point is in a shaded part of the figure is $\frac{\text{area of shaded part}}{\text{area of whole figure}}$. Suppose two points are chosen.
  a. What is the probability that both points will be in the shaded part?
  b. What is the probability that one point will be in the shaded part and the other point will *not* be in the shaded part?

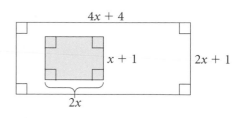

Need Help?

If two events A and B are independent, then $P(A \text{ and } B) = P(A) \cdot P(B)$.

Multiply or divide. (*Hint:* Remember that $\dfrac{\frac{a}{b}}{\frac{c}{d}} = \dfrac{a}{b} \div \dfrac{c}{d}$.)

47. $\dfrac{3m^3 - 3m}{4m^2 + 4m - 8} \cdot (6m^2 + 12m)$

48. $\dfrac{t^2 - r^2}{t^2 + tr - 2r^2} \cdot \dfrac{t^2 + 3tr + 2r^2}{t^2 + 2tr + r^2}$

49. $\dfrac{5x^2}{y^2 - 25} \div \dfrac{5xy - 25x}{y^2 - 10y + 25}$

50. $\dfrac{2a^2 - ab - 6b^2}{2b^2 + 9ab - 5a^2} \div \dfrac{2a^2 - 7ab + 6b^2}{a^2 - 4b^2}$

51. $\dfrac{\frac{3m}{m - 1}}{\frac{6m^2}{m - 2}}$

52. $\dfrac{\frac{3x}{x^2 - 1}}{\frac{6}{x^2 - x - 2}}$

53. $\dfrac{\frac{w - 3}{w^2 - 4}}{\frac{w^2 - 9}{w - 2}}$

Standardized Test Prep

Multiple Choice

54. Simplify $(2x - 5) \cdot \dfrac{2x}{2x^2 - 9x + 10}$.

  A. 1
  B. $\dfrac{2x}{x - 2}$
  C. $\dfrac{x - 5}{-4x + 5}$
  D. $\dfrac{2x - 5}{-8x - 10}$

55. Simplify $\dfrac{a^2 - 9}{a^2} \div \dfrac{a + 3}{a}$.

  F. -3
  G. $\dfrac{a - 3}{a}$
  H. $\dfrac{a(a - 3)}{a^2}$
  I. $\dfrac{a(a^2 - 9)}{a^2(a + 3)}$

56. Which expression is equivalent to $\dfrac{r^2 - 1}{r} \div (2r^2 - 2)$?

  A. $\dfrac{r^2 - 1}{r} \cdot \dfrac{1}{2}(r^2 - 1)$
  B. $\dfrac{r^2 - 1}{r} \cdot \dfrac{2}{r^2 - 1}$

  C. $\dfrac{r^2 - 1}{r} \cdot \left(\dfrac{1}{2r^2} - 2\right)$
  D. $\dfrac{r^2 - 1}{r} \cdot \dfrac{1}{2r^2 - 2}$

57. Which CANNOT be the first step in multiplying $\dfrac{x^2 - 2x - 3}{x + 3}$ by $\dfrac{2x + 6}{2x + 2}$?

  F. Multiply the numerators.
  G. Find the reciprocal of $\dfrac{2x + 6}{2x + 2}$.
  H. Factor each polynomial.
  I. Multiply the denominators.

Short Response

58. Simplify $\dfrac{x^2 - 1}{x} \cdot \dfrac{3x}{x - 1}$. Write the product in factored form. Show your work.

Take It to the NET
Online lesson quiz at
www.PHSchool.com
Web Code: aea-1204

Mixed Review

Lesson 12-3   **Simplify each expression.**

59. $\dfrac{5b - 25}{10}$

60. $\dfrac{36k^3}{48k^4}$

61. $\dfrac{7m - 14}{3m - 6}$

62. $\dfrac{7q^5}{28q}$

63. $\dfrac{15t^2 - 27}{24}$

64. $\dfrac{6m^3}{12m - 18m^2}$

65. $\dfrac{5a^2}{10a^4 - 15a^2}$

66. $\dfrac{2z^2 - 11z - 21}{z^2 - 6z - 7}$

67. $\dfrac{4c^2 - 36c + 81}{4c^2 - 2c - 72}$

Lesson 11-2   **Assume a and b are legs of a right triangle, and c is the hypotenuse. Find the length of the missing side of each right triangle. If necessary, round to the nearest tenth.**

68. $a = 2, b = 8$

69. $a = 3.1, b = 4.3$

70. $a = \sqrt{7}, c = \sqrt{32}$

71. $a = \sqrt{10}, b = \sqrt{111}$

72. $a = \dfrac{1}{5}, b = \dfrac{1}{12}$

73. $a = 2\dfrac{1}{3}, b = 6\dfrac{2}{3}$

Lesson 10-2   **Graph each function. Label the axis of symmetry and the vertex.**

74. $y = x^2 + 10x - 2$

75. $y = x^2 - 10x - 2$

76. $y = 2x^2 + x + 5$

Dividing Polynomials

Lesson Preview

What You'll Learn

OBJECTIVE
▼ 1 To divide polynomials

... And Why

To find the length of a rectangle, as in Example 3

✓ Check Skills You'll Need

(For help, go to Lessons 9-1 and 9-3.)

Write each polynomial in standard form.

1. $9a - 4a^2 + 1$ **2.** $3x^2 - 6 + 5x - x^3$ **3.** $-2 + 8t$

Find each product.

4. $(2x + 4)(x + 3)$ **5.** $(-3n - 4)(n - 5)$ **6.** $(3a^2 + 1)(2a - 7)$

OBJECTIVE

▼ 1

Dividing Polynomials

ⓘTEXT Interactive lesson includes instant self-check, tutorials, and activities.

To divide a polynomial by a monomial, divide each term of the polynomial by the monomial divisor.

1 EXAMPLE Dividing a Polynomial by a Monomial

Divide $8x^3 + 4x^2 - 12x$ by $2x^2$.

$$(8x^3 + 4x^2 - 12x) \div 2x^2 = (8x^3 + 4x^2 - 12x)\frac{1}{2x^2} \quad \text{Multiply by the reciprocal of } 2x^2.$$

$$= \frac{8x^3}{2x^2} + \frac{4x^2}{2x^2} - \frac{12x}{2x^2} \quad \text{Use the Distributive Property.}$$

$$= 4x^1 + 2x^0 - \frac{6}{x} \quad \text{Use the division rules for exponents.}$$

$$= 4x + 2 - \frac{6}{x} \quad \text{Simplify.}$$

✓ Check Understanding **1** Divide.

a. $(3m^3 - 6m^2 + m) \div 3m^2$ **b.** $(8t^5 + 16t^3 - 4t^2 + 2t) \div 4t^2$

The process of dividing a polynomial by a binomial is similar to long division. For example, consider dividing 737 by 21.

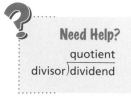

Need Help?

$\dfrac{\text{quotient}}{\text{divisor}\,)\overline{\text{dividend}}}$

$$\begin{array}{r} 35 \\ 21\overline{)737} \\ \underline{63} \\ 107 \\ \underline{105} \\ 2 \end{array}$$

1. **Divide:** 21 can go into 73 about 3 times.
2. **Multiply** 3 × 21, then subtract from 73.
3. **Bring down** the 7. Divide: 107 ÷ 21 ≈ 5.
4. **Multiply** 5 × 21, and then subtract from 107.
5. **The remainder** is 2.

$737 \div 21 = 35\frac{2}{21}$

You can summarize the process for long division as

"Divide, multiply, subtract, bring down, and repeat as necessary."

In the division above, the answer is written as a mixed number: $35\frac{2}{21}$ means $35 + \frac{2}{21}$. In dividing polynomials, write the answer as quotient $+ \frac{\text{remainder}}{\text{divisor}}$.

When the divisor and dividend are in standard form, divide the first term of the dividend by the first term of the divisor to find the first term of the quotient.

2 EXAMPLE   Dividing a Polynomial by a Binomial

Divide $2y^2 + 3y - 40$ by $y + 5$.

Step 1 Begin the long division process.

$\downarrow$

Align terms by their degrees.
So put **2y** above **3y** of the dividend.

$$
\begin{array}{r}
2y \\
y + 5 \overline{)\,2y^2 + 3y - 40} \\
\underline{2y^2 + 10y} \\
-7y - 40
\end{array}
$$

Divide: Think $2y^2 \div y = 2y$.
Multiply: $2y(y + 5) = 2y^2 + 10y$. Then subtract.
Bring down -40.

Step 2 Repeat the process: divide, multiply, subtract, and bring down.

$$
\begin{array}{r}
2y - 7 \\
y + 5 \overline{)\,2y^2 + 3y - 40} \\
\underline{2y^2 + 10y} \\
-7y - 40 \\
\underline{-7y - 35} \\
-5
\end{array}
$$

Divide: $-7y \div y = -7$.
Multiply: $-7(y + 5) = -7y - 35$. Then subtract.
The remainder is -5.

• The answer is $2y - 7 + \dfrac{-5}{y + 5}$, or $2y - 7 - \dfrac{5}{y + 5}$.

Need Help?

When subtracting the polynomial $-7y - 35$ from $-7y - 40$, think

$$
\begin{array}{r}
-7y - 40 \\
\underline{-(-7y - 35)}
\end{array}
$$

is

$$
\begin{array}{r}
-7y - 40 \\
\underline{+(7y + 35)} \\
-5
\end{array}
$$

✓ **Check Understanding** **2** Divide.

a. $(2b^2 - b - 3) \div (b + 1)$
b. $(6m^2 - 5m - 7) \div (2m + 1)$

When the dividend is in standard form and a power is missing, add a term of that power with 0 as its coefficient. For example, rewrite $4b^3 + 5b - 3$, as $4b^3 + 0b^2 + 5b - 3$.

3 EXAMPLE   Dividing Polynomials With a Zero Coefficient

Geometry The width and area of a rectangle are shown in the figure. What is the length?

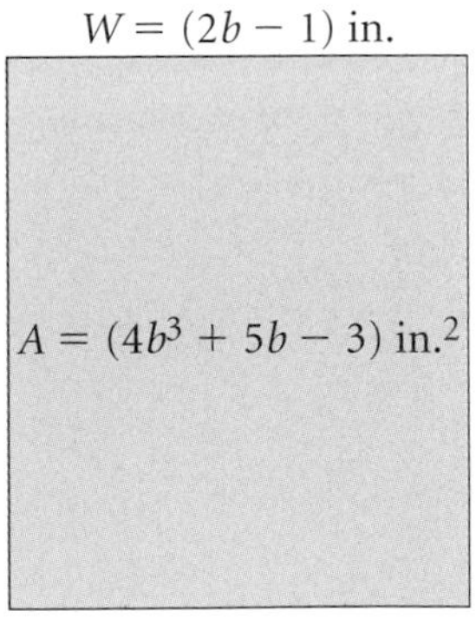

$W = (2b - 1)$ in.

Since $A = \ell w$, divide the area by the width to find the length.

$$
\begin{array}{r}
2b^2 + b + 3 \\
2b - 1 \overline{)\,4b^3 + 0b^2 + 5b - 3} \\
\underline{4b^3 - 2b^2} \\
2b^2 + 5b \\
\underline{2b^2 - b} \\
6b - 3 \\
\underline{6b - 3} \\
0
\end{array}
$$

Rewrite the dividend with 0b².

$A = (4b^3 + 5b - 3)$ in.²

• The length of the rectangle is $(2b^2 + b + 3)$ in.

✓ **Check Understanding** **3** Divide.

a. $(t^4 + t^2 + t - 3) \div (t - 1)$
b. $(c^3 - 4c + 12) \div (c + 3)$

Need Help?

To review standard form, see Lesson 9-1.

To use the process for long division, write any divisor or dividend in standard form before you begin to divide.

4 EXAMPLE Reordering Terms and Dividing Polynomials

Divide $-3x + 4 + 9x^2$ by $1 + 3x$.

Rewrite $-3x + 4 + 9x^2$ as $9x^2 - 3x + 4$ and $1 + 3x$ as $3x + 1$. Then divide.

$$
\begin{array}{r}
3x - 2 \\
3x + 1 \overline{)\,9x^2 - 3x + 4} \\
\underline{9x^2 + 3x} \\
-6x + 4 \\
\underline{-6x - 2} \\
6
\end{array}
$$

The answer is $3x - 2 + \dfrac{6}{3x + 1}$.

✓ Check Understanding   **4** Divide.

a. $(10x - 1 + 8x^2) \div (1 + 2x)$ b. $(9 - 6a^2 - 11a) \div (3a - 2)$

Key Concepts

Summary	**Dividing a Polynomial by a Polynomial**

Step 1 Arrange the terms of the dividend and divisor in standard form.

Step 2 Divide the first term of the dividend by the first term of the divisor. This is the first term of the quotient.

Step 3 Multiply the first term of the quotient by the divisor and place the product under the dividend.

Step 4 Subtract this product from the dividend.

Step 5 Bring down the next term.

Repeat Steps 2–5 as necessary until the degree of the remainder is less than the degree of the divisor.

EXERCISES

For more practice, see *Extra Practice*.

Practice and Problem Solving

A Practice by Example

Divide.

Example 1
(page 662)

1. $(x^6 - x^5 + x^4) \div x^2$

2. $(12x^8 - 8x^3) \div 4x^4$

3. $(9c^4 + 6c^3 - c^2) \div 3c^2$

4. $(n^5 - 18n^4 + 3n^3) \div n^3$

5. $(8q^2 - 32q) \div 2q^2$

6. $(-7t^5 + 14t^4 - 28t^3 + 35t^2) \div 7t^2$

Example 2
(page 663)

7. $(x^2 - 5x + 6) \div (x - 2)$

8. $(2t^2 + 3t - 11) \div (t - 3)$

9. $(n^2 - 5n + 4) \div (n - 4)$

10. $(y^2 - y + 2) \div (y + 2)$

11. $(3x^2 - 10x + 3) \div (x - 3)$

12. $(-4q^2 - 22q + 12) \div (2q + 1)$

Example 3
(page 663)

13. $(5t^2 - 500) \div (t + 10)$

14. $(2w^3 + 3w - 15) \div (w - 1)$

15. $(3b^3 - 10b^2 + 4) \div (3b - 1)$

16. $(c^3 - c^2 - 1) \div (c - 1)$

17. $(t^3 - 6t - 4) \div (t + 2)$

18. $(n^3 - 25n - 50) \div (n + 2)$

19. Geometry The width of a rectangle is $(r - 5)$ cm and the area is $(r^3 - 24r - 5)$ cm^2. What is the length?

20. Geometry The base of a triangle is $(c + 2)$ ft and the area is $(2c^3 + 16)$ ft^2. What is the height? $\left(\textit{Hint:}\text{ The formula for the area of a triangle is } A = \tfrac{1}{2}bh.\right)$

Example 4
(page 664)

Divide.

21. $(49 + 16b + b^2) \div (b + 4)$

22. $(a^2 - 6 + 3a) \div (4 + a)$

23. $(39w + 14 + 10w^2) \div (72 + w)$

24. $(4t + t^2 - 9) \div (4 + t)$

25. $(-13x + 2x^3 - 6 - x^2) \div (x - 3)$

26. $(6 - q + 3q^3 - 4q^2) \div (q - 2)$

B Apply Your Skills

27. $(6x^4 + 4x^3 - x^2) \div 2x^3$

28. $(c^3 + 11c^2 - 15c + 8) \div c$

29. $(8b + 2b^3) \div (b - 1)$

30. $(4y + y^3 - 7) \div (y - 5)$

31. $(56a^2 + 4a - 12) \div (2a + 1)$

32. $(5t^4 - 10t^2 + 6) \div (t + 5)$

33. $(3k^3 - 0.9k^2 - 1.2k) \div 3k$

34. $(-7s + 6s^2 + 5) \div (2s + 3)$

35. $(-2z^3 - z + z^2 + 1) \div (z + 1)$

36. $(6m^3 + 3m + 70) \div (m + 4)$

37. $(64c^3 - 125) \div (5 - 4c)$

38. $(21 - 5r^4 - 10r^2 + 2r^6) \div (r^2 - 3)$

39. $(2t^4 - 2t^3 + 3t - 1) \div (2t^3 + 1)$

40. $(z^4 + z^2 - 2) \div (z + 3)$

41. a. Open-Ended Write a binomial and a trinomial using the same variable.
    b. Divide the trinomial by the binomial.

42. Use the function rule $y = \frac{2x + 5}{x + 3}$.
    a. Rewrite the function rule as a quotient plus a remainder.
    b. Make a table of values and graph the function.
    c. What are the vertical and horizontal asymptotes?

43. Writing Suppose you divide a polynomial by a binomial. Explain how you know if the binomial is a factor of the polynomial.

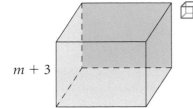

44. Geometry The volume of the rectangular prism shown at the left is $m^3 + 8m^2 + 19m + 12$. Find the area of the base of the prism.

45. a. Find $(d^2 - d + 1) \div (d + 1)$.
    b. Find $(d^3 - d^2 + d - 1) \div (d + 1)$.
    c. Find $(d^4 - d^3 + d^2 - d + 1) \div (d + 1)$.
    d. Patterns Predict the result of dividing $d^5 - d^4 + d^3 - d^2 + d - 1$ by $d + 1$.
    e. Verify your prediction by dividing the polynomials.

46. Critical Thinking Find the value of k if $x + 3$ is a factor of $x^2 - x - k$.

47. a. Solve $d = rt$ for t.
    b. Use your answer from part (a) to find an expression for the time it takes to travel a distance of $t^3 - 6t^2 + 5t + 12$ miles at a rate of $t + 1$ miles per hour.

C Challenge

Divide.

48. $(4a^3b^4 - 6a^2b^5 + 10a^2b^4) \div 2ab^2$

49. $(15x^2 + 7xy - 2y^2) \div (5x - y)$

50. $(90r^6 + 28r^5 + 45r^3 + 2r^4 + 5r^2) \div (9r + 1)$

51. $(2b^6 + 2b^5 - 4b^4 + b^3 + 8b^2 - 3) \div (b^3 + 2b^2 - 1)$

52. In Lesson 12-2, you saw horizontal and vertical asymptotes of rational functions. Some rational functions have asymptotes that are neither horizontal nor vertical. Consider the function $f(x) = \frac{x^2 + 2x - 5}{x + 5}$.

　　a. Divide $x^2 + 2x - 5$ by $x + 5$.

　　b. Rewrite the function using the quotient.

　　c. As $|x|$ increases, the remainder will become smaller, approaching zero, though never reaching it. So an asymptote is defined by the quotient without the remainder. Write an equation of that asymptote.

　　d. Graph the original equation and the asymptote.

Standardized Test Prep

Multiple Choice

53. Which of the following expressions equals $(3x^3 - 4x - 1) \div (x + 1)$?

　　A. $3x^2 - 3x - 7 + \frac{6}{x + 1}$ 　　　　　**B.** $3x^2 - 3x - 7 - \frac{8}{x + 1}$

　　C. $3x^2 - 3x - 1$ 　　　　　　　　　　　**D.** $3x^2 - 7x + 8$

54. What is the remainder when $x^2 - 4$ is divided by $x - 3$?

　　F. -13 　　　　**G.** 5 　　　　**H.** $\frac{-13}{x - 3}$ 　　　　**I.** $\frac{5}{x + 3}$

55. Which of the following must be true for $\left(x^2 + 2x + 1\right) \div (x + 3)$?

　　I. The remainder is negative.

　　II. The dividend is in standard form.

　　III. The quotient is larger than the divisor for positive values of x.

　　A. I only 　　　　**B.** II only 　　　　**C.** I and II 　　　　**D.** II and III

Take It to the NET

Online lesson quiz at
www.PHSchool.com
Web Code: aea-1205

Short Response

56. The volume of a rectangular prism is $2x^3 + 5x^2 + x - 2$. The height of the prism is $2x - 1$, and the length of the prism is $x + 2$. Find the width of the prism. Show your work.

Extended Response

57. a. Write the function $y = \frac{3x + 10}{x + 4}$ as a quotient plus a remainder.

　　b. Make a table and find the vertical and horizontal asymptotes. Graph the function.

Mixed Review

Lesson 12-4 　　**Multiply or divide.**

58. $\dfrac{n^2 + 7n - 8}{n - 1} \cdot \dfrac{n^2 - 4}{n^2 + 6n - 16}$ 　　　　　**59.** $\dfrac{6t^2 - 30t}{2t^2 - 53t - 55} \cdot \dfrac{6t^2 + 35t + 11}{18t^2}$

60. $\dfrac{3c^2 - 4c - 32}{2c^2 + 17c + 35} \div \dfrac{c - 4}{c + 5}$ 　　　　**61.** $\dfrac{x^2 + 9x + 20}{x^2 + 5x - 24} \div \dfrac{x^2 + 15x + 56}{x^2 + x - 12}$

Lesson 11-3 　　**Find the distance between each pair of points. If necessary, round to the nearest tenth.**

62. $(1, 2), (4, 6)$ 　　　　**63.** $(-1, 2), (4, -6)$ 　　　　**64.** $(7, 5), (-8, 5)$

65. $(7, 5), (-9, -3)$ 　　　**66.** $(-1, 5), (-2, -7)$ 　　　**67.** $(0, -5), (-6, 10)$

Lesson 10-3 　　**Find the value of each expression. If the value is irrational, round to the nearest hundredth.**

68. $\sqrt{28.9}$ 　　**69.** $\sqrt{289}$ 　　**70.** $-\sqrt{161.29}$ 　　**71.** $\sqrt{4000}$ 　　**72.** $\sqrt{40}$

Adding and Subtracting Rational Expressions

Lesson Preview

What You'll Learn

OBJECTIVE 1
To add and subtract rational expressions with like denominators

OBJECTIVE 2
To add and subtract rational expressions with unlike denominators

... And Why

To find the time of a round-trip flight, as in Example 5

✓ Check Skills You'll Need

(For help, go to Lessons 1-5 and 9-5.)

Simplify each expression.

1. $\frac{4}{9} + \frac{2}{9}$ **2.** $\frac{3}{7} - \frac{5}{7}$ **3.** $\frac{1}{2} + \left(-\frac{5}{2}\right)$

4. $\frac{5}{6} + \frac{2}{9}$ **5.** $\frac{1}{4} - \frac{1}{3}$ **6.** $\frac{5}{12} - \frac{3}{4}$

7. $\frac{4x}{9} + \frac{2x}{9}$ **8.** $\frac{7x}{12} - \frac{x}{12}$ **9.** $\frac{7}{12y} - \frac{1}{12y}$

Factor each quadratic expression.

10. $x^2 + 3x + 2$ **11.** $y^2 + 7y + 12$ **12.** $t^2 - 4t + 4$

---

iTEXT Interactive lesson includes instant self-check, tutorials, and activities.

OBJECTIVE 1

Adding and Subtracting Rational Expressions With Like Denominators

Adding rational expressions with like denominators is like adding rational numbers with like denominators. If a, b, and c represent polynomials (with $c \neq 0$), then $\frac{a}{c} + \frac{b}{c} = \frac{a + b}{c}$.

1 EXAMPLE Adding Expressions With Like Denominators

Add $\frac{2}{x + 3}$ and $\frac{5}{x + 3}$.

$$\frac{2}{x + 3} + \frac{5}{x + 3} = \frac{2 + 5}{x + 3} \quad \text{Add the numerators.}$$

$$= \frac{7}{x + 3} \quad \text{Simplify the numerator.}$$

✓ Check Understanding   **1** Add.

a. $\frac{3}{x + 2} + \frac{2}{x + 2}$ **b.** $\frac{y}{y - 5} + \frac{3y}{y - 5}$ **c.** $\frac{5n}{n + 1} + \frac{2n}{n + 1}$

Similarly, you can subtract rational expressions with like denominators.

2 EXAMPLE Subtracting Expressions With Like Denominators

Subtract $\frac{2n + 1}{2n^2 + 5n - 3}$ from $\frac{3n + 4}{2n^2 + 5n - 3}$.

$$\frac{3n + 4}{2n^2 + 5n - 3} - \frac{2n + 1}{2n^2 + 5n - 3} = \frac{3n + 4 - (2n + 1)}{2n^2 + 5n - 3} \quad \text{Subtract the numerators.}$$

$$= \frac{3n + 4 - 2n - 1}{2n^2 + 5n - 3} \quad \text{Use the Distributive Property.}$$

$$= \frac{n + 3}{2n^2 + 5n - 3} \quad \text{Simplify the numerator.}$$

$$= \frac{n + 3^1}{(2n - 1)_1(n + 3)} \quad \text{Factor the denominator. Divide out the common factor } n + 3.$$

$$= \frac{1}{2n - 1} \quad \text{Simplify.}$$

✔ **Check Understanding** ② Subtract.

a. $\dfrac{4}{t-2} - \dfrac{5}{t-2}$

b. $\dfrac{7b-2}{3b+6} - \dfrac{b+7}{3b+6}$

c. $\dfrac{2c+1}{5m+2} - \dfrac{3c-4}{5m+2}$

OBJECTIVE

2 | **Adding and Subtracting Rational Expressions With Unlike Denominators**

To add or subtract rational expressions with different denominators, you can write the expressions with the least common denominator (LCD), which is the least common multiple (LCM) of the denominators.

LCM of Whole Numbers	LCM of Variable Expressions
$4 = 2 \cdot 2$	$4x = 2 \cdot 2 \cdot \quad x$
$6 = 2 \cdot \quad 3$	$6x^2 = 2 \cdot \quad 3 \cdot x \cdot x$
$\text{LCM} = 2 \cdot 2 \cdot 3 = 12$	$\text{LCM} = 2 \cdot 2 \cdot 3 \cdot x \cdot x = 12x^2$

3 EXAMPLE **Adding Expressions With Monomial Denominators**

Add $\dfrac{2}{3x} + \dfrac{1}{6}$.

Step 1 Find the LCD of $\dfrac{2}{3x}$ and $\dfrac{1}{6}$.

$3x = 3 \cdot x$ **Factor each denominator.**

$6 = 2 \cdot 3$

$\text{LCD} = 2 \cdot 3 \cdot x = 6x$.

Step 2 Rewrite using the LCD and add.

$\dfrac{2}{3x} + \dfrac{1}{6} = \dfrac{2 \cdot 2}{2 \cdot 3x} + \dfrac{1 \cdot x}{6 \cdot x}$ **Rewrite each fraction using the LCD.**

$\quad = \dfrac{4}{6x} + \dfrac{x}{6x}$ **Simplify numerators and denominators.**

$\quad = \dfrac{4+x}{6x}$ **Add the numerators.**

✔ **Check Understanding** ③ Add or subtract.

a. $\dfrac{3}{7y^4} + \dfrac{2}{3y^2}$

b. $\dfrac{4}{25x} - \dfrac{49}{100}$

c. $\dfrac{5}{12b} + \dfrac{15}{36b^2}$

You can also find the LCD of rational expressions that have polynomials with two or more terms in the denominator.

4 EXAMPLE **Adding Expressions With Polynomial Denominators**

Add $\dfrac{5}{c+2}$ and $\dfrac{6}{c-3}$.

Step 1 Find the LCD of $c + 2$ and $c - 3$.
Since there are no common factors, the LCD is $(c + 2)(c - 3)$.

Step 2 Rewrite using the LCD and add.

$\dfrac{5}{c+2} + \dfrac{6}{c-3} = \dfrac{5(c-3)}{(c+2)(c-3)} + \dfrac{6(c+2)}{(c+2)(c-3)}$ **Rewrite the fractions using the LCD.**

$\quad = \dfrac{5c-15}{(c+2)(c-3)} + \dfrac{6c+12}{(c+2)(c-3)}$ **Simplify each numerator.**

$\quad = \dfrac{5c-15+6c+12}{(c+2)(c-3)}$ **Add the numerators.**

$\quad = \dfrac{11c-3}{(c+2)(c-3)}$ **Simplify the numerator.**

✔ **Check Understanding** ④ Add.

a. $\dfrac{5}{t+4} + \dfrac{3}{t-1}$ b. $\dfrac{m}{2m+1} + \dfrac{3}{m-1}$ c. $\dfrac{-2}{a+2} + \dfrac{3a}{2a-1}$

You can combine rational expressions to investigate real-world situations.

⑤ **EXAMPLE** Real-World 🌐 Problem Solving

2500 miles
New York
Los Angeles

Air Travel The ground speed for jet traffic from Los Angeles to New York City can be about 15% faster than the ground speed from New York City to Los Angeles. This difference is due to a strong westerly wind at high altitudes. If r is a jet's ground speed from New York City to Los Angeles, write and simplify an expression for the round-trip air time. The two cities are about 2500 miles apart.

NYC to LA time: $\dfrac{2500}{r}$ time $= \dfrac{\text{distance}}{\text{rate}}$

LA to NYC time: $\dfrac{2500}{1.15r}$ time $= \dfrac{\text{distance}}{\text{rate}}$ **15% more than a number is 115% of the number.**

An expression for the total time is $\dfrac{2500}{r} + \dfrac{2500}{1.15r}$.

$\dfrac{2500}{r} + \dfrac{2500}{1.15r} = \dfrac{2875}{1.15r} + \dfrac{2500}{1.15r}$ **Rewrite using the LCD, 1.15r.**

$= \dfrac{5375}{1.15r}$ **Add the numerators.**

$\approx \dfrac{4674}{r}$ **Simplify.**

✔ **Check Understanding** ⑤ **Air Travel** The distance between Atlanta, Georgia, and Albuquerque, New Mexico, is about 1270 miles. The ground speed for jet traffic from Atlanta to Albuquerque can be about 12% faster than the ground speed from Albuquerque to Atlanta. Use r for a jet's ground speed. Write and simplify an expression for the round-trip air time.

EXERCISES

For more practice, see *Extra Practice.*

Practice and Problem Solving

Ⓐ Practice by Example

Example 1
(page 667)

Add or subtract.

1. $\dfrac{5}{2m} + \dfrac{4}{2m}$
2. $\dfrac{4}{6t-1} + \dfrac{3}{6t-1}$
3. $\dfrac{n}{n+3} + \dfrac{2}{n+3}$
4. $\dfrac{5}{c-5} + \dfrac{9}{c-5}$
5. $\dfrac{s^2+3}{4s^2+2} + \dfrac{s^2-2}{4s^2+2}$
6. $\dfrac{5c}{2c+7} + \dfrac{c-28}{2c+7}$

Example 2
(page 667)

7. $\dfrac{1}{2-b} - \dfrac{4}{2-b}$
8. $\dfrac{5}{t^2+1} - \dfrac{6}{t^2+1}$
9. $\dfrac{3t}{2t-3} - \dfrac{5t}{2t-3}$
10. $\dfrac{2y+1}{y-1} - \dfrac{y+2}{y-1}$
11. $\dfrac{3n+2}{n+4} - \dfrac{n-6}{n+4}$
12. $\dfrac{3}{b-3} - \dfrac{b}{b-3}$

Example 3
(page 668)

Find the LCD of each pair of expressions.

13. $\dfrac{1}{2}; \dfrac{4}{x^2}$
14. $\dfrac{b}{6}; \dfrac{2b}{9}$
15. $\dfrac{1}{z}; \dfrac{3}{7z}$
16. $\dfrac{8}{5b}; \dfrac{12}{7b^3c}$

Add or subtract.

17. $\dfrac{7}{3a} + \dfrac{2}{5}$
18. $\dfrac{4}{x} - \dfrac{2}{3}$
19. $\dfrac{6}{5x^8} + \dfrac{4}{3x^6}$
20. $\dfrac{3}{8m^3} + \dfrac{1}{12m^2}$
21. $\dfrac{27}{n^3} - \dfrac{9}{7n^2}$
22. $\dfrac{9}{4x^2} + \dfrac{9}{5}$

Example 4
(page 668)

Add.

23. $\dfrac{9}{m+2} + \dfrac{8}{m-7}$

24. $\dfrac{a}{a+3} + \dfrac{4}{a+5}$

25. $\dfrac{a}{a+3} + \dfrac{a+5}{4}$

26. $\dfrac{c}{c+5} + \dfrac{4}{c+3}$

27. $\dfrac{5}{t^2} + \dfrac{4}{t+1}$

28. $\dfrac{3}{2a+1} + \dfrac{6}{2a-1}$

Example 5
(page 669)

29. Exercise Jane walks one mile from her house to her grandparents' house. Then she returns home, walking with her grandfather. Her return rate is 70% of her normal walking rate. Let r represent her normal walking rate.
   a. Write an expression for the amount of time Jane spends walking.
   b. Simplify your expression.
   c. Suppose Jane's normal walking rate is 3 mi/h. About how much time does she spend walking?

Ⓑ Apply Your Skills

Add or subtract.

30. $\dfrac{y^2 + 2y - 1}{3y + 1} - \dfrac{2y^2 - 3}{3y + 1}$

31. $\dfrac{h^2 + 1}{2t^2 - 7} + \dfrac{h}{2t^2 - 7}$

32. $\dfrac{r - 5}{9 + p^3} - \dfrac{2k + 1}{9 + p^3}$

33. $\dfrac{2 - x}{xy^2z} - \dfrac{5 + z}{xy^2z}$

34. $\dfrac{k}{2m^2} + \dfrac{3k}{2m}$

35. $\dfrac{12}{ab} - \dfrac{15}{bc}$

36. $\dfrac{c^2}{ab} - \dfrac{a^2}{bc}$

37. $9 + \dfrac{x - 3}{x + 2}$

38. $\dfrac{t}{2t - 3} - 11$

39. $\dfrac{x}{x^2 - 9} - \dfrac{x}{x^2 + 6x + 9}$

40. $\dfrac{k - 24}{k^2 - 3k - 18} - \dfrac{3}{k + 3} + \dfrac{k + 1}{k - 6}$

41. Error Analysis A student wrote that $\dfrac{2}{x + 3} + \dfrac{3}{x + 1} = \dfrac{5}{2x + 4}$. What error did the student make?

42. Rowing A rowing team practices rowing 2 mi upstream and 2 mi downstream. The team can row downstream 25% faster than they can row upstream.
   a. Let r represent their rate upstream. Write and simplify an expression for the amount of time they spend rowing.
   b. Let d represent their rate downstream. Write and simplify an expression for the amount of time they spend rowing.
   c. Critical Thinking Do the expressions you wrote in parts (a) and (b) represent the same time? Explain.

43. Writing When adding or subtracting rational expressions, will the answer be in simplest form if you use the LCD? Explain.

44. Open-Ended Write two rational expressions with different denominators. Find the LCD and add the two expressions.

For $f(x) = 8x$, $g(x) = \dfrac{1}{x}$, and $h(x) = \dfrac{4}{x - 5}$, perform the indicated operation.

Samples

$f(x) + g(x) = 8x + \dfrac{1}{x}$

$\qquad = \dfrac{8x}{1}\left(\dfrac{x}{x}\right) + \dfrac{1}{x}$

$\qquad = \dfrac{8x^2}{x} + \dfrac{1}{x}$

$\qquad = \dfrac{8x^2 + 1}{x}$

$f(x) \div g(x) = 8x \div \dfrac{1}{x}$

$\qquad = 8x\left(\dfrac{x}{1}\right)$

$\qquad = 8x^2$

45. $f(x) - g(x)$

46. $f(x) \cdot g(x)$

47. $g(x) - h(x)$

48. $f(x) \cdot h(x)$

49. $g(x) \div h(x)$

50. $h(x) \div f(x)$

Ⓒ Challenge

Simplify each expression.

51. $\dfrac{7d - 2}{d^2 + 2d - 8} - \dfrac{4}{d + 4} - \dfrac{d}{d - 2}$

52. $\dfrac{7x - 10}{x^3 + x^2 - 10x} - \dfrac{1}{x + 5}$

53. $\dfrac{x^2}{x^2 + x - 12} - \dfrac{x}{x + 4} \cdot \dfrac{3}{x - 3}$

54. $\dfrac{2}{a - 5} \cdot \dfrac{a - 1}{a + 2} - \dfrac{a - 2}{2 + a} \cdot \dfrac{3}{5 - a}$

Multiple Choice

55. Subtract $\frac{2x}{3x-2}$ from $\frac{5x}{3x-2}$.

    A. -2 **B.** $\frac{-3x}{3x-2}$ **C.** $\frac{7x}{3x-2}$ **D.** $\frac{3x}{3x-2}$

56. What is the least common denominator of $\frac{x}{x^2-1}$ and $\frac{-2}{x-1}$?

    F. $x+1$ **G.** $x-1$ **H.** x^2-1 **I.** $(x^2-1)(x-1)$

57. A band director found that he could line up the musicians in the brass section in rows of 4, 5, or 8. What is the least number of brass players in the band?

    A. 16 players   **B.** 24 players   **C.** 32 players   **D.** 40 players

Short Response

58. The members of a bicycle club rode a 20-mile round-trip route. On the way back, they had a tail wind and averaged 3 mi/h faster than on the first 10 miles of the trip.

    a. Use r for the rate. Write an expression for the total ride time. Simplify the expression.

    b. Suppose the bicyclists averaged a rate of 12 mi/h for the first half of the ride. How long did the round trip take? Show your work.

Take It to the NET

Online lesson quiz at
www.PHSchool.com
Web Code: aea-1206

Mixed Review

Lesson 12-5

Divide.

59. $(2x^4 + 8x^3 - 4x^2) \div 4x^2$ **60.** $(10b + 5b^3) \div (b+2)$

Lesson 11-5

Solve each radical equation. Check your answers. If there is no solution, write *no solution*.

61. $x = \sqrt{5x+6}$ **62.** $n = \sqrt{24-5n}$ **63.** $\sqrt{16y} = -8$

Lesson 10-4

Solve each equation by finding square roots. Round to the nearest tenth. If the equation has no solution, write *no solution*.

64. $a^2 - 48 = 0$ **65.** $2n^2 = 30$ **66.** $3p^2 + 60 = 0$

Algebra at Work

··················· Electrician

More than half a million men and women work as electricians. All are highly skilled technicians licensed by the states in which they work. Electricians use formulas containing rational expressions. For example, when a circuit connected in parallel contains two resistors with resistances R_1 and R_2 ohms, the total resistance R_T (in ohms) of the circuit can be found using the formula $\frac{1}{R_T} = \frac{1}{R_1} + \frac{1}{R_2}$.

Take It to the NET For more information about a career as an electrician, go to **www.PHSchool.com**.
Web Code: aeb-2031

Solving Rational Equations

Lesson Preview

What You'll Learn

OBJECTIVE 1 To solve rational equations

OBJECTIVE 2 To solve proportions

. . . And Why

To find the time it will take two people to do a job, as in Example 3

✓ Check Skills You'll Need

(For help, go to Lessons 4-1 and 12-6.)

Solve each proportion.

1. $\frac{1}{x} = \frac{3}{5}$ **2.** $\frac{3}{t} = \frac{5}{2}$ **3.** $\frac{m}{3} = \frac{27}{m}$

Find the LCD of each group of expressions.

4. $\frac{3}{4n}, \frac{1}{2}, \frac{2}{n}$ **5.** $\frac{1}{3x}, \frac{2}{5}, \frac{4}{3x}$ **6.** $\frac{1}{8y}, \frac{1}{y^2}, \frac{5}{6}$

New Vocabulary • rational equation

OBJECTIVE 1 Solving Rational Equations

TEXT Interactive lesson includes instant self-check, tutorials, and activities.

A **rational equation** contains one or more rational expressions. One method for solving rational equations is similar to the method you learned in Chapter 2 for solving equations with rational numbers.

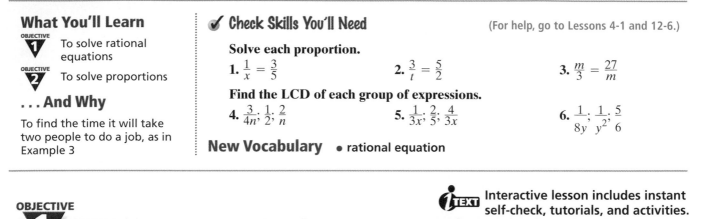

$\frac{1}{2}x + \frac{3}{10} = \frac{1}{5}$ The denominators are 2, 10, and 5. The LCD is 10.

$10\left(\frac{1}{2}x + \frac{3}{10}\right) = 10\left(\frac{1}{5}\right)$ Multiply each side by 10.

$^5\cancel{10}\left(\frac{1}{\cancel{2}_1}x\right) + {}^1\cancel{10}\left(\frac{3}{\cancel{10}_1}\right) = {}^2\cancel{10}\left(\frac{1}{\cancel{5}_1}\right)$ Use the Distributive Property.

$5x + 3 = 2$ No fractions! This equation is easier to solve.

1 EXAMPLE Solving Equations With Rational Expressions

Solve $\frac{1}{2x} + \frac{3}{10} = \frac{1}{5x}$. Check the solution.

$\frac{1}{2x} + \frac{3}{10} = \frac{1}{5x}$ The denominators are 2x, 10, and 5x. The LCD is 10x.

$10x\left(\frac{1}{2x} + \frac{3}{10}\right) = 10x\left(\frac{1}{5x}\right)$ Multiply each side by 10x.

$^5\cancel{10x}\left(\frac{1}{\cancel{2x}_1}\right) + {}^1\cancel{10}x\left(\frac{3}{\cancel{10}_1}\right) = {}^2\cancel{10x}\left(\frac{1}{\cancel{5x}_1}\right)$ Use the Distributive Property.

$5 + 3x = 2$ No rational expressions! Now you can solve.

$3x = -3$ Subtract 5 from each side.

$x = -1$ Divide each side by 3, and then simplify.

Check See if -1 makes $\frac{1}{2x} + \frac{3}{10} = \frac{1}{5x}$ true.

$\frac{1}{2(-1)} + \frac{3}{10} \overset{?}{=} \frac{1}{5(-1)}$

$-\frac{5}{10} + \frac{3}{10} = -\frac{1}{5}$ ✓

✓ Check Understanding

1 Solve each equation. Check your solution.

a. $\frac{1}{3} + \frac{1}{3x} = \frac{1}{6}$ **b.** $\frac{4}{c} = \frac{3}{2c} - \frac{1}{5}$

To solve some rational equations, you need to factor a quadratic expression.

2 EXAMPLE Solving by Factoring

Solve $\frac{5}{x^2} = \frac{6}{x} - 1$. Check the solution.

$$x^2\left(\frac{5}{x^2}\right) = x^2\left(\frac{6}{x} - 1\right)$$ **Multiply each side by the LCD, x^2.**

$${}^1x^2\left(\frac{5}{{}_1x^2}\right) = {}^xx^2\left(\frac{6}{x_1}\right) - x^2(1)$$ **Use the Distributive Property.**

$$5 = 6x - x^2$$ **Simplify.**

$$x^2 - 6x + 5 = 0$$ **Collect terms on one side.**

$$(x - 5)(x - 1) = 0$$ **Factor the quadratic expression.**

$$(x - 5) = 0 \quad \text{or} \quad (x - 1) = 0$$ **Use the Zero-Product Property.**

$$x = 5 \quad \text{or} \quad x = 1$$ **Solve.**

Check $\frac{5}{5^2} \stackrel{?}{=} \frac{6}{5} - 1$ $\frac{5}{1^2} \stackrel{?}{=} \frac{6}{1} - 1$

$\frac{1}{5} = \frac{1}{5}$ ✓ $5 = 5$ ✓

✔ **Check Understanding** ② Solve each equation. Check your solution.

a. $\frac{5}{m} = \frac{2}{m^2} + 2$ **b.** $t - 2 = \frac{8 - 2t}{t - 1}$

You can solve a work problem by finding the part of the job each person does in one unit of time (hour or minute). Find the part of the job each person does, and then write an equation.

3 EXAMPLE Work-Rate Problem

Volunteerism Max can wash and wax a car in 60 min. His older sister Kayla can do the same job in 45 min. How long will the car take them if they work together?

Define Let n = the time to complete the job if they work together (in minutes).

Relate   fraction of job   fraction of job   fraction of
         Max can do   +   Kayla can do   =   job completed
         in 1 minute   in 1 minute   in 1 minute

Write $\frac{1}{60}$ + $\frac{1}{45}$ = $\frac{1}{n}$

$$180n\left(\frac{1}{60} + \frac{1}{45}\right) = 180n\left(\frac{1}{n}\right)$$ **Multiply each side by the LCD, $180n$.**

$$3n + 4n = 180$$ **Use the Distributive Property.**

$$7n = 180$$ **Simplify.**

$$n = \frac{180}{7}, \text{ or } 25\frac{5}{7}$$ **Simplify.**

It will take the two of them about 26 minutes to wash the car working together.

Check Max will do $\frac{180}{7} \cdot \frac{1}{60} = \frac{3}{7}$ of the job, and Kayla will do $\frac{180}{7} \cdot \frac{1}{45} = \frac{4}{7}$ of the job. Together, they will do $\frac{3}{7} + \frac{4}{7} = 1$, or the whole job.

Real-World Connection

Many student groups hold car washes to raise money.

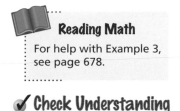

Reading Math

For help with Example 3, see page 678.

✔ **Check Understanding** ③ Peggy can pick a bushel of apples in 45 min. Peter can pick a bushel of apples in 75 min. How long will it take them to pick a bushel if they work together?

Some rational equations are proportions. You can solve them by using cross products.

4 EXAMPLE **Solving a Rational Proportion**

Solve $\frac{2}{x} = \frac{1}{x + 4}$. Check the solution.

Need Help?

If $\frac{a}{b} = \frac{c}{d}$, then $ad = bc$.

$$\frac{2}{x} = \frac{1}{x + 4}$$

$2(x + 4) = x(1)$	Write cross products.
$2x + 8 = x$	Use the Distributive Property.
$x = -8$	Solve for x.

Check $\quad \frac{2}{x} = \frac{1}{x + 4}$

$$\frac{2}{-8} \stackrel{?}{=} \frac{1}{-8 + 4}$$

$$-\frac{1}{4} = -\frac{1}{4} \checkmark$$

✓ **Check Understanding** ④ Solve each equation. Check your solution.

a. $\frac{3}{a} = \frac{5}{a - 2}$ **b.** $\frac{n}{5} = \frac{4}{n + 1}$

The process of cross multiplying or multiplying by the LCD may give an extraneous solution to an equation, or a solution that makes a denominator in the original equation equal zero. An extraneous solution solves a new equation but not the original one. So you must check your solutions.

5 EXAMPLE **Checking to Find an Extraneous Solution**

Solve $\frac{-2}{x - 2} = \frac{x - 4}{x^2 - 4}$.

$$\frac{-2}{x - 2} = \frac{x - 4}{x^2 - 4}$$

$-2(x^2 - 4) = (x - 2)(x - 4)$	Write cross products.
$-2x^2 + 8 = x^2 - 6x + 8$	Simplify each side of the equation.
$0 = 3x^2 - 6x$	Collect terms on one side.
$0 = 3x(x - 2)$	Factor.
$0 = 3x$ or $0 = x - 2$	Use the Zero-Product Property.
$x = 0 \qquad x = 2$	Solve.

Check $\quad \frac{-2}{x - 2} = \frac{x - 4}{x^2 - 4}$

$$\frac{-2}{0 - 2} \stackrel{?}{=} \frac{0 - 4}{0^2 - 4} \qquad\qquad \frac{-2}{2 - 2} \stackrel{?}{=} \frac{2 - 4}{2^2 - 4}$$

$$\frac{-2}{-2} \stackrel{?}{=} \frac{-4}{-4} \qquad\qquad \frac{-2}{0} = \frac{-2}{0} \qquad \text{Undefined!}$$

$$1 = 1 \checkmark$$

The equation has one solution, 0.

✓ **Check Understanding** ⑤ Solve each equation. Check your solutions.

a. $\frac{2}{c^2} = \frac{2}{c^2 + 1}$ **b.** $\frac{w^2}{w - 1} = \frac{1}{w - 1}$

EXERCISES

For more practice, see *Extra Practice*.

Practice and Problem Solving

A **Practice by Example**

Examples 1, 2
(pages 672, 673)

Solve each equation. Check your solutions.

1. $\frac{1}{2} + \frac{2}{x} = \frac{1}{x}$

2. $5 + \frac{2}{p} = \frac{17}{p}$

3. $\frac{3}{a} - \frac{5}{a} = 2$

4. $y - \frac{6}{y} = 5$

5. $\frac{5}{2s} + \frac{3}{4} = \frac{9}{4s}$

6. $\frac{1}{t-2} = \frac{t}{8}$

7. $\frac{2}{c-2} = 2 - \frac{4}{c}$

8. $\frac{5}{3p} + \frac{2}{3} = \frac{5+p}{2p}$

9. $\frac{8}{x+3} = \frac{1}{x} + 1$

10. $\frac{v+2}{v} + \frac{4}{3v} = 11$

11. $\frac{4}{3(c+4)} + 1 = \frac{2c}{c+4}$

12. $\frac{a}{a+4} = 3 - \frac{4}{a+4}$

13. $\frac{z}{z+2} = 3 - \frac{2}{z+2}$

14. $\frac{a}{a+3} = \frac{2a}{a-3} - 1$

15. $\frac{z}{z+2} - \frac{1}{z} = 1$

Example 3
(page 673)

16. Gardening Marian can weed a garden in 3 hours. Robin can weed the same garden in 4 hours. How long will the weeding take them if they work together?

17. David can unload a delivery truck in 20 min. Allie can unload a delivery truck in 35 min. How long will the unloading take them if they work together?

Examples 4, 5
(page 674)

Solve each equation. Check your solutions. If there is no solution, write *no solution*.

18. $\frac{5}{x+1} = \frac{x+2}{x+1}$

19. $\frac{4}{c+4} = \frac{c}{c+25}$

20. $\frac{3}{m-1} = \frac{2m}{m+4}$

21. $\frac{2x+4}{x-3} = \frac{3x}{x-3}$

22. $\frac{30}{x+3} = \frac{30}{x-3}$

23. $\frac{x+2}{x+4} = \frac{x-2}{x-1}$

B **Apply Your Skills**

Solve each equation. Check your solutions.

24. $\frac{2r}{r-4} - 2 = \frac{4}{r+5}$

25. $6 - \frac{2}{b} = \frac{-5}{b-3}$

26. $\frac{r+1}{r-1} = \frac{r}{3} + \frac{2}{r-1}$

27. $\frac{3}{s-1} + 1 = \frac{12}{s^2-1}$

28. $\frac{d}{d+2} - \frac{2}{2-d} = \frac{d+6}{d^2-4}$

29. $\frac{u+1}{u} + \frac{1}{2u} = 4$

30. $\frac{s}{3s+2} + \frac{s+3}{2s-4} = \frac{-2s}{3s^2-4s-4}$

31. $\frac{u+1}{u+2} = \frac{-1}{u-3} + \frac{u-1}{u^2-u-6}$

32. Two pipes fill a storage tank in 9 hours. The larger pipe fills the tank three times as fast as the smaller one. How long would it take the larger pipe to fill the tank alone?

33. A teacher assigned the equation $\frac{40}{x} = \frac{15}{x-20}$. Carlos studied the equation and said, "I'll start by finding the LCD." Ingrid studied the equation and said, "I'll start by cross multiplying."
  a. Solve the equation using Carlos's method and then Ingrid's method.
  b. Writing Which method do you prefer? Explain why.
  c. Critical Thinking Will Ingrid's method work for all rational equations? Explain.

34. Find the value of each variable. $\begin{bmatrix} \frac{5a}{3} & \frac{7}{3b} \\ 2c-15 & \frac{5}{2d} + \frac{3}{4} \\ \overline{35c} & \end{bmatrix} = \begin{bmatrix} 2 + \frac{7a}{6} & 9 \\ \frac{1}{5c} & \frac{9}{4d} \end{bmatrix}$

35. a. Write two functions using the expressions on the two sides of the equation $\frac{6}{x^2} + 1 = \frac{(x+7)^2}{6}$. Graph the functions.
  b. Find the coordinates of the points of intersection.
  c. Are the *x*-values of the points of intersection solutions to the equation? Explain.

Problem Solving Hint

For Exercise 32, making a table may help you organize the information in the question.

Lesson 12-7 Solving Rational Equations **675**

Circuit connected in series.

Circuit connected in parallel.

Real-World 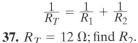 **Connection**

The resistance of a conductor is the opposition it gives to the flow of electrical current through it.

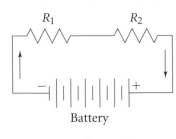 **Electricity** Lamps can be connected to a battery in a circuit in series or in parallel. You can calculate the total resistance R_T in a circuit if you know the resistance in each lamp. Resistance is measured in ohms (Ω).

Circuit Connected in Series

Battery

$$R_T = R_1 + R_2$$

Circuit Connected in Parallel

Battery

$$\frac{1}{R_T} = \frac{1}{R_1} + \frac{1}{R_2}$$

36. Find R_T.

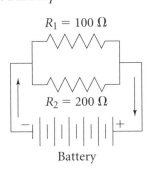

Battery

37. $R_T = 12\ \Omega$; find R_2.

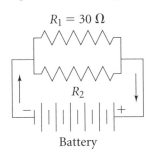

Battery

38. Find R_T. (*Hint*: The lamps in this circuit are connected in series *and* in parallel.)

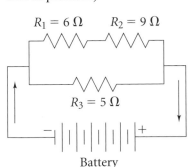

Battery

39. $R_T = 10\ \Omega$; find R_2.

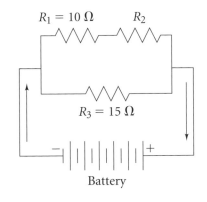

Battery

40. Open-Ended Write a rational equation that has 3 as a solution.

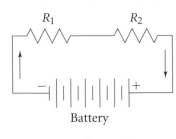 **41. Travel** A plane flies 450 mi/h. It can travel 980 miles with a wind in the same amount of time as it travels 820 mi against the wind. Solve the equation $\frac{980}{450 + s} = \frac{820}{450 - s}$ to find the speed s of the wind.

C Challenge **Solve each equation. Be sure to check your answers.**

42. $\frac{x - 6}{x + 3} + \frac{2x}{x - 3} = \frac{4x + 3}{x + 3}$

43. $\frac{n}{n - 2} + \frac{n}{n + 2} = \frac{n}{n^2 - 4}$

44. $\frac{2}{r} + \frac{1}{r^2} + \frac{r^2 + r}{r^3} = \frac{1}{r}$

45. $\frac{3}{t} - \frac{t^2 - 2t}{t^3} = \frac{4}{t^2}$

46. It takes Jon 75 min to paint a room. It takes Jeff 60 min and Jackie 80 min each to paint the same room. How long will the painting take if all three work together?

Real-World 🌐 **Connection**

Many chemistry classes include a lab on testing acidity.

47. Chemistry A chemist has one solution that is 80% acid and a second solution that is 30% acid. The chemist needs to mix some of both solutions to make 50 liters of a solution that is 62% acid. Let s = the number of liters of the 80% solution used in the mixture.

    a. Write an expression for the amount of acid in s liters of the 80% solution.

    b. Write an expression for the number of liters of the 30% acid used in the mixture.

    c. Write an expression for the amount of acid in a 30% acid solution.

    d. Write an equation that combines the amount of acid in each solution to make the total amount of acid in 50 liters of 62% acid solution.

    e. Solve the equation you wrote in part (d).

    f. How many liters of each solution will the chemist need to make 50 liters of 62% acid solution?

48. Sumi can wash the windows of an office building in $\frac{3}{4}$ the time it takes her apprentice. One day they worked on a building together for 2 h 16 min, and then Sumi continued alone. It took 4 h 32 min more to complete the job. How long would it take her apprentice to wash all the windows alone?

Standardized Test Prep

Multiple Choice

49. Which is a solution of $\frac{2}{n} + \frac{1}{2} = \frac{1}{n}$?

    A. -4 **B.** -2 **C.** 2 **D.** 4

50. Which inequality contains both solutions of $x = \frac{1}{2} + \frac{3}{x}$?

    F. $-1 < x < 3$ **G.** $-2 < x \le 2$ **H.** $-2 \le x < 0$ **I.** $-3 \le x \le -1$

51. What is the least common denominator of $\frac{1}{x}$, $\frac{x}{3}$, and $\frac{3}{2x}$?

    A. $2x$ **B.** $3x$ **C.** $6x$ **D.** $6x^2$

Short Response

52. You are trying to find the number you would add to both the numerator and denominator of $\frac{3}{16}$ to make a fraction equal to $\frac{1}{2}$. Write a rational equation that can be used to find this number. Then solve the equation to find the number and check your solution.

Mixed Review

Lesson 12-6   **Add or subtract.**

53. $\dfrac{5}{x^2y^2z} - \dfrac{8}{x^2y^2z}$ **54.** $\dfrac{3h^2}{2t^2 - 8} + \dfrac{h}{t - 2}$ **55.** $\dfrac{k - 11}{k^2 + 6k - 40} - \dfrac{5}{k - 4}$

Lesson 11-6   **Graph each function either by translating the graph of $y = \sqrt{x}$ or by making a table of values.**

56. $f(x) = -2\sqrt{x}$ **57.** $y = \sqrt{x + 7}$ **58.** $f(x) = \sqrt{x - 2} - 8$

59. $y = \sqrt{0.25x}$ **60.** $y = \sqrt{2x} + 3$ **61.** $y = \sqrt{4x - 2} - 2$

Lesson 10-5   **Solve each equation by factoring.**

62. $x^2 + 23x + 90 = 0$ **63.** $x^2 - 19x + 880 = 0$ **64.** $x^2 + 22x - 230 = 0$

65. $x^2 + 2x - 48 = 0$ **66.** $x^2 + 52 = -17x$ **67.** $x^2 + 92x - 9 = -100$

Example 3 shows one method for solving a work problem. Here is another way to solve the same problem.

Max can wash and wax a car in 60 min. His older sister Kayla can do the same job in 45 min. How long will the car take them if they work together?

You can use a formula, $rt = 1$, to solve this problem. In this formula,
$t =$ the time (in minutes) it takes to complete a job and
$r =$ the rate for doing the job (in job per minute).

Max can do the job in 60 min, so his rate is $\frac{1}{60}$ job per minute (job/min).

Kayla can do the job in 45 min, so her rate is $\frac{1}{45}$ job/min.

Their combined rate is $r = \left(\frac{1}{60} + \frac{1}{45}\right)$ job/min.

The following table contains all the information.

	Rate	Time	Work
Max	$\frac{1}{60}$	60	$\left(\frac{1}{60}\right)(60) = 1$
Kayla	$\frac{1}{45}$	45	$\left(\frac{1}{45}\right)(45) = 1$
Max and Kayla	$\frac{1}{60} + \frac{1}{45}$	t	$\left(\frac{1}{60} + \frac{1}{45}\right)t = 1$

Now you can solve the equation to find the time t the job will take Max and Kayla working together.

$\left(\frac{1}{60} + \frac{1}{45}\right)t = 1$	**Substitute.**
$180\left(\frac{1}{60} + \frac{1}{45}\right)t = 180 \cdot 1$	**Multiply each side by the LCD of 60 and 45, which is 180.**
$(3 + 4)t = 180$	**Use the Distributive Property.**
$7t = 180$	**Simplify within the parentheses.**
$t = \frac{180}{7}$ or $25\frac{5}{7}$	**Divide each side by 7.**

It will take Max and Kayla together about 26 minutes to wash and wax the car.

EXERCISES

Test your understanding by solving the problems below using either the method shown here or the one shown on page 673.

1. Dawn can clean the garage in 15 minutes. Phil can clean the garage in 10 minutes.
   a. Find the rate in terms of job/min for Dawn and for Phil.
   b. What is their rate if they are working together?
   c. How long will the job take them if they work together?

2. Working together, Maureen and Nan can prepare and paint a room in 6 hours. Working alone, Maureen can prepare and paint the room in 10 hours. How long will it take Nan to prepare and paint the room when she works alone?

12-8

Counting Methods and Permutations

Lesson Preview

What You'll Learn

OBJECTIVE 1
To use the multiplication counting principle

OBJECTIVE 2
To find permutations

. . . And Why

To find the number of possible six-letter passwords, as in Example 5

✔ **Check Skills You'll Need** (For help, go to Lessons 4-5 and 4-6.)

You roll a number cube. Find each probability.

1. P(even number)
2. P(prime number)

3. P(a number greater than 5)
4. P(a negative number)

You roll a blue number cube and a yellow number cube. Find each probability.

5. P(blue 1 and yellow 2)
6. P(blue even and yellow odd)

New Vocabulary ● Multiplication Counting Principle ● permutation

---

OBJECTIVE 1

Using the Multiplication Counting Principle

iTEXT Interactive lesson includes instant self-check, tutorials, and activities.

Investigation: Determining Order

Suppose you have to read the following works over the summer for English class next year.

1. In how many different orders can you read the books?

2. Describe how you determined the number of different ways you could order the books.

3. Suppose you choose one of the orders at random. What is the probability that you will read the books in alphabetical order by title? By author?

You can find the possible orders of objects by making an organized list. Another way is to make a tree diagram. Both methods help you see if you have thought of all of the possibilities.

Using a Tree Diagram

Suppose you have three shirts and two pair of pants that coordinate well. Make a tree diagram to find the number of possible outfits you have.

Shirts	Pants	Outfits
Shirt 1 ⟶	Pants 1 ⟶	Shirt 1, Pants 1
	Pants 2 ⟶	Shirt 1, Pants 2
Shirt 2 ⟶	Pants 1 ⟶	Shirt 2, Pants 1
	Pants 2 ⟶	Shirt 2, Pants 2
Shirt 3 ⟶	Pants 1 ⟶	Shirt 3, Pants 1
	Pants 2 ⟶	Shirt 3, Pants 2

● There are six possible outfits.

✓ Check Understanding **1** **a.** Suppose you have two T-shirts and four pairs of shorts you could bring for gym class. Make a tree diagram to find the number of possible outfits for gym.
b. **Critical Thinking** Would you want to use a tree diagram to find the number of outfits for five T-shirts and eight pairs of shorts? Explain.

Recall that when one event does not affect the result of a second event, the events are *independent*. When events are independent, you can find the number of outcomes using the Multiplication Counting Principle.

🔑 Key Concepts

Rule	**Multiplication Counting Principle**

If there are *m* ways to make a first selection and *n* ways to make a second selection, there are *m* × *n* ways to make the two selections.

Example For five shirts and eight pairs of shorts, the number of possible outfits is 5 · 8 = 40.

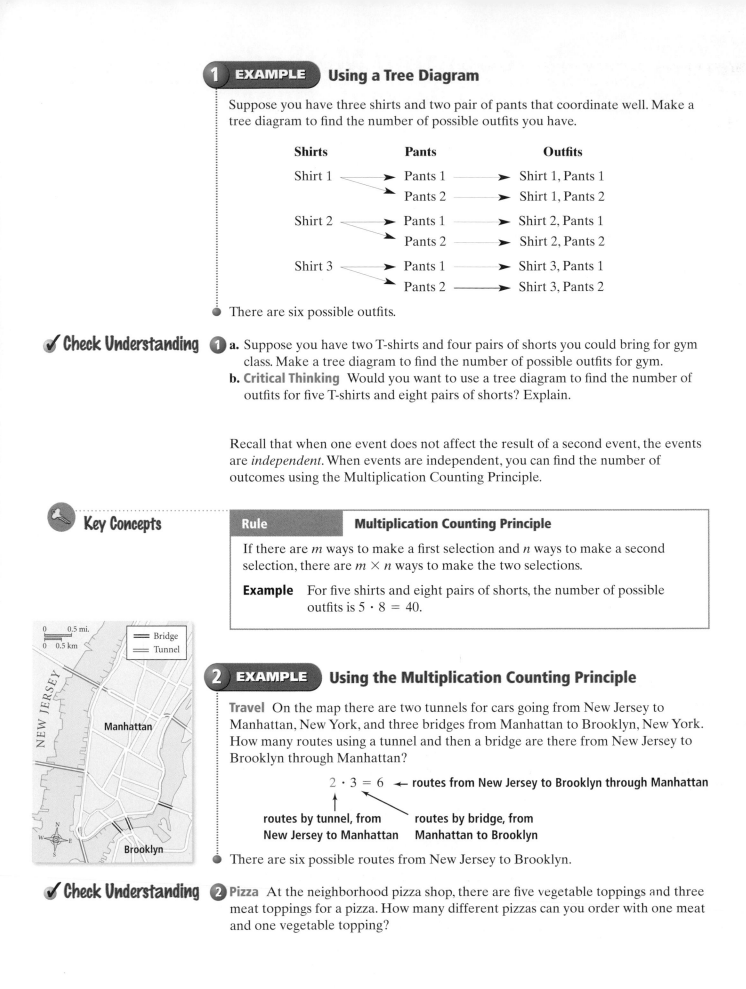

2 **EXAMPLE** **Using the Multiplication Counting Principle**

Travel On the map there are two tunnels for cars going from New Jersey to Manhattan, New York, and three bridges from Manhattan to Brooklyn, New York. How many routes using a tunnel and then a bridge are there from New Jersey to Brooklyn through Manhattan?

2 · 3 = 6 ← **routes from New Jersey to Brooklyn through Manhattan**

routes by tunnel, from **routes by bridge, from**
New Jersey to Manhattan **Manhattan to Brooklyn**

● There are six possible routes from New Jersey to Brooklyn.

✓ Check Understanding **2** **Pizza** At the neighborhood pizza shop, there are five vegetable toppings and three meat toppings for a pizza. How many different pizzas can you order with one meat and one vegetable topping?

One kind of counting problem is to find the number of possible arrangements of the objects in a set. Here are the possible arrangements for the letters A, B, and C without repeating any letters.

ABC   BAC   CAB   ACB   BCA   CBA

Each of the arrangements is a permutation. A **permutation** is an arrangement of objects in a specific order.

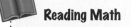

Reading Math

A short way to write the product in Example 3 is 9!, read "nine factorial." For positive integers, factorial means the product of integers from the given number to 1.

3 **EXAMPLE** **Counting Permutations**

Baseball How many different batting orders can you have with 9 baseball players?

There are 9 choices for the first batter, 8 for the second, 7 for the third, and so on.

$9 \cdot 8 \cdot 7 \cdot 6 \cdot 5 \cdot 4 \cdot 3 \cdot 2 \cdot 1 = 362{,}880$ **Use a calculator.**

There are 362,880 possible batting orders.

✓ **Check Understanding** **3** **Swimming** A swimming pool has eight lanes. In how many ways can eight swimmers be assigned lanes for a race?

In how many ways can you select a right, center, and left fielder from eight players on a baseball team? To answer this question, you need to find the number of permutations of 8 objects (players) arranged 3 at a time.

🔑 **Key Concepts**

Definition	**Permutation Notation**

The expression $_nP_r$ represents the number of permutations of n objects arranged r at a time.

n will be the first factor.

$$_nP_r = n(n-1)(n-2)\ldots$$

Stop when you have r factors.

Example $_8P_3$ represents 8 objects (players) chosen 3 at a time, or $8 \cdot 7 \cdot 6 = 336$.

4 **EXAMPLE** **Using Permutation Notation**

Simplify $_7P_4$.

Method 1 Use pencil and paper.

$_7P_4 = 7 \cdot 6 \cdot 5 \cdot 4$ **The first factor is 7, and there are 4 factors.**

$= 840$ **Simplify.**

Method 2 Use a graphing calculator. Use MATH to select nPr in the PRB screen.

$_7P_4 = 840$

7 nPr 4
840

💻 **Take It to the NET**

Graphing Calculator procedures online at **www.PHSchool.com**
Web Code: aee-2116

✓ **Check Understanding** **4** Simplify each expression.

a. $_9P_3$ **b.** $_7P_3$ **c.** $_5P_2$

In some situations, order matters, but repetition is allowed. In that case, use the Multiplication Counting Principle. However, when repetition is not allowed, use permutations to find the number of arrangements.

5 EXAMPLE **Real-World Problem Solving**

Computers Suppose you use six different letters to make a computer password. Find the number of possible six-letter passwords.

There are 26 letters in the alphabet. You are finding the number of permutations of 26 letters arranged 6 at a time.

$$_{26}P_6 = 26 \cdot 25 \cdot 24 \cdot 23 \cdot 22 \cdot 21 \qquad \textbf{Use a calculator.}$$
$$= 165,765,600$$

There are 165,765,600 six-letter passwords in which letters do not repeat.

✓ **Check Understanding** **5 a.** Suppose your cousin needs to choose a four-digit number to use with a new debit card. Find the number of possible four-digit numbers without repeating a digit.
  b. Critical Thinking Is a six-letter password or a six-digit number harder for someone to guess? Explain.

EXERCISES

For more practice, see *Extra Practice*.

Practice and Problem Solving

A Practice by Example

Example 1
(page 680)

1. Job Interview James must wear a shirt and tie for a job interview. He has two dress shirts and five ties. Use a tree diagram to find the number of shirt-tie choices he has.

2. Catering Suppose your grandparents are planning an anniversary party. The caterer offers the following choices for a menu. Guests can have either spinach salad or chef's salad, and either vegetable soup or chicken soup. The main course is chicken, beef, or salmon. Use a tree diagram to find the number of possible menus.

Example 2
(page 680)

3. Telephones A seven-digit telephone number can begin with any digit except 0 or 1.
  a. How many possible choices are there for the first digit? The second digit? The third digit? The seventh digit?
  b. How many different seven-digit telephone numbers are possible?

4. Use the diagram and the Multiplication Counting Principle to find each of the following:
  a. the number of routes from A to C
  b. the number of routes from A to D

A B—C D

Example 3
(page 681)

5. Sports In ice-skating competitions, the order in which competitors skate is determined by a drawing. Suppose there are ten skaters in the finals. How many different orders are possible for the final program?

6. Suppose you are lining up with four cousins for a photo. How many different arrangements are possible?

Example 4
(page 681)

Simplify each expression.

7. $_8P_4$ **8.** $_9P_4$ **9.** $_6P_4$ **10.** $_5P_4$

11. $_7P_7$ **12.** $_7P_6$ **13.** $_7P_5$ **14.** $_7P_2$

Example 5
(page 682)

15. On a bookshelf there are ten books: five novels, two volumes of short stories, and three biographies. In how many ways can you select four books to read in order?

16. A student council has 24 members. A 3-person committee must arrange a car wash. Each person on the committee will have a task: one person will find a location, another person will organize publicity, and the third person will schedule workers. In how many different ways can three students be chosen and given a job?

B   **Apply Your Skills**

Which is greater?

17. $_8P_6$ or $_6P_2$ **18.** $_9P_7$ or $_9P_2$ **19.** $_{10}P_3$ or $_8P_4$

Use the tiles at the left for Exercises 20 and 21.

20. a. How many vowels are there? How many consonants are there?
     b. In how many ways can you choose at random a vowel and then a consonant?
     c. Critical Thinking Would your answer to part (b) be different if you chose a consonant first and then a vowel? Explain.

21. a. What is the number of possible arrangements in which you can select three letters?
     b. Find the probability that you select C, A, and then R.

22. a. Lena wants a password that uses the four letters of her name. How many permutations are possible using each letter only once?
     b. A four-letter password with no repeated letters is assigned randomly from the alphabet. What is the probability that it uses the letters L, E, N, and A?
     c. Writing Is creating a password based on your name a good idea? Explain your reasoning.

Simplify each expression.

23. $\dfrac{_5P_3}{_5P_2}$ **24.** $\dfrac{_4P_3}{_4P_2}$ **25.** $\dfrac{_7P_3}{_7P_2}$

26. a. Suppose your cousin needs to choose a four-digit number to use with a new debit card, and repetition is allowed. Find the number of possible four-digit numbers with repetition.
     b. Critical Thinking Is it easier to guess a password with or without repetition? Explain.

27. License Plates In Indiana, a regular license plate has two numbers that are fixed by county, then one letter, and then four numbers.
     a. How many different license plates are possible in each county?
     b. There are 92 counties in Indiana. How many license plates are possible in the entire state?

28. a. Open-Ended Use the letters of your last name. If any letters are repeated, use only one of them. For example, for the last name Bell, use the letters B, E, and L. In how many ways can the resulting letters be arranged?
     b. In how many ways can two different letters be selected and arranged from your last name?

29. Travel The International Airline Transportation Association (IATA) assigns three-letter codes to each airport. For example, LAX is the code for the Los Angeles International Airport. Letters can be repeated within a code.
  a. How many possible codes are there?
  b. Of the possible codes, the IATA has kept 50 codes for internal purposes. How many codes are available for airports?

30. Radio Stations The call letters of radio and television stations in the United States generally begin with the letter W east of the Mississippi River and the letter K west of the Mississippi. Repetition of letters is allowed.
  a. How many different call letters are possible if each station uses a W or K followed by three letters?
  b. How many different call letters are possible if each station uses a W or K followed by four letters?

Real-World Connection

NASDAQ (NAZ dak) started as an acronym for National Association of Securities Dealers Automated Quotations. Today its volume of trade is larger than the New York Stock Exchange.

31. Stock Exchange The companies listed on the New York Stock Exchange have a one- to three-letter ticker symbol. The companies listed on the NASDAQ exchange have a four- or five-letter symbol. Letters can be repeated in a ticker symbol.
  a. How many companies can be listed on the New York Stock Exchange?
  b. How many companies can be listed on the NASDAQ Exchange?
  c. Which stock exchange can list more companies, and how many more?

C Challenge

32. You know there are 3!, or 6, arrangements of 3 objects. Consider the number of clockwise arrangements of objects placed in a loop, without a beginning or end.

ABC, BCA, and CAB are all part of the same clockwise loop arrangement.

  a. Find the number of clockwise loop arrangements of the ABC.
  b. Use the diagram at the right to help find the number of loop arrangements of ABCD.
  c. Write an expression for the number of clockwise loop arrangements for n objects.

33. Reasoning Suppose $_nP_r = 210$ and $r = 3$. What is the value of n?

34. A three-digit number is formed by randomly selecting from the digits 1, 2, 3, 4, and 5 without replacement.
  a. How many different three-digit numbers can be formed?
  b. How many different numbers with three odd digits can be formed?
  c. Find the probability that the number formed has three odd digits.
  d. Find the probability that the number formed has at least one even digit.

35. Critical Thinking Assume a and b are positive integers. Is the statement $(a - b)! = a! - b!$ true or false? If it is true, explain why. If it is false, give a counterexample.

Standardized Test Prep

Gridded Response

36. The school cafeteria has lunches of one entrée, one vegetable, one salad, and one dessert. The menu has choices of two entrées, 3 vegetables, 3 salads, and 4 desserts. How many different lunches are there?

37. You are planning your schedule for next year. You already know your classes for the last three periods. There are four choices for period 1, two choices for period 2, and 2 choices for period 3. How many combinations are there for the first three periods?

38. Southside High School T-shirts come in two styles, three colors, and four sizes. A student wants to buy a large or extra large black T-shirt. How many choices does the student have?

39. Simplify $_4P_3$.

Take It to the NET
Online lesson quiz at
www.PHSchool.com
Web Code: aea-1208

Mixed Review

Lesson 12-7

Solve each equation. Check your solution.

40. $\dfrac{1}{x} + \dfrac{1}{2x} = 5$

41. $\dfrac{2}{n} + \dfrac{1}{n+1} = \dfrac{11}{n^2+n}$

42. $\dfrac{m}{2} = \dfrac{24-m}{m}$

43. $\dfrac{10}{3v+6} = \dfrac{3v}{v+2} + \dfrac{v^2}{3v+6}$

44. $\dfrac{3w}{w-1} - \dfrac{2w}{w+3} = \dfrac{8w+40}{w^2+2w-3}$

45. $\dfrac{h-5}{h+4} + \dfrac{h+1}{h+3} = \dfrac{-6h-6}{h^2+7h+12}$

Lesson 11-7

Suppose $\triangle ABC$ has right angle C. Find the lengths of the other sides to the nearest whole number.

46. $m\angle A = 45°, BC = 5$

47. $m\angle A = 32°, AB = 64$

48. $m\angle B = 75°, AC = 20$

49. $m\angle B = 8°, BC = 48$

Lesson 10-6

Solve by completing the square. If there is no real solution, write *no solution*.

50. $x^2 + 12x + 1 = 0$

51. $x^2 + 6x + 20 = 0$

52. $x^2 + 8x = 11$

53. $x^2 + 7x + 1 = 13$

54. $2x^2 + 8x + 7 = 9$

55. $x^2 - 18x + 65 = 0$

✓ Checkpoint Quiz 2   Lessons 12-4 through 12-8

iTEXT Instant self-check quiz online and on CD-ROM

Find each product or quotient.

1. $\dfrac{x^2-4}{x+3} \cdot \dfrac{x^2+7x+12}{x-2}$

2. $\dfrac{z+5}{z} \div \dfrac{3z+15}{4z}$

3. $\dfrac{a^3+2a^2-1}{a-3}$

Find each sum or difference.

4. $\dfrac{9}{x-3} - \dfrac{4}{x-3}$

5. $\dfrac{8}{m+2} - \dfrac{6}{3-m}$

6. $\dfrac{6}{t} + \dfrac{3}{t^2}$

Solve each equation.

7. $\dfrac{9}{t} + \dfrac{3}{2} = 12$

8. $\dfrac{10}{z+4} = \dfrac{30}{2z+3}$

9. $c - \dfrac{8}{c} = -7$

10. Hiking Suppose there are four different trails up a mountain.
    a. In how many ways can someone climb up and down the mountain?
    b. In how many ways can someone climb up and down the mountain if that person does not want to take the same trail in both directions?

Combinations

Lesson Preview

What You'll Learn

OBJECTIVE 1 To find combinations

OBJECTIVE 2 To find probability with counting techniques

...And Why

To find the number of different possible 12-person juries, as in Example 2

✓ **Check Skills You'll Need** (For help, go to Lessons 12-8 and 4-6.)

Evaluate each expression.

1. $_5P_3$ **2.** $_6P_3$ **3.** $_7P_3$ **4.** $_7P_4$

A and B are independent events. Find $P(A$ and $B)$ for the given probabilities.

5. $P(A) = \frac{1}{3}, P(B) = \frac{3}{4}$ **6.** $P(A) = \frac{1}{8}, P(B) = \frac{5}{9}$

7. $P(A) = \frac{9}{10}, P(B) = \frac{5}{6}$ **8.** $P(A) = 0.35, P(B) = 0.2$

New Vocabulary • combination

OBJECTIVE

1   **Combinations**

 Interactive lesson includes instant self-check, tutorials, and activities.

Suppose you are making a sandwich with three of these ingredients: turkey, cheese, tomato, and lettuce. Below are the permutations of the four ingredients chosen three at a time.

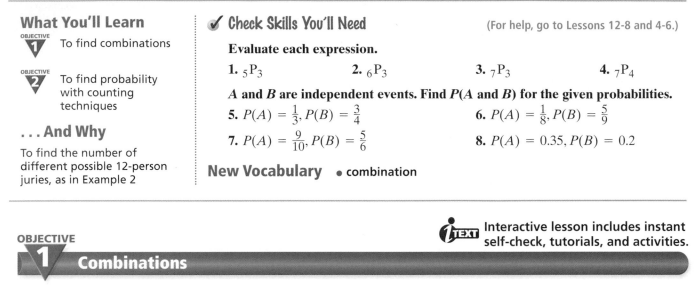

turkey cheese **tomato**
turkey **tomato** cheese
cheese **tomato** turkey
cheese turkey **tomato**
tomato turkey cheese
tomato cheese turkey

turkey cheese lettuce
turkey lettuce cheese
cheese lettuce turkey
cheese turkey lettuce
lettuce turkey cheese
lettuce cheese turkey

turkey **tomato** lettuce
turkey lettuce **tomato**
tomato lettuce turkey
tomato turkey lettuce
lettuce turkey **tomato**
lettuce **tomato** turkey

cheese **tomato** lettuce
cheese lettuce **tomato**
tomato lettuce cheese
tomato cheese lettuce
lettuce cheese **tomato**
lettuce **tomato** cheese

For most people, the *order* of the ingredients within the sandwich does not matter. Ignoring order, there are only four different sandwiches. Each sandwich type is a **combination,** a collection of objects without regard to order.

Every combination of three ingredients has $_3P_3$ or 6 permutations, which are considered the same. Dividing the total number of permutations, $_4P_3$ or 24, by 6 gives the number of different sandwiches without regard to order.

number of different sandwiches =

$$= \frac{\text{number of permutations of ingredients } (_4P_3)}{\text{number of permutations of ingredients in one sandwich } (_3P_3)}$$

$$= \frac{4 \cdot 3 \cdot 2}{3 \cdot 2 \cdot 1}$$

$$= 4$$

Key Concepts

Definition	Combination Notation

The expression $_nC_r$ represents the number of combinations of n objects arranged r at a time.

$$_nC_r = \frac{_nP_r}{_rP_r} = \frac{n(n-1)(n-2)\ldots}{r(r-1)(r-2)\ldots} \quad \begin{array}{l}\leftarrow r \text{ factors, starting with } n \\ \leftarrow r \text{ factors, starting with } r\end{array}$$

Example $_4C_3 = \frac{_4P_3}{_3P_3} = \frac{4 \cdot 3 \cdot 2}{3 \cdot 2 \cdot 1} = 4$

---

1 EXAMPLE Counting Combinations

Simplify $_8C_5$.

$\begin{aligned}
_8C_5 &= \frac{_8P_5}{_5P_5} && \text{Write using permutation notation.} \\
&= \frac{8 \cdot 7 \cdot 6 \cdot 5 \cdot 4}{5 \cdot 4 \cdot 3 \cdot 2 \cdot 1} && \text{Write the product represented by the notation.} \\
&= 56 && \text{Simplify.}
\end{aligned}$

✓ **Check Understanding** ❶ Simplify each expression.

a. $_4C_2$ **b.** $_7C_3$ **c.** $_{10}C_4$

You can use combinations to model real-world situations.

2 EXAMPLE Real-World 🌐 Problem Solving

Real-World 🌐 Connection

Most civil and criminal cases in the United States are tried by a judge with a jury of 12 people.

Juries Twenty people report for jury duty. How many different twelve-person juries can be chosen?

The order in which jury members are listed once the jury members are chosen does not distinguish one jury from another. You need the number of combinations of 20 potential jurors chosen 12 at a time. Evaluate $_{20}C_{12}$.

Method 1 Use pencil and paper.

$\begin{aligned}
_{20}C_{12} &= \frac{_{20}P_{12}}{_{12}P_{12}} \\
&= \frac{20 \cdot 19 \cdot 18 \cdot 17 \cdot 16 \cdot 15 \cdot 14 \cdot 13 \cdot 12 \cdot 11 \cdot 10 \cdot 9}{12 \cdot 11 \cdot 10 \cdot 9 \cdot 8 \cdot 7 \cdot 6 \cdot 5 \cdot 4 \cdot 3 \cdot 2 \cdot 1} \\
&= 125{,}970 \qquad \text{Use a calculator.}
\end{aligned}$

Method 2 Use a graphing calculator.
Use MATH to select nCr in the PRB screen.
$_{20}C_{12} = 125{,}970$

```
20 nCr 12
              125970
```

There are 125,970 different twelve-person juries that can be chosen from a group of 20 people.

✓ **Check Understanding** ❷ **a.** For your history report, you can choose to write about two of a list of five presidents of the United States. Use $_nC_r$ notation to write the number of combinations possible for your report.

     b. Calculate the number of combinations of presidents on whom you could report.

     c. **Critical Thinking** Explain why you should model this situation with combinations, not permutations.

Some probability problems can be solved using permutations.

3 EXAMPLE **Using Permutations in Probability**

Music Suppose you have six new CDs (two rock, two rhythm and blues, and two jazz) to put on a rack. If you choose the CDs at random, what is the probability that the first one is jazz and the second one is rhythm and blues?

number of ways to select jazz then rhythm and blues $= 2 \cdot 2$ **Use the Multiplication Counting Principle.**

number of ways to order 6 CDs arranged 2 at a time $= {}_6P_2$

$P(\text{jazz, then rhythm and blues}) = \dfrac{\text{number of ways to select jazz, then rhythm and blues}}{\text{number of ways to order all 6 CDs}}$

$= \dfrac{2 \cdot 2}{{}_6P_2}$ **Substitute.**

$= \dfrac{4}{30}$ **Simplify the numerator, Find ${}_6P_2$.**

$= \dfrac{2}{15}$ **Simplify.**

The probability that you choose jazz, and then rhythm and blues, is $\frac{2}{15}$.

✔ **Check Understanding** **3** Suppose you have three novels and two history books to read over the summer. If you choose books at random, what is the probability that you first choose a novel, and then a history book?

You can rewrite the probability formula using combination notation, where f is the number of favorable items, t is the total number of items, and r is the number of items being chosen.

$$P(\text{event}) = \frac{\text{number of favorable outcomes}}{\text{total number of outcomes}} = \frac{{}_fC_r}{{}_tC_r}$$

4 EXAMPLE **Using Combinations in Probability**

Money Suppose you have six Virginia quarters and four Connecticut quarters in a change purse. You choose three quarters without looking. What is the probability that all the quarters you choose have a boat on them?

There are 10 quarters in all. The six Virginia quarters have boats on them.

$\begin{array}{l}\text{number of}\\\text{favorable outcomes}\end{array} = {}_6C_3$ **number of ways to choose 3 quarters from the 6 quarters with boats on them**

$\begin{array}{l}\text{number of}\\\text{possible outcomes}\end{array} = {}_{10}C_3$ **number of ways to choose 3 quarters from 10 possible quarters**

Real-World 🌐 **Connection**

The United States Mint began issuing quarters for each state in 1999.

$P(3 \text{ quarters with boats})$

$= \dfrac{\text{number of favorable outcomes}}{\text{total number of outcomes}}$ **Use the definition of probability.**

$= \dfrac{{}_6C_3}{{}_{10}C_3}$ **Substitute.**

$= \dfrac{20}{120} = \dfrac{1}{6}$ **Simplify each expression. Simplify fraction.**

The probability that you choose three quarters with boats is $\frac{1}{6}$, or about 17%.

✓ **Check Understanding** **4** **a.** Suppose you have the quarters in Example 4. You choose four quarters at random. How many combinations are possible?
b. How many combination have only trees?
c. What is the probability that all of the quarters have trees?

EXERCISES

For more practice, see *Extra Practice*.

Practice and Problem Solving

A **Practice by Example**

Simplify each expression.

Example 1
(page 687)

1. $_6C_6$ **2.** $_6C_5$ **3.** $_6C_4$ **4.** $_6C_3$ **5.** $_6C_2$

6. $_6C_1$ **7.** $_8C_6$ **8.** $_8C_2$ **9.** $_7C_5$ **10.** $_7C_2$

Example 2
(page 687)

11. Law For some civil cases, at least nine of twelve jurors must agree on a verdict. How many combinations of nine jurors are possible on a twelve-person jury?

12. For your birthday you received a gift certificate from a music store for three CDs. There are eight you would like to have. If you select the CDs at random, how many different groups of three CDs could you select?

Example 3
(page 688)

13. The colors red, orange, yellow, green, blue, indigo, and violet are written on slips of paper and placed in a hat. What is the probability that the slips will be chosen in the order of the colors of a rainbow (the order listed above)?

Example 4
(page 688)

14. The letters A, B, C, D, E, F, G, H, I, and J are written on slips of paper and placed in a hat. Two letters are then drawn from the hat.
a. What is the number of possible combinations of two letters?
b. How many combinations consist only of the vowels A, E, or I?
c. What is the probability that the letters chosen would consist only of vowels?
d. What is the probability that the letters chosen would be only B, C, D, or F?

15. a. The class president plans to randomly select a committee of three people from three boys and five girls. How many committees are possible?
b. How many possible committees have all boys?
c. What is the probability that the committee will have all boys?
d. Critical Thinking What is the probability that the committee will have no boys?

B **Apply Your Skills**

Find the number of combinations of letters taken three at a time that can be formed from each set of cards.

16. A B C D E   **17.** P Q R

18. E F G H I J K   **19.** M N O P

Classify each situation as a permutation or a combination problem. Explain.

20. A locker contains eight books. You select three books at random. How many different sets of books could you select?

21. You take four books out of the library to read during spring vacation. In how many different orders can you read the four books?

22. a. Geometry Draw four points on your paper like those in Figure 1. Draw line segments so that every point is joined to every other point.
   b. How many segments did you draw?
   c. Find the number of segments using combinations. You are joining four points, two at a time.
   d. How many segments would you need to join each point to all the others in Figure 2?

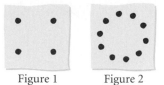

Figure 1   Figure 2

23. A famous problem known as the handshake problem asks, "If ten people in a room shake hands with everyone else in the room, how many different handshakes occur?"
   a. Is this a combination or a permutation problem? Justify your answer.
   b. Solve the problem.
   c. Critical Thinking Is the handshake problem similar to the problem in Exercise 22 part (d)? Explain.

24. Locks A lock like the one at the left is called a combination lock. However, mathematically speaking, it should be called a permutation lock! This is because the order of the numbers *is* important. Suppose a three-number sequence opens the lock, and no numbers are repeated.
   a. How many different sequences are possible?
   b. How many sequences use 32 as the first number?
   c. What is the probability that the sequence of numbers that opens this lock uses 32 as the first number?
   d. Explain why the lock is unlikely to be opened by someone who does not know the correct sequence.

25. Writing Explain the difference between a permutation and a combination.

Simplify each expression.

26. $_2C_2 + {_2C_1} + {_2C_0}$

27. $_3C_3 + {_3C_2} + {_3C_1} + {_3C_0}$

28. a. How many different 3-digit numbers are possible using 2, 3, 5, and 7 if you do not repeat any digits?
   b. What is the probability that a number selected at random is even?

29. Open-Ended Write and solve two problems: one that can be solved using permutations and one that can be solved using combinations.

30. Twelve computer monitors are stored in a warehouse. The warehouse manager knows that three monitors are defective, but the report telling him which ones are defective is missing. He selects five monitors at random to begin testing.
   a. How many different choices of five monitors does the manager have?
   b. In how many ways could he happen to select five monitors that include the defective ones?
   c. What is the probability that he will find the three defective monitors when he tests the first five monitors?

Challenge

Determine whether each statement is *sometimes*, *always*, or *never* true.

31. $_nC_1 = n$ **32.** $_3C_x > x$ **33.** $_nC_{(n-1)} = n$

34. The numerals 3, 4, 5, 6, 7, 10, 12, and 13 are written on slips of paper and placed in a hat. Three slips of paper are then drawn from the hat. What is the probability that the numbers will form a Pythagorean triple?

35. On a particular test, you must answer seven out of ten questions. You also must answer at least four of the first six questions.
   a. In how many ways can you choose four of the first six questions?
   b. How many questions are left after you have answered four of the first six questions? How many must you still answer?
   c. In how many ways can you choose questions to finish the test?
   d. How many different ways are there of completing the test (meeting all its requirements)?

36. a. Graph the function $f(x) = {}_xC_2$ using the replacement set $\{2, 3, 4, 5\}$.
   b. **Critical Thinking** What is $f(x)$? Explain.
   c. **Critical Thinking** Explain why you should not connect the points you graphed in part (a).

Multiple Choice

37. A florist has twelve different flowers to choose from to make a bouquet. In how many different ways can the florist choose three of these flowers?
   A. 36   **B.** 220   **C.** 1320   **D.** 1728

38. What is ${}_5C_3 - {}_8C_2$?
   F. -18 **G.** -2 **H.** -1 **I.** 4

39. Suppose a teacher gives a four-question true-or-false quiz. The correct answers are F, T, T, and F. If a student guesses the answers, how many of the outcomes have exactly 2 correct answers?
   A. 1   **B.** 4   **C.** 6   **D.** 16

Short Response

40. The Pizza Palace offers five different toppings, but you have just enough money for a two-topping pizza. How many different two-topping pizzas can you choose? Is this a combination or a permutation? Explain.

Mixed Review

Lesson 12-8

Simplify each expression.

41. ${}_4P_2$ **42.** ${}_7P_6$ **43.** ${}_7P_4$ **44.** ${}_9P_1$ **45.** ${}_{23}P_1$

46. License Plates In North Carolina, a regular license plate for cars and light trucks has seven characters: three letters followed by four digits. The letters G, I, O, Q, and U are not used. How many different license plates are possible?

Lessons 12-7 and 11-5

Solve each equation. Check your solution. If there is no real solution, write *no solution.*

47. $\frac{4}{x} + \frac{x}{x-4} = 1$ **48.** $\sqrt{r-7} = \sqrt{2r+4}$ **49.** $\frac{2}{z} - \frac{3}{2z} = 5$

50. $\sqrt{3v+10} = v$ **51.** $\frac{1}{a+2} + \frac{1}{a-2} = \frac{10}{a-2}$ **52.** $\sqrt{16m} = \sqrt{m^2}$

Lesson 10-7

Use the Quadratic Formula to solve each equation. If necessary, round answers to the nearest hundredth.

53. $2x^2 + 12x - 11 = 0$ **54.** $x^2 - 7x + 2 = 0$ **55.** $x^2 + 4x - 8 = 0$

56. $-9x^2 + x + 15 = 0$ **57.** $-x^2 - 3x + 18 = 0$ **58.** $1.5x^2 - 20x - 1 = 0$

Answering the Question Asked

When answering a question, be sure to answer the question that is asked. Read the question carefully and identify the quantity that you are asked to find.

1 EXAMPLE

What is the y-intercept of the graph of $y = \frac{6}{x+2} - 4$?

A. -4 **B.** -2 **C.** -1 **D.** -0.5

The question is asking for the y-intercept. To find the y-intercept, let $x = 0$. Therefore $y = \frac{6}{0+2} - 4 = \frac{6}{2} - 4 = 3 - 4 = -1$. The correct answer is C.

In Example 1, notice that the answer for A is the horizontal asymptote, the answer for B is the vertical asymptote, and the answer for D is the x-intercept. Usually answer choices only have meaning for a given question, so you must be careful to answer the question asked.

2 EXAMPLE

If $5x^2 - x + 4$ is divided by $x + 1$, what is the remainder?

F. $5x - 6$ **G.** $5x + 1$ **H.** 10 **I.** 0

Use long division.

$$
\begin{array}{r}
5x - 6 \\
x + 1 \overline{)5x^2 - x + 4} \\
\underline{5x^2 + 5x} \\
-6x + 4 \\
\underline{-6x - 6} \\
10
\end{array}
$$

Choice F is the quotient, and you might be tempted to choose it. The question, however, is asking for the remainder. Choice H is the remainder. That is the correct answer to the question.

EXERCISES

1. What is the remainder when $3x^3 - 2x^2 - 4$ is divided by $x^2 - 2$?
    A. $6x - 8$ **B.** $6x + 8$ **C.** $3x + 2$ **D.** $3x - 2$

2. What is the horizontal asymptote of $y = \frac{3}{x+2} + 2$?
    F. $y = -2$ **G.** $y = 2$ **H.** $y = 0.5$ **I.** $y = 1.5$

3. If $\frac{4x}{3} + \frac{4x}{5} = 1$, what is the value of $4x$?
    A. $\frac{15}{32}$ **B.** $\frac{15}{8}$ **C.** 4 **D.** 8

Chapter Review

Vocabulary

asymptote (p. 644)
combination (p. 686)
constant of variation (p. 637)
inverse variation (p. 637)

multiplication counting principle
(p. 680)
permutation (p. 681)
rational equation (p. 672)

rational expression (p. 652)
rational function (p. 644)

Reading Math
Understanding
Vocabulary

Take It to the NET
Online vocabulary quiz
at **www.PHSchool.com**
Web Code: aej-1251

Choose the correct vocabulary term to complete each sentence.

1. A(n) __?__ is in simplest form if the numerator and the denominator have no common factors other than 1.

2. The y-axis is a vertical __?__ of the function $y = \frac{1}{x}$.

3. A(n) __?__ is an arrangement of some or all of a set of objects in a specific order.

4. The first step in solving a(n) __?__ is to find the least common denominator.

5. An equation of the form $y = \frac{k}{x}$, where k is a constant, is called a(n) __?__.

Skills and Concepts

12-1 Objectives

▼ To solve inverse variations (p. 636)

▼ To compare direct and inverse variation (p. 638)

When two quantities are related so that their product is constant, they form an **inverse variation.** An inverse variation can be written $xy = k$, where k is the **constant of variation.**

Suppose y varies inversely with x. Write an equation for each inverse variation.

6. $x = 6$ when $y = 1$ **7.** $x = 90$ when $y = 0.1$ **8.** $x = 88$ when $y = 0.05$

Each pair of points is on the graph of an inverse variation. Find the missing value.

9. $(9, x)$ and $(3, 12)$ **10.** $(4, 2.65)$ and $(y, 4.24)$ **11.** $(r, 100)$ and $(75, 25)$

Do the data in each table represent a direct variation or an inverse variation? Write an equation to model the data in each table.

12.

x	y
2	35
5	14
10	7

13.

x	y
3	24.6
5	41
10	82

14.

x	y
1	3
4	$\frac{3}{4}$
9	$\frac{1}{3}$

12-2 Objectives

▼ To graph rational functions (p. 644)

▼ To identify types of functions (p. 647)

A **rational function** has a polynomial of at least degree 1 in the denominator. The graph of a rational function may have asymptotes. A line is an **asymptote** of a graph if the graph of the function gets closer to the line as x or y gets larger in absolute value.

Identify the asymptotes of each function. Then graph the function.

15. $y = \frac{8}{x}$ **16.** $xy = 20$ **17.** $y = \frac{6}{x - 5}$ **18.** $y = \frac{3}{x} + 2$

19. Open-Ended Write the equation of a rational function with a graph that is in three quadrants only.

20. Writing Explain why the function $f(x) = \frac{5}{x+3}$ has asymptotes.

12-3 and 12-4 Objectives

▼ To simplify rational expressions (p. 652)

▼ To multiply rational expressions (p. 657)

▼ To divide rational expressions (p. 658)

A **rational expression** is an expression with a variable in the denominator. The **domain** of a variable is all real numbers excluding the values for which the denominator is zero. A rational expression is in simplest form when the numerator and denominator have no common factors other than 1.

You can multiply and divide rational expressions.

$\frac{a}{b} \cdot \frac{c}{d} = \frac{ac}{bd}$ where b and d are nonzero.

$\frac{a}{b} \div \frac{c}{d} = \frac{a}{b} \cdot \frac{d}{c}$ where b, c, and d are nonzero.

Simplify each expression.

21. $\frac{x^2 - 4}{x + 2}$

22. $\frac{5x}{20x + 15}$

23. $\frac{6x - 18}{x - 3}$

24. $\frac{-3t}{t^3 - t^2}$

25. $\frac{z + 2}{2z^2 + z - 6}$

26. $\frac{x^2 - 3x - 10}{x^2 - x - 20}$

Multiply or divide.

27. $\frac{8}{m - 3} \cdot \frac{3m}{m + 1}$

28. $\frac{4t - 12}{t^2 - 9} \cdot (3t + 9)$

29. $\frac{4n + 8}{3n} \div \frac{4}{9n}$

30. $\frac{2e + 1}{8e - 4} \div \frac{4e^2 + 4e + 1}{4e - 2}$

12-5 Objectives

▼ To divide polynomials (p. 662)

To divide a polynomial by a monomial, divide each term by the monomial divisor. To divide a polynomial by another polynomial, use long division. When dividing polynomials, write the answer as quotient $+ \frac{\text{remainder}}{\text{divisor}}$.

Divide.

31. $(14x^2 - 28x) \div 7x$

32. $(24x^6 + 32x^5 - 8x^2) \div 8x^2$

33. $(50x^5 - 7x^4 + x^2) \div x^3$

34. $(x^2 + 8x + 2) \div (x + 1)$

35. $(x^2 + 8x - 16) \div (x + 4)$

36. $(8x^3 - 22x^2 - 5x + 12) \div (4x + 3)$

12-6 Objectives

▼ To add and subtract rational expressions with like denominators (p. 667)

▼ To add and subtract rational expressions with unlike denominators (p. 668)

You can add and subtract rational expressions. Restate each expression with the LCD as the denominator, and then add or subtract the numerators.

If a, b, and c represent polynomials (with $c \neq 0$),

then $\frac{a}{c} + \frac{b}{c} = \frac{a + b}{c}$.

Add or subtract.

37. $\frac{8x}{x - 7} - \frac{4}{x - 7}$

38. $\frac{6}{7x} + \frac{1}{4}$

39. $\frac{9}{3x - 1} + \frac{5x}{2x + 3}$

40. $\frac{7m}{m^2 - 1} - \frac{10}{m + 1}$

41. What is the LCD of $\frac{1}{4}, \frac{2}{x}, \frac{5x}{3x - 2}$, and $\frac{3}{8x}$?

    A. $96x^3 - 64x^2$ **B.** $12x + 2$ **C.** $24x^2 - 16x$ **D.** $27x^2 - 6x - 8$

You can use the least common denominator (LCD) to solve **rational equations.** Check possible solutions to make sure each answer satisfies the original equation.

Solve each equation. Check your solution.

42. $\frac{1}{2} + \frac{3}{t} = \frac{5}{8}$

43. $9 + \frac{1}{t} = \frac{1}{4}$

44. $\frac{3}{m-4} + \frac{1}{3(m-4)} = \frac{6}{m}$

45. $\frac{2c}{c-4} - 2 = \frac{4}{c+5}$

46. $\frac{5}{2x-3} = \frac{7}{3x}$

47. $\frac{2}{x} = \frac{2}{x^2} + \frac{1}{2}$

48. Business A new photocopier can make 72 copies in 2 min. When an older photocopier is working, the two photocopiers can make 72 copies in 1.5 min. How long will it take the older photocopier working alone to make 70 copies?

You can find the number of different outcomes using the **multiplication counting principle.** If there are m ways to make a first selection and n ways to make a second selection, there are $m \times n$ ways to make the two selections.

A **permutation** is an arrangement of objects in a definite order. To calculate $_nP_r$, the number of permutations of n objects taken r at a time, use the following formula.

$$_nP_r = n(n-1)(n-2)\ldots \leftarrow r \text{ factors starting with } n$$

Simplify each expression.

49. $_5P_3$ **50.** $_8P_4$ **51.** $_6P_4$ **52.** $_5P_2$ **53.** $_9P_4$

54. a. Telephones Before 1995, three-digit area codes could begin with any number except 0 or 1. The middle number was either 0 or 1, and the last number could be any digit. How many possible area codes were there?

     b. Beginning in 1995, area codes were not limited to having 0 or 1 as the middle number. How many new area codes became available?

A **combination** is an arrangement of objects without regard to order.

To find $_nC_r$, the combinations of n objects taken r at a time, use the following formula:

$$_nC_r = \frac{_nP_r}{_rP_r} = \frac{n(n-1)(n-2)\ldots}{r(r-1)(r-2)\ldots} \quad \begin{array}{l} \leftarrow r \text{ factors starting with } n \\ \leftarrow r \text{ factors starting with } r \end{array}$$

Simplify each expression.

55. $_6C_5$ **56.** $_{10}C_4$ **57.** $_9C_2$ **58.** $_{11}C_3$ **59.** $_5C_4$

60. Nutrition You want to have three servings of dairy products without having the same food more than once. Milk, yogurt, cottage cheese, and cheddar cheese are in the refrigerator. How many different combinations can you have?

61. A group of 15 friends wants to go to an amusement park. Unfortunately, there are only 10 seats available on the bus they would take. How many combinations of 10 friends could take the bus to the amusement park?

Chapter Test

Find the constant of variation k for each inverse variation.

1. $y = 5$ when $x = 6$

2. $y = 78$ when $x = 0.1$

3. $y = 2.4$ when $x = -10$

4. $y = 5.3$ when $x = 9.1$

5. Which point is *not* on the same graph of an inverse variation as the others?

   A. $(3, 12)$ **B.** $(-9, -4)$

   C. $(6, 6)$ **D.** $(-18, 2)$

6. It took you 1.5 hours to drive to a concert at 40 miles per hour. How long will it take you to drive back at 50 miles per hour?

Identify the asymptotes of each function. Then graph the function.

7. $y = \dfrac{6}{x}$ **8.** $xy = 20$

9. $y = \dfrac{1}{x} + 3$ **10.** $y = \dfrac{4}{x} + 3$

11. Writing Explain how direct variations and inverse variations are similar and different. Include an example of each.

Multiply or divide.

12. $\dfrac{3}{x - 2} \cdot \dfrac{x^2 - 4}{12}$ **13.** $\dfrac{5x}{x^2 + 2x} \div \dfrac{30x^2}{x + 2}$

14. $\dfrac{4w}{3w - 5} \cdot \dfrac{7}{2w}$ **15.** $\dfrac{6c - 2}{c + 5} \div \dfrac{3c - 9}{c}$

16. Open-Ended Write a rational expression for which 6 and 3 are restricted from the domain.

Divide.

17. $\left(12x^4 + 9x^3 - 10x^2\right) \div 3x^3$

18. $\left(x^4 - 16\right) \div (x + 2)$

19. $\left(4x^4 - 6x^3 + x + 7\right) \div (2x - 1)$

20. $\left(6x^3 - 11x^2 - 16x + 13\right) \div (3x + 2)$

21. If three people working together can clean an office suite in two hours, how long will it take a crew of four people to clean the office?

Solve each equation. Check your solution.

22. $\dfrac{v}{3} + \dfrac{v}{v + 5} = \dfrac{-4}{v + 5}$

23. $\dfrac{16}{x + 10} = \dfrac{8}{2x - 1}$

24. $\dfrac{2}{3} + \dfrac{t + 6}{t - 3} = \dfrac{18}{2(t - 3)}$

Add or subtract.

25. $\dfrac{5}{t} + \dfrac{t}{t + 1}$

26. $\dfrac{9}{n} - \dfrac{8}{n + 1}$

27. $\dfrac{2y}{y^2 - 9} - \dfrac{1}{y - 3}$

28. $\dfrac{4b - 2}{3b} + \dfrac{b}{b + 2}$

Classify each situation as a permutation or a combination problem. Explain your choice. Then solve the problem.

29. The 30-member debate club needs a president and treasurer. How many different pairs are possible?

30. How many different ways can you choose two books from the six books on your shelf?

31. You have enough money for two extra pizza toppings. If there are six possible toppings, how many different pairs of toppings can you choose?

Find the number of combinations of letters taken four at a time that can be formed from each set of letters.

32. A E I O U Y   **33.** E Q U A T I O N

34. L E A R N   **35.** A B C D E F G

Simplify each expression.

36. $_4C_3$ **37.** $_8P_6$

38. $_{10}P_7$ **39.** $_5C_2$

40. You have 5 kinds of wrapping paper and 4 different bows. How many different combinations of paper and a bow can you have?

41. Probability There are 15 books on your summer reading list. Three of them are plays, one is poetry, and the rest are novels. What is the probability that you will choose two novels and a play if you choose the books at random?

Standardized Test Prep

Take It to the NET
Online end-of-course test
at www.PHSchool.com
Web Code: aea-1254

Multiple Choice

For Exercises 1–42, choose the correct letter.

1. If $\frac{2x}{3} = 5$, $\frac{2y - 2}{4} = 3$, and $\frac{z}{2} + \frac{z}{3} = 5$, which of the following is true?
   A. $x > y$ B. $y < z$
   C $x = z$ D. $z > x$

2. **Business** A manufacturing company spends $1200 each day on plant costs plus $7 per item for labor and materials. The items sell for $23 each. How many items must the company sell in one day to equal its daily costs?
   F. 52   G. 75   H. 150   I. 200

3. A rectangle has a perimeter of 72 in. The length is 3 in. more than twice the width. What is the length of the rectangle in inches?
   A. 11   B. 22   C. 25   D. 36

4. The test scores of one student are 79, 82, 83, 87, and 94. Find the mean of these scores.
   F. 15   G. 83   H. 85   I. 94

5. **Consumer** Russell wants to purchase a computer that costs $1575. With a better disk drive, the cost of the computer will go up 8%. How much will an upgraded computer cost?
   A. $1701   B. $1449
   C. $1458.33   D. $1712

6. A and B are independent events. If $P(A) = \frac{5}{6}$ and $P(A \text{ and } B) = \frac{1}{8}$, what is $P(B)$?
   F. $\frac{1}{10}$ G. $\frac{3}{20}$ H. $\frac{1}{5}$ I. $\frac{1}{4}$

7. Which relations are functions?

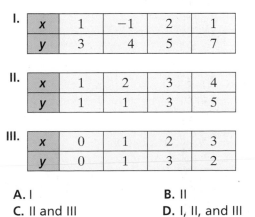

   I.
x	1	−1	2	1
y	3	4	5	7

   II.
x	1	2	3	4
y	1	1	3	5

   III.
x	0	1	2	3
y	0	1	3	2

   A. I   B. II
   C. II and III   D. I, II, and III

8. What is the value of $f(x) = \frac{-3}{x - 1}$ for $x = -1$?
   F. 2   G. $\frac{3}{2}$ H. undefined   I. $-\frac{3}{2}$

9. Which function is modeled by the table?

x	−1	1	3	5
y	−5	−1	3	7

   A. $y = 2x$ B. $y = 2x - 3$
   C. $y = \frac{1}{2}x$ D. $y = \frac{1}{2}x + 3$

10. Find the sixth term of the sequence 14, 9, 4, . . .
    F. −13   G. −11   H. −1   I. 1

11. A parachutist opens her parachute at 800 ft. Her rate of change in altitude is −30 ft/s. Which equation represents her altitude a in feet t seconds after she opens her parachute?
    A. $a = 30t$ B. $a = 800 - 30t$
    C. $a = 800 + 30t$ D. $a = -30t$

12. What is the slope of a line perpendicular to $3x + 2y = 7$?
    F. $-\frac{3}{2}$ G. $-\frac{2}{3}$ H. $\frac{2}{3}$ I. $\frac{3}{2}$

13. What is true of the graphs of the two lines $3y - 8 = -5x$ and $3x = 2y - 18$?
    A. no intersection   B. intersect at $(2, -6)$
    C. intersect at $(-2, 6)$ D. identical

14. What is the solution of the system $-2x - 3y = -15$ and $3x + 2y = 0$?
    F. $(-6, 9)$ G. $(-6, -9)$ H. $(6, -9)$ I. $(6, 9)$

15. Which of the following points are solutions of $4y - 3x \leq 8$?
    I. $(0, 2)$ II. $\left(-3, \frac{1}{4}\right)$
    III. $(5, -17.6)$ IV. $\left(-4, \frac{2}{5}\right)$
    A. I only   B. IV only
    C. II and IV   D. I and III

16. Which statement is true for every solution of the following system?
    $$2y > x + 4$$
    $$3y + 3x > 13$$
    F. $x \leq -3$ G. $y < 5$
    H. $x > 4$ I. $y > 1$

17. Simplify $(2.5 \times 10^4)(3.0 \times 10^{-15})$.
    A. 7.5×10^{19} B. 7.5×10^{-19}
    C. 7.5×10^{11} D. 7.5×10^{-11}

18. Evaluate $a^2b^3c^{-1}$ for $a = 2$, $b = -1$, and $c = -2$.
    F. -2 G. 2 H. 4 I. 8

19. Simplify $\frac{20x^2y^4}{30x^5y^2}$.

    A. $\frac{4x^7y^6}{6}$

    B. $\frac{2y^2}{3x^3}$

    C. $\frac{3y^6}{2x^7}$

    D. $\frac{2}{3}x^{10}y^8$

20. **Interest** Suppose you deposit $1000 in an account paying 5.5% interest, compounded annually. Which expression represents the value of the investment after 10 years?
    F. $1000 \cdot 1.55^{10}$ G. $1000 \cdot 1.055^{10}$
    H. $1000 \cdot 0.055^{10}$ I. $1000 \cdot 10^{1.055}$

21. Simplify $\left(3x^2 - 7x - 2\right) - (8x - 3)$.
    A. $3x^2 + x - 5$ B. $-5x^3 + 1$
    C. $3x^2 - 5x - 5$ D. $3x^2 - 15x + 1$

22. Find the greatest common factor (GCF) of the polynomial $12x^5 + 4x^3 - 16x^2$.
    F. $4x^3$ G. x^3 H. $4x^2$ I. $-2x$

23. What is the standard form of the product $(3x - 1)(5x + 3)$?
    A. $15x^2 + 2x - 3$ B. $15x^2 + 2x + 3$
    C. $15x^2 + 4x + 3$ D. $15x^2 + 4x - 3$

24. Simplify $(2x - 3)(5x + 4)$.
    F. $10x^2 - 12$ G. $10x^2 - 7x - 12$
    H. $10x^2 + 23x - 12$ I. $10x^2 - 7x + 12$

25. Factor $x^2 + 3x - 10$.
    A. $(x - 2)(x + 5)$ B. $(x + 2)(x - 5)$
    C. $(x - 2)(x - 5)$ D. $-(x + 2)(x - 5)$

26. What is the maximum value of y in $y = -3x^2 - 6x - 1$?
    F. -2 G. -1 H. 1 I. 2

27. Find the solutions of $2x^2 + 5x + 3 = 0$.
    A. $-3, -1$ B. $-3, -2$
    C. $\frac{3}{2}, 1$ D. $-\frac{3}{2}, -1$

28. Which are the solutions of $x^2 + 4x - 5 = 0$?
    F. $x = 1$ and $x = 5$
    G. $x = -1$ and $x = 5$
    H. $x = 1$ and $x = -5$
    I. $x = -1$ and $x = -5$

29. How many solutions are there to the quadratic equation $2x^2 + 5x + 1 = 0$?
    A. 0 B. 1 C. 2 D. many

30. What are the solutions of the equation $x^2 - 6x - 11 = 0$?
    F. -8 and 3 G. $3 \pm 4\sqrt{5}$
    H. 8 and -3 I. $3 \pm 2\sqrt{5}$

31. A support wire from the top of a tower is 100 ft long. It is anchored at a spot 60 ft from the base of the tower. Find the height of the tower.
    A. 160 ft   B. 80 ft
    C. 40 ft   D. $4\sqrt{10}$ ft

32. Each leg of a right isosceles triangle is 8 cm long. What is the length of the hypotenuse to the nearest tenth?
    F. 27.7 cm   G. 16 cm
    H. 13.9 cm   I. 11.3 cm

33. Solve the equation $4 + \sqrt{y - 3} = 11$.
    A. 52   B. 46   C. 14   D. 10

34. Triangle DEF is a right triangle with a right angle at F. Which of the following is false?
    F. $\sin D = \frac{EF}{DE}$ G. $\cos D = \frac{DE}{DF}$
    H. $\sin E = \frac{DF}{DE}$ I. $\cos E = \frac{EF}{DE}$

35. The pair of points, $(2, 5)$ and $(x, 10)$ are on the graph of an inverse variation. Find x.
    A. 0   B. 1   C. 4   D. 5

36. **Travel** In the equation $d = rt$, the time t varies inversely with the rate r for a given distance d. If a trip takes 3 hours at 50 mi/h, find the time for the same trip when the rate is 60 mi/h.
    F. 3.6 hours   G. 3.3 hours
    H. 2.5 hours   I. 2.3 hours

37. **Bakery** A baker can shape 2 loaves of bread in 5 minutes. How many loaves can the baker shape in an hour?
    A. 120   B. 12   C. 60   D. 24

38. Which expression is equal to $\frac{3x - 9}{x^2 - 6x + 9}$?
    F. $\frac{1}{3}x - \frac{1}{3}$ G. $\frac{3}{x - 3}$
    H. $\frac{1}{x + 3}$ I. $x^2 + \frac{1}{3}x - \frac{1}{3}$

39. Identify the vertical asymptote of $y = \frac{8}{x - 10}$.
    A. $x = 7$ B. $x = 8$ C. $x = 9$ D. $x = 10$

40. Divide $\frac{x - 4}{x^2 + 2x} \div \frac{x^2 - 16}{x^2 - x}$.
    F. $\frac{x - 1}{x^2 + 6x + 8}$ G. $\frac{1}{x^2 + x - 4}$
    H. $\frac{x^2 - 6x + 4}{x^2 + x - 4}$ I. 1

41. Divide $\frac{5}{m^3}$ by $\frac{10}{m^2}$.
    A. $\frac{m}{2}$ B. $\frac{2}{m}$ C. $\frac{50}{m^5}$ D. $\frac{1}{2m}$

42. Multiply $\frac{x - 1}{x + 3} \cdot \frac{x - 3}{x^2 - 1}$.
    F. $\frac{x - 1}{x^2 - 1}$ G. $\frac{x - 3}{x^2 + 4x + 3}$
    H. $\frac{x - 3}{x + 3}$ I. $\frac{x - 3}{x^2 + 2x - 3}$

Quantitative Comparison

Compare the boxed quantity in Column A with the boxed quantity in Column B. Choose the best answer.

A. The quantity in Column A is greater.
B. The quantity in Column B is greater.
C. The two quantities are equal.
D. The relationship cannot be determined from the information given.

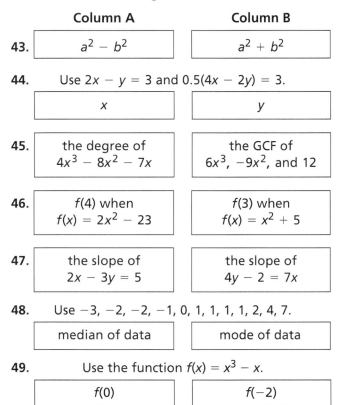

	Column A	Column B
43.	$a^2 - b^2$	$a^2 + b^2$

44. Use $2x - y = 3$ and $0.5(4x - 2y) = 3$.

	x	y

45.	the degree of $4x^3 - 8x^2 - 7x$	the GCF of $6x^3$, $-9x^2$, and 12

46.	$f(4)$ when $f(x) = 2x^2 - 23$	$f(3)$ when $f(x) = x^2 + 5$

47.	the slope of $2x - 3y = 5$	the slope of $4y - 2 = 7x$

48. Use $-3, -2, -2, -1, 0, 1, 1, 1, 1, 2, 4, 7$.

median of data	mode of data

49. Use the function $f(x) = x^3 - x$.

$f(0)$	$f(-2)$

Short Response

50. Find the value of $_{10}P_3$.

51. Simplify $\dfrac{4x + 10}{2x^2 + 7x + 5}$.

52. Factor $4x^2 - 12x + 9$.

53. Geometry What is the length of the diagonal of a rectangle with sides 6 cm and 10 cm?

54. Writing What are extraneous solutions? In what type of equations do they occur?

55. Probability A bag contains 5 green cubes and 7 yellow cubes. You pick two cubes without replacing the first one.
 a. What is the probability of choosing a yellow cube and then a green cube?
 b. What is the probability of choosing two yellow cubes?

56. Evaluate the expression $a(bc)^4$ for $a = -2$, $b = -1$, and $c = 4$.

57. Solve $\dfrac{x}{6} + \dfrac{1}{2} = \dfrac{3}{x}$.

58. The product of two positive integers is 45. The first is 4 less than the second. Find the integers.

59. The solution of the system $ax - 3y = 13$ and $x - by = 8$ is $(2, -3)$. Find a and b.

60. Transportation In 1996, the City Council of New York City voted to increase the number of taxis in the city from 11,787 to 12,187. What was the percent of increase?

61. Find the asymptotes, the x-intercept, and the y-intercept of the graph of $y = \dfrac{5}{x - 2} + 1$.

62. Serena bought a sweatshirt on sale for \$32. The regular price was \$42. What was the percent of decrease, to the nearest tenth of a percent?

63. Do the equations $x - 2 = 5$ and $\dfrac{x}{x - 7} - \dfrac{2}{x - 7} = \dfrac{5}{x - 7}$ have the same solution(s)?

64. Suppose $x - 472 = 1634$. Find the value of $x + 472$.

Extended Response

65. There is a linear relationship between the total length ℓ of a certain species of snake and the tail length (t) of this snake. Here are the measurements for two snakes of this species. Snake 1: $\ell = 150$ mm and $t = 19$ mm; Snake 2: $\ell = 300$ mm and $t = 40$ mm. Use the ordered pairs (ℓ, t).
 a. Find a linear equation for these data points.
 b. Use this linear equation to estimate the tail length of a snake with a total length of 200 mm.
 c. Use this linear equation to estimate the total length of a snake with a tail length of 61 mm.

66. Geometry In $\triangle ABC$, $\angle C$ is a right angle, $AB = 7$, and $m\angle B = 28°$. What are the lengths of $\overline{BC}$ and $\overline{AC}$ to the nearest hundredth?

67. The table shows the closing prices of a stock over a period of 5 days. Graph this relation and determine whether it is a linear function. Explain why or why not.

Day	1	2	3	4	5
Price	12	$12\frac{1}{2}$	$12\frac{1}{4}$	13	$13\frac{1}{4}$

Good Vibrations

Applying Functions When you pluck a guitar string, it vibrates at a frequency corresponding to the note being played. In an acoustic guitar the hollow chamber and vibration of the wood shell amplify the sound produced by the strings. Electric guitars rely on electromagnetic pickups to detect the string's vibration and relay a signal to an amplifier. You can use the frequencies of musical notes to calculate the length of a guitar string.

Bridge

Electric Plucking

In 1952 Gibson introduced a solid-body electric guitar incorporating design elements by guitarist Les Paul.

Activity 1

Materials: pencil, paper or poster board

Cut a 70-cm length of 6-cm wide paper or poster board. This paper will represent the length of a string from nut to bridge. (See diagram and photo.)

a. Use the frequency 220.0 cycles/s and length 70 cm to find the constant k for the A string on page 701.

b. Use the value of k and the frequencies in the diagram to calculate the positions of each of the frets shown. Draw the frets on your model.

Building a Guitar

A master guitar maker invests about 120 hours of intensive work to build a guitar. The tonal properties of the wood used for the soundboard are crucial to the sound the guitar produces.

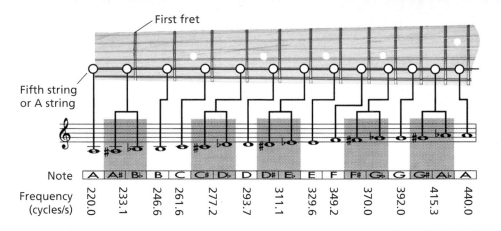

First fret

Fifth string or A string

Note	A	A# Bb	B	C	C# Db	D	D# Eb	E	F	F# Gb	G	G# Ab	A
Frequency (cycles/s)	220.0	233.1	246.6	261.6	277.2	293.7	311.1	329.6	349.2	370.0	392.0	415.3	440.0

Musical Interlude

When you pluck the A string, it vibrates according to the equation below. Pressing a string against a fret changes its length and consequently its frequency.

$f = \dfrac{k}{L}$, where

f = frequency of string vibration (cycles/s)

k = constant

L = length of string (cm)

Activity 2

a. The distance from C to G is 7 frets, which corresponds to 7 half-steps or 3.5 full steps. The C and G notes form a musical interval called a perfect fifth. Calculate the ratio of the frequency of G to the frequency of C.

b. Locate other perfect fifths and calculate each frequency ratio. What do you notice?

c. Calculate the frequency ratio of an octave (6 steps) and of a major third (2 steps).

d. **Make a Conjecture** Predict the ratio of a perfect fourth (2.5 steps). Check your prediction by calculating the ratio.

Activity 3

Materials: graphing calculator or graphing utility

Use your model from Activity 1.

a. Plot the points (Frequency, String Length).

b. Plot the points (Fret Number, Frequency).

c. **Reasoning** Which of the sets of points plotted above lie on the graph of an inverse function? Explain.

Fifth string or A string

Frets

Neck

First fret

Nut

Headstock

Guitars Through Time

Guitars date from as early as the 1500s. The acoustic guitar at the left, from 1627, has wire strings, which produce greater volume. The electric guitar above, from 1958, has two volume controls and one tone control.

Take It to the NET For more information about guitars, go to www.PHSchool.com.
Web Code: aee-1253

Extra Practice

● **Lesson 1-1** Define variables and write an equation to model each situation.

1. The total length of the edges of a cube is 12 times the length of an edge.

2. The total cost of lunch is $5.50 times the number of people at the table.

3. The area of a rectangle is 12 cm times the length of the rectangle.

4. The cost of a telephone call is 75 cents plus 25 cents times the number of minutes.

● **Lesson 1-2** Simplify each expression.

5. $4 + 3 \cdot 8$ **6.** $2 \cdot 3^2 - 7$ **7.** $6 \cdot (5 - 2) - 9$ **8.** $2 - 12 \div 3$

9. $4^2 + 8 \div 2$ **10.** $\frac{1}{2} \div \frac{4}{3}$ **11.** $-6 \cdot 4.2 - 5 \div 2$ **12.** $9 - (3 + 1)^2$

13. $2 + 6 \cdot 8 \div 4$ **14.** $6 + 8 \div 2 - 3$ **15.** $10 \div 5 \cdot 2 + 6$ **16.** $5 + 4 \cdot (8 - 6)^2$

● **Lesson 1-3** Use <, =, or > to compare.

17. $0.45 \ \blacksquare \ 0.54$ **18.** $-1.08 \ \blacksquare \ -1.008$ **19.** $\frac{3}{7} \ \blacksquare \ \frac{11}{25}$ **20.** $1.4 \ \blacksquare \ \frac{18}{11}$

21. $0.444 \ldots \ \blacksquare \ \frac{4}{9}$ **22.** $\frac{4}{13} \ \blacksquare \ \frac{4}{15}$ **23.** $0.101101110 \ldots \ \blacksquare \ \frac{1}{9}$ **24.** $\pi \ \blacksquare \ \frac{22}{7}$

● **Lessons 1-4 to 1-8** Simplify each expression.

25. $22 + (-33)$ **26.** $45 + (-54)$ **27.** $-\frac{4}{3} - \frac{4}{5}$ **28.** $\frac{4}{13} - \frac{4}{13}$

29. $|12 - 21|$ **30.** $|12| - |-21|$ **31.** $-(-(11 - 22))$ **32.** $\left| \frac{2}{3} + \frac{4}{5} \right|$

33. $(-2)(44)$ **34.** $(-3)^2$ **35.** -3^2 **36.** $\left(\frac{3}{2} \right)\left(-\frac{22}{33} \right)$ **37.** $\frac{3^2}{2^3}$ **38.** $\frac{-5^2}{(-5)^2}$

39. $81 \div (-9)$ **40.** $\frac{4^2}{5^2}$ **41.** $\frac{2 \cdot 3 + 4}{2(3 + 4)}$ **42.** $1 + \frac{1}{2 + \frac{1}{3}}$ **43.** $\left(\frac{5}{7} \right)^2$ **44.** $\frac{2}{3} \div \frac{4}{9}$

45. $\begin{bmatrix} -3 & 0 \\ 11 & -5 \end{bmatrix} + \begin{bmatrix} -4 & 6 \\ -8 & 13 \end{bmatrix}$ **46.** $\begin{bmatrix} 6 & 12 \\ -9 & 7 \end{bmatrix} - \begin{bmatrix} 8 & -6 \\ 15 & 0 \end{bmatrix}$ **47.** $\begin{bmatrix} 4.2 & 0.6 \\ 1.7 & 9.5 \end{bmatrix} + \begin{bmatrix} 5.8 & -3.5 \\ 0.2 & 4.9 \end{bmatrix}$

Simplify each expression.

48. $-4(a + 3)$ **49.** $-12\left(\frac{4}{3}x - 1 \right)$ **50.** $5 + 6(m + 1)$ **51.** $\frac{4}{9}(18 - 9t)$

52. $1 + 3 + 5 + 7$ **53.** $1 - 3 + 5 - 7$ **54.** $-3(7w) + 7(3w)$ **55.** $2(1 - d) - (2d + 1)$

56. $6c + 2(4c - 3)$ **57.** $5(2 - j) + (2j - 3)$ **58.** $\frac{1}{3}(12 - 6r)$ **59.** $6\left(\frac{1}{2} - \frac{2}{3}y \right)$

● **Lesson 1-9** Graph the points on the same coordinate plane.

60. $(2, 0)$ **61.** $(-4, -1)$ **62.** $(0, -2)$ **63.** $\left(-1, -1\frac{1}{4} \right)$ **64.** $\left(\frac{1}{2}, \frac{1}{2} \right)$ **65.** $(3, 3.5)$

66. Make a scatter plot of the data. Describe the trend of the data.

Cover Price and Number of Pages of Some Magazines

Cover Price	$2.25	$2.50	$3.75	$3.00	$4.95	$1.95	$2.95	$2.50
Number of Pages	208	68	122	124	234	72	90	90

● **Lessons 2-1 to 2-3** Solve each equation.

1. $h - 4 = 10$ **2.** $8p - 3 = 13$ **3.** $8j - 5 + j = 67$ **4.** $6t = -42$

5. $-n + 8.5 = 14.2$ **6.** $6(t + 5) = -36$ **7.** $m - 9 = 11$ **8.** $\frac{1}{2}(s + 5) = 7.5$

9. $\frac{s}{3} = 8$ **10.** $7h + 2h - 3 = 15$ **11.** $\frac{7}{12}x = \frac{3}{14}$ **12.** $3r - 8 = -32$

13. $8g - 10g = 4$ **14.** $-3(5 - t) = 18$ **15.** $3(c - 4) = -9$ **16.** $\frac{3}{8}z = 9$

17. $0.1(h + 20) = 3$ **18.** $\frac{3m}{5} = 6$ **19.** $4 - y = 10$ **20.** $8q + 2q = -7.4$

Define a variable and write an equation for each situation. Then solve.

21. Your test scores for the semester are 87, 84, and 85. Can you raise your test average to 90 with your next test?

22. You spend $\frac{1}{2}$ of your allowance each week on school lunches. Each lunch costs $1.25. How much is your weekly allowance?

● **Lesson 2-4** Solve each equation. If the equation is an identity, write *identity*. If it has no solution, write *no solution*.

23. $6t = 6$ **24.** $5m + 3 = 9m - 1$ **25.** $8d = 4d - 8$

26. $4h + 5 = 9h$ **27.** $2(3x \quad 6) = 3(2x - 4)$ **28.** $7t = 80 + 9t$

29. $w - 9 = 4w$ **30.** $m + 3m = 4$ **31.** $-b + 4b = 8b - b$

32. $-p = p - 4$ **33.** $-(h + 7) = -8h$ **34.** $6p + 1 = 3(2p + 1)$

35. $10z - 5 + 3z = 8 - z$ **36.** $3(g - 1) + 7 = 3g + 4$ **37.** $17 - 20q = (-13 - 5q)4$

● **Lesson 2-5**

38. **Transportation** A bus traveling 40 mi/h and a car traveling 50 mi/h cover the same distance. The bus travels 1 h more than the car. How many hours did each travel?

● **Lesson 2-6** Solve each equation for the given variable.

39. $A = \ell w; w$ **40.** $C = \frac{W + t}{V}; t$ **41.** $h = \frac{r}{t}(p - m); r$ **42.** $P = 2\ell + 2w; \ell$

43. $V = \pi r^2 h; h$ **44.** $m = \frac{t}{b - a}; t$ **45.** $y = bt - c; b$ **46.** $g = 1.9\frac{m}{r^2}; m$

● **Lesson 2-7** Find the mean, median, and mode for each set of data.

47. 36, 42, 35, 40, 35, 51, 41, 35   **48.** 1.2, 0.9, 0.7, 1.1, 0.8, 1.3, 0.6   **49.** 5, 8, 6, 8, 3, 5, 8, 6, 5, 9

50. A student surveyed the members of the drama club. She included a question about age. Her results are below.

Ages of Drama Club Members
14 18 16 15 17 14 15 18 15
13 14 15 18 14 17 16 14 16

a. Make a stem-and-leaf plot for the data.
b. What is the median age of the drama club members?

● **Lessons 3-1 to 3-4** Solve each inequality. Graph and check your solution.

1. $-8w < 24$

2. $9 + p \leq 17$

3. $\frac{r}{4} > -1$

4. $7y + 2 \leq -8$

5. $t - 5 \geq -13$

6. $9h > -108$

7. $8w + 7 > 5$

8. $\frac{s}{6} \leq 3$

9. $\frac{6c}{5} \geq -12$

10. $-8\ell + 3.7 \leq 31.7$

11. $9 - t \leq 4$

12. $m + 4 \geq 8$

13. $y + 3 < 16$

14. $n - 6 \leq 8.5$

15. $12b - 5 > -29$

16. $4 - a > 15$

17. $4 - x \leq 3$

18. $1 - 4d \geq 4 - d$

19. $n + 7 \leq 3n - 1$

20. $\frac{s}{2} + 1 < s + 2$

21. $3 - \frac{2x}{3} > 5$

22. $8r - \frac{r}{6} > \frac{1}{6} - 8$

23. $1.4 + 2.4x < 0.6$

24. $x - 2 < 3x - 4$

25. The booster club raised $102 in their car wash. They want to buy $18 soccer balls for the soccer team. Write and solve an inequality to find how many soccer balls they can buy.

26. You earn $7.50 per hour and need to earn $35. Write and solve an inequality to find how many hours you must work.

● **Lesson 3-5** Solve each compound inequality.

27. $8 < w + 3 < 10$

28. $-6 < t - 1 < 6$

29. $6m - 15 \leq 9$ or $10m > 84$

30. $9j - 5j \geq 20$ and $8j > -36$

31. $37 < 3c + 7 < 43$

32. $3 < 5 + 6h < 10$

33. $1 + t < 4 < 2 + t$

34. $2 + 3w < -1 < 3w + 5$

35. $2x - 3 \leq x$ and $2x + 1 \geq x + 3$

36. $3n - 7 > n + 1$ or $4n - 5 < 3n - 3$

● **Lesson 3-6** Choose a variable and write an absolute value inequality that represents each set of numbers.

37. all real numbers less than 2 units from 0

38. all real numbers more than 0.5 units from 4.5

39. all real numbers less than 1 unit from -4

40. all real numbers 3 or more units from -1

41. all real numbers less than or equal to 5 units from 3

Solve each inequality. Graph and check your solution.

42. $|x| < 5$

43. $|t| > 1$

44. $|t| - 5 \leq 3$

45. $|-6m + 2| > 20$

46. $|3c| - 1 \geq 11$

47. $|8 - w| \leq 8$

48. $|2b + 3| < 7$

49. $|c - 5| \leq 6$

50. $|n| + 4 \leq 5$

51. Write an absolute value inequality that has numbers between 2 and 3 as the solutions.

52. Holes with radius 3 cm must be drilled in sheets of metal. The radius must have an error no more than 0.01 cm. Write an absolute value inequality whose solutions are acceptable radii.

● **Lessons 4-1 and 4-2** Solve each proportion.

1. $\frac{3}{4} = \frac{-6}{m}$ **2.** $\frac{t}{7} = \frac{3}{21}$ **3.** $\frac{9}{j} = \frac{3}{16}$ **4.** $\frac{2}{5} = \frac{w}{65}$

5. $\frac{s}{15} = \frac{4}{45}$ **6.** $\frac{9}{4} = \frac{x}{10}$ **7.** $\frac{10}{q} = \frac{8}{62}$ **8.** $\frac{3}{2} = \frac{18}{y}$

9. $\frac{5}{9} = \frac{t}{3}$ **10.** $\frac{6}{m} = \frac{3}{5}$ **11.** $\frac{c}{8} = \frac{13.5}{36}$ **12.** $\frac{7}{9} = \frac{35}{x}$

13. Architecture A blueprint scale is 1 in. : 4 ft. On the plan, the garage is 2 in. by 3 in. What are the actual dimensions of the garage?

14. The ratio of the weights of two pieces of pottery is 3 : 5. The weight of the lighter piece is 4.3 lb. Find the weight of the heavier.

15. The scale on a map is 1 in. : 15 mi. The distance between two cities is 25 mi. Find the distance in inches between the cities on the map.

● **Lesson 4-3** Write an equation to model each question and solve.

16. What is 10% of 94?   **17.** What percent of 10 is 4?   **18.** 147 is 14% of what?

19. What percent of 1.2 is 6?   **20.** 13.2 is 55% of what?   **21.** What is 0.4% of 800?

22. What is 75% of 68?   **23.** 5 is 200% of what?   **24.** What percent of 54 is 28?

25. 114 is 95% of what?   **26.** What percent of 20 is 31?   **27.** What is 35% of 15?

● **Lesson 4-4** Find each percent of change. Describe each as a percent of increase or decrease. Round to the nearest percent.

28. $4.50 to $5.00   **29.** 56 in. to 65 in.   **30.** 18 oz to 12 oz

31. 1 s to 3 s   **32.** 8 lb to 5 lb   **33.** 6 km to 6.5 km

34. 39 h to 40 h   **35.** 7 ft to 2 ft   **36.** 0.2 mL to 0.45 mL

37. $\frac{1}{2}$ tsp to $\frac{1}{8}$ tsp   **38.** 18 kg to 20 kg   **39.** 55 min to 50 min

Find the percent error of each measurement. Round to the nearest tenth of a percent.

40. 18 mm   **41.** 1.8 cm   **42.** 18.0 cm   **43.** 3 mm

● **Lesson 4-5** The results of rolling a number cube 54 times are at the right. Use the results to find each probability.

6 3 4 5 1 1 5 5 3 6 3 2 1 3 3 3 2 1
2 3 6 3 3 4 5 1 2 2 6 3 3 6 5 4 5 3
2 5 1 4 5 2 6 2 5 2 1 2 5 3 2 4 6 3

44. $P(3)$ **45.** $P(4)$ **46.** $P(\text{not } 5)$

47. $P(7)$ **48.** $P(\text{even number})$ **49.** $P(\text{not } 1)$

● **Lesson 4-6** You roll a blue number cube and a red number cube. Find each probability.

50. $P(\text{blue 3 and red 2})$ **51.** $P(\text{blue odd and red 6})$ **52.** $P(\text{blue 5 and red less than 4})$

You have 3 green marbles, 5 red marbles, and 1 yellow marble in a bag. You pick two marbles from the bag. You pick the second one without replacing the first one. Find each probability.

53. $P(\text{red then green})$ **54.** $P(\text{yellow then red})$ **55.** $P(\text{two greens})$

● **Lesson 5-1** Sketch a graph to describe each situation. Label each section of the graph.

  1. the number of apples on a tree over one year

  2. the amount of milk in your bowl as you eat cereal

  3. the energy you use in a 24-h period

  4. your distance from home plate after your home run

● **Lesson 5-2** Find the range of each function when the domain is $\{-4, -1, 0, 3\}$.

  5. $y = 6x - 5$ **6.** $y = |x| - 2$ **7.** $y = x^2 + 3x + 1$

  8. $y = \frac{1}{2}x + 8$ **9.** $y = -x^2 - x$ **10.** $y = \frac{2}{3}x$

  11. $y = |x - 2|$ **12.** $y = 2x^2 - 5$ **13.** $y = |4 - x|$

  Use a mapping diagram to determine whether each relation is a function.

  14. $\{(1, 2), (2, 3), (3, 4), (4, 5), (5, 6)\}$ **15.** $\{(5, 2), (1, 3), (4, 7), (5, 6), (0, 4)\}$

  16. $\{(3.4, 2), (5.6, 2), (0.1, 2), (2.8, 2)\}$ **17.** $\{(6, 7), (5, 2), (7, 7), (4, 3), (0, 0)\}$

● **Lesson 5-3** Graph each function.

  18. $y = 2x + 1$ **19.** $y = 4 - x$ **20.** $y = |x| - 3$

● **Lessons 5-3 and 5-4** Write a function rule for each table.

21.

x	f(x)
−3	−1
−1	1
1	3
3	5

22.

x	f(x)
0	0
3	6
6	12
9	18

23.

x	f(x)
21	14
25	18
29	22
33	26

24.

x	f(x)
−8	−4
−6	−3
−4	−2
−2	−1

25. a. Write a sentence and an equation to describe the relationship between the number of notebooks and the price.
    b. If you have $5, can you buy a notebook for each of your classes? Explain.

Notebooks	Price
1	$0.99
2	$1.98
3	$2.97

● **Lesson 5-5** Graph the direct variation that includes the given point. Write the equation of the line.

  26. $(5, 4)$ **27.** $(7, 7)$ **28.** $(-3, -10)$

  29. $(4, -8)$ **30.** $(-2, 9)$ **31.** $(11, 1)$

  32. The stretch s of a spring is directly proportional to the force F. A force of 2 newtons produces a stretch of 3 cm. Find the force that produces a stretch of 4.5 cm.

● **Lesson 5-6** Find the second and fifth terms of each sequence.

  33. $A(n) = 22 + (n - 1)11$ **34.** $A(n) = -2 + (n - 1)(-2)$

  35. $A(n) = -2 + (n - 1)$ **36.** $A(n) = 1 + 4(n - 1)$

Chapter 6 Extra Practice

● **Lesson 6-1** Find the rate of change for each situation.

1. growing from 1.4 m to 1.6 m in one year

2. bicycling 3 mi in 15 min and 7 mi in 55 min

3. growing 22.4 mm in 14 s

4. reading 8 pages in 9 min and 22 pages in 30 min

● **Lessons 6-2 to 6-4** Find the slope and y-intercept.

5. $y = 6x + 8$
6. $3x + 4y = -24$
7. $2y = 8$
8. $y = \frac{-3}{4}x - 8$

Find the x- and y-intercepts for each equation.

9. $6x + y = 12$
10. $y = -7x$
11. $y = \frac{1}{2}x + 3$
12. $-2y = 5x - 12$

Write the equation in point-slope form for the line through the given point with the given slope.

13. $(4, 6); m = -5$
14. $(3, -1); m = 1$
15. $(8, 5); m = \frac{1}{2}$
16. $(0, -6); m = \frac{4}{3}$

17. $(-2, 7); m = 2$
18. $(-5, -9); m = -3.5$
19. $(4, 0); m = 7$
20. $(6, -4); m = -\frac{1}{5}$

Graph each equation.

21. $y = 2x - 3$
22. $x + 4y = 8$
23. $y - 5 = -2(x + 1)$
24. $x + 3 = 0$

25. $4x - 3y = 12$
26. $y = -1$
27. $y = \frac{2}{3}x - 4$
28. $y + 1 = -\frac{1}{2}(x + 2)$

A line passes through the given points. Write an equation for the line in slope-intercept form.

29. $(2, 5)$ and $(4, 8)$
30. $(1, 6)$ and $(7, 3)$
31. $(-2, 4)$ and $(3, 9)$
32. $(1, 6)$ and $(9, -4)$

33. $(0, -7)$ and $(-1, 0)$
34. $(7, 0)$ and $(3, -4)$
35. $(0, 0)$ and $(-7, 1)$
36. $(10, 0)$ and $(0, 7)$

● **Lesson 6-5** Write an equation in standard form that satisfies the given conditions.

37. parallel to $y = 4x + 1$, through $(-3, 5)$

38. perpendicular to $y = -x - 3$, through $(0, 0)$

39. perpendicular to $3x + 4y = 12$, through $(7, 1)$

40. parallel to $2x - y = 6$, through $(-6, -9)$

41. perpendicular to $y = -2x + 5$, through $(4, -10)$

42. parallel to $2y = 5x + 12$, through $(2, -1)$

43. parallel to the x-axis and through $(4, -1)$

44. through $(4, 44)$ and parallel to the y-axis

● **Lesson 6-6**

45. a. Graph the (ages, grades) data of some students in a school at the right.
   b. Draw a trend line.
   c. Find the equation of the line of best fit.

$(10, 6), (16, 10), (15, 10), (18, 12), (17, 11),$
$(17, 12), (19, 12), (16, 11), (11, 7), (15, 9), (13, 8)$

● **Lesson 6-7** Graph each equation by translating $y = |x|$ or $y = -|x|$.

46. $y = |x| + 1$
47. $y = |x + 2|$
48. $y = |x - 2|$
49. $y = -|x - 1|$

50. $y = -|x + 1|$
51. $y = -|x| + 1$
52. $y = |x + 0.5|$
53. $y = |x| - 4$

● **Lesson 7-1 Solve each system by graphing.**

1. $x - y = 7$

$3x + 2y = 6$

2. $y = 2x + 3$

$y = -\frac{3}{2}x - 4$

3. $y = -2x + 6$

$3x + 4y = 24$

● **Lesson 7-2 Solve each system by using substitution.**

4. $x - y = 13$

$y - x = -13$

5. $3x - y = 4$

$x + 5y = -4$

6. $x + y = 4$

$y = 7x + 4$

● **Lesson 7-3 Solve each system by elimination.**

7. $x + y = 19$

$x - y = -7$

8. $-3x + 4y = 29$

$3x + 2y = -17$

9. $3x + y = 3$

$-3x + 2y = -30$

10. $6x + y = 13$

$y - x = -8$

11. $4x - 9y = 61$

$10x + 3y = 25$

12. $4x - y = 105$

$x + 7y = -10$

● **Lesson 7-4 Write a system of equations to model each problem and solve.**

13. Suppose you have 12 coins that total 32 cents. Some of the coins are nickels and the rest are pennies. How many of each coin do you have?

14. Claire bought three bars of soap and five sponges for $2.31. Steve bought five bars of soap and three sponges for $3.05. Find the cost of each item.

15. The perimeter of a rectangular lot is 74 feet. The cost of fencing along the two lengths is $1 per foot, and the cost of fencing along the two widths is $3.50 per foot. Find the dimensions of the lot if the total cost of the fencing is $159.

16. A chemist wants to make a 10% solution of fertilizer. How much water and how much of a 30% solution should the chemist mix to get 30 L of a 10% solution?

17. Fruit drink A consists of 6% pure fruit juice and drink B consists of 15% pure fruit juice. How much of each kind of drink should you mix together to get 4 L of a 10% concentration of fruit juice?

18. A motor boat traveled 12 miles with the current, turned around, and returned 12 miles against the current to its starting point. The trip with the current took 2 hours and the trip against the current took 3 hours. Find the speed of the boat and the speed of the current.

● **Lesson 7-5 Graph each linear inequality.**

19. $y < x$

20. $y < x - 4$

21. $y > -6x + 5$

22. $y \leq 14 - x$

23. $y \geq \frac{1}{4}x - 3$

24. $2x + 3y \leq 6$

● **Lesson 7-6 Solve each system by graphing.**

25. $y \leq 5x + 1$

$y > x - 3$

26. $y > 4x + 3$

$y \geq -2x - 1$

27. $y > -x + 2$

$y > x - 4$

28. $y < -2x + 1$

$y > -2x - 3$

29. $y \leq 5$

$y \geq -x + 1$

30. $y \leq 5x - 2$

$y > 3$

● **Lessons 8-1 to 8-5** Simplify each expression. Use only positive exponents.

1. $(2t)^{-6}$

2. $5m^5m^{-8}$

3. $(4.5)^4(4.5)^{-2}$

4. $(m^7t^{-5})^2$

5. $(x^2n^4)(n^{-8})$

6. $(w^{-2}j^{-4})^{-3}(j^7j^3)$

7. $(t^6)^3(m)^2$

8. $(3n^4)^2$

9. $\dfrac{r^5}{g^{-3}}$

10. $\dfrac{1}{a^{-4}}$

11. $\dfrac{w^7}{w^{-6}}$

12. $\dfrac{6}{t^{-4}}$

13. $\dfrac{a^2b^{-7}c^4}{a^5b^3c^{-2}}$

14. $\dfrac{(2t^5)^3}{4t^8t^{-1}}$

15. $\left(\dfrac{a^6}{a^7}\right)^{-3}$

16. $\left(\dfrac{c^5c^{-3}}{c^{-4}}\right)^{-2}$

Evaluate each expression for $m = 2, t = -3, w = 4,$ and $z = 0$.

17. t^m

18. t^{-m}

19. $(w \cdot t)^m$

20. $w^m \cdot t^m$

21. $(w^z)^m$

22. w^mw^z

23. $z^{-t}(m^t)^z$

24. $w^{-t}t^t$

Write each number in scientific notation.

25. 34,000,000

26. 0.00063

27. 1500

28. 0.0002

29. 360,000

30. 6,200,000,000

31. 0.05

32. 0.000000000891

Write each number in standard notation.

33. 8.05×10^6

34. 3.2×10^{-7}

35. 9.0×10^8

36. 4.25×10^{-4}

37. 2.35×10^2

38. 6.3×10^4

39. 2.001×10^{-5}

40. 5.2956×10^3

● **Lesson 8-6** Find the common ratio of each sequence. Then find the next two terms.

41. $12, 18, 27, \ldots$

42. $2, 1, 0.5, \ldots$

43. $-1, -0.2, -0.04, \ldots$

44. $-2, -4, -8, \ldots$

45. $2, 6, 18, \ldots$

46. $1.2, -0.6, 0.3, \ldots$

47. $30, 10, \frac{10}{3}, \ldots$

48. $-2.25, -9, -36, \ldots$

● **Lesson 8-7** Evaluate each function for the domain $\{-1, 0, 1, 2\}$. As the values of the domain increase, do the values of the function *increase* or *decrease*?

49. $y = 3^x$

50. $y = \left(\frac{3}{4}\right)^x$

51. $y = 1.5^x$

52. $y = \frac{1}{2} \cdot 3^x$

53. $y = -3 \cdot 7^x$

54. $y = -(4)^x$

55. $y = 3 \cdot \left(\frac{1}{5}\right)^x$

56. $y = 2^x$

57. $y = 2 \cdot 3^x$

58. $y = (0.8)^x$

59. $y = 2.5^x$

60. $y = -4 \cdot (0.2)^x$

● **Lesson 8-8** Identify each function as *exponential growth* or *exponential decay*. Then identify the growth factor or decay factor.

61. $y = 8^x$

62. $y = \frac{3}{4} \cdot 2^x$

63. $y = 9 \cdot \left(\frac{1}{2}\right)^x$

64. $y = 4 \cdot 9^x$

65. $y = 0.65^x$

66. $y = 3 \cdot 1.5^x$

67. $y = \frac{2}{5} \cdot \left(\frac{1}{4}\right)^x$

68. $y = 0.1 \cdot 0.9^x$

Write an exponential function to model each situation. Find each amount after the specified time.

69. \$200 principal, 4% compounded annually for 5 years

70. \$1000 principal, 3.6% compounded monthly for 10 years

71. \$3000 investment, 8% loss each year for 3 years

Extra Practice

● **Lesson 9-1** Simplify. Write each answer in standard form.

1. $(5x^3 + 3x^2 - 7x + 10) - (3x^3 - x^2 + 4x - 1)$ **2.** $(x^2 + 3x - 2) + (4x^2 - 5x + 2)$

3. $(4m^3 + 7m - 4) + (2m^3 - 6m + 8)$ **4.** $(8t^2 + t + 10) - (9t^2 - 9t - 1)$

5. $(-7c^3 + c^2 - 8c - 11) - (3c^3 + 2c^2 + c - 4)$ **6.** $(6v + 3v^2 - 9v^3) + (7v - 4v^2 - 10v^3)$

7. $(s^4 - s^3 - 5s^2 + 3s) - (5s^4 + s^3 - 7s^2 - s)$ **8.** $(9w - 4w^2 + 10) + (8w^2 + 7 + 5w)$

9. The sides of a rectangle are $4t - 1$ and $5t + 9$. Write an expression for the perimeter of the rectangle.

10. Three consecutive integers are $n - 1, n,$ and $n + 1$. Write an expression for the sum of the three integers.

● **Lesson 9-2** Simplify each product.

11. $4b(b^2 + 3)$ **12.** $9c(c^2 - 3c + 5)$ **13.** $8m(4m - 5)$ **14.** $5k(k^2 + 8k)$

15. $5r^2(r^2 + 4r - 2)$ **16.** $2m^2(m^3 + m - 2)$ **17.** $-3x(x^2 + 3x - 1)$ **18.** $-x(1 + x + x^2)$

Find the GCF of the terms of each polynomial. Factor.

19. $t^6 + t^4 - t^5 + t^2$ **20.** $3m^2 - 6 + 9m$ **21.** $16c^2 - 4c^3 + 12c^5$ **22.** $8v^6 + 2v^5 - 10v^9$

23. $6n^2 - 3n^3 + 2n^4$ **24.** $5r + 20r^3 + 15r^2$ **25.** $9x^6 + 5x^5 + 4x^7$ **26.** $4d^8 - 2d^{10} + 7d^4$

● **Lessons 9-3 and 9-4** Simplify each product. Write in standard form.

27. $(5c + 3)(-c + 2)$ **28.** $(3t - 1)(2t + 1)$ **29.** $(w + 2)(w^2 + 2w - 1)$ **30.** $(3t + 5)(t + 1)$

31. $(2n - 3)(2n + 4)$ **32.** $(b + 3)(b + 7)$ **33.** $(3x + 1)^2$ **34.** $(5t + 4)^2$

35. $(w - 1)(w^2 + w + 1)$ **36.** $(a + 4)(a - 4)$ **37.** $(3y - 2)(3y + 2)$ **38.** $(w^2 + 2)(w^2 - 2)$

39. **Geometry** A rectangle has dimensions $3x - 1$ and $2x + 5$. Write an expression for the area of the rectangle as a product and in standard form.

40. Write an expression for the product of the two consecutive odd integers $n - 1$ and $n + 1$.

● **Lessons 9-5 to 9-7** Factor each expression.

41. $x^2 - 4x + 3$ **42.** $3x^2 - 4x + 1$ **43.** $v^2 + v - 2$ **44.** $5t^2 - t - 18$

45. $m^2 + 9m - 22$ **46.** $x^2 - 2x - 15$ **47.** $2n^2 + n - 3$ **48.** $2h^2 - 5h - 3$

49. $m^2 - 25$ **50.** $9y^2 - 1$ **51.** $9y^2 + 6y + 1$ **52.** $p^2 + 2p + 1$

53. $x^2 + 6x + 9$ **54.** $25x^2 - 9$ **55.** $4t^2 + t - 3$ **56.** $9c^2 - 169$

57. $4m^2 - 121$ **58.** $3v^2 + 10v - 8$ **59.** $4g^2 + 4g + 1$ **60.** $-w^2 + 5w - 4$

61. $9t^2 + 12t + 4$ **62.** $12m^2 - 5m - 2$ **63.** $36s^2 - 1$ **64.** $c^2 - 10c + 25$

● **Lesson 9-8** Factor each expression.

65. $3y^3 + 9y^2 - y - 3$ **66.** $3u^3 + u^2 - 6u - 2$ **67.** $w^3 - 3w^2 + 3w - 9$ **68.** $4z^3 + 2z^2 - 2z - 1$

69. $3x^3 + 8x^2 - 3x$ **70.** $y^5 - 9y$ **71.** $2p^3 - 4p^2 + 2p - 4$ **72.** $3y^3 - 3y^2 - 6y$

Extra Practice

● **Lessons 10-1 and 10-2** Without graphing, describe how each graph differs from the graph of $y = x^2$.

1. $y = 3x^2$ **2.** $y = -4x^2$ **3.** $y = -0.5x^2$ **4.** $y = 0.2x^2$

5. $y = x^2 - 4$ **6.** $y = x^2 + 1$ **7.** $y = 2x^2 + 5$ **8.** $y = -0.3x^2 - 7$

Identify the axis of symmetry and the vertex of each function.

9. $y = 3x^2$ **10.** $y = -2x^2 + 1$ **11.** $y = 0.5x^2 - 3$

12. $y = -x^2 + 2x + 1$ **13.** $y = 3x^2 + 6x$ **14.** $y = \frac{3}{4}x^2$

15. $y = 2x^2 - 9$ **16.** $y = -5x^2 + x + 4$ **17.** $y = x^2 - 8x$

Graph each quadratic inequality.

18. $y > x^2 - 4$ **19.** $y < 2x^2 + x$ **20.** $y \le x^2 + x - 2$

● **Lesson 10-3** Find the square roots of each number.

21. 25   **22.** $\frac{4}{9}$ **23.** 64   **24.** $\frac{25}{36}$ **25.** 0.81   **26.** 900

27. 144   **28.** 324   **29.** $\frac{16}{225}$ **30.** 0.0001   **31.** 3600   **32.** $\frac{1}{9}$

● **Lessons 10-4 to 10-7** Solve each equation. If the equation has no solution, write *no solution*.

33. $x^2 = 36$ **34.** $x^2 + x - 2 = 0$ **35.** $c^2 - 100 = 0$

36. $9d^2 = 25$ **37.** $(x - 4)^2 = 100$ **38.** $3x^2 = 27$

39. $2x^2 - 54 = 284$ **40.** $7n^2 = 63$ **41.** $h^2 + 4 = 0$

42. $x^2 + 6x - 2 = 0$ **43.** $x^2 - 5x = 7$ **44.** $x^2 - 10x + 3 = 0$

45. $2x^2 - 4x + 1 = 0$ **46.** $3x^2 + x + 5 = 0$ **47.** $\frac{1}{2}x^2 - 3x - 8 = 0$

48. $x^2 + 8x + 4 = 0$ **49.** $x^2 - 2x - 6 = 0$ **50.** $-3x^2 + x - 7 = 0$

51. $x^2 + 5x + 6 = 0$ **52.** $d^2 - 144 = 0$ **53.** $c^2 + 6 = 2 - 4c$

54. $x^2 + 4x = 2x^2 - x + 6$ **55.** $3x^2 + 2x - 12 = x^2$ **56.** $r^2 + 4r + 1 = r$

57. $d^2 + 2d + 10 = 2d + 100$ **58.** $3c^2 + c - 10 = c^2 - 5$ **59.** $t^2 - 3t - 10 = 0$

60. Agriculture You are planting a rectangular garden. It is 5 feet longer than 3 times its width. The area of the garden is 250 ft². Find the dimensions of the garden.

● **Lesson 10-8** Find the number of solutions of each equation.

61. $3x^2 + 4x - 7 = 0$ **62.** $5x^2 - 4x = -6$ **63.** $x^2 - 20x + 101 = 1$

64. $2x^2 - 8x + 9 = 4$ **65.** $4x^2 - 5x + 6 = 0$ **66.** $x^2 - 2x + 7 = 0$

● **Lesson 10-9** Graph each set of data. Which model is most appropriate for each set?

67. $(2, 4), (4, 4), (1, 2), (5, 1.5)$ **68.** $(3, 8), (4, 6), (5, 5), (6, 4), (7, 3)$ **69.** $(0, 7), (1, 3), (3, 0.5), (2, 1)$

● **Lessons 11-1 and 11-4 Simplify each radical expression.**

1. $\dfrac{\sqrt{27}}{\sqrt{81}}$

2. $\sqrt{\dfrac{25}{4}}$

3. $\sqrt{\dfrac{50}{9}}$

4. $\dfrac{\sqrt{72}}{\sqrt{50}}$

5. $\sqrt{75} - 4\sqrt{75}$

6. $\sqrt{5}(\sqrt{20} - \sqrt{80})$

7. $\sqrt{25} \cdot \sqrt{4}$

8. $\sqrt{6}(\sqrt{6} - 3)$

9. $3\sqrt{300} + 2\sqrt{27}$

10. $5\sqrt{2} \cdot 3\sqrt{50}$

11. $\sqrt{8} - 4\sqrt{2}$

12. $\sqrt{27} \cdot \sqrt{3}$

13. $\dfrac{\sqrt{3c^2}}{\sqrt{27}}$

14. $\dfrac{\sqrt{z^3}}{\sqrt{5z}}$

15. $\sqrt{\dfrac{44x^4}{11}}$

16. $(\sqrt{5} + 1)(\sqrt{5} - 1)$

17. $(\sqrt{3} + \sqrt{2})^2$

18. $\dfrac{1}{\sqrt{2} + 1}$

19. $\dfrac{2}{\sqrt{2} - 2}$

20. $\dfrac{\sqrt{3} + 1}{\sqrt{2} + 1}$

● **Lesson 11-2 Determine whether the given lengths are sides of a right triangle.**

21. $4, 5, 7$

22. $6, 8, 10$

23. $6, 9, 13$

24. $10, 13, 17$

25. $15, 36, 39$

26. $3, 7, 10$

27. $8, 15, 17$

28. $\sqrt{3}, \sqrt{4}, \sqrt{5}$

For the values given, a and b are legs of a right triangle. Find the length of the hypotenuse. If necessary, round to the nearest tenth.

29. $a = 6, b = 8$

30. $a = 5, b = 9$

31. $a = 4, b = 10$

32. $a = 9, b = 1$

● **Lesson 11-3 Find the distance between each pair of points. If necessary, round your answer to the nearest tenth. Then find the midpoint of each segment.**

33. $A(1, 3), B(2, 8)$

34. $R(6, -2), S(-7, -10)$

35. $G(4, 0), H(5, -1)$

36. $A(-4, 1), B(3, 5)$

37. $G(11, 7), H(-7, -11)$

38. $R(1, -6), S(4, -2)$

39. $R(-8, -4), S(5, 7)$

40. $A(0, 6), B(-2, 9)$

41. $G(5, 10), H(0, 0)$

● **Lesson 11-5 Solve each radical equation. Check your solution.**

42. $\sqrt{3x + 4} = 1$

43. $6 = \sqrt{8x - 4}$

44. $2x = \sqrt{14x - 6}$

45. $\sqrt{2x + 5} = \sqrt{3x + 1}$

46. $2x = \sqrt{6x + 4}$

47. $\sqrt{5x + 11} = \sqrt{7x - 1}$

48. $\sqrt{3x - 2} = x$

49. $\sqrt{x + 7} = x + 1$

50. $\sqrt{x + 3} = \dfrac{x + 9}{5}$

● **Lesson 11-6 Find the domain of each function. Then graph the function.**

51. $y = \sqrt{x + 5}$

52. $y = \sqrt{x} - 2$

53. $y = \sqrt{x + 1}$

54. $y = \sqrt{x} - 4$

55. $y = \sqrt{x - 3}$

56. $y = \sqrt{x} + 6$

● **Lesson 11-7 Use $\triangle ABC$ to find the value of each expression.**

57. $\sin A$

58. $\cos A$

59. $\tan A$

60. $\sin B$

61. $\cos B$

62. $\tan B$

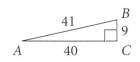

Find the value of each expression. Round to the nearest ten-thousandth.

63. $\sin 72°$

64. $\cos 29°$

65. $\tan 48°$

66. $\tan 52°$

67. A forester is 50 m from the base of a tree and measures the angle between the ground and the top of the tree. If the angle is 76°, find the height of the tree. Round your answer to the nearest meter.

● **Lesson 12-1** Find the constant of variation k for each inverse variation.

1. $y = 10$ when $x = 7$ 　　　 **2.** $y = -8$ when $x = 12$ 　　　 **3.** $y = 0.2$ when $x = 4$

4. $y = 4$ when $x = -5$ 　　　 **5.** $y = 0.1$ when $x = 6$ 　　　 **6.** $y = -3$ when $x = -7$

Each pair of points is on the graph of an inverse variation. Find the missing value.

7. $(5.4, 3)$ and $(2, y)$ 　　　 **8.** $(x, 4)$ and $(5, 6)$ 　　　 **9.** $(3, 6)$ and $(9, y)$

10. $(100, 2)$ and $(x, 25)$ 　　　 **11.** $(6, 1)$ and $(x, -2)$ 　　　 **12.** $(8, y)$ and $(-2, 4)$

● **Lesson 12-2** Identify the asymptotes of each function. Then graph the function.

13. $y = \frac{6}{x}$ 　　 **14.** $y = \frac{8}{x + 2}$ 　　 **15.** $y = \frac{4}{x} - 3$ 　　 **16.** $y = \frac{5}{x + 1} + 3$

17. $y = \frac{5}{x} - 1$ 　　 **18.** $y = \frac{2}{x - 1}$ 　　 **19.** $y = \frac{3}{x} + 4$ 　　 **20.** $y = \frac{2}{x + 1} - 1$

● **Lessons 12-3 to 12-6** Simplify each expression.

21. $\frac{4t^2}{16t}$ 　　 **22.** $\frac{c - 5}{c^2 - 25}$ 　　 **23.** $\frac{4m - 12}{m - 3}$ 　　 **24.** $\frac{a^2 + 2a - 3}{a + 3}$

25. $\frac{4}{x} - \frac{3}{x}$ 　　 **26.** $\frac{6t}{5} + \frac{4t}{5}$ 　　 **27.** $\frac{6}{c} + \frac{4}{c^2}$ 　　 **28.** $\frac{6}{3d} - \frac{4}{3d}$

29. $\frac{5s^4}{10s^3}$ 　　 **30.** $\frac{4n^2}{7} \cdot \frac{14}{2n^3}$ 　　 **31.** $\frac{8b^2 - 4b}{3b^2} \div \frac{2b - 1}{9b}$ 　　 **32.** $\frac{v^5}{v^3} \cdot \frac{4v^{-1}}{v^2}$

33. $\frac{5}{t + 4} + \frac{3}{t - 4}$ 　 **34.** $\frac{8}{m^2 + 6m + 5} + \frac{4}{m + 1}$ 　 **35.** $\frac{3y}{4y - 8} \div \frac{9y}{2y^2 - 4y}$ 　 **36.** $\frac{4}{d^2} - \frac{3}{d^3}$

Divide.

37. $(2x^3 - x^2 - 13x - 6) \div (x - 3)$ 　　　 **38.** $(3x^3 - 3) \div (x + 1)$

39. $(3x^3 + 5x^2 - 22x + 24) \div (x + 4)$ 　　　 **40.** $(3x^3 - 3) \div (x - 1)$

● **Lesson 12-7** Solve each equation. Check your answer.

41. $\frac{1}{4} + \frac{1}{x} = \frac{3}{8}$ 　　 **42.** $\frac{4}{m} - 3 = \frac{2}{m}$ 　　 **43.** $\frac{1}{b - 3} = \frac{1}{4b}$ 　　 **44.** $\frac{4}{x - 1} = \frac{3}{x}$

45. $\frac{4}{n} + \frac{5}{9} = 1$ 　　 **46.** $\frac{x}{x + 2} = \frac{x - 3}{x + 1}$ 　　 **47.** $t - \frac{8}{t} = \frac{17}{t}$ 　　 **48.** $\frac{x + 2}{x + 5} = \frac{x - 4}{x + 4}$

49. $\frac{4}{c + 1} - \frac{2}{c - 1} = \frac{3c + 6}{c^2 - 1}$ 　　 **50.** $\frac{4}{m + 3} = \frac{6}{m - 3}$ 　　 **51.** $\frac{4}{t + 5} + 1 = \frac{15}{t^2 - 25}$

● **Lessons 12-8 and 12-9** Simplify each expression.

52. $_6C_4$ 　　 **53.** $_7P_2$ 　　 **54.** $_{10}C_5$ 　　 **55.** $_8C_7$ 　　 **56.** $_{12}P_6$ 　　 **57.** $_9C_7$

58. How many four-letter groups can be made with the letters A, B, C, and D if no letter can be repeated?

59. Two people are running for president, three are running for vice-president, and two are running for speaker. How many election results are possible?

60. a. Suppose your bank assigns a four-digit personal identification number for your bank card. The first digit cannot be zero. How many different numbers are possible?

   b. What is the probability that the number you are given is 4861?

Skills Handbook

Problem Solving Strategies

You may find one or more of these strategies helpful in solving a word problem.

STRATEGY	WHEN TO USE IT
Draw a Diagram	The problem describes a picture or diagram.
Try, Check, Revise	Solving the problem directly is too complicated.
Look for a Pattern	The problem describes a relationship.
Make a Table	The problem has data that need to be organized.
Solve a Simpler Problem	The problem is complex or has numbers that are too cumbersome to use at first.
Use Logical Reasoning	You need to reach a conclusion using given information.
Work Backward	You need to find the number that led to the result in the problem.

Problem Solving: Draw a Diagram

> **EXAMPLE**
>
> Two cars started from the same point. One traveled east at 45 mi/h and the other west at 50 mi/h. How far apart were the cars after 5 hours?
>
> Draw a diagram. 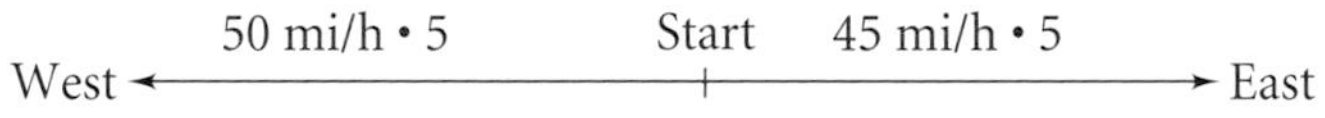
>
> West ← 50 mi/h • 5 —— Start —— 45 mi/h • 5 → East
>
> The first car traveled 45 · 5 or 225 mi. The second car traveled 50 · 5 or 250 mi.
>
> The diagram shows that the two distances should be added: 225 + 250 = 475 mi.
>
> ● After 5 hours, the cars were 475 mi apart.

EXERCISES

1. Jason, Lee, Melda, Aaron, and Bonnie want to play one another in tennis. How many games will be played?

2. A playground, a zoo, a picnic area, and a flower garden will be in four corners of a new park. Straight paths will connect each of these areas to all the other areas. How many pathways will be built?

3. Pedro wants to tack 4 posters on a bulletin board. He will tack the four corners of each poster, overlapping the sides of each poster a little bit. What is the least number of tacks that Pedro can use?

Problem Solving: Try, Check, Revise

When you are not sure how to start, guess an answer and then test it. In the process of testing a guess, you may see a way of revising your guess to get closer to the answer or to get the exact answer.

EXAMPLE

Maria bought books and CDs as gifts. Altogether she bought 12 gifts and spent $84. The books cost $6 each and the CDs cost $9 each. How many of each gift did she buy?

Trial	6 books	**Test**	$6 \cdot \$6 =$	$\$36$
	6 CDs		$6 \cdot \$9 =$	$\underline{+\$54}$
				$\$90$

Revise your guess. You need fewer CDs to bring the total cost down.

Trial	7 books	**Test**	$7 \cdot \$6 =$	$\$42$
	5 CDs		$5 \cdot \$9 =$	$\underline{+\$45}$
				$\$87$

The cost is still too high.

Trial	8 books	**Test**	$8 \cdot \$6 =$	$\$48$
	4 CDs		$4 \cdot \$9 =$	$\underline{+\$36}$
				$\$84$

Maria bought 8 books and 4 CDs.

EXERCISES

1. Find two consecutive odd integers whose product is 323.

2. Find three consecutive integers whose sum is 81.

3. Find four consecutive integers whose sum is 138.

4. Mika bought 9 rolls of film to take 180 pictures on a field trip. Some rolls had 36 exposures and the rest had 12 exposures. How many of each type did Mika buy?

5. Tanya is 18 years old. Her brother Shawn is 16 years younger. How old will Tanya be when she is 3 times as old as Shawn?

6. Steven has 100 ft of fencing and wants to build a fence in the shape of a rectangle to enclose the largest possible area. What should be the dimensions of the rectangle?

7. The combined ages of a mother, her son, and her daughter are 61 years. The mother is 22 years older than her son and 31 years older than her daughter. How old is each person?

8. Kenji traveled 210 mi in a two-day bicycle race. He biked 20 mi farther on the first day than he did on the second day. How many miles did Kenji travel each day?

9. Darren is selling tickets for the school play. Regular tickets are $4 each, and student tickets are $3 each. Darren sells a total of 190 tickets and collects $650. How many of each kind of ticket did he sell?

Problem Solving: Look for a Pattern and Make a Table

Some problems describe relationships that involve regular sequences of numbers or other things. To solve the problem you need to be able to recognize and describe the pattern that gives the relationship for the numbers or things. One way to organize the information given is to make a table.

EXAMPLE

A tree farm is planted as shown at the right. The dots represent trees. The lot will be enlarged by adding larger squares. How many trees will be in the fifth square?

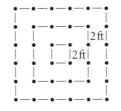

Make a table to help find a pattern.

Square position	1st	2nd	3rd	4th	5th
Number of trees	4	12	20	■	■

Pattern: 8 more trees are planted in each larger square.

The fourth square will have 28 trees. The fifth square will have 36 trees.

EXERCISES

1. Kareem made a display of books at a book fair. One book was in the first row, and each of the other rows had two more books than the row before it. How many books does Kareem have if he has nine rows?

2. Chris is using green and white tiles to cover her floor. If she uses tiles in the pattern G, W, G, G, W, G, G, W, G, G, what will be the color of the twentieth tile?

3. Jay read one story the first week of summer vacation, 3 stories the second week, 6 stories the third week, and 10 stories the fourth week. He kept to this pattern for eight weeks. How many stories did he read the eighth week?

4. Jan has 6 coins, none of which is a half dollar. The coins have a value of $.85. What coins does she have?

5. Sam is covering a wall with rows of red, white, and blue siding. The red siding is cut in 1.8-m strips, the white in 2.4-m strips, and the blue in 1.2-m strips. What is the shortest length that Sam can cover with uncut strips to form equal rows of each color?

6. A train leaves a station at 8:00 A.M. and averages 40 mi/h. Another train leaves the same station one hour later and averages 50 mi/h traveling in the same direction on a parallel track. At what time will the second train catch up with the first train? How many miles would each train have traveled by that time?

7. The soccer team held a car wash and earned $200. They charged $7 per truck and $5 per car. In how many different ways could the team have earned the $200?

8. Students are going to march in a parade. There will be one first-grader, two second-graders, three third-graders, and so on through the twelfth grade. How many students will march in the parade?

Problem Solving: Solve a Simpler Problem

By solving one or more simpler problems you can often find a pattern that will help solve a more complicated problem.

> ### EXAMPLE
>
> How many different rectangles are in a strip with 10 squares?
>
>
> Begin with one square, and then add one square at a time. Determine whether there is a pattern.
>
> | Squares in the strip: | 1 | 2 | 3 | 4 | 5 |
> |---|---|---|---|---|---|
> | Number of rectangles: | 1 | 3 | 6 | 10 | 15 |
> | Pattern: | | $1 + 2 = 3$ | $3 + 3 = 6$ | $6 + 4 = 10$ | $10 + 5 = 15$ |
>
> Now continue the pattern.
>
> | Squares in the strip: | 6 | 7 | 8 | 9 | 10 |
> |---|---|---|---|---|---|
> | Number of rectangles: | 21 | 28 | 36 | 45 | 55 |
>
> Pattern: $15 + 6 = 21$ $21 + 7 = 28$ $28 + 8 = 36$ $36 + 9 = 45$ $45 + 10 = 55$
>
> There are 55 rectangles in a strip with 10 squares.

EXERCISES

1. Lockers in the east wing of Hastings High School are numbered 1–120. How many contain the digit 8?

2. What is the sum of all the numbers from 1 to 100? (*Hint:* What is $1 + 100$? What is $2 + 99$?)

3. Suppose your heart beats 70 times per minute. At this rate, how many times had it beaten by the time you were 10?

4. For a community project you have to create the numbers 1 through 148 using large cardboard digits covered with glitter, which you make by hand. How many cardboard digits will you make?

5. There are 64 teams competing in the state soccer championship. If a team loses a game it is eliminated. How many games have to be played in order to get a single champion team?

6. You work in a supermarket. Your boss asks you to arrange oranges in a pyramid for a display. The pyramid's base should be a square with 25 oranges. How many layers of oranges will be in your pyramid? How many oranges will you need?

7. Kesi has her math book open. The product of the two page numbers on the facing pages is 1056. What are the two page numbers?

8. There are 12 girls and 11 boys at a school party. A photographer wants to take a picture of each boy with each girl. How many photographs must the photographer set up?

Problem Solving: Use Logical Reasoning

Some problems can be solved without the use of numbers. They can be solved by the use of logical reasoning, given some information.

EXAMPLE

Joe, Melissa, Liz and Greg play different sports. Their sports are running, basketball, baseball, and tennis. Liz's sport does not use a ball. Joe hit a home run in his sport. Melissa is the sister of the tennis player. Which sport does each play?

Make a table to organize what you know.

	Running	Basketball	Baseball	Tennis	
Joe	✗	✗	✓	✗	← A home run means Joe plays baseball.
Melissa				✗	← Melissa cannot be the tennis player.
Liz	✓	✗	✗	✗	← Liz must run, since running does not
Greg					involve a ball.

Use logical reasoning to complete the table.

	Running	Basketball	Baseball	Tennis	
Joe	✗	✗	✓	✗	
Melissa	✗	✓	✗	✗	
Liz	✓	✗	✗	✗	
Greg	✗	✗	✗	✓	← The only option for Greg is tennis.

● Greg plays tennis, Melissa plays basketball, Liz runs, and Joe plays baseball.

EXERCISES

1. Juan has a dog, a horse, a bird, and a cat. Their names are Bo, Cricket, K.C., and Tuffy. Tuffy and K.C. cannot fly or be ridden. The bird talks to Bo. Tuffy runs from the dog. What is each pet's name?

2. A math class has 25 students. There are 13 students who are only in the band, 4 students who are only on the swimming team, and 5 students who are in both groups. How many students are not in either group?

3. Annette is taller than Heather but shorter than Garo. Tanya's height is between Garo's and Annette's. Karin would be the shortest if it weren't for Alexa. List the names in order from shortest to tallest.

4. The Robins, Wrens, and Sparrows teams played one another twice in basketball. The Robins won 3 of their games. The Sparrows won 2 of their games. How many games did each team win and lose?

5. The girls' basketball league uses a telephone tree when it needs to cancel its games. The leader takes 1 min to call 2 players. These 2 players take 1 min to call 2 more players, and so on. How many players will be called in 6 min?

6. Miss White, Miss Gray, and Miss Black are wearing single-colored dresses that are white, gray, and black. Miss Gray remarks to the woman wearing a black dress that no woman's dress color matches her last name. What color dress is each woman wearing?

Problem Solving: Work Backward

To solve some problems, you need to start with the end result and work backward to the beginning.

EXAMPLE

On Monday, Rita withdrew $150 from her savings account. On Wednesday, she deposited $400 into her account. She now has $1000. How much was in her account on Monday before she withdrew the money?

money in account now	$1000
Undo the deposit.	$-\$400$
	$\$600$
Undo the withdrawal.	$+\$150$
	$\$750$

● Rita had $750 in her account on Monday before withdrawing money.

EXERCISES

1. Ned gave Connie the following puzzle: I am thinking of a number. I doubled it, then tripled the result. The final result was 36. What is my number?

2. Fernando gave Maria the following puzzle: I am thinking of a number. I divide it by 3. Then I divide the result by 5. The final result is 8. What is my number?

3. A teacher lends pencils to students. She gave out 7 pencils in the morning, collected 5 before lunch, and gave out 3 after lunch. At the end of the day she had 16 pencils. How many pencils did the teacher have at the start of the day?

4. This week Sandy withdrew $350 from her savings account. She made a deposit of $125, wrote a check for $ 275, and made a deposit of $150. She now has $225 in her account. How much did she have in her account at the beginning of the week?

5. Jeff paid $12.50, including a $1.60 tip, for a taxi ride from his home to the airport. City Cab charges $1.90 for the first mile plus $.15 for each additional $\frac{1}{6}$ mile. How many miles is Jeff's home from the airport?

6. Ben sold $\frac{1}{4}$ as many tickets to the fund-raiser as Charles. Charles sold 3 times as many as Susan. Susan sold 4 fewer than Tom. Tom sold 12 tickets. How many did Ben sell?

7. Two cars start traveling towards each other. One car averages 30 mi/h and the other 40 mi/h. After 4 h the cars are 10 mi apart. How far apart were the cars when they started?

8. Nina has a dentist appointment at 8:45 A.M. She wants to arrive 10 min early. Nina needs to allow 25 min to travel to the appointment and 45 min to dress and have breakfast. What is the latest time Nina should get up?

9. Jordan spent the day exploring her neighborhood and ended up at the park 2 mi east and 1 mi north of the center of town. She started from her house and walked $\frac{1}{2}$ mi north. Next she walked 3 mi west and then $1\frac{1}{2}$ mi south. Finally, she walked $\frac{1}{4}$ mi east to the park. Where is Jordan's house in relation to the center of town?

Prime Numbers and Composite Numbers

A prime number is a whole number greater than 1 that has exactly two factors, the number 1 and itself.

Prime number	2	5	17	29
Factors	1, 2	1, 5	1, 17	1, 29

A composite number is a number that has more than two factors. The number 1 is neither prime nor composite.

Composite number	6	15	48
Factors	1, 2, 3, 6	1, 3, 5, 15	1, 2, 3, 4, 6, 8, 12, 16, 24, 48

1 EXAMPLE

Is 51 prime or composite?

$51 = 3 \cdot 17$ **Try to find factors other than 1 and 51.**

● 51 is a composite number.

You can use a factor tree to find the prime factors of a number. When all the factors are prime numbers, it is called the prime factorization of the number.

2 EXAMPLE

Use a factor tree to write the prime factorization of 28.

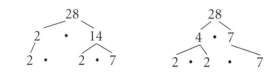

The order of listing the factors may be different, but the end result is the same.

● The prime factorization of 28 is $2 \cdot 2 \cdot 7$.

EXERCISES

Is each number prime or composite?

1. 9	**2.** 16	**3.** 34	**4.** 61	**5.** 7	**6.** 13
7. 12	**8.** 40	**9.** 57	**10.** 64	**11.** 120	**12.** 700
13. 39	**14.** 23	**15.** 63	**16.** 19	**17.** 522	**18.** 101

List all the factors of each number.

19. 46	**20.** 32	**21.** 11	**22.** 65	**23.** 27	**24.** 29
25. 205	**26.** 123	**27.** 24	**28.** 162	**29.** 88	**30.** 204
31. 183	**32.** 6	**33.** 98	**34.** 92	**35.** 59	**36.** 47

Use a factor tree to write the prime factorization of each number.

37. 18	**38.** 20	**39.** 27	**40.** 54	**41.** 64	**42.** 96
43. 100	**44.** 125	**45.** 84	**46.** 150	**47.** 121	**48.** 226

Factors and Multiples

A common factor is a number that is a factor of two or more numbers. The greatest common factor (GCF) is the greatest number that is a common factor of two or more numbers.

1 EXAMPLE

Find the GCF of 24 and 64.

Method 1 List all the factors of each number.

Factors of 24   1, 2, 3, 4, 6, 8, 12, 24   **Find the common factors: 1, 2, 4, 8.**

Factors of 64   1, 2, 4, 8, 16, 32, 64   **The greatest common factor is 8.**

GCF (24, 64) = 8

Method 2 Use the prime factorization of each number.

$24 = 2 \cdot 2 \cdot 2 \cdot 3$ **Find the prime factorization of each number.**

$64 = 2 \cdot 2 \cdot 2 \cdot 2 \cdot 2 \cdot 2$

$GCF = 2 \cdot 2 \cdot 2 = 8$ **Use each factor the number of times it appears as a common factor.**

A common multiple is a number that is a multiple of two or more numbers. The least common multiple (LCM) is the least number that is a common multiple of two or more numbers.

2 EXAMPLE

Find the LCM of 12 and 18.

Method 1 List the multiples of each number.

Multiples of 12   12, 24, 36, . . .   **List a number of multiples until you find**

Multiples of 18   18, 36, . . .   **the first common multiple.**

LCM (12, 18) = 36

Method 2 Use the prime factorization of each number.

$12 = 2 \cdot 2 \cdot 3$

$18 = 2 \cdot 3 \cdot 3$

$LCM = 2 \cdot 2 \cdot 3 \cdot 3 = 36$ **Use each prime factor the greatest number of times it appears in either number.**

EXERCISES

Find the GCF of each set of numbers.

1. 12 and 22   **2.** 7 and 21   **3.** 24 and 48   **4.** 17 and 51

5. 9 and 12   **6.** 10 and 25   **7.** 21 and 49   **8.** 27 and 36

9. 10, 30, and 25   **10.** 56, 84, and 140   **11.** 42, 63, and 105   **12.** 20, 28, and 40

Find the LCM of each set of numbers.

13. 16 and 20   **14.** 14 and 21   **15.** 11 and 33   **16.** 8 and 9

17. 5 and 12   **18.** 54 and 84   **19.** 48 and 80   **20.** 25 and 36

21. 10, 15, and 25   **22.** 6, 7, and 12   **23.** 5, 8, and 20   **24.** 18, 21, and 36

Divisibility

An integer is divisible by another integer if the remainder is zero. You can use the following tests to determine whether a number is divisible by the numbers below.

Number	Divisibility Test
2	The ones' digit is 0, 2, 4, 6, or 8.
3	The sum of the digits is divisible by 3.
4	The number formed by the last two digits is divisible by 4.
5	The ones' digit is 0 or 5.
6	The number is divisible by 2 and by 3.
8	The number formed by the last three digits is divisible by 8.
9	The sum of the digits is divisible by 9.
10	The ones' digit is 0.

EXAMPLE

Use the divisibility tests to determine the numbers by which 2116 is divisible.

2: Yes; the ones' digit is 6.
3: No; the sum of the digits is $2 + 1 + 1 + 6 = 10$, which is not divisible by 3.
4: Yes; the number formed by the last two digits is 16, which is divisible by 4.
5: No; the ones' digit is 6, *not* 0 or 5.
6: No; 2116 is not divisible by 3.
8: No; the number formed by the last three digits is 116, which is *not* divisible by 8.
9: No; the sum of the digits is $2 + 1 + 1 + 6 = 10$, which is not divisible by 9.
10: No; the ones' digit is 6, *not* 0.

● 2116 is divisible by 2 and 4.

EXERCISES

Determine whether each number is divisible by 2, 3, 4, 5, 6, 8, 9, or 10.

1. 236   **2.** 72   **3.** 105   **4.** 108   **5.** 225   **6.** 364

7. 1234   **8.** 4321   **9.** 7848   **10.** 3366   **11.** 1421   **12.** 1071

13. 78,765   **14.** 30,303   **15.** 4104   **16.** 700   **17.** 868   **18.** 1155

19. Reasoning Since 435 is divisible by both 3 and 5, it is also divisible by what number?

20. Find a number greater than 1000 that is divisible by 4, 5, and 9.

21. Critical Thinking If *a* is divisible by 2, what can you conclude about $a + 1$? Justify your answer.

Using Estimation

To make sure the answer to a problem is reasonable, you can estimate before you calculate. If the answer is close to your estimate, the answer is probably correct.

1 EXAMPLE

Estimate to find whether each answer is reasonable.

a. Calculation   **Estimate**

$126.91	≈	$130
$14.05	≈	$10
+$25.14	≈	+$30
$266.10		$170

The answer is not close to the estimate. It is *not* reasonable. The calculation is *incorrect*.

b. Calculation   **Estimate**

372.85	≈	370
−227.31	≈	−230
145.54		140

The answer is close to the estimate. It *is* reasonable. The calculation is *correct*.

For some situations, like estimating a grocery bill, you may not need an exact answer. A *front-end estimate* will give you a good estimate that is usually closer to the exact answer than an estimate you would get by rounding. Add the front-end digits, estimate the sum of the remaining digits by rounding, and then combine sums.

2 EXAMPLE

Tomatoes cost $3.54, squash costs $2.75, and lemons cost $1.20. Estimate the total cost of the produce.

Add the front-end digits.	3.54	→	0.50	**Estimate by rounding.**
	2.75	→	0.80	
	+1.20	→	+ 0.20	
	6	+	1.50 = 7.50	

The total cost is about $7.50.

EXERCISES

Estimate by rounding.

1. the sum of $15.70, $49.62, and $278.01

2. 563 − 125

3. the sum of $163.90, $107.21, and $33.56

4. 824 − 467

Use front-end estimation.

5. $1.65 + $5.42 + $9.89

6. 1.369 + 7.421 + 2.700

7. 9.563 − 2.480

8. 1.17 + 3.92 + 2.26

9. 8.611 − 1.584

10. $2.52 + $3.04 + $5.25

Estimate using a method of your choice.

11. Ticket prices at an amusement park cost $11.25 for adults and $6.50 for children under 12. Estimate the cost for three children and one adult.

12. Esmeralda has a new checking account. So far, she has deposited $177, $250, and $193. She has also written a check for $26.89. Estimate her current balance.

Simplifying Fractions

A fraction can name a part of a group or region. The region below is divided into 10 equal parts and 6 of the equal parts are shaded.

 $\dfrac{6}{10}$ ← Numerator
← Denominator   **Read: six tenths**

A fraction can have many names. Different names for the same fraction are called equivalent fractions. You can find an equivalent fraction for any given fraction by multiplying the numerator and denominator of the given fraction by the same number.

1 EXAMPLE

Write five equivalent fractions for $\frac{3}{5}$.

$\dfrac{3}{5} = \dfrac{3 \cdot 2}{5 \cdot 2} = \dfrac{6}{10}$ $\dfrac{3}{5} = \dfrac{3 \cdot 3}{5 \cdot 3} = \dfrac{9}{15}$ $\dfrac{3}{5} = \dfrac{3 \cdot 4}{5 \cdot 4} = \dfrac{12}{20}$ $\dfrac{3}{5} = \dfrac{3 \cdot 5}{5 \cdot 5} = \dfrac{15}{25}$ $\dfrac{3}{5} = \dfrac{3 \cdot 6}{5 \cdot 6} = \dfrac{18}{30}$

The fraction $\frac{3}{5}$ is in simplest form because its numerator and denominator are relatively prime, that is, their only common factor is the number 1. To write a fraction in simplest form, divide its numerator and denominator by their greatest common factor (GCF).

2 EXAMPLE

Write $\frac{6}{24}$ in simplest form.

Step 1 Find the GCF of 6 and 24.

$6 = 2 \cdot 3$ **Multiply the common prime factors.**

$24 = 2 \cdot 2 \cdot 2 \cdot 3$ **GCF = 2 · 3 = 6.**

Step 2 Divide the numerator and denominator of $\frac{6}{24}$ by the GCF, 6.

$\dfrac{6}{24} = \dfrac{6 \div 6}{24 \div 6} = \dfrac{1}{4}$ **simplest form**

EXERCISES

Write five equivalent fractions for each fraction.

1. $\frac{4}{7}$ **2.** $\frac{9}{16}$ **3.** $\frac{3}{8}$ **4.** $\frac{8}{17}$ **5.** $\frac{5}{6}$ **6.** $\frac{7}{10}$

Complete each statement.

7. $\frac{3}{7} = \frac{\blacksquare}{21}$ **8.** $\frac{5}{8} = \frac{20}{\blacksquare}$ **9.** $\frac{11}{12} = \frac{44}{\blacksquare}$ **10.** $\frac{12}{16} = \frac{\blacksquare}{4}$ **11.** $\frac{50}{100} = \frac{1}{\blacksquare}$

12. $\frac{5}{9} = \frac{\blacksquare}{27}$ **13.** $\frac{3}{8} = \frac{\blacksquare}{24}$ **14.** $\frac{5}{6} = \frac{20}{\blacksquare}$ **15.** $\frac{12}{20} = \frac{\blacksquare}{5}$ **16.** $\frac{75}{150} = \frac{1}{\blacksquare}$

Which fractions are in simplest form?

17. $\frac{4}{12}$ **18.** $\frac{3}{16}$ **19.** $\frac{5}{30}$ **20.** $\frac{9}{72}$ **21.** $\frac{11}{22}$ **22.** $\frac{24}{25}$

Write in simplest form.

23. $\frac{8}{16}$ **24.** $\frac{7}{14}$ **25.** $\frac{6}{9}$ **26.** $\frac{20}{30}$ **27.** $\frac{8}{20}$ **28.** $\frac{12}{40}$

29. $\frac{15}{45}$ **30.** $\frac{14}{56}$ **31.** $\frac{10}{25}$ **32.** $\frac{9}{27}$ **33.** $\frac{45}{60}$ **34.** $\frac{20}{35}$

Fractions and Decimals

You can write a fraction as a decimal.

1 EXAMPLE

Write $\frac{3}{5}$ as a decimal.

$$\begin{array}{r} 0.6 \\ 5\overline{)3.0} \\ -3.0 \end{array}$$ **Divide the numerator by the denominator.**

The decimal for $\frac{3}{5}$ is 0.6.

You can write a decimal as a fraction.

2 EXAMPLE

Write 0.38 as a fraction.

$0.38 = 38$ hundredths $= \frac{38}{100} = \frac{19}{50}$

Some fractions have decimal forms that do not end, but do repeat.

3 EXAMPLE

Write $\frac{3}{11}$ as a decimal.

Divide the numerator by the denominator. The remainders 8 and 3 keep repeating. Therefore 2 and 7 will keep repeating in the quotient.

$\frac{3}{11} = 0.2727\ldots = 0.\overline{27}$

$$\frac{3}{11} = 11\overline{)3.0000\ldots} \quad \begin{array}{r} 0.2727 \\ \hline 22 \\ \overline{80} \\ 77 \\ \overline{30} \\ 22 \\ \overline{80} \\ 77 \\ \overline{3} \end{array}$$

You can write a repeating decimal as a fraction.

4 EXAMPLE

Write 0.363636 . . . as a fraction.

Let $\quad x = 0.363636\ldots$

Then $\quad 100x = 36.36363636\ldots$ **When 2 digits repeat, multiply by 100.**

$\quad\quad 99x = 36$ **Subtract the first equation from the second.**

$\quad\quad\quad x = \frac{36}{99}$ or $\frac{4}{11}$ **Divide each side by 99.**

EXERCISES

Write as a decimal.

1. $\frac{3}{10}$ **2.** $\frac{13}{12}$ **3.** $\frac{4}{20}$ **4.** $\frac{25}{75}$ **5.** $\frac{5}{7}$ **6.** $4\frac{3}{25}$

7. $\frac{5}{9}$ **8.** $5\frac{7}{8}$ **9.** $\frac{2}{7}$ **10.** $\frac{3}{15}$ **11.** $\frac{16}{100}$ **12.** $2\frac{2}{5}$

Write as a fraction in simplest form.

13. 0.07 **14.** 0.25 **15.** 0.875 **16.** 0.4545 . . . **17.** 6.333 . . . **18.** 7.2626 . . .

19. 0.77 . . . **20.** 3.1313 . . . **21.** 0.375 **22.** 0.8333 . . . **23.** 6.48 **24.** 0.8

Adding and Subtracting Fractions

You can add and subtract fractions when they have the same denominator.
Fractions with the same denominator are called like fractions.

1 EXAMPLE

a. Add $\frac{4}{5} + \frac{3}{5}$.

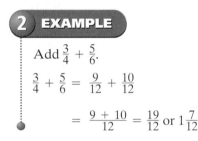

b. Subtract $\frac{5}{9} - \frac{2}{9}$.

$$\frac{4}{5} + \frac{3}{5} = \frac{4+3}{5} = \frac{7}{5} = 1\frac{2}{5}$$

← Add or subtract the numerators and keep the same denominator. →

$$\frac{5}{9} - \frac{2}{9} = \frac{5-2}{9} = \frac{3}{9} = \frac{1}{3}$$

Fractions with unlike denominators are called unlike fractions. To add or subtract fractions with unlike denominators, find the least common denominator (LCD) and write equivalent fractions with the same denominator. Then add or subtract the like fractions.

2 EXAMPLE

Add $\frac{3}{4} + \frac{5}{6}$.

$$\frac{3}{4} + \frac{5}{6} = \frac{9}{12} + \frac{10}{12}$$

Find the LCD. The LCD is the same as the least common multiple (LCM). The LCD of 4 and 6 is 12.

$$= \frac{9+10}{12} = \frac{19}{12} \text{ or } 1\frac{7}{12}$$

Write equivalent fractions with the same denominator.

To add or subtract mixed numbers, add or subtract the fractions. Then add or subtract the whole numbers. Sometimes when subtracting mixed numbers you may have to regroup.

3 EXAMPLE

Subtract $5\frac{1}{4} - 3\frac{2}{3}$.

$$5\frac{1}{4} - 3\frac{2}{3} = 5\frac{3}{12} - 3\frac{8}{12}$$

Write equivalent fractions with the same denominator.

$$= 4\frac{15}{12} - 3\frac{8}{12}$$

Write $5\frac{3}{12}$ as $4\frac{15}{12}$ so you can subtract the fractions.

$$= 1\frac{7}{12}$$

Subtract the fractions. Then subtract the whole numbers.

EXERCISES

Add. Write each answer in simplest form.

1. $\frac{2}{7} + \frac{3}{7}$ **2.** $\frac{3}{8} + \frac{7}{8}$ **3.** $\frac{6}{5} + \frac{9}{5}$ **4.** $\frac{4}{9} + \frac{8}{9}$ **5.** $6\frac{2}{3} + 3\frac{4}{5}$

6. $1\frac{4}{7} + 2\frac{3}{14}$ **7.** $4\frac{5}{6} + 1\frac{7}{18}$ **8.** $2\frac{4}{5} + 3\frac{6}{7}$ **9.** $4\frac{2}{3} + 1\frac{6}{11}$ **10.** $3\frac{7}{9} + 5\frac{4}{11}$

11. $8 + 1\frac{2}{3}$ **12.** $8\frac{1}{5} + 3\frac{3}{4}$ **13.** $11\frac{3}{8} + 2\frac{1}{16}$ **14.** $9\frac{1}{12} + 8\frac{3}{4}$ **15.** $33\frac{1}{3} + 23\frac{2}{5}$

Subtract. Write each answer in simplest form.

16. $\frac{7}{8} - \frac{3}{8}$ **17.** $\frac{9}{10} - \frac{3}{10}$ **18.** $\frac{17}{5} - \frac{2}{5}$ **19.** $\frac{11}{7} - \frac{2}{7}$ **20.** $\frac{5}{11} - \frac{4}{11}$

21. $8\frac{5}{8} - 6\frac{1}{4}$ **22.** $3\frac{2}{3} - 1\frac{8}{9}$ **23.** $8\frac{5}{6} - 5\frac{1}{2}$ **24.** $12\frac{3}{4} - 4\frac{5}{6}$ **25.** $17\frac{2}{7} - 8\frac{2}{9}$

26. $7\frac{3}{4} - 3\frac{3}{8}$ **27.** $4\frac{1}{12} - 1\frac{11}{12}$ **28.** $5\frac{5}{8} - 2\frac{7}{16}$ **29.** $11\frac{2}{3} - 3\frac{5}{6}$ **30.** $25\frac{5}{8} - 17\frac{15}{16}$

Multiplying and Dividing Fractions

To multiply two or more fractions, multiply the numerators, multiply the denominators, and simplify the product, if necessary.

1 EXAMPLE

Multiply $\frac{3}{7} \cdot \frac{5}{6}$.

$$\frac{3}{7} \cdot \frac{5}{6} = \frac{3 \cdot 5}{7 \cdot 6} = \frac{15}{42} = \frac{15 \div 3}{42 \div 3} = \frac{5}{14}$$

Sometimes you can simplify before multiplying.

$$\frac{\cancel{3}^{1}}{7} \cdot \frac{5}{\cancel{6}_{2}} = \frac{5}{14}$$ **Divide a numerator and a denominator by a common factor.**

To multiply mixed numbers, change the mixed numbers to improper fractions and multiply the fractions. Write the product as a mixed number.

2 EXAMPLE

Multiply $2\frac{4}{5} \cdot 1\frac{2}{3}$.

$$2\frac{4}{5} \cdot 1\frac{2}{3} = \frac{14}{_{1}\cancel{5}} \cdot \frac{\cancel{5}^{1}}{3} = \frac{14}{3} = 4\frac{2}{3}$$

To divide fractions, change the division problem to a multiplication problem. Remember that $8 \div \frac{1}{4}$ is the same as $8 \cdot 4$.

To divide mixed numbers, change the mixed numbers to improper fractions and divide the fractions.

3 EXAMPLE

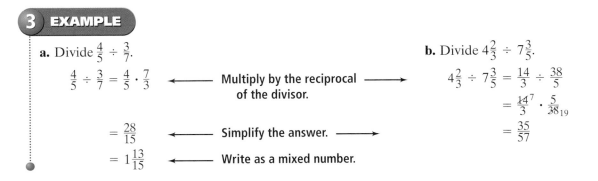

a. Divide $\frac{4}{5} \div \frac{3}{7}$.

$$\frac{4}{5} \div \frac{3}{7} = \frac{4}{5} \cdot \frac{7}{3}$$ ⟵ Multiply by the reciprocal of the divisor. ⟶

$$= \frac{28}{15}$$ ⟵ Simplify the answer. ⟶

$$= 1\frac{13}{15}$$ ⟵ Write as a mixed number.

b. Divide $4\frac{2}{3} \div 7\frac{3}{5}$.

$$4\frac{2}{3} \div 7\frac{3}{5} = \frac{14}{3} \div \frac{38}{5}$$

$$= \frac{\cancel{14}^{7}}{3} \cdot \frac{5}{\cancel{38}_{19}}$$

$$= \frac{35}{57}$$

EXERCISES

Multiply. Write your answers in simplest form.

1. $\frac{2}{5} \cdot \frac{3}{4}$ **2.** $\frac{3}{7} \cdot \frac{4}{3}$ **3.** $1\frac{1}{2} \cdot 5\frac{3}{4}$ **4.** $3\frac{4}{5} \cdot 10$ **5.** $5\frac{1}{4} \cdot \frac{2}{3}$

6. $4\frac{1}{2} \cdot 7\frac{1}{2}$ **7.** $3\frac{2}{3} \cdot 6\frac{9}{10}$ **8.** $6\frac{1}{2} \cdot 7\frac{2}{3}$ **9.** $2\frac{2}{5} \cdot 1\frac{1}{6}$ **10.** $4\frac{1}{9} \cdot 3\frac{3}{8}$

11. $3\frac{1}{5} \cdot 1\frac{7}{8}$ **12.** $7\frac{5}{6} \cdot 4\frac{1}{2}$ **13.** $1\frac{2}{3} \cdot 5\frac{9}{10}$ **14.** $3\frac{3}{4} \cdot 5\frac{1}{3}$ **15.** $1\frac{2}{3} \cdot 3\frac{9}{16}$

Divide. Write your answers in simplest form.

16. $\frac{3}{5} \div \frac{1}{2}$ **17.** $\frac{4}{5} \div \frac{9}{10}$ **18.** $2\frac{1}{2} \div 3\frac{1}{2}$ **19.** $1\frac{4}{5} \div 2\frac{1}{2}$ **20.** $3\frac{1}{6} \div 1\frac{3}{4}$

21. $5 \div \frac{3}{8}$ **22.** $\frac{4}{9} \div \frac{3}{5}$ **23.** $\frac{5}{8} \div \frac{3}{4}$ **24.** $2\frac{1}{5} \div 2\frac{1}{2}$ **25.** $6\frac{1}{2} \div \frac{1}{4}$

26. $1\frac{3}{4} \div 4\frac{3}{8}$ **27.** $\frac{8}{9} \div \frac{2}{3}$ **28.** $\frac{1}{5} \div \frac{1}{3}$ **29.** $2\frac{2}{5} \div 7\frac{1}{5}$ **30.** $7\frac{2}{3} \div \frac{2}{9}$

Fractions, Decimals, and Percents

Percent means per hundred. 50% means 50 per hundred. $50\% = \frac{50}{100} = 0.50$

You can write fractions as percents by writing the fractions as decimals first. Then move the decimal point two places to the right and write a percent sign.

1 EXAMPLE

Write each number as a percent.

a. $\frac{3}{5}$

$\frac{3}{5} = 0.6$

b. $\frac{7}{20}$

$\frac{7}{20} = 0.35$

c. $\frac{2}{3}$

$\frac{2}{3} = 0.66\overline{6}$

Move the decimal point two places to the right and write a percent sign.

$0.6 = 60\%$

$0.35 = 35\%$

$0.66\overline{6} = 66.\overline{6}\% \approx 66.7\%$

You can write percents as decimals by moving the decimal point two places to the left and removing the percent sign.

You can write a percent as a fraction with the denominator of 100. You then simplify it, if possible.

2 EXAMPLE

Write each number as a decimal and as a fraction or mixed number.

a. 25%

$25\% = 0.25$

$25\% = \frac{25}{100} = \frac{1}{4}$

b. $\frac{1}{2}\%$

$\frac{1}{2}\% = 0.5\% = 0.005$

$\frac{1}{2}\% = \frac{\frac{1}{2}}{100} = \frac{1}{2} \div 100$

$= \frac{1}{2} \cdot \frac{1}{100} = \frac{1}{200}$

c. 360%

$360\% = 3.6$

$360\% = \frac{360}{100} = \frac{18}{5} = 3\frac{3}{5}$

EXERCISES

Write each number as a percent. If necessary, round to the nearest tenth.

1. 0.56   **2.** 0.09   **3.** 6.02   **4.** 5.245

5. 8.2   **6.** 0.14   **7.** $\frac{1}{7}$ **8.** $\frac{9}{20}$

9. $\frac{1}{9}$ **10.** $\frac{5}{6}$ **11.** $\frac{3}{4}$ **12.** $\frac{7}{8}$

Write each number as a decimal.

13. 7%   **14.** 8.5%   **15.** 0.9%   **16.** 250%   **17.** 83%   **18.** 110%

19. 15%   **20.** 72%   **21.** 0.03%   **22.** 36.2%   **23.** 365%   **24.** 101%

Write each number as a fraction or mixed number in simplest form.

25. 19%   **26.** $\frac{3}{4}\%$ **27.** 450%   **28.** $\frac{4}{5}\%$ **29.** 64%   **30.** $\frac{2}{3}\%$

31. 24%   **32.** 845%   **33.** $\frac{3}{8}\%$ **34.** 480%   **35.** 60%   **36.** 350%

37. 2%   **38.** 16%   **39.** 66%   **40.** $\frac{4}{7}\%$ **41.** 125%   **42.** 84%

Exponents

You can express $2 \cdot 2 \cdot 2 \cdot 2 \cdot 2$ as 2^5. The raised number 5 shows the number of times 2 is used as a factor. The number 2 is the base. The number 5 is the exponent.

$2^5 \leftarrow$ **exponent**
$\uparrow$ **base**

Factored Form	Exponential Form	Standard Form
$2 \cdot 2 \cdot 2 \cdot 2 \cdot 2$	2^5	32

A number with an exponent of 1 is the number itself: $8^1 = 8$.
Any number, except 0, with an exponent of 0 is 1: $5^0 = 1$.

1 EXAMPLE

Write using exponents.

a. $8 \cdot 8 \cdot 8 \cdot 8 \cdot 8$ **b.** $2 \cdot 9 \cdot 9 \cdot 9 \cdot 9 \cdot 9 \cdot 9$ **c.** $6 \cdot 6 \cdot 10 \cdot 10 \cdot 10 \cdot 6 \cdot 6$

Count the number of times the number is used as a factor.

$= 8^5$ $= 2 \cdot 9^6$ $= 6^4 \cdot 10^3$

2 EXAMPLE

Write in standard form.

a. 2^3 **b.** $8^2 \cdot 3^4$ **c.** $10^3 \cdot 15^2$

Write in factored form and multiply.

$2 \cdot 2 \cdot 2 - 8$ $8 \cdot 8 \cdot 3 \cdot 3 \cdot 3 \cdot 3 = 5184$ $10 \cdot 10 \cdot 10 \cdot 15 \cdot 15 = 225,000$

In powers of 10, an exponent tells how many zeros are in the equivalent standard form.

$10^1 = 10$

$10^2 = 10 \cdot 10 = 100$

$10^3 = 10 \cdot 10 \cdot 10 = 1000$

$10^4 = 10 \cdot 10 \cdot 10 \cdot 10 = 10,000$

$10^5 = 10 \cdot 10 \cdot 10 \cdot 10 \cdot 10 = 100,000$

$10^6 = 10 \cdot 10 \cdot 10 \cdot 10 \cdot 10 \cdot 10 = 1,000,000$

You can use exponents to write numbers in expanded form.

3 EXAMPLE

Write 739 in expanded form using exponents.

$739 = 700 + 30 + 9 = (7 \cdot 100) + (3 \cdot 10) + (9 \cdot 1) = (7 \cdot 10^2) + (3 \cdot 10^1) + (9 \cdot 10^0)$

EXERCISES

Write using exponents.

1. $6 \cdot 6 \cdot 6 \cdot 6$ **2.** $7 \cdot 7 \cdot 7 \cdot 7 \cdot 7$ **3.** $5 \cdot 2 \cdot 2 \cdot 2 \cdot 2$

4. $3 \cdot 3 \cdot 3 \cdot 3 \cdot 3 \cdot 14 \cdot 14$ **5.** $4 \cdot 4 \cdot 3 \cdot 3 \cdot 2$ **6.** $3 \cdot 5 \cdot 5 \cdot 7 \cdot 7 \cdot 7$

Write in standard form.

7. 4^3 **8.** 9^4 **9.** 12^2 **10.** $6^2 \cdot 7^1$ **11.** $11^2 \cdot 3^3$

Write in expanded form using exponents.

12. 658   **13.** 1254   **14.** 7125   **15.** 83,401   **16.** 294,863

Measuring and Classifying Angles

An angle is a geometric figure formed by two rays with a common endpoint. The rays are sides of the angle and the endpoint is the vertex of the angle. An angle is measured in degrees. The symbol for an angle is $\angle$.

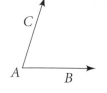

The angle picture at the right can be named in three different ways: $\angle A$, $\angle BAC$, or $\angle CAB$.

Angles can be classified by their measures.

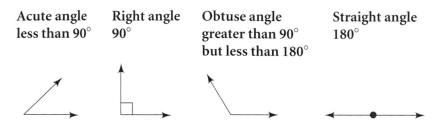

Acute angle	Right angle	Obtuse angle	Straight angle
less than 90°	90°	greater than 90° but less than 180°	180°

EXAMPLE

Measure the angle. Is it *acute*, *right*, *obtuse* or *straight*?

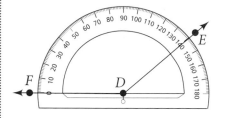

Line up side DF through $0°$ with the vertex at the center of the protractor. Read the scale number through which side DE passes.

● The measure of the angle is $140°$. The angle is obtuse.

EXERCISES

Measure each angle. Is the angle *acute*, *right*, *obtuse*, or *straight*?

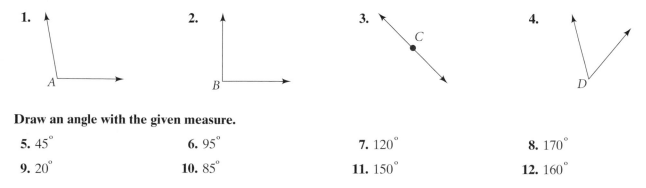

Draw an angle with the given measure.

5. $45°$	**6.** $95°$	**7.** $120°$	**8.** $170°$
9. $20°$	**10.** $85°$	**11.** $150°$	**12.** $160°$

13. Open-Ended Draw a triangle. Use a protractor to find the measure of each angle of your triangle.

Perimeter, Area, and Volume

The perimeter of a figure is the distance around the figure. The area of a figure is
the number of square units contained in the figure. The volume of a space figure is
the number of cubic units contained in the space figure.

1 EXAMPLE

Find the perimeter of each figure.

a.

5 in.
3 in.
4 in.

Add the measures of the sides.
$3 + 4 + 5 = 12$
The perimeter is 12 in.

b.

3 cm
4 cm

Use the formula $P = 2\ell + 2w$.
$P = 2(3) + 2(4)$
$= 6 + 8 = 14$
The perimeter is 14 cm.

2 EXAMPLE

Find the area of each figure.

a.

5 in.
6 in.

Use the formula $A = bh$.
$A = 6 \cdot 5 = 30$
The area is 30 in.^{2}.

b.

6 in.
7 in.

Use the formula $A = \frac{1}{2}(bh)$.
$A = \frac{1}{2}(7 \cdot 6) = 21$
The area is 21 in.^{2}.

3 EXAMPLE

Find the volume of each figure.

a.

6 in.
3 in.
5 in.

Use the formula $V = Bh$.
(B = area of the base
$= 3 \cdot 5 = 15$).
$V = 15 \cdot 6 = 90$ in.^{3}
The volume is 90 in.^{3}.

b.

5 in.
2 in.

Use the formula $V = \pi r^2 h$.
$V = 3.14 \cdot 2^2 \cdot 5$
$= 3.14 \cdot 4 \cdot 5 = 62.8$ in.^{3}
The volume is 62.8 in.^{3}.

EXERCISES

For Exercises 1–2, find the perimeter of each figure. For Exercises 3–4, find the
area of each figure.

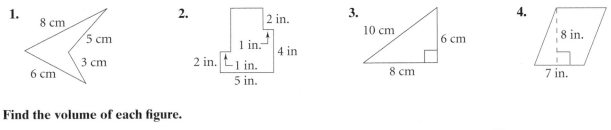

1.
8 cm
5 cm
3 cm
6 cm

2.
2 in.
1 in.
4 in
2 in.
1 in.
5 in.

3.
10 cm
6 cm
8 cm

4.
8 in.
7 in.

Find the volume of each figure.

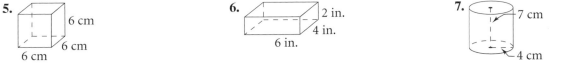

5.
6 cm
6 cm
6 cm

6.
2 in.
4 in.
6 in.

7.
7 cm
4 cm

Translations

A translation is a transformation that moves a figure so that every point in the figure moves the same direction and the same distance. Each translated figure is an image of the original figure. If point A is on the original figure, the corresponding point on the image is A'.

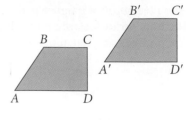

1 EXAMPLE

Graph the image of $\triangle ABC$ after a translation of 4 units right and 2 units down.

To get from $A(-6, 1)$ to $A'(-2, -1)$ by a translation, move
4 units to the right: add 4 to the x-value, $-6 + 4 = -2$,
and 2 units down: add -2 to the y-value, $-1 + (-2) = -1$.

Similarly, the coordinates of B' are $(3, 3)$ and of C' are $(2, 0)$.

You can describe a translation using arrow ($\rightarrow$) notation. The translation from A to A' in Example 1 can be written $A(-6, 1) \rightarrow A'(-2, -1)$.

2 EXAMPLE

Write a rule to describe the translation of $\triangle PQR$ to $\triangle P'Q'R'$.

Use any point on the figure and its image to find the horizontal and vertical translations. Try $P(3, 2)$ and its image $P'(-2, 5)$.

horizontal translation: $-2 - 3 = -5$ 5 units left
vertical translation: $5 - 2 = 3$ 3 units up

The rule for the translation is $(x, y) \rightarrow (x - 5, y + 3)$.

EXERCISES

The vertices of a triangle are given. Graph the triangle and its image after a translation of the specified number of units in each direction.

1. $P(2, 5)$, $Q(5, 6)$, $R(5, 0)$; 4 units right, 5 units down

2. $U(0, 0)$, $V(-5, -3)$, $W(-6, 0)$; 2 units left, 2 units up

Write a rule to describe each translation.

3. $A(4, -4) \rightarrow A'(2, -5)$

4. $G(-1, 9) \rightarrow G'(1, -9)$

5. $M(-2, 0) \rightarrow M'\left(2, \frac{1}{2}\right)$

6. $D(2, 4) \rightarrow D'(-3, 5)$

7. $Q(7, -3) \rightarrow Q'(9, 2)$

8. $W(6, -4) \rightarrow W'(2, 2)$

9.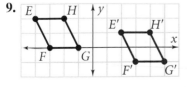

10.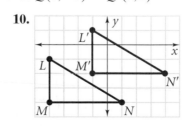

11.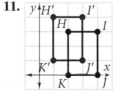

Reflections

A reflection is a transformation that flips a figure over a line, called a line of reflection. The picture at the right shows $\triangle DEF$ and its reflection over the line of reflection ℓ. The image is $\triangle D'E'F'$.

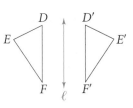

1 EXAMPLE

Reflect the point $P(2, 5)$ over the line $y = 2$. What are the coordinates of its image P''?

● The coordinates of P' are $(2, -1)$.

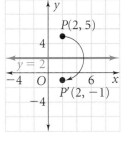

2 EXAMPLE

The vertices of $\triangle ABC$ are $A(-7, 0)$, $B(-5, 6)$, and $C(-3, 4)$. Graph the image of the triangle after a reflection over the line $x = 1$.

To get from $A(-7, 0)$ to $A'(9, 0)$, point A is reflected the same distance on the other side of the line $x = 1$. The coordinates of the other two vertices in the reflected image are $B'(7, 6)$ and $C'(5, 4)$.

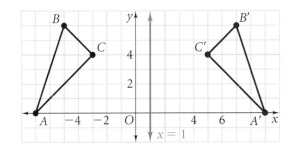

EXERCISES

Graph each point and its image after a reflection over the specified line.

1. $K(2, 3); x = 1$

2. $D(-3, 1); y = -2$

3. $Z(2, 5);$ x-axis

The vertices of various figures are given. Graph both the figure and its image after a reflection over the specified line.

4. $R(2, 4), S(-1, 3), T(2, 0); y = -2$

5. $C(1, 4), D(1, 7), E(-2, 7); x = 3$

6. $H(-5, 5),\ I(6, 0),\ J(0, 0);$ y-axis

7. $K(-2, -3), L(-7, -3), M(-7, -5), N(-2, -5);$ x-axis

The reflected image of each figure is shown in red. Identify the line of reflection.

8.

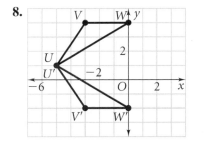

9.

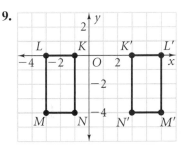

Rotations

A rotation is a transformation that turns a figure about a fixed point, called the *center of rotation*. You can rotate a figure up to 360°. All rotations shown on this page are counterclockwise.

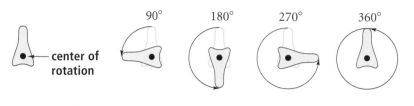

90°   180°   270°   360°

center of rotation

1 EXAMPLE

Find the image of $P(1, 2)$ after a rotation of 90° about the origin.

● The coordinates of P' are $(-2, 1)$.

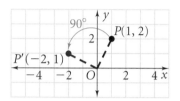

2 EXAMPLE

The vertices of $\triangle ABC$ are $A(0, 2)$, $B(-2, 0)$, and $C(2, 2)$. Find the coordinates of the image of $\triangle ABC$ after a rotation of 180° about the origin.

● The vertices of the image are $A'(0, -2)$, $B'(2, 0)$, and $C'(-2, -2)$.

EXERCISES

Graph each point. Then rotate it the given number of degrees counterclockwise about the given center of rotation and graph the new point.

1. $D(2, 4)$; 90° about the origin

2. $G(-3, -1)$; 180° about $(0, 0)$

3. $Z(4, -2)$; 90° about $(2, 0)$

4. $M(-3, 2)$; 180° about $(2, 3)$

The vertices of a triangle are given. On separate coordinate planes, graph each triangle and its image after a rotation of (a) 90° and (b) 180° about the origin.

5. $A(2, 0), B(7, 2), C(7, 0)$

6. $E(0, 3), F(-5, 4), G(-3, 0)$

7. $L(-2, -1), M(-5, -1), N(-2, -5)$

8. $Q(0, -2), R(0, 0), S(2, 0)$

The triangles in the exercises below were formed by rotating the triangle at the left counterclockwise about the origin. What is each angle of rotation?

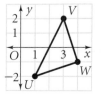

9.

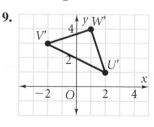

10.

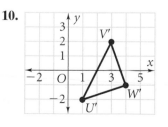

Line Plots

A line plot is created by placing a mark above a number line corresponding to the location of each data item. Line plots have two main advantages:

- You can see the frequency of data items.

- You can see how the data items compare.

EXAMPLE

The table at the right gives the heights (in inches) of a group of twenty-five adults. Display the data in a line plot. Describe the data shown in the line plot.

Height of Adults (inches)

59	60	63	63	64
64	64	65	65	65
67	67	67	67	68
68	68	69	70	70
71	72	73	73	77

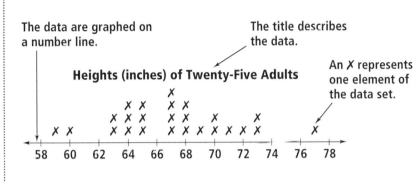

The data are graphed on a number line.

The title describes the data.

An *X* represents one element of the data set.

Heights (inches) of Twenty-Five Adults

The line plot shows that most of the heights are concentrated around 67 inches, the maximum value is 77, and the minimum value is 59.

EXERCISES

Display each set of data in a line plot.

1. 3, 6, 4, 3, 6, 0, 4, 5, 0, 4, 6, 1, 5, 1, 0, 5, 5, 6, 5, 3

2. 19, 18, 18, 18, 19, 20, 19, 18, 18, 17, 18, 20, 19, 17

Draw a line plot for each frequency table.

3.

Number	1	2	3	4	5	6
Frequency	4	1	0	5	7	2

4.

Number	12	13	15	16	18	19
Frequency	2	5	1	3	6	3

5. Olympics Here are the numbers of gold medals won by different countries during the 1998 Winter Olympics (Bulgaria had the least with 1 gold medal and Germany had the most with 12 gold medals).
1, 1, 2, 2, 2, 2, 3, 3, 5, 5, 6, 6, 9, 10, 12
Display the data in a line plot. Describe the data shown in the line plot.

Bar Graphs

Bar graphs are used to compare amounts. The horizontal axis shows the categories and the vertical axis shows the amounts. A multiple bar graph includes a key.

EXAMPLE

Draw a bar graph for the data in the table below.

Median Household Income

State	1995	1997	1999
Calif.	$40,457	$41,203	$43,744
Conn.	$43,993	$45,657	$50,798
Ind.	$36,496	$40,367	$40,929
Tex.	$35,024	$36,408	$38,978
Utah	$39,879	$44,401	$46,094

SOURCE: U.S. Census Bureau

The categories (in the first column) are placed on the horizontal scale. The amounts (in the second, third, and fourth columns) are placed on the vertical scale.

Graph the data for each state. Use the values in the top row to create the key.

The highest projected income is $50,798. So a reasonable range for the vertical scale is 0 to $55,000.

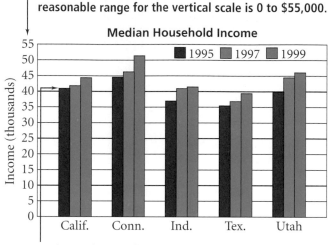

To draw a bar on the graph, estimate its placement based on the vertical scale.

EXERCISES

1. Draw a bar graph for the data in the table below.

Highest Temperatures

City	March	June	August
Juneau, AK	61	86	83
Denver, CO	84	104	101
Atlanta, GA	89	101	102
Honolulu, HI	88	92	93
Detroit, MI	81	104	100
Buffalo, NY	81	96	99
Houston, TX	91	103	107

2. a. Critical Thinking If one more column of data were added to the table in the example, how would the bar graph be different?

  b. If one more row of data were added to the table in the example, how would the bar graph be different?

Histograms

A histogram is a bar graph that shows the frequency, or number of times, a data item occurs. Histograms often combine data into intervals of equal size. The intervals do not overlap.

EXAMPLE

The data at the right show the number of hours of battery life for different brands of batteries used in portable CD players. Use the data to make a histogram.

Hours of Battery Life

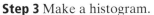

12 9 10 14 10 11
10 18 21 10 14 22

Step 1 Decide on an interval size.

The data start at 9 hours and go to 22 hours. Use equal-sized intervals of 4 hours, beginning with 8 hours. So the first interval will be 8–11.

Step 2 Make a frequency table.

Battery Life

Hours	Tally	Frequency
8–11	⊮ I	6
12–15	III	3
16–19	I	1
20–23	II	2

Step 3 Make a histogram.

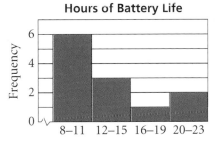

Hours of Battery Life

EXERCISES

1. Students answered a survey question about how long it takes to get ready in the morning. The histogram at the right shows the survey results.

   a. Which interval indicates the answers most students gave?

   b. How many students answered the survey question?

   c. Why might no students have given an answer in the interval 50–59?

   d. **Critical Thinking** With the information you have, could you redraw the histogram with intervals half their current size? Explain why or why not.

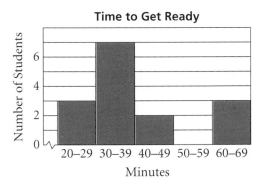

Time to Get Ready

2. a. An internet company surveyed their users. The first 25 people who responded gave the ages shown at the right. What intervals would you use to make a histogram?

   b. Make a frequency table for the data.

   c. Make a histogram.

Age of Internet Users

25, 43, 65, 12, 8, 30, 44, 68, 18, 21,
25, 33, 37, 54, 61, 29, 31, 38, 22, 48,
19, 34, 55, 14, 21

3. a. **Data Collection** Survey your class to find out what day of the month they were born. For example, 12 if a student's birthday is August 12th.

   b. What intervals would you use to make a histogram?

   c. Make a frequency table for the data.

   d. Make a histogram.

Line Graphs

Line graphs are used to display the change in a set of data over a period of time. A multiple-line graph shows change in more than one category of data over time. You can use a line graph to look for trends and make predictions.

EXAMPLE

Graph the data in the table below.

Households with VCR and Cable TV (millions)

Year	1985	1990	1995	1996	1997	1998
VCR	18	63	77	79	82	83
Cable TV	36	52	60	63	64	66

SOURCE: Television Bureau of Advertising, Inc., *Trends in Television*

Since the data show changes over time for two sets of data, use a double line graph. The horizontal scale displays years. The vertical scale displays the number of households for each category, VCR and cable TV.

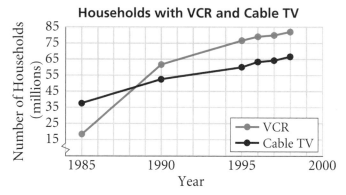

Notice that there is a *break* in the vertical scale, which goes from 0 to 85. A zigzag line is used to indicate a break from 0 to 15 since there is no data to graph in this part of the *y*-axis.

EXERCISES

Graph the following data.

1.

Market Shares (percent)

Year	1994	1995	1996	1997	1998	1999	2000
Rap/Hip Hop	7.9	6.7	8.9	10.1	9.7	10.8	12.9
Pop	10.3	10.1	9.3	9.4	10.0	10.3	11.0

SOURCE: The Recording Industry of America

2.

Percents of Schools with Internet Access

Year	1995	1996	1997	1998	1999
Elementary	46	61	75	88	94
Secondary	65	77	89	94	98

SOURCE: U.S. National Center for Education Statistics

Circle Graphs

A circle graph is an efficient way to present certain types of data. The graphs show data as percents or fractions of a whole. The total must be 100% or 1. Circle graphs are used to show the parts of the whole. The angles at the center are central angles, and each angle is proportional to the percent or fraction of the total.

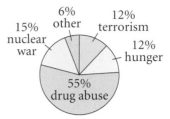

What Do You Think Is the Number One Problem in the World Today?

Source: *The Second Kids' World Almanac*

EXAMPLE

The table below shows the number of people in the United States who have at least one grandchild under the age of 18. Draw a circle graph for the data.

Ages of U.S. Grandparents

Age	People (millions)
44 and under	3.6
45–54	10.3
55–64	15.0
65 and over	18.2

Step 1 Add to find the total number.

$3.6 + 10.3 + 15.0 + 18.2 = 47.1$ (million)

Step 2 For each central angle, set up a proportion to find the measure. Use a calculator to solve each proportion.

$\frac{3.6}{47.1} = \frac{a}{360°}$ $\frac{10.3}{47.1} = \frac{b}{360°}$ $\frac{15.0}{47.1} = \frac{c}{360°}$ $\frac{18.2}{47.1} = \frac{d}{360°}$

$a \approx 27.5°$ $b \approx 78.7°$ $c \approx 114.6°$ $d \approx 139.1°$

Step 3 Use a compass to draw a circle. Draw the approximate central angles with a protractor.

Step 4 Label each sector. Add any necessary information.

Ages of U.S. Grandparents

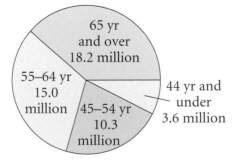

EXERCISES

1. a. Use the data in the table to draw a circle graph.
   b. Approximately what percent of students ride the bus?
   c. Approximately how many times more students walk than ride in a car?

Transportation Mode	Walk	Bicycle	Bus	Car
Number of Students	252	135	432	81

2. Data Collection Survey your class to find out how they get to school. Use the data to draw a circle graph.

Box-and-Whisker Plots

To show how data items are spread out, you can arrange a set of data in order from least to greatest. The maximum, minimum, and median give you some information about the data. You can better describe the data by dividing it into fourths.

The lower quartile is the median of the lower half of the data. The upper quartile is the median of the upper half of the data. If the data set has an odd number of items, the median is not included in either the upper half or the lower half.

The data below describes the highway gas mileage (mi/gal) for several cars.

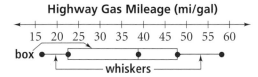

minimum | median = 38.5 | | maximum

17   19   27   37   40   42   52   58

lower quartile $\frac{19 + 27}{2} = 23$ upper quartile $\frac{42 + 52}{2} = 47$

A box-and-whisker plot is a visual representation of data. The box-and-whisker plot below displays the gas mileage information.

Highway Gas Mileage (mi/gal)

15 20 25 30 35 40 45 50 55 60

box   whiskers

The box represents the data from the lower quartile to the upper quartile. The vertical line segment represents the median. Horizontal line segments called whiskers show the spread of the data to the minimum and to the maximum.

EXERCISES

Create a box-and-whisker plot for each data set.

1. {3, 2, 3, 4, 6, 6, 7}

2. {1, 1.5, 1.7, 2, 6.1, 6.2, 7}

3. {1, 2, 5, 6, 9, 12, 7, 10}

4. {65, 66, 59, 61, 67, 70, 67, 66, 69, 70, 63}

5. {29, 32, 40, 31, 33, 39, 27, 42}

6. {3, 3, 5, 7, 1, 10, 10, 4, 4, 7, 9, 8, 6}

7. {1, 1.2, 1.3, 4, 4.1, 4.2, 7}

8. {1, 3.8, 3.9, 4, 4.3, 4.4, 7, 5}

9. Jobs Below are the number of hours a student worked each week at her summer job. When she applied for the job, she was told that the typical work week was 29 hours.

$$29, 25, 21, 20, 17, 16, 15, 33, 33, 30, 15$$

a. Make a box-and-whisker plot for the data.
b. How many weeks are above the upper quartile? What are the numbers of hours worked?
c. What is the median number of hours she worked? What is the mean? Compare them to the typical work week.

10. Writing In what ways are histograms and box-and-whisker plots alike, and in what ways are they different?

Choosing an Appropriate Graph

The type of data you want to display can suggest an appropriate graph. You can have data by categories (qualitative data), such as states (page 736), years (page 739), or mode of transportation (page 739). You may also have measurement data (quantitative data), such as height (page 735), time to get ready in the morning (page 737), or gas mileage (page 740).

The table below lists some common types of graphs and how they are frequently used.

Graph	Use
Bar Graph	To display frequency of categories
Circle Graph	To show categories as part of a whole
Line Graph	To show trends over time
Line Plot, Histogram, Stem-and-Leaf Plot	To display frequency distribution of measurement data
Box-and-Whisker Plot	To summarize the distribution of measurement data
Scatter Plot	To display possible relationships in data pairs

1 EXAMPLE

Would you use a line graph or a circle graph to display the percent of fiction books published each year for the last ten years?

A circle graph shows percents, but it would not allow you to show the change over time. A line graph would be more appropriate.

EXERCISES

Choose the appropriate graph to display each set of data. Explain your choice.

1. circle graph or bar graph
   how much the average family spends on rent, food, transportation, utilities, and entertainment in October

2. bar graph or line graph
   the number of runners in the Olympic marathon for each of the last five Olympic games

3. scatter plot or double bar graph
   the ages of twelve cars and their levels of emissions

4. double box-and-whisker plot or scatter plot
   the heights of men and women playing professional basketball in 2004

Open-Ended For each type of graph, describe a set of data that would be appropriate.

5. stem-and-leaf plot
6. double line graph
7. circle graph

Misleading Graphs

There are many ways to graph data that show the data accurately. There are also ways to graph data that are misleading. One way that is misleading is graphing data that has less than the whole vertical axis, but doesn't point this out with the use of a break symbol on the axis.

1 EXAMPLE

What impression does the graph at the right give? What is actually true about the data?

Company Revenues

The graph implies that company revenues are growing quickly. Actually, company revenues are increasing more slowly.

Another way a graph can mislead is by using shapes that increase in both height and width, which implies a much bigger increase has happened, since the area increases much more than the height alone.

2 EXAMPLE

What makes the graph at the right misleading? Explain.

Books Read in Two Years

Looking at the vertical axis, you can see that the number of books read increased by one third. However, the bar on the right increased not only in height, but width. The area of the second bar is more than two times the area of the first bar. This gives the impression that the increase was much greater than it really was.

EXERCISES

For each graph below, (a) explain how the graph is misleading, and (b) explain how to redraw the graph so it is not misleading.

1. **Times for 10-Mile Run**

2. **Towels Sold**

3. Choose one of the graphs on this page. Redraw the graph to display the data accurately.

Probability Distributions

A probability distribution is a function that gives the probability of each event in a sample space. You can use a table or a graph to show a probability distribution.

1 EXAMPLE

Experimental Probability Use the data in the table below to make a graph of the probability distribution.

What Is Your Favorite Color?

Color	Percent
Red	27
Blue	35
Green	17
Black	21

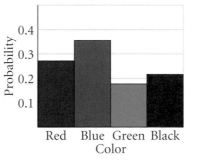

What Is Your Favorite Color?

EXERCISES

Use the data in each table to make a graph of each probability distribution.

1. **How Many Siblings Do You Have?**

Number	Percent
0	38
1	41
2	17
3 or more	4

2. **Where Do People Live in the U.S.?**

Region	Percent
Northeast	19.0
Midwest	22.9
South	35.6
West	22.5

3. **Theoretical Probability** Suppose you roll two number cubes to find the sum of the numbers.
   a. Show the probability distribution in a table and a graph.
   b. Find the mean and the range of the distribution.
   c. What is the probability that the sum is 10?
   d. What is the probability that the sum is 7?
   e. What is the probability that the sum is less than 9?

4. **Theoretical Probability** Use the spinner at the right.
   a. Show the probability distribution in a table for getting each color.
   b. Show the probability distribution in a graph.
   c. What is the probability that you will spin green?
   d. What is the probability that you will spin blue or red?

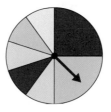

5. **Critical Thinking** What is the sum of the probabilities in a probability distribution? Explain.

Simulations

On page 218, you learned how to simulate a problem using random numbers generated by a graphing calculator or computer program. You can also simulate some probability problems using a coin, spinner, or number cube.

1 EXAMPLE

Describe a simulation you could use to model each situation.

a. About 10% of the members of Congress in the House of Representatives represent California. What is the probability that three representatives chosen at random are all from California?

There are not two equally likely outcomes, so using a coin is not a good choice.

A spinner lets you represent outcomes that are not equally likely. Here, there are two outcomes: either a representative is from California (10%) or not (90%). So a spinner that models this situation would have a region with the central angle of 36°, showing 10% of the area of the circle.

Each three spins of the spinner would be one trial.

b. One fifth of the students in a school choose blue as a favorite color. What is the probability that four students all prefer blue?

One way to simulate this problem is using a number cube. Choose one number to represent the one fifth of students who prefer blue, and four numbers to represent the four fifths of the students who don't. Ignore the extra number when it is rolled, and do not count that roll in any trial. One choice is to have 1 represent liking blue, 2–5 represent not liking blue, and ignore any 6s that are rolled. Each four rolls of the number cube would be one trial.

EXERCISES

Describe a simulation could you use to represent each situation.

1. Half of the books sold in one bookstore are trade paperbacks. What is the probability that the next six books sold will be trade paperbacks?

2. For a woman aged 25 or more, there is a 25% chance that she has at least a bachelor's degree from college. What is the probability that four out of 10 women over age 25 all have at least a bachelor's degree?

3. By weight, about 38% of the pumpkins grown in the United States come from Illinois. What is the probability that three pumpkins selected at random all come from Illinois?

4. About two thirds of school-aged students have access to a computer at home. What is the probability that six students do not have access to a computer at home?

5. A basketball player has made 82 of her last 100 free throws. What is the probability that she will make her next five free throws?

6. **Open-Ended** Write a probability problem you could solve using a simulation.

Conducting a Survey

Statisticians collect information about specific groups. Any group of objects or people is a population. When a population is too large to survey, they study a sample, or part, of the population to find out characteristics of the population.

Three kinds of samples, random, systematic, and stratified, are explained in the table below.

Name	Sampling Method	Example
Random	Survey a population at random.	Survey people whose names are drawn out of a hat.
Systematic	Select a number n at random. Then survey every nth person.	Select the number 5 at random. Survey every fifth person.
Stratified	Separate a population into smaller groups, each with a certain characteristic. Then survey at random within each group.	Separate a high school into four groups by grade level. Survey a random sample of students from each grade.

When statisticians survey a sample of a population, they try to write questions that are as unbiased as possible. Biased questions can make assumptions that may or may not be true. They can also make one answer seem better than another.

1 EXAMPLE

Determine whether each question is biased or not. Explain.

a. What kind of pet do you own?

This question is biased. It assumes you own a pet.

b. Do you prefer exciting action movies or sedate foreign films?

This question is biased. It makes action movies seem more appealing than foreign films.

c. What is your favorite food?

This question is unbiased. It does not try to persuade your answer.

EXERCISES

Tell whether each survey plan describes a good sample and, if so, which method of sampling is used.

1. A candidate calls every 50th name in the phone book to find out how the person likes the candidate.

2. A factory tests the quality of the last 25 out of 1000 shirts made.

3. A bindery selects 10 of the 450 packages of inserts at random to see if all the inserts were printed properly.

Determine whether each question is biased or not. Explain.

4. What toppings do you like on pizza?

5. Where would you most like to go for a vacation?

Interpreting Statistical Results

One-variable Data Suppose you survey 50 people and 30% of them like the color blue best. The size of your sample affects the confidence you should have in the result. You can use the margin of error formula to interpret the result.

1 EXAMPLE

Find the margin of error for your survey of 50 people.

margin of error $= \pm\dfrac{1}{\sqrt{n}}$ **Use the margin of error formula.**

$\qquad = \pm\dfrac{1}{\sqrt{50}}$ **Substitute 50 for n, the size of the sample.**

$\qquad \approx \pm 0.1414$ **Use a calculator.**

The margin of error is about $\pm 14\%$, so about 16% to 44% of the population you sampled is likely to prefer blue.

Two-variable Data Suppose you compare people's height and shoe size. You can use a line of best fit (or trend line) to predict shoe size for various heights.

Predictions within the range of data values (called interpolating) are more reliable than predictions beyond the range of data values (called extrapolating).

2 EXAMPLE

Use the scatter plot at the right. What size shoe would you predict a woman 6 ft 3 in. tall would wear? A woman 7 ft tall?

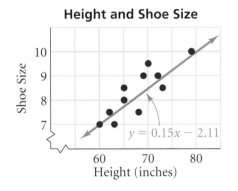

Height and Shoe Size

A woman 6 ft 3 in. tall is 75 inches tall. Use the line of best fit; the shoe size would likely be $y = 0.15(75) - 2.11 \approx 9$.

A woman 7 ft tall is 84 in. The shoe size would likely be $y = 0.15(84) - 2.11 \approx 10.5$. This is an extrapolation, so it is a less reliable result.

EXERCISES

Find the margin of error for each sample size.
Round to the nearest percent.

1. 100 people   **2.** 500 people   **3.** 1000 people   **4.** 10,000 people

5. Critical Thinking What sample size will produce a margin of error of $\pm 5\%$?

6. Use the scatter plot in Example 2. What would be the shoe size of a woman 5 ft 7 in. tall?

7. Critical Thinking What height would you predict a woman wearing size 9.5 shoes would be?

8. a. Data Collection Find data that you could display in a scatter plot.
   b. Use your scatter plot to make a prediction about a value not included in one data set.

Spreadsheets

You can use a spreadsheet to evaluate formulas. Spreadsheets use the symbols
$+$ for addition and $-$ for subtraction, but different symbols for other operations.

Multiplication: $* \rightarrow$ $\quad\quad 10 * 2 = 10 \cdot 2 = 20$

Division: $/ \rightarrow$ $\quad\quad 10 / 2 = 10 \div 2 = 5$

Exponent: $\wedge \rightarrow$ $\quad\quad 10 \wedge 2 = 10^2 = 100$

EXAMPLE

Evaluate the formula $P = 2\ell + 2w$ for $\ell = 3$ and for whole-number values of w from 8 to 11.

Enter the values of ℓ and w into the first two columns. Cell A2 has the value of ℓ. Cell B2 has the first value of w. In cell C2, enter the expression $= 2*A2 + 2*B2$ to find the perimeter of a figure with length 3 and width 8.

Column names

	A	B	C
1	L	W	2L + 2W
2		3	8	= 2*A2 + 2* B2
3		3	9	
4		3	10	
5		3	**11**	

Row numbers

Cell B5

The spreadsheet evaluates the expression automatically.

Copy the expression in cell C2 into cells C3, C4, and C5. The spreadsheet automatically updates for the values of ℓ and w in rows 3, 4, and 5.

✗	✓	= 2*A2 + 2* B2
	A	B	C
1	L	W	2L + 2W
2		3	8	**22**
3		3	9	24
4		3	10	26
5		3	11	28

EXERCISES

Suppose the values of a, b, and c are in cells A2, B2, and C2 of a spreadsheet. Write the expression you would use to enter each formula in the spreadsheet.

1. $P = a + b + c$
2. $T = \dfrac{3a + 5b}{8}$
3. $R = \frac{1}{2}bc$
4. $A = c^2$

5. You deposit $200 in an account that earns 6% compounded annually for three years. The spreadsheet below shows the balance at the end of each year.

	A	B	C	D	E
1	Year	Start of Year	Rate	Interest	End of Year
2	1st	$200.00	0.06	$12.00	$212.00
3	2nd	$212.00	0.06	$12.72	$224.72
4	3rd	$224.72	0.06	$13.48	$238.20

a. In which cell of the spreadsheet would you find the formula $= B3 * C3$?
b. In which cell of the spreadsheet would you find the formula $= B4 + D4$?

Tables

Table 1 Measures

United States Customary	Metric

Length

12 inches (in.) = 1 foot (ft)	10 millimeters (mm) = 1 centimeter (cm)
36 in. = 1 yard (yd)	100 cm = 1 meter (m)
3 ft = 1 yard	1000 mm = 1 meter
5280 ft = 1 mile (mi)	1000 m = 1 kilometer (km)
1760 yd = 1 mile	

Area

144 square inches (in.^2) = 1 square foot (ft^2)	100 square millimeters (mm^2) = 1 square centimeter (cm^2)
9 ft^2 = 1 square yard (yd^2)	10,000 cm^2 = 1 square meter (m^2)
43,560 ft^2 = 1 acre (a)	10,000 m^2 = 1 hectare (ha)
4840 yd^2 = 1 acre	

Volume

1728 cubic inches (in.^3) = 1 cubic foot (ft^3)	1000 cubic millimeters (mm^3) = 1 cubic centimeter (cm^3)
27 ft^3 = 1 cubic yard (yd^3)	1,000,000 cm^3 = 1 cubic meter (m^3)

Liquid Capacity

8 fluid ounces (fl oz) = 1 cup (c)	1000 milliliters (mL) = 1 liter (L)
2 c = 1 pint (pt)	1000 L = 1 kiloliter (kL)
2 pt = 1 quart (qt)	
4 qt = 1 gallon (gal)	

Weight or Mass

16 ounces (oz) = 1 pound (lb)	1000 milligrams (mg) = 1 gram (g)
2000 pounds = 1 ton (t)	1000 g = 1 kilogram (kg)
	1000 kg = 1 metric ton

Temperature

32°F = freezing point of water	0°C = freezing point of water
98.6°F = normal body temperature	37°C = normal body temperature
212°F = boiling point of water	100°C = boiling point of water

Time	
60 seconds (s) = 1 minute (min)	365 days = 1 year (yr)
60 minutes = 1 hour (h)	52 weeks (approx.) = 1 year
24 hours = 1 day (d)	12 months = 1 year
7 days = 1 week (wk)	10 years = 1 decade
4 weeks (approx.) = 1 month (mo)	100 years = 1 century

Table 2 📖 Reading Math Symbols

Symbol	Meaning	Page
·	multiplication sign, times ($\times$)	p. 4
=	equals	p. 5
( )	parentheses for grouping	p. 9
a^n	nth power of a	p. 9
%	percent	p. 11
[ ]	brackets for grouping	p. 12
. . .	and so on	p. 17
$-a$	opposite of a	p. 17
π	pi, an irrational number, approximately equal to 3.14	p. 18
<	is less than	p. 19
>	is greater than	p. 19
$\lvert a \rvert$	absolute value of a	p. 20
°	degree(s)	p. 26
$\begin{bmatrix} 1 & 2 \\ 3 & 4 \end{bmatrix}$	matrix	p. 27
$\frac{1}{a}, a \neq 0$	reciprocal of a	p. 40
(x, y)	ordered pair	p. 59
$\stackrel{?}{=}$	Is the statement true?	p. 75
$\triangle ABC$	triangle ABC	p. 100
$\approx$	is approximately equal to	p. 119
$\leq$	is less than or equal to	p. 134
$\geq$	is greater than or equal to	p. 134
{ }	set braces	p. 160
$a:b$	ratio of a to b	p. 182
$\neq$	is not equal to	p. 182
AB	length of $\overline{AB}$; distance between points A and B	p. 189
$\overline{AB}$	segment with endpoints A and B	p. 189
$\cong$	is congruent to	p. 190
$\angle A$	angle A	p. 190
$P(\text{event})$	probability of the event	p. 211
$f(x)$	f of x; the function value at x	p. 243
x_1, x_2, etc.	specific values of the variable x	p. 264
y_1, y_2, etc.	specific values of the variable y	p. 264
$\overleftrightarrow{AB}$	line through points A and B	p. 284
m	slope of a linear function	p. 290
b	y-intercept of a linear function	p. 291
a^{-n}	$\frac{1}{a^n}, a \neq 0$	p. 394
$\sqrt{x}$	nonnegative square root of x	p. 524
$\pm$	plus or minus	p. 524
$\sin A$	sine of $\angle A$	p. 621
$\cos A$	cosine of $\angle A$	p. 621
$\tan A$	tangent of $\angle A$	p. 621
$\bar{x}$	mean of data values of x	p. 620
$m\angle A$	measure of angle A	p. 625
$_nP_r$	permutations of n things taken r at a time	p. 681
$_nC_r$	combinations of n things taken r at a time	p. 687
^	raised to a power (in a spreadsheet formula)	p. 747
*	multiply (in a spreadsheet formula)	p. 747
/	divide (in a spreadsheet formula)	p. 747

Tables

Table 3 Squares and Square Roots

Number n	Square n^2	Positive Square Root $\sqrt{n}$	Number n	Square n^2	Positive Square Root $\sqrt{n}$	Number n	Square n^2	Positive Square Root $\sqrt{n}$
1	1	1.000	51	2601	7.141	101	10,201	10.050
2	4	1.414	52	2704	7.211	102	10,404	10.100
3	9	1.732	53	2809	7.280	103	10,609	10.149
4	16	2.000	54	2916	7.348	104	10,816	10.198
5	25	2.236	55	3025	7.416	105	11,025	10.247
6	36	2.449	56	3136	7.483	106	11,236	10.296
7	49	2.646	57	3249	7.550	107	11,449	10.344
8	64	2.828	58	3364	7.616	108	11,664	10.392
9	81	3.000	59	3481	7.681	109	11,881	10.440
10	100	3.162	60	3600	7.746	110	12,100	10.488
11	121	3.317	61	3721	7.810	111	12,321	10.536
12	144	3.464	62	3844	7.874	112	12,544	10.583
13	169	3.606	63	3969	7.937	113	12,769	10.630
14	196	3.742	64	4096	8.000	114	12,996	10.677
15	225	3.873	65	4225	8.062	115	13,225	10.724
16	256	4.000	66	4356	8.124	116	13,456	10.770
17	289	4.123	67	4489	8.185	117	13,689	10.817
18	324	4.243	68	4624	8.246	118	13,924	10.863
19	361	4.359	69	4761	8.307	119	14,161	10.909
20	400	4.472	70	4900	8.367	120	14,400	10.954
21	441	4.583	71	5041	8.426	121	14,641	11.000
22	484	4.690	72	5184	8.485	122	14,884	11.045
23	529	4.796	73	5329	8.544	123	15,129	11.091
24	576	4.899	74	5476	8.602	124	15,376	11.136
25	625	5.000	75	5625	8.660	125	15,625	11.180
26	676	5.099	76	5776	8.718	126	15,876	11.225
27	729	5.196	77	5929	8.775	127	16,129	11.269
28	784	5.292	78	6084	8.832	128	16,384	11.314
29	841	5.385	79	6241	8.888	129	16,641	11.358
30	900	5.477	80	6400	8.944	130	16,900	11.402
31	961	5.568	81	6561	9.000	131	17,161	11.446
32	1024	5.657	82	6724	9.055	132	17,424	11.489
33	1089	5.745	83	6889	9.110	133	17,689	11.533
34	1156	5.831	84	7056	9.165	134	17,956	11.576
35	1225	5.916	85	7225	9.220	135	18,225	11.619
36	1296	6.000	86	7396	9.274	136	18,496	11.662
37	1369	6.083	87	7569	9.327	137	18,769	11.705
38	1444	6.164	88	7744	9.381	138	19,044	11.747
39	1521	6.245	89	7921	9.434	139	19,321	11.790
40	1600	6.325	90	8100	9.487	140	19,600	11.832
41	1681	6.403	91	8281	9.539	141	19,881	11.874
42	1764	6.481	92	8464	9.592	142	20,164	11.916
43	1849	6.557	93	8649	9.644	143	20,449	11.958
44	1936	6.633	94	8836	9.695	144	20,736	12.000
45	2025	6.708	95	9025	9.747	145	21,025	12.042
46	2116	6.782	96	9216	9.798	146	21,316	12.083
47	2209	6.856	97	9409	9.849	147	21,609	12.124
48	2304	6.928	98	9604	9.899	148	21,904	12.166
49	2401	7.000	99	9801	9.950	149	22,201	12.207
50	2500	7.071	100	10,000	10.000	150	22,500	12.247

Table 4 Trigonometric Ratios

Angle	Sine	Cosine	Tangent	Angle	Sine	Cosine	Tangent
1°	0.0175	0.9998	0.0175	46°	0.7193	0.6947	1.0355
2°	0.0349	0.9994	0.0349	47°	0.7314	0.6820	1.0724
3°	0.0523	0.9986	0.0524	48°	0.7431	0.6691	1.1106
4°	0.0698	0.9976	0.0699	49°	0.7547	0.6561	1.1504
5°	0.0872	0.9962	0.0875	50°	0.7660	0.6428	1.1918
6°	0.1045	0.9945	0.1051	51°	0.7771	0.6293	1.2349
7°	0.1219	0.9925	0.1228	52°	0.7880	0.6157	1.2799
8°	0.1392	0.9903	0.1405	53°	0.7986	0.6018	1.3270
9°	0.1564	0.9877	0.1584	54°	0.8090	0.5878	1.3764
10°	0.1736	0.9848	0.1763	55°	0.8192	0.5736	1.4281
11°	0.1908	0.9816	0.1944	56°	0.8290	0.5592	1.4826
12°	0.2079	0.9781	0.2126	57°	0.8387	0.5446	1.5399
13°	0.2250	0.9744	0.2309	58°	0.8480	0.5299	1.6003
14°	0.2419	0.9703	0.2493	59°	0.8572	0.5150	1.6643
15°	0.2588	0.9659	0.2679	60°	0.8660	0.5000	1.7321
16°	0.2756	0.9613	0.2867	61°	0.8746	0.4848	1.8040
17°	0.2924	0.9563	0.3057	62°	0.8829	0.4695	1.8807
18°	0.3090	0.9511	0.3249	63°	0.8910	0.4540	1.9626
19°	0.3256	0.9455	0.3443	64°	0.8988	0.4384	2.0503
20°	0.3420	0.9397	0.3640	65°	0.9063	0.4226	2.1445
21°	0.3584	0.9336	0.3839	66°	0.9135	0.4067	2.2460
22°	0.3746	0.9272	0.4040	67°	0.9205	0.3907	2.3559
23°	0.3907	0.9205	0.4245	68°	0.9272	0.3746	2.4751
24°	0.4067	0.9135	0.4452	69°	0.9336	0.3584	2.6051
25°	0.4226	0.9063	0.4663	70°	0.9397	0.3420	2.7475
26°	0.4384	0.8988	0.4877	71°	0.9455	0.3256	2.9042
27°	0.4540	0.8910	0.5095	72°	0.9511	0.3090	3.0777
28°	0.4695	0.8829	0.5317	73°	0.9563	0.2924	3.2709
29°	0.4848	0.8746	0.5543	74°	0.9613	0.2756	3.4874
30°	0.5000	0.8660	0.5774	75°	0.9659	0.2588	3.7321
31°	0.5150	0.8572	0.6009	76°	0.9703	0.2419	4.0108
32°	0.5299	0.8480	0.6249	77°	0.9744	0.2250	4.3315
33°	0.5446	0.8387	0.6494	78°	0.9781	0.2079	4.7046
34°	0.5592	0.8290	0.6745	79°	0.9816	0.1908	5.1446
35°	0.5736	0.8192	0.7002	80°	0.9848	0.1736	5.6713
36°	0.5878	0.8090	0.7265	81°	0.9877	0.1564	6.3138
37°	0.6018	0.7986	0.7536	82°	0.9903	0.1392	7.1154
38°	0.6157	0.7880	0.7813	83°	0.9925	0.1219	8.1443
39°	0.6293	0.7771	0.8098	84°	0.9945	0.1045	9.5144
40°	0.6428	0.7660	0.8391	85°	0.9962	0.0872	11.4301
41°	0.6561	0.7547	0.8693	86°	0.9976	0.0698	14.3007
42°	0.6691	0.7431	0.9004	87°	0.9986	0.0523	19.0811
43°	0.6820	0.7314	0.9325	88°	0.9994	0.0349	28.6363
44°	0.6947	0.7193	0.9657	89°	0.9998	0.0175	57.2900
45°	0.7071	0.7071	1.0000	90°	1.0000	0.0000	

Tables

Properties and Formulas

Chapter 1

Order of Operations
1. Perform any operation(s) inside grouping symbols.
2. Simplify powers.
3. Multiply and divide in order from left to right.
4. Add and subtract in order from left to right.

Identity Property of Addition
For every real number n, $n + 0 = n$.

Inverse Property of Addition
For every real number n, there is an additive inverse $-n$ such that $n + (-n) = 0$.

Identity Property of Multiplication
For every real number n, $1 \cdot n = n$.

Multiplication Property of Zero
For every real number n, $n \cdot 0 = 0$.

Multiplication Property of -1
For every real number n, $-1 \cdot n = -n$.

Inverse Property of Multiplication
For every nonzero real number a, there is a multiplicative inverse $\frac{1}{a}$ such that $a\left(\frac{1}{a}\right) = 1$.

Distributive Property
For every real number a, b, and c:
$a(b + c) = ab + ac$
$(b + c)a = ba + ca$
$a(b - c) = ab - ac$
$(b - c)a = ba - ca$

Commutative Property of Addition
For every real number a and b, $a + b = b + a$.

Commutative Property of Multiplication
For every real number a and b, $a \cdot b = b \cdot a$.

Associative Property of Addition
For every real number a, b, and c,
$(a + b) + c = a + (b + c)$.

Associative Property of Multiplication
For every real number a, b, and c,
$(a \cdot b) \cdot c = a \cdot (b \cdot c)$.

Chapter 2

Addition Property of Equality
For every real number a, b, and c, if $a = b$, then $a + c = b + c$.

Subtraction Property of Equality
For every real number a, b, and c, if $a = b$, then $a - c = b - c$.

Multiplication Property of Equality
For every real number a, b, and c, if $a = b$, then $a \cdot c = b \cdot c$.

Division Property of Equality
For every real number a, b, and c, with $c \neq 0$, if $a = b$, then $\frac{a}{c} = \frac{b}{c}$.

Chapter 3
The following properties of inequality are also true for $\geq$ and $\leq$.

Addition Property of Inequality
For every real number a, b, and c,
if $a > b$, then $a + c > b + c$;
if $a < b$, then $a + c < b + c$.

Subtraction Property of Inequality
For every real number a, b, and c,
if $a > b$, then $a - c > b - c$;
if $a < b$, then $a - c < b - c$.

Multiplication Property of Inequality
For every real number a and b, and for $c > 0$,
if $a > b$, then $ac > bc$;
if $a < b$, then $ac < bc$.

For every real number a and b, and for $c < 0$,
if $a > b$, then $ac < bc$;
if $a < b$, then $ac > bc$.

Division Property of Inequality
For every real number a and b, and for $c > 0$,
if $a > b$, then $\frac{a}{c} > \frac{b}{c}$;

if $a < b$, then $\frac{a}{c} < \frac{b}{c}$.

For every real number a and b, and for $c < 0$,
if $a > b$, then $\frac{a}{c} < \frac{b}{c}$;

if $a < b$, then $\frac{a}{c} > \frac{b}{c}$.

Reflexive Property of Equality
For every real number a, $a = a$.

Symmetric Property of Equality
For every real number a and b,
if $a = b$, then $b = a$.

Transitive Property of Equality
For every real number a, b, and c,
if $a = b$ and $b = c$, then $a = c$.

Transitive Property of Inequality
For every real number a, b, and c,
if $a < b$ and $b < c$, then $a < c$.

Chapter 4

Cross Products of a Proportion
If $\frac{a}{b} = \frac{c}{d}$, then $ad = bc$.

Percent Error Formula
$$\text{percent error} = \frac{\text{greatest possible error}}{\text{measurement}}$$

Probability Formula
$$P(\text{event}) = \frac{\text{number of favorable outcomes}}{\text{number of possible outcomes}}$$

Probability of Complement Formula
$P(\text{event}) + P(\text{not event}) = 1$;
$P(\text{not event}) = 1 - P(\text{event})$

Probability of Two Independent Events
If A and B are independent events,
$P(A \text{ and } B) = P(A) \cdot P(B)$.

Probability of Two Dependent Events
If A and B are dependent events,
$P(A \text{ then } B) = P(A) \cdot P(B \text{ after } A)$.

Chapter 5

Arithmetic Sequence
The form for the rule of an arithmetic sequence is
$A(n) = a + (n - 1)d$, where $A(n)$ is the nth term, a is
the first term, $n - 1$ is the term number, and d is the
common difference.

Chapter 6

Slope
$$\text{slope} = \frac{\text{vertical change}}{\text{horizontal change}} = \frac{\text{rise}}{\text{run}}$$

Slope-Intercept Form of a Linear Equation
The slope-intercept form of a linear equation is
$y = mx + b$, where m is the slope and b is the
y-intercept.

Standard Form of a Linear Equation
The standard form of a linear equation is
$Ax + By = C$, where A, B, and C are real numbers
and A and B are not both zero.

Point-Slope Form of a Linear Equation
The point-slope form of the equation of a nonvertical
line that passes through the point (x_1, y_1) with slope m
is $y - y_1 = m(x - x_1)$.

Slopes of Parallel Lines
Nonvertical lines are parallel if they have the same
slope and different y-intercepts. Any two vertical
lines are parallel.

Slopes of Perpendicular Lines
Two lines are perpendicular if the product of their
slopes is -1. A vertical and a horizontal line are
perpendicular.

Chapter 7

Solutions of Systems of Linear Equations
A system of linear equations can have one solution,
no solution, or infinitely many solutions:
- If the lines have different slopes, the lines intersect,
  so there is one solution.
- If the lines have the same slopes and different
  y-intercepts, the lines are parallel, so there are
  no solutions.
- If the lines have the same slopes and the same
  y-intercepts, the lines are the same, so there are
  infinitely many solutions.

Chapter 8

Zero as an Exponent
For every nonzero number a, $a^0 = 1$.

Negative Exponent
For every nonzero number a and integer n, $a^{-n} = \frac{1}{a^n}$.

Scientific Notation
A number in scientific notation is written as the
product of two factors in the form $a \times 10^n$, where n is
an integer and $1 \le a < 10$.

Multiplying Powers with the Same Base

For every nonzero number a and integers m and n,
$a^m \cdot a^n = a^{m+n}$.

Dividing Powers with the Same Base

For every nonzero number a and integers m and n,
$\frac{a^m}{a^n} = a^{m-n}$.

Raising a Power to a Power

For every nonzero number a and integers m and n,
$(a^m)^n = a^{mn}$.

Raising a Product to a Power

For every nonzero number a and b and integer n,
$(ab)^n = a^n b^n$.

Raising a Quotient to a Power

For every nonzero number a and b and integer n,
$\left(\frac{a}{b}\right)^n = \frac{a^n}{b^n}$.

Geometric Sequence

The form for the rule of a geometric sequence is
$A(n) = a \cdot r^{n-1}$, where $A(n)$ is the nth term, a is the first term, $n-1$ is the term number, and r is the common ratio.

Exponential Growth and Decay

An exponential function has the form $y = a \cdot b^x$, where a is a nonzero constant, b is greater than 0 and not equal to 1, and x is a real number.

- The function $y = a \cdot b^x$ models exponential growth for $a > 0$ and $b > 1$. b is the growth factor.
- The function $y = a \cdot b^x$ models exponential decay for $a > 0$ and $0 < b < 1$. b is the decay factor.

Chapter 9

Factoring Special Cases

For every nonzero number a and b:
$a^2 - b^2 = (a + b)(a - b)$
$a^2 + 2ab + b^2 = (a + b)(a + b) = (a + b)^2$
$a^2 - 2ab + b^2 = (a - b)(a - b) = (a - b)^2$

Chapter 10

Graph of a Quadratic Function

The graph of $y = ax^2 + bx + c$, where $a \neq 0$, has the line $x = \frac{-b}{2a}$ as its axis of symmetry. The x-coordinate of the vertex is $\frac{-b}{2a}$.

Zero-Product Property

For every real number a and b, if $ab = 0$,
then $a = 0$ or $b = 0$.

Quadratic Formula

If $ax^2 + bx + c = 0$ and $a \neq 0$,
then $x = \frac{-b \pm \sqrt{b^2 - 4ac}}{2a}$.

Property of the Discriminant

For the quadratic equation $ax^2 + bx + c = 0$, where $a \neq 0$, the value of the discriminant $b^2 - 4ac$ tells you the number of solutions.

- If $b^2 - 4ac > 0$, there are two real solutions.
- If $b^2 - 4ac = 0$, there is one real solution.
- If $b^2 - 4ac < 0$, there are no real solutions.

Chapter 11

Multiplication Property of Square Roots

For every number $a \geq 0$ and $b \geq 0$, $\sqrt{ab} = \sqrt{a} \cdot \sqrt{b}$.

Division Property of Square Roots

For every number $a \geq 0$ and $b > 0$, $\sqrt{\frac{a}{b}} = \frac{\sqrt{a}}{\sqrt{b}}$.

The Pythagorean Theorem

In a right triangle, the sum of the squares of the lengths of the legs is equal to the square of the length of the hypotenuse. $a^2 + b^2 = c^2$

The Converse of the Pythagorean Theorem

If a triangle has sides of lengths a, b, and c, and $a^2 + b^2 = c^2$, then the triangle is a right triangle with hypotenuse of length c.

The Distance Formula

The distance d between any two points (x_1, y_1) and (x_2, y_2) is $d = \sqrt{(x_2 - x_1)^2 + (y_2 - y_1)^2}$.

The Midpoint Formula

The midpoint M of a line segment with endpoints $A(x_1, y_1)$ and $B(x_2, y_2)$ is $\left(\frac{x_1 + x_2}{2}, \frac{y_1 + y_2}{2}\right)$.

Trigonometric Ratios

sine of $\angle A = \frac{\text{length of leg opposite } \angle A}{\text{length of hypotenuse}}$

cosine of $\angle A = \frac{\text{length of leg adjacent to } \angle A}{\text{length of hypotenuse}}$

tangent of $\angle A = \frac{\text{length of leg opposite } \angle A}{\text{length of leg adjacent to } \angle A}$

Chapter 12

Multiplication Counting Principle

If there are m ways to make a first selection and n ways to make a second selection, there are $m \times n$ ways to make the two selections.

Permutation Notation

The expression $_nP_r$ stands for the number of permutations of n objects chosen r at a time.

$$_nP_r = n(n-1)(n-2)\ldots \} \, r \text{ factors}$$

Combination Notation

The expression $_nC_r$ stands for the number of combinations of n objects chosen r at a time.

$$_nC_r = \frac{_nP_r}{_rP_r} = \frac{n(n-1)(n-2)\ldots}{r(r-1)(r-2)\ldots}$$

Formulas of Geometry

You will use a number of geometric formulas as you work through your algebra book. Here are some perimeter, area, and volume formulas.

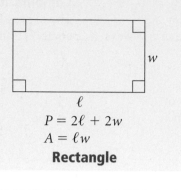

$P = 2\ell + 2w$
$A = \ell w$
Rectangle

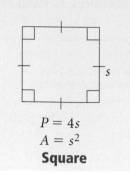

$P = 4s$
$A = s^2$
Square

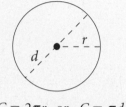

$C = 2\pi r \quad \text{or} \quad C = \pi d$
$A = \pi r^2$
Circle

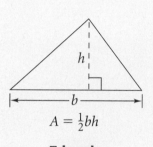

$A = \frac{1}{2}bh$
Triangle

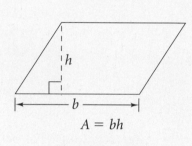

$A = bh$
Parallelogram

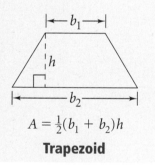

$A = \frac{1}{2}(b_1 + b_2)h$
Trapezoid

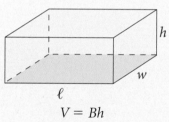

$V = Bh$
$V = \ell wh$
Rectangular Prism

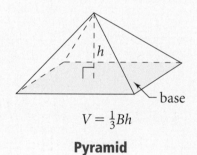

$V = \frac{1}{3}Bh$
Pyramid

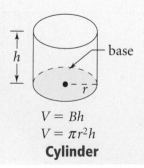

$V = Bh$
$V = \pi r^2 h$
Cylinder

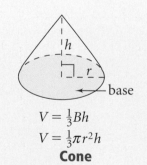

$V = \frac{1}{3}Bh$
$V = \frac{1}{3}\pi r^2 h$
Cone

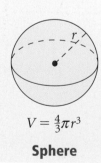

$V = \frac{4}{3}\pi r^3$
Sphere

English/Spanish Illustrated Glossary

A

Absolute value (p. 20)   The distance that a number is from zero on a number line.

-7 is 7 units from 0, so $|-7| = 7$.

Valor absoluto (p. 20)   La distancia a la que un número está del cero en una recta numérica.

Absolute value equation (p. 325)   Equation whose graph forms a V that opens up or down.

Ecuación de valor absoluto (p. 325)   La ecuación cuya gráfica forma una V que se abre hacia arriba o hacia abajo.

$y = |3 - x|$

Additive inverse (p. 24)   The opposite of a number. Additive inverses sum to 0.

-5 and 5 are additive inverses because $-5 + 5 = 0$.

Inversos aditivos (p. 24)   Un número y su opuesto. La suma de inversos aditivos es igual a 0.

Algebraic expression (p. 4)   A mathematical phrase that can include numbers, variables, and operation symbols.

$7 + x$ is an algebraic expression.

Expresión algebraica (p. 4)   Proposición matemática que incluye números, variables y símbolos de operaciones.

Angle of depression (p. 624)   An angle from the horizontal down to a line of sight. It is used to measure heights indirectly.

Ángulo de depresión (p. 624)   Ángulo con que se miden indirectamente las alturas. También, un ángulo de la horizontal hacia la línea de vista.

Angle of elevation (p. 623)   An angle from the horizontal up to a line of sight. It is used to measure heights indirectly.

Ángulo de elevación (p. 623)   Ángulo con que se miden las alturas indirectamente. También, un ángulo de la horizontal hacia la línea de vista.

Arithmetic sequence (p. 269)   A number sequence formed by adding a fixed number to each previous term.

$4, 7, 10, 13, \ldots$ is an arithmetic sequence.

Progresión aritmética (p. 269)   Sucesión numérica que se obtiene al sumar un número constante a cada término consecutivo.

Asymptote (p. 644)   A line the graph of a function gets closer to as x or y gets larger in absolute value.

Asíntota (p. 644)   Línea recta a la que la gráfica de una función se acerca indefinidamente, mientras el valor absoluto de x o y se aumenta.

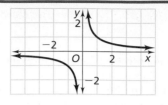

The y-axis is a vertical asymptote for $y = \frac{1}{x}$. The x-axis is a horizontal asymptote for $y = \frac{1}{x}$.

Axis of symmetry (p. 511)   The line that divides a parabola into two matching halves.

Eje de simetría (p. 511)   Línea recta que divide una parábola en dos mitades exactamente iguales.

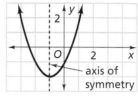

axis of symmetry

B

Base (p. 9)   A number that is multiplied repeatedly.

Base (p. 9)   El número que se multiplica repetidas veces.

$4^5 = 4 \cdot 4 \cdot 4 \cdot 4 \cdot 4$. The base 4 is used as a factor 5 times.

Binomial (p. 457)   A polynomial of two terms.

Binomio (p. 457)   Polinomio compuesto de dos términos.

$3x + 7$ is a binomial.

C

Coefficient (p. 49)   The numerical factor when a term has a variable.

Coeficiente (p. 49)   Factor numérico de un término que contiene una variable.

In the expression $2x + 3y + 16$, 2 and 3 are coefficients.

Combination (pp. 686–687)   An arrangement of some or all of a set of objects without regard to order. The number of combinations

$$= \frac{\text{total number of permutations}}{\text{number of times the objects in each group are repeated}}.$$ You can use the notation $_nC_r$ to write the number of combinations of n objects chosen r at a time.

Combinación (pp. 686–687)   Grupo que contiene algunos o todos los objetos de un conjunto, cualquiera que sea su orden. El número de combinaciones

$$= \frac{\text{número total de permutaciones}}{\text{número de veces que se repiten los objetos de cada grupo}}.$$ La notación $_nC_r$ expresa el número de combinaciones de n objetos escogidos r en un momento dado.

The number of combinations 10 things can be taken 4 at a time:

$$_{10}C_4 = \frac{_{10}P_4}{_4P_4} = \frac{10 \cdot 9 \cdot 8 \cdot 7}{4 \cdot 3 \cdot 2 \cdot 1} = 210$$

Common difference (p. 269) The fixed number added to each term of an arithmetic sequence.

Diferencia común (p. 269) Número constante que se suma a cada término para formar una progresión aritmética.

The common difference is 3 in the arithmetic sequence 4, 7, 10, 13, . . .

Common ratio (p. 424) The fixed number used to find terms in a geometric sequence.

Razón común (p. 424) Número constante que resulta se usa para hallar los términos en una progresión geométrica.

The common ratio is $\frac{1}{3}$ in the geometric sequence $9, 3, 1, \frac{1}{3}, \ldots$

Complement of an event (p. 212) All possible outcomes that are not in the event.

$P(\text{complement of event}) = 1 - P(\text{event})$

Complemento de un suceso (p. 212) Todos los resultados posibles que no se dan en el suceso.

$P(\text{complemento de suceso}) = 1 - P(\text{suceso})$

The complement of rolling a 1 or a 2 on a number cube is rolling a 3, 4, 5, or 6.

Completing the square (p. 541) A method of solving quadratic equations. Completing the square turns every quadratic equation into the form $x^2 = c$.

Completación del cuadrado (p. 541) Método para solucionar ecuaciones cuadráticas. Cuando se completa el cuadrado se transforma la ecuación cuadrática a la fórmula $x^2 = c$.

$x^2 + 6x - 7 = 11$ is rewritten as $(x + 3)^2 = 25$ by completing the square.

Compound inequalities (p. 161) Two inequalities that are joined by *and* or *or*.

Desigualdades compuestas (p. 161) Dos desigualdades que están enlazadas por medio de una *y* o una *o*.

$5 < x$ and $x < 10$

$14 < x$ or $x \geq -3$

Compound interest (p. 438) Interest paid on both the principal and the interest that has already been paid.

Interés compuesto (p. 438) Interés calculado tanto sobre el capital como sobre los intereses ya pagados.

For an initial deposit of $1000 at a 6% interest rate with interest compounded quarterly, the function $y = 1000\left(\frac{0.06}{4}\right)^{4x}$ gives the account balance y after x years.

Conclusion (p. 586) In a conditional, the part following *then*. *See* **conditional**.

Conclusión (p. 586) En un enunciado condicional, la parte que sigue a *entonces*. *Ver* **conditional**.

In the conditional "If an animal has four legs, then it is a horse," the conclusion is "it is a horse."

Conditional (p. 586) An "if-then" statement.

Condicional (p. 586) Un enunciado de la forma "si-entonces."

If an animal has four legs, then it is a horse.

English/Spanish Glossary

Conjecture (p. 268) Conclusion reached by inductive reasoning.

Conjetura (p. 268) Conclusión a la que se llega mediante razonamiento inductivo.

Conjugates (p. 601) The sum and the difference of the same two terms.

$\left(\sqrt{3} + 2\right)$ and $\left(\sqrt{3} - 2\right)$ are conjugates.

Valores conjugados (p. 601) La suma y resta de los mismos dos términos.

Consecutive integers (p. 104) Integers that differ by one.

$-5, -4,$ and -3 are three consecutive integers.

Números enteros consecutivos (p. 104) Número enteros cuya diferencia es 1.

Constant (p. 49) A term that has no variable factor.

In the expression $4x + 13y + 17, 17$ is a constant term.

Constante (p. 49) Término que tiene un valor fijo.

Constant of variation for direct variation (p. 262) The nonzero constant k in the function $y = kx$.

For the function $y = 24x, 24$ is the constant of variation.

Constante de variación en variaciones directas (p. 262) La constante k cuyo valor no es cero en la función $y = kx$.

Constant of variation for inverse variation (p. 637) The nonzero constant k in the function $y = \frac{k}{x}$.

For the equation $y = \frac{8}{x}, 8$ is the constant of variation.

Constante de variación en variaciones inversas (p. 637) La constante k cuyo valor no es cero en la función $y = \frac{k}{x}$.

Converse (p. 586) The statement obtained by reversing the *if* and *then* parts of an if-then statement.

The converse of "If I was born in Houston, then I am a Texan," would be "If I am a Texan, then I was born in Houston."

Expresión recíproca (p. 586) La que se obtiene al invertir los componentes *si* y *entonces* de un enunciado condicional.

Coordinate plane (p. 59) A plane formed by two number lines that intersect at right angles.

Plano de coordenadas (p. 59) Se forma cuando dos rectas numéricas se cortan formando ángulos rectos.

Coordinates (p. 59) The numbers that make an ordered pair and identify the location of a point.

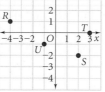

The coordinates of R are $(-4, 1)$.

Coordenadas (p. 59) Números ordenados por pares que determinan la posición de un punto sobre un plano.

Correlation coefficient (p. 319) A number that tells how closely the equation of best fit models the data. The value r of the correlation coefficient is in the range $-1 \le r \le 1$.

Coeficiente de correlación (p. 319) Valor que indica qué tan bien la ecuación más adecuada modela los datos. El valor r del coeficiente de correlación está dentro del rango $-1 \le r \le 1$.

```
LinReg
  y=ax+b
  a=.0134039132
  b=−.3622031627
  r²=.886327776
  r=.9414498267
■
```

The correlation coefficient for the data points $(68, 0.5)$, $(85, 0.9)$, $(100, 0.9)$, and $(108, 1.1)$ is approximately 0.94.

Cosine (p. 621) In a right triangle, such as $\triangle ABC$ with right $\angle C$, cosine of $\angle A = \dfrac{\text{length of side adjacent to } \angle A}{\text{length of hypotenuse}}$ or $\cos A = \dfrac{b}{c}$.

Coseno (p. 621) En $\triangle ABC$ con $\angle C$ recto, el coseno de $\angle A = \dfrac{\text{longitud del lado adyacente a } \angle A}{\text{longitud de la hipotenusa}}$, o $\cos A = \dfrac{b}{c}$.

$\cos A = \dfrac{4}{5}$

Counterexample (p. 18) Any example that proves a statement false.

Contraejemplo (p. 18) Todo ejemplo que pruebe la falsedad de un enunciado.

Statement: All apples are red.

Counterexample: A Granny Smith apple is green.

Cross products (p. 183) In a proportion, $\frac{a}{b} = \frac{c}{d}$, the products of ad and bc. These products are equal.

Productos en equis (p. 183) En una proporción, $\frac{a}{b} = \frac{c}{d}$, los productos de ad y bc. Estos productos son iguales.

$\dfrac{3}{4} = \dfrac{6}{8}$

The cross products are $3 \cdot 8$ and $4 \cdot 6$.
$3 \cdot 8 = 24$ and $4 \cdot 6 = 24$

D

Decay factor (p. 440) The base b in the exponential function $y = ab^x$, where $0 < b < 1$.

Factor decremental (p. 440) La base b en la función exponencial $y = ab^x$ donde $0 < b < 1$.

The decay factor of the function $y = 5(0.3)^x$ is 0.3.

Deductive reasoning (p. 56) A process of reasoning logically from given facts to a conclusion.

Razonamiento deductivo (p. 56) Proceso de razonar lógicamente para llegar a una conclusión a partir de datos dados.

Degree of a monomial (p. 457) The sum of the exponents of the variables of a monomial.

Grado de un monomio (p. 457) La suma de los exponentes de sus variables.

$-4x^3y^2$ is a monomial of degree 5.

Degree of a polynomial (p. 457) The degree of the term with the greatest exponent for a polynomial in one variable.

The degree of $3x^2 + x - 9$ is 2.

Grado de un polinomio (p. 457) El valor mayor del exponente de cualquiera de sus variables.

Dependent events (p. 221) Two events in which the occurrence of one event affects the probability of the second event.

If you pick a marble from a bag and pick another without replacing the first, the events are dependent events.

Sucesos dependientes (p. 221) Cuando el resultado de un suceso influye en la probabilidad de que ocurra el segundo suceso, los sucesos son dependientes.

Dependent variable (p. 248) A variable that provides the output values of a function.

In the equation $y = 3x$ the value of y depends upon the value of x.

Variable dependiente (p. 248) Variable de la que dependen los valores de salid de una función.

Direct variation (p. 262) A linear function that can be expressed in the form $y = kx$, where $k \neq 0$.

$y = 18x$ is a direct variation.

Variación directa (p. 262) Función lineal que puede expresarse como $y = kx$, donde $k \neq 0$.

Discriminant (p. 554) The quantity $b^2 - 4ac$ is the discriminant of $ax^2 + bx + c = 0$.

The discriminant of $2x^2 + 9x - 2 = 0$ is 65.

Discriminante (p. 554) La cantidad $b^2 - 4ac$ es el discriminante de $ax^2 + bx + c = 0$.

Distance Formula (p. 591) The distance d between any two points (x_1, y_1) and (x_2, y_2) is

$$d = \sqrt{(x_2 - x_1)^2 + (y_2 - y_1)^2}.$$

The distance between $(-2, 4)$ and $(4, 5)$ is

$$d = \sqrt{(4 - (-2))^2 + (5 - 4)^2}$$
$$= \sqrt{(6)^2 + (1)^2}$$
$$= \sqrt{37}$$

Fórmula de distancia (p. 591) La distancia d entre dos puntos cualesquiera (x_1, y_1) y (x_2, y_2) es

$$d = \sqrt{(x_2 - x_1)^2 + (y_2 - y_1)^2}.$$

Distributive property (p. 47) For every real number a, b, and c:

$a(b + c) = ab + ac \quad (b + c)a = ba + ca$

$a(b - c) = ab - ac \quad (b - c)a = ba - ca$

$3(19 + 4) = 3(19) + 3(4)$

$(19 + 4)3 = 19(3) + 4(3)$

$7(11 - 2) = 7(11) - 7(2)$

$(11 - 2)7 = 11(7) - 2(7)$

Propiedad distributiva (p. 47) Para cada número real a, b, y c:

$a(b + c) = ab + ac \quad (b + c)a = ba + ca$

$a(b - c) = ab - ac \quad (b - c)a = ba - ca$

Domain (p. 241) The set of all first coordinates in the ordered pairs of a relation.

In the function $f(x) = x + 22$, the domain is all real numbers.

Dominio (p. 241) Conjunto que comprende todas las primeras coordenadas de los pares ordenados de una relación.

E

Element (p. 27) An item in a matrix.

Elemento (p. 27) Componente de una matriz.

$\begin{bmatrix} 5 & -2 \\ 7 & 3 \end{bmatrix}$ 5, 7, −2, and 3 are the four elements of the matrix.

Elimination method (p. 353) A method for solving a system of linear equations. You add or subtract the equations to eliminate a variable.

Eliminación (p. 353) Método para resolver un sistema de ecuaciones lineales. Se suman o se restan las ecuaciones para eliminar una variable.

$3x + y = 19$
$\underline{2x - y = 1}$
$x + 0 = 18 \qquad x = 18$
$2(18) - y = 1 \rightarrow$ Substitute 18 for x
$36 - y = 1 \qquad$ in the second
 equation.
$y = 35 \rightarrow$ Solve for y.

Equation (p. 5) A mathematical sentence that uses an equal sign.

Ecuación (p. 5) Enunuado matemático que tiene el signo de igual.

$x + 5 = 3x - 7$

Equivalent equations (p. 75) Equations that have the same solution.

Ecuaciones equivalentes (p. 75) Ecuaciones que tienen la misma solución.

$\frac{9}{3} = 3$ and $\frac{9}{3} + a = 3 + a$ are equivalent equations.

Equivalent inequalities (p. 161) Equivalent inequalities have the same set of solutions.

Desigualdades equivalentes (p. 161) Las desigualdades equivalentes tienen el mismo conjunto de soluciones.

$x + 4 < 7$ and $x < 3$ are equivalent inequalities.

Evaluate (p. 10) Substitute a given number for each variable, and then simplify.

Evaluar (p. 10) Método de sustituir cada variable por un número dado para luego simplificar la expresión.

To evaluate $3x + 4$ for $x = 2$, substitute 2 for x and simplify.
$3(2) + 4$
$6 + 4$
10

Event (p. 211) Any group of outcomes in a situation involving probability.

Suceso (p. 211) En la probabilidad, cualquier grupo de resultados.

When rolling a number cube, there are six possible outcomes. Rolling an even number is an event with three possible outcomes, 2, 4, and 6.

Experimental probability (p. 212) The ratio of the number of times an event actually happens to the number of times the experiment is done.

$$P(\text{event}) = \frac{\text{number of times an event happens}}{\text{number of times the experiment is done}}$$

Probabilidad experimental (p. 212) La relación entre el número de veces que un suceso sucede en la realidad y el número de veces que se hace el experimento.

$$P(\text{suceso}) = \frac{\text{número de veces que sucede un suceso}}{\text{número de veces que se hace el experimento}}$$

A baseball player's batting average shows how likely it is that a player will get a hit, based on previous times at bat.

Exponent (p. 9) A number that shows repeated multiplication.

Exponente (p. 9) Denota el número de veces que debe multiplicarse.

$3^4 = 3 \cdot 3 \cdot 3 \cdot 3$

The exponent 4 indicates that 3 is used as a factor four times.

Exponential decay (p. 440) A situation modeled with a function of the form $y = ab^x$, where $a > 0$ and $0 < b < 1$.

Decremento exponencial (p. 440) Para $a > 0$ y $0 < b < 1$, la función $y = ab^x$ representa el decremento exponencial.

$y = 5(0.1)^x$

Exponential function (p. 430) A function that repeatedly multiplies an initial amount by the same positive number. You can model all exponential functions using $y = ab^x$, where a is a nonzero constant, $b > 0, b \neq 1$.

Función exponencial (p. 430) Función que multiplica repetidas veces una cantidad inicial por el mismo número positivo. Todas las funciones exponenciales se pueden representar mediante $y = ab^x$, donde a es una constante con valor distinto de cero, $b > 0$ y $b \neq 1$.

$y = 4.8(1.1)^x$

Exponential growth (p. 437) A situation modeled with a function of the form $y = ab^x$, where $a > 0$ and $b > 1$.

Incremento exponencial (p. 437) Para $a > 0$ y $b > 1$, la función $y = ab^x$ representa el incremento exponencial.

$y = 100(2)^x$

Extraneous solution (p. 609) An apparent solution of the equation that does not satisfy the original equation.

Solución extraña (p. 609) Solución aparente de una ecuación que no satisface la ecuación original.

$\frac{b}{b+4} = 3 - \frac{4}{b+4}$

Multiply by $(b+4)$.

$b = 3(b+4) - 4$
$b = 3b + 12 - 4$
$-2b = 8$
$b = -4$

Replace b with -4 in the original equation. The denominator is 0, and so -4 is an extraneous solution.

Extremes of a proportion (p. 183) In the proportion, $\frac{a}{b} = \frac{c}{d}$, a and d are the extremes.

The product of the extremes of $\frac{x}{4} = \frac{x+3}{2}$ is $2x$.

Valores extremos de una proporción (p. 183) En la proporción $\frac{a}{b} = \frac{c}{d}$, a y d son los valores extremos.

F

Factor by grouping (p. 496) A method of factoring that uses the distributive property to remove a common binomial factor of two pairs of terms.

The expression $7x(x-1) + 4(x-1)$ can be factored as $(7x+4)(x-1)$.

Factor común por agrupación de términos (p. 496) Método de factorización que aplica la propiedad distributiva para sacar un factor común de dos pares de términos en un binomio.

Function (p. 242) A relation that assigns exactly one value in the range to each value of the domain.

Earned income is a function of the number of hours worked. If you earn $4.50/h, then your income is expressed by the function $f(h) = 4.5h$.

Función (p. 242) La relación que asigna exactamente un valor del recorrido a cada valor del dominio.

Function notation (p. 243) To write a rule in function notation, you use the symbol $f(x)$ in place of y.

$f(x) = 3x - 8$ is in function notation.

Notación de una función (p. 243) Para expresar una regla en notación de función se usa el símbolo $f(x)$ en lugar de y.

Function rule (p. 243) An equation that describes a function.

$y = 4x + 1$ is a function rule.

Regla de una función (p. 243) Ecuación que describe una función.

G

Geometric sequence (p. 424) A number sequence formed by multiplying a term in a sequence by a fixed number to find the next term.

$9, 3, 1, \frac{1}{3}, \ldots$ is an example of a geometric sequence.

Progresión geométrica (p. 424) Tipo de sucesión numérica formada al multiplicar un término por un número constante, para hallar el siguiente término.

Greatest possible error (p. 205) One half of the measuring unit, for any measurement.

~~ock is measured as 3.8 g. The mass~~ possible error is one half The g~0.05 g. 0 ¹

Máximo error posible (p. 205) Para una medición dada, la mitad de la unidad de medida.

Growth factor (p. 437) The number b in an exponential growth function of the form $y = ab^x$, where $b > 1$.

The growth factor of $y = 7(1.3)^x$ is 1.3.

Factor incremental (p. 437) Para la función exponencial incremental $y = ab^x$, donde $b > 1$, b es el factor incremental.

H

Hypotenuse (p. 584) The side opposite the right angle in a right triangle. It is the longest side in the triangle.

c is the hypotenuse.

Hipotenusa (p. 584) En un triángulo rectángulo, el lado opuesto al ángulo recto. Es el lado más largo del triángulo.

Hypothesis (p. 586) The part following *if* in a conditional. *See* **conditional**.

In the conditional "If an animal has four legs, then it is a horse," the hypothesis is "an animal has four legs."

Hipótesis (p. 586) En un enunciado condicional, la parte que sigue a siguiente *si*. *Ver* **conditional**.

I

Identity (p. 98) An equation that is true for every value.

$5 - 14x = 5\left(1 - \frac{14}{5}x\right)$ is an identity because it is true for any value of x.

Identidad (p. 98) Una ecuación que es verdadera para todos los valores.

Independent events (p. 220) Two events for which the outcome of one does not affect the other.

Picking a colored marble from a bag, and then replacing it and picking another marble, are two independent events.

Sucesos independientes (p. 220) Dos sucesos son independientes si el resultado de uno de ellos no influye en el resultado del otro.

Independent variable (p. 248) A variable that provides the input values of a function.

In the equation $y = 3x$, x is the independent variable.

Variable independiente (p. 248) Variable de la que dependen los valores de entrada de una función.

Inductive reasoning (p. 268) Making conclusions based on observed patterns.

Razonamiento inductivo (p. 268) Sacar conclusiones a partir de patrones observados.

Inequality (p. 19) A mathematical sentence that compares the values of two expressions using an inequality symbol.

$3 < 7$

Desigualdad (p. 19) Expresión matemática que compara el valor de dos expresiones con el símbolo de desigualdad.

Infinitely many solutions (p. 342) The number of solutions of a system of equations in which the graphs of the equations are the same line.

The system $2x + 4y = 8$ and $y = -\frac{1}{2}x + 2$ has infinitely many solutions.

Infinitamente muchas soluciones (p. 342) Cuando las gráficas de las ecuaciones de un sistema son la misma recta.

Integers (p. 16) Whole numbers and their opposites.

$\ldots -3, -2, -1, 0, 1, 2, 3, \ldots$

Números enteros (p. 16) Números que constan exclusivamente de una o más unidades, y sus opuestos.

Interest period (p. 438) The length of time over which interest is calculated.

Periodo de interés (p. 438) Plazo para el cual se calcula el interés a pagar.

Inverse operations (p. 75) Operations that undo one another.

Addition and subtraction are inverse operations. Multiplication and division are inverse operations.

Operaciones inversas (p. 75) Las operaciones que se cancelan una a la otra.

Inverse variation (p. 637) A function that can be written in the form $xy = k$ or $y = \frac{k}{x}$. The product of the quantities remains constant, so as one quantity increases, the other decreases.

The length x and the width y of a rectangle with a fixed area vary inversely. If the area is 40, $xy = 40$.

Variación inversa (p. 637) Función que puede expresarse como $xy = k$ ó $y = \frac{k}{x}$. El producto de las cantidades permanece constante, de modo que al aumentar una cantidad, disminuye la otra.

Irrational number (p. 18) A number that cannot be written as a ratio of two integers. Irrational numbers in decimal form are nonterminating and nonrepeating.

$\sqrt{11}$ and π are irrational numbers.

Número irracional (p. 18) Número que no puede expresarse como cociente de dos números enteros. Los números irracionales en forma decimal no tienen término y no se repiten.

English/Spanish Glossary

Leg (p. 584)   Each of the sides that form the right angle of a right triangle.

a and *b* are legs.

Cateto (p. 584)   Cada uno de los dos lados que forman el ángulo recto en un triángulo rectángulo.

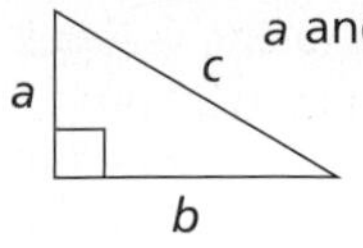

Like radicals (p. 600)   Radical expressions with the same radicands.

$3\sqrt{7}$ and $-5\sqrt{7}$ are like radicals.

Radicales semejantes (p. 600)   Expresiones radicales con los mismos radicandos.

Like terms (p. 49)   Terms with exactly the same variable factors in a variable expression.

$4y$ and $16y$ are like terms.

Términos semejantes (p. 49)   Términos con los mismos factores variables en una expresión variable.

Line of best fit (p. 319)   The most accurate trend line on a scatter plot showing the relationship between two sets of data.

Recta de mayor aproximación (p. 319)   La recta de tendencia en un diagrama de puntos que más se acerca a los puntos que representan la relación de los datos.

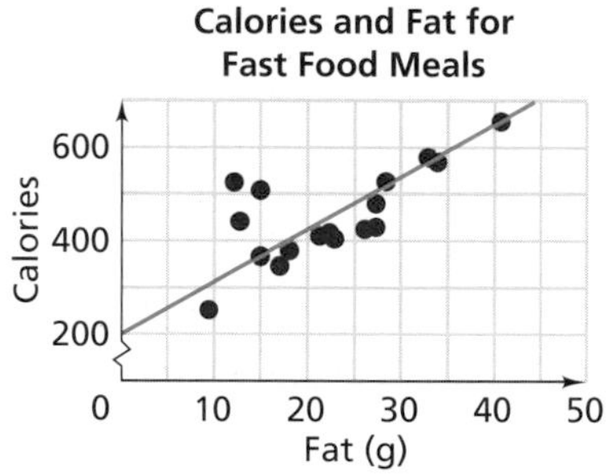

Calories and Fat for Fast Food Meals

Linear equation (p. 291)   An equation whose graph forms a straight line.

Ecuación lineal (p. 291)   Ecuación cuya gráfica es una línea recta.

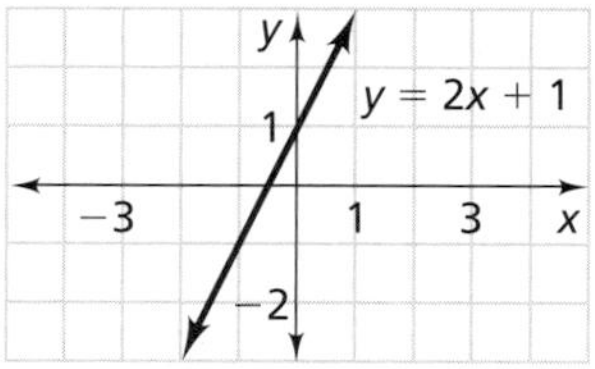

$y = 2x + 1$

Linear inequality (p. 371)   A mathematical sentence that describes a region of the coordinate plane having a boundary line. Each point in the region is a solution of the inequality.

$y > x + 1$

Desigualdad lineal (p. 371)   Expresión matemática que describe una región del plano de coordenadas que tiene una recta límite. Cada punto de la región es una solución de la desigualdad.

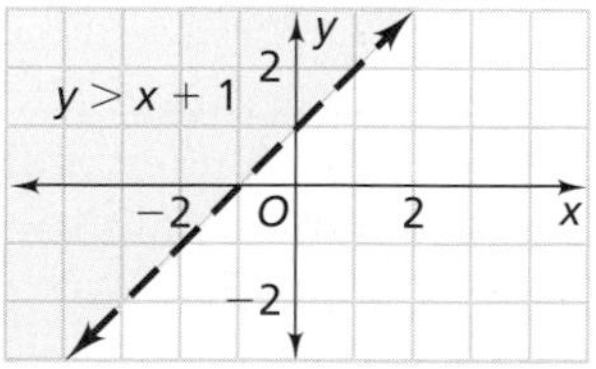

Literal equation (p. 111)   An equation involving two or more variables.

$4x + 2y = 18$ is a literal equation.

Ecuación literal (p. 111)   Ecuación que incluye dos o más variables.

Matrix (p. 27)   A rectangular arrangement of numbers. The number of rows and columns of a matrix determines its size. Each item in a matrix is an element.

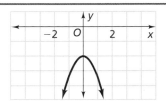 is a 2×3 matrix.

Matriz (p. 27)   Conjunto de números dispuestos en forma de rectángulo. La cantidad de líneas horizontales y verticales de una matriz determina su tamaño. Cada cifra de la matriz es un elemento.

Maximum (p. 511)   The y-coordinate of the vertex of a parabola that opens downward.

Valor máximo (p. 511)   La coordenada y del vértice en una parábola que se abre hacia abajo.

Since the parabola opens downward, the y-coordinate of the vertex is the function's maximum value.

Mean (p. 118)   To find the mean of a set of numbers, find the sum of the numbers and divide the sum by the number of items.
The mean is $\frac{\text{sum of data items}}{\text{number of data items}}$.

In the data set 12, 11, 12, 10, 13, 12, and 7, the mean is
$$\frac{12 + 11 + 12 + 10 + 13 + 12 + 7}{7} = 11.$$

Media (p. 118)   Para encontrar la media de un conjunto de números, se suman todos los números y el resultado se divide por la cantidad de números sumados.
La media es $\frac{\text{suma de los datos}}{\text{cantidad de números sumados}}$.

Means of a proportion (p. 183)   In the proportion, $\frac{a}{b} = \frac{c}{d}$, b and c are the means.

The product of the means of $\frac{x}{4} = \frac{x + 3}{2}$ is $4(x + 3)$ or $4x + 12$.

Valores medios de una proporción (p. 183)   En la proporción, $\frac{a}{b} = \frac{c}{d}$, b y c son los valores medios.

Measure of central tendency (p. 118)   Mean, median, and mode. They are used to organize and summarize a set of data.

For examples, see mean, median, and mode.

Medida de tendencia central (p. 118)   Se usa para organizar y resumir un conjunto de datos. La media, la mediana y la moda son medidas de tendencia central.

Median (p. 118)   The middle value in an ordered set of numbers.

In the data set 7, 10, 11, 12, 12, 12, and 13, the median is 12.

Mediana (p. 118)   El valor del medio en un conjunto ordenado de números.

Midpoint (p. 593) The point M that divides a segment $\overline{AB}$ into two equal segments, $\overline{AM}$ and $\overline{MB}$.

Punto medio (p. 593) El punto M que divide un segmento $\overline{AB}$ en dos segmentos iguales, $\overline{AM}$ y $\overline{MB}$.

M is the midpoint of $\overline{XY}$.

X   M   Y

Midpoint Formula (p. 593) The midpoint M of a line segment with endpoints $A(x_1, y_1)$ and $B(x_2, y_2)$ is $\left(\dfrac{x_1 + x_2}{2}, \dfrac{y_1 + y_2}{2} \right)$.

Fórmula del punto medio (p. 593) El punto medio M de un segmento con puntos extremos $A(x_1, y_1)$ y $B(x_2, y_2)$ es $\left(\dfrac{x_1 + x_2}{2}, \dfrac{y_1 + y_2}{2} \right)$.

The midpoint of a segment with endpoints $A(3, 5)$ and $B(7, 1)$ is $(5,3)$.

Minimum (p. 511) The y-coordinate of the vertex of a parabola that opens upward.

Valor mínimo (p. 511) La coordenada y del vértice en una parábola que se abre hacia arriba.

Since the parabola opens upward, the y-coordinate of the vertex is the function's minimum value.

Mode (p. 118) The data item that occurs the greatest number of times in a data set. A data set may have no mode, one mode, or more than one mode.

Moda (p. 118) El dato que ocurre el mayor número de veces en un conjunto de datos. El conjunto de datos puede no tener moda, o tener una o más modas.

In the data set 7, 7, 9, 10, 11, and 13, the mode is 7.

Monomial (p. 456) An expression that is a number, a variable, or a product of a number and one or more variables.

Monomio (p. 456) Expresión algebraica que puede ser un número, una variable, o el producto de un número y una o más variables.

$9, n,$ and $-5xy^2$ are examples of monomials.

Multiplication counting principle (p. 680) If there are m ways to make the first selection and n ways to make the second selection, there are $m \times n$ ways to make the two selections.

Principio de conteo en multiplicación (p. 680) Si hay m maneras de hacer la primera selección y n maneras de hacer la segunda selección, quiere decir que hay $m \times n$ maneras de hacer las dos selecciones.

For 5 shirts and 8 pairs of shorts, the number of possible outfits is $5 \cdot 8 = 40$.

Multiplicative inverse (p. 41)   Given a nonzero rational number $\frac{a}{b}$, the multiplicative inverse, or reciprocal, is $\frac{b}{a}$. The product of a nonzero number and its multiplicative inverse is 1.

$\frac{3}{4}$ is a multiplicative inverse of $\frac{4}{3}$ because $\frac{3}{4} \times \frac{4}{3} = 1$.

Inverso multiplicativo (p. 41)   Dado un número racional $\frac{a}{b}$ distinto de cero, el inverso multiplicativo, o recíproco, es $\frac{b}{a}$. El producto de un número distinto de cero y su inverso multiplicativo es 1.

N

Natural numbers (p. 16)   The counting numbers.

$1, 2, 3, \ldots$

Números naturales (p. 16)   Los números que se emplean para contar.

Negative correlation (p. 61)   The relationship between two sets of data, in which one set of data decreases as the other set of data increases.

Correlación negativa (p. 61)   Relación entre dos conjuntos de datos en la que uno de los conjuntos decrece a medida que el otro se incrementa.

Negative reciprocal (p. 312)   A number of the form $-\frac{b}{a}$, where $\frac{a}{b}$ is a nonzero rational number. The product of a number and its negative reciprocal is -1.

$\frac{2}{5}$ and $-\frac{5}{2}$ are negative reciprocals because $\left(\frac{2}{5}\right)\left(-\frac{5}{2}\right) = -1$.

Recíproco negativo (p. 312)   El recíproco negativo de un número racional $\frac{a}{b}$ cuyo valor no es cero es $-\frac{b}{a}$. El producto de un número y su recíproco negativo es -1.

Negative square root (p. 524)   A number of the form $-\sqrt{b}$, which is the negative square root of b.

-7 is the negative square root of $\sqrt{49}$.

Raíz cuadrada negativa (p. 524) $-\sqrt{b}$ es la raíz cuadrada negativa de b.

No correlation (p. 61)   There does not appear to be a relationship between two sets of data.

Sin correlación (p. 61)   No hay relación entre dos conjuntos de datos.

No solution (p. 342)   When the graphs of the equations in a system are parallel with no point of intersection.

There is no solution to the system of equations $x + y = 5$ and $x + y = -3$.

Sin solución (p. 342)   Cuando las gráficas de las ecuaciones de un sistema son paralelas y no existe entre ellas ningún punto de intersección.

English/Spanish Glossary

Open sentence (p. 5) An equation that contains one or more variables.

$5 + x = 12$ is an open sentence.

Ecuación abierta (p. 5) Ecuación que contiene una o más variables.

Opposite (p. 20) A number that is the same distance from zero on the number line as a given number, but lies in the opposite direction.

-3 and 3 are opposites.

Opuestos (p. 20) Dos números son opuestos si están a la misma distancia del cero en la recta numérica, en sentidos opuestos.

Order of operations (p. 10)

1. Perform any operation(s) inside grouping symbols.

2. Simplify powers.

3. Multiply and divide in order from left to right.

4. Add and subtract in order from left to right.

$$6 - (4^2 - [2 \cdot 5]) \div 3$$
$$= 6 - (16 - 10) \div 3$$
$$= 6 - 6 \div 3$$
$$= 6 - 2$$
$$= 4$$

Orden de las operaciones (p. 10)

1. Se hacer las operaciones que están dentro de símbolos de agrupación.

2. Se simplifican todos los términos que tengan exponentes.

3. Se hacen las multiplicaciones y divisiones en orden de izquierda a derecha.

4. Se hacen las sumas y restas en orden de izquierda a derecha.

Ordered pair (p. 59) Two numbers that identify the location of a point.

The ordered pair $(4, -1)$ identifies the point 4 units to the right on the x-axis and 1 unit down on the y-axis.

Par ordenado (p. 59) Un par ordenado de números denota la localización de un punto en un plano de coordenadas.

Origin (p. 59) The point at which the axes of the coordinate plane intersect.

Origen (p. 59) Punto de intersección de los ejes del plano de coordenadas.

Outcome (p. 211) The result of a single trial in a probability experiment.

The outcomes of rolling a number cube are $1, 2, 3, 4, 5,$ and 6.

Resultado (p. 211) Lo que se obtiene al hacer una sola prueba en un experimento de probabilidad.

Outlier (p. 118) A data value that is much higher or lower than the other data values in the set.

For the set of values 2, 5, 3, 7, 12, the data value 12 is an outlier.

Valor extralimitado (p. 118) Valor que es mucho mayor o mucho menor que los demás valores de un conjunto.

P

Parabola (p. 510) The graph of a quadratic function.

Parábola (p. 510) La gráfica de una función cuadrática.

Parallel lines (p. 311) Two lines in the same plane that never intersect. Parallel lines have the same slope.

Rectas paralelas (p. 311) Dos rectas situadas en el mismo plano que nunca se cruzan. Las rectas paralelas tienen la misma pendiente.

Lines ℓ and m are parallel.

Percent error (p. 206) The ratio of the greatest possible error to the measurement.

Error porcentual (p. 206) El valor del máximo error posible dividido por el valor de la medida obtenida.

The diameter of a CD is measured as 12.1 cm. The greatest possible error is 0.05 cm. The percent error is $\frac{0.05}{12.1} \approx 0.4\%$.

Percent of change (p. 204) The ratio of the amount of change to the original amount expressed as a percent.

Porcentaje de cambio (p. 204) La cantidad de cambio dividida por la cantidad original y expresada como un porcentaje.

The price of a sweater was $20. The price increases $2. The percent of change is $\frac{2}{20} = 10\%$.

Percent of decrease (p. 204) The percent of change found when the original amount decreases.

Porcentaje de disminución (p. 204) El porcentaje de cambio que resulta cuando la cantidad original disminuye.

The price of a sweater was $22. The price decreases $2. The percent of change is $\frac{2}{22} \approx 9\%$.

Percent of increase (p. 204) The percent of change found when the original amount increases.

Porcentaje de aumento (p. 204) El porcentaje de cambio que resulta cuando la cantidad original aumenta.

See example for percent of change.

Perfect square trinomial (p. 490) Any trinomial of the form $a^2 + 2ab + b^2$ or $a^2 - 2ab + b^2$.

Trinomio cuadrado perfecto (p. 490) Todo trinomio de la forma $a^2 + 2ab + b^2$ ó $a^2 - 2ab + b^2$.

$(x + 3)^2 = x^2 + 6x + 9$

English/Spanish Glossary

Perfect squares (p. 525)   Numbers whose square roots are integers.

Cuadrado perfecto (p. 525)   Número cuya raíz cuadrada es un número entero.

The numbers $1, 4, 9, 16, 25, 36, \ldots$ are perfect squares because they are the squares of integers.

Permutation (p. 681)   An arrangement of some or all of a set of objects in a specific order. You can use the notation $_nP_r$ to express the number of permutations, where n equals the number of objects available and r equals the number of selections to make.

Permutación (p. 681)   Disposición de algunos o de todos los objetos de un conjunto en un orden determinado. El número de permutaciones se puede expresar con la notación $_nP_r$, donde n es igual al número total de objetos y r es igual al número de selecciones que han de hacerse.

How many ways can 5 children be arranged three at a time?

$_5P_3 = 5 \cdot 4 \cdot 3 = 60$ arrangements

Perpendicular lines (p. 312)   Lines that intersect to form right angles. Two lines are perpendicular if the product of their slopes is -1.

Rectas perpendiculares (p. 312)   Rectas que forman ángulos rectos en su intersección . Dos rectas son perpendiculares si el producto de sus pendientes es -1.

Lines ℓ and m are perpendicular.

Point-slope form (p. 304)   A linear equation of a nonvertical line written as $y - y_1 = m(x - x_1)$. The line passes through the point (x_1, y_1) with slope m.

Forma punto-pendiente (p. 304)   La ecuación lineal de una recta no vertical que pasa por el punto (x_1, y_1) con pendiente m está dada por $y - y_1 = m(x - x_1)$.

An equation with a slope of $-\frac{1}{2}$ passing through $(2, -1)$ would be written $y + 1 = -\frac{1}{2}(x - 2)$ in point-slope form.

Polynomial (p. 457)   A monomial or the sum or difference of two or more monomials. A quotient with a variable in the denominator is not a polynomial.

Polinomio (p. 457)   Un monomio o la suma o diferencia de dos o más monomios. Un cociente con una variable en el denominador no es un polinomio.

$2x^2, 3x + 7, 28$, and $-7x^3 - 2x^2 + 9$ are all polynomials.

Positive correlation (p. 61)   The relationship between two sets of data in which both sets of data increase together.

Correlación positiva (p. 61)   La relación entre dos conjuntos de datos en la que ambos conjuntos se incrementan a la vez.

Power (p. 9)   The base and the exponent of an expression of the form a^n.

Potencia (p. 9)   La base y el exponente de una expresión de la forma a^n.

5^4

Principal square root (p. 524) A number of the form $\sqrt{b}$. The expression $\sqrt{b}$ is called the principal (or positive) square root of b.

5 is the principal square root of $\sqrt{25}$.

Raíz cuadrada principal (p. 524) La expresión $\sqrt{b}$ se llama raíz cuadrada principal de b.

Probability (p. 211) How likely it is that an event will occur (written formally as P (event)).

You have 4 red marbles and 3 white marbles. The probability that you select one red marble, and then, without replacing it, randomly select another red marble is $P(\text{red}) = \frac{4}{7} \cdot \frac{3}{6} = \frac{2}{7}$.

Probabilidad (p. 211) La probabilidad de un suceso, o P(suceso), expresa que posibilidad hay de que el suceso ocurra.

Properties of equality (pp. 74 and 76) For all real numbers $a, b,$ and c:

Addition: If $a = b$, then $a + c = b + c$.

Subtraction: If $a = b$, then $a - c = b - c$.

Multiplication: If $a = b$, then $a \cdot c = b \cdot c$.

Division: If $a = b$, and $c \neq 0$, then $\frac{a}{c} = \frac{b}{c}$.

Since $\frac{2}{4} = \frac{1}{2}, \frac{2}{4} + 5 = \frac{1}{2} + 5$.

Since $\frac{9}{3} = 3, \frac{9}{3} - 6 = 3 - 6$.

Propiedades de una igualdad (pp. 74 y 76) Para todos los números reales a, b y c:

Suma: Si $a = b$, entonces $a + c = b + c$.

Resta: Si $a = b$, entonces $a - c - b \quad c$.

Multiplicación: Si $a = b$, entonces $a \cdot c = b \cdot c$.

División: Si $a = b$, y $c \neq 0$, entonces $\frac{a}{c} = \frac{b}{c}$.

Proportion (p. 183) An equation that states that two ratios are equal.
$$\frac{a}{b} = \frac{c}{d} \text{ where } b \neq 0 \text{ and } d \neq 0$$

$\frac{7.5}{9} = \frac{5}{6}$

Proporción (p. 183) Es una ecuación que establece que dos relaciones son iguales.
$$\frac{a}{b} = \frac{c}{d} \text{ por } b \neq 0 \text{ y } d \neq 0$$

Pythagorean Theorem (p. 585) In any right triangle, the sum of the squares of the lengths of the legs is equal to the square of the length of the hypotenuse: $a^2 + b^2 = c^2$.

$3^2 + 4^2 = 5^2$

Teorema de Pitágoras (p. 585) En un triángulo rectángulo, la suma de los cuadrados de los catetos es igual al cuadrado de la hipotenusa: $a^2 + b^2 = c^2$.

Q

Quadrants (p. 59) The four parts into which the coordinate plane is divided by its axes.

Cuadrantes (p. 59) El plano de coordenadas está dividido por sus ejes en cuatro regiones llamadas cuadrantes.

English/Spanish Glossary

Quadratic equation (p. 530) An equation you can write in the standard form $ax^2 + bx + c = 0$, where $a \neq 0$.

$4x^2 + 9x - 5 = 0$

Ecuación cuadrática (p. 530) Ecuación que puede expresarse de la forma $ax^2 + bx + c = 0$, en la que $a, b,$ y c son números reales y $a \neq 0$.

Quadratic formula (p. 547) If $ax^2 + bx + c = 0$ and $a \neq 0$, then
$$x = \frac{-b \pm \sqrt{b^2 - 4ac}}{2a}.$$

Fórmula cuadrática (p. 547) Si $ax^2 + bx + c = 0$ y $a \neq 0$, entonces
$$x = \frac{-b \pm \sqrt{b^2 - 4ac}}{2a}.$$

$2x^2 + 10x + 12 = 0$

$$x = \frac{-b \pm \sqrt{b^2 - 4ac}}{2a}$$

$$x = \frac{-10 \pm \sqrt{10^2 - 4(2)(12)}}{2(2)}$$

$$x = \frac{-10 \pm \sqrt{4}}{4}$$

$$x = \frac{-10 + 2}{4} \text{ or } \frac{-10 - 2}{4}$$

$x = -2 \text{ or } -3$

Quadratic function (p. 510) A function of the form $y = ax^2 + bx + c$, where $a \neq 0$. The graph of a quadratic function is a parabola, a U-shaped curve that opens up or down.

$y = 5x^2 - 2x + 1$ is a quadratic function.

Función cuadrática (p. 510) La función $y = ax^2 + bx + c$, en la que $a \neq 0$. La gráfica de una función cuadrática es una parábola, o curva en forma de U que se abre hacia arriba o hacia abajo.

R

Radical equation (p. 607) An equation that has a variable in a radicand.

$\sqrt{x} - 2 = 12$

$\sqrt{x} = 14$

Ecuación radical (p. 607) Ecuación que tiene una variable en un radicando.

Radical expression (p. 578) Expression that contains a radical.

$\sqrt{3}, \sqrt{5x},$ and $\sqrt{x - 10}$ are examples of radical expressions.

Expresión radical (p. 578) Expresiones que contienen radicals.

Radicand (p. 524) The expression under the radical sign.

The radicand of the radical expression $\sqrt{x + 2}$ is $x + 2$.

Radicando (p. 524) La expresión que aparece debajo del signo radical.

Range (p. 120) The difference between the greatest and the least data values for a set of data.

For the set $2, 5, 8, 12$, the range is $12 - 2 = 10$.

Rango (p. 120) Diferencia entre el valor mayor y el menor en un conjunto de datos.

Range (p. 241) The set of all the second coordinates of a function.

Recorrido (p. 241) El conjunto de todos los valores de salida de una función.

In the function $f(x) = |x|$, the range is the set of all nonnegative numbers.

Rate (p. 182) A ratio of a to b where a and b represent quantities measured in different units.

Razón (p. 182) La relación que existe entre a y b cuando a y b son cantidades medidas con distintas unidades.

Traveling 125 miles in 2 hours results in the rate $\frac{125 \text{ miles}}{2 \text{ hours}}$ or 62.5 mi/h.

Rate of change (p. 282) The relationship between two quantities that are changing. The rate of change is also called slope.

$\text{rate of change} = \dfrac{\text{change in the dependent variable}}{\text{change in the independent variable}}$

Tasa de cambio (p. 282) Permite ver la relación entre dos cantidades que cambian. La tasa de cambio se llama también pendiente.

$\text{tasa de cambio} = \dfrac{\text{cambio en la variable dependiente}}{\text{cambio en la variable independiente}}$

Video rental for 1 day is $1.99. Video rental for 2 days is $2.99.

$$\text{rate of change} = \frac{2.99 - 1.99}{2 - 1}$$
$$= \frac{1.00}{1}$$
$$= 1$$

Ratio (p. 182) A comparison of two numbers by division.

Razón (p. 182) Comparación de dos números por división.

$\frac{5}{7}$ and $7:3$ are ratios.

Rational equation (p. 672) An equation containing rational expressions.

Ecuación racional (p. 672) Ecuación que contiene expresiones racionales.

$\frac{1}{x} = \frac{3}{2x - 1}$ is a rational equation.

Rational expression (p. 652) A ratio of two polynomials. The value of the variable cannot make the denominator equal to 0.

Expresión racional (p. 652) Un razón de dos polinomios. El valor de la variable no puede hacer el denominador igual a 0.

$\dfrac{3}{x^3 + x}$ when $x \neq 0$

Rational function (p. 640) A function that can be written in the form $f(x) = \frac{\text{polynomial}}{\text{polynomial}}$. The value of the variable cannot make the denominator equal to 0.

Función racional (p. 640) Función que puede expresarse de forma $f(x) = \frac{\text{polinomio}}{\text{polinomio}}$. El valor de la variable no puede hacer el denominador igual a 0.

$y = \dfrac{x}{x^2 + 2}$

English/Spanish Glossary

Rational number (p. 17) A real number that can be written as a ratio of two integers. Rational numbers in decimal form are terminating or repeating.

$\frac{2}{3}$, 1.548, and 2.292929 . . . are all rational numbers.

Número racional (p. 17) Número real que puede expresarse como el cociente de dos números enteros. Los números racionales en forma decimal son exactos o periódicos.

Rationalize (p. 581) Rewrite as a rational number. Rationalizing the denominator of a radical expression may be necessary to obtain the simplest radical form.

$$\frac{2}{\sqrt{5}} = \frac{2}{\sqrt{5}} \cdot \frac{\sqrt{5}}{\sqrt{5}} = \frac{2\sqrt{5}}{\sqrt{25}} = \frac{2\sqrt{5}}{5}$$

Racionalizar (p. 581) Escribir una expresión matemática en forma de número racional. A veces es necesario racionalizar el denominador de una expresión radical a fin de obtener la forma radical más simple.

Real number (p. 18) A number that is either rational or irrational.

$5, -3, \sqrt{11}, 0.666\ldots, 5\frac{4}{11}, 0$, and π are all real numbers.

Número real (p. 18) El conjunto de números racionales e irracionales.

Reciprocal (p. 41) Given a nonzero rational number $\frac{a}{b}$, the reciprocal, or multiplicative inverse, is $\frac{b}{a}$. The product of a nonzero number and its reciprocal is 1.

$\frac{2}{5}$ and $\frac{5}{2}$ are reciprocals because $\frac{2}{5} \times \frac{5}{2} = 1$.

Recíproco (p. 41) El recíproco, o inverso multiplicativo, de un número racional $\frac{a}{b}$ cuyo valor no es cero es $\frac{b}{a}$. El producto de un número y su valor recíproco es 1.

Relation (p. 241) Any set of ordered pairs.

$\{(0, 0), (2, 3), (2, -7)\}$ is a relation.

Relación (p. 241) Cualquier grupo de pares ordenados.

S

Sample space (p. 211) All possible outcomes of an event.

When tossing two coins one at a time, the sample space is $(H, H), (T, T),$ $(H, T), (T, H)$.

Espacio de muestra (p. 211) El conjunto de todos los resultados posibles de un suceso.

Scale (p. 191) The ratio of a distance in a drawing to the actual distance.

For a drawing in which a 2-in. length represents an actual length of 18 ft, the scale is 1 in. : 9 ft.

Escala (p. 191) Proporción entre las distancias expresadas en un dibujo y las distancias reales.

Scale drawing (p. 191) An enlarged or reduced drawing similar to an actual object or place.

Dibujo a escala (p. 191) Dibujo que muestra de mayor o menor tamaño un objeto o lugar dado.

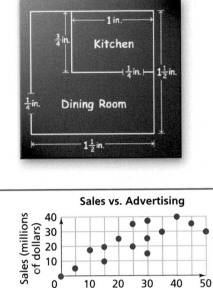

Scatter plot (p. 61) A graph that relates data of two different sets. The two sets of data are displayed as ordered pairs.

Diagrama de puntos (p. 61) Gráfica que muestra la relación entre dos conjuntos. Los datos de ambos conjuntos se presentan como pares ordenados.

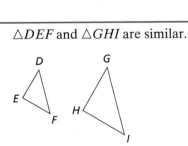

The scatter plot displays the amount spent on advertising (in thousands of dollars) versus product sales (in millions of dollars).

Scientific notation (p. 400) A number expressed in the form $a \times 10^n$, where n is an integer and $1 < a < 10$.

Notación científica (p. 400) Un número expresado en forma de $a \times 10^n$, donde n es un número entero y $1 < a < 10$.

3.4×10^6

Sequence (p. 269) A number pattern.

Progresión (p. 269) Sucesión de números.

$-4, 5, 14, 23$ is a sequence.

Similar figures (p. 191) Figures that have the same shape, but not necessarily the same size.

Figuras semejantes (p. 191) Figuras que tienen la misma forma pero no necesariamente el mismo tamaño.

$\triangle DEF$ and $\triangle GHI$ are similar.

Simple interest (p. 201) Interest paid only on the principal.

Interés simple (p. 201) Intéres basado en el capital solamente.

The interest on $1000 at 6% for 5 years is $1000(0.06)5 = 300.

Simplify (p. 9) Replace an expression with its simplest name or form.

Simplificar (p. 9) Reemplazar una expresión por su versión o forma más simple.

$$\frac{3 + 5}{8}$$

English/Spanish Glossary

Sine (p. 425) In a right triangle, such as $\triangle ABC$, with right $\angle C$,

sine of $\angle A = \dfrac{\text{length of side opposite } \angle A}{\text{length of hypotenuse}}$ or $\sin A = \dfrac{a}{c}$.

Seno (p. 425) En $\triangle ABC$ con $\angle C$ recto,

el seno de $\angle A = \dfrac{\text{longitud del lado opuesto a } \angle A}{\text{longitud de la hipotenusa}}$, o sen $A = \dfrac{a}{c}$.

A $\sin A = \frac{4}{5}$

3 5

C 4 B

Slope (p. 284) The ratio of the vertical change to the horizontal change.

slope $= \dfrac{\text{vertical change}}{\text{horizontal change}} = \dfrac{y_2 - y_1}{x_2 - x_1}$, where $x_2 - x_1 \neq 0$

Pendiente (p. 284) La razón del cambio vertical al cambio horizontal.

pendiente $= \dfrac{\text{cambio vertical}}{\text{cambio horizontal}} = \dfrac{y_2 - y_1}{x_2 - x_1}$, donde $x_2 - x_1 \neq 0$

The slope of the line below is $\frac{2}{4} = \frac{1}{2}$.

Slope-intercept form (p. 292) A linear equation of a nonvertical line written as $y = mx + b$, where m is the slope and b is the y-intercept.

Forma pendiente-ordenada (p. 292) La ecuación lineal de una recta no vertical expresada como $y = mx + b$, donde m es la pendiente y b es el punto donde la recta corta el eje y.

$y = 8x + 2$

Solution of a system of linear equations (p. 340) Any ordered pair in a system that makes all the equations of that system true.

Solución de un sistema (p. 340) Todo par ordenado de un sistema que hace verdaderas todas las ecuaciones de ese sistema.

$(2, 1)$ is a solution of the system
$y = 2x - 3$
$y = x - 1$
because the ordered pair makes each equation true.

Solution of a system of linear inequalities (p. 377) Any ordered pair that makes all of the inequalities in the system true.

Solución de un sistema de desigualdades lineales (p. 377) Todo par ordenado que hace verdaderas todas las desigualdades del sistema.

The shaded purple area shows the solution of the system
$y > 2x - 5$
$3x + 4y < 12$.

Solution of an equation (p. 75) Any value or values that make an equation true.

Solución de una ecuación (p. 75) Cualquier valor o valores que hagan verdadera una ecuación.

In the equation $y + 22 = 11$, -11 is the solution.

Solution of an inequality (one variable) (p. 134) Any value or values of a variable in the inequality that makes an inequality true.

Solución de una desigualdad (una variable) (p. 134) Cualquier valor o valores de una variable de la desigualdad que hagan verdadera la desigualdad.

The solution of the inequality $x < 9$ is all numbers less than 9.

Solution of an inequality (two variables) (p. 371) Any ordered pair that makes the inequality true.

Solución de una desigualdad (dos variables) (p. 371) Cualquier par ordenado que haga verdadera la desigualdad.

Each ordered pair in the pink area and on the solid pink line is a solution of $3x - 5y \leq 10$.

Square root (p. 524) A number b such that $a^2 = b$. $\sqrt{b}$ is the principal square root. $-\sqrt{b}$ is the negative square root.

Raíz cuadrada (p. 524) Si $a^2 = b$, entonces a es la raíz cuadrada de b. $\sqrt{b}$ es la raíz cuadrada principal. $-\sqrt{b}$ es la raíz cuadrada negativa.

-3 and 3 are square roots of 9.

Square root function (p. 614) A function that contains the independent variable in the radicand.

Función de raíz cuadrada (p. 614) Una función que contiene la variable independiente en el radicando.

$y = \sqrt{2x}$ is a square root function.

Standard form of a linear equation (p. 298) The form of a linear equation $Ax + By = C$, where A, B, and C are real numbers and A and B are not both zero.

Forma normal de una ecuación lineal (p. 298) La forma normal de una ecuación lineal es $Ax + By = C$, donde A, B y C son números reales, y donde A y B no son ambos iguales a cero.

$6x - y = 12$

Standard form of a polynomial (p. 457) The form of a polynomial in which the degree of the terms decreases from left to right (also *descending order*).

Forma normal de un polinomio (p. 457) Cuando el grado de los términos de un polinomio disminuye de izquierda a derecha, está en forma normal, o en orden descendente.

$15x^3 + x^2 + 3x - 9$

Standard form of a quadratic equation (p. 530) The form of a quadratic equation written $ax^2 + bx + c = 0$.

Forma normal de una ecuación cuadrática (p. 530) Cuando una ecuación cuadrática se expresa de forma $ax^2 + bx + c = 0$.

$-x^2 + 2x + 9 = 0$

Standard form of a quadratic function (p. 510) The form of a quadratic function written $y = ax^2 + bx + c$, where $a \neq 0$.

Forma normal de una función cuadrática (p. 510) Cuando una ecuación cuadrática se expresa como $y = ax^2 + bx + c$, donde $a \neq 0$.

$y = 2x^2 - 5x + 2$

Stem-and-leaf plot (p. 120)   A display of data made by using the digits of the values.

Diagrama de tallo y hojas (p. 120)   Un arreglo de los datos que use los dígitos de los valoves.

Substitution method (p. 347)   A method of solving a system of equations by replacing one variable with an equivalent expression containing the other variable.

$y = 2x + 5$
$x + 3y = 7$
$x + 3(2x + 5) = 7$

Método de sustitución (p. 347)   Método para resolver un sistema de ecuaciones en el que se reemplaza una variable por una expresión equivalente que contenga la otra variable.

System of linear equations (p. 340)   Two or more linear equations using the same variables.

$y = 5x + 7, y = \frac{1}{2}x - 3$

Sistema de ecuaciones lineales (p. 340)   Dos o más ecuaciones lineales que usen las mismas variables.

System of linear inequalities (p. 375)   Two or more linear inequalities using the same variables.

$y \leq x + 11, y < 5x$

Sistema de desigualdades lineales (p. 375)   Dos o más desigualdades lineales que usen las mismas variables.

T

Tangent (p. 621)   In a right triangle, such as $\triangle ABC$ with right $\angle C$, tangent of $\angle A = \dfrac{\text{length of side opposite } \angle A}{\text{length of side adjacent to } \angle A}$, or $\tan A = \frac{a}{b}$.

Tangente (p. 621)   En $\triangle ABC$, con $\angle C$ recto, tangente de $\angle A = \dfrac{\text{longitud del lado opuesto a } \angle A}{\text{longitud del lado adyacente a } \angle A}$, o la $\tan A = \frac{a}{b}$.

$\tan A = \frac{4}{3}$

Term (p. 49)   A number, variable, or the product or quotient of a number and one or more variables.

The expression $5x + \frac{y}{2} - 8$ has three terms: $5x, \frac{y}{2},$ and -8.

Término (p. 49)   Un número, una variable o el producto o cociente de un número y una o más variables.

Term of a sequence (p. 269)   Any number in a sequence.

-4 is the first term of the sequence $-4, 5, 14, 23$.

Término de una progresión (p. 269)   Todos los números de una progresión.

Theoretical probability (p. 211) The ratio of the number of favorable outcomes to the number of possible outcomes if all outcomes have the same chance of happening.

$$P(\text{event}) = \frac{\text{number of favorable outcomes}}{\text{number of possible outcomes}}$$

Probabilidad teórica (p. 211) Si cada resultado tiene la misma probabilidad de darse, la probabilidad teórica de un suceso se calcula como el cociente del número de resultados favorables y el número de resultados posibles.

$$P(\text{suceso}) = \frac{\text{número de resultados favorables}}{\text{número de resultados posibles}}$$

In tossing a coin, the probabilities of getting a head or tail are equally likely. The likelihood of getting a head is $P(\text{head}) = \frac{1}{2}$.

Translation (p. 325) A transformation that shifts a graph horizontally, vertically, or both.

Traslación (p. 325) Proceso de rotar una gráfica horizontalmente, verticalmente o en ambos sentidos.

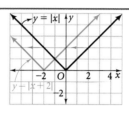

$y = |x + 2|$ is a translation of $y = |x|$.

Trend line (p. 61) A line on a scatter plot drawn near the points. It shows a correlation.

Línea de tendencia (p. 61) Línea de un diagrama de puntos que se traza cerca de los puntos para mostrar una correlación.

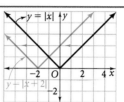

Positive   Negative   No Correlation

Trigonometric ratios (p. 621) The ratios of the sides of a right triangle. *See* **cosine**, **sine**, and **tangent**.

Razones trigonométricas (p. 621) Las razones de los lados de un triángulo rectángulo. *Ver* **coseno**, **seno**, y **tangente**.

Trinomial (p. 457) A polynomial of three terms.

Trinomio (p. 457) Polinomio compuesto de tres términos.

$$3x^2 + 2x - 5$$

U

Uniform motion (p. 104) The motion of an object moving at a constant rate.

Movimiento uniforme (p. 104) El movimiento de un objeto que se mueve a una velocidad constante.

Unit analysis (p. 182) The process of selecting conversion factors to produce the appropriate units.

Análisis de unidades (p. 182) Proceso de seleccionar factores de conversión para producir las unidades apropiadas.

To change ten feet to yards, multiply by the conversion factor $\frac{1\ \text{yd}}{3\ \text{ft}}$.

$$10\ \text{ft}\left(\frac{1\ \text{yd}}{3\ \text{ft}}\right) = 3\tfrac{1}{3}\ \text{yd}$$

English/Spanish Glossary

Unit rate (p. 182)   A rate with a denominator of 1.

Razón en unidades (p. 182)   Razón cuyo denominador es 1.

The unit rate for 120 miles driven in 2 hours is 60 mi/h.

Unlike radicals (p. 600)   Radical expressions that do not have the same radicands.

Radicales desemejantes (p. 600)   Expresiones radicales que no tienen radicandos semejantes.

$\sqrt{2}$ and $\sqrt{3}$ are unlike radicals.

Variable (p. 4)   A symbol, usually a letter, that represents one or more numbers.

Variable (p. 4)   Símbolo, generalmente una letra, que representa uno o más valores.

x is a variable in the equation $9 - x = 3$.

Vertex (p. 511)   The highest or lowest point on a parabola. The axis of symmetry intersects the parabola at the vertex.

Vértice (p. 511)   El punto más alto o más bajo de una parábola. El punto de intersección del eje de simetría y la parábola.

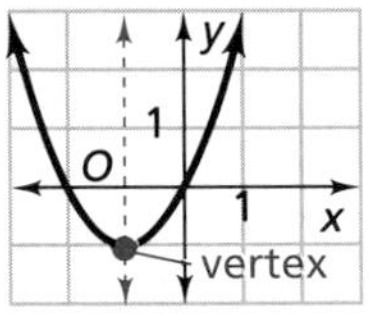

Vertical-line test (p. 242)   A method used to determine if a relation is a function or not. If a vertical line passes through a graph more than once, the graph is not the graph of a function.

Prueba de la línea vertical (p. 242)   Método que permite determinar si una relación es o no es una función. Si una línea vertical pasa por la gráfica más de una vez, la gráfica no es de función.

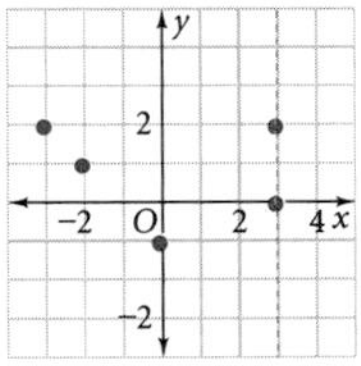

A line would pass through $(3, 0)$ and $(3, 2)$, so the relation is not a function.

Whole numbers (p. 17)   The nonnegative integers.

Números enteros positivos (p. 17)   Todos los números enteros que no son negativos.

$0, 1, 2, 3, \ldots$

---

x-axis (p. 59)   The horizontal axis of the coordinate plane.

Eje x (p. 59)   El eje horizontal del plano de coordenadas.

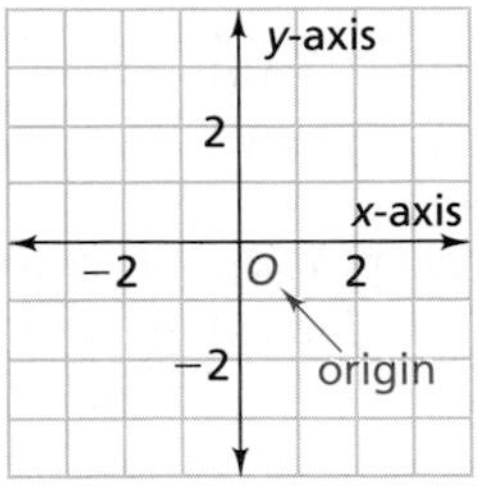

x-coordinate (p. 59) The location on the x-axis of a point in the coordinate plane.

In the ordered pair $(4, -1)$, 4 is the x-coordinate.

Coordenada x (p. 59) La coordenada x de un punto muestra la localización del punto sobre el eje x en el plano de coordenadas.

x-intercept (p. 298) The x-coordinate of the point where a line crosses the x-axis.

The x-intercept of $3x + 4y = 12$ is 3.

Abscisa al origen (p. 298) La coordenada horizontal del punto donde una recta cruza el eje x.

Y

y-axis (p. 59) The vertical axis of the coordinate plane.

Eje y (p. 59) El eje vertical del plano de coordenadas.

y-coordinate (p. 59) The location on the y-axis of a point in the coordinate plane.

In the ordered pair $(4, -1)$, -1 is the y-coordinate.

Coordenada y (p. 59) La coordenada y de un punto muestra la localización del punto sobre el eje y en el plano de coordenadas.

y-intercept (p. 290) The y-coordinate of the point where a line crosses the y-axis.

The y-intercept of $y = 5x + 2$ is 2.

Ordenada al origen (p. 290) La coordenada vertical del punto donde una recta cruza el eje y.

Z

Zero-product property (p. 536) For all real numbers a and b, if $ab = 0$, then $a = 0$ or $b = 0$.

$x(x + 3) = 0$
$x = 0$ or $x + 3 = 0$
$x = 0$ or $x = -3$

Propiedad del producto cero (p. 536) Para todos los números reales a y b, si $ab = 0$, entonces $a = 0$ ó $b = 0$.

English/Spanish Glossary

Answers to Instant Check System™

Chapter 1

Diagnosing Readiness   p. 2

1. $\frac{4}{5}$ **2.** $\frac{5}{7}$ **3.** $\frac{3}{7}$ **4.** $\frac{1}{7}$ **5.** $\frac{12}{13}$ **6.** $\frac{7}{24}$ **7.** $\frac{6}{11}$ **8.** $1\frac{9}{20}$ **9.** $\frac{23}{39}$
10. $12\frac{23}{40}$ **11.** $4\frac{7}{12}$ **12.** $1\frac{5}{6}$ **13.** $13\frac{13}{28}$ **14.** 9^5 **15.** $8 \cdot 7^6$
16. $2^2 \cdot 3^6$ **17.** $\approx 2{,}650{,}000$ **18.** Texas; $\approx 1{,}000{,}000$

Lesson 1-1   pp. 2–6

Check Skills You'll Need **1.** $\div$ **2.** $-$ **3.** $+$ **4.** $\times$ **5.** $-$
6. $+$ **7.** $\times$ **8.** $\div$ **9.** 21 **10.** 5 **11.** 4 **12.** 50

Check Understanding **1a.** $\frac{4 \cdot 2}{c}$ **b.** $t - 15$ **2.** Let n be
the number. **a.** $n - 9$ **b.** $2n + 31$ **c.** $\frac{1}{2}n\left(\frac{1}{3}n\right)$
3a. $c = 15n$ **b.** Each CD costs $10.99.
4. Answers may vary. Sample: $e =$ money earned,
$s =$ money saved, $s = \frac{1}{2}e$

Lesson 1-2   pp. 9–12

Check Skills You'll Need **1.** 16 **2.** 49 **3.** 25 **4.** 81 **5.** 8
6. 3 **7.** 11 **8.** 1 **9.** 32 **10.** 10

Check Understanding **1a.** 4 **b.** 10 **c.** 29 **d.** 134
2a. 3 **b.** 8 **c.** 6 **d.** 45 **3.** $26.20 **4a.** 26 **b.** 10.5
5a. 1764 **b.** 1134 **c.** 15,876 **6a.** 95 **b.** 21 **c.** 29
7. 63,000 ft^2

Lesson 1-3   pp. 17–20

Check Skills You'll Need **1.** $\frac{1}{2}$ **2.** $\frac{1}{20}$ **3.** $\frac{13}{4}$ **4.** $\frac{13}{40}$ **5.** 0.4
6. 0.375 **7.** $0.\overline{6}$ **8.** $3.\overline{5}$

Check Understanding **1a.** integers, rational numbers
b. rational numbers **c.** rational numbers
d. natural numbers, whole numbers, integers,
rational numbers **2.** rational numbers **3a.** true
b. False; answers may vary. Sample: $\frac{3}{1} = 3$ is a
whole number. **4.** $-\frac{2}{3}, -\frac{5}{8}, \frac{1}{12}$ **5a.** 5 **b.** 4 **c.** 3.7
d. $\frac{5}{7}$

Lesson 1-4   pp. 24–27, 31

Check Skills You'll Need **1.** 6 **2.** 17 **3.** 14 **4.** 59 **5.** 1.3
6. 5.2 **7.** 10.9 **8.** 17.1 **9.** $\frac{4}{5}$ **10.** $1\frac{2}{9}$ **11.** $1\frac{1}{4}$ **12.** $\frac{5}{8}$

Check Understanding **1a.** -2 **b.** -2 **c.** -11 **d.** 6
2a. -11 **b.** -17.4 **c.** $-1\frac{1}{4}$ **d.** $\frac{1}{18}$ **3.** $-15 + 18 = 3$,
rise of 3° **4a.** -11.4 **b.** -9.1 **c.** 15.6 **d.** 14.59
5. Choices of variable may vary.
Sample: $c =$ change in temp., $-14 + c$; $-25°F$

6a. $\begin{bmatrix} -4 \\ 1.5 \\ -16 \end{bmatrix}$ **b.** $\begin{bmatrix} -9 & \frac{1}{8} \\ 1\frac{1}{4} & -1 \end{bmatrix}$

Checkpoint Quiz 1 **1.** $b + 4$; 2 **2.** $\frac{c}{2}$; 1.25 **3.** $4.3a$; 12.9
4. $b + c + 2a$; 6.5 **5.** $b + 17$; 15 **6.** $3c$; 7.5
7. $24 - a$; 21 **8.** $b + 2a$; 4 **9.** No; the statement is
not true for nonpositive numbers.
10. whole numbers

Lesson 1-5   pp. 32–34

Check Skills You'll Need **1.** -6 **2.** 7 **3.** -3.79 **4.** $\frac{7}{19}$
5. 1 **6.** 6 **7.** 5 **8.** $\frac{1}{2}$

Check Understanding **1a.** -4 **b.** -5 **c.** -11 **d.** 5
2a. -1 **b.** 14 **c.** 4 **d.** 3 **3a.** -8 **b.** 12 **c.** 8.0
d. $-\frac{1}{18}$ **4a.** 1 **b.** 1 **c.** 6 **d.** 6 **5a.** -5 **b.** 5 **c.** 9
d. 5 **6.** ABC: $32.47; PQR: $15.46

Lesson 1-6   pp. 37–41

Check Skills You'll Need **1.** -8 **2.** -25 **3.** -24 **4.** -72
5. 8, 10, 12 **6.** 0, -2, -4 **7.** 3, 0, -3 **8.** 0, 6, 12

Check Understanding **1a.** -24 **b.** 50 **c.** 39.2 **d.** $-\frac{1}{2}$
2a. -56 **b.** 336 **c.** -56 **3a.** $-24.75°F$ **b.** 15.25°F
4a. -64 **b.** 16 **c.** 0.09 **d.** $-\frac{9}{16}$ **5a.** -6 **b.** 4
c. -1 **d.** 13 **6a.** $-4\frac{1}{2}$ **b.** $-\frac{1}{5}$ **c.** $29\frac{1}{2}$ **7.** -10

Lesson 1-7   pp. 47–49

Check Skills You'll Need **1.** 33 **2.** -22 **3.** 1 **4.** -1 **5.** $3t$
6. $-4m$

Check Understanding **1a.** 1339 **b.** 2121 **c.** 2352
d. 1485 **2.** $17.70 **3a.** $6m + 30$ **b.** $6 - 14t$
c. $1.2 + 3.3c$ **4a.** $-2x - 1$ **b.** $-7 + 5b$
c. $-3 + 8a$ **5a.** $13y$ **b.** $2t$ **c.** $-12w^3$ **d.** $9d$
6a. $-2(t + 7)$ **b.** $14(8 + w)$

Lesson 1-8   pp. 54–56, 58

Check Skills You'll Need **1.** 19 **2.** -30 **3.** 26 **4.** 140
5. -1 **6.** 3 **7.** $1 + x$ **8.** $5t - 8$ **9.** $-7m$

Check Understanding **1a.** Ident. Prop. of Mult.; m is
mult. by the mult. identity, 1. **b.** Assoc. Prop. of
Add.; the grouping of the terms changes.
c. Assoc. Prop. of Mult.; the grouping of the
factors changes. **d.** Ident. Prop. of Add.; the
ident. for add., 0, is added. **e.** Comm. Prop. of
Mult.; the order of the factors changes.

f. Comm. Prop. of Add.; the order of the terms changes. **2.** $8.80

3a. $5a + 6 + a$

$= 5a + a + 6$	Comm. Prop. of Add.
$= (5a + a) + 6$	Assoc. Prop. of Add.
$= (5a + 1a) + 6$	Ident. Prop. of Mult.
$= (5 + 1)a + 6$	Dist. Prop.
$= 6a + 6$	addition

b. $2(3t - 1) + 2$

$= 6t - 2 + 2$	Dist. Prop.
$= 6t + (-2) + 2$	def. of subtr.
$= 6t + [(-2) + 2]$	Assoc. Prop. of Add.
$= 6t + 0$	Inv. Prop. of Add.
$= 6t$	Ident. Prop. of Add.

Checkpoint Quiz 2 1. $13 + 5t$ **2.** 160 **3.** 42 **4.** -49
5. $-12 - 9w$ **6.** $5 + 4m$ **7.** 1.5 **8.** -2.5
9. $-5x + 5y$
10a. $9t + 3(t + 4)$

$= 9t + 3t + 12$	Dist. Prop.
$= (9t + 3t) + 12$	Assoc. Prop. of Add.
$= (9 + 3)t + 12$	Dist. Prop.
$= 12t + 12$	Add.

b. -24

Lesson 1-9   pp. 59–62

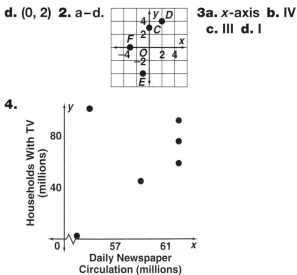

Check Skills You'll Need 1.

2. **3.**

4. **5.** 1 **6.** -2.5 **7.** 3.5 **8.** -4

Check Understanding 1a. $(3, -3)$ **b.** $(-1, 1)$ **c.** $(4, 1)$
d. $(0, 2)$ **2.** a–d.   **3a.** x-axis **b.** IV
c. III **d.** I

4.

5a. 4-year-old car with an asking price of $14,900
b. $5000

Chapter 2

Diagnosing Readiness   p. 72

1. $0.45n = 3.60$ **2.** $3s = 124$ **3.** 34 **4.** 10 **5.** 5
6. 30 **7.** 3 **8.** -10 **9.** 8 **10.** -8 **11.** 7.14 **12.** 16.4
13. $-\frac{9}{20}$ **14.** $-\frac{7}{15}$ **15.** 17 **16.** -3 **17.** 576
18. -2.75 **19.** $16k^2$ **20.** $13xy$ **21.** $2t + 2$
22. $12x - 4$

Lesson 2-1   pp. 74–77

Check Skills You'll Need 1. x **2.** n **3.** c **4.** m **5.** $-2, \frac{1}{2}$
6. $2, -\frac{1}{2}$ **7.** $-\frac{3}{5}, \frac{5}{3}$ **8.** $\frac{3}{5}, -\frac{5}{3}$

Check Understanding 1a. 12 **b.** 11.6 **c.** -4 **2a.** 1
b. $-\frac{5}{12}$ **c.** -24 **3.** $268.19 **4a.** 30 **b.** -54 **c.** 100
5a. -32 **b.** -40 **c.** $1\frac{1}{3}$ **6a.** 4 **b.** -10 **c.** $-1\frac{3}{5}$

Lesson 2-2   pp. 81–83

Check Skills You'll Need 1. 19; Add. Prop. of Eq.
2. 5.2; Subtr. Prop. of Eq. **3.** 14; Add. Prop. of Eq.
4. 33; Add. Prop. of Eq. **5.** 32; Mult. Prop. of Eq.
6. 3; Div. Prop. of Eq. **7.** $\frac{1}{5}$; **8.** -9; **9.** $3\frac{3}{4}$

Check Understanding 1a. 5 **b.** $-1\frac{2}{3}$ **c.** 243 **2.** 18 bulbs
3a. -5 **b.** 3 **c.** 7

4.

$\frac{3}{5}w + 9 - 9 = -1 - 9$	Subtr. Prop. of Eq.
$\frac{3}{5}w = -10$	Simplify.
$\frac{3}{5}w \cdot \frac{5}{3} = -10 \cdot \frac{5}{3}$	Mult. Prop. of Eq.
$w = -16\frac{2}{3}$	Simplify.

5.

$-9 - 4m + 9 = 3 + 9$	Add. Prop. of Eq.
$-4m = 12$	Simplify.
$\frac{-4m}{-4} = \frac{12}{-4}$	Div. Prop. of Eq.
$m = -3$	Simplify.

Lesson 2-3   pp. 88–91, 94

Check Skills You'll Need 1. $-n$ **2.** $8b - 2$ **3.** $9w - 45$
4. $-10b + 120$ **5.** $-3x + 12$ **6.** $30 - 5w$ **7.** 43
8. 26 **9.** -45 **10.** -35

Check Understanding 1a. 8 **b.** 3 **c.** 3 **d.** 4 **2.** 135 ft
3a. -1 **b.** -1 **4a.** $\frac{5}{6}$ **b.** 624 **5a.** 28 **b.** 4

Checkpoint Quiz 1 1. 1 **2.** 33 **3.** 20 **4.** $2\frac{1}{2}$ **5.** 120
6. -2 **7.** $-19\frac{1}{5}$ **8.** -16 **9.** $\frac{3}{5}$ **10.** $154.00

Lesson 2-4   pp. 96–98

Check Skills You'll Need 1. $4x$ **2.** $-4x$ **3.** 0 **4.** 0 **5.** -2
6. -5 **7.** -7 **8.** $\frac{1}{3}$

788 Answers to Instant Check System

Check Understanding **1a.** $-\frac{4}{7}$ **b.** -2 **c.** $-\frac{5}{2}$ **d.** 10
2. at least 15 bottles **3a.** no solution **b.** identity

Lesson 2-5 pp. 103–105

Check Skills You'll Need **1.** $25q$ **2.** 2ℓ **3.** $34h$ **4.** $5x$
5. $3.99n$

Check Understanding **1.** 5 cm **2a.** Let $x =$ the first
integer. **b.** $x + 1$ is the second integer and $x + 2$
is the third integer. **c.** $3x + 3 = 48$, 15, 16, 17
3a. $3\frac{2}{3}$ h **b.** $1\frac{2}{3}$ h **4.** 1h **5.** John: 38 mi/h; Sarah:
50 mi/h

Lesson 2-6 pp. 111–113, 115

Check Skills You'll Need **1.** 180 mi **2.** 32 cm **3.** 28 m^2

Check Understanding **1.** $w = \frac{P}{2} - \ell$ **2.** $x = \frac{y + 4}{3}$
3. $p = \frac{m - d}{h}$; $h \neq 0$ **4.** $n = 4F - 148$;
92 chirps/min

Checkpoint Quiz 2 **1.** $-\frac{3}{4}$ **2.** $-14\frac{2}{7}$ **3.** $-2\frac{13}{21}$ **4.** 5
5. -13 **6.** 4 **7.** $y = \frac{35 - 2x}{7}$ **8.** $y = \frac{5x - 15}{2}$
9. $y = 12 - \frac{8}{9}x$ **10.** first car: 5 h, second car: 4 h

Lesson 2-7 pp. 118–121

Check Skills You'll Need **1.** 1.9, 2.4, 3.6, 7.5, 9.8
2. 58, 72, 98, 144, 195, 235 **3.** $-12, -8, -3, 0, 7, 14$
4. $-4\frac{3}{8}, -3\frac{2}{3}, -2\frac{5}{8}, 2\frac{1}{2}, 4\frac{1}{2}, 6\frac{1}{4}$ **5.** 5 **6.** 7

Check Understanding **1a.** about $6.53/h; about $6.38/h;
$6.25/h **b.** Median; the mean is still larger than 8
of 10 wages. **2.** No; you would need at least a 104
to have a 92 average. **3.** Maine: mean = 0.4°F,
range = 13°F; Michigan: mean = 4.4°F,
range = 34°F. On average, Maine was colder. The
temperatures for Michigan were more spread out.

4.
```
0 | 2 8 8
1 | 4
2 | 6
3 | 5
4 | 3 3 5
6 | 0
4 | 3 means 4.3
```
5a. city: 28 mi/gal;
highway: 32 mi/gal;
b. city: 23 mi/gal; 31 mi/gal;
highway: 32 mi/gal; 38 mi/gal
c. city: 15 mi/gal;
highway: 14 mi/gal

Chapter 3

Diagnosing Readiness p. 132

1. > **2.** = **3.** > **4.** < **5.** 7 **6.** -4 **7.** 1 **8.** 2 **9.** 3
10. -12 **11.** 32.4 **12.** 23 **13.** 29.5 **14.** -28
15. -12 **16.** 48 **17.** 5 **18.** -24 **19.** -10 **20.** 1.85
21. -24 **22.** -2 **23.** 3 **24.** -4 **25.** 3 **26.** $\frac{1}{2}$ **27.** $\frac{5}{2}$
28. 4.1 **29.** 48

Lesson 3-1 pp. 134–136

Check Skills You'll Need **1–5.**
6. > **7.** < **8.** = **9.** = **10.** > **11.** <

Check Understanding **1a.** no **b.** yes **c.** yes **d.** yes
2a. no **b.** no **c.** yes **d.** yes

3a.
b.
c.
4a–b. Choice of
variable may vary. **a.** $x \geq 2$ **b.** $x < 0$ **5a.** No;
speeds cannot be negative, so you can't use all
real numbers. **b.** No; answers may vary.
Sample: Hourly wages are not likely to be in
hundreds of dollars.

Lesson 3-2 pp. 140–142

Check Skills You'll Need **1.** > **2.** < **3.** > **4.** 9 **5.** -2
6. -9 **7.** $\frac{1}{6}$

Check Understanding **1.** $m > 2$;
2. $n \leq 5$;
3. $t \geq 5$;
4. at least 53 blankets

Lesson 3-3 pp. 146–149, 151

Check Skills You'll Need **1.** 16 **2.** $-\frac{2}{3}$ **3.** -6 **4.** 6.4
5. -18 **6.** 18 **7.** $x \leq -1$ **8.** $x > 3$

Check Understanding **1a.** $b > 2$;
b. $d \geq 2\frac{1}{2}$;
c. $y \leq -1.5$;
2a. $k < 4$;
b. $t > -\frac{1}{2}$;
c. $w \leq -10$;
3a. $t > 4$;
b. $w \leq -4$;
c. $n > -3$;
4. $0.4c > 327$; 818 calendars

Checkpoint Quiz 1 **1.** $c > 5$;
2. $x < -6$;

3. $p \le -6$; [number line: $-10\ -8\ -6\ -4\ -2\ 0\ 2$]

4. $y \ge 2$; [number line: $-1\ 0\ 1\ 2\ 3\ 4$]

5. $g < -8$; [number line: $-12\ -10\ -8\ -6\ -4\ -2\ 0\ 2$]

6. $b \le -5$; [number line: $-8\ -6\ -4\ -2\ 0\ 2$]

7a. yes **b.** no **c.** yes **d.** no **8a.** no **b.** no **c.** no
d. yes **9a.** $m + 38 + 50 \ge 180$ **b.** $m \ge 92$
10a. $1.50p \le 20$ **b.** 13 plants

Lesson 3-4 pp. 153–155

Check Skills You'll Need 1. -2 **2.** no solution **3.** $-3\frac{1}{3}$
4. identity **5.** $1\frac{2}{9}$ **6.** -11 **7.** 40 cm **8.** 13 in.

Check Understanding 1a. $x \ge -6$ **b.** $t < 1$ **c.** $n > 3$
d. $k \le -2$ **2.** $2(12) + 2w \le 40$, so the banner's
width must be 8 feet or less. **3a.** $p < -1$
b. $m \le -3$ **c.** $b > 3$ **4.** $b > 3$ **5.** $x \le 2\frac{1}{4}$

Lesson 3-5 pp. 161–163, 166

Check Skills You'll Need 1. [number line: $6\ 7\ 8\ 9\ 10\ 11\ 12$]

2. [number line: $-6\ -5\ -4\ -3\ -2\ -1$]

3. [number line: $5\ 6\ 7\ 8\ 9\ 10\ 11\ 12\ 13\ 14$]

4. 6 **5.** -3 **6.** 14 **7.** 3

Check Understanding 1a. $n > -2$ and $n < 9$ or
$-2 < n < 9$; [number line: $-4\ -2\ 0\ 2\ 4\ 6\ 8\ 10$]

b. $3.50 \le b \le 6$; [number line: $0\ 1\ 2\ 3\ 4\ 5\ 6\ 7$]

2a. $-2 \le x < 5$; [number line: $-4\ -2\ 0\ 2\ 4\ 6$]

b. $-1 < x < 4$; [number line: $-2\ -1\ 0\ 1\ 2\ 3\ 4\ 5$]

c. $-4 \le n < -2$; [number line: $-5\ -4\ -3\ -2\ -1\ 0\ 1$]

3a. $6.7 \le p \le 8.5$ **b.** $5.2 \le p \le 7$. No; readings in
this range are unlikely if the first readings are high.

4. $n \le -5$ or $n \ge 3$; [number line: $-6\ -4\ -2\ 0\ 2\ 4\ 6$]

5. $x < 2$ or $x \ge 3$; [number line: $-1\ 0\ 1\ 2\ 3\ 4$]

Checkpoint Quiz 2

1. $d < -3$ [number line: $-5\ -4\ -3\ -2\ -1\ 0\ 1$]

2. $n \ge -2$ [number line: $-4\ -3\ -2\ -1\ 0\ 1\ 2\ 3\ 4$]

3. $-2 \le m \le 1$ [number line: $-3\ -2\ -1\ 0\ 1\ 2$]

4. $s < 2$ [number line: $-1\ 0\ 1\ 2\ 3$]

5. $p > 4$ [number line: $-2\ 0\ 2\ 4\ 6\ 8$]

6. $x \le -4$ or $x > 4$ [number line: $-6\ -4\ -2\ 0\ 2\ 4\ 6$]

7. $c < 8$ **8.** $65 \le t \le 75$
9. $2(15) + 2(w) \le 48$, $w \le 9$ **10.** $x \ge -19$

Lesson 3-6 pp. 167–169

Check Skills You'll Need 1. 15 **2.** 3 **3.** 6 **4.** -7 **5.** 24
6. 2 **7.** $=$ **8.** $>$ **9.** $<$ **10.** $>$ **11.** $>$ **12.** $=$

Check Understanding 1a. $-1, 1$ **b.** $-5, 5$ **c.** $-2, 2$
d. No; an absolute value cannot be negative.
2a. $-4, 8$ **b.** no solution **c.** $-2, 2$
3a. $w < -7$ or $w > 3$, [number line: $-8\ -6\ -4\ -2\ 0\ 2\ 4\ 6$]

b. all real numbers **4.** 33.81 oz to 33.91 oz,
inclusive

Chapter 4

Diagnosing Readiness p. 180

1. $\frac{2}{5}$ **2.** $\frac{9}{16}$ **3.** $3\frac{1}{5}$ **4.** 3 **5.** 75% **6.** 62.5% **7.** 1250%
8. 0.2% **9.** 70% **10.** $n - 22$ **11.** $p + 40$ **12.** $20m$
13. $z + 17$ **14.** $6 - 3n$ **15.** $0.4t + 2$ **16.** $-8x + 8$
17. $25a + 200$ **18.** $-10 + 2.5c$ **19.** $-b - 12$
20. 24 **21.** -10 **22.** $1\frac{1}{5}$ **23.** $9\frac{3}{4}$ **24.** $-1\frac{1}{4}$ **25.** $-\frac{1}{10}$
26. $\frac{2}{3}$ **27.** $1\frac{4}{11}$

Lesson 4-1 pp. 182–185

Check Skills You'll Need 1. $\frac{7}{12}$ **2.** $\frac{4}{7}$ **3.** $\frac{3}{4}$ **4.** 5 **5.** $\frac{3}{4}$ **6.** $\frac{1}{2}$

Check Understanding 1a. 3.75¢/oz, 2.5¢/oz **b.** 64-oz
2. 13.2 ft/min **3a.** $6\frac{2}{3}$ **b.** $6\frac{6}{7}$ **c.** 5.4 **4a.** $8\frac{1}{3}$ **b.** 33.6
c. 48 **5a.** $\frac{2}{35} = \frac{x}{60}$ **b.** ≈ 3.4 **6a.** 5 **b.** -8.75
c. -21 **d.** -5

Lesson 4-2 pp. 189–191, 195

Check Skills You'll Need 1. $\frac{6}{7}$ **2.** $\frac{3}{4}$ **3.** $\frac{1}{2}$ **4.** $2\frac{4}{5}$ **5.** $2\frac{2}{15}$
6. $6\frac{2}{3}$ **7.** $1\frac{1}{9}$ **8.** 10 **9.** $\frac{3}{5}$

Check Understanding 1. 15 cm **2a.** 9.75 ft **b.** 42 ft
3a. about 21 mi **b.** 3.5 in.

Checkpoint Quiz 1 1. 2880 **2.** $6.00/h **3.** 10.5
4. -20 **5.** 4.4 **6.** 33.6 min **7.** 3.125 cm **8.** 4.5 ft
9. 35 ft **10.** $36\frac{2}{3}$ mi

Lesson 4-3 pp. 197–200

Check Skills You'll Need 1. 5.4 **2.** 25.84 **3.** $\frac{1}{6}$ **4.** $\frac{1}{54}$
5. 0.7, 70% **6.** 0.23, 23% **7.** 0.4, 40% **8.** 0.65, 65%
9. 0.875, 87.5% **10.** 0.4375, 43.75% **11.** 0.16, 16%

12. 0.85, 85%

Check Understanding 1. 75% **2.** 12 **3.** 36 h
4a. $\frac{85}{100} = \frac{x}{320}$, 272 **b.** $\frac{60}{100} = \frac{393}{x}$, 655 **5a.** 84
b. 0.5% **c.** 2000% **d.** 3,000,000 **6a.** 140 **b.** 222
c. 33 **d.** 52 **7a.** $19 **b.** $37

Lesson 4-4 pp. 204–206

Check Skills You'll Need 1. $\frac{x}{20} = \frac{20}{100}$, 4 **2.** $\frac{8}{20} = \frac{x}{100}$, 40%
3. $\frac{18}{x} = \frac{90}{100}$, 20 **4.** $\frac{27}{x} = \frac{90}{100}$, 30 **5.** 16 **6.** 32

Check Understanding 1a. 8% **b.** 7% **2.** 1899%
3. 0.5 cm **4.** 86.25 ft^2, 106.25 ft^2 **5a.** about 0.3%
b. about 0.03% **6.** about 66%

Lesson 4-5 pp. 211–213, 217

Check Skills You'll Need 1. 32% **2.** 9% **3.** 22.5% **4.** 18%

Check Understanding 1. $\frac{2}{7}$ **2.** increases **3.** 98%
4. about 35,260 light bulbs

Checkpoint Quiz 2 1. 120 **2.** 80% **3.** 24 **4.** 70 **5.** 25%
6. 50% **7.** 11.25 ft^2, 19.25 ft^2 **8.** 10% **9.** $\frac{2}{7}$
10. 2352 bicycles

Lesson 4-6 pp. 219–221

Check Skills You'll Need 1. $\frac{1}{3}$ **2.** $\frac{1}{3}$ **3.** $\frac{1}{6}$ **4.** 0 **5.** $\frac{1}{6}$ **6.** $\frac{1}{4}$
7. $1\frac{3}{5}$

Check Understanding 1. $\frac{1}{18}$ **2.** $\frac{4}{225}$ **3.** $\frac{4}{105}$ **4a.** $\frac{2}{39}$ **b.** $\frac{2}{39}$
c. No; according to the Comm. Prop. of Mult.,
the order of the terms does not change the
result.

Chapter 5

Diagnosing Readiness p. 234

1. Let n = number of pens and t = total price;
$t = 0.59n$. **2.** Let h = height of house and t =
height of tower; $t = h + 200$. **3.** Let s = length of
a side and p = perimeter; $p = 3s$. **4.** −7 **5.** −18
6. 2 **7.** −1

8–11.

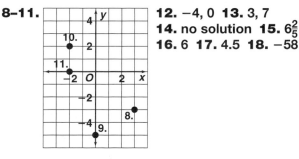

12. −4, 0 **13.** 3, 7
14. no solution **15.** $6\frac{2}{5}$
16. 6 **17.** 4.5 **18.** −58

Lesson 5-1 pp. 236–237

Check Skills You'll Need 1. C **2.** D **3.** E **4.** A **5.** (0, 0)
6. (−4, −2) **7.** (−3, 3)

Check Understanding 1–2. Labels may vary. Samples
are given.

1.

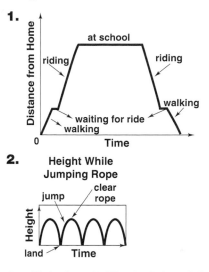

2.

3a. III **b.** I **c.** II The height of the water in A will
increase at a steady rate. The rate that the water
rises in B will decrease steadily because it gets
wider from the bottom to the top. The rate that
the water rises in C will decrease as it gets wider
and then increase as it gets narrower towards
the top.

Lesson 5-2 pp. 241–243, 246

Check Skills You'll Need

1. 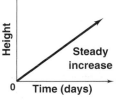 **5.** −17 **6.** −1 **7.** 108

Check Understanding 1. {−2, −1, 4}, {−2, 1, 3}
2a. function **b.** not a function **3a.** not a function
b. function **4a.** 5.2 **b.** 0.41 **c.** −0.1
5a. {−8, −6, −1} **b.** {−20, 0, 8} **c.** {1, 5, 26}

Checkpoint Quiz 1 1–3. Graphs may vary. Samples
are given. **1.**

Instant Check System™ Answers

2.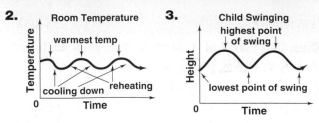

Room Temperature

warmest temp

cooling down / reheating

Temperature / Time

3. Child Swinging

highest point of swing ↓

lowest point of swing

Height / Time

b. Tables may vary. Sample:

x	f(x)
−2	3
−1	0
0	−1
1	0
2	3

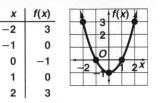

4. Yes; it passes the vertical line test. **5.** −2.4
6. 2.13 **7.** 1.7 **8.** 1.08 **9.** 33.4 **10.** −1.8

Lesson 5-3 — pp. 247–249

Check Skills You'll Need

1. **2.** **3.**

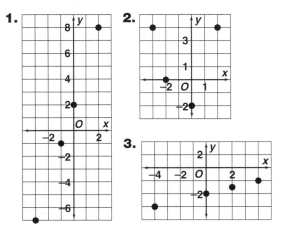

Check Understanding

1. Tables may vary. Sample:

x	f(x)
0	4
1	7
−1	1
−2	−2

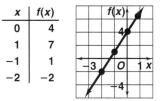

2a. Tables may vary. Sample:

c	P(c)
0	300
100	550
200	800
300	1050
500	1550

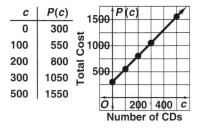

b. as many as 99 CDs

3a. Tables may vary. Sample:

x	y
−2	1
−1	0
0	−1
1	0
2	1

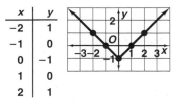

Lesson 5-4 — pp. 254–255

Check Skills You'll Need **1–6.** Tables may vary. Samples are given.

1.

x	f(x)
−1	−6
0	−1
1	4
2	9
3	14

2.

x	y
−2	10
−1	7
0	4
1	1
2	−2

3.

t	g(t)
−2	−7.4
−1	−7.2
0	−7
1	−6.8
2	−6.6

4.

x	y
−2	−7
−1	−3
0	1
1	5
2	9

5.

x	f(x)
−2	8
−1	7
0	6
1	5
2	4

6.

d	c(d)
−2	−1.1
−1	−0.1
0	0.9
1	1.9
2	2.9

7. 3 **8.** −2 **9.** 4

Check Understanding **1a.** $f(x) = x − 2$ **b.** $y = 2x$
c. $y = x + 2$ **2a.** $C(x) = 1.19x$ **b.** \$14.28
3. $p(n) = 15n − 199$

Lesson 5-5 — pp. 261–264, 267

Check Skills You'll Need **1.** $q = \frac{m}{n}$ **2.** $r = \frac{d}{t}$ **3.** $y = −\frac{ax}{b}$
4. 7.5 **5.** 20 **6.** 5 **7.** 10 **8.** 14.4 **9.** 81

Check Understanding **1a.** yes; $\frac{2}{7}$ **b.** no **c.** yes; 7.5
2. $y = 2x$ **3.** $y = 12x$ **4a.** no **b.** yes; $y = 1.5x$
5. 2.5 lb

Checkpoint Quiz 2

1.

x	y
−1	−3
0	1
1	5

2.

x	y
−2	−1
0	0
2	1

$\frac{1}{2}$

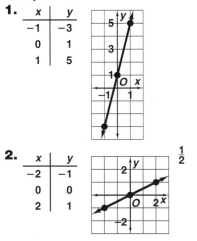

3.

x	f(x)
−1	3
0	0
1	−3

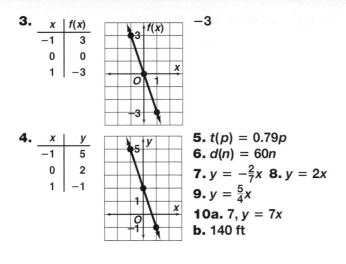

−3

4.

x	y
−1	5
0	2
1	−1

5. $t(p) = 0.79p$
6. $d(n) = 60n$
7. $y = -\frac{2}{7}x$ **8.** $y = 2x$
9. $y = \frac{5}{4}x$
10a. 7, $y = 7x$
b. 140 ft

Lesson 5-6   pp. 268–270

Check Skills You'll Need 1. 12, 15, 18 **2.** 15, 22, 29
3. −2.6, −5.6, −8.6 **4.** 14 **5.** −17 **6.** −1.9

Check Understanding 1a. "Multiply the previous term
by 3"; 243, 729. **b.** "Add 6 to the previous term";
33, 39. **c.** "Multiply the previous term by −2"; 32,
−64. **2a.** 12 **b.** −5 **3a.** −5, 10, 28
b. 6.3, 31.3, 61.3

Chapter 6

Diagnosing Readiness   p. 280

1. 2 **2.** 5 **3.** $\frac{1}{12}$ **4.** 7 **5.** 7

6.

Average Life Span
of American Currency

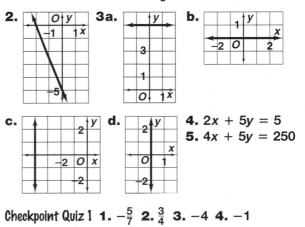

Time (years) — Value of currency ($)

7. 1 **8.** 3 **9.** 3
10. $y = \frac{1}{2}x + 2$
11. $y = 3x - 2$
12. $y = -x - 2$

13.

14.

15.

Lesson 6-1   pp. 282–285

Check Skills You'll Need 1. −12 **2.** 12 **3.** −5 **4.** 5 **5.** 2
6. $-\frac{1}{3}$ **7.** −3 **8.** $\frac{3}{5}$ **9.** $\frac{1}{4}$ **10.** −1

Check Understanding 1a. 15 **b.** No; the rate of
change for each consecutive pair of days does
not have to be the same. **2.** 50 mi/h **3a.** $\frac{3}{5}$ **b.** $-\frac{1}{6}$
4a. 1 **b.** $-\frac{3}{2}$ **c.** $\frac{d-b}{c-a}$ **5a.** 0 **b.** undefined

Lesson 6-2   pp. 291–293

Check Skills You'll Need 1. 15 **2.** −11 **3.** 6 **4.** 5
5. $y = 4x + 5$ **6.** $y = -2x + 7$ **7.** $y = -4x - 3$

Check Understanding 1a. $m = -2; b = 1$ **b.** $m = \frac{7}{6};$
$b = -\frac{3}{4}$ **c.** $m = -\frac{4}{5}; b = 0$ **2.** $y = -3x + 4$
3. $y = \frac{1}{2}x + 1$

4.   **5.**

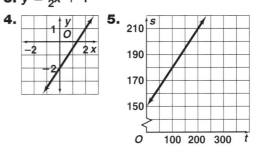

Lesson 6-3   pp. 298–300, 303

Check Skills You'll Need 1. $y = -3x + 5$
2. $y = 2x + 10$ **3.** $y = x - 6$ **4.** $y = -5x + 2$
5. $y = -\frac{1}{3}x + \frac{1}{9}$ **6.** $y = \frac{2}{5}x + \frac{4}{5}$
7. $625x + 850 = 775$ **8.** $4 = 2x - 50$
9. $900 - 222x = 1000$

Check Understanding 1. $-3; \frac{4}{3}$

2.   **3a.**   **b.**

c.   **d.**   **4.** $2x + 5y = 5$
5. $4x + 5y = 250$

Checkpoint Quiz 1 1. $-\frac{5}{7}$ **2.** $\frac{3}{4}$ **3.** −4 **4.** −1
5. $121.75 billion

6. 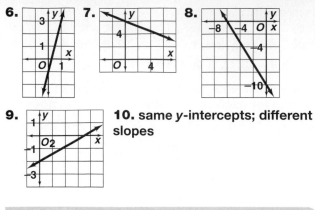 **7.** **8.**

9. **10.** same y-intercepts; different slopes

Lesson 6-4   pp. 304–307

Check Skills You'll Need 1. -2 **2.** $\frac{1}{2}$ **3.** 2 **4.** $-3x + 15$
5. $5x + 10$ **6.** $-\frac{4}{9}x + \frac{8}{3}$

Check Understanding

1. **2.** $y + 8 = \frac{2}{5}(x - 10)$
3a. $y + 5 = \frac{8}{3}(x + 1)$
b. $y = \frac{8}{3}x - 2\frac{1}{3}$
c. They are the same.

4. Yes; answers may vary. Sample:
$y - 5 = \frac{2}{5}(x - 19)$
5. Yes; answers may vary. Sample:
$y - 3030 = -\frac{50}{3}(x - 68)$

Lesson 6-5   pp. 311–313

Check Skills You'll Need 1. $\frac{2}{1}$ **2.** $\frac{3}{4}$ **3.** $-\frac{5}{2}$ **4.** $-\frac{5}{7}$ **5.** $\frac{5}{3}$; 4
6. $\frac{5}{3}$; -8 **7.** 6; 0 **8.** 6; 2

Check Understanding 1. Yes; same slope, different
y-intercept **2.** $y = 3x - 12$ **3.** $y = -\frac{4}{3}x + 9\frac{1}{3}$
4. $y = 2x + 4$

Lesson 6-6   pp. 318–320, 324

Check Skills You'll Need

1. **2.**

Check Understanding

1. 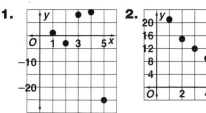 Answers may vary. Sample:
$y = 14x + 166$; 362 calories

---

2. $y = 0.33x - 25.35$; 0.9751360069

Checkpoint Quiz 2 1. $y - 4 = -\frac{1}{4}(x - 3)$
2. $y + 3 = 18x$ **3.** $y = -5$ **4.** $y + 6 = -\frac{2}{3}(x - 2)$
5. $y - 4 = -(x - 5)$
6. $y - 6 = -\frac{3}{2}(x + 2)$ **7.** $y - 2 = \frac{1}{4}x$
8. $y - 2 = -\frac{3}{2}(x + 6)$ **9.** Answers may vary.
Sample: $y = 5.33x + 1.34$ **10.** $y = -6.07x + 62.71$

Lesson 6-7   pp. 325–327

Check Skills You'll Need 1. 5 **2.** 5 **3.** 18 **4.** 12

5.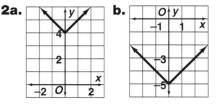

x	y
0	6
1	5
2	4
3	3

6.

x	y
0	1
1	2
2	3
3	4

7.

x	y
0	1
1	2
-1	0
-2	1

Check Understanding 1a. Answers may vary. Sample:
same shape, different y-intercepts 0 and 3
b. Answers may vary. Sample: same shape,
different y-intercepts 0 and -3

2a. **b.**

3a. $y = |x| + 2$ **b.** $y = |x| - 5$

4a. **b.**

5a. $y = |x - 5|$ **b.** $y = |x + 7|$

Chapter 7

Diagnosing Readiness   p. 338

1. identity **2.** 1 **3.** no solution **4.** 3 **5.** $\frac{3}{2}$
6. no solution **7.** $y = \frac{3}{2}x + 1$ **8.** $y = -\frac{1}{5}x + 2$
9. $y = -x - 4$
10. $-10 < x < 3$;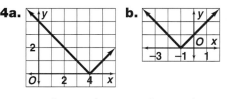
11. $x < 12$ or $x > 60$

12a. $C(t) = 39.50t$ **b.** \$118.50 **c.** 6

13.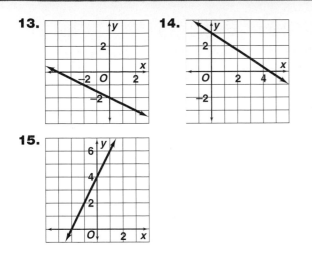

14.

15.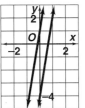

Lesson 7-1   pp. 340–342

Check Skills You'll Need   **1.** $1\frac{2}{3}$ **2.** $3\frac{1}{2}$ **3.** 7

5.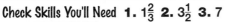

Check Understanding

1a. (−1, 4);   **b.** (−2, 3);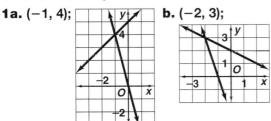

2. after 6 days; 17 cm
3. If the slopes are the same, but the y-intercepts are different, the system will have no solution.
4. all the ordered pairs (x, y) such that $y = \frac{1}{5}x + 9$

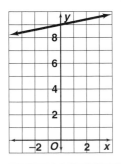

Lesson 7-2   pp. 347–349, 352

Check Skills You'll Need   **1.** $-4\frac{2}{3}$ **2.** $1\frac{1}{2}$ **3.** 15   **4.** no   **5.** no

Check Understanding   **1.** (3, 6)   **2.** (2.3, 1.6)
3. 3 cm by 12 cm

Checkpoint Quiz 1

1. (1, −1); 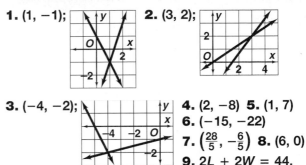   **2.** (3, 2);

3. (−4, −2);   **4.** (2, −8)   **5.** (1, 7)
6. (−15, −22)
7. $\left(\frac{28}{5}, -\frac{6}{5}\right)$ **8.** (6, 0)
9. $2L + 2W = 44$,
$3W = L$; 5.5 cm by 16.5 cm   **10.** $p + c = 420$,
$c = p + 250$; 85 acres pumpkins, 335 acres corn

Lesson 7-3   pp. 353–356

Check Skills You'll Need   **1.** (8, 29)   **2.** (2, −6)   **3.** (3, −4)

Check Understanding   **1.** (2, 3)   **2.** 30 adult; 34 student
3. (1, −2)   **4.** 85 cards, 135 gift wrap   **5.** (1, −2)

Lesson 7-4   pp. 362–365

Check Skills You'll Need   **1.** 3.25 h   **2.** 275 mi

Check Understanding   **1.** 32 kg 50% alloy; 8 kg 25% alloy   **2.** 3850 copies   **3.** 440 mi/h; 40 mi/h

---

Lesson 7-5   pp. 370–372, 376

Check Skills You'll Need   **1.** never   **2.** always
3. sometimes   **4.** $y = \frac{2}{3}x - 3$ **5.** $y = -3x + 6$
6. $y = \frac{3}{4}x + \frac{1}{4}$

Check Understanding

1.   **2.**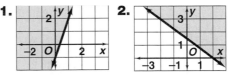

3. Answers may vary. Sample: 6 lb hamburger and 2 lb chicken, 3 lb hamburger and 6 lb chicken, 5 lb hamburger and 3 lb chicken

Checkpoint Quiz 2   **1.** (11, −4)   **2.** (−9, 1)   **3.** (3.5, 10)
4. no solution   **5.** $\left(15, -\frac{1}{2}\right)$ **6.** $n + d = 21$,
$0.05n + 0.10d = 1.70$; 8 nickels, 13 dimes
7. $y = 200 + 0.35x$, $y = 1.20x$;
about 236 ice cream cones
8. $x + y = 4$, $x - y = 3$; 0.5 mi/h, 3.5 mi/h

9.   **10.**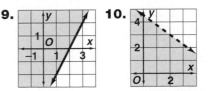

Lesson 7-6   pp. 377–380

Check Skills You'll Need   **1.** (2, 0);

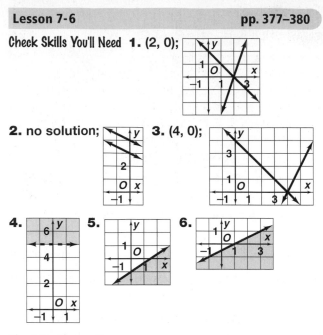

2. no solution;   **3.** (4, 0);

4.   **5.**   **6.**

Check Understanding

1.   **2a.** $y \geq \frac{1}{2}x - 1$ and $y < 2$
b. $y \leq -\frac{2}{3}x$ and $x > -3$

3.   **4a.** Answers may vary. Sample: 2 20¢ stamps and 6 34¢ stamps; 4 20¢ stamps and 5 34¢ stamps **b.** no **c.** You cannot have a negative or fractional number of stamps.

Chapter 8

Diagnosing Readiness   p. 392

1. 0.7 **2.** 6.4 **3.** 0.008 **4.** 3.5 **5.** $0.\overline{27}$ **6.** 49
7. 5.027 **8.** 0.75 **9.** 4 **10.** 100 **11.** 49 **12.** 17
13. -31 **14.** \$120 **15.** \$800 **16.** {$-24.5, -8, 0$}
17. {$-32.875, 10, 18$} **18.** {$-11, -1, 16.5$}
19. 9, 11 **20.** 14, 20 **21.** 31, 37

Lesson 8-1   pp. 394–396

Check Skills You'll Need   **1.** 8 **2.** $\frac{1}{16}$ **3.** 4 **4.** -27 **5.** -27
6. 3 **7.** $\frac{1}{2}$ **8.** -1 **9.** 4

Check Understanding   **1a.** $\frac{1}{81}$ **b.** 1 **c.** $-\frac{1}{64}$ **d.** $\frac{1}{7}$ **e.** $-\frac{1}{9}$
2a. $\frac{11}{m^5}$ **b.** $\frac{7t^2}{s^4}$ **c.** $2a^3$ **d.** $\frac{1}{n^5v^2}$ **3a.** $-\frac{1}{8}$ **b.** $-\frac{1}{50}$ **c.** $\frac{1}{16}$
d. $-12\frac{1}{2}$ **4.** 600; 5400; for $x = -2$, the population is 600, 2 months before the population is 5400. For $x = 0$, it is the population when time is 0.

Lesson 8-2   pp. 400–402

Check Skills You'll Need   **1.** 60,000 **2.** 0.07 **3.** 820,000
4. 0.003 **5.** 34 **6.** 524 **7.** 367.8

Check Understanding   **1a.** yes **b.** No; 52 > 10. **c.** No; 0.04 < 1. **2a.** 2.67×10^5 **b.** 4.6205×10^7
c. 3.25×10^{-5} **d.** 9.0×10^{-9} **e.** 436 is 436 times greater than 1, and $436 = 4.36 \times 10^2$. Then $(4.36 \times 10^2) \cdot 10^9 = 4.36 \times 10^{11}$.
3a. 3,200,000,000,000 **b.** 50,700 **c.** 0.00056
d. 0.083 **4.** electron, proton, neutron
5. $60.2 \times 10^{-5}, 61 \times 10^{-2}, 0.067 \times 10^3, 63 \times 10^4$
6a. 1.5×10^4 **b.** 8×10^{-10}

Lesson 8-3   pp. 405–407

Check Skills You'll Need   **1.** t^7 **2.** $(6 - m)^3$ **3.** $(r + 5)^5$
4. 5^3s^3 **5.** -625 **6.** 625 **7.** 1 **8.** $\frac{1}{625}$

Check Understanding   **1a.** 5^9 **b.** 2^1 **c.** 7^5 **2a.** a^6
b. $7n^6$ **c.** $36y$ **3a.** a^6b **b.** $28x^2y^7$ **c.** $\frac{7m^3}{n^2}$
4a. 1.5×10^{12} **b.** 4.5×10^2 **c.** 6.3×10^{-14}
5. about 2.56×10^{13} red blood cells

Lesson 8-4   pp. 411–413, 416

Check Skills You'll Need   **1.** 3^6 **2.** 2^{12} **3.** 5^{28} **4.** 7^3 **5.** x^6
6. a^6 **7.** $\frac{1}{y^6}$ **8.** $\frac{1}{n^6}$
Check Understanding   **1.** $a^{28}; \frac{1}{a^{28}}$ **2a.** n^{17} **b.** $\frac{1}{t^{12}}$ **c.** a^{18}
3a. $16z^4$ **b.** $\frac{1}{16g^{10}}$ **c.** 81 **4a.** $81c^{26}$ **b.** $864a^{18}b^6$
c. $\frac{5400n^3}{m^3}$ **5a.** 5.22×10^5 joules
b. about 1.7×10^8 h

Checkpoint Quiz 1 p. 416 **1.** $\frac{1}{45}$ **2.** r^{20} **3.** $6x^{17}$ **4.** $\frac{mq^2}{n^4}$
5. $\frac{1}{a}$ **6.** $\frac{64m^6}{9}$ **7.** $6m^9$ **8.** $\frac{27t^6}{8}$ **9.** 500; 2000; 16,000
10a. 6.8×10^3 km **b.** about 5.81×10^8 km^2
c. 145,000,000 km^2

Lesson 8-5   pp. 417–419

Check Skills You'll Need   **1.** $\frac{1}{4}$ **2.** 5 **3.** $\frac{3}{5}$ **4.** 31 **5.** $\frac{2}{5}$ **6.** $\frac{4}{15}$
7. $\frac{2}{7}$ **8.** $\frac{2}{7}$ **9.** $\frac{y}{3}$ **10.** $\frac{2y^2}{x}$ **11.** $\frac{c}{4}$ **12.** $\frac{4}{n^2}$
Check Understanding   **1a.** $\frac{1}{b^5}$ **b.** z^5 **c.** $\frac{1}{a^2b^2}$ **d.** $\frac{n}{m^4}$
e. $\frac{xz^7}{y^5}$ **2a.** 2.5×10^{-6} **b.** 3.0×10^{16} **c.** $3.\overline{3} \times 10^2$
d. about 1.18×10^{-2} tons **3a.** $\frac{9}{x^4}$ **b.** $\frac{x^3}{y^6}$ **c.** $\frac{t^{14}}{64}$
4a. $\frac{64}{27}$ **b.** -32 **c.** $\frac{s}{2r}$ **d.** $\frac{m^2}{49a^2}$

Lesson 8-6
pp. 424–427

Check Skills You'll Need 1. 2 **2.** -2 **3.** -1.2 **4.** 3.5
5. 32, 64 **6.** 108, 324 **7.** 3.2, 6.4 **8.** 12.5, 6.25

Check Understanding 1a. $\frac{1}{5}$ **b.** 2 **c.** $\frac{3}{2}$ **2a.** 81, 243, 729
b. 7.5, -3.75, 1.875 **c.** 17.6, 35.2, 70.4
3a. arithmetic **b.** geometric **c.** arithmetic
4a. 4; 972; 708,588 **b.** -2; -6250; $-97,656,250$
5. $A(n) = 200 \cdot 0.56^{n-1}$; 35.1 cm

Lesson 8-7
pp. 430–432, 435

Check Skills You'll Need

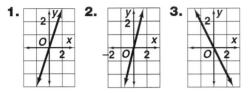

4. 9 **5.** $\frac{1}{125}$ **6.** 162 **7.** $\frac{2}{9}$ **8.** $\frac{3}{2}$ **9.** 90

Check Understanding 1a. $\frac{1}{16}$, 1, 64 **b.** $\frac{2}{5}$, 10, 1250
c. $-\frac{2}{9}$, -2, -54 **2.** 40,960 animals

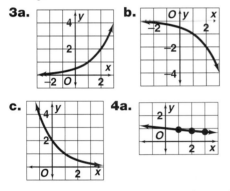

b. $f(0) = 1$, so copies are made at the same size
of the original, or at 100%.

CheckPoint Quiz 2 1. 3^{12} **2.** $\frac{y^{15}}{x^{10}}$ **3.** $\frac{4n^{12}}{25m^6}$ **4.** $\frac{1}{t^{10}}$
5. geometric **6.** geometric **7.** arithmetic
8a. -100 **b.** $-\frac{1}{5}$ or -0.2
c. $A(n) = -100 \cdot (-0.2)^{n-1}$ **d.** -0.16; -0.0064
9a. $A(n) = 40 \cdot (0.85)^{n-1}$ **b.** 209 mm
10a. 1.08×10^8 **b.** 2.49×10^8 **c.** about \$2.31

Lesson 8-8
pp. 437–441

Check Skills You'll Need 1. \$100 **2.** \$64.80 **3.** \$225
4. \$352.80 **5.** \$324

Check Understanding 1a. $y = 4512 \cdot 1.025^x$ **b.** about
4859 students **2a.** \$5994.03 **b.** \$5994.03
c. $(1 + r)$ is the same as 100% + 100r% written
as a decimal. **3a.** \$4817.75 **b.** \$210.23; \$220.99;
\$256.67 **4a.** 4 half-lives **b.** 25 mCi; 12.5 mCi
c. 15 mCi; 3.75 mCi **5a.** 604,000 **b.** 0.982
c. $y = 604,000 \cdot (0.982)^x$ **d.** about 420,017 people

Chapter 9

Diagnosing Readiness
p. 454

1. 1, 2, 3, 4, 6, 12 **2.** 1, 2, 4, 7, 8, 14, 28, 56 **3.** 1, 31
4. 1, 3, 9, 27 **5.** 1, 2, 5, 10, 11, 22, 55, 110 **6.** 1, 5,
13, 65 **7.** 1, 2, 5, 10, 25, 50 **8.** 1, 2, 4, 5, 8, 10, 20,
25, 40, 50, 100, 200 **9.** 1, 11 **10.** 1, 2, 3, 6, 7, 14,
21, 42 **11.** 1, 2, 3, 6, 11, 22, 33, 66 **12.** 1, 73
13. $3x^2 - 4x$ **14.** $2b + 6$ **15.** $3y^2 - 11y$
16. $-\frac{2}{3}w^2 + \frac{7}{6}w$ **17.** $7z - 66$ **18.** $4x^2 - 2x$
19. $-6t^2 + 10t$ **20.** $-p^2 - 2p$ **21.** $49w^2$ **22.** $25n^3$
23. $9z^4$ **24.** $10t^7$ **25.** $16y^6$ **26.** $81a^2b^2$ **27.** $4x^4$
28. $36p^8$ **29.** x^2y^4 **30.** $3c$ **31.** $-\frac{1}{4t^3}$ **32.** $2a^2$

Lesson 9-1
pp. 456–458

Check Skills You'll Need 1. $19t$ **2.** $39g$ **3.** $-8k$ **4.** $11b - 6$
5. $-3n^2$ **6.** $7x^2$

Check Understanding 1. 0; the degree of a nonzero
constant is 0. **2a.** $-9x^4 + 6x^2 + 7$; fourth
degree trinomial **b.** $-y^3 + 3y - 4$; cubic trinomial
c. $-4v + 8$; linear binomial **3a.** $20m^2 + 9$
b. $4t^2 + 5$ **c.** $16w^3 + 8w^2 + 4$
d. $11p^3 + 17p^2 + 13p$ **4a.** $-8v^3 + 13v^2 - 4v$
b. $28d^3 - 30d^2 - 3d$ **c.** $-2x^2 + 4x - 7$

Lesson 9-2
pp. 462–463

Check Skills You'll Need 1. 906 **2.** 287 **3.** 4536
4. $24 + 20x$ **5.** $-16y - 8$ **6.** $25v - 5$ **7.** $7p - 14$
8. $54 - 9x$ **9.** $-8q + 2$

Check Understanding 1a. $20b^3 + 4b^2 + 24b$
b. $-21h^3 + 56h^2 + 7h$ **c.** $2x^3 - 12x^2 + 10x$
2a. $5v^3$ **b.** 3 **c.** $2b$ **3a.** $4x(2x - 3)$ **b.** $5d(d^2 + 2)$
c. $6m(m^2 - 2m - 4)$

Lesson 9-3
pp. 467–469, 472

Check Skills You'll Need 1. $4r^2 - 4r$ **2.** $6h^3 + 48h^2 - 18h$
3. $2y^5 - 7y^2$ **4.** $x^3 + 8x^2 + 2x + 1$ **5.** $8t^3 + t + 6$
6. $5w^2 - 27w$ **7.** $-2b^2 - 15b$
8. $7m^3 + 27m^2 - 6m$ **9.** $d^5 - 4d^3 - 18d^2$

Check Understanding 1a. $12h^2 + 4h - 21$ **b.** $40m^2 + 11m - 2$ **c.** $63a^2 - 20a - 32$ **2a.** $6x^2 + 23x + 20$ **b.** $6x^2 + 7x - 20$ **c.** $6x^2 - 7x - 20$
d. $6x^2 - 23x + 20$ **3a.** $25x^2 + 28x + 16$
b. $x^2 + 2x - 2$ **4.** $12n^3 - 10n^2 + 34n - 56$

Checkpoint Quiz 1 1. $9x^2 + 10x + 1$ **2.** $6b^2 - 13b + 9$
3. $4g^4 + 8g^3 + 7g^2 + 32g - 36$ **4.** $-48k^3 + 42k^2$
5. $x^2 - 2x - 15$ **6.** $12n^5 + 2n^4 - 30n^2 - 5n$
7. $36w^2 - 11w$ **8.** $2(6y^2 - 5)$ **9.** $5t(t^5 + 5t^2 - 2)$
10. $9v^2(2v^2 + 3v + 4)$

Lesson 9-4   pp. 474–477

Check Skills You'll Need **1.** $49x^2$ **2.** $9v^2$ **3.** $16c^2$ **4.** $25g^6$
5. $j^2 + 12j + 35$ **6.** $6b^2 - 34b + 48$
7. $20y^2 - 3y - 2$ **8.** $x^2 - x - 12$
9. $8c^4 - 78c^2 - 20$ **10.** $54y^4 - 21y^2 - 3$

Check Understanding **1a.** $t^2 + 12t + 36$
b. $25y^2 + 10y + 1$ **c.** $49m^2 - 28mp + 4p^2$
d. $81c^2 - 144c + 64$ **2a.** $\frac{1}{9}A^2 + \frac{4}{9}AB + \frac{4}{9}B^2$
b. $\frac{1}{9}$ **c.** $\frac{4}{9}$ **d.** $\frac{4}{9}$ **3a.** 961 **b.** 841 **c.** 9604
d. 41,209 **4a.** $d^2 - 121$ **b.** $c^4 - 64$ **c.** $81v^6 - w^8$
5a. 396 **b.** 399 **c.** 3599 **d.** 8091

Lesson 9-5   pp. 481–483

Check Skills You'll Need **1.** 1, 2, 3, 4, 6, 8, 12, 24 **2.** 1, 2,
3, 4, 6, 12 **3.** 1, 2, 3, 6, 9, 18, 27, 54 **4.** 1, 3, 5, 15
5. 1, 2, 3, 4, 6, 9, 12, 18, 36 **6.** 1, 2, 4, 7, 8, 14, 28,
56 **7.** 1, 2, 4, 8, 16, 32, 64 **8.** 1, 2, 3, 4, 6, 8, 12, 16,
24, 32, 48, 96

Check Understanding **1a.** $(g + 5)(g + 2)$ **b.** $(v + 20)\cdot$
$(v + 1)$ **c.** $(a + 10)(a + 3)$ **2a.** $(k - 5)(k - 5)$
b. $(x - 2)(x - 9)$ **c.** $(q - 12)(q - 3)$ **3a.** $(m + 10)\cdot$
$(m - 2)$ **b.** $(p - 8)(p + 5)$ **c.** $(y + 7)(y - 8)$
4a. $(x + 8y)(x + 3y)$ **b.** $(v + 8w)(v - 6w)$
c. $(m - 20n)(m + 3n)$

Lesson 9-6   pp. 486–487

Check Skills You'll Need **1.** $6x$ **2.** 7 **3.** 2 **4.** $(x + 1)(x + 4)$
5. $(y - 7)(y + 4)$ **6.** $(t - 5)(t - 6)$

Check Understanding **1a.** $(2y + 1)(y + 2)$
b. $(3n - 1)(2n - 7)$ **c.** $(2y - 1)(y - 2)$
2a. $(5d + 1)(d - 3)$ **b.** $(2n + 3)(n - 1)$
c. $(5p - 9)(4p + 1)$ **3a.** $2(v - 1)(v - 5)$
b. $2(2y + 1)(y + 3)$ **c.** $6(3k + 1)(k - 1)$

Lesson 9-7   pp. 490–492, 495

Check Skills You'll Need **1.** $9x^2$ **2.** $25y^2$ **3.** $225h^4$
4. $4a^2b^4$ **5.** $c^2 - 36$ **6.** $p^2 - 22p + 121$
7. $16d^2 + 56d + 49$

Check Understanding **1a.** $(x + 4)^2$ **b.** $(n + 8)^2$
c. $(n - 8)^2$ **2a.** $(3g - 2)^2$ **b.** $(2t + 9)^2$
c. $(2t - 9)^2$ **3a.** $(x + 6)(x - 6)$
b. $(m + 10)(m - 10)$ **c.** $(p + 7)(p - 7)$
4a. $(3v + 2)(3v - 2)$ **b.** $(5x + 8)(5x - 8)$
c. $(2w + 7)(2w - 7)$ **5a.** $2(2y + 5)(2y - 5)$
b. $3(c + 5)(c - 5)$ **c.** $7(2k + 1)(2k - 1)$

Checkpoint Quiz 2 **1.** $k^2 - 14k + 49$ **2.** $25t^2 +$
$90t + 81$ **3.** $h^2 - 22h + 121$ **4.** $(v + 10)^2$
5. $(p - 10)(p + 4)$ **6.** $(k - 12)(k - 5)$

7. $(2x + 11)(x + 1)$ **8.** $(5m + 7)(2m + 1)$
9. $3(w + 2)(w - 4)$ **10.** $(3t + 5)(3t - 5)$

Lesson 9-8   pp. 496–498

Check Skills You'll Need **1.** 2 **2.** $3r$ **3.** $5h$ **4.** $4m$
5. $v^3 + 3v^2 + 5v + 15$ **6.** $2q^3 - 10q^2 - 4q + 20$
7. $6t^2 - 7t - 20$ **8.** $4x^3 + 7x^2 + 10x - 3$

Check Understanding **1a.** $(5t^3 + 6)(t + 4)$
b. $(w^2 - 7)(2w + 1)$ **2.** $3m(3m^2 + 2)(5m - 1)$
3a. $(9d + 5)(7d + 1)$ **b.** $(11k + 5)(k + 4)$
c. $(4y - 7)(y + 10)$ **4a.** Answers may vary.
Sample: $2g$, $(3g + 4)$, and $(g + 2)$ **b.** m, $(3m + 1)$,
and $(m + 3)$

Chapter 10

Diagnosing Readiness   p. 508

1. -13 **2.** $-\frac{7}{2}$ **3.** -9 **4.** $-\frac{1}{2}$ **5.** -23 **6.** -3 **7.** -108
8. 26 **9.** 0 **10.** 49 **11.** -67 **12.** 25 **13.** 24 **14.** 144

15. **16.**

17.

18. $x^2 - x - 6$ **19.** $4y^2 + 8y + 3$ **20.** $3x^2 +$
$5x - 28$ **21.** $(2x + 1)^2$ **22.** $(5x - 3)(x + 7)$
23. $(4x - 3)(2x - 1)$ **24.** $(m - 9)(m + 2)$
25. $(6y - 5)(2y + 3)$ **26.** $(x - 9)^2$

Lesson 10-1   pp. 510–513

Check Skills You'll Need **1.** -24 **2.** 18 **3.** 12 **4.** 35

5. **6.** **7.**

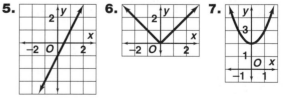

Check Understanding **1a.** (4, 3); max. **b.** (−3, −3); min.

2.

x	$f(x) = -2x^2$	(x, y)
0	$-2(0)^2 = 0$	$(0, 0)$
1	$-2(1)^2 = -2$	$(1, -2)$
2	$-2(2)^2 = -8$	$(2, -8)$

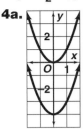

3. $y = \frac{1}{2}x^2$, $y = x^2$, $y = -2x^2$

4a.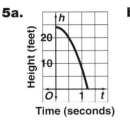

The graph of $y = x^2 - 4$ has the same shape as the graph of $y = x^2$, and it is shifted down 4 units.

b. Positive values of c shift the vertex up. Negative values of c shift the vertex down.

5a.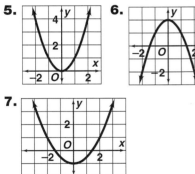

b. Time must be nonnegative.

Lesson 10-2   pp. 517–519

Check Skills You'll Need 1. $\frac{1}{3}$ **2.** $-\frac{2}{3}$ **3.** $-3\frac{1}{2}$ **4.** 6

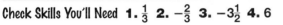

5. **6.**

7.

Check Understanding

1. 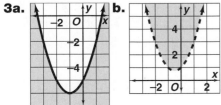 **2a.** 1.5 s **b.** 40 ft

3a. 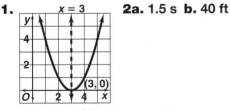 **b.**

Lesson 10-3   pp. 524–526

Check Skills You'll Need 1. 121 **2.** 144 **3.** -144 **4.** 2.25
5. 0.36 **6.** $\frac{1}{4}$ **7.** $\frac{4}{9}$ **8.** $\frac{16}{25}$

Check Understanding 1a. 7 **b.** ± 6 **c.** -11 **d.** $\frac{1}{5}$
2a. irrational **b.** rational **c.** irrational **d.** rational
3. -11 and -10 **4.** 4.22 **5.** 156.5 ft

Lesson 10-4   pp. 529–531, 534

Check Skills You'll Need 1. 6 **2.** -9 **3.** ± 11 **4.** 1.2
5. 0.5 **6.** ± 1.1 **7.** $\frac{1}{2}$ **8.** $\pm \frac{1}{3}$ **9.** $\frac{7}{10}$

Check Understanding

1a. 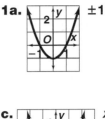 ± 1 **b.** 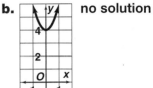 no solution

c. 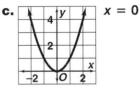 $x = 0$

2a. ± 5 **b.** 0 **c.** no solution **3.** about 14 ft

Checkpoint Quiz 1

1. 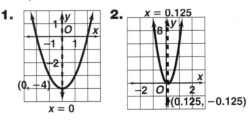 **2.** $x = 0.125$

3.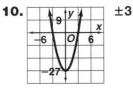

4a. 0.75 s **b.** 15 ft **5.** 10 **6.** ± 0.6 **7.** -2 **8.** ± 8
9. ± 5

10. ± 3

Lesson 10-5   pp. 536–537

Check Skills You'll Need 1. -1 **2.** 104 **3.** $-2\frac{5}{7}$
4. $(2c + 1)(c + 14)$ **5.** $(3p + 2)(p + 10)$
6. $(4x + 3)(x - 6)$

Check Understanding 1a. $-7, 4$ **b.** $\frac{5}{3}, 2$ **c.** $-\frac{3}{2}, \frac{11}{4}$
2. $-4, 3$ **3.** 6 **4.** 9 in. $\times$ 10 in. $\times$ 2 in.

Lesson 10-6   pp. 541–543

Check Skills You'll Need 1. $d^2 - 8d + 16$
2. $x^2 + 22x + 121$ **3.** $k^2 - 16k + 64$ **4.** $(b + 5)^2$
5. $(t + 7)^2$ **6.** $(n - 9)^2$

Check Understanding 1. 121 **2.** $19, -13$
3a. $-0.70, -4.30$ **b.** $12.74, 1.26$ **4a.** $-1.65, 3.65$
b. $2.56, -1.96$

Lesson 10-7   pp. 547–550

Check Skills You'll Need 1. 9 **2.** $\frac{49}{4}$ **3.** $\frac{81}{4}$ **4.** $6, 4$
5. $2, -18$ **6.** $1, -5$ **7.** $-7, 8$

Check Understanding 1a. $4, -2$ **b.** $13, -9$ **2a.** $0.67, 1$
b. $1.22, -0.94$ **3a.** $0 = -16t^2 + 38.4t + 3.5$
b. $t \approx 2.5$; 2.5 s **4a.** Quadratic formula; the
equation cannot be factored easily. **b.** Factoring;
the equation is easily factorable. **c.** Square roots;
there is no x term.

Lesson 10-8   pp. 554–555, 558

Check Skills You'll Need 1. -80 **2.** 72 **3.** -283 **4.** $2.18,$
0.15 **5.** $0.39, -0.64$ **6.** $7, 5$

Check Understanding 1a. 0 **b.** 2 **c.** 0 **2.** yes

Checkpoint Quiz 2 1. $-3, 7$ **2.** $-3, -9$ **3.** $-5, 10$
4. $0.4, -2.4$ **5.** $5.7, -0.7$ **6.** $11, -3$ **7.** $1, -\frac{3}{4}$
8. no solution **9.** $1, 0.5$ **10.** 0

Lesson 10-9   pp. 559–563

Check Skills You'll Need

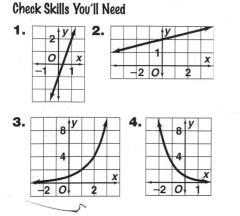

5. 6.

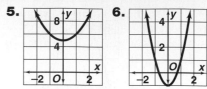

Check Understanding

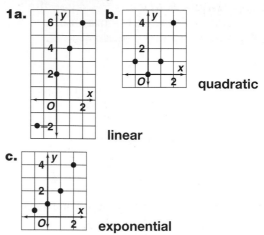

1a.   **b.**   quadratic

         linear

c.   exponential

2a. exponential; $y = 4 \cdot 1.1^x$ **b.** linear; $y = \frac{1}{2}x + \frac{1}{2}$
c. quadratic; $y = -\frac{1}{2}x^2$ **3a.** quadratic
b. $y = 5000x^2$

Chapter 11

Diagnosing Readiness   p. 576

1. $2.8\overline{3}$ or $2\frac{5}{6}$ **2.** 51.75 **3.** 1.825 **4.** -0.75 **5.** $204.\overline{6}$
6. 3 **7.** 3 **8.** 13 **9.** 30 **10.** 4 **11.** 45 **12.** 17 **13.** 3
14. 66 **15.** 11 **16.** 2 **17.** 15 **18.** $\frac{3}{5}$ **19.** -0.06
20. 6.32 **21.** 9.17 **22.** 10.20 **23.** 1.79 **24.** 2 **25.** 2
26. 0 **27.** 1 **28.** 2 **29.** 2

Lesson 11-1   pp. 578–581

Check Skills You'll Need 1. 1 **2.** 1 **3.** 3 **4.** 4 **5.** 2 **6.** 13
7. 5 **8.** 7

Check Understanding 1a. $5\sqrt{2}$ **b.** $-50\sqrt{3}$ **c.** $3\sqrt{2}$
2a. $3n\sqrt{3}$ **b.** $-2a^4\sqrt{15a}$ **c.** $xy^2\sqrt{y}$ **3a.** 26
b. $15c\sqrt{2}$ **c.** $60a^2\sqrt{2a}$ **4.** 6 mi **5a.** 4 **b.** $\frac{5p\sqrt{p}}{q}$
c. $\frac{5\sqrt{3}}{4t}$ **6a.** $3\sqrt{2}$ **b.** $\frac{4}{5}$ **c.** $3x$ **7a.** $\sqrt{3}$ **b.** $\frac{\sqrt{10t}}{6t}$
c. $\frac{\sqrt{70m}}{10}$

Lesson 11-2   pp. 584–587

Check Skills You'll Need 1. 61 **2.** 65 **3.** $25t^2$ **4.** $-6, 6$
5. $-5, 5$ **6.** $-7, 7$ **7.** $-2\sqrt{5}, 2\sqrt{5}$ **8.** $-4\sqrt{5}, 4\sqrt{5}$
9. $-4\sqrt{3}, 4\sqrt{3}$

Check Understanding 1. 25 cm **2.** 6.9 mi **3.** yes **4.** no

Lesson 11-3   pp. 591–593, 597

Check Skills You'll Need 1. 5 **2.** 5.4 **3.** 8.5 **4.** 8.6 **5.** 10 **6.** 2 **7.** −6 **8.** −6.5

Check Understanding 1. ≈4.5 units **2a.** ≈27.2 units **b.** $(RS)^2 = (RT)^2 + (ST)^2$ or $(\sqrt{130})^2 = (\sqrt{40})^2 + (\sqrt{90})^2$ **3.** $(1, \frac{1}{2})$ **4.** $(-6, 2\frac{1}{2})$

Checkpoint Quiz 1 1. $4\sqrt{10}$ **3.** $\frac{2}{3}$ **5.** 7.5 cm **7.** 8.6 ft **9.** no

Lesson 11-4   pp. 600–602

Check Skills You'll Need 1. $2\sqrt{13}$ **2.** $10\sqrt{2}$ **3.** $12\sqrt{6}$ **4.** $5x\sqrt{5}$ **5.** $\frac{\sqrt{33}}{11}$ **6.** $\frac{\sqrt{10}}{4}$ **7.** $\frac{\sqrt{30x}}{2x}$

Check Understanding 1a. $-7\sqrt{5}$ **b.** $-4\sqrt{10}$ **2a.** $8\sqrt{5}$ **b.** $-3\sqrt{3}$ **3a.** $2\sqrt{5} + 5\sqrt{2}$ **b.** $2x\sqrt{3} - 11\sqrt{2x}$ **c.** $5a + 3\sqrt{5a}$ **4a.** $-33 - 21\sqrt{2}$ **b.** $23 + 8\sqrt{7}$ **5a.** $2(\sqrt{7} - \sqrt{5})$ **b.** $-2(\sqrt{10} - 2\sqrt{2})$ **c.** $\frac{-5(\sqrt{11} + \sqrt{3})}{8}$ **6.** 55 in.

Lesson 11-5   pp. 607–609

Check Skills You'll Need 1. 1 **2.** 4 **3.** 4 **4.** 3 **5.** $x + 1$ **6.** $2x - 5$

Check Understanding 1a. 25 **b.** 81 **c.** 38 **2a.** about 67 ft **b.** No; $h - 2r$ decreases as r increases. **3.** 5 **4a.** A principal square root must be a nonnegative number. **b.** 2 **5.** no solution

Lesson 11-6   pp. 614–615, 619

Check Skills You'll Need

1. 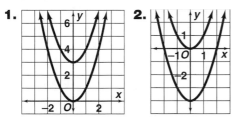 **2.**

3. 2 **4.** 0 **5.** 11

Check Understanding 1. $x \geq 7$

2a.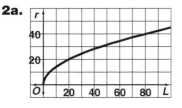

b. 361.25 ft

3. 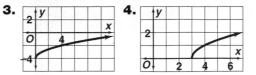 **4.**

Checkpoint Quiz 2 1. $-8\sqrt{7}$ **2.** $4 - 5\sqrt{2}$ **3.** $2\sqrt{5} + 15$ **4.** $3\sqrt{2}$ **5.** $5 + 2\sqrt{6}$ **6.** $4\sqrt{3} + 2\sqrt{10} - 9\sqrt{2} - 3\sqrt{15}$ **7.** 256 **8.** 8 **9.** 5 **10.** It is translated 2 units left.

Lesson 11-7   pp. 621–624

Check Skills You'll Need 1. $\frac{3}{5}; \frac{4}{5}; \frac{4}{3}$ **2.** $\frac{5}{13}; \frac{12}{13}; \frac{12}{5}$ **3.** 20 **4.** 6.8 **5.** 25 **6.** 7.28

Check Understanding 1a. $\frac{12}{13}; \frac{5}{13}; \frac{12}{5}$ **b.** They are equal. **2a.** 0.9397 **b.** 0.3420 **c.** 2.7475 **3a.** 6.9 **b.** 5.6 **4.** about 270 ft **5.** 745,000 ft

Chapter 12

Diagnosing Readiness   p. 634

1. $1\frac{1}{6}$ **2.** $\frac{9}{13}$ **3.** $\frac{47}{50}$ **4.** $\frac{5}{12}$ **5.** $\frac{3}{10}$ **6.** $\frac{1}{10}$ **7.** $\frac{2}{5}$ **8.** $\frac{3}{5}$ **9.** $3w^2x$ **10.** r^2s^2 **11.** $\frac{5}{2}k^4$ **12.** 100 **13.** no solution **14.** 1 **15.** $x \geq 0$ **16.** $x \geq 0$ **17.** $x \leq \frac{10}{3}$

Lesson 12-1   pp. 636–639

Check Skills You'll Need 1. 5 **2.** −7 **3.** $\frac{1}{3}$ **4.** 4 **5.** $y = 2x$ **6.** $y = 0.5x$ **7.** $y = -0.25x$ **8.** $y = 0.4x$

Check Understanding 1. $xy = 18$ **2a.** 15 **b.** 5 **3a.** $5.\overline{3}$ ft **b.** 120 lb **4a.** inverse variation; $xy = 36$ **b.** direct variation; $y = 4x$ **5a.** Direct variation, since the ratio $\frac{\text{cost}}{\text{sweater}}$ is constant at $15 each. **b.** Inverse variation, since the total number of miles walked each day is a constant product of 5.

Lesson 12-2   pp. 644–648

Check Skills You'll Need 1. −10; −8; −5 **2.** 8, 4, 13 **3.** $\frac{1}{9}$, 1, 27

4.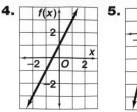

5.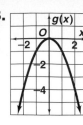

6.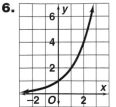

Check Understanding

1a.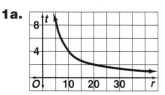

b. Speed and time are both positive values, so graphing it in the first quadrant only makes sense.

2a. asymptote $x = -2$; **b.** asymptote $x = 3$;

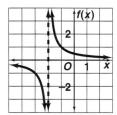 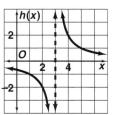

3a. $x = -2, y = -3$;   **b.** $x = 4, y = 1$;

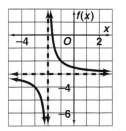 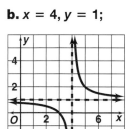

4a. an absolute value function with vertex $(-4, 0)$
b. a graph of exponential growth **c.** a rational function with asymptotes $x = -1$ and $y = 0$

Lesson 12-3   pp. 652–654, 656

Check Skills You'll Need 1. 4 **2.** $-\frac{5}{8}$ **3.** $\frac{5}{7}$
4. $(x + 4)(x - 3)$ **5.** $(x + 4)(x + 2)$
6. $(x - 5)(x + 3)$ **7.** $(x + 4)^2$ **8.** $(x + 3)(x - 4)$
9. $(x - 3)(x - 4)$

Check Understanding 1a. $\frac{3}{5b}$ **b.** $\frac{4c^2}{c + 2}$ **c.** 2 **d.** 4
2a. $\frac{3}{x - 5}$ **b.** $\frac{2}{z - 3}$ **c.** $\frac{8}{2a + 1}$ **d.** $\frac{c - 3}{c + 3}$ **3a.** -1

b. $-\frac{1}{m + 8}$ **c.** $-\frac{4}{r + 4}$ **d.** $-\frac{2}{3}$ **4a.** 51 min **b.** $\frac{30rh}{r + h}$

Checkpoint Quiz 1 **1.** 3 **2.** -2 **3.** 4
4. $x = 0, y = 0$; **5.** $x = 4, y = 0$;

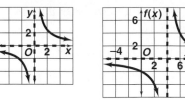 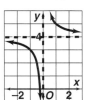

6. $x = 0, y = 4$; **7.** $6(x - 2)$ **8.** $\frac{c + 3}{c - 3}$ **9.** $\frac{1}{k + 4}$

10. Answers may vary.
Sample: $\frac{15}{x - 3}$

Lesson 12-4   pp.657–659

Check Skills You'll Need 1. r^{10} **2.** b^7 **3.** c^5 **4.** $6x^9$
5. $5n^4$ **6.** $-45a^5$ **7.** $(2c + 1)(c + 7)$
8. $(15t - 11)(t - 1)$ **9.** $(2q + 1)(q + 5)$

Check Understanding 1a. $\frac{-12}{a^5}$ **b.** $\frac{(x - 5)(x - 7)}{x(x + 3)}$ **2.** $-\frac{1}{x}$
3a. $3(c - 1)(c + 1)$ **b.** $2v(v - 5)$ **c.** $\frac{4(m + 2)}{m + 1}$ **4a.** $\frac{1}{b}$
b. $\frac{5(7m - 10)}{7(m - 10)}$ **c.** $\frac{3n + 2}{2n - 3}$ **5a.** $-\frac{1}{10x^2}$ **b.** $\frac{y + 3}{(y + 2)^2}$
c. $\frac{1}{z + 4}$

Lesson 12-5   pp. 662–664

Check Skills You'll Need 1. $-4a^2 + 9a + 1$ **2.** $-x^3 +$
$3x^2 + 5x - 6$ **3.** $8t - 2$ **4.** $2x^2 + 10x + 12$
5. $-3n^2 + 11n + 20$ **6.** $6a^3 - 21a^2 + 2a - 7$

Check Understanding 1a. $m - 2 + \frac{1}{3m}$ **b.** $2t^3 + 4t -$
$1 + \frac{1}{2t}$ **2a.** $2b - 3$ **b.** $3m - 4 - \frac{3}{2m + 1}$
3a. $t^3 + t^2 + 2t + 3$ **b.** $c^2 - 3c + 5 - \frac{3}{c + 3}$
4a. $4x + 3 - \frac{4}{2x + 1}$ **b.** $-2a - 5 - \frac{1}{3a - 2}$

Lesson 12-6   pp. 667–669

Check Skills You'll Need 1. $\frac{2}{3}$ **2.** $-\frac{2}{7}$ **3.** -2 **4.** $1\frac{1}{18}$
5. $-\frac{1}{12}$ **6.** $-\frac{1}{3}$ **7.** $\frac{2x}{3}$ **8.** $\frac{x}{2}$ **9.** $\frac{1}{2y}$ **10.** $(x + 2)(x + 1)$
11. $(y + 3)(y + 4)$ **12.** $(t - 2)^2$

Check Understanding 1a. $\frac{5}{x + 2}$ **b.** $\frac{4y}{y - 5}$ **c.** $\frac{7n}{n + 1}$
2a. $-\frac{1}{t - 2}$ **b.** $\frac{2b - 3}{b + 2}$ **c.** $\frac{-c + 5}{5m + 2}$ **3a.** $\frac{9 + 14y^2}{21y^4}$
b. $\frac{16 - 49x}{100x}$ **c.** $\frac{5b + 5}{12b^2}$ **4a.** $\frac{8t + 7}{(t + 4)(t - 1)}$
b. $\frac{m^2 + 5m + 3}{(2m + 1)(m - 1)}$ **c.** $\frac{3a^2 + 2a + 2}{(a + 2)(2a - 1)}$

5. $\frac{1270}{r} + \frac{1270}{1.12r} \approx \frac{2404}{r}$

Lesson 12-7 pp. 672–685

Check Skills You'll Need 1. $1\frac{2}{3}$ **2.** $1\frac{1}{5}$ **3.** $-9, 9$ **4.** $4n$
5. $15x$ **6.** $24y^2$

Check Understanding 1a. -2 **b.** $-\frac{25}{2}$ **2a.** $\frac{1}{2}, 2$ **b.** $-2, 3$
3. $28\frac{1}{8}$ min **4a.** -3 **b.** $-5, 4$ **5a.** no solution
b. -1

Lesson 12-8 pp. 679–682, 685

Check Skills You'll Need 1. $\frac{1}{2}$ **2.** $\frac{1}{2}$ **3.** $\frac{1}{6}$ **4.** 0 **5.** $\frac{1}{36}$ **6.** $\frac{1}{4}$

Check Understanding
1a. Shirt 1 → Shorts 1 → Shirt 1, Shorts 1
　　　　　　 → Shorts 2 → Shirt 1, Shorts 2
　　　　　　 → Shorts 3 → Shirt 1, Shorts 3
　　　　　　 → Shorts 4 → Shirt 1, Shorts 4
　 Shirt 2 → Shorts 1 → Shirt 2, Shorts 1
　　　　　　 → Shorts 2 → Shirt 2, Shorts 2
　　　　　　 → Shorts 3 → Shirt 2, Shorts 3
　　　　　　 → Shorts 4 → Shirt 2, Shorts 4
There are eight possible outfits.
b. Answers may vary. Sample: No, because it
would take a lot of room to make such a diagram.
2. 15 pizzas **3.** 40,320 ways **4a.** 504 **b.** 210 **c.** 20
5a. 5040 **b.** A six-letter password; there are more
possible passwords, since 26 > 10.

Checkpoint Quiz 2 1. $(x + 2)(x + 4)$ **2.** $\frac{4}{3}$
3. $a^2 + 5a + 15 + \frac{44}{a - 3}$ **4.** $\frac{5}{x - 3}$ **5.** $\frac{14m - 12}{(m + 2)(m - 3)}$
6. $\frac{6t + 3}{t^2}$ **7.** $\frac{6}{7}$ **8.** -9 **9.** $-8, 1$ **10a.** 16 **b.** 12

Lesson 12-9 pp. 686–689

Check Skills You'll Need 1. 60 **2.** 120 **3.** 210 **4.** 840
5. $\frac{1}{4}$ **6.** $\frac{5}{72}$ **7.** $\frac{3}{4}$ **8.** 0.07

Check Understanding 1a. 6 **b.** 35 **c.** 210 **2a.** $_5C_2$ **b.** 10
c. Order does not matter. **3.** $\frac{3}{10}$ **4a.** 210 **b.** 1
c. $\frac{1}{210}$

Selected Answers

Chapter 1

Lesson 1-1   pp. 6–8

EXERCISES 1. $p + 4$ **3.** $12 - m$ **9–11.** Choice of variable for the number may vary. **9.** $2n + 2$ **11.** $9 - n$ **17.** $c = $ total cost, $n = $ number of cans, $c = 0.70n$ **19.** $\ell = $ total length in feet, $n = $ number of tents, $\ell = 60n$ **21–23.** Choices of variables may vary. Samples are given. **21.** $w = $ number of workers, $r = $ number of radios, $r = 13w$ **23.** $n = $ number of sales, $t = $ total earnings, $t = 0.4n$ **25.** $9 + k - 17$ **27.** $37t - 9.85$ **35–37.** Answers may vary. Samples are given. **35.** the difference of 3 and t **37.** the quotient of y and 5 **39.** Choices of variables may vary. Sample is given. $n = $ number of days, $c = $ change in height (m), $c = 0.165n$ **55.** 1.04 **57.** 1.46

Lesson 1-2   pp. 12–15

EXERCISES 1. 59 **3.** 7 **7.** 21 **9.** 124 **13.** $37.09 **15.** 22 **17.** 44 **21.** 704 **23.** 185 **29.** 18 **31.** 0 **35.** 8 cm^3 **37.** 21 ft^3 **41.** 15 **43.** 111 **57.** 9 **59.** 135 **65.** $.16 **67a.** 523.60 cm^3 **b.** 381.70 cm^3 **c.** about 73% **69.** 127 **71.** 10 **73a.** 23.89 in.^{3} **b.** 2.0 in.^{3} **c.** 47.38 in.^{2} **89.** $c + 2$ **91.** $t - 21$ **93.** 50% **95.** 95% **99.** 18.9 **101.** 60.3 **103–105.** Answers may vary. Samples are given. **103.** 55, 100, 250 **105.** 60, 150, 240

Lesson 1-3   pp. 20–23

EXERCISES 1. integers, rational numbers **3.** rational numbers **11.** Answers may vary. Sample: -17 **13.** Answers may vary. Sample: 0.3 **15.** whole numbers **17.** whole numbers **19.** true **21.** False; answers may vary. Sample: 6 **25.** $<$ **27.** $=$ **29.** $-9\frac{3}{4}, -9\frac{2}{3}, -9\frac{7}{12}$ **31.** $-1.01, -1.001, -1.0009$ **35.** 9 **37.** 0.5 **43.** Answers may vary. Sample: $\frac{5}{1}$ **45.** Answers may vary. Sample: $\frac{1034}{1000}$ **47.** natural numbers, whole numbers, integers, rational numbers **49.** rational numbers **51.** $=$ **53.** $<$ **57.** 6 **59.** a **69.** sometimes **71.** always **86.** 33 **87.** 48 **88.** 315 **89.** 7 **90.** 0 **91.** $7\frac{1}{2}$ **92.** 25 **93.** 4 **94.** 195 **95–98.** Choices of variables may vary. **95.** $n = $ number of tickets, $6.25n$ **96.** $i = $ cost of item, $i + 3.98$ **97.** $n = $ number of hours, $d = $ distance traveled, $d = 7n$ **98.** $c = $ total cost, $n = $ number of books, $c = 3.5n$

Lesson 1-4   pp. 27–31

EXERCISES 1. $6 + (-3)$; 3 **3.** $-5 + 7$; 2 **5.** 15 **7.** -19 **25.** $-47 + 12 = -35$, 35 ft **27.** $-6 + 13 = 7$, 7°F **29.** -1.7 **31.** -8.7 **37.** Choices of variable may vary. $c = $ change in amount of money, $74 + c$

a. $92 **b.** $45 **c.** $27 **39.** $\begin{bmatrix} -18.2 \\ 11.6 \\ 19.1 \end{bmatrix}$ **41.** $\begin{bmatrix} 1.8 & 22 \\ -\frac{1}{2} & 7 \end{bmatrix}$

43. -13 **45.** $11\frac{19}{24}$ **57.** 6.3 million people **59a.** $\frac{100}{442} = \frac{50}{221}$ **b.** 0.23 **c.** about 23% **61.** -2 **63.** -5 **71.** -13.7 **73.** 8.7 **81.** $7 **105.** $<$ **107.** $<$ **111.** 9 **113.** 18

Lesson 1-5   pp. 34–36

EXERCISES 1. -1

3. -6 **9.** -4 **11.** -10 **21.** 3 **23.** 6

29. -10 **31.** 1 **37.** $50.64 **39.** -1.5 **41.** 5.5 **53.** false; $2 - (-1) = 3$, $3 \not< 2$ or -1 **57.** $[-\frac{1}{4} \quad 0 \quad -3]$

73. -9 **75.** -4.1 **77.** $\begin{bmatrix} 1.2 \\ -2.5 \\ 5.2 \end{bmatrix}$ **79–81.** Choices

of variables may vary. **79.** $t = $ total cost, $p = $ pounds of pears, $t = 1.19p$ **81.** $c = $ check ($), $s = $ your share, $s = \frac{c}{6}$

Lesson 1-6   pp. 41–44

EXERCISES 1. -15 **3.** 15 **13.** -12 **15.** -15 **25.** -64 **27.** 4 **33.** 8 **35.** 81 **41.** -4 **43.** 6 **49.** -7 **51.** 0 **55.** -15 **57.** $-\frac{6}{25}$ **59.** 18 **61.** $-\frac{8}{15}$ **73.** $-\frac{5}{6}$ **75.** $-\frac{1}{5}$ **77.** $-4\frac{1}{2}$ **79.** $\frac{1}{5}$ **85.** 31¢ **91.** $\begin{bmatrix} -15 & 21 \\ \frac{2}{3} & -9 \end{bmatrix}$ **93.** $\left[-12 \quad -2\frac{2}{3}\right]$ **97a.** $a = 5000 - 25t$ **b.** 312.5 ft **c.** 4687.5 ft **115.** -20 **117.** 9.8 **121.** 56 **123.** $\frac{3}{4}$ **125.** 121 **127.** $34.93

Technology   p. 45

1. $\begin{bmatrix} -1 & 10 \\ 8 & 9 \end{bmatrix}$ **3.** $\begin{bmatrix} -1 & 17 \\ 1 & -16 \end{bmatrix}$ **11.** $\begin{bmatrix} -3 & -7 & 3 \\ -6 & -8 & 9 \\ 12 & 16 & 19 \end{bmatrix}$

13. $\begin{bmatrix} -6 & -28 & -12 \\ -32 & -23 & 26 \\ 48 & 10 & 53 \end{bmatrix}$

Lesson 1-7 pp. 50–53

EXERCISES 1. 2412 **3.** 5489 **9.** $3.96 **11.** $29.55
15. $7t - 28$ **17.** $3m + 12$ **27.** $-x - 3$ **29.** $-3 - x$
35. $-3t$ **37.** $7x$ **43.** $3(m - 7)$ **45.** $2(b + 9)$
49. 44,982 **51.** 14.021 **65.** $2\frac{1}{4}\left(5\frac{1}{2} - k\right)$
67. $\frac{11}{20}\left(b - \frac{13}{30}\right)$ **68.** $\frac{17}{z - 34}$ **75.** $-76p^2 - 20p - 9$
77. $1.5m - 12.5v$ **105.** -68 **107.** 4 **115.** 12.127
117. 45.7 **123a.** $4 + \frac{m}{3}$ **b.** 7; 5; 8

Lesson 1-8 pp. 56–58

EXERCISES 1. Ident. Prop. of Add.; 0, the identity
for addition, is added. **3.** Ident. Prop. of Mult.;
1, the identity for multiplication, is multiplied.
11. 7400 **13.** 4200 **17a.** def. of subtr. **b.** Dist.
Prop. **c.** addition
19. $25 \cdot 1.7 \cdot 4$
  $= 25 \cdot 4 \cdot 1.7$ Comm. Prop. of Mult.
  $= (25 \cdot 4) \cdot 1.7$ Assoc. Prop. of Mult.
  $= 100 \cdot 1.7$ mult.
  $= 170$ mult.
21. $8 + 9m + 7$
  $= 9m + 8 + 7$ Comm. Prop. of Add.
  $= 9m + (8 + 7)$ Assoc. Prop. of Add.
  $= 9m + 15$ add.
25. $2 + g\left(\frac{1}{g}\right) = 2 + 1$ Inv. Prop. of Mult.
     $= 3$ add.
27. $(3^2 - 2^3)(8759) = (9 - 8)(8759)$ mult.
        $= [9 + (-8)](8759)$ def. of subtr.
        $= 1(8759)$ add.
        $= 8759$ Ident. Prop. of Mult.
33. no **35.** yes **41.** No; $(5 - 3) - 1 = 2 - 1 = 1$,
while $5 - (3 - 1) = 5 - 2 = 3$. **43.** No;
$16 \div (4 \div 2) = 16 \div 2 = 8$, while $(16 \div 4) \div 2 =$
$4 \div 2 = 2$. **59.** $6 + 5k$ **61.** $-10p - 35$
65. $7 + [m + (-17)]$ **67.** $\frac{1}{2}\left(\frac{b}{4}\right)$ **69.** 7 **71.** $-\frac{1}{4}$

Lesson 1-9 pp. 62–65

EXERCISES 1. (4, 5) **3.** (−5, 0)

5–8. 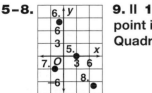   **9.** II **11.** IV **13.** I **15.** No; the
point is on the y-axis, not in
Quadrant III.

17. neg. correlation **19.** no correlation **21.** (5, 0)
23. (−3, −2), (1, 3), (2, −4)

---

25. 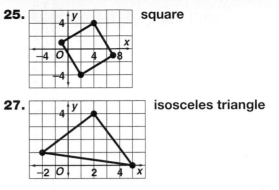   square

27. isosceles triangle

29. Neg. correlation; the more classes you take,
the more work you have, so the less free time you
have. **31.** No correlation; baby's length at birth is
not related to its birthday.
47. $x - 4(2x + 1) - 3$
   $= x - 8x - 4 - 3$ Dist. Prop.
   $= 1x - 8x - 4 - 3$ Ident. Prop. of Mult.
   $= 1x + (-8x) + (-4) + (-3)$ def. of subtr.
   $= [1x + (-8x)] + [(-4) + (-3)]$ Assoc. Prop.
              of Add.
   $= [1 + (-8)]x + (-4) + (-3)$ Dist. Prop.
   $= -7x + (-4) + (-3)$ add.
   $= -7x + (-7)$ add.
   $= -7x - 7$ def. of subtr.
49. $8b + 7a - 4b - 9a$
   $= 8b + 7a + (-4b) + (-9a)$ def. of subtr.
   $= 8b + (-4b) + 7a + (-9a)$ Comm. Prop. of
              Add.
   $= [8b + -4b] + [7a + -9a]$ Assoc. Prop. of
              Add.
   $= [8 + (-4)]b + [7 + (-9)]a$ Dist. Prop.
   $= 4b + (-2)a$ add.
   $= 4b - 2a$ def. of subtr.
51. $\begin{bmatrix} 9 & -13 \\ 19 & -1 \end{bmatrix}$ **53.** $\begin{bmatrix} 3.1 & -0.7 & 21 \\ -4.9 & -4.7 & -2.1 \\ -1 & -7 & 8 \end{bmatrix}$
55. true **57.** true

Chapter Review pp. 67–69

1. term **2.** evaluate **3.** algebraic expression
4. rational **5.** absolute value **6.** matrix
7. reciprocal **8.** rational number **9.** x-coordinate
10. scatter plot **11.** neg. correlation **12.** power
13. Let $n =$ the number, $5 + 3n$. **14.** Let $n =$ the
number, $30 - n$. **15.** Let $n =$ the number, $\frac{7}{n}$.
16. Let $n =$ the number, $n(12)$. **17.** 9 **18.** 64
19. 4 **20.** 8 **21.** real numbers, rational numbers
22. real numbers, irrational numbers **23.** real
numbers, rational numbers **24.** real numbers,
rational numbers, natural numbers, whole
numbers, integers **25.** real numbers, rational
numbers, natural numbers, whole numbers,
integers **26.** -17 **27.** -5 **28.** 9.9 **29.** 24.9

30. -12 **31.** 0 **32.** 10 **33.** -40 **34.** $-\frac{5}{9}$ **35.** 2
36. $-\frac{5}{4}$ **37.** $\frac{23}{18}$ **38.** $4m + 3$ **39.** $b + 10$
40. $-5w + 20$ **41.** $36 - 27j$ **42.** $-3 + 10y$
43. $-2r + 1$ **44.** $35b + 5$ **45.** $7 - 25v$ **46.** $9t - \frac{6}{5}$
47. $-18 + 9m$ **48.** $-4 + x$ **49.** $10g + 1.5$
50. Assoc. Prop. of Add. **51.** Ident. Prop. of Add.
52. Comm. Prop. of Mult. **53.** Dist. Prop.
54. $19 + 56\left(\frac{1}{56}\right) = 19 + 1$ Inv. Prop. of Mult.
$\qquad\qquad\qquad = 20$ add.
55. $-12p + 45 - 7p$
$\quad = -12p + 45 + (-7p)$ def. of subtr.
$\quad = -12p + (-7p) + 45$ Comm. Prop. of Add.
$\quad = [-12 + (-7)]p + 45$ Dist. Prop.
$\quad = -19p + 45$ add.
56. $24abc - 24bac$
$\quad = 24abc - 24abc$ Comm. Prop. of Mult.
$\quad = 24abc + (-24abc)$ def. of subtr.
$\quad = [24 + (-24)]abc$ Dist. Prop.
$\quad = (0)abc$ Inv. Prop. of Add.
$\quad = 0$ Mult. Prop. of Zero
57. $4 \cdot 13 \cdot 25 \cdot 1$
$\quad = 4 \cdot 25 \cdot 13 \cdot 1$ Comm. Prop. of Mult.
$\quad = (4 \cdot 25) \cdot (13 \cdot 1)$ Assoc. Prop. of Mult.
$\quad = 100 \cdot 13$ mult.
$\quad = 1300$ mult.
58. $(-4, 1)$ **59.** $(2, -2)$ **60.** $(3, 0)$ **61.** $(-1, -1)$

62.
63.

64.
65a.

b. pos. correlation

Chapter 2

Lesson 2-1   pp. 77–80

EXERCISES 1. 8 **3.** 13 **11.** 4 **13.** -57
19. $38\frac{3}{4} + g = 41\frac{1}{2}; 2\frac{3}{4}$ in. **21.** 500 **23.** -18
29. -9 **31.** -10 **41.** -15 **43.** 8 **53.** No; 96.26 is close to 100 and 62.74 is close to 60, so the difference is close to 40. **57.** $-\frac{3}{8}$ **71.** $189 =$

$e - 1048$; 1237 engineers **73.** $17x = 106.25$, $\$6.25$
77. 44 **79.** 92 **91.** A **92.** C **93.** B **94.** D
95. $5a - 15$ **96.** $-12 - 2y$ **97.** $9 + \frac{1}{2}m$
98. $8ac - 10c$ **99.** 6 **100.** 41 **101.** -13

Lesson 2-2   pp. 84–86

EXERCISES 1. -10 **3.** -1 **17.** $2n + 4028 = 51{,}514$; 23,743 books **19.** $39.95 + 0.35m = 69.70$; 85 min **21.** -16 **23.** -85 **37.** Add. Prop. of Eq., Simplify., Mult. Prop. of Eq., Simplify. **39.** Subtr. Prop. of Eq., Simplify., Div. Prop. of Eq., Simplify. **41.** 75 **43.** 1
53. $7 - 3k - 7 = -14 - 7$ Subtr. Prop. of Eq.
$\qquad\quad -3k = -21$ Simplify.
$\qquad\quad \frac{-3k}{-3} = \frac{-21}{-3}$ Div. Prop. of Eq.
$\qquad\qquad k = 7$ Simplify.
55. $\frac{-y}{2} + 14 - 14 = -1 - 14$ Subtr. Prop. of Eq.
$\qquad\quad \frac{-y}{2} = -15$ Simplify.
$\qquad\quad \frac{-y}{2}(-2) = -15(-2)$ Mult. Prop. of Eq.
$\qquad\qquad y = 30$ Simplify.
57. $0.8c - 500 = 4650$; $\$6437.50$ **59.** 43 **61.** 2
67. 15.5 **69.** 31.5 **71.** The neg. sign was dropped; -1. **87.** 12 **88.** 15 **89.** -9 **90.** 6 **91.** 33 **92.** $11\frac{2}{5}$
93. 6 **94.** 4 **95.** 6 **96.** -11 **97.** 12

Lesson 2-3   pp. 91–94

EXERCISES 1. 9 **3.** $5\frac{4}{7}$ **11.** $x + 9 + x = 25$; 8 ft by 9 ft **13.** 8 **21.** 11 **23.** 46 **31.** 21 **33.** 3.5 **39.** 2
41. 5 **55.** $4\frac{2}{3}$ **57.** 92 mi **61.** 25 **75.** 16 **77.** -19
83. 150 **85.** 90 **89.** 27 **91.** -4

Lesson 2-4   pp. 98–100

EXERCISES 1. 9 **3.** 3 **17.** 200 min **19.** 8 ft
21a. Answers may vary. Sample:
$\quad 0: \quad 9 = 9$
$\quad 3: \quad -9 = -9$
$\quad -4: \quad 33 = 33$
$\quad -6: \quad 45 = 45$ **b.** identity
23. no solution **25.** identity **29.** 0 **31.** 10
39. $1200 + 9b = 25b$; 75 bags **41.** $a = 3, b = 5$, $c = 7, d = 11$ **43.** $a = 3, b = 6, c = 5, d = \frac{1}{3}$
45. The student subtracted y from both sides instead of adding y to both sides; 5.3. **65.** -4
67. $-6\frac{2}{3}$ **71.** $-\frac{4}{5}, -\frac{5}{8}, -\frac{3}{5}$ **73.** $8.02, 8.1, 8.3$

Lesson 2-5   pp. 107–110

EXERCISES 1a. Let w = width **b.** $\ell = w + 3$
c. $2w + 2(w + 3) = 30$; 6 **d.** 9 in. **3.** 9 cm; 18 cm

5. C **7a.** Let n = the first integer. **b.** 2 **c.** $n + 2$
d. $n + n + 2 = 56$; 27, 29 **11.** $1\frac{17}{30}$ h **13a.** x; $3 - x$
b. $320x = 280(3 - x)$, $1\frac{2}{5}$ h **15.** 15 mi/h; 20 mi/h
17. 14 cm **19.** $-31, -29, -27$ **41.** 0 **43.** $-\frac{1}{3}$
47. -12 **49.** 54

Lesson 2-6   pp. 111–113

EXERCISES 1. $r = \frac{C}{2\pi}$ **3.** $\ell = \frac{p}{2} - w$ **9.** $y = -2x + 5$
11. $y = -4x + 3$ **17.** $x = \frac{c}{d}$ **19.** $z = a + y$
25a. $H = \frac{N}{7L}$ **b.** 11 ft **27a.** $p = \frac{I}{rt}$ **b.** \$3000 **c.** If
the interest at 3.5% for 4 yr is \$420, the principal
is \$3000.00. **29.** $b = \frac{A}{h}$ **31.** $p = \frac{r + b}{a}$
41a. $n = \frac{S}{180} + 2$ **b.** 5; 7; 4; 9 **51.** 71, 72, 73
53. $[-60 \; 9]$ **55.** $\begin{bmatrix} -15.6 & 27 & 3 \\ 0 & 24 & -28.5 \end{bmatrix}$

Extension   pp. 116–117

1. $SA = 2\pi rh + 2\pi r^2$ **3.** 340 in.^{2} **9.** $V = \ell wh$
11. 282.74 ft^3

Lesson 2-7   pp. 121–123

EXERCISES 1. 12; 11; 10; median **3.** 63; 52; none;
median **5.** 5.9 **7.** 125 **9.** 18 **11.** 20

15.
```
15 | 3 7
16 |
17 | 5 6
18 | 4 6
15 | 3 means 15.3
```
17.
```
0 | 2 8
1 | 4
2 | 2 6
3 | 5
4 | 3 5
0 | 2 means 0.2
```

19. Type A: 0.30, 0.31, 0.23 and 0.31, 0.18; Type B:
0.42, 0.44, 0.31, 0.23 **21.** $-3.1, -2, -1$ and -2, 15
37. $x = y - 4$ **39.** $x = \frac{y - 4}{10}$ **41.** -144 **43.** $-\frac{2}{3}$

Chapter Review   pp. 125–127

1. identity **2.** solution **3.** inverse operations
4. Solutions of equivalent equations
5. consecutive integers **6.** C **7.** D **8.** A **9.** B
10. 16 **11.** -36 **12.** 31 **13.** 24 **14.** 26 **15.** 4.25
16. 12 **17.** 2 **18.** 4 **19.** 3 **20.** 5 **21.** 3 **22.** 2
23. 11 **24.** $\frac{1}{2}$ **25.** -9 **26.** 18 **27.** -12 **28.** 9
29. -10 **30.** Let x = number of people;
$6x + 3 = 27$; 4 people
31.
$$314 = -n + 576$$
$$314 - 576 = -n + 576 - 576 \quad \text{Subtr. Prop. of Eq.}$$
$$-262 = -n \qquad\qquad\qquad \text{Simplify.}$$
$$-1(-262) = -1(-n) \qquad \text{Mult. Prop. of Eq.}$$
$$262 = n \qquad\qquad\qquad \text{Simplify.}$$

32.
$$-\tfrac{1}{4}w - 1 = 6$$
$$-\tfrac{1}{4}w - 1 + 1 = 6 + 1 \quad \text{Add. Prop. of Eq.}$$
$$-\tfrac{1}{4}w = 7 \qquad\qquad \text{Simplify.}$$
$$-4(-\tfrac{1}{4}w) = -4(7) \quad \text{Mult. Prop. of Eq.}$$
$$w = -28 \qquad \text{Simplify.}$$
33.
$$3h - 4 = 5$$
$$3h - 4 + 4 = 5 + 4 \quad \text{Add. Prop. of Eq.}$$
$$3h = 9 \qquad\qquad \text{Simplify.}$$
$$\tfrac{3h}{3} = \tfrac{9}{3} \qquad\qquad \text{Div. Prop. of Eq.}$$
$$h = 3 \qquad\qquad \text{Simplify.}$$
34. -125 **35.** 6 **36.** -7 **37.** -18 **38.** 4 **39.** $-\frac{1}{2}$
40. $\frac{3}{2}$ **41.** 2 **42.** 0 **43.** 0 **44.** $\frac{3}{2}$ **45.** -2 **46.** no
solution **47.** identity **48.** 20 **49.** 10 **50.** identity
51. no solution **52.** $2x + 2(x - 6) = 72$; width =
15 cm, length = 21 cm **53.** $4.25x + 2.50 = 15.25$;
3 games **54.** $b = \frac{2A}{h}$ **55.** $x = \frac{y - b}{m}$ **56.** $d = \frac{C}{\pi}$
57a. $I = \frac{E}{R}$ **b.** 40 amperes **58.** 1.9 h or 1 h 54 min
59. 36.75 m **60.** 193, 194, 195 **61.** $-68, -66, -64$
62. 6.75 h or 6 h 45 min **63.** 52 **64.** 85, 85, 87
65. 30.6, 27, 24 **66.** 2.3, 2.3, 2.3 **67.** 42.1, 42, 37
68. 3.8 km **69.** 19 items **70.** 6 people
71. 18, 18.4, 19.9

Chapter 3

Lesson 3-1   pp. 136–138

EXERCISES 1. yes **3.** yes **5.** no **9a.** no **b.** no **c.**
yes **11a.** no **b.** no **c.** no **15.** C **17.** D
19.
```
—+—+—⊕—+—+—+→
 -1 0  1  2  3
```
21.
```
+—+—+—+—●—+—+→
-7 -6 -5 -4 -3 -2
```
27–35. Choice of variable may vary. **27.** $x > -3$
29. $x \geq 1$ **33.** Let s = number of students. $s \leq 48$
35. Let w = safe number of watts. $w \leq 60$ **39.**
b is greater than 0. **41.** z is greater than or equal
to -5.6. **51.** Answers may vary. Sample:
For $x = -1$, $3(-1) + 1 = -3 + 1 = -2$. $-2 \not> 0$.
55. $b \leq -5$
```
←—●—+—+—+—+—+—+→
 -6 -5 -4 -3 -2 -1 0
```
57. $a < 5$
```
←—+—+—+—⊕—+→
  2  3  4  5  6
```
59.
```
←—+—⊕—+—+—+→
 -2 -1 0  1  2
```
61.
```
←—+—+—+—●—+—+→
  0  1  2  3  4  5
```
63.
```
←—+—+—+—+—●—+—+→
 -2 0  2  4  6  8
```
64. "At least" is translated
as $\geq$. "At most" is translated as $\leq$. **65.** $x \geq 2451$
81. $y = 5x + 4$ **87.** $I = \frac{V}{R}$ **89.** $b = P - a - c$
91. Commutative Property of Multiplication

Lesson 3-2   pp. 142–144

EXERCISES 1. 5 **3.** 4.3 **5.** $t < 1$
```
←—+—+—+—⊕—+→
 -2 -1 0  1  2
```

7. $d \geq 10$
-8 9 10 11 12 13

21. $\frac{5}{3}$ **23.** $w \leq 5$;
3 4 5 6 7 8

25. $b > -7$;
-8 -6 -4 -2 0 2

39. $s + 637 \leq 2000$, \$1363 **41.** $r + 17 + 12 \geq 50$, 21 reflectors **43.** Subtract 9 from each side.
45. $w \geq 11$ **47.** $y < 3.1$ **71.** at least \$15.50
75. $x \geq 1$ **77.** $t \leq -3$ **99.** Let $c =$ length of octopus in feet. $c \leq 10$ **101.** Let $a =$ average. $a \geq 90$ 103. 13 **105.** -12 **113.** 7 **115.** 31

Lesson 3-3 pp. 149–151

EXERCISES 1. $t \geq -4$;
-6 -4 -2 0 2

3. $w \leq -2$;
-3 -2 -1 0 1

17. $t < -3$;
-5 -4 -3 -2 -1 0 1

19. $w \leq -5$;
-8 -6 -4 -2 0 2

29. $4.5c \geq 300$, 67 cars **31–33.** Answers may vary. Samples are given. **31.** $-2, -3, -4, -5$
33. $-3, -4, -5, -6$ **39.** Multiply each side by -4 and reverse the inequality symbol. **41.** Divide each side by 5. **45.** -2 **47.** 4 **51.** x and y are equal. **53–55.** Estimates may vary. **53.** $j > -6$
55. $s \geq 28$ **59.** $d \leq -7$ **61.** $s < -\frac{1}{4}$ **75.** Yes; in each case, y is greater than 6. **91.** $w < -\frac{1}{8}$
93. $d > 4$ **99.** $n = -2$ **101.** Prop. of Opposites **103.** Ident. Prop. of Add.

Lesson 3-4 pp. 155–158

EXERCISES 1. $d \leq 4$ **3.** $x > -2\frac{1}{2}$

11. $27 \geq 2s + 8$ and $s \leq 9.5$, so the two equal sides must be no longer than 9.5 cm. **13.** $j \geq 1$
15. $h > 5$ **23.** $t \leq -1$ **25.** $n \geq 2$ **35.** $q \leq -2$
37. $x < 1\frac{1}{3}$ **41.** Subtract 7 from each side.

43. Add 2 to each side, then multiply each side by -5, and reverse the inequality sign.

47. $6 - (r + 3) < 15$, $r > -12$ **49.** $3(z + 2) > 12$, $z > 2$ **53a.** maximum **b.** no more than 135
55. E **57.** A **61.** $r < 5\frac{1}{2}$ **63.** $s \leq 4.4$ **79.** Add $2x$ to each side rather than subtract $2x$, so $x \leq \frac{2}{5}$.
93. $y \geq -8$ **95.** $t \geq -3$ **101.** -16 **103.** 24

Extension p. 160

1. 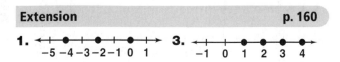
-5 -4 -3 -2 -1 0 1 **3.**
-1 0 1 2 3 4

Lesson 3-5 pp. 163–165

EXERCISES 1. $-4 < x$ and $x < 6$ or $-4 < x < 6$;
-6 -4 -2 0 2 4 6 8

3. $23 < c < 23.5$;
22 23 24

5. $-5 < j < 5$;
-10 -5 0 5 10

7. $2 < n \leq 6$;
-2 0 2 4 6 8

21. $x < 3$ or $x > 7$;
-2 0 2 4 6 8

23. $b < 100$ or $b > 300$;
0 100 300

25. $k < -5$ or $k > -1$;
-6 -5 -4 -3 -2 -1 0 1

27. $a \leq 4$ or $a > 5$;
2 3 4 5 6 7

35. $x < -3$ or $x \geq 2$ **37.** $-4 \leq x \leq 3$
39. $h < -7$ or $h > 4$ **41.** $r < 16$ or $r > 25$
45. all real numbers except 5 **47.** $2.5 < x < 7.5$
49. $7 < x < 49$ **51.** $66 \leq C \leq 88$ **53.** Charlotte: $29 \leq C \leq 90$, Detroit: $15 \leq D \leq 83$ **65.** $n \leq 3$
67. $x = -1$ **69.** identity

Lesson 3-6 pp. 167–169

EXERCISES 1. $-2, 2$ **3.** $-\frac{1}{2}, \frac{1}{2}$ **13.** $3, 13$ **15.** $-3, 1$
23. $k < -2.5$ or $k > 2.5$;
-4 -3 -2 -1 0 1 2 3 4

25. $-8 < x < 2$;
-8 -6 -4 -2 0 2

35. between 12.18 mm and 12.30 mm, inclusive

37. $-9, 9$ **39.** $-1\frac{1}{2}, 1\frac{1}{2}$ **53.** $|n| > 7.5$

55. $|n + 1| \geq 3$ **57.** 39%, 45% **63.** $|x - 2| = 4$

65. $|x - 12\frac{1}{2}| = 3\frac{1}{2}$ **87.** $-282 \leq e \leq 20,320$

89. -3 **91.** 5 **95.** $-2.5, -2, 0, 3, \pi$ **97.** 0.001, 0.009, 0.01, 0.011

Extension p. 173

1. Symmetric Prop. of Equality **7.** Add. Prop. of Ineq., Add. Prop. of Ineq., Transitive Prop. of Ineq.

Chapter Review pp. 175–177

1. C **2.** B **3.** A **4.** C **5.** D **6.**
-1 0 1 2 3 4

7.
-6 -5 -4 -3 -2 -1 0 1

8.

9.

10. $n < -2$ **11.** $n \geq -3.5$ **12.** $n > -6$ **13.** $n \geq 2$
14. Let p = number of people, $p \geq 600$.
15. Let n = number of people, $n \leq 15$. **16.** Let t = temperature in degrees Fahrenheit, $t < 32$.

17. $h > -1$;

18. $t < -5$;

19. $m \geq -3$;

20. $w \geq -2$;

21. $q > -2.5$;

22. $y > -14$;

23. $n \leq 15$;

24. $d \geq 4$;

25. $-2 \leq t$;

26. $0 < c$;

27. $2.5 \geq u$;

28. $-9 < p$;

29. $3.50 + 2.75 + x \leq 12.00$, $x \leq 5.75$
30. $7.25h \geq 200$, $h \geq 27.586$
You must work at least 28 h.

31. $n > -2$ **32.** $k \leq -\frac{1}{2}$ **33.** $b < 40$ **34.** $c \leq -2$
35. $m < -6$ **36.** $t > 3$ **37.** $x \geq 2$ **38.** $y \leq -56$
39. $x < \frac{8}{3}$ **40.** $190 + 0.04x \geq 500$, $x \geq 7750$

41.
42.

43.

44. $-2 \leq z < 4$,

45. $-\frac{5}{2} \leq d < 4$,

46. $-\frac{3}{2} \leq b < 0$,

47. $t \leq -2$ or $t \geq 7$,

48. $2 \leq a < 5$,

49. $2 \leq a < 4$,
50. $75 \leq t \leq 89$

51. $|n + 2| > 3$
52. $|n - 12| \leq 5$ **53.** 5 or -5
54. $n \leq -6$ or $n \geq 2$ **55.** $-3 \leq x \leq 3$
56. $-9.6 < m < 9.6$ **57.** $x < 3$ or $x > 4$
58. 6.5 or -12.5 **59.** 8 **60.** all real numbers
61. no solution **62.** $k < -7$ or $k > -3$
63. -5 or 1 **64.** $z \leq -0.25$ or $z \geq 0.25$
65. $2.74 \leq d \leq 2.86$ **66.** $19.6 \leq \ell \leq 20.4$

Chapter 4

Lesson 4-1 pp. 185–188

EXERCISES 1. \$9.50/h **3.** 131 cars/week **7.** A
9. B **11.** 480 **13.** 10,800 **15.** 11.25 **17.** 25.2
31. 105.6 km **33.** $8\frac{11}{12}$ **35.** $-3\frac{1}{2}$ **39.** 18.75
41. 18.25 **45.** 15 mi/h **47.** 1 mi/h **51.** 10.5 mm
53. 3 **55.** -16 **61.** -8.4 **63.** about 750 students
67. 4 people/mi², 2485 people/mi², 78 people/mi²

71. 48 v **83.**

85.

89. s = students, $s \geq 235$ **91.** w = weight (lb),
$w > 20$ **93.**
95. 6 **97.** -5

Lesson 4-2 pp. 192–195

EXERCISES 1. $\overline{AB} \cong \overline{PQ}$, $\overline{BC} \cong \overline{QR}$, $\overline{CA} \cong \overline{RP}$;
$\angle A \cong \angle P$, $\angle B \cong \angle Q$, $\angle C \cong \angle R$ **3.** 3.125 ft
5. 80 in. **9.** 4.8 ft **11.** 87.5 mi **13.** 325.5 mi
17. 4 in. by 6 in. **19.** 2 in. by 3 in. **21.** 33.75 in.
25. 9 ft by 12 ft **27.** 216 ft² **33.** $a = 8$, $b = 6$,
$c = 10$ **35.** 400,400 km **41.** 4.5
43. $-22\frac{6}{7}$ **45.** $b < -4$ **47.** $m < -4$

Lesson 4-3 pp. 200–202

EXERCISES 1. 50% **3.** $33\frac{1}{3}$% **7.** 8 **9.** 21
13. $\frac{40}{100} = \frac{20}{x}$, 50 **15.** $\frac{15}{100} = \frac{24}{x}$, 160
21. $25 = 0.50x$; 50 **23.** $45 = n \cdot 60$; 75%
27. 200% **29.** 300% **33.** 100 **35.** 150
39. $\frac{75}{100} = \frac{3}{x}$, 4 **41.** $x = 0.002(900)$, 1.8
45. 62; 50% is 61 and 51.3% > 50%. **47.** 73; 10%
is 74 and 9.79% < 10%. **49.** \$297.00 **51.** \$3896.00
53a. \$74.25 **b.** 3.75% **c.** 6 yr **55.** \$1250.00
57. 2 yr **67.** $13\frac{1}{3}$ mi **69.** 90 mi

71. $b < -4$;

73. $h > -21$;

EXERCISES 1. 50%; increase **3.** 25%; increase **13.** 39% **15.** 0.5 ft **17.** 0.005 g **19.** 19.25 cm^2, 29.25 cm^2 **21.** 46.75 in.^{2}, 61.75 in.^{2} **25.** 25% **27.** 12.5% **29a.** 48 cm^3 **b.** 74.375 cm^3 **c.** 28.125 cm^3 **d.** 26.375 cm^3 **e.** 55% **31.** 22%; decrease **33.** 175%; increase **39.** 2% **41.** 1 mm **45.** 24.5 cm^2, 25.5 cm^2 **47.** 54.1 in.^{2}, 54.3 in.^{2} **49.** 11% **61–63.** Equations may vary. **61.** $\frac{x}{100} = \frac{13}{15}$, 87% **63.** $\frac{x}{100} = \frac{96}{32}$, 300% **67.** $q \geq -17$

EXERCISES 1. $\frac{1}{2}$ **3.** $\frac{1}{6}$ **11.** $\frac{5}{6}$ **13.** 1 **15.** 24% **17.** 15% **23.** $\frac{1}{6}$ **25.** $\frac{1}{3}$ **27.** $\frac{1}{2}$ **29.** $\frac{1}{450}$ **33.** 1% **37a.** $\frac{3}{4}$ **b.** $\frac{2}{5}$ **c.** $\frac{3}{20}$ **39.** $\frac{3}{16}$ **41.** $\frac{7}{16}$ **43.** $\frac{1}{3}$ **55.** 25%; increase **57.** 40%; increase

61. $-3 \leq t \leq 4$;

```
←+——●—+—+—+—+—+—+—●—→
  -4-3-2-1 0 1 2 3 4
```

63. $h < 2$ or $h > 5$;

```
←+—+—⊕—+—+—+—⊕—+—→
  0 1 2 3 4 5 6
```

67. 6.17, 5, 5 **69.**

```
3 | 4 7 9
4 | 1 9
6 | 5
7 | 1
```

1. Answers may vary. Sample: Yes, as long as they are 40% of the data, any 4 numbers will suffice.

EXERCISES 1. $\frac{1}{36}$ **3.** $\frac{1}{18}$ **9.** $\frac{4}{81}$ **11.** $\frac{1}{9}$ **15.** $\frac{2}{11}$ **17.** $\frac{1}{55}$ **21.** $\frac{2}{7}$ **23.** $\frac{1}{6}$ **25.** $\frac{1}{9}$ **31.** Indep.; the data set hasn't changed. **33a.** 0.58 **b.** 0.003248 **35.** 0.0036 **37.** $\frac{1}{10}$ **51.** $\frac{4}{21}$ **53.** $\frac{8}{21}$ **55.** 2 **57.** No solution; abs. value can't be negative.

1. Not good; not everyone in a barber shop or salon is a teenager. **3.** No; the sample was biased toward athletic activities such as biking.

1. rate **2.** cross products **3.** percent of change **4.** greatest possible error **5.** an outcome **6.** complement of an event **7.** independent **8.** sample space **9.** unit rate **10.** percent of increase **11.** 150 mi/h **12.** 3.41 mi/h **13.** 0.23 mi/h **14.** 2 **15.** 2.3 **16.** −6 **17.** 20 **18.** 6 **19.** 5 **20.** 7.5 m **21.** 19.5 m **22.** 36 ft **23.** 12.9 **24.** 2.5 **25.** 800% **26.** 850 **27.** 3.75% **28.** $220 **29.** about 13%; increase **30.** 25%; decrease **31.** about 33%; decrease **32.** Answers may vary. Sample: It costs a restaurant $.11 to make a cup of tea, which it sells for $.75. The percent of increase is about 582%. **33.** about 5.4% **34.** 0 **35.** $\frac{5}{6}$ **36.** $\frac{1}{3}$ **37.** $\frac{1}{6}$ **38a.** $\frac{1}{4}$ **b.** Sample: P(not 3 heads) means the chances of getting 0, 1, 2, or 4 heads. **39.** $\frac{11}{14}$ **40.** dependent; $\frac{2}{45}$ **41.** independent; $\frac{1}{20}$ **42.** Answers may vary. Sample: In probability, two events are dependent if the outcome of one influences the outcome of the other. In everyday language, if one person is dependent on another, the first person relies on the second for support. **43.** Indep.; the result of one number cube does not affect the other. **44.** Dep.; once you select one sock, there are fewer socks when you make the second selection.

Chapter 5

EXERCISES 1. Labels may vary. Sample is given.

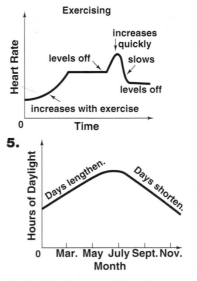

9. C; the temperature increases steadily and then alternates cooling and warming as the oven turns off and on during a cooking cycle.

11a.

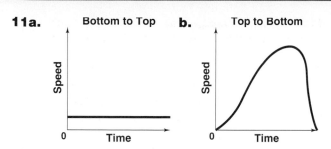

Bottom to Top   **b.**   Top to Bottom

No; the graphs are different because you have a constant speed traveling up but not down.

15a.

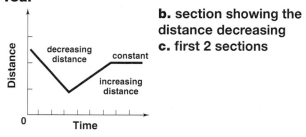

b. section showing the distance decreasing
c. first 2 sections

27. $\frac{1}{36}$ **29.** $\frac{1}{12}$ **33.** $x < 8$ **35.** $x > -4$
39. 17   **41.** -15

Lesson 5-2   pp. 244–246

EXERCISES 1. {4, 5, 6}, {3, 6, 7, 19} **3.** {−2, 2, 3}, {−3, −2, 3} **7.** yes **9.** no **11.** no **13.** yes **15.** 4 **17.** 9 **23.** {0.5, 53} **25.** {−27, −7, −2, 8, 48} **27.** no **29.** yes; {−4, −1, 0, 3}; {−4} **35.** {−13.8, −1, 5} **37.** {−0.75, 0, 12.69} **39.** no **55.** 30 mi **57.** 7.5 mi **61.** 33.5, 33.5, none, 3 **63.** $\frac{52}{9}$, 5, 5, 11

Lesson 5-3   pp. 249–252

EXERCISES 1. C **3.** B
5–7. Tables may vary. Samples are given.

5.

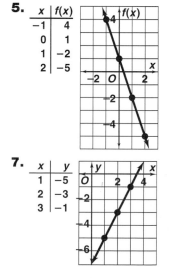

x	f(x)
−1	4
0	1
1	−2
2	−5

7.

x	y
1	−5
2	−3
3	−1

13a. $M = 3.5\,h$
d. (Answers may vary. Sample is given.) about 8.5 h

15.

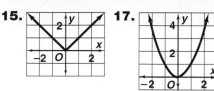

17.

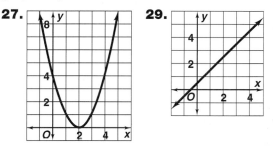

25. Answers may vary. Sample: Make a table to find values for $f(x)$ when $x = -2$, 0, and 2. Then graph the ordered pairs $(x, f(x))$ and join the graphed points with a line.

27.

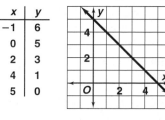

29.

41a. $.71 **b.** about 12 min **43.** B **53.** {−5, 1, 11.5} **55.** {−6.5, 4, 10} **63.** No sol.; $9 = 10 - 1$ and $|b|$ cannot be −1. **65.** −7, 7 **71.** 48 km **73.** 100.8 km

---

Technology   p. 253

EXERCISES 1. {−9, 6, 15, 27} **3.** $y = 3$, $x = 1.5$ **5.** $y = 2.16$, $x = -1.8$

Lesson 5-4   pp. 256–259

EXERCISES 1. B **3.** C **11.** $d(n) = 45n$ **13.** $e(n) = 6.37n$ **17a.** $f(x) = 0.19x$ **b.** $1.52 **19.** $f(x) = 1000x$ **21a.** $C(a) = 10a + 1$ **b.** $31 **c.** 61; the total cost of 12 books
25–27. Tables may vary. Samples are given.

25.

x	f(x)
−2	−1
0	0
2	1
4	2

$f(x) = \frac{1}{2}x$

27.

x	y
−1	3
0	2
1	1
2	0
3	−1

$y = -x + 2$

43. Tables may vary. Sample is given.

x	y
−1	6
0	5
2	3
4	1
5	0

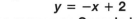

49. 2%; increase
51. 83%; decrease

Lesson 5-5   pp. 264–267

EXERCISES 1. no **3.** yes; −2 **11.** $y = \frac{1}{5}x$ **13.** $y = \frac{9}{5}x$ **23.** Choices of variables may vary.

$E(h) = 7.10h$ **25.** no **27a.** $\frac{50}{20}$ or $\frac{5}{2}$ **b.** $\frac{50}{20} = \frac{130}{x}$, 52 lb
29. $y = \frac{1}{6}x$ **31.** $y = -\frac{36}{25}x$ **33.** $y = 9x$
41.

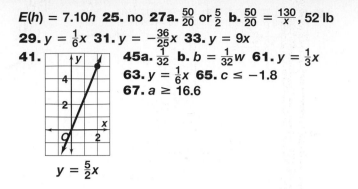

$y = \frac{5}{2}x$

45a. $\frac{1}{32}$ **b.** $b = \frac{1}{32}w$ **61.** $y = \frac{1}{3}x$
63. $y = \frac{1}{6}x$ **65.** $c \le -1.8$
67. $a \ge 16.6$

Lesson 5-6   pp. 270–272

EXERCISES 1. "Add 2 to the previous term"; 12, 14. **3.** "Add 2 to the first term, 3 to the second term and continue, adding 1 more each time"; 18, 24. **13.** 3 **15.** −11 **23.** −3, 15, 39 **25.** 17, 44, 80 **35.** $3\frac{1}{4}$, $3\frac{1}{2}$ **37.** $\frac{4}{27}$, $\frac{4}{81}$ **47.** \$4500, \$4350, \$4200, \$4050, \$3900; the balance after 4 payments **49.** No; there is no common difference. **51.** No; there is no common difference. **57.** 4.5, −4.5, −22.5 **59.** 1, $2\frac{3}{5}$, $5\frac{4}{5}$ **63.** value of new term = value of previous term + 6 **65.** value of new term = value of previous term − 2.5 **83.** $y = 24x$ **85.** $y = 0.14x$ **91.** {−19, −3, 9} **93.** {2, 4, 10}

Chapter Review

1. C **2.** D **3.** A **4.** E **5.** B **6.** G **7.** F
8. Answers may vary. Sample: A computer rental costs \$2.50/h. If you start with a fixed amount of money, the longer you work on the computer, the less money you will have left.
9. Answers may vary. Sample: A residential thermostat senses when the temperature in the room falls below the set level. The heater is turned on until the temperature is 3°F above the set level. The heater is then turned off. The graph shows the air temperature rising while the heater is working, and falling after the heater is turned off.
10. Answers may vary. Sample: An elevator is on the second floor. Someone gets in, goes to the 11th floor, and gets off.
11–14. Answers may vary. Samples are given.
11.

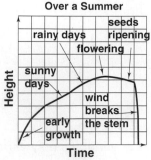

Height of a Sunflower Over a Summer

12.

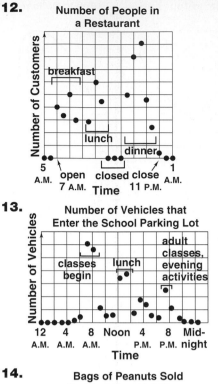

Number of People in a Restaurant

13.

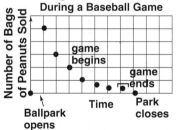

Number of Vehicles that Enter the School Parking Lot

14.

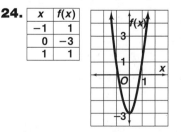

Bags of Peanuts Sold During a Baseball Game

15. {−23, −7, −3, 13} **16.** {1, 3, 3.5, 5.5}
17. {1, 2, 17, 26} **18.** {−10, 2, 5, 17} **19.** no
20. yes **21.** yes **22.** no **23.** A relation is a function when each value of the domain corresponds to exactly one value of the range.
24–27. Tables may vary. Samples are given.
24.

x	f(x)
−1	1
0	−3
1	1

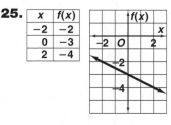

25.

x	f(x)
−2	−2
0	−3
2	−4

26.

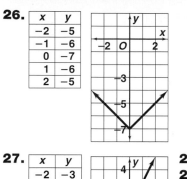

x	y
-2	-5
-1	-6
0	-7
1	-6
2	-5

27.

x	y
-2	-3
-1	-1
0	1
1	3

28. $f(x) = x + 1$
29. $f(x) = -x$
30. $f(x) = x + 3.5$
31. $S(r) = 0.1r$
32. $c = 27 + 0.2b$
33. yes; -3 **34.** no
35. no **36.** yes; $\frac{2}{5}$

37. $y = \frac{1}{5}x$ **38.** $y = x$ **39.** $y = 2x$ **40.** $y = -3x$
41. yes; $y = -2x$ **42.** no **43.** yes: $y = \frac{1}{6}x$
44. 68.4 kg **45.** 132.5 lb **46.** "Add -9 to the previous term"; 63, 54, 45. **47.** "Add 3 to the previous term"; 17, 20, 23. **48.** "Add 11 to the previous term"; 56, 67, 78. **49.** $-\frac{1}{2}$; 7, $6\frac{1}{2}$, 6
50. -2; -4, -6, -8 **51.** 13; 53, 66, 79
52. 3, 13, 17 **53.** 10, 25, 31 **54.** 4.5, 12, 15
55. -2, -17, -23 **56.** yes; 42, 49, 56 **57.** no

Chapter 6

Lesson 6-1 pp. 282–289

EXERCISES 1. 3; the temperature increases 3°F each hour. **3.** $-\frac{1}{15}$ gal/mi **7.** $\frac{1}{2}$ **9.** $\frac{2}{3}$ **11.** 2 **13.** $-\frac{3}{2}$
23. undefined **25.** undefined **27.** $\frac{9}{10}$ in./month
29. 30 mi/hr **31.** $\frac{1}{6}$ **33.** -20

37.

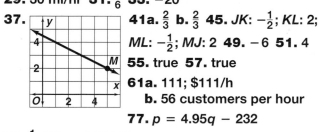

41a. $\frac{2}{3}$ **b.** $\frac{2}{3}$ **45.** JK: $-\frac{1}{2}$; KL: 2;
ML: $-\frac{1}{2}$; MJ: 2 **49.** -6 **51.** 4
55. true **57.** true
61a. 111; $111/h
    b. 56 customers per hour
77. $p = 4.95q - 232$

79. $\frac{1}{2}$ **83.** -4 **85.** 7

Technology p. 290

1a. $y = 2x + 1$ **b.** $y = \frac{1}{2}x + 1$ **3.** Answers may vary. Sample: Changing m affects the slope of the graph. **5.** (0, 1); (0, -2); (0, 2)

Lesson 6-2 pp. 294–296

EXERCISES 1. -2; 1 **3.** 1; $-\frac{5}{4}$ **11.** $y = 3x + \frac{2}{9}$
13. $y = 1$ **23.** $y = \frac{3}{4}x + 2$ **25.** $y = \frac{1}{2}x + \frac{1}{2}$

29.

$y = \frac{2}{3}x - 1$

31.

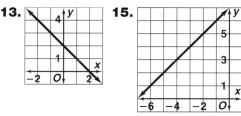

$y = 2x + 5$

41. -3; 2
43. 9; $\frac{1}{2}$

51. **53.**

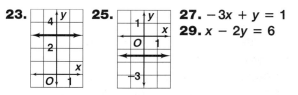

$y = -2x$ $y = 5x - 6$

59. no **61.** no **63.** I
65a. $d = 7p$
b. 84 dog years
69. $y = 2x - 1$
71. $y = -\frac{1}{2}x + 8$
87. $-\frac{9}{7}$ **89.** $\frac{9}{2}$

91. 4.8 billion

Lesson 6-3 pp. 301–303

EXERCISES 1. 18; 9 **3.** -6; 30 **11.** C

13. **15.**

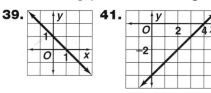

19. horizontal **21.** horizontal

23. **25.**

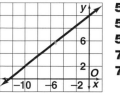

27. $-3x + y = 1$
29. $x - 2y = 6$

37a. Answers may vary. Sample: x = time walking; y = time running **b.** $3x + 8y = 15$

39. **41.**

47a. $3x + 7y = 28$
49. $y = \frac{4}{5}x + 10$

51. $y = -\frac{4}{5}x - 3$
57. $-3x$ instead of $3x$
59. $y = -2$ **61.** $x = -2$
71. no **73.** $\frac{1}{36}$ **75.** 4
77. -0.5

EXERCISES 1. 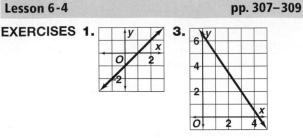 **3.**

11. $y - 2 = -\frac{5}{3}(x - 4)$ **13.** $y + 7 = -\frac{3}{2}(x + 2)$
9–21. Answers may vary for the point indicated by the equation. **19.** $y = 1(x + 1); y = x + 1$
21. $y + 2 = -\frac{6}{5}(x - 4); y = -\frac{6}{5}x + \frac{14}{5}$ **31.** Yes; answers may vary. Sample: $y - 9 = -2(x + 4)$
33. no **35.** no **37–39.** Answers may vary for point indicated by the equation. **37.** $y + 3 = \frac{2}{5}(x - 1)$ **39.** $y - 4 = \frac{3}{2}(x - 1); -3x + 2y = 5$
55. $y = -2.6x + 315.6$ **57.** y-intercept changes

71. **73.**

77. $\frac{2}{6}; \frac{3}{2}; \frac{11}{6}$ **79.** $-0.05; -3.35; -3.4$

EXERCISES 1. $\frac{1}{2}$ **3.** 1 **7.** no, different slopes
9. yes, same slopes and different y-intercepts
13. $y = 6x$ **15.** $y = -2x - 1$ **19.** $-\frac{1}{2}$ **21.** $-\frac{5}{7}$
25. $y = -\frac{1}{2}x$ **27.** $y = 3x - 10$ **31.** $y = \frac{5}{4}x + 1$
33. parallel **35.** neither **43.** $y = -\frac{4}{5}x - \frac{19}{5}$;
$y = -\frac{4}{5}x + \frac{3}{5}$ **45.** $y = -\frac{1}{2}x; y = 2x$ **49.** about $\frac{5}{4}$
51. Answers may vary. Sample: $\frac{5}{4} \cdot \left(-\frac{1}{2}\right) \neq -1$
55. No; the slopes are not neg. reciprocals.
57. False; the product of two positive numbers can't be -1. **61.** The slope of $\overleftrightarrow{JK}$ is $\frac{1}{5}$. The slope of $\overleftrightarrow{KL}$ is -2. The slope of $\overleftrightarrow{LM}$ is $\frac{1}{6}$. The slope of $\overleftrightarrow{JM}$ is -4. The quadrilateral is not a parallelogram.
81. $y = -4x - 8$ **83.** $y + 9 = -\frac{2}{3}(x + 1)$
87. $-9; -17; -25$ **89.** yes **91.** yes

EXERCISES 1–3. Trend lines may vary. Samples are given. **1.** $y - 52.5 = 2(x - 91)$
3. $y - 16.4 = 0.64(x - 69.9)$
7. $y = -1.06x + 92.31; -0.9701709306$
9. $y = -2.29x + 613.93; -0.8108238756$

13a.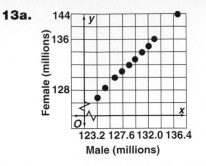

b. Answers may vary. Sample: $y = 0.9386x + 13,790$ **c.** 143,800,000 **d.** Answers may vary. Sample: No, the year is too far in the future.
17. $y = 0.37x - 28.66; \$12.04$ billion
19a. $(2, 3)$ and $(6, 6); y = 0.75x + 1.5$
b. $y = 0.75x + 1.21$ **25.** $y - 5 = -x$
27. $y + 4 = -\frac{1}{2}(x - 3)$ **31.** $x < 5$ **33.** $x \leq -5$

EXERCISES 1. Answers may vary. Sample: same shape, shifted 3 units up **3.** Answers may vary. Sample: same shape, shifted 7 units down

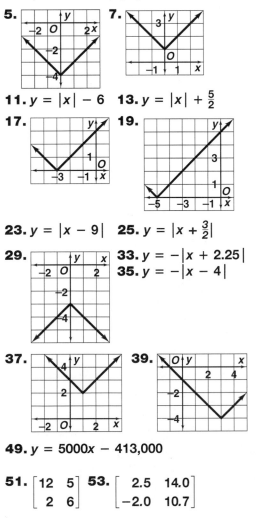

5. **7.**

11. $y = |x| - 6$ **13.** $y = |x| + \frac{5}{2}$
17. **19.**

23. $y = |x - 9|$ **25.** $y = |x + \frac{3}{2}|$
29. **33.** $y = -|x + 2.25|$
35. $y = -|x - 4|$

37. **39.**

49. $y = 5000x - 413,000$

51. $\begin{bmatrix} 12 & 5 \\ 2 & 6 \end{bmatrix}$ **53.** $\begin{bmatrix} 2.5 & 14.0 \\ -2.0 & 10.7 \end{bmatrix}$

1. perpendicular lines **2.** parallel lines
3. translation **4.** slope **5.** *y*-intercept **6.** 8 oz/mo
7. 3.375 in./wk **8.** 5; the speed is 5 mi/h. **9.** −1.25;
gasoline decreases 1.25 gal for each hour of
driving time. **10.** 150; the height is at a
constant level of 150 ft. **11.** $\frac{1}{4}$ **12.** undefined **13.** 1

14. $y = -3$ **15.** $y = -7x + \frac{1}{2}$

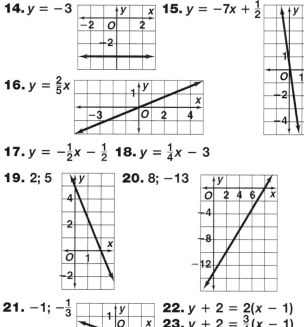

16. $y = \frac{2}{5}x$

17. $y = -\frac{1}{2}x - \frac{1}{2}$ **18.** $y = \frac{1}{4}x - 3$

19. 2; 5 **20.** 8; −13

21. $-1; -\frac{1}{3}$ **22.** $y + 2 = 2(x - 1)$
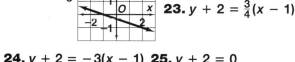 **23.** $y + 2 = \frac{3}{4}(x - 1)$

24. $y + 2 = -3(x - 1)$ **25.** $y + 2 = 0$
26. $y - 3 = \frac{1}{3}(x - 4)$ or $y - 1 = \frac{1}{3}(x + 2)$
27. $y + 4 = -\frac{6}{5}(x - 5)$ or $y - 2 = -\frac{6}{5}x$
28. $y = \frac{1}{2}(x + 1)$ or $y + 1 = \frac{1}{2}(x + 3)$
29a. $p = 0.25s + 75$

b. **c.** $275 **d.** 75; weekly salary
when no sales are made
30. $y + 1 = 5(x - 2)$ or
$y = 5x - 11$ **31.** $y - 5 = \frac{1}{3}(x - 3)$ or $y = \frac{1}{3}x + 4$

32. $y + 5 = 9x$ or $y = 9x - 5$
33. $y - 10 = -\frac{1}{8}(x - 4)$ or $y = -\frac{1}{8}x + 10\frac{1}{2}$
34a. Answers may vary. Sample: $y = 1.28x - 60.2$
b. For sample in (a): 80.6 lb/person

35. **36.** **37.** B **38.** D

39. C **40.** A

Chapter 7

EXERCISES 1. Yes, (−1, 5) makes both equations
true. **3.** Yes, (−1, 5) makes both equations true.

5. (0, 2); 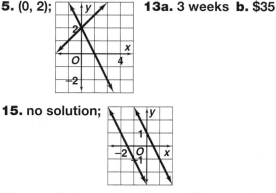 **13a.** 3 weeks **b.** $35

15. no solution;

19. no solution; same slope, different *y*-int.
21. one solution; different slopes **23.** A

25. (20, 60); 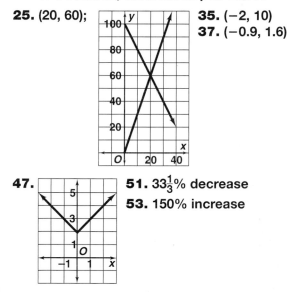 **35.** (−2, 10)
37. (−0.9, 1.6)

47. 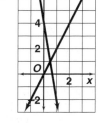 **51.** $33\frac{1}{3}$% decrease
53. 150% increase

EXERCISES 1. D **3.** B **5–13.** Coordinates given
in alphabetical order. **5.** (9, 28) **7.** $\left(6\frac{1}{3}, -\frac{1}{3}\right)$
11. (2, 0) **13.** (6, −2) **17.** 4 cm by 13 cm
19. (15, 15) **21.** (−4, 4) **23.** 80 acres flax,
160 acres sunflowers
25. estimate: $\left(\frac{1}{2}, 1\right)$; ; $\left(\frac{1}{2}, 1\right)$

35. (2, 4) **37.** (2, −4)

51. (12, 10);

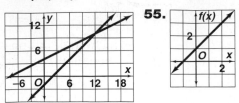

55.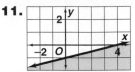

Lesson 7-3   pp. 356–359

EXERCISES 1. (1, 3) **3.** (5, −17) **7a.** $x + y = 20$, $x − y = 4$ **b.** 12 and 8 **9.** (−5, 1) **11.** $\left(-2, -\frac{5}{2}\right)$
15a. $30w + \ell = 17.65$, $20w + 3\ell = 25.65$
b. \$.39 for a wallet size, \$5.95 for an 8 × 10
17. (−1, −3) **19.** (2, −2) **23–25.** Choice of method may vary. Samples are given. **23.** (−1, −2); substitution; both solved for y **25.** (10, 2); substitution; one eq. solved for x **33.** (10, −6)
35. (−15, −1) **39.** 9 **51.** (6, 26) **53.** (9, −5) **55.** $\frac{2}{9}$
57. 71 **59.** −44

Technology   pp. 360–361

1. [77] **3.** $\begin{bmatrix} 624 & -2008 \\ 1442 & -512 \\ 125 & -1297 \end{bmatrix}$ **5.** (5.6, 1.3)

7. (9.8, −36.6)

Lesson 7-4   pp. 365–368

EXERCISES 1a. $4a + 5b = 6.71$
b. $5a + 3b = 7.12$ **c.** pen: \$1.19, pencil: \$.39

3a.

a	b	24
$0.04a$	$0.08b$	$0.05(24)$

b. $a + b = 24$; $0.04a + 0.08b = 1.2$ **c.** 18 kg A, 6 kg B **5.** 600 games **7a.** $s + c = 2.75$
b. $s − c = 1.5$ **c.** 2.125 mi/h **d.** 0.625 mi/h
9–11. Answers may vary. Samples are given.
9. Substitution; one eq. is solved for t.
11. Elimination; subtract to eliminate m.
15a. $t = 99 − 3.5m$; $t = 0 + 2.5m$; $t = 41.25°$, $m = 16.5$ min **b.** After 16.5 min, the temp. of either piece will be 41.25°C. **19a.** 42 mi/h
b. 12mi/h **29.** (4, 1) **31.** $\left(3, \frac{3}{2}\right)$ **33.** 1 **35.** −2
39. $−8 < n \le 3$

Lesson 7-5   pp. 373–376

EXERCISES 1. no **3.** yes **7.** A **9.** B
11.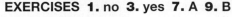

19. $y \le \frac{2}{3}x − \frac{7}{3}$;   **21.** $y \le \frac{2}{3}x − \frac{8}{3}$;

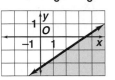

23a. $3x + 5y \le 48$

b. 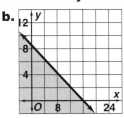   **c.** Answers may vary. Sample: 8 blue and 4 gold, 2 blue and 8 gold, 12 blue and 2 gold **d.** No; you cannot buy −2 rolls of paper.

25. 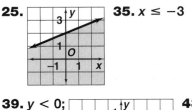   **35.** $x \le −3$

39. $y < 0$; 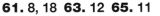   **43.** $y < x + 2$
55. about 775 games
57. 5 **59.** 11

61. 8, 18 **63.** 12 **65.** 11

Lesson 7-6   pp. 380–384

EXERCISES 1. no **3.** no **5.**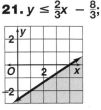

17. $y \ge -\frac{1}{2}x − 2$ and $y \le \frac{1}{2}x + 2$

19. $y \le -\frac{2}{3}x − 4$ and $y \ge \frac{1}{5}x − 3$
21.

23. $x + y \ge 50$, $4x + 3y \le 180$

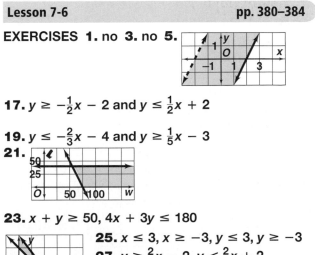

25. $x \le 3$, $x \ge −3$, $y \le 3$, $y \ge −3$
27. $y \ge \frac{2}{3}x − 2$, $y < \frac{2}{3}x + 2$
31a. triangle **b.** (2, 2), (−4, −1), (−4, 2) **c.** 9 units^2

35a. $x \geq 1$, $10.99x + 4.99y \leq 45$

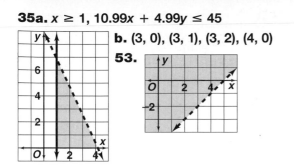

b. (3, 0), (3, 1), (3, 2), (4, 0)

53.

59. $\frac{5}{2}$ **61.** -8 **63.** $-\frac{1}{5}$ **65.** $\frac{10}{9}$ **69.** $f(x) = x + 6$

Technology   p. 385

1.

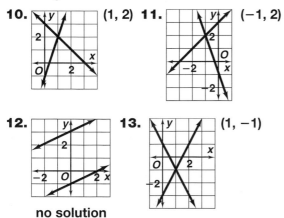

Chapter Review   pp. 387–389

1. elimination **2.** solution of the system of linear equations **3.** system of linear inequalities **4.** solution of the inequality **5.** substitution **6.** A **7.** No; (2, 5) only satisfies one equation. **8.** Infinitely many; the equations are equivalent. **9.** Answers may vary. Sample: systems with noninteger solutions

10. (1, 2) **11.** (−1, 2)

12. **13.** (1, −1)

no solution

14. (−2, 5) **15.** $\left(-4\frac{1}{2}, -6\right)$ **16.** $\left(-1\frac{1}{9}, -\frac{5}{9}\right)$ **17.** (2, 2)

18. Answers may vary. Sample: There is no solution when you get a false equation such as $0 = 2$. There are infinitely many solutions when you get a true equation such as $5 = 5$.

19a. $x + y = 24$, $4x + 5y = 100$ **b.** (20, 4) **c.** 20 4-point, 4 5-point **20.** (−6, 23) **21.** (1, −1) **22.** (6, 4) **23.** $\left(5\frac{5}{11}, 1\frac{7}{11}\right)$ **24.** $x + y = 34$, $2x + 4y = 110$; 13 chickens and 21 cows **25.** $10\frac{2}{3}$ fl oz **26.** 63° and 27° **27.** 18 ft by 39 ft

28. $1.29 **29.** 154 km/h

30. **31.**

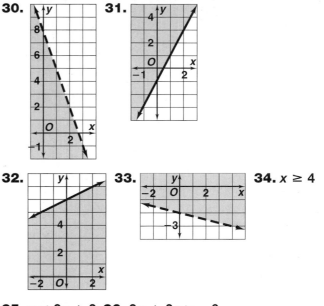

32. **33.** **34.** $x \geq 4$

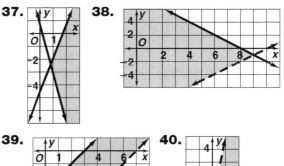

35. $y \leq 3x + 3$ **36.** $2x + 3y \geq -6$

37. **38.**

39. **40.**

41. $y \leq 3$, $y > x$ **42.** $y > -2x + 2$, $y > \frac{4}{5}x - 4$
43. $x > -1$, $y \leq x + 5$ **44.** $y \leq -\frac{2}{3}x + 3$,
$y \geq -\frac{1}{2}x - 1$ **45.** Answers may vary.
Sample: $x \geq -1$, $y \leq 5$, $x \leq 5$, $x + y \leq 7$, $y \geq -1$

Chapter 8

Lesson 8-1   p. 397–399

EXERCISES 1. -1 **3.** $\frac{1}{25}$ **13.** -2 **15.** 0; -3
17. $3a$ **19.** x^7 **33.** $\frac{1}{25}$ **35.** $-\frac{1}{9}$ **45a.** $20.48; $.32
b. No; the value of the allowance rapidly becomes very great. **47.** pos. **51.** 10^{-1} **53.** 10^{-3}
57. 0.000001 **59.** 0.03 **61a.** $5^{-2}, 5^{-1}, 5^0, 5^1, 5^2$
b. 5^4 **c.** $\frac{a^n}{1}$ **63.** 45 **65.** 40 **69.** $\frac{2}{9}$ **71.** $\frac{1}{16}$

73.

a	4	$\frac{1}{3}$	6	$\frac{7}{8}$	2
a^{-1}	$\frac{1}{4}$	3	$\frac{1}{6}$	$\frac{8}{7}$	0.5

75. A, B, D

77. No; $3x^{-2} \cdot 3x^2 = 9 \cdot x^0 = 9$. The product of reciprocals should be 1. **79a.** 1 correct, 0.4096; 2 correct, 0.1536; 3 correct, 0.0256; 4 correct, 0.0016 **b.** 0 or 1 **95.** 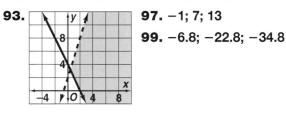 **99.** $y = 5x - 2$ **101.** $y = -\frac{3}{11}x - 17$

Lesson 8-2   pp. 402–404

EXERCISES 1. No; $55 > 10$. **3.** No; $0.9 < 1$. **34.** 5400 **36.** 1×10^1 **53.** 4 **55.** $\frac{2}{3}$

58.

Lesson 8-3   pp. 407–410

EXERCISES 1. 2^{10} or 1024 **3.** 1 **7.** c^5 **9.** $\frac{10}{t^7}$ **17.** $45x^7y^6$ **19.** $x^{10}y^2$ **23.** 6×10^9 **25.** 3.4×10^{-5} **29.** 1.08×10^{21} dollars **31.** 9 **33.** -3 **41.** $4x^4$ **43.** $4c^4$ **45.** $12a^7$ **47.** $3^4 \cdot 2^2$ **49.** 8.0×10^5 **51.** 1.2×10^{-4} **59.** 7.65×10^{14} **61.** 7.039305×10^{-7} **63.** about 6.7×10^{33} molecules **65.** x^3 **67.** $5c^3$ **85.** 1.28×10^6 **87.** 9.0×10^{-5}

93.   **97.** -1; 7; 13

99. -6.8; -22.8; -34.8

Lesson 8-4   pp. 413–415

EXERCISES 1. c^{10} **7.** $\frac{1}{t^{14}}$ **9.** $625y^4$ **11.** $49a^2$ **17.** x^{16} **19.** 1 **23.** 1.6×10^{11} **25.** 8×10^{-30} **31.** 8.57375×10^{-10} m^3 **33.** -4 **35.** -3 **41.** The student who wrote $x^5 + x^5 = 2x^5$ is correct; x^5 times x^5 is x^{10}. **43.** $243x^3$ **45.** $30x^2$ **51a.** $24x^2$; $96x^2$ **b.** 4 times **c.** $8x^3$; $64x^3$ **d.** 8 times **53.** $(ab)^5$ **55.** $(2xy)^2$ **59a.** about 5.15×10^{14} m^2 **b.** about 3.60×10^{14} m^2 **c.** about 1.37×10^{18} m^3 **75.** a^8b^3 **77.** $-4t^5$ **79.** $\left(4\frac{2}{3}, 1\frac{1}{3}\right)$ **81.** $(-9, -5)$ **83.** 6 **85.** $-\frac{9}{11}$

Lesson 8-5   pp. 420–422

EXERCISES 1. 7 **3.** -3 **5.** $\frac{1}{4}$ **7.** $\frac{1}{c^3}$ **13.** 5×10^7 **15.** 6×10^2 **19a.** 3.86×10^{11} h; 2.65×10^8 people

---

b. about 1457 h **c.** about 4.0 h **21.** $\frac{9}{25}$ **23.** $\frac{32x^5}{y^5}$ **29.** $\frac{3}{2}$ **31.** $\frac{9}{4}$ **37.** 5^3 simplifies to 125. **39.** Each term should be raised to the 4th power and simplified. **43.** $\frac{1}{16m^{12}}$ **45.** a^6 **53.** $\frac{a^5c^5}{b^3}$ **55.** 5 **63a.** The student treated $\frac{5^4}{5}$ as $\left(\frac{5}{5}\right)^4$. **b.** 125 **65.** $\left(\frac{m}{n}\right)^7$ **67.** 10^{10} **75.** dividing powers with the same base, def. of neg. exponent **77.** mult. powers with the same base **91.** $27y^6$ **93.** $\frac{t^{20}}{r^8}$ **99.** $(0, 0)$ 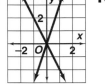 **101.** $(3, 5)$

Lesson 8-6   pp. 427–429

EXERCISES 1. 4 **3.** 0.1 **7.** 40, 80, 160 **9.** 20.25, 30,375, 45.5625 **13.** geometric **15.** geometric **19.** 5; 135; 10,935 **21.** 5; -135; $-10,935$ **25.** $A(n) = 6 \cdot 0.5^{n-1}$; 0.375 **27.** $A(n) = 7 \cdot (1.1)^{n-1}$; 9.317 **29a.** $A(n) = 100 \cdot (0.64)^{n-1}$ **b.** about 10.74 cm **31.** 1, 0.2, 0.04; $A(n) = 625 \cdot (0.2)^{n-1}$ **33.** 1, -0.5, 0.25; $A(n) = 16 \cdot (-0.5)^{n-1}$ **37.** arithmetic; 3, 1, -1 **39.** geometric; 1.125, 0.5625, 0.28125 **41a.** $A(n) = 36 \cdot (0.9)^{n-1}$ **b.** 6; $n = 1$ corresponds to the first swing, because $A(1) = 36$. **c.** 21.3 cm **55.** a^4 **57.** $\frac{1}{x^{10}z^{20}}$ **63.** 2.467×10^{-3} **65.** $y = \frac{8}{3}x$ **67.** $y = -\frac{7}{6}x$

Lesson 8-7   pp. 432–435

EXERCISES 1. 216 **3.** 2.5 **9.** \$160,000; \$320,000 **11.** \$16,000, \$32,000 **13.** C **15.** B **17.** C

19.   **21.**

25. 0.04, 0.2, 1, 5, 25, 125; increase **27.** 100, 10, 1, 0.1, 0.01, 0.001; decrease

37a.

x	y
1	-2
2	4
3	-8
4	16
5	-32

39. $f(t) = 200 \cdot t^2$ **41.** $f(x) = 100x^2$ **57.** -3; 567, -1701, 5103 **59.** $-\frac{1}{3}; \frac{1}{3}, -\frac{1}{9}, \frac{1}{27}$ **63.** $y = 3x + 1$ **65.** $y = 0.4x - 3.8$

Technology p. 436

1a. $y = 26.87(0.83)^x$
b.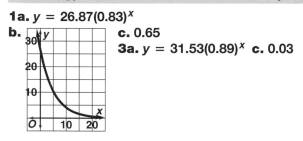
c. 0.65
3a. $y = 31.53(0.89)^x$ **c.** 0.03

Lesson 8-8 pp. 441–446

EXERCISES 1. 20; 2 **3.** 10,000; 1.01 **7.** 1.05
9. 1.0875 **11.** 0.75%, 0.25% **13.** 1.125%; 0.375%
17. $16,661.35 **19.** $28,338.18 **21a.** 3 half-lives
b. 3.125 mCi **23.** 0.1 **25.** 0.9 **27.** exp. decay
29. exp. decay **31.** $y = 130,000 \cdot (1.01)^x$; about
142,179 people **33.** $y = 2400 \cdot (1.07)^x$; $4721.16
35a. $y = 584 \cdot (1.065)^x$; $2057.81 **37.** Neither; it is
not just one straight line. **39.** Neither; it
decreases and and then increases, unlike an
exponential function.
41. exponential function

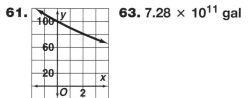

45. 4 half-lives
47a. $y = 6,284,000 \cdot (1.01)^x$
b. 7,667,674 people **49.** 88%
51. 46.1%

61. **63.** 7.28×10^{11} gal

Chapter Review

1. exponential growth **2.** growth factor
3. Scientific notation **4.** exponential decay
5. decay factor **6.** Compound interest
7. common ratio **8.** interest period **9.** geometric
sequence **10.** exponential function **11.** $\frac{d^6}{b^4}$ **12.** $\frac{y^8}{x^2}$
13. $\frac{7h^3}{k^8}$ **14.** $\frac{q^4}{p^2}$ **15.** $\frac{625}{16}$ or $39\frac{1}{16}$ **16.** $-\frac{1}{8}$ **17.** $-\frac{1}{8}$
18. $\frac{1}{49y^4}$ **19.** $\frac{9x^2}{w^4y^7}$ **20.** 36 **21.** $\frac{4}{9}$ **22.** $\frac{9}{8}$ or $1\frac{1}{8}$ **23.** 1
24. 108 **25.** C **26.** No; for values other than 0,
$(-3b)^4 = 81b^4 \neq -12b^4$. **27.** No; 950 > 10.
28. No; 72.35 > 10. **29.** yes **30.** No; 0.84 < 1.
31. 2.793×10^6 mi **32.** 1.89×10^8 cars and
trucks **33.** $2d^5$ **34.** $q^{12}r^4$ **35.** $-20c^4m^2$ **36.** 1.34^2
or 1.7956 **37.** $\frac{243x^2y^{14}}{64}$ **38.** $-\frac{4}{3r^{10}z^8}$

39. about 7.8×10^3 pores **40.** Answers may
vary. Sample: Simplify $(2a^{-2})^{-2}(-3a)^2$; $\frac{9a^6}{4}$.
41. $\frac{1}{w^3}$ **42.** $\frac{1}{64}$ **43.** $7x^2$ **44.** $\frac{n^{35}}{v^{21}}$ **45.** $\frac{c^3}{e^{11}}$
46. 2×10^{-3} **47.** 2.5×10^1 **48.** 5×10^{-5}
49. 3×10^3 **50.** Answers may vary. Sample:
Simplify and use div. prop: $\left(\frac{a^2}{2}\right)^{-3}$; use raising a
quot. to a power prop.: $\frac{a^{-6}}{2^{-3}}$; use the def. of neg.
exp.: $\frac{2^3}{a^6}$ or $\frac{8}{a^6}$ **51.** 0.1 **52.** 3 **53.** $-\frac{1}{2}$
54. geometric; $\frac{25}{4}, \frac{25}{16}, \frac{25}{64}$ **55.** neither; $-30, -25,$
-19 **56.** arithmetic; 42, 49, 56 **57.** 6, 12, 24, 48
58. 7.5, 5.625, 4.21875 **59a.** 2430 bacteria
b. about 180 min **60.** $a = 100$, $b = 1.025$
61. $a = 32$, $b = 0.75$ **62.** $a = 0.4$, $b = 2$
63. growth; 3 **64.** growth; 1.5 **65.** decay; 0.32
66. decay; $\frac{1}{4}$

67. **68.** **69.** **70.**

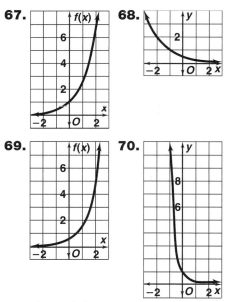

71. about 8.2 mg

Chapter 9

Lesson 9-1 pp. 459–461

EXERCISES 1. 1 **3.** 0 **9.** quadratic trinomial
11. cubic trinomial **15.** $-3x^2 + 4x$; quadratic
binomial **17.** $c^2 + 4c - 2$; quadratic trinomial
21. $8m^2 + 15$ **23.** $8w^2 - 3w + 4$ **29.** $b + 1$
31. $7n^4 + n^3$ **35.** $18y^2 + 5y$ **37.** $-7z^3 + 6z^2 +$
$2z - 5$ **39.** $28c - 16$ **43.** $-x^4 + x^3 + 15x$
45. $-h^{10} - 5h^9 + 8h^5 + 2h^4$ **49.** $5x + 18$
51. No; both terms of a binomial cannot be
constants. **63.** 2 **65.** 5 **67.** exponential growth
69. exponential growth **71.** 7^{18} **73.** $36x^5$
79. $y = |x| + 5$ **81.** $y = |x| - 12$

Lesson 9-2   pp. 463–465

EXERCISES 1. $8m^2 + 48m$ **3.** $63k^2 + 36k$ **13.** 3
15. 12 **19.** $2(3x - 2)$ **21.** $5(2x^3 - 5x^2 + 4)$
25. Karla; Kevin multiplied $-2x$ by 3 instead of -3.
27. $-12a^3 + 15a^2 - 27a$ **29.** $-60c^3 + 36c^2 - 48c$
33a. $A = 16\pi x^2 - 4x^2$ **b.** $A = 4x^2(4\pi - 1)$
35. $24x(x^2 - 4x + 2)$ **37.** $x^2(5x^2 + 4x + 3)$
51. $-3x^2 + 10$ **53.** $5g^2 - g$ **57.** $\frac{1}{5}$ **59.** $-\frac{1}{8}$
65. (3, 2) **67.** (1, 6)

Lesson 9-3   pp. 469–472

EXERCISES 1. 30 **3.** 7 **5.** $x^2 + 7x + 10$
7. $k^2 + k - 42$ **11.** $r^2 + 2r - 24$ **13.** $x^2 - x - 42$
21. $-2x^2 + 5x + 48$ **23.** $a^3 - 6a^2 + 9a - 4$
25. $3k^3 + 19k^2 - 33k + 56$ **27.** $2t^3 - 17t^2 +$
$36t - 15$ **29.** $48w^3 - 28w^2 - 2w + 2$ **31.** $p^2 +$
$p - 56$ **33.** $25c^2 - 40c - 9$ **39a.** $2x^2 + 12x + 16$
b. $12x + 16$ **c.** 10 ft by 5 ft **43.** $1.5x^2 + 2.5x - 1$
45. $n^3 + 15n^2 + 56n$ **65.** $3c^2 - 27c$ **67.** $3y^2 - 10y$
73. $x(3x - 11)$ **75.** $n^2(9 - n)$ **81.** $\frac{1}{27}$ **83.** $\frac{1}{3w^5}$

Lesson 9-4   pp. 477–479

EXERCISES 1. $c^2 + 2c + 1$ **3.** $4v^2 + 44v + 121$
11. 9801 **13.** 91,204 **15.** $x^2 - 16$ **17.** $d^2 - 49$
21. 899 **23.** 2496 **27.** $(10x + 15)$ units^2
29. $25p^2 - 10pq + q^2$ **31.** $x^2 - 14xy + 49y^2$
45. $p^2 - 81q^2$ **47.** $49b^2 - 64c^2$ **65.** $2x^2 - 23x +$
66 **67.** $3y^2 + 4y + 1$ **73.** 8.713×10^3
75. 6.8952×10^4

Lesson 9-5   pp. 483–485

EXERCISES 1. 5 **3.** 7 **5.** $(r + 3)(r + 1)$ **7.** $(k + 3)$
$(k + 2)$ **17.** 5 **19.** 9 **21.** $(x + 4)(x - 1)$ **23.** $(y + 5) \cdot$
$(y - 4)$ **31.** B **33.** $(t + 9v)(t - 2v)$ **35.** $(p - 8q) \cdot$
$(p - 2q)$ **39–41.** Answers may vary. Samples are
given. **39.** 18; $(x - 6)(x + 3)$, 28; $(x - 7)(x + 4)$,10;
$(x - 5)(x + 2)$ **41.** 7; $(x + 4)(x + 3)$, 8; $(x + 6)(x + 2)$,
13; $(x + 12)(x + 1)$ **43.** $(k + 2)(k + 8)$ **45.** $(n - 4) \cdot$
$(n + 14)$ **55.** $4x^2 + 12x + 5$; $(2x + 1)(2x + 5)$
73. $w^2 - 12w + 36$ **75.** $4q^2 + 28q + 49$
81. 6 weeks **83a.** 81 basic players, 48 deluxe
players **b.** \$9719.19

85.
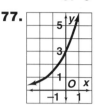

Lesson 9-6   pp. 487–489

EXERCISES 1. $(2n + 1)(n + 7)$ **3.** $(11w - 3)(w - 1)$
13. $(2t - 3)(t + 1)$ **15.** $(2q + 3)(q - 7)$
29. Answers may vary. Sample: 18; $(5m - 4) \cdot$
$(3m + 6)$, 54; $(5m - 2)(3m + 12)$, 117; $(5m - 1) \cdot$
$(3m + 24)$ **33.** $(9p + 4)(6p + 7)$ **35.** $(7x - 2) \cdot$
$(2x - 7)$ **45.** $(7p - 3q)(7p + 12q)$ **46.** $54h(2g - 1) \cdot$
$(g - 1)$ **55.** $(t - 4)(t - 3)$ **57.** $(m - 3)(m - 12)$
63. 7921 **65.** 815,409 **67.** 1599 **69.** 39,996 **71.** $\frac{1}{2}$,
4, 16 **73.** $\frac{1}{81}$, $\frac{1}{3}$, 3

77.

Lesson 9-7   pp. 493–495

EXERCISES 1. $(c + 5)^2$ **3.** $(h + 6)^2$ **7.** $(2m + 5)$
9. $(5g - 4)$ **11.** $(8r - 9)^2$ **13.** $(x + 2)(x - 2)$
23. $(7y + 2)(7y - 2)$ **25.** $(2m + 9)(2m - 9)$
31. $3(m + 2)(m - 2)$ **33.** $3(x + 8)^2$ **39.** 11, 9
41. 15, 5 **45.** $25(2v + w)(2v - w)$ **47.** $7(2c + 5d)^2$
55a. $4(x + 5)(x - 5)$ **b.** $4(x + 5)(x - 5)$
73. $(2d + 1)(d + 5)$ **75.** $(2t + 1)(2t + 7)$ **83.** 29;
37; 45; $-11 + 8n$ **85.** 0.02; 0.002; 0.0002;
$2000 \cdot \left(\frac{1}{10}\right)^n$ **91a.** $y = 11.4x + 64.8$ **b.** 93 **c.** 79

Lesson 9-8   pp. 499–501

EXERCISES 1. $2m^2$; 3 **3.** $2z^2$; -5 **5.** $(2n^2 + 1) \cdot$
$(3n + 4)$ **7.** $(3t + 1)(3t - 1)(3t + 5)$ **11.** $2(2v^2 + 1) \cdot$
$(3v - 8)$ **13.** $2(m^2 + 2)(10m - 9)$ **17.** $(6p + 5) \cdot$
$(2p + 1)$ **19.** $(6n - 1)(3n + 10)$ **27.** $5k$, $(k + 2)$, and
$(k + 4)$ **29.** $2(10t^2 - 11)(3t - 10)$ **31.** $4(3x - 7y) \cdot$
$(x + 2y)$ **35.** $(7w^2 - 4)(2w + 7)$ **37.** $2(2t^2 + 3) \cdot$
$(11t - 1)$ **39.** $2w$, $(6w + 5)$, and $(7w + 1)$
55. $(r + 3)^2$ **57.** $2(t + 3)^2$ **63.** b^4 **65.** t^{15}
71. 1.6×10^{21} **73.** 4.9×10^{-11} **79.** (1, 5) **81.** (0.5, 5)

Chapter Review   pp. 503–505

1. A **2.** D **3.** E **4.** C **5.** B **6.** $-6y^2 + 8y + 2$;
quadratic trinomial **7.** $9h^2 + 1$; quadratic
binomial **8.** $3k^5 + k$; fifth degree binomial
9. $7t^2 + 8t + 9$; quadratic trinomial **10.** x^2y^2;
fourth degree monomial **11.** $x^3 + x^2 + 5$; cubic
trinomial **12.** Answers may vary.
Sample: $3z^4 - 5z^2 + 1$; 4 **13.** $-b^5 + 2b^3 + 6$
14. $8g^4 - 5g^2 + 11g + 5$
15. $7x^3 + 8x^2 - 3x + 12$ **16.** $t^3 - 5t^2 + 12t - 8$
17. $4y^2 + 3y + 4$
18. $7w^5 - 5w^4 - 7w^3 + w^2 + 3w - 3$
19. $-40x^2 + 16x$ **20.** $35g^3 + 15g^2 - 45g$

21. $-40t^4 + 24t^3 - 32t^2$ **22.** $5m^3 + 15m^2$
23. $-6w^4 - 8w^3 + 20w^2$ **24.** $-3b^3 + 5b^2 + 10b$
25. $3x$; $3x(3x^3 + 4x^2 + 2)$
26. $4t^2$; $4t^2(t^3 - 3t + 2)$
27. $10n^3$; $10n^3(4n^2 + 7n - 3)$
28. 2; $2(k^4 + 2k^3 - 3k - 4)$ **29.** $3d$; $3d(d - 2)$
30. $2m^2$; $2m^2(5m^2 - 6m + 2)$ **31.** 5; $5(2v - 1)$
32. $4w$; $4w(3w^2 + 2w + 5)$
33. $3d^3$; $3d^3(6d^2 + 2d + 3)$ **34.** 12; if the GCF of
x and y is 3, the GCF of $4x$ and $4y$ is $4 \cdot 3$ or 12.
35. Kim; 4, m, and n are factors of both
monomials. The GCF is their product.
36. $x^2 + 8x + 15$ **37.** $15v^2 - 29v - 14$
38. $6b^2 + 11b - 10$ **39.** $-k^2 + 5k - 4$
40. $p^3 + 3p^2 + 3p + 2$ **41.** $4a^2 - 21a + 5$
42. $y^3 - 9y^2 + 18y + 8$ **43.** $3x^2 + 10x + 8$
44. $-2h^3 + 11h^2 - 6h + 5$ **45.** $q^2 - 8q + 16$
46. $4k^6 + 20k^3 + 25$ **47.** $64 - 9t^4$ **48.** $4m^4 - 25$
49. $w^2 - 16$ **50.** $16g^4 - 25h^8$ **51.** $(2x + 1)(x + 4)$;
$2x^2 + 9x + 4$ **52.** No; $(x - y)^2 = x^2 - 2xy + y^2 \neq$
$x^2 - y^2$. **53.** $(x + 2)(x + 1)$ **54.** $(y - 7)(y - 2)$
55. $(x - 5) \cdot (x + 3)$ **56.** $(2w - 3)(w + 1)$
57. $(b - 3)(b - 4)$ **58.** $(2t - 1)(t + 2)$
59. $(x + 6)(x - 1)$ **60.** $2(3x + 2)(x + 1)$
61. $(7x + 2)(3x - 4)$ **62.** $(3x - 2)(x + 1)$
63. $(15y + 1)(y + 1)$ **64.** $(15y - 1)(y - 1)$
65. $(q + 1)^2$ **66.** $(b + 4)(b - 4)$ **67.** $(x - 2)^2$
68. $(2t + 11)(2t - 11)$ **69.** $(2d - 5)^2$ **70.** $(3c + 1)^2$
71. $(3k + 5)(3k - 5)$ **72.** $(x + 3)^2$ **73.** $6(2y + 1) \cdot$
$(2y - 1)$ **74.** $\frac{1}{2}d + 1$ **75.** The factors are equal.
76. No; only the square $(5u + 6)^2$ would have
$25u^2$ and 36 as the first and last terms, however
$2(5u)(6) \neq 65u$. **77.** $4x^2$; -2 **78.** $3k^2$; -2
79. $24y^2$; -4 **80.** $10n^3$; 7 **81.** $(3x^2 + 4)(2x + 1)$
82. $5y^2(2y + 3)(2y - 3)$ **83.** $3(3g - 1)(g + 2)$
84. $(3c - d)(2c - d)$ **85.** $(11k + 1)(k + 2)$
86. $3(u + 6)(u + 1)$ **87.** $(5p + 3)(3p + 1)$
88. $3(u - 6)(u - 1)$ **89.** $(h^2 - 3)(15h + 11)$
90. $(5x + 7)(6x^2 - 1)$ **91.** $4s^2t(3s - 1)(s + 2)$
92. $(x^2 + 2)(2x + 7)$ **93.** $2p$, $(p + 5)$, and $(3p + 4)$

Chapter 10

Lesson 10-1   pp. 513–516

EXERCISES 1. (2, 5); max. **3.** (2, 1); min.
5.
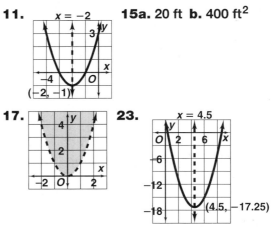
11. $f(x) = \frac{1}{3}x^2$, $f(x) = x^2$,
$f(x) = 5x^2$
13. $f(x) = -\frac{2}{3}x^2$, $f(x) = -2x^2$,
$f(x) = -4x^2$

15.
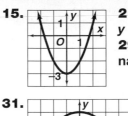
21. E **23.** F **27.** The graph of
$y = 2x^2$ is narrower.
29. The graph of $y = 1.5x^2$ is
narrower.

31.   **35.**
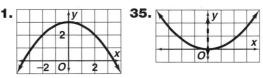

41. M **43.** M **55.** $(3a^2 - 2)(5a - 6)$
57. $(y + 2)(y - 2)(y + 3)$ **61.** $9n^2 - 63n$
63. $12m^6 - 4m^5 + 20m^2$

Lesson 10-2   pp. 520–523

EXERCISES 1. $x = 0$, (0, 4) **3.** $x = 4$, (4, −25)
5. B **7.** C

11.   **15a.** 20 ft **b.** 400 ft^2

17.   **23.** $x = 4.5$

33. Answers may vary. Sample: **33.** $y = -3x^2$
37a. \$12.50 **b.** \$10,000 **39.** 26 units^2
51. C **53.** F **57.** $c^2 - 5c - 36$ **59.** $20t^2 + 17t + 3$

Lesson 10-3   pp. 526–528

EXERCISES 1. 13 **3.** $\frac{1}{3}$ **13.** irrational
15. irrational **17.** 5 and 6 **19.** −12 and −11
21. 3.46 **23.** 107.47 **25.** 0.93 **27.** 0 **29.** $\pm\frac{3}{7}$
41. $-\frac{2}{5}$ **43.** 1.26
67.   **73.** $9t^2 - 25$ **75.** $x^2 + 26x + 169$
81. −2 **83.** $-\frac{3}{4}$

Lesson 10-4   pp. 531–534

EXERCISES

1. 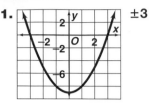 ±3

11. ±21 **13.** 0 **19.** $x^2 = 256$; 16 m **21.** $\pi r^2 = 80$;
5.0 cm **23.** none **25.** one **29.** $\pm\frac{3}{7}$ **31.** ±2.8
41. 6.3 ft **51.** 3 **53.** 40 **59.** $(x + 4)(x + 1)$
61. $(a + 5)(a - 2)$ **65.** 3.6135×10^6
67. -8.12×10^0 **69.** 701,000

Technology	p. 535

1. 10.78, 13.22 **3.** −2, 1.5 **5.** 0.28, 17.72 **7.** −12, 6

Lesson 10-5	pp. 538–540

EXERCISES 1. 3, 7 **3.** 0, −1 **7.** 1, −4 **9.** 0, 8
13. −3, −5 **15.** 0, 6 **23.** 5 **25.** base: 10 ft, height:
22 ft **27.** $2q^2 + 22q + 60 = 0$; −6, −5
29. $4y^2 + 12y + 9 = 0$; $-\frac{3}{2}$ **35.** 8 in. × 10 in.
41. 0, 4, 6 **43.** 0, 3 **57.** $x^2 = 320$; 17.9 ft
59. $(2x + 3)(x + 5)$ **61.** $(4t - 3)(t + 2)$

Lesson 10-6	pp. 544–546

EXERCISES 1. 49 **3.** 400 **7.** 4, −12 **9.** −5, −17
13. 7, −5 **15.** 11, 1 **19.** 1 **21.** $\frac{81}{100}$ **23.** 5, −1
25a. $(2x + 1)(x + 1)$ **b.** $2x^2 + 3x + 1 = 28$ **c.** 3
27. −3, −4 **29.** 6, 2 **39.** 5.16, −1.16
41. 5.6 ft by 14.2 ft **51.** −6, −5 **53.** $-\frac{8}{3}, \frac{8}{3}$
57. $(t - 11)^2$ **59.** $(4c + 3)^2$ **65.** r^{12} **67.** $-y$

Lesson 10-7	pp. 550–552

EXERCISES 1. −1, −1.5 **3.** 1.5 **11.** 10.42, 1.58
13. 1.14, −0.77 **17a.** $0 = -16t^2 + 50t + 3.5$
b. $t \approx 3.2$; 3.2 s **19.** Factoring or square roots;
the equation is easily factorable and there is no
x term. **21.** Quadratic formula; the equation
cannot be factored. **25.** 0.87, −1.54 **27.** 1.28,
−2.61 **33a.** 7 ft × 8 ft **b.** $x(x + 1) = 60$,
7.26 ft × 8.26 ft **37.** 13.44 cm and 7.44 cm
47. 1.54, 8.46 **49.** 0.06, −6.06 **51.** $(3z - 2)(z + 4)$
53. $(6v - 5)(2v + 7)$ **55.** $(5t + 3)(3t + 2)$

Lesson 10-8	pp. 556–558

EXERCISES 1. A **3.** B **5.** 1 **7.** 2 **17.** No; the
discriminant is negative. **19.** 0 **21.** 2

25a. $S = -0.75p^2 + 54p$ **b.** no **c.** $36 **31.** no
33. yes; 1, −1.25 **49.** 0.5, −1.5 **51.** 0.61, −0.27
55. $1093.81 **57.** $6104.48 **59.** arithmetic
61. arithmetic

Lesson 10-9	pp. 563–566

EXERCISES

1. 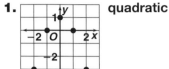 quadratic

7. quadratic; $y = 1.5x^2$ **9.** quadratic; $y = 2.8x^2$

13a. 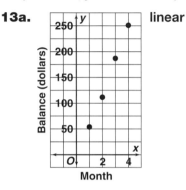 linear

b. 65, 64, 64; yes **c.** 64 **d.** $y = 64x - 5$ **15a.** 41,
123, 206 **b.** 82, 83 **c.** $d = 41t^2$ **d.** 256.25 cm
19. $y = 0.875x^2 - 0.435x + 1.515$
21. $y = 2.125x^2 - 4.145x + 2.955$
27a. quadratic **b.** $d = 13.6t^2$ **c.** 54.4 ft **35.** 0

37.

43. 0.125 **45.** $\frac{2}{27}$

Extension	p. 567

**1. Both graphs have the same shape, go through
the origin, and lie in Quadrants I and III. The
graph of** $y = x^3$ **is narrower than the graph of**
$y = \frac{1}{3}x^3$. **3. Yes; the sign of** a **changes which
quadrants the graphs are in, and the larger** $|a|$,
the narrower the graph.

5a.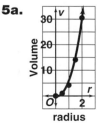

b. about 1.3 ft

1. parabola **2.** completing the square
3. principal square root **4.** vertex **5.** discriminant
6–9. Answers may vary. Samples are given.

6. $y = -2x^2$ **7.** $y = 2x^2$ **8.** $y = x^2$ **9.** $y = \frac{1}{2}x^2$

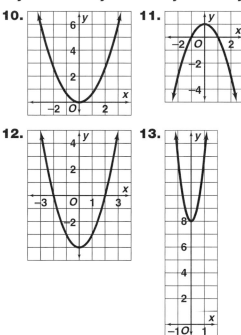

14. min. **15.** max. **16.** min. **17.** max.

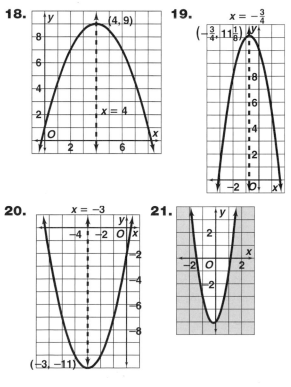

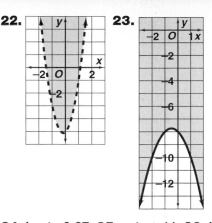

24. irrat.; 9.27 **25.** rat.; −11 **26.** irrat.; ±0.71
27. irrat.; 1.60 **28.** rat.; $-\frac{2}{5}$ **29.** irrat.; −6.86
30. rat.; 0.6 **31.** irrat.; 11.83 **32.** rat.; −1 **33.** rat.;
14 **34.** 2, −2 **35.** 5, −5 **36.** 0 **37.** no solution
38. $x^2 + 7x + 12 = 0$; −4, −3 **39.** $5x^2 - 10x = 0$;
0, 2 **40.** $x^2 - 9x + 20 = 0$; 4, 5 **41.** $x^2 + \frac{5}{2}x - \frac{3}{2} = 0$;
$-3, \frac{1}{2}$ **42.** $x^2 - \frac{5}{6}x - 1 = 0$; $-\frac{2}{3}, 1\frac{1}{2}$
43. $x^2 - 5x + 4 = 0$; 1, 4 **44.** −6.74, 0.74
45. 0.38, 2.62 **46.** −2, $-1\frac{1}{2}$ **47.** 2.3 in.
48. 10 ft × 17 ft **49.** 2 **50.** 2 **51.** 0 **52.** 1
53. −1.84, 1.09 **54.** 0.5, 3 **55.** 0.13, 7.87
56. −5.48, 5.48 **57.** −5, 5; use factoring, because
the equation is easily factorable. **58.** −4.12, 0.78;
use the quadratic formula, because the trinomial
does not factor easily. **59.** 4, 5; use factoring,
because the equation is easily factorable.
60. 3; use factoring, because the equation is
easily factorable. **61.** −15, 15; use square roots,
because the equation has no x term. **62.** −8.47,
0.47; complete the square, because the equation
is in the form $x^2 + bx = c$. **63.** 18 ft; 324 ft^2
64. 1.5 s

65. 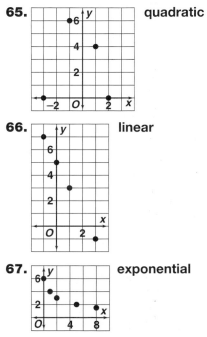 quadratic

66. linear

67. exponential

Selected Answers

68. 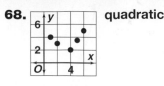 quadratic

69. $y = 5(2)^x$ **70.** $y = 3x - 2$ **71.** $y = (x + 1)^2$
72. $y = \frac{1}{2}(10^x)$

Chapter 11

Lesson 11-1 pp. 578–581

EXERCISES 1. $10\sqrt{2}$ **3.** $5\sqrt{3}$ **13.** $\frac{20}{}$ **15.** $11\sqrt{2}$
25. 3 mi **27.** 17 mi **29.** $\frac{3\sqrt{3}}{2}$ **31.** $\frac{2\sqrt{30}}{11}$ **37.** $\frac{3}{2}$
39. $-2\sqrt{5}$ **45.** $\sqrt{5}$ **47.** $\frac{2\sqrt{10n}}{5n}$ **53.** not simplest
form; radical in the denominator of a fraction
55. Simplest form; radicand has no perfect-
square factors other than 1. **57.** 30 **59.** $\frac{3\sqrt{2}}{4}$
69. $-3 \pm 3\sqrt{2}$ **71.** $\frac{2 \pm \sqrt{10}}{3}$ **85.** exponential;
$y = 4(2.5)^x$

87.

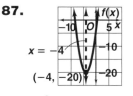

91. $3v^2 - v - 9$ **93.** $-3b^2 - 23b - 21$

Lesson 11-2 pp. 587–590

EXERCISES 1. 10 **3.** 17 **7.** 4 **9.** 12 **17.** no
19. yes **23.** no **25.** yes **27.** $\frac{4}{15}$ or 0.3 **29.** 6
33. yes **35.** yes **37.** 4.2 cm **39.** 559.9 **41.** 9.7
45. 12.8 ft **49.** A figure is a square; the figure is a
rectangle; if a figure is a rectangle then the figure
is a square; false. **51.** An angle is a right angle;
its measure is 90°; if the measure of an angle is
90°, then it is a right angle; true. **53.** 6 in. **67.** $\frac{\sqrt{6}}{3}$
69. $2b^2\sqrt{10b}$ **73.** 8 and 9 **75.** 11 and 12
77. irrational **79.** rational **81.** $12a^2 + 15a$
83. $-10p^4 + 26p^3$

Lesson 11-3 pp. 594–597

EXERCISES 1. 15 **3.** 10 **7.** 16 **9.** (1, 6) **11.** (0, 0)
15. (−4, 4) **17.** 10.6 **19.** $AB \approx 4.1$; $BC \approx 3.2$;
$AC = 5$ **21.** $RS \approx 3.2$; $ST \approx 5.7$; $RT \approx 5.1$
25a. $OR = \sqrt{29}$, $ST = \sqrt{29}$ **b.** $\frac{5}{2}$; $\frac{5}{2}$ **c.** yes
31a. 38.1 mi **b.** 20 mi, 21.2 mi **c.** 15 min, 16 min
33a. $R(-27, -5)$ **b.** $PR = \sqrt{13} \approx 3.6$ $RQ =$
$\sqrt{13} \approx 3.6$ **49.** 10.2 **51.** 3.5 **55.** −10, 10 **57.** −5,
5 **61.** $v^2 + 2v - 35$ **63.** $8w^4 + 19w^2 + 11$

Extension pp. 598–599

1. 7.1 cm **3.** 9.9 ft **5.** 28.4 ft **7.** $x \approx 6.9$ cm;
$y = 8$ cm **9.** $x \approx 5.2$ m; $y = 6$ m

Lesson 11-4 pp. 600–602

EXERCISES 1. $5\sqrt{6}$ **3.** $-2\sqrt{5}$ **7.** yes **9.** no
11. $-3\sqrt{3}$ **13.** $-2\sqrt{5}$ **17.** $9 + \sqrt{3}$ **19.** $3\sqrt{5} +$
$2\sqrt{3}$ **23.** $58 - 10\sqrt{30}$ **25.** $43 + 4\sqrt{30}$
29. $-6\sqrt{2}$ **31.** $\frac{3(\sqrt{10} + \sqrt{5})}{5}$ **35.** $-\frac{4}{3}$; -1.3
37. 7.4 ft **39.** $6\sqrt{2} + 6\sqrt{3}$ or $6(\sqrt{2} + \sqrt{3})$
41. $8 + 2\sqrt{15}$ **47.** $\frac{\sqrt{10}}{5}$ **49.** $(10 + 10\sqrt{2})$ units
55. 9.1% **57.** 15.5% **77.** 6.7 units **79.** (3, 5)
81. 0, 7 **83.** −9, −3 **87.** $b^2 + 22b + 121$
89. $25g^2 - 49$

Lesson 11-5 pp. 607–609

EXERCISES 1. 4 **3.** 36 **7.** 576 ft **9.** 4.5 **11.** 7
15. 2 **17.** none **21.** 3 **23.** no solution **29a.** 25
b. 11.25 **33.** 1600 ft **35.** no solution **37.** 1, 6
63. $3\sqrt{2} + 4\sqrt{3}$ **65.** 32 **69.** 8.4, −0.4 **71.** −10.7,
0.7 **75.** $(m - 13)(m - 1)$ **77.** $(2p + 1)(p + 7)$

Lesson 11-6 pp. 616–619

EXERCISES 1. $x \geq 2$ **3.** $x \geq 0$

11.

x	$f(x)$
0	0
1	2
4	4

17. D **19.** C

21.

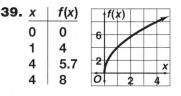

31. $x \leq 4$; $y \geq 0$ **35.** Translate
the graph of $y = \sqrt{x}$ 10 units
down. **37.** Translate the graph
of $y = \sqrt{x}$ 9 units right.

39.

x	$f(x)$
0	0
1	4
4	5.7
4	8

47. B **49.** A **55.** False; only combine like terms.
57. False; $x = -1$. **71.** 7 **73.** 14.76 **77.** $4 - \sqrt{39}$,
$4 + \sqrt{39}$ **79.** $\frac{-1 - \sqrt{11}}{3}$, $\frac{-1 + \sqrt{11}}{3}$
83. $(3x - 5)(x + 2)$ **85.** $2(x - 8)(x + 3)$

Extension
p. 620

1. 10 **2.** 5 **3.** 2 **4.** 343 **5.** 4 **6.** 16 **7.** 125 **8.** 256
9. x^2 **10.** b **11.** $m^{\frac{2}{3}}$ **12.** m **13.** $a^{\frac{7}{6}}$ **14.** $k^{\frac{5}{4}}$
15. $216y^{\frac{21}{2}}$ **16.** $27c^6$

Lesson 11-7
pp. 621–624

EXERCISES 1. $\frac{3}{5}$ **3.** $\frac{3}{4}$ **7.** 0.5299 **9.** 1.2799
13. 10.4 **15.** 38.1 **19.** about 172 ft **21.** about
0.4 mi **23.** $B = 15$; $\sin A = \frac{8}{17}$; $\cos A = \frac{15}{17}$;
$\tan A = \frac{8}{15}$ **25.** $AC \approx 6$; $AB \approx 8$ **27.** $BC \approx 6$;
$AB \approx 18$ **29.** about 55 m **31a.** 1,720,000 ft
b. 326 mi **33.** about 6.8 m **35.** 4.5 **37.** $q \approx 6.1$;
$r \approx 7.9$ **39a.** about 252 ft **b.** about 377 ft
41. about 203 ft

51.
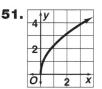

55. 0 **57.** $(n - 20)(n + 20)$
59. $(10p - 7)(10p + 7)$

Chapter Review
pp. 629–631

1. conjugates **2.** legs **3.** rationalize
4. extraneous solution **5.** like radicals
6. Pythagorean Theorem **7.** sine **8.** angle of
elevation **9.** distance formula **10.** midpoint
11. $48\sqrt{2}$ **12.** $\frac{2\sqrt{21}}{11}$ **13.** $20c^2\sqrt{6}$ **14.** $\frac{10\sqrt{13}}{13}$
15. $10\sqrt{2}$ cm by $70\sqrt{2}$ cm **16.** 5.8 **17.** 17.8
18. 14.8 **19.** 9.8 **20.** yes **21.** yes **22.** about 85 ft
23. 5 units **24.** 8.2 units **25.** 10.8 units
26. Answers may vary. Sample:

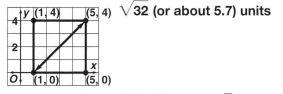 $\sqrt{32}$ (or about 5.7) units

27. (0.5, 5.5) **28.** $\left(5\frac{1}{2}, 4\frac{1}{4}\right)$ **29.** $2\sqrt{7}$ **30.** $30\sqrt{5}$
31. $\sqrt{6}$ **32.** $2\sqrt{5}$ **33.** $10 - 10\sqrt{2}$
34. $-1 + 2\sqrt{14}$ **35.** $53 + 8\sqrt{15}$ **36.** $17\sqrt{7}$
37. $\sqrt{6} + \sqrt{3}$ **38.** 2 **39.** 16 **40.** 8 **41.** 81 **42.** 1
43. 7 **44.** $5\sqrt{5}$ cm **45.** 2.93 in.

46.
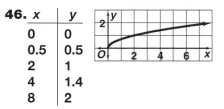

x	y
0	0
0.5	0.5
2	1
4	1.4
8	2

47.

x	y
0	0
1	$\frac{1}{2}$
4	1
9	$1\frac{1}{2}$

48.

x	y
0	0
$\frac{1}{2}$	1
2	2
8	4

49.

x	y
0	1
1	2
4	3
9	4

50. $x \geq 0$; **51.** $x \geq 2$;

52. $x \geq -1$; **53.** $x \geq 0$;

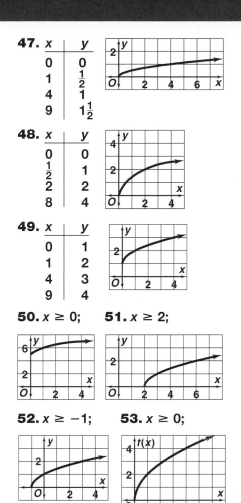

54. $AC \approx 10$; $BC \approx 7$ **55.** $AB \approx 29$; $AC \approx 28$
56. $AB \approx 10$; $BC \approx 6$ **57.** $AC \approx 24$; $BC \approx 5$
58. about 55 ft

Chapter 12

Lesson 12-1
pp. 640–642

EXERCISES 1. $xy = 18$ **3.** $xy = 56$ **11.** 15 **13.** 7
23. $13.\overline{3}$ mi/h **25.** inverse variation; $xy = 60$
27. Direct variation; the ratio $\frac{\text{cost}}{\text{pound}}$ is constant at
$1.79. **29.** Inverse variation; the product of the
length and width remains constant with an area
of 24 square units. **31.** 1.1; $rt = 1.1$ **33.** 1; $ab = 1$
37. Inverse variation; the product of the rate and
the time is always 150. **39.** 121 ft **41.** direct
variation; $y = 0.4x$; 8 **43.** inverse variation;
$xy = 48$; 0.5 **47.** 10.2 L **57.** $\frac{15}{17}$ **59.** $\frac{8}{17}$ **63.** 12.0
65. 10.6 **69.** $(5x + 2)(3x + 7)$

Technology   p. 643

1.

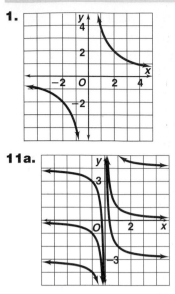

11a.

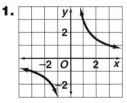

b. Adding translates the graph up, subtracting translates the graph down.

Lesson 12-2   pp. 648–650

EXERCISES

1.

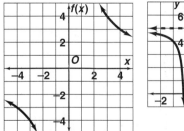

7. 2 **9.** 2 **11.** $x = -1, y = 0$ **13.** $x = 0, y = 2$
15. $x = 0;$ **21.** $x = 0, y = 5;$

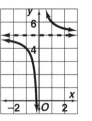

27. absolute value function with vertex (4, 0)
29. line with slope $\frac{1}{4}$, y-int. 0 **35.** moves graph
1 unit to the left **37.** lowers graph 15 units
43. $x = 0, y = 0;$

---

53. 17.8 lumens; 1.9$\overline{7}$ lumens **69.** $xy = 16$
71. $xy = 21.08$ **73.** 1 **75.** $3(d - 6)(d + 6)$
77. $(t^2 + 3)(t - 1)$

Extension   p. 651

1. -1 **3.** gets very small; gets very large
5. 0 **7.** 2

Lesson 12-3   pp. 654–656

EXERCISES 1. $\frac{2a + 3}{4}$ **3.** $\frac{1}{3}$ **7.** $\frac{2}{3}$ **9.** $\frac{1}{m - 7}$ **17.** $\frac{-4}{t + 1}$
19. $-\frac{1}{2}$ **23.** 13 min **25.** $\frac{2r - 1}{r + 5}$ **27.** $\frac{5t - 4}{3t - 1}$
35a. i. $\frac{2b + 4h}{bh}$ **ii.** $\frac{2h + 2r}{rh}$ **b.** $\frac{4}{9}; \frac{4}{9}$ **39.** $\frac{1}{4}$
41. $\frac{t + 3}{3(t + 2)}$
55. vertical asymptote: $x = 4$

horizontal asymptote: $y = 0;$

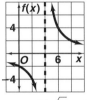

57. $10\sqrt{2}$ **59.** $2\sqrt{2}$ **61.** $y = x^2, y = -2x^2,$
$y = 3x^2$

Lesson 12-4   pp. 657–659

EXERCISES 1. $\frac{35x}{36}$ **3.** $\frac{40}{3a^5}$ **7.** $\frac{2c}{c - 1}$ **9.** $\frac{9}{t}$
13. $4(t + 1)(t + 2)$ **15.** $\frac{(x - 1)(x - 2)}{3}$ **17.** $-\frac{2d - 5}{6d^2}$
19. $\frac{1}{s + 4}$ **21.** 6 **23.** $-\frac{1}{3}$ **27.** $\frac{11}{7k - 15}$ **29.** $t + 3$
31. $\frac{3t - 5}{7t^2}$ **39.** $132.96 **41.** $\frac{x - 2}{4(x + 7)}$ **43.** $\frac{2}{a + 5}$
59. $\frac{b - 5}{2}$ **61.** $\frac{7}{3}$ **69.** 5.3 **71.** 11
75.

Lesson 12-5   pp. 664–666

EXERCISES 1. $x^4 - x^3 + x^2$ **3.** $3c^2 + 2c - \frac{1}{3}$
7. $x - 3$ **9.** $n - 1$ **13.** $5t - 50$
15. $b^2 - 3b - 1 + \frac{3}{3b - 1}$ **19.** $(r^2 + 5r + 1)$ cm
21. $b + 12 + \frac{1}{b + 4}$ **23.** $10w - 681 + \frac{49,046}{w + 72}$
27. $3x + 2 - \frac{1}{2x}$ **29.** $2b^2 + 2b + 10 + \frac{10}{b - 1}$

47a. $t = \frac{d}{r}$ **b.** $t^2 - 7t + 12$
59. $\frac{(t - 5)(3t + 1)(2t + 11)}{(2t - 55)(t + 1)(3t)}$ **61.** $\frac{(x + 5)(x + 4)^2}{(x + 7)(x + 8)^2}$
63. 9.4 **65.** 17.9 **69.** 17 **71.** 63.25

Lesson 12-6   pp. 669–671

EXERCISES 1. $\frac{9}{2m}$ **3.** $\frac{n + 2}{n + 3}$ **13.** $2x^2$ **15.** $7z$
17. $\frac{35 + 6a}{15a}$ **19.** $\frac{18 + 20x^2}{15x^8}$ **23.** $\frac{17m - 47}{(m + 2)(m - 7)}$
25. $\frac{a^2 + 12a + 15}{4(a + 3)}$ **31.** $\frac{h^2 + h + 1}{2t^2 - 7}$ **33.** $\frac{-3 - x - z}{xy^2z}$
45. $\frac{8x^2 - 1}{x}$ **47.** $\frac{-3x - 5}{x(x - 5)}$ **59.** $\frac{x^2}{2} + 2x - 1$ **61.** 6
63. no solution **65.** ±3.9

Lesson 12-7   pp. 675–677

EXERCISES 1. −2 **3.** −1 **17.** ≈12.7 min
19. 10, −10 **21.** 4 **25.** $\frac{1}{2}$, 2 **27.** −5, 2 **37.** 20 Ω
39. 20 Ω **53.** $-\frac{3}{x^2y^2z}$ **55.** $\frac{-4k - 61}{(k - 4)(k + 10)}$
57.

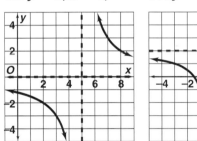

63. 8, 11 **65.** −8, 6

Lesson 12-8   pp. 682–685

EXERCISES

1. 10 choices
Shirt 1 → Tie 1 → S1, T1
          → Tie 2 → S1, T2
          → Tie 3 → S1, T3
          → Tie 4 → S1, T4
          → Tie 5 → S1, T5
Shirt 2 → Tie 1 → S2, T1
          → Tie 2 → S2, T2
          → Tie 3 → S2, T3
          → Tie 4 → S2, T4
          → Tie 5 → S2, T5
3a. 8, 10, 10, 10 **b.** 8,000,000 telephone numbers
5. 3,628,800 orders **7.** 1680 **9.** 360 **15.** 5040
17. $_8P_6$ **19.** $_8P_4$ **21a.** 24 **b.** $\frac{1}{24}$ **23.** 3 **25.** 5
27a. 260,000 license plates **b.** 23,920,000 license plates **29a.** 17,576 codes **b.** 17,526 codes **41.** 3
43. −10, 1 **47.** $BC \approx 34, AC \approx 54$ **49.** $AB \approx 48$,
$AC \approx 7$ **51.** no solution **53.** $-\frac{7}{2} \pm \frac{\sqrt{97}}{2}$

Lesson 12-9   pp. 689–691

EXERCISES 1. 1 **3.** 15 **11.** 220 **13.** $\frac{1}{5040}$ **15a.** 56
b. 1 **c.** $\frac{1}{56}$ **d.** $\frac{5}{28}$ **17.** 1 **19.** 4 **21.** permutation,
since order *is* important **27.** 8 **41.** 12 **43.** 840
47. 2 **49.** $\frac{1}{10}$ **53.** −6.81, 0.81 **55.** −5.46, 1.46

Chapter Review   pp. 693–695

1. rational expression **2.** asymptote
3. permutation **4.** rational equation **5.** inverse
variation **6.** $xy = 6$ **7.** $xy = 9$ **8.** $xy = 4.4$ **9.** 4
10. 2.5 **11.** 18.75 **12.** inverse; $xy = 70$
13. direct; $y = 8.2x$ **14.** inverse; $xy = 3$
15. $y = 0, x = 0$;   **16.** $y = 0, x = 0$;

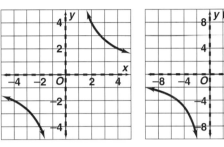

17. $y = 0, x = 5$;   **18.** $y = 2, x = 0$;

19. Answers may vary. Sample: $y = \frac{1}{x + 1}$
20. The graph of $f(x) = \frac{5}{x + 3}$ gets closer and
closer to the lines $x = -3$ and $y = 0$. **21.** $x - 2$
22. $\frac{x}{4x + 3}$ **23.** 6 **24.** $\frac{-3}{t(t - 1)}$ **25.** $\frac{1}{2z - 3}$ **26.** $\frac{x + 2}{x + 4}$
27. $\frac{24m}{(m - 3)(m + 1)}$ **28.** 12 **29.** $3(n + 2)$
30. $\frac{1}{2(2e + 1)}$ **31.** $2x - 4$ **32.** $3x^4 + 4x^3 - 1$
33. $50x^2 - 7x + \frac{1}{x}$ **34.** $x + 7 - \frac{5}{x + 1}$
35. $x + 4 - \frac{32}{x + 4}$ **36.** $2x^2 - 7x + 4$ **37.** $\frac{8x - 4}{x - 7}$
38. $\frac{7x + 24}{28x}$ **39.** $\frac{15x^2 + 13x + 27}{(3x - 1)(2x + 3)}$ **40.** $\frac{-3m + 10}{(m + 1)(m - 1)}$
41. C **42.** 24 **43.** $-\frac{4}{35}$ **44.** 9 **45.** −14 **46.** −21
47. 2 **48.** ≈ 6 min **49.** 60 **50.** 1680 **51.** 360
52. 20 **53.** 3024 **54a.** 160 possible area codes
b. 640 new area codes **55.** 6 **56.** 210 **57.** 36
58. 165 **59.** 5 **60.** 4 combinations
61. 3003 ways

Extra Practice

CHAPTER 1 **1.** Let T = total length, e = edge length; $T = 12e$. **3.** Let A = area, ℓ = length; $A = 12\ell$. **5.** 28 **7.** 9 **17.** < **19.** < **25.** −11 **27.** $-\frac{32}{15}$ **49.** $-16x + 12$ **51.** $8 - 4t$

60–65.

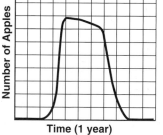

CHAPTER 2 **1.** 14 **3.** 8 **21.** t = test score; $\frac{87 + 84 + 85 + t}{4} = 90$; no **23.** 1 **25.** −2 **39.** $\frac{A}{\ell}$ **41.** $\frac{ht}{p - m}$
47. mean = 39.375
median = 38
mode = 35
49. mean = 6.3
median = 6
modes = 5, 8

CHAPTER 3 **1.** $w > -3$;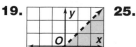
27. $5 < w < 7$ **29.** $m \le 4$ or $m > 8.4$ **37.** $|x| < 2$ **39.** $|x + 4| < 1$ **43.** $t > 1$ or $t < -1$;

CHAPTER 3 **1.** −8 **3.** 48 **17.** $10x = 4, 40\%$ **19.** $1.2x = 6, 500\%$ **29.** 16% increase **31.** 200% increase **41.** 2.8%
43. 16.7% **45.** $\frac{5}{54}$ **47.** 0 **51.** $\frac{1}{12}$ **53.** $\frac{5}{24}$ **55.** $\frac{1}{12}$

CHAPTER 5 **1.**

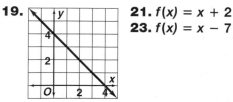

5. {−29, −11, −5, 13} **7.** {5, −1, 1, 19} **15.** no **17.** yes

19.

21. $f(x) = x + 2$
23. $f(x) = x - 7$

27.

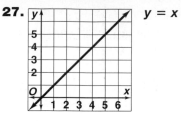

$y = x$

33. 33, 66 **35.** −1, 2

CHAPTER 6 **1.** 0.2 m/yr **3.** 1.6 mm/s
5. slope = 6, y-intercept = 8
7. slope = 0, y-intercept = 4
9. x-intercept = 2, y-intercept = 12
11. x-intercept = −6, y-intercept = 3
13. $y - 6 = -5(x - 4)$ **15.** $y - 5 = \frac{1}{2}(x - 8)$

21.

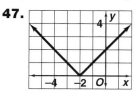

29. $y = \frac{3}{2}x + 2$
31. $y = x + 6$
37. $4x - y = -17$
39. $4x - 3y = 25$

45a–b.

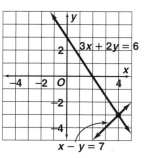

c. grade = 0.720 · age − 1.118

47.

CHAPTER 7 **1.** (4, −3);

5. $x = 1, y = -1$
7. $x = 6, y = 13$
9. $x = 4, y = -9$
13. $x + y = 12$,
$5x + y = 32$, 5 nickels, 7 pennies
15. $2x + 2y = 74$,
$7x + 2y = 159$, length: 20 ft, width: 17 ft

19.

25.

CHAPTER 8 1. $\frac{1}{64t^6}$ **3.** $(4.5)^2$ **17.** 9 **19.** 144
25. 3.4×10^7 **27.** 1.5×10^3 **33.** 8,050,000
35. 900,000,000 **41.** 1.5; 40.5, 60.75
43. 0.2; -0.008, -0.0016
49. $\{\frac{1}{3}, 1, 3, 9\}$; increase **51.** $\{\frac{2}{3}, 1, \frac{3}{2}, \frac{9}{4}\}$; increase
61. exponential growth; growth factor = 8
63. exponential decay; decay factor = $\frac{1}{2}$
69. $y = 200(1.04)^x$; \$243.33
71. $y = 3000(0.92)^x$; \$2336.06

CHAPTER 9 1. $2x^3 + 4x^2 - 11x + 11$
3. $6m^3 + m + 4$ **11.** $4b^3 + 12b$ **13.** $32m^2 - 40m$
19. $t^2(t^4 - t^3 + t^2 + 1)$ **21.** $4c^2(3c^3 - c + 4)$
27. $-5c^2 + 7c + 6$ **29.** $w^3 + 4w^2 + 3w - 2$
39. $(3x - 1)(2x + 5)$, $6x^2 + 13x - 5$
41. $(x - 3)(x - 1)$ **43.** $(v - 1)(v + 2)$
65. $(y + 3)(3y^2 - 1)$ **67.** $(w - 3)(w^2 + 3)$

CHAPTER 10 1. narrower **3.** wider and reflected
over the x-axis **9.** $x = 0$, $(0, 0)$ **11.** $x = 0$, $(0, -3)$

19.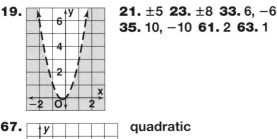
21. ± 5 **23.** ± 8 **33.** 6, -6
35. 10, -10 **61.** 2 **63.** 1

67. 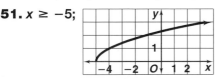 quadratic

CHAPTER 11 1. $\frac{\sqrt{3}}{3}$ **3.** $\frac{5\sqrt{2}}{3}$ **21.** no; $16 + 25 \neq 49$
23. no; $6^2 + 9^2 \neq 13^2$ **29.** 10 **31.** 10.8
33. 5.1; $(\frac{3}{2}, \frac{11}{2})$ **35.** 1.4; $(\frac{9}{2}, -\frac{1}{2})$ **43.** 5 **45.** 4

51. $x \geq -5$;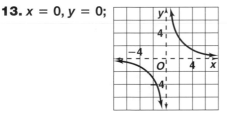

57. $\frac{9}{41}$ **59.** $\frac{9}{40}$ **63.** 0.9511 **65.** 1.1106 **67.** 201 m

CHAPTER 12 1. 70 **3.** 0.8 **7.** 8.1 **9.** 2
13. $x = 0$, $y = 0$;

21. $\frac{t}{4}$ **23.** 4 **37.** $2x^2 + 5x + 2$ **39.** $3x^2 - 7x + 6$
41. 8 **43.** -1 **53.** 42 **55.** 8

Algebra Skills Handbook

p. 714 **1.** 10 games **3.** 9 tacks

p. 715 **1.** 17 and 19, or -19 and -17 **3.** 33, 34, 35,
and 36 **5.** 24 years old **7.** mother: 38 yr; son:
16 yr; daughter: 7 yr **9.** regular tickets: 80;
student tickets: 110

p. 716 **1.** 81 books **3.** 36 stories **5.** 7.2 m
7. 6 ways

p. 717 **1.** 21 lockers **3.** about 370,000,000 times
5. 63 games **7.** 32 and 33

p. 718 **1.** dog: K. C.; horse: Bo; bird: Cricket; cat:
Tuffy **3.** Alexa, Karin, Heather, Annette, Tanya,
Garo **5.** 126 players

p. 719 **1.** 6 **3.** 21 pencils **5.** 11 mi **7.** 290 mi
9. $4\frac{3}{4}$ mi east, 2 mi north

p. 710 **1.** composite **3.** composite **5.** prime
7. composite **9.** composite **11.** composite
13. composite **15.** composite **17.** composite
19. 1, 2, 23, 46 **21.** 1, 11 **23.** 1, 3, 9, 27 **25.** 1, 5,
41, 205 **27.** 1, 2, 3, 4, 6, 8, 12, 24 **29.** 1, 2, 4, 8, 11,
22, 44, 88 **31.** 1, 3, 61, 183 **33.** 1, 2, 7, 14, 49, 98
35. 1, 59 **37.** $2 \cdot 3 \cdot 3$ **39.** $3 \cdot 3 \cdot 3$ **41.** $2 \cdot 2 \cdot 2 \cdot 2 \cdot 2 \cdot 2$
43. $2 \cdot 2 \cdot 5 \cdot 5$ **45.** $2 \cdot 2 \cdot 3 \cdot 7$ **47.** $11 \cdot 11$

p. 721 **1.** 2 **3.** 24 **5.** 3 **7.** 7 **9.** 5 **11.** 21 **13.** 80
15. 33 **17.** 60 **19.** 240 **21.** 150 **23.** 40

p. 722 **1.** 2, 4 **3.** 3, 5 **5.** 3, 5, 9 **7.** 2 **9.** 2, 3, 4, 6, 8,
9 **11.** none **13.** 3, 5 **15.** 2, 3, 4, 6, 8, 9 **17.** 2, 4
19. 15 **21.** Answers may vary. Sample: $a + 1$ is
not divisible by 2. Dividing by 2 will leave a
remainder of 1.

p. 723 **1.** \$350 **3.** \$300 **5.** \$17.00 **7.** 7.10 **9.** 7.00
11. \$30.80

p. 724 **1.** $\frac{8}{14}, \frac{12}{21}, \frac{16}{28}, \frac{20}{35}, \frac{24}{42}$ **3.** $\frac{6}{16}, \frac{9}{24}, \frac{12}{32}, \frac{15}{40}, \frac{18}{48}$
5. $\frac{10}{12}, \frac{15}{18}, \frac{20}{24}, \frac{25}{30}, \frac{30}{36}$ **7.** 9 **9.** 48 **11.** 2 **13.** 9 **15.** 3
17. no **19.** no **21.** no **23.** $\frac{1}{2}$ **25.** $\frac{2}{3}$ **27.** $\frac{2}{5}$ **29.** $\frac{1}{3}$
31. $\frac{2}{5}$ **33.** $\frac{3}{4}$

p. 725 **1.** 0.3 **3.** 0.2 **5.** $0.\overline{714285}$ **7.** $0.\overline{5}$
9. $0.\overline{285714}$ **11.** $0.1\overline{6}$ **13.** $\frac{7}{100}$ **15.** $\frac{7}{8}$ **17.** $6\frac{1}{3}$ **19.** $\frac{7}{9}$
21. $\frac{3}{8}$ **23.** $6\frac{12}{25}$

p. 726 **1.** $\frac{5}{7}$ **3.** 3 **5.** $10\frac{7}{15}$ **7.** $6\frac{2}{9}$ **9.** $6\frac{7}{33}$ **11.** $9\frac{2}{3}$
13. $13\frac{7}{16}$ **15.** $56\frac{11}{15}$ **17.** $\frac{3}{5}$ **19.** $1\frac{2}{7}$ **21.** $2\frac{3}{8}$ **23.** $3\frac{1}{3}$
25. $9\frac{4}{63}$ **27.** $2\frac{1}{6}$ **29.** $7\frac{5}{6}$

p. 727 **1.** $\frac{3}{10}$ **3.** $8\frac{5}{8}$ **5.** $3\frac{1}{2}$ **7.** $25\frac{3}{10}$ **9.** $2\frac{4}{5}$ **11.** 6
13. $9\frac{5}{6}$ **15.** $5\frac{15}{16}$ **17.** $\frac{8}{9}$ **19.** $\frac{18}{25}$ **21.** $13\frac{1}{3}$ **23.** $\frac{5}{6}$ **25.** 26
27. $1\frac{1}{3}$ **29.** $\frac{1}{3}$

p. 728 **1.** 56% **3.** 602% **5.** 820% **7.** 14.3%

9. 11.1% **11.** 75% **13.** 0.07 **15.** 0.009 **17.** 0.83
19. 0.15 **21.** 0.0003 **23.** 3.65 **25.** $\frac{19}{100}$ **27.** $4\frac{1}{2}$
29. $\frac{16}{25}$ **31.** $\frac{6}{25}$ **33.** $\frac{3}{800}$ **35.** $\frac{3}{5}$ **37.** $\frac{1}{50}$ **39.** $\frac{33}{50}$ **41.** $1\frac{1}{4}$

p. 729 **1.** 6^4 **3.** $5 \cdot 2^4$ **5.** $4^2 \cdot 3^2 \cdot 2$ **7.** 64 **9.** 144
11. 3267 **13.** $(1 \cdot 10^3) + (2 \cdot 10^2) + (5 \cdot 10^1) + (4 \cdot 10^0)$
15. $(8 \cdot 10^4) + (3 \cdot 10^3) + (4 \cdot 10^2) + (1 \cdot 10^0)$

p. 730 **1.** 100°, obtuse **3.** 180°, straight
5–12. Check students' work. **13.** Check students'
work.

p. 731 **1.** 22 cm **3.** 24 cm² **5.** 216 cm³
7. 351.68 cm³

p. 732 **1.**

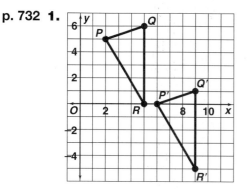

3. $(x, y) \rightarrow (x - 2, y - 1)$ **5.** $(x, y) \rightarrow (x + 4, y + \frac{1}{2})$
7. $(x, y) \rightarrow (x + 2, y + 5)$ **9.** $(x, y) \rightarrow (x + 6, y - 1)$
11. $(x, y) \rightarrow (x - 1, y + 1)$

p. 733 **1.**

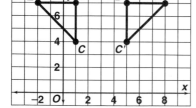

3.

5.

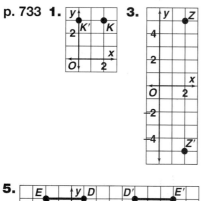

7.

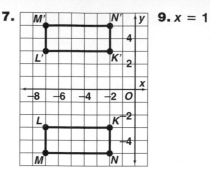

9. $x = 1$

p. 734 **1.**

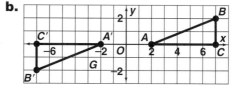

3.

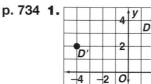

5a.

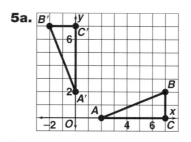

b.

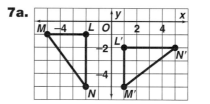

7a.

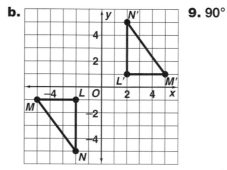

b.

9. 90°

p. 735 **1.**

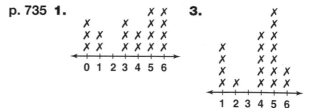

3.

830 Selected Answers

5.

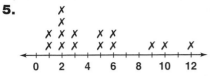

The line plot shows that most of the numbers are concentrated around 2, the maximum is 12, and the minimum is 1.

p. 736 1.

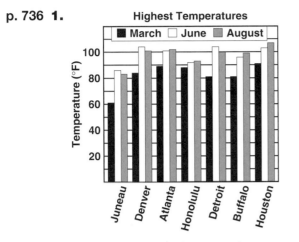

p. 737 1a. 30–39 **b.** 15 students **c.** Answers may vary. Sample: If it actually took 50–59 minutes, the student might estimate by saying 1 hour.
d. No; you don't know where inside each interval the answers are.

p. 738 1.

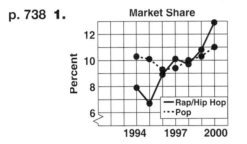

The rap/hip hop category is growing faster.

p. 739 1a.

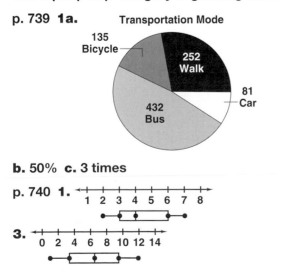

b. 50% **c.** 3 times

p. 740 1.

3.

9a. **b.** 2; 33, 33

c. 21 h; 23 h; both are much less than the 29-h typical week.

p. 741 1. Circle graph; the categories seem to cover how an average family spends all of its money in October. A circle graph also shows the percentage of a category more easily than a bar graph. **3.** Scatter plot; the levels of emissions most likely increase as the age of a car increases. A double bar graph would only be used if the data had an additional subject.

p. 742 1a. The graph implies that the runner's time on the 10-mile run was more than cut in half in six weeks, while actually the runner's time decreased by about 14%. **b.** Add a break on the vertical axis, or redraw the graph with the vertical axis starting at zero.

p. 743 1.

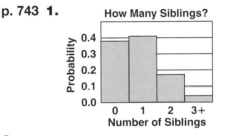

3a.

Rolling Two
Number Cubes

Sum	Probability
2	$\frac{1}{36}$
3	$\frac{2}{36}$
4	$\frac{3}{36}$
5	$\frac{4}{36}$
6	$\frac{5}{36}$
7	$\frac{6}{36}$
8	$\frac{5}{36}$
9	$\frac{4}{36}$
10	$\frac{3}{36}$
11	$\frac{2}{36}$
12	$\frac{1}{36}$

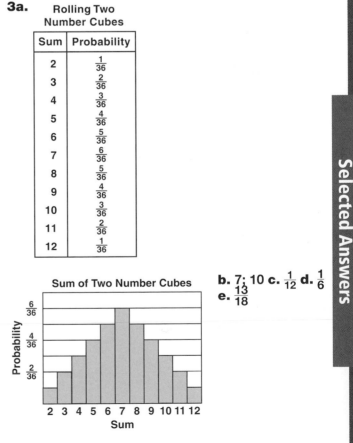

b. 7; 10 **c.** $\frac{1}{12}$ **d.** $\frac{1}{6}$
e. $\frac{13}{18}$

p. 744 **1.** Use a coin. Let heads represent a book being a trade paperback. Flip the coin six times to represent one trial. Six rolls represent one trial. Count the number of trials that had only heads.

p. 745 **1.** Good sample; it uses the systematic method. **3.** Good sample; it is a random sample. **5.** Not biased; the question makes no assumptions and does not attempt to persuade you.

p. 746 **1.** ±10% **3.** ±3% **5.** 400 **7.** about 6 ft 5 in. tall

p. 747 **1.** = A2 + B2 + C2 **3.** = 1/2 * B2 * C2 **5.a.** D3 **b.** E4

Index

B

Back-to-back stem-and-leaf plot, 121, 122
Bar graphs, 736
Base
  defined, 9
  for exponent, 11, 729
Bauelos, Romana Acosta, 273
Best fit, line of, 319–324, 329, 333, 334, 436, 495
Binomials
  dividing polynomials by, 663, 665
  dividing trinomials by, 665
  as factors of trinomials, 480
  multiplying, 466–472, 474–480, 504, 508
  square of, 474–476, 477, 478, 479
Box-and-whisker plots, 740
Boyle's Law, 641
Brackets, 12, 45
Break-even point, finding, 363–364

C

Calculator. *See also* Graphing calculators.
  angle of depression, 624
  angle of elevation, 623
  combinations, 687
  compound interest, 439
  distance, 592
  evaluating, 438
  exercises, 207, 409, 526, 527, 542, 543, 564, 625–627
  exponential growth, 438
  golden ratio, 602
  hints, 12, 319, 341, 400, 408, 438, 525, 592
  permutations, 681
  Pythagorean Theorem, 585
  quadratic equation, 531
  quadratic formula, 548
  scientific notation, 400
  simplifying, 12, 409, 519
  square roots, 525, 526, 527, 531, 542, 543, 548, 579
  trigonometric ratios, 622–624
Careers. *See* Connections.
CD-ROM. *See* iText.
Celsius temperature, 43, 71, 112, 113
Center, of circle, 593
Central tendency, measures of, 118–123
Certain event, 211
Challenge Exercises. *See* Enrichment.
Change
  percent of, 204–209, 228, 229, 230
  rate of, 282–289, 331
Chapter Review, 67–69, 125–127, 175–177, 227–229, 275–277, 331–333, 387–389, 447–449, 503–505, 569–571, 629–631, 693–695
Chapter Test, 70, 128, 178, 230, 278, 334, 390, 450, 506, 572, 632, 696
Check for reasonableness, 76, 82, 97, 99, 154, 349, 354, 537, 563, 673

Check Skills You'll Need. *See* Instant Check System.
Check solutions, 75
Check Understanding. *See* Instant Check System.
Checkpoint Quiz. *See* Instant Check System.
Chu Shih-Chieh, 501
Cierva, Juan de la, 540
Circle
  area of, 116–117
  center of, 593, 594
  circumference of, 113, 127, 640
  expressions for the area of, 471
  pi (π) defined by, 18
  and probability, 214, 215
  radius of, 531, 532
Circle graphs, 739
Classification
  of angles, 730
  of combinations, 696
  of numbers, 17–19, 20–21, 68
  of permutations, 696
  of polynomials, 457
Closure properties, 57
Cobb, Jewel Plummer, 416
Coefficient
  correlation, 319–320, 333
  defined, 49
  zero, 663
Combination(s), 686–691, 695
  classifying, 696
  counting, 687, 695
  defined, 686, 695
  using in probability, 688–689
Combination notation, 687
Common difference, 269, 272, 277
Common ratio, 424–429, 449
Communication. *See* Critical Thinking, Investigation, Reading Math, Writing.
Commutative Property
  of Addition, 54, 55, 56, 69
  of Multiplication, 49, 54, 69
Compatible numbers, 199
Complement of an event, 212, 214
Completing the square, 541–546, 570, 685
Composite numbers, 454, 720
Compound events, probability of, 219–224
Compound inequalities, 161–166, 177, 338
Compound interest, 438–439, 449, 558, 660, 698
Computers
  exercises, 144, 403, 415, 420, 682, 697
  simulations, 218
  spreadsheets, 100, 334, 338, 456, 557
Conclusion, 586
Conditional, 586
Congruent triangles, 100
Conjecture, 268, 271, 275, 277. *See also* Make a Conjecture.

Conjugates, 601–602, 630
Connections
  Careers
    airline pilot, 94
    archaeologist, 35, 595
    auto mechanic, 606
    businessperson, 368
    carpenter, 79, 89, 93, 99, 543
    cartographer, 224
    cartoonist, 21
    cell physiologist, 416
    demographer, 551, 564
    electrical engineer, 577
    electrician, 251, 671
    firefighter, 585, 617
    helicopter pilot, 594
    marketing director, 159
    mathematician, 501
    mechanic, 79, 606
    medical researcher, 443
    nutritionist, 64
    photographer, 649
    physician, 209
    physician's assistant, 78
    police officer, 615
    quality control inspector, 169
    recording engineer, 248
    surveyor, 641
    urban planner, 313
    wildlife manager, 122
    woodworker, 543
    zoologist, 379
  Interdisciplinary
    art, 29, 101, 195, 231, 602
    astronomy, 194, 401, 404, 407, 408, 422, 423, 448, 450
    biology, 265, 277, 287, 404, 407, 431, 433, 449, 478
    botany, 127
    chemistry, 29, 162, 366, 401, 408, 440, 442, 489, 603, 677
    civics, 202
    geography, 415
    geology, 408
    history, 14, 42, 53. *See also* Point in Time.
    language arts, 239, 250
    music, 5, 271, 358, 391
    physics, 8, 130, 245, 264, 265, 413, 428, 435, 527, 533, 555, 556, 564, 565, 583, 586, 587, 588, 611, 616, 671
    science, 22, 127, 164, 229, 277, 309, 409
    zoology, 379, 562
  Mathematics
    geometry, 9, 14, 15, 51, 63, 64, 70, 75, 79, 85, 92, 97, 98, 100, 103, 108, 109, 111, 114, 126, 144, 156, 158, 165, 166, 179, 190, 193, 194, 215, 250, 251, 265, 288, 296, 302, 316, 322, 349, 350, 366, 367, 375, 382, 388, 408, 409, 414, 428, 459, 460, 464, 468, 470, 471, 477, 491, 494, 500, 504, 505, 506, 515, 532, 533, 535, 538, 539, 545, 551, 571, 572, 589, 593, 594, 595, 596, 604, 610, 632, 640, 660, 663, 665, 690, 699
    Mental Math, 50, 56, 63, 94, 136, 156, 349, 476–477, 493, 532, 556
    number theory, 272, 478

Index

Index

Transformed formulas, 111–115, 280
Transitive Property of Equality, 173
Translation, 325–329, 333, 732
    of graphs of square root functions, 615, 631
    horizontal, 327, 333, 615, 631
    vertical, 326, 333, 615, 631
Trapezoid(s)
    area of, 12, 15, 70, 113, 470, 533
    midpoints of segments of, 596
Tree diagram, 680
Trend. *See* correlation.
Trend line, 61, 62, 64, 318–324, 334
Triangle(s)
    area of, 64, 111, 251, 665
    congruent, 100
    45-45-90, 598
    Pascal's, 271, 501
    perimeter of, 101, 109, 110, 156, 165
    proportions in, 189–190, 194, 195
    right. *See* Right triangles.
    Sierpinski's, 428
    similar, 190
    sum of angles of, 92
    30-60-90, 599
Triangle Inequality Theorem, 144
Triangular numbers, 464
Trigonometric ratios, 621–627, 631
    cosine, 621–622, 631
    defined, 621, 631
    finding, 621–622, 625–627
    sine, 621–622, 631
    solving problems using, 623–624
    table of, 751
    tangent, 621–622, 623, 624, 631
Trinomial(s)
    dividing by binomials, 665
    factoring, 480–491, 493–495, 497–501, 504–505
    factoring by grouping, 497–501
    multiplication of, 469
    perfect-square, 490–491, 493–495, 505
    square of, 478
Try, Check, Revise, 715
Two-step equation, 81–85, 126, 132

U

Uniform motion, 104
Unit analysis, 182
Unit fractions, 53
Unit rates, 182–183
Unlike fractions, 726
Unlike radicals, 600
Update
    data, 27, 128, 319, 320, 321, 324, 333, 334, 564
Use Logical Reasoning, 718

V

Value, absolute. *See* Absolute value.
Variable(s), 4–8
    on both sides of equation, 96–101
    defined, 4, 68
    defining in terms of another, 103
    dependent, 248, 276
    independent, 248, 276
    as test-taking strategy, 274
    transforming equations with only variables, 112
Variation
    constant of, 262, 277, 637, 640, 693, 696
    direct, 261–267, 277, 638–639, 640, 641, 696
    inverse, 636–642, 693, 696
Venn diagram, 18
Vermeer, Jan, 231
Vertex
    defined, 511, 569, 730
    identifying, 511, 513, 520, 521
Vertical angles, 97
Vertical asymptote, 645–646, 648, 649
Vertical line, 285, 286, 299
Vertical-line test, 242, 244, 245, 276
Vertical motion formula, 549, 550, 551
Vertical translation, 326, 333, 615, 631
Vinci, Leonardo da, 195
Volume
    of air in lungs, 114
    of cube, 414
    of cylinder, 14, 113, 465, 572, 610, 631
    defined, 731
    finding percent error in calculating, 206
    formulas for, 13, 14, 113, 114, 465, 471, 567, 572, 610, 631, 665
    percent error in calculating, 206, 207, 208
    of rectangular prism, 113, 409, 471, 498, 501, 505, 665
    of rectangular solid, 660
    and similarity, 194
    of sphere, 14, 567

W

Whole numbers, 17–18, 20–21
Working backward, 208, 209, 375, 446, 608, 719
Writing
    algebraic expressions, 4–8, 42, 180
    decimals as percents, 180, 728
    equations, 5–6, 72, 89, 97, 99, 104–106, 234, 300
    equations from graphs, 292
    equations of parallel lines, 312, 313, 333

    equations using tables, 306
    Exercises, 7, 13, 14, 22, 29, 35, 42, 51, 57, 64, 70, 79, 85, 100, 109, 114, 122, 128, 137, 144, 150, 156, 164, 171, 178, 187, 194, 201, 208, 215, 222, 229, 230, 239, 245, 250, 257, 265, 270, 271, 276, 278, 288, 296, 302, 303, 316, 322, 344, 350, 358, 366, 374, 383, 386, 388, 390, 397, 403, 409, 415, 421, 427, 434, 443, 448, 450, 460, 464, 470, 478, 484, 488, 493, 500, 506, 514, 522, 527, 533, 538, 545, 551, 557, 564, 571, 572, 582, 588, 595, 605, 610, 611, 616, 617, 619, 632, 641, 649, 655, 660, 665, 670, 675, 683, 690, 694, 696, 699
    Extended Responses, 174
    fractions as percent, 180, 728
    function rules, 254–259, 338
    function rules from tables, 254, 257, 259
    Gridded-Responses, 66
    linear equations, 291–292, 306–307
    linear equations from data, 306–307
    linear equations in standard form, 300
    numbers in scientific notation, 400–401
    percents as decimals, 180, 728
    percents as fractions, 180, 728
    Short Responses, 124
    systems of equations, 362–368
    systems of linear inequalities, 379–380, 389

X

x-axis, 59, 69
x-coordinate, 59, 60, 62, 69
x-intercept, 298–299, 529

Y

y-axis, 59, 69
y-coordinate, 59, 60, 62, 69, 560
y-intercept, 291, 292, 299

Z

Zero
    dividing by, 41
    as exponent, 394–399, 447
    Multiplication Property of, 38, 55
Zero coefficient, 663
Zero pair, 81
Zero-Product Property, 536–540, 570, 673

Acknowledgments

Staff Credits

The people who made up the High School Mathematics team—representing design services, editorial, editorial services, market research, marketing services, online services & multimedia development, production services, project office, and publishing processes—are listed below. Bold type denotes the core team members.

Leora Adler, Carolyn Artin, Stephanie Bradley, **Peter Brooks,** Amy D. Breaux, Judith Buice, Ronit Carter, **Lisa J. Clark,** Bob Cornell, Sheila DeFazio, Marian DeLollis, Jo DiGiustini, Delphine Dupee, Emily Ellen, Janet Fauser, Debby Faust, Suzanne Feliciello, Frederick Fellows, Jonathan Fisher, **Paula Foye,** Paul Frisoli, Patti Fromkin, Melissa Garcia, Jonathan Gorey, Jennifer Graham, Barbara Hardt, Daniel R. Hartjes, Richard Heater, Kerri Hoar, Jayne Holman, Karen Holtzman, Angela Husband, Carolyn Lock, Kevin Jackson-Mead, Al Jacobson, Misty-Lynn Jenese, Diahanne Lucas, Cathie Maglio, Cheryl Mahan, Barry Maloney, Ann McSweeney, **Eve Melnechuk,** Meredith Mascola, Sandy Morris, **Cindy Noftle,** Marsha Novak, **Marie Opera,** Jill Ort, Michael Oster, Steve Ouellette, Dorothy M. Preston, Rashid Ross, Donna Russo, **Malti Sharma, Dennis Slattery,** Emily Soltanoff, **Deborah Sommer,** Kathryn Smith, Lisa Smith-Ruvalcaba, Mark Tricca, Nate Walker, Diane Walsh, **Joe Will,** Amy Winchester, Carol Zacny

Cover Design
Brainworx Studio

Cover Photos
Fern, Corbis; Rollercoaster, Robin Smith/Stone/ Getty Images, Inc.

Technical Illustration
Nesbitt Graphics, Inc.

Photo Research
Sue McDermott, Magellan Visual Research

Illustration

Argosy Illustration: 104, 105, 106, 157, 282, 295
Kim Barnes: 344
Ken Batelman: 381, 522, 531, 624
John Edwards and Associates: 244, 264, 308, 396, 401, 415
Ellen Korey-Lie: 63
Annette LeBlanc: 171
Ron Magnes: 109
Lisa Manning: 112, 123
Steve McEntee: 364
Morgan Cain & Associates: 27, 61, 64, 136, 182, 194, 539, 545
Matthew Pippin: 51
Roberto Portocarrero: 320
Brucie Rosch: 8, 17, 22; 34, 74, 120, 140, 193b, 201, 202, 357, 444, 456, 533
Phil Scheuer: 29
Kathryn Smith: 223, 358, 686

Neil Stewart: 438, 439
Roberta Warshaw: 6, 259, 315, 618, 660, 669, 679, 683
J/B Woolsey and Associates: 191t, 192, 232, 233
XNR Productions: 138, 158, 187, 191b, 193t, 322, 680

Photography

Front matter: Page ix, Bob Daemmrich/The Image Works; **vii,** Hal Beral/Visuals Unlimited; **viii,** Michelle Bridwell/PhotoEdit; **x,** Frank Lane/Parfitt/Stone/Getty Images, Inc.; **xi,** Rob Atkins/The Image Bank/Getty Images, Inc.; **xii,** Joseph McBride/Stone/Getty Images, Inc.; **xiii,** Wilfried Krecichwost/Stone/Getty Images, Inc.; **xiv,** Jeff Greenberg/Omni-Photo Communications, Inc.; **xv,** Ron Kimball; **xvi,** R. D. Rubic/Precision Chromes, Inc.; **xvii,** Zefa/London/Corbis Stock Market; **xviii,** Nancy Richmond/The Image Works

Chapter 1: Pages 2, 3, Chris Noble/Stone/Getty Images, Inc.; **5,** Jon Riley/Stone/Getty Images, Inc.; **7,** Bob Daemmrich/Stock Boston; **12,** Steve Bronstein/The Image Bank/Getty Images, Inc.; **13,** PhotoEdit; **14 both,** The Granger Collection; **17,** Arnulf Husmo/Stone/Getty Images, Inc.; **20,** Dugald Bremner/Stone/Getty Images, Inc.; **21,** © Bill Amend/Universal Press Syndicate; **26,** John Elk, III/Stock Boston; **29,** Russ Lappa; **30,** © 1980 by Thaves. Distributed from www.thecomics.com; **35,** Hal Beral/Visuals Unlimited; **39,** Nicholas Devore III/Bruce Coleman, Inc.; **43,** Courtesy of Cedar Point/Photo by Dan Feicht; **48,** Corbis; **51,** Alan Thornton/Stone/Getty Images, Inc.; **53,** British Museum/Michael Holford; **55,** Russ Lappa; **59,** Klaus Lahnstein/Stone/Getty Images, Inc.; **62,** Russ Lappa; **64,** Bill Aron/PhotoEdit

Chapter 2: Pages 72, 73, Bohemian Nomad Picturemakers/Corbis; **76,** Howard Grey/FPG/Getty Images, Inc.; **79,** ©Baloo/Rothco; **82,** Russ Lappa; **85,** SuperStock; **89,** Kevin R. Norris/Stone/Getty Images, Inc.; **92,** VCL/Alistair Berg/FPG/Getty Images, Inc.; **94,** David Frazier/Stone/Getty Images, Inc.; **97,** Michelle Bridwell/PhotoEdit; **99,** Russ Lappa; **105,** The Image Works; **114,** Chuck Piper/Visuals Unlimited; **119,** R. Krubner/H. Armstrong Roberts; **122,** Fred Whitehouse/Animals Animals/Earth Scenes; **130,** Philip Gatward/Dorling Kindersley; **130–131,** Philip Gatward /Dorling Kindersley; **131 tr,** Michael Dinneen/AP/Wide World Photos; **131 br,** Philip Gatward/Dorling Kindersley; **131 tl, 131 bl,** Jane Stockman/Dorling Kindersley

Chapter 3: Pages 132, 133, V.C.L./FPG/Getty Images, Inc.; **136,** Tony Freeman/PhotoEdit; **138,** Poulides/Thatcher/Stone/Getty Images, Inc.; **142,** Karl Weatherly/Corbis; **143,** Clive Brunskill/Allsport/Getty Images, Inc.; **144,** Corbis Stock Market; **148,** Jon Chomitz; **150,** Doug Sokell/Visuals Unlimited; **154,** Russ Lappa; **157,** Robin L. Sachs/PhotoEdit; **158,** Stone/Getty Images, Inc.; **159,** Mug Shots/Corbis Stock Market; **162,** Bob Daemmrich/Stock Boston; **165,** Michael Newman/PhotoEdit; **169,** Bob Daemmrich/The Image Works

Chapter 4: Pages 180, 181, David Madison/Stone/Getty Images, Inc.; **183,** Frank Lane/Parfitt/Stone/Getty Images, Inc.; **184,** Reuters New Media, Inc./Corbis; **186,** Charles Gupton/Corbis Stock Market; **189 both,** Russ Lappa; **198,** Larry Ulrich/Stone/Getty Images, Inc.; **200,** Wolfgang Kaehler/Corbis; **205,** Don Mason/Corbis Stock Market; **206,** Russ Lappa; **208,**

NOAA; **209,** Mulvehill/The Image Works; **210 both, 212,** Russ Lappa; **213,** Lawrence Migdale/Stock Boston; **215,** PhotoEdit; **216,** Duomo Photography, Inc.; **220,** Russ Lappa; **222,** Mark Thayer; **223,** Peter Timmermans/Stone/Getty Images, Inc.; **224,** Bob Daemmrich; **232,** Jim Mone/AP/Wide World Photos; **232–233,** The Brearley Collection; **233,** © 1992 Ron Vesely/MLBPhotos

Chapter 5: Pages 234, 235, Getty Images, Inc.; **237 l,** Kit Kittle/Corbis; **237 r,** PhotoDisc, Inc.; **239 all,** Russ Lappa; **241,** Daryl Balfour/Stone/Getty Images, Inc.; **245,** Michael Newman/PhotoEdit; **248,** Stephen Frisch/Stock Boston; **255,** Seth Resnick/Stock Boston; **258,** SuperStock; **263,** Rob Atkins/The Image Bank/Getty Images, Inc.; **265,** Jim West/The Image Works; **271,** David Young-Wolff/PhotoEdit; **273,** UPI/Bettman

Chapter 6: Pages 280, 281, SuperStock; **284 l,** Martyn Goddard/Corbis; **284 r,** Chris Cheadle/Stone/Getty Images, Inc.; **286,** Joseph McBride/Stone/Getty Images, Inc.; **288,** David H. Wells/The Image Works; **291,** Ryan McVay/PhotoDisc, Inc./Getty Images, Inc.; **293,** Mark Thayer; **295 b,** Reprinted by permission: Tribune Media Services; **295 t,** Willie Maldonado/ Stone/Getty Images, Inc.; **296,** Tim Davis/Stone/Getty Images, Inc.; **297 both,** NASA; **300,** Myrleen Ferguson/PhotoEdit; **302,** Kenneth W. Fink/Photo Researchers, Inc.; **306,** Tom Stock/Stone/Getty Images, Inc.; **311,** Alan Thornton/Stone/Getty Images, Inc.; **313,** Charles Gupton/Stock Boston; **315,** Zoom/Allsport/Getty Images, Inc.; **321,** Mike Powell/Allsport/Getty Images, Inc.; **327,** Russ Lappa; **337 br,** Peter Hayman/Dorling Kindersley; **337 t,** Geoff Brightling/Dorling Kindersley; **337 bl,** Shaun Egan/Stone/Getty Images, Inc.

Chapter 7: Pages 338, 339, AP/Wide World Photos; **341,** SuperStock; **349,** Annie Griffiths Belt/Corbis; **350,** Wilfried Krecichwost/Stone/Getty Images, Inc.; **354,** Robert Brenner/PhotoEdit; **357 l,** Tony Freeman/PhotoEdit; **357 the rest,** Prentice Hall; **358,** Corel Corp.; **362,** Index Stock Imagery; **366,** Don Johnson/Corbis Stock Market; **367,** Steve McCutcheon/Visuals Unlimited; **368,** Brian Smith/Stock Boston; **372,** Spencer Grant/Picture Cube; **373,** Tamara Reynolds/Stone/Getty Images, Inc.; **374,** Aaron Stevenson/Silver Burdett Ginn; **379,** Steven Kline/Bruce Coleman, Inc.; **380 t,** Silver Burdett Ginn; **380 b,** Leonard de Selva/Corbis; **382,** John Eastcott, Frank Pedrick/The Image Works; **383,** Omni-Photo Communications

Chapter 8: Pages 392, 393, John Lund/Stone/Getty Images, Inc.; **403,** Frans Lanting/Minden Pictures; **404,** Bill Amend/Universal Press Syndicate; **407,** Andrew Syred/Science Photo Library/Photo Researchers, Inc.; **409,** Maxine Hall/Corbis; **413,** The Granger Collection; **416,** Courtesy of Dr. Jewel Plummer Cobb; **421 m,** Jessica Wecker/Photo Researchers, Inc.; **421 t,** PhotoDisc, Inc.; **421 b,** Chris Koonts/Transparencies, Inc.; **426,** Richard Megna/Fundamental Photographs; **428,** Richard Megna/Fundamental Photographs; **431,** John Carnemolla/ANT Photo Library; **432,** Corbis; **435,** PhotoEdit; **437,** Jeff Greenberg/Omni-Photo Communications, Inc.; **440,** Jonathan Nourok/PhotoEdit; **443,** Phototake; **452,** Dave King/Dorling Kindersley; **453 l,** Tim Flach/Getty Images, Inc.; **453 r,** David Madison/Getty Images, Inc.

Chapter 9: Pages 454, 455, Mark Bacon/Alamy.com; **456,** The Image Bank/Getty Images, Inc.; **460,** Chuck Savage/Corbis Stock Market; **464,** Patrick Ingrand/Stone/Getty Images, Inc.; **471,** Cesar Lucas Abreu/The Image Bank/Getty Images, Inc.; **475,** Ron Kimball; **478,** Lynn M. Stone; **501,** Needham Research Institute

Chapter 10: Pages 508, 509, NASA; **511,** Richard Megna/Fundamental Photographs; **513,** James H. Robinson/Animals Animals/Earth Scenes; **514 l,** Stone/Getty Images, Inc.; **514 r,** Prentice Hall; **515,** C Squared Studios/PhotoDisc/Getty Images, Inc.; **519,** R. D. Rubic/Precision Chromes, Inc.; **521,** Agence Vandystadt/Allsport; **522,** Jose Carrillo/PhotoEdit; **526,** David Austen/Stone/Getty Images, Inc.; **527 t,** NASA; **527 b,** Reprinted by permission: Tribune Media Services; **531,** Gene Peach/The Picture Cube/Index Stock Imagery; **532,** A. Ramey/Stock Boston; **538,** Michael Keller/FPG International/Getty Images, Inc.; **540 l,** The Granger Collection; **540 r,** UPI/Corbis/Bettman; **543,** Michael Pole/Corbis; **547,** Andy Lyons/Allsport/Getty Images, Inc.; **551,** *Close to Home* by John McPherson/Universal Press Syndicate; **552,** SuperStock; **555,** Jeff Sherman/FPG International/Getty Images, Inc.; **557,** SuperStock; **562,** Animals Animals/Earth Scenes; **565,** Russ Lappa; **574,** NASA

Chapter 11: Pages 576, 577, AFP/Corbis; **579,** Telegraph Colour Library/FPG International/Getty Images, Inc.; **585,** Spencer Jones/FPG International/Getty Images, Inc.; **588,** AFP/Corbis; **595,** Wesley Bocxe/Photo Researchers, Inc.; **602,** © ABC/Mondrian Estate/Holtzman Trust/Haags Gemeentemuseum; **605,** © Tribune Media Services, Inc. All Rights Reserved. Reprinted with permission.; **606,** Ron Sherman/Stock Boston; **608,** Zefa/London/Corbis Stock Market; **611,** David Young Wolff/PhotoEdit; **615,** PhotoEdit; **617,** Kelly-Mooney Photography/Corbis; **618,** David Young-Wolff/PhotoEdit; **623,** Joe McDonald/Bruce Coleman, Inc.; **626,** Eye Ubiquitous/Corbis

Chapter 12: Pages 634, 635, John William Banagan/The Image Bank/Getty Images, Inc.; **636,** Nancy Richmond/The Image Works; **638,** David Young-Wolff/PhotoEdit; **641 l,** Bruce Roberts/Photo Researchers, Inc.; **641 r,** *Close to Home* by John McPherson/Universal Press Syndicate; **649,** Mark Joseph/Stone/Getty Images, Inc.; **653,** Antman/The Image Works; **655,** SuperStock; **670,** Bob Daemmrich/The Image Works; **671,** Frank Pedrick/The Image Works; **673,** Billy E. Barnes/PhotoEdit; **676 both, 677,** Richard Haynes; **682,** Billy E. Barnes/PhotoEdit; **687,** J. Pickerell/The Image Works; **688 both,** U.S. Mint; **690 t,** David Young-Wolff/PhotoEdit; **690,** Prentice Hall School Division; **700,** Neal Preston/Corbis; **700–701 the rest,** Dorling Kindersley